Sexuality Law

Sexuality Law

Arthur S. Leonard

PROFESSOR OF LAW, NEW YORK LAW SCHOOL

Patricia A. Cain

VICE PROVOST AND ALIBER FAMILY CHAIR IN LAW, UNIVERSITY OF IOWA

CAROLINA ACADEMIC PRESS

Durham, North Carolina

ISBN 0-89089-624-0
LCCN 2005932332

Carolina Academic Press
700 Kent Street
Durham, North Carolina 27701
Telephone (919) 489-7486
Fax (919) 493-5668
www.cap-press.com

Printed in the United States of America

#62883197

As with all my writing, I dedicate my contribution to this book to my domestic partner and friend, Tim Nenno.

ASL

I dedicate my contribution to this book to Jean Love, partner and colleague, in law and life.
PAC

Contents

Table of Cases

The principal cases are in bold type. Cases cited or discussed in the text are in roman type.

Preface

Some law schools began to offer courses on lesbian/gay legal issues in the 1980s, under a variety of titles, such as Sexual Privacy Law, Sexuality and Law, Sexual Minorities and the Law. As there were no textbooks, professors put together their own teaching materials from various sources. In those pre-internet days, that meant lots of photocopying and physical cutting and pasting.

The pioneers teaching in this field included Thomas B. Stoddard at New York University, E. Carrington Boggan at New York Law School, Rhonda Rivera at Ohio State University, and Mary C. Dunlap and Thomas Coleman at several California law schools. The classes were small, with many students reluctant to take the course out of fear that the presence of such a course title on their transcript would harm their employment chances.

When Boggan first offered the course at New York Law School under the title "Homosexuality and the Law," no students enrolled. When he offered the same course the following year as "Sexual Privacy Law," he had a full house.

When Arthur Leonard took over the New York Law School course upon Boggan's retirement, Tom Stoddard's teaching materials from N.Y.U. provided his starting point for creating a new set of materials. By the 1990s, casebooks began to appear, so professors had a choice of continuing to assemble materials on their own or to adopt the first published casebook, an N.Y.U. press paperback offered by William B. Rubenstein, then the director of the American Civil Liberties Union's Lesbian and Gay Rights and AIDS Projects, who was teaching the course on an adjunct basis at various schools. Soon a second book emerged, co-authored by Nan Hunter of Brooklyn Law School and William Eskridge of Yale, and Rubenstein's book migrated to a different publisher for a new hardbound edition. The two books had very different philosophies; Rubenstein's focusing on sexual orientation law while Hunter & Eskridge broadly surveyed gender, sexuality and the law.

Now we are excited to present the third published casebook in the field, Sexuality Law. Each of us has been teaching this course under various names and configurations and at various schools for many years, sometimes with our own materials and sometimes with one of the published casebooks. When Carolina Academic Press invited us to put together a new casebook in the area, we thought about ways to make it distinctively useful for instructors and students. We decided our focus would fall somewhere between the narrower focused approach on homosexuality and the broadly-encompassing gender. This book seeks to incorporate relevant material beyond sexual orientation, embracing legal issues raised by varying gender identities. We tried to introduce some practical issues that haven't necessarily been covered elsewhere, such as tax issues for same-sex couples, and to inject a public interest lawyering perspective. We also decided that as we both prefer to teach from cases that have been lightly edited so as to leave in the full flavor and context of the original opinion, we would follow that principle in presenting cases for this book.

One of the biggest challenges we faced was deciding when to "close" the book to new developments. Completion of this project was several times delayed as we awaited important forthcoming rulings by the United States Supreme Court and various lower courts, most notably the Massachusetts Supreme Judicial Court's ruling on same-sex marriage. Finally we just came to accept that the book would never be completed if we kept waiting for the next major ruling to come along, and we decided to cut things off with the beginning of April 2005. Subsequent developments will be noted in the Teachers Manual and in periodic updates. This is a field where new developments are frequently occurring and a timely text is important, but a termination point must be reached. For example, just shortly after we "closed" the book, Connecticut enacted the nation's second Civil Union law and Canada and Spain took final legislative steps to make same-sex marriage available. We decided not to engage in extensive rewriting in Chapter IV to account for these developments, which had been anticipated a bit in the text.

Our schools have been very supportive of our work on sexuality law in general and "Sexuality Law" in particular. Arthur Leonard wishes to acknowledge New York Law School faculty research grants supporting the work on this book. Patricia Cain acknowledges Provost Michael J. Hogan, University of Iowa, for supporting a research leave from the Provost's office that enabled her to finish work on this project.

This book, like law and life themselves, is never-ending. Welcome to the fascinating unfolding story of Sexuality Law.

Arthur S. Leonard, New York Law School
Patricia Cain, University of Iowa College of Law

Sexuality Law

Chapter One

An Introduction

A. General Introduction:
What is Sexuality?

This book brings together materials from a variety of legal disciplines to explore the interaction of legal policy and human sexuality. Before looking at cases, statutes, and specific policy issues, however, it is worth spending some time thinking about human sexuality to help define the field of study. What do we mean by "sexuality"?

According to the American Psychological Association, "sexuality" has four components: (1) biological sex; (2) gender identity; (3) social sex role; and (4) sexual orientation. Biological sex is thought to refer to the physical attributes of being either male or female, whether measured by chromosomes or genitalia. There are in fact five physical criteria for measuring biological sex: (1) chromosomal sex, (2) gonadal sex, (3) hormonal sex, (4) internal accessory reproductive structures, (5) and external sex organs. While most individuals possess all five criteria generally associated with being either male or female, such consistency is not true for all people. Our understanding of biological sex is challenged by these non-conformists.

Feminists, riding on the shoulders of Simone de Beauvoir, have been telling us for years that sex is different from gender, that one may be born of the "second sex," but one is socially constructed to be a woman. Thus, gender identity refers to how one views oneself, as a man or as a woman. Feminists would likely say that "social sex role" is an oxymoron, because if the role is one created by society, then it is a *gender* role, not a *sex* role. Thus, "gender role identity" would be a more accurate term. A butch lesbian, for example, may well identify as a woman, but view herself as more masculine than feminine. And finally, sexual orientation usually refers to one's preference or attraction to a person of the same or opposite sex, as well as one's sexual behavior with sexual partners. It might be more inclusive to say that the fourth component is sexual behavior, a concept broader than sexual orientation. Finally, "sexual identity" is a term that is fairly interchangeable with the term "sexuality" and includes one's self concept of biological sex, gender role, and sexual orientation. Some theorists, however, use the term "sexual identity" as a synonym for "sexual orientation."

All of these concepts are currently contested both within the academy and within identity communities struggling for political and social change. For example, the traditional division of biological sex into two discrete categories (male and female) is under attack by academicians in the sciences who suggest either that biological sex is more appropriately conceived as a continuum or that, at the least, it consists of more than two simple categories of female and male. This bifurcation of sex is also seriously questioned by self-designated "queer activists," who support the rights of transsexuals and intersexed persons to exist outside of these two distinct categories. To date, federal and state law in the United States has generally been unwilling to consider any possibility other than the traditional division into the categories male and female.

Once sex has been determined, certain expectations about gender identity, gender role, and sexual orientation follow as a matter of societal custom. "Normal" gender identity in mainstream American culture has been thought to require the alignment of biological sex (i.e., being female) with gender identity (i.e. identifying as a woman). Women, in turn, are then expected to behave in typical feminine roles. And, of course, they are expected to engage in heterosexual sexual behavior with persons of the opposite sex, known as men, who are supposed to be masculine.

Sexual orientation is perhaps the most complex and the most contested concept of all. It includes affection, sexual desire, and sexual behavior. Heterosexuality means that one is primarily attracted to and sexually active with a member of the opposite sex. Homosexuality means that one is primarily attracted to and sexually active with a member of the same sex. However, it is possible to have attraction and desire without sexual activity. For example, both heterosexual and homosexual persons can be celibate. And some individuals do not fit comfortably within the two distinct categories, since it is possible to have affection and attraction for one sex and sexual behavior with the other sex, or to have both attraction to and behavior with both sexes.

The LGBT civil rights movement is rich with debates over whether same-sex relationships are a matter of sexual preference or sexual orientation. Persons who identify as bisexual have been particularly difficult for the movement. Is same-sex sexuality a choice, a social construction, or a hard-wired biological necessity? Are bisexuals born as bisexual or are they simply evidence that we all have that capacity, although individual life experiences determine which way each of us will swing? There are no clear answers to these questions.

This course will explore the legal questions that have been raised about all four components of sexuality. Its primary emphasis, however, will be on cases in which the four components do not line up in accord with the expectations of our dominant culture. These cases present instances of sexual diversity or "difference" from the norm. The people who inhabit these "different" spaces are often referred to as gay men, lesbians, bisexuals, transgendered persons, intersexuals or, more inclusively, as members of sexual minorities. A prime example would be the case of the butch lesbian, a case in which biological sex (female) does not line up with the expected gender role (feminine) or with the sexual orientation that is expected of females (attraction to and sexual mating with males).

We will consider how these variations in human sexuality, both in terms of identity and in the behaviors with which they are associated, are affected by legal doctrine and practice. The interaction of law and sexuality is complex, and the attitudes of lawmakers towards sexual issues heavily affects the shaping of legal doctrines and their application in particular situations. What legislators and judges think they know and believe about the scientific issues will influence the legal doctrines they either invent or apply to persons presenting situations where sexual variation appears to matter.

Thus, some consideration of the various attitudes towards sexual diversity is also a necessary prelude to considering the legal issues. What follows barely scratches the surface of the voluminous literature on human sexuality and the enormous range of theories and opinions about why people experience and enact their sexuality in the way that they do, and focuses heavily on legal regulation of sexuality. At the end of this section is a brief list of books that the reader might wish to consult for a more in-depth consideration of the topic.

B. A Brief History of Sexual Minorities and the Law

Prior to the 19th century, a narrow focus on behavior was characteristic of the legal treatment of sexuality. The idea that an individual might be a "homosexual" or a "transsexual" as a distinct type of person had not yet emerged, and status-related terms to refer to such individuals were not used. Instead, the law focused on prohibiting or regulating particular acts, regardless of the identity of the actors. This approach can be found in the Bible, which assumes heterosexuality as a universal norm and appears, according to many of its interpreters, to treat all non-procreative sexual activity (and all extra-marital procreative activity) as sinful behavior inspired by idolatry. The principal text usually cited to condemn homosexuality is found in the Priestly Code in Leviticus, Chapter 18, and may have been primarily aimed at the ritual prostitution, both heterosexual and homosexual, that was incorporated into the idol-worshiping faiths of Middle Eastern people from whom the Hebrews wished to differentiate themselves. Later references in the Christian scriptures clearly go beyond ritual prostitution, but no statement about variant sexuality is attributed to Jesus.

Certainly a focus on behavior was the approach taken by government and religious authorities when confronted by evidence of extra-marital sexual behavior or any form of anal or oral sex, even between marital partners. Before the English Reformation, regulation of sexual activity in England was left to the authorities of the established Catholic Church, who dealt with "sin" on their own terms. During the Reformation, with its disestablishment of the Catholic Church, King Henry VIII directed Parliament to enact statutes to take the place of canon law, and thus England's first sodomy statute was enacted in 1533. It forbade all anal sexual intercourse involving persons with each other or with animals, regardless of the sex of the actors involved. Other statutes involving lewdness and disorderly conduct came to be construed to forbid oral sex or any contact of a sexual nature outside of marriage.

The American Revolution was fought, at least in part, to secure for the residents of the thirteen colonies the "rights of Englishmen." Under the United States Constitution of 1787, English legal doctrines then in existence were taken to be the law in the new nation unless or until displaced by subsequent legislative enactment or judicial development. Thus, at the time of independence, the same sexual behavior that was unlawful in England was considered unlawful in the United States as a matter of state common law. During the 19th century, many English common law principles in this sphere were displaced by state statutes, some borrowing from the language of the Statute of Henry VIII, some using less archaic language. The kinds of phrases one finds in laws of the 19th century mirror the attitudes of legislators towards the acts involved: "abominable and detestable crime against nature, not fit to be mentioned among Christians" is a typical example. (Sodomy laws provide one of the most striking examples of laws derived from religious doctrine, yet no court has ever accepted the argument that their enactment violates the Establishment Clause of the First Amendment of the Bill of Rights.)

The reference to a "crime against nature" derives from a "natural law" tradition that had arisen during the 18th century to provide a non-sectarian rationale for various principles of law and morality that had previously been Biblically-rooted. The natural law tradition seized upon the common understanding of "natural" functions of body parts, and from that understanding derived principles of natural and unnatural acts. The penis was seen as an organ for the purpose of excretion of liquid waste to cleanse the body and ejaculation of semen for the purpose of impregnating women in order to perpetuate humanity with new offspring. Under this view, any use of the penis for purposes not directly tied to these two "natural" functions was seen as "unnatural" and thus morally wrong, worthy of condemnation, and to be prevented or punished by the state. (The Biblical prohibition on masturbation certainly contributed to a view that non-procreative ejaculation was wrong.) Similarly, any manipulation of female genitals for the purpose of non-procreative sexual pleasure was considered an "unnatural" use of a body part that had been "created" for reproductive purposes. The pleasurable sensations arising out of the manipulation of genitals were considered to be part of nature's plan to stimulate reproductive activity, and condemned as ends in themselves.

The combination and interaction of these religious and philosophical views provided the intellectual bedrock, (1) for laws in all the states forbidding: (a) fornication (heterosexual sex between persons not married to each other), (b) sodomy (originally just anal sex but extended by interpretation in many jurisdictions to include oral sex in which the penis played a role), and (c) contraception (outlawed in many jurisdictions); and (2) for the general condemnation by spokespersons for public morality, such as religious ministers and moral philosophers, of masturbation, although it was rare to find masturbation the subject of criminal law. Such laws could fall heavily on those attracted sexually to members of their own sex, since by definition any sexual activity in which they might engage with a desired partner would fall under moral and perhaps legal condemnation. These laws were premised, of course, on the idea that the behavior in question was an instance of sin or immorality by a person who was otherwise "normal," and thus worthy of severe punishment. In most jurisdictions, these sex offenses, whether or not consensual, were serious felonies calling for long prison terms or other severe punishments.

The modern concept of "sexuality" as a distinct characteristic or set of characteristics of people emerged toward the middle of the 19th century, a time when the scientific study of humanity was becoming more systematized and began to advance significantly from speculation to actual examination. However, the tools of 20th century social science had not yet been invented, and the tendency of 19th century scholars of sexuality was to base conclusions on sometimes haphazard or adventitious observations of the world around them.

Influence of Darwin

Charles Darwin's theories placed a central focus on sexual behavior as an engine of evolutionary development of species, and undoubtedly helped to generate an intensified focus on both sexual behavior and expression as important aspects of human existence. By the middle of the 19th century, reflecting the urge to classify and categorize that is so evident in Darwin's work, various observers had begun to suggest that labels be placed on people whose focus of sexual desire was towards members of their own physical sex. "Homosexual" was only one of several such terms that emerged into use in the scientific literature, but by early in the 20th century it had become generally accepted, soon to be joined by "heterosexual," "bisexual" and "transsexual," as "scientific" terms intended to label people having particular characteristics with respect to their sexuality. In other words, an important conceptual shift had begun, in which people's identity began to be defined on the basis of how they expressed their sexual nature. Thus, one might speak of a "homosexual" or a "lesbian" as a person having a particular set of characteristics that justified classifying her as part of a group sharing those characteristics.

Social Construction Thesis

It seems clear in retrospect, although it was not necessarily clear at the time, that such categories are "socially constructed," in that they are a product of theorizing about the place in society occupied by people with particular orientations, preferences and behaviors. In the same sense, identities premised on residency in a particular place are also "socially constructed." When you say that you are an "American" or a "Californian," you are using a socially constructed category, a convention of conceptual organization, by which you are classifying yourself according to characteristics that the society in which you live considers salient for some reason, but the categorization clearly has a relationship to real, essential facts about your place of origin or current residence. Another socially constructed category is "blonde," in the sentence "They say blondes have more fun." The sentence incorporates an understanding that women can be classified into groups according to their hair color, and that particular groups thus defined allegedly have more "fun" than groups of women having other hair colors. That a particular woman has blond hair is a physical fact, part of her essential reality, but that this would mark her as a member of a particular group is a matter of social convention. Some people might find hair color to be a fact irrelevant to any scheme of categorization for any purpose, while others might attribute great significance to such a classification. Some socially constructed categories, such as citizenship status, have clearly understandable significance for matters of public policy in terms of entitlement for various benefits or protection of various rights, although one might disagree with how the law deals with any particular aspect of citizenship rights.

There was no scientific consensus early on about the determinants of the various aspects of sexuality, among which one might include not only sexual activity but modes of dress, physical gestures, living arrangements, and other aspects of personality and behavior commonly seen as associated with gender roles (the social presentation of gender identity). Some speculated that various deviations from the statistical norms of social convention were due to mental defects or illnesses or psychological maladjustments, others looked for explanations in the newly emerging science of genetics and inheritance, and still others clung to the age-old explanations of deviant behavior grounded in demonic possession (the Devil made her do it!) or wilful criminality.

Freud and the Early Sexologists

By the early 20th century, Sigmund Freud and his followers were devising elaborate psychological explanations for variant sexuality, usually centered on family relationships.

In a letter to an American mother who had written for advice about her son, who had been engaging in homosexual activity, Freud stated that homosexuality was not an illness or a vice, not something to be condemned or punished, but rather a case of arrested development. It was an article of faith among many of Freud's followers that all persons were born with the potential for erotic attraction without respect to sex, and that a "normal" psychological adjustment would result in the mature adult being firmly heterosexual in orientation. Anything that interrupted the "normal" development of a heterosexual orientation might cause the individual to become fixated on a bisexual or homosexual orientation, which was described as being immature or undeveloped. A goal of Freudian psychotherapy for "homosexuals" was to reanimate the development process by getting the subject to uncover repressed memories of traumatic incidents in their earlier life that may have caused their sexual development to become prematurely halted, and to bring the individual to a fully developed heterosexual orientation by dealing analytically with the trauma. That Freudian psychologists were unable to achieve a full heterosexual orientation for their patients did not cause them to doubt their theories.

Explanations for the variety of human sexuality continued to stimulate debate throughout the century, especially as evidence emerged that the amount of sexual diversity was larger than had been previously spoken about and documented. The new emphasis on genetics in the life sciences gave rise to a growing belief that diverse sexuality had some basis in genetic diversity. This belief began to gather more support in the second half of the 20th century as the newly-respectable field of sexology began to produce surprising data.

The Kinsey Reports

The major breakthrough in the public discourse on human sexuality in the United States came with the publication of two books in the decade following World War II: *Sexual Behavior in the Human Male*, by Kinsey, Pomeroy & Martin (1948), and *Sexual Behavior in the Human Female*, by Kinsey, Pomeroy, Martin & Gebhard (1953). These books were based on wide-ranging surveys undertaken under the leadership of Dr. Alfred C. Kinsey during the two decades prior to the war, in which thousands of people submitted to lengthy face-to-face interviews with specially trained interviewers seeking to probe their beliefs, feelings and experiences of sex. Popularly called the "Kinsey Reports" (although much of the scientific apparatus of the publications was contributed by Dr. Kinsey's collaborators), these books suggested that sexual diversity was far more widespread in the population than anyone had previously suggested. For example, the books asserted, to the amazement of most readers, that 37% of all adult males in America had engaged in at least one sexual activity with another member of the same sex leading to an orgasm, and that perhaps as many as one in ten of the adult male population was "mainly homosexual" in orientation for at least three years. The figures for women were less striking but nonetheless significant in showing the extent of same-sex desire and experience among women.

Perhaps more significantly, the Kinsey books suggested a "continuum" of sexual orientation that departed from the popular wisdom that every person was either homosexual or heterosexual, by documenting a surprising amount of bisexual behavior, and by showing that at different times in their lives people acted in different ways. Kinsey derived a scale to describe human sexual orientation ranging from 0 to 6, with 0 representing people who reported that all their sexual fantasies and actual experiences involved members of the opposite sex, and 6 representing the converse. Kinsey found that most people fell between 0 and 6 rather than at the polar extremes.

That is, it was rare to find somebody who, despite a self-identification as heterosexual, had never fantasized erotically about another member of the same sex, or to find a self-identified homosexual who had never fantasized erotically about a member of the opposite sex, and most "homosexuals" reported some actual sexual experience with members of the opposite sex. Of course, what caused the most consternation among the public was Kinsey's assertion that more than a third of adult males had actually engaged at least once in a sexual experience resulting in an orgasm with another man.

The Kinsey books aroused furious rebuttals, and social scientists in particular criticized the research methodology for making no attempt to interview a randomly selected sample of the population, thus casting significant doubt on the accuracy of Kinsey's statistics. (Kinsey talked with anybody who would talk to him, and so his samples tended to be overly weighted toward Caucasian college students, prisoners, and more "liberated" folk who were willing to talk about their sex lives at a time when such talk was not really "socially acceptable.") While the columns of numbers in numerous tables included in the Kinsey books looked authoritative, subsequent researchers who took great pains to derive their data from random selection of their survey subjects have never come close to replicating Kinsey's results. In *Sex and Reason* (1992), Judge Richard Posner summarized the evidence published up to that date and found that "most estimates of the number of male homosexuals are in fact between 2 and 5 percent," and noted that all studies seemed to find that lesbians made up an even smaller percentage of all women. Some studies have suggested that as few as one percent of the adult population are "exclusively homosexual" in their sexual behavior, and only a slightly larger percentage are mainly oriented towards the same sex for most of their adult life.

The Illness Model of Sexual Variation

Despite their methodological failings, the Kinsey books achieved an important breakthrough in making it respectable to research and publish about human sexuality, and the floodgates were opened during the decades after World War II, as the field of sex research emerged as a distinct scientific discipline, attracting experts from the fields of psychology, medicine, sociology, genetics, and anatomy to a field previously dominated by moral philosophers, psychiatrists, criminologists and theologians. Conventional wisdom among many educated people by the middle of the 20th century was that sexual diversity was primarily a psychological phenomenon involving "arrested development" of sexual identity, as described above. This theory led to several generations of psychiatrists and psychologists who believed that homosexuality was a medical problem that could yield to therapy, and various kinds of therapy were attempted to "change" homosexuals into heterosexuals. Viewing homosexuality as a medical problem had the benefit (for homosexuals) of winning sympathy for law reform, most notably with the American Law Institute in the United States and the Wolfendon Committee (a Parliamentary committee established to recommend changes in the criminal law) in England, both of which recommended removing criminal penalties for consensual adult sex outside of marriage (including anal and oral sex). The Defense Department officially accepted the psychological theory during World War II, premising its decision to attempt to "screen out" and reject homosexuals on the contention that they suffered from a personality disorder that would make them unfit for military service, and Congress accepted the idea during the 1950s when it amended the immigration law specifically to exclude persons "afflicted with psychopathic personality," a term that expert witnesses assured them would mandate the exclusion of any homosexuals "diagnosed" as such by the Public Health Service. During the 1960s, reacting to litigation attacking the "psychopathic personality" nomenclature as unconstitutionally vague, Congress added the phrase "sexual deviation" to the list of excludable conditions. The American Psychiatric Association listed "homosexuality" as a mental illness in its official compilation, the Diagnostic & Statistical Manual (DSM).

Birth of the Homophile Movement

The Kinsey books presented a sharp challenge to this orthodoxy, by suggesting that sexual diversity was much more common than generally believed, and was characteristic of a wide range of otherwise "normal" people. A research psychologist in California, Dr. Evelyn Hooker, advanced this view with studies during the 1950s showing that panels of "expert" psychologists, accustomed to diagnosing mental conditions by interpreting test subjects' verbal responses to ink blot ("Rorschach") tests, could not distinguish in blind tests between the responses of self-identified homosexuals and self-identified heterosexuals of comparable demographic backgrounds (age, education, race). Hooker opined that sexual diversity was a matter of "difference" rather than "defect" or "illness." Her views, and those of other researchers, helped to bolster the slowly emerging self-identity and organization of homosexuals in the United States and Europe during the 1950s and 1960s, as they began to form organizations dedicated to educating society and seeking social and legal changes in the status of homosexuals.

In the United States, the early gay liberation organizations focused on securing decriminalization of homosexual conduct, an end to discrimination in military and civilian government employment (a 1953 Eisenhower administration executive order banned the employment of homosexuals in the civil service), and the removal of homosexuality from the lexicon of psychiatric illness. As noted above, the American Law Institute accepted the conventional wisdom that homosexuality was an illness as a justification to recommend decriminalizing homosexual acts, but it took its action before Dr. Hooker's studies were published and began to change the opinions of some psychiatric authorities. After the ALI's Model Penal Code was disseminated to the states, some legislative reforms took place. Illinois in 1961 became the first state to adopt the Model Penal Code with its sex crimes provisions intact, thus repealing the state's criminal sodomy law as applied to consensual sex in private between adults. The Model Penal Code also introduced new verbiage; the old "crime against nature" or "sodomy," which was still to be a crime if committed without consent, with minors, or in public, was now called "deviate sexual intercourse" with the explanation that "deviate" referred to a deviation from the statistical norm without implying a normative judgment.

Gay Liberation Movement

The early "homophile" organizations in the United States were small, secretive groups that did not attract much public attention during the 1950s. During the 1960s, spurred by the visible and active movements for racial and sexual civil rights, the organizations became a bit bolder, staging some public demonstrations and engaging in let-

ter-writing campaigns in support of reforms. But a major transformation in the movement was sparked by several days of demonstrations in New York City's Greenwich Village late in June 1969, when a police raid of a bar, the Stonewall, aroused angry protests
and violence from the bar patrons. A new spirit of resistance led to the formation of the
Gay Liberation Front and Gay Activists Alliance, more public demonstrations (including annual marches in support of "gay rights" in major American cities, mainly during
the month of June), and efforts to form a wider array of organizations dedicated to advancing the rights of sexual minorities. The early 1970s saw the formation of such organizations as the National Gay Task Force (later renamed the National Gay and Lesbian
Task Force) and Lambda Legal Defense and Education Fund, the first public-interest
law firm dedicated entirely to gay rights issues.

By 1973, gay liberationists had been able to persuade a majority of the members of the
American Psychiatric Association, participating in a national mail referendum, to support
a decision by the organization's executive board (which had itself been responsive both to
a political lobbying campaign and to the newly-emerging evidence about the mental
health of homosexuals) to remove "homosexuality" from the DSM, although the organization voted to retain a category called ego-dystonic homosexuality, referring to a person
who was very disturbed about his sexual orientation and desired therapy to achieve a firm
adjustment to heterosexuality; in the 1990s, this category was removed when a majority of
the psychiatrists became convinced that "conversion therapy" was a fraud. The American
Psychological Association soon followed suit, and the American Bar Association, reacting
to these developments, called for the decriminalization of consensual adult sex and passage of laws forbidding sexual orientation discrimination. By the end of the 1970s, enough
states had adopted the Model Penal Code that a significant portion of the United States
population lived in jurisdictions where same-sex intercourse between consenting adults in
private was legal. Also by the end of the 1970s, the Surgeon General of the United States,
Julius Richmond, responding to the American Psychiatric Association's actions, had concluded that it was professionally insupportable for PHS psychiatrists to participate in "diagnosing" homosexuals for purposes of the immigration law, thereby throwing a wrench
into the operation of the statutory exclusion policy, and ten years later Congress amended
the Immigration and Nationality Act to overhaul the medical exclusions and remove "psychopathic personality" and "sexual deviation" from the list of excludable conditions.

While a majority of the professions of psychiatry and psychology had by the 1970s
come to embrace a non-disease view of homosexuality, there remained persistent opposition, both within those professions and among the general public. Some persisted (and
still persist) in believing that sexual diversity is entirely a matter of choice that can and
should be influenced by social policy, including the retention of criminal penalties, exclusion from various professions, and the maintenance of social policy incentives for individuals to "chose" a heterosexual way of life. Those holding this view also tend to be
predisposed against civil rights legislation incorporating protection for homosexuals, on
the view that homosexuality, unlike race or sex, is not an "immutable" physical characteristic, and that any social expression of acceptance or condonation of homosexuality
would cause more impressionable youngsters to follow that errant path. (Of course,
there are also many who have come to reject the idea of immutable or essential personal
characteristics entirely, having concluded that race and, to some extent, sex are themselves socially constructed categories with blurred boundaries.) Others, especially within
the psychiatric profession, continue to hold to the view that homosexuality is a mental
illness, that therapy to convert the homosexual to a heterosexual adjustment should be
available, and argue that the majority of their profession has cruelly abandoned homo-

sexuals by eschewing such conversion therapy. Some of those taking this view still cling to the family dynamics explanations that were advanced earlier in the 20th century, and many continue to base their views on their clinical experiences involving exposure to numerous individuals who are unhappy at discovering homosexual feelings and are eager to conform to social norms by achieving a heterosexual adjustment.

The Debate over Cause:
Nature or Nurture

Dr. Hooker's findings during the 1950s begged a very important question for many people. She may have proved to the satisfaction of psychiatric authorities that homosexuality was not an illness, but then what was it? Why did some percentage of the population have a "sexual orientation" (a term just then coming into wider usage in place of "sexual preference") different from the majority? Why did some people have a gender identity different from their anatomical sex, an issue that was just coming to the fore in the late 1950s as modern surgery had advanced to the point of attempting gender-reassignment procedures?

What was the "cause" for sexual diversity? Would it be found in early childhood experience and the emulation of role models such as parents, grandparents, siblings, teachers or other authority figures? Would it be found in a particular constellation of family functioning and parental styles, such as the "distant father" and "overprotective, smothering mother" of some mid-20th-century psychiatric theories of male homosexuality? Would it be found in the genes, in the hormonal balance during pregnancy, in the trauma of the birth process, in specific events occurring during early childhood? Was it, as some said, entirely a matter of learned behaviors and free choices made by individuals, of impressionable teens being seduced by the perceived glamor or tantalizing danger of the "gay lifestyle," or yet another example of the wilful nonconformity characteristic of rebellious youth? Or was it some complex interaction of several or even all of these factors, which might differ dramatically from person to person? Although many researchers came to hold strong beliefs about particular theories to explain how aspects of human sexuality developed, nobody was able to produce an overall theory that both explained all variation and could be proven through a scientific method. The search for such explanations was complicated further by the possibility that men and women experienced sexuality differently, such that explanations that might appear to make sense for one sex could break down or merely seem irrelevant when applied to the other, or that even within each biological sex different individuals developed their sexuality in different ways.

During the 1980s, the organization Parents and Friends of Lesbians and Gay Men (PFLAG) commissioned a survey of the leading sex researchers in the United States, focused on whether sexual orientation was determined by biology or by environmental factors, including both the physical environment as well as interactions with other people, especially parents and other caretakers early in life. Almost all of the experts answered "all of the above" or "a complex interaction and combination" and indicated that nobody was yet in a position to state authoritatively how human sexual orientation was determined in any particular individual, although most of them agreed that genetics would ultimately be proved to be an important factor. Correlations could be shown, but causation could not be explained. And that remained true as the 21st century began.

Since the 1970s, however, there have been significant developments of knowledge, mainly in support of theories that human sexuality probably has a physical basis and that differences in gender identity and sexual orientation are probably at least *partly* determined by genetic influences. This is unsurprising in light of the degree to which research has managed to establish links between genes and many different aspects of human personality and behavior, although without providing clear explanations about how a particular gene affects a particular behavior. Scientists now generally say that for any complex human phenomenon, more than one gene is likely to be involved, and the interaction of the organism with the outside world is also likely to play a role. Little in the way of behavior could be said to be solely dictated by genes, but much of human behavior was seen to have at least some physical basis.

Perhaps the most persuasive evidence came from studies of families to determine the prevalence of homosexuality among siblings. Researchers found, for example, that it was much more likely that identical twins were both gay than that fraternal twins were both gay. Identical twins have the identical genetic inheritance, having developed from the splitting of an ovum early in pregnancy. Fraternal twins share the same parents, but develop from two separate eggs fertilized by two separate sperm, and so there is more genetic variation possible at conception than with identical twins, but presumably identical and fraternal twins will be more alike than sibling brothers conceived and gestated sequentially, since the period of pregnancy may have its own physical impact as a result of conditions in the womb (levels of hormones, interaction with the mother's circulatory system, etc.), and most twins, whether identical or fraternal, are raised within the same family group, subject to the same socio-psychological dynamics of early childhood. If diversity in sexuality was a phenomenon totally attributable to genes, one would expect that identical twins would always express their sexuality identically. That a bit fewer than half of the pairs of identical twins studied had the same sexual orientation suggests that genetic influence provides only part of the explanation. Identical twins also share the same time in the womb and are born in close—almost simultaneous—sequence (after all, one must emerge first, if only by seconds), but that is true as well for fraternal twins.

Interestingly, there is also a high correlation of sexual orientation among fraternal twins, about half as high as among identical twins, and about twice as high as among non-twin brothers. This suggests that the time in the womb has its own impact. But, of course, children born at the same time and raised in the same household are also experiencing the same parents and siblings and other environmental factors of early childhood, which, if they have some effect on sexual identity development, would suggest that even adopted children raised together would have a higher correlation of sexuality than would be predicted from a random selection of children of the same age raised separately. (Non-twin sequentially-born brothers are both likely to be gay at a higher rate than the incidence of homosexuality in the population as a whole—perhaps the most persuasive of these findings in suggesting that a common genetic ancestry plays some role in sexual orientation). Twins studies have supported the theory that genetics plays a role, that prenatal biology probably plays some role, and that post-natal environment plays some role in influencing the development of sexual identity, and some scientists even hazard percentages in discussing this, but nobody is in a position yet to say why or how with certainty.

Dr. Dean Hamer, a researcher at the National Institutes of Health, claimed that he had identified an area on the X-chromosome that seemed to be associated with an inherited disposition to homosexual orientation, which he identified as a sex-linked trait based on a correlation he had established through population research showing a heightened incidence of homosexual orientation in the sons of women who had gay brothers (the "gay uncle" phenomenon). Other researchers had difficulty replicating Hamer's results which, in any event, had nothing to say about whether lesbian identity has a genetic basis. (Hamer did not document a lesbian aunt phenomenon, for example.) Subsequent to Hamer's announcement, other researchers began to identify particular physical traits that marked gay men or lesbians as being different from heterosexual men or women, and in some cases more like members of the opposite sex. For example, Dr. Simon LeVay identified a particular brain structure (through the examination of brains donated for research after death) that showed measurement correlations between self-identified gay men (who had died from AIDS) and women of indeterminate sexual orientation that were closer than the correlations between gay men and men whose orientation was believed to be heterosexual. Once again, other researchers found it difficult to replicate these results. Another study found that transsexuals' brains were in a measurable respect more like the brains of the sex with which their owners identified than the anatomical sex into which they were born, although the research did not show whether this was a genetically-determined phenomenon or the result of the brain adapting to the individual's lived gender identity. Other researchers found that lesbians had a different hearing capacity than non-lesbian women, while yet others identified particular physical features in which homosexuals appeared to be more like members of the opposite sex than heterosexual members of their own sex.

Because both Dr. Hamer and Dr. LeVay identified themselves as being gay, some critics raised issues of bias or wishful thinking in their interpretation of their data. Others saw the Hamer and LeVay results as confirming the twins studies in finding some genetic influence in the determination of sexual orientation.

None of these observed differences and similarities in physically measurable traits provided any direct explanation of why or how sexual diversity occurs, but they tended to support the argument that sexual diversity is not solely a psychological manifestation. They also tended to discredit older theories suggesting that a homosexual orientation could be explained entirely by the personality types and early life interactions between children and their parents, and they helped to bolster Dr. Kinsey's conclusions about sexual diversity being a significant natural phenomenon, even if his prevalence numbers could never be replicated in later studies.

At the same time that more attention was being focused on genetic or physical explanations for homosexuality, new schools of thought were developing that questioned these explanations. Influenced by social theorists such as Michel Foucault, theorists began to challenge the 19th century categorical notions that classifications of people according to such concepts as "sexual orientation" had any essential meaning in regard to an "objective reality" apart from the particular culture in which they lived. These questions mirrored the questions that feminist theorists had been raising about the category "woman"—was it biological or socially constructed? Similarly, debate raged furiously among "queer scholars" during the 1980s about whether sexual orientation itself was a socially-constructed phenomenon or a physical reality. (Is "the homosexual" real, or just a social convention?) Historical and ethnographic studies looking at different cultures and different historical periods uncovered evidence of people having engaged in same-sex activities, but having varied widely in the way they talked and thought about themselves. Most of the evidence tended to show that the concept of "the homosexual" as a distinct category of human being, is largely an artifact of Western Civilization of the past 150 years, and is not commonly found in other cultures (except to the extent they have been influenced by Western Civilization) or at earlier times. This led to propositions about "the homosexual" being an invention of 19th century scientists, an invention that had no objective reality or existence apart from such scientific theories. One book by a social construction advocate was titled *A Hundred Years of Homosexuality*, arguing that prior to the mid-19th century emergence of the concept, there had been no "homosexuals" as such. This "social constructivist" view harmonized with notions of sexual fluidity embraced by many feminist scholars, and with the trend identified by some social observers of increased sexual experimentation among young people, especially on college campuses.

While the "social construction versus essentialism" debate continues, the more extreme versions of social constructionism, i.e, that sexuality is so fluid it has *no* fixed meaning, has begun to fade. The evidence that certain physical differences correlate with sexual orientation is mounting. As the project of mapping the human genome goes forward, there appears to be some sort of genetic factor playing some role with regard to almost every aspect of human personality and behavior. As a counter to this "hard science" data, social construction theory usefully reminds us that the view of the world embraced by a particular society is peculiar to a particular time and place, that classifying and labeling conventions may superimpose concepts that accord imperfectly with and oversimplify reality, that knowledge is limited and complex phenomena are not easily explained, and that as much as we think we know about a topic as multifaceted as human sexuality, there is probably more that we do not know.

Legal Consideration of Sexuality

How has United States law dealt with human sexuality?

Until 1961, when Illinois adopted the Model Penal Code provisions on sex crimes, the law throughout the United States treated various homosexual sex acts as criminal, but this was largely incidental to outlawing particular kinds of sexual activity regardless of the genders of the participants. As states began to revise their laws in light of the Model Penal Code recommendations, some followed Illinois' lead to reform, while others continued to maintain criminal penalties. A few states, especially after the Supreme Court identified a constitutional right of privacy for the sexual intimacies of married couples (see, e.g. *Griswold v. Connecticut*, 381 U.S. 479 (1965)), cut back their sodomy laws to apply only to unmarried persons or to persons of the same sex. As legal activists began to bring lawsuits challenging the existence of these laws, the courts were forced to grapple with the asserted justifications for them, and to test them against newly emerging conceptions of human sexuality. As is frequently the case, the courts lagged behind the social scientists in assimilating the newest scientific insights.

C. Sexual Minorities in the Courts

The remainder of this chapter is devoted to three major United States Supreme Court decisions that lay the groundwork for consideration of the constitutional rights of sexual minorities. They all concern claims by gay people that a particular state law or policy violates their constitutional rights protected by the 14th Amendment of the federal Constitution. In addition, there is one decision by the highest court of a state addressing the willingness of the state to recognize the reality of transgender existence by taking official note of a "sex change."

In 1986 the Supreme Court addressed the constitutional status of gay people for the first time in *Bowers v. Hardwick*, embracing an analysis of the Due Process Clause that was to set the pattern for much of the federal constitutional litigation about gay rights for at least a decade.

An organized legal movement for gay rights had emerged in the mid-1960s, seeking to build upon the Supreme Court's privacy decisions in cases such as *Griswold v. Connecticut* (1965), which struck down a state law banning the sale or use of contraceptives to prevent pregnancy, and *Stanley v. Georgia* (1969), which invalidated a criminal conviction for private possession of obscene materials. In both cases, the Supreme Court suggested that liberty protected by the Due Process Clause from inadequately justified governmental invasion included a right of privacy that was broad enough to encompass personal preference in matters of sexual expression. This trend continued in cases like *Roe v. Wade* (1973) and *Carey v. Population Services International* (1977), in which the court found the constitutional privacy right was broad enough to protect a woman's right to terminate her pregnancy or a teenager's right to obtain contraceptives.

Gay rights proponents challenged the laws that criminalized their sex lives by building on these precedents, with mixed results. In some cases, state courts proved receptive to the arguments and invalidated sodomy laws or limited their application in New York, Iowa, and Massachusetts. In other cases, the efforts failed, most spectacularly in *Doe v. Commonwealth's Attorney for City of Richmond* (1975), where a three-judge federal court rejected a constitutional challenge to Virginia's sodomy law and the Supreme Court summarily affirmed the ruling in 1976, without taking time to hear oral argument and receive briefs on the merits. The degree of precedential weight to be given this decision was a point of controversy in the lower courts until *Bowers* made it irrelevant in 1986.

Two cases reached the Supreme Court in the mid-1980s presenting the sodomy law issue, *Baker v. Wade* from Texas, in which the 5th Circuit rejected a challenge to that state's Homosexual Conduct Law, and *Bowers v. Hardwick* from Georgia, in which the 11th Circuit suggested that the state's felony sodomy law might violate the Due Process Clause. The Court granted certiorari in *Bowers*, and reversed, denied rehearing, and then denied certiorari in *Baker v. Wade*. From 1986 until 2003, *Bowers* stood as the Supreme Court's statement on the privacy rights of gay people under the Due Process Clause.

But lower federal courts and some state courts decided that *Bowers* was also significant in deciding how to address equality claims raised by gay litigants in a wide variety of contexts. As these courts construed it, *Bowers* stood for the proposition that "homosexuals" were not entitled to protection under the 14th Amendment, whether the issue was privacy or equal protection, because it accepted the argument that societal moral disapproval of a particular group—or at least of the conduct that in some way defined the group—could justify government disfavor for that group. This rationale was particularly prominent in cases challenging military regulations providing for expulsion of gay service members.

The gay rights movement after *Bowers* turned more towards state court and legislative strategies, and began to win enactment of local ordinances and some state laws banning sexual orientation discrimination while achieving some victories invalidating sodomy laws under state constitutions. As more "gay rights" laws were enacted, those opposed to any kind of "special rights" (in the form of legal civil rights protection) for sexual minorities petitioned for referenda to overturn these laws. By the early 1990s a new referendum strategy had emerged, seeking to amend state constitutions and municipal charters to prohibit the enactment of laws to protect the civil rights of sexual minorities. In 1992, almost identically worded referenda of this sort were on the ballot in Oregon and Colorado. The Oregon measure was defeated, but the Colorado measure, called Amendment 2, was enacted, triggering a lawsuit that resulted in the Court's 1996 decision in *Romer v. Evans*.

In *Romer v. Evans*, the Court tore at the conceptual underpinnings of *Bowers* without directly confronting that decision (or even mentioning it), as it signaled the Court's discomfort with the idea that majority moral disapproval could suffice to justify unequal treatment. And *Romer* clearly signaled to the lower federal and state courts that *Bowers* could not be relied upon to reject the equal protection claims of sexual minorities without more serious analysis of the merits of a claim.

In 2003, in *Lawrence v. Texas*, the court overruled *Bowers* and, building on the implications of its decision in *Romer*, established what may become a new framework for the constitutional analysis of gay rights claims. Using expansive language about the liberty interest protected under the Due Process Clause, the Court declared that *Bowers* had been inconsistent with its own sexual privacy precedents of the 1960s and 1970s, and was wrong when it was decided. However, as in *Romer*, the Court's discussion did not expose a clear, precise doctrinal basis for its ruling, so it is uncertain how *Lawrence* will function as a precedent when courts confront the many issues that sexual minority litigants are likely to raise.

Understanding this sequence of three Supreme Court opinions is the necessary foundation for the study of sexual minority rights as they will unfold in American constitutional law during the first part of the 21st century. We have added to this trilogy the Maryland Court of Appeals decision in Matter of Heilig in order to surface basic legal questions raised by the phenomenon of gender identity variation. The Supreme Court has yet to address constitutional issues raised by gender identity and expression in the context of transsexuality, having denied several certiorari petitions in significant cases. The most basic question is whether, and under what circumstances, the law will accept the proposition that a person's gender identity may differ from their anatomical sex at birth. The Heilig decision provides a thoughtful basis for beginning to address that question.

In reading the gay rights trilogy of *Bowers*, *Romer* and *Lawrence*, take special note of the differing ways in which these opinions characterize the constitutional landscape that existed when *Bowers* was argued in 1986 and the changes in constitutional doctrine over the following period. This sequence of cases provides an extraordinary example of the maleability of constitutional doctrine, derived from an open-textured document that articulates broad, general principles, and provides as well an opportunity for reflecting on different theories of constitutional interpretation.

Bowers v. Hardwick
478 U.S. 186 (1986)

Justice WHITE delivered the opinion of the Court.

In August 1982, respondent was charged with violating the Georgia statute criminalizing sodomy[1] by committing that act with another adult male in the bedroom of respondent's home. After a preliminary hearing, the District Attorney decided not to present the matter to the grand jury unless further evidence developed.

Respondent then brought suit in the Federal District Court, challenging the constitutionality of the statute insofar as it criminalized consensual sodomy.[2] He asserted that he was a practicing homosexual, that the Georgia sodomy statute, as administered by the defendants, placed him in imminent danger of arrest, and that the statute for several reasons violates the Federal Constitution. The District Court granted the defendants' motion to dismiss for failure to state a claim...

A divided panel of the Court of Appeals for the Eleventh Circuit reversed. Relying on our decisions in Griswold v. Connecticut, 381 U.S. 479 (1965), Eisenstadt v. Baird, 405 U.S. 438 (1972), Stanley v. Georgia, 394 U.S. 557 (1969), and Roe v. Wade, 410 U.S. 113 (1973), the court [held] that the Georgia statute violated respondent's fundamental rights because his homosexual activity is a private and intimate association that is beyond the reach of state regulation by reason of the Ninth Amendment and the Due Process Clause of the Fourteenth Amendment. The case was remanded for trial, at which, to prevail, the State would have to prove that the statute is supported by a compelling interest and is the most narrowly drawn means of achieving that end. Because other Courts of Appeals have arrived at judgments contrary to that of the Eleventh Circuit in this case, we granted the State's petition for certiorari. We agree with the State that the Court of Appeals erred, and hence reverse its judgment.

This case does not require a judgment on whether laws against sodomy between consenting adults in general, or between homosexuals in particular, are wise or desirable. It raises no question about the right or propriety of state legislative decisions to repeal their laws that criminalize homosexual sodomy, or of state court decisions invalidating those laws on state constitutional grounds. The issue presented is whether the Federal Constitution confers a fundamental right upon homosexuals to engage in sodomy and hence invalidates the laws of the many States that still make such conduct illegal and have done so for a very long time. The case also calls for some judgment about the limits of the Court's role in carrying out its constitutional mandate.

We first register our disagreement with the Court of Appeals and with respondent that the Court's prior cases have construed the Constitution to confer a right of privacy that extends to homosexual sodomy and for all intents and purposes have decided this case. The reach of this line of cases was sketched in Carey v. Population Services International, 431 U.S. 678, 685 (1977). Pierce v. Society of Sisters, 268 U.S. 510 (1925), and Meyer v. Nebraska, 262 U.S. 390 (1923), were described as dealing with child rearing and education; Prince v. Massachusetts, 321 U.S. 158 (1944), with family relationships; Skinner v. Oklahoma ex rel. Williamson, 316 U.S. 535 (1942), with procreation;

---

1. Ga.Code Ann. § 16-6-2 (1984) provides, in pertinent part, as follows: "(a) A person commits the offense of sodomy when he performs or submits to any sexual act involving the sex organs of one person and the mouth or anus of another...."(b) A person convicted of the offense of sodomy shall be punished by imprisonment for not less than one nor more than 20 years...."

2. John and Mary Doe were also plaintiffs in the action. They alleged that they wished to engage in sexual activity proscribed by § 16-6-2 in the privacy of their home and that they had been "chilled and deterred" from engaging in such activity by both the existence of the statute and Hardwick's arrest. The District Court held, however, that because they had neither sustained, nor were in immediate danger of sustaining, any direct injury from the enforcement of the statute, they did not have proper standing to maintain the action.... The only claim properly before the Court, therefore, is Hardwick's challenge to the Georgia statute as applied to consensual homosexual sodomy. We express no opinion on the constitutionality of the Georgia statute as applied to other acts of sodomy.

Loving v. Virginia, 388 U.S. 1 (1967), with marriage; Griswold v. Connecticut and Eisenstadt v. Baird with contraception; and Roe v. Wade with abortion. The latter three cases were interpreted as construing the Due Process Clause of the Fourteenth Amendment to confer a fundamental individual right to decide whether or not to beget or bear a child.

Accepting the decisions in these cases and the above description of them, we think it evident that none of the rights announced in those cases bears any resemblance to the claimed constitutional right of homosexuals to engage in acts of sodomy. No connection between family, marriage, or procreation on the one hand and homosexual activity on the other has been demonstrated, either by the Court of Appeals or by respondent. Moreover, any claim that these cases nevertheless stand for the proposition that any kind of private sexual conduct between consenting adults is constitutionally insulated from state proscription is unsupportable. Indeed, the Court's opinion in Carey twice asserted that the privacy right, which the Griswold line of cases found to be one of the protections provided by the Due Process Clause, did not reach so far.

[R]espondent would have us announce a fundamental right to engage in homosexual sodomy. This we are quite unwilling to do. It is true that despite the language of the Due Process Clauses of the Fifth and Fourteenth Amendments, which appears to focus only on the processes by which life, liberty, or property is taken, the cases are legion in which those Clauses have been interpreted to have substantive content, subsuming rights that to a great extent are immune from federal or state regulation or proscription. Among such cases are those recognizing rights that have little or no textual support in the constitutional language. Striving to assure itself and the public that announcing rights not readily identifiable in the Constitution's text involves much more than the imposition of the Justices' own choice of values on the States and the Federal Government, the Court has sought to identify the nature of the rights qualifying for heightened judicial protection. In Palko v. Connecticut, 302 U.S. 319, 325, 326 (1937), it was said that this category includes those fundamental liberties that are "implicit in the concept of ordered liberty," such that "neither liberty nor justice would exist if [they] were sacrificed." A different description of fundamental liberties appeared in Moore v. East Cleveland, 431 U.S. 494, 503 (1977) (opinion of POWELL, J.), where they are characterized as those liberties that are "deeply rooted in this Nation's history and tradition."

It is obvious to us that neither of these formulations would extend a fundamental right to homosexuals to engage in acts of consensual sodomy. Proscriptions against that conduct have ancient roots. Sodomy was a criminal offense at common law and was forbidden by the laws of the original thirteen States when they ratified the Bill of Rights. In 1868, when the Fourteenth Amendment was ratified, all but 5 of the 37 States in the Union had criminal sodomy laws. In fact, until 1961,[3] all 50 States outlawed sodomy, and today, 24 States and the District of Columbia continue to provide criminal penalties for sodomy performed in private and between consenting adults. Against this background, to claim that a right to engage in such conduct is "deeply rooted in this Nation's history and tradition" or "implicit in the concept of ordered liberty" is, at best, facetious.

---

3. In 1961, Illinois adopted the American Law Institute's Model Penal Code, which decriminalized adult, consensual, private, sexual conduct. Criminal Code of 1961, ss 11-2, 11-3, 1961 Ill.Laws 1985, 2006 (codified as amended at Ill.Rev.Stat., ch. 38, PP 11-2, 11-3 (1983) (repealed 1984). See American Law Institute, Model Penal Code s 213.2 (Proposed Official Draft 1962).

Nor are we inclined to take a more expansive view of our authority to discover new fundamental rights. The Court is most vulnerable and comes nearest to illegitimacy when it deals with judge-made constitutional law having little or no cognizable roots in the language or design of the Constitution. That this is so was painfully demonstrated by the face-off between the Executive and the Court in the 1930s, which resulted in the repudiation of much of the substantive gloss that the Court had placed on the Due Process Clause of the Fifth and Fourteenth Amendments. There should be, therefore, great resistance to expand the substantive reach of those Clauses, particularly if it requires redefining the category of rights deemed to be fundamental. Otherwise, the Judiciary necessarily takes to itself further authority to govern the country without express constitutional authority. The claimed right pressed on us today falls far short of overcoming this resistance.

Respondent, however, asserts that the result should be different where the homosexual conduct occurs in the privacy of the home. He relies on Stanley v. Georgia, 394 U.S. 557 (1969), where the Court held that the First Amendment prevents conviction for possessing and reading obscene material in the privacy of his home: "If the First Amendment means anything, it means that a State has no business telling a man, sitting alone in his house, what books he may read or what films he may watch."

Stanley did protect conduct that would not have been protected outside the home, and it partially prevented the enforcement of state obscenity laws; but the decision was firmly grounded in the First Amendment. The right pressed upon us here has no similar support in the text of the Constitution, and it does not qualify for recognition under the prevailing principles for construing the Fourteenth Amendment. Its limits are also difficult to discern. Plainly enough, otherwise illegal conduct is not always immunized whenever it occurs in the home. Victimless crimes, such as the possession and use of illegal drugs do not escape the law where they are committed at home. Stanley itself recognized that its holding offered no protection for the possession in the home of drugs, firearms, or stolen goods. And if respondent's submission is limited to the voluntary sexual conduct between consenting adults, it would be difficult, except by fiat, to limit the claimed right to homosexual conduct while leaving exposed to prosecution adultery, incest, and other sexual crimes even though they are committed in the home. We are unwilling to start down that road.

Even if the conduct at issue here is not a fundamental right, respondent asserts that there must be a rational basis for the law and that there is none in this case other than the presumed belief of a majority of the electorate in Georgia that homosexual sodomy is immoral and unacceptable. This is said to be an inadequate rationale to support the law. The law, however, is constantly based on notions of morality, and if all laws representing essentially moral choices are to be invalidated under the Due Process Clause, the courts will be very busy indeed. Even respondent makes no such claim, but insists that majority sentiments about the morality of homosexuality should be declared inadequate. We do not agree, and are unpersuaded that the sodomy laws of some 25 States should be invalidated on this basis.[4] Accordingly, the judgment of the Court of Appeals is Reversed.

Chief Justice BURGER, concurring.

I write separately to underscore my view that in constitutional terms there is no such thing as a fundamental right to commit homosexual sodomy. As the Court notes, the

---

4. Respondent does not defend the judgment below based on the Ninth Amendment, the Equal Protection Clause or the Eighth Amendment.

proscriptions against sodomy have very "ancient roots." Decisions of individuals relating to homosexual conduct have been subject to state intervention throughout the history of Western Civilization. Condemnation of those practices is firmly rooted in Judeao-Christian moral and ethical standards. Homosexual sodomy was a capital crime under Roman law. See Code Theod. 9.7.6; Code Just. 9.9.31. See also D. Bailey, Homosexuality in the Western Christian Tradition 70–81 (1975). During the English Reformation when powers of the ecclesiastical courts were transferred to the King's Courts, the first English statute criminalizing sodomy was passed. 25 Hen. VIII, c. 6. Blackstone described "the infamous crime against nature" as an offense of "deeper malignity" than rape, an heinous act "the very mention of which is a disgrace to human nature," and "a crime not fit to be named." Blackstone's Commentaries. The common law of England, including its prohibition of sodomy, became the received law of Georgia and the other Colonies. In 1816 the Georgia Legislature passed the statute at issue here, and that statute has been continuously in force in one form or another since that time. To hold that the act of homosexual sodomy is somehow protected as a fundamental right would be to cast aside millennia of moral teaching. This is essentially not a question of personal "preferences" but rather of the legislative authority of the State. I find nothing in the Constitution depriving a State of the power to enact the statute challenged here.

Justice POWELL, concurring.

I agree with the Court that there is no fundamental right—i.e., no substantive right under the Due Process Clause—such as that claimed by respondent. This is not to suggest, however, that respondent may not be protected by the Eighth Amendment. The Georgia statute at issue in this case authorizes a court to imprison a person for up to 20 years for a single private, consensual act of sodomy. In my view, a prison sentence for such conduct—certainly a sentence of long duration—would create a serious Eighth Amendment issue. Under the Georgia statute a single act of sodomy, even in the private setting of a home, is a felony comparable in terms of the possible sentence imposed to serious felonies such as aggravated battery, first degree arson, and robbery. In this case, however, respondent has not been tried, much less convicted and sentenced.[5] Moreover, respondent has not raised the Eighth Amendment issue below. For these reasons this constitutional argument is not before us.

Justice BLACKMUN, with whom Justice BRENNAN, Justice MARSHALL, and Justice STEVENS join, dissenting.

This case is no more about "a fundamental right to engage in homosexual sodomy," as the Court purports to declare, than Stanley v. Georgia was about a fundamental right to watch obscene movies, or Katz v. United States, 389 U.S. 347 (1967), was about a fundamental right to place interstate bets from a telephone booth. Rather, this case is about "the most comprehensive of rights and the right most valued by civilized men,"

---

5. It was conceded at oral argument that, prior to the complaint against respondent Hardwick, there had been no reported decision involving prosecution for private homosexual sodomy under this statute for several decades...Moreover, the State has declined to present the criminal charge against Hardwick to a grand jury...The history of nonenforcement suggests the moribund character today of laws criminalizing this type of private, consensual conduct. Some 26 states have repealed similar statutes. But the constitutional validity of the Georgia statute was put in issue by respondent, and for the reasons stated by the Court, I cannot say that conduct condemned for hundreds of years has now become a fundamental right.

namely, "the right to be let alone." Olmstead v. United States, 277 U.S. 438, 478 (1928) (Brandeis, J., dissenting).

The statute at issue, Ga.Code Ann. § 16-6-2, denies individuals the right to decide for themselves whether to engage in particular forms of private, consensual sexual activity. The Court concludes that § 16-6-2 is valid essentially because "the laws of...many States...still make such conduct illegal and have done so for a very long time." But the fact that the moral judgments expressed by statutes like § 16-6-2 may be "natural and familiar...ought not to conclude our judgment upon the question whether statutes embodying them conflict with the Constitution of the United States." Like Justice Holmes, I believe that "[i]t is revolting to have no better reason for a rule of law than that so it was laid down in the time of Henry IV. It is still more revolting if the grounds upon which it was laid down have vanished long since, and the rule simply persists from blind imitation of the past." Holmes, The Path of the Law, 10 Harv.L.Rev. 457, 469 (1897). I believe we must analyze respondent's claim in the light of the values that underlie the constitutional right to privacy. If that right means anything, it means that, before Georgia can prosecute its citizens for making choices about the most intimate aspects of their lives, it must do more than assert that the choice they have made is an "'abominable crime not fit to be named among Christians.'" Herring v. State, 119 Ga. 709, 721 (1904).

In its haste to reverse the Court of Appeals and hold that the Constitution does not "confe[r] a fundamental right upon homosexuals to engage in sodomy," the Court relegates the actual statute being challenged to a footnote and ignores the procedural posture of the case before it. The majority has distorted the question this case presents.

First, the Court's almost obsessive focus on homosexual activity is particularly hard to justify in light of the broad language Georgia has used. Unlike the Court, the Georgia Legislature has not proceeded on the assumption that homosexuals are so different from other citizens that their lives may be controlled in a way that would not be tolerated if it limited the choices of those other citizens. Rather, Georgia has provided that "[a] person commits the offense of sodomy when he performs or submits to any sexual act involving the sex organs of one person and the mouth or anus of another." The sex or status of the persons who engage in the act is irrelevant as a matter of state law. In fact, to the extent I can discern a legislative purpose for Georgia's 1968 enactment of § 16-6-2, that purpose seems to have been to broaden the coverage of the law to reach heterosexual as well as homosexual activity.[6] I therefore see no basis for the Court's decision to treat this case as an "as applied" challenge, or for Georgia's attempt, both in its brief and at oral argument, to defend solely on the grounds that it prohibits homosexual activity. Michael Hardwick's standing may rest in significant part on Georgia's apparent willingness to enforce against homosexuals a law it seems not to have any desire to enforce against heterosexuals. But his claim that § 16-6-2 involves an unconstitutional intrusion into his privacy and his right of intimate association does not depend in any way on his sexual orientation.

---

6. Until 1968, Georgia defined sodomy as "the carnal knowledge and connection against the order of nature, by man with man, or in the same unnatural manner with woman." Ga. Crim. Code § 26-5901 (1933). In Thompson v. Aldredge, 187 Ga. 467, 200 S.E. 799 (1939), the Georgia Supreme Court held that § 26-5901 did not prohibit lesbian activity. And in Riley v. Garrett, 219 Ga. 345, 133 S.E.2d 367 (1963), the Georgia Supreme Court held that § 26-5901 did not prohibit heterosexual cunnilingus. Georgia passed the act-specific statute currently in force "perhaps in response to the restrictive court decisions such as Riley." Note, The Crimes Against Nature, 16 J.Pub.L. 159, 167, n. 47 (1967).

Second, I disagree with the Court's refusal to consider whether § 16-6-2 runs afoul of the Eighth or Ninth Amendments or the Equal Protection Clause of the Fourteenth Amendment. Respondent's complaint expressly invoked the Ninth Amendment, and he relied heavily before this Court on Griswold v. Connecticut, which identifies that Amendment as one of the specific constitutional provisions giving "life and substance" to our understanding of privacy. More importantly, the procedural posture of the case requires that we affirm the Court of Appeals' judgment if there is any ground on which respondent may be entitled to relief. I need not reach either the Eighth Amendment or the Equal Protection Clause issues because I believe that Hardwick has stated a cognizable claim that § 16-6-2 interferes with constitutionally protected interests in privacy and freedom of intimate association. But neither the Eighth Amendment nor the Equal Protection Clause is so clearly irrelevant that a claim resting on either provision should be peremptorily dismissed.[7] With respect to the Equal Protection Clause's applicability, I note that Georgia's exclusive stress before this Court on its interest in prosecuting homosexual activity despite the gender-neutral terms of the statute may raise serious questions of discriminatory enforcement. The legislature having decided that the sex of the participants is irrelevant to the legality of the acts, I do not see why the State can defend on the ground that individuals singled out for prosecution are of the same sex as their partners. Thus, under the circumstances of this case, a claim under the Equal Protection Clause may well be available without having to reach the more controversial question whether homosexuals are a suspect class. The Court's cramped reading of the issue before it makes for a short opinion, but it does little to make for a persuasive one.

"Our cases long have recognized that the Constitution embodies a promise that a certain private sphere of individual liberty will be kept largely beyond the reach of government." In construing the right to privacy, the Court has proceeded along two somewhat distinct, albeit complementary, lines. First, it has recognized a privacy interest with reference to certain decisions that are properly for the individual to make. Second, it has recognized a privacy interest with reference to certain places without regard for the particular activities in which the individuals who occupy them are engaged. The case before us implicates both the decisional and the spatial aspects of the right to privacy.

The Court concludes today that none of our prior cases dealing with various decisions that individuals are entitled to make free of governmental interference "bears any resemblance to the claimed constitutional right of homosexuals to engage in acts of sodomy that is asserted in this case." While it is true that these cases may be characterized by their connection to protection of the family, the Court's conclusion that they extend no further than this boundary ignores the warning in Moore v. East Cleveland against "clos[ing] our eyes to the basic reasons why certain rights associated with the

---

7. In Robinson v. California, 370 U.S. 660 (1962), the Court held that the Eighth Amendment barred convicting a defendant due to his "status" as a narcotics addict, since that condition was "apparently an illness which may be contracted innocently or involuntarily."....

Despite historical views of homosexuality, it is no longer viewed by mental health professionals as a "disease" or disorder. But, obviously, neither is it simply a matter of deliberate personal election. Homosexual orientation may well form part of the very fiber of an individual's personality.... [T]he Eighth Amendment may pose a constitutional barrier to sending an individual to prison for acting on that attraction regardless of the circumstances. An individual's ability to make constitutionally protected "decisions concerning sexual relations," Carey v. Population Services International, 431 U.S. 678, 711 (1977) (POWELL, J.), is rendered empty indeed if he or she is given no real choice but a life without any physical intimacy.

family have been accorded shelter under the Fourteenth Amendment's Due Process Clause." We protect those rights not because they contribute, in some direct and material way, to the general public welfare, but because they form so central a part of an individual's life. "[T]he concept of privacy embodies the 'moral fact that a person belongs to himself and not others nor to society as a whole.'" Thornburgh, 106 S.Ct., at 2187, n. 5 (STEVENS, J., concurring), quoting Fried, Correspondence, 6 Phil. & Pub. Affairs 288–89 (1977). And so we protect the decision whether to marry precisely because marriage "is an association that promotes a way of life, not causes; a harmony in living, not political faiths; a bilateral loyalty, not commercial or social projects." Griswold, 381 U.S., at 486. We protect the decision whether to have a child because parenthood alters so dramatically an individual's self-definition, not because of demographic considerations or the Bible's command to be fruitful and multiply. And we protect the family because it contributes so powerfully to the happiness of individuals, not because of a preference for stereotypical households. The Court [has] recognized that the "ability independently to define one's identity that is central to any concept of liberty" cannot truly be exercised in a vacuum; we all depend on the "emotional enrichment of close ties with others."

Only the most willful blindness could obscure the fact that sexual intimacy is "a sensitive, key relationship of human existence, central to family life, community welfare, and the development of human personality," Paris Adult Theatre I v. Slaton, 413 U.S. 49, 63 (1973). The fact that individuals define themselves in a significant way through their intimate sexual relationships with others suggests, in a Nation as diverse as ours, that there may be many "right" ways of conducting those relationships, and that much of the richness of a relationship will come from the freedom an individual has to choose the form and nature of these intensely personal bonds.

In a variety of circumstances we have recognized that a necessary corollary of giving individuals freedom to choose how to conduct their lives is acceptance of the fact that different individuals will make different choices. "A way of life that is odd or even erratic but interferes with no rights or interests of others is not to be condemned because it is different." The Court claims that its decision today merely refuses to recognize a fundamental right to engage in homosexual sodomy; what the Court really has refused to recognize is the fundamental interest all individuals have in controlling the nature of their intimate associations with others.

The behavior for which Hardwick faces prosecution occurred in his own home, a place to which the Fourth Amendment attaches special significance. Even when our understanding of the contours of the right to privacy depends on "reference to a 'place,' the essence of a Fourth Amendment violation is 'not the breaking of [a person's] doors, and the rummaging of his drawers,' but rather is 'the invasion of his indefeasible right of personal security, personal liberty and private property.'" California v. Ciraolo, 106 S.Ct. 1809, 1819 (1986) (POWELL, J., dissenting), quoting Boyd v. United States, 116 U.S. 616, 630 (1886).

The Court's interpretation of the pivotal case of Stanley v. Georgia is entirely unconvincing. Stanley held that Georgia's undoubted power to punish the public distribution of constitutionally unprotected, obscene material did not permit the State to punish the private possession of such material. According to the majority here, Stanley relied entirely on the First Amendment, and thus, it is claimed, sheds no light on cases not involving printed materials. But that is not what Stanley said. Rather, the Stanley Court anchored its holding in the Fourth Amendment's special protection for the individual in his home: "'The makers of our Constitution undertook to secure conditions favorable to the pursuit of happiness. They recognized the significance of man's spiritual nature, of his feelings and of his intellect. They knew that only a part of the pain, pleasure and satisfactions of life are to be found in material things. They sought to protect Americans in their beliefs, their thoughts, their emotions and their sensations.' * * * "These are the rights that appellant is asserting in the case before us. He is asserting the right to read or observe what he pleases—the right to satisfy his intellectual and emotional needs in the privacy of his own home." Id., at 564–65, quoting Olmstead v. United States, 277 U.S., at 478 (Brandeis, J., dissenting).

The central place that Stanley gives Justice Brandeis' dissent in Olmstead, a case raising no First Amendment claim, shows that Stanley rested as much on the Court's understanding of the Fourth Amendment as it did on the First. Indeed, in Paris Adult Theatre the Court suggested that reliance on the Fourth Amendment not only supported the Court's outcome in Stanley but actually was necessary to it: "If obscene material unprotected by the First Amendment in itself carried with it a 'penumbra' of constitutionally protected privacy, this Court would not have found it necessary to decide Stanley on the narrow basis of the 'privacy of the home,' which was hardly more than a reaffirmation that 'a man's home is his castle.'" "The right of the people to be secure in their houses," expressly guaranteed by the Fourth Amendment, is perhaps the most "textual" of the various constitutional provisions that inform our understanding of the right to privacy, and thus I cannot agree with the Court's statement that "[t]he right pressed upon us here has no support in the text of the Constitution." Indeed, the right of an individual to conduct intimate relationships in the intimacy of his or her own home seems to me to be the heart of the Constitution's protection of privacy.

The Court's failure to comprehend the magnitude of the liberty interests at stake in this case leads it to slight the question whether petitioner, on behalf of the State, has justified Georgia's infringement on these interests. I believe that neither of the two general justifications that petitioner has advanced warrants dismissing respondent's challenge for failure to state a claim.

First, petitioner asserts that the acts made criminal by the statute may have serious adverse consequences for "the general public health and welfare," such as spreading communicable diseases or fostering other criminal activity. Inasmuch as this case was dismissed by the District Court on the pleadings, it is not surprising that the record before us is barren of any evidence to support petitioner's claim.[8] I see no justification for the Court's attempt to equate the private, consensual sexual activity at issue here with the "possession in the home of drugs, firearms, or stolen goods," to which Stanley refused to extend its protection. None of the behavior so mentioned in Stanley can properly be viewed as "[v]ictimless." Nothing in the record before the Court provides any justification for finding the activity forbidden by § 16-6-2 to be physically dangerous, either to the persons engaged in it or to others.[9]

---

8. Even if a court faced with a challenge to § 16-6-2 were to apply simple rational-basis scrutiny to the statute, Georgia would be required to show an actual connection between the forbidden acts and the ill effects it seeks to prevent. The connection between the acts prohibited by § 16-6-2 and the harms identified by petitioner in his brief before this Court is a subject of hot dispute, hardly amenable to dismissal.

9. Although I do not think it necessary to decide today issues that are not even remotely before us, it does seem to me that a court could find simple, analytically sound distinctions between certain private, consensual sexual conduct, on the one hand, and adultery and incest (the only two vaguely specific "sexual crimes" to which the majority points) on the other. Notably, the Court makes no effort to explain why it has chosen to group private, consensual homosexual activity with

The core of petitioner's defense, however, is that respondent and others who engage in the conduct prohibited by § 16-6-2 interfere with Georgia's exercise of the "'right of the Nation and of the States to maintain a decent society,'" Paris Adult Theatre, quoting Jacobellis v. Ohio, 378 U.S. 184, 199 (1964) (Warren, C.J., dissenting). Essentially, petitioner argues, and the Court agrees, that the fact that the acts described in § 16-6-2 "for hundreds of years, if not thousands, have been uniformly condemned as immoral" is a sufficient reason to permit a State to ban them today.

I cannot agree that either the length of time a majority has held its convictions or the passions with which it defends them can withdraw legislation from this Court's scrutiny. As Justice Jackson wrote so eloquently for the Court in West Virginia Board of Education v. Barnette, 319 U.S. 624, 641–42, (1943), "we apply the limitations of the Constitution with no fear that freedom to be intellectually and spiritually diverse or even contrary will disintegrate the social organization. Freedom to differ is not limited to things that do not matter much. That would be a mere shadow of freedom. The test of its substance is the right to differ as to things that touch the heart of the existing order." It is precisely because the issue raised by this case touches the heart of what makes individuals what they are that we should be especially sensitive to the rights of those whose choices upset the majority.

The assertion that "traditional Judeo-Christian values proscribe" the conduct involved cannot provide an adequate justification. That certain, but by no means all, religious groups condemn the behavior at issue gives the State no license to impose their judgments on the entire citizenry. The legitimacy of secular legislation depends instead on whether the State can advance some justification for its law beyond its conformity to religious doctrine. Thus, far from buttressing his case, petitioner's invocation of Leviticus, Romans, St. Thomas Aquinas, and sodomy's heretical status during the Middle Ages undermines his suggestion that § 16-6-2 represents a legitimate use of secular coercive power.[10] A State can no more punish private behavior because of religious intolerance than it can punish such behavior because of racial animus. "The Constitution cannot control such prejudices, but neither can it tolerate them. Private biases may be outside the reach of the law, but the law cannot, directly or indirectly give them effect." Palmore v. Sidoti, 466 U.S. 429, 433 (1984). No matter how uncomfortable a certain group may make the majority of this Court, we have held that "[m]ere public intolerance or animosity cannot constitutionally justify the deprivation of a person's physical liberty." O'Connor v. Donaldson, 422 U.S. 563, 575 (1975).

Nor can § 16-6-2 be justified as a "morally neutral" exercise of Georgia's power to "protect the public environment," Paris Adult Theatre I. Certainly, some private behavior can affect the fabric of society as a whole. Reasonable people may differ about whether particular sexual acts are moral or immoral, but "we have ample evidence for

---

adultery and incest rather than with private, consensual heterosexual activity by unmarried persons or, indeed, with oral or anal sex within marriage.

10. The theological nature of the origin of Anglo-American antisodomy statutes is patent. It was not until 1533 that sodomy was made a secular offense in England. 25 Hen. VIII, cap. 6. Until that time, the offense was, in Sir James Stephen's words, "merely ecclesiastical." 2 J. Stephen, A History of the Criminal Law of England 430 (1883). Pollock and Maitland similarly observed that "[t]he crime against nature was so closely connected with heresy that the vulgar had but one name for both." 2 F. Pollock & F. Maitland, The History of English Law 554 (1895). The transfer of jurisdiction over prosecutions for sodomy to the secular courts seems primarily due to the alteration of ecclesiastical jurisdiction attendant on England's break with the Roman Catholic Church, rather than to any new understanding of the sovereign's interest in preventing or punishing the behavior involved. Cf. E. Coke, The Third Part of the Institutes of the Laws of England, ch. 10 (4th ed. 1797).

believing that people will not abandon morality, will not think any better of murder, cruelty and dishonesty, merely because some private sexual practice which they abominate is not punished by the law." H.L.A. Hart, Immorality and Treason. Petitioner and the Court fail to see the difference between laws that protect public sensibilities and those that enforce private morality. Statutes banning public sexual activity are entirely consistent with protecting the individual's liberty interest in decisions concerning sexual relations: the same recognition that those decisions are intensely private which justifies protecting them from governmental interference can justify protecting individuals from unwilling exposure to the sexual activities of others. But the mere fact that intimate behavior may be punished when it takes place in public cannot dictate how States can regulate intimate behavior that occurs in intimate places. This case involves no real interference with the rights of others, for the mere knowledge that other individuals do not adhere to one's value system cannot be a legally cognizable interest, let alone an interest that can justify invading the houses, hearts, and minds of citizens who choose to live their lives differently.

It took but three years for the Court to see the error in its analysis in Minersville School District v. Gobitis, 310 U.S. 586 (1940), and to recognize that the threat to national cohesion posed by a refusal to salute the flag was vastly outweighed by the threat to those same values posed by compelling such a salute. I can only hope that here, too, the Court soon will reconsider its analysis and conclude that depriving individuals of the right to choose for themselves how to conduct their intimate relationships poses a far greater threat to the values most deeply rooted in our Nation's history than tolerance of nonconformity could ever do. Because I think the Court today betrays those values, I dissent.

Justice STEVENS, with whom Justice BRENNAN and Justice MARSHALL join, dissenting.

Like the statute that is challenged in this case, the rationale of the Court's opinion applies equally to the prohibited conduct regardless of whether the parties who engage in it are married or unmarried, or are of the same or different sexes. Sodomy was condemned as an odious and sinful type of behavior during the formative period of the common law. That condemnation was equally damning for heterosexual and homosexual sodomy. Moreover, it provided no special exemption for married couples. The license to cohabit and to produce legitimate offspring simply did not include any permission to engage in sexual conduct that was considered a "crime against nature."

The history of the Georgia statute before us clearly reveals this traditional prohibition of heterosexual, as well as homosexual, sodomy. Indeed, at one point in the 20th century, Georgia's law was construed to permit certain sexual conduct between homosexual women even though such conduct was prohibited between heterosexuals. The history of the statutes cited by the majority as proof for the proposition that sodomy is not constitutionally protected similarly reveals a prohibition on heterosexual, as well as homosexual, sodomy.

Because the Georgia statute expresses the traditional view that sodomy is an immoral kind of conduct regardless of the identity of the persons who engage in it, I believe that a proper analysis of its constitutionality requires consideration of two questions: First, may a State totally prohibit the described conduct by means of a neutral law applying without exception to all persons subject to its jurisdiction? If not, may the State save the statute by announcing that it will only enforce the law against homosexuals?

That the governing majority in a State has traditionally viewed a particular practice as immoral is not a sufficient reason for upholding a law prohibiting the practice; neither history nor tradition could save a law prohibiting miscegenation from constitutional attack. Individual decisions by married persons, concerning the intimacies of their physical relationship, even when not intended to produce offspring, are a form of "liberty" protected by the Due Process Clause of the Fourteenth Amendment. Moreover, this protection extends to intimate choices by unmarried as well as married persons. As I wrote some years ago:

> "These cases do not deal with the individual's interest in protection from unwarranted public attention, comment, or exploitation. They deal, rather, with the individual's right to make certain unusually important decisions that will affect his own, or his family's, destiny. The Court has referred to such decisions as implicating 'basic values,' as being 'fundamental,' and as being dignified by history and tradition. The character of the Court's language in these cases brings to mind the origins of the American heritage of freedom—the abiding interest in individual liberty that makes certain state intrusions on the citizen's right to decide how he will live his own life intolerable. Guided by history, our tradition of respect for the dignity of individual choice in matters of conscience and the restraints implicit in the federal system, federal judges have accepted the responsibility for recognition and protection of these rights in appropriate cases." Fitzgerald v. Porter Memorial Hospital, 523 F.2d 716, 719–20 (CA7 1975) (footnotes omitted), cert. denied, 425 U.S. 916 (1976).

Society has every right to encourage its individual members to follow particular traditions in expressing affection for one another and in gratifying their personal desires. It, of course, may prohibit an individual from imposing his will on another to satisfy his own selfish interests. It also may prevent an individual from interfering with, or violating, a legally sanctioned and protected relationship, such as marriage. And it may explain the relative advantages and disadvantages of different forms of intimate expression. But when individual married couples are isolated from observation by others, the way in which they voluntarily choose to conduct their intimate relations is a matter for them— not the State—to decide. The essential "liberty" that animated the development of the law in cases like Griswold, Eisenstadt, and Carey surely embraces the right to engage in non-reproductive, sexual conduct that others may consider offensive or immoral.

Our prior cases thus establish that a State may not prohibit sodomy within "the sacred precincts of marital bedrooms," or, indeed, between unmarried heterosexual adults. In all events, it is perfectly clear that the State of Georgia may not totally prohibit the conduct proscribed by § 16-6-2.

If the Georgia statute cannot be enforced as it is written, the State must assume the burden of justifying a selective application of its law. Either the persons to whom Georgia seeks to apply its statute do not have the same interest in "liberty" that others have, or there must be a reason why the State may be permitted to apply a generally applicable law to certain persons that it does not apply to others.

The first possibility is plainly unacceptable. Every free citizen has the same interest in "liberty" that the members of the majority share. From the standpoint of the individual, the homosexual and the heterosexual have the same interest in deciding how he will live his own life, and, more narrowly, how he will conduct himself in his personal and voluntary associations with his companions. State intrusion into the private conduct of either is equally burdensome.

The second possibility is similarly unacceptable. A policy of selective application must be supported by a neutral and legitimate interest—something more substantial than a habitual dislike for, or ignorance about, the disfavored group. Neither the State nor the Court has identified any such interest in this case. The Court has posited as a justification for the Georgia statute "the presumed belief of a majority of the electorate in Georgia that homosexual sodomy is immoral and unacceptable." But the Georgia electorate has expressed no such belief—instead, its representatives enacted a law that presumably reflects the belief that all sodomy is immoral and unacceptable. Unless the Court is prepared to conclude that such a law is constitutional, it may not rely on the work product of the Georgia Legislature to support its holding. The record of non-enforcement, in this case and in the last several decades, belies the Attorney General's representations about the importance of the State's selective application of its generally applicable law.

The Court orders the dismissal of respondent's complaint even though the State's statute prohibits all sodomy; even though that prohibition is concededly unconstitutional with respect to heterosexuals; and even though the State's post hoc explanations for selective application are belied by the State's own actions. At the very least, I think it clear at this early stage of the litigation that respondent has alleged a constitutional claim sufficient to withhold a motion to dismiss.

* * *

Romer v. Evans
517 U.S. 620 (1996)

Justice KENNEDY delivered the opinion of the Court.

One century ago, the first Justice Harlan admonished this Court that the Constitution "neither knows nor tolerates classes among citizens." *Plessy v. Ferguson*, 163 U.S. 537, 559 (1896) (dissenting opinion). Unheeded then, those words now are understood to state a commitment to the law's neutrality where the rights of persons are at stake. The Equal Protection Clause enforces this principle and today requires us to hold invalid a provision of Colorado's Constitution.

I.

The enactment challenged in this case is an amendment to the Constitution of the State of Colorado, adopted in a 1992 statewide referendum. The parties and the state courts refer to it as "Amendment 2," its designation when submitted to the voters. The impetus for the amendment and the contentious campaign that preceded its adoption came in large part from ordinances that had been passed in various Colorado municipalities. For example, the cities of Aspen and Boulder and the city and County of Denver each had enacted ordinances which banned discrimination in many transactions and activities, including housing, employment, education, public accommodations, and health and welfare services. Denver Rev. Municipal Code, Art. IV, §§ 28-91 to 28-116 (1991); Aspen Municipal Code § 13-98 (1977); Boulder Rev.Code §§ 12-1-1 to 12-1-11 (1987). What gave rise to the statewide controversy was the protection the ordinances afforded to persons discriminated against by reason of their sexual orientation. See Boulder Rev.Code § 12-1-1 (defining "sexual orientation" as "the choice of sexual partners, i.e., bisexual, homosexual or heterosexual"); Denver Rev. Municipal Code, Art. IV, § 28-92 (defining "sexual orientation" as "[t]he status of an individual as to his or her heterosexuality, homosexuality or bisexuality"). Amendment 2 repeals these ordinances to the extent they prohibit discrimination on the basis of "homosexual, lesbian or bisexual orientation, conduct, practices or relationships." Colo. Const., Art. II, § 30b.

Yet Amendment 2, in explicit terms, does more than repeal or rescind these provisions. It prohibits all legislative, executive or judicial action at any level of state or local government designed to protect the named class, a class we shall refer to as homosexual persons or gays and lesbians. The amendment reads:

"No Protected Status Based on Homosexual, Lesbian or Bisexual Orientation. Neither the State of Colorado, through any of its branches or departments, nor any of its agencies, political subdivisions, municipalities or school districts, shall enact, adopt or enforce any statute, regulation, ordinance or policy whereby homosexual, lesbian or bisexual orientation, conduct, practices or relationships shall constitute or otherwise be the basis of or entitle any person or class of persons to have or claim any minority status, quota preferences, protected status or claim of discrimination. This Section of the Constitution shall be in all respects self-executing."

Soon after Amendment 2 was adopted, this litigation to declare its invalidity and enjoin its enforcement was commenced in the District Court for the City and County of Denver. Among the plaintiffs (respondents here) were homosexual persons, some of them government employees. They alleged that enforcement of Amendment 2 would subject them to immediate and substantial risk of discrimination on the basis of their sexual orientation. Other plaintiffs (also respondents here) included the three municipalities whose ordinances we have cited and certain other governmental entities which had acted earlier to protect homosexuals from discrimination but would be prevented by Amendment 2 from continuing to do so. Although Governor Romer had been on record opposing the adoption of Amendment 2, he was named in his official capacity as a defendant, together with the Colorado Attorney General and the State of Colorado.

The trial court granted a preliminary injunction to stay enforcement of Amendment 2, and an appeal was taken to the Supreme Court of Colorado. Sustaining the interim injunction and remanding the case for further proceedings, the State Supreme Court held that Amendment 2 was subject to strict scrutiny under the Fourteenth Amendment because it infringed the fundamental right of gays and lesbians to participate in the political process. *Evans v. Romer*, 854 P.2d 1270 (Colo.1993) (*Evans I*). To reach this conclusion, the state court relied on our voting rights cases, *e.g., Reynolds v. Sims*, 377 U.S. 533 (1964); *Carrington v. Rash*, 380 U.S. 89 (1965); *Harper v. Virginia Bd. of Elections*, 383 U.S. 663 (1966); *Williams v. Rhodes*, 393 U.S. 23 (1968), and on our precedents involving discriminatory restructuring of governmental decision-making, see, *e.g., Hunter v. Erickson*, 393 U.S. 385 (1969); *Reitman v. Mulkey*, 387 U.S. 369 (1967); *Washington v. Seattle School Dist. No. 1*, 458 U.S. 457 (1982); *Gordon v. Lance*, 403 U.S. (1971). On remand, the State advanced various arguments in an effort to show that Amendment 2 was narrowly tailored to serve compelling interests, but the trial court found none sufficient. It enjoined enforcement of Amendment 2, and the Supreme Court of Colorado, in a second opinion, affirmed the ruling. 882 P.2d 1335 (1994) (*Evans II*). We granted certiorari and now affirm the judgment, but on a rationale different from that adopted by the State Supreme Court.

II.

The State's principal argument in defense of Amendment 2 is that it puts gays and lesbians in the same position as all other persons. So, the State says, the measure does no more than deny homosexuals special rights. This reading of the amendment's language is implausible. We rely not upon our own interpretation of the amendment but upon the authoritative construction of Colorado's Supreme Court. The state court, deeming it unnecessary to determine the full extent of the amendment's reach, found it invalid even on a modest reading of its implications. The critical discussion of the amendment, set out in *Evans I,* is as follows:

> The immediate objective of Amendment 2 is, at a minimum, to repeal existing statutes, regulations, ordinances, and policies of state and local entities that barred discrimination based on sexual orientation. The 'ultimate effect' of Amendment 2 is to prohibit any governmental entity from adopting similar, or more protective statutes, regulations, ordinances, or policies in the future unless the state constitution is first amended to permit such measures.

Sweeping and comprehensive is the change in legal status effected by this law. So much is evident from the ordinances the Colorado Supreme Court declared would be void by operation of Amendment 2. Homosexuals, by state decree, are put in a solitary class with respect to transactions and relations in both the private and governmental spheres. The amendment withdraws from homosexuals, but no others, specific legal protection from the injuries caused by discrimination, and it forbids reinstatement of these laws and policies.

The change Amendment 2 works in the legal status of gays and lesbians in the private sphere is far reaching, both on its own terms and when considered in light of the structure and operation of modern anti-discrimination laws. That structure is well illustrated by contemporary statutes and ordinances prohibiting discrimination by providers of public accommodations. "At common law, innkeepers, smiths, and others who 'made profession of a public employment,' were prohibited from refusing, without good reason, to serve a customer." *Hurley v. Irish-American Gay, Lesbian and Bisexual Group of Boston, Inc.,* 515 U.S. 557, 571 (1995). The duty was a general one and did not specify protection for particular groups. The common-law rules, however, proved insufficient in many instances, and it was settled early that the Fourteenth Amendment did not give Congress a general power to prohibit discrimination in public accommodations, *Civil Rights Cases,* 109 U.S. 3, 25 (1883). In consequence, most States have chosen to counter discrimination by enacting detailed statutory schemes.

Colorado's state and municipal laws typify this emerging tradition of statutory protection and follow a consistent pattern. The laws first enumerate the persons or entities subject to a duty not to discriminate. The list goes well beyond the entities covered by the common law. The Boulder ordinance, for example, has a comprehensive definition of entities deemed places of "public accommodation." They include "any place of business engaged in any sales to the general public and any place that offers services, facilities, privileges, or advantages to the general public or that receives financial support through solicitation of the general public or through governmental subsidy of any kind." Boulder Rev.Code § 12-1-1(j) (1987). The Denver ordinance is of similar breadth, applying, for example, to hotels, restaurants, hospitals, dental clinics, theaters, banks, common carriers, travel and insurance agencies, and "shops and stores dealing with goods or services of any kind," Denver Rev. Municipal Code, Art. IV, § 28-92 (1991).

These statutes and ordinances also depart from the common law by enumerating the groups or persons within their ambit of protection. Enumeration is the essential device used to make the duty not to discriminate concrete and to provide guidance for those who must comply. In following this approach, Colorado's state and local governments have not limited anti-discrimination laws to groups that have so far been given the protection of heightened equal protection scrutiny under our cases. Rather, they set forth an extensive catalog of traits which cannot be the basis for discrimination, including age, military status, marital status, pregnancy, parenthood, custody of a minor child, political affiliation, physical or mental disability of an individual or of his or her associates—and, in recent times, sexual orientation. Aspen Municipal Code § 13-98(a)(1) (1977); Boulder Rev.Code §§ 12-1-1 to 12-1-4 (1987); Denver Rev. Municipal Code, Art. IV, §§ 28-92 to 28-119 (1991); Colo.Rev.Stat. §§ 24-34-401 to 24-34-707 (1988 and Supp.1995).

Amendment 2 bars homosexuals from securing protection against the injuries that these public-accommodations laws address. That in itself is a severe consequence, but there is more. Amendment 2, in addition, nullifies specific legal protections for this targeted class in all transactions in housing, sale of real estate, insurance, health and welfare services, private education, and employment. See, *e.g.*, Aspen Municipal Code §§ 13-98(b), (c) (1977); Boulder Rev.Code §§ 12-1-2, 12-1-3 (1987); Denver Rev. Municipal Code, Art. IV, §§ 28-93 to 28-95, 28-97 (1991).

Not confined to the private sphere, Amendment 2 also operates to repeal and forbid all laws or policies providing specific protection for gays or lesbians from discrimination by every level of Colorado government. The State Supreme Court cited two examples of protections in the governmental sphere that are now rescinded and may not be reintroduced. The first is Colorado Executive Order D0035 (1990), which forbids employment discrimination against "'all state employees, classified and exempt' on the basis of sexual orientation." Also repealed, and now forbidden, are "various provisions prohibiting discrimination based on sexual orientation at state colleges." The repeal of these measures and the prohibition against their future re-enactment, demonstrate that Amendment 2 has the same force and effect in Colorado's governmental sector as it does elsewhere and that it applies to policies as well as ordinary legislation.

Amendment 2's reach may not be limited to specific laws passed for the benefit of gays and lesbians. It is a fair, if not necessary, inference from the broad language of the amendment that it deprives gays and lesbians even of the protection of general laws and policies that prohibit arbitrary discrimination in governmental and private settings. At some point in the systematic administration of these laws, an official must determine whether homosexuality is an arbitrary and, thus, forbidden basis for decision. Yet a decision to that effect would itself amount to a policy prohibiting discrimination on the basis of homosexuality, and so would appear to be no more valid under Amendment 2 than the specific prohibitions against discrimination the state court held invalid.

If this consequence follows from Amendment 2, as its broad language suggests, it would compound the constitutional difficulties the law creates. The state court did not decide whether the amendment has this effect, however, and neither need we. In the course of rejecting the argument that Amendment 2 is intended to conserve resources to fight discrimination against suspect classes, the Colorado Supreme Court made the limited observation that the amendment is not intended to affect many anti-discrimination laws protecting non-suspect classes. In our view that does not resolve the issue. In any event, even if, as we doubt, homosexuals could find some safe harbor in laws of general application, we cannot accept the view that Amendment 2's prohibition on specific legal protections does no more than deprive homosexuals of special rights. To the contrary, the amendment imposes a special disability upon those persons alone. Homosexuals are forbidden the safeguards that others enjoy or may seek without constraint. They can obtain specific protection against discrimination only by enlisting the citizenry of Colorado to amend the State Constitution or perhaps, on the State's view, by trying to pass helpful laws of general applicability. This is so no matter how local or discrete the harm, no matter how public and widespread the injury. We find nothing special in the protections Amendment 2 withholds. These are protections taken for granted by most people either because they already have them or do not need them; these are protections against exclusion from an almost limitless number of transactions and endeavors that constitute ordinary civic life in a free society.

III.

The Fourteenth Amendment's promise that no person shall be denied the equal protection of the laws must coexist with the practical necessity that most legislation classifies for one purpose or another, with resulting disadvantage to various groups or persons. *Personnel Administrator of Mass. v. Feeney,* 442 U.S. 256 (1979); *F.S. Royster Guano Co. v. Virginia,* 253 U.S. 412, 415 (1920). We have attempted to reconcile the principle with the reality by stating that, if a law neither burdens a fundamental right nor targets a suspect class, we will uphold the legislative classification so long as it bears a rational relation to some legitimate end. See, *e.g., Heller v. Doe,* 509 U.S. 312, 319–20 (1993).

Amendment 2 fails, indeed defies, even this conventional inquiry. First, the amendment has the peculiar property of imposing a broad and undifferentiated disability on a single named group, an exceptional and, as we shall explain, invalid form of legislation. Second, its sheer breadth is so discontinuous with the reasons offered for it that the amendment seems inexplicable by anything but animus toward the class it affects; it lacks a rational relationship to legitimate state interests.

Taking the first point, even in the ordinary equal protection case calling for the most deferential of standards, we insist on knowing the relation between the classification adopted and the object to be attained. The search for the link between classification and objective gives substance to the Equal Protection Clause; it provides guidance and discipline for the legislature, which is entitled to know what sorts of laws it can pass; and it marks the limits of our own authority. In the ordinary case, a law will be sustained if it can be said to advance a legitimate government interest, even if the law seems unwise or works to the disadvantage of a particular group, or if the rationale for it seems tenuous. See *New Orleans v. Dukes,* 427 U.S. 297 (1976) (tourism benefits justified classification favoring pushcart vendors of certain longevity); *Williamson v. Lee Optical of Okla., Inc.,* 348 U.S. 483 (1955) (assumed health concerns justified law favoring optometrists over opticians); *Railway Express Agency, Inc. v. New York,* 336 U.S. 106 (1949) (potential traffic hazards justified exemption of vehicles advertising the owner's products from general advertising ban); *Kotch v. Board of River Port Pilot Comm'rs for Port of New Orleans,* 330 U.S. 552 (1947) (licensing scheme that disfavored persons unrelated to current river boat pilots justified by possible efficiency and safety benefits of a closely knit pilotage system). The laws challenged in the cases just cited were narrow enough in scope and grounded in a sufficient factual context for us to ascertain some relation between the classification and the purpose it served. By requiring that the classification bear a rational relationship to an independent and legitimate legislative end, we ensure that classifications are not drawn for the purpose of disadvantaging the group burdened by the law.

Amendment 2 confounds this normal process of judicial review. It is at once too narrow and too broad. It identifies persons by a single trait and then denies them protection across the board. The resulting disqualification of a class of persons from the right to seek specific protection from the law is unprecedented in our jurisprudence. The absence of precedent for Amendment 2 is itself instructive; "discriminations of an unusual character especially suggest careful consideration to determine whether they are obnoxious to the constitutional provision." *Louisville Gas & Elec. Co. v. Coleman,* 277 U.S. 32, 37–38 (1928).

It is not within our constitutional tradition to enact laws of this sort. Central both to the idea of the rule of law and to our own Constitution's guarantee of equal protection is the principle that government and each of its parts remain open on impartial terms to all who seek its assistance. "'Equal protection of the laws is not achieved through indiscriminate imposition of inequalities.'" *Sweatt v. Painter*, 339 U.S. 629, 635 (1950) (quoting *Shelley v. Kraemer*, 334 U.S. 1, 22 (1948)). Respect for this principle explains why laws singling out a certain class of citizens for disfavored legal status or general hardships are rare. A law declaring that in general it shall be more difficult for one group of citizens than for all others to seek aid from the government is itself a denial of equal protection of the laws in the most literal sense. "The guaranty of 'equal protection of the laws is a pledge of the protection of equal laws.'" *Skinner v. Oklahoma ex rel. Williamson*, 316 U.S. 535, 541 (1942) (quoting *Yick Wo v. Hopkins*, 118 U.S. 356, 369 (1886)).

Davis v. Beason, 133 U.S. 333 (1890), not cited by the parties but relied upon by the dissent, is not evidence that Amendment 2 is within our constitutional tradition, and any reliance upon it as authority for sustaining the amendment is misplaced. In *Davis*, the Court approved an Idaho territorial statute denying Mormons, polygamists, and advocates of polygamy the right to vote and to hold office because, as the Court construed the statute, it "simply excludes from the privilege of voting, or of holding any office of honor, trust or profit, those who have been convicted of certain offences, and those who advocate a practical resistance to the laws of the Territory and justify and approve the commission of crimes forbidden by it." To the extent *Davis* held that persons advocating a certain practice may be denied the right to vote, it is no longer good law. To the extent it held that the groups designated in the statute may be deprived of the right to vote because of their status, its ruling could not stand without surviving strict scrutiny, a most doubtful outcome. To the extent *Davis* held that a convicted felon may be denied the right to vote, its holding is not implicated by our decision and is unexceptionable.

A second and related point is that laws of the kind now before us raise the inevitable inference that the disadvantage imposed is born of animosity toward the class of persons affected. "If the constitutional conception of 'equal protection of the laws' means anything, it must at the very least mean that a bare desire to harm a politically unpopular group cannot constitute a *legitimate* governmental interest." *Department of Agriculture v. Moreno*, 413 U.S. 528, 534 (1973). Even laws enacted for broad and ambitious purposes often can be explained by reference to legitimate public policies which justify the incidental disadvantages they impose on certain persons. Amendment 2, however, in making a general announcement that gays and lesbians shall not have any particular protections from the law, inflicts on them immediate, continuing, and real injuries that outrun and belie any legitimate justifications that may be claimed for it. We conclude that, in addition to the far-reaching deficiencies of Amendment 2 that we have noted, the principles it offends, in another sense, are conventional and venerable; a law must bear a rational relationship to a legitimate governmental purpose, *Kadrmas v. Dickinson Public Schools*, 487 U.S. 450, 462 (1988), and Amendment 2 does not.

The primary rationale the State offers for Amendment 2 is respect for other citizens' freedom of association, and in particular the liberties of landlords or employers who have personal or religious objections to homosexuality. Colorado also cites its interest in conserving resources to fight discrimination against other groups. The breadth of the amendment is so far removed from these particular justifications that we find it impossible to credit them. We cannot say that Amendment 2 is directed to any identifiable legitimate purpose or discrete objective. It is a status-based enactment divorced from any factual context from which we could discern a relationship to legitimate state interests; it is a classification of persons undertaken for its own sake, something the Equal Protection Clause does not permit. "Class legislation is obnoxious to the prohibitions of the Fourteenth Amendment." *Civil Rights Cases,* 109 U.S., at 24.

We must conclude that Amendment 2 classifies homosexuals not to further a proper legislative end but to make them unequal to everyone else. This Colorado cannot do. A State cannot so deem a class of persons a stranger to its laws. Amendment 2 violates the Equal Protection Clause, and the judgment of the Supreme Court of Colorado is affirmed. *It is so ordered.*

Justice SCALIA, *with whom* THE CHIEF JUSTICE *and Justice* THOMAS *join, dissenting.*

The Court has mistaken a Kulturkampf for a fit of spite. The constitutional amendment before us here is not the manifestation of a "'bare desire to harm'" homosexuals, but is rather a modest attempt by seemingly tolerant Coloradans to preserve traditional sexual mores against the efforts of a politically powerful minority to revise those mores through use of the laws. That objective, and the means chosen to achieve it, are not only unimpeachable under any constitutional doctrine hitherto pronounced (hence the opinion's heavy reliance upon principles of righteousness rather than judicial holdings); they have been specifically approved by the Congress of the United States and by this Court.

In holding that homosexuality cannot be singled out for disfavorable treatment, the Court contradicts a decision, unchallenged here, pronounced only 10 years ago, see *Bowers v. Hardwick,* 478 U.S. 186 (1986), and places the prestige of this institution behind the proposition that opposition to homosexuality is as reprehensible as racial or religious bias. Whether it is or not is *precisely* the cultural debate that gave rise to the Colorado constitutional amendment (and to the preferential laws against which the amendment was directed). Since the Constitution of the United States says nothing about this subject, it is left to be resolved by normal democratic means, including the democratic adoption of provisions in state constitutions. This Court has no business imposing upon all Americans the resolution favored by the elite class from which the Members of this institution are selected, pronouncing that "animosity" toward homosexuality is evil. I vigorously dissent.

I.

Let me first discuss Part II of the Court's opinion, its longest section, which is devoted to rejecting the State's arguments that Amendment 2 "puts gays and lesbians in the same position as all other persons," and "does no more than deny homosexuals special rights." The Court concludes that this reading of Amendment 2's language is "implausible" under the "authoritative construction" given Amendment 2 by the Supreme Court of Colorado.

In reaching this conclusion, the Court considers it unnecessary to decide the validity of the State's argument that Amendment 2 does not deprive homosexuals of the "protection afforded by general laws and policies that prohibit arbitrary discrimination in governmental and private settings." I agree that we need not resolve that dispute, because the Supreme Court of Colorado has resolved it for us. In the case below, the Colorado court stated:

It is significant to note that Colorado law currently proscribes discrimination against persons who are not suspect classes, including discrimination based on age, § 24-34-402(1)(a), 10A C.R.S. (1994 Supp.); marital or family status, § 24-

34-502(1)(a), 10A C.R.S. (1994 Supp.); veterans' status, § 28-3-506, 11B C.R.S. (1989); and for any legal, off-duty conduct such as smoking tobacco, § 24-34-402.5, 10A C. R.S. (1994 Supp.). Of course Amendment 2 is not intended to have any effect on this legislation, but seeks only to prevent the adoption of anti-discrimination laws intended to protect gays, lesbians, and bisexuals.

The Court utterly fails to distinguish this portion of the Colorado court's opinion. Colorado Rev. Stat. § 24-34-402.5 (Supp.1995), which this passage authoritatively declares not to be affected by Amendment 2, was respondents' primary example of a generally applicable law whose protections would be unavailable to homosexuals under Amendment 2. The clear import of the Colorado court's conclusion that it is not affected is that "general laws and policies that prohibit arbitrary discrimination" would continue to prohibit discrimination on the basis of homosexual conduct as well. This analysis, which is fully in accord with (indeed, follows inescapably from) the text of the constitutional provision, lays to rest such horribles, raised in the course of oral argument, as the prospect that assaults upon homosexuals could not be prosecuted. The amendment prohibits special treatment of homosexuals, and nothing more. It would not affect, for example, a requirement of state law that pensions be paid to all retiring state employees with a certain length of service; homosexual employees, as well as others, would be entitled to that benefit. But it would prevent the State or any municipality from making death-benefit payments to the "life partner" of a homosexual when it does not make such payments to the long-time roommate of a non-homosexual employee. Or again, it does not affect the requirement of the State's general insurance laws that customers be afforded coverage without discrimination unrelated to anticipated risk. Thus, homosexuals could not be denied coverage, or charged a greater premium, with respect to auto collision insurance; but neither the State nor any municipality could require that distinctive health insurance risks associated with homosexuality (if there are any) be ignored.

Despite all of its hand wringing about the potential effect of Amendment 2 on general anti-discrimination laws, the Court's opinion ultimately does not dispute all this, but assumes it to be true. The only denial of equal treatment it contends homosexuals have suffered is this: They may not obtain *preferential* treatment without amending the State Constitution. That is to say, the principle underlying the Court's opinion is that one who is accorded equal treatment under the laws, but cannot as readily as others obtain *preferential* treatment under the laws, has been denied equal protection of the laws. If merely stating this alleged "equal protection" violation does not suffice to refute it, our constitutional jurisprudence has achieved terminal silliness.

The central thesis of the Court's reasoning is that any group is denied equal protection when, to obtain advantage (or, presumably, to avoid disadvantage), it must have recourse to a more general and hence more difficult level of political decision-making than others. The world has never heard of such a principle, which is why the Court's opinion is so long on emotive utterance and so short on relevant legal citation. And it seems to me most unlikely that any multilevel democracy can function under such a principle. For *whenever* a disadvantage is imposed, or conferral of a benefit is prohibited, at one of the higher levels of democratic decision-making (*i.e.*, by the state legislature rather than local government, or by the people at large in the state constitution rather than the legislature), the affected group has (under this theory) been denied equal protection. To take the simplest of examples, consider a state law prohibiting the award of municipal contracts to relatives of mayors or city councilmen. Once such a law is passed, the group composed of such relatives must, in order to get the benefit of city contracts, persuade the state legislature—unlike all other citizens, who need only persuade the municipality. It is ridiculous to consider this a denial of equal protection, which is why the Court's theory is unheard of.

The Court might reply that the example I have given is *not* a denial of equal protection only because the same "rational basis" (avoidance of corruption) which renders constitutional the *substantive discrimination* against relatives (*i.e.*, the fact that they alone cannot obtain city contracts) also automatically suffices to sustain what might be called the *electoral-procedural discrimination* against them (*i.e.*, the fact that they must go to the state level to get this changed). This is of course a perfectly reasonable response, and would explain why "electoral-procedural discrimination" has not hitherto been heard of: A law that is valid in its substance is automatically valid in its level of enactment. But the Court cannot afford to make this argument, for as I shall discuss next, there is no doubt of a rational basis for the substance of the prohibition at issue here. The Court's entire novel theory rests upon the proposition that there is something *special*—something that cannot be justified by normal "rational basis" analysis—in making a disadvantaged group (or a non-preferred group) resort to a higher decision-making level. That proposition finds no support in law or logic.

II

I turn next to whether there was a legitimate rational basis for the substance of the constitutional amendment—for the prohibition of special protection for homosexuals.[11] It is unsurprising that the Court avoids discussion of this question, since the answer is so obviously yes. The case most relevant to the issue before us today is not even mentioned in the Court's opinion: In *Bowers v. Hardwick*, 478 U.S. 186 (1986), we held that the Constitution does not prohibit what virtually all States had done from the founding of the Republic until very recent years—making homosexual conduct a crime. That holding is unassailable, except by those who think that the Constitution changes to suit current fashions. But in any event it is a given in the present case: Respondents' briefs did not urge overruling *Bowers,* and at oral argument respondents' counsel expressly disavowed any intent to seek such overruling. If it is constitutionally permissible for a State to make homosexual conduct criminal, surely it is constitutionally permissible for a State to enact other laws merely *disfavoring* homosexual conduct. (As the Court of Appeals for the District of Columbia Circuit has aptly put it: "If the Court [in *Bowers*] was unwilling to object to state laws that criminalize the behavior that defines the class, it is hardly open to conclude that state sponsored discrimination against the class is invidious. After all, there can hardly be more palpable discrimination against a class than making the conduct that defines the class criminal." *Padula v. Webster,* 822 F.2d 97, 103 (1987).) And *a fortiori* it is constitutionally permissible for a State to adopt a provision *not even* disfavoring homosexual conduct, but merely prohibiting all levels of state government from bestowing *special protections* upon homosexual conduct. Respondents (who, unlike the Court, cannot afford the luxury of ignoring inconvenient precedent) counter *Bowers* with the argument that a greater-includes-the-lesser rationale cannot justify Amend-

---

11. The Court evidently agrees that "rational basis"—the normal test for compliance with the Equal Protection Clause—is the governing standard. The trial court rejected respondents' argument that homosexuals constitute a "suspect" or "quasi-suspect" class, and respondents elected not to appeal that ruling to the Supreme Court of Colorado. And the Court implicitly rejects the Supreme Court of Colorado's holding, *Evans v. Romer,* 854 P.2d 1270, 1282 (1993), that Amendment 2 infringes upon a "fundamental right" of "independently identifiable class[es]" to "participate equally in the political process."

ment 2's application to individuals who do not engage in homosexual acts, but are merely of homosexual "orientation." Some Courts of Appeals have concluded that, with respect to laws of this sort at least, that is a distinction without a difference. See *Equality Foundation of Greater Cincinnati, Inc. v. Cincinnati*, 54 F.3d 261, 267 (C.A.6 1995) ("For purposes of these proceedings, it is virtually impossible to distinguish or separate individuals of a particular *orientation* which predisposes them toward a particular sexual conduct from those who actually *engage* in that particular type of sexual conduct"); *Steffan v. Perry*, 41 F.3d 677, 689–90 (C.A.D.C.1994). The Supreme Court of Colorado itself appears to be of this view. See 882 P.2d, at 1349–50 ("Amendment 2 targets this class of persons based on four characteristics: sexual orientation; conduct; practices; and relationships. Each characteristic provides a potentially different way of identifying that class of persons who are gay, lesbian, or bisexual. These four characteristics are not truly severable from one another because each provides nothing more than a different way of identifying *the same class of persons*") (emphasis added).

But assuming that, in Amendment 2, a person of homosexual "orientation" is someone who does not engage in homosexual conduct but merely has a tendency or desire to do so, *Bowers* still suffices to establish a rational basis for the provision. If it is rational to criminalize the conduct, surely it is rational to deny special favor and protection to those with a self-avowed tendency or desire to engage in the conduct. Indeed, where criminal sanctions are not involved, homosexual "orientation" is an acceptable stand-in for homosexual conduct. A State "does not violate the Equal Protection Clause merely because the classifications made by its laws are imperfect," *Dandridge v. Williams*, 397 U.S. 471, 485 (1970). Just as a policy barring the hiring of methadone users as transit employees does not violate equal protection simply because *some* methadone users pose no threat to passenger safety, see *New York City Transit Authority v. Beazer*, 440 U.S. 568 (1979), and just as a mandatory retirement age of 50 for police officers does not violate equal protection even though it prematurely ends the careers of many policemen over 50 who still have the capacity to do the job, see *Massachusetts Bd. of Retirement v. Murgia*, 427 U.S. 307 (1976) *(per curiam)*, Amendment 2 is not constitutionally invalid simply because it could have been drawn more precisely so as to withdraw special anti-discrimination protections only from those of homosexual "orientation" who actually engage in homosexual conduct. As Justice KENNEDY wrote, when he was on the Court of Appeals, in a case involving discharge of homosexuals from the Navy: "Nearly any statute which classifies people may be irrational as applied in particular cases. Discharge of the particular plaintiffs before us would be rational, under minimal scrutiny, not because their particular cases present the dangers which justify Navy policy, but instead because the general policy of discharging all homosexuals is rational." *Beller v. Middendorf*, 632 F.2d 788, 808–9, n. 20 (C.A.9 1980).

Moreover, even if the provision regarding homosexual "orientation" *were* invalid, respondents' challenge to Amendment 2—which is a facial challenge—must fail. "A facial challenge to a legislative Act is, of course, the most difficult challenge to mount successfully, since the challenger must establish that no set of circumstances exists under which the Act would be valid." It would not be enough for respondents to establish (if they could) that Amendment 2 is unconstitutional as applied to those of homosexual "orientation"; since, under *Bowers*, Amendment 2 is unquestionably constitutional as applied to those who engage in homosexual conduct, the facial challenge cannot succeed. Some individuals of homosexual "orientation" who do not engage in homosexual acts might successfully bring an as-applied challenge to Amendment 2, but so far as the record indicates, none of the respondents is such a person. See App. 4-5 (complaint describing each of the individual respondents as either "a gay man" or "a lesbian").[12]

III

The foregoing suffices to establish what the Court's failure to cite any case remotely in point would lead one to suspect: No principle set forth in the Constitution, nor even any imagined by this Court in the past 200 years, prohibits what Colorado has done here. But the case for Colorado is much stronger than that. What it has done is not only unprohibited, but eminently reasonable, with close, congressionally approved precedent in earlier constitutional practice.

First, as to its eminent reasonableness. The Court's opinion contains grim, disapproving hints that Coloradans have been guilty of "animus" or "animosity" toward homosexuality, as though that has been established as un-American. Of course it is our moral heritage that one should not hate any human being or class of human beings. But I had thought that one could consider certain conduct reprehensible—murder, for example, or polygamy, or cruelty to animals—and could exhibit even "animus" toward such conduct. Surely that is the only sort of "animus" at issue here: moral disapproval of homosexual conduct, the same sort of moral disapproval that produced the centuries-old criminal laws that we held constitutional in *Bowers*. The Colorado amendment does not, to speak entirely precisely, prohibit giving favored status to people who are *homosexuals;* they can be favored for many reasons—for example, because they are senior citizens or members of racial minorities. But it prohibits giving them favored status *because of their homosexual conduct*—that is, it prohibits favored status *for homosexuality.*

But though Coloradans are, as I say, *entitled* to be hostile toward homosexual conduct, the fact is that the degree of hostility reflected by Amendment 2 is the smallest conceivable. The Court's portrayal of Coloradans as a society fallen victim to pointless, hate-filled "gay-bashing" is so false as to be comical. Colorado not only is one of the 25 States that have repealed their anti-sodomy laws, but was among the first to do so. But the society that eliminates criminal punishment for homosexual acts does not necessarily abandon the view that homosexuality is morally wrong and socially harmful; often, abolition simply reflects the view that enforcement of such criminal laws involves unseemly intrusion into the intimate lives of citizens.

There is a problem, however, which arises when criminal sanction of homosexuality is eliminated but moral and social disapprobation of homosexuality is meant to be retained. The Court cannot be unaware of that problem; it is evident in many cities of the country, and occasionally bubbles to the surface of the news, in heated political disputes over such matters as the introduction into local schools of books teaching that homosexuality is an optional and fully acceptable "alternative life style." The problem (a problem,

---

12. The Supreme Court of Colorado stated: "We hold that the portions of Amendment 2 that would remain if only the provision concerning sexual orientation were stricken are not autonomous and thus, not severable," 882 P.2d, at 1349. That statement was premised, however, on the proposition that "[the] four characteristics [described in the Amendment—sexual orientation, conduct, practices, and relationships] are not truly severable from one another because each provides nothing more than a different way of identifying *the same class of persons." Id.,* at 1349–50 (emphasis added). As I have discussed above, if that premise is true—if the entire class affected by the Amendment takes part in homosexual conduct, practices, and relationships—*Bowers* alone suffices to answer all constitutional objections. Separate consideration of persons of homosexual "orientation" is necessary only if one believes (as the Supreme Court of Colorado did not) that that is a distinct class.

that is, for those who wish to retain social disapprobation of homosexuality) is that, because those who engage in homosexual conduct tend to reside in disproportionate numbers in certain communities, and, of course, care about homosexual-rights issues much more ardently than the public at large, they possess political power much greater than their numbers, both locally and statewide. Quite understandably, they devote this political power to achieving not merely a grudging social toleration, but full social acceptance, of homosexuality. See, *e.g.*, Jacobs, The Rhetorical Construction of Rights: The Case of the Gay Rights Movement, 1969–1991, 72 Neb. L.Rev. 723, 724 (1993) ("The task of gay rights proponents is to move the center of public discourse along a continuum from the rhetoric of disapproval, to rhetoric of tolerance, and finally to affirmation").

By the time Coloradans were asked to vote on Amendment 2, their exposure to homosexuals' quest for social endorsement was not limited to newspaper accounts of happenings in places such as New York, Los Angeles, San Francisco, and Key West. Three Colorado cities—Aspen, Boulder, and Denver—had enacted ordinances that listed "sexual orientation" as an impermissible ground for discrimination, equating the moral disapproval of homosexual conduct with racial and religious bigotry. The phenomenon had even appeared statewide: The Governor of Colorado had signed an executive order pronouncing that "in the State of Colorado we recognize the diversity in our pluralistic society and strive to bring an end to discrimination in any form," and directing state agency-heads to "ensure non-discrimination" in hiring and promotion based on, among other things, "sexual orientation." I do not mean to be critical of these legislative successes; homosexuals are as entitled to use the legal system for reinforcement of their moral sentiments as is the rest of society. But they are subject to being countered by lawful, democratic countermeasures as well.

That is where Amendment 2 came in. It sought to counter both the geographic concentration and the disproportionate political power of homosexuals by (1) resolving the controversy at the statewide level, and (2) making the election a single-issue contest for both sides. It put directly, to all the citizens of the State, the question: Should homosexuality be given special protection? They answered no. The Court today asserts that this most democratic of procedures is unconstitutional. Lacking any cases to establish that facially absurd proposition, it simply asserts that it *must* be unconstitutional, because it has never happened before.

As I have noted above, this is proved false every time a state law prohibiting or disfavoring certain conduct is passed, because such a law prevents the adversely affected group—whether drug addicts, or smokers, or gun owners, or motorcyclists—from changing the policy thus established in "each of [the] parts" of the State. What the Court says is even demonstrably false at the constitutional level. The Eighteenth Amendment to the Federal Constitution, for example, deprived those who drank alcohol not only of the power to alter the policy of prohibition *locally* or through *state legislation,* but even of the power to alter it through *state constitutional amendment* or *federal legislation.* The Establishment Clause of the First Amendment prevents theocrats from having their way by converting their fellow citizens at the local, state, or federal statutory level; as does the Republican Form of Government Clause prevent monarchists.

But there is a much closer analogy, one that involves precisely the effort by the majority of citizens to preserve its view of sexual morality statewide, against the efforts of a geographically concentrated and politically powerful minority to undermine it. The Constitutions of the States of Arizona, Idaho, New Mexico, Oklahoma, and Utah *to this day* contain provisions stating that polygamy is "forever prohibited." Polygamists, and those who have a polygamous "orientation," have been "singled out" by these provisions for much more severe treatment than merely denial of favored status; and that treatment can only be changed by achieving amendment of the state constitutions. The Court's disposition today suggests that these provisions are unconstitutional, and that polygamy must be permitted in these States on a state-legislated, or perhaps even local-option, basis — unless, of course, polygamists for some reason have fewer constitutional rights than homosexuals.

The United States Congress, by the way, *required* the inclusion of these antipolygamy provisions in the Constitutions of Arizona, New Mexico, Oklahoma, and Utah, as a condition of their admission to statehood. Idaho adopted the constitutional provision on its own, but the 51st Congress, which admitted Idaho into the Union, found its Constitution to be "republican in form *and...in conformity with the Constitution of the United States.*" Thus, this "singling out" of the sexual practices of a single group for statewide, democratic vote — so utterly alien to our constitutional system, the Court would have us believe — has not only happened, but has received the explicit approval of the United States Congress.

I cannot say that this Court has explicitly approved any of these state constitutional provisions; but it has approved a territorial statutory provision that went even further, depriving polygamists of the ability even to achieve a constitutional amendment, by depriving them of the power to vote. In *Davis v. Beason*, 133 U.S. 333 (1890), Justice Field wrote for a unanimous Court:

> In our judgment, §501 of the Revised Statutes of Idaho Territory, which provides that 'no person who is a bigamist or polygamist or who teaches, advises, counsels, or encourages any person or persons to become bigamists or polygamists, or to commit any other crime defined by law, or to enter into what is known as plural or celestial marriage, or who is a member of any order, organization or association which teaches, advises, counsels, or encourages its members or devotees or any other persons to commit the crime of bigamy or polygamy, or any other crime defined by law is permitted to vote at any election, or to hold any position or office of honor, trust, or profit within this Territory,' *is not open to any constitutional or legal objection.*"

To the extent, if any, that this opinion permits the imposition of adverse consequences upon mere abstract advocacy of polygamy, it has, of course, been overruled by later cases. But the proposition that polygamy can be criminalized, and those engaging in that crime deprived of the vote, remains good law. See *Richardson v. Ramirez*, 418 U.S. 24, 53 (1974). *Beason* rejected the argument that "such discrimination is a denial of the equal protection of the laws." Among the Justices joining in that rejection were the two whose views in other cases the Court today treats as equal protection lodestars — Justice Harlan, who was to proclaim in *Plessy v. Ferguson*, 163 U.S. 537, 559 (1896) (dissenting opinion), that the Constitution "neither knows nor tolerates classes among citizens," and Justice Bradley, who had earlier declared that "class legislation...[is] obnoxious to the prohibitions of the Fourteenth Amendment," *Civil Rights Cases*, 109 U.S. 3, 24 (1883).

This Court cited *Beason* with approval as recently as 1993, in an opinion authored by the same Justice who writes for the Court today. That opinion said: "[A]dverse impact will not always lead to a finding of impermissible targeting. For example, a social harm may have been a legitimate concern of government for reasons quite apart from discrimination....See, *e.g.,...Davis v. Beason*, 133 U.S. 333 (1890)." *Church of Lukumi Babalu Aye, Inc. v. Hialeah*, 508 U.S. 520, 535 (1993). It remains to be explained how §501 of the Idaho Revised Statutes was not an "impermissible targeting" of polygamists, but (the much more mild) Amendment 2 is an "impermissible targeting" of homosexuals. Has the Court concluded that the perceived social harm of polygamy is a "legitimate concern of government," and the perceived social harm of homosexuality is not?

IV

I strongly suspect that the answer to the last question is yes, which leads me to the last point I wish to make: The Court today, announcing that Amendment 2 "defies conventional [constitutional] inquiry," and "confounds [the] normal process of judicial review," employs a constitutional theory heretofore unknown to frustrate Colorado's reasonable effort to preserve traditional American moral values. The Court's stern disapproval of "animosity" towards homosexuality might be compared with what an earlier Court (including the revered Justices Harlan and Bradley) said in *Murphy v. Ramsey*, 114 U.S. 15 (1885), rejecting a constitutional challenge to a United States statute that denied the franchise in federal territories to those who engaged in polygamous cohabitation:

> Certainly no legislation can be supposed more wholesome and necessary in the founding of a free, self-governing commonwealth, fit to take rank as one of the co-ordinate States of the Union, than that which seeks to establish it on the basis of the idea of the family, as consisting in and springing from the union for life of one man and one woman in the holy estate of matrimony; the sure foundation of all that is stable and noble in our civilization; the best guaranty of that reverent morality which is the source of all beneficent progress in social and political improvement.

I would not myself indulge in such official praise for heterosexual monogamy, because I think it no business of the courts (as opposed to the political branches) to take sides in this culture war.

But the Court today has done so, not only by inventing a novel and extravagant constitutional doctrine to take the victory away from traditional forces, but even by verbally disparaging as bigotry adherence to traditional attitudes. To suggest, for example, that this constitutional amendment springs from nothing more than "'a bare desire to harm a politically unpopular group,'" is nothing short of insulting. (It is also nothing short of preposterous to call "politically unpopular" a group which enjoys enormous influence in American media and politics, and which, as the trial court here noted, though composing no more than 4% of the population had the support of 46% of the voters on Amendment 2.)

When the Court takes sides in the culture wars, it tends to be with the knights rather than the villains—and more specifically with the Templars, reflecting the views and values of the lawyer class from which the Court's Members are drawn. How that class feels about homosexuality will be evident to anyone who wishes to interview job applicants at virtually any of the Nation's law schools. The interviewer may refuse to offer a job because the applicant is a Republican; because he is an adulterer; because he went to the wrong prep school or belongs to the wrong country club; because he eats snails; because he is a womanizer; because she wears real-animal fur; or even because he hates the Chicago Cubs. But if the interviewer should wish not to be an associate or partner of an applicant because he disapproves of the applicant's homosexuality, *then* he will have violated the pledge which the Association of American Law Schools requires all its member schools to exact from job interviewers: "assurance of the employer's willingness" to hire homosexuals. Bylaws of the Association of American Law Schools, Inc. §6-4(b); Executive Committee Regulations of the Association of American Law Schools §6.19, in 1995 Handbook, Association of American Law Schools. This law-school view of what "prejudices" must be stamped out may be contrasted with the more plebeian attitudes that apparently still prevail in the United States Congress, which has been unresponsive to repeated attempts to extend to homosexuals the protections of federal civil rights laws, and which took the pains to exclude them specifically from the Americans with Disabilities Act of 1990.

Today's opinion has no foundation in American constitutional law, and barely pretends to. The people of Colorado have adopted an entirely reasonable provision which does not even disfavor homosexuals in any substantive sense, but merely denies them preferential treatment. Amendment 2 is designed to prevent piecemeal deterioration of the sexual morality favored by a majority of Coloradans, and is not only an appropriate means to that legitimate end, but a means that Americans have employed before. Striking it down is an act, not of judicial judgment, but of political will. I dissent.

Lawrence v. Texas
539 U.S. 558 (2003)

Justice KENNEDY delivered the opinion of the Court.

Liberty protects the person from unwarranted government intrusions into a dwelling or other private places. In our tradition the State is not omnipresent in the home. And there are other spheres of our lives and existence, outside the home, where the State should not be a dominant presence. Freedom extends beyond spatial bounds. Liberty presumes an autonomy of self that includes freedom of thought, belief, expression, and certain intimate conduct. The instant case involves liberty of the person both in its spatial and more transcendent dimensions.

I

The question before the Court is the validity of a Texas statute making it a crime for two persons of the same sex to engage in certain intimate sexual conduct.

In Houston, Texas, officers of the Harris County Police Department were dispatched to a private residence in response to a reported weapons disturbance. They entered an apartment where one of the petitioners, John Geddes Lawrence, resided. The right of the police to enter does not seem to have been questioned. The officers observed Lawrence and another man, Tyron Garner, engaging in a sexual act. The two petitioners were arrested, held in custody over night, and charged and convicted before a Justice of the Peace. [The convictions were sustained on appeal by the state courts.]

The complaints described their crime as "deviate sexual intercourse, namely anal sex, with a member of the same sex (man)." Tex. Penal Code Ann. §21.06(a) (2003) provides: "A person commits an offense if he engages in deviate sexual intercourse with another individual of the same sex." The statute defines "[d]eviate sexual intercourse" as follows: "(A) any contact between any part of the genitals of one person and the mouth or anus of another person; or (B) the penetration of the genitals or the anus of another person with an object."

We granted certiorari to consider three questions: "1. Whether Petitioners' criminal convictions under the Texas 'Homosexual Conduct' law—which criminalizes sexual intimacy by same-sex couples, but not identical behavior by different-sex couples—violate the Fourteenth Amendment guarantee of equal protection of laws? "2. Whether Petitioners' criminal convictions for adult consensual sexual intimacy in the home violate their vital interests in liberty and privacy protected by the Due Process Clause of the Fourteenth Amendment? "3. Whether *Bowers v. Hardwick,* 478 U.S. 186 (1986), should be overruled?"

The petitioners were adults at the time of the alleged offense. Their conduct was in private and consensual.

II

We conclude the case should be resolved by determining whether the petitioners were free as adults to engage in the private conduct in the exercise of their liberty under the Due Process Clause of the Fourteenth Amendment to the Constitution. For this inquiry we deem it necessary to reconsider the Court's holding in *Bowers*.

There are broad statements of the substantive reach of liberty under the Due Process Clause in earlier cases, but the most pertinent beginning point is our decision in *Griswold v. Connecticut,* 381 U.S. 479 (1965). In *Griswold* the Court invalidated a state law prohibiting the use of drugs or devices of contraception and counseling or aiding and abetting the use of contraceptives. The Court described the protected interest as a right to privacy and placed emphasis on the marriage relation and the protected space of the marital bedroom. After *Griswold* it was established that the right to make certain decisions regarding sexual conduct extends beyond the marital relationship. In *Eisenstadt v. Baird,* 405 U.S. 438 (1972), the Court invalidated a law prohibiting the distribution of contraceptives to unmarried persons. The case was decided under the Equal Protection Clause; but with respect to unmarried persons, the Court went on to state the fundamental proposition that the law impaired the exercise of their personal rights. It quoted from the statement of the Court of Appeals finding the law to be in conflict with fundamental human rights, and it followed with this statement of its own:

> "It is true that in *Griswold* the right of privacy in question inhered in the marital relationship....If the right of privacy means anything, it is the right of the *individual,* married or single, to be free from unwarranted governmental intrusion into matters so fundamentally affecting a person as the decision whether to bear or beget a child."

The opinions in *Griswold* and *Eisenstadt* were part of the background for the decision in *Roe v. Wade,* 410 U.S. 113 (1973). Although the Court held the woman's rights were not absolute, her right to elect an abortion did have real and substantial protection as an exercise of her liberty under the Due Process Clause. The Court cited cases that protect spatial freedom and cases that go well beyond it. *Roe* recognized the right of a woman to make certain fundamental decisions affecting her destiny and confirmed once more that the protection of liberty under the Due Process Clause has a substantive dimension of fundamental significance in defining the rights of the person.

In *Carey v. Population Services Int'l,* 431 U.S. 678 (1977), the Court confronted a New York law forbidding sale or distribution of contraceptive devices to persons under 16 years of age. Although there was no single opinion for the Court, the law was invalidated. Both *Eisenstadt* and *Carey,* as well as the holding and rationale in *Roe,* confirmed that the reasoning of *Griswold* could not be confined to the protection of rights of married adults. This was the state of the law with respect to some of the most relevant cases when the Court considered *Bowers v. Hardwick.*

The facts in *Bowers* had some similarities to the instant case. A police officer, whose right to enter seems not to have been in question, observed Hardwick, in his own bedroom, engaging in intimate sexual conduct with another adult male. The conduct was in violation of a Georgia statute making it a criminal offense to engage in sodomy. One difference between the two cases is that the Georgia statute prohibited the conduct whether or not the participants were of the same sex, while the Texas statute, as we have seen, applies only to participants of the same sex. Hardwick was not prosecuted, but he brought an action in federal court to declare the state statute invalid. He alleged he was a practicing homosexual and that the criminal prohibition violated rights guaranteed to him by the Constitution. The Court, in an opinion by Justice White, sustained the Georgia law. Chief Justice Burger and Justice Powell joined the opinion of the Court and filed separate, concurring opinions. Four Justices dissented.

The Court began its substantive discussion in *Bowers* as follows: "The issue presented is whether the Federal Constitution confers a fundamental right upon homosexuals to engage in sodomy and hence invalidates the laws of the many States that still make such conduct illegal and have done so for a very long time." That statement, we now conclude, discloses the Court's own failure to appreciate the extent of the liberty at stake. To say that the issue in *Bowers* was simply the right to engage in certain sexual conduct demeans the claim the individual put forward, just as it would demean a married couple were it to be said marriage is simply about the right to have sexual intercourse. The laws involved in *Bowers* and here are, to be sure, statutes that purport to do no more than prohibit a particular sexual act. Their penalties and purposes, though, have more far-reaching consequences, touching upon the most private human conduct, sexual behavior, and in the most private of places, the home. The statutes do seek to control a personal relationship that, whether or not entitled to formal recognition in the law, is within the liberty of persons to choose without being punished as criminals.

This, as a general rule, should counsel against attempts by the State, or a court, to define the meaning of the relationship or to set its boundaries absent injury to a person or abuse of an institution the law protects. It suffices for us to acknowledge that adults may choose to enter upon this relationship in the confines of their homes and their own private lives and still retain their dignity as free persons. When sexuality finds overt expression in intimate conduct with another person, the conduct can be but one element in a personal bond that is more enduring. The liberty protected by the Constitution allows homosexual persons the right to make this choice.

Having misapprehended the claim of liberty there presented to it, and thus stating the claim to be whether there is a fundamental right to engage in consensual sodomy, the *Bowers* Court said: "Proscriptions against that conduct have ancient roots." In academic writings, and in many of the scholarly *amicus* briefs filed to assist the Court in this case, there are fundamental criticisms of the historical premises relied upon by the majority and concurring opinions in *Bowers.* We need not enter this debate in the attempt to reach a definitive historical judgment, but the following considerations counsel against adopting the definitive conclusions upon which *Bowers* placed such reliance.

At the outset it should be noted that there is no longstanding history in this country of laws directed at homosexual conduct as a distinct matter. Beginning in colonial times there were prohibitions of sodomy derived from the English criminal laws passed in the first instance by the Reformation Parliament of 1533. The English prohibition was understood to include relations between men and women as well as relations between men and men. Nineteenth-century commentators similarly read American sodomy, buggery, and crime-against-nature statutes as criminalizing certain relations between men and women and between men and men. The absence of legal prohibitions focusing on homosexual conduct may be explained in part by noting that according to some scholars the concept of the homosexual as a distinct category of person did not emerge until the late 19th century. See, e.g., J. Katz, The Invention of Heterosexuality 10 (1995); J. D'Emilio & E. Freedman, Intimate Matters: A History of Sexuality in America 121 (2d ed. 1997) (" The modern terms *homosexuality* and *heterosexuality* do not apply to an era that had not yet articulated these distinctions"). Thus early American sodomy laws were not directed at homosexuals as such but instead sought to prohibit non-procreative sexual activity more generally. This does not suggest approval of homosexual conduct. It does tend to show that this particular form of conduct was not thought of as a separate category from like conduct between heterosexual persons.

Laws prohibiting sodomy do not seem to have been enforced against consenting adults acting in private. A substantial number of sodomy prosecutions and convictions for which there are surviving records were for predatory acts against those who could not or did not consent, as in the case of a minor or the victim of an assault. As to these, one purpose for the prohibitions was to ensure there would be no lack of coverage if a predator committed a sexual assault that did not constitute rape as defined by the criminal law. Thus the model sodomy indictments presented in a 19th-century treatise addressed the predatory acts of an adult man against a minor girl or minor boy. Instead of targeting relations between consenting adults in private, 19th-century sodomy prosecutions typically involved relations between men and minor girls or minor boys, relations between adults involving force, relations between adults implicating disparity in status, or relations between men and animals.

To the extent that there were any prosecutions for the acts in question, 19th-century evidence rules imposed a burden that would make a conviction more difficult to obtain even taking into account the problems always inherent in prosecuting consensual acts committed in private....The longstanding criminal prohibition of homosexual sodomy upon which the *Bowers* decision placed such reliance is as consistent with a general condemnation of non-procreative sex as it is with an established tradition of prosecuting acts because of their homosexual character.

The policy of punishing consenting adults for private acts was not much discussed in the early legal literature. We can infer that one reason for this was the very private nature of the conduct. Despite the absence of prosecutions, there may have been periods in which there was public criticism of homosexuals as such and an insistence that the criminal laws be enforced to discourage their practices. But far from possessing "ancient roots," American laws targeting same-sex couples did not develop until the last third of the 20th century. The reported decisions concerning the prosecution of consensual, homosexual sodomy between adults for the years 1880–1995 are not always clear in the details, but a significant number involved conduct in a public place. It was not until the 1970's that any State singled out same-sex relations for criminal prosecution, and only nine States have done so. Post-*Bowers* even some of these States did not adhere to the policy of suppressing homosexual conduct. Over the course of the last decades, States with same-sex prohibitions have moved toward abolishing them. In summary, the historical grounds relied upon in *Bowers* are more complex than the majority opinion and the concurring opinion by Chief Justice Burger indicate. Their historical premises are not without doubt and, at the very least, are overstated.

It must be acknowledged, of course, that the Court in *Bowers* was making the broader point that for centuries there have been powerful voices to condemn homosexual conduct as immoral. The condemnation has been shaped by religious beliefs, conceptions of right and acceptable behavior, and respect for the traditional family. For many persons these are not trivial concerns but profound and deep convictions accepted as ethical and moral principles to which they aspire and which thus determine the course of their lives. These considerations do not answer the question before us, however. The issue is whether the majority may use the power of the State to enforce these views on the whole society through operation of the criminal law. "Our obligation is to define the liberty of all, not to mandate our own moral code." *Planned Parenthood of Southeastern Pa. v. Casey,* 505 U.S. 833, 850 (1992).

Chief Justice Burger joined the opinion for the Court in *Bowers* and further explained his views as follows: "Decisions of individuals relating to homosexual conduct have been subject to state intervention throughout the history of Western civilization. Condemnation of those practices is firmly rooted in Judeao-Christian moral and ethical standards." As with Justice White's assumptions about history, scholarship casts some doubt on the sweeping nature of the statement by Chief Justice Burger as it pertains to private homosexual conduct between consenting adults. See, *e.g.,* Eskridge, Hardwick and Historiography, 1999 U. Ill. L.Rev. 631, 656. In all events we think that our laws and traditions in the past half century are of most relevance here. These references show an emerging awareness that liberty gives substantial protection to adult persons in deciding how to conduct their private lives in matters pertaining to sex. "[H]istory and tradition are the starting point but not in all cases the ending point of the substantive due process inquiry." *County of Sacramento v. Lewis,* 523 U.S. 833, 857 (1998) (KENNEDY, J., concurring).

This emerging recognition should have been apparent when *Bowers* was decided. In 1955 the American Law Institute promulgated the Model Penal Code and made clear that it did not recommend or provide for "criminal penalties for consensual sexual relations conducted in private." It justified its decision on three grounds: (1) The prohibitions undermined respect for the law by penalizing conduct many people engaged in; (2) the statutes regulated private conduct not harmful to others; and (3) the laws were arbitrarily enforced and thus invited the danger of blackmail. ALI, Model Penal Code, Commentary 277–80 (Tent. Draft No. 4, 1955). In 1961 Illinois changed its laws to conform to the Model Penal Code. Other States soon followed.

In *Bowers* the Court referred to the fact that before 1961 all 50 States had outlawed sodomy, and that at the time of the Court's decision 24 States and the District of Columbia had sodomy laws. Justice Powell pointed out that these prohibitions often were being ignored, however. Georgia, for instance, had not sought to enforce its law for decades. 106 S.Ct. 2841 ("The history of non-enforcement suggests the moribund character today of laws criminalizing this type of private, consensual conduct").

The sweeping references by Chief Justice Burger to the history of Western civilization and to Judeo-Christian moral and ethical standards did not take account of other authorities pointing in an opposite direction. A committee advising the British Parliament recommended in 1957 repeal of laws punishing homosexual conduct. The Wolfenden Report: Report of the Committee on Homosexual Offenses and Prostitution (1963). Parliament enacted the substance of those recommendations 10 years later. Sexual Offences Act 1967, § 1.

Of even more importance, almost five years before *Bowers* was decided the European Court of Human Rights considered a case with parallels to *Bowers* and to today's case. An adult male resident in Northern Ireland alleged he was a practicing homosexual who desired to engage in consensual homosexual conduct. The laws of Northern Ireland forbade him that right. He alleged that he had been questioned, his home had been searched, and he feared criminal prosecution. The court held that the laws proscribing the conduct were invalid under the European Convention on Human Rights. *Dudgeon v. United Kingdom,* 45 Eur. Ct. H.R. (1981) & ¶ 52. Authoritative in all countries that are members of the Council of Europe (21 nations then, 45 nations now), the decision is at odds with the premise in *Bowers* that the claim put forward was insubstantial in our Western civilization.

In our own constitutional system the deficiencies in *Bowers* became even more apparent in the years following its announcement. The 25 States with laws prohibiting the relevant conduct referenced in the *Bowers* decision are reduced now to 13, of which 4 enforce their laws only against homosexual conduct. In those States where sodomy is still proscribed, whether for same-sex or heterosexual conduct, there is a pattern of non-enforcement with respect to consenting adults acting in private. The State of Texas admitted in 1994 that as of that date it had not prosecuted anyone under those circumstances. *State v. Morales,* 869 S.W.2d 941, 943.

Two principal cases decided after *Bowers* cast its holding into even more doubt. In *Planned Parenthood of Southeastern Pa. v. Casey,* 505 U.S. 833 (1992), the Court reaffirmed the substantive force of the liberty protected by the Due Process Clause. The *Casey* decision again confirmed that our laws and tradition afford constitutional protection to personal decisions relating to marriage, procreation, contraception, family relationships, child rearing, and education. In explaining the respect the Constitution demands for the autonomy of the person in making these choices, we stated as follows:

> "These matters, involving the most intimate and personal choices a person may make in a lifetime, choices central to personal dignity and autonomy, are central to the liberty protected by the Fourteenth Amendment. At the heart of liberty is the right to define one's own concept of existence, of meaning, of the universe, and of the mystery of human life. Beliefs about these matters could not define the attributes of personhood were they formed under compulsion of the State."

Persons in a homosexual relationship may seek autonomy for these purposes, just as heterosexual persons do. The decision in *Bowers* would deny them this right.

The second post-*Bowers* case of principal relevance is *Romer v. Evans,* 517 U.S. 620 (1996). There the Court struck down class-based legislation directed a homosexuals as a violation of the Equal Protection Clause. *Romer* invalidated an amendment to Colorado's constitution which named as a solitary class persons who were homosexuals, lesbians, or bisexual either by "orientation, conduct, practices or relationships," and deprived them of protection under state anti-discrimination laws. We concluded that the provision was "born of animosity toward the class of persons affected" and further that it had no rational relation to a legitimate governmental purpose.

As an alternative argument in this case, counsel for the petitioners and some *amici* contend that *Romer* provides the basis for declaring the Texas statute invalid under the Equal Protection Clause. That is a tenable argument, but we conclude the instant case requires us to address whether *Bowers* itself has continuing validity. Were we to hold the statute invalid under the Equal Protection Clause some might question whether a prohibition would be valid if drawn differently, say, to prohibit the conduct both between same-sex and different-sex participants.

Equality of treatment and the due process right to demand respect for conduct protected by the substantive guarantee of liberty are linked in important respects, and a decision on the latter point advances both interests. If protected conduct is made criminal and the law which does so remains unexamined for its substantive validity, its stigma might remain even if it were not enforceable as drawn for equal protection reasons. When homosexual conduct is made criminal by the law of the State, that declaration in and of itself is an invitation to subject homosexual persons to discrimination both in the public and in the private spheres. The central holding of *Bowers* has been brought in question by this case, and it should be addressed. Its continuance as precedent demeans the lives of homosexual persons.

The stigma this criminal statute imposes, moreover, is not trivial. The offense, to be sure, is but a class C misdemeanor, a minor offense in the Texas legal system. Still, it remains a criminal offense with all that imports for the dignity of the persons charged. The petitioners will bear on their record the history of their criminal convictions. Just this Term we rejected various challenges to state laws requiring the registration of sex offenders. We are advised that if Texas convicted an adult for private, consensual homosexual conduct under the statute here in question the convicted person would come within the registration laws of a least four States were he or she to be subject to their jurisdiction. This underscores the consequential nature of the punishment and the state-sponsored condemnation attendant to the criminal prohibition. Furthermore, the Texas criminal conviction carries with it the other collateral consequences always following a conviction, such as notations on job application forms, to mention but one example.

The foundations of *Bowers* have sustained serious erosion from our recent decisions in *Casey* and *Romer*. When our precedent has been thus weakened, criticism from other sources is of greater significance. In the United States criticism of *Bowers* has been substantial and continuing, disapproving of its reasoning in all respects, not just as to its historical assumptions. See, *e.g.,* C. Fried, Order and Law: Arguing the Reagan Revolution —A Firsthand Account 81–84 (1991); R. Posner, Sex and Reason 341–50 (1992). The courts of five different States have declined to follow it in interpreting provisions in their own state constitutions parallel to the Due Process Clause of the Fourteenth Amendment [reciting cases from Arkansas, Georgia, Montana, Tennessee and Kentucky].

To the extent *Bowers* relied on values we share with a wider civilization, it should be noted that the reasoning and holding in *Bowers* have been rejected elsewhere. The European Court of Human Rights has followed not *Bowers* but its own decision in *Dudgeon v. United Kingdom*. See *P.G. & J.H. v. United Kingdom*, App. No. 00044787/98, & ¶ 56 (Eur.Ct.H. R., Sept. 25, 2001); *Modinos v. Cyprus*, 259 Eur. Ct. H.R. (1993); *Norris v. Ireland*, 142 Eur. Ct. H.R. (1988). Other nations, too, have taken action consistent with an affirmation of the protected right of homosexual adults to engage in intimate, consensual conduct. See Brief for Mary Robinson [U.N. Commissioner for Human Rights and former President of Ireland] et al. as *Amici Curiae* 11–12. The right the petitioners seek in this case has been accepted as an integral part of human freedom in many other countries. There has been no showing that in this country the governmental interest in circumscribing personal choice is somehow more legitimate or urgent.

The doctrine of *stare decisis* is essential to the respect accorded to the judgments of the Court and to the stability of the law. It is not, however, an inexorable command. In *Casey* we noted that when a Court is asked to overrule a precedent recognizing a constitutional liberty interest, individual or societal reliance on the existence of that liberty cautions with particular strength against reversing course. The holding in *Bowers,* however, has not induced detrimental reliance comparable to some instances where recognized individual rights are involved. Indeed, there has been no individual or societal reliance on *Bowers* of the sort that could counsel against overturning its holding once there are compelling reasons to do so. *Bowers* itself causes uncertainty, for the precedents before and after its issuance contradict its central holding.

The rationale of *Bowers* does not withstand careful analysis. In his dissenting opinion in Bowers Justice STEVENS came to these conclusions:

> Our prior cases make two propositions abundantly clear. First, the fact that the governing majority in a State has traditionally viewed a particular practice as immoral is not a sufficient reason for upholding a law prohibiting the practice; neither history nor tradition could save a law prohibiting miscegenation from constitutional attack. Second, individual decisions by married persons, concerning the intimacies of their physical relationship, even when not intended to produce offspring, are a form of 'liberty' protected by the Due Process Clause of the Fourteenth Amendment. Moreover, this protection extends to intimate choices by unmarried as well as married persons. 478 U.S., at 216 (footnotes and citations omitted).

Justice STEVENS' analysis, in our view, should have been controlling in *Bowers* and should control here.

Bowers was not correct when it was decided, and it is not correct today. It ought not to remain binding precedent. *Bowers v. Hardwick* should be and now is overruled.

The present case does not involve minors. It does not involve persons who might be injured or coerced or who are situated in relationships where consent might not easily be refused. It does not involve public conduct or prostitution. It does not involve whether the government must give formal recognition to any relationship that homosexual persons seek to enter. The case does involve two adults who, with full and mutual consent from each other, engaged in sexual practices common to a homosexual lifestyle. The petitioners are entitled to respect for their private lives. The State cannot demean their existence or control their destiny by making their private sexual conduct a crime. Their right to liberty under the Due Process Clause gives them the full right to engage in their conduct without intervention of the government. "It is a promise of the Constitution that there is a realm of personal liberty which the government may not enter." *Casey, supra,* at 847. The Texas statute furthers no legitimate state interest which can justify its intrusion into the personal and private life of the individual.

Had those who drew and ratified the Due Process Clauses of the Fifth Amendment or the Fourteenth Amendment known the components of liberty in its manifold possibilities, they might have been more specific. They did not presume to have this insight. They knew times can blind us to certain truths and later generations can see that laws once thought necessary and proper in fact serve only to oppress. As the Constitution endures, persons in every generation can invoke its principles in their own search for greater freedom.

Justice O'CONNOR, concurring in the judgment.

The Court today overrules *Bowers v. Hardwick*. I joined *Bowers,* and do not join the Court in overruling it. Nevertheless, I agree with the Court that Texas' statute banning same-sex sodomy is unconstitutional. Rather than relying on the substantive component of the Fourteenth Amendment's Due Process Clause, as the Court does, I base my conclusion on the Fourteenth Amendment's Equal Protection Clause.

The Equal Protection Clause of the Fourteenth Amendment "is essentially a direction that all persons similarly situated should be treated alike." *Cleburne v. Cleburne Living Center, Inc.,* 473 U.S. 432, 439 (1985); see also *Plyler v. Doe,* 457 U.S. 202, 216 (1982). Under our rational basis standard of review, "legislation is presumed to be valid and will be sustained if the classification drawn by the statute is rationally related to a legitimate state interest." *Cleburne;* see also *Department of Agriculture v. Moreno,* 413 U.S. 528, 534 (1973); *Romer v. Evans,* 517 U.S. 620, 632–33 (1996); *Nordlinger v. Hahn,* 505 U.S. 1, 11–12 (1992).

Laws such as economic or tax legislation that are scrutinized under rational basis review normally pass constitutional muster, since "the Constitution presumes that even improvident decisions will eventually be rectified by the democratic processes." We have consistently held, however, that some objectives, such as "a bare...desire to harm a politically unpopular group," are not legitimate state interests. *Department of Agriculture v. Moreno,* at 534. When a law exhibits such a desire to harm a politically unpopular group, we have applied a more searching form of rational basis review to strike down such laws under the Equal Protection Clause.

We have been most likely to apply rational basis review to hold a law unconstitutional under the Equal Protection Clause where, as here, the challenged legislation inhibits personal relationships. In *Moreno,* for example, we held that a law preventing those households containing an individual unrelated to any other member of the household from receiving food stamps violated equal protection because the purpose of the law was to "'discriminate against hippies.'" The asserted governmental interest in preventing food stamp fraud was not deemed sufficient to satisfy rational basis review. In *Eisenstadt,* we refused to sanction a law that discriminated between married and unmarried persons by prohibiting the distribution of contraceptives to single persons. Likewise, in *Cleburne,* we held that it was irrational for a State to require a home for the mentally disabled to obtain a special use permit when other residences—like fraternity houses and apartment buildings —did not have to obtain such a permit. And in *Romer,* we disallowed a state statute that "impos[ed] a broad and undifferentiated disability on a single named group"—specifically, homosexuals. The dissent apparently agrees that if these cases have *stare decisis* effect, Texas' sodomy law would not pass scrutiny under the Equal Protection Clause, regardless of the type of rational basis review that we apply. Texas treats the same conduct differently based solely on the participants. Those harmed by this law are people who have a same-sex sexual orientation and thus are more likely to engage in behavior prohibited by §21.06.

The Texas statute makes homosexuals unequal in the eyes of the law by making particular conduct—and only that conduct—subject to criminal sanction. It appears that prosecutions under Texas' sodomy law are rare. This case shows, however, that prosecutions under §21.06 *do* occur. And while the penalty imposed on petitioners in this case was relatively minor, the consequences of conviction are not. And the effect of Texas' sodomy law is not just limited to the threat of prosecution or consequence of conviction. Texas' sodomy law brands all homosexuals as criminals, thereby making it more difficult for homosexuals to be treated in the same manner as everyone else. Indeed, Texas itself has previously acknowledged the collateral effects of the law, stipulating in a prior challenge to this action that the law "legally sanctions discrimination against [homosexuals] in a variety of ways unrelated to the criminal law," including in the areas of "employment, family issues, and housing." *Morales,* 826 S.W.2d 201, 203 (Tex.App.1992).

Texas attempts to justify its law, and the effects of the law, by arguing that the statute satisfies rational basis review because it furthers the legitimate governmental interest of the promotion of morality. In *Bowers,* we held that a state law criminalizing sodomy as applied to homosexual couples did not violate substantive due process. We rejected the argument that no rational basis existed to justify the law, pointing to the government's interest in promoting morality. The only question in front of the Court in *Bowers* was whether the substantive component of the Due Process Clause protected a right to engage in homosexual sodomy. *Bowers* did not hold that moral disapproval of a group is a rational basis under the Equal Protection Clause to criminalize homosexual sodomy when heterosexual sodomy is not punished.

This case raises a different issue than *Bowers:* whether, under the Equal Protection Clause, moral disapproval is a legitimate state interest to justify by itself a statute that bans homosexual sodomy, but not heterosexual sodomy. It is not. Moral disapproval of this group, like a bare desire to harm the group, is an interest that is insufficient to satisfy rational basis review under the Equal Protection Clause. Texas' invocation of moral disapproval as a legitimate state interest proves nothing more than Texas' desire to criminalize homosexual sodomy. But the Equal Protection Clause prevents a State from creating "a classification of persons undertaken for its own sake."

Texas argues, however, that the sodomy law does not discriminate against homosexual persons. Instead, the State maintains that the law discriminates only against homosexual conduct. While it is true that the law applies only to conduct, the conduct targeted by this law is conduct that is closely correlated with being homosexual. Under such circumstances, Texas' sodomy law is targeted at more than conduct. It is instead directed toward gay persons as a class. "After all, there can hardly be more palpable discrimination against a class than making the conduct that defines the class criminal." *Romer,* at 641 (SCALIA, J., dissenting).

Indeed, Texas law confirms that the sodomy statute is directed toward homosexuals as a class. In Texas, calling a person a homosexual is slander *per se* because the word "homosexual" "impute[s] the commission of a crime." *Plumley v. Landmark Chevrolet, Inc.,* 122 F.3d 308, 310 (C.A.5 1997) (applying Texas law). The State has admitted that because of the sodomy law, *being* homosexual carries the presumption of being a criminal. See *Morales,* 826 S.W.2d, at 202–3 ("[T]he statute brands lesbians and gay men as criminals and thereby legally sanctions discrimination against them in a variety of ways unrelated to the criminal law"). Texas' sodomy law therefore results in discrimination against homosexuals as a class in an array of areas outside the criminal law. In *Romer v. Evans,* we refused to sanction a law that singled out homosexuals "for disfavored legal status." The same is true here. The Equal Protection Clause "'neither knows nor tolerates classes among citizens.'" *Id.,* at 623 (quoting *Plessy v. Ferguson,* 163 U.S. 537, 559 (1896) (Harlan, J. dissenting)).

A State can of course assign certain consequences to a violation of its criminal law. But the State cannot single out one identifiable class of citizens for punishment that does not apply to everyone else, with moral disapproval as the only asserted state interest for the law. Whether a sodomy law that is neutral both in effect and application would violate the substantive component of the Due Process Clause is an issue that need not be decided today. I am confident, however, that so long as the Equal Protection Clause requires a sodomy law to apply equally to the private consensual conduct of homosexuals and heterosexuals alike, such a law would not long stand in our democratic society. . . . That this law as applied to private, consensual conduct is unconstitutional under the Equal Protection Clause does not mean that other laws distinguishing between heterosexuals and homosexuals would similarly fail under rational basis review. Texas cannot assert any legitimate state interest here, such as national security or preserving the traditional institution of marriage. Unlike the moral disapproval of same-sex relations—the asserted state interest in this case—other reasons exist to promote the institution of marriage beyond mere moral disapproval of an excluded group.

A law branding one class of persons as criminal solely based on the State's moral disapproval of that class and the conduct associated with that class runs contrary to the values of the Constitution and the Equal Protection Clause, under any standard of review. I therefore concur in the Court's judgment that Texas' sodomy law banning "deviate sexual intercourse" between consenting adults of the same sex, but not between consenting adults of different sexes, is unconstitutional.

Justice SCALIA, with whom THE CHIEF JUSTICE and Justice THOMAS join, dissenting.

"Liberty finds no refuge in a jurisprudence of doubt." *Planned Parenthood of Southeastern Pa. v. Casey* (1992). That was the Court's sententious response, barely more than a decade ago, to those seeking to overrule *Roe v. Wade* (1973). The Court's response today, to those who have engaged in a 17-year crusade to overrule *Bowers v. Hardwick* (1986), is very different. The need for stability and certainty presents no barrier.

Most of the rest of today's opinion has no relevance to its actual holding—that the Texas statute "furthers no legitimate state interest which can justify" its application to petitioners under rational-basis review. Though there is discussion of "fundamental proposition[s]," and "fundamental decisions," nowhere does the Court's opinion declare that homosexual sodomy is a "fundamental right" under the Due Process Clause; nor does it subject the Texas law to the standard of review that would be appropriate (strict scrutiny) if homosexual sodomy *were* a "fundamental right." Thus, while overruling the *outcome* of *Bowers,* the Court leaves strangely untouched its central legal conclusion: "[R]espondent would have us announce...a fundamental right to engage in homosexual sodomy. This we are quite unwilling to do." Instead the Court simply describes petitioners' conduct as "an exercise of their liberty"—which it undoubtedly is —and proceeds to apply an unheard-of form of rational-basis review that will have far-reaching implications beyond this case.

I

I begin with the Court's surprising readiness to reconsider a decision rendered a mere 17 years ago in *Bowers v. Hardwick.* Today, the widespread opposition to *Bowers,* a decision resolving an issue as "intensely divisive" as the issue in *Roe [v. Wade],* is offered as a reason in favor of *overruling* it. Gone, too, is any "enquiry" (of the sort conducted in *Casey*) into whether the decision sought to be overruled has "proven 'unworkable.'" Today's approach to *stare decisis* invites us to overrule an erroneously decided precedent (including an "intensely divisive" decision) *if:* (1) its foundations have been "eroded" by subsequent decisions; (2) it has been subject to "substantial and continuing" criticism; and (3) it has not induced "individual or societal reliance" that counsels against overturning. The problem is that *Roe* itself—which today's majority surely has no disposition to overrule—satisfies these conditions to at least the same degree as *Bowers.*

(1) A preliminary digressive observation with regard to the first factor: The Court's claim that *Planned Parenthood v. Casey* "casts some doubt" upon the holding in *Bowers* (or any other case, for that matter) does not withstand analysis. As far as its holding is concerned, *Casey* provided a *less* expansive right to abortion than did *Roe, which was al-*

ready on the books when Bowers *was decided.* And if the Court is referring not to the holding of *Casey,* but to the dictum of its famed sweet-mystery-of-life passage ("'At the heart of liberty is the right to define one's own concept of existence, of meaning, of the universe, and of the mystery of human life'"): That "casts some doubt" upon either the totality of our jurisprudence or else (presumably the right answer) nothing at all. I have never heard of a law that attempted to restrict one's "right to define" certain concepts; and if the passage calls into question the government's power to regulate *actions based on* one's self-defined "concept of existence, etc.," it is the passage that ate the rule of law.

I do not quarrel with the Court's claim that *Romer* "eroded" the "foundations" of *Bowers'* rational-basis holding. But *Roe* and *Casey* have been equally "eroded" by *Washington v. Glucksberg,* 521 U.S. 702, 721 (1997), which held that *only* fundamental rights which are "deeply rooted in this Nation's history and tradition" qualify for anything other than rational basis scrutiny under the doctrine of "substantive due process." *Roe* and *Casey,* of course, subjected the restriction of abortion to heightened scrutiny without even attempting to establish that the freedom to abort *was* rooted in this Nation's tradition.

(2) *Bowers,* the Court says, has been subject to "substantial and continuing [criticism], disapproving of its reasoning in all respects, not just as to its historical assumptions." Exactly what those non-historical criticisms are, and whether the Court even agrees with them, are left unsaid, although the Court does cite two books. Of course, *Roe* too (and by extension *Casey*) had been (and still is) subject to unrelenting criticism, including criticism from the two commentators cited by the Court today.

(3) That leaves, to distinguish the rock-solid, unamendable disposition of *Roe* from the readily overrulable *Bowers,* only the third factor. "[T]here has been," the Court says, "no individual or societal reliance on *Bowers* of the sort that could counsel against overturning its holding...." It seems to me that the "societal reliance" on the principles confirmed in *Bowers* and discarded today has been overwhelming. Countless judicial decisions and legislative enactments have relied on the ancient proposition that a governing majority's belief that certain sexual behavior is "immoral and unacceptable" constitutes a rational basis for regulation. See, *e.g., Williams v. Pryor,* 240 F.3d 944 (C.A.11 2001) (citing *Bowers* in upholding Alabama's prohibition on the sale of sex toys on the ground that "[t]he crafting and safeguarding of public morality...indisputably is a legitimate government interest under rational basis scrutiny"); *Milner v. Apfel,* 148 F.3d 812 (C.A.7 1998) (citing *Bowers* for the proposition that "[l]egislatures are permitted to legislate with regard to morality...rather than confined to preventing demonstrable harms"); *Holmes v. California Army National Guard* 124 F.3d 1126 (C.A.9 1997) (relying on *Bowers* in upholding the federal statute and regulations banning from military service those who engage in homosexual conduct); *Owens v. State,* 352 Md. 663 (1999) (relying on *Bowers* in holding that "a person has no constitutional right to engage in sexual intercourse, at least outside of marriage"); *Sherman v. Henry,* 928 S.W.2d 464 (Tex.1996) (relying on *Bowers* in rejecting a claimed constitutional right to commit adultery). We ourselves relied extensively on *Bowers* when we concluded, in *Barnes v. Glen Theatre, Inc.,* 501 U.S. 560, 569 (1991), that Indiana's public indecency statute furthered "a substantial government interest in protecting order and morality"(plurality opinion). State laws against bigamy, same-sex marriage, adult incest, prostitution, masturbation, adultery, fornication, bestiality, and obscenity are likewise sustainable only in light of *Bowers'* validation of laws based on moral choices. Every single one of these laws is called into question by today's decision; the Court makes no effort to cabin the scope of its decision to exclude them from its holding. The impossibility of distinguishing homosexual-

ity from other traditional "morals" offenses is precisely why *Bowers* rejected the rational-basis challenge.[2] What a massive disruption of the current social order, therefore, the overruling of *Bowers* entails. Not so the overruling of *Roe*, which would simply have restored the regime that existed for centuries before 1973, in which the permissibility of and restrictions upon abortion were determined legislatively State-by-State. To tell the truth, it does not surprise me, and should surprise no one, that the Court has chosen today to revise the standards of *stare decisis* set forth in *Casey*. It has thereby exposed *Casey*'s extraordinary deference to precedent for the result-oriented expedient that it is.

II

Having decided that it need not adhere to *stare decisis*, the Court still must establish that *Bowers* was wrongly decided and that the Texas statute, as applied to petitioners, is unconstitutional. Texas Penal Code Ann. § 21.06(a) (2003) undoubtedly imposes constraints on liberty. So do laws prohibiting prostitution, recreational use of heroin, and, for that matter, working more than 60 hours per week in a bakery. But there is no right to "liberty" under the Due Process Clause, though today's opinion repeatedly makes that claim. The Fourteenth Amendment *expressly allows* States to deprive their citizens of "liberty," so long as "due process of law" is provided: "No state shall…deprive any person of life, liberty, or property, *without due process of law.*" (Emphasis added).

Our opinions applying the doctrine known as "substantive due process" hold that the Due Process Clause prohibits States from infringing *fundamental* liberty interests, unless the infringement is narrowly tailored to serve a compelling state interest. We have held repeatedly, in cases the Court today does not overrule, that *only* fundamental rights qualify for this so-called "heightened scrutiny" protection—that is, rights which are "'deeply rooted in this Nation's history and tradition.'"All other liberty interests may be abridged or abrogated pursuant to a validly enacted state law if that law is rationally related to a legitimate state interest.

Bowers held, first, that criminal prohibitions of homosexual sodomy are not subject to heightened scrutiny because they do not implicate a "fundamental right" under the Due Process Clause. The Court today does not overrule this holding. Not once does it describe homosexual sodomy as a "fundamental right" or a "fundamental liberty inter-

---

2. While the Court does not overrule *Bowers*' holding that homosexual sodomy is not a "fundamental right," it is worth noting that the "societal reliance" upon that aspect of the decision has been substantial as well. See 10 U.S.C. § 654(b)(1) ("A member of the armed forces shall be separated from the armed forces if the member has engaged in a homosexual act or acts"); *Marcum v. McWhorter*, 308 F.3d 635 (C.A.6 2002) (relying on *Bowers* in rejecting a claimed fundamental right to commit adultery); *Mullins v. Oregon*, 57 F.3d 789 (C.A.9 1995) (relying on *Bowers* in rejecting a grandparent's claimed "fundamental liberty interes[t]" in the adoption of her grandchildren); *Doe v. Wigginton*, 21 F.3d 733 (C.A.6 1994) (relying on *Bowers* in rejecting a prisoner's claimed "fundamental right" to on-demand HIV testing); *Schowengerdt v. United States*, 944 F.2d 483 (C.A.9 1991) (relying on *Bowers* in upholding a bisexual's discharge from the armed services); *Charles v. Baesler*, 910 F.2d 1349 (C.A.6 1990) (relying on *Bowers* in rejecting fire department captain's claimed "fundamental" interest in a promotion); *Henne v. Wright*, 904 F.2d 1208 (C.A.8 1990) (relying on *Bowers* in rejecting a claim that state law restricting surnames that could be given to children at birth implicates a "fundamental right"); *Walls v. Petersburg*, 895 F.2d 188 (C.A.4 1990) (relying on *Bowers* in rejecting substantive-due-process challenge to a police department questionnaire that asked prospective employees about homosexual activity); *High Tech Gays v. Defense Industrial Security Clearance Office*, 895 F.2d 563 (C.A.9 1990) (relying on *Bowers*' holding that homosexual activity is not a fundamental right in rejecting—on the basis of the rational-basis standard—an equal-protection challenge to the Defense Department's policy of conducting expanded investigations into backgrounds of gay and lesbian applicants for secret and top-secret security clearance).

est," nor does it subject the Texas statute to strict scrutiny. Instead, having failed to establish that the right to homosexual sodomy is "'deeply rooted in this Nation's history and tradition,'" the Court concludes that the application of Texas's statute to petitioners' conduct fails the rational-basis test, and overrules *Bowers'* holding to the contrary.

III

The Court's description of "the state of the law" at the time of *Bowers* only confirms that *Bowers* was right. The Court points to *Griswold,* but that case *expressly disclaimed* any reliance on the doctrine of "substantive due process," and grounded the so-called "right to privacy" in penumbras of constitutional provisions *other than* the Due Process Clause. *Eisenstadt* likewise had nothing to do with "substantive due process"; it invalidated a Massachusetts law prohibiting the distribution of contraceptives to unmarried persons solely on the basis of the Equal Protection Clause. Of course *Eisenstadt* contains well known dictum relating to the "right to privacy," but this referred to the right recognized in *Griswold*—a right penumbral to the *specific* guarantees in the Bill of Rights, and not a "substantive due process" right.

Roe recognized that the right to abort an unborn child was a "fundamental right" protected by the Due Process Clause. The *Roe* Court, however, made no attempt to establish that this right was "'deeply rooted in this Nation's history and tradition'"; instead, it based its conclusion that "the Fourteenth Amendment's concept of personal liberty is broad enough to encompass a woman's decision whether or not to terminate her pregnancy" on its own normative judgment that anti-abortion laws were undesirable. We have since rejected *Roe's* holding that regulations of abortion must be narrowly tailored to serve a compelling state interest, see *Planned Parenthood v. Casey,* 505 U.S., at 876—and thus, by logical implication, *Roe's* holding that the right to abort an unborn child is a "fundamental right."

After discussing the history of antisodomy laws, the Court proclaims that, "it should be noted that there is no longstanding history in this country of laws directed at homosexual conduct as a distinct matter." This observation in no way casts into doubt the "definitive [historical] conclusion" on which *Bowers* relied: that our Nation has a longstanding history of laws prohibiting *sodomy in general*—regardless of whether it was performed by same-sex or opposite-sex couples. It is (as *Bowers* recognized) entirely irrelevant whether the laws in our long national tradition criminalizing homosexual sodomy were "directed at homosexual conduct as a distinct matter." Whether homosexual sodomy was prohibited by a law targeted at same-sex sexual relations or by a more general law prohibiting both homosexual and heterosexual sodomy, the only relevant point is that it *was* criminalized—which suffices to establish that homosexual sodomy is not a right "deeply rooted in our Nation's history and tradition." The Court today agrees that homosexual sodomy was criminalized and thus does not dispute the facts on which *Bowers actually* relied.

Next the Court makes the claim, again unsupported by any citations, that "[l]aws prohibiting sodomy do not seem to have been enforced against consenting adults acting in private." The key qualifier here is "acting in private"—since the Court admits that sodomy laws *were* enforced against consenting adults (although the Court contends that prosecutions were "infrequent"). I do not know what "acting in private" means; surely consensual sodomy, like heterosexual intercourse, is rarely performed on stage. If all the Court means by "acting in private" is "on private premises, with the doors closed and windows covered," it is entirely unsurprising that evidence of enforcement would be hard to come by. (Imagine the circumstances that would enable a search warrant to be obtained for a residence on the ground that there was probable cause to believe that consensual sodomy was then and there occurring.) Surely that lack of evidence would not sustain the proposition that consensual sodomy on private premises with the doors closed and windows covered was regarded as a "fundamental right," even though all other consensual sodomy was criminalized. There are 203 prosecutions for consensual, adult homosexual sodomy reported in the West Reporting system and official state reporters from the years 1880–1995. See W. Eskridge, Gaylaw: Challenging the Apartheid of the Closet 375 (1999) (hereinafter Gaylaw). There are also records of 20 sodomy prosecutions and 4 executions during the colonial period. J. Katz, Gay/Lesbian Almanac 29, 58, 663 (1983). *Bowers'* conclusion that homosexual sodomy is not a fundamental right "deeply rooted in this Nation's history and tradition" is utterly unassailable.

Realizing that fact, the Court instead says: "[W]e think that our laws and traditions in the past half century are of most relevance here. These references show *an emerging awareness* that liberty gives substantial protection to adult persons in deciding how to conduct their private lives *in matters pertaining to sex.*" (emphasis added). Apart from the fact that such an "emerging awareness" does not establish a "fundamental right," the statement is factually false. States continue to prosecute all sorts of crimes by adults "in matters pertaining to sex": prostitution, adult incest, adultery, obscenity, and child pornography. Sodomy laws, too, have been enforced "in the past half century," in which there have been 134 reported cases involving prosecutions for consensual, adult, homosexual sodomy. In relying, for evidence of an "emerging recognition," upon the American Law Institute's 1955 recommendation not to criminalize " 'consensual sexual relations conducted in private,' " the Court ignores the fact that this recommendation was "a point of resistance in most of the states that considered adopting the Model Penal Code." In any event, an "emerging awareness" is by definition not "deeply rooted in this Nation's history and tradition[s]," as we have said "fundamental right" status requires. Constitutional entitlements do not spring into existence because some States choose to lessen or eliminate criminal sanctions on certain behavior. Much less do they spring into existence, as the Court seems to believe, because *foreign nations* decriminalize conduct. The *Bowers* majority opinion *never* relied on "values we share with a wider civilization," but rather rejected the claimed right to sodomy on the ground that such a right was not " 'deeply rooted in *this Nation's* history and tradition.' " (emphasis added). *Bowers'* rational-basis holding is likewise devoid of any reliance on the views of a "wider civilization." The Court's discussion of these foreign views (ignoring, of course, the many countries that have retained criminal prohibitions on sodomy) is therefore meaningless dicta.

IV

I turn now to the ground on which the Court squarely rests its holding: the contention that there is no rational basis for the law here under attack. This proposition is so out of accord with our jurisprudence—indeed, with the jurisprudence of *any* society we know—that it requires little discussion.

The Texas statute undeniably seeks to further the belief of its citizens that certain forms of sexual behavior are "immoral and unacceptable"—the same interest furthered by criminal laws against fornication, bigamy, adultery, adult incest, bestiality, and obscenity. *Bowers* held that this *was* a legitimate state interest. The Court today reaches the opposite conclusion. The Court embraces instead Justice STEVENS' declaration in his *Bowers* dissent, that "the fact that the governing majority in a State has traditionally viewed a particular practice as immoral is not a sufficient reason for upholding a law prohibiting the practice." This effectively decrees the end of all morals legislation. If, as the Court asserts, the promotion of majoritarian sexual morality is not even a *legitimate* state interest, none of the above-mentioned laws can survive rational-basis review.

V

Finally, I turn to petitioners' equal-protection challenge: On its face §21.06(a) applies equally to all persons. Men and women, heterosexuals and homosexuals, are all subject to its prohibition of deviate sexual intercourse with someone of the same sex. To be sure, §21.06 does distinguish between the sexes insofar as concerns the partner with whom the sexual acts are performed: men can violate the law only with other men, and women only with other women. But this cannot itself be a denial of equal protection, since it is precisely the same distinction regarding partner that is drawn in state laws prohibiting marriage with someone of the same sex while permitting marriage with someone of the opposite sex.

The objection is made, however, that the antimiscegenation laws invalidated in *Loving v. Virginia*, 388 U.S. 1, 8 (1967), similarly were applicable to whites and blacks alike, and only distinguished between the races insofar as the *partner* was concerned. In *Loving*, however, we correctly applied heightened scrutiny, rather than the usual rational-basis review, because the Virginia statute was "designed to maintain White Supremacy." No purpose to discriminate against men or women as a class can be gleaned from the Texas law, so rational-basis review applies. That review is readily satisfied here by the same rational basis that satisfied it in *Bowers*—society's belief that certain forms of sexual behavior are "immoral and unacceptable." This is the same justification that supports many other laws regulating sexual behavior that make a distinction based upon the identity of the partner—for example, laws against adultery, fornication, and adult incest, and laws refusing to recognize homosexual marriage.

Justice O'CONNOR argues that the discrimination in this law which must be justified is not its discrimination with regard to the sex of the partner but its discrimination with regard to the sexual proclivity of the principal actor. Of course the same could be said of any law. A law against public nudity targets "the conduct that is closely correlated with being a nudist," and hence "is targeted at more than conduct"; it is "directed toward nudists as a class." But be that as it may. Even if the Texas law *does* deny equal protection to "homosexuals as a class," that denial *still* does not need to be justified by anything more than a rational basis, which our cases show is satisfied by the enforcement of traditional notions of sexual morality.

Justice O'CONNOR simply decrees application of "a more searching form of rational basis review" to the Texas statute. The cases she cites do not recognize such a standard, and reach their conclusions only after finding, as required by conventional rational-basis analysis, that no conceivable legitimate state interest supports the classification at issue. Nor does Justice O'CONNOR explain precisely what her "more searching form" of rational-basis review consists of. It must at least mean, however, that laws exhibiting "'a...desire to harm a politically unpopular group'" are invalid *even though* there may be a conceivable rational basis to support them.

This reasoning leaves on pretty shaky grounds state laws limiting marriage to opposite-sex couples. Justice O'CONNOR seeks to preserve them by the conclusory statement that "preserving the traditional institution of marriage" is a legitimate state interest. But "preserving the traditional institution of marriage" is just a kinder way of describing the State's *moral disapproval* of same-sex couples. Texas's interest in §21.06 could be recast in similarly euphemistic terms: "preserving the traditional sexual mores of our society." In the jurisprudence Justice O'CONNOR has seemingly created, judges can validate laws by characterizing them as "preserving the traditions of society" (good); or invalidate them by characterizing them as "expressing moral disapproval" (bad).

* * *

Today's opinion is the product of a Court, which is the product of a law-profession culture, that has largely signed on to the so-called homosexual agenda, by which I mean the agenda promoted by some homosexual activists directed at eliminating the moral opprobrium that has traditionally attached to homosexual conduct. I noted in an earlier opinion (*Romer*)the fact that the American Association of Law Schools (to which any reputable law school *must* seek to belong) excludes from membership any school that refuses to ban from its job-interview facilities a law firm (no matter how small) that does not wish to hire as a prospective partner a person who openly engages in homosexual conduct.

One of the most revealing statements in today's opinion is the Court's grim warning that the criminalization of homosexual conduct is "an invitation to subject homosexual persons to discrimination both in the public and in the private spheres." It is clear from this that the Court has taken sides in the culture war, departing from its role of assuring, as neutral observer, that the democratic rules of engagement are observed. Many Americans do not want persons who openly engage in homosexual conduct as partners in their business, as scoutmasters for their children, as teachers in their children's schools, or as boarders in their home. They view this as protecting themselves and their families from a lifestyle that they believe to be immoral and destructive. The Court views it as "discrimination" which it is the function of our judgments to deter. So imbued is the Court with the law profession's anti-anti-homosexual culture, that it is seemingly unaware that the attitudes of that culture are not obviously "mainstream"; that in most States what the Court calls "discrimination" against those who engage in homosexual acts is perfectly legal; that proposals to ban such "discrimination" under Title VII have repeatedly been rejected by Congress; and that in some cases such "discrimination" is a constitutional right.

Let me be clear that I have nothing against homosexuals, or any other group, promoting their agenda through normal democratic means. Social perceptions of sexual and other morality change over time, and every group has the right to persuade its fellow citizens that its view of such matters is the best. That homosexuals have achieved some success in that enterprise is attested to by the fact that Texas is one of the few remaining States that criminalize private, consensual homosexual acts. But persuading one's fellow citizens is one thing, and imposing one's views in the absence of democratic majority will is something else. I would no more *require* a State to criminalize homosexual acts — or, for that matter, display *any* moral disapprobation of them — than I would *forbid* it to do so. What Texas has chosen to do is well within the range of traditional democratic action, and its hand should not be stayed through the invention of a brand-new "constitutional right" by a Court that is impatient of democratic change. It is indeed true that "later generations can see that laws once thought necessary and proper in fact serve only to oppress;" and when that happens, later generations can repeal those laws. But it is the premise of our system that those judgments are to be made by the people, and not imposed by a governing caste that knows best.

One of the benefits of leaving regulation of this matter to the people rather than to the courts is that the people, unlike judges, need not carry things to their logical conclusion. The people may feel that their disapprobation of homosexual conduct is strong enough to disallow homosexual marriage, but not strong enough to criminalize private homosexual acts—and may legislate accordingly. The Court today pretends that it possesses a similar freedom of action, so that we need not fear judicial imposition of homosexual marriage, as has recently occurred in Canada (in a decision that the Canadian Government has chosen not to appeal). See *Halpern v. Toronto,* 2003 WL 34950 (Ontario Ct.App.). At the end of its opinion—after having laid waste the foundations of our rational-basis jurisprudence—the Court says that the present case "does not involve whether the government must give formal recognition to any relationship that homosexual persons seek to enter." Do not believe it. More illuminating than this bald, unreasoned disclaimer is the progression of thought displayed by an earlier passage in the Court's opinion, which notes the constitutional protections afforded to "personal decisions relating to *marriage,* procreation, contraception, family relationships, child rearing, and education," and then declares that "[p]ersons in a homosexual relationship may seek autonomy for these purposes, just as heterosexual persons do" (emphasis added). Today's opinion dismantles the structure of constitutional law that has permitted a distinction to be made between heterosexual and homosexual unions, insofar as formal recognition in marriage is concerned. If moral disapprobation of homosexual conduct is "no legitimate state interest" for purposes of proscribing that conduct; and if, as the Court coos (casting aside all pretense of neutrality), "[w]hen sexuality finds overt expression in intimate conduct with another person, the conduct can be but one element in a personal bond that is more enduring"; what justification could there possibly be for denying the benefits of marriage to homosexual couples exercising "[t]he liberty protected by the Constitution"? Surely not the encouragement of procreation, since the sterile and the elderly are allowed to marry. This case "does not involve" the issue of homosexual marriage only if one entertains the belief that principle and logic have nothing to do with the decisions of this Court. Many will hope that, as the Court comfortingly assures us, this is so.

The matters appropriate for this Court's resolution are only three: Texas's prohibition of sodomy neither infringes a "fundamental right" (which the Court does not dispute), nor is unsupported by a rational relation to what the Constitution considers a legitimate state interest, nor denies the equal protection of the laws. I dissent.

Justice THOMAS, dissenting.

I join Justice SCALIA's dissenting opinion. I write separately to note that the law before the Court today "is…uncommonly silly." *Griswold v. Connecticut,* 381 U.S. 479, 527 (1965) (Stewart, J., dissenting). If I were a member of the Texas Legislature, I would vote to repeal it. Punishing someone for expressing his sexual preference through non-commercial consensual conduct with another adult does not appear to be a worthy way to expend valuable law enforcement resources.

Notwithstanding this, I recognize that as a member of this Court I am not empowered to help petitioners and others similarly situated. My duty, rather, is to "decide cases 'agreeably to the Constitution and laws of the United States.'" And, just like Justice Stewart, I "can find [neither in the Bill of Rights nor any other part of the Constitution a] general right of privacy," or as the Court terms it today, the "liberty of the person both in its spatial and more transcendent dimensions."

* * *

The following case provides an opportunity to consider the legal treatment of another sexual minority, transgendered people, whose cases present issues that sometimes overlap those presented by lesbians, gay men and bisexuals, and sometimes present completely different concerns. To enhance readability and produce a text of manageable length, extensive citations and discussions of scientific authority have been significantly abridged from the original opinion by the court.

In re Heilig

816 A.2d 68 (Md. Ct. App. 2003)

WILNER, Judge.

Petitioner was born in Pennsylvania in 1948. His birth certificate, issued by the Department of Health of that State, records his name as Robert Wright Heilig and his sex as male. In March, 2001, Mr. Heilig filed a petition in the Circuit Court for Montgomery County, in which he alleged that he was then a Maryland resident and that he was "transitioning from male to female." Invoking the equitable jurisdiction of the court, he asked for an order that would change his name to Janet Heilig Wright and change his "sexual identity" designation from male to female. [While granting a name change, the Circuit Court declined to order a change of "sexual identity," and was upheld by the Court of Special Appeals.] The appellate court concluded that, even if the Circuit Court had equitable jurisdiction to grant the relief requested, such relief could not be granted to the petitioner because he had not shown that any purported change in his sexual status was in fact permanent. In default of such evidence, the court stated, the petitioner "has not established a strong case on the equities."

Background

Perhaps because there was no opposition to the petition, the factual evidence was rather skimpy. Attached to the petition was a copy of petitioner's birth certificate and two letters, each addressed "To Whom It May Concern." The first, from Dr. Michael Dempsey, an endocrinologist, stated that petitioner had been under his care for eighteen months as a "transgendered person," that her treatment consisted of female hormones and anti-androgens "designed to maintain her body chemistry and bring about anatomical changes within typical female norms," that the hormonal therapy had resulted in "hormonal castration," and that, in Dr. Dempsey's medical opinion, the gender designation on petitioner's driver's license and other documents should be changed to female to " accurately reflect both her appearance and the hormonal changes of her body."[1] The second letter, from a licensed social worker named Ellen Warren, stated that petitioner "is in psychotherapeutic treatment…as a transsexual woman," that it was Ms. Warren's professional opinion that petitioner's name and gender should be legally changed to reflect "her true gender identity, which is female," and that such change was "in accordance with the Standards of Care of the Harry Benjamin International Gender Dysphoria Association."

---

1. The letter from Dr. Dempsey used the feminine pronoun in describing petitioner. Because of our conclusion that petitioner has not yet established an entitlement to a determination that his gender has been effectively changed from male to female, we shall use the masculine pronoun. We do so not to disparage petitioner's undoubtedly sincere belief that his transition is, indeed, complete, but simply to be consistent with our conclusion that he has yet to offer sufficient evidence to warrant that determination as a legal matter. We note that, in the petition and other papers filed with the Circuit Court, petitioner also used the masculine pronoun to describe himself.

A court master, completely misconstruing the nature of the requested relief, placed in the court file and presumably sent to petitioner a document asking what authority a Maryland court had "over the Secretary of State for Pennsylvania" and for petitioner to "indicate how petition complies with Health-Gen Article §4-214(b)(5)." Petitioner responded with a memorandum urging that, although the court had no authority over officials from other States, it did have equity jurisdiction to entertain petitions for change of name and gender filed by Maryland residents. Petitioner acknowledged that, because he was not born in Maryland and did not have a Maryland birth certificate, he was unable to take direct advantage of §4-214(b)(5), but contended that, under equal protection principles, he was entitled to a determination from a court of competent jurisdiction that his gender had changed. The hearing conducted by the Circuit Court dealt entirely with the issue of jurisdiction. The only evidence presented in support of the petition, apart from the two letters attached to it, was a form letter from the Maryland Motor Vehicle Administration establishing that, upon review and recommendation by its Medical Advisory Board, the Administration does recognize "transitional gender status change" and will issue a new driver's license reflecting that change, and a copy of the fifth version of the Standards of Care for Gender Identity Disorders adopted by the Harry Benjamin International Gender Dysphoria Association.

Discussion

Transsexualism: Medical Aspects

One of the dominant themes of transsexualism, which, to some extent, is reflected in the two letters and the Standards offered by petitioner, is the belief that sex/gender is not, in all instances, a binary concept—all male or all female. *See* Leslie Pearlman, *Transsexualism as Metaphor: The Collision of Sex and Gender,* 43 Buffalo L. Rev. 835, 842–43 (1995); Julie A. Greenberg, *Defining Male and Female: Intersexuality and the Collision Between Law and Biology,* 41 Ariz. L. Rev. 265, 275–76 (1999). Transsexuals, as petitioner claims to be, seek to achieve recognition of the view that a person's gender/sex is determined by his or her personal sexual identity rather than by physical characteristics alone.[2] Sex reassignment surgery, under that view, merely harmonizes a person's physical characteristics with that identity.

This Opinion is not intended to be a medical text. Apart from our own incompetence to write such a text, it appears that some of the concepts that underlie the views espoused by transsexuals who seek recognition of gender change are the subject of debate, in both the medical and legal communities. The literature, in both communities, is extensive and daunting, and, unguided by expert testimony, there is no way that we could evaluate it properly. It is, however, necessary to understand those underlying concepts in order to determine what gender is and whether, or how, it may be changed.

There is a recognized medical viewpoint that gender is not determined by any single criterion, but that the following seven factors may be relevant:

(1) Internal morphologic sex (seminal vesicles/prostate or vagina/uterus/fallopian tubes);

(2) External morphologic sex (genitalia);

---

2. In the context before us, the terms "sex" and "gender" are not necessarily synonymous for all purposes, and, indeed, the perceived distinctions between them, to some extent, lie at the core of transsexualism. The term "sex" is often used to denote anatomical or biological sex, whereas "gender" refers to a person's psychosexual individuality or identity.

(3) Gonadal sex (testes or ovaries);

(4) Chromosomal sex (presence or absence of Y chromosome);

(5) Hormonal sex (predominance of androgens or estrogens);

(6) Phenotypic sex (secondary sex characteristics, e.g. facial hair, breasts, body type); and

(7) Personal sexual identity.

Blackburn notes that the initial development of a fetus is asexual. SUSAN TUCKER BLACKBURN, MATERNAL, FETAL, & NEONATAL PHYSIOLOGY: A CLINICAL PERSPECTIVE 19–24 (2d ed. 2002). The fetus first forms rudimentary sexual organs—gonads, genital ridge, and internal duct system—that later develop into sexually differentiated organs: testes or ovaries, penis/scrotum or clitoris/labia, and fallopian tubes or seminal vesicles/vas deferens, respectively. This initial differentiation, according to Blackburn, is governed by the presence or absence of a Y chromosome inherited from the father. If present, the Y chromosome triggers the development of testes, which begin to produce male hormones that influence much of the fetus's further sexual development. Those hormones cause the development of male genitalia and inhibit the development of the fetus's primitive fallopian tube system. If the Y chromosome is not present, the fetus continues on what has been characterized as the "default" path of sexual development. The gonads develop into ovaries, and, freed from the inhibiting influence of male hormones, the fetus's primordial duct system develops into fallopian tubes and a uterus.

Most often, it appears, a fetus's sexual development is uneventful, and, because all of the sexual features are consistent and indicate one gender or the other, the person becomes easily identifiable as either male or female. When this development is changed or interrupted, however, the situation may become less clear, and people may be born with sexual features that are either ambiguous (consistent with *either* sex) or incongruent (seemingly inconsistent with their "assigned" sex).

Individuals who have biological features that are ambiguous or incongruent are sometimes denoted as intersexed or hermaphroditic. The variety of intersexed conditions encompasses virtually every permutation of variance among the seven factors considered in determining gender. These various ambiguities, moreover, may occur both within a specific factor (e.g., ambiguous, unclassifiable genitalia) or between two or more different factors (e.g., chromosomal sex is incongruent with morphological sex). Generally, these conditions are classified into three "theoretical types": male pseudohermaphroditism, female pseudohermaphroditism, and true hermaphroditism. The true hermaphrodite consists of an individual with at least some ovarian tissue and some testicular tissue, and is the most rare. Female pseudohermaphrodites often have XX chromosomes and ovaries, but exhibit "masculinized" external genitalia. The "masculinization" of the genitalia can take many forms, including the enlargement of the clitoris or swelling of the labia (thus resembling a scrotum).

Male pseudohermaphroditism describes an individual who is chromosomally male (XY) and has testes, but who also has external genitalia that have become feminized. In one condition, called androgen insensitivity syndrome (AIS), the feminization of the genitalia is the result of the body's inability to respond to the developmental influences of androgen. Without the effects of the male hormone, the genitalia develop along the "default" path of feminity. This process continues through puberty, resulting in a person with (undescended) testes and male chromosomes who is very feminine. Because the condition may be detectable only upon an internal examination, it is often undiagnosed until puberty, when the presumed woman fails to menstruate.

A condition that produces similar results is known as 5-alpha-reductase deficiency (5AR). Like AIS, the individual with 5AR deficiency has testes but fails to respond to androgen in the womb, resulting in feminine external genitalia. With the onset of puberty, however, the individual *does* begin to respond to the increased production of testosterone, and the body begins to masculinize. The individual grows tall and muscular, begins to grow facial hair, and the genitals become more masculine. Some of these types of ambiguities, as noted above, may go largely unnoticed by the individual manifesting them, and may go undiagnosed for years.

In other cases, the individual's sexual ambiguity may be the result of a mistaken "sex assignment" at birth. The official designation of a person as male or female usually occurs at or immediately after birth, and is often based on the appearance of the external genitalia. Sometimes, when the genitalia are abnormal, doctors have erred in determining the baby's sex, mistaking an enlarged clitoris for a small penis, or *vice versa*. The criteria for determining sex at birth, one researcher has argued, are simply too rudimentary to be entirely accurate.

In the past, it was not uncommon, if a doctor examining the neonatal child observed what appeared to be ambiguous genitalia and concluded that the genitalia so observed would be incapable of functioning in the male capacity, for the doctor to recommend that the child be surgically altered and raised as a girl. It was previously believed that a person was psychosexually neutral at birth, and that subsequent psychosexual development was dependent on the appearance of the genitals. Thus, it was assumed, the altered male would psychologically respond, adapt to the new genitalia, and develop into a functional and healthy female.

That view appears no longer to be generally accepted. Individuals who have undergone such surgical alterations as a result of abnormal genitalia often have rejected their "assigned" gender and ultimately request that the alterations be surgically negated so that they may assume their original gender. In this regard, the medical community seems to have concluded that human brains are not psychosexually neutral at birth but are "predisposed and biased to interact with environmental, familial, and social forces in either a male or female mode."[3]

The medical community's experience with patients born with ambiguous genitalia has led many researchers to believe that the brain "differentiates" *in utero* to one gender or the other and that, once the child's brain has differentiated, that child cannot be made into a person of the other gender simply through surgical alterations. Some scientists have argued that such medical developments now offer a robust biological explanation of transsexualism—that the brain has differentiated to one sex while the rest of the body has differentiated to another.

Transsexualism was once regarded as a form of sexual or psychological deviance and, in some quarters, is still considered so today. *See, e.g., Hartin v. Bureau of*

---

3. As a result of this more recent experience and knowledge, doctors and clinicians seem now to be more skeptical about surgical alteration of ambiguous genitalia in very young children. Some doctors and advocates have proposed a moratorium on all surgical reconstruction prior to the patient becoming capable of consenting Others argue that surgical alteration of the genitalia should be an absolute last resort, performed only if all available alternatives fail.

Records, 75 Misc.2d 229, 347 N.Y.S.2d 515, 518 (N.Y.Sup.Ct.1973) (where the New York Board of Health described sex reassignment surgery as "an experimental form of psychotherapy by which mutilating surgery is conducted on a person with the intent of setting his mind at ease, and that nonetheless, does not change the body cells governing sexuality."); *Corbett v. Corbett,* [1970] 2 All E.R. 33, 2 W.L.R. 1306 (Probate, Divorce, and Admiralty Div. 1970) (finding litigant's transsexualism to be a "psychological abnormality"); *Maggert v. Hanks,* 131 F.3d 670, 671 (7th Cir.1997) (in describing transsexual wishing to undergo sex reassignment surgery, court observed that "[s]omeone eager to undergo this mutilation is plainly suffering from a profound psychiatric disorder.").

Recent studies have suggested that this condition may be associated with certain conditions in the womb and certain processes in the developing pre-natal brain. As noted, there is evidence suggesting that the brain differentiates into "male" and "female" brains, just as the fetus's rudimentary sex organs differentiate into "male" and "female" genitalia. These studies, the authors assert, "clearly support the paradigm that in transsexuals sexual differentiation of the brain and genitals may go into opposite directions and point to a neurobiological basis of gender identity disorder." Researchers theorize that the developing brain may differentiate in response to hormonal levels in the womb—"intrauterine adrogen exposure." This hypothesis has been tested with animals. Research has indicated, for instance, that the sexual differentiation of primates may be manipulated by controlling prenatal hormone exposure. Such experimental results have been cited by at least one court. *See Doe v. McConn,* 489 F.Supp. 76, 78 (S.D.Tex.1980) (describing the results of experiments discussed above).

The studies imply that transsexualism may be more similar to other physiological conditions of sexual ambiguity, such as androgen insensitivity syndrome, than to purely psychological disorders. The ultimate conclusion of such studies, which, as noted, is the central point sought to be made by transsexuals, is that the preeminent factor in determining gender is the individual's own sexual identity as it has developed in the brain. Regardless of its cause, the accounts from transsexuals themselves are startlingly consistent. *See, e.g., In re Estate of Gardiner,* 42 P.3d 120 (Kan.2002); *Littleton v. Prange,* 9 S.W.3d 223, 224 (Tex.Ct.App.1999); *M.T. v. J.T.,* 140 N.J.Super. 77, 355 A.2d 204, 205 (App.Div.1976). They grow up believing that they are not the sex that their body indicates they are. They believe that they have mistakenly grown up with the wrong genitalia. These disconcerting feelings often begin early in childhood, as early as three or four years. *See, e.g., Littleton, supra,* 9 S.W.3d at 224; *M.T., supra,* 355 A.2d at 205 (where the expert witness testified that "[t]here was… 'very little disagreement' on the fact that gender identity generally is established 'very, very firmly, almost immediately, by the age of 3 to 4 years.'"); *Doe v. McConn,* 489 F.Supp. 76, 78 (S.D.Tex.1980) ("Most, if not all, specialists in gender identity are agreed that the transsexual condition establishes itself very early, before the child is capable of elective choice in the matter"). These individuals often rebel against any attempt to impose social gender expectations that are inconsistent with what they believe they are-they may refuse to wear the "appropriate" clothes and refuse to participate in activities associated with their assigned gender. *See, e.g., M.T., supra,* 355 A.2d at 205. That kind of behavior has become one of the determining factors for a diagnosis of gender identity disorder.

A transsexual wishing to transition to a different gender has limited options. Generally, the options consist of psychotherapy, living as a person of the desired sex, hormonal treatment, and sex reassignment surgery. Although psychotherapy may help the transsexual deal with the psychological difficulties of transsexualism, courts have recognized that psychotherapy is not a "cure" for transsexualism. Because transsexualism is universally recognized as inherent, rather than chosen, psychotherapy will never succeed in "curing" the patient:

> "Most, if not all, specialists in gender identity are agreed that the transsexual condition establishes itself very early, before the child is capable of elective choice in the matter, probably in the first two years of life; some say even earlier, before birth during the fetal period. These findings indicate that the transsexual has not made a choice to be as he is, but rather that the choice has been made for him through many causes preceding and beyond his control. Consequently, it has been found that attempts to treat the true adult transsexual psychotherapeutically have consistently met with failure."

McConn, supra, 489 F.Supp. at 78.

Hormonal treatment has been shown to be more effective, and, for the male-to-female transsexual, results in breast growth, feminine body fat distribution, a decrease in body hair, and softening of the skin. Although most of these effects are reversible upon termination of the treatment, the individual's breast growth may not reverse entirely. Hormonal treatment for female-to-male transsexuals results in deepening of the voice, enlargement of the clitoris, breast atrophy, increased upper body strength, weight gain, increased facial and body hair, baldness, increased sexual arousal, and decreased hip fat.

Surgical options for the male-to-female transsexual include orchiectomy (removal of gonads), vaginoplasty (construction of vagina), and mammoplasty (construction of breasts). Some patients elect to undergo additional cosmetic surgeries to enhance other secondary sex features, such as facial structure or voice tone. Surgical options for the female-to-male transsexual include mastectomy, hysterectomy, vaginectomy, and phalloplasty. As most health insurance companies currently exclude coverage for transsexual treatment, the out-of-pocket cost is often prohibitively expensive. One commentator has asserted that a male-to-female operation costs an average of $37,000, whereas the average female-to-male operation costs $77,000. Aaron C. McKee, *The American Dream—2.5 Kids and a White Picket Fence: The Need for Federal Legislation to Protect the Insurance Rights of Infertile Couples*, 41 Washburn L.J. 191, 198 (2001). Another estimate describes the cost as "easily reach[ing] $100,000." *Maggert, supra*, 131 F.3d at 672. Contributing to the much higher cost of female-to-male sex reassignment surgery is the increased technical difficulty of phalloplasty, estimates for which range from $30,000 to $150,000. *See* Shana Brown, *Sex Changes and "Opposite Sex" Marriage: Applying the Full Faith and Credit Clause to Compel Interstate Recognition of Transgendered Persons' Amended Legal Sex for Marital Purposes*, 38 San Diego L. Rev. 1113, 1127 n. 79 (2001); Patricia A. Cain, *Stories From the Gender Garden: Transsexuals and Anti-Discrimination Law*, 75 Denv. U. L. Rev. 1321, 1334 n. 59 (1998). The procedure may require several operations.

Estimates of the number of intersexed individuals vary considerably, from 1 per 37,000 people to 1 per 2,000. It seems to be a guess, although Dreger suggests that "the frequency of births in which the child exhibits a condition which today could count as 'intersexual' or 'sexually ambiguous' is significantly higher than most people outside the medical field (and many inside) assume it is."

In reviewing the medical literature, we have avoided making pronouncements of our own, but have simply recounted some of the assertions and conclusions that appear in that literature—assertions and conclusions which, when presented in the form of testimony in court, have evoked differing responses from the courts, both in the United States and elsewhere. Notwithstanding that this remains an evolving field, in which final conclusions as to some aspects may be premature, the current medical thinking does seem to support at least these relevant propositions: (1) that external genitalia are not the sole medically recognized determinant of gender; (2) that the medically recognized determinants of gender may sometimes be either ambiguous or incongruent; (3) that due to mistaken assumptions made by physicians of an infant's ambiguous external genitalia at or shortly after birth, some people are mislabeled at that time as male or female and thereafter carry an official gender status that is medically incorrect; (4) that at least some of the medically recognized determinants of gender are subject to being altered in such a way as to make them inconsistent with the individual's officially declared gender and consistent with the opposite gender; and (5) whether or not a person's psychological gender identity is physiologically based, it has received recognition as one of the determinants of gender and plays a powerful role in the person's psychic makeup and adaptation.

For our purposes, the relevance of these propositions lies in the facts that (1) gender itself is a fact that may be established by medical and other evidence, (2) it may be, or possibly may become, other than what is recorded on the person's birth certificate, and (3) a person has a deep personal, social, and economic interest in having the official designation of his or her gender match what, in fact, it always was or possibly has become.[4] The issue then becomes the circumstances under which a court may declare one's gender to be other than what is officially recorded and the criteria to be used in making any such declaration.

We agree that, in the circumstances of this case, a declaratory judgment would have been inappropriate, as no one has contested petitioner's claim that he had successfully transitioned to become a woman and was entitled to be declared as such. Of greater importance, we disagree with the intermediate appellate court's conclusion that there is no other basis of jurisdiction to consider the petition and, should the case for it be made, to grant the relief requested by petitioner. The Circuit Court has Constitutionally-based, and statutorily recognized, equitable jurisdiction to consider and rule upon the petition. [Omitted here is a lengthy analysis of equity jurisdiction's development in Maryland, showing the expansive nature of a court's authority to determine issues of status that are necessary to resolve legal controversies.]

The statute referenced by petitioner—§4-214(b)(5) of the 'Health-General' Article—has significant relevance in this regard. It provides that "[u]pon receipt of a certified copy of an order of a court of competent jurisdiction indicating the sex of an individual born in this State has been changed by surgical procedure and whether such individual's name has been changed, the Secretary shall amend the certificate of birth of the individual as prescribed by regulation." Although petitioner was not seeking relief under that statute and, because he was not born in Maryland and has no Maryland birth certificate, would not be entitled to relief under it, the statute, along with other statutes in the subtitle of which it is a part, evidences a clear recognition by the General Assembly that a person's gender can be changed and that there are courts with jurisdiction to consider and determine whether that has occurred.

It appears that 22 States and the District of Columbia have enacted statutes expressly enabling a person who has undergone a change in gender to have his or her birth certificate amended to reflect the change. Most of those statutes require a court order based

---

4. Indeed, that interest has received recognition as a "right" under the European Convention for the Protection of Human Rights and Fundamental Freedoms. *See Goodwin v. United Kingdom,* [2002] 2 FCR 577, 67 BMLR 199 (European Court of Human Rights (Grand Chamber) 2002).

on evidence of a surgical procedure, although a few allow an amendment without a court order and three do not require a surgical procedure. About 20 States have statutes dealing generally with amendments to birth certificates but which do not speak expressly, one way or the other, to gender changes. Only one State — Tennessee — statutorily forbids a change in birth certificate by reason of gender change. *See* Tenn.Code Ann. § 68-3-203 (2002).

Viewed against this background, it is clear that, in enacting § 4-214(b)(5), the Legislature necessarily recognized the jurisdiction of the Circuit Courts to consider and grant petitions to declare a change in gender; indeed, that section could have no other rational meaning.

The fact that § 4-214(b)(5) directly operates only with respect to a Maryland birth certificate does not detract in the least from the legislative recognition of jurisdiction to entertain and grant petitions such as the one before us. Obviously, the Legislature cannot direct officials in other States to change birth certificates issued in those States but may deal only with birth certificates issued or issuable in Maryland, and that is the thrust of the statute. The jurisdiction of Maryland courts is not limited by the birthplace of the parties seeking relief, however, so by recognizing the authority of the Circuit Courts to enter gender-change declarations with respect to persons born in Maryland, it necessarily recognizes as well their jurisdiction to enter such orders on behalf of anyone properly before the court. Indeed, any other conclusion would raise serious Constitutional issues under the Equal Protection and Privileges and Immunities Clause of the 14th Amendment to the United States Constitution.

As should be evident, we do not rest our holding that the Circuit Court had jurisdiction over Mr. Heilig's petition solely on the basis of § 4-214(b)(5), but rather on the conclusion that his action fell within the general equity jurisdiction of the court. Section 4-214(b)(5) simply recognizes the existence of that jurisdiction. *Nor do we opine on what the collateral effect of any judgment attesting to a change in gender might be.*[5] We hold only that the court had jurisdiction to consider and rule upon the petition.[6]

---

5. As pointed out in *Goodwin v. United Kingdom,* [2002] 2 FCR 577, 67 BMLR 199 (Eur. Ct. H.R. (Grand Chamber) 2002), the issue of a transsexual's true gender can arise in many different contexts and have a wide variety of collateral consequences. It may affect or determine, for example, the validity of a marriage, whether a birth certificate may be amended, entitlement to pension or insurance rights that distinguish by gender, whether distinctions in employment are, as to a particular individual, permissible or unlawful, application of the law of rape or other offenses in which gender may be an element or issue, medical treatment and housing assignment upon incarceration or other institutional confinement, entitlement to participate in certain amateur or professional sports, and housing and work assignments available for persons in military service. In Comment, *Transsexuals in Limbo: The Search for a Legal Definition of Sex,* 31 Md. L. Rev. 236, 247–51 (1971), the unnamed author noted the possible effect of gender change on various estate and trust issues, questioning, for example, whether a male to female transsexual would still qualify for a legacy to the testator's "son." Most cases in which the gender of a transsexual is at issue have arisen in the context of marriage, and the prevailing sentiment in the United States seems to be that, absent legislation to the contrary, marriage between a transsexual and a person of the transsexual's initial assigned gender is not permitted, even when the transsexual has undergone surgery. Many of the courts expressing that view have followed the lead of the English court in *Corbett v. Corbett,* [1970] 2 All E.R. 33, 2 W.L.R. 1306 (Probate, Divorce, and Admiralty Div. 1970), which initially set the law for England in this regard. Based on the medical evidence presented in that case, the Corbett court concluded that "the biological sexual constitution of an individual is fixed at birth (at the latest), and cannot be changed, either by the natural development of organs of the opposite sex, or by medical or surgical means," and "[t]he only cases where the term 'change of sex' is appropriate are those in which a mistake as to sex is made at birth and subsequently revealed by further medical investigation." *See In re Ladrach,* 32

What Must Be Shown?

Most courts and other agencies that have dealt with establishing the gender of trans-sexuals have done so in particular contexts and have set the requirements for such recognition accordingly. To warrant amending a birth certificate, Maryland (and most States that permit such a change at all) requires by statute a finding that gender *has been changed* "by surgical procedure."[7] Those courts that have permitted transsexuals to marry someone of their former gender have also uniformly required surgery as a condition to recognizing a change in gender.

Surgery seems to be a requirement for recognition of gender change in other contexts as well. The Social Security Administration apparently will alter its records to record a change of gender but requires "[c]linical or medical records or other combination of documents showing the sex change surgery has been completed." In the Federal prison system, pre-operative transsexuals are housed with inmates of their birth gender, but post-operative transsexuals are housed with inmates of their acquired gender. *See Farmer v. Haas*, 990 F.2d 319, 320 (7th Cir. 1993). It has been reported, although there seems to be no official documentation, that the State Department will issue a temporary passport with a change of gender upon a certified letter from a

---

Ohio Misc.2d 6, 513 N.E.2d 828 (Probate Ct.1987). In *Frances B. v. Mark B.*, 78 Misc.2d 112, 355 N.Y.S.2d 712 (N.Y.Sup.Ct.1974), the court based its rejection of a marriage on the fact that, under New York law, physical incapacity for a sexual relationship was a ground for annulment. It thus concluded that, as a female to male transsexual, even after surgery, was incapacitated in that regard, the transsexual's marriage to a woman was invalid. *See also Littleton v. Prange*, 9 S.W.3d 223 (Tex.Ct.App.1999) (biologically, post-operative female transsexual still a male); *In re Estate of Gardiner*, 42 P.3d 120 (Kan.2002) (same); *but compare M.T. v. J.T.*, 140 N.J.Super. 77, 355 A.2d 204 (App.Div.1976) (rejecting Corbett and recognizing as valid a marriage involving post-operative transsexual).

The holding in *Corbett* was reexamined but confirmed in England in *Bellinger v. Bellinger*, [2001] EWCA Civ. 1140, [2002] Fam. 150 (C.A.2001). That view is not shared in other countries, however, including at least two that are regarded as common law countries. Australia and New Zealand recognize such marriages when the transsexual has undergone surgery. *See In re Kevin*, 28 Fam. L.R. 158 (Family Ct. of Australia 2001); *Attorney General v. Otahuhu Family Court*, [1995] 1 N.Z.L.R. 603 (High Court Wellington, N.Z. 1994). In *Goodwin v. United Kingdom, supra* [2002] 2 F.C.R. 577, 67 BMLR 199 (Eur. Ct. H.R. (Grand Chamber) 2002), the European Court of Human Rights noted a report indicating that 20 European countries (Austria, Belgium, Denmark, Estonia, Finland, France, Germany, Greece, Iceland, Italy, Latvia, Luxembourg, the Netherlands, Norway, Slovakia, Spain, Sweden, Switzerland, Turkey, and the Ukraine) also permitted a post-operative transsexual to marry a person of his/her original gender and concluded that England's refusal to recognize such marriages violated the personal rights of the transsexual under Articles 8 and 12 of the Convention for the Protection of Human Rights and Fundamental Freedoms (Art. 8: Everyone has the right to respect for his private…life; Art. 12: Men and women of marriageable age have the right to marry and to found a family, according to the national laws governing the exercise of this right). This is an issue that is not before us in this case and upon which we express no opinion.

6. The question may be raised, of what use is a judgment declaring that a person's gender has been changed if we do not specify the effect of such a judgment? The answer is that courts rarely specify the collateral effect of their judgments, unless it is raised as a justiciable issue. The question in a case, ordinarily, is simply whether a party is entitled to the judgment, not what the party may do with it. What effect a judgment has depends on the law governing what the judgment holder seeks to do, and that is true in this regard as well.

7. It appears to be undisputed that no surgery, however extensive, can make a transsexual fertile in his/her "new" gender. Neither male-to-female nor female-to-male transsexuals are capable of conceiving children once sex reassignment surgery has been completed. The fact that §4-214(b)(5) recognizes that surgery *can* effect a change in gender indicates, at least in the context of amending birth certificates, that infertility is not a basis for refusing to recognize the change.

physician stating that the applicant is about to undergo sex reassignment surgery and will issue a regular new passport showing such a change upon a certified letter stating that the applicant has undergone such surgery. *See* Greenberg, *supra*, 41 ARIZ. L. REV. at 315.

The statutes or regulations that make surgery a condition to recognition of gender change rarely, if ever, specify the kind of surgery that will suffice, although in the court cases there is usually considerable evidence regarding the nature and effect of any surgery that is undertaken and both the medical and legal literature describe it as well. The point, or relevance, of the requirement of surgery seems to lie in the assumption that, if the person has undergone sex reassignment surgery, the change has been effected, in that at least (1) the person's external genitalia have been brought into consistency with that indicative of the new gender and with other determinants of gender, and (2) the change is regarded as permanent and irreversible. Hormonal therapy alone, which usually can be terminated or perhaps even reversed, has not, to our knowledge, been recognized as effecting either a sufficient change or a permanent one.

Almost all courts have recognized that the question of whether and how gender can be changed is one where the law depends upon and, to a large extent, must follow medical facts (medical facts, in this context, to include relevant psychological facts). Any reasoned legal conclusion respecting an asserted change in one's gender must therefore be based on admissible evidence of medical fact—the factors that actually should be considered in determining gender and what the person's gender status is when viewed in the context of those factors. We have examined the literature available to us and recounted some of the evidence that other courts have found relevant, but only to establish the basis for our conclusion that the court has jurisdiction over petitions seeking recognition of gender change. None of what we have recounted is evidence in this case and therefore does not establish, by itself, petitioner's entitlement to the order he seeks.

This is, clearly, an evolving area. As noted, aside from the two unsworn letters attached to the petition and the Standards of Care of the Harry Benjamin International Gender Dysphoria Association, no medical evidence was presented to the Circuit Court with respect to petitioner's gender status. Because we believe (1) that the court had jurisdiction to consider the petition, and (2) that, on the record before it, the court erred in broadly concluding, apparently as a matter of law, that gender was not subject to modification or adjustment, we shall direct that the case be remanded for the court to consider admissible evidence relevant to the issue and to make a determination of whether the relief requested by petitioner should be granted based on that evidence. As the seeker of relief, petitioner has the burden of establishing his entitlement to it, and it will therefore be incumbent upon him to present sufficient medical evidence of both the relevant criteria for determining gender and of the fact that, applying that criteria, he has completed a permanent and irreversible change from male to female.

Notes and Questions

1. Compare the language of the judges in the preceding cases. Compare their apparent understanding (or lack of understanding) of the issues faced by the sexual minority parties in their cases. What is the appropriate role of judicial empathy for the parties in making important constitutional decisions?

2. Many lower federal courts gave *Bowers v. Hardwick* extraordinary weight in due process and equal protection litigation, while many state courts were hostile to the decision, rejecting it as a precedent for state constitutional law and striking down sodomy laws on privacy theories developed under their own state constitutions. To what extent does the Supreme Court's 2003 decision in *Lawrence*, overruling *Bowers* and stating that it was "wrong" when it was decided, cancel out the precedential value of the intervening federal court decisions that had rejected claims based on the precedent of *Bowers*? Note the portion of Justice Scalia's dissent in Lawrence where he describes the many lower court rulings that had relied on *Bowers* to adjudicate constitutional privacy claims.

3. *Bowers* rejected the "claim" that "homosexuals" have a right to "privacy" when engaging in "sodomy." Although the Supreme Court overruled *Bowers* in *Lawrence*, in so doing did it strike down the Texas Homosexual Conduct Law based on a "right of privacy."? What was the relevance of *Romer v. Evans*, an equal protection decision, to the outcome in *Lawrence*?

4. *Heilig* marks a significant break with recent appellate rulings in the United States on gender identity issues. Appellate courts in Texas and Kansas, in decisions cited in *Heilig*, had recently ruled that for purposes of law, sex change procedures are merely cosmetic and that an individual remains in their assigned gender of birth for purposes of state marriage law. In both cases, that meant retroactively invalidating marriages entered into by a party to the case and a deceased person, working a forfeiture of legal rights of the surviving marital partner. Does the constitutional "liberty" that Justice Kennedy describes in *Lawrence* have any bearing on the question presented in *Heilig*, or in the transgender marriage cases from Kansas and Texas?

5. Based on your reading so far, do you believe that the issues presented by sexual orientation and gender identity should be seen as distinct and different, or do they interrelate sufficiently that legislatures and courts should consider them as integral aspects of a larger realm of human sexuality? What would that mean for purposes of development of new legal rules, statutes or regulations?

Further Reading

Ronald Bayer, Homosexual and American Psychiatry: The Politics of Diagnosis (Princeton, 1987 [revised second edition]).

Alan P. Bell, Martin S. Weinberg, & Sue K. Hammersmith, Sexual Preference: Its Development in Men and Women (Indiana, 1981).

Sandra L. Bem, Probing the Promise of Androgyny in Beyond Sex-Role Stereotypes (Alexandra G, Kaplan and Joan P. Bean, eds) at 48 (Little Brown 1976).

John E. Boswell, Christianity, Social Tolerance, and Homosexuality: Gay People in Western Europe From the Beginning of the Christian Era to the Fourteenth Century (Chicago, 1980).

Chandler Burr, A Separate Creation: The Search for the Biological Origins of Sexual Orientation (Hyperion 1996).

Judith Butler, Gender Trouble (Routledge 1990).

John. D'Emilio & Estelle B. Freedman, Intimate Matters: A History of Sexuality in America (Harper & Row, 1988).

Lillian Faderman, Odd Girls and Twilight Lovers (New York: Columbia University Press, 1991).

Anne Fausto-Sterling, Myths of Gender: Biological Theories About Women and Men (rev. ed. 1992).

Michel Foucault, The History of Sexuality, Volume I: An Introduction (New York: Random House, 1978).

John C. Gonsiorek & James D. Weinrich, eds, Homosexuality: Research Implications for Public Policy (Sage, 1991)

David F. Greenberg, The Construction of Homosexuality (Chicago, 1988).

Janet E. Halley, Sexual Orientation and the Politics of Biology: A Critique of the Argument from Immutability, 46 Stanford Law Review 503 (1994).

Dean H. Hamer & Peter Copeland, The Science of Desire: The Search for the Gay Gene and the Biology of Behavior (Simon & Schuster 1995).

Richard A. Isay, Being Homosexual: Gay Men and Their Development (Farrar, Straus & Giroux, 1989).

Simon LeVay, Queer Science: The Use and Abuse of Research Into Homosexuality (MIT 1996).

Simon LeVay, The Sexual Brain (MIT 1993).

Kenneth Lewes, The Psychoanalytic Theory of Male Homosexuality (Simon & Schuster, 1988).

Ethel Spector Person, Sexuality as the Mainstay of Identity in Women: Sex and Sexuality (Catharine R. Stimpson and Ethel Pector Person, eds.) at 36–61 (1980).

Shane Phelan, "(Be)Coming Out: Lesbian Identity and Politics," Signs: Journal of Women in Culture and Society 18 (Summer 1993): 765–90.

Richard A. Posner, Sex and Reason (Harvard, 1992).

Adrienne Rich, "Compulsory Heterosexuality and Lesbian Existence," Signs: Journal of Women in Culture and Society 5 (Summer 1980): 631–60.

Eve Kosofsky Sedgwick, Epistemology of the Closet (Berkeley: University of California Press, 1990).

Edward Stein, The Mismeasure of Desire: The Science, Theory, and Ethics of Sexual Orientation (Oxford 2001).

Edward Stein, ed., Forms of Desire: Sexual Orientation and the Social Constructionist Controversy (Routledge 1992).

J.D. Weinrich, Sexual Landscapes: Why We Are What We Are, Why We Love Whom We Love (Scribners, 1987).

Heather Wishik and Carol Pierce, Sexual Orientation and Identity (New Dynamics 1991).

Chapter Two

What Is the Meaning of *Lawrence & Romer?*

The U.S. Supreme Court's rulings in *Romer v. Evans* and *Lawrence v. Texas* marked a significant turning point in the law governing the constitutional rights of sexual minorities in the United States. *Romer* was the first case in which the Supreme Court ruled affirmatively on an equal protection claim brought by gay plaintiffs, and Lawrence was the first case in which the Supreme Court ruled affirmatively on a due process claim brought by gay claimants. In addition, of course, *Lawrence* overruled *Bowers v. Hardwick*, a case that had been frequently cited by the federal appeals and district courts, as well as many state courts, in rejecting constitutional claims by gay litigants. Consequently, a question of first importance for constitutional principles governing claims by sexual minorities is: What is the meaning of *Lawrence* and what is the meaning of *Romer* as precedents for subsequent litigation?

The following sequence of opinions is intended to pose this question in the context of actual litigation that raises both the equal protection and due process issues. It concerns the constitutionality of a Florida statutory provision that forbids "homosexuals" (defined as those actually engaging in homosexual conduct) from adopting children. The following description of the enactment of the statute is taken from 11th Circuit Judge Rosemary Barkett's dissenting opinion in the case:

> The Florida statute was enacted after an organized and relentless anti-homosexual campaign led by Anita Bryant, a pop singer who sought to repeal a January 1977 ordinance of the Dade County Metropolitan Commission prohibiting discrimination against homosexuals in the areas of housing, public accommodations, and employment. Bryant organized a drive that collected the 10,000 signatures needed to force a public referendum on the ordinance. In the course of her campaign, which the Miami Herald described as creating a "witch-hunting hysteria more appropriate to the 17th century than the 20th," Bryant referred to homosexuals as "human garbage." She also promoted the insidious myth that schoolchildren were vulnerable to molestation at the hands of homosexual schoolteachers who would rely on the ordinance to avoid being dismissed from their positions.

In response to Bryant's efforts, Senator Curtis Peterson introduced legislation in the Florida Senate banning both adoptions by and marriage between homosexuals. The legislative history reveals the very close and utterly transparent connection between Bryant's campaign and the Peterson bills. At the May 3, 1977 hearings of the Senate Judiciary Civil Committee, for example, Senator Peterson observed that "it is a possible problem, constantly in the news." Senator George Firestone commented that "this [gay rights controversy] has totally polarized [my] community unnecessarily." And Senator Don Chamberlin explicitly tied the Bryant campaign to the proposed ban on homosexual adoption, arguing that the latter would never have arisen without the ruckus over the Dade County antidiscrimination ordinance. The impetus for Florida's adoption ban exactly parallels the impetus for the state constitutional amendment struck down in *Romer*.

The Florida legislature's intention to stigmatize and demean homosexuals is further confirmed by the passage, on May 30, 1977, of a House amendment that allowed for public disclosure of the reasons for a denial of an application for adoption. The explicit purpose of this amendment was to protect non-homosexual prospective parents whose applications were denied for reasons other than sexual orientation from the stigma of being thought to be homosexual. The Senate provided added coverage against stigmatization for non-homosexual applicants with its May 31 amendment requiring courts, when dismissing a petition for adoption, to state with specificity the reasons for doing so.

Throughout all of these proceedings, it could hardly be said that there was any discussion of the "best interests of the child" standard. The only legislator who bothered to inject the concept was Senator Chamberlin, who tried to block the bill, noting that there was no incompatibility at all between homosexuals and the best interests of children. Another senator simply stated that "we have a responsibility to provide children with a wholesome atmosphere."

As the House and Senate gave their final approval to the Peterson bills on May 31, Senator Peterson stated that his bills were a message to homosexuals that "[w]e're really tired of you. We wish you would go back into the closet." On June 8, 1977, exactly one day after Dade County voters repealed the antidiscrimination ordinance, the Governor of Florida signed the Peterson bills into law, in what can only be seen as a deliberate acknowledgment of the orchestration between Bryant's campaign and the legislature's actions. In short, the legislative history shows that anti-gay animus was the major factor—indeed the sole factor—behind the law's promulgation.

Several lawsuits were instituted to challenge the constitutionality of the adoption restriction. Despite some initial success at the trial level in the state courts, the Florida appellate courts rebuffed the challenges, finding that the law was subject to only the least demanding rational basis scrutiny, and that the legislature could have believed that it was preferable for adoptive children to be placed in traditional married-parent heterosexual families, on the theory that children do best with opposite-sex parental role models. After *Romer v. Evans* was decided, a new challenge was mounted in federal district court, contending that a more demanding scrutiny of Florida's justifications for the law was required. The appeal to the 11th Circuit of the federal district court's rejection of that lawsuit was pending when *Lawrence v. Texas* was decided. What follows is the decision by the 11th Circuit's three-judge panel, followed by opinions issued by two members of the court in response to the full Circuit's vote denying en banc rehearing. The Supreme Court denied a petition for certiorari on January 10, 2005, putting off the opportunity to clarify the scope of its ruling.

Lofton v. Secretary, Department of Children and Family Services

358 F.3d 804 (11th Cir. 2004),
petition for rehearing en banc denied, 377 F.3d 1275 (2004),
petition for certiorari denied, 125 S.Ct. 869 (2005)

BIRCH, Circuit Judge:

In this appeal, we decide the states' rights issue of whether Florida Statute §63.042(3), which prevents adoption by practicing homosexuals, is constitutional as enacted by the Florida legislature and as subsequently enforced. The district court granted summary judgment to Florida over an equal protection and due process challenge by homosexual persons desiring to adopt. We AFFIRM.

I. BACKGROUND

A. *The Challenged Florida Statute*

Since 1977, Florida's adoption law has contained a codified prohibition on adoption by any "homosexual" person. 1977 Fla. Laws, ch. 77-140, §1, Fla. Stat. §63.042(3) (2002). For purposes of this statute, Florida courts have defined the term "homosexual" as being "limited to applicants who are known to engage in current, voluntary homosexual activity," thus drawing "a distinction between homosexual orientation and homosexual activity." *Fla. Dep't of Health & Rehab. Servs. v. Cox,* 627 So.2d 1210, 1215 (Fla.Dist.Ct.App.1993), *aff'd in relevant part,* 656 So.2d 902, 903 (Fla.1995). During the past twelve years, several legislative bills have attempted to repeal the statute, and three separate legal challenges to it have been filed in the Florida courts. To date, no attempt to overturn the provision has succeeded. We now consider the most recent challenge to the statute.

B. *The Litigants*

Six plaintiffs-appellants bring this case. The first, Steven Lofton, is a registered pediatric nurse who has raised from infancy three Florida foster children, each of whom tested positive for HIV at birth. By all accounts, Lofton's efforts in caring for these children have been exemplary, and his story has been chronicled in dozens of news stories and editorials as well as on national television. We confine our discussion of that story to those facts relevant to the legal issues before us and properly before us in the record. John Doe, also named as a plaintiff-appellant in this litigation, was born on 29 April 1991. Testing positive at birth for HIV and cocaine, Doe immediately entered the Florida foster care system. Shortly thereafter, Children's Home Society, a private agency, placed Doe in foster care with Lofton, who has extensive experience treating HIV patients. At eighteen months, Doe sero-reverted and has since tested HIV negative. In September of 1994, Lofton filed an application to adopt Doe but refused to answer the application's inquiry about his sexual preference and also failed to disclose Roger Croteau, his cohabiting partner, as a member of his household. After Lofton refused requests from the Department of Children and Families ("DCF") to supply the missing information, his application was rejected pursuant to the homosexual adoption provision. Shortly thereafter, in early 1995, William E. Adams, Jr., a professor of law who had participated in one of the previous legal challenges to Fla. Stat. §63.042(3), wrote to the American Civil Liberties Union

("ACLU") and informed it that Lofton and Croteau would make "excellent test plaintiffs." R3-108 at 3. Two years later, in light of the length of Doe's stay in Lofton's household, DCF offered Lofton the compromise of becoming Doe's legal guardian. This arrangement would have allowed Doe to leave the foster care system and DCF supervision. However, because it would have cost Lofton over $300 a month in lost foster care subsidies and would have jeopardized Doe's Medicaid coverage, Lofton declined the guardianship option unless it was an interim stage toward adoption. Under Florida law, DCF could not accommodate this condition, and the present litigation ensued.

Plaintiff-appellant Douglas E. Houghton, Jr., is a clinical nurse specialist and legal guardian of plaintiff-appellant John Roe, who is eleven years old. Houghton has been Roe's caretaker since 1996 when Roe's biological father, suffering from alcohol abuse and frequent unemployment, voluntarily left Roe, then four years old, with Houghton. That same year, Houghton was appointed co-guardian of Roe along with one Robert Obeso (who otherwise has no involvement in this case). After Roe's biological father consented to termination of his parental rights, Houghton attempted to adopt Roe. Because of Houghton's homosexuality, however, he did not receive a favorable preliminary home study evaluation, which precluded him from filing the necessary adoption petition in state circuit court. Fla. Stat. §§ 63.092(3), 63.112(2)(b).

Plaintiff-appellants Wayne Larue Smith and Daniel Skahen, an attorney and real estate broker residing together in Key West, became licensed DCF foster parents after completing a requisite ten-week course in January of 2000. Since then, they have cared for three foster children, none of whom has been available for adoption. On 1 May 2000, Smith and Skahen submitted applications with DCF to serve as adoptive parents. On their adoption applications, both Smith and Skahen indicated that they are homosexuals. On 15 May 2000, they received notices from DCF stating that their applications had been denied because of their homosexuality. Unlike Lofton and Houghton, neither of whose cohabiting partners seeks to join their respective adoptions, Smith and Skahen seek to adopt jointly.

C. Procedural History

Appellants filed suit in the United States District Court for the Southern District of Florida. Their complaint alleged that the statute violates appellants' fundamental rights and the principles of equal protection. Jointly, appellants asked the district court to declare Fla. Stat. § 63.042(3) unconstitutional and to enjoin its enforcement. The district court denied a request for class certification and granted summary judgment in favor of the state on all counts, thereby upholding the statute. It is from this judgment that appellants now appeal.

Appellants assert three constitutional arguments on appeal. First, appellants argue that the statute violates Lofton, Houghton, Doe, and Roe's rights to familial privacy, intimate association, and family integrity under the Due Process Clause of the Fourteenth Amendment. Second, appellants argue that the Supreme Court's recent decision in *Lawrence v. Texas*, 539 U.S. 558 (2003), recognized a fundamental right to private sexual intimacy and that the Florida statute, by disallowing adoption by individuals who engage in homosexual activity, impermissibly burdens the exercise of this right. Third, appellants allege that, by categorically prohibiting only homosexual persons from adopting children, the statute violates the Equal Protection Clause of the Fourteenth Amendment. Each of these challenges raises questions of first impression in this circuit.

II. Discussion

A. *Summary Judgment Standard*

We review a summary judgment decision *de novo* and apply the same legal standard used by the district court. In conducting our review, we view all evidence and factual inferences in the light most favorable to the nonmoving party. Summary judgment is proper where "there is no genuine issue as to any material fact" and "the moving party is entitled to a judgment as a matter of law." Fed.R.Civ.P. 56(c). However, "the mere existence of *some* alleged factual dispute between the parties will not defeat an otherwise properly supported motion for summary judgment." Only factual disputes that are material under the substantive law governing the case will preclude entry of summary judgment.

B. *Florida's Adoption Scheme*

Appellants' challenge cannot be viewed apart from the context in which it arises. Under Florida law, "adoption is not a right; it is a statutory privilege." *Cox*, 627 So.2d at 1216. Unlike biological parentage, which precedes and transcends formal recognition by the state, adoption is wholly a creature of the state. *Cf. Smith v. Org. of Foster Families for Equal. & Reform*, 431 U.S. 816, 845 (1977) (noting that, unlike the natural family, which has "its origins entirely apart from the power of the State," the foster parent-child relationship "has its source in state law and contractual arrangements"); *Lindley v. Sullivan*, 889 F.2d 124, 131 (7th Cir.1989) ("Because of its statutory basis, adoption differs from natural procreation in a most important and striking way.").

In formulating its adoption policies and procedures, the State of Florida acts in the protective and provisional role of *in loco parentis* for those children who, because of various circumstances, have become wards of the state. Thus, adoption law is unlike criminal law, for example, where the paramount substantive concern is not intruding on individuals' liberty interests, *see, e.g., Lawrence*, 539 U.S. 558; *Roe v. Wade*, 410 U.S. 113 (1973), and the paramount procedural imperative is ensuring due process and fairness. Adoption is also distinct from such contexts as government-benefit eligibility schemes or access to a public forum, where equality of treatment is the primary concern. *See, e.g., Rosenberger v. Rector & Visitors of Univ. of Va.*, 515 U.S. 819 (1995); *Adarand Constructors, Inc. v. Pena*, 515 U.S. 200 (1995). By contrast, in the adoption context, the state's overriding interest is the best interests of the children whom it is seeking to place with adoptive families. *In re Adoption of H.Y.T.*, 458 So.2d 1127, 1128 (Fla.1984) (noting that, in Florida adoption proceedings, "the court's primary duty is to serve the best interests of the child—the object of the proceeding"). Florida, acting *parens patriae* for children who have lost their natural parents, bears the high duty of determining what adoptive home environments will best serve all aspects of the child's growth and development.

Because of the primacy of the welfare of the child, the state can make classifications for adoption purposes that would be constitutionally suspect in many other arenas. For example, Florida law requires that, in order to adopt any child other than a special needs child, an individual's primary residence and place of employment must be located in Florida. Fla. Stat. § 63.185. In screening adoption applicants, Florida considers such factors as physical and mental health, income and financial status, duration of marriage, housing, and neighborhood, among others. Fla. Admin. Code Ann. r. 65C-16.005(3) (2003). Similarly, Florida gives preference to candidates who demonstrate a commitment to "value, respect, appreciate, and educate the child regarding his or her racial and ethnic heritage." Moreover, prospective adoptive parents are required to sign an affidavit of good moral character. Many of these preferences and requirements, if employed outside the adoption arena, would be unlikely to withstand constitutional scrutiny. *See, e.g., Troxel v. Granville*, 530 U.S. 57, 68 (2000) (recognizing that, absent neglect or abuse, the state may not "inject itself into the private realm of the family to further question the ability of that parent to make the best decisions concerning the rearing of that parent's children"); *Supreme Court of Va. v. Friedman*, 487 U.S. 59, 70 (1988) (invalidating as unconstitutional Virginia's residency requirement for waive-in admission to the state bar).

The decision to adopt a child is not a private one, but a public act. *Cox*, 627 So.2d at 1216. At a minimum, would-be adoptive parents are asking the state to confer official recognition—and, consequently, the highest level of constitutional insulation from subsequent state interference, *see Troxel*, 530 U.S. at 65—on a relationship where there exists no natural filial bond. In many cases, they also are asking the state to entrust into their permanent care a child for whom the state is currently serving as *in loco parentis*. In doing so, these prospective adoptive parents are electing to open their homes and their private lives to close scrutiny by the state. Florida's adoption application requires information on a variety of private matters, including an applicant's physical and psychiatric medical history, previous marriages, arrest record, financial status, and educational history. In this regard, Florida's adoption scheme is like any "complex social welfare system that necessarily deals with the intimacies of family life." *Bowen v. Gilliard*, 483 U.S. 587, 602 (1987) (quoting *Califano v. Jobst*, 434 U.S. 47, 55 n. 11 (1977)). Accordingly, such intrusions into private family matters are on a different constitutional plane than those that "seek[ ] to foist orthodoxy on the unwilling by banning or criminally prosecuting" nonconformity. *Califano*, 434 U.S. at 55 n. 11; *cf. Lindley*, 889 F.2d at 131 (declining to find a privacy interest in adopting a child because state law "requires adopters to submit their personal lives to intensive scrutiny before the adoption may be approved").

In short, a person who seeks to adopt is asking the state to conduct an examination into his or her background and to make a determination as to the best interests of a child in need of adoption. In doing so, the state's overriding interest is not providing individuals the opportunity to become parents, but rather identifying those individuals whom it deems most capable of parenting adoptive children and providing them with a secure family environment. Indicative of the strength of the state's interest—indeed duty— in this context is the fact that appellants have not cited to us, nor have we found, a single precedent in which the Supreme Court or one of our sister circuits has sustained a constitutional challenge to an adoption scheme or practice by any individual other than a natural parent, and even many challenges by natural parents have failed. *See, e.g., Lehr v. Robertson*, 463 U.S. 248 (1983); *Quilloin v. Walcott*, 434 U.S. 246 (1978). Of course, despite their highly sensitive nature, adoption schemes are by no means immune from constitutional scrutiny, and we now consider the constitutionality of the Florida statute.

C. Appellants' Due Process Challenges

1. Fundamental Right to "Family Integrity"

Neither party disputes that there is no fundamental right to adopt, nor any fundamental right to be adopted. Both parties likewise agree that adoption is a privilege created by statute and not by common law. Because there is no fundamental right to adopt or to be adopted, it follows that there can be no fundamental right to apply for adoption.

Nevertheless, appellants argue that, by prohibiting homosexual adoption, the state is refusing to recognize and protect constitutionally protected parent-child relationships between Lofton and Doe and between Houghton and Roe. Noting that the Supreme Court has identified "the interest of parents in the care, custody, and control of their children" as "perhaps the oldest of the fundamental liberty interests recognized by this Court," *Troxel*, 530 U.S. at 65, appellants argue that they are entitled to a similar constitutional liberty interest because they share deeply loving emotional bonds that are as close as those between a natural parent and child. They further contend that this liberty interest is significantly burdened by the Florida statute, which prevents them from obtaining permanency in their relationships and creates uncertainty about the future integrity of their families. Only by being given the opportunity to adopt, appellants assert, will they be able to protect their alleged right to "family integrity."

Although the text of the Constitution contains no reference to familial or parental rights, Supreme Court precedent has long recognized that "the Due Process Clause of the Fourteenth Amendment protects the fundamental right of parents to make decisions concerning the care, custody, and control of their children." A corollary to this right is the "private realm of family life which the state cannot enter that has been afforded both substantive and procedural protection." *Smith v. Org. of Foster Families for Equal. & Reform*, 431 U.S. 816, 842 (1977). Historically, the Court's family and parental-rights holdings have involved biological families. *See, e.g., Troxel*, 530 U.S. 57 (2000); *Wisconsin v. Yoder*, 406 U.S. 205 (1972); *Stanley v. Illinois*, 405 U.S. 645 (1972); *Pierce v. Soc'y of Sisters*, 268 U.S. 510 (1925); *Meyer v. Nebraska*, 262 U.S. 390 (1923). The Court itself has noted that "the usual understanding of 'family' implies biological relationships, and most decisions treating the relation between parent and child have stressed this element." *Smith*, 431 U.S. at 843. Appellants, however, seize on a few lines of *dicta* from *Smith*, in which the Court acknowledged that "biological relationships are not [the] exclusive determination of the existence of a family," and noted that "[a]doption, for instance, is recognized as the legal equivalent of biological parenthood." Extrapolating from *Smith*, appellants argue that parental and familial rights should be extended to individuals such as foster parents and legal guardians and that the touchstone of this liberty interest is not biological ties or official legal recognition, but the emotional bond that develops between and among individuals as a result of shared daily life.

We do not read *Smith* so broadly. In *Smith*, the Court considered whether the appellee foster families possessed a constitutional liberty interest in "the integrity of their family unit" such that the state could not disrupt the families without procedural due process. Although the Court found it unnecessary to resolve that question, Justice Brennan, writing for the majority, did note that the importance of familial relationships stems not merely from blood relationships, but also from "the emotional attachments that derive from the intimacy of daily association." The *Smith* Court went on, however, to discuss the "important distinctions between the foster family and the natural family," particularly the fact that foster families have their genesis in state law. The Court stressed that the parameters of whatever potential liberty interest such families might possess would be defined by state law and the justifiable expectations it created. The Court found that the expectations created by New York law—which accorded only limited recognition to foster families—supported only "the most limited constitutional 'liberty' in the foster family." Basing its holding on other grounds, the Court concluded that the procedures provided under New York law were "adequate to protect whatever liberty interest appellees may have."

Here, we find that under Florida law neither a foster parent nor a legal guardian could have a justifiable expectation of a permanent relationship with his or her child free from state oversight or intervention.... Lofton and Houghton entered into relationships to be a foster parent and legal guardian, respectively, with an implicit understanding that these relationships would not be immune from state oversight and would be permitted to continue only upon state approval. The emotional connections between Lofton and his foster child and between Houghton and his ward originate in arrangements that have been subject to state oversight from the outset. We conclude that Lofton, Doe, Houghton, and Roe could have no justifiable expectation of permanency in their relationships. Nor could Lofton and Houghton have developed expectations that they would be allowed to adopt, in light of the adoption provision itself.

Even if Florida law did create an expectation of permanency, appellants misconstrue the nature of the liberty interest that it would confer upon them. The resulting liberty interest at most would provide *procedural* due process protection in the event the state were to attempt to remove Doe or Roe. Such a procedural right does not translate, however, into a substantive right to be free from state inference. Nor does it create an affirmative right to be accorded official recognition as "parent" and "child." In sum, Florida's statute by itself poses no threat to whatever hypothetical constitutional protection foster families and guardian-ward relationships may possess.

We conclude that appellants' right-to-family-integrity argument fails to state a claim. There is no precedent for appellants' novel proposition that long-term foster care arrangements and guardianships are entitled to constitutional protection akin to that accorded to natural and adoptive families.

2. Fundamental Right to "Private Sexual Intimacy"

Laws that burden the exercise of a fundamental right require strict scrutiny and are sustained only if narrowly tailored to further a compelling government interest. *See, e.g., Zablocki v. Redhail,* 434 U.S. 374, 388 (1978); *Shapiro v. Thompson,* 394 U.S. 618, 634 (1969). Appellants argue that the Supreme Court's recent decision in *Lawrence v. Texas,* 539 U.S. 558 (2003), which struck down Texas's sodomy statute, identified a hitherto unarticulated fundamental right to private sexual intimacy. They contend that the Florida statute, by disallowing adoption to any individual who chooses to engage in homosexual conduct, impermissibly burdens the exercise of this right.

We begin with the threshold question of whether *Lawrence* identified a new fundamental right to private sexual intimacy. *Lawrence's* holding was that substantive due process does not permit a state to impose a criminal prohibition on private consensual homosexual conduct. The effect of this holding was to establish a greater respect than previously existed in the law for the right of consenting adults to engage in private sexual conduct. Nowhere, however, did the Court characterize this right as "fundamental." *Cf. id.* (Scalia, J., dissenting) (observing that "nowhere does the Court's opinion declare that homosexual sodomy is a 'fundamental right' under the Due Process Clause"). Nor did the Court locate this right directly in the Constitution, but instead treated it as the by-product of several different constitutional principles and liberty interests.

We are particularly hesitant to infer a new fundamental liberty interest from an opinion whose language and reasoning are inconsistent with standard fundamental-rights analysis. The Court has noted that it must "exercise the utmost care whenever [it is] asked to break new ground" in the field of fundamental rights, *Washington v. Glucksberg,* 521 U.S. 702, 720 (1997), which is precisely what the *Lawrence* petitioners and their *amici curiae* had asked the Court to do. That the Court declined the invitation is apparent from the absence of the "two primary features" of fundamental-rights analysis in its opinion. First, the *Lawrence* opinion contains virtually no inquiry into the question of whether the petitioners' asserted right is one of "those fundamental rights and liberties which are, objectively, deeply rooted in this Nation's history and tradition and implicit in the concept of ordered liberty, such that neither liberty nor justice would exist if they were sacrificed."[1] Second, the opinion notably never provides the "'careful description' of the asserted fundamental liberty interest" that is to accompany fundamental-rights analysis. Rather, the constitutional liberty interests on which the Court relied were invoked, not with "careful description," but with sweeping generality. Most significant, however, is the fact that the *Lawrence* Court never applied strict scrutiny, the proper standard when fundamental rights are implicated, but instead invalidated the Texas statute on rational-basis grounds, holding that it "furthers no legitimate state interest which can justify its intrusion into the personal and private life of the individual."

We conclude that it is a strained and ultimately incorrect reading of *Lawrence* to interpret it to announce a new fundamental right. Accordingly, we need not resolve the second prong of appellants' fundamental-rights argument: whether exclusion from the statutory privilege of adoption because of appellants' sexual conduct creates an impermissible burden on the exercise of their asserted right to private sexual intimacy.

Moreover, the holding of *Lawrence* does not control the present case. Apart from the shared homosexuality component, there are marked differences in the facts of the two cases. The Court itself stressed the limited factual situation it was addressing in *Lawrence*:

> The present case does not involve minors. It does not involve persons who might be injured or coerced or who are situated in relationships where consent might not easily be refused. It does not involve public conduct or prostitution. It does not involve whether the government must give formal recognition to any relationship that homosexual persons seek to enter. The case does involve two adults who, with full and mutual consent from each other, engaged in sexual practices common to a homosexual lifestyle.

Lawrence, 123 S.Ct. at 2484. Here, the involved actors are not only consenting adults, but minors as well. The relevant state action is not criminal prohibition, but grant of a statutory privilege. And the asserted liberty interest is not the negative right to engage in private conduct without facing criminal sanctions, but the affirmative right to receive official and public recognition. Hence, we conclude that the *Lawrence* decision cannot be extrapolated to create a right to adopt for homosexual persons.

D. *Appellants' Equal Protection Challenge*

1. Rational-Basis Review

The Equal Protection Clause of the Fourteenth Amendment proclaims that "[n]o State shall…deny to any person within its jurisdiction the equal protection of laws." U.S. Const. amend. XIV, § 1. The central mandate of the equal protection guarantee is

---

1. The Court did devote considerable attention to history and tradition. This examination, however, was for the purpose of challenging the historical premises relied upon by the *Bowers* Court, and it focused on whether there has been a history of enacting, and regularly enforcing, laws specifically directed at private homosexual conduct. Notably absent from this discussion was the critical inquiry for purposes of fundamental-rights analysis: whether there has been a deeply rooted tradition and history of *protecting* the right to homosexual sodomy or the right to private sexual intimacy.

that "[t]he sovereign may not draw distinctions between individuals based solely on differences that are irrelevant to a legitimate governmental objective." *Lehr v. Robertson*, 463 U.S. 248, 265 (1983). Equal protection, however, does not forbid legislative classifications. *Nordlinger v. Hahn*, 505 U.S. 1, 10 (1992). "It simply keeps governmental decisionmakers from treating differently persons who are in all relevant respects alike." Unless the challenged classification burdens a fundamental right or targets a suspect class, the Equal Protection Clause requires only that the classification be rationally related to a legitimate state interest. *Romer v. Evans*, 517 U.S. 620, 631 (1996). As we have explained, Florida's statute burdens no fundamental rights. Moreover, all of our sister circuits that have considered the question have declined to treat homosexuals as a suspect class. Because the present case involves neither a fundamental right nor a suspect class, we review the Florida statute under the rational-basis standard.

Rational-basis review, "a paradigm of judicial restraint," does not provide "a license for courts to judge the wisdom, fairness, or logic of legislative choices." *F.C.C. v. Beach Communications, Inc.,* 508 U.S. 307, 313–14 (1993). The question is simply whether the challenged legislation is rationally related to a legitimate state interest. *Heller v. Doe*, 509 U.S. 312, 320 (1993). Under this deferential standard, a legislative classification "is accorded a strong presumption of validity," *id.* at 319, and "must be upheld against equal protection challenge if there is any reasonably conceivable state of facts that could provide a rational basis for the classification," *id.* at 320. This holds true "even if the law seems unwise or works to the disadvantage of a particular group, or if the rationale for it seems tenuous." *Romer*, 517 U.S. at 632. Moreover, a state has "no obligation to produce evidence to sustain the rationality of a statutory classification." *Heller*, 509 U.S. at 320. Rather, "the burden is on the one attacking the legislative arrangement to negative every conceivable basis which might support it, whether or not the basis has a foundation in the record." *Id.* at 320–21.

2. Florida's Asserted Rational Bases

Florida contends that the statute is only one aspect of its broader adoption policy, which is designed to create adoptive homes that resemble the nuclear family as closely as possible. Florida argues that the statute is rationally related to Florida's interest in furthering the best interests of adopted children by placing them in families with married mothers and fathers. Such homes, Florida asserts, provide the stability that marriage affords and the presence of both male and female authority figures, which it considers critical to optimal childhood development and socialization. In particular, Florida emphasizes a vital role that dual-gender parenting plays in shaping sexual and gender identity and in providing heterosexual role modeling. Florida argues that disallowing adoption into homosexual households, which are necessarily motherless or fatherless and lack the stability that comes with marriage, is a rational means of furthering Florida's interest in promoting adoption by marital families. Florida also asserts that the statute is rationally related to its interest in promoting public morality both in the context of child rearing and in the context of determining which types of households should be accorded legal recognition as families. Appellants respond that public morality cannot serve as a legitimate state interest. Because of our conclusion that Florida's interest in promoting married-couple adoption provides a rational basis, it is unnecessary for us to resolve the question. We do note, however, the Supreme Court's conclusion that there is not only a legitimate interest, but "a substantial government interest in protecting order and morality," *Barnes v. Glen Theatre, Inc.,* 501 U.S. 560, 569 (1991), and its observation that "[i]n a democratic society legislatures, not courts, are constituted to respond to the will and consequently the moral values of the people." *Gregg v. Georgia,* 428 U.S. 153, 175 (1976) (plurality opinion). We also note that our own recent precedent has unequivocally affirmed the furtherance of public morality as a legitimate state interest. *See, e.g., Williams v. Pryor,* 240 F.3d 944, 949 (11th Cir.2001) ("The crafting and safeguarding of public morality has long been an established part of the States' plenary police power to legislate and indisputably is a legitimate government interest under rational basis scrutiny."); *see also id.* at 949 n. 3 ("In fact, the State's interest in public morality is sufficiently substantial to satisfy the government's burden under the more rigorous intermediate level of constitutional scrutiny applicable in some cases.").]

Florida clearly has a legitimate interest in encouraging a stable and nurturing environment for the education and socialization of its adopted children. *See, e.g., Palmore v. Sidoti,* 466 U.S. 429, 433 (1984) ("The State, of course, has a duty of the highest order to protect the interests of minor children, particularly those of tender years."); *Stanley,* 405 U.S. at 652 (noting that "protect [ing] the moral, emotional, mental, and physical welfare of the minor" is a "legitimate interest[ ], well within the power of the State to implement"). It is chiefly from parental figures that children learn about the world and their place in it, and the formative influence of parents extends well beyond the years spent under their roof, shaping their children's psychology, character, and personality for years to come. In time, children grow up to become full members of society, which they in turn influence, whether for good or ill. The adage that "the hand that rocks the cradle rules the world" hardly overstates the ripple effect that parents have on the public good by virtue of their role in raising their children. It is hard to conceive an interest more legitimate and more paramount for the state than promoting an optimal social structure for educating, socializing, and preparing its future citizens to become productive participants in civil society—particularly when those future citizens are displaced children for whom the state is standing *in loco parentis.*

More importantly for present purposes, the state has a legitimate interest in encouraging this optimal family structure by seeking to place adoptive children in homes that have both a mother and father. Florida argues that its preference for adoptive marital families is based on the premise that the marital family structure is more stable than other household arrangements and that children benefit from the presence of both a father and mother in the home. Given that appellants have offered no competent evidence to the contrary, we find this premise to be one of those "unprovable assumptions" that nevertheless can provide a legitimate basis for legislative action. *Paris Adult Theatre I v. Slaton,* 413 U.S. 49, 62–63 (1973). Although social theorists from Plato to Simone de Beauvoir have proposed alternative child-rearing arrangements, none has proven as enduring as the marital family structure, nor has the accumulated wisdom of several millennia of human experience discovered a superior model. *See, e.g.,* Plato, *The Republic,* Bk. V, 459d–461e; Simone de Beauvoir, *The Second Sex* (H.M. Parshley trans., Vintage Books 1989) (1949). Against this "sum of experience," it is rational for Florida to conclude that it is in the best interests of adoptive children, many of whom come from troubled and unstable backgrounds, to be placed in a home anchored by both a father and a mother. *Paris Adult Theatre I,* 413 U.S. at 63.

3. Appellants' Arguments

Appellants offer little to dispute whether Florida's preference for marital adoptive families is a legitimate state interest. Instead, they maintain that the statute is not rationally related to this interest. Arguing that the statute is both overinclusive and underinclusive, appellants contend that the real motivation behind the statute cannot be the best interest of adoptive children.

In evaluating this argument, we note from the outset that "it is entirely irrelevant for constitutional purposes whether the conceived reason for the challenged distinction actually motivated the legislature." *Beach Communications,* 508 U.S. at 315; *see also City of Renton v. Playtime Theatres, Inc.,* 475 U.S. 41, 48 (1986) ("It is a familiar principle of constitutional law that this Court will not strike down an otherwise constitutional statute on the basis of an alleged illicit legislative motive."). Instead, the question before us is whether the Florida legislature *could* have reasonably believed that prohibiting adoption into homosexual environments would further its interest in placing adoptive children in homes that will provide them with optimal developmental conditions. *See Panama City Med. Diagnostic Ltd. v. Williams,* 13 F.3d 1541, 1545 (11th Cir.1994) ("The task is to determine if any set of facts may be reasonably conceived of to justify the legislation."). Unless appellants' evidence, which we view on summary judgment review in the light most favorable to appellants, can negate every plausible rational connection between the statute and Florida's interest in the welfare of its children, we are compelled to uphold the statute. *See Vance v. Bradley,* 440 U.S. 93, 111 (1979) ("In an equal protection case of this type, however, those challenging the legislative judgment must convince the court that the legislative facts on which the classification is apparently based could not reasonably be conceived to be true by the governmental decisionmaker."). We turn now to appellants' specific arguments.

a. Adoption by Unmarried Heterosexual Persons

Appellants note that Florida law permits adoption by unmarried individuals and that, among children coming out the Florida foster care system, 25% of adoptions are to parents who are currently single. Their argument is that homosexual persons are similarly situated to unmarried persons with regard to Florida's asserted interest in promoting married-couple adoption. According to appellants, this disparate treatment lacks a rational basis and, therefore, disproves any rational connection between the statute and Florida's asserted interest in promoting adoption into married homes. Citing *City of Cleburne v. Cleburne Living Ctr., Inc.,* 473 U.S. 432 (1985), appellants argue that the state has not satisfied *Cleburne*'s threshold requirement that it demonstrate that homosexuals pose a unique threat to children that others similarly situated in relevant respects do not.

We find appellants' reading of *Cleburne* to be an unwarranted interpretation. In *Cleburne,* the Supreme Court invalidated under the rational-basis test a municipal zoning ordinance requiring a group home for the mentally retarded to obtain a special use permit. The municipality argued that it had a legitimate interest in (1) protecting the residents of the home from a nearby flood plain, (2) limiting potential liability for acts of residents of the home, (3) maintaining low-density land uses in the neighborhood, (4) reducing congestion in neighborhood streets, and (5) avoiding fire hazards. The Court, however, found that the municipality failed to distinguish how these concerns applied particularly to mentally retarded residents of the home and not to a number of other persons who could freely occupy the identical structure without a permit, such as boarding houses, fraternity houses, and nursing homes. The Court concluded that the purported justifications for the ordinance made no sense in light of how it treated other groups similarly situated. Appellants have overstated *Cleburne*'s holding by asserting that it places a burden on the State of Florida to show that homosexuals pose a greater threat than other unmarried adults who are allowed to adopt. The *Cleburne* Court reasserted the unremarkable principle that, when a statute imposes a classification on a particular group, its failure to impose the same classification on "other groups similarly situated in relevant respects" can be probative of a lack of a rational basis.

This case is distinguishable from *Cleburne*. The Florida legislature could rationally conclude that homosexuals and heterosexual singles are not "similarly situated in relevant respects." It is not irrational to think that heterosexual singles have a markedly greater probability of eventually establishing a married household and, thus, providing their adopted children with a stable, dual-gender parenting environment. Moreover, as the state noted, the legislature could rationally act on the theory that heterosexual singles, even if they never marry, are better positioned than homosexual individuals to provide adopted children with education and guidance relative to their sexual development throughout pubescence and adolescence. In a previous challenge to Florida's statute, a Florida appellate court observed:

> [W]hatever causes a person to become a homosexual, it is clear that the state cannot know the sexual preferences that a child will exhibit as an adult. Statistically, the state does know that a very high percentage of children available for adoption will develop heterosexual preferences. As a result, those children will need education and guidance after puberty concerning relationships with the opposite sex. In our society, we expect that parents will provide this education to teenagers in the home. These subjects are often very embarrassing for teenagers and some aspects of the education are accomplished by the parents telling stories about their own adolescence and explaining their own experiences with the opposite sex. It is in the best interests of a child if his or her parents can personally relate to the child's problems and assist the child in the difficult transition to heterosexual adulthood. Given that adopted children tend to have some developmental problems arising from adoption or from their experiences prior to adoption, it is perhaps more important for adopted children than other children to have a stable heterosexual household during puberty and the teenage years.

Cox, 627 So.2d at 1220. "It could be that the assumptions underlying these rationales are erroneous, but the very fact that they are arguable is sufficient, on rational-basis review, to immunize the legislative choice from constitutional challenge." *Heller*, 509 U.S. at 333. Although the influence of environmental factors in forming patterns of sexual behavior and the importance of heterosexual role models are matters of ongoing debate, they ultimately involve empirical disputes not readily amenable to judicial resolution—as well as policy judgments best exercised in the legislative arena. For our present purposes, it is sufficient that these considerations provide a reasonably conceivable rationale for Florida to preclude all homosexuals, but not all heterosexual singles, from adopting.

The possibility, raised by appellants, that some homosexual households, including those of appellants, would provide a better environment than would some heterosexual single-parent households does not alter our analysis. The Supreme Court repeatedly has instructed that neither the fact that a classification may be overinclusive or underinclusive nor the fact that a generalization underlying a classification is subject to exceptions renders the classification irrational. "[C]ourts are compelled under rational-basis review to accept a legislature's generalizations even when there is an imperfect fit between means and ends." *Id.* at 321, 113 S.Ct. at 2643. We conclude that there are plausible rational reasons for the disparate treatment of homosexuals and heterosexual singles under Florida adoption law and that, to the extent that the classification may be imperfect, that imperfection does not rise to the level of a constitutional infraction.

b. Current Foster Care Population

Appellants make much of the fact that Florida has over three thousand children who are currently in foster care and, consequently, have not been placed with permanent adoptive families. According to appellants, because excluding homosexuals from the pool of prospective adoptive parents will not create more eligible married couples to reduce the backlog, it is impossible for the legislature to believe that the statute advances the state's interest in placing children with married couples.

We do not agree that the statute does not further the state's interest in promoting nuclear-family adoption because it may delay the adoption of some children. Appellants misconstrue Florida's interest, which is not simply to place children in a permanent home as quickly as possible, but, when placing them, to do so in an optimal home, i.e., one in which there is a heterosexual couple or the potential for one. According to appellants' logic, every restriction on adoptive-parent candidates, such as income, in-state residency, and criminal record—none of which creates more available married couples— are likewise constitutionally suspect as long as Florida has a backlog of unadopted foster children. The best interests of children, however, are not automatically served by adoption into *any* available home merely because it is permanent. Moreover, the legislature could rationally act on the theory that not placing adoptees in homosexual households increases the probability that these children eventually will be placed with married-couple families, thus furthering the state's goal of optimal placement. Therefore, we conclude that Florida's current foster care backlog does not render the statute irrational.

c. Foster Care and Legal Guardianship

Noting that Florida law permits homosexuals to become foster parents and permanent guardians, appellants contend that this fact demonstrates that Florida must not truly believe that placement in a homosexual household is not in a child's best interests. We do not find that the fact that Florida has permitted homosexual foster homes and guardianships defeats the rational relationship between the statute and the state's asserted interest. We have not located and appellants have not cited any precedent indicating that a disparity between a law and its enforcement is a relevant consideration on rational-basis review, which only asks whether the legislature could have reasonably thought that the challenged law would further a legitimate state interest. Thus, to the extent that foster care and guardianship placements with homosexuals are the handiwork of Florida's executive branch, they are irrelevant to the question of the *legislative* rationale for Florida's adoption scheme. To the extent that these placements are the product of an intentional legislative choice to treat foster care and guardianships differently than adoption, the distinction is not an irrational one. Indeed, it bears a rational relationship to Florida's interest in promoting the nuclear-family model of adoption since foster care and guardianship have neither the permanence nor the societal, cultural, and legal significance as does adoptive parenthood, which is the legal equivalent of natural parenthood. Fla. Stat. §63.032(2).

Foster care and legal guardianship are designed to address a different situation than permanent adoption, and "the legislature must be allowed leeway to approach a perceived problem incrementally." *Beach Communications,* 508 U.S. at 316. The fact that "[t]he legislature may select one phase of one field and apply a remedy there, neglecting the others," does not render the legislative solution invalid. *Id.* We conclude that the rationality of the statute is not defeated by the fact that Florida permits homosexual persons to serve as foster parents and legal guardians.

d. Social Science Research

Appellants cite recent social science research and the opinion of mental health professionals and child welfare organizations as evidence that there is no child welfare basis for excluding homosexuals from adopting. They argue that the cited studies show that the parenting skills of homosexual parents are at least equivalent to those of heterosexual parents and that children raised by homosexual parents suffer no adverse outcomes. Appellants also point to the policies and practices of numerous adoption agencies that permit homosexual persons to adopt.

In considering appellants' argument, we must ask not whether the latest in social science research and professional opinion *support* the decision of the Florida legislature, but whether that evidence is so well established and so far beyond dispute that it would be irrational for the Florida legislature to believe that the interests of its children are best served by not permitting homosexual adoption. Also, we must credit any conceivable rational reason that the legislature might have for choosing not to alter its statutory scheme in response to this recent social science research.

We must assume, for example, that the legislature might be aware of the critiques of the studies cited by appellants—critiques that have highlighted significant flaws in the studies' methodologies and conclusions, such as the use of small, self-selected samples; reliance on self-report instruments; politically driven hypotheses; and the use of unrepresentative study populations consisting of disproportionately affluent, educated parents. Alternatively, the legislature might consider and credit other studies that have found that children raised in homosexual households fare differently on a number of measures, doing worse on some of them, than children raised in similarly situated heterosexual households. Or the legislature might consider, and even credit, the research cited by appellants, but find it premature to rely on a very recent and still developing body of research, particularly in light of the absence of longitudinal studies following child subjects into adulthood and of studies of adopted, rather than natural, children of homosexual parents.

We do not find any of these possible legislative responses to be irrational. Openly homosexual households represent a very recent phenomenon, and sufficient time has not yet passed to permit any scientific study of how children raised in those households fare as adults. Scientific attempts to study homosexual parenting in general are still in their nascent stages and so far have yielded inconclusive and conflicting results. Thus, it is hardly surprising that the question of the effects of homosexual parenting on childhood development is one on which even experts of good faith reasonably disagree. Given this state of affairs, it is not irrational for the Florida legislature to credit one side of the debate over the other. Nor is it irrational for the legislature to proceed with deliberate caution before placing adoptive children in an alternative, but unproven, family structure that has not yet been conclusively demonstrated to be equivalent to the marital family structure that has established a proven track record spanning centuries. Accordingly, we conclude that appellants' proffered social science evidence does not disprove the rational basis of the Florida statute.

e. *Romer v. Evans*

Finally, we disagree with appellants' contention that *Romer* requires us to strike down the Florida statute. In *Romer,* the Supreme Court invalidated Amendment 2 to the Colorado state constitution, which prohibited all legislative, executive, or judicial action designed to protect homosexual persons from discrimination. 517 U.S. 620, 624 (1996). The constitutional defect in Amendment 2 was the disjunction between the "[s]weeping and comprehensive" classification it imposed on homosexuals and the state's asserted bases for the classification— respect for freedom of association and conservation of resources to fight race and gender discrimination. The Court concluded that the Amendment's "sheer breadth is so discontinuous with the reasons offered for it that the amendment seems inexplicable by anything but animus toward the class it affects."

Unlike Colorado's Amendment 2, Florida's statute is not so "[s]weeping and comprehensive" as to render Florida's rationales for the statute "inexplicable by anything but animus" toward its homosexual residents. Amendment 2 deprived homosexual persons of "protections against exclusion from an almost limitless number of transactions and endeavors that constitute ordinary civic life in a free society." In contrast to this "broad and undifferentiated disability," the Florida classification is limited to the narrow and discrete context of access to the statutory privilege of adoption and, more importantly, has a plausible connection with the state's asserted interest. Moreover, not only is the effect of Florida's classification dramatically smaller, but the classification itself is narrower. Whereas Amendment 2's classification encompassed both conduct *and* status, Florida's adoption prohibition is limited to conduct, *see Cox,* 627 So.2d at 1215. Thus, we conclude that *Romer* 's unique factual situation and narrow holding are inapposite to this case.

III. CONCLUSION

We exercise great caution when asked to take sides in an ongoing public policy debate, such as the current one over the compatibility of homosexual conduct with the duties of adoptive parenthood. The State of Florida has made the determination that it is not in the best interests of its displaced children to be adopted by individuals who "engage in current, voluntary homosexual activity," and we have found nothing in the Constitution that forbids this policy judgment. Thus, any argument that the Florida legislature was misguided in its decision is one of legislative policy, not constitutional law. The legislature is the proper forum for this debate, and we do not sit as a superlegislature "to award by judicial decree what was not achievable by political consensus." *Thomasson v. Perry,* 80 F.3d 915, 923 (4th Cir.1996). The judgment of the district court is AFFIRMED.

[The appellants filed a motion for reconsideration en banc. The twelve active judges of the 11th Circuit voted 6-6 on the motion, thus rejecting it since a majority vote is required to grant reconsideration. 377 F.3d 1275 (July 21, 2004). No opinion was issued for the en banc court, but Judge Birch, author of the panel decision, issued a "concurring opinion," mainly devoted to responding to the arguments made by Judge Barkett in her "dissenting opinion." Judge Barnett spoke for herself and two other judges in arguing that the Florida law is unconstitutional. Three other judges voted for review, arguing that the statute raised significant constitutional questions that should be resolved by the en banc court. Reproduced below are parts of Judge Barkett's dissent and Judge Birch's rejoinder.]

BARKETT, Circuit Judge, Dissenting from the Denial of Rehearing En Banc:

[The panel opinion] finds constitutional 1977 Fla. Laws, ch. 77-140, § 1, Fla. Stat. § 63.042(3) (2003), which provides that "[n]o person eligible to adopt under this statute may adopt if that person is a homosexual." Florida is the only state in the union to have such a categorical statutory prohibition targeted solely against homosexuals. This provision finds, as a matter of law, hundreds of thousands of Florida citizens unfit to serve as adoptive parents solely because of constitutionally protected conduct. There is no comparable bar in Florida's adoption statute that applies to any other group. Neither child molesters, drug addicts, nor domestic abusers are categorically barred by the statute from serving as adoptive parents. In a very real sense, Florida's adoption statute treats homosexuals less favorably than even those individuals with characteristics that may pose a threat to the well-being of children.

While Florida claims that it has singled out homosexuals because it wishes to limit adoptions to married couples, the statute in this case says absolutely nothing about married couples. In fact, Florida's adoption statute expressly provides for single persons to adopt. A full twenty-five percent of adoptions out of foster care in Florida are by single people; in the district covering Miami-Dade County, this figure is over forty percent. This is only the first and most glaring of numerous gaps between the state's ban on homosexual adoption and its purported justification. Under Florida law, for example, single persons who are homosexuals but are "not practicing" may adopt. Florida also permits homosexuals (whether sexually active or not) to serve as foster parents on a *permanent* basis, and the state acknowledges that such foster care placements involve a state of "*de facto* permanency." Finally, Florida permits homosexuals to serve as legal guardians.

The ban on homosexual adoption at issue here violates the Equal Protection Clause of the Fourteenth Amendment because Florida's proffered rational basis is expressly refuted by the state's own law and practice and because a class consisting of all homosexual citizens was targeted solely on the basis of impermissible animus. Thus, as argued in Section I below, even under the lowest standard of review—rational basis—Florida's statute fails to survive equal protection analysis under the Supreme Court's precedents in *Eisenstadt, Moreno, Cleburne,* and *Romer.*

The state's ban on homosexual adoption also violates the Due Process Clause by conditioning access to the statutory privilege of adoption on surrender of the right to engage in private intimate sexual conduct protected by *Lawrence v. Texas.* As argued in Section II below, in upholding the Florida statute, *Lofton* directly conflicts with an entire body of substantive due process jurisprudence, culminating in the Supreme Court's decision in *Lawrence.*

I. Equal Protection

A. The Rational Basis Test Established in the Analogous Cases of *Romer, Cleburne, Moreno,* and *Eisenstadt* Requires that We Invalidate this Statute.

The Equal Protection Clause "is essentially a direction that all persons similarly situated should be treated alike." *Cleburne,* 473 U.S. at 439. Yet because of the practical need for legislators to draw distinctions among groups, a classification that neither burdens a fundamental right nor targets a suspect class will be analyzed using rational basis scrutiny, which means that it will be upheld provided that it "bears a rational relation to some legitimate end." *Romer,* 517 U.S. at 631. Although this is a deferential form of review, a court must still identify legitimate state interests and find a "relationship between the classification adopted and the object to be attained."

The classification at issue in this case burdens personal relationships and exudes animus against a politically unpopular group. Under these circumstances, statutes have consistently failed rational basis review. Summarizing these cases, Justice O'Connor observed in her concurrence in *Lawrence* that

> [l]aws such as economic or tax legislation that are scrutinized under rational basis review normally pass constitutional muster, since the Constitution presumes that even improvident decisions will eventually be rectified by the de-

mocratic processes. We have consistently held, however, that some objectives, such as a bare…desire to harm a politically unpopular group, are not legitimate state interests. *When a law exhibits such a desire to harm a politically unpopular group, we have applied a more searching form of rational basis review to strike down such laws under the Equal Protection Clause.*

Lawrence, 123 S.Ct. at 2484–85 (O'Connor, J., concurring) (emphasis added). Justice O'Connor went on to explain how this principle has been applied by the Court in prior equal protection cases:

> *We have been most likely to apply rational basis review to hold a law unconstitutional under the Equal Protection Clause where, as here, the challenged legislation inhibits personal relationships.* In *Department of Agriculture v. Moreno,* for example, we held that a law preventing those households containing an individual unrelated to any other member of the household from receiving food stamps violated equal protection because the purpose of the law was to discriminate against hippies. The asserted governmental interest in preventing food stamp fraud was not deemed sufficient to satisfy rational basis review. In *Eisenstadt v. Baird,* we refused to sanction a law that discriminated between married and unmarried persons by prohibiting the distribution of contraceptives to single persons. Likewise, in *Cleburne v. Cleburne Living Center,* we held that it was irrational for a State to require a home for the mentally disabled to obtain a special use permit when other residences—like fraternity houses and apartment buildings— did not have to obtain such a permit. And in *Romer v. Evans,* we disallowed a state statute that impos[ed] a broad and undifferentiated disability on a single named group— specifically, homosexuals. *The dissent apparently agrees that if these cases have* stare decisis *effect, Texas' sodomy law would not pass scrutiny under the Equal Protection Clause, regardless of the type of rational basis review that we apply.*

Id., 123 S.Ct. at 2484–85 (emphasis added). An examination of these cases bears out Justice O'Connor's point and their direct application here. Regardless of how one labels the rational-basis review employed in these cases, Florida's ban on gay adoption is simply not compatible with them.

All four of these precedents involved legislation targeting politically unpopular groups to varying degrees: "hippies" (*Moreno*), unmarried users of birth control (*Eisenstadt*), the mentally disabled (*Cleburne*), and homosexuals (*Romer*). Moreover, in each case, the Court invalidated a law that had the effect of inhibiting personal relationships of one sort or another: among mentally disabled or unrelated persons who wished to share a common living space (*Cleburne* and *Moreno*); among unmarried individuals who wished to engage in intimate relations (*Eisenstadt*); and among individuals who wished to live without fear of state-sanctioned discrimination prompted solely by their attachment to persons of the same sex (*Romer*).

In *Moreno,* the Supreme Court found that excluding individuals unrelated to other household members from the federal food stamp program was not rationally related to the government's asserted interest in minimizing administrative fraud. In so finding, the Court observed that

> even if we were to accept as rational the Government's wholly unsubstantiated assumptions concerning the differences between 'related' and 'unrelated' households we still could not agree with the Government's conclusion that the denial of essential federal food assistance to all otherwise eligible households

containing unrelated members constitutes a rational effort to deal with these concerns.

Id. at 535–36. The Court pointed out that the statute already contained anti-fraud provisions and that it provided for strict criminal penalties. Furthermore, the Court found that in "practical effect," the statute did not operate to further the prevention of fraud, since it only precluded groups that lived as one economic unit, shared common cooking facilities, and customarily purchased food in common. The Court found that individuals with the financial means to alter their living arrangements could avoid the exclusion by sidestepping any one of the three conditions. For example, two wealthy unrelated individuals living together could manage to purchase their groceries separately. In so doing, they would effectively create two separate households, both eligible for assistance, and thereby evade the application of the statute. This being the case, it could not truthfully be said that the purpose of the exclusion was to eliminate the operation of fraud in the food stamp program. Instead, the statute irrationally punished "only those persons who are so desperately in need of aid that they cannot even afford to alter their living arrangements so as to retain their eligibility."

In *Eisenstadt,* the Court invalidated on rational basis grounds a Massachusetts statute banning the distribution of contraceptives to unmarried persons. The state's highest court had defined the statute's purposes as the deterrence of premarital sex and the promotion of community health needs by regulating the distribution of potentially harmful articles. The Supreme Court looked behind the facial legitimacy of the state's proffered justifications and refused to accept that either rationale could "reasonably be regarded" as the purpose of the statute. 405 U.S. at 448–49. The Court found that the first purpose, deterring premarital sex, was "dubious" considering that Massachusetts law did not limit the distribution of contraceptives when used to prevent the spread of disease rather than to prevent pregnancy. And in allowing married persons to use contraceptives, the state's law made no effort to limit illicit sexual relations between married and unmarried persons. Thus, the proffered rational basis was "illogical to the point of irrationality."

The Court concluded that "the Massachusetts statute is thus so riddled with exceptions that deterrence of premarital sex cannot reasonably be regarded as its aim." The *Eisenstadt* Court also discounted the state's promotion of health argument as "both discriminatory and overbroad," and a transparent effort to escape the reach of the Court's holding in *Griswold v. State of Connecticut,* 381 U.S. 479 (1965). The Court held on equal protection grounds that "whatever the rights of the individual to access to contraceptives may be, the rights must be the same for the unmarried and the married alike."

In *Cleburne,* the Court heard an equal protection challenge to a Texas city's zoning ordinance that required a special use permit in residential areas for the operation of a home for the mentally disabled. The city argued that the ordinance was justified by the "negative attitude of the majority of property owners" toward institutions for the mentally disabled and by "the fears of elderly residents" living near the institution. 473 U.S. at 448. It also defended the measure as an effort to serve the best interests of the mentally disabled themselves, arguing that the institution would be threatened by its location near a junior high school whose students might harass the residents, its setting on a flood plain, and its size and capacity. Finally, the city pointed to concerns over street congestion, fire hazards, neighborhood serenity, and potential liability arising out of the conduct of the mentally disabled.

Again applying rational basis review, the Supreme Court first rejected the city's attempt to justify the statute by reference to a supposed communal aversion to the mentally disabled. "[M]ere negative attitudes, or fear, unsubstantiated by factors which are properly cognizable in a zoning proceeding," the Court found, "are not permissible bases for treating a home for the mentally retarded differently from apartment houses, multiple dwellings, and the like." With respect to the city's other arguments, the Court "did not discount the legitimacy of these interests, but rather found that, in creating the means used to carry out these interests, the city had adopted a classification that had no rational basis." The city's fears that junior high school students would harass the residents could not be credited because the junior high school itself had thirty mentally retarded students in attendance. The concern of a possible flood was not tenable because the zoning ordinance allowed nursing homes, homes for the elderly, sanitariums, and hospitals to be located in the same area without permits. The city's fear of legal liability could not be credited because fraternities and boarding houses did not require a permit. Moreover, fear of over-crowding in the institution was not reasonable when the city did not require permits to protect against crowding in other facilities. Finally, there was no reason to believe that the institution would contribute to street congestion more than any other similar institution. What the Court said of this last argument applied with equal force to all of the city's other rationales:

> [T]his record does not clarify how…the characteristics of the intended occu-pants of the Featherston home rationally justify denying to those occupants what would be permitted to groups occupying the same site for different purposes.

After discounting any connection between plausible legitimate government interests and the statute in question, the Court concluded that "[t]he short of it is that requiring the permit in this case appears to us to rest on an irrational prejudice against the men-tally retarded." In *Cleburne,* as in *Eisenstadt,* the Supreme Court indicated that it simply disbelieved that the purposes articulated by the state had any rational relationship to the ordinance and refused to accept the facial legitimacy of the city's proffered reasons. The Court held that none of the goals fit the class of persons targeted except by way of con-firming that animus towards the mentally disabled had been the major impetus behind the statute.

Finally, in *Romer* the Court extended rational basis review to the area of anti-homo-sexual discrimination. Colorado argued that the amendment struck down in that case was justified by the state's interests in protecting the associational rights of landlords and employers with moral objections to homosexuality and in "conserving resources to fight discrimination against other groups." 517 U.S. at 635. The Court found it "impos-sible to credit" these proffered purposes. Noting that rational basis inquiry was meant to "ensure that classifications are not drawn for the purpose of disadvantaging the group burdened by the law," the Court held that

> [e]ven laws enacted for broad and ambitious purposes often can be explained by reference to legitimate public policies which justify the incidental disadvan-tages they impose on certain persons. Amendment 2, however, in making a general announcement that gays and lesbians shall not have any particular pro-tections from the law, inflicts on them immediate, continuing, and real injuries that *outrun* and *belie* any legitimate justifications that may be claimed for it.

Id. at 635 (emphasis added). Because the amendment bore no credible relationship to the state's proffered legitimate justifications, the Court accepted "the inevitable infer-ence that the disadvantage imposed is born of animosity toward the class of persons af-fected." And it concluded that, whatever else might be said of the amendment, it "offended" the "conventional and venerable" principle that "a law must bear a rational relationship to a legitimate governmental purpose."

In all four cases, the Court concluded that the asserted justifications were not rationally related to the classification. Thus, the Court *inferred* that animus was the motivation behind the legislation and established that such a motivation could not constitute a legitimate state interest.[2] As Justice O'Connor noted in *Lawrence*, "if these cases have *stare decisis* effect, Texas' sodomy law would not pass scrutiny under the Equal Protection Clause, regardless of the type of rational basis review that we apply." So too does Florida's law fail to survive any form of rational basis review. Here, there is no question that a politically unpopular group is being targeted, that the challenged legislation inhibits personal relationships, and that there is no legitimate rational relationship between Florida's proffered justifications and its sweeping categorical adoption ban against homosexuals.

B. Subjected to the Identical Analysis Used in *Eisenstadt, Cleburne, Moreno,* and *Romer,* the Florida Ban Would be Unconstitutional.

Like the justifications for the statutes in the cases discussed above, Florida's proffered justifications for the categorical ban here are false, do not rationally relate to the best interests of children, and are simply pretexts for impermissible animus and prejudice against homosexuals.

[After quoting the relevant passage summarizing the state's arguments in the panel opinion, Judge Barkett writes:] This rhetoric boils down to the argument that Florida prohibits homosexuals from being considered as adoptive parents because it wishes to place children with married couples. It wishes to do so for two alleged reasons: (1) to provide "stability" in the home, which the panel apparently believes can only be provided by married couples representing the "nuclear" family model; and (2) to properly shape heterosexual "sexual and gender identity," which the panel asserts should be accomplished by married couples.

Like the proffered reasons in *Eisenstadt,* which were "so riddled with exceptions" that the state's asserted goal could not "reasonably be regarded as its aim," 405 U.S. at 449, the state's proffered rational basis for the statute here (providing adopted children with married couples as parents) cannot be legitimately credited because it fails the equal protection requirement that "all persons similarly situated should be treated alike." *Cle-*

---

2. Judge Birch incorrectly claims that I have argued that these cases stand for the proposition that rational-basis review should focus on the *actual* reasons for enacting a statute. On the contrary, I recognize that if Florida's *post hoc* justifications were able to rationally account for its ban on homosexual adoption, then Florida's law might be constitutional notwithstanding some evidence in the legislative record that the state's actual motivation was animus. Thus, the suggestion that I have invented some alternative "animus/analysis" theory is a complete distortion of my position. Instead, I merely contend that the Supreme Court's decisions in *Eisenstadt, Moreno, Cleburne,* and *Romer* require that we examine Florida's post hoc rationales to determine if there is some conceivable legitimate government interest that can plausibly account for Florida's law. There is nothing novel about this kind of analysis. As Judge Birch himself recognizes, in certain circumstances, a court may *infer* that a statute is motivated by animus or irrational prejudice when the proffered rationales cannot rationally explain the actual operation of the statute. Because animus and irrational prejudice are not legitimate governmental purposes, such a statute will fail rational-basis scrutiny. I have simply applied these principles to the facts of this case, as I am required to do in faithfully applying Supreme Court precedent. As I explain in detail below, I do not believe Judge Birch has offered any plausible explanation for Florida's categorical determination that homosexuals are *inherently* and *always* unfit to serve as adoptive parents. I fail to see how any objective observer could think such a law is rational and consistent with the most basic, minimal notions of equal protection under law.

burne, 473 U.S. at 439. As noted at the beginning of this dissent, it is plainly false that Florida has established a preference for "married mothers and fathers" as adoptive parents. The 1977 statute prohibiting homosexual adoption expresses no preference whatsoever for married couples, expressly permitting an "unmarried adult" to adopt. Moreover, the DCF administrative regulations that are inextricably tied to Florida's adoption statutes do not prefer married over single candidates for adoption. In short, the Florida legislature never did, and the Florida executive no longer does, express a preference for married over unmarried couples or singles in the area of adoption. The fact that Florida places children for adoption with single parents directly and explicitly contradicts Florida's post hoc assertion that the ban is justified by the state's wish to place children for adoption only with "families with married mothers and fathers." This contradiction alone is enough to prove that the state's alleged reasons are "illogical to the point of irrationality." *Eisenstadt*, 405 U.S. at 451.

However, instead of acknowledging this glaring gap between the ban on homosexual adoption and the state's purported justification, as did the Supreme Court in invalidating the statutes in *Eisenstadt, Moreno, Cleburne,* and *Romer,* the *Lofton* panel stretches mightily to construct a hypothetical to bridge this gap. "It is not irrational," the panel opines, "to think that heterosexual singles have a markedly greater probability of eventually establishing a married household and, thus, providing their adopted children with a stable, dual-gender parenting environment." The panel's contrived hypothetical offering blatantly ignores not only the absence of any preference in Florida's statute for married couples but also the realities of the adoption process. Evaluations of prospective parents are based on present, not "eventual," status and conditions. Florida does not ask for a commitment of plans to marry someday in the future and permits single adults to adopt without making inquiry into whether they have immediate, or even long-range, marriage plans or prospects. Indeed, that many individuals choose to adopt outside of marriage is an indication that adoption and commitment to a permanent adult relationship are completely separate decisions. Moreover, experience leads one to believe that single heterosexuals who adopt are less likely to marry in the future, not more likely. Finally, this speculative hypothesis also fails to take account of "non-practicing homosexuals" who are not likely to marry but can adopt under Florida law. The Supreme Court found the state's arguments in *Eisenstadt* to be a futile and transparent move to escape the reach of the Court's decision in *Griswold.* The hypothetical posited by the *Lofton* panel demonstrates a comparable and equally transparent attempt to ignore the equal protection cases applicable here.

In addition to its failure to meaningfully distinguish homosexuals from single heterosexuals, the panel never explains why it is rational to believe that homosexuals, as a class, are unable to provide stable homes and appropriate role models for children. With respect to the first of these arguments, there is absolutely no record evidence to show that homosexuals are incapable of providing the permanent family life sought by Florida. To the contrary, as the facts in this case suggest, many children throughout the country are lovingly and successfully cared for by homosexuals in their capacity as biological parents, foster parents, or legal guardians. Yet another disturbing aspect of Florida's ban is that, while permitting single persons to adopt, this statute could conceivably ban the homosexual partner of a biological parent from adopting the partner's biological child. Furthermore, it is not marriage that guarantees a stable, caring environment for children but the character of the individual caregiver.[3] Indeed, given the re-

---

3. The most recent U.S. Census Bureau statistics indicate that about 50% of first marriages for men under age 45 may end in divorce. The figures for the first marriages of women in the same age

ality of foster care in Florida, the statute actually operates to impede, rather than promote, the placement of a child into a permanent family. Florida's statute expresses a clear intent "to protect and promote the well-being of persons being adopted…and to provide to all children who can benefit by it a permanent family life." Fla. Stat. § 63.022(3) (2003). Yet, Florida's foster care system has a backlog of more than 3,400 children in it, far more than the number of married couples eligible to adopt. Given this backlog, the state's ban on gay adoption does nothing to increase the number of children being adopted, whether by married couples or anyone else. The state is evidently willing to allow children to live with the potential uncertainties of several foster-care placements rather than enjoy the security and certainty of an adoptive home with one or two caring parents who are also homosexual.[4]

Nor does the panel offer a reason for why it is rational to credit the state's second argument: that homosexuals are incapable of providing good role models. The panel claims that "[heterosexual] children will need education and guidance after puberty concerning relationships with the opposite sex.…It is in the best interests of a child if his or her parents can personally relate to the child's problems and assist the child in the difficult transition to heterosexual adulthood." Is the panel suggesting that heterosexual parents are necessary in order to tell children about their own dating experiences after puberty? For anyone who has been a parent, this will no doubt seem a very strange,

---

group range between 44 and 52%. Rose M. Kreider and Jason M. Fields, "Number, Timing, and Duration of Marriages and Divorces: Fall 1996," *Current Population Reports* (P70-80) at 18. Washington, DC: U.S. Census Bureau, 2001. These statistics are confirmed by the findings of the National Center for Health Statistics, which released a report in 2001 finding that 43% of first marriages end in separation or divorce within fifteen years. Matthew Bramlett & William Mosher, "First Marriage Dissolution, Divorce, and Remarriage: United States," *Advance Data from Vital and Health Statistics* (2001). As of 2001, Florida ranked with Mississippi as the state with the sixth highest divorce rate in the nation. U.S. Census Bureau, *Statistical Abstract of the United States* (2003) at 100. This ranking includes the District of Columbia but not California, Colorado, Indiana, and Louisiana, which did not report divorce statistics to the Census Bureau. As Florida Statute § 63.042(1)(b) makes explicit, the fact that two persons are married does not make them fit parents or tell us how or even whether they will fulfill the responsibilities of caring for children. There is nothing selective about the institution of marriage; all kinds of persons who would not be regarded as suitable adoptive parents are admitted to the responsibilities of marriage, and marriage does not insulate spouses or children from the neglect and abuse that occur within it. In its annual national report on child abuse and neglect mandated under the Child Abuse and Prevention and Treatment Act ("CAPTA"), the U.S. Department of Health and Human Resources found that 81% of the perpetrators were parents defined as birth parents, adoptive parents, and stepparents. Similarly, in Florida, the report indicates that 78% of all reported child maltreatment cases were committed by parents. *See* Admin. for Children & Families, U.S. Dep't of Health & Human Serv., *Child Maltreatment 2002: Reports from the States to the National Child Abuse and Neglect Data Systems—National Statistics on Child Abuse and Neglect* (2004). In 2002, a total of 121,834 cases of domestic violence were reported to police law enforcement agencies in the state of Florida. Of that number, 26% (31,874) of the victims were spouses while 8% (9,190) of the victims were children. *See* Fla. Statistical Analysis Ctr., Fla. Dep't of Law Enforcement, *Florida Uniform Crime Report* (1992–2002).

4. In its August 2001 "Child and Family Services Review Final Assessment," the U.S. Department of Health and Human Services found that Florida failed to meet the national standard for stability of foster care placements (measured in terms of the percentage of children who experience more than two placements during their first twelve months of placement). The same assessment found that, in over 40% of the cases reviewed, Florida failed to meet its own statutorily specified permanency goals for children in its foster care system. (Florida law requires that a permanent living situation be sought for each child who has remained in out-of-home care for twelve consecutive months, and that progress towards this permanency goal be reviewed on a biannual basis.) Admin. for Children & Families (Region IV), U.S. Dep't of Health & Human Serv., *Child and Family Services Review Final Assessment* (2001) at 14–17.

even faintly comical, claim. There is certainly no evidence that the ability to share one's adolescent dating experiences (or lack thereof) is an important, much less essential, facet of parenting. The difficult transition to adulthood is a common human experience, not an experience unique to human beings of a particular race, gender, or sexual orientation. It is downright silly to argue that parents must have experienced everything that a child will experience in order to guide them. Indeed, that will generally not be the case. For example, immigrant parents help their children adjust to a world and culture they have not known. It cannot be suggested that such individuals are unfit to parent any more than it could be suggested that a mother is unfit to parent a son or that a white person is unfit to parent an African-American child. Furthermore, the panel's argument completely neglects to consider the situation of gay children of heterosexual parents. Children simply need parents who will love and support them.

In addition to this contrived argument about teenage dating advice, the panel suggests that placing children with homosexual parents may make it more likely that children will become homosexual, referring cryptically to the "vital role that dual-gender parenting plays in *shaping sexual and gender identity* and in providing heterosexual role modeling." In our democracy, however, it is not the province of the State, even if it were *able* to do so, to dictate or even attempt to influence how its citizens should develop their sexual and gender identities. This approach views homosexuality in and of itself as a social harm that must be discouraged, and so demeans the dignity of homosexuals, something that *Lawrence* specifically proscribes.

Finally, the panel also intimates in dicta that Florida has a legitimate interest in defending public morality by expressing disapproval of homosexuality. But moral disapproval of disfavored groups "is an interest that is insufficient to satisfy rational basis review under the Equal Protection Clause." *Lawrence*, 123 S.Ct. at 2486 (O'Connor, J., concurring). *Moreno* established that "if the constitutional conception of 'equal protection of the laws' means anything, it must at the very least mean that a bare…desire to harm a politically unpopular group cannot constitute a legitimate government interest." As the *Lawrence* Court made clear, "[o]ur obligation is to define the liberty of all, not to mandate our own moral code."

Nor may the state hide behind a suggestion that it is attempting to protect children from disapproval at large in society. Florida courts have specifically rejected moral disapprobation of homosexuality as a justification for granting custody of a child to one or another biological parent. *See Maradie v. Maradie*, 680 So.2d 538 (Fla.Dist.Ct.App.1996) (holding that a lower court's finding as to the effect of a homosexual environment on a child is not a proper subject of judicial notice, and that it requires reversal and remand for a new custody determination); *Jacoby v. Jacoby*, 763 So.2d 410 (Fla.Dist.Ct.App.2000) (citing *Palmore v. Sidoti*, 466 U.S. 429, 433 (1984), and holding that a lower court's reliance on perceived biases against homosexuality is an improper basis for a residential custody determination).

Ultimately, the breadth of the categorical adoption ban "outrun[s] and belie [s]" the state's asserted justifications. *Romer*, 517 U.S. at 635. As *Cleburne* discounted the state's asserted reason of protecting the public from fraud because the state had adequate anti-fraud provisions with strict penalties, Florida's rationale should likewise be discounted, given that Florida has explicitly tailored provisions to protect children placed in adoptive homes. The adoption statute accords everyone other than homosexuals the benefit of an individualized consideration that is directed toward the best interests of the child. Child abusers, terrorists, drug dealers, rapists and murderers are not categorically barred by the adoption statute from consideration for adoptive parenthood in Florida. On the other hand, individuals who take children into their care, including unwanted children, such as those who are HIV-positive, and who have raised them with loving care for years are categorically barred from adopting if they happen to be homosexual. In the context of adoption, this disparity of treatment on the face of the statute amounts to the purest form of irrationality.

Just as troubling, even where a foster relationship is comparable to the most stable and caring of biological parent-child relationships, the state may remove a child from that relationship simply because the parent is a homosexual.[5] In light of these considerations, it is no exaggeration to say that the best interests of the child not only fail to justify or support the ban on homosexual adoption, but that those interests are actually subordinated to the state's evident need to discriminate on the basis of sexual orientation.

The Equal Protection Clause does not permit a classification of persons undertaken for its own sake. "[C]lass legislation…[is] obnoxious to the prohibitions of the Fourteenth Amendment…." *Civil Rights Cases*, 3 S.Ct. 18, 30 (1883). When there is no reason to believe that the disadvantaged class is different, in relevant respects, from similarly situated classes, the Supreme Court has held that irrational prejudice can be inferred as the basis for a classification. *Cleburne*, 473 U.S. at 449–50. Here, irrational prejudice can be inferred as the basis for this classification because there is no difference in relevant respects between single heterosexual persons and single homosexual persons with reference to the state's purported justification for the ban in the statute. Moreover, when all the proffered rationales for a law are clearly and manifestly implausible, a reviewing court may infer that animus is the only explicable basis. *Romer*, 517 U.S. at 632, 635. Since Florida's rationale is not plausible given that single persons may adopt, the inference is obvious that Florida's decision to single out homosexuals is based solely on anti-gay animus. Unsurprisingly, animus is just what the legislative history of Florida's ban confirms.

C. Legislative History

[This portion of the opinion is reproduced in substantial part in the introduction to this chapter. Omitted is a brief passage in which Judge Barkett argues that the legislative history confirms an inference that the legislature acted from animus rather than from the reasons articulated by the state in defending this lawsuit.]

II. Substantive Due Process

Although I believe that this case can be resolved solely on equal protection grounds, without considering *Lawrence*, I address the independent basis of substantive due process because *Lofton* incorrectly concludes that *Lawrence* did not recognize a fundamental right to or liberty interest in sexual privacy. *Lawrence* held that consenting adults have a right under the Due Process Clause to engage in private sexual conduct, including homosexual conduct. Because Florida's law punishes the exercise of this right by denying all active homosexuals the ability to be considered as adoptive parents, we are required to subject Florida's law to heightened scrutiny—not the cursory, attempted rational-basis analysis the panel employs. In addition to its failure to apply heightened scrutiny, the panel makes further errors of law in attempting to evade the application of *Lawrence*. It makes erroneous statements about the proper use of history and tradition

---

5. In response to the ACLU's June 2001 request for a guarantee that Doe would not be taken away from Lofton, the DCF responded that it "is left with no legal alternative but to make appropriate efforts to place [Doe] for adoption."

in a substantive due process analysis, and mistakenly claims that *Lawrence* does not apply here because adoption is a privilege and not a right, and because Florida's statute is a civil rather than criminal law. These reasons are not only unsupported by, but are directly contrary to, Supreme Court precedent.

A. *Lawrence* Reaffirmed a Fundamental Right or Liberty Interest
   to Engage in Private Intimate Sexual Conduct.

The doctrine of substantive due process requires, first, that *every* law must address in a relevant way only a legitimate governmental purpose.[6] In other words, no law may be arbitrary and capricious but rather must address a permissible state interest in a way that is rationally related to that interest. As a consequence, any law challenged as violating a fundamental right or liberty interest must survive rational-basis review.

However, the Supreme Court has found that some decisions are so fundamental and central to human liberty that they are protected as part of a right to privacy under the Due Process Clause, and that the government may constitutionally restrict these decisions only if it has *more* than an ordinary run-of-the-mill governmental purpose. Included within this right to privacy is the ability to make decisions about private sexual matters.

In invalidating the sodomy statute at issue in *Lawrence,* the Court reaffirmed this right of sexual privacy, finding that private homosexual conduct is likewise encompassed within it. The Court stated that the Due Process Clause gives homosexuals "the full right to engage in [private sexual] conduct without intervention of the government." *Lawrence,* 123 S.Ct. at 2484. There can be no doubt that the Court's conclusion here is a binding holding. From the outset of its opinion, the Court stated that it had granted certiorari specifically to consider "[w]hether Petitioners' criminal convictions for *adult consensual sexual intimacy in the home* violate their *vital interests in liberty and privacy protected by the Due Process Clause of the Fourteenth Amendment?*" *Id.* at 2476 (emphasis added). While the Court also granted certiorari to address whether Texas's sodomy statute violated the Equal Protection Clause, the Court explicitly decided to rest its holding on a substantive due process analysis. Accordingly, the Court wrote that the "case should be resolved by determining whether the petitioners were free as adults to engage in the private [sexual] conduct in the exercise of their liberty under the Due Process Clause of the Fourteenth Amendment."

In resolving this issue, the Court retraced its substantive due process jurisprudence by discussing the fundamental rights cases of *Griswold, Eisenstadt, Roe,* and *Carey* and emphasized the breadth of their holdings as involving private decisions regarding intimate physical relationships. Beginning with *Griswold,* the *Lawrence* Court found that its prior decisions confirmed "that the protection of liberty under the Due Process Clause has a substantive dimension of fundamental significance in defining the rights of the person" and "that the right to make certain decisions regarding sexual conduct extends beyond the marital relationship." Because of the existence of this right to make private decisions regarding sexual conduct, the *Lawrence* Court was compelled to overrule the anomaly of *Bowers,* which had failed to acknowledge this right in permitting Georgia to

---

6. Judge Birch is mistaken that I view substantive due process as always synonymous with fundamental-rights analysis. I agree that rational-basis review is also part of the doctrine of substantive due process. The source of my disagreement with Judge Birch is based on his attempt to artificially downgrade the *Lawrence* decision to a rational-basis holding, which fails to provide a coherent and plausible interpretation of the entire opinion.

criminalize sodomy. *Lawrence* found that at the time of *Bowers* the Court's prior hold-ings had already made "abundantly clear" that individuals have a right to make deci-sions "'concerning the intimacies of their physical relationship[s], even when not in-tended to produce offspring.'"[7] On this basis, the Court concluded that "*Bowers* was not correct when it was decided, and it is not correct today."[8]

In overruling *Bowers*, *Lawrence* found that *Bowers* "misapprehended the claim of lib-erty there presented" when it framed the issue before it as whether the Constitution protects "a fundamental right to engage in consensual sodomy":

> To say that the issue in *Bowers* was simply the right to engage in certain sexual conduct demeans the claim the individual put forward, just as it would de-mean a married couple were it to be said marriage is simply about the right to have sexual intercourse. *The laws involved in Bowers and here are, to be sure, statutes that purport to do no more than prohibit a particular sexual act. Their penalties and purposes, though, have more far-reaching consequences, touching upon the most private human conduct, sexual behavior, and in the most private of places, the home.*

Lawrence, 123 S.Ct. at 2478 (emphasis added). Just as marriage involves much more than simply the right to have sexual intercourse, the right to participate in a homosex-ual relationship extends far beyond the ability to engage in homosexual sodomy. *Bowers* was therefore wrong to have focused on a particular sexual act instead of upon the right to sexual privacy which encompasses acts of adult consensual sexual intimacy.

Lawrence indicated that the question that *Bowers* should have asked is whether adults have a right to engage in "private [sexual] conduct in the exercise of their liberty under the Due Process Clause of the Fourteenth Amendment." In answering this question, *Lawrence* expressly adopted the reasoning of Justice Stevens' dissent in *Bowers*:

> [I]ndividual decisions by married persons, *concerning the intimacies of their physical relationship*, even when not intended to produce offspring, are a form of 'liberty' protected by the Due Process Clause of the Fourteenth Amendment.

---

7. In overruling *Bowers*, *Lawrence* explained that "our laws and tradition afford constitutional protection to personal decisions relating to marriage, procreation, contraception, family relation-ships, child rearing, and education.... 'These matters, involving the most intimate and personal choices a person may make in a lifetime, choices central to personal dignity and autonomy, are cen-tral to the liberty protected by the Fourteenth Amendment. At the heart of liberty is the right to de-fine one's own concept of existence, of meaning, of the universe, and of the mystery of human life. Beliefs about these matters could not define the attributes of personhood were they formed under compulsion of the State.'" The Court unequivocally stated that "[p]ersons in a homosexual relation-ship may seek autonomy for these purposes, just as heterosexual persons do. The decision in *Bowers* would deny them this right."

8. Given the *Lawrence* Court's statement in 2003, I fail to understand Judge Birch's reliance on a footnote from the Supreme Court's 1977 decision in *Carey*, where the Court indicated in dicta that it had not "definitively answered" the extent to which the Due Process Clause protects the private sexual conduct of consenting adults. Obviously, *Carey* does not resolve in any way the meaning of a case that comes twenty-six years later. Nor does it prevent *Lawrence* from answering the very ques-tion posed in *Carey*'s footnote. As I discuss extensively in this dissent, *Lawrence* does precisely this in affirming the right of consenting adults to make private sexual decisions. As I also explain, this could not have been a new right. *Carey*'s footnote notwithstanding, the *Lawrence* Court determined that its pre-*Bowers* decisions, properly understood from its later vantage point, had already recog-nized a right to sexual privacy. This is the only way to make sense of the *Lawrence* Court's statements that *Bowers* was "not correct when it was decided," and that its decisions before *Bowers* had already made "abundantly clear" that adults have a right to make decisions "concerning the intimacies of their physical relationship[s]."

> Moreover, this protection extends to intimate choices by unmarried as well as married persons.

Id. at 2483 (emphasis added). Because the private conduct at issue in *Lawrence* also concerned the "intimacies" of a "physical relationship," the Court held that the petitioners have a right to engage in private sexual conduct without government interference.

The *Lawrence* Court's answer to its question of whether adults have a right to engage in private sexual conduct—the question it granted certiorari to answer and which it found was necessary to resolve the case—is binding precedent and should control the outcome here. While the *Lofton* panel concedes that "substantive due process does not permit a state to impose a criminal prohibition on private consensual homosexual conduct," it fails to consider the ramifications of such a holding. Without defining what other kind of right it could be, *Lofton* maintains that "it is a strained and ultimately incorrect reading of *Lawrence* to interpret it to announce a new fundamental right." Indeed, *Lawrence* did not establish a *new* fundamental right. Rather, given the Court's statement that *Bowers* was not correct when it was decided, the *Lawrence* Court *reiterated the longstanding right* of consenting adults to engage in private sexual conduct.

B. *Lofton*'s Arguments for Why Lawrence is a Rational Basis Case are Unsupported by any Supreme Court Precedents.

In addition to its insistence that *Lawrence* did not announce a "new" right to sexual privacy, the panel offers four arguments for its skewed reading of *Lawrence* as a pure rational-basis decision. First, it claims that *Lawrence* did not "locate this right [to sexual privacy] directly in the Constitution." Second, it argues that *Lawrence* failed to provide the "careful description" of the asserted right required by *Glucksberg*. Third, the panel claims that *Lawrence* failed to identify a history and tradition of affirmative protection of the right to engage in homosexual conduct. Finally, the panel argues that *Lawrence* could not have recognized a fundamental right or liberty interest entitled to heightened scrutiny because of a single sentence in the opinion indicating that the Texas sodomy statute furthered no legitimate state interest.

Regarding the panel's first argument, as noted earlier, the *Lawrence* Court stated that the petitioners' "*right to liberty under the Due Process Clause* gives them the full right to engage in their [private sexual] conduct without intervention of the government." The Court could not have been more clear that the petitioners' right to engage in private sexual conduct was located in the Due Process Clause. Thus, the panel's argument that *Lawrence* did not "locate this right directly in the Constitution" is meritless.

The panel's second argument that *Lawrence* did not provide the "careful description" of the right required by *Glucksberg* is also untenable given that the *Lawrence* Court was at pains to describe how *Bowers* had misframed the question in that case in terms of whether there was a fundamental right to engage in consensual homosexual sodomy. As indicated above, *Lawrence* explained that the narrow framing of the question in *Bowers* "demean[ed] the claim" set forth and "disclose[d] the Court's own failure to appreciate the extent of the liberty at stake" in that case. The *Lawrence* Court explained that "[t]he laws involved in *Bowers* and here are, to be sure, statutes that *purport to do no more than prohibit a particular sexual act.* Their penalties and purposes, though, have more far-reaching consequences, touching upon the most private human conduct, sexual behavior, and in the most private of places, the home." (emphasis added). Thus, *Lawrence* demonstrates that the "careful description" of a liberty interest required by *Glucksberg* will not necessarily be synonymous with framing the liberty interest in the most narrow fashion possible. The panel has ignored this important clarification of the *Glucksberg* analysis required by the Court's subsequent decision in *Lawrence*. Inexplicably, given its purported interest in a "careful description" of the asserted right, the panel also fails to recognize that part of *Lawrence* in which the Court clearly states what the right at issue is and is not about for purposes of guiding future courts:

> The present case does not involve minors. It does not involve persons who might be injured or coerced or who are situated in relationships where consent might not easily be refused. It does not involve public conduct or prostitution. It does not involve whether the government must give formal recognition to any relationship that homosexual persons seek to enter. The case does involve two adults who, with full and mutual consent from each other, engaged in sexual practices common to a homosexual lifestyle.[9]

Third, the panel further ignores how *Lawrence* clarifies *Glucksberg*'s treatment of the role of history and tradition in identifying a fundamental right or liberty interest. The panel misreads *Glucksberg* to say that the only relevant historical inquiry is whether there has been a tradition of laws affirmatively protecting the conduct at issue. The panel then argues that while *Lawrence* "devote[d] considerable attention to history and tradition," it did so only to demonstrate that there had not been a "history of enacting, and regularly enforcing, laws specifically directed at private homosexual conduct." Apparently in the panel's view, this was a superfluous inquiry, devoid of legal meaning. According to the panel, the Supreme Court should have asked "whether there has been a deeply rooted tradition and history of *protecting* the right to homosexual sodomy or the right to private sexual intimacy."

The panel's belief that a history of state non-interference in the private sexual lives of homosexual adults cannot, as a matter of law, serve as the basis for recognizing a right to sexual privacy is entirely unsupported by any Supreme Court case. The panel has simply made up a new constitutional requirement that there must be a history of affirmative legislative protection before a right can be judicially protected under the Due Process Clause. Such a requirement ignores not only *Lawrence,* but an entire body of Supreme Court jurisprudence. Had the Supreme Court required affirmative governmental protection of an asserted liberty interest, all of the Court's privacy cases would have been decided differently. Equally significantly, the panel fails to heed the *Lawrence* Court's instruction that "[h]istory and tradition are the starting point but not in all cases the ending point of the substantive due process inquiry." As *Lawrence* stated:

> [W]e think that our laws and traditions in the past half century are of most relevance here. These references show an emerging awareness that liberty gives substantial protection to adult persons in deciding how to conduct their private lives in matters pertaining to sex.

Thus, *Lawrence* elucidates the *Glucksberg* discussion of the proper use of history and tradition in more than one sense. In addition to clarifying that history and tradition do not themselves resolve the due process inquiry, *Lawrence* establishes that recent trends and practices are as important as more distant ones in defining the existence and scope

---

9. Judge Birch makes inconsistent use of this passage. On the one hand, he uses it to argue that *Lawrence* cannot possibly extend to the facts of the instant case—an argument that is untenable. On the other hand, he overlooks this passage when it comes to arguing that *Lawrence* did not provide a careful description of the scope of the right at issue.

of a liberty interest. The panel's discussion of history and tradition is outdated in both of these respects.

Fourth and finally, the panel insists that, no matter how hard *Lawrence* tries, it cannot have involved a liberty interest that requires heightened scrutiny because of a single reference to the phrase "legitimate state interest" towards the end of the *Lawrence* opinion. The sentence in question stated that "[t]he Texas statute furthers no legitimate state interest which can justify its intrusion into the personal and private life of the individual." The panel misconstrues even this solitary fragment of the *Lawrence* opinion. The mere presence of the phrase "legitimate state interest" does not mean that heightened scrutiny is not applicable, as can be seen by its use in conjunction with the application of heightened scrutiny. As the Supreme Court has explained, "[w]here certain *fundamental rights* are involved, the Court has held that regulation limiting these rights may be justified only by a compelling state interest, and that legislative enactments must be narrowly drawn to express only the *legitimate state interests* at stake." Once the *Lawrence* Court found that the Texas sodomy statute completely proscribed the petitioners' substantive right under the Due Process Clause, and that the law lacked any legitimate purpose, its inquiry was at an end. Heightened scrutiny requires a compelling state interest. The *Lawrence* Court clearly found that there was not even a conceivable legitimate state interest that could have sustained the Texas law.

The only way to avoid the conclusion that *Lawrence* recognized a fundamental right or liberty interest that requires heightened scrutiny is to deliberately refuse to give meaning to the overwhelming bulk of the words, phrases, sentences, and paragraphs used in *Lawrence*. Under the panel's view, *Lawrence* is a one-sentence opinion with pages and pages of irrelevant *dicta*. I submit that it is the panel in *Lofton* that constructs a "strained and ultimately incorrect reading of *Lawrence*."

C. Florida's Adoption Ban is Subject to Heightened Scrutiny Because It Significantly Burdens the Right Identified in *Lawrence*.

Every precedent teaches that when the government directly burdens a fundamental right or liberty interest of the nature affirmed in *Lawrence*, heightened scrutiny applies. The panel argues essentially that, even if *Lawrence* affirmed a fundamental right or liberty interest, heightened scrutiny is not appropriate here, first, because adoption is a privilege and not a right under state law and, second, because Florida's ban is the product of a civil rather than a criminal law.

With respect to the panel's first argument, the Supreme Court long ago rejected the rights/privileges distinction. *See, e.g., Shapiro v. Thompson,* 394 U.S. 618, 627 n.6, 638 (1969) (invalidating law that conditioned receipt of welfare benefits, a statutory privilege, on one-year residency requirement as an unconstitutional burden on right to interstate travel, and noting that "[t]his constitutional challenge cannot be answered by the argument that public assistance benefits are a 'privilege' and not a 'right.' "), *overruled in part on other grounds by Edelman v. Jordan,* 415 U.S. 651 (1974). Therefore, contrary to the panel's suggestions, the refusal to extend a government benefit or privilege on non-discriminatory terms may indeed unconstitutionally burden the exercise of a fundamental right or liberty interest.

The panel's second argument is also mistaken. The need to closely scrutinize Florida's justifications for burdening this right is not diminished because the burden in this case is the product of a civil statute, rather than a criminal law. Once a fundamental right or liberty interest has been established, the Supreme Court has stated that heightened scrutiny applies not only when a state punishes its exercise by means of a criminal statute, but also when a civil law directly and substantially burdens that protected right.

For example, the Court in *Zablocki* applied heightened scrutiny in striking down a civil law that prevented individuals who had not made child support payments from receiving a marriage license. The Court found that the government was unable to show that the law was justified by "sufficiently important state interests" or that it was "closely tailored to effectuate only those interests." The Court explained that heightened scrutiny was appropriate because the law had "directly and substantially" burdened the right of poor people to marry.

Similarly, in *Shapiro*, the Court struck down the civil laws of various jurisdictions which required that residents live within the jurisdiction for a year before receiving welfare benefits. Even though the laws involved the receipt of a government benefit (welfare payments) rather than a right, the Court expressly rejected the application of rational-basis review. Instead, because the law "penalized" the fundamental right to interstate travel, the Court asked whether the law was "necessary" to achieve a "compelling governmental interest."

Together, *Zablocki* and *Shapiro* stand for the proposition that a court must analyze a civil law under heightened scrutiny when it either penalizes or severely burdens the exercise of a fundamental right. I submit that if heightened scrutiny was required given the nature of the civil burdens in *Zablocki* and *Shapiro*, then such scrutiny must, a fortiori, apply in this case. After all, in *Zablocki*, a person could marry after making his or her delinquent child support payment. And in *Shapiro*, a resident would be eligible to receive welfare payments (a government benefit like the ability to adopt) after living in the relevant jurisdiction for a year. But a person exercising his or her *Lawrence* right in Florida may *never* adopt. The categorical nature of this ban, which burdens the right to form intimate relationships only when it is exercised by homosexuals, requires the same close analysis that the Court gave to the laws analyzed in *Zablocki* and *Shapiro* and warrants the very same result. None of the three cases newly cited by Judge Birch in his Special Concurrence in an attempt to fill the gaps in the panel opinion rebuts this conclusion.

In sum, given the *Lawrence* Court's recognition of the fundamental nature of the liberty interest of consenting adults to engage in homosexual relationships, Florida's statute must be subjected to heightened scrutiny. The statute in this case imposes a direct, substantial and severe burden on the right recognized in *Lawrence*. Florida's adoption ban forces a choice between the right to participate in a consensual, private, intimate relationship and consideration for parenthood through adoption. In effect, under the Florida statute, homosexual men and women must forgo the consideration given to all others to be adoptive parents in order to engage in conduct protected by the Fourteenth Amendment. The Constitution does not permit such a choice unless, under heightened scrutiny, a compelling and narrowly tailored justification has been found. As demonstrated above, not only is there no compelling interest to justify the Florida adoption ban, but the law is not even rationally related to the governmental purposes asserted. As such, Florida's ban on homosexual adoption fails both heightened scrutiny and rational basis review.

BIRCH, Circuit Judge, Specially Concurring in the Denial of Rehearing En Banc:

After a review of the Supreme Court's decisions in *Eisenstadt, Moreno, Cleburne,* and *Romer,* the vociferous dissent by my sister jurist (for whom I have great respect and affection), liberally quoting from Justice O'Connor's *concurring* opinion in *Lawrence,* concludes that under a rational basis analysis or, alternatively, an animus-motivated analysis, the Florida adoption statute at issue is constitutionally flawed. I would offer the following additional considerations to balance those suggested by Judge Barkett's spirited and well-crafted dissent.

The *Lofton* panel's analysis and approach in this case was premised on a fundamental principal or philosophy, articulated well by Justice Felix Frankfurter in his concurring opinion in *Dennis v. United States*, 341 U.S. 494, 525 (1951), when he observed:

> Courts are not representative bodies. They are not designed to be a good reflex of a democratic society....Their essential quality is detachment, founded on independence. History teaches that the independence of the judiciary is jeopardized when courts become embroiled in the passions of the day and assume primary responsibility in choosing between competing political, economic and social pressures.

The dissent, instead of approaching the issue as the panel did in this case by asking "[W]hether the Florida legislature *could* have reasonably believed that prohibiting adoption into homosexual environments would further its interest in placing adoptive children in homes that will provide them with optimal developmental conditions," seeks to disparage a fundamental rationale of the Florida *legislature*. Both the Florida attorney general and a Florida appellate court, specifically considering an equal protection challenge to the statute, articulated a rational and arguable basis for the statute: "[W]hatever causes a person to become a homosexual, it is clear that the state cannot know the sexual preferences that a child will exhibit as an adult. Statistically, the state does know that a very high percentage of children available for adoption will develop heterosexual preferences." *Fla. Dep't of Health & Rehab. Servs. v. Cox*, 627 So.2d 1210, 1229 (Fla.Dist.Ct.App.1993). Stated differently, the mainstream of contemporary American family life consists of heterosexual individuals. Can it be seriously contended that an arguably rational basis does not exist for placing adoptive children in the *mainstream* of American family life? And that to do so is irrational? I think not. In fact, the Congress of the United States in determining what is in the best interests of other special needs children, the handicapped, has passed laws focused on educationally *mainstreaming* such children. *See, e.g.*, 20 U.S.C. § 1412(a)(5)(A) ("To the maximum extent appropriate, children with disabilities, including children in public or private institutions or other care facilities, are educated with children who are not disabled").

It is also worthy to note that the dissent would focus on conduct by Florida's *executive branch* (the Department of Children and Family Services ["the Department"]) and Florida's *judicial branch* (citing just two isolated custody determinations), which the dissent argues is inconsistent with the *legislature's* arguably rational bases. Recall that the Supreme Court has held: "It could be that the assumptions underlying these rationales are erroneous, but the very fact that they are *arguable* is sufficient, on rational-basis review, to immunize the legislative choice from constitutional challenge." *Heller v. Doe*, 509 U.S. 312, 333 (1993) (emphasis mine). Moreover, post-legislation conduct, including the passage of regulations, by the executive agency that must find placements for parentless children, which may be at times inconsistent with the spirit, if not the letter, of a legislative enactment, should not weigh heavily in the calculus of rational basis review. The executive branch, acting through unelected bureaucrats who, while undoubtedly concerned about the best interests of their wards, often are motivated by other concerns such as coping with inadequate resources and an unmanageable number of unplaced children. As the *Lofton* panel recognized:

> The central mandate of the equal protection guarantee is that "[t]he sovereign may not draw distinctions between individuals based solely on differences that

are irrelevant to a legitimate governmental objective." Equal protection, however, does not forbid legislative classifications." It simply keeps governmental decisionmakers from treating differently persons who are in all relevant respects alike." Unless the challenged classification burdens a fundamental right or targets a suspect class, the Equal Protection Clause requires only that the classification be rationally related to a legitimate state interest. *Romer v. Evans,* 517 U.S. 620, 631 (1996). As we have explained, Florida's statute burdens no fundamental rights. Moreover, all of our sister circuits that have considered the question have declined to treat homosexuals as a suspect class. Because the present case involves neither a fundamental right nor a suspect class, we review the Florida statute under the rational-basis standard. Rational-basis review, "a paradigm of judicial restraint," does not provide "a license for courts to judge the wisdom, fairness, or logic of legislative choices." The question is simply whether the challenged legislation is rationally related to a legitimate state interest. Under this deferential standard, a legislative classification "is accorded a strong presumption of validity," and "must be upheld against equal protection challenge if there is any reasonably conceivable state of facts that could provide a rational basis for the classification." This holds true "even if the law seems unwise or works to the disadvantage of a particular group, or if the rationale for it seems tenuous." Moreover, a state has "no obligation to produce evidence to sustain the rationality of a statutory classification." Rather, "the burden is on the one attacking the legislative arrangement to negative every conceivable basis which might support it, whether or not the basis has a foundation in the record."

The dissent also sets up a "straw man" when it suggests: "[t]he panel also intimates in dicta that Florida has a legitimate interest in defending public morality by expressing disapproval of homosexuality." The footnote was not motivated by some sort of homophobic agenda, but only acknowledged the argument advanced by Florida's counsel that public morality was a rational basis and thus the panel stated, given our finding of a mainstreaming rationale as a rational basis, that "it is unnecessary for us to resolve the question [of a public morality basis]."

Turning now from the dissent's attack on the rational basis predicate to its alternative "animus/analysis" challenge, I offer the following perspectives in counter-balance to the arguments by the dissent. The dissent advances a second equal protection argument in favor of striking down the Florida adoption statute's categorical prohibition against practicing homosexual citizens. As I understand the dissent's argument, once it is demonstrated that the motivation propelling a piece of legislation is animus, a different sort of analysis from a traditional "any-existing-rational-basis-will-justify" approach must be employed, as putatively mandated by Supreme Court precedents in *Romer, Cleburne, Moreno* and *Eisenstadt.* Under this "animus/analysis," a court is required to examine whether the proffered reasons for the statute are pretextual—particularly in light of what the State (including its executive branch [here the Department] and judicial branch [courts awarding custody to homosexual parents, etc.]) does that is contradictory to the statute.

While a principled argument can be made on this equal protection animus/analysis that might result in invalidation of this statute, the *Lofton* panel was not willing to embrace that more adventurous leap and preferred to stay with a more traditional analytical approach that ignored the actual legislative history and instead searched for any rational basis.

The real point of disagreement between the *Lofton* panel and the dissent is whether rational-basis review should always uphold a law as long as there exists some "conceivable" rational basis—or whether there are certain instances that call for a "more searching" form of rational-basis review that examines the actual motivations underlying the law. Accordingly, I offer the counter-argument to the dissent's "heightened rational-basis review" theory.

The dissent's interpretation of *Romer, Cleburne, Moreno* and *Eisenstadt*—and its theory that these precedents call for a "more searching" form of rational-basis review—is summarized well in the following passage:

> In all four cases, the Court concluded that the asserted justifications were not rationally related to the classification. Thus, the Court inferred that animus was the motivation behind the legislation and established that such a motivation could not constitute a legitimate state interest.

Aside from Justice O'Connor's *Lawrence* concurrence, I have found in the Supreme Court's language no explicit support for the theory that rational-basis review should examine the actual motivation behind legislation (assuming that such a thing can be divined with any accuracy). I also note the Supreme Court's own observation that "it is entirely irrelevant for constitutional purposes whether the conceived reason for the challenged distinction actually motivated the legislature." *F.C.C. v. Beach Communications. Inc.,* 508 U.S. 307, 315; *see also City of Renton v. Playtime Theatres, Inc.,* 475 U.S. 41, 48 (1986) ("It is a familiar principle of constitutional law that this Court will not strike down an otherwise constitutional statute on the basis of an alleged illicit legislative motive.").

Moreover, my review of the cases cited by the dissent fails to convince me that those opinions applied a "heightened" form of review as the dissent contends. In that vein, I offer my more conventional and measured reading of each of those precedents.

The *Romer* Court found Colorado's Amendment 2—a "sweeping and comprehensive" measure that imposed a "broad and undifferentiated disability" on the state's homosexual residents—to be "inexplicable by anything but animus" because the breadth of the Amendment so exceeded its proffered rationales. 517 U.S. 620 (1996). As I understand it, the fatal defect in Amendment 2 was not that the Court determined that *actual* animus motivated passage of the Amendment. Indeed, in contrast to the dissent's scrutiny of the legislative history of the Florida statute, the *Romer* Court never examined the actual history of the plebiscite vote that led to passage of Amendment 2, nor the accompanying campaign rhetoric or the "intent" of the electorate.

Instead, the Court found the proffered rationales so implausible that the Court *inferred* that animus was the only conceivable (as opposed to actual) rationale. In its pivotal language, the Court stated:

> The primary rationale the State offers for Amendment 2 is respect for other citizens' freedom of association, and in particular the liberties of landlords or employers who have personal or religious objections to homosexuality. Colorado also cites its interest in conserving resources to fight discrimination against other groups. The breadth of the amendment is so far removed from these particular justifications that we find it impossible to credit them. We cannot say that Amendment 2 is directed to any identifiable legitimate purpose or discrete objective. It is a status-based enactment divorced from any factual context from which we could discern a relationship to legitimate state interests; it

is a classification of persons undertaken for its own sake, something the Equal Protection Clause does not permit.

Id. *at 635.*

In sum, I read *Romer* to stand for the proposition that when all the proffered rationales for a law are clearly and manifestly implausible, a reviewing court may infer that animus is the only explicable basis. And animus *alone* cannot constitute a legitimate government interest.

In *City of Cleburne*, the Supreme Court invalidated, under the rational-basis test, a municipal zoning ordinance requiring a group home for the mentally retarded to obtain a special use permit. Although the municipality offered various justifications for the ordinance, the Court could not discern how these justifications applied particularly to mentally retarded residents—but not to other groups of persons who could freely occupy the identical structure without a permit, such as boarding houses, fraternity houses, and nursing homes.

Cleburne stands primarily for the proposition that irrational prejudice is not a legitimate state interest. And irrational prejudice can be inferred as the basis for a classification when there is no reason to believe that the disadvantaged class is different, in relevant respects, from similarly situated classes.

I would also note this recent gloss that the Court gave *Cleburne* in *Bd. of Trustees of the Univ. of Alabama v. Garrett*:

> The [*Cleburne*] Court's reasoning was that the city's purported justifications for the ordinance made no sense in light of how the city treated other groups similarly situated in relevant respects. Although the group home for the mentally retarded was required to obtain a special use permit, apartment houses, other multiple-family dwellings, retirement homes, nursing homes, sanitariums, hospitals, boarding houses, fraternity and sorority houses, and dormitories were not subject to the ordinance.

531 U.S. 356, 366 n.4 (2001). *Garrett* also expressly rejected the theory that, under *Cleburne,* the mere presence of animus can fatally taint a statute against a rational-basis challenge:

> Justice Breyer suggests that *Cleburne* stands for the broad proposition that state decisionmaking reflecting "negative attitudes" or "fear" necessarily runs afoul of the Fourteenth Amendment. Although such biases may often accompany irrational (and therefore unconstitutional) discrimination, their presence alone does not a constitutional violation make. As we noted in *Cleburne:* "[M]ere negative attitudes, or fear, *unsubstantiated by factors which are properly cognizable* in a zoning proceeding, are not permissible bases for treating a home for the mentally retarded differently...."

Id. at 367 (emphasis added in *Garrett).*

In *Moreno,* the Court found that Section 3(a) the Federal Food Stamp Act, which forbade assistance to any "household" wherein one member was unrelated to any other member, was not rationally related to any legitimate state interest, including the proffered reasons, such as fraud prevention. This led to the Court to conclude that the only plausible rationale for the provision was to prevent hippie communes from taking advantage of food stamp assistance. And this, by itself, was not a sufficient basis to sustain the provision: "a bare congressional desire to harm a politically unpopular group cannot constitute a legitimate governmental interest…*without reference to some independent considerations in the public interest.*" (emphasis mine).

I call particular attention to a later gloss on *Moreno* expressly disclaiming the theory that *Moreno* stands for something more than traditional rational-basis review:

> [In *Moreno,*] we upheld an equal protection challenge to a provision of the Food Stamp Act and concluded that 'a bare congressional desire to harm a politically unpopular group cannot constitute a legitimate governmental interest.' This statement is *merely an application of the usual rational-basis test:* if a statute is not rationally related to any legitimate governmental objective, it cannot be saved from constitutional challenge by a defense that relates it to an illegitimate governmental interest. Accordingly, in *Moreno* itself we examined the challenged provision under the rational-basis standard of review.

Lyng v. United Auto. Workers of America, 485 U.S. 360, 370 n.8 (emphasis mine).

In *Eisenstadt,* the issue was whether a Massachusetts law that prevented dispensation of contraceptives to unmarried persons unless the purpose was to prevent disease violated the Equal Protection clause by treating married and unmarried persons differently. In *Eisenstadt,* as in *Romer,* the fatal defect was not a determination that actual animus motivated the law, but that the proffered rationales were implausible. As I understand it, the *Eisenstadt* Court was not, as the dissent suggests, looking at the actual motivations behind the statute. Instead, the Court simply found that the proffered reasons did not rationally relate to the scope of the legislation and, accordingly, the classification failed rational-basis review.

The *Lofton* panel concluded its analysis with the following observation: "Florida has made the determination that it is not in the best interests of its displaced children to be adopted by [homosexuals]…and we have found nothing in the Constitution that forbids this policy judgment. Thus, any argument that the Florida legislature was misguided in its decision is one of legislative policy, not constitutional law. The legislature is the proper forum for this debate." The dissent would have this court impose its putatively superior judgment on this policy issue and legislate from the bench. Such a breach of the separation of powers and departure from deference to the elected lawmakers of Florida, we have rejected. Only where the laws of Florida can be demonstrated to be irrational on any arguable basis or constitute a clear deprivation of a citizen's fundamental rights should this court substitute its judgment for that of the Florida legislature. Thus, I turn to the alternative analysis by one of the dissents that finds such a fundamental right having been articulated in the Supreme Court's decision in *Lawrence.*

The right to privacy that is the touchstone for a right to sexual intimacy by consenting adults (hereinafter "RSI/CA") has its Supreme Court lineage and trajectory through the decisions in *Griswold, Eisenstadt, Roe v. Wade,* and *Carey,* and culminating with *Lawrence* (2003) (which leveled the only speed-bump in that trajectory, *Bowers*). There seems to be only one problem with this theory, albeit in the form of a footnote:

> [T]he Court has not definitely answered the difficult question whether and to what extent the Constitution prohibits state statutes regulating private consensual sexual behavior among adults, and we do not purport to answer that question now.

Carey, 431 U.S. at 688 n.5, 97 S.Ct. at 2018 n.5 (internal punctuation and citation omitted).

I suggest that the answer to *Carey's* "difficult question" was not provided to us in *Lawrence* when viewed through an objective lens. I find that the most coherent lens through which to read *Lawrence* and its often enigmatic language is to recall that most of that language is devoted to explaining why the Court was not bound by its prior decision in *Bowers.* Perhaps the best way to explain this reading is to begin with the dissent's chief critique of the *Lofton* panel's interpretation of *Lawrence.* The dissent posits that the *Lofton* panel failed to recognize that *Lawrence* unequivocally held that consenting adults have a *substantive* due process right to engage in private intimate sexual conduct. This statement highlights well where the dissent and the *Lofton* panel part company. The first task in faithfully applying precedent, including that of the Supreme Court, is to look to the actual holding of the relevant precedent. That task requires examining the facts that were before the deciding court and ascertaining what conclusions of law were *necessarily* reached in disposing of the case.

A word-count approach as apparently employed by the dissent, in addition to being too formalistic, is problematic in practice. For example, my own unscientific survey of the words, phrases, sentences, and paragraphs used in *Lawrence* reveals not only language from which can be inferred a RSI/CA, but even stronger language from which we might infer any number of new rights, or even a new mandate in conducting constitutional review. *See, e.g.,* 123 S.Ct. at 2475 ("The instant case involves liberty of the person both in its spatial and more transcendent dimensions."); *id.* at 2481 ("At the heart of liberty is the right to define one's own concept of existence, of meaning, of the universe, and of the mystery of human life. Beliefs about these matters could not define the attributes of personhood were they formed under compulsion of the State.") (quoting *Planned Parenthood of Southeastern Pa. v. Casey,* 505 U.S. 833, 851 (1992)); *id.* at 2483 ("[T]imes can blind us to certain truths and later generations can see that laws once thought necessary and proper in fact serve only to oppress. As the Constitution endures, persons in every generation can invoke its principles in their own search for greater freedom.").

I realize these are outer examples, but they point to the importance of attentiveness to context in interpreting precedent—and in distinguishing binding language from advisory *dicta.* It was this distinction that the *Lofton* panel carefully made in construing *Lawrence* and its holding: "*Lawrence's* holding was that substantive due process does not permit a state to impose a criminal prohibition on private consensual homosexual conduct." I would add that this holding relied on two predicate legal conclusions: (1) that *stare decisis* did not require that *Bowers's* precedent be followed and (2) that Texas's sodomy prohibition did not further a legitimate state interest. It was necessary for the Court to reach the first conclusion because *Bowers* had upheld Georgia's sodomy statute against, *inter alia,* a rational-basis challenge. And the second conclusion was all that was required to resolve the dispositive question of whether the Texas sodomy law was constitutional.

To read *Lawrence's* holding any broader [sic] would be to assume that the Court departed from the established principle of minimalism in deciding constitutional matters. Of course, the Court will so depart from time to time, usually when announcing a new rule of constitutional law that will require frequent application by the lower courts. And those decisions are typically accompanied with clear guideposts for applying the new rule. *Lawrence* does not appear to be such a case. We find in the opinion no such guideposts; there is no description of the scope of this putative fundamental right, no standard of review for scrutinizing infringements on that right, no balancing test, and so on.

What we do find in the *Lawrence* opinion by way of mandate is that *Bowers* is no longer to be treated as good law. Indeed, *Bowers* is its constant point of reference, and the unrelenting thrust of *Lawrence's* analysis is to show that *Bowers* should not have reached the result it did. This begins in the first paragraph of the majority opinion's analysis, where the Court announced, "[W]e deem it necessary to reconsider the Court's holding in *Bowers*." Virtually the entire remainder of the opinion is focused upon explaining *Bowers's* shortcomings, culminating in the pronouncement that "*Bowers* was not correct when it was decided, and it is not correct today. It ought not to remain binding precedent. *Bowers v. Hardwick* should be and now is overruled." Having cleared *Bowers* from the books, the Court's analysis spends a mere two paragraphs on the facts of the *Lawrence* case—and disposes of the case in a single sentence: "The Texas statute furthers no legitimate state interest which can justify its intrusion into the personal and private life of the individual."

An important point bears noting here. To say that *Lawrence* overruled *Bowers* is not to say that every question *Bowers* answered in the negative should now be answered in the affirmative (or vice versa).[10] For example, although the *Lawrence* Court specifically noted that *Bowers* misframed the issue as one of whether there is a right to engage in sodomy, the Court never identified how *Bowers* should in fact have framed the inquiry—much less what the precise answer to that inquiry should have been. We see this pattern throughout the *Lawrence* opinion. The opinion contains extensive critique of *Bowers's* answers to the questions raised in that case—but virtually no definitive answers to those questions, much less rules of law. Another example is *Lawrence's* history discussion. After noting *Bowers's* misframing of its inquiry, the Court went on to point out some of the "fundamental criticisms of the historical premises relied upon by the majority and concurring opinions in *Bowers*." Here, again, the Court only pointed to shortcomings in *Bowers's* analysis, but did not reach any conclusions itself, noting that "[w]e need not enter this debate in the attempt to reach a definitive historical judgment, but the following considerations counsel against adopting the definitive conclusions upon which *Bowers* placed such reliance."

In short, the critique of *Bowers* provides the necessary context for understanding the great bulk of *Lawrence's* language—including much of the language that the dissent quotes in support of its RSI/CA argument. For example, the dissent's main premise— that *Lawrence* "held that consenting adults have a right under the Due Process Clause to engage in private sexual conduct, including homosexual conduct," relies heavily on the Court's analysis of the privacy cases preceding *Bowers,* namely, *Griswold, Eisenstadt, Roe,* and *Carey.*

Far from engaging in an extensive analysis, the Court spent less than a page surveying these precedents. More importantly, rather than put any definitive gloss on these precedents, the Court canvassed them in order to point out that "[t]his was the state of the law with respect to some of the most relevant cases when the Court considered *Bowers*."

And so I return to my opening suggestion that the most coherent and objective lens through which to read *Lawrence* is to recall that the purpose of the vast bulk of its analysis was to call into question and ultimately overrule *Bowers*. Of course, this still leaves open the thorny question of to what extent the *Griswold* line of cases—which no

---

10. For an even narrower interpretation of the extent to which *Bowers* was overruled, *see* Justice Scalia's dissent. Because the resolution of the instant case only required reaching the rational basis of the challenged statute, it was Justice Scalia's suggestion that *Lawrence* only overruled the rational-basis aspect of *Bowers's* holding, but left intact its fundamental-rights holding.

longer must be reconciled with *Bowers*—establish a RSI/CA, as well as what standard of review that right would trigger. The question is further complicated by *Carey*'s footnote 5, which not only disavowed that those precedents had definitely established such a right, but also rejected the argument that strict scrutiny was the appropriate standard.

The dissent would have our court create a new fundamental substantive due process right where none has existed before. The *Lofton* panel and this court's rejection of *en banc* review has declined such an activist approach and has sought to "exercise the utmost care whenever…asked to break new ground" in the field of fundamental rights. *Washington v. Glucksberg,* 521 U.S. 702, 720 (1997). I submit that the latter is the best advised course—particularly in this area where the Court appears to be breaking new ground, but has crafted its opinions to avoid fashioning bright-line rules and to limit its holdings to the facts of the immediate case. In my view, the most judicious way to follow such precedents is to apply their holdings to cases involving the same facts and permit the Supreme Court itself to clarify the gray areas it has apparently (and perhaps intentionally) left for another day. It may well be that the Court in time takes its jurisprudence in the direction that the dissent advocates. But that, in my opinion, is a step for the Supreme Court to take.

The *Lofton* panel chose not to expand *Lawrence* through inference and extrapolation, but rather applied the holding of *Lawrence* to the facts at hand. Our reading finds its legitimacy in the following passage from *Lawrence,* a passage in which the Court clearly limited the scope of its holding:

> The present case does not involve minors. It does not involve persons who might be injured or coerced or who are situated in relationships where consent might not easily be refused. It does not involve public conduct or prostitution. It does not involve whether the government must give formal recognition to any relationship that homosexual persons seek to enter. The case does involve two adults who, with full and mutual consent from each other, engaged in sexual practices common to a homosexual lifestyle. The petitioners are entitled to respect for their private lives. The State cannot demean their existence or control their destiny by making their private sexual conduct a crime. Their right to liberty under the Due Process Clause gives them the full right to engage in their conduct without intervention of the government. "It is a promise of the Constitution that there is a realm of personal liberty which the government may not enter." The Texas statute furthers no legitimate state interest which can justify its intrusion into the personal and private life of the individual.

As the *Lofton* panel explains, this case is different from *Lawrence* because this is not a criminal prosecution, because the state is not attempting to intervene in the private lives of any adults, because adoption is not a private act but a public one, and because, when it permits people to adopt, the state confers official status on them as adoptive parents. This case is different from *Lawrence,* the *Lofton* panel opinion points out, because Florida's statute does further a legitimate state interest. It furthers the legitimate interest the state has in encouraging what it deems to be the optimal family structure, a home that has both a mother and a father, or at least one parent in the heterosexual mainstream of American family life. The plaintiffs did not seriously contest the legal sufficiency of that state interest, but instead argued that the Florida law is not rationally related to that interest, an argument that the panel opinion thoroughly addresses.

The dissent places great emphasis on the fact that the Court announced at the beginning of its opinion that "the case should be resolved by determining whether the petitioners were free as adults to engage in [their] private conduct in the exercise of their liberty under the Due Process Clause of the Fourteenth Amendment to the Constitution." According to it, this language, along with the Court's other references to due process "liberty," requires that we interpret *Lawrence* as affirming a fundamental or substantive due process right to private consensual adult intimacy. It contends that this, in turn, requires that we subject the challenged Florida statute to "heightened scrutiny."

Then the dissent makes two related assumptions. First, it conflates substantive due process analysis and fundamental rights analysis—or at least treats the two as interchangeable. Second, it assumes that *Lawrence*'s references to "liberty under the Due Process Clause" are tantamount to acknowledgment of a constitutional right deserving strict scrutiny protection. Upon close scrutiny, neither assumption is sound.

Admittedly, there is considerable overlap between substantive due process analysis and fundamental rights analysis. And the Supreme Court has at times used the term "substantive due process" as shorthand for its fundamental rights analysis. But a careful reading of the Court's precedents indicates that its fundamental rights jurisprudence is but one subset of the various doctrines that emanate from the concept of substantive due process.

As our Chief Judge has noted, "In its application, substantive due process is a puzzling concept." *McKinney v. Pate*, 20 F.3d 1550, 1567 (11th Cir.1994) (Edmondson, J., concurring). And even if I had the chutzpah to try, this would hardly be the place to solve that puzzle. I will, however, sketch a few principles that underlie my belief that there is no contradiction between the notion that *Lawrence* employed substantive due process analysis and the *Lofton* panel's conclusion that *Lawrence*'s holding was a rational-basis holding.

As an initial matter, I would suggest that rational-basis review—like every standard of review that scrutinizes the substance of state action for irrationality and arbitrariness—is itself a form of substantive due process review. Although it is rarely classified as such, I find no other plausible constitutional source for its substantive review of state and federal legislative acts. Indeed, "the touchstone of due process is protection of the individual against arbitrary action of government." *County of Sacramento v. Lewis*, 523 U.S. 833, 845 (1998). And it has long been understood that the concept of due process protects against not only procedural arbitrariness, but also substantive arbitrariness.

As I understand it, this substantive scrutiny of governmental action is the primary source of the Court's jurisprudence regarding fundamental, or unenumerated, rights (hereinafter, simply "fundamental rights"). However, the concept of substantive due process underlies other doctrines outside the field of fundamental rights. For example, I note that just last term the Court reaffirmed its line of cases holding that there are "substantive constitutional limitations" on the size and severity of civil punitive damage awards. *State Farm Mutual Auto. Ins. Co. v. Campbell*, 538 U.S. 408, 416 (2003). Another example is the "shocks the conscience" test, under which courts consider whether the substance of actions by governmental officers is fatally arbitrary.

I note these examples to underscore my point that rational-basis review likewise is a form of substantive review, albeit a deferential one, that protects against the arbitrary and irrational exercise of legislative power in enacting economic and social legislation. Accordingly, unlike the dissent, I do not find any incompatibility between (a) the *Lawrence* Court's assertion that "the case should be resolved by determining whether the petitioners were free as adults to engage in [their] private conduct in the exercise of their liberty under the Due Process Clause of the Fourteenth Amendment to the Constitution" and (b) the *Lofton* panel's conclusion that the Court ultimately based its holding on rational-basis grounds.

With regard to the dissent's second implicit assumption, I would submit that the mere fact that a liberty interest receives substantive protection under the Due Process Clause does not automatically trigger strict scrutiny. Based on its interpretation that *Lawrence* recognizes a substantive liberty interest, the dissent contends that any burden to that liberty interest requires strict scrutiny. Its chief exhibits are various lines from *Lawrence* that allude to the petitioners' liberty under the Due Process clause. The dissent translates these general references to "liberty" under the Due Process Clause into a specific due process right to engage in private sexual conduct. The dissent appears to be: (multiple references to Due Process liberty) + (decision finding Texas sodomy statute unconstitutional) = (holding that there is a substantive due process right to sexual intimacy). But even if I were persuaded that *Lawrence* announced, or "reaffirmed," a substantive due process right to sexual intimacy, I still am not convinced that burdens on this right necessarily would require strict scrutiny. First, as the *Lofton* panel observed, the *Lawrence* Court itself never applied, nor used any of the language of, strict scrutiny. Second, with all due respect, as cryptic as some of the Supreme Court's substantive due process precedents are, my recent review of them convinces me of this much: the mere presence of a substantive liberty interest does not automatically trigger strict scrutiny, as the dissent seems to suggest.

Indeed, even cursory research has revealed several instances in which the Court identified a substantive right under the Fourteenth Amendment—and yet did not require strict scrutiny. I note briefly two examples. The most recent is *Sell v. United States,* 539 U.S. 166 (2003), issued only days before the *Lawrence* opinion. The *Sell* Court vacated the conviction of a murder defendant who had been administered anti-psychotic medication against his wishes in order to render him competent to stand trial. What I find significant is that the Court identified a *"constitutionally protected liberty interest* in avoiding the unwanted administration of antipsychotic drugs," *id.* at 178 (emphasis mine), and then proceeded to articulate a standard of review lower than strict scrutiny—"necessary significantly to further important governmental trial-related interests," *id.* at 179.

The second case I note is *City of Chicago v. Morales,* 527 U.S. 41 (1999). There, the plurality opinion recognized, in language similar to that employed in *Lawrence,* that "the freedom to loiter for innocent purposes is part of the 'liberty' protected by the Due Process Clause of the Fourteenth Amendment." I call attention to the fact that, despite using this substantive due process language, the *Morales* plurality never hinted at the applicability of strict scrutiny (and instead struck down Chicago's gang loitering statute on vagueness grounds—a decision that nevertheless was predicated on the existence of this "constitutionally protected liberty" to loiter innocently.

In sum, a closer and careful reading of *Lawrence* and other relevant precedents indicate that, even if *Lawrence's dicta* did acknowledge a constitutional liberty interest in private sexual intimacy, this liberty interest does not rise to the level of a fundamental right nor does it necessarily trigger strict scrutiny.

I will conclude on a purely personal note. If I were a legislator, rather than a judge, I would vote in favor of considering otherwise eligible homosexuals for adoptive parenthood. In reviewing the record in this case one can only be impressed by the courage, tenacity and devotion of Messrs. Lofton and Houghton for the children placed in their care. For these children, these men are the only parents they have ever known. Thus, I consider the policy decision of the Florida legislature to be misguided and trust that over time attitudes will change and it will see the best interest of these children in a different light. Nevertheless, as compelling as this perspective is to me, I will not allow my personal views to conflict with my judicial duty—conduct that apparently fewer and fewer citizens, commentators and Senators seem to understand or appreciate. And, I hasten to add, the vast majority of federal judges, including each and every judge of the Eleventh Circuit, are similarly sensitive to separate their personal preferences from their duty to follow precedent as they understand it.

Notes and Questions

1. Having read the various arguments of the *Lofton* panel, Judge Barkett's dissent, and Judge Birch's concurrence, how would you answer the following questions? What was the holding of *Romer v. Evans*? What was the holding of *Lawrence v. Texas*? In cases involving sexual orientation discrimination by a government agency, what level of scrutiny is to be applied to the government's challenged policy? In cases that impose some sort of disability or burden on members of sexual minorities because of their propensity to engage in the conduct that was found to be constitutionally protected from criminal prosecution in *Lawrence*, what level of scrutiny is to be applied to the government's challenged policy?

2. Judges Birch and Barkett resumed their argument about the holding and scope of *Lawrence* just a week later in *Williams v. Attorney General of Alabama*, 378 F.3d 1232 (11th Cir. 2004), cert. denied, 125 S.Ct. 1335 (2005). Reversing a decision by the U.S. District Court for the Northern District of Alabama, a three-judge panel voted 2-1 that the Due Process Clause does not include a right of sexual privacy for adults and therefore a state law criminalizing the sale of "sex toys" can be sustained by the state's interest in promoting morality. In dissent, Judge Barkett insisted that the court had repeated the error of *Bowers v. Hardwick* in defining the question for decision too narrowly and had ignored all the salient parts of the Supreme Court's holding in *Lawrence*, including its rejection of "morality" as a rational basis for a criminal statute that burdens the right of adults to conduct their private, consensual sexual activities. (The majority had conceded that prohibiting the sale of sex toys burdens the ability of adults in Alabama to use them as part of their sexual activities, even though the statute did not criminalize use or possession.) The Supreme Court's denial of certiorari once again forestalled a definitive resolution of this argument.

3. In Chapter Five of this book, you will consider various arguments about how children are or might be affected by being raised in a household headed by a same-sex couple. The *Lofton* panel decision alludes to various studies that have been introduced into evidence in a range of cases, including challenges to the Florida adoption statute, challenges to a similar New Hampshire adoption statute that was subsequently repealed after New Hampshire had enacted a law forbidding discrimination on the basis of sexual orientation, and more traditional litigation concerning rights to child custody or visitation. What is the relevance of such studies to the constitutional issues being considered by the court? What evidentiary standards should judges use in deciding whether proffered, purportedly scientific studies are admissible on factual issues whose determination is important for the case? The footnote references to actual studies have been

edited out of the opinions in this chapter, but it is noteworthy that Judge Birch cited, without comment or explication and as supporting the contention that children raised by same-sex couples do "worse" on some measures than other children, a study co-authored by a person who was sanctioned and expelled from membership in a professional organization because of the disreputable methodology of studies he conducted purporting to document negative stereotypes about homosexuals.

4. Judge Birch's opinions are not the only ones issued in the aftermath of *Lawrence* that attributed a narrow holding to that opinion. In *State of Kansas v. Limon*, 83 P.3d 229 (Kan.Ct.App., Jan. 30, 2004), review granted, May 25, 2004, a three-judge panel of the Kansas Court of Appeals held that *Lawrence* was essentially irrelevant to the question whether Kansas could impose a significantly harsher criminal sanction on oral sex between gay teens than non-gay teens, and during 2004 courts in Arizona and New Jersey treated *Lawrence* as essentially irrelevant to the question whether those states had violated the constitutional rights of gay people by denying them the right to marry. *See Lewis v. Harris*, 2003 WL 23191114 (N.J.Super.Ct., Nov. 5, 2003), appeal pending; *Standhardt v. Superior Court*, 77 P.3d 451 (Az.Ct.App. 2003), review den'd, May 26, 2004.

5. On the other hand, some courts have given *Lawrence* a broader reading. The Massachusetts Supreme Judicial Court cited and relied on *Lawrence* in ruling that same-sex couples are constitutionally entitled to marry in Massachusetts, *Goodridge v. Department of Public Health*, 798 N.E.2d 941 (Mass. Sup.Ct. 2003), although that case was decided solely on state constitutional grounds. More to the point, a federal trial court in Pennsylvania relied on *Lawrence* to rule that a federal obscenity statute was unconstitutional in its application to the sale of obscene matter to consenting adults for private use, since it was grounded solely on "morality" justifications that could no longer serve to validate content-based restrictions on speech, *United States v. Extreme Associates, Inc.*, 352 F. Supp. 2d 578 (W.D. Pa. 2005).

6. The most prominently enforced sodomy law in the United States is found in Article 125 of the Uniform Code of Military Justice, governing the conduct of military personnel. To what extent does *Lawrence* affect its continued enforceability? This question had not been answered by the federal appellate courts as of the end of 2004, but military appeals courts have found a substantial "military exception" to *Lawrence*. See *U.S. v. Marcum*, 60 M.J. 198 (Ct.App., Armed Forces, 2004). The first reported case in which a military appeals court refused to uphold a sodomy prosecution involved heterosexual adults engaging in consensual activity in private where one of the participants was a civilian. *U.S. v. Bullock*, ARMY 20030534 (U.S. Army Court of Criminal Appeals, Nov. 30, 2004) (unpublished disposition).

Chapter Three

Government Regulation of Sexual Conduct

The Supreme Court's decision in *Lawrence v. Texas* (2003) appears to establish a "floor" of constitutional protection for sexual conduct. Although the precise holding of the Court may be disputed, at the very least the Court held that the legislature's moral disapproval of homosexuality did not provide a rational basis for making the homosexual conduct described in the Texas statute a crime. A more expansive reading, focused on the Court's description of why *Bowers v. Hardwick* was "wrong" when it was decided, could find that the Court had recognized constitutional protection as an aspect of "liberty" under the 14th (and presumably the 5th) Amendment for private, consensual adult sexual conduct. The Court described the protected conduct, in part, in terms of what it was not:

> The present case does not involve minors. It does not involve persons who might be injured or coerced or who are situated in relationships where consent might not easily be refused. It does not involve public conduct or prostitution.

This suggests that the concerns for individual liberty that the Court articulated in *Lawrence* might play out differently in a constitutional analysis where the conduct involves minors or persons in relationships where consent issues are difficult, where conduct arguably takes place in public, contains elements of compensation, or involves the possibility of physical or psychological injury. In other words, the "decriminalization" of private, noncommercial acts of consensual sodomy between adults directly addresses only a small portion of the full range of human sexual conduct and expression. Indeed, it fails to address directly the issue of sexual intercourse between unmarried adults of the opposite sex, conduct that was not covered by the challenged statute, but that was still declared criminal as "fornication" in the laws of some other states, such as Virginia, at the time of the *Lawrence* decision. It also fails to address directly the issue of adultery, still a crime in some jurisdictions, in which a married person has sex with an adult to whom he or she is not married. And it does not address directly other statutes under which same-sex conduct might be treated differently than opposite-sex conduct.

As extensively discussed in *Lawrence* and in the various opinions in *Lofton* considered in Chapter II, both *Lawrence* and *Bowers v. Hardwick* were decided against the backdrop of several decades of "sexual privacy" decisions by the Supreme Court. In *Lawrence*, Justice Kennedy identified the beginning of this sequence of cases as *Griswold v. Connecticut*, 381 U.S. 479 (1965), in which the Court found that a fundamental right of marital privacy, constructed from the "penumbras" that "emanate" from various provisions of the Bill of Rights and also inherent in the concept of "liberty" specified in the Due Process Clause, would shield a married couple's decision to use contraceptives in order to be able to have sexual intercourse without fear of pregnancy. Although this was the Court's first express identification of "privacy" as a constitutional doctrine in the realm of sexual practice (as opposed to the kind of privacy addressed in criminal cases about searches by law enforcement authorities), prior cases, most notably *Skinner v. Oklahoma*, 316 U.S. 535 (1942), could be cited as an example of the Court's recognition that there are constitutional limitations on the state's ability to interfere with the individual's sexual expression. In *Skinner*, Justice William O. Douglas, writing for the Court, found an equal protection violation in Oklahoma's imposition of involuntary sterilization on individuals who repeatedly committed blue collar type crimes involving "moral turpitude" without prescribing the same treatment for equally culpable white collar crimes, noting the importance of the physical capacity to reproduce. (A concurring opinion by Chief Justice Harlan Fiske Stone preferred to invalidate the law using a Due Process analysis, identifying the right to reproduce as a "personal liberty" protected by the 14th Amendment.)

After *Griswold*, the Court ruled in *Eisenstadt v. Baird*, 405 U.S. 438 (1972), that unmarried persons enjoy the same constitutional protection for the right to use contraceptives as married persons, indicating that the privacy right identified in *Griswold* was an individual right, not a right peculiar just to married couples. In *Roe v. Wade*, 410 U.S. 113 (1973), the Court held that the previously-identified right of privacy (referred to by some commentators as a right of "sexual privacy") was broad enough to encompass a woman's decision to terminate her pregnancy, and that the state's compelling interest in preserving potential life only became strong enough to overcome this right once the fetus had sufficiently developed in the third trimester of pregnancy to be theoretically capable of independent existence outside the womb. In *Carey v. Population Services International*, 431 U.S. 678 (1977), carrying *Eisenstadt* even one step further, the Court held that minors also enjoyed the right to obtain and use contraceptives. In a footnote, however, the Court noted that it had not yet described the outer limits of the privacy right involved in the case. In *Bowers*, the Court placed "homosexual sodomy" outside those outer limits, in an opinion that seemed reluctant to recognize the previously declared right of privacy as having any scope beyond the cases previously decided, but the Court's description of the liberty interest in *Lawrence* disagreed with that conclusion, albeit reflecting the change in doctrinal terminology introduced by *Planned Parenthood of Southeastern Pa. v. Casey*, 505 U.S. 833 (1992), in which a plurality opinion stated that the Court was reaffirming "the essential holding" of *Roe v. Wade*, but tacitly abandoned the terminology of "privacy," describing the constitutional right involved solely in terms of personal liberty.

This chapter addresses some remaining issues of government regulation of sexual conduct against this historical backdrop, after *Lawrence v. Texas*. What are the bounds of the "private" sphere in which conduct is protected from government regulation? What conduct anticipatory to private sexual conduct can be regulated by government on grounds of concern for public order or public morality? How is consent to be defined, and to what extent can the government presume that particular individuals are unable to consent? For example, should the government be able to forbid sexual activity between prison inmates, regardless of "consent"? And to what extent may the government continue to treat homosexual conduct differently from heterosexual conduct, in circumstances involving minors, lack of legal consent, or public activity? Many of these questions remain open in the absence of definitive post-*Lawrence* rulings by state high courts or the U.S. Supreme Court. In considering the materials that follow, think about how the holdings of the courts might be affected by the application of the Lawrence precedent, both as described by the *Lofton* majority and by dissenting 11th Circuit Judge Barkett.

A. Public vs. Private

In *Lawrence*, the defendants were apprehended while engaged in sexual activity in a private apartment. The nature of their relationship, if any, was not reflected in the trial record, although the rhetoric of the Court's opinion intimated—incorrectly, as it happens—that the two men might have been domestic partners.

Where should courts draw the line in determining whether particular conduct of a sexual nature is taking place in public or in private, and what kind of conduct of a sexual nature can take place in a "public setting" without incurring law enforcement penalties? Although one need not be a member of a sexual minority to engage in sexual conduct in a public place, law enforcement actions against public sexual conduct usually have a disproportionate effect on sexual minorities. Those who are "in the closet" about their sexuality are more likely to seek anonymous sexual encounters in public or quasi-public settings, and even those who are relatively open about their sexuality may have a preference for sexual activity in a variety of settings outside the private bedroom.

Group sexual activity immediately raises the issue of a public vs. private distinction. Does consensual sexual activity among adults in a private place lose its protected aspect if more than two adults are involved? Is the private aspect lost if the participants are careless enough to allow others to learn of their activities inadvertently?

Lovisi v. Slayton
539 F.2d 349 (4th Cir. 1976)(en banc)
cert. denied, 429 U.S. 977 (1976)

HAYNSWORTH, Chief Judge.

The petitioners in this habeas corpus proceeding, Aldo and Margaret Lovisi, husband and wife, were convicted in the state court of sodomy with each other in violation of Va.Code Ann. sec. 18.1-212. They challenged the constitutionality of the statute, as applied to them. After a [habeas corpus] hearing, the district judge concluded that the Lovisis had waived their constitutional right to privacy in their marital conduct and, consequently, their right to contest their state convictions of sodomy with one another by carelessly exposing erotic photographs to Mrs. Lovisi's young daughters. We affirm.

From time to time the Lovisis had placed advertisements in a magazine, "Swinger's Life," in which they sought contact with others interested in erotic sexual experiences. Earl Romeo Dunn answered one such advertisement, and the three met together on three occasions. The last occasion was in the Lovisis' home in Virginia Beach, Virginia. The three engaged in sexual activity in the Lovisis' bedroom, during which Margaret Lovisi performed fellatio upon her husband and upon Dunn. Polaroid pictures were made of this activity, and Mrs. Lovisi's daughters by a former marriage, then 13 and 11 years old, testified that they were present in the bedroom at the time, described what they saw and testified that they took the Polaroid pictures. Dunn and Lovisi denied the presence of the young girls and testified that they took the pictures, sometimes with the aid of a time-delay device.

The general verdict of guilty in the state court did not resolve the dispute in the testimony about the presence of the young girls and their taking the pictures. The district judge was disinclined to accept the disputed testimony of the girls, but he did find that the Lovisis had relinquished their right of privacy by carelessly exposing pictures of their sexual activity to the girls. The entire matter had come to light when one of the girls appeared in school with a picture, subsequently destroyed, said to have been of her and of an adult male, both completely unclothed. This resulted in the execution of a search warrant, and the policeman testified that hundreds of erotic pictures were found in the house. Lovisi, however, testified that the pictures taken of himself and his wife and their companions were kept in a box in a gun cabinet which, as described by him, was quite insecure, and these were among the pictures seized by the police.

The Constitution recognizes a right of privacy with respect to those rights regarded as "fundamental" or "implicit in the concept of ordered liberty." Roe v. Wade, 410 U.S. 113, 152 (1973). The personal intimacies of marriage, the home, procreation, motherhood, childbearing and the family have been held "fundamental" by the Supreme Court and, hence, have been encompassed within the protected rights of privacy. We may thus assume that the marital intimacies shared by the Lovisis when alone and in their own bedroom are within their protected right of privacy. What they do in the privacy of the marital boudoir is beyond the power of the state to scrutinize. The question we face, however, is whether they preserve any right of privacy when they admit others to observe their intimacies.

Married couples engage in acts of sexual intimacy. That they do is no secret. Though they converse with friends or write books about their sexual relations, recounting in explicit detail their own intimacies and techniques, they remain protected in their expectation of privacy within their own bedroom. State law protects them from unwelcome intruders, and the federal constitution protects them from the state in the guise of an unwelcome intruder.

What the federal constitution protects is the right of privacy in circumstances in which it may reasonably be expected. Once a married couple admits strangers as onlookers, federal protection of privacy dissolves. It matters not whether the audience is composed of one, fifty, or one hundred, or whether the onlookers pay for their titillation. If the couple performs sexual acts for the excitation or gratification of welcome onlookers, they cannot selectively claim that the state is an intruder. They possess the freedom to follow their own inclinations in privacy, but once they accept onlookers, whether they are close friends, chance acquaintances, observed "peeping Toms" or paying customers, they may not exclude the state as a constitutionally forbidden intruder.

The answer to the question when the right of privacy is lost cannot turn upon numbers, preserved, if there is one onlooker or two, but not if there are three, or preserved if there are ten, but not if there are eleven. Nor should it turn upon the fact that the onlookers, however many, are not only passive observers but are participants themselves in sexual activity, some of it with one or more of the partners to the marriage. In either such event, the married couple has welcomed a stranger to the marital bedchamber, and what they do is no longer in the privacy of their marriage. The presence of the onlooker, Dunn, in the Lovisis' bedroom dissolved the reasonable expectation of privacy shared by the Lovisis when alone. Hence, we affirm the district court's refusal to issue the writ. AFFIRMED.

[In a brief addendum, the court noted that after it had approved the above decision but before it was released, the Supreme Court had granted summary affirmance in Doe v. Commonwealth's Attorney for City of Richmond, E.D.Va., 403 F.Supp. 1199, affirmed, 96 S.Ct. 1489 (1976), holding that Virginia's law against consensual sodomy did not violate the federal constitution, even as applied to the conduct of consenting adults in private.]

WINTER, with whom CRAVEN and BUTZNER, concur (dissenting):

We accept as settled law the majority's assumption that marital intimacies shared by the Lovisis when alone and in their own bedroom are within their protected right of privacy. We reject, however, the majority's implied premise that this marital right of privacy is restricted to those situations in which it is enjoyed in secret. In this regard, the majority's opinion is unsupported either by reason or by authority.

That there exists a marital right of privacy need not be merely assumed; it is positive law. We conclude that certainly within the marital relationship, and perhaps in some instances even without, the nature and kind of consensual sexual intimacy is beyond the power of the state to regulate or even to inquire. If the state may not restrict marital sexual relations to those whose object or risk is that of procreation, we think that the state is powerless to brand as sodomitic other consensual sexual practice within the marital relationship.

Given the premise that a sufficient state interest to regulate or to inquire into consensual marital intimacies does not exist, we turn to the question of whether this marital right of privacy exists only if the consensual conduct is carried on in secrecy. We think that existence of the right is not conditioned upon secrecy.

The marital right of privacy, a term which lends itself to confusion since the term carries with it connotations of secrecy, is not founded solely upon the Fourth Amendment. In Fourth Amendment cases, a voluntary relinquishment of one's reasonable expectation of secrecy, such as a consent to search, waives the right. Cf. *Poe v. Ullman*, 367 U.S. at 551–52 (Harlan, J., dissenting). The marital right of privacy has a base broader than the Fourth Amendment alone and the cases recognizing the right pitch it on grounds that belie that secrecy is a necessary element.

Certainly *Meyer v. Nebraska*, *Pierce v. Society of Sisters*, and *Skinner v. Oklahoma*, the foundations from which the right of marital privacy was developed, had nothing to do with secrecy. Their outcome depended upon the nature of the activity sought to be regulated and the relationship of that activity to a protected right. In *Griswold*, the Court invalidated Connecticut's ban on the use of contraceptives at the behest of a doctor who was permitted to assert the rights of his patients who came to him for advice about contraceptives. These patients were admitting an outsider into their marital intimacies by seeking counseling and advice about contraception, yet they were not held to have lost their right to constitutional protection. Most recently, in *Roe v. Wade*, the Court, in upholding a woman's exercise of her right to "privacy" by having an abortion, explicitly noted that "(t)he pregnant woman cannot be isolated in her privacy." 410 U.S. at 159. Not only was the developing fetus involved, but the abortion would have to be performed by a doctor, probably with the assistance of others.

Based on these authorities, we conclude that secrecy is not a necessary element of the right and that therefore the right exists, whether or not exercised in secret. We are at a loss to understand how or why the majority concludes otherwise. Its conclusion is unsupported by any authority; nor do we think it supported by reason. The majority assumes that the Lovisis have a constitutional right to practice marital sodomy in secret, and further suggests that this right would not be lost or "waived" if they talked or wrote about their sexual activities. Presumably this protection would extend to non-obscene but explicit photographs and movies even if sold on a commercial basis; yet, if a husband and wife were to seek certain types of medical help in an attempt to save a marriage endangered by sexual maladjustment, or if due to economic necessity, or for any other reason, they share a bedroom with other family members, under the majority's holding the state may prosecute them for certain types of consensual marital acts. Surely these absurd results suggest that the presence of Dunn is irrelevant to the question before us. What would not be punishable sodomy in Dunn's absence is not rendered punishable sodomy by his presence, although his presence may, of course, give rise to other prosecution for other crimes.

When the state chooses to regulate the public sexual conduct of married persons, it must choose means less intrusive to the marital relationship than the bald criminalization of the marital sexual intimacies themselves. In his dissenting opinion in *Poe v. Ullman*, 367 U.S. 497 (1961), Mr. Justice Harlan stressed that even assuming that the state was entitled to reach a moral judgment that the use of contraceptives by married couples was immoral and that the state could implement its policy by prohibiting the sale of contraceptives to be used by married persons, the state could not criminalize the act of using contraceptives: Though the State has argued the Constitutional permissibility of the moral judgment underlying this statute, neither its brief, nor its argument, nor anything in any of the opinions of its highest court in these or other cases even remotely suggests a justification for the obnoxiously intrusive means it has chosen to effectuate that policy.

Similarly, while the state may punish public exposure of marital sexual conduct, it may not choose means which make the act of sexual conduct the dominant characteristic of the offense.

CRAVEN, Circuit Judge (dissenting):

I dissent because I think it is dangerous to withdraw from any citizen the protection of the Constitution because he or she is amoral, immoral or just plain nasty. The point I make is a factual one. It will not be understood without knowing what the case is about, and to make that clear I begin by stating what it is not about. It is not about group sex. It is not about sexual activity, deviant or otherwise, in public. The Lovisis attack their charges and convictions under a statute making their conduct with each other while married criminal whether or not in public and without regard to the presence or participation of a third person.

Most of the court's opinion consists of a narrative of the sort found in "adult" bookstores. Had the case been properly tried in the Virginia state court, we would not even know this sordid story because Dunn's participation is irrelevant and highly prejudicial to the question of the Lovisis' guilt of a violation of Virginia's crime against nature by their conduct with each other. Just as a jury cannot forget such evidence erroneously received, neither, apparently, can we.

The great freedoms enumerated in the first ten amendments are known to all Americans by name, e. g., speech, press, religion, etc. What may be the greatest of all, antedating the Constitution as well as the Bill of Rights, has not yet been christened. "Liberty" is too much.

The "right of privacy," apt in some cases, is a misleading misnomer in others including this one. This freedom may be termed more accurately "the right to be let alone," or personal autonomy, or simply "personhood." One thing for sure: it is not limited to the conduct of persons in private. Marriage, normally a public ceremony, is protected. Mrs. Roe does not lose her right to be let alone to abort because her doctor permits the intrusion of a nurse to assist him. Baird may not be prosecuted for failure to be discreet and secret in lecturing students on contraception.

It is therefore unclear to me why the Lovisis forfeit their right to be let alone in their conjugal relationship because they allowed a third person to be present. The only valid reason I can think of is a moral value judgment that deviant sex is so odious that not even the Constitution may be successfully interposed to protect a husband and wife so despicably disposed. However right the court may be as to morals, I do not believe it to be a proper principle of constitutional law.

If there is any more fundamental right of personhood than the conjugal relationship of husband and wife, it does not occur to me. I do not believe it to be within the power of the state to make consensual physical contact between husband and wife criminal; and when convictions are predicated upon that fact alone, the writ must issue.

In order to deny the Lovisis their constitutional right to be let alone in their conduct with each other, the court has amended the indictment in the state court so as to charge the Lovisis with lewd and lascivious behavior in the presence of another and indecent exposure. I agree that they are guilty of both offenses, but I believe this court has not the power to validate convictions of offenses not charged.

I would hold that the Lovisis are protected by the right to be let alone from a conviction of violating the Virginia crime against nature statute with each other, and I would reverse and remand with instructions to issue the writ. Judge Winter and Judge Butzner authorize me to say that they join in these views.

Notes and Questions

1. Does the 4th Circuit's constitutional analysis hold up after *Lawrence v. Texas*? What justification does the state have for making it a crime for a husband and wife to engage in sexual activity with a third consenting adult present in the room?

2. In light of *Lawrence*'s methodology in analyzing the 14th Amendment Due Process claim, does it advance the analysis in *Lovisi* to speak in terms of "privacy" rather than "liberty." Would the Supreme Court today likely consider the conduct of the Lovisis together with Mr. Dunn to come within the protected sphere of "liberty" articulated in *Lawrence*?

State of Idaho v. Limberhand
788 P.2d 857 (Idaho App. 1990)

WALTERS, Chief Judge.

Mr. Limberhand was arrested for participating in obscene live conduct, I.C. § 18-4104, after an undercover officer observed him masturbating in a closed toilet stall, in a public restroom at a rest area along Interstate 90 in northern Idaho. He moved to suppress all evidence obtained by the officers, on the ground that the undercover officer's observations of him in the rest stop toilet stall constituted an illegal search in violation of the United States and Idaho Constitutions.

The magistrate's findings may be summarized as follows. In early June, 1987, the Idaho Department of Law Enforcement and the Idaho State Police conducted an investigation at the eastbound rest area of Interstate 90, near Huetter, Idaho, in Kootenai County, in response to reports of homosexual activity. The investigation involved approximately eight police agents, unmarked police vehicles and an undercover officer wearing a body transmitter. The police obtained no warrant for search or surveillance activity connected with this investigation.

The men's restroom at the Huetter rest area included two enclosed toilet stalls, each provided with doors containing locks. A metal partition separated the stalls. About three feet above the floor level, a hole with a diameter of approximately four inches had been made through the common partition, evidently with a cutting torch. The hole was not an aspect of the design of the stalls and neither the police nor Limberhand had any part in cutting the hole. No evidence was submitted to explain the hole's origin or purpose.

On June 5, 1987, Idaho State Police Officer Komosinski—equipped with a transmitter—operated as an undercover agent at the rest area. Komosinski entered the restroom and found it unoccupied. He noticed the hole in the partition between the two toilet stalls. He plugged the hole with toilet paper—for reasons not disclosed by the record—and left the restroom. A short time thereafter, Komosinski observed an individual, later identified as the defendant, Limberhand, enter the restroom. After waiting one to two minutes, Komosinski reentered the restroom and noted that Limberhand occupied one of the stalls, had closed the door, and that his feet were in an appropriate position for an individual seated on the toilet. Komosinski testified that he had observed no suspicious conduct from Limberhand at any time up to this point.

Komosinski stood outside the adjacent stall and observed that the toilet paper he had placed in the hole was gone. No evidence was submitted regarding how the toilet paper had disappeared. Komosinski then entered the adjacent stall, sat down on the toilet, turned his head and looked through the hole to observe Limberhand's crotch area. Komosinski observed Limberhand already engaged in masturbating. Komosinski testified that he then repositioned himself to better observe Limberhand, in particular, by bending down so he could see Limberhand's face. In accordance with the officers' preconceived plan—established in order to avoid detection of their undercover operation—Komosinski initiated a conversation with Limberhand, for the purpose of luring him away from the restroom area for arrest by inviting Limberhand to accompany him to a nearby motel. Limberhand turned down Komosinski's proposition. As Komosinski left the stall, he told Limberhand that if Limberhand changed his mind, he would be waiting outside. Komosinski again looked into the restroom a short time later and noted Limberhand still in the stall. Limberhand left the restroom shortly thereafter, walked by Komosinski, made no physical or verbal indication that he had changed his mind and got into his vehicle. He remained seated in his vehicle until Komosinski entered his own vehicle to depart from the area. When Komosinski left the rest stop, Limberhand followed. They travelled east on the Interstate at about fifty miles per hour until a uniformed police officer in a patrol car stopped Limberhand before Limberhand could take any exit from the Interstate. The police arrested Limberhand for violation of I.C. §18-4104 [committing an act of "obscene live conduct in a public place," a misdemeanor]. While conducting a search at the jail following Limberhand's arrest, the police found marijuana on Limberhand's person.

Limberhand moved to suppress Komosinski's testimony, arguing that the officer's peering into the restroom stall constituted an unwarranted search in violation of the fourth amendment....The magistrate agreed with Limberhand's argument, holding that there was a reasonable expectation of privacy in a public restroom stall and that a police officer peering through a hole in the stall constituted a search. The magistrate held further that the state has the burden of proving that a warrantless search was reasonable and that, failing to do so, the search was illegal pursuant to the United States and Idaho Constitutions.

The focal point of this case is whether the police conduct constituted a search. The Idaho appellate courts have not defined the scope of privacy interest in a public restroom stall. Limberhand contends an individual maintains a reasonable expectation of privacy in such a location. With regard to expectations of privacy, vis-a-vis warrantless police searches, our Supreme Court recently noted that both the fourth amendment and art. 1, § 17 of the Idaho Constitution are designed to protect a person's legitimate expectation of privacy, "which society is prepared to recognize as 'reasonable.'" *State v. Thompson*, 760 P.2d 1162, 1165 (Idaho 1988). The test for review of an individual's subjective expectation of privacy has been further characterized by the United States Supreme Court as whether "the individual's expectation, viewed objectively, is 'justifiable' under the circumstances." *United States v. Knotts*, 460 U.S. 276, 281 (1983).

The record indicates that the door to the stall Limberhand occupied was closed at all relevant times. Furthermore, the position of his feet as observed from outside the stall indicated that he was using the toilet in an appropriate manner. The record does not indicate that Limberhand exhibited conduct inconsistent with a subjective expectation of privacy. From these facts, the magistrate reasonably inferred Limberhand did not desire his conduct to be viewed by the public but was utilizing the features of the stall to prevent exposure. We conclude Limberhand maintained a subjective expectation of privacy.

The state argues that Limberhand's subjective expectation of privacy in a stall with a four-inch hole in the partition is not one society is willing to accept as reasonable. The state correctly points out that the reasonableness of such an expectation depends on the facts of each case. It appears that many jurisdictions have ruled on an individual's privacy expectations in public restroom stalls. Many cases turn on the door structure or design of the stall when determining the privacy interest involved. However, focusing on the stall design diminishes the underlying intent of the *Katz* decision and the overall protection guaranteed by the fourth amendment. In *Katz*, the Court examined the privacy interests of a public telephone booth and concluded that telephone conversations within a booth are constitutionally protected. The majority opinion in *Katz* states:

> For the Fourth Amendment protects people, not places. What a person knowingly exposes to the public, even in his own home or office, is not a subject of Fourth Amendment protection...But what he seeks to preserve as private even in an area accessible to the public, may be constitutionally protected.

In elucidating how the Court utilized the notion that the fourth amendment "protects people, not places" in *Katz*, Justice Harlan explained:

> The point is not that [a telephone] booth is "accessible to the public" at other times but that it is a temporarily private place whose momentary occupants' expectations of freedom from intrusion are recognized as reasonable.

Thus, it has been determined that the expectation of privacy is generated by the nature of the activity involved rather than by the precise physical characteristics of the stall. *Kroehler v. Scott*, 391 F.Supp. 1114 (E.D.Pa.1975) (determining whether toilet stalls had doors is not a crucially material inquiry). The activities associated with the use of a toilet are private, based on widely accepted social norms. We acknowledge that the privacy interest in a public telephone booth is auditory while the privacy interest generated within a bathroom stall is to be free from visual intrusion. Otherwise we find no constitutional distinction between a public telephone booth and a public restroom stall with regard to the privacy expectation generated within. Regardless of the four-inch hole in the partition, Limberhand's expectation of privacy within the toilet stall is one we believe society would recognize as objectively reasonable.

Next we must determine whether the officer's conduct violated Limberhand's expectation of privacy. The state maintains that viewing that which any member of the public may view is not constitutionally protected. The state also notes, correctly, that the fourth amendment precludes unreasonable government intrusion into a person's expectation of privacy. However, the scope of the protection is determined by the privacy interest at stake. It is clear beyond question that, after Katz, clandestine or surreptitious surveillance into a closed restroom stall constitutes a fourth amendment search.

Here, we need not intimate any view regarding whether the police engaged in clandestine conduct. Suffice it to say once it is resolved that there is a cognizable expectation of privacy, the invasion of that privacy interest—including a visual one—will be a search subject to constitutional requirements. In this case, Officer Komosinski's unwarranted act of peering through the hole into the next stall was a search for the purposes of the United States and Idaho Constitutions. Therefore, we conclude that Limberhand maintained a reasonable expectation of privacy and that Komosinski violated that expectation when he looked into the neighboring stall occupied by Limberhand.

We recognize that circumstances may exist where there may be a diminished expectation of privacy within a toilet stall, see, e.g., State v. Holt, supra (during an ongoing investigation, an officer observed an individual peering through small holes in the partition. The officer then looked back through the hole, observed the defendant masturbating, walked to the front of the doorless stall and again observed as the individual continued to masturbate). Under other circumstances, police conduct could be considered reasonable, see e.g., People v. Mercado (airport security officer investigating report of two men in single, closed stall in restroom; heard two low voices conversing in the stall; could see through space between the door and frame of stall that one man was seated on the toilet tank with his feet on the bowl; could see there were no crutches or wheelchair in the stall; ascertained the men were not using the stall for its intended purpose and suspected the men were engaged in "drug crime" or "sex crime;" held, based on articulated, objective facts and reasonable inferences that may be drawn therefrom, that the officer had probable cause to believe it was more probable than not that criminal activity was taking place inside the stall; officer's conduct in peering over top of partition and observing drug transaction was justified and was not unreasonable under fourth amendment).

Here, the state proffers but one argument to justify the officer's warrantless search—the state contends that whatever the officer observed, it was in plain or open view. "Plain view" is not so much an exception to the warrant requirement as it is an exclusion from the requirements of the fourth amendment. If a police officer is where he has a right to be, and he sees something in plain view, the observation is not a search. This doctrine is applicable when (1) the officer's vantage point is lawfully gained, (2) the incriminating evidence discovered is a by-product of other permissible police activity, and (3) the incriminating nature of matters viewed are immediately apparent to the officer...We are concerned only with the second element, that is, whether the evidence was gained as a result of permissible police activity.

The Idaho Supreme Court has interpreted the plain view doctrine as not validating the seizure of evidence in plain view, "if the plain view observation had its genesis in a

Fourth Amendment violation." *State v. Allgood*, 98 Idaho 525, 527, 567 P.2d 1276, 1278 (1977). We have already stated that Limberhand had a reasonable expectation of privacy...We have also held that the officer's conduct—peering through the partition hole—intruded upon that privacy interest. If that particular police conduct is impermissible under the fourth amendment, the officer's testimony—regarding his observations of Limberhand's activities—is inadmissible. This analysis is problematic because the exact police conduct urged by the state to be legal under the plain view doctrine is the same conduct that may be determined to be constitutionally impermissible. We choose not to take the incongruous step of utilizing the plain view doctrine to legitimize unconstitutional police conduct. From the facts found by the magistrate, it is unclear whether the incriminating evidence discovered was a by-product of permissible police activity. Accordingly, we conclude that the state failed to demonstrate that its conduct was justified under the plain view doctrine.

The state submits that this is an appropriate case to draw a distinction between "plain view" and "open view." It argues that when an officer makes an observation from a non-intrusive vantage point to that which is knowingly exposed to the public, the object is not subject to any reasonable expectation of privacy. We agree, noting, however, that this distinction begs the first question under the plain view doctrine of whether the officer's vantage point was lawfully gained. Assuming, arguendo, that the open view distinction is legally significant in this case, an officer is only permitted the scope of observation ascribed to a reasonably respectful citizen....

Clearly, a "reasonably respectful citizen" could not avoid seeing the hole and whatever was on the other side. The permissible scope of the observation would depend on the location of the hole in relation to the citizen's line of sight while using the adjoining stall in a normal way. However, there are two "observations" critical to this case: first, the observation of the "crotch area," and, second, the eye contact with Limberhand, such that Limberhand would know he was being watched (an essential element of either I.C. § 18-4104 or § 18-4105). The magistrate did not make findings as to whether these observations required Officer Komosinski to position himself to obtain a view not available to a "reasonably respectful citizen."

Accordingly, we vacate the order of the district court reversing the Magistrate's suppression and dismissal ruling. We remand the case to the district court with directions to further remand it to the magistrate for additional findings on the question of whether the officer's observation of Limberhand was within a permissible scope as outlined above. Since the state has the burden of proof to show the reasonableness of the warrantless search in this case, if the record is inadequate for the magistrate to make the required findings, then the suppression order should stand.

Questions

1. Do you agree with the court that the question whether particular sexual conduct is taking place "in public" should turn on the expectation of the "sexual performer"?

2. To what extent should any constitutional protection be extended to those who engage in sexual activity in public restrooms, parks, parked cars, or other settings where their activity could come to the attention of unwilling viewers?

3. What exactly counts as sexual activity?

People v. Ramsden

2003 WL 21398303
Court of Appeals of Michigan
(Unpublished Disposition)

PER CURIAM.

Defendant was convicted of performing oral sex on another male in a public rest-room at a state highway rest area [in violation of M.C.L. sec. 750.338]. Defendant's conduct was observed by two state police troopers who were able to observe the activity after they stood on an outside picnic table and looked into an open window, thereby enabling them to view the inside common area of the restroom.

Defendant first argues that the officers' conduct violated his rights under both the Fourth Amendment, U.S. Const, Am IV, and the state constitution, Const 1963, art 1, § 11, and, therefore, the trial court erred in denying his motion to suppress the evidence of the officers' observations and dismiss the case. Defendant argues that the officers violated his reasonable expectation of privacy.

The record establishes that two female police troopers stood on top of a picnic table and looked into the men's restroom through an open window. The trooper who testified at the suppression hearing had witnessed illegal sexual activity in that restroom in the past, but had no evidence that illegal activity was occurring at that particular time. From the window, the trooper was only able to observe the sides of the restroom stalls and the common areas of the restroom. The window, although eight or nine feet above the ground, did not provide an overhead view of the stalls. From her position, the trooper first observed a codefendant push open a stall door. She saw that another man was already inside that stall because his feet were visible. The codefendant entered the stall. The codefendant was facing the inside of the stall, with his back side sticking out. The door to the stall was left open. The codefendant began moving his pelvic area back and forth. Something caught the codefendant's attention and he turned around. As the codefendant stood in the common area, he stroked his exposed penis. From her observations of the two men in the stall, the trooper concluded that the man who was originally inside the stall was performing oral sex on the codefendant.

After the codefendant left, defendant approached the same previously occupied stall, also leaving the door open. Only one person had left that stall, leading the trooper to believe that the other man still occupied the stall. Defendant got down on his knees within the stall, with his back side sticking out of the stall. From her observations, the trooper concluded that defendant was performing oral sex on the other man in the stall. At that point, defendant and the other two men were arrested.

Apart from her direct observations as described above, the trooper testified that she was also able to observe the activity inside the stall through a mirror in the common area directly in front of the stall. The trial court denied defendant's motion to suppress, concluding that defendant did not have a reasonable expectation of privacy with regard to his activities in the public restroom, but ruled that the officer could only testify to observations made without the aid of the mirror.

The first question that must be addressed when deciding any challenge under the Fourth Amendment is whether the defendant has standing to challenge the officers' conduct. The constitutional protections against unreasonable searches and seizures, U.S. Const, Am IV, Const 1963, art 1, § 11, are personal and those rights may only be properly invoked by persons whose own protections were infringed by a search or seizure. Therefore, defendant must establish his standing to challenge the officers' conduct in this case. The burden is on the defendant to establish standing and a court should consider the totality of the circumstances in deciding this question. Standing is determined by whether the defendant had an expectation of privacy in the place or object that was searched and whether that expectation is one that society recognizes as reasonable. *People v. Lee Smith,* 420 Mich. 1, 28; 360 NW2d 841 (1984); see also *Rakas v. Illinois,* 439 U.S. 128, 143; 99 S Ct 421; 58 L.Ed.2d 387 (1978), and *People v. Hunt,* 77 Mich.App 590, 593; 259 NW2d 147 (1977).

This Court has previously considered whether a reasonable expectation of privacy exists in public restrooms. This Court has recognized that a limited expectation of privacy exists in public restrooms, but that that expectation generally extends only to the enclosed stall, not common areas. Thus, while surveillance devices over a bathroom stall have been found to be unreasonable, cameras used to monitor the common areas of a public restroom are not deemed unreasonable under the Fourth Amendment. See *People v. Lynch,* 179 Mich.App 63, 68–69; 445 NW2d 803 (1989); *People v. Heydenberk,* 171 Mich.App 494; 430 NW2d 760 (1988); *People v. Kalchik,* 160 Mich.App 40; 407 NW2d 627 (1987); *People v. Dezek,* 107 Mich.App 78, 84, 89–90; 308 NW2d 652 (1981); *People v. Abate,* 105 Mich.App 274, 275–76, 283; 306 NW2d 476 (1981).

In *Kalchik, supra* at 48–49, this Court explained:

As noted by the *Dezek* panel, a bathroom stall, such as at issue herein, does not afford complete privacy, but an occupant of the stall would reasonably expect to enjoy such privacy as the design of the stall afforded, i.e., to the extent that defendant's activities were performed beneath a partition and could be viewed by one using the common area of the restroom, the defendant had no subjective expectation of privacy, and, even if he did, it would not be an expectation which society would recognize as reasonable. On the other hand, defendant did have an actual, subjective expectation that he would not be viewed from overhead. We find this expectation to be a reasonable one. Here, even though defendant's expectation of privacy may be only partial, it is nevertheless entitled to constitutional protection.

In *Heydenberk,* this Court upheld the use of video cameras in a men's public restroom at a highway rest area. One camera was installed under a sink and showed only the area under the sinks and the stalls. Anyone standing at the urinals was not visible. A second camera was placed above the entrance to the bathroom and showed only the common areas within the restroom. The defendant was caught on tape engaging in sexual acts in the common areas of the restroom by the camera placed over the main entrance. This Court held that the defendant did not have a reasonable expectation of privacy when he was engaged in sexual activities in the area of the bathroom readily observable by anyone who entered the restroom. Any expectation of privacy was unreasonable on those facts.

In a case factually similar to this case, *People v. Lillis,* 181 Mich.App 315, 316–18; 448 NW2d 818 (1989), this Court held that a police trooper did not act unreasonably where he first boosted himself up to look into the window of a public restroom at a highway rest stop. The trooper observed the defendant and another male engage in sexual activity in the common area of the restroom, outside of the stalls. The trooper normally checked the restrooms when inspecting the premises as part of his regular patrol. By looking into the window, the trooper could see the inside common area outside of the stalls, but not the urinals. Because the trooper observed the defendant engaged in sexual activity in the common area of the restroom, the defendant had no reasonable expectation of privacy under the Fourth Amendment.

The above cases demonstrate that, as applied to public restrooms, Fourth Amendment protections extend only to the enclosed stalls where a person using the stall would not expect his activities to be viewed by others. To the extent that a person using a public restroom performs acts visible from within the common areas of the restroom, he does not have a reasonable expectation of privacy.

In the case at bar, the troopers looked into a window that enabled them to observe the inside common areas of the restroom. The window was far enough away from the stalls, and the sides of the stalls, that the troopers were not able to look directly into the stalls. Therefore, this case is distinguishable from the cases barring overhead video or surveillance equipment of the stall areas. Because the officers' testimony was based upon their observations of the common areas of the restroom, and because defendant does not have a reasonable expectation of privacy with respect to conduct observable from the common areas, trial court did not err in denying defendant's motion to suppress.

Defendant also argues that his expectation of privacy was further violated because the troopers involved were both female. We disagree. In *Lillis, supra* at 319, this Court held that even though the trooper had to hoist himself up to a window to observe the defendant in the common areas of the restroom, that did not have any bearing on the Fourth Amendment question. The Court stated:

> The manner by which Trooper Day observed defendant has no bearing on whether defendant had a reasonable expectation of privacy in the rest room's common area. The determination whether a defendant had a reasonable expectation of privacy in the area searched must be made without regard to the manner in which the area was searched. The constitutionality of the challenged police conduct may be examined only after a determination has been made that the defendant had a reasonable expectation of privacy in the area searched. [*People v] Smith,* [420 Mich. 1, 28; 360 NW2d 841 (1984)]. [*Lillis, supra* at 318–19.]

We similarly conclude that defendant cannot challenge the use of troopers of the opposite gender to check the men's restroom unless the conduct at issue infringed upon an interest that is constitutionally protected. As discussed previously, defendant has failed to show that his constitutionally protected interests in the restroom were infringed. Accordingly, the fact that the troopers who observed defendant's activities were female does not afford a basis for relief. For this same reason, defendant also lacks standing to challenge the troopers' conduct on the basis that it allegedly violated the state's law against window peeping. MCL 750.167(1)(c).

Next, defendant argues that the evidence was insufficient to support a conviction for gross indecency between males and, therefore, trial court erred in denying his motion for a directed verdict. We disagree.

MCL 750.338 prohibits the following conduct:

> Any male person who, in public or in private, commits or is a party to the commission of or procures or attempts to procure the commission by any male person of any act of gross indecency with another male person shall be guilty of a felony[.]

An act of fellatio between two males, committed in a public place, violates M.C.L. § 750.338 as an act of gross indecency. *People v. Lino,* 447 Mich. 567, 571, 576; 527 NW2d 434 (1994).

Viewed in a light most favorable to the prosecution, the trooper's testimony regarding her observations of defendant's conduct in the open restroom stall, and the circumstances surrounding that conduct, was sufficient to enable a rational trier of fact to conclude beyond a reasonable doubt that defendant was performing oral sex on another male in a public place. The trial court did not err in denying defendant's motion for a directed verdict. Contrary to what defendant argues, the record does not indicate that the trooper violated the court's suppression order which precluded the trooper from testifying about observations made only with the aid of the mirror.

Defendant also argues that the trial court erred by allowing the trooper to offer opinion testimony that defendant was engaged in sexual activity. We disagree. The testimony was admissible under MRE 701, which allows a lay witness to offer testimony in the form of an opinion or inference when the testimony is rationally based on the witness' perception of an incident and is helpful to either a clear understanding of the witness' testimony or relevant to an issue of fact.

[Omitted is the court's discussion of why it rejected the defendant's argument that the statute was unconstitutionally vague.]

Defendant also argues that the trial court should have sua sponte dismissed this case on the basis that the troopers did not have probable cause to look into the men's restroom and, therefore, their conduct amounted to an illegal search. Because defendant did not raise this issue in the trial court, we review the issue for plain error affecting defendant's substantial rights.

As discussed in part I of this opinion, the Fourth Amendment's protection against unreasonable searches and seizures first requires a defendant to show that he has standing based upon a legally protected interest in the place or object searched. Because we have concluded in part I that defendant did not have a reasonable expectation of privacy, defendant cannot establish plain error predicated on the troopers' conduct.

Next, defendant argues that M.C.L. § 750.338 was selectively enforced against him, depriving him of equal protection under the law. We disagree. Under both the state and federal constitutions, equal protection of the law is guaranteed. US Const, Am XIV; Const 1963, art 1, § 2. The guarantees under both constitutions afford similar protections. *In re Hawley*, 238 Mich.App 509, 511; 606 NW2d 50 (1999). The Equal Protection Clause requires that persons under similar circumstances be treated alike; it does not require that persons under different circumstances must be treated the same.

Three different statutes prohibit gross indecency between males, between females, and between a male and a female, respectively. See M.C.L. § 750.338, 750.338a and 750.338b. Defendant argues that these statutes are selectively enforced.

A prosecution may violate the Equal Protection Clause if the following standards are satisfied:

> First, it must be shown that the defendants were "singled" out for prosecution while others similarly situated were not prosecuted for the same conduct. Second, it must be established that this discriminatory selection in prosecution was based on an impermissible ground such as race, sex, religion or the exercise of a fundamental right. [*In re Hawley, supra* at 513, quoting *People v. Ford*, 417 Mich. 66, 102; 331 NW2d 878 (1982).]

Here, the record does not support defendant's claim that others similarly situated were not prosecuted for the same conduct. There was testimony that sexual activity in the men's restroom was a problem at this particular rest area, but there was no testimony that a similar problem existed with the women's restroom. The record also does not contain any evidence that females were observed engaging in public sexual activity in the women's restroom and were not arrested or prosecuted. Accordingly, we find no merit to defendant's argument that the troopers improperly singled him out by failing to investigate the women's restroom on the night defendant was arrested, or that he was selectively prosecuted because females committing the same acts were not prosecuted. Furthermore, although defendant maintains that there are more published appellate decisions addressing M.C.L. §750.338, rather than the other gross indecency statutes, that does not establish that he was singled out for prosecution. Thus, a plain error has not been shown.

Questions

1. Are these decisions logically consistent with each other? Is the action of the state trooper in *Limberhand* any more or less "respectful" of the privacy rights of the defendant than the action of the troopers in *Ramsden*? Who has the better argument as to reasonable expectation of privacy in these cases?

2. At the level of policy, should it be a crime to engage in solo masturbation in a public toilet? Should it be a crime to engage in oral sex with a willing partner in a public restroom closed toilet stall? Should it be a crime to engage in oral sex with a willing partner in a "public place" such as a restroom in a commercial or government building, on a beach, or in a park, under circumstances where it is possible that an objecting member of the public may enter the vicinity and observe the conduct? What are your reasons for reaching these conclusions?

B. Solicitation

When the Model Penal Code drafters addressed the issue of sex crimes, they determined that the legitimate interest of government pertained to conduct in the public sphere, and urged decriminalization of non-commercial consensual adult conduct in private. However, they concluded that the state had legitimate concerns with public conduct anticipatory to private sexual activity, such as public loitering for purposes of finding a sex partner or public solicitation. If private consensual sexual conduct enjoys protection from law enforcement, what is the justification for punishing solicitation unaccompanied by inappropriate public conduct?

Pryor v. Municipal Court
599 P.2d 636 (Cal. 1979)

TOBRINER, Justice.

Defendant Don Pryor seeks prohibition to bar his trial on a charge of violating Penal Code §647, subdivision (a). This section declares that a person is guilty of disorderly conduct, a misdemeanor, "Who solicits anyone to engage in or who engages in Lewd or dissolute conduct in any public place or in any place open to the public or exposed to public view." We agree with defendant that the phrase "lewd or dissolute conduct" as construed by past decisions is unconstitutionally vague.... [R]ejecting prior interpretations of this statute, we adopt a limited and specific construction consistent with the present action of § 647, subdivision (a), in the California penal statutes; we construe that section to prohibit only the solicitation or commission of conduct in a public place or one open to the public or exposed to public view, which involves the touching of the genitals, buttocks, or female breast, for purposes of sexual arousal, gratification, annoyance or offense, by a person who knows or should know of the presence of persons who may be offended by the conduct. As so construed, § 647, subdivision (a), complies with constitutional standards; we therefore deny defendant's petition for writ of prohibition.

On May 1, 1976, defendant solicited an undercover police officer to perform an act of oral copulation. He was arrested. Defendant was charged with violating Penal Code § 647, subdivision (a), by soliciting a lewd or dissolute act. At trial, the officer testified that he parked his car a few feet from where defendant was standing. Defendant came over, and after a brief conversation, suggested oral sex acts. Looking at a nearby parking lot, defendant said "We could probably sit and park in the parking lot." The officer suggested instead that they go to his home. Defendant agreed, entered the car, and was arrested.

Defendant's version of the incident differs only in that he denies making any statement about the parking lot, but maintains instead that the only situs discussed was the officer's home. Thus both defendant and the officer agree that defendant, while in a public place, solicited an act of oral sex; they disagree only whether defendant suggested the act itself occur in a public place. Over defendant's objection, the trial court instructed the jury that oral copulation between males is "lewd or dissolute" as a matter of law. The court further instructed over objection that "If the solicitation occurred in a public place, it is immaterial that the lewd act was intended to occur in a private place." Despite these instructions, which virtually compelled the jury to find defendant guilty, the jury deadlocked and the court declared a mistrial. Defendant then filed the instant petition for writs of prohibition and mandate with this court... We issued an alternative writ of prohibition "limited to the proceedings in the municipal court related to retrial of the charge of violating § 647, subdivision (a) of the Penal Code."

The statutory terms "lewd" and "dissolute" are not technical legal terms, but words of common speech. In ordinary usage, they do not imply a definite and specific referent, but apply broadly to conduct which the speaker considers beyond the bounds of propriety. Thus, speaking of the term "lewd," the court in *Morgan v. City of Detroit* (E.D.Mich.1975) 389 F.Supp. 922, 930, observed that all definitions of that term in ordinary usage are "subjective," dependent upon the speaker's "social, moral, and cultural bias." The term "dissolute" is, if anything, even less specific; while "lewd" implies a sexual act, "dissolute" can refer to nonsexual acts which exceed subjective limits of propriety.

Finding, therefore, that the facial language... is not sufficiently certain to bring the statute into compliance with due process standards, we turn to examine legislative history as a guide to its construction. The Legislature enacted present § 647, subdivision (a) in 1961 to replace former § 647, subdivision 5, which provided that "Every lewd or dissolute person... is a vagrant, and is punishable (as a misdemeanant)." That earlier enactment formed part of California's vagrancy law, a venerable but archaic form of status crime which dates from the economic crisis occasioned by the Black Death in early 14th century England. As Justice Frankfurter noted, vagrancy statutes were purposefully cast in vague language; "(d)efiniteness is designedly avoided so as to allow the net to be cast at large, to enable men to be caught who are vaguely unde-sirable in the eyes of the police and prosecution...." (*Winters v. New York* (1948) 333 U.S. 507, 540.)

Our 1960 decision in *In re Newbern*, 53 Cal.2d 786, 350 P.2d 116, holding the "com-mon drunk" provision of the California Vagrancy Law void for vagueness, and an analysis of vagrancy statutes by Professor Arthur Sherry (Sherry, Vagrants, Rogues, and Vagabonds Old Concepts in Need of Revision (1960) 48 Cal.L.Rev. 557) prompted the 1961 revision of §647. That revision changed the criminal proscription from status ("lewd or dissolute person") to behavior ("lewd or dissolute conduct"). It also added, for the first time, a spe-cific proscription against solicitation; decisions under the former law treated solicitation simply as evidence that the solicitor was leading a lewd or dissolute life.

The legislative history, however, suggests no intent to change the definition of "lewd or dissolute" established by the decisions under the former vagrancy statute. The leg-islative history reveals §647, subdivision (a), to be the lineal descendant of the archaic vagrancy statutes which were designedly drafted to grant police and prosecutors a vague and standardless discretion. Under these circumstances, we cannot look to legislative history to supply §647, subdivision (a), with a clear and definite content; such con-struction must come, if at all, from judicial interpretation of the statute.

Turning to the cases which have construed §647, subdivision (a) and its predecessor is like opening a thesaurus. The cases do not define "lewd or dissolute" by pointing to specific acts, but by pejorative adjectives. "(T)he words 'lewd' and 'dissolute' are syn-onymous, and mean lustful, lascivious, unchaste, wanton, or loose in morals and con-duct." (CALJIC (misdemeanor) No. 16.402, quoted in *People v. Williams* (1976) 59 Cal.App.3d 225, 229; see *People v. Babb* (1951) 229 P.2d 843.) "Dissolute" behavior is that which is "'loosed from restraint, unashamed, lawless, loose in morals and conduct, recklessly abandoned to sensual pleasures, profligate, wanton, lewd, debauched.'" (*People v. Jaurequi*, 298 P.2d 896, 900; *People v. Scott* (1931) 296 P. 601.) A dissolute per-son is one who is "'indifferent to moral restraint'" and "'given over to dissipation....'" (*People v. Jaurequi*, 298 P.2d 896, 900.) The terms "lewd" and "dissolute" ordinarily in-clude conduct found "disgusting, repulsive, filthy, foul, abominable (or) loathsome" under contemporary community standards.

This impressive list of adjectives and phrases confers no clarity upon the terms "lewd" and "dissolute". Indeed, "the very phrases and synonyms through which mean-ing is purportedly ascribed serve to obscure rather than to clarify those terms." To in-struct the jury that a "lewd or dissolute" act is one which is morally "loose," or "law-less," or "foul" piles additional uncertainty upon the already vague words of the statute. In short, vague statutory language is not rendered more precise by defining it in terms of synonyms of equal or greater uncertainty.

The California cases to date have produced neither a clear nor a consistent definition of the term "lewd or dissolute conduct". The decisions have also failed to adopt possible interpretations of the statute which would narrow its scope and in that manner increase its specificity. Refusing to confine the phrase "lewd or dissolute conduct" to sexual con-duct, the courts have applied the term "dissolute" to sustain the conviction under for-mer §647, subdivision 5, of a defendant who was addicted to narcotics, of a defendant who gave inflammatory speeches, and to sustain juvenile court jurisdiction over a minor who sold marijuana on the ground that he was "in danger of leading a dissolute life." Courts also have rejected invitations to limit the statute to public conduct or to conduct otherwise illegal. Thus the statute as construed by prior California decisions appears to reach any public conduct, or public solicitation to public or private conduct, if that conduct might be described as "lustful," "loose in morals," "disgusting," or by other epithetical adjectives.

We conclude that California decisions do not provide a specific content for the uncertain language of § 647, subdivision (a). Such vague statutory language, resulting in inadequate notice of the reach and limits of the statutory proscription, poses a specially serious problem when the statute concerns speech, for uncertainty concerning its scope may then chill the exercise of protected First Amendment rights. Section 647, subdivision (a), we observe, does not proscribe lewd, dissolute, or obscene solicitations; it bans any public solicitation, however discreet or diffident, of lewd or dissolute conduct. Cases have extended that ban to solicitations seeking private, lawful, and consensual conduct.

But what private, consensual, lawful sexual acts are nonetheless lewd or dissolute, such that public solicitation of them is criminal? The answer of the prior cases—such acts as are lustful, lascivious, unchaste, wanton, or loose in morals and conduct—is no answer at all. Some jurors would find that acts of extramarital intercourse fall within that definition; some would draw the line between intercourse and other sexual acts; others would distinguish between homosexual and heterosexual acts. Thus one could not determine what actions are rendered criminal by reading the statute or even the decisions which interpret it. He must gauge the temper of the community, and predict at his peril the moral and sexual attitudes of those who will be called to serve on the jury.

Vague statutory language also creates the danger that police, prosecutors, judges and juries will lack sufficient standards to reach their decisions, thus opening the door to arbitrary or discriminatory enforcement of the law. The danger of discriminatory enforcement assumes particular importance in the context of the present case. Three studies of law enforcement in Los Angeles County indicate that the overwhelming majority of arrests for violation of Penal Code § 647, subdivision (a), involved male homosexuals. A perusal of those studies suggests both that the police selected techniques and locations of enforcement deliberately designed to detect a disproportionate number of male homosexual offenders, and that they arrested male homosexuals for conduct which, if committed by two women or by a heterosexual pair, did not result in arrest. (See Project, The Consenting Adult Homosexual and the Law: An Empirical Study of Enforcement and Administration in Los Angeles County (1966) 13 UCLA L.Rev. 643; Copilow & Coleman, Enforcement of Section 647(a) of the California Penal Code by the Los Angeles Police Department (1972); Toy, Update: Enforcement of Section 647(a) of the California Penal Code by the Los Angeles Police Department (1974).) [The 1972 and 1974 studies were privately printed, and are attached as exhibits to the amicus curiae brief of the National Committee for Sexual Civil Liberties.] The city attorney's brief in response to the petition for writ of prohibition states that since January of 1977 the city attorney's office has followed specific guidelines in deciding whether to prosecute cases under section 647, subdivision (a). The guidelines indicate that solicitation seeking private conduct will form the basis of a prosecution only if the solicitation is offensive, or the person solicited is under 18. Although these guidelines represent a substantial improvement in even-handed law enforcement when compared to past practices, their very detail and the extent to which they depart from judicial decisions construing section 647, subdivision (a), emphasizes the vast discretion granted the prosecutorial authorities under the statute.

We conclude that §647, subdivision (a), as construed by prior California decisions, does not meet constitutional standards of specificity. That conclusion, however, does not dispose of this case. The judiciary bears an obligation to "construe enactments to give specific content to terms that might otherwise be unconstitutionally vague." Thus we have declared that "A statute will not be held void for uncertainty if any reasonable and practical construction can be given to its language." If by fair and reasonable interpretation we can construe §647, subdivision (a), to sustain its validity, we must adopt such interpretation, even if that course requires us to depart from prior precedent which fastened an unconstitutionally broad interpretation on the statute. We believe that such a construction can be derived from analysis of the role of §647, subdivision (a), in the structure of the California penal law.

We begin with the portion of the statute proscribing "solicitation" of lewd or dissolute conduct. The term "solicitation" itself is not unconstitutionally vague. Instead our difficulties stem from the decisions in *People v. Mesa*, 265 Cal.App.2d 746, and *People v. Dudley*, 250 Cal.App.2d Supp. 955, holding that public solicitation of private conduct falls within the statutory compass. *Mesa* and *Dudley*, however, were decided at a time when many forms of private consensual sexual acts were illegal. With the enactment of the Brown Act, however, most such acts are no longer within the purview of the criminal law. Thus, as the Los Angeles City Attorney states in a brief filed in this case, we conclude that *Mesa* and *Dudley* are inconsistent with the protection of private conduct afforded by the Brown Act and are no longer viable; we believe §647 subdivision (a), must be limited to the solicitation of criminal sexual conduct. More specifically, we hold that this section prohibits only solicitations which propose the commission of conduct itself banned by §647, subdivision (a), that is, lewd or dissolute conduct which occurs in a public place, a place open to the public, or a place exposed to public view.

By so limiting the reach of the statute, we avoid two substantial constitutional problems. First, we need not attempt the probably impossible task of defining with constitutional specificity which forms of private lawful conduct, protected by the Brown Act, are lewd or dissolute conduct, the solicitation of which is proscribed by this statute. Second, we avoid the First Amendment issues which, as we noted earlier, attend a statute which prohibits solicitation of lawful acts. A statute which by judicial construction prohibits only the solicitation of criminal acts does not abridge freedom of speech.

Turning to the portion of the statute banning "lewd or dissolute conduct," we hold that the terms "lewd" and "dissolute" are synonymous and refer to sexually motivated conduct.... The final step is to define specifically the sexually motivated conduct proscribed by the section. We proceed by deriving the function of this section in the penal statutes pertaining to sexual conduct. Section 647, subdivision (a), unlike statutes which ban sexual assault or exploitation of minors, is limited to conduct in public view. The statute thus serves the primary purpose of protecting onlookers who might be offended by the proscribed conduct.

Two other statutes partially serve that same purpose. Penal Code §314, subdivision 1, prohibits indecent exposure "in any public place, or in any place where there are present other persons to be offended or annoyed thereby...." Section 311.6 prohibits "obscene live conduct to or before an assembly or audience...in any public place or in any place exposed to public view, or in any place open to the public or to a segment thereof...." Neither statute, however, is directed at sexual conduct, as distinguished from indecent exposure, when such conduct is not intended to arouse the prurient interest of an audience. Section 647, subdivision (a), we believe, serves the function of filling this gap in the penal law.

Clearly, the statute cannot be construed to ban all sexually motivated public conduct, for such a sweeping prohibition would encompass much innocent and nonoffensive behavior. A constitutionally specific definition must be limited to conduct of a type likely to offend. Although the varieties of sexual expression are almost infinite, virtually all such offensive conduct will involve the touching of the genitals, buttocks, or female breast, for "purposes of sexual arousal, gratification, or affront." The quoted phrase... serves not only to define the reach of the law but also to add a requirement of specific intent, a feature which has often served to avert a determination that a statute is unconstitutionally vague.

Even if conduct occurs in a location that is technically a public place, a place open to the public, or one exposed to public view, the state has little interest in prohibiting that conduct if there are no persons present who may be offended. The scope of § 647, subdivision (a), should be limited accordingly.

Under the construction we have established in this opinion, § 647, subdivision (a), prohibits only the solicitation or commission of a sexual touching, done with specific intent when persons may be offended by the act. It does not impose vague and farreaching standards under which the criminality of an act depends upon the moral views of the judge or jury, does not prohibit solicitation of lawful acts, and does not invite discriminatory enforcement. We are confident that the statute, as so construed, is not unconstitutionally vague.

Since § 647, subdivision (a), is constitutional as construed, defendant is not entitled to a writ of prohibition to bar his trial on the charge of violating that provision. Accordingly, the alternative writ of prohibition is discharged and the petition for a peremptory writ is denied. Because defendant Pryor by this proceeding secured a favorable interpretation of § 647, subdivision (a), he shall recover costs in the matter.

CLARK, Justice, concurring and dissenting.

Retroactive application of the narrow construction of Penal Code § 647, subdivision (a), announced today provides a windfall to defendants validly convicted under the statute. The injustice of so applying today's decision may be illustrated by the following example. Prior to the enactment of the Brown Act, one man solicits another, publicly, to commit sodomy, the act to be performed privately, and is convicted of violating § 647, subdivision (a). At that time the Legislature unquestionably intended such solicitation to be punishable under the statute. Then, as now, legislative prohibition of such conduct was constitutional. (See *Doe v. Commonwealth's Attorney for City of Richmond* (1976) 425 U.S. 901, affirming 403 F.Supp. 1199.) Nevertheless, the criminal would be entitled to "relief" under today's holding. The majority create a remedy for which there is no wrong.

[Note: For a relatively contemporary decision along the same lines from another jurisdiction, see *People v. Uplinger*, 58 N.Y.2d 936 (1983), *certiorari dismissed as improvi-
dently granted*, 467 U.S. 246 (1984).]

Harden v. Zinnemann

2003 WL 21802250
California Court of Appeal, 3rd District
(Unpublished Disposition)

NICHOLSON, Acting P.J.

Convicted twice of soliciting a lewd act in a public place and ordered to register as a
sex offender, Fred Harden applied for a license to sell real estate. The Department of Real
Estate (Department), acting through its commissioner, denied the application. Harden
petitioned the trial court for a writ of administrative mandamus, which the trial court
granted, ordering the Department to issue the license. The Department appeals. We conclude substantial evidence supports the denial of the license and therefore reverse.

FACTS RELATING TO CRIMINAL CONVICTIONS

On November 18, 1996, an undercover detective of the Pleasanton Police Department, acting on a complaint from Pleasanton Sports Park maintenance workers of lewd
activity in park restrooms, parked his car in the vicinity of one of those restrooms. The
restroom is located about 40 yards from a children's playground. At the time, there were
two children playing there. Harden, grabbing and rubbing his penis through the front
of his pants, approached the detective's car and engaged the detective in conversation.
The detective suggested they "try the bathroom" and Harden agreed. Harden entered
the restroom, and the detective followed. Harden exposed his semi-erect penis and
turned toward the detective. The detective entered a stall, and Harden followed. At that
point, the detective gave the bust signal, and Harden was arrested.

In Alameda County Municipal Court, Harden pled no contest to a violation of Penal
Code section 647, subdivision (a), misdemeanor solicitation of a lewd act in a public
place. The court placed defendant on probation for three years, with conditions that he,
among other things, obey all laws and stay away from Pleasanton Sports Park.

On May 19, 1997, just three months after Harden was placed on probation in
Alameda County, he went to Concord's Hillcrest Park, which had a reputation for lewd
conduct in the restrooms. Harden parked his car near a restroom. He exited his car and
stared at an undercover officer who was sitting on the lawn near the restroom. Harden
went into the restroom and the undercover officer followed. The officer went to the urinal adjacent to where Harden was standing and observed that Harden was stroking his
erect penis. Harden turned toward the officer. The officer asked: "What's up?" And
Harden replied: "It's hot." Harden pulled his shirt up and his pants down, exposing his
abdomen and genital area. The officer asked: "What are you doing? You're hot?" And
Harden said: "Hot and sweaty." After a pause, Harden began to replace his clothing, but
he left his penis exposed. Harden told the officer he had to leave but would return. As
they were walking out of the restroom, Harden turned and grabbed the officer's genital
area through his pants. The officer quickly backed away. Harden was arrested as he was
leaving the park. As he was being escorted away, Harden said: "I know I've got a problem. I've been arrested for this before."

Harden pled no contest in the Contra Costa Municipal Court to another violation of Penal Code section 647, subdivision (a). He was placed on probation for three years and ordered to register as a sex offender pursuant to Penal Code section 290.

EVIDENCE CONCERNING MITIGATION AND REHABILITATION

Harden testified at the administrative hearing that he went through a difficult divorce in 1991 and was emotionally distraught. He also lost his business to bankruptcy. He claimed that during the six months prior to the hearing he had worked hard to put his life back together. Harden went through counseling twice, after his divorce and after his second conviction to comply with a probation condition. He presented no further material evidence of rehabilitation.

PROCEDURE

In February 2001, Harden applied to the Department for a license to sell real estate. In July 2001, the Department, through Deputy Real Estate Commissioner Les R. Bettencourt, filed a notice that Harden's application would be denied, citing his convictions. A hearing was held in October 2001, and the administrative law judge issued a proposed decision in November 2001. The administrative law judge concluded the Department had failed to show Harden's convictions were substantially related to the qualifications, functions, and duties of a real estate salesperson and recommended that the license be granted. In December 2001, Real Estate Commissioner Paula Reddish Zinnemann notified Harden she did not adopt the proposed decision of the administrative law judge and would conduct her own independent review of the evidence before deciding whether to issue the license. After considering the evidence and receiving further written arguments, the commissioner denied Harden's application for a real estate salesperson's license.

In her decision, the commissioner found: "As a real estate licensee, [Harden] would have unrestricted access via lock-box keys and open houses to the homes of others. [Harden] could also have access to unsupervised children at those homes. Given the nature of [Harden's] two criminal convictions, his registration under Section 290 of the Penal Code and his potential access to the homes and children of real estate clients, [Harden's] criminal convictions involve moral turpitude and are substantially related to the qualifications, functions, and duties of a real estate licensee. [Harden's] convictions are recent and his second conviction occurred at a time when [Harden] was still on probation as a result of his first conviction. In committing the acts that led to his second conviction, [Harden] violated the terms and conditions of his probation. [Harden] has not presented evidence of rehabilitation from his criminal convictions sufficient to meet his burden of establishing that he is entitled to a real estate license. Given the recency of those convictions and [Harden's] violation of the terms and conditions of his probation, additional time is necessary for [Harden] to establish that he is in fact rehabilitated."

Harden petitioned the trial court for mandamus relief, and the trial court, rejecting the commissioner's conclusions, granted the petition. The court stated:

1. Harden's crimes involved moral turpitude.

2. The crimes do not establish a substantial relationship between Harden's conduct and the qualifications, functions, and duties of a real estate salesperson.

3. The criminal court's requirement that Harden register as a sex offender does not establish a substantial relationship between Harden's conduct and the qualifications, functions, and duties of a real estate salesperson.

4. The record does not indicate Harden engaged in improper conduct involving children.

5. The record does not support an inference that Harden would engage in lewd conduct in his conduct of a real estate salesperson.

6. The Department abused its discretion in denying Harden a license.

DISCUSSION

The real estate commissioner may refuse to issue a license to an applicant who has "[e]ntered a plea of guilty or nolo contendere to, or been found guilty of, or been convicted of, a felony or a crime involving moral turpitude...." (Bus. & Prof.Code, § 10177, subd. (b).) Conviction alone, however, does not support refusal to issue the license unless the crime substantially relates to the qualifications, functions, or duties of real estate salesperson. (Bus. & Prof.Code, § 480, subd. (a)(3); *Loder v. Municipal Court* (1976) 17 Cal.3d 859, 874.)

Here, it is undisputed that Harden's crimes involved moral turpitude. (Bus. & Prof.Code, § 10177, subd. (b).) Harden argues, in support of the trial court's judgment, only that the crimes did not substantially relate to the qualifications, functions, or duties of a real estate salesperson. (Bus. & Prof.Code, § 480, subd. (a)(3).) We therefore turn to that question—whether Harden's crimes substantially relate to the qualifications, functions, or duties of a real estate salesperson. In doing so, we do not consider the crimes merely in the abstract but, instead, in their factual context.

Harden wastes much energy arguing that (1) his conduct as reflected in evidence presented during the administrative hearing did not violate Penal Code section 647, subdivision (a), (2) authorities commonly engage in overreaching when charging violations of this statute, and (3) he should not have been required to register as a sex offender. His convictions and requirement to register are conclusive proof in this forum that he committed the acts supporting the convictions and registration requirement. We therefore disregard Harden's irrelevant assertions to the contrary.

The commissioner found that Harden's conduct was substantially related to the qualifications, functions, and duties of a real estate salesperson. The record supports this finding. As shown by Harden's convictions, he has solicited lewd acts in public parks, where children congregate. During one such incident, children were nearby. Furthermore, the court order that he register as a sex offender conclusively establishes he committed the second offense "as a result of sexual compulsion or for purposes of sexual gratification." As the commissioner noted, a person licensed to sell real estate has access to people's homes via lock boxes and other means of entry. Based on his former conduct, it cannot be said Harden will not use this opportunity, under the right circumstances, to engage in lewd conduct. The commissioner's concern for the sanctity of the home and for unsupervised (and, in our view, even supervised) children is valid. (See *Oliver v. United States* (1984) 466 U.S. 170, 178 [80 L.Ed.2d 214, 224] [sanctity of home merits protection].)

Furthermore, Harden did not successfully allay these concerns with his largely conclusionary and self-serving assertion of rehabilitation. The commissioner noted how recent the crimes were, his violation of probation, and the lack of evidence concerning rehabilitation. An unsupported claim that for six months he had worked hard to put his life back together does not overcome the commissioner's conclusion as a matter of law under the substantial evidence standard for two reasons. First, the commissioner was justified in concluding that six months of work was insufficient to show real rehabilitation. And second, Harden offered no support for his assertion—no third-party character evidence, no expert averment to his purported rehabilitation, nothing to inspire confidence in his bare claim. The fact that Harden has not been arrested again since the second conviction also does not overcome, as a matter of law, the commissioner's finding that Harden did not show he is rehabilitated.

Harden chides the Department for pointing out that his crimes took place in public restrooms and that during commission of one of the crimes there were children in the park who could have walked into the restroom while Harden was engaging in lewd conduct. He scolds: "This argument panders to the basest prejudices of our society—that homosexuals are somehow likely to corrupt our children." Contrary to Harden's attempt to characterize this argument as discrimination against homosexuals, the Department's argument is well-taken. Engaging in lewd conduct in a public place, especially a place available to children, is despicable and threatens the innocence of nearby children, regardless of the sexual proclivities of the person engaging in the conduct. In fact, in the November 1996 incident, Harden began grabbing and rubbing his penis through his pants while outside of the restroom, which was only 40 yards from where two children were playing.

Accordingly, we reject defendant's diversionary assertion that the denial of his license was the result of prejudice and conclude the Department's denial of his license was supported by substantial evidence. The trial court erred in concluding otherwise.

Disposition

The judgment is reversed. The trial court is directed to enter judgment in favor of the Department. The Department shall recover its costs on appeal.

Robie, J.

I concur in the result. I write separately to emphasize that Harden's sexuality should have no bearing on this court's decision. There is nothing in the record to support the inference in the majority opinion that Harden is somehow a danger or threat to children.

Harden was twice convicted of soliciting lewd acts in public restrooms. In committing his second crime, he violated the probation he was granted for his first conviction. He must now register as a sex offender pursuant to Penal Code section 290. It simply does not matter that the acts Harden solicited were homosexual rather than heterosexual.

The commissioner acted within the bounds of reason in finding Harden's conduct justified denying him a license to sell real estate, particularly since Harden consistently has sought to deny culpability for these offenses and show any rehabilitation. Harden only offered some brief testimony about the "state of [his] personal life" which, under the circumstances, the commissioner was justified in finding insufficient.

Notes and Questions

1. Does the decision in *Pryor* strike the appropriate balance between respect for privacy and a legitimate concern by the state to preserve public order and protect the public from exposure to conduct that some may find offensive? Is the later a legitimate state interest?

2. Were the arrests of Mr. Harden appropriate under the Pryor decision's interpretation of the sexual solicitation statute?

3. The *Harden* case is included here not only to show that the police enforcement activities described in cases such as Pryor still go on, but also to suggest possible consequences, other than direct punishment, of imposing criminal liability for sexual solicitation. Are you satisfied that the Commissioner made the correct decision in denying Harden a license to be a real estate broker?

C. Non-Marital Sex

Consider how the principles developed in cases concerning reproduction (sterilization, contraception, abortion) might apply to claims that the government has violated constitutional rights when it directly prohibits particular kinds of sexual activity. In the United States, virtually every kind of sexual activity other than vaginal intercourse between a man and a woman who are married to each other has been prohibited at one time or another by almost all of the states. During the 19th century, statutory prohibitions of fornication, prostitution, adultery, and anal or oral sex existed in virtually all the states, and some jurisdictions even criminalized any kind of sexual touching or groping, regardless of whether it was consensual or took place in private. Of course, non-consensual sexual activity, public sexual activity, and sexual activity involving minors was also universally condemned. Same-sex activity was not singled out for particular treatment, as the more broadly inclusive statutes clearly applied regardless of the gender of the actors.

The twentieth century brought liberalizing trends, and the Model Penal Code at mid-century proposed decriminalizing most private, consensual sex between adults. However, the Model Penal Code's sex crimes provisions received uneven acceptance from the states. In many jurisdictions, such as New York, enactment of the code brought extensive legislative revision to retain many of the traditional sex crimes, and some states rejected the Model Penal Code entirely.

In light of *Eisenstadt* and *Lawrence*, what is the validity of laws that remain on the books in some states that forbid sexual intercourse between persons not married to each other? During the oral argument of *Bowers v. Hardwick*, counsel for the state of Georgia conceded that it would violate the constitution to prosecute an unmarried opposite-sex couple for engaging in anal or oral sex in private, and the trial court had dismissed as co-plaintiffs a heterosexual couple (for whom acts of anal or oral sex would have been just as forbidden by the statute as the oral sex between men for which Michael Hardwick was arrested), on the ground of lack of standing due to the expressed disinclination of law enforcement authorities to enforce the sodomy law against heterosexuals. And yet, at the time of the *Hardwick* argument, numerous heterosexuals were serving prison sentences in Georgia on charges of sodomy, as well as fornication, according to a survey undertaken by the ACLU.

In *Eisenstadt*, the Supreme Court ruled that the state could not constitutionally ban sales of contraceptives to unmarried persons while allowing such sales for married persons (as the state was required to do under *Griswold*). In *Lawrence*, the Court found that signaling moral disapproval for homosexual acts was not a legitimate state interest to support making such acts a crime. In light of these rulings, what legitimate justifications might states advance for continuing to keep laws against fornication and/or cohabitation on the books? Such laws are primarily used as "fallbacks" when prosecutions for rape or prostitution fail due to credible evidence of consent or lack of payment for services. Would such use provide a sufficient justification to keep the laws on the books? Alternatively, since sexually-transmitted diseases would undoubtedly become quite rare if everybody confined their sexual activity to committed, monogamous relations, either legally-married or same-sex-partnered in jurisdictions where same-sex marriage is not available, might a state rely on public health concerns as justification for outlawing fornication?

State v. Saunders
381 A.2d 333 (N.J. 1977)

PASHMAN, J.

[Defendants Charles Saunders and Bernard Busy were indicted on charges of rape, assault with intent to rape and armed robbery. The prosecution stemmed from a "pick-up" of some women by the two men when they were driving about during the early morning hours in Newark. The women, who had been arrested for prostitution in the past, denied that they had consented to have sex with the men or requested any compensation. The men's testimony was to the contrary. Their defense at trial to the rape charge was consent. They admitted having sex with the complainants, to whom they were not married. The trial judge *sua sponte* charged the jury that this would violate the fornication law. The jury convicted them of fornication, and the trial court rejected a constitutional challenge to the law.]

I

...In charging the jury, the judge defined the crime of fornication as "an act of illicit sexual intercourse by a man, married or single, with an unmarried woman." He placed the burden on the State to prove that the act occurred, but he made no reference to proof of the marital status of the complainants. Defense counsel objected to the fornication charge. He disputed the court's conclusion that fornication was truly a lesser included offense of rape, since one of its elements required proof that the woman be unmarried. The trial judge responded that his "recollection" was that both women had testified that they were not married. Defendant's counsel disagreed, although he was not certain. Counsel for Busby also objected on the ground that fornication was not a lesser included offense of rape.

The jury deliberated for about 20 minutes before seeking further advice from the court concerning the relationship between fornication and the other crimes. The court suggested that the jury consider the charges in descending order of gravity, starting with rape and considering fornication only if it found the defendants not guilty of the more serious offenses. At the urging of defense counsel, the judge stated that a verdict of guilty on the fornication charge would necessarily include a finding of consent by the women, precluding a conviction for rape or assault. The prosecutor made no objection to this additional clarification. Shortly thereafter, the jury returned its verdict of guilty on the two fornication counts and not guilty on all other counts.

Defendant was fined $50 and his co-defendant, who had spent seven months in jail awaiting trial, was sentenced to "time spent." Despite undisputed evidence of widespread nonenforcement of N.J.S.A. 2A:110-1, the trial judge found an insufficient showing of selective and purposeful discrimination based on an arbitrary or invidious classification. He stated that "the very nature of the crime makes enforcement difficult" and held further that defendant's conviction did not deny him equal protection or due process. The Appellate Division affirmed the decision.

III

Right of Privacy

The right of privacy is not explicitly mentioned in either the New Jersey or United States Constitutions. However, both documents have been construed to include such a right. However, the precise scope of the interests protected by the right of privacy are not easily defined. As the [U.S. Supreme] Court noted in *Carey* [v. Population Services International], the interests which have been held to fall within the protections of the right have been "personal" ones; they have included those "relating to marriage, *Loving v. Virginia*, 388 U.S. 1 (1967); procreation, *Skinner v. Oklahoma*, 316 U.S. 535 (1942); contraception, *Eisenstadt v. Baird*, 405 U.S. at 453-53 (White, J., concurring in result); family relationships, *Prince v. Massachusetts*, 321 U.S. 158, 166 (1944); and child rearing and education, *Pierce v. Society of Sisters*, 268 U.S. 510, 535 (1925); *Meyer v. Nebraska*, 262 U.S. 390, 399 (1923)." Although the Court in *Carey* observed that the "decision whether or not to beget or bear a child is at the very heart of this cluster of constitutionally protected choices," we believe that the right of privacy is not confined to the private situations involved in each of these decisions. Indeed, the Court's references in *Roe v. Wade* to cases having nothing to do with such decisions should effectively dispel any such notion. While *Carey* certainly emphasizes the importance of a person's choice regarding whether or not to have children, it indicates that the constitutional basis for the protection of such decisions is their relationship to individual autonomy. Mr. Justice Brennan observed that such personal choices concern "the most intimate of human activities and relationships," adding that "decisions whether to accomplish or to prevent conception are among the most private and sensitive."

This view of the right of privacy is consistent with the approach taken by this Court in our recent decision in *In re Quinlan*. There we held, as a matter of State constitutional law, that this important right was broad enough to encompass the freedom to make a personal choice as to the continuance of artificial life-support mechanisms. Though Chief Justice Hughes noted for the Court that the right of privacy had theretofore been primarily associated with decisions involving contraception and family life, he also found that its underlying concern was with the protection of personal decisions, and that it might be included within "the class of what have been called rights of 'personality.'" Our *Quinlan* decision could not have been predicated on privacy grounds if the class of cognizable privacy interests was limited to personal decisions concerning procreative matters.

Any discussion of the right of privacy must focus on the ultimate interest which protection the Constitution seeks to ensure the freedom of personal development. Whether one defines that concept as a "right to 'intimacy' and a freedom to do intimate things," or "a right to the 'integrity' of one's 'personality,'" see Henkin, "Privacy and Autonomy," 74 Colum.L.Rev. 1410, 1419 (1974), the crux of the matter is that governmental regulation of private personal behavior under the police power is sharply limited. As Mr. Justice Brandeis stated so eloquently in his dissent in *Olmstead v. United States*, 277 U.S. 438 (1928):

> The makers of our Constitution undertook to secure conditions favorable to the pursuit of happiness. They recognized the significance of man's spiritual

nature, of his feelings and of his intellect. They knew that only a part of the pain, pleasure and satisfactions of life are found in material things. They sought to protect Americans in their beliefs, their thoughts, their emotions and their sensations. They conferred, as against the government, the right to be let alone the most valued by civilized men.

We conclude that the conduct statutorily defined as fornication involves, by its very nature, a fundamental personal choice. Thus, the statute infringes upon the right of privacy. Although persons may differ as to the propriety and morality of such conduct and while we certainly do not condone its particular manifestations in this case, such a decision is necessarily encompassed in the concept of personal autonomy which our Constitution seeks to safeguard.

We recognize that the conduct prohibited by this statute has never been explicitly treated by the Supreme Court as falling within the right of privacy. Nevertheless, our decision today is consistent with the tenor and thrust of the Court's more recent decisions. We therefore join with other courts which have held that such sexual activities between adults are protected by the right of privacy. See *State v. Pilcher*, 242 N.W.2d 348 (Sup.Ct.Iowa 1976).

Finally, we note that our doubts as to the constitutionality of the fornication statute are also impelled by this Court's development of a constitutionally mandated "zone" of privacy protecting individuals from unwarranted governmental intrusion into matters of intimate personal and family concern. It is now settled that the right of privacy guaranteed under the Fourteenth Amendment has an analogue in our State Constitution. Although the scope of this State right is not necessarily broader in all respects, the lack of constraints imposed by considerations of federalism permits this Court to demand stronger and more persuasive showings of a public interest in allowing the State to prohibit sexual practices than would be required by the United States Supreme Court.

Yet our inquiry cannot end here. Having found that the statute impinges upon the fundamental right of privacy, we must go on to consider whether that impingement can be justified by some compelling state interest. In an attempt to justify the statute's infringement of protected rights, the State cites its interests in preventing venereal disease and an increase in the number of illegitimate children, and in protecting the marital relationship and public morals by preventing illegitimacy.

Perhaps the strongest reason favoring the law is its supposed relationship to the furtherance of the State's salutary goal of preventing venereal disease. We do not question the State's compelling interest in preventing the spread of such diseases. Nor do we dispute the power of the State to regulate activities which may adversely affect the public health. However, we do not believe that the instant enactment is properly designed with that end in mind.

First, while we recognize that the statute would substantially eliminate venereal diseases if it could successfully deter people from engaging in the prohibited activity, we doubt its ability to achieve that result. The risk of contracting venereal disease is surely as great a deterrent to illicit sex as the maximum penalty under this act: a fine of $50 and/or imprisonment in jail for six months. Furthermore, if the State's interest in the instant statute is that it is helpful in preventing venereal disease, we conclude that it is counterproductive. To the extent that any successful program to combat venereal disease must depend upon affected persons coming forward for treatment, the present statute operates as a deterrent to such voluntary participation. The fear of being prosecuted for the "crime" of fornication can only deter people from seeking such necessary treatment. We similarly fail to comprehend how the State's interest in preventing the propagation of il- legitimate children will be measurably advanced by the instant law. If the unavailability of contraceptives is not likely to deter people from engaging in illicit sexual activities, it follows that the fear of unwanted pregnancies will be equally ineffective.

The last two reasons offered by the State as compelling justifications for the enact- ment, that it protects the marital relationship and the public morals by preventing illicit sex, offer little additional support for the law. Whether or not abstention is likely to in- duce persons to marry, this statute can in no way be considered a permissible means of fostering what may otherwise be a socially beneficial institution. If we were to hold that the State could attempt to coerce people into marriage, we would undermine the very independent choice which lies at the core of the right of privacy.

This is not to suggest that the State may not regulate, in an appropriate manner, ac- tivities which are designed to further public morality. Our conclusion today extends no further than to strike down a measure which has as its objective the regulation of pri- vate morality. To the extent that N.J.S.A. 2A:110-1 serves as an official sanction of cer- tain conceptions of desirable lifestyles, social mores or individualized beliefs, it is not an appropriate exercise of the police power.

Fornication may be abhorrent to the morals and deeply held beliefs of many persons. But any appropriate "remedy" for such conduct cannot come from legislative fiat. Pri- vate personal acts between two consenting adults are not to be lightly meddled with by the State. The right of personal autonomy is fundamental to a free society. Persons who view fornication as opprobrious conduct may seek strenuously to dissuade people from engaging in it. However, they may not inhibit such conduct through the coercive power of the criminal law. As aptly stated by Sir Francis Bacon, "(t)he sum of behavior is to re- tain a man's own dignity without intruding on the liberty of others." The fornication statute mocks the dignity of both offenders and enforcers. Surely police have more pressing duties than to search out adults who live a so-called "wayward" life. Surely the dignity of the law is undermined when an intimate personal activity between consent- ing adults can be dragged into court and "exposed." More importantly, the liberty which is the birthright of every individual suffers dearly when the State can so grossly intrude on personal autonomy.

CLIFFORD, J., dissenting.

Bluntly put, this case is a wretched vehicle for addressing the questions which coun- sel for the respective parties would have us answer. It seems somehow incongruous to use the soaring phrases of Mr. Justice Brandeis in *Olmstead v. United States* as support for the proposition that the State of New Jersey is powerless to prohibit indiscriminate group fornicating by or indeed, among complete strangers exhibiting remarkable dex- terity in the confined quarters of a parked automobile on a deserted lot in Newark.

As an abstract proposition, certainly, I am inclined to ground any determination of the statute's invalidity on the State constitution, and on the authority of *In re Quinlan*. I hold to the view (and as I read the other opinions, so do all the other members of this Court) that absent a compelling state interest the State may not regulate a person's pri- vate decisions which have merely incidental effects on others. In application that princi- ple leads to the conclusion that if two people freely determine that they wish to have sexual relations in a setting inoffensive to and only incidentally affecting others, the State is without authority to interfere through the criminal process with that decision, despite the fact that such decision may be in violation of conventional community standards of morality. And that includes the grubby little exercise in self-gratification involved here.

But I think we need not, and I would not, get to the constitutional issue, at least not at this point. It is quite clear that a substantial issue is present as to whether fornication is a lesser included offense of rape. In some other jurisdictions to convict for fornication the State must show that the female participant is unmarried and that both parties consented to the act, neither of which requirements is a constituent element of a rape conviction. In the instant case the record leaves doubt as to the marital status of one of the complaining witnesses. In addition, a jury's determination that the State has failed to prove beyond a reasonable doubt the complaining witnesses' lack of consent does not equate with an affirmative finding of consent. Further, defense counsel was unaware that the possibility of a fornication conviction was to be submitted to the jury until after summations had been completed; hence he had no opportunity to introduce evidence bearing on these issues or to argue them to the jury.

While the foregoing brief discussion is obviously not, nor is it intended to be, exhaustive, nevertheless it does demonstrate a respectable basis for rejecting the "lesser included offense" position adopted by the trial court over defendant's objection. I would think the point sufficiently worth pursuing as to require further briefs, putting the constitutional issue aside for now. I therefore dissent from the judgment of the Court. Justice MOUNTAIN joins in this opinion. [This decision and some ensuing lower court decisions persuaded the New Jersey legislature to reform its sex crimes laws to decriminalize private, consensual sexual activity between adults, including same-sex conduct.]

Martin v. Ziherl
607 S.E.2d 367 (Va. 2005)

Justice ELIZABETH B. LACY.

In this appeal we consider whether *Zysk v. Zysk*, 239 Va. 32, 404 S.E.2d 721 (1990), which disallows tort recovery for injuries suffered while participating in an illegal activity, precludes Muguet S. Martin from maintaining a tort action against Kristopher Joseph Ziherl for injuries allegedly inflicted during sexual intercourse, a criminal act of fornication proscribed by Code § 18.2-344, in light of the decision of the Supreme Court of the United States in *Lawrence v. Texas*, 539 U.S. 558 (2003), holding unconstitutional a Texas penal statute prohibiting certain sexual acts.

Martin and Ziherl were unmarried adults in a sexually active relationship from approximately October 31, 2001 through November 3, 2003. Martin experienced a vaginal outbreak in June 2003, which her physician diagnosed as herpes. Martin filed a motion for judgment against Ziherl alleging that he knew he was infected with the sexually transmitted herpes virus when he and Martin were engaged in unprotected sexual conduct, knew that the virus was contagious, and failed to inform Martin of his condition. In the two-count motion for judgment, Martin asserted claims of negligence, intentional battery and intentional infliction of emotional distress and sought compensatory and punitive damages.

Ziherl filed a demurrer asserting that Martin's injuries were caused by her participation in an illegal act and therefore, under *Zysk*, the motion for judgment did not state a claim upon which relief could be granted. Following a hearing, the trial court applied

Zysk and sustained Ziherl's demurrer holding that *Lawrence* did not "strike down" Code § 18.2-344 and that valid reasons such as the protection of public health and encouraging marriage for the procreation of children are "rationally related to achieve the objective of the statute." We awarded Martin an appeal.

Martin asserts that the reasoning of the Supreme Court of the United States in *Lawrence* renders Virginia's statute criminalizing the sexual intercourse between two unmarried persons, Code § 18.2-344, unconstitutional. The issue in *Lawrence,* as stated by the Court, was "whether the petitioners were free as adults to engage in the private conduct in the exercise of their liberty under the Due Process Clause of the Fourteenth Amendment to the Constitution."

Acknowledging that the Texas court properly considered *Bowers* [*v. Hardwick*] as "then being authoritative," the Supreme Court reexamined its prior decision and concluded that "*Bowers* was not correct when it was decided, and is not correct today." The Court explained that the liberty interest at issue was not a fundamental right to engage in certain conduct but was the right to enter and maintain a personal relationship without governmental interference. The Court determined that the statutes proscribing certain acts between persons of the same sex sought to control a personal relationship that is "within the liberty of persons to choose without being punished as criminals." The Court explained that the constitution protects the liberty interests of persons to maintain a personal relationship "in the confines of their homes and their own private lives" and that an element of that relationship is its "overt expression in intimate conduct."

In overruling *Bowers,* the Court also stated that the analysis of Justice Stevens in his dissenting opinion in *Bowers* should have been applied in that case and "should control" in *Lawrence.* That analysis is:

> Our prior cases make two propositions abundantly clear. First, the fact that the governing majority in a State has traditionally viewed a particular practice as immoral is not a sufficient reason for upholding a law prohibiting the practice; neither history nor tradition could save a law prohibiting miscegenation from constitutional attack. Second, individual decisions by married persons, concerning the intimacies of their physical relationship, even when not intended to produce offspring, are a form of "liberty" protected by the Due Process Clause of the Fourteenth Amendment. Moreover, this protection extends to intimate choices by unmarried as well as married persons.

Applying Justice Stevens' analysis, the Court stated, "The State cannot demean their existence or control their destiny by making their private sexual conduct a crime. Their right to liberty under the Due Process Clause gives them the full right to engage in their conduct without intervention of the government."

We find no relevant distinction between the circumstances in *Lawrence* and the circumstances in the present case. As described in Justice Stevens' rationale adopted by the Court in *Lawrence,* decisions by married or unmarried persons regarding their intimate physical relationship are elements of their personal relationships that are entitled to due process protection. Using this rationale, the Supreme Court found that the Texas statute criminalizing a specific sexual act between two persons of the same sex violated the Due Process Clause of the Fourteenth Amendment because such statute improperly abridged a personal relationship that was within the liberty interest of persons to choose. We find no principled way to conclude that the specific act of intercourse is not an element of a personal relationship between two unmarried persons or that the Virginia statute criminalizing intercourse between unmarried persons does not improperly abridge a personal relationship that is within the liberty interest of persons to choose. Because Code § 18.2-334, like the Texas statute at issue in *Lawrence*, is an attempt by the state to control the liberty interest which is exercised in making these personal decisions, it violates the Due Process Clause of the Fourteenth Amendment.

Ziherl argues, and the trial court held, that Code § 18.2-344 withstands constitutional scrutiny because "[v]alid public reasons for the law exist," including protection of public health and "encouraging that children be born into a family consisting of a married couple." Regardless of the merit of the policies referred to by the trial court, the Supreme Court in *Lawrence* indicated that such policies are insufficient to sustain the statute's constitutionality.

The Supreme Court did not consider the liberty right vindicated in *Lawrence* as a fundamental constitutional right which could be infringed only if the statute in question satisfied the strict scrutiny test. Rather, the Court applied a rational basis test, but held that "[t]he Texas statute furthers no legitimate state interest which can justify its intrusion into the personal and private life of the individual." This statement is not limited to state interests offered by the state of Texas in support of its statute, but sweeps within it all manner of states' interests and finds them insufficient when measured against the intrusion upon a person's liberty interest when that interest is exercised in the form of private, consensual sexual conduct between adults. As we have said, this same liberty interest is invoked in this case when two unmarried adults make the choice to engage in the intimate sexual conduct proscribed by Code § 18.2-344. Thus, as in *Lawrence*, the Commonwealth's interests do not warrant such encroachment on personal liberty.

Therefore, applying the reasoning of *Lawrence* as Martin asks us to do, leads us to conclude that Code § 18.2-344 is unconstitutional because by subjecting certain private sexual conduct between two consenting adults to criminal penalties it infringes on the rights of adults to "engage in the private conduct in the exercise of their liberty under the Due Process Clause of the Fourteenth Amendment to the Constitution." *Id.* at 564, 123 S.Ct. 2472.

It is important to note that this case does not involve minors, non-consensual activity, prostitution, or public activity. The *Lawrence* court indicated that state regulation of that type of activity might support a different result. Our holding, like that of the Supreme Court in *Lawrence*, addresses only private, consensual conduct between adults and the respective statutes' impact on such conduct. Our holding does not affect the Commonwealth's police power regarding regulation of public fornication, prostitution, or other such crimes.

We now turn to the application of *Zysk* to this case. The rule applied in *Zysk* was that "a party who consents to and participates in an immoral and illegal act cannot recover damages from other participants for the consequence of that act." 239 Va. at 34. We adhere to that rule. However, in light of our determination regarding the constitutionality of Code § 18.2-344, the sexual activity between Martin and Ziherl was not illegal and "the fact that the governing majority in a State has traditionally viewed a particular practice as immoral is not a sufficient reason for upholding a law prohibiting the practice." *Lawrence*, 539 U.S. at 577. Therefore, *Zysk* is no longer controlling precedent to the extent that its holding applies to private, consensual sexual intercourse.

Notes and Questions

1. In *Doe v. Duling*, 603 F.Supp. 960 (E.D.Va. 1985), vacated, 782 F.2d 1202 (4th Cir. 1986), a federal district court found in response to a declaratory judgment action that Virginia's fornication and cohabitation statutes were unconstitutional. The decision was vacated, however, on the ground that the plaintiffs, who had never been prosecuted, lacked standing to challenge the statute. More recently, Utah citizens seeking a declaration that the Utah fornication and sodomy laws are unconstitutional as applied to consenting heterosexual adults was thrown out of court on standing and procedural grounds, as was a challenge focused solely on the sodomy law. *W.N.J. and J.A.S.and J.O.H.N. and D.M.W. v. Yocum*, 257 F.3d 1171 (10th Cir. 2001); *D.L.S. v. State*, 374 F.3d 971 (10th Cir. 2004). In a portion of the decision in *Martin v. Ziherl* omitted above, the court found that standing to raise the constitutionality of the law was not a problem, due to its direct impact on the pending case.

2. Laws outlawing fornication and/or cohabitation used to be widespread. They have been repealed in some jurisdictions as a result of the overall reform of sex crime laws when states adopted the Model Penal Code, but remain in force in many states. Although law enforcement officials do not appear to place a high priority on enforcing fornication laws, they have been held to serve as statements of public policy that may be relevant in other contexts, including (1) divorce proceedings, (2) defamation cases, in which an imputation that a woman is unchaste (i.e., has engaged in fornication) may be held defamatory per se as a reflection on her character, (3) employment cases, in which a discharge for refusal to have sex with the boss could be held tortious as a violation of the public policy against fornication, as well as in the torts context shown above. For an interesting example of the third category, see *Mitchem v. Counts*, 523 S.E.2d 246 (Va. 2000). Is it appropriate for society to declare conduct criminal so that a public policy disfavoring the conduct can be invoked in non-criminal litigation contexts?

3. One of the few remaining enforcement purposes of a fornication law is to serve as a possible "lesser included offense" in prosecutions for rape or prostitution. For a recent example, see *State of Utah v. Houston*, 9 P.3d 188 (Utah Ct. App. 2000), where the defendant was acquitted by the jury of rape and forcible sodomy charges, but was convicted of fornication and sodomy, the jury believing his defense that the sexual activity was consensual. The defendant and the complainant were Mormon Church missionaries, engaged to be married, who had vowed not to have sex with each other prior to their marital vows. While sleeping outdoors, the defendant apparently misinterpreted a physical gesture by the complainant as an invitation to have sex; oral and anal sex followed and complainant never protested. She later asserted that she was paralyzed with fear brought on by youthful experiences of sexual assault. The defendant testified he would not have engaged in sex had he not thought that the complainant was inviting him to do so. Does the defendant's conviction on these facts serve a legitimate law enforcement purpose?

4. There is a significant difference under our legal system between maintaining that a particular law is "bad policy" and that it is "unconstitutional." Are you persuaded that fornication and cohabitation laws are unconstitutional? Why? See Note, Constitutional Barriers to Civil and Criminal Restrictions on Pre- and Extramarital Sex, 104 Harv. L. Rev. 1660 (May 1991).

5. The *Saunders* decision presents an interesting example of the role for state constitutional law in considering the validity of state criminal statutes. In a concurring opin-

ion omitted here, a member of the court concurred solely on state constitutional grounds, finding that the New Jersey constitution provided broader protection for individual privacy in sexual matters than had yet been recognized in the federal courts. State courts are free to construe protections for individual rights derived from state constitutions as broader than analogous federal constitutional rights, and many state constitutions differ from the federal constitution in their specifications of individual rights. An important "side effect" of using state constitutional principles to invalidate a statute is that the decision will not be subject to review by the United States Supreme Court, which lacks jurisdiction in the absence of a federal question. Before the Supreme Court overruled *Bowers v. Hardwick*, state constitutional privacy would likely have provided the best basis to challenge the constitutionality of a state law against fornication. For an example of a successful challenge, see *In re J.M.*, 575 S.E.2d 441 (Ga. 2003), where the Georgia Supreme Court, having previously invalidated the state's sodomy law on state constitutional grounds, proceeded to do the same to the state's fornication law.

D. Commercial Prostitution

Prostitution laws can be found in every state in the United States, imposing criminal sanctions for the performance of sex for pay. In forty-nine states, these are a matter of state law as well as local ordinance. In Nevada, the state authorizes localities to decide whether to ban prostitution, and a few have decided to allow it, under tightly regulated conditions. The United States differs in this from many Western European countries, which allow prostitution as a regulated commercial activity. In Great Britain, the Wolfenden Committee noted that prostitution in private was not a criminal offense under British law, and recommended against criminalization, but argued in favor of continuing to penalize public solicitation by prostitutes from a concern over public order and morality, noting the criminality that sometimes accompanies public solicitation for prostitution. The Model Penal Code, on the other hand, continues to impose criminal penalties for prostitution.

The one significant variation between state laws is in the treatment of the prostitute as opposed to the customer. While some jurisdictions punish both, some only punish the prostitute. Is this appropriate as a matter of policy? Is it constitutional as a matter of equal protection? What is the relevance of the concerns articulated in *Lawrence v. Texas* about personal liberty in evaluating the continued constitutionality of laws penalizing prostitution?

Roe v. Butterworth
958 F. Supp. 1569 (S.D. Fla. 1997)

GONZALEZ, District Judge

Petitioner challenges the constitutionality of Chapter 796, Florida Statutes, and seeks declaratory and injunctive relief against Robert Butterworth, acting as Attorney General of the State of Florida. Petitioner brings her claims under the Fifth and Fourteenth Amendments to the United States Constitution.

Petitioner is a former employee of the "most prestigious and famous escort service in south Florida and the United States." According to Petitioner, during her employment as a call girl, she "dated and engaged in sexual activity for hire with some of the most powerful and well known businessmen in the United States and the World as well as numerous diverse professionals such as doctors, lawyers, reverends and ministers, professors and even State Circuit Court and Federal Judges," most of whom were married. Petitioner is interested in returning to her career as a prostitute, but has refrained from doing so at the prompting of her attorney, and out of fear of prosecution.

Florida defines prostitution as "the giving or receiving of the body for sexual activity for hire but excludes sexual activity between spouses." Fla.Stat. §796.07(1)(a). "Sexual activity" is defined as "oral, anal, or vaginal penetration by, or union with, the sexual organ of another; anal or vaginal penetration of another by any other object; or the handling or fondling of the sexual organ of another for the purpose of masturbation." Fla.Stat. §796.07(1)(d). Section 796.07 also makes it unlawful for any person to "purchase the services of any person engaged in prostitution." Fla.Stat. §796(2)(h)(i). Violation of Section 796.07 constitutes the commission of a misdemeanor. Fla.Stat. §796.07(4).

Petitioner alleges that sections 796.02 through 796.08 "to the extent they prohibit and make criminal prostitution and acts related thereto, are unconstitutional because they directly violate the Petitioner's Fifth and Fourteenth Amendment rights to due process and equal protection and her fundamental right of privacy, and pursuant to that right[, the right] to control her own reproductive organs whether in a private or commercial transaction."

If, as Petitioner asserts, the conduct in which she wishes to engage falls within the zone of privacy protected by the Fifth and Fourteenth Amendments to the United States Constitution, the Court must engage in a two part analysis. Initially, the Court must determine whether the challenged legislation burdens the exercise of Petitioner's right of privacy. If the Court answers this question in the affirmative, it must strictly scrutinize the legislation to determine if it is narrowly tailored to achieve a compelling state interest. If the Court concludes that the activity in which Petitioner seeks to engage does not fall within the ambit of her fundamental right of privacy, or that the legislation does not burden any fundamental right, the Court must determine whether the statute is rationally related to a legitimate governmental interest.

Even before it determines what level of review to apply, however, the Court must identify the exact nature of the right Petitioner asserts. In large part, the Court's conclusion will turn upon the level of specificity with which it views Petitioner's claim; the Court must determine whether to view Petitioner's claim at a very general level—as a unitary whole—or at a more specific level. In other words, is the issue in this case whether Petitioner has a constitutional right to engage in prostitution? Or should that activity be broken down into its constituent parts?

There remains a strong precedent in favor of selecting the most specific level of tradition possible for adjudicating this case—*Bowers v. Hardwick*, 478 U.S. 186 (1986). In *Bowers*, the Court rejected Hardwick's challenge to Georgia's anti-sodomy law. Hardwick, who had been arrested for committing an act of sodomy with another adult male in the privacy of his own bedroom, argued that the statute violated his constitutional right to privacy. In his dissent, Justice Blackmun argued that Hardwick's claim should be viewed at a very general level as "'the right to be let alone.'" The Court, however, rejected Justice Blackmun's formulation, and instead framed the issue as "whether the Federal Constitution confers a fundamental right upon homosexuals to engage in sodomy." Thus, the Court viewed Hardwick's claim at a very specific level, taking into consideration all of the relevant facts of which the State complained. Thus, it is clear that the Court does not inevitably limit its inquiry to general, overriding principles of privacy.

Initially, Petitioner presented her claim as a coherent activity. Later, perhaps in response to this Court's recognition that Petitioner's claim could be based upon "some smaller subset of personal rights," she directed greater attention to this alternative theory. Petitioner has, however, included arguments supporting each approach in her memoranda. Because the Court believes that it would be helpful to explore both of Petitioner's approaches, it will consider each in turn.

A. What constitutes a fundamental right?

It is never easy for a court to determine whether a particular activity, previously unaddressed by the Supreme Court, falls within one of the "unenumerated rights" created by the Constitution. Some restrictions on the state were made unmistakably clear by the framers. As for other restrictions upon state legislation, the Constitution has at times appeared miserly, only begrudgingly revealing her mysteries. The unenumerated rights upon which the states are forbidden from intruding are most often found as stemming from the Due Process Clauses of the Fourteenth Amendment. Read literally, the Due Process Clause seems to be a procedural provision, merely limiting the manner in which a state may deprive a person of "life, liberty, or property". For at least 109 years, however, "the Clause has been understood to contain a substantive component as well, one 'barring certain government actions regardless of the fairness of the procedures used to implement them." The due process clause of the Fourteenth Amendment "affords not only a procedural guarantee against deprivation of 'liberty,' but likewise protects substantive aspects of liberty against unconstitutional restrictions by the State." *Kelley v. Johnson,* 425 U.S. 238, 244 (1976).

In evaluating Petitioner's claim, the Court must ask whether the liberty she asserts is "so rooted in the traditions and conscience of our people as to be ranked as fundamental." *Snyder v. Massachusetts,* 291 U.S. 97, 105 (1934) (Cardozo, J.). Only if the right involved "is of such a character that it cannot be denied without violating those 'fundamental principles of liberty and justice which lie at the base of all our civil and political institutions,'" will it be deemed fundamental. In determining whether a right is so "implicit in the concept of ordered liberty" as to warrant constitutional protection, the Court should refer to this Nation's history, and basic underlying values. *Palko v. Connecticut,* 302 U.S. 319, 325 (1937). Also, the Court must maintain a "wise appreciation of the great roles that the doctrines of federalism and separation of powers have played in establishing and preserving American freedoms." After referring to these sources of guidance, a fundamental right will only be found if the Court concludes that the liberty asserted is of such importance that "neither liberty nor justice would exist if [it] were sacrificed." *Palko v. Connecticut,* 302 U.S. at 326.

At issue in this case is the Due Process Clause's substantive guarantee of liberty, which has been interpreted as including a right of privacy protecting "the personal intimacies of the home, the family, marriage, motherhood, procreation,...child rearing," and education. These protected intimacies were, for a long time, limited to the marital relationship. The Court's opinion in *Eisenstadt v. Baird,* however, made clear that this right "to be let alone" means more.

Recognizing that the interpretation of the Due Process Clause is not a precise science, the Supreme Court has admonished lower courts to exercise extreme caution before extending that Clause's reach. Such circumspection is dictated by the nature of the government the Constitution established. Under our representative democracy, courts must be particularly careful to leave important political decisions in the hands of the majority. Thus, the Court has warned:

> The Court is most vulnerable and comes nearest to illegitimacy when it deals with judge-made constitutional law having little or no cognizable roots in the language or design of the Constitution. That this is so was painfully demonstrated by the face-off between the Executive and the Court in the 1930's, which resulted in the repudiation of much of the substantive gloss that the Court had placed on the Due Process Clauses of the Fifth and Fourteenth Amendments. There should be, therefore, great resistance to expand the substantive reach of those Clauses, particularly if it requires redefining the category of rights deemed to be fundamental. Otherwise, the Judiciary necessarily takes to itself further authority to govern the country without express constitutional authority.

Bowers v. Hardwick, 478 U.S. at 194–95

B. Does Petitioner have a fundamental right to engage in prostitution?

Petitioner argues that prostitution is so well established in the traditions and history of this society as to come within the protection of Due Process Clause's guarantee of privacy. Her supporting references to "evidence" reach back millions of years to the development of Homo Erectus. She also refers to ancient Greek history, Roman Mythology, the Bible, biblical scholars such as St. Thomas Aquinas and St. Augustine, and the history of the old American West. Petitioner has submitted ample evidence to establish that prostitution has an extensive and lengthy history; this is no surprise. Yet she has utterly failed to show either that the act of engaging in prostitution is "implicit in the concept of ordered liberty" such that "neither liberty nor justice would exist if [it] were sacrificed," or that it is so "deeply rooted in this Nations's history and tradition" as to be deemed fundamental. Indeed, such an argument "is, at best, facetious." *Bowers v. Hardwick,* 478 U.S. at 194.

Longevity alone does not bring an activity within the protection of the Constitution. If it did, every activity that has long been denounced by civilized societies—and they are myriad—would gain constitutional protection from state interference. Murder, robbery, extortion, bigamy, incest, theft, and many other crimes have been committed since before histories were recorded. Yet, because societies considered them destructive, immoral, indecent, or generally evil, they have all been prohibited at one time or another. The same is undoubtedly true of prostitution.

Petitioner does not contest the long standing history of state and criminal laws prohibiting prostitution in this country. Today, every state in the Union, as well as the federal government, has some form of penal statute prohibiting prostitution. Such a well established history of prohibition strongly supports the conclusion that this society has not traditionally valued the practice of prostitution.

Petitioner's references to the Bible are also completely unavailing. The Bible is replete with negative references to "harlots," "prostitutes" and "whores," both in the Old and New Testament. The mere fact that "harlots" may not have been "systematically repressed," or that particular prostitutes, such as Rehab, were even revered, falls far short of establishing that the institution of prostitution is "implicit in the concept of ordered liberty."

Petitioner's own exhibits demonstrate the public opprobrium that has been leveled towards prostitution throughout history. Indeed, the main thrust of Petitioner's argument is that such malevolent judgments, so common throughout history, stem from antiquated and hypocritical attitudes and ethics. While such an argument shows that societal norms do not mesh with Petitioner's liberalized ideals, it does nothing to advance her claim that the right to engage in prostitution is constitutionally protected.

Petitioner's reliance on the privacy of the home or other closed quarters also fails to persuade this Court that prostitution is constitutionally protected. While the Supreme Court has given a more expansive reading to the right of privacy when a challenged ordinance seeks to reach within an individual's home, the Court has also made clear that the privacy of one's home does not render an individual immune from prosecution. Even "[v]ictimless crimes...do not escape the law where they are committed at home." Various Justices of the Supreme Court, both in separate opinions and on behalf of the Court, have stated that the states may appropriately criminalize prostitution. *See e.g. Barnes v. Glen Theatre, Inc.*, 501 U.S. 560, 594 (1991) (White, J., dissenting) ("the State clearly has the authority to criminalize prostitution and obscene behavior"); *Id.*, 501 U.S. at 575 (Scalia, J., concurring); *Id.*, 501 U.S. at 584 (Souter, J., concurring); *Paris Adult Theatre I v. Slaton*, 413 U.S. 49, 68 n. 15 (1973) ("The state statute books are replete with constitutionally unchallenged laws against prostitution,...although [this] crime[ ] may only directly involve 'consenting adults.' "); *Hoke v. United States*, 227 U.S. 308, 321 (1913) ("There is unquestionably a control in the states over the morals of their citizens, and, it may be admitted, it extends to making prostitution a crime.").

Various justices have also expressed the view that other extra-marital sexual crimes are valid and enforceable. *See Carey v. Population Services, Int'l*, 431 U.S. 678, 702 (1977) (White, J., concurring) ("I do not regard the opinion, however, as declaring unconstitutional any state law forbidding extramarital sexual relations."); *Paris Adult Theatre I*, 413 U.S. at 68 n. 15 ("Statutes making bigamy a crime surely cut into an individual's freedom to associate, but few today seriously claim such statutes violate the First Amendment or any other constitutional provision."); *Griswold v. Connecticut*, 381 U.S. at 498 (Goldberg, J., concurring) ("The State of Connecticut does have statutes, the constitutionality of which is beyond doubt, which prohibit adultery and fornication."); *Id.*, at 505 (White, J., concurring) ("the State's policy against all forms of promiscuous or illicit sexual relationships...[is] concededly a permissible and legitimate legislative goal."); *Poe v. Ullman*, 367 U.S. at 552 (Harlan, J., dissenting) ("I would not suggest that adultery, homosexuality, fornication and incest are immune from criminal enquiry, however privately practiced."), *quoted in* Catherine D. Perry, "Right of Privacy Challenges to Prostitution Statutes," 58 Wash.U.Law.Quarterly 439, 456 n. 120. Even Justice Blackmun, dissenting in *Bowers v. Hardwick*, suggested that the a state could legitimately enforce such laws. 478 U.S. at 209 n. 4.

Petitioner has utterly failed to show that this society has ever recognized a right to engage in prostitution; instead, she has painted a picture of consistent and long standing denunciation. While she has shown that the roots of prostitution reach well back into ancient history, she has failed to show that "neither liberty nor justice would exist if [it] were sacrificed." Therefore, following the reasoning and analysis of the Supreme Court in *Bowers v. Hardwick*, the Court concludes that Petitioner has failed to show that the right of privacy, as delineated by the Supreme Court, includes the right to engage in prostitution.

C. Is engaging in sex a fundamental right?

Whether the right of privacy includes the right to engage in extra-marital sexual relations between consenting, heterosexual adults is a much more difficult question, and one which the Supreme Court has refused to resolve. The lower courts that have considered this issue have reached different conclusions.

Petitioner states unequivocally that "[t]he United States Supreme Court has repeatedly, without fail, ruled that the right to have sex is a fundamental constitutional right independent of *Roe v. Wade* and *Casey.*" This conclusion, however, is not supported by even the most strained reading of the cases Petitioner cites. In fact, as pointed out above, several of those cases contain statements suggesting that the Supreme Court would uphold the constitutionality of adultery and fornication statutes. Nonetheless, a strong argument can be made that the right to personal intimacy and privacy is broad enough to protect from state intrusion or interference the consensual sexual relations of heterosexual adults. Fortunately, the Court need not consider that argument at this time, for even assuming the existence of such a fundamental right, Petitioner's challenge to Florida's prostitution statute fails.

As a general matter, when a state law abridges a fundamental personal liberty "the State may prevail only upon showing a subordinating interest which is compelling." This strict level of review, however, is not triggered automatically. Only where a state law "imposes an undue burden" on the exercise of a fundamental right "does the power of the State reach into the heart of the liberty interest protected by the Due Process Clause." If a state law has only incidental effects upon the exercise of a fundamental right, a court will not review that law at the strictest level of scrutiny. Instead, the state need only show that the statute is rationally related to a legitimate state purpose.

Petitioner has not shown that the challenged statute has placed a "substantial obstacle in the path" of her decision to engage in consensual sexual activities, nor has she raised such a claim on behalf of another. Chapter 769 of the Florida Statutes simply does not prevent Petitioner from engaging in sex. On the contrary, Petitioner apparently has so little trouble obtaining willing partners for sexual intercourse that they are willing to pay her for the privilege. Thus, Petitioner has not shown even a marginal infringement of the claimed fundamental right.

Petitioner's true complaint is that she is forbidden from profiting financially from engaging in sex. In essence, she argues that "the right to purchase and sell labor is part of the liberty protected by [the Fourteenth] [A]mendment." Viewed in this light, Petitioner's claim fits neatly within the economic due process line of cases announced by the Supreme Court during the early part of this century. Obviously, it is beyond the power of this Court to breathe new life into these long discredited cases. As the law stands today, "a state is free to adopt whatever economic policy may reasonably be deemed to promote public welfare." If the means selected "have a reasonable relation to a proper legislative purpose, and are neither arbitrary nor discriminatory, the requirements of due process are satisfied, and judicial determination to that effect renders a court *functus officio.*" It is not the function of a court to sit as a super legislature judging the "wisdom or desirability of legislative policy determinations made in areas that neither affect fundamental rights nor proceed along suspect lines." Following the dictate of these cases, the Court is bound to give great deference to the State's economic regulations, and presume the existence of facts supporting the legislature's judgment. Thus, the Court's inquiry is "restricted to the issue whether any state of facts either known or which could reasonably be assumed, affords support" for the challenged statute. *United States v. Carolene Products Co.,* 304 U.S. 144, 154 (1938). (Petitioner argues that there is no precedent for criminalizing a legal act merely because it is performed for consideration. Respondent, however, has pointed to two—the sale of children and the sale of organs. Respondent's Memorandum at 26, citing Fla.Stat. §§ 873.01 and 63.212. Petitioner makes a feeble effort to distinguish the latter example, stating that "we are merely talking about assets of an estate, not fundamental constitutional rights or liberty interests."

Yet the Fourteenth Amendment to the Constitution provides that no state shall "deprive any person of life, liberty, or property, without due process of law." United States Const., 14th Amend, §1. Petitioner seems to believe that the framers of the Constitution somehow intended to provide less protection for property rights than they did for liberty interests. This may be Petitioner's personal preference, but it is not supported by the text of the Constitution.)

The dictate of these cases is clear: this Court shall not second guess the collective decision of the citizens of Florida to prohibit the sale or purchase of sexual services. So long as any reasonable basis for this prohibition can be advanced or even hypothesized, the law must be declared valid. In summary, the Court holds that: (1) there is no constitutionally protected right to engage in prostitution; and (2) even assuming that the fundamental right of privacy includes consensual heterosexual sexual relations between adults, Petitioner has failed to show that Chapter 796 of the Florida Statutes interferes with that right.

Petitioner has raised both a due process and equal protection challenge to Florida Statutes Chapter 796. The latter challenge is based upon the fact that Fla.Stat. §796.07(1)(a) excludes married couples from its reach. Petitioner also seems to argue that the entire statutory scheme impermissibly discriminates against women. Having already determined that no fundamental right is denied by Chapter 796, the Court must determine whether Petitioner is a member of a suspect class, or otherwise entitled to a heightened degree of review under the equal protection clause. If she is not, the Court will evaluate both Petitioner's Due Process and Equal Protection claims under the rational basis test. On its face, Chapter 796 applies equally to males and females, and is not facially discriminatory. Thus, in order to prevail on her claim, Petitioner must show that the statute is applied in a discriminatory manner. Additionally, Petitioner must prove that any disproportionate application of the law or impermissible classification was intentional.

The intent requirement is not satisfied even if the legislature was aware that the enactment of the challenged statute would result in discrimination. Discriminatory intent requires more than a mere "awareness of consequences." Instead, "'[d]iscriminatory purpose' implies that the decision-maker selected or reaffirmed a particular course of action at least in part 'because of,' not merely 'in spite of,' its adverse effects upon an identifiable group." Even if Petitioner shows that discriminatory intent was one of the State's motivating factors, the State may still "rebut the presumption of unconstitutional action" by showing that the discriminatory purpose did not cause the disparate impact, or by showing that the State would have reached the same result regardless of the discriminatory purpose.

Petitioner has provided no evidence, either in the form of statistics or otherwise, supporting the conclusion that discrimination was a motivating factor behind either the passage or application of Florida Statutes Chapter 796. She has provided voluminous exhibits in an effort to establish that prostitution statutes have a discriminatory impact on women, and are based on outmoded, patriarchal, and chauvinistic beliefs; but she has failed to prove the direct intent to discriminate against women. Because Petitioner has failed to show either the violation of a fundamental right, or the presence of intentional discrimination in this case, the Court must determine whether the challenged statute is rationally related to a legitimate state purpose.

Of course, were Petitioner able to prove that Chapter 796 of the Florida Statutes was enacted merely to discriminate against women—to impose male domination, to demean or degrade women, or to discriminatorily "protect" women in a paternalistic manner, as Petitioner argues—she would be successful in her claim. Petitioner, however, has utterly failed to establish that this is the case, and there are far too many logical explanations behind the passage of that statute to take her assertions seriously.

Petitioner claims that Chapter 769 violates the equal protection clause by treating married and unmarried couples unequally. The Florida Legislature, however, is free to treat dissimilarly situated people differently. As stated by the Supreme Court:

> Evils in the same field may be of different dimensions and proportions, requiring different remedies. Or so the legislature may think. Or the reform may take one step at a time, addressing itself to the phase of the problem which seems most acute to the legislative mind. The legislature may select one phase of one field and apply a remedy there, neglecting the others.

Williamson v. Lee Optical of Oklahoma Inc., 348 U.S. at 489.

Under the rational basis test, the Court will only overturn a statute when "the varying treatment of different persons is so unrelated to the achievement of any combination of legitimate purposes that [the Court] can only conclude that the legislature's actions were irrational." Additionally, "the burden is not upon the state to establish the rationality of its restriction, but is upon the challenger to show that the restriction is wholly arbitrary." Finally, "[a] classification having some reasonable basis does not offend [the Equal Protection Clause] merely because it is not made with mathematical nicety or because in practice it results in some inequality." Instead, "if any state of facts reasonably can be conceived that would sustain it, the existence of that state of facts at the time the law was enacted must be assumed."

Applying this standard, the Court finds that the challenged statute is rationally related to a number of legitimate governmental interests. First, Respondent has a particularly strong interest in protecting the sanctity and strength of family and marital relationships. The Constitution "protects the sanctity of the family [and marriage] precisely because institution of the family is deeply rooted in this Nation's history and tradition." *Moore v. City of East Cleveland,* 431 U.S. 494, 503 (1977), *quoted in Michael H. v. Gerald D.,* 491 U.S. at 124. This special constitutional protection provides a strong justification for the State's decision to exclude married couples from the effects of the challenged statute. It also justifies the criminal prohibition against prostitution, as most patrons of prostitutes are married men. J. James, J. Withers, M. Haft, S. Theiss & M. Owen, *The Politics of Prostitution at* 49 (2d ed.1977), *cited in* Perry, "Right of Privacy Challenges to Prostitution Statutes," at 469 n. 222. Petitioner herself has admitted that most of her customers were married. It is unquestionable that a spouse's relationship with a prostitute would have a disastrous effect on most marriages, and it is reasonable for the legislature to conclude that such an affair would lead to greater marital strife than mere adultery. Thus, the challenged provisions are reasonably related to the legitimate government purpose of protecting the institutions of marriage and the family.

The state also has a "substantial," if not compelling interest in protecting the morals of its citizens. Such a function lies at the very foundation of the "social contract" underlying all civilized democracies. The Supreme Court has recognized the States' legitimate interest in protecting the "social interest in order and morality," *Roth v. United States,* 354 U.S. 476, 485 (1957), and has supported "the right of the Nation and of the States to maintain a decent society...." *Paris Adult Theatre I v. Slaton,* 413 U.S. at 59–60.

"This Nation's laws are constantly based on notions of morality," *Bowers v. Hardwick,* 478 U.S. at 196; such laws are crucial to a stable and conscientious society. Because every individual's concept of morality may differ, the only legitimate basis for imposing a particular set of mores upon a population is democratic consensus; and the only limitation our Constitution places on this rule of the majority is to insure that such laws are applied to all with an even hand, and that certain fundamental rights are not infringed. Petitioner, however, would have this Court follow a different course by allowing her to impose her mores—which are shared by a diminutive minority—upon the majority. This the Court cannot do, for while our Constitutional system may be "counter-majoritarian" in certain instances, it is not "pro-minoritarian."

It is reasonable to believe that the majority of citizens of the State of Florida condemn the act of prostitution as "immoral and unacceptable," and it is not this Court's place to tell them that they are wrong. While this moral judgment obviously will offend and aggravate a few, including Petitioner, it does not implicate the Fourteenth Amendment. The dictate of the Constitution is clear: "[f]or protection against abuses by legislatures the people must resort to the polls, not to the courts." *Williamson v. Lee Optical of Oklahoma Inc.*, 348 U.S. at 487. Numerous other legitimate interests support the legislation at issue in this case, including: crime prevention; protection of public health and welfare; protection of juveniles; and protection of the character of the State's communities.

Petitioner's arguments stridently attacking the prudence of Florida's prostitution statute simply are insufficient to overcome her burden in this case, and are more suitable for consideration by the Legislature. This Court will not engage in an extensive, probing, analysis into the logic underlying the Legislature's decision to enact the challenged prohibition. Instead, the proper course is to recognize that a state legislature can do whatever it sees fit to do unless it is restrained by some express prohibition in the Constitution of the United States or of the State, and that Courts should be careful not to extend such prohibitions beyond their obvious meaning by reading into them conceptions of public policy that the particular Court may happen to entertain.

In an effort to inject some life into the merits of her argument, Petitioner attempts to metamorphosize the State into some evil spirited Orwellian behemoth bent on the destruction of women's rights. Yet her argument belies a basic misunderstanding of the social contract which forms the basis of our government. In our constitutional system, states do not exist as independent entities unaccountable to those whom they govern. Instead, they are communal bodies, through which their constituent members express their common will. It is the very essence of our democratic republic that citizens can influence and direct the political process by casting ballots. Thus, if any law is "a direct and arrogant slap in the face to all women and men in Florida," it is a slap inflicted by those men and women upon themselves. When citizens become unhappy with their government, it is incumbent upon them to make their will known to their representatives.

Notes and Questions

1. Do you agree that the commercial aspect of prostitution necessarily takes it outside the realm of private conduct that should be held beyond state criminal prosecution? Although the Supreme Court's decision in *Lawrence* disavowed ruling on the issue of commercial sex, what effect would that case have on this decision? For post-*Lawrence* rulings by state courts rejecting federal constitutional attacks on prostitution or related solicitation laws, see *People v. Williams*, 811 N.E.2d 1197 (App.Ct.Ill. 2004) and *State of*

Louisiana v. Thomas, 891 So.2d 1233 (La. 2005). In Thomas, the Lousiana Supreme Court upheld a law under which solicitation for oral sex for compensation would be more severely punished than solicitation for vaginal intercourse, rejecting the idea that *Lawrence* requires a different result because *Lawrence* was not, in its view, an equal protection case. The court held that morality concerns can justify unequal treatment.

2. Some feminist scholars have argued that sex within marriage may itself be a form of prostitution in light of the power dynamics within that social institution. See Catharine MacKinnon, Feminism Unmodified: Discourses on Life and Law (1987). Others have argued that maintaining criminal laws against prostitution serves to oppress poor women who may be forced into prostitution from economic necessity; a regulatory regime could at least extend public concern to protecting their health and safety. *See* Sylvia A. Law, Commercial Sex: Beyond Decriminalization, 73 S. Cal. L. Rev. 523 (March 2000); Kenneth Shuster, On the "Oldest Profession": A Proposal in Favor of Legalized but Regulated Prostitution, 5 U. Fla. J. L. & Pub. Pol'y 1 (1992). It has long been a violation of federal law to transport a person across state lines for purposes of prostitution. Does such a prohibition serve a useful function as part of Congress's power to regulate commerce among the states?

3. In *Cherry v. Koch*, 491 N.Y.S.2d 934 (N.Y. Supreme Ct., Kings County 1985), modified, 514 N.Y.S.2d 30 (N.Y. App. Div., 2nd Dept. 1987), a man who suffered from physical disabilities argued that the only way he could enjoy sexual fulfillment was by hiring prostitutes, and that the state had no rational basis for denying him this opportunity, but the court was unsympathetic. Would Fred Cherry have a stronger argument today in light of *Lawrence v. Texas*?

E. Minors

The following case involves oral sex between 18 year old and 14 year old males, in an institutional setting. The events occurred prior to the Supreme Court's decision in *Lawrence v. Texas*, and the Kansas courts upheld a felony sodomy conviction of the 18 year old, relying on *Bowers v. Hardwick*. Had the younger party been female, the maximum prison term would have been significantly shorter, under a state law that provided shorter prison terms for cases involving teenagers of the opposite sex who were close in age, one over the age of consent and one under. (Such laws are colloquially referred to as "Romeo and Juliet" laws, because the "star-crossed lovers" in the Shakespeare play were teenagers.) The difference in treatment was challenged as violating equal protection. The Supreme Court remanded for reconsideration after deciding Lawrence, and the Kansas Court of Appeals reaffirmed the conviction, as follows:

State v. Limon
83 P.3d 229 (Kan. App. 2004)
review granted, May 25, 2004

GREEN, J.

Matthew Limon, an 18-year-old male adult, and M.A.R., a 14-year-old boy, both resided at a school for the developmentally disabled. M.A.R. told police that Limon had performed one instance of oral sex on him. M.A.R. further told the police that Limon performed oral sex on him until he asked Limon to stop. Limon was later charged with criminal sodomy under K.S.A. 21-3505(a)(2). Limon moved to dismiss the complaint, arguing that he should have been charged with unlawful voluntary sexual relations under K.S.A.2002 Supp. 21-3522. He further argued that because he could not be charged under K.S.A.2002 Supp. 21-3522, as it applied only to heterosexual sex, this statute violated his right to equal protection.... The trial court sentenced Limon to 206 months' imprisonment [taking into account two prior convictions of sexual misbehavior].

It is a basic rule that every reasonable construction must be applied to save a statute from unconstitutionality. "When the constitutionality of a statute is challenged, the statute comes before the court cloaked in a presumption of constitutionality." *State v. Baker,* 711 P.2d 759 (1985), *rev. denied* 238 Kan. 878 (1986) (citing *State ex rel. Schneider v. Liggett,* 576 P.2d 221 [Kans. 1978]). "Before a statute may be stricken down, it must clearly appear the statute violates the Constitution. Moreover, it is the court's duty to uphold the statute under attack, if possible, rather than defeat it, and, if there is any reasonable way to construe the statute as constitutionally valid, that should be done." *Bair v. Peck,* 811 P.2d 1176 (1991).

Limon first contends that because gay teenagers are excluded from the protection of K.S.A.2002 Supp. 21-3522, the statute violates the Equal Protection Clause of the Fourteenth Amendment to the United States Constitution. Although the Equal Protection Clause guarantees equality before the law, *Norvell v. Illinois,* 373 U.S. 420, 423, 10 L.Ed.2d 456, 83 S.Ct. 1366 (1963), it does not require the law to treat all persons exactly alike. *Tigner v. Texas,* 310 U.S. 141, 147, 84 L.Ed. 1124, 60 S.Ct. 879 (1940).

Statutes by necessity are directed to less than universal situations. If this were not so, statutes would be ineffective because they would fail to take into account factual differences. As a result, a mere showing that different persons or classes are treated differently is not sufficient to establish an equal protection violation. Moreover, legislatures are presumed to have acted within their constitutional power in making a classification. Chief Justice Warren, speaking for a unanimous Court in rejecting the claim that the exemptions in a Maryland law violated equal protection, stated: "State legislatures are presumed to have acted within their constitutional power despite the fact that, in practice, their laws result in some inequality. A statutory discrimination will not be set aside if any state of facts reasonably may be conceived to justify it. [Citations omitted.]" *McGowan v. Maryland,* 366 U.S. 420, 425–26 (1961).

Our Supreme Court, in determining the appropriate level of scrutiny to apply in an equal protection claim, stated: "[I]t appears that the legislature's purpose in creating the classification need not be established. The classification must, however, bear a rational relationship to a legitimate objective." *Stephenson v. Sugar Creek Packing,* 250 Kan. 768, 774, 830 P.2d 41 (1992). As a result, the question to be answered is whether the challenged classification has a rational basis. If the answer is yes, our inquiry is over.

Limon relies on the recent United States Supreme Court decision in *Lawrence v. Texas,* 539 U.S. ——, 156 L.Ed.2d 508, in support of his equal protection claim. Nevertheless, *Lawrence* is factually and legally distinguishable from the present case. In explaining that homosexual acts, illegal under Texas law, are protected by the Fourteenth Amendment's Due Process Clause of the United States Constitution, Justice Kennedy stated:

"The case does involve two adults who, with full and mutual consent from each other, engaged in sexual practices common to a homosexual lifestyle. The petitioners are entitled to respect for their private lives. The State cannot demean their existence or control their destiny by making their private sexual conduct a crime. Their right to liberty under the Due Process Clause gives them the full right to engage in their conduct without intervention of the government."

From this language, the major premise that underlies the *Lawrence* holding is clearly apparent: No state may prohibit adults from engaging in private consensual sexual practices common to a homosexual lifestyle. This major premise may be reconstructed to state: All adults may legally engage in private consensual sexual practices common to a homosexual lifestyle.

Reference is made to all adults in the above proposition; children are excluded from the proposition. As a result, all children are excluded from the class that "may legally engage in private consensual sexual practices common to a homosexual lifestyle," and all persons who "may legally engage in private consensual sexual practices common to a homosexual lifestyle" are excluded from the class of children. Moreover, in declaring that the majority's decision did not encompass children, Justice Kennedy stated:

"The present case does not involve minors. It does not involve persons who might be injured or coerced or who are situated in relationships where consent might not easily be refused. It does not involve public conduct or prostitution. It does not involve whether the government must give formal recognition to any relationship that homosexual persons seek to enter."

Because the present case involved a 14-year-old developmentally disabled child, it is factually distinguishable from *Lawrence.*

In addition, the present case is legally distinguishable from *Lawrence.* For example, the *Lawrence* majority overruled *Bowers v. Hardwick,* 478 U.S. 186, which refused to extend to homosexuals the privacy right to be free from the criminalization of homosexual sex. In so doing, the *Lawrence* Court declared that private consensual homosexual acts between adults are protected by the Fourteenth Amendment's Due Process Clause. Nevertheless, as pointed out by the State in its brief, Limon is not asserting a *Lawrence*-like due process challenge. Instead, Limon makes an equal protection challenge to K.S.A.2002 Supp. 21-3522. As a result, the law and facts are distinguishable from *Lawrence.*

Limon was convicted of criminal sodomy under K.S.A. 21-3505(a)(2). This subsection states: "Criminal sodomy is...sodomy with a child who is 14 or more years of age but less than 16 years of age." This subsection prohibits sodomy with a child within the stated age limitations without regard to the age of the offender or to the sex of the participants. As a result, K.S.A. 21-3505(a)(2) is gender neutral. A violation of K.S.A. 21-3505(a)(2) is a severity level 3, person felony. K.S.A. 21-3505(c).

On the other hand, K.S.A.2002 Supp. 21-3522(a)(2) reads:

"(a) Unlawful voluntary sexual relations is engaging in voluntary:...(2) sodomy...with a child who is 14 years of age but less than 16 years of age and the offender is less than 19 years of age and less than four years of age older than the child and child and the offender are the only parties involved *and are members of the opposite sex.*" (Emphasis added.)

In addition to the age restrictions placed on the parties and to the requirement that the parties' age difference be less than 4 years, K.S.A.2002 Supp. 21-3522(a)(2) requires that the sodomy be consensual and that the parties be members of the opposite sex. Unlike K.S.A. 21-3505(a)(2), K.S.A.2002 Supp. 21-3522(a)(2) is gender specific. Under K.S.A.2002 Supp. 21-3522(a)(2), unlawful voluntary sexual relations (involving sodomy) is a severity level 9, person felony. K.S.A.2002 Supp. 21-3522(b)(2).

Limon contends that excluding gay teenagers from the protections of K.S.A.2002 Supp. 21-3522 does not rationally advance any purpose that the statute could be expected to serve. In considering Limon's challenge to the constitutionality of K.S.A.2002 Supp. 21-3522, we are reminded of a statement made by Justice Douglas: "It is no requirement of equal protection that all evils of the same genus be eradicated or none at all." *Railway Express v. New York,* 336 U.S. 106, 110 (1949).

By classifying same-sex persons as ineligible for prosecution under K.S.A.2002 Supp. 21-3522, the Kansas Legislature has made an implicit fact-finding that same-sex sex acts are different from heterosexual sex acts. Generally, sex acts, including sodomy, between a child and an adult are illegal, unless the child is married to the adult when the sex acts occurred. The question we must address is whether the legislature can punish those adults who engage in heterosexual sodomy with a child less severely than those adults who engage in homosexual sodomy with a child. The answer is yes. The legislature could have rationally determined that heterosexual sodomy between a child and an adult could be put in a class by itself and could be dealt with differently than homosexual sodomy between a child and an adult.

The unequal position of children and their dependence, both physically and mentally, make them a proper subject for legislative protection. Our Supreme Court has noted: "The State has a compelling interest in the well-being of its children and particularly in their protection from all forms of cruelty, neglect, degradation, and inhumanity." *State v. Wilson,* 987 P.2d 1060 (1999); see also 42 Am.Jur.2d, Infants § 36 ("It is the policy of the law to look after the interests of infants, who are considered incapable of looking after their own affairs, to protect them from their own folly and improvidence, and to prevent adults from taking advantage of them.").

Protective legislation is permissible even though based on a classification which may seem unreasonable. For example, laws based on a sexual classification are normally considered inherently unreasonable. Sexual classifications, however, have been upheld where their purpose was to protect the morals of women. Shortly after the turn of the 20th century, laws made it illegal to sell liquor to women. See *Cronin v. Adams,* 192 U.S. 108, 114–15 (1904); *Eskridge v. Division of Alcoholic Beverage Control,* 105 A.2d 6 (N.J. 1954); see also *Randles v. State Liquor Control Bd.,* 206 P.2d 1209 (Wash. 1949) (prohibiting the sale of liquor to women except under certain conditions). Likewise, state legislatures have used the same rationale in making it illegal to furnish alcoholic liquor, to sell tobacco products, and to provide pornographic material to a child. As in the case of selling liquor to women, these laws were designed to protect the morals of children. See *Cronin,* 192 U.S. at 115. Such statutes are valid even though they may turn on a classification which is generally considered unreasonable. As a result, a classification that would normally be deemed unreasonable may be allowed when the legislature acts to protect a class and a rational basis exists for the protection of that class.

In enacting K.S.A.2002 Supp. 21-3522, the legislature could have reasonably determined that to prevent the gradual deterioration of the sexual morality approved by a majority of Kansans, it would encourage and preserve the traditional sexual mores of society. Moreover, traditional sexual mores have played a significant role in the sexual development of children. During early adolescence, children are in the process of trying to figure out who they are. A part of that process is learning and developing their sexual identity. As a result, the legislature could well have concluded that homosexual sodomy between children and young adults could disturb the traditional sexual development of children.

Although the record reveals that M.A.R., the victim, had only one same-sex encounter with Limon, Limon labels M.A.R. as either homosexual or bisexual in his brief. Labeling M.A.R. in this way is unfair. For instance, if M.A.R.'s sexual identity was not well defined before his homosexual encounter with Limon, M.A.R. might have become confused about his sexual identity. In this case, M.A.R. was a 14-year-old developmentally disabled minor. Moreover, the record does not show that M.A.R. was either homosexual or bisexual.

Because the penalty for heterosexual sodomy with a child under K.S.A.2002 Supp. 21-3522 is less severe than the penalty for homosexual sodomy with a child under K.S.A. 21-3505(a)(2), K.S.A.2002 Supp. 21-3522 is designed to discourage voluntary sexual behavior between young adults and children which deviates from traditional sexual mores.

Obviously, K.S.A.2002 Supp. 21-3522 contains a classification component: "members of the opposite sex." Nevertheless, the classification is proper because it is rationally related to the purpose of protecting and preserving the traditional sexual mores of society and the historical sexual development of children.

In addition, traditional sexual mores concerning marriage and procreation have been important to the very survival of the human race. In rejecting the statutory right to sterilize a convicted felon, Justice Douglas declared: "Marriage and procreation are fundamental to the very existence and survival of the race." *Skinner v. Oklahoma*, 316 U.S. 535 (1942). Throughout history, governments have extolled the virtues of procreation as a way to furnish new workers, soldiers, and other useful members of society. The survival of society requires a continuous replenishment of its members.

On the other hand, sexual acts between same-sex couples do not lead to procreation on their own. As the State correctly points out in its brief, "protecting and advancing the family has been a legitimate governmental aim" throughout written history. Moreover, the family is commonly recognized as the unit for the procreation and the rearing of children.

Additionally, sexual contact between minors and young adults can lead to unwanted pregnancies. Rearing children is not an overnight occurrence. Parents have a common law, as well as a statutory, duty to furnish support to their minor child. This duty applies equally to parents of a child born out of wedlock. *State ex. rel. Hermesmann v. Seyer*, 847 P.2d 1273 (Kans. 1993). When a child is born from a relationship between a minor and a young adult, the minor is often unable to financially support the newborn child. In many cases, the minor is still a dependent. As a result, the financial burden to support the newborn child properly falls to the young adult. Obviously, the young adult cannot furnish adequate financial support for the newborn child while he or she is incarcerated. The legislature could well have concluded that incarcerating the young adult parent for a long period would be counterproductive to the requirement that a parent has a duty to provide support to his or her minor child. See *State v. Crawford*, 908 P.2d

638 (1995) (holding that defendant's obligation to raise her children along with several other factors justified a downward sentence departure).

On the other hand, same-sex relationships do not generally lead to unwanted pregnancies. As a result, the need to release the same-sex offender from incarceration is absent. Equal protection is satisfied because K.S.A.2002 Supp. 21-3522 is rationally related to the State's legitimate interest in getting a young adult parent involved in providing financial support for the newborn child.

The State has argued that lessening the penalty for heterosexual activity between adults and children as opposed to homosexual activity between adults and children may reduce the spread of sexually transmitted diseases. The legislature could well have considered that same-sex sexual acts between males might increase their risk of contracting certain infectious diseases. Medical literature is replete with articles suggesting that certain health risks are more generally associated with homosexual activity than with heterosexual activity. Accordingly, we determine that K.S.A.2002 Supp. 21-3522(a)(2) is rationally related to the State's legitimate interest in public health.

Next, Limon maintains that his punishment under K.S.A. 21-3505(a)(2) is significantly more severe than the punishment administered to individuals who commit unlawful voluntary heterosexual sex acts under K.S.A.2002 Supp. 21-3522(a)(2). We agree. Nevertheless, "[w]hatever views may be entertained regarding severity of punishment, whether one believes in its efficacy or its futility, [citation omitted,] these are peculiarly questions of legislative policy." *Gore v. United States,* 357 U .S. 386, 393 (1958). Moreover, in stating that the authority to fix or to impose a particular penalty for a crime rests with the legislature, our Supreme Court has declared: "The power to prescribe the penalty to be imposed for the commission of a crime rests exclusively with the legislature, not the courts." *State v. Keeley,* 694 P.2d 422 (Kans. 1985). Because we have previously determined that the line drawn by the Kansas Legislature has a rational basis, K.S.A.2002 Supp. 21-3522(a)(2) does not violate the Equal Protection Clause.

In addition, in a footnote, Limon maintains that his conviction and sentence violate the Eighth Amendment to the United States Constitution by punishing him based on his status as a teenager having a same-sex sexual orientation. In support of his argument, Limon cites *Robinson v. California,* 370 U.S. 660 (1962). Nevertheless, unlike *Robinson,* where the United States Supreme Court struck down a statute that made it an offense for a person to "be addicted to the use of narcotics," same-sex sexual orientation has not been shown to be a condition or illness that would compel a young adult to engage in sodomy with a child. See *Powell v. Texas,* 392 U.S. 514 (1968) (White, J., concurring). In *Powell,* the defendant, a chronic alcoholic, was convicted of being drunk in public. In determining that the statute making public drunkenness an offense did not amount to cruel and unusual punishment, the Court concluded that the offense of public drunkenness consisted not of the condition of being a chronic alcoholic. Instead, the offense consisted of defendant's conduct of being drunk while in public, a situation over which defendant had some control.

Finally, Limon argues that his sentence of 206 months is disproportionate to the crime of criminal sodomy under K.S.A. 21-3505(a)(2). Nevertheless, Limon fails to show that his sentence, due in large part to his prior adjudications for aggravated criminal sodomy, is unconstitutionally disproportionate to the offense of criminal sodomy, a severity level 3 person felony. Violation of K.S .A. 21-3505(a)(2) constitutes a felony of the same severity level as a violation of K.S.A. 21-3504(a)(1) (sexual intercourse with a child of 14 or 15 years of age). See K.S.A. 21-3504(c). To insist that Limon's sentence, based on his two prior adjudications for aggravated criminal sodomy, is cruel and unusual flies in the face of reason. Because Limon's sentence does not come within the ban against cruel and unusual punishment under the Eighth Amendment, Limon's argument fails.

Limon further argues that had he been a female engaging in this illegal activity, the activity would have been covered under K.S.A.2002 Supp. 21-3522. As a result, Limon contends that because K.S.A.2002 Supp. 21-3522 unconstitutionally discriminates on the basis of gender, the statute should be subject to a heightened scrutiny. Limon relies on *Loving v. Virginia*, 388 U.S. 1, (1967), and *McLaughlin v. Florida*, 379 U.S. 184 (1964). Nevertheless, *Loving* and *McLaughlin* do not bear the weight of reliance which Limon places on these cases.

When one contrasts the freedom to marry someone of one's own choosing with the right to engage in homosexual sodomy, a clear distinction is apparent. In *Loving*, the Court pointed out that "[t]here can be no doubt that restricting the freedom to marry solely because of racial classification violates the central meaning of the Equal Protection Clause." 388 U.S. at 12. Later, the *Loving* Court stated that the Virginia miscegenation statutes deprived the Lovings of liberty without due process of law in violation of the Due Process Clause of the Fourteenth Amendment. The *Loving* Court declared that the Virginia law was "designed to maintain White Supremacy." As a result, because the classification in *Loving* was based on race, a strict scrutiny review was applied. *McLaughlin* is also distinguishable from the present case. Like *Loving*, the statute in *McLaughlin* made a classification based on race. As a result, the *McLaughlin* Court determined that "rigid scrutiny" should apply. The classifications in both *Loving* and *McLaughlin* were based on race. Race is one of those characteristics over which an individual has no control. The mere fact of being of a certain race is constitutionally irrelevant. *Edwards v. California*, 314 U.S. 160, 184–85 (1941) (Jackson, J., concurring). As a result, a classification based on race is generally considered to be inherently unreasonable and unjustifiable.

On the other hand, the *Lawrence* Court refused to hold that homosexuality was constitutionally irrelevant and deserving of a strict scrutiny review. Unlike the individuals in *Loving* and *McLaughlin*, who had no control over their race, the offense with which Limon was charged was not based on his sexual orientation or his gender, but was based on his conduct of engaging in sodomy with a child, conduct over which Limon had some control. To say otherwise, we would have to believe that an adult with an irresistible urge to engage in sodomy with a child should not be punished for such behavior. As a result, *Loving* and *McLaughlin* are clearly distinguishable from the present case.

Further, Limon's "had he been a female" argument is flawed. There has been no evidence that limiting the applicability of K.S.A.2002 Supp. 21-3522 to members of the opposite sex was motivated by a gender bias. Although K.S.A.2002 Supp. 21-3522 is gender specific, it creates no discernible difference between the sexes. For instance, K.S.A.2002 Supp. 21-3522 neither disadvantages nor advantages men or women. The statute places both men and women under the same restrictions and similarly excludes them from the statute's applicability when they engage in same-sex sex acts. We determine that the classification embodied in K.S.A.2002 Supp. 21-3522 is not quasi-suspect. As a result, Limon's argument that K.S.A.2002 Supp. 21-3522 discriminates based on gender fails.

Limon maintains that *Romer v. Evans*, 517 U.S. 620 (1996), controls the disposition of his argument that K.S.A.2002 Supp. 21-3522 discriminates against gay teenagers. We disagree. In *Romer*, the United States Supreme Court determined that a Colorado constitutional amendment prohibiting government action designed to protect homosexuals from discrimination violated the Equal Protection Clause. Applying a rational basis standard of review, the Court invalidated the amendment. In invalidating the amendment, the *Romer* Court focused on the apparent animosity toward gay people in enacting the amendment. The Court stated that the amendment drew a classification "for the purpose of disadvantaging the group burdened by the law."

Unlike *Romer*, the instant case deals with two criminal statutes: K.S.A. 21-3505 and K.S.A.2002 Supp. 21-3522. As stated earlier, Limon was charged with criminal sodomy under K.S.A. 21-3505(a)(2). This subsection of the statute does not disadvantage gay teenagers burdened by the law. K.S.A. 21-3505(a)(2) is gender neutral. It prohibits sodomy with a child within the stated age limitations without regard to the age of the offender or to the sex of the participants. Lack of consent is not an element under K.S.A. 21-3505(a)(2). Moreover, if there is no consent, aggravated criminal sodomy can be charged. K.S.A. 21-3506(a)(3).

Kansas, like other states, prohibits sex offenses such as rape, sodomy, indecent liberties with a child, and sexual battery. The severity level of these offenses depends on the sexual act of the defendant and on the age of the victim, not on the status of the offender. As a result, K.S.A. 21-3505(a)(2) is based on the conduct of engaging in sodomy with a child and not based on the offender's sexual orientation or gender. On the other hand, in *Romer*, the challenged legislation concerned the sexual orientation of the class, which is a significant difference between *Romer* and the present case.

Likewise, K.S.A.2002 Supp. 21-3522(a)(2) does not disadvantage gay teenagers burdened by the law. Sodomy with a child is punishable under both K.S.A. 21-3505(a)(2) and K.S.A.2002 Supp. 21-3522(a)(2). Although sodomy is punished harsher under K.S.A. 21-3505(a)(2) than under K.S.A.2002 Supp. 21-3522(a)(2), the legislature may enact laws punishing one class less severely than another class for the same crime. For instance, youthful offenders are not subject to the same penalties as adult offenders. In addition, first-time offenders are not subject to the same length of sentence as mature recidivists.

As discussed earlier, the courts have upheld classifications protecting children based on their physical and mental immaturity. Moreover, many of those classifications have been upheld by the courts based solely on protecting the morals of children. Because we have previously determined that a rational basis exists for placing adult heterosexual sex acts with children in a class by themselves and that these acts may be dealt with differently than adult homosexual sex acts with children, Limon's reliance on *Romer* is misplaced.

As a final point, Limon contends that the language "and are members of the opposite sex" should be eliminated from K.S.A.2002 Supp. 21-3522 so that both same-sex and opposite-sex couples could be sentenced under this statute. Because we have already determined that the statute withstands rational basis review, it is unnecessary to address this issue any further. Nevertheless, we wish to make clear that even if the statute were declared unconstitutional, the proper remedy would be to strike down the entire statute. In addressing the issue of whether a statute can stand after a portion of it has been declared unconstitutional, our Supreme Court has stated:

> "Whether the court may sever an unconstitutional provision from a statute and
> leave the remainder in force and effect depends on the intent of the legislature.
> If from examination of a statute it can be said that the act would have been

passed without the objectional portion and if the statute would operate effectively to carry out the intention of the legislature with such portion stricken, the remainder of the valid law will stand." *State ex rel. Tomasic v. Unified Gov. of Wyandotte Co./Kansas City,* 955 P.2d 1136 (Kans. 1998).

Upon examination of K.S.A.2002 Supp. 21-3522, we cannot say that the statute would have passed without the language "and are members of the opposite sex." The history of the statute, coupled with its clear wording, reveals that the legislature intended to impose this penalty only on young couples of the opposite sex. The striking of the language "and are members of the opposite sex" would alter the statute from gender specific, which clearly was the intent of the legislature, to gender neutral. Moreover, the striking of the previously mentioned language would enlarge the statute beyond its obvious statutory limits or boundaries. As a result, the remedy suggested by Limon would require us to make a statutory revision that would replace the intent of the legislature, which we cannot do.

MALONE, J., concurring: [Malone concurred solely on the basis that the legislature could have had a health reason for treating same-sex conduct differently than opposite-sex conduct.]

PIERRON, J.: Dissenting.

The purpose of the Romeo and Juliet law was apparently to reflect the judgment that consensual sex between males and females of the specified ages should have a less severe punishment than consensual sex between older males (usually) and young females. A violation of K.S.A.2002 Supp. 21-3522(a)(2) (the Romeo and Juliet provision) is a severity level 9 person felony. A violation of K.S.A. 21-3505(a)(2) (criminal sodomy) is a severity level 3 person felony. With no previous criminal record a level 9 crime has a sentencing range of 5 to 7 months with presumptive probation. A level 3 crime has a range of 55 to 61 months with presumptive imprisonment.

Had Limon been of the opposite sex from M.A.R., with his criminal history and crime severity level, his sentence range would have been 13 to 15 months' imprisonment. Since he was the same sex as M.A.R., the sentence range was 206 to 228 months. The court imposed a sentence of 206 months—17 years and 2 months.

Limon does *not* contend there should be no punishment for his acts. This was reemphasized at oral argument by his counsel. It is the great difference in punishment, based on the sex of the participants, that is challenged. This is important to remember because the State and the majority often appear to approach this appeal as if the issue was whether same-sex sexual relations between adults and minors should be decriminalized. As will be seen, this leads to what appear to be inappropriate arguments being put forward in defense of the disparate sentences.

The State presents three threshold arguments: (1) The facts of the instant case are significantly different from those in *Lawrence,* making *Lawrence* inapplicable; (2) the *Lawrence* Court excluded sex with minors from the scope of the ruling; and (3) "[t]his court cannot interfere with the legislative function because that function is left to the legislative branch pursuant to the separation-of-powers doctrine."

The threshold issues raised by the State do not prevent a review of this case in light of the *Lawrence* decision. In applying *Lawrence,* we must apply principles of a decision dealing with consensual acts between adults to our case of consensual acts between a young adult and a minor. Our focus is not on whether the act involved is criminal; due to the age of one of the participants, it is. The issue we must resolve is if it is constitutional that the sentence for the commission of an identical act can be more than 15 times as long because the participants were of the same sex.

We first turn, as did the *Lawrence* Court, to the core holdings in *Planned Parenthood of Southeastern Pa. v. Casey*, 505 U.S. 833 (1992), and *Romer v. Evans*, 517 U.S. 620 (1996). *Casey* appears to have limited applicability as it deals with personal autonomy issues involved in a reproductive freedom context. Our case involves criminal activity with a minor. *Casey*, however, does indicate that matters involving sexual morality are not the exclusive domain of legislatures.

The issues involved in *Romer* are more to the point. There, the Court struck down legislation aimed specifically at homosexuals, which deprived them of rights in the political process. The basis for that decision was the Equal Protection Clause of the Fourteenth Amendment to the United States Constitution. *Romer* appears to stand for the proposition that legislation impacting on sexuality is subject to analysis for constitutionality when it discriminates between different classes or groups of citizens. This is particularly true in a criminal justice context where the stakes can be quite high, even when the penalties may not seem great. In the instant case, where we are talking about many years of incarceration, it is certainly true.

Lawrence, which dealt with a criminal prosecution, was decided on the basis of the Due Process Clauses of the Fifth and Fourteenth Amendments. Justice O'Connor, in her concurrence, also implicated the Equal Protection Clause. The Fourteenth Amendment provides that no state shall "deprive any person of life, liberty, or property, without due process of law; nor deny any person within its jurisdiction the equal protection of the laws." Sections 1 and 2 of the Bill of Rights of the Kansas Constitution provide a state counterpart to the federal provision. "[T]hese two provisions are given much the same effect as the clauses of the Fourteenth Amendment relating to due process and equal protection of the law." *Farley v. Engelken*, 740 P.2d 1058 (Kans. 1987).

The United States Supreme Court applies three levels of scrutiny or review when examining legislative enactments which treat differently classified persons unequally to determine if there is a denial of constitutional due process or equal protection. Classifications involving "suspect" classes or fundamental rights are examined under "strict scrutiny," which shifts the presumption against a statute's usually presumed constitutionality and requires the State to demonstrate that the classification is necessary to serve a compelling state interest. Fundamental rights recognized by the Supreme Court include marriage, contraception, voting, and travel. The suspect classes which the Court has recognized include alienage, race, and ancestry. A less stringent standard is "heightened scrutiny," which applies to "quasi-suspect" classes, such as gender, and requires the classification to substantially further a legitimate legislative purpose. The least stringent test is the "rational basis" test. Under this test the State must only show the statutory classification bears some rational relationship to a valid legislative purpose in order to discriminate. The rational basis test, which was used by the Supreme Court in *Lawrence*, should also be used here. This gives the greatest amount of deference to the legislature.

The legislative judgment on the immorality of homosexuality is argued extensively in the State's brief and the legislators' *amicus* brief as a justification for the widely differing penalties. The applicable arguments in the State's brief are clearly titled: "C. The State Legislates, and Its Legislation is Often Based Upon a Pre-Existing Morality" and "I. It Is Left To The Legislature—And Not This Court—To Legislate Morality." The applicable argument in the legislators' brief is also aptly titled: "The Kansas Legislature, And Not The Judiciary, Is Charged With The Obligation To Make Moral Decisions About What Conduct Should Be Criminalized, And Should Not Be Second Guessed Where Neither A Fundamental Right Nor A Suspect Classification Is Involved."

Of course, morality is often involved in the formation of criminal law. The problem with the State's argument is the implication that morality judgments by the legislature are the only considerations in cases of this kind and that the legislature is the only branch of government with any input as to what can be considered criminal. This is not the law. Simply because a majority of the legislature thinks something is immoral does not mean it can make it criminal and be free from having that decision reviewed by the courts. As noted earlier, the deference of the courts to legislative judgments does not extend to the rare instances where that branch exceeds the limits of the people's constitutional protections. *Lawrence* is only the most recent example of the duty of the courts to protect the constitutional rights of all people and not just those with whose code of morality we fully agree.

The act involved here is criminal. But if the penalty for the act is not the same for all, the difference must be justified on some rational basis. Simple moral disapproval or dislike of a certain group does not satisfy the constitutional requirements which courts must apply. "Our obligation is to define the liberty of all, not to mandate our own moral code." *Casey*, 505 U.S. at 850. "[A] bare...desire to harm a politically unpopular group" is not a valid justification that will meet the requirements to show a legitimate state interest. *United States Dept. of Agriculture v. Moreno*, 413 U.S. 528, 534 (1973). Legislative disapproval of homosexuality alone is not enough to justify any measures the legislature might choose to express its disapproval. Under the rational basis test, there must be a showing that the measures adopted have a rational relationship to a legitimate legislative concern.

In its brief the State contends it has no need of "costly experts," nor has it taken any "heroic steps," such as presenting any arguments from the law's legislative history, to support the rationality of the provision involved. Clearly, there was nothing in the way of expert testimony presented supporting the measure, and the legislative history appears to have nothing in support of the provision at issue. What is presented by the State to establish a rational basis for the law, other than the general moral judgment, are three arguments accurately summarized by their headings: "It is Rational for the State to Value Relationships that May Culminate in Marriage over Relationships that cannot culminate in Marriage"; "It is Rational for the State to Value Human Relationships Less Likely to Spread Disease Pathogens"; and "It is Rational for the State to Value Relationships Leading to Pro-creation."

We must examine the reasons asserted by the State to determine if they provide a rational basis for enacting the discriminatory sentence provision. The State argues that the responses of government to problems of this kind may sometimes seem to be "illogical and unscientific." The State appears to contend that almost any argument presented in support of a legislative enactment must be found to supply a rational basis for the law, even if it appears to be irrational. The State rather overstates the degree of deference that should be and is granted to implied legislative findings. A rational basis must be rational and supported by a reasonable cause and effect relationship to qualify. Otherwise, judicial review would be meaningless. We grant deference, not blind acquiescence, to legislative findings.

Two of the reasons given by the State, those of encouraging marriage and human procreation, are very odd justifications for having much greater criminal penalties for a male performing oral sodomy on a male minor than for a female performing the same act on the same minor. As a matter of legislative policy in Kansas, marriage and procreation between adults and minors are *dis* couraged. Although skillfully defended at oral argument by the State, it is incomprehensible that this law has anything to do with encouraging marriage and procreation between the victim and the assailant, or anyone else, as is apparently claimed by the State and approved by the majority. At least, no connection has been shown.

There is a facial connection between penalizing consensual criminal sexual relations with a minor and concerns about venereal diseases. However, there is no reasonable support presented for much greater criminal punishments for any homosexual acts than for any heterosexual acts.

One must first note the obvious fact that there is no difference in the penalties imposed under the Kansas law based on whether the defendant actually does or does not have a venereal disease. This is a very important omission if the law was truly concerned about venereal disease. Perhaps even more unusual is that under the law a female infected with every venereal disease yet identified, and engaging in acts quite likely to infect or actually infecting a male minor, will receive a much lighter sentence. A disease-free male engaging in sex with another male in a manner not likely to spread disease if it was present will receive a much heavier sentence. Perversely, under the law, a male with a venereal disease who infects and impregnates an underage female will also receive a much lighter sentence. We must also recognize the inapplicability of much of this rationale as it applies to female-with-female sex, which usually has an extremely low potential for spreading venereal disease but receives the higher penalty.

The State and the majority attempt to draw a nexus by pointing to the higher incidence of AIDS among homosexuals than the population in general. However, no attempt is made to draw a connection between punishing any particular individual and the likelihood of that person spreading a disease. Group guilt is not a favored concept in American law. What is the rationality of a law that would punish persons 15 times longer because they may belong to a group that has a higher incidence of AIDS, notwithstanding the fact that there is no evidence the defendant had AIDS or any other disease? This is especially puzzling when, as noted above, a person who actually has AIDS and engages in sex with a minor will receive a much lighter sentence if the defendant is of the opposite sex from the minor.

It is difficult to conclude that any concern over the spread of disease is factually and logically related enough to establish a rational basis for the huge difference in sentences.

As noted earlier, the issue in this appeal is not whether the act is criminal; it is. The issue in this appeal is whether two different people, with the same criminal history, performing the same act, can constitutionally receive vastly different sentences based on the sexes of the parties involved. The majority's attempt to divert attention from the real issue by setting up a straw man argument that has never been made, and has been specifically denied and repudiated by Limon, contributes nothing to a valid analysis of this issue.

The majority also attempts to tie this case in with society's attempts to protect children from being involved in pornography or being provided with alcohol or tobacco. Again, the case is not about the illegality of the acts involved. Society should protect minors from premature sexual activity, which is conceded by Limon. On the other hand, the majority ignores the fact that the very statutes it cites concerning pornography and supplying minors with alcohol or tobacco do not provide penalties 15 times longer depending on whether the defendant was the same sex as the minor. In fact, in the majority's examples, all defendants receive the same penalty regardless of their sex.

Perhaps most unsettling about the majority's attempt to strengthen the State's case is its injection of an unsupported argument not found in the record on appeal, in the brief of the State, or in the *amicus* brief of the 25 legislators, the argument concerning encouraging and protecting "traditional sexual mores of society." What is the basis for this statement?

More confusing is the majority's argument concerning parental responsibility and unwanted pregnancies. The law and its legislative history make no reference to any of this analysis. The legislative testimony about the heterosexual applications of the Romeo and Juliet law made no mention of the desirability of getting the assailant involved in supporting any child who might be conceived. And what has any of this to do, under the facts of this case, with punishing unlawful oral sex, which not only "generally" but *never* causes pregnancies?

The reason none of these arguments seem to fit is that they do not. The purpose of the law is not to accomplish any of the stated aims other than to punish homosexuals more severely than heterosexuals for doing the same admittedly criminal acts. As we stated in the first appeal on this matter, even as we affirmed the lower court, the argument that this statute is not aimed at homosexuals cannot be made with a straight face.

If there is a rational relationship between the stated concerns and the difference in penalties, it has not been demonstrated in the record on appeal or in the briefs of the appellee and the *amicus curiae*. The portion of K.S.A.2002 Supp. 21-3522, the Romeo and Juliet law, which effectively mandates a substantially higher sentence for the same acts, based on whether the defendant is of the same sex as the victim, is a violation of the Due Process Clause of the Fifth and Fourteenth Amendments to the United States Constitution referenced in the *Lawrence* decision.

Assuming the unconstitutional language is stricken, the highest Kansas crime for which Limon can be convicted for the acts which occurred is under K.S.A.2002 Supp. 21-3522. We should reverse and remand to the trial court for resentencing for a conviction under K.S.A.2002 Supp. 21-3522. Striking the entire statute, as suggested by the majority, would not correct the injustice to Limon created by the unconstitutional discrimination. It would also thwart the legislative intent of providing the relief contemplated by the legislature to heterosexual situations, which no one challenges as being inappropriate.

Carved in stone above the pillars in front of the United States Supreme Court building are the words "Equal Justice Under Law." In bronze letters on the north interior wall of the Kansas Judicial Center we read "Within These Walls The Balance Of Justice Weighs Equal." There are reasons why we remind ourselves so graphically of the importance of equal justice. Persons in power and authority have historically been tempted to discriminate against people they do not like or understand. If these personal and political dislikes become law and exceed the bounds of constitutionality, the courts have been given the duty to be the final protectors of our ideal of equality under the law. This blatantly discriminatory sentencing provision does not live up to American standards of equal justice.

Notes and Questions

1. There is a general social consensus that sex between minors and adults is harmful and should be against the law. All parties to *Limon* agreed on this, the only disputed

point being whether gay sex involving minors may be punished by a drastically more harsh sentence than non-gay sex, especially in a case where the participants were relatively close in age. Are you persuaded by the majority's holding that the state has a rational basis for treating Matthew Limon more harshly for having sex with an underaged boy than he would have been treated for having sex with an underage girl? Which of the justifications cited by the court are persuasive?

2. Do you agree with the general social consensus that minors should not be allowed to engage in sexual activity and that there cannot be true consent for a sexual act between a minor and an adult? Age of consent laws, which impose an irrefutable presumption of lack of consent when one party is younger than the uniformly established age of consent and the other is older than that age, are premised on the belief that minors are not capable of giving informed consent to engaging in sex, and that sexual acts involve both physical and emotional risks to the participants. In most jurisdictions, various exceptions to the age of consent laws may cast doubt on some of the beliefs underlying them. In many states, for example, the law imposes lesser criminal sanctions for sex between an adult and a minor if the adult is barely above the age of majority and the minor is only slightly below that age, and may impose minimal or no criminal penalties for apparently consensual acts between two minors. Another fact that may raise questions about the assumptions underlying age of consent laws is that the age varies among the states, from a low of 14 to a high of 18. In the New York metropolitan area, the three contiguous states have ages of consent of 16, 17, and 18, but there is no evidence that the level of maturity of teenagers varies accordingly. In Europe, the trend in recent years has been towards reforming the age of consent downwards to 16, and eliminating differences between the age for men and for women and for gay sex (which in some countries had a higher age of consent than non-gay sex). The alternatives would be either to remove the presumption and allow defendants to prove that the sex was consensual and that the minor was intellectually and emotionally capable of consenting, or to get rid of a uniform age entirely and leave the issue of consent involving minors solely to ad hoc adjudication. Thus far, legislators seem disinclined to take up the issue and depart from the existing regime of a presumption that cannot be rebutted.

3. As a means of detecting incidents of child abuse, the state of Kansas passed a statute requiring licensed professionals such as physicians, nurses, social workers, psychologists, and sexuality educators, to report to the state any incidents involving adolescents under age 16 where the professional had reason to suspect that injurious activity was involved. In an advisory opinion, the state's Attorney General indicated that because it was presumed that sexual activity was harmful to minors, any indication that a person under sixteen had engaged in sexual activity must be reported to the state. Is this interpretation constitutional? See *Aid for Women v. Foulston*, 327 F.Supp.2d 1273 (D. Kans. 2004).

F. Consensual Painful Sex

One genre of sexual activity that has enjoyed little public approbation is sexual activity in which the consensual participants introduce pain as an essential component. Examples are described in detail in the following opinion by England's Law Lords on the question whether such activity should be subject to criminal punishment. In both England and the United States, groups of persons who enjoy participating in such activities have begun to agitate for "reform" of the laws to tolerate "safe" sadomasochistic sexual activity.

Regina v. Brown
1 A.C. 212 (U.K., House of Lords)
1994

LORD TEMPLEMAN

My Lords, the appellants were convicted of assaults occasioning actual bodily harm contrary to section 47 of the Offences against the Person Act 1861. Three of the appellants were also convicted of wounding contrary to section 20 of the Act of 1861. The incidents which led to each conviction occurred in the course of consensual sadomasochistic homosexual encounters. The Court of Appeal upheld the convictions and certified the following point of law of general public importance: "Where A wounds or assaults B occasioning him actual bodily harm in the course of a sado-masochistic encounter, does the prosecution have to prove lack of consent on the part of B before they can establish A's guilt under section 20 or section 47 of the Offences against the Person Act 1861?" In the present case each appellant pleaded guilty when the trial judge ruled that consent of the victim was no defence.

In the present case each of the appellants intentionally inflicted violence upon another (to whom I refer as "the victim") with the consent of the victim and thereby occasioned actual bodily harm or in some cases wounding or grievous bodily harm. Each appellant was therefore guilty of an offence under section 47 or section 20 of the Act of 1861 unless the consent of the victim was effective to prevent the commission of the offence or effective to constitute a defence to the charge.

In some circumstances violence is not punishable under the criminal law. When no actual bodily harm is caused, the consent of the person affected precludes him from complaining. There can be no conviction for the summary offence of common assault if the victim has consented to the assault. Even when violence is intentionally inflicted and results in actual bodily harm, wounding or serious bodily harm, the accused is entitled to be acquitted if the injury was a foreseeable incident of a lawful activity in which the person injured was participating. Surgery involves intentional violence resulting in actual or sometimes serious bodily harm but surgery is a lawful activity. Other activities carried on with consent by or on behalf of the injured person have been accepted as lawful notwithstanding that they involve actual bodily harm or may cause serious bodily harm. Ritual circumcision, tattooing, ear-piercing and violent sports including boxing are lawful activities.

In earlier days some other forms of violence were lawful and when they ceased to be lawful they were tolerated until well into the 19th century. Duelling and fighting were at first lawful and then tolerated provided the protagonists were voluntary participants. But where the results of these activities was the maiming of one of the participants, the defence of consent never availed the aggressor; see *Hawkins' Pleas of the Crown*, 8th ed. (1824), vol. 1, ch. 15. A maim was bodily harm whereby a man was deprived of the use of any member of his body which he needed to use in order to fight, but a bodily injury was not a maim merely because it was a disfigurement. The act of maim was unlawful because the King was deprived of the services of an able-bodied citizen for the defence of the realm. Violence which maimed was unlawful despite consent to the activity which produced the maiming. In these days there is no difference between maiming on the one hand and wounding or causing grievous bodily harm on the other hand except with regard to sentence.

When duelling became unlawful, juries remained unwilling to convict but the judges insisted that persons guilty of causing death or bodily injury should be convicted despite the consent of the victim. Similarly, in the old days, fighting was lawful provided the protagonists consented because it was thought that fighting inculcated bravery and skill and physical fitness. The brutality of knuckle fighting, however, caused the courts to declare that such fights were unlawful even if the protagonists consented. Rightly or wrongly the courts accepted that boxing is a lawful activity.

The appellants and their victims in the present case were engaged in consensual homosexual activities. The attitude of the public towards homosexual practices changed in the second half of this century. Change in public attitudes led to a change in the law. The Wolfenden Report (Report of the Committee on Homosexual Offences and Prostitution (1957) (Cmnd. 247)) declared that the function of the criminal law in relation to homosexual behaviour "is to preserve public order and decency, to protect the citizen from what is offensive or injurious, and to provide sufficient safeguards against exploitation and corruption of others, particularly those who are specially vulnerable because they are young, weak in body or mind, inexperienced, or in a state of special physical, official or economic dependence:" paragraph 13 of chapter 2.

In response to the Wolfenden Report and consistently with its recommendations, Parliament enacted section 1 of the Sexual Offences Act 1967 which provided, inter alia, as follows: "(1) Notwithstanding any statutory or common law provision...a homosexual act in private shall not be an offence provided that the parties consent thereto and have attained the age of 21 years. (2) An act which would otherwise be treated for the purposes of this Act as being done in private shall not be so treated if done — (a) when more than two persons take part or are present;...(6) It is hereby declared that where in any proceedings it is charged that a homosexual act is an offence the prosecutor shall have the burden of proving that the act was done otherwise than in private or otherwise than with the consent of the parties or that any of the parties had not attained the age of 21 years. (7) For the purposes of this section a man shall be treated as doing a homosexual act if, and only if, he commits buggery with another man or commits an act of gross indecency with another man or is a party to the commission by a man of such an act."

The offence of gross indecency was created by section 13 of the Sexual Offences Act 1956 in the following terms: "It is an offence for a man to commit an act of gross indecency with another man, whether in public or private, or to be a party to the commission by a man of an act of gross indecency with another man, or to procure the commission by a man of an act of gross indecency with another man."

By the Act of 1967, Parliament recognised and accepted the practice of homosexuality. Subject to exceptions not here relevant, sexual activities conducted in private between not more than two consenting adults of the same sex or different sexes are now lawful. Homosexual activities performed in circumstances which do not fall within section 1(1) of the Act of 1967 remain unlawful. Subject to the respect for private life embodied in the Act of 1967, Parliament has retained criminal sanctions against the practice, dissemination and encouragement of homosexual activities.

My Lords, the authorities dealing with the intentional infliction of bodily harm do not establish that consent is a defence to a charge under the Act of 1861. They establish that the courts have accepted that consent is a defence to the infliction of bodily harm in the course of some lawful activities. The question is whether the defence should be extended to the infliction of bodily harm in the course of sado-masochistic encounters. The Wolfenden Committee did not make any recommendations about sado-masochism and Parliament did not deal with violence in 1967. The Act of 1967 is of no assistance for present purposes because the present problem was not under consideration.

The question whether the defence of consent should be extended to the consequences of sado-masochistic encounters can only be decided by consideration of policy and public interest. Parliament can call on the advice of doctors, psychiatrists, criminologists, sociologists and other experts and can also sound and take into account public opinion. But the question must at this stage be decided by this House in its judicial capacity in order to determine whether the convictions of the appellants should be upheld or quashed.

Counsel for some of the appellants argued that the defence of consent should be extended to the offence of occasioning actual bodily harm under section 47 of the Act of 1861 but should not be available to charges of serious wounding and the infliction of serious bodily harm under section 20. I do not consider that this solution is practicable. Sado-masochistic participants have no way of foretelling the degree of bodily harm which will result from their encounters. The differences between actual bodily harm and serious bodily harm cannot be satisfactorily applied by a jury in order to determine acquittal or conviction.

Counsel for the appellants argued that consent should provide a defence to charges under both section 20 and section 47 because, it was said, every person has a right to deal with his body as he pleases. I do not consider that this slogan provides a sufficient guide to the policy decision which must now be made. It is an offence for a person to abuse his own body and mind by taking drugs. Although the law is often broken, the criminal law restrains a practice which is regarded as dangerous and injurious to individuals and which if allowed and extended is harmful to society generally. In any event the appellants in this case did not mutilate their own bodies. They inflicted bodily harm on willing victims. Suicide is no longer an offence but a person who assists another to commit suicide is guilty of murder or manslaughter.

The assertion was made on behalf of the appellants that the sexual appetites of sadists and masochists can only be satisfied by the infliction of bodily harm and that the law should not punish the consensual achievement of sexual satisfaction. There was no evidence to support the assertion that sado-masochist activities are essential to the happiness of the appellants or any other participants but the argument would be acceptable if sado-masochism were only concerned with sex, as the appellants contend. In my opinion sado-masochism is not only concerned with sex. Sado-masochism is also concerned with violence. The evidence discloses that the practices of the appellants were unpredictably dangerous and degrading to body and mind and were developed with increasing barbarity and taught to persons whose consents were dubious or worthless.

A sadist draws pleasure from inflicting or watching cruelty. A masochist derives pleasure from his own pain or humiliation. The appellants are middle-aged men. The victims were youths some of whom were introduced to sado-masochism before they attained the age of 21. In his judgment in the Court of Appeal, Lord Lane C.J. said that two members of the group of which the appellants formed part, namely one Cadman and the appellant Laskey: "were responsible in part for the corruption of a youth K.... It is some comfort at least to be told, as we were, that K. has now it seems settled into a normal heterosexual relationship. Cadman had befriended K. when the boy was 15 years old. He met him in a cafeteria and, so he says, found out that the boy was interested in homosexual activities. He introduced and encouraged K. in 'bondage affairs.'

He was interested in viewing and recording on videotape K. and other teenage boys in homosexual scenes…One cannot overlook the danger that the gravity of the assaults and injuries in this type of case may escalate to even more unacceptable heights."

The evidence disclosed that drink and drugs were employed to obtain consent and increase enthusiasm. The victim was usually manacled so that the sadist could enjoy the thrill of power and the victim could enjoy the thrill of helplessness. The victim had no control over the harm which the sadist, also stimulated by drink and drugs might inflict. In one case a victim was branded twice on the thigh and there was some doubt as to whether he consented to or protested against the second branding. The dangers involved in administering violence must have been appreciated by the appellants because, so it was said by their counsel, each victim was given a code word which he could pronounce when excessive harm or pain was caused. The efficiency of this precaution, when taken, depends on the circumstances and on the personalities involved. No one can feel the pain of another. The charges against the appellants were based on genital torture and violence to the buttocks, anus, penis, testicles and nipples. The victims were degraded and humiliated, sometimes beaten, sometimes wounded with instruments and sometimes branded. Bloodletting and the smearing of human blood produced excitement. There were obvious dangers of serious personal injury and blood infection. Prosecuting counsel informed the trial judge against the protests of defence counsel, that although the appellants had not contracted Aids, two members of the group had died from Aids and one other had contracted an H.I.V. infection although not necessarily from the practices of the group. Some activities involved excrement. The assertion that the instruments employed by the sadists were clean and sterilised could not have removed the danger of infection, and the assertion that care was taken demonstrates the possibility of infection. Cruelty to human beings was on occasions supplemented by cruelty to animals in the form of bestiality. It is fortunate that there were no permanent injuries to a victim though no one knows the extent of harm inflicted in other cases. It is not surprising that a victim does not complain to the police when the complaint would involve him in giving details of acts in which he participated. Doctors of course are subject to a code of confidentiality.

In principle there is a difference between violence which is incidental and violence which is inflicted for the indulgence of cruelty. The violence of sado-masochistic encounters involves the indulgence of cruelty by sadists and the degradation of victims. Such violence is injurious to the participants and unpredictably dangerous. I am not prepared to invent a defence of consent for sado-masochistic encounters which breed and glorify cruelty and result in offences under sections 47 and 20 of the Act of 1861.

The appellants' counsel relied on article 8 of the Convention which is in these terms: "1. Everyone has the right to respect for his private and family life, his home and his correspondence. "2. There shall be no interference by a public authority with the exercise of this right except such as is in accordance with the law and is necessary in a democratic society in the interests of natural security, public safety or the economic well-being of the country, for the prevention of disorder or crime, for the protection of health or morals, or for the protection of the rights and freedoms of others."

It is not clear to me that the activities of the appellants were exercises of rights in respect of private and family life. But assuming that the appellants are claiming to exercise those rights I do not consider that article 8 invalidates a law which forbids violence which is intentionally harmful to body and mind.

Society is entitled and bound to protect itself against a cult of violence. Pleasure derived from the infliction of pain is an evil thing. Cruelty is uncivilised. I would answer the certified question in the negative and dismiss the appeals of the appellants against conviction.

LORD JAUNCEY OF TULLICHETTLE

The facts giving rise to the charges came to light as a result of police investigation into other matters. It was common ground that the receivers had neither complained to the police nor suffered any permanent injury as a result of the activities of the appellants. Although the incidents giving rise to each charge were the subject of a video-recording, these recordings were made not for sale at a profit but for the benefit of those members of the "ring," if one may so describe it, who had not had the opportunity of witnessing the events in person. Your Lordships were further informed that the activities of the appellants, who are middle aged men, were conducted in secret and in a highly controlled manner, that code words were used by the receiver when he could no longer bear the pain inflicted upon him and that when fish-hooks were inserted through the penis they were sterilised first. None of the appellants however had any medical qualifications and there was, of course, no referee present such as there would be in a boxing or football match.

The basic argument propounded by all the appellants was that the receivers having in every case consented to what was inflicted upon them no offence had been committed against sections 20 or 47 of the Offences against the Person Act 1861. All the appellants recognised however that so broad a proposition could not stand up and that there must be some limitation upon the harm which an individual could consent to receive at the hand of another. The line between injuries to the infliction of which an individual could consent and injuries to whose infliction he could not consent must be drawn, it was argued, where the public interest required. Thus except in the case of regulated sports the public interest required that injuries should not be inflicted in public where they might give rise to a breach of the peace.

I must say a word about hostility. It was urged upon your Lordships that hostility on the part of the inflicter was an essential ingredient of assault and that this ingredient was necessarily lacking when injury was inflicted with the consent of the receiver. It followed that none of the activities in question constituted assault. The answer to this submission is to be found in the judgment of the Court of Appeal in *Wilson v. Pringle* [1987] Q.B. 237 where it was said, at p. 253, that hostility could not be equated with ill-will or malevolence. The judgment went on to state: "Take the example of the police officer in *Collins v. Wilcock* [1984] 1 W.L.R. 1172. She touched the woman deliberately, but without an intention to do more than restrain her temporarily. Nevertheless, she was acting unlawfully and in that way was acting with hostility." If the appellant's activities in relation to the receivers were unlawful they were also hostile and a necessary ingredient of assault was present.

Be that as it may, in considering the public interest it would be wrong to look only at the activities of the appellants alone, there being no suggestion that they and their associates are the only practitioners of homosexual sado-masochism in England and Wales. This House must therefore consider the possibility that these activities are practised by others and by others who are not so controlled or responsible as the appellants are claimed to be. Without going into details of all the rather curious activities in which the appellants engaged it would appear to be good luck rather than good judgment which has prevented serious injury from occurring. Wounds can easily become septic if not properly treated, the free flow of blood from a person who is H.I.V. positive or who has Aids can infect another and an inflicter who is carried away by sexual excitement or by drink or drugs could very easily inflict pain and injury beyond the level to which the receiver had consented. Your Lordships have no information as to whether such situations have occurred in relation to other sado-masochistic practitioners. It was no doubt these dangers which caused Lady Mallalieu to restrict her propositions in relation to the public interest to the actual rather than the potential result of the activity. In my view such a restriction is quite unjustified. When considering the public interest potential for harm is just as relevant as actual harm. Furthermore, the possibility of proselytisation and corruption of young men is a real danger even in the case of these appellants and the taking of video recordings of such activities suggests that secrecy may not be as strict as the appellants claimed to your Lordships. If the only purpose of the activity is the sexual gratification of one or both of the participants what then is the need of a video recording?

My Lords I have no doubt that it would not be in the public interest that deliberate infliction of actual bodily harm during the course of homosexual sado-masochistic activities should be held to be lawful.

LORD LOWRY

My Lords, I, too, would answer the certified question in the negative and dismiss the appeals. In stating my own further reasons for this view I shall address myself exclusively to the cases in which, as has been informally agreed, one person has acted upon another in private, occasioning him actual bodily harm but nothing worse.

The appellants' main point is that, contrary to the view of the trial judge and the Court of Appeal, the consent of the victim, as I shall call the willing recipient of the sado-masochistic treatment, constitutes a defence to the charges of assault occasioning actual bodily harm contrary to section 47 of the Offences against the Person Act 1861 and of wounding contrary to section 20 of the Act of 1861 (no more than actual bodily harm being occasioned) or, to put it another way, that, when the victim consents, no such offence of assault or wounding as I have described takes place.

Under the law which formerly held sway, consent was a defence to a charge of common assault but not to a charge of mayhem or maiming. Everyone agrees that consent remains a complete defence to a charge of common assault and nearly everyone agrees that consent of the victim is not a defence to a charge of inflicting really serious personal injury (or "grievous bodily harm"). The disagreement concerns offences which occasion actual bodily harm: the appellants contend that the consent of the victim is a defence to one charged with such an offence, while the respondent submits that consent is not a defence. I agree with the respondent's contention for reasons which I now explain.

The Act of 1861 was one of several laudable but untidy Victorian attempts to codify different areas of the law. It follows that the indications to be gathered from the Act of 1861 are not precise. Nevertheless, I consider that it contains fairly clear signs that, with regard to the relevance of the victim's consent as a defence, assault occasioning actual bodily harm and wounding which results in actual bodily harm are not offences "below the line," to be ranked with common assault as offences in connection with which the victim's consent provides a defence, but offences "above the line," to be ranked with inflicting grievous bodily harm and the other more serious offences in connection with which the victim's consent does not provide a defence.

Does the second part of the Court of Criminal Appeal's judgment therefore stand condemned in all respects? My Lords, I suggest not. It clearly indicates the view of the court that assault, occasioning actual bodily harm, is malum in se, an offence for which, absent one of the recognised exceptions, the accused will be convicted, even though the victim consents.

In adopting this conclusion I follow closely my noble and learned friends, Lord Templeman and Lord Jauncey. What the appellants are obliged to propose is that the deliberate and painful infliction of physical injury should be exempted from the operation of statutory provisions the object of which is to prevent or punish that very thing, the reason for the proposed exemption being that both those who will inflict and those who will suffer the injury wish to satisfy a perverted and depraved sexual desire. Sado-masochistic homosexual activity cannot be regarded as conducive to the enhancement or enjoyment of family life or conducive to the welfare of society. A relaxation of the prohibitions in sections 20 and 47 can only encourage the practice of homosexual sado-masochism, with the physical cruelty that it must involve (which can scarcely be regarded as a "manly diversion"), by withdrawing the legal penalty and giving the activity a judicial imprimatur. As well as all this, one cannot overlook the physical danger to those who may indulge in sado-masochism. In this connection, and also generally, it is idle for the appellants to claim that they are educated exponents of "civilised cruelty." A proposed *general* exemption is to be tested by considering the likely *general* effect. This must include the probability that some sado-masochistic activity, under the powerful influence of the sexual instinct, will get out of hand and result in serious physical damage to the participants and that some activity will involve a danger of infection such as these particular exponents do not contemplate for themselves. When considering the danger of infection, with its inevitable threat of Aids, I am not impressed by the argument that this threat can be discounted on the ground that, as long ago as 1967, Parliament, subject to conditions, legalised buggery, now a well known vehicle for the transmission of AIDS.

So far as I can see, the only counter-argument is that to place a restriction on sado-masochism is an unwarranted interference with the private life and activities of persons who are indulging in a lawful pursuit and are doing no harm to anyone except, possibly, themselves. This approach, which has characterised every submission put forward on behalf of the appellants, is derived from the fallacy that what is involved here is the restraint of a lawful activity as opposed to the refusal to relax existing prohibitions in the Act of 1861. If in the course of buggery, as authorised by the Act of 1967, one participant, either with the other participant's consent or not, deliberately causes actual bodily harm to that other, an offence against section 47 has been committed. The Act of 1967 provides no shield. The position is as simple as that, and there is no legal right to cause actual bodily harm in the course of sado-masochistic activity.

As your Lordships have observed, the appellants have sought to fortify their argument by reference to the European Convention on Human Rights. Article 8(1) of the Convention states that everyone has the right to respect for his private and family life, his home and his correspondence. The attempt to rely on this article is another example of the appellants' reversal of the onus of proof of legality, which disregards the effect of sections 20 and 47. I would only say, in the first place, that article 8 is not part of our law. Secondly, there has been no legislation which, being post-Convention and ambiguous, falls to be construed so as to conform with the Convention rather than to contradict it; and thirdly, if one is looking at article 8(2), no public authority can be said to have interfered with a *right* (to indulge in sado-masochism) by enforcing the provisions of the Act of 1861. If, as appears to be the fact, sado-masochistic acts inevitably involve the occasioning of at least actual bodily harm, there cannot be a *right* under our law to indulge in them.

For all these reasons I would answer "No" to the certified question and would dismiss the appeals.

LORD MUSTILL (dissent)

My Lords, this is a case about the criminal law of violence. In my opinion it should be a case about the criminal law of private sexual relations, if about anything at all. Right or wrong, the point is easily made. The speeches already delivered contain summaries of the conduct giving rise to the charges under the Offences against the Person Act 1861 now before the House, together with other charges in respect of which the appellants have been sentenced, and no longer appeal. Fortunately for the reader my Lords have not gone on to describe other aspects of the appellants' behaviour of a similar but more extreme kind which was not the subject of any charge on the indictment. It is sufficient to say that whatever the outsider might feel about the subject matter of the prosecutions—perhaps horror, amazement or incomprehension, perhaps sadness—very few could read even a summary of the other activities without disgust. The House has been spared the video tapes, which must have been horrible. If the criminality of sexual deviation is the true ground of these proceedings, one would have expected that these above all would have been the subject of attack. Yet the picture is quite different.

The conduct of the appellants and of other co-defendants was treated by the prosecuting authorities in three ways. First, there were those acts which fell squarely within the legislation governing sexual offences. These are easily overlooked, because attention has properly been concentrated on the charges which remain in dispute, but for a proper understanding of the case it is essential to keep them in view. Thus, four of the men pleaded guilty either as principals or as aiders and abettors to the charges of keeping a disorderly house. Laskey also pleaded guilty to two counts of publishing an obscene article. The articles in question were video tapes of the activities which formed the subject of some of the counts laid under the Act of 1861.

The pleas of guilty to these counts, which might be regarded as dealing quite comprehensively with those aspects of Laskey's sexual conduct which impinged directly on public order attracted sentences of four years reduced on appeal to eighteen months' imprisonment and three months' imprisonment respectively. Other persons, not before the House, were dealt with in a similar way.

The two remaining categories of conduct comprised private acts. Some were prosecuted and are now before the House. Others, which I have mentioned, were not. If repugnance to general public sentiments of morality and propriety were the test, one would have expected proceedings in respect of the most disgusting conduct to be prosecuted with the greater vigour. Yet the opposite is the case. Why is this so? Obviously because the prosecuting authorities could find no statutory prohibition apt to cover this conduct. Whereas the sexual conduct which underlies the present appeals, although less extreme, could at least arguably be brought within sections 20 and 47 of the Act of 1861 because it involved the breaking of skin and the infliction of more than trifling hurt.

I must confess that this distribution of the charges against the appellants at once sounds a note of warning. It suggests that the involvement of the Act of 1861 was adventitious. This impression is reinforced when one considers the title of the statute under which the appellants are charged, "Offences *against* the Person." Conduct infringing sections 18, 20 and 47 of the Act of 1861 comes before the Crown Courts every day. Typically it involves brutality, aggression and violence, of a kind far removed from the appellants' behaviour which, however worthy of censure, involved no animosity, no aggression, no personal rancour on the part of the person inflicting the hurt towards the recipient and no protest by the recipient. In fact, quite the reverse. Of course we must give effect to the statute if its words capture what the appellants have done, but in deciding whether this is really so it is in my opinion legitimate to assume that the choice of the Offences against the Person Act 1861 as the basis for the relevant counts in the indictment was made only because no other statute was found which could conceivably be brought to bear upon them.

I approach the appeal on the basis that the convictions on charges which seem to me so inapposite cannot be upheld unless the language of the statute or the logic of the decided cases positively so demand. Unfortunately, as the able arguments which we have heard so clearly demonstrate, the language of the statute is opaque, and the cases few and unhelpful.

I must accept that the existing case law does not sustain a step-by-step analysis of the type proposed above. This being so I have considered whether there is some common feature of those cases in which consent has been held ineffectual whose presence or absence will furnish an immediate solution when the court is faced with a new situation. The only touchstone of this kind suggested in argument was the notion of "hostility " without which, as Mr. Kershen maintained, no offence of violence can be made out. This argument, which equates hostility with antagonism, is attractive because antagonism felt by the perpetrator against the recipient, and expressed in terms of violence, is present in the great majority of the offences dealt with by the courts under the Act of 1861. Nevertheless I cannot accept it as a statement of the existing law which leads automatically to a conclusion on the present appeals. It is true that counsel was able to cite a series of cases on indecent conduct with consenting children, in which the absence of hostility formed a ground for holding that indecent assaults were not proved. It is however clear to my mind that whatever precise meaning the word was intended to bear in the judgments there delivered it must have been different from the one for which Mr. Kershen now contends. The facts were far removed from the present, for the accused persons did nothing to the children but merely persuaded them to do certain acts. They used no force, nor inflicted any physical harm. It is not surprising that no assault was made out, and the decisions do no more than furnish a useful reminder of the care to be taken before punishing repugnant sexual conduct under laws aimed at violence. Furthermore this theory does not fit the situations at the upper end of the scale. The doctor who hastens the end of a patient to terminate his agony acts with the best intentions, and quite without hostility to him in any ordinary sense of the word, yet there is no doubt that notwithstanding the patient's consent he is guilty of murder. Nor has it been questioned on the argument of the present appeal that someone who inflicts serious harm, because (for example) he is inspired by a belief in the efficacy of a pseudo-medical treatment, or acts in conformity with some extreme religious tenet, is guilty of an offence notwithstanding that he is inspired only by a desire to do the best he can for the recipient. Hostility cannot, as it seems to me, be a crucial factor which in itself determines guilt or innocence, although its presence or absence may be relevant when the court has to decide as a matter of policy how to react to a new situation.

I thus see no alternative but to adopt a much narrower and more empirical approach, by looking at the situations in which the recipient consents or is deemed to consent to the infliction of violence upon him, to see whether the decided cases teach us how to react to this new challenge. I will take them in turn.

1. Death

With the exception of a few exotic specimens which have never come before the courts, euthanasia is in practice the only situation where the recipient expressly consents to being killed. As the law stands today, consensual killing is murder. Why is this so? Professor Glanville Williams suggests (*Textbook of Criminal Law*, 2nd ed., pp. 579–80) that the arguments in support are transcendental, and I agree. Believer or atheist, the observer grants to the maintenance of human life an overriding imperative, so strong as to outweigh any consent to its termination. Some believers and some atheists now dissent from this view, but the controversy as to the position at common law does not illuminate our present task, which is to interpret a statute which is aimed at non-lethal violence.

Nor is anything gained by study of duelling, an activity in which the recipient did not consent to being killed (quite the reverse) but did consent to running the risk. The 19th century authorities were not too concerned to argue the criminality of the practice as between principals, but to stamp out this social evil by involving in the criminality those others, such as seconds and surgeons, who helped to perpetuate it. A series of 19th century cases, such as *Rex v. Rice* (1803) 3 East 581, reiterated that the dueller who inflicted the fatal wound was guilty of murder, whether he was the challenger or not, and regardless of the fact that the deceased willingly took the risk but by then it was already very old law—certainly as old as *Rex v. Taverner* (1616) 3 Bulstr. 171 where Coke C.J. and Croke J. expounded the heinousness of the offence with copious reference to the ancients and to Holy Scripture. Killing in cold blood was the sin of Cain, and that was that. There is nothing to help us here.

2. Maiming

The act of maiming consisted of "such a hurt of any part of a man's body whereby he is rendered less able, in fighting, either to defend himself or to annoy his adversary." (*Hawkins' Pleas of the Crown*, 8th ed., vol. 1, ch. 15, p. 107). Maiming was a felony at common law. Self-maiming was also a crime, and consent was no defence to maiming by another. Maiming was also, in certain circumstances, a statutory offence under a series of Acts, now repealed, beginning in 1670 with the so-called "Coventry Act (22 & 23 Car. 2, c. 1), " and continuing as part of a more general prohibition of serious offences against the person until an Act of 1803 (43 Geo. 3, c. 58). Then it seems to have disappeared. There is no record of anyone being indicted for maim in modern times, and I doubt whether maiming would have been mentioned in the present case but for the high authority of Sir James Fitzjames Stephen who as late as 1883, in article 206 of the third edition of his *Digest of the Criminal Law*, stated that "Everyone has a right to consent to the infliction upon himself of bodily harm not amounting to a maim." No reported decision or statute was cited in support of this proposition, and the reasoning (according to a footnote) rested upon the assertion that below the level of maiming an injury was no more than an assault, to which consent was a defence.

My Lords, I cannot accept that this antique crime any longer marks a watershed for the interrelation of violence and consent. In the first place the crime is obsolete. The Act of 1861 says nothing about it, as it must have done if Parliament had intended to perpetuate maiming as a special category of offence. Furthermore, the rationale of maiming as a distinct offence is now quite out of date. Apparently the permanent disablement of an adult male was criminal because it cancelled him as a fighting unit in the service of his king. I think it impossible to apply this reasoning to the present case.

Finally, the practical results of holding that maim marks the level at what consent ceases to be relevant seem to me quite unacceptable. The point cannot be better made than in terms of the only illustration given by Stephen J. in article 206 of his work: "It is a maim to strike out a front tooth. It is not a maim to cut off a man's nose." Evidently consent would be a defence in the latter instance, but not in the former. This is not in my view a sound basis for a modern law of violence.

3. Prize-fighting, sparring and boxing

Far removed as it is from the present appeal, I must take a little time over prize-fighting, for it furnishes in *Reg. v. Coney*, 8 Q.B.D 534 one of the very few extended judicial analyses of the relationship between violence and consent. By the early part of the 19th century it was firmly established that prize-fighting was unlawful notwithstanding the consent of the fighters. It nevertheless continued to flourish. It is therefore not surprising to find that the few and meagrely reported early cases at nisi prius were concerned with the efforts of the courts to stamp out the practice by prosecuting those who were thought to encourage it by acting as seconds or promoters, or just by being present. Although it was at that stage taken for granted that the activity was criminal per se, it is significant that in almost all the cases the accused were charged with riot, affray or unlawful assembly, and that emphasis was given to the tendency of prize-fights to attract large and unruly crowds. We encounter the same theme when at a later stage the courts were forced to rationalise the distinction between prize-fighting (unlawful) and sparring between amateurs (lawful). Of these cases much the most important was *Coney*, 8 Q.B.D. 534. Burke and Mitchell fought in a ring of posts and ropes on private land a short distance from a highway. Upwards of one hundred people were present. There was no evidence that the fight was for money or reward.

Two issues arose. First, whether the fighting between Burke and Mitchell was an assault. If it was not, none of the accused were guilty of any offence. Second, whether the direction as to the participation of the other three appellants as aiders and abettors was correct. The court was divided on the second issue. But on the first all the judges were agreed that if the proceedings constituted a prize-fight then Burke and Mitchell were guilty of assault irrespective of the fact that they had agreed to fight.

Even at first sight it is clear that this decision involved something out of the ordinary, for the accused were charged, not with any of the serious offences of violence under the Act of 1861 but with common assault; and as all concerned in the argument of the present appeal have agreed, in common with the judges in *Coney* itself (8 Q.B.D. 534), consent is usually a defence to such a charge. Furthermore it seems that the degree of harm actually inflicted was thought to be immaterial, for no reference was made to it in the case or (except tangentially) in the judgments of the court. What then was the basis for holding that a prize-fight stood outside the ordinary rules of criminal violence? Of the eleven judges only five went further than to say that the law was well established. Their reasons were as follows. (1) Prize-fighting is a breach of the peace. The parties may consent to the infliction of blows as a civil wrong, but cannot prevent a breach of the peace from being criminal; (2) The participants are at risk of suffering ferocity and severe punishment, dreadful injuries and endangerment of life, and are encouraged to take the risk by the presence of spectators. It is against the public interest that these risks should be run, whether voluntarily or not; (3) Fists are dangerous weapons like pistols, and prize-fighting should be proscribed for the same reasons as duelling.

My Lords, there is nothing here to found a general theory of consensual violence. The court simply identifies a number of reasons why as a matter of policy a particular activity of which consent forms an element should found a conviction for an offence where the level of violence falls below what would normally be the critical level. As Stephen J. made clear, the question whether considerations of policy are strong enough to take the case outside the ordinary law depends on whether "the injury is of such nature, or is inflicted under such circumstances, that its infliction is injurious to the public." Precisely the same reliance on an empirical or intuitive reference to public policy in substitution for any theory of consent and violence are seen in discussions of amateur sparring with fists and other sports which involve the deliberate infliction of harm.

Thus, although consent is present in both cases the risks of serious violence and public disorder make prize-fighting something which "the law says shall not be done," whereas the lesser risk of injury, the absence of the public disorder, the improvement of the health and skills of the participants, and the consequent benefit to the public at large combine to place sparring into a different category, which the law says "may be done."

That the court is in such cases making a value-judgment, not dependant upon any general theory of consent is exposed by the failure of any attempt to deduce why professional boxing appears to be immune from prosecution. For money, not recreation or personal improvement, each boxer tries to hurt the opponent more than he is hurt himself, and aims to end the contest prematurely by inflicting a brain injury serious enough to make the opponent unconscious, or temporarily by impairing his central nervous system through a blow to the midriff, or cutting his skin to a degree which would ordinarily be well within the scope of section 20. The boxers display skill, strength and courage, but nobody pretends that they do good to themselves or others. The onlookers derive entertainment, but none of the physical and moral benefits which have been seen as the fruits of engagement in manly sports. I intend no disrespect to the valuable judgment of McInerney J. in *Pallante v. Stadiums Pty. Ltd.* (No. 1) [1976] V.R. 331 when I say that the heroic efforts of that learned judge to arrive at an intellectually satisfying account of the apparent immunity of professional boxing from criminal process have convinced me that the task is impossible. It is in my judgment best to regard this as another special situation which for the time being stands outside the ordinary law of violence because society chooses to tolerate it.

4. *"Contact" sports*

Some sports, such as the various codes of football, have deliberate bodily contact as an essential element. They lie at a mid-point between fighting, where the participant knows that his opponent will try to harm him, and the milder sports where there is at most an acknowledgement that someone may be accidentally hurt. In the contact sports each player knows and by taking part agrees that an opponent may from time to time inflict upon his body (for example by a rugby tackle) what would otherwise be a painful battery. By taking part he also assumes the risk that the deliberate contact may have unintended effects, conceivably of sufficient severity to amount to grievous bodily harm. But he does not agree that this more serious kind of injury may be inflicted deliberately. This simple analysis conceals a number of difficult problems, which are discussed in a series of Canadian decisions on the subject of ice hockey, a sport in which an ethos of physical contact is deeply entrenched. The courts appear to have started with the proposition that some level of violence is lawful if the recipient agrees to it, and have dealt with the question of excessive violence by enquiring whether the recipient could really have tacitly accepted a risk of violence at the level which actually occurred. These deci-

sions do not help us in the present appeal, where the consent of the recipients was express, and where it is known that they gladly agreed, not simply to some degree of harm
but to everything that was done. What we need to know is whether, notwithstanding
the recipient's implied consent, there comes a point at which it is too severe for the law
to tolerate. Whilst common sense suggests that this must be so, and that the law will not
license brutality under the name of sport, one of the very few reported indications of
the point at which tolerable harm becomes intolerable violence is in the direction to the
jury given by Bramwell L.J. in *Reg. v. Bradshaw*, 14 Cox C.C. 83 that the act (in this case
a charge at football) would be unlawful if intended to cause "serious hurt." This accords
with my own instinct, but I must recognise that a direction at nisi prius, even by a great
judge, cannot be given the same weight as a judgment on appeal, consequent upon full
argument and reflection.

5. Surgery

Many of the acts done by surgeons would be very serious crimes if done by anyone
else, and yet the surgeons incur no liability. Actual consent, or the substitute for consent
deemed by the law to exist where an emergency creates a need for action, is an essential
element in this immunity; but it cannot be a direct explanation for it, since much of the
bodily invasion involved in surgery lies well above any point at which consent could
even arguably be regarded as furnishing a defence. Why is this so? The answer must in
my opinion be that proper medical treatment, for which actual or deemed consent is a
prerequisite, is in a category of its own.

6. Lawful correction

It is probably still the position at common law, as distinct from statute, that a parent
or someone to whom the parent has delegated authority may inflict physical hurt on his
or her child, provided that it does not go too far and is for the purpose of correction
and not the gratification of passion or rage. These cases have nothing to do with consent, and are useful only as another demonstration that specially exempt situations can
exist and that they can involve an upper limit of tolerable harm.

7. Dangerous pastimes; bravado; mortification

For the sake of completeness I should mention that the list of situations in which one
person may agree to the infliction of harm, or to the risk of infliction of harm, by another includes dangerous pastimes, bravado (as where a boastful man challenges another to try to hurt him with a blow) and religious mortification. These examples have
little in common with one another and even less with the present case. They do not appear to be discussed in the authorities although dangerous pastimes are briefly mentioned and I see no advantage in exploring them here.

8. Rough horseplay

The law recognises that community life (and particularly male community life), such
as exists in the school playground, in the barrack-room and on the factory floor, may
involve a mutual risk of deliberate physical contact in which a particular recipient may
come off worst, and that the criminal law cannot be too tender about the susceptibilities
of those involved. I think it hopeless to attempt any explanation in terms of consent.
Once again it appears to me that as a matter of policy the courts have decided that the
criminal law does not concern itself with these activities, provided that they do not go
too far. It also seems plain that as the general social appreciation of what is tolerable and

of the proper role of the state in regulating the lives of individuals changes with the passage of time, so we shall expect to find that the assumptions of the criminal justice system about what types of conduct are properly excluded from its scope, and about what is meant by going "too far," will not remain constant.

9. Prostitution

Prostitution may well be the commonest occasion for the voluntary acceptance of the certainty, as distinct from the risk, of bodily harm. It is very different from the present case. There is no pretence of mutual affection. The prostitute, as beater or beaten, does it for money. The dearth of reported decisions on the application of the Act of 1861 clearly shows how the prosecuting authorities have (rightly in my view) tended to deal with such cases, if at all, as offences against public order.

10. Fighting

I doubt whether it is possible to give a complete list of the situations where it is conceivable that one person will consent to the infliction of physical hurt by another, but apart from those already mentioned only one seems worth considering; namely, what one may call "ordinary" fighting.

I am very willing to recognise that the public interest may sometimes operate in one direction and sometimes in the other. But even if it be correct that fighting in private to settle a quarrel is so much against the public interest as to make it automatically criminal even if the fighter is charged only with assault (a proposition which I would wish to examine more closely should the occasion arise), I cannot accept that the infliction of bodily harm, and especially the private infliction of it, is invariably criminal absent some special factor which decrees otherwise. I prefer to address each individual category of consensual violence in the light of the situation as a whole. Sometimes the element of consent will make no difference and sometimes it will make all the difference. Circumstances must alter cases.

For these reasons I consider that the House is free, as the Court of Appeal in the present case was not, to consider entirely afresh whether the public interest demands the interpretation of the Act of 1861 in such a way as to render criminal under section 47 the acts done by the appellants.

Public policy

The purpose of this long discussion has been to suggest that the decks are clear for the House to tackle completely anew the question whether the public interest requires section 47 of the Act of 1861 to be interpreted as penalising an infliction of harm which is at the level of actual bodily harm, but not grievous bodily harm; which is inflicted in private (by which I mean that it is exposed to the view only of those who have chosen to view it); which takes place not only with the consent of the recipient but with his willing and glad co-operation; which is inflicted for the gratification of sexual desire, and not in a spirit of animosity or rage; and which is not engaged in for profit.

My Lords, I have stated the issue in these terms to stress two considerations of cardinal importance. Lawyers will need no reminding of the first, but since this prosecution has been widely noticed it must be emphasised that the issue before the House is not whether the appellants' conduct is morally right, but whether it is properly charged under the Act of 1861. When proposing that the conduct is not rightly so charged I do not invite your Lordships' House to endorse it as morally acceptable. Nor do I pronounce in favour of a libertarian doctrine specifically related to sexual matters. Nor in the least do I suggest that ethical pronouncements are meaningless, that there is no difference between right and wrong, that sadism is praiseworthy, or that new opinions on sexual morality are necessarily superior to the old, or anything else of the same kind. What I do say is that these are questions of private morality; that the standards by which they fall to be judged are not those of the criminal law; and that if these standards are to be upheld the individual must enforce them upon himself according to his own moral standards, or have them enforced against him by moral pressures exerted by whatever religious or other community to whose ethical ideals he responds. The point from which I invite your Lordships to depart is simply this, that the state should interfere with the rights of an individual to live his or her life as he or she may choose no more than is necessary to ensure a proper balance between the special interests of the individual and the general interests of the individuals who together comprise the populace at large. Thus, whilst acknowledging that very many people, if asked whether the appellants' conduct was wrong, would reply "Yes, repulsively wrong," I would at the same time assert that this does not in itself mean that the prosecution of the appellants under sections 20 and 47 of the Offences against the Person Act 1861 is well founded.

This point leads directly to the second. As I have ventured to formulate the crucial question, it asks whether there is good reason to impress upon section 47 an interpretation which penalises the relevant level of harm irrespective of consent, i.e., to recognise sado-masochistic activities as falling into a special category of acts, such as duelling and prize-fighting, which "the law says shall not be done." This is very important, for if the question were differently stated it might well yield a different answer. In particular, if it were to be held that as a matter of law all infliction of bodily harm above the level of common assault is incapable of being legitimated by consent, except in special circumstances, then we would have to consider whether the public interest required the recognition of private sexual activities as being in a specially exempt category. This would be an altogether more difficult question and one which I would not be prepared to answer in favour of the appellants, not because I do not have my own opinions upon it but because I regard the task as one which the courts are not suited to perform, and which should be carried out, if at all, by Parliament after a thorough review of all the medical, social, moral and political issues, such as was performed by the Wolfenden Committee. Thus, if I had begun from the same point of departure as my noble and learned friend, Lord Jauncey of Tullichettle, I would have arrived at a similar conclusion; but differing from him on the present state of the law, I venture to differ.

Let it be assumed however that we should embark upon this question. I ask myself, not whether as a result of the decision in this appeal, activities such as those of the appellants should *cease* to be criminal, but rather whether the Act of 1861 (a statute which I venture to repeat once again was clearly intended to penalise conduct of a quite different nature) should in this new situation be interpreted so as to *make* it criminal. Why should this step be taken? Leaving aside repugnance and moral objection, both of which are entirely natural but neither of which are in my opinion grounds upon which the court could properly create a new crime, I can visualise only the following reasons.

(1) Some of the practices obviously created a risk of genito-urinary infection, and others of septicaemia. These might indeed have been grave in former times, but the risk of serious harm must surely have been greatly reduced by modern medical science.

(2) The possibility that matters might get out of hand, with grave results. It has been acknowledged throughout the present proceedings that the appellants' activities were performed as a pre-arranged ritual, which at the same time enhanced their excitement and minimised the risk that the infliction of injury would go too far. Of course things might go wrong and really serious injury or death might ensue. If this happened, those responsible would be punished according to the ordinary law, in the same way as those who kill or injure in the course of more ordinary sexual activities are regularly punished. But to penalise the appellants' conduct even if the extreme consequences do not ensue, just because they might have done so would require an assessment of the degree of risk, and the balancing of this risk against the interests of individual freedom. Such a balancing is in my opinion for Parliament, not the courts; and even if your Lordships' House were to embark upon it the attempt must in my opinion fail at the outset for there is no evidence at all of the seriousness of the hazards to which sado-masochistic conduct of this kind gives rise. This is not surprising, since the impressive argument of Mr. Purnell for the respondents did not seek to persuade your Lordships' to bring the matter within the Act of 1861 on the ground of special risks, but rather to establish that the appellants are liable *under the general law* because the level of harm exceeded the critical level marking off criminal from non-criminal consensual violence which he invited your Lordships to endorse.

(3) I would give the same answer to the suggestion that these activities involved a risk of accelerating the spread of auto-immune deficiency syndrome, and that they should be brought within the Act of 1861 in the interests of public health. The consequence would be strange, since what is currently the principal cause for the transmission of this scourge, namely consenting buggery between males, is now legal. Nevertheless, I would have been compelled to give this proposition the most anxious consideration if there had been any evidence to support it. But there is none, since the case for the respondent was advanced on an entirely different ground.

(4) There remains an argument to which I have given much greater weight. As the evidence in the present case has shown, there is a risk that strangers (and especially young strangers) may be drawn into these activities at an early age and will then become established in them for life. This is indeed a disturbing prospect, but I have come to the conclusion that it is not a sufficient ground for declaring these activities to be criminal under the Act of 1861. The element of the corruption of youth is already catered for by the existing legislation; and if there is a gap in it which needs to be filled the remedy surely lies in the hands of Parliament, not in the application of a statute which is aimed at other forms of wrongdoing. As regards proselytisation for adult sado-masochism the argument appears to me circular. For if the activity is not itself so much against the public interest that it ought to be declared criminal under the Act of 1861 then the risk that others will be induced to join in cannot be a ground for making it criminal.

Leaving aside the logic of this answer, which seems to me impregnable, plain humanity demands that a court addressing the criminality of conduct such as that of the present should recognise and respond to the profound dismay which all members of the community share about the apparent increase of cruel and senseless crimes against the defenceless. Whilst doing so I must repeat for the last time that in the answer which I propose I do not advocate the decriminalisation of conduct which has hitherto been a crime; nor do I rebut a submission that a new crime should be created, penalising this conduct, for Mr. Purnell has rightly not invited the

House to take this course. The only question is whether these consensual private acts are offences against the existing law of violence. To this question I return a negative response.

Accordingly I would allow these appeals and quash such of the convictions as are now before the House.

LORD SLYNN OF HADLEY (dissent)

The determination of the appeal does not depend on bewilderment or revulsion or whether the right approach for the House in the appeal ought to be liberal or otherwise. The sole question is whether when a charge of assault is laid under the two sections in question, consent is relevant in the sense either that the prosecution must prove a lack of consent on the part of the person to whom the act is done or that the existence of consent by such person constitutes a defence for the person charged.

If, as seems clear on previous authority, it was a general rule of the common law that any physical touching could constitute a battery, there was an exception where the person touched expressly or impliedly consented.

The law has recognised cases where consent, expressed or implied, can be a defence to what would otherwise be an assault and cases where consent cannot be a defence. The former include surgical operations, sports, the chastisement of children, jostling in a crowd, but all subject to a reasonable degree of force being used, tattooing and earpiercing; the latter include death and maiming. None of these situations, in most cases pragmatically accepted, either covers or is analogous to the facts of the present case.

It is, however, suggested that the answer to the question certified flows from the decisions in three cases.

The first is *Reg. v. Coney*, 8 Q.B.D. 534. This is a somewhat remarkable case in that not only the two participants in a prize-fight but a number of observers were convicted of a common assault. The case was said to be relevant to the present question since it was decided that consent was not a defence to common assault. It is, however, accepted in the present appeal that consent can be a defence to common assault. Moreover it is plain from the judgment as a whole that a fight of this kind, since in public, either did, or had a direct tendency to, create a breach of the peace. This emphasis on the risk of a breach of the peace and the great danger to the combatants is to be found in all of the judgments in the case.

The second case is *Rex v. Donovan* [1934] 2 K.B. 498. Here the, appellant, in private for his sexual gratification, caned a girl, who consented and was paid. The appeal was allowed because the question of consent was not left to the jury yet it was said that if the act done was itself unlawful, consent to the act could not be a defence. This, however, was a long way from Coney, upon which the essential passage in the judgment was largely based, where the act was held to be unlawful in all circumstances regardless of consent. In Donovan there was accepted to be an issue for the jury as to whether the prosecution had proved that the girl had not consented and whether the consent was immaterial.

The third case is Attorney-General's Reference (No. 6 of 1980) [1981] Q.B. 715. Here two youths fought following an argument. There was one bystander but no suggestion of public disorder as in Coney. If the judgment had been limited to the fact that the fight took place in public then there would clearly have been a possibility of a breach of the peace being caused; but the court laid down that even consensual fighting in private constitutes an assault on the basis that consent is no defence where "people...try to cause or...cause each other actual bodily harm for no good reason." I am not satisfied that fighting in private is to be treated always and necessarily as so much contrary to the public interest that consent cannot be a defence. In any event I think that the question of consent in regard to a fight needs special consideration. If someone is attacked and fights back he is not to be taken as consenting in any real sense. He fights to defend himself. If two people agree to fight to settle a quarrel the persons fighting may accept the risk of being hurt; they do not consent to serious hurt, on the contrary the whole object of the fight is to avoid being hurt and to hurt the opponent. It seems to me that the notion of "consent" fits ill into the situation where there is a fight. It is also very strange that a fight in private between two youths where one may, at most, get a bloody nose should be unlawful, whereas a boxing match where one heavyweight fighter seeks to knock out his opponent and possibly do him very serious damage should be lawful.

Accordingly I do not consider that any of these three cases is conclusive in resolving the present question.

Three propositions seem to me to be clear.

It is "inherent in the conception of assault and battery that the victim does not consent:" Glanville Williams, "Consent and Public Policy" [1962] Crim.L.R. 74, 75. Secondly, consent must be full and free and must be as to the actual level of force used or pain inflicted. Thirdly, there exist areas where the law disregards the victim's consent even where that consent is freely and fully given. These areas may relate to the person (e.g. a child); they may relate to the place (e.g. in public); they may relate to the nature of the harm done. It is the latter which is in issue in the present case.

I accept that consent cannot be said simply to be a defence to any act which one person does to another. A line has to be drawn as to what can and as to what cannot be the subject of consent. In this regard it is relevant to recall what was said by Stephen J. in *Reg. v. Coney*, 8 Q.B.D. 534, 549. Even though he was referring to the position at common law, his words seem to me to be of relevance to a consideration of the statute in question. "In cases where life and limb are exposed to no serious danger in the common course of things, I think that consent is a defence to a charge of assault, even when considerable force is used, as, for instance, in cases of wrestling, single-stick, sparring with gloves, football, and the like; but in all cases the question whether consent does or does not take from the application of force to another its illegal character, is a question of degree depending upon circumstances."

I do not think a line can simply be drawn between "maiming" and death on the one hand and everything else on the other hand. The rationale for negating consent when maiming occurred has gone. It is, however, possible to draw the line, and the line should be drawn, between really serious injury on the one hand and less serious injuries on the other. I do not accept that it is right to take common assault as the sole category of assaults to which consent can be a defence and to deny that defence in respect of all other injuries. In the first place the range of injuries which can fall within "actual bodily harm" is wide—the description of two beatings in the present case show that one is much more substantial than the other. Further, the same is true of wounding where the test is whether the skin is broken and where it can be more or less serious. I can see no significant reason for refusing consent as a defence for the lesser of these cases of actual bodily harm and wounding.

If a line has to be drawn, as I think it must, to be workable, it cannot be allowed to fluctuate within particular charges and in the interests of legal certainty it has to be accepted that consent can be given to acts which are said to constitute actual bodily harm and wounding. Grievous bodily harm I accept to be different by analogy with and as an extension of the old cases on maiming. Accordingly, I accept that other than for cases of grievous bodily harm or death, consent can be a defence. This in no way means that the acts done are approved of or encouraged. It means no more than that the acts do not constitute an assault within the meaning of these two specific sections of the Offences against the Person Act 1861.

None of the convictions in the present cases have been on the basis that grievous bodily harm was caused. Whether some of the acts done in these cases might have fallen within that category does not seem to me to be relevant for present purposes.

Even if the act done constitutes common assault, actual bodily harm or wounding, it remains to be established that the act was done otherwise than in public and that it was done with full consent. I do not accept the suggested test, as to whether an offence is committed, to be whether there is expense to the state in the form of medical assistance or social security payments. It seems to me better to ask whether the act was done in private or in public: is the public harmed or offended by seeing what is done or is a breach of the peace likely to be provoked? Nor do I consider that "hostility" in the sense of "aggression" is a necessary element to an assault. It is sufficient if what is done is done intentionally and against the will of the person to whom it is done. These features in themselves constitute "hostility."

In the present cases there is no doubt that there was consent; indeed there was more than mere consent. Astonishing though it may seem, the persons involved positively wanted, asked for, the acts to be done to them, acts which it seems from the evidence some of them also did to themselves. All the accused were old enough to know what they were doing. The acts were done in private. Neither the applicants nor anyone else complained as to what was done. The matter came to the attention of the police "coincidentally;" the police were previously unaware that the accused were involved in these practices though some of them had been involved for many years. The acts did not result in any permanent or serious injury or disability or any infection and no medical assistance was required even though there may have been some risk of infection, even injury.

My conclusion is thus that as the law stands, adults can consent to acts done in private which do not result in serious bodily harm, so that such acts do not constitute criminal assaults for the purposes of the Act of 1861.

I agree that in the end it is a matter of policy. It is a matter of policy in an area where social and moral factors are extremely important and where attitudes can change. In my opinion it is a matter of policy for the legislature to decide. If society takes the view that this kind of behaviour, even though sought after and done in private, is either so new or so extensive or so undesirable that it should be brought now for the first time within the criminal law, then it is for the legislature to decide. It is not for the courts in the interests of "paternalism," or in order to protect people from themselves, to introduce, into existing statutory crimes relating to offences *against* the person, concepts which do not properly fit there.

I would therefore answer the question certified on the basis that where a charge is brought in respect of acts done between adults in private under section 20 of the Offences against the Person Act 1861 in respect of wounding and under section 47 in respect of causing actual bodily harm, it must be proved by the prosecution that the person to whom the act was done did not consent to it.

Accordingly I consider that these appeals should be allowed and the convictions set aside.

Notes and Questions

1. The defendants took an appeal to the European Court of Human Rights, which concluded that Article 8 of the European Convention on Human Rights was not violated by their prosecution. See *Laskey v. United Kingdom*, 24 E.H.R.R. 39 (1997).

2. American courts have generally taken the view that consent is not a defense to a prosecution for assault in connection with sadomasochistic activities. See, e.g., *People v. Samuels*, 58 Cal. Rptr. 439 (1967); *Commonwealth v. Appleby*, 402 N.E.2d 1051 (Mass. 1980); *State v. Collier*, 372 N.W.2d 303 (Iowa Ct. App. 1985). But the New York Appellate Division, 1st Dept., has intimated that consent may be a relevant issue to place before the jury, vacating a conviction in *People v. Jovanovic*, 700 N.Y.S.2d 156 (1999), because the trial court rejected the introduction of some evidence going to the issue of consent. Oliver Jovanovic, then a graduate student at Columbia University, met another student, a woman, through an internet chatroom. They exchanged email messages about their mutual interest and experiences with sadomasochistic sex. They had a date, during which Jovanovic tied up the woman and performed some of the acts they had communicated about. She later claimed that she had not consented to everything that he did, and pressed criminal charges against him. He was convicted at trial, but the cited decision vacated the conviction and remanded for retrial.

3. Should consensual sadomasochistic sexual activities, engaged in by adults in private, be subject to criminal prosecution in situations where no serious injuries have been inflicted? How would a court draw the line between a "serious" injury and a "nonserious" injury without statutory guidance? What sorts of cases are likely to come up for prosecution? In the British case, a videotape of the activities in question fell into the hands of police during an investigation totally unrelated to sexual activity, and the prosecution went forward without any of the participants having complained of their treatment. American prosecutions usually involve a victim who denies having consented to some or all of the activities. Certainly, in the absence of consent, normal rules of criminal law should apply. But lines are hard to draw.

4. Consider the prosecution of Roger Van of Wayne, Nebraska. Van, an accomplished sexual sadist, maintained a presence on the Internet in forums devoted to sadomasochistic sex. He was approached through email by a man from Houston, Texas, who was seeking to undergo a highly punitive sadomasochistic experience. Van and the man exchanged about 300 emails over a three month period, thoroughly discussing what would take place. Finally, the man turned up as arranged at Van's house, which featured a basement dungeon. They had a conversation in which the man reiterated his desire to be placed in a permanent slave relationship and punished along the lines of their prior email correspondence. Their agreement included that there was no "safe word" to terminate the activity, and that there were no restrictions on what Van could do. Indeed, the man specifically requested that Van "mark him" as a slave. After one day of punitive treatment, the man reconsidered and asked to be released, but Van, believing this was "in the game," punished him harder and threat-

ened him with death if he tried to escape. Van and his partner placed the man under restraint, subjected him to branding, body shaving, and beatings of varying intensity over a period of nine days until Van's partner, convinced that the man no longer wished to continue the experience, helped him to "escape." The man later testified that when Van discovered that he was trying to summon help using the computer, he was warned that he would be killed if he attempted to escape. Van was prosecuted and convicted on felony charges, and sentenced to a lengthy prison term. The prosecutor argued that consent was irrelevant, and consent by prearrangement was Van's entire defense, since he did not deny any of the allegations about what he actually did to the victim. Should he have been convicted? Since he was sentenced after the Supreme Court decided *Lawrence v. Texas*, would he have a valid constitutional liberty claim as a defense? *State of Nebraska v. Van*, 688 N.W.2d 600 (Nebraska Supreme Ct. 2004).

5. For a thorough analysis of the legal and policy issues, see Monica Pa, Beyond the Pleasure Principle: The Criminalization of Consensual Sadomasochistic Sex, 11 Texas Journal of Women and the Law 51 (Fall 2001).

6. Would it violate the constitution for a state to enact and enforce a law making it a crime to sell or distribute "sex toys,"defined as "any device designed or marketed as useful primarily for the stimulation of human genital organs"? Sex toys are widely used by S/M practitioners, but also by ordinary folks as masturbatory and sexual aids. Could such a statute be challenged on a "privacy" or "autonomy" or "liberty" theory as facially unconstitutional due to the burden that such a prohibition might place on the ability of adults to obtain sex toys for their private, solitary and/or consensual use? *See Williams v. Attorney General*, 378 F.3d 1232 (11th Cir. 2004), cert. denied, 125 S.Ct. S.Ct. 1335 (2005).

G. Adultery

Despite the lack of criminal enforcement, laws against adultery remain on the books in many jurisdictions. Like laws against consensual sodomy, laws against adultery have frequently served ancillary purposes, being cited by employers as grounds for discipline or discharge for immorality, or being invoked in divorce proceedings where fault might be at issue in states that have not embraced no-fault divorce, or where evidence of adultery may be weighed heavily by courts in determining which parent is better qualified to have custody on "morality" grounds.

Public health concerns have also been cited in connection with adultery laws, since a "cheating" spouse might well acquired a sexually-transmitted disease and transmit it to his or her innocent spouse, rather than arouse suspicions by suggesting the use of barrier contraception in a relationship where birth control might not have been an issue previously, either due to voluntary sterilization, menopause, or complete trust by the other spouse in the monogamous relationship. During the AIDS epidemic, the question whether doctors should warn the spouses of their HIV-positive patients generated significant debate among medical ethicists, for example. How do these potential justifications of adultery laws stand up in light of *Lawrence v. Texas*? Is that precedent narrow enough to be essentially irrelevant in considering the continued viability of adultery laws?

Oliverson v. West Valley City
875 F.Supp. 1465 (D. Utah 1995)

BOYCE, J.:

[The court adopted the following opinion by the magistrate to whom the case had been referred for fact-finding and a recommended verdict.]

The plaintiff, Gary Oliverson, a police officer employed by West Valley City, Utah, filed the instant suit against West Valley City and various officials of the City as well as against the Attorney General of the State of Utah and the Director of Utah Peace Officer Standards and Training (P.O.S.T.). Plaintiff challenged the constitutionality of the Utah fornication (Utah Code Ann. § 76-7-104), sodomy (Utah Code Ann. § 76-5-403) and adultery (Utah Code Ann. § 76-7-103) statutes. The plaintiff has now made a motion for partial summary judgment as to the Utah adultery statute.

FACTS

The plaintiff was a West Valley City police officer during times relevant to this action. The plaintiff, while married, had sexual relations with a woman or women not his wife. The relations included sexual intercourse and sodomy. As part of the relief plaintiff seeks, he asks this court to order removal from his employment file all the references to charges, discipline, or suspension that resulted in part from a violation of the Utah adultery statute. Plaintiff has since divorced the woman to whom he was married at the time. Plaintiff alleges the sexual acts were performed in private, were consensual, non-prostitutional or commercial, and heterosexual. The female participant was an unmarried adult. The conduct occurred during non-duty hours. Plaintiff was, as a result of the conduct, suspended for thirty (30) days without pay by West Valley City and the suspension noted in plaintiff's employment file. The West Valley City Civil Service Commission upheld plaintiff's suspension. The plaintiff's P.O.S.T. certificate was revoked for forty (40) days based on a consent order. Plaintiff contends the adverse actions were in part the result of plaintiff's violation of the Utah adultery statute.

CONSTITUTIONALITY OF THE UTAH ADULTERY STATUTE

History

The offense of adultery was not a common law crime, under English law, but it was punished by the ecclesiastical courts which had adjunct authority to the common law courts. 4 William Blackstone, Commentaries 65. It was a crime in the British colonies, where ecclesiastical courts had no jurisdiction, and in the United States. The sexual penetration for adultery is defined the same as in rape. As Honore notes, "In many societies adultery is one of the most serious crimes, and often carries the death penalty." In Hebraic law the Seventh Commandment forbade adultery. Subsequent Hebraic codes also penalized adultery. Leviticus 20:10 stated: "And the man that committeth adultery with another man's wife, even he that committeth adultery with his neighbor's wife, the adulterer and the adulteress shall surely be put to death."

Roman law also severely punished adultery. Code of Justinian, I. IX T.T.XI; Dig. 48. 5.14. See also Annette Lawson, Adultery, 41-42 (1988). Article 118 of the Argentine Penal Code (1963) punished adultery: § 502 of the Austrian Penal Code (1911) punished adultery as a petty misdemeanor. Section 172 of the German Penal Code of 1871

(1961) punished adultery and § 193 of the 1962 German Penal Code (Draft) punished adultery by one year penal custody. At one time Scotland imposed criminal sanctions for adultery. Gordon, Criminal Law, (Scot) 16 (1967). See also § 241, Korean Penal Code, (1960). Section 172 of the Canadian Penal Code imposes criminal sanctions for adulterous conduct that corrupts a child. In England, Australia and other common law countries adulterous conduct may be a basis for a claim of provocation to reduce murder to manslaughter, thereby giving some recognition to the concept that adulterous conduct can provoke an innocent spouse to act with sufficient heat of passion or emotional disturbance for such person to lose control and commit a violent act. In France adultery that causes a homicide is a "crime passionnel" which may result in an acquittal on a homicide charge or a reduced sentence. Rowan, Crime Passionnel, Ch. 4, in Famous European Crimes (1956); Bresler, supra, Ch.17. Adultery is a frequently prosecuted crime in Switzerland, Bresler, supra. at 157.

These employments of the criminal law to punish the practice of adultery support the conclusion that a wide variety of cultures and judicial systems have found adulterous conduct sufficiently injurious to justify some form of sanction and to be conduct which society was not only unwilling to approve but to attach an opprobrious criminal status. The American experience is somewhat different but historically there is even greater support for the criminalization of adulterous behavior. The Laws and Liberties of Massachusetts, 1658 5-6 (Leg. cl. ed.1982) provided punishment of death for forms of adultery. Friedman, Crime and Punishment in American History, 13 (1993) observes that during the colonial period in the United States adultery was a crime "almost everywhere." Virginia law, Statutes of Virginia, Vol. 1 at 433 [Act II of March 1657–58] also punished adultery. Friedman, supra at 40 reflects New Hampshire's adultery statute in 1701 [where] adultery included the sanction that required a person to sit with a hangman's noose around one's neck and to be "severely whipt." In the nineteenth century, criminal statutes against adultery were common. From 1750 to 1796, 4.3% of the criminal indictments were for sexual offenses including adultery.

Using the fact of adultery as the unwritten law to excuse homicide also occurred in the United States. The unwritten law of justifiable homicide was actually written in Texas and in Utah. Friedman notes "In most states, adultery laws were still part of the penal code in 1900." Enforcement of adultery laws was significant in Massachusetts in the early twentieth century.

In 1840 in *Commonwealth v. Elwell*, 2 Met.190 (Mass. 1840) the venerable Chief Justice Shaw, speaking for the court, upheld an indictment for adultery charging both a married woman and an unmarried man. Both could be prosecuted for adultery. Certainly, adultery statutes and prosecutions under such provisions were common in the United States in the eighteenth and nineteenth centuries and at the time of the adopting of the Bill of Rights as well as at the time of the approval of the Fourteenth Amendment. See Hocheimer, Criminal Law, § 239 (2d ed.1904); Clark's Criminal Law, § 125 at 312 (1894); May's Criminal Law, § 195 (2d ed. 1893). There is no historical support for a contention that the framers of the Constitution or its relevant amendments would have intended the Bill of Rights or the Fourteenth Amendment to abrogate state adultery laws.

Since that time, most states have continued to maintain adultery statutes as a part of their criminal law. Prosecutions have decreased but they are still reported in appellate cases and legislatures retain the offense in criminal codes. The statutes vary from jurisdiction to jurisdiction. Adultery is still recognized as a basis to reduce a homicide from murder to manslaughter in many jurisdictions.

The Model Penal Code, American Law Institute Commentaries note on adultery and fornication observes "sexual intercourse out of wedlock is a crime in several American jurisdictions," Commentaries pt. II at 430 (1980), noting that in 18 jurisdictions a single act of sexual intercourse between unmarried persons is punished as a crime. "As of the date, simple adultery constituted a criminal offense in thirty states." The statutes take various forms from state to state. Adultery has been punished as a felony in states other than Utah. Oklahoma punishes the offense by five years imprisonment. Okla. Stat. Ann. tit. 21, 871, 872 1983). The Model Penal Code Council voted to remove any offense of adultery from the MPC, although the Advisory Committee had maintained an offense that would have covered some form of adulterous conduct. The reasons for the action of the MPC Council, Commentaries, at 436–38, are not without justification, however, the reasons are those of legislative choice and not based on constitutional analysis.

Adultery as a Criminal Offense in Utah

Adultery was not a crime in Utah prior to 1887. The reason might be assumed to be that to prosecute adultery would open the door to criminal prosecution of polygamous relationships. This is exactly what occurred when Congress made adultery a crime in Utah by the Edmunds-Tucker Law "Anti Polygamy Acts" of March 3, 1887. The Utah Territorial Legislature did not make adultery a crime until 1892. The Act of March 3, 1887 enacted by Congress (and the identical territorial statute) punished adultery as a felony (three years imprisonment). The man was guilty of adultery if he was married and had intercourse with an unmarried woman or if the man was unmarried and had intercourse with a married woman. The woman was only guilty of adultery if she was married and had a relationship with a man outside of marriage. A woman who was unmarried did not commit the offense of adultery by having intercourse with a married man. The statute was retained in the Utah Criminal Code after statehood. It was re-adopted in subsequent codifications. The offense was characterized as not being a continuing offense, but each act was a separate offense.

A later general codification of Utah criminal law continued the Utah adultery statute in the same form as originally enacted by Congress during the territorial period. However, in 1973 the adultery statute was modified and made a class A misdemeanor. Utah Code Ann. §76-7-103 (1992) now provides: (1). A married person commits adultery when he voluntarily has sexual intercourse with a person other than his spouse. (2). Adultery is a class B misdemeanor. In 1991 the criminal penalty in the adultery statute was reduced from a class A misdemeanor to a Class B misdemeanor. In 1971 the gender differentiation that discriminated against married men was eliminated. Any married person who has sexual intercourse with anyone other than the person's spouse is guilty of adultery.

The history of the enforcement of the Utah adultery law records a number of appellate decisions. It is apparent that in Utah there has been substantial congressional, territorial and state legislative support for the criminalization of adulterous conduct. Although Congressional action against adultery in the Utah Territory was aimed at polygamy, it is also difficult to see how polygamy prohibitions could withstand a constitutional challenge if adulterous conduct were a constitutional right. To declare adultery a constitutional right would therefore be a significant change in constitutional doctrine and could support the right to engage in polygamy.

Privacy Interests

The plaintiff contends the Utah adultery statute violates a privacy interest protected by the Fourteenth Amendment. The defendant refers to *Whalen v. Roe*, 429 U.S. 589,

598–600 (1977), a decision on medical privacy, and contends the constitutional privacy right involves two interests: decision-making autonomy and freedom of disclosure. This general analysis may be correct, but both of these arguments fail in the adultery context. First, in *Whalen*, the decision-making autonomy right was the individual right to privacy with regard to records of certain prescription drugs and the Supreme Court upheld the requirement of a New York law that required providing the state with a copy of prescriptions written for certain drugs. The individual privacy interest did not prevail. The case does not support the plaintiff, but supports the exercise of state police power. In the case of adultery, the decision to engage in the act must involve two persons. There is no individual autonomy. Further, even the right of privacy attendant to the decision to have an abortion is not absolute, but subject in certain contexts to state interests and requirements. The freedom of disclosure is not involved in the act of adultery since the joint nature of the act inherently involves disclosure beyond one person. There is no marital union, no privacy protected by familial interests; indeed the act has for centuries been viewed as totally antithetical to the family. It is a physical sexual act involving two persons not having any obligation to each other. The Utah law does not compel disclosure of anything. It precludes the act in the first instance. The privacy is in conduct like that of deceit or theft and similar to that of conspiracy, not that of a marriage relationship. See Lawson, Adultery, supra, ch. 1, "What is Adultery?" at 35–62. The author suggests a relationship between adultery and theft. It is suggested here that adultery is akin to a conspiratorial act in violation of the family.

In essence the plaintiff's claim of privacy is that the Constitution gives him an unfettered right as a married man to engage in sexual intercourse outside of his marital relationship. The Fourth Amendment clearly protects privacy interests, but only from "unreasonable" intrusion. The Constitution itself does not mention any right of privacy and no general right to privacy exists under the constitution, and must be found implicit in Constitutional provisions. Generally, privacy interests are protected by state tort law. The constitutional analysis of a privacy right is a delicate one. In Schneider, State Interest Analysis in Fourteenth Amendment Privacy Law: An Essay on Constitutionalization of Social Issues, 57 Law & Contemp. Probs. 79, 81 (1988), it is observed, "Constitutional privacy has an artificial meaning most easily understood by looking at the specific rights it has been held to encompass." Most of the privacy right concepts under the Fourteenth Amendment have developed through family and reproductive rights cases. "[T]he right has some extension to marriage, procreation, contraception, family relationship, and child rearing and education." Roe, 410 U.S. at 152–53. See *Griswold v. Connecticut*; *Eisenstadt v. Baird*; *Carey v. Population Serv. Int'l.*; *Planned Parenthood v. Danforth*; *Webster v. Reproductive Health Sery.*; *Planned Parenthood v. Casey*. However, privacy interests have not been extended to matters that only involve a mere subjective interest that is not one that society would consider, objectively, as warranting protection. *Bowers v. Hardwick*; *Katz v. United States*. The right to privacy has been limited to specific areas and matters warranting special protection. Even in areas where privacy is protected, not all aspects of a relationship are free from state intrusion or regulation.

To some extent balancing is essential. Modern life is urbanized and communal and requires restriction of some individual interests in order for all citizens to be able to enjoy a reasonable life. Harmony dictates some limitation on individual interests. An absolute right of privacy would be a form of anarchy. The privacy interest to be protected, therefore, must be significant if not fundamental. Further, the privacy interest must be balanced against public interest.

It would appear the right of privacy as constitutional doctrine is a narrow concept still in the process of doctrinal evolution. In this circuit it has been recognized as a part of the right of familial association. None of the cases from the Tenth Circuit support recognition of a privacy right to an adulterous relationship. The privacy interests protected by the Supreme Court and other federal courts' cases are inapposite to the conduct associated with adultery. In *Potter v. Murray City*, 760 F.2d at 1070, the court rejected polygamy as a protected privacy right and found no authority for such an extension. The court cited to *Paris Adult Theater I v. Slaton*. In that case the Supreme Court said: "Finally, petitioners argue that conduct which directly involves 'consenting adults' only has, for that sole reason, a special claim to constitutional protection. Our Constitution establishes a broad range of conditions on the exercise of power by the States, but for us to say that our Constitution incorporates the proposition that conduct involving consenting adults only is always beyond state regulation is a step we are unable to take."

In a note to the opinion the court cited to many instances where activity between consenting adults was outside of constitutional protection e.g., "bigamy." The court cited to *Caminetti v. United States* (1917), prohibiting transportation of a woman across a state line for "immoral purposes" under the language of the then Mann Act. The Supreme Court has recognized other areas of privacy protected by the Constitution. The right of association in the context of political activities is protected. The Court has also recognized a privacy interest in association in family living circumstances against arbitrary government restrictions.

An examination of these decisions shows no support for a conclusion of a constitutional right in plaintiff to engage in adulterous conduct. The decisions of the Supreme Court and other courts on privacy are narrowly drawn to protect fundamental or historical interests of personal privacy. Extramarital sexual relationships are not within the penumbra of the various constitutional provisions or the articulated privacy interests protected by the Constitution.

… [I]n *Eisenstadt v. Baird*, the defendant challenged his conviction under Massachusetts law for providing a woman with contraceptive foam. At one point the plurality opinion noted the statute had "a dubious relation to the State's criminal prohibition on fornication." The opinion did not suggest the State's fornication statute was unconstitutional and that, therefore, there was a right of access to the contraceptives. The opinion referring to *Griswold* did observe that, "If the right of privacy means anything, it is the right of the individual, married or single, to be free from unwarranted governmental intrusion into matters so fundamentally affecting a person as the decision whether to bear or beget a child." The key here is "unwarranted" intrusion. Some intrusion in this area has been recognized, as later cases have allowed. This language will not support a conclusion that a person has a right to extramarital intercourse under the power to control one's procreation. Such an argument is a non-sequitur. It is the unwarranted governmental intrusion into prevention of pregnancy that the person has a claim to avoid. There is no argument in *Baird* that a person has a right to adultery, but rather the use of contraception cannot be arbitrarily denied. The case does not support the plaintiff's contention of a privacy right for a married person to engage in extramarital sex. Finally, *Baird* does not invoke a due process analysis considering privacy but one of equal protection of the law.

An examination of substantive due process concepts is helpful. When speaking of substantive due process the requirement is of a fundamental right. This involves only personal rights that can be deemed fundamental or implicit in the concept of ordered liberty or deeply rooted in the nation's history and tradition. Applying the above factors a substantive due process claim of a right to adultery must fail. The practice of adultery has never been seen as implicit in the concept of ordered liberty. The same is true of any claim that the "right" is deeply rooted in this nation's history or tradition. The historical development of the criminalization of adultery is directly opposite to any aspect of an historical right.

The claim of the right to commit adultery cannot be considered "fundamental." A similar claim was considered in *Bowers v. Hardwick*. Defendant challenged the Georgia sodomy statute which punished an act of sodomy with another adult male. The Supreme Court upheld the constitutionality of the Georgia statute. The court found that there was no "fundamental right" to engage in homosexual sodomy. The court said the family and reproductive privacy cases did not confer a right of privacy to engage in sodomy. The rights announced in *Carey*, *Griswold*, *Eisenstadt* and *Roe v. Wade* did not bear "any resemblance to the claimed constitutional right" to engage in homosexual sodomy. "Moreover, any claim that these cases nevertheless stand for the proposition that any kind of private sexual conduct between consenting adults is constitutionally insulated from state proscription is unsupportable." The court observed that the proscriptions against such conduct "have ancient roots." The court cautioned that the judiciary "is most vulnerable and comes nearest to illegitimacy when it deals with judge-made constitutional law having little or no cognizable roots in the language or design of the Constitution." The court also rejected a claim for a different result when the act takes place in private. The court concluded the asserted interest was not fundamental and the fact it may be based on notions of morality did not defeat constitutionality. "The law, however, is constantly based on notions of morality, and if all laws representing essentially moral choices are to be invalidated under the Due Process Clause, the courts will be very busy indeed."

Justice Burger, concurring, noted the question of the wisdom of such legislation was for the "legislative authority." Therefore, it cannot be said there is a fundamental right for married persons to have sexual intercourse outside of the marital relationship. The concept of privacy as articulated in the decisions of the Supreme Court does not provide support for plaintiff's argument. This conclusion is also supported by lower state and federal court decisions that have focused more directly on the constitutionality of adultery legislation.

Congress has made adultery a military crime, 10 U.S.C. §§ 133, 134. The offense is frequently presented in military courts. In *United States v. Henderson*, 34 MJ 174 (CMA 1992) the court held consensual heterosexual fellatio that was punished under military law did not violate an accuser's right to privacy. "Adultery is a transgression against the marriage relation which relation the law endeavors to protect." 2 C.J.S. Adultery, § 4 at 610. An adulterous relationship imposes costs on the non-involved spouse. Costs may also be incurred by the errant spouse. Emotional costs may be substantial. It may lead to unwanted children and greater problems of child support. It may also lead to the destruction of a family and even serious violence. A state also has an interest in preventing disease and adultery may be more deterrable than fornication. The adulterer whose liaison produces offspring may not have a protectable interest in the child. Adultery does not guarantee special status towards a child produced from the liaison. See *Michael H. v. Gerald D.*, 491 U.S. 110 (1989). Adultery in the case of many will lead to divorce and breakup of a family unit as a positive social and economic unit and force in society. The results can be tragic and the social costs may impact innocent children and relatives.

Annette Lawson's major work on Adultery shows adultery to have serious and endangering social and psychological consequences. It is not a victimless crime. There can be substantial adverse social costs. The state has an interest in avoiding the deficits and damages of the adulterous affair. The fact that adultery may occur with some frequency is no justification for a constitutional restriction on the criminalization of adultery any more than on embezzlement or numerous other violations of trust which frequently occur. What is perceived as acceptable sexual conduct may be a product of fashion and a temporary social phenomenon and may change from other circumstances just a few years before.

Whether under the circumstances a strict scrutiny or a rational basis standard applies for constitutional review is not material to the resolution of this issue. The State of Utah and the defendants have a compelling state interest in preventing adultery. Law Professor Martha A. Fineman of Columbia University, in "Our Sacred Institution: The Ideal of the Family in American Law and Society," 1993 Utah L.Rev. 387, notes that in regulating intimacy, the norms of the nuclear family have been firmly supported by the law. Professor Fineman notes changes that have taken place, but the "family as a legal, functional, and symbolic institution in America is based" on natural law. It has "tremendous societal value which helps to explain why it alone continues to serve as the only legitimate referent for our political and public discussions about intimacy, sexuality, and morality, as well as defining for us what are appropriate 'family' policies and needed law reforms." Therefore, if this is so, it is appropriate for a state legislature to criminalize adultery in support of legitimate family interests.

Equal Protection

Plaintiff contends the Utah adultery statute violates his right to equal protection of the laws under the Fourteenth Amendment. As noted before, plaintiff has no fundamental right to engage in adulterous conduct. The classification of adultery is not a suspect classification. Therefore, the only question is whether the classification of prohibited conduct under the Utah adultery statute is rationally based. As noted before, there is an interest of the State of Utah in preventing adultery. Whether to use the criminal law to that end is a matter particularly within the legislative judgment as to whether it will accomplish the desired result. Given the special interest of the state, it is rational to classify adultery as a crime. There is no merit to plaintiff's equal protection argument.

Free Speech

The plaintiff contends that the Utah adultery statute infringes on plaintiff's First Amendment right of free expression and that he may challenge the statute as being overbroad. Assuming that adultery does involve some aspect of speech, if so, it is minimal and does not involve "pure speech." Therefore, under *Broadrick v. Oklahoma* the plaintiff may only challenge the statute as it applies to him, that is an act of sexual intercourse of a married man with an unmarried woman not his wife.

Some conduct may involve speech. However, the conduct must be communicative or symbolic. In *United States v. O'Brien*, 391 U.S. 367 (1968), the court refused to find a statute prohibiting the destruction or mutilation of a selective service card to infringe on free speech. The Supreme Court did not accept the position that such conduct was speech simply because the actor intended a message: "We cannot accept the view that an apparently limitless variety of conduct can be labeled 'speech' whenever the person engaging in the conduct intends thereby to express an idea." 391 U.S. at 376. The conduct must be intended to communicate before a speech interest is involved. Thus, an act of wearing an armband is conduct sending a message. *Tinker v. Des Moines Community School District*, 393 U.S. 503, 505–7 (1969). The same is true as to burning a flag as a protest message. *Texas v. Johnson*, 472 U.S. 38 (1982); *United States v. Eichman*, 496 U.S. 310 (1990). There must be a speech aspect to the conduct before it may claim First

Amendment protection. In *Madsen v. Women's Health Center Inc.*, 114 S.Ct. 2516 (1994) the court upheld the use of injunctive relief to control conduct associated with the exercise of speech. This would protect speech but disallow intrusive conduct unnecessary to effective speech.

The Utah adultery statute does not regulate any speech or expression. It prohibits only sexual intercourse. No speech communication between persons is prohibited. No caring caresses, statements of affection or sensual interest, or manifestations of pleasure are prohibited. The plaintiff's indication that the statement "I love you" may be barred is in error. The Utah law does not sanction words but only limits conduct. The plaintiff has offered absolutely no evidence that his sexual escapades were to communicate something. It appears it was simply to satisfy his sexual appetites. Therefore, no speech element is involved in this case. Plaintiff has not shown any speech as part of his conduct, but addresses the issue only hypothetically. As noted in *Broadrick*, plaintiff has no standing to make such a claim. Penetration of the female sexual organ by the male organ is required for the crime, nothing else except the status of the parties is required to make out the offense. That was the act that was involved in this case. The Utah statute on its face reaches no farther. Therefore, plaintiff's First Amendment speech argument is without merit.

Notes and Questions

1. For similar recent decisions, see *Marcum v. McWhorter*, 308 F.3d 635 (6th Cir. 2002); *Mercure v. Van Buren Township*, 81 F. Supp. 2d 814 (E.D. Mich. 2000), *City of Sherman v. Henry*, 928 S.W.2d 464 (Tex. Supreme Ct. 1996), cert. denied, 519 U.S. 1156 (1997). In *Sherman*, the Texas Supreme Court noted that 25 states and the District of Columbia maintained criminal adultery statutes as of 1996.

2. Does the state have any legitimate justification for criminalizing adultery, as that conduct is defined in the above opinion? In *City of Sherman*, the court found adultery to be grounds for discharge from public employment as a police officer, even though Texas had decriminalized adultery, on the ground that it was not constitutionally protected conduct.

3. The state is said to have a strong interest in protecting the institution of marriage as a fundamental unit of society. Does the criminalization of extra-marital sex effectively accomplish this purpose? Should the right of privacy attach to consensual sexual activity between adults where one or both are married to other people? Why or why not? For a consideration of these issues, see Coleman, "Who's Been Sleeping in My Bed? You and Me, and the State Makes Three," 24 Indiana L. Rev. 399 (1991); Note, Constitutional Barriers to Civil and Criminal Restrictions on Pre- and Extramarital Sex, 104 Harv. L. Rev. 1660 (May 1991).

H. Cross-Dressing in Public

The following case considers whether persons identifying themselves as pre-operative transsexuals or transvestites may be subject to criminal prosecution for appearing in public dressed as a member of the opposite biological sex. Although the courts do not speak in terms of the 8th Amendment, many of the considerations in deciding these cases seem similar to arguments made by some of the U.S. Supreme Court justices in *Robinson v. California*, 370 U.S. 660 (1962). *Robinson* involved a prosecution under a California law that made it a crime for anybody to be present in the state of California who was addicted to controlled substances (narcotics). The Court held that it was a violation of the constitutional prohibition of cruel and unusual punishment, found in the 8th Amendment of the Bill of Rights, for a state to impose criminal penalties on somebody for his or her "status" or state-of-being, as opposed to punishment for prohibited conduct. Clearly, the statute was being used to go after people whom the police knew were using narcotics, but who were never "caught in the act." A dissenting opinion contended that implicit in the definition of the crime was the requirement to prove that the individual in question had used illegal drugs in the past, and therefore the punishment was not solely directed at status. In addition, the usual punishment in such cases was to remand the individual to a treatment facility to cure the addiction, rather than to a punitive setting. Of course, there is a significant distinction between the law at issue in Robinson and that in the cases below, since appearing in public as a cross-dresser involves conduct.

To what extent does the guarantee against deprivation of "liberty" without due process of law confer upon individuals a right to appear as they wish to appear without government interference? What rational justification might a state advance for forbidding cross-dressing in public?

City of Chicago v. Wilson
389 N.E.2d 522 (Ill. 1978)

THOMAS J. MORAN, Justice.

Following a bench trial in the circuit court of Cook County, the defendants, Wallace Wilson and Kim Kimberley, were convicted of having violated section 192-8 of the Municipal Code of the city of Chicago (Code), which prohibits a person from wearing clothing of the opposite sex with the intent to conceal his or her sex. Each defendant was fined $100....

Defendants were arrested on February 18, 1974, minutes after they emerged from a restaurant where they had had breakfast. Defendant Wilson was wearing a black knee-length dress, a fur coat, nylon stockings and a black wig. Defendant Kimberley had a bouffant hair style and was wearing a pants suit, high-heeled shoes and cosmetic makeup. Defendants were taken to the police station and were required to pose for pictures in various stages of undress. Both defendants were wearing brassieres and garter belts; both had male genitals. Prior to trial, defendants moved to dismiss the complaint on the grounds that §192-8 was unconstitutional in that it denied them equal protection of the law and infringed upon their freedom of expression and privacy. This motion was denied. At trial, the defendants testified that they were transsexuals, and were, at the time of their arrests, undergoing psychiatric therapy in preparation for a sex reassignment operation. As part of this therapy, both defendants stated, they were required to wear female clothing and to adopt a female life-style. Kimberley stated that he had explained this to the police at the time of his arrest. Both defendants said they had been transsexuals all of their lives and thought of themselves as females.

Section 192-8 of the Code provides: "Any person who shall appear in a public place *
* * in a dress not belonging to his or her sex, with intent to conceal his or her sex, * * *
shall be fined not less than twenty dollars nor more than five hundred dollars for each
offense." Defendants contend that § 192-8 is unconstitutionally vague, overly broad,
and denies them equal protection under the law on account of sex. They argue that the
section is overly broad, both on its face and as applied to them, in that it denies them
freedom of expression protected by the first amendment and personal liberties protected by the ninth and fourteenth amendments of the United States Constitution. The
city asserts that § 192-8 is neither vague nor overly broad and that the section does not
deny defendants equal protection under the law. We find that the above-cited section, as
applied to defendants here, is unconstitutional, and in so doing we do not, therefore,
reach the issues of vagueness and equal protection.

The existence of unspecified constitutionally protected freedoms cannot be doubted.
E. g., *Roe v. Wade* (1973), 410 U.S. 113; *Griswold v. Connecticut* (1965), 381 U.S. 479. In
Kelley v. Johnson (1976), 425 U.S. 238, the Supreme Court was confronted with the
question of whether one's choice of appearance was constitutionally protected from
governmental infringement. At issue was an order promulgated by petitioner, the commissioner of police for Suffolk County, New York, which order established hair-groom-
ing standards for male members of the police force. The court acknowledged that the
due process clause of the fourteenth amendment "affords not only a procedural guarantee against deprivation of 'liberty,' but likewise protects substantive aspects of liberty
against unconstitutional restrictions by the State." The court observed, however, that its
prior cases offered little, if any, guidance on whether the citizenry at large has some sort
of liberty interest in matters of personal appearance. It assumed for purposes of its
opinion that such did exist.

In determining the scope of that interest and the justification that would warrant
its infringement, the court distinguished claims asserted by individuals of a uniformed
police department from claims by the citizenry at large, noting that the distinction
was "highly significant." The court held that, in the context of the case before it, the
burden rested with the respondent police officer to demonstrate that there was no rational connection between the regulation and the police department's legitimate function of promoting safety of persons and property. After analyzing the need for unifor-
mity and discipline within the ranks of the police department, the court concluded
that the challenged order was rationally related to two legitimate objectives: first, "to
make police officers readily recognizable to the members of the public," and second, to
foster the "espirit de corps which such similarity is felt to inculcate within the police
force itself." Mr. Justice Powell, who specially concurred, noted that "(w)hen the State
has an interest in regulating one's personal appearance * * * there must be a weighing
of the degree of infringement of the individual's liberty interest against the need for
the regulation."

This court has long recognized restrictions on the State's power to regulate matters
pertinent to one's choice of a life-style which has not been demonstrated to be harmful to society's health, safety or welfare. E. g., *People v. Fries* (1969) 250 N.E.2d 149
(statute requiring the wearing of a motorcycle helmet held invalid); *City of Chicago v.
Drake Hotel Co.* (1916) 113 N.E. 718 (ordinance prohibiting public dancing in restaurants held invalid); *Town of Cortland v. Larson* (1916) 113 N.E. 51 (ordinance prohibiting the private possession of liquor held invalid); *City of Zion v. Behrens* (1914)
104 N.E. 836 (ordinance prohibiting smoking in public parks and on public streets
held invalid).

In *Haller Sign Works v. Physical Culture Training School* (1911) 94 N.E. 920, a case which involved the regulation of billboards for aesthetic purposes, this court noted: "The citizen has always been supposed to be free to determine the style and architecture of his house, the color of the paint that he puts thereon, the number and character of trees he will plant, the style and quality of the clothes that he and his family will wear, and it has never been thought that the Legislature could invade private rights so far as to prescribe the course to be pursued in these and other like matters, although the highly cultured may find on every street in every town and city many things that are not only open to criticism but shocking to the aesthetic taste."

The notion that the State can regulate one's personal appearance, unconfined by any constitutional strictures whatsoever, is fundamentally inconsistent with "values of privacy, self-identity, autonomy, and personal integrity that * * * the Constitution was designed to protect." *Kelley v. Johnson* (1976), 425 U.S. 238, 251 (Marshall, J., dissenting).

Finding that the Constitution provides an individual some measure of protection with regard to his choice of appearance answers only the initial issue. Resolution of the second issue is more difficult: to determine the circumstances under which the interest can be infringed. It is at this juncture that *Kelley*, and cases subsequent thereto, offer little guidance. With the exception of one Federal decision *Williams v. Kleppe* (1st Cir. 1976), 539 F.2d 803, all of the cases subsequent to *Kelley* have involved regulations set in the context of an organized governmental activity. Such circumstance is distinguished from that in which a regulation, as here, controls the dress of the citizens at large. This distinction, as noted in *Kelley*, is "highly significant."

Even though one's choice of appearance is not considered a "fundamental" right, the State is not relieved from showing some justification for its intrusion. As *Kelley* suggests, the degree of protection to be accorded an individual's choice of appearance is dependent upon the context in which the right is asserted. It is, therefore, incumbent upon the court to analyze both the circumstances under which the right is asserted and the reasons which the State offers for its intrusion.

In this court, the city has asserted four reasons for the total ban against cross-dressing in public: (1) to protect citizens from being misled or defrauded; (2) to aid in the description and detection of criminals; (3) to prevent crimes in washrooms; and (4) to prevent inherently antisocial conduct which is contrary to the accepted norms of our society. The record, however, contains no evidence to support these reasons. If we assume that the ordinance is, in part, directed toward curbing criminal activity, the city has failed to demonstrate any justification for infringing upon the defendants' choice of public dress under the circumstances of this case.

Both defendants testified that they are transsexuals and were, at the time of their arrest, undergoing psychiatric therapy in preparation for a sex-reassignment operation. (For a general discussion of the therapy required prior to sex-reassignment surgery, see Comment, *M. P. v. J. T.*: An Enlightened Perspective on Transsexualism, 6 Cap.U.L.Rev. 403, 407–10 (1977); Note, The Law and Transsexualism: A Faltering Response to a Conceptual Dilemma, 7 Conn.L.Rev. 288, 296 n. 28 (1975); Comment, Transsexualism, Sex Reassignment Surgery and the Law, 56 Cornell L.Rev. 963, 972–74 (1971) (wherein it is noted that cross-dressing is recommended as part of a sex-reassignment preoperative therapy program).) Neither of the defendants was engaged in deviate sexual conduct or any other criminal activity. Absent evidence to the contrary, we cannot assume that individuals who cross-dress for purposes of therapy are prone to commit crimes.

The city's fourth reason (as noted above) for prohibiting the defendants' choice of public dress is apparently directed at protecting the public morals. In its brief, however, the city has not articulated the manner in which the ordinance is designed to protect the public morals. It is presumably believed that cross-dressing in public is offensive to the general public's aesthetic preference. There is no evidence, however, that cross-dressing, when done as a part of a preoperative therapy program or otherwise, is, in and of itself, harmful to society. In this case, the aesthetic preference of society must be balanced against the individual's well-being.

Through the enactment of § 17(1)(d) of the Vital Records Act, which authorizes the issuance of a new certificate of birth following sex-reassignment surgery, the legislature has implicitly recognized the necessity and validity of such surgery. It would be inconsistent to permit sex-reassignment surgery yet, at the same time, impede the necessary therapy in preparation for such surgery. Individuals contemplating such surgery should, in consultation with their doctors, be entitled to pursue the therapy necessary to insure the correctness of their decision.

Inasmuch as the city has offered no evidence to substantiate its reasons for infringing on the defendants' choice of dress under the circumstances of this case, we do not find the ordinance invalid on its face; however, we do find that § 192-8 as applied to the defendants is an unconstitutional infringement of their liberty interest. The judgments of the appellate court and the circuit court are reversed and the cause is remanded to the circuit court with directions to dismiss.

WARD, Chief Justice, dissenting:

The majority states that it does not find the ordinance to be unconstitutional on its face, but it concludes that the ordinance was unconstitutional as applied to these defendants. That conclusion is founded on the premise that the defendants' conduct was part of a psychiatrically prescribed program to prepare them for sex-reassignment surgery. The only testimony in support of the defendants' claim was that of the defendants themselves. No psychiatrist was called to testify that the defendants had been diagnosed as transsexuals or that cross-dressing had been prescribed as preoperative therapy. No letter or statement was offered in evidence. Neither defendant named the psychiatrist from whom he was receiving treatment. Indeed, the defendant Wilson, on cross-examination, testified that he didn't know what sex-reassignment surgery would involve and said he did not know the doctor who would perform it.

The majority ignores a basic consideration that the credibility to be given the defendants' testimony was for the trial judge and proceeds to discuss therapy in preparation for sex-reassignment surgery. That is a subject of sensitivity and importance, but I consider it is not reached here. UNDERWOOD and RYAN, JJ., join in this dissent.

Notes and Questions

1. To similar effect, see *D.C. and M.S. v. City of St. Louis*, 795 F.2d 652 (8th Cir. 1986).

2. Do cases involving criminal penalties for cross-dressing in public implicate the issue of "status offenses," as the concept was developed in *Robinson v. California*? Would it violate the 8th Amendment to penalize a preoperative transsexual man for dressing as

a woman, or a transvestite for wearing clothing of the opposite sex? Imagine the following scenario: A masculine appearing middle-aged businessman dressed in a three-piece male suit is crossing the main street in Chicago when he is struck by a truck. Emergency medical assistance arrives and attendants cut away part of his clothing in the process of lifting him to a stretcher. This process reveals that he is wearing feminine undergarments. Has he violated the Chicago ordinance? Would it be appropriate to punish him for doing so?

3. Would it be constitutional for a municipality to make it a criminal offense for a genital man dressed as a woman to use a public restroom that is labelled for use by women? What policy justifications might be advanced in support of such a law? What arguments in opposition? Would it make a difference whether the man had been diagnosed with gender dysphoria, was receiving hormone treatments as part of a program of gender reassignment, and was cross-dressing under the care of a psychiatrist or psychologist? Access to restrooms is a significant health and safety matter. How should it be resolved in the employment context, where female employees may object to a genital male who identifies as a woman using "their" restroom, while the employee in question would feel uncomfortable—even unsafe—using the "male" restroom. See chapter 6.

Chapter Four

Recognition of Same-Sex Relationships

A. Marriage

State statutes define which families shall be legally recognized under state law. Almost all states have statutes that define the marital relationship as one between one man and one woman. These definitions control a host of secondary benefits (e.g., the right to inherit) and secondary burdens (e.g. obligations of support). As of 2004, only one state (Massachusetts) recognized marriage between persons of the same sex, and the status of marriages involving transsexuals was highly contested. Two states (Vermont and California) recognized certain relationships between same-sex couples and granted them the same basic rights and responsibilities that are given to married couples under state law. In Vermont the relationship is called a "civil union." In California, the relationship is called a "domestic partnership."

Until 1996, the federal government had normally accepted state definitions of marriage for purposes of determining whether couples were entitled to the numerous rights, benefits and privileges (and, in some cases, subject to duties) under federal law where marital status was relevant. For example, filing status under the Internal Revenue Code (married or single) has always been determined on the basis of whether one was married or not under state law. In 1996, the federal government, for the first time, adopted by statute a definition of marriage, in response to the Hawaii litigation mentioned in this chapter, under which the federal government will not recognize same-sex marriages for any purpose. The constitutionality of this statute, called The Defense of Marriage Act (DOMA), has been questioned, prompting calls for passage of a federal constitutional amendment defining marriage as an institution restricted to one man and one woman.

In the early 1970s, during the first wave of gay rights litigation, same-sex couples began turning to the courts to challenge their exclusion from the legal institution of marriage. In these early cases, couples relied heavily on the fourteenth amendment, which the Supreme Court applied to strike down anti-miscegenation laws in 1967. In more recent years, most same-sex marriage litigation in the United States has relied solely on state constitutions, reflecting a strategic concern by the plaintiffs to avoid having their cases removed to the more conservative federal courts.

1. Access to Marriage as a Fundamental Right

Loving v. Virginia
388 U.S. 1 (1967)

Mr. Chief Justice WARREN delivered the opinion of the Court.

This case presents a constitutional question never addressed by this Court: whether a statutory scheme adopted by the State of Virginia to prevent marriages between persons solely on the basis of racial classifications violates the Equal Protection and Due Process Clauses of the Fourteenth Amendment. For reasons which seem to us to reflect the central meaning of those constitutional commands, we conclude that these statutes cannot stand consistently with the Fourteenth Amendment.

In June 1958, two residents of Virginia, Mildred Jeter, a Negro woman, and Richard Loving, a white man, were married in the District of Columbia pursuant to its laws. Shortly after their marriage, the Lovings returned to Virginia and established their marital abode in Caroline County. At the October Term, 1958, of the Circuit Court of Caroline County, a grand jury issued an indictment charging the Lovings with violating Virginia's ban on interracial marriages. On January 6, 1959, the Lovings pleaded guilty to the charge and were sentenced to one year in jail; however, the trial judge suspended the sentence for a period of 25 years on the condition that the Lovings leave the State and not return to Virginia together for 25 years. He stated in an opinion that:

> 'Almighty God created the races white, black, yellow, malay and red, and he placed them on separate continents. And but for the interference with his arrangement there would be no cause for such marriages. The fact that he separated the races shows that he did not intend for the races to mix.'

After their convictions, the Lovings took up residence in the District of Columbia. On November 6, 1963, they filed a motion in the state trial court to vacate the judgment and set aside the sentence on the ground that the statutes which they had violated were repugnant to the Fourteenth Amendment....On January 22, 1965, the state trial judge denied the motion to vacate the sentences, and the Lovings perfected an appeal to the Supreme Court of Appeals of Virginia.

The Supreme Court of Appeals upheld the constitutionality of the antimiscegenation statutes and, after modifying the sentence, affirmed the convictions. The Lovings appealed this decision...

The two statutes under which appellants were convicted and sentenced are part of a comprehensive statutory scheme aimed at prohibiting and punishing interracial marriages. The Lovings were convicted of violating sec. 20—58 of the Virginia Code:

> 'Leaving State to evade law.—If any white person and colored person shall go out of this State, for the purpose of being married, and with the intention of returning, and be married out of it, and afterwards return to and reside in it, cohabiting as man and wife, they shall be punished as provided in s 20—59, and the marriage shall be governed by the same law as if it had been solemnized in this State. The fact of their cohabitation here as man and wife shall be evidence of their marriage.'

Section 20—59, which defines the penalty for miscegenation, provides:

'Punishment for marriage.—If any white person intermarry with a colored person, or any colored person intermarry with a white person, he shall be guilty of a felony and shall be punished by confinement in the penitentiary for not less than one nor more than five years.'...

Virginia is now one of 16 States which prohibit and punish marriages on the basis of racial classifications. Penalties for miscegenation arose as an incident to slavery and have been common in Virginia since the colonial period....

I.

In upholding the constitutionality of these provisions in the decision below, the Supreme Court of Appeals of Virginia referred to its 1955 decision in *Naim v. Naim*, 197 Va. 80, 87 S.E.2d 749, as stating the reasons supporting the validity of these laws. In *Naim*, the state court concluded that the State's legitimate purposes were 'to preserve the racial integrity of its citizens,' and to prevent 'the corruption of blood,' 'a mongrel breed of citizens,' and 'the obliteration of racial pride,' obviously an endorsement of the doctrine of White Supremacy. Id., at 90, 87 S.E.2d, at 756. The court also reasoned that marriage has traditionally been subject to state regulation without federal intervention, and, consequently, the regulation of marriage should be left to exclusive state control by the Tenth Amendment.

While the state court is no doubt correct in asserting that marriage is a social relation subject to the State's police power,...the State does not contend in its argument before this Court that its powers to regulate marriage are unlimited notwithstanding the commands of the Fourteenth Amendment. Nor could it do so in light of *Meyer v. State of Nebraska*, 262 U.S. 390 (1923), and *Skinner v. State of Oklahoma*, 316 U.S. 535 (1942). Instead, the State argues that the meaning of the Equal Protection Clause, as illuminated by the statements of the Framers, is only that state penal laws containing an interracial element as part of the definition of the offense must apply equally to whites and Negroes in the sense that members of each race are punished to the same degree. Thus, the State contends that, because its miscegenation statutes punish equally both the white and the Negro participants in an interracial marriage, these statutes, despite their reliance on racial classifications do not constitute an invidious discrimination based upon race. The second argument advanced by the State assumes the validity of its equal application theory. The argument is that, if the Equal Protection Clause does not outlaw miscegenation statutes because of their reliance on racial classifications, the question of constitutionality would thus become whether there was any rational basis for a State to treat interracial marriages differently from other marriages. On this question, the State argues, the scientific evidence is substantially in doubt and, consequently, this Court should defer to the wisdom of the state legislature in adopting its policy of discouraging interracial marriages.

Because we reject the notion that the mere 'equal application' of a statute containing racial classifications is enough to remove the classifications from the Fourteenth Amendment's proscription of all invidious racial discriminations, we do not accept the State's contention that these statutes should be upheld if there is any possible basis for concluding that they serve a rational purpose. The mere fact of equal application does not mean that our analysis of these statutes should follow the approach we have taken in cases involving no racial discrimination...In these cases, involving distinctions not drawn according to race, the Court has merely asked whether there is any rational foundation for the discriminations, and has deferred to the wisdom of the state legislatures. In the case at bar, however, we deal with statutes containing racial classifications, and the fact of equal application does not immunize the statute from the very heavy burden of justification which the Fourteenth Amendment has traditionally required of state statutes drawn according to race....

There can be no question but that Virginia's miscegenation statutes rest solely upon distinctions drawn according to race. The statutes proscribe generally accepted conduct if engaged in by members of different races. Over the years, this Court has consistently repudiated '(d)istinctions between citizens solely because of their ancestry' as being 'odious to a free people whose institutions are founded upon the doctrine of equality.'... At the very least, the Equal Protection Clause demands that racial classifications, especially suspect in criminal statutes, be subjected to the 'most rigid scrutiny,' *Korematsu v. United States*, 323 U.S. 214, 216 (1944), and, if they are ever to be upheld, they must be shown to be necessary to the accomplishment of some permissible state objective, independent of the racial discrimination which it was the object of the Fourteenth Amendment to eliminate. Indeed, two members of this Court have already stated that they 'cannot conceive of a valid legislative purpose * * * which makes the color of a person's skin the test of whether his conduct is a criminal offense.' *McLaughlin v. Florida*, supra, 379 U.S. at 198 (Stewart, J., joined by Douglas, J., concurring).

There is patently no legitimate overriding purpose independent of invidious racial discrimination which justifies this classification. The fact that Virginia prohibits only interracial marriages involving white persons demonstrates that the racial classifications must stand on their own justification, as measures designed to maintain White Supremacy. We have consistently denied the constitutionality of measures which restrict the rights of citizens on account of race. There can be no doubt that restricting the freedom to marry solely because of racial classifications violates the central meaning of the Equal Protection Clause.

II.

These statutes also deprive the Lovings of liberty without due process of law in violation of the Due Process Clause of the Fourteenth Amendment. The freedom to marry has long been recognized as one of the vital personal rights essential to the orderly pursuit of happiness by free men.

Marriage is one of the 'basic civil rights of man,' fundamental to our very existence and survival. *Skinner v. State of Oklahoma*, 316 U.S. 535, 541 (1942). To deny this fundamental freedom on so unsupportable a basis as the racial classifications embodied in these statutes, classifications so directly subversive of the principle of equality at the heart of the Fourteenth Amendment, is surely to deprive all the State's citizens of liberty without due process of law. The Fourteenth Amendment requires that the freedom of choice to marry not be restricted by invidious racial discriminations. Under our Constitution, the freedom to marry or not marry, a person of another race resides with the individual and cannot be infringed by the State.

These convictions must be reversed. It is so ordered.

Notes and Questions

1. The Lovings did not attempt to marry in the state of Virginia because they knew the state law forbade interracial marriages. Instead they went to Washington, D.C., and

entered into a legal marriage there, and moved back to Virginia, where they initially resided with Mrs. Loving's parents. Why should Virginia have cared about the Lovings' actions in D.C.?

2. Suppose Richard and Mildred Loving had not only married in D.C., but had also made D.C. their legal place of residence. If one year later they return to Virginia to visit family and friends, could the local authorities arrest them during this visit?

3. Are state constitutional amendments or laws that ban marriages between persons of the same sex the same or different from laws that banned interracial marriages prior to the Supreme Court's decision in *Loving v. Virginia*?

4. In subsequent cases, the Court held that the fundamental right of marriage trumped state interests in prohibiting the remarriage of a father who had fallen behind in child support payments to his first wife, *Zablocki v. Redhail*, 434 U.S. 374 (1978), or whatever interest the state might have in preventing prison inmates from marrying, *Turner v. Safley*, 482 U.S. 78 (1987). The prison case, *Turner v. Safley*, presents a particularly interesting argument in light of the interests states have articulated in opposing same-sex marriage. The state argued that because prisoners did not have rights to conjugal visits with their spouses, the marriage of an inmate could not be physically consummated and produce children, which the state defined as the essential purpose of marriage. The Supreme Court disagreed, enumerating an impressive list of other reasons why people marry and why the state sanctions marriage. Justice O'Connor, writing for the Court, explained:

> First, inmate marriages, like others, are expressions of emotional support and public commitment. These elements are an important and significant aspect of the marital relationship. In addition, many religions recognize marriage as having spiritual significance...Finally, marital status often is a precondition to the receipt of government benefits (e.g., Social Security benefits), property rights (e.g., tenancy by the entirety, inheritance rights), and other, less tangible benefits...

482 U.S. at 94.

5. Is marriage protected as a fundamental right *because* of these additional benefits listed by Justice O'Connor or is marriage protected for some other reason and these additional benefits are merely ones that tend to flow from the marital status? Or, put another way, does one have a fundamental right to social security benefits for one's spouse? See Patricia A. Cain, Imagine There's No Marriage, 16 Quinnipiac L. Rev. 27 (1996), pointing out that to the extent the fundamental right to marry is derived from the Court's privacy jurisprudence, it would appear to be a right that prevents the state from unduly interfering in a relationship, but would not necessarily require the state to provide positive benefits.

Baker v. Nelson

191 N.W. 2d 185 (Minn. 1971)
appeal dismissed 409 U.S. 810 (1972)

PETERSON, Justice.

The questions for decision are whether a marriage of two persons of the same sex is authorized by state statutes and, if not, whether state authorization is constitutionally compelled.

Petitioners, Richard John Baker and James Michael McConnell, both adult male persons, made application to respondent, Gerald R. Nelson, clerk of Hennepin County

District Court, for a marriage license, pursuant to Minn.St. 517.08. Respondent declined to issue the license on the sole ground that petitioners were of the same sex, it being undisputed that there were otherwise no statutory impediments to a heterosexual marriage by either petitioner.

The trial court...ruled that respondent was not required to issue a marriage license to petitioners and specifically directed that a marriage license not be issued to them. This appeal is from those orders. We affirm.

Petitioners contend, first, that the absence of an express statutory prohibition against same-sex marriages evinces a legislative intent to authorize such marriages. We think, however, that a sensible reading of the statute discloses a contrary intent.

Minn.St. c. 517, which governs 'marriage,' employs that term as one of common usage, meaning the state of union between persons of the opposite sex. It is unrealistic to think that the original draftsmen of our marriage statutes, which date from territorial days, would have used the term in any different sense. The term is of contemporary significance as well, for the present statute is replete with words of heterosexual import such as 'husband and wife' and 'bride and groom'...

We hold, therefore, that Minn.St. c. 517 does not authorize marriage between persons of the same sex and that such marriages are accordingly prohibited.

Petitioners contend, second, that Minn.St. c. 517, so interpreted, is unconstitutional. There is a dual aspect to this contention: The prohibition of a same-sex marriage denies petitioners a fundamental right guaranteed by the Ninth Amendment to the United States Constitution, arguably made applicable to the states by the Fourteenth Amendment, and petitioners are deprived of liberty and property without due process and are denied the equal protection of the laws, both guaranteed by the Fourteenth Amendment.

These constitutional challenges have in common the assertion that the right to marry without regard to the sex of the parties is a fundamental right of all persons and that restricting marriage to only couples of the opposite sex is irrational and invidiously discriminatory. We are not independently persuaded by these contentions and do not find support for them in any decisions of the United States Supreme Court.

The institution of marriage as a union of man and woman, uniquely involving the procreation and rearing of children within a family, is as old as the book of Genesis. *Skinner v. Oklahoma*, 316 U.S. 535, 541 (1942), which invalidated Oklahoma's Habitual Criminal Sterilization Act on equal protection grounds, stated in part: 'Marriage and procreation are fundamental to the very existence and survival of the race.' This historic institution manifestly is more deeply founded than the asserted contemporary concept of marriage and societal interests for which petitioners contend. The due process clause of the Fourteenth Amendment is not a charter for restructuring it by judicial legislation.

Griswold v. Connecticut, 381 U.S. 479 (1965), upon which petitioners rely, does not support a contrary conclusion. A Connecticut criminal statute prohibiting the use of contraceptives by married couples was held invalid, as violating the due process clause of the Fourteenth Amendment. The basic premise of that decision, however, was that the state, having authorized marriage, was without power to intrude upon the right of privacy inherent in the marital relationship. Mr. Justice Douglas, author of the majority opinion, wrote that this criminal statute 'operates directly on an intimate relation of husband and wife,' 381 U.S. 482, and that the very idea of its enforcement by police search of 'the sacred precincts of marital bedrooms for telltale signs of the use of contraceptives * * * is repulsive to the notions of privacy surrounding the marriage relationship,' 381 U.S. 485. In a separate opinion for three justices, Mr. Justice Goldberg similarly abhorred this state disruption of 'the traditional relation of the family—a relation as old and as fundamental as our entire civilization.' 381 U.S. 496.

The equal protection clause of the Fourteenth Amendment, like the due process clause, is not offended by the state's classification of persons authorized to marry. There is no irrational or invidious discrimination....

Loving v. Virginia, 388 U.S. 1 (1967), upon which petitioners additionally rely, does not militate against this conclusion. Virginia's antimiscegenation statute, prohibiting interracial marriages, was invalidated solely on the grounds of its patent racial discrimination. As Mr. Chief Justice Warren wrote for the court (388 U.S. 12, 87 S.Ct. 1824, 18 L.Ed.2d 1018):

> 'Marriage is one of the 'basic civil rights of man,' fundamental to our very existence and survival.... To deny this fundamental freedom on so unsupportable a basis as the racial classifications embodied in these statutes, classifications so directly subversive of the principle of equality at the heart of the Fourteenth Amendment, is surely to deprive all the State's citizens of liberty without due process of law. The Fourteenth Amendment requires that the freedom of choice to marry not be restricted by invidious racial discriminations.

Loving does indicate that not all state restrictions upon the right to marry are beyond reach of the Fourteenth Amendment. But in commonsense and in a constitutional sense, there is a clear distinction between a marital restriction based merely upon race and one based upon the fundamental difference in sex.

We hold, therefore, that Minn.St. c. 517 does not offend the... Ninth, or Fourteenth Amendments to the United States Constitution. Affirmed.

Notes and Questions

1. *Loving v. Virginia* held that restrictions on marriage that use race as a classification are subject to strict scrutiny. What was the classification being challenged in *Baker v. Nelson*? What level of scrutiny did the Minnesota Supreme Court use? What justification for the classification did the state offer?

2. Similar "right to marry" cases were brought in other states during the 1970s with similar outcomes. See, e.g., *Jones v. Hallohan*, 501 S.W.2d 588 (Ky. App. 1973); *Singer v. Hara*, 522 P.2d 1187 (Wash. App. 1974), rev. denied, 84 Wash. 2d. 1008 (1974). See also *Burkett v. Zablocki*, 54 F.R.D. 626 (E.D. Wis. 1972)(marriage license denied to two women who brought suit in federal district court; case dismissed for failure to submit briefs on legal issue). See also *Adams v. Howerton*, 673 F.2d 1036 (9th Cir. 1982)(male couple obtained marriage license from county clerk in Boulder, Colorado, and were "married" by a minister; but marriage was not recognized by federal immigration law and thus alien "spouse" was not allowed to stay in the country). In *Singer v. Hara*, the plaintiffs raised an important state claim in addition to their federal claim, arguing that the state's Equal Rights Amendment, which had just recently been added to the state constitution by public referendum after heated debate, required the state to allow same-sex marriages. The Equal Rights Amendment added to the Washington Constitution a

provision banning discrimination on account of sex. The Washington Court of Appeals found that the proponents of the ERA had stoutly denied that the amendment was intended to require same-sex marriages, which the opponents had argued in attempting to defeat its passage.

3. The *Baker* case was "appealed" to the United States Supreme Court. An appeal is not the same thing as a *writ of certiorari*. Under current appellate procedures, the Supreme Court has discretion to grant or deny *writs of certiorari*. Most decisions about whether to hear an appeal are discretionary. An affirmative vote by four of the nine justices is required before a *writ* will be granted. However, before 1988, the Court was obligated to hear appeals from state courts whenever the state court had upheld a state statute that was being challenged on the basis of federal law. To avoid this mandatory jurisdiction, often the Court would find that the case did not raise a substantial enough issue under federal law and would "dismiss" the appeal "for want of a substantial federal question." The appeal in *Baker v. Nelson* was dismissed on this basis. Do you agree that there was no substantial federal question raised in the case? What precedential weight does this dismissal have?

2. Is Same-sex Marriage a Crime?

The Woman Who Married The Woman
Davenport Gazette, December 29, 1842

We mentioned yesterday that a woman dressed in the disguise of a man was arrested for marrying a woman named Mrs. Donnelly. Strange as this may appear, it is true. She has worn the trowsers, coat, hat, boots and all for some years past, and has worked at the tinsmith trade in town for a long period "on her on hook," carrying a budget on her back, with all the utensils necessary for mending old pots and kettles.

It is also stated on very good authority that she voted the Whig ticket, in the eighth ward, at the late election. She has passed under the notorious and unfortunate cognomen of John Smith, and was married by the Rev. Mr. Stillwell, minister of the North Methodist Church, some four weeks since, to Mrs. Donnelly, a widow lady, mother to a chubby cheek boy in trowsers. They lived together as man and wife since then; but Mr. Smith on all occasions went to bed with his trowsers on.

Mrs. Smith, for this was her name by marriage, was dissatisfied with the matrimonial state and complained to a friend of her's [sic], Micheal [sic] McGuire. Mr. McGuire, from the conversation, was led to believe that there was a mystery about the affair and protested that he would ferret it out.

A day or two subsequently to this, Mr. John Smith called at Mc's house, and enquired "any pots or kettles to mend?" "Divil'a one," said Mike; "come in my lad, I've a word to say to yourself." In walked John Smith, and Mike eyed the gentleman very sharp. "A purty trick we have been playing isn't it madam," exclaimed Mike, with a shrewd shake with his left eye.—"Madam! Don't Madam me," roared Smith, greatly excited.

"Yes, I will," said Mike, in an angry tone, "and I'll know whether you are one or not;" at this moment Mike seized hold of John Smith and tore open his coat and vest, and— saw to his great surprise that Mr. Smith was a woman.

These are the facts that led to the arrest. There is no law on the statute books, however, which covers the offence, and yesterday she was discharged from custody.

— *Albany Argus*

3. Litigating for the Right to Same-sex Marriage in the United States

Note
Litigating for the Right to Marry: *Baehr* to *Baker*
1990–2000

In December 1990, Nina Baehr and her partner Genora Dancel, along with two other same-sex couples, applied for marriage licenses in Honolulu, Hawaii, and were denied. The following April, Hawaii became the third state in the United States to enact statewide civil rights protections for gay men and lesbians. One month later, Baehr and the other marriage license applicants sued Hawaii's Director of Health, John Lewin, claiming that the state's denial of their marriage application violated their fundamental right to marry as well as their equal protection rights under the Hawaii constitution. The trial judge dismissed their claim and they appealed. In May of 1993, the Hawaii Supreme Court surprised people throughout the country by reversing the trial judge and remanding for a trial. The court ruled favorably on a state constitutional equal protection argument, but rejected a fundamental rights argument, finding that Hawaii's due process clause operated in the same way as the federal due process clause, and explaining that there was no fundamental right to "same-sex marriage." ("[W]e do not believe that a right to same-sex marriage is so rooted in the traditions and collective conscience of our people that failure to recognize it would violate the fundamental principles of liberty and justice that lie at the base of all our civil and political institutions.") In the view of the majority (3 judges out of 5, with one judge in the majority only concurring in the result in a separate opinion), restricting marriage to opposite sex couples constituted sex discrimination and was thus subject to Hawaii's equal rights amendment, which made sex a "suspect classification" in Hawaii. The state could sustain the discrimination only by satisfying the compelling state interest test. See *Baehr v. Lewin*, 852 P.2d 44 (Haw. 1993).

At about the same time in the District of Columbia, Craig Dean and Patrick Gill challenged the D.C. law regarding marriage, claiming that failure to grant them a marriage license violated the D.C. Human Rights Act, which prohibited discrimination on the basis of gender and on the basis of sexual orientation. They also claimed that their right to marry was a fundamental right protected by the United States Constitution. In 1995, the D.C. Court of Appeals ruled against them, reasoning that the Human Rights Act was never intended to apply to marriage and that same-sex marriage was not a fundamental right. The court cited *Baehr* with approval regarding the fundamental right issue, and distinguished the sex discrimination issue by viewing *Baehr* as limited to a question of interpretation of the Hawaii state constitution and not applying to the statutory construction issue raised under the Human Rights Act. See *Dean v. District of Columbia*, 653 A.2d 307 (D.C. 1995).

In the meantime, the lawyers in the Hawaii litigation prepared for trial over the issue of whether the state could satisfy its burden in proving that the discrimination in the marriage statute was necessary under the compelling state interest test. A trial was held in October 1996, during which the plaintiffs and the state were each allowed to produce testimony by four expert witnesses on the only argument the state sought to advance in justification of excluding same-sex couples from marriage: that opposite-sex couples presented a superior setting for raising children. On December 3, 1996, Judge Kevin Chang ruled that the state had failed to justify its denial of marriage licenses to same-sex couples, ordering an end to sex discrimination in marriage. Specifically, he found that excluding same-sex couples from marrying actually disadvantaged the children whom they might be raising, by depriving them of the protection and benefits from having two parents who were married to each other. Based on his review of the expert testimony, Judge Chang found that the state failed to show that same-sex couples could not provide a satisfactory setting for raising children. The enforcement of the decision was delayed, pending appeal to the State Supreme Court by the state's new Health Director, Miike. (The name of the case was changed to *Baehr v. Miike* to reflect this change.)

The state legislature reacted to these developments by passing a pair of statutes, one of which placed on the state ballot in 1998 a proposed constitutional amendment that would reserve to the legislature the power to restrict who could marry on the basis of sex, and the other of which established a new legal status, "reciprocal beneficiary," that would provide some of the rights and benefits of marriage. This new status was opened to same-sex couples and certain other couples.

On November 3, 1998, the people of Hawaii voted to amend their Constitution in order to authorize the state legislature to adopt a restrictive definition of marriage. The legislature had already enacted a statute (§572-1) making it clear that their intent was to restrict marriage to one man and one woman. The presumed effect of the new constitutional amendment was to trump the sex discrimination holding in *Baehr v. Lewin*. However, the Supreme Court requested additional briefing by the parties on the exact effect of the constitutional amendment.

On December 9, 1999, the Supreme Court of Hawaii finally issued its ruling in the case. After taking judicial notice of the fact that the marriage amendment to the Hawaii Constitution had been ratified in November of 1998, the Court stated:

> "The marriage amendment validated HRS §572-1 by taking the statute out of the ambit of the equal protection clause of the Hawaii Constitution....Accordingly, whether or not in the past it was violative of the equal protection clause, HRS §572-1 no longer is. In light of the marriage amendment, HRS §572-1 must be given full force and effect."

A similar challenge to the Alaska marriage statute was initially successful. See *Brause v. Bureau of Vital Statistics*, 1998 WL 88743 (Alaska Super. Ct. 1998)(holding that the right to marry is fundamental and thus restriction to opposite-sex couples can only be justified by compelling state interest). Shortly thereafter the legislature passed a law to amend the Alaska constitution to prohibit same-sex marriage. That amendment was ratified on Nov. 3, 1998, the same date that Hawaiians ratified their constitutional amendment against same-sex marriage.

Note the difference between the constitutional amendments in Hawaii and Alaska. The Alaska amendment makes same-sex marriages unconstitutional. Thus the legislature in Alaska could not enact a same-sex marriage statute, even if it were inclined to do so. Any such statute would be in violation of the Alaska constitution. By contrast, the Hawaii constitution does not prohibit same-sex marriages. Instead, the Hawaii constitutional amendment provides that the legislature is to have the final word on whether the state will recognize same-sex marriages. The current state statute, HRS §572-1, authorizes only opposite-sex marriages. But if the Hawaii legislature were to change its mind, it could enact a statute recognizing same-sex marriages without violating the Hawaii Constitution.

Well before the trial court ruling in *Baehr*, forces around the country opposed to same-sex marriage began to mobilize. They lobbied state legislatures to adopt anti-marriage bills. By the time Judge Chang had ruled in favor of the plaintiffs, fifteen states had enacted statutes that proclaimed same-sex marriages void in the state even if valid in another state. Congress, too, became involved in the debate, enacting legislation that would limit the ability of legally-married same-sex couples to obtain the many federal benefits that are provided to opposite-sex spouses. Section 3 of the Defense of Marriage Act (DOMA) defines 'marriage' and 'spouse' under federal law to refer only to heterosexual couples:

> In determining the meaning of any Act of Congress, or of any ruling, regulation, or interpretation of administrative bureaus and agencies of the United States, the word "marriage" means only a legal union between one man and one woman as husband and wife, and the word "spouse" refers only to a person of the opposite sex who is a husband or a wife.

DOMA contains another provision directed at spousal benefits that Hawaiian same-sex spouses might claim in states other than Hawaii. Section 2 of DOMA allows sister states to refuse to recognize lawful same-sex marriages by providing that:

> No State...shall be required to give effect to any public act, record, or judicial proceeding of any other State...respecting a relationship between persons of the same sex that is treated as a marriage under the laws of such other State... or a right or claim arising from such a relationship.

The vote on DOMA was swift and lopsided. Representative Robert Barr of Georgia introduced the bill in May 1996. Within weeks the House Judiciary Committee held hearings on the bill and approved it by a vote of 20 to 10. On July 12, the House voted in favor of the bill 342 to 67. The Senate vote followed on September 10, 85 to 14. President Clinton signed the bill on September 21, 1996, thus effectively taking the issue of same-sex marriage out of debate in the pending presidential election between himself and Senator Robert Dole, who had also endorsed DOMA.

The litigation in Hawaii was extremely important even though none of the plaintiffs in that case ultimately won the right to marry. The Hawaii Supreme Court became the first court anywhere in the world to rule that same-sex couples might be entitled to marry, and Judge Chang became the first judge ever to rule, after a full trial on the merits, that the state lacked any compelling reason to exclude same-sex couples from marrying.

The case brought the issue of same-sex marriage to the attention of the American people and started a national debate. The backlash was quick and fierce. By 1999, despite the fact that no state had yet accorded legal recognition to same-sex marriages, at least 30 states and the federal government had enacted legislation declaring such marriages void. Two states, Hawaii and Alaska, had adopted constitutional amendments addressing the issue and more states were considering constitutional amendments. Right-to-marry litigation, relying on state constitutional arguments, would now have to be carefully planned to avoid states that might respond with a constitutional amendment prohibiting same-sex marriages.

The next key case of import was litigated in the state of Vermont. Mary Bonauto of GLAD (Gay and Lesbian Advocates and Defenders), located in Boston, and Susan Murray and Beth Robinson of Langrock Sperry & Wool in Middlebury, Vermont, represented three couples who claimed the right to marry under Vermont law. Vermont was thought to be a good state for this litigation because of language in the state constitution guaranteeing to every "person, family, or set of persons" common benefits. In addition, the Vermont legislature had enacted legislation protecting gay men and lesbians from discrimination and had codified the Vermont Supreme Court's decision permitting the adoption of a child by the mother's lesbian partner. Additionally, the Vermont populace had the reputation of being independent and fair-minded. As explained by the lawyers:

> As the first state to prohibit slavery by constitution, and one of the few states which, from its inception, extended the vote to male citizens who did not own land, the State of Vermont has long been at the forefront of this nation's march toward full equality for all of its citizens. In July 1997, three same-sex couples challenged Vermont to act as a leader yet again, this time in affording full civil rights to the State's gay and lesbian citizens. Stan Baker and Peter Harrigan, Nina Beck and Stacy Jolles, and Holly Puterbaugh and Lois Farnham were denied marriage licenses by their respective town clerks in the summer of 1997. They sued the State of Vermont and the towns, arguing that the marriage statutes allowed them to marry, and that if the law did purport to limit marriage to different sex unions it would be unconstitutional. The trial court dismissed their claims in December 1997, and the couples appealed to the Vermont Supreme Court. The court heard oral arguments on the case on November 18, 1998.
>
> The Appellants' primary constitutional claim is based on the "Common Benefits Clause" of the Vermont Constitution, which prohibits the State from passing laws for the particular "emolument or advantage" of a "part only of [the] community." The Vermont Supreme Court has used an analytical framework similar to federal equal protection law in applying the Common Benefits Clause, although in some cases that court has scrutinized classifications more closely than might be required under federal law.
>
> In contrast to the State of Hawaii in *Baehr v. Lewin*, where the State argued that its laws did not discriminate, the State of Vermont articulated its rationales in support of the discriminatory marriage laws at the outset of the *Baker v. State* litigation, affording the couples the first real opportunity to flesh out in some depth not only the appropriate level of scrutiny, but also the State's lack of an adequate justification under any standard. The couples' opening brief delves into the State's explanations for its discriminatory laws in some depth, arguing that even absent heightened scrutiny, the State could not justify its discriminatory marriage laws. The opening brief also lays out three arguments for heightened scrutiny, based on the State's gender discrimination, sexual orientation discrimination, and impingement on a fundamental right—the right to marry.

See Mary Bonauto, Susan M. Murray, Beth Robinson, The Freedom to Marry for Same-Sex Couples: The Opening Appellate Brief of Plaintiffs Stan Baker et al. in *Baker et al. v. State of Vermont*, 5 MICH. J. GENDER & L. 409 at 412 (1999).

On December 20, 1999, the Vermont court ruled in favor of the same-sex couples.

> We conclude that under the Common Benefits Clause of the Vermont Constitution...plaintiffs may not be deprived of the statutory benefits and protections afforded persons of the opposite sex who choose to marry. We hold that the State is constitutionally required to extend to same-sex couples the common benefits and protections that flow from marriage under Vermont law. Whether this ultimately takes the form of inclusion within the marriage laws themselves or a parallel "domestic partnership" system or some equivalent statutory alternative, rests with the Legislature. Whatever system is chosen, however, must conform with the constitutional imperative to afford all Vermonters the common benefit, protection, and security of the law.

Baker v. Vermont, 744 A.2d 864 at 867 (Vt. 1999).

In reaching its conclusion, the Court analyzed the various interests set forth by the state to justify excluded same-sex couples from marriage. The state's primary asserted justification was the role of procreation and child-rearing in marriage. After noting that many same-sex couples were in fact rearing children, the Vermont Supreme Court responded to the state's argument as follows:

> The legal benefits and protections flowing from a marriage license are of such significance that any statutory exclusion must necessarily be grounded on public concerns of sufficient weight, cogency, and authority that the justice of the deprivation cannot seriously be questioned. Considered in light of the extreme logical disjunction between the classification and the stated purposes of the law—protecting children and "furthering the link between procreation and child-rearing"—the exclusion falls substantially short of this standard. The laudable governmental goal of promoting a commitment between married couples to promote the security of their children and the community as a whole provides no reasonable basis for denying the legal benefits and protections of marriage to same-sex couples, who are no differently situated with respect to this goal than their opposite-sex counterparts. Promoting a link between procreation and child-rearing similarly fails to support the exclusion.

On April 26, 2000, the Vermont legislature responded to the *Baker* decision by enacting a statute that created a new legal status, a "civil union." The legislature elected to reserve the institution of marriage to opposite-sex couples, but declared that the "state has a strong interest in promoting stable and lasting families, including families based upon a same-sex couple." To carry out that interest, the legislature has provided that same-sex couples may enter a "civil union" that parallels marriage. Specifically, the new law provides:

> Parties to a civil union shall have all the same benefits, protections and responsibilities under law, whether they derive from statute, administrative or court rule, policy, common law or any other source of civil law, as are granted to spouses in a marriage. [15 Vermont Statutes Annotated §1204]

Baker v. Vermont was a milestone in the battle for recognizing same-sex marriages, as it marked the first time that a state's highest appellate court ruled on the merits that same-sex couples were entitled to the benefits of marriage. (The Hawaii Supreme Court ruling had fallen short by remanding for trial on the state's asserted justifications, because the trial judge had initially granted a motion to dismiss. In Baker, the trial judge had granted summary judgment, so the Supreme Court was positioned to issue a ruling on the merits without having to remand for trial.) The court correctly understood that the benefits provided by the state to married couples should not be uniformly denied to same-sex couples. In earlier cases across the United States, gay and lesbian plaintiffs had argued that employer-provided benefits (e.g., spousal health care, family bereavement leave) should not be denied them solely because they were not married to their partners. They lost most of these cases because courts were willing to draw the line between married couples and unmarried couples. Litigation has continued in many states to challenge the denial of benefits, benefit by benefit. In more recent times, some cases have been successful. Litigating benefit by benefit is time-consuming and costly. In *Baker*, by contrast, a single action resulted in the equal availability of all spousal benefits to same-sex couples in the state, provided they were willing to engage in a civil union.

Question for Discussion

"Right to marry" litigation has escalated in recent years. Both in the United States and around the globe, lesbian and gay rights activists argue in courts and legislatures for the right to marry. In addition to the specific legal arguments that are necessary for successful constitutional challenges to discriminatory marriage statutes, activists make broad policy arguments to justify same-sex marriages. Not all activists remain convinced that battling for same-sex marriage is the right thing to do. Professor Janet Halley has challenged us to think more carefully about this project, pointing out the inherent connection between arguing for legal recognition of a status and subjecting that status to state regulation:

> ...[B]y my count, we in the U.S. have four basic modes of justification for same-sex marriage. Two are explicit: Recognition and Rights. Each of these modes of justification is typically proposed as simple and internally coherent, but each is actually internally heterogeneous, and moreover each disguises while depending on a supplementary rhetoric of justification. That supplementary rhetoric is sometimes Regulation, and it is almost always Normalisation. I think this hidden complexity makes the project of seeking same-sex marriage normatively much more dubious than it might appear. Janet Halley, *Recognition, Rights, Regulation, Normalisation: Rhetorics of Justification in the Same-Sex Marriage Debate*, in Legal Recognition of Same-Sex Partnerships (Wintemute and Andenaes, eds) at 97 (2001).

Do you agree?

Goodridge v. Department of Public Health
798 N.E.2d 941 (Mass. 2003)

Marshall, C.J.

Marriage is a vital social institution. The exclusive commitment of two individuals to each other nurtures love and mutual support; it brings stability to our society. For those who choose to marry, and for their children, marriage provides an abundance of legal, financial, and social benefits. In return it imposes weighty legal, financial, and social obligations. The question before us is whether, consistent with the Massachusetts Constitution, the Commonwealth may deny the protections, benefits, and obligations conferred by civil marriage to two individuals of the same sex who wish to marry. We conclude that it may not. The Massachusetts Constitution affirms the dignity and equality of all individuals. It forbids the creation of second-class citizens. In reaching our conclusion we have given full deference to the arguments made by the Commonwealth. But it has failed to identify any constitutionally adequate reason for denying civil marriage to same-sex couples.

We are mindful that our decision marks a change in the history of our marriage law. Many people hold deep-seated religious, moral, and ethical convictions that marriage should be limited to the union of one man and one woman, and that homosexual conduct is immoral. Many hold equally strong religious, moral, and ethical convictions that same-sex couples are entitled to be married, and that homosexual persons should be treated no differently than their heterosexual neighbors. Neither view answers the question before us. Our concern is with the Massachusetts Constitution as a charter of governance for every person properly within its reach. "Our obligation is to define the liberty of all, not to mandate our own moral code." *Lawrence v. Texas,* 539 U.S. 558, — —, 123 S.Ct. 2472, 2480, 156 L.Ed.2d 508 (2003)...

Whether the Commonwealth may use its formidable regulatory authority to bar same-sex couples from civil marriage is a question not previously addressed by a Massachusetts appellate court. It is a question the United States Supreme Court left open as a matter of Federal law in *Lawrence, supra* at 2484, where it was not an issue. There, the Court affirmed that the core concept of common human dignity protected by the Fourteenth Amendment to the United States Constitution precludes government intrusion into the deeply personal realms of consensual adult expressions of intimacy and one's choice of an intimate partner. The Court also reaffirmed the central role that decisions whether to marry or have children bear in shaping one's identity. The Massachusetts Constitution is, if anything, more protective of individual liberty and equality than the Federal Constitution; it may demand broader protection for fundamental rights; and it is less tolerant of government intrusion into the protected spheres of private life.

Barred access to the protections, benefits, and obligations of civil marriage, a person who enters into an intimate, exclusive union with another of the same sex is arbitrarily deprived of membership in one of our community's most rewarding and cherished institutions. That exclusion is incompatible with the constitutional principles of respect for individual autonomy and equality under law.

The plaintiffs are fourteen individuals from five Massachusetts counties. As of April 11, 2001, the date they filed their complaint, the plaintiffs Gloria Bailey, sixty years old, and Linda Davies, fifty-five years old, had been in a committed relationship for thirty years; the plaintiffs Maureen Brodoff, forty-nine years old, and Ellen Wade, fifty-two years old, had been in a committed relationship for twenty years and lived with their twelve year old daughter; the plaintiffs Hillary Goodridge, forty-four years old, and Julie Goodridge, forty-three years old, had been in a committed relationship for thirteen years and lived with their five year old daughter; the plaintiffs Gary Chalmers, thirty-five years old, and Richard Linnell, thirty-seven years old, had been in a committed relationship for thirteen years and lived with their eight year old daughter and Richard's mother; the plaintiffs Heidi Norton, thirty-six years old, and Gina Smith, thirty-six years old, had been in a committed relationship for eleven years and lived with their two sons, ages five years and one year; the plaintiffs Michael Horgan, forty-one years old, and Edward Balmelli, forty-one years old, had been in a committed relationship for seven years; and the plaintiffs David Wilson, fifty-seven years old, and Robert Compton, fifty-one years old, had been in a committed relationship for four years and had cared for David's mother in their home after a serious illness until she died.

The plaintiffs include business executives, lawyers, an investment banker, educators, therapists, and a computer engineer. Many are active in church, community, and school groups. They have employed such legal means as are available to them—for example, joint adoption, powers of attorney, and joint ownership of real property—to secure aspects of their relationships. Each plaintiff attests a desire to marry his or her partner in order to affirm publicly their commitment to each other and to secure the legal protections and benefits afforded to married couples and their children.

The Department of Public Health (department) is charged by statute with safeguarding public health.... Among its responsibilities, the department oversees the registry of vital records and statistics (registry), which "enforce[s] all laws" relative to the issuance of marriage licenses and the keeping of marriage records,... and which promulgates policies and procedures for the issuance of marriage licenses by city and town clerks and registers.... The registry is headed by a registrar of vital records and statistics (registrar), appointed by the Commissioner of Public Health (commissioner) with the approval of the public health council and supervised by the commissioner.

In March and April, 2001, each of the plaintiff couples attempted to obtain a marriage license from a city or town clerk's office. As required under G.L. c. 207, they completed notices of intention to marry on forms provided by the registry,... and presented these forms to a Massachusetts town or city clerk, together with the required health forms and marriage license fees.... In each case, the clerk either refused to accept the notice of intention to marry or denied a marriage license to the couple on the ground that Massachusetts does not recognize same-sex marriage. Because obtaining a marriage license is a necessary prerequisite to civil marriage in Massachusetts, denying marriage licenses to the plaintiffs was tantamount to denying them access to civil marriage itself, with its appurtenant social and legal protections, benefits, and obligations.

On April 11, 2001, the plaintiffs filed suit in the Superior Court against the department and the commissioner seeking a judgment that "the exclusion of the [p]laintiff couples and other qualified same-sex couples from access to marriage licenses, and the legal and social status of civil marriage, as well as the protections, benefits and obligations of marriage, violates Massachusetts law."... The plaintiffs alleged violation of the laws of the Commonwealth, including but not limited to their rights under (various sections) of the Massachusetts constitution. The department, represented by the Attorney General, admitted to a policy and practice of denying marriage licenses to same-sex couples. It denied that its actions violated any law or that the plaintiffs were entitled to relief. The parties filed cross motions for summary judgment.

A Superior Court judge ruled for the department. In a memorandum of decision and order dated May 7, 2002, he dismissed the plaintiffs' claim that the marriage statutes should be construed to permit marriage between persons of the same sex, holding that the plain wording of G.L. c. 207, as well as the wording of other marriage statutes, precluded that interpretation. Turning to the constitutional claims, he held that the marriage exclusion does not offend the liberty, freedom, equality, or due process provisions of the Massachusetts Constitution, and that the Massachusetts Declaration of Rights does not guarantee "the fundamental right to marry a person of the same sex." He concluded that prohibiting same-sex marriage rationally furthers the Legislature's legitimate interest in safeguarding the "primary purpose" of marriage, "procreation." The Legislature may rationally limit marriage to opposite-sex couples, he concluded, because those couples are "theoretically...capable of procreation," they do not rely on "inherently more cumbersome" noncoital means of reproduction, and they are more likely than same-sex couples to have children, or more children.

After the complaint was dismissed and summary judgment entered for the defendants, the plaintiffs appealed. Both parties requested direct appellate review, which we granted.

Although the plaintiffs refer in passing to "the marriage statutes," they focus, quite properly, on G.L. c. 207, the marriage licensing statute, which controls entry into civil marriage. As a preliminary matter, we summarize the provisions of that law.

General Laws c. 207 is both a gatekeeping and a public records statute. It sets minimum qualifications for obtaining a marriage license and directs city and town clerks, the registrar, and the department to keep and maintain certain "vital records" of civil marriages. The gatekeeping provisions of G.L. c. 207 are minimal. They forbid marriage of individuals within certain degrees of consanguinity, §§ 1 and 2, and polygamous marriages. They prohibit marriage if one of the parties has communicable syphilis, and restrict the circumstances in which a person under eighteen years of age may marry. The statute requires that civil marriage be solemnized only by those so authorized.

The record-keeping provisions of G.L. c. 207 are more extensive. Marriage applicants file standard information forms and a medical certificate in any Massachusetts city or town clerk's office and tender a filing fee. The clerk issues the marriage license, and when the marriage is solemnized, the individual authorized to solemnize the marriage adds additional information to the form and returns it (or a copy) to the clerk's office. (This completed form is commonly known as the "marriage certificate"). The clerk sends a copy of the information to the registrar, and that information becomes a public record.

In short, for all the joy and solemnity that normally attend a marriage, G.L. c. 207, governing entrance to marriage, is a licensing law. The plaintiffs argue that because nothing in that licensing law specifically prohibits marriages between persons of the same sex, we may interpret the statute to permit "qualified same sex couples" to obtain marriage licenses, thereby avoiding the question whether the law is constitutional.... This claim lacks merit.

We interpret statutes to carry out the Legislature's intent, determined by the words of a statute interpreted according to "the ordinary and approved usage of the language." *Hanlon v. Rollins*, 286 Mass. 444, 447, 190 N.E. 606 (1934). The everyday meaning of "marriage" is "[t]he legal union of a man and woman as husband and wife," Black's Law Dictionary 986 (7th ed.1999), and the plaintiffs do not argue that the term "marriage" has ever had a different meaning under Massachusetts law.

We conclude, as did the [trial] judge, that G.L. c. 207 may not be construed to permit same-sex couples to marry.[1]

The larger question is whether, as the department claims, government action that bars same-sex couples from civil marriage constitutes a legitimate exercise of the State's authority to regulate conduct, or whether, as the plaintiffs claim, this categorical marriage exclusion violates the Massachusetts Constitution. We have recognized the long-standing statutory understanding, derived from the common law, that "marriage" means the lawful union of a woman and a man. But that history cannot and does not foreclose the constitutional question.

The plaintiffs' claim that the marriage restriction violates the Massachusetts Constitution can be analyzed in two ways. Does it offend the Constitution's guarantees of equality before the law? Or do the liberty and due process provisions of the Massachusetts Constitution secure the plaintiffs' right to marry their chosen partner? In matters implicating marriage, family life, and the upbringing of children, the two constitutional concepts frequently overlap, as they do here. See, e.g., *Perez v. Sharp*, 32 Cal.2d 711, 728, 198 P.2d 17 (1948) (analyzing statutory ban on interracial marriage as equal protection

---

1. We use the terms "same sex" and "opposite sex" when characterizing the couples in question, because these terms are more accurate in this context than the terms "homosexual" or "heterosexual," although at times we use those terms when we consider them appropriate. Nothing in our marriage law precludes people who identify themselves (or who are identified by others) as gay, lesbian, or bisexual from marrying persons of the opposite sex. See *Baehr v. Lewin*, 74 Haw. 530, 543 n. 11, 547 n. 14, 852 P.2d 44 (1993).

violation concerning regulation of fundamental right). See also *Lawrence, supra* at 2482 ("Equality of treatment and the due process right to demand respect for conduct protected by the substantive guarantee of liberty are linked in important respects, and a decision on the latter point advances both interests")...

We begin by considering the nature of civil marriage itself. Simply put, the government creates civil marriage. In Massachusetts, civil marriage is, and since pre-Colonial days has been, precisely what its name implies: a wholly secular institution. No religious ceremony has ever been required to validate a Massachusetts marriage.

Civil marriage is created and regulated through exercise of the police power. "Police power" (now more commonly termed the State's regulatory authority) is an old-fashioned term for the Commonwealth's lawmaking authority, as bounded by the liberty and equality guarantees of the Massachusetts Constitution and its express delegation of power from the people to their government. In broad terms, it is the Legislature's power to enact rules to regulate conduct, to the extent that such laws are "necessary to secure the health, safety, good order, comfort, or general welfare of the community" (citations omitted).

Without question, civil marriage enhances the "welfare of the community." It is a "social institution of the highest importance." Civil marriage anchors an ordered society by encouraging stable relationships over transient ones. It is central to the way the Commonwealth identifies individuals, provides for the orderly distribution of property, ensures that children and adults are cared for and supported whenever possible from private rather than public funds, and tracks important epidemiological and demographic data.

Marriage also bestows enormous private and social advantages on those who choose to marry. Civil marriage is at once a deeply personal commitment to another human being and a highly public celebration of the ideals of mutuality, companionship, intimacy, fidelity, and family. "It is an association that promotes a way of life, not causes; a harmony in living, not political faiths; a bilateral loyalty, not commercial or social projects." *Griswold v. Connecticut,* 381 U.S. 479, 486, 85 S.Ct. 1678, 14 L.Ed.2d 510 (1965). Because it fulfils yearnings for security, safe haven, and connection that express our common humanity, civil marriage is an esteemed institution, and the decision whether and whom to marry is among life's momentous acts of self-definition.

Tangible as well as intangible benefits flow from marriage. The marriage license grants valuable property rights to those who meet the entry requirements, and who agree to what might otherwise be a burdensome degree of government regulation of their activities. The Legislature has conferred on "each party [in a civil marriage] substantial rights concerning the assets of the other which unmarried cohabitants do not have." (Citations omitted).

The benefits accessible only by way of a marriage license are enormous, touching nearly every aspect of life and death. The department states that "hundreds of statutes" are related to marriage and to marital benefits. With no attempt to be comprehensive, we note that some of the statutory benefits conferred by the Legislature on those who enter into civil marriage include, as to property: joint Massachusetts income tax filing; tenancy by the entirety (a form of ownership that provides certain protections against creditors and allows for the automatic descent of property to the surviving spouse without probate); extension of the benefit of the homestead protection (securing up to $300,000 in equity from creditors) to one's spouse and children; automatic rights to inherit the property of a deceased spouse who does not leave a will; the rights of elective share and of dower (which allow surviving spouses certain property rights where the decedent spouse has not made adequate provision for the survivor in a will).

Where a married couple has children, their children are also directly or indirectly, but no less auspiciously, the recipients of the special legal and economic protections obtained by civil marriage. Notwithstanding the Commonwealth's strong public policy to abolish legal distinctions between marital and nonmarital children in providing for the support and care of minors, the fact remains that marital children reap a measure of family stability and economic security based on their parents' legally privileged status that is largely inaccessible, or not as readily accessible, to nonmarital children. Some of these benefits are social, such as the enhanced approval that still attends the status of being a marital child. Others are material, such as the greater ease of access to family-based State and Federal benefits that attend the presumptions of one's parentage.

It is undoubtedly for these concrete reasons, as well as for its intimately personal significance, that civil marriage has long been termed a "civil right." See, e.g., *Loving v. Virginia*.

Without the right to marry—or more properly, the right to choose to marry—one is excluded from the full range of human experience and denied full protection of the laws for one's "avowed commitment to an intimate and lasting human relationship." *Baker v. State, supra* at 229, 744 A.2d 864. Because civil marriage is central to the lives of individuals and the welfare of the community, our laws assiduously protect the individual's right to marry against undue government incursion. Laws may not "interfere directly and substantially with the right to marry." *Zablocki v. Redhail, supra* at 387, 98 S.Ct. 673. See *Perez v. Sharp,* 32 Cal.2d 711, 714 (1948) ("There can be no prohibition of marriage except for an important social objective and reasonable means").[2]

Unquestionably, the regulatory power of the Commonwealth over civil marriage is broad, as is the Commonwealth's discretion to award public benefits. Individuals who have the choice to marry each other and nevertheless choose not to may properly be denied the legal benefits of marriage. But that same logic cannot hold for a qualified individual who would marry if she or he only could.

For decades, indeed centuries, in much of this country (including Massachusetts) no lawful marriage was possible between white and black Americans. That long history availed not when the Supreme Court of California held in 1948 that a legislative prohibition against interracial marriage violated the due process and equality guarantees of the Fourteenth Amendment, *Perez v. Sharp,* 32 Cal.2d 711, 728, 198 P.2d 17 (1948), or when, nineteen years later, the United States Supreme Court also held that a statutory bar to interracial marriage violated the Fourteenth Amendment, *Loving v. Virginia,* 388 U.S. 1, 87 S.Ct. 1817, 18 L.Ed.2d 1010 (1967). As both *Perez* and *Loving* make clear, the

---

2. The department argues that this case concerns the rights of couples (same-sex and opposite-sex), not the rights of individuals. This is incorrect. The rights implicated in this case are at the core of individual privacy and autonomy. See, e.g., *Loving v. Virginia,* 388 U.S. 1, 12, 87 S.Ct. 1817, 18 L.Ed.2d 1010 (1967) ("Under our Constitution, the freedom to marry or not marry, a person of another race resides with the individual and cannot be infringed by the State"); *Perez v. Sharp,* 32 Cal.2d 711, 716, 198 P.2d 17 (1948) ("The right to marry is the right of individuals, not of racial groups"). See also *A.Z. v. B.Z.,* 431 Mass. 150, 162, 725 N.E.2d 1051 (2000), quoting *Moore v. East Cleveland,* 431 U.S. 494, 499, 97 S.Ct. 1932, 52 L.Ed.2d 531 (1977) (noting "freedom of personal choice in matters of marriage and family life"). While two individuals who wish to marry may be equally aggrieved by State action denying them that opportunity, they do not "share" the liberty and equality interests at stake.

right to marry means little if it does not include the right to marry the person of one's choice, subject to appropriate government restrictions in the interests of public health, safety, and welfare. In this case, as in *Perez* and *Loving,* a statute deprives individuals of access to an institution of fundamental legal, personal, and social significance—the institution of marriage—because of a single trait: skin color in *Perez* and *Loving,* sexual orientation here. As it did in *Perez* and *Loving,* history must yield to a more fully developed understanding of the invidious quality of the discrimination.

The Massachusetts Constitution protects matters of personal liberty against government incursion as zealously, and often more so, than does the Federal Constitution, even where both Constitutions employ essentially the same language. That the Massachusetts Constitution is in some instances more protective of individual liberty interests than is the Federal Constitution is not surprising. Fundamental to the vigor of our Federal system of government is that "state courts are absolutely free to interpret state constitutional provisions to accord greater protection to individual rights than do similar provisions of the United States Constitution."

The individual liberty and equality safeguards of the Massachusetts Constitution protect both "freedom from" unwarranted government intrusion into protected spheres of life and "freedom to" partake in benefits created by the State for the common good. Both freedoms are involved here. Whether and whom to marry, how to express sexual intimacy, and whether and how to establish a family—these are among the most basic of every individual's liberty and due process rights. See, e.g., *Lawrence, supra*; *Loving v. Virginia, supra.* And central to personal freedom and security is the assurance that the laws will apply equally to persons in similar situations. "Absolute equality before the law is a fundamental principle of our own Constitution." The liberty interest in choosing whether and whom to marry would be hollow if the Commonwealth could, without sufficient justification, foreclose an individual from freely choosing the person with whom to share an exclusive commitment in the unique institution of civil marriage.

The plaintiffs challenge the marriage statute on both equal protection and due process grounds. With respect to each such claim, we must first determine the appropriate standard of review. Where a statute implicates a fundamental right or uses a suspect classification, we employ "strict judicial scrutiny." For all other statutes, we employ the " 'rational basis' test." For due process claims, rational basis analysis requires that statutes "bear[ ] a real and substantial relation to the public health, safety, morals, or some other phase of the general welfare." For equal protection challenges, the rational basis test requires that "an impartial lawmaker could logically believe that the classification would serve a legitimate public purpose that transcends the harm to the members of the disadvantaged class."

The department argues that no fundamental right or "suspect" class is at issue here, and rational basis is the appropriate standard of review. For the reasons we explain below, we conclude that the marriage ban does not meet the rational basis test for either due process or equal protection. Because the statute does not survive rational basis review, we do not consider the plaintiffs' arguments that this case merits strict judicial scrutiny.

The department posits three legislative rationales for prohibiting same-sex couples from marrying: (1) providing a "favorable setting for procreation"; (2) ensuring the optimal setting for child rearing, which the department defines as "a two-parent family with one parent of each sex"; and (3) preserving scarce State and private financial resources. We consider each in turn.

The judge in the Superior Court endorsed the first rationale, holding that "the state's interest in regulating marriage is based on the traditional concept that marriage's primary purpose is procreation." This is incorrect. Our laws of civil marriage do not privilege procreative heterosexual intercourse between married people above every other form of adult intimacy and every other means of creating a family. General Laws c. 207 contains no requirement that the applicants for a marriage license attest to their ability or intention to conceive children by coitus. Fertility is not a condition of marriage, nor is it grounds for divorce. People who have never consummated their marriage, and never plan to, may be and stay married. See *Franklin v. Franklin,* 154 Mass. 515, 516, 28 N.E. 681 (1891) ("The consummation of a marriage by coition is not necessary to its validity"). People who cannot stir from their deathbed may marry. See G.L. c. 207, § 28A. While it is certainly true that many, perhaps most, married couples have children together (assisted or unassisted), it is the exclusive and permanent commitment of the marriage partners to one another, not the begetting of children, that is the sine qua non of civil marriage.[3]

Moreover, the Commonwealth affirmatively facilitates bringing children into a family regardless of whether the intended parent is married or unmarried, whether the child is adopted or born into a family, whether assistive technology was used to conceive the child, and whether the parent or her partner is heterosexual, homosexual, or bisexual.

The "marriage is procreation" argument singles out the one unbridgeable difference between same-sex and opposite-sex couples, and transforms that difference into the essence of legal marriage. Like "Amendment 2" to the Constitution of Colorado, which effectively denied homosexual persons equality under the law and full access to the political process, the marriage restriction impermissibly "identifies persons by a single trait and then denies them protection across the board." *Romer v. Evans,* 517 U.S. 620, 633, 116 S.Ct. 1620, 134 L.Ed.2d 855 (1996). In so doing, the State's action confers an official stamp of approval on the destructive stereotype that same-sex relationships are inherently unstable and inferior to opposite-sex relationships and are not worthy of respect.

The department's first stated rationale, equating marriage with unassisted heterosexual procreation, shades imperceptibly into its second: that confining marriage to opposite-sex couples ensures that children are raised in the "optimal" setting. Protecting the welfare of children is a paramount State policy. Restricting marriage to opposite-sex couples, however, cannot plausibly further this policy. "The demographic changes of the past century make it difficult to speak of an average American family. The composition of families varies greatly from household to household." Massachusetts has responded supportively to "the changing realities of the American family,"...and has moved vigorously to strengthen the modern family in its many variations.

The department has offered no evidence that forbidding marriage to people of the same sex will increase the number of couples choosing to enter into opposite-sex mar-

---

3. It is hardly surprising that civil marriage developed historically as a means to regulate heterosexual conduct and to promote child rearing, because until very recently unassisted heterosexual relations were the only means short of adoption by which children could come into the world, and the absence of widely available and effective contraceptives made the link between heterosexual sex and procreation very strong indeed. Punitive notions of illegitimacy, see *Powers v. Wilkinson,* 399 Mass. 650, 661, 506 N.E.2d 842 (1987), and of homosexual identity, see *Lawrence, supra* at 2478–79, further cemented the common and legal understanding of marriage as an unquestionably heterosexual institution. But it is circular reasoning, not analysis, to maintain that marriage must remain a heterosexual institution because that is what it historically has been. As one dissent acknowledges, in "the modern age," "heterosexual intercourse, procreation, and child care are not necessarily conjoined." *Post* at 382, 798 N.E.2d at 995–996 (Cordy, J., dissenting).

riages in order to have and raise children. There is thus no rational relationship between the marriage statute and the Commonwealth's proffered goal of protecting the "optimal" child rearing unit. Moreover, the department readily concedes that people in same-sex couples may be "excellent" parents. These couples (including four of the plaintiff couples) have children for the reasons others do—to love them, to care for them, to nurture them. But the task of child rearing for same-sex couples is made infinitely harder by their status as outliers to the marriage laws. While establishing the parentage of children as soon as possible is crucial to the safety and welfare of children,...same-sex couples must undergo the sometimes lengthy and intrusive process of second-parent adoption to establish their joint parentage. While the enhanced income provided by marital benefits is an important source of security and stability for married couples and their children, those benefits are denied to families headed by same-sex couples.

In this case, we are confronted with an entire, sizeable class of parents raising children who have absolutely no access to civil marriage and its protections because they are forbidden from procuring a marriage license. It cannot be rational under our laws, and indeed it is not permitted, to penalize children by depriving them of State benefits because the State disapproves of their parents' sexual orientation.

The third rationale advanced by the department is that limiting marriage to opposite-sex couples furthers the Legislature's interest in conserving scarce State and private financial resources. The marriage restriction is rational, it argues, because the General Court logically could assume that same-sex couples are more financially independent than married couples and thus less needy of public marital benefits, such as tax advantages, or private marital benefits, such as employer-financed health plans that include spouses in their coverage.

An absolute statutory ban on same-sex marriage bears no rational relationship to the goal of economy. First, the department's conclusory generalization— that same-sex couples are less financially dependent on each other than opposite-sex couples—ignores that many same-sex couples, such as many of the plaintiffs in this case, have children and other dependents (here, aged parents) in their care. The department does not contend, nor could it, that these dependents are less needy or deserving than the dependents of married couples. Second, Massachusetts marriage laws do not condition receipt of public and private financial benefits to married individuals on a demonstration of financial dependence on each other; the benefits are available to married couples regardless of whether they mingle their finances or actually depend on each other for support.

The department suggests additional rationales for prohibiting same-sex couples from marrying, which are developed by some amici. It argues that broadening civil marriage to include same-sex couples will trivialize or destroy the institution of marriage as it has historically been fashioned. Certainly our decision today marks a significant change in the definition of marriage as it has been inherited from the common law, and understood by many societies for centuries. But it does not disturb the fundamental value of marriage in our society.

Here, the plaintiffs seek only to be married, not to undermine the institution of civil marriage. They do not want marriage abolished. They do not attack the binary nature of marriage, the consanguinity provisions, or any of the other gate-keeping provisions of the marriage licensing law. Recognizing the right of an individual to marry a person of the same sex will not diminish the validity or dignity of opposite-sex marriage, any more than recognizing the right of an individual to marry a person of a different race devalues the marriage of a person who marries someone of her own race.[4] If anything, extending civil marriage to same-sex couples reinforces the importance of marriage to individuals and communities. That same-sex couples are willing to embrace marriage's solemn obligations of exclusivity, mutual support, and commitment to one another is a testament to the enduring place of marriage in our laws and in the human spirit.

We also reject the argument suggested by the department, and elaborated by some amici, that expanding the institution of civil marriage in Massachusetts to include same-sex couples will lead to interstate conflict. We would not presume to dictate how another State should respond to today's decision. But neither should considerations of comity prevent us from according Massachusetts residents the full measure of protection available under the Massachusetts Constitution. The genius of our Federal system is that each State's Constitution has vitality specific to its own traditions, and that, subject to the minimum requirements of the Fourteenth Amendment, each State is free to address difficult issues of individual liberty in the manner its own Constitution demands.

Several amici suggest that prohibiting marriage by same-sex couples reflects community consensus that homosexual conduct is immoral. Yet Massachusetts has a strong affirmative policy of preventing discrimination on the basis of sexual orientation. See G.L. c. 151B (employment, housing, credit, services); G.L. c. 265, § 39 (hate crimes); G.L. c. 272, § 98 (public accommodation); G.L. c. 76, § 5 (public education).

The department has had more than ample opportunity to articulate a constitutionally adequate justification for limiting civil marriage to opposite-sex unions. It has failed to do so.

The marriage ban works a deep and scarring hardship on a very real segment of the community for no rational reason. The absence of any reasonable relationship between, on the one hand, an absolute disqualification of same-sex couples who wish to enter into civil marriage and, on the other, protection of public health, safety, or general welfare, suggests that the marriage restriction is rooted in persistent prejudices against persons who are (or who are believed to be) homosexual. "The Constitution cannot control such prejudices but neither can it tolerate them. Private biases may be outside the reach of the law, but the law cannot, directly or indirectly, give them effect." *Palmore v. Sidoti*, 466 U.S. 429, 433, 104 S.Ct. 1879, 80 L.Ed.2d 421 (1984) (construing Fourteenth Amendment). Limiting the protections, benefits, and obligations of civil marriage to opposite-sex couples violates the basic premises of individual liberty and equality under law protected by the Massachusetts Constitution.

We declare that barring an individual from the protections, benefits, and obligations of civil marriage solely because that person would marry a person of the same sex violates the Massachusetts Constitution. We vacate the summary judgment for the department. We remand this case to the Superior Court for entry of judgment consistent with this opinion. Entry of judgment shall be stayed for 180 days to permit the Legislature to take such action as it may deem appropriate in light of this opinion. *So ordered.*

---

4. Justice Cordy suggests that we have "transmuted the 'right' to marry into a right to change the institution of marriage itself," *post* at 365, 798 N.E.2d at 984 (Cordy, J., dissenting), because marriage is intimately tied to the reproductive systems of the marriage partners and to the "optimal" mother and father setting for child rearing. *Id.* That analysis hews perilously close to the argument, long repudiated by the Legislature and the courts, that men and women are so innately and fundamentally different that their respective "proper spheres" can be rigidly and universally delineated. An abundance of legislative enactments and decisions of this court negate any such stereotypical premises.

Notes and Questions

1. The court's decision reflected a vote of 4-3 by the justices, with the dissenters producing lengthy, impassioned arguments, some of which are referenced and responded to in Chief Justice Marshall's opinion.

2. In response to the court's ruling, the Massachusetts legislature considered adopting civil unions, as Vermont had done, to cure the constitutionality of the opposite-sex only marriage statute. In an advisory opinion, responding to an inquiry from the Massachusetts Senate, the Supreme Judicial Court said that creating civil unions would not satisfy the Massachusetts constitution. The continued exclusion of same-sex couples from civil marriage would be unconstitutional. Alluding to the U.S. Supreme Court's famous decision in Brown v. Board of Education, which had declared racial segregation of public schools unconstitutional and rejected the long-standing "separate but equal" doctrine, the Massachusetts court asserted that civil unions would be a futile attempt to establish a "separate but equal" institution for same-sex couples, and that separate was rarely truly equal. See *Opinions of the Justices to the Senate*, 802 N.E.2d 565 (Mass. 2004). On May 17, 2004, at the expiration of the 180 day stay, same-sex couples began to marry in Massachusetts. However, the Massachusetts legislature, assembled as a constitutional convention, approved an amendment to the state constitution that would restrict marriage to opposite-sex couples and authorize the establishment of civil unions as an alternative legal structure for same-sex couples. The proposed amendment cannot come to a vote until November 2006, and then only if it has been approved in identical form by a new session of the legislature.

3. Although the Massachusetts Supreme Judicial Court did not specify that its decision was valid only for Massachusetts residents, Governor Mitt Romney, seizing upon a provision of Massachusetts marriage law dating from 1913 (and evidently intended, among other things, to prevent interracial couples from coming to Massachusetts to marry), instructed the state officials charged with issuing marriage licenses that they could not issue licenses to same-sex couples whose state of residence would not allow or recognize same-sex marriages. Although a few local authorities initially rejected this instruction and issued licenses to out-of-state couples, within a few weeks they had ceased doing so under threats of lawsuit by the state's attorney general. Gay & Lesbian Advocates & Defenders then filed suit against the state on behalf of out-of-state couples, asserting that the 1913 statute was no longer valid and violated the *Goodridge* ruling. See *Cote-Whitacre v. Department of Public Health*, 18 Mass. L. Rptr. 190 (Mass. Super. 2004), upholding the denial of marriage certificates to nonresidents whose home states would not recognize the marriage. The case has been appealed to the Supreme Judicial Court of Massachusetts and the Court has agreed to hear the appeal.

4. *Litigation in New Jersey*: A test case, similar to *Goodridge*, has been filed in New Jersey by lawyers from Lambda Legal Defense and Education Fund. See *Lewis et al. v. Harris* (filed June 26, 2002). On November 5, 2003, the trial court rejected the plaintiffs' argument that the right to same-sex marriage is guaranteed in the New Jersey Constitution, and concluded that the definition of marriage was a matter for the legislature to decide. See 2003 WL 23191114. The case is currently on appeal. Oral arguments were made before the intermediate appellate court on December 7, 2004.

5. *Litigation in California*: In early 2004, the mayor of San Francisco determined that excluding same-sex couples from marriage was in violation of the California constitu-

tion. There was no litigation and no one made legal arguments before a court. Mayor Gavin Newsom, after attending President George W. Bush's January 20 state of the union address, in which the president called for a constitutional amendment to prevent same-sex marriages throughout the country, decided that it was his duty as a public official to uphold the existing constitutional guarantee of equality rather than to enforce discriminatory marriage laws. On February 12, 2004, Del Martin and Phyllis Lyon, partners for over 50 years, and early pioneers in the fight for sex equality and lesbian rights, were the first same-sex couple to be issued a marriage license by the City of San Francisco. Thousands of same-sex couples flocked to the city, requiring extra shifts of work for municipal employees and the deputizing of additional persons to perform the marriage ceremonies. Litigation immediately ensued. Opponents filed suit to stop the issuing of licenses to lesbian and gay couples and proponents filed suit claiming a constitutional right to marry. The City and County of San Francisco also filed suit, asking that the State of California be compelled to record and recognize the marriage licenses issued to same-sex couples.

Section 300 of the California Family Code provides that "[m]arriage is a personal relation arising out of a civil contract between a man and a woman..." Section 308.5, added by the voters in March 2000 when they passed Proposition 22, provides that only a marriage between a man and a woman is valid in California. The Attorney General for the State, the person responsible for defending California law, determined that the matter of the constitutionality of statutes limiting marriage to opposite sex couples was of utmost importance and requested an opinion from the California Supreme Court on this issue.

On March 11, 2004, the California Supreme Court halted the issuance of marriage licenses to same-sex couples, pending its consideration of whether the mayor had authority to direct city officers to issue the licenses. On August 12, in *Lockyer v. City and County of San Francisco*, 95 P.3d 459, the court unanimously ruled that the mayor lacked such authority, and by 5-2 vote ruled that the 4,037 licenses that had been issued to same-sex couples between February 12 and March 11 and that the marriages that had been performed were void and of no legal effect. The court ordered the city to contact all the couples and to offer to refund the fees they had paid. However, the court disclaimed any ruling on the underlying question of whether same-sex couples are entitled to marry in California, as new lawsuits had been filed on the question and were then pending in the Superior Court in San Francisco.

Six California "right to marry' lawsuits were consolidated and argued together before the Superior Court of San Francisco County. On March 14, 2005, the judge handed down his opinion in favor of the contestants, holding that California statutes restricting marriage to persons of the opposite sex unconstitutional under the equal protection clause of the California Constitution. See *Marriage Cases*, 2005 WL 583129 (2005).

6. *Litigation in the State of Washington*: Six same-sex couples filed suit against King County seeking the issuance of marriage licenses and claiming the right to marry under the Washington constitution. On August 4, 2003, Judge William Downing ruled in favor of the couples, observing:

> The social issue before the Court is one about which people of the highest intellect, the deepest morality and the broadest public vision maintain divergent opinions, strongly held in good faith and all worthy of great respect. Resolving their disagreement is, to be frank, a matter too big to be addressed to a lone individual and this author would naturally like nothing better than to stop at this point and, with a warm and sincere pat on the back, to send all parties

off to the State Supreme Court or the State legislature or both. Regrettably or not, such an abdication of responsibility is not an option. As this case and this debate pass by this way station, some impressions and conclusions must be recorded.

When the court is asked to sit in judgment of a law, it is not to consider whether, in its view, the law is wise or consistent with sound policy. These are matters for the people and their chosen legislators to weigh. The court's role is limited to holding the challenged law up to the state and federal constitutions —the foundations of our rule of law—to see if it satisfies the constitutional requirements. Rather than its own personal preferences, the court is required to apply a consistent, principled and reasoned analysis in evaluating the statute's constitutionality. Through this brilliant design, the constitutions empower the courts to ensure both that no group is singled out for special privileges and also that no minority is deprived of rights to which its members should be entitled. At the same time, respect for democratic lawmaking is maintained.

Proper respect for the separation of powers requires that, as to most laws subjected to challenge, the court will show great deference to the legislature. In most such cases, the court applies what is called "rational basis" review. Under this type of review, a statute will be found constitutional if it can be said that it is rationally related to a legitimate state goal or purpose.

Some challenged laws, however, call for what is called a "heightened scrutiny" by the courts. When the statute in question burdens a "fundamental right" or a "suspect class", it must pass a more rigorous test in order to satisfy the constitutions. The goal or purpose being sought must be deemed a "compelling state interest" and the means implemented toward that goal must be "narrowly tailored" toward that end.

The Court must examine the question of whether or not a fundamental right of the plaintiffs' is being burdened. There is a fundamental difference in the parties' approach to identifying the putative fundamental right upon which this analysis should focus. Should the Court focus on the broad right to marry or should it, instead, focus on the more narrowly drawn right to marry someone of the same sex?

This is a crucial question because all agree that precedent firmly establishes the broad right to marry as a fundamental right. *Loving v. Virginia*, 388 U.S. 1, 87 S. Ct. 1817, 18 L. Ed. 2d 1010 (1967). However, no case stands for the proposition that that narrowly defined right, standing by itself, constitutes a fundamental right.

This is not surprising as a fundamental right is generally described as one that is "deeply rooted in this Nation's history and tradition" and "implicit in the concept of ordered liberty." *Washington v. Glucksberg*, 521 U.S. 702, 720–21 (1997).

In seeking to label the right at issue in this case, it is instructive to examine the way in which the earlier key "right to marry" cases were argued and decided.

There was no deeply rooted tradition of interracial marriage at the time of the U.S. Supreme Court's consideration of anti-miscegenation statutes in *Loving v. Virginia*, supra; yet, the Court analyzed the issue of their constitutionality in terms of the broad right to marry and found that right to have been infringed. There was no deeply rooted tradition of marriage while delinquent in child support payments at the time of the U.S. Supreme Court's consideration of statutes prohibiting this in *Zablocki v. Redhail*, 434 U.S. 374 (1978); yet, the Court analyzed the issue of their constitutionality in terms of the broad right to marry and found that right to have been infringed. There was no deeply rooted tradition of inmate marriage at the time of the U.S. Supreme Court's consideration of statutes restricting this in *Turner v. Safley*, 482 U.S. 78 (1987); yet, the Court analyzed the issue of their constitutionality in terms of the broad right to marry and found that right to have been infringed....

In *Turner*, supra, it was specifically argued that the Court should focus its attention on "inmate marriage" as opposed to the broader right to marry. The Court rejected this approach.

It may be argued that the marriage contemplated in *Turner*, like those in *Zablocki* and *Loving*, was a heterosexual marriage. Yet, the hallmarks of the marital relationship to which the inmates and their intendeds aspired, are not linked to a capacity to procreate. It is to a non-coital relationship but one that was a supportive, committed, spiritually significant marriage with government benefits and property rights that the Supreme Court deemed them to have a fundamental right.

Recently, in looking at this same issue, the Massachusetts Supreme Court concluded "it is the exclusive and permanent commitment of the marriage partners to one another, not the begetting of children, that is the sine qua non of civil marriage." *Goodridge v. Department of Public Health*, 440 Mass. 309, 332, 798 N.E.2d 941 (2003).

The recent trend, both in our society and in the Supreme Court, has been to focus even more on the fundamental liberty of personal autonomy in connection with one's intimate affairs and family relations. In building on its 1992 analysis in *Planned Parenthood of Southeastern Pa. v. Casey*, 505 U.S. 833 (1992), the U. S. Supreme Court had this to say just last year:

> The Casey decision again confirmed that our laws and traditions afford constitutional protection to personal decisions relating to marriage, procreation, contraception, family relationships, child rearing, and education. In explaining the respect the Constitution demands for the autonomy of the person in making these choices, we stated as follows:
>
> > "These matters, involving the most intimate and personal choices a person may make in a lifetime, choices central to personal dignity and autonomy, are central to the liberty protected by the Fourteenth Amendment. At the heart of liberty is the right to define one's own concept of existence, of meaning, of the universe, and of the mystery of human life. Beliefs about these matters could not define the attributes of personhood were they formed under compulsion of the State."

Lawrence v. Texas, 123 S. Ct. at 2481. To this eloquent description of just what it is that is fundamental about fundamental rights, the Court added this: "Persons in a homosexual relationship may seek autonomy for these reasons just as heterosexual persons do." 123 S. Ct. at 2482.

Leaping backwards now, more than a century ago the United States Supreme Court characterized marriage as "the most important relation in life" and "the foundation of the family and of society, without which there would be neither civilization nor progress." *Maynard v. Hill*, 125 U.S. 190, 211, 8 S. Ct. 723, 31 L. Ed. 654 (1888).

That, then, is the right being asserted by the plaintiffs here—the autonomous right to have such a "most important relation" in their lives and, in that relationship, to be able to make their own unique contribution to the foundation of society. That right—a right that is unquestionably burdened by the statutes in question—is the fundamental right to marry.

Judge Downing then analyzed the state's justifications for refusing to grant licenses to same-sex couples and found all of them to be wanting, both under heightened scrutiny and also under rational basis review. *Anderson v. King County*, 2004 WL 1738447 (Wash., King Co. Super. Ct., Aug. 4, 2004). See also *Castle v. State*, 2004 WL 1985215 (Wash. Super. September 7, 2004)(similarly holding state statute prohibiting same-sex marriage violates privileges and immunities clause). Both of these cases are on appeal to the state Supreme Court and the effect of the trial court decisions has been stayed, pending the outcome on appeal.

7. *Litigation in Oregon*: Over 3000 marriage licenses have been issued to same-sex couples, although a court stopped the practice in Multnomah County (Portland) shortly after it had begun. An appeals court has ordered the state to register the licenses even though their validity is the subject of a separate lawsuit to be heard by the Oregon Supreme Court. See *Li v. State*, 2004 WL 1258167 (Ore. Cir. April 20, 2004)(holding that the Oregon constitution requires equal access to benefits by same-sex couples). On July 28, the Oregon Supreme Court agreed that it would hear the constitutional claim without going through the intermediate appeals court. However, on November 3, Oregon voters amended the state constitution to prohibit recognition of same-sex marriages. The amendment provided: "Only marriage between one man and one woman is valid or legally recognized as marriage." How should this amendment affect the Oregon Supreme Court's deliberations in the *Li* case?

8. *Litigation in other states*: As of December, 2004, "right to marry" cases had been filed in a number of other states, including Arizona, Connecticut, Florida, Indiana, Maryland and New York. The Arizona and Indiana courts have definitively ruled against same-sex marriage, see *Standhardt v. Superior Court*, 77 P.3d 451 (Ariz. Ct. App. 2003)(ruling against same-sex marriage), review denied (May 25, 2004); *Morrison v. Sadler*, 821 N.E.2d 15 (Ind. App. 2005). There are several New York cases currently in litigation. Several trial courts have upheld the constitutionality of the marriage statute. See, e.g., Shields v. Madigan, 783 N.Y.S.2d 279 (N.Y. Sup. Ct. 2004); Seymour v. Holcomb, 2005 WL 440509 (N.Y. Sup. Ct. 2005). But at least one trial court has ruled the statute unconstitutional on both equal protection and due process grounds. Hernandez v. Robles, 2005 WL 363778 (N.Y. Sup. Ct. 2005).

9. *The backlash*: As the push for same-sex marriage increased during 2004, opponents of same-sex marriage mounted a counter attack, building on their earlier success following Congressional enactment of DOMA in 1996. Between 1996 and 2004, thirty-seven states followed Congress by enacting state versions of DOMA, often referred to as baby or mini-DOMAs. A true mini-DOMA not only bans recognition of same-sex marriage within the state by limiting marriage to one man and one woman, but also separately provides that same-sex marriages, even if valid in other jurisdic-

tions, will not be recognized within the state. Some of these states (e.g., Nebraska, Nevada, and Oregon) placed these provisions directly in the state constitution rather than in the statute books. Three states had enacted similar statutory provisions before 1996 (Hawaii, Maryland, and North Carolina). Thus, by the end of 2004, there were only ten states in which the recognition of foreign same-sex marriages was not specifically addressed by a statute or by a provision in the state constitution. Yet, a number of those ten states (e.g., Vermont and Wyoming) have statutes clearly defining marriage as a relationship between a man and a woman. See Vt. Stat. Ann. Tit. 15 §8; Wyo. Stat. §20-1-101. At the general elections held November 2, 2004, a dozen states added amendments to their state constitutions prohibiting same-sex marriages. Some of these amendments went further to forbid other forms of legal recognition of unmarried couples.

4. Marriage Developments in Other Countries

a. The Netherlands

In April 2001, the Netherlands became the first country to enact legislation authorizing same-sex marriage. As in the United States, same-sex marriage activists had pursued litigation asking the Dutch courts to recognize same-sex marriage. In the only case to reach the Dutch Supreme Court, the Court ruled that excluding same-sex couples from marriage was justified because the law presumes that a woman's husband is the father of her children. That single special rule for married couples was inappropriate for same-sex couples and thus apparently the denial of all marriage benefits was justified. That decision was handed down in 1990. By 1994 the Dutch parliament was seriously studying the issues raised by state recognition of same-sex marriage, or, in the alternative, recognition of a form of domestic partnership. Ultimately, the parliament passed a domestic partnership law, known as the Dutch Registered Partnership Act, which went into effect in 1998. The act provided that registered partners enjoyed most of the same benefits and obligations as married couples. The primary exception was in the area of parenting. Partners were unable to adopt children jointly. If a person with a child entered into a registered partnership with another person, that person was accorded no parental status. In order to overcome these shortcomings, same-sex marriage activists continued to lobby the Dutch parliament. A bill recognizing same-sex marriages was adopted in early December 2000 and signed into law on December 1. The act took effect on April 1, 2001. To take advantage of the Dutch law, at least one of the partners must be either a Dutch national or domiciliary.

There are two differences between same-sex and opposite-sex marriages in the Netherlands. First of all, a same-sex partner will not be presumed to be the biological parent of any child born of the mother during the term of the marriage. The partner does automatically obtain joint custody of the child by virtue of the marriage and the partner can easily adopt the child. Thus, the distinction is a minor one in practice. The other difference involves foreign adoptions. While opposite-sex couples are free to adopt children from other countries, a same-sex couple is more restricted. This distinction was thought necessary because it was not clear how foreign countries might respond to Dutch same-sex marriages. International treaties that speak of spouses and spousal rights were obviously adopted at a time when the only possible spouses were persons of the opposite sex. It will take some time to sort out questions regarding the extra-territorial effect of Dutch same-sex marriages.

See generally Yuval Merin, Equality for Same-Sex Couples: The Legal Recognition of Gay Partnerships in Europe and the United States, pp. 114–29 (2002).

b. Belgium

In 2003, Belgium followed the lead of the Netherlands and enacted same-sex marriage legislation. See Developments in the Law—The Law of Marriage and the Family, Inching Down the Aisle: Differing Paths Toward the Legalization of Same-Sex Marriage in the Unites States and Europe, 116 Harv. L. Rev. 2004 (2003).

c. Canada

On July 12, 2002, the Superior Court of Justice in Ontario, Canada issued its ruling in *Halpern v. Canada*, holding that the common law rule limiting marriage to a union of one man and one woman violated the equality rights of gay men and lesbians under the Canadian Charter of Rights and Freedoms. The three judges who heard the case disagreed as to remedy. One judge (LaForme) ruled that that the definition of marriage must be opened immediately to include same-sex unions and concluded that the "marriages" of the claimants were valid. The second judge (Blair) ruled that it should be up to Parliament to determine the appropriate remedy, but if Parliament failed to enact a constitutional remedy within 24 months, then the definition of marriage would be changed to include same-sex couples. The third judge (Smith) agreed that the common law rule violated the equality rights of the claimants and also agreed that Parliament should have 24 months to "fix" the rule, but thought it inappropriate to decide at the current time what the court should do if Parliament failed to act appropriately. Instead, she would prefer to review Parliament's action (or inaction) whenever it occurs and to determine the constitutional consequences at that time.

The case was appealed. On June 10, 2003, the Ontario Court of Appeal upheld the substantive ruling that the exclusion of same-sex couples from the institution of marriage violated the equality provision in the Canadian Charter of Rights and Freedoms. But the court disagreed with the 24 month suspension and held that the ruling was to be effective immediately. The City of Toronto at once began issuing marriage licenses to same-sex couples. Perhaps even more importantly, the court ruled that the marriages of two of the couples in the case, that had previously taken place at the Metropolitan Community Church in Toronto on January 14, 2001, were valid, making them the first valid same-sex marriages in the modern world.

Similar litigation moved forward in the province of British Columbia. See *EGALE Canada Inc. v. Canada*, [2001] B.C.J. No. 1995, rev'd, [2003] B.C.C.A. No. 251. The British Columbia appellate court agreed with the Ontario courts that prohibiting same-sex couples from marrying violated the charter. Initially the court agreed with the 24 month suspension of the ruling's effect, but once the Ontario ruling was made effective, the British Columbia court followed suit. By the end of 2003, the two most populous provinces in Canada recognized same-sex marriage. American same-sex couples flocked to both provinces to marry because, for the first time marriage licenses were freely available, and, unlike the situation in Holland, were available to nonresidents.

On March 19, 2004, the appeals court in the province of Quebec handed down a decision that made Quebec the third province to recognize same-sex marriages, and later in the year, a Supreme Court justice in Yukon Territory opined that it was intolerable that the Charter Rights of same-sex couples vary from province to province, in light of the federal government's decision not to appeal the prior rulings to the national supreme court, and ordered the Yukon government to issue licenses, declaring a nation-wide precedent. The federal legislature is considering legislation that would make same-sex marriage available throughout all ten provinces in Canada and asked the Supreme Court of Canada for advice (called a "Reference") about the constitutionality of the proposed law (e.g., will it infringe religious liberty). The Supreme Court has ruled that the law would be constitutional and it is expected to pass in 2005.

For a detailed description of Canada's move toward marriage equality for same-sex couples, see R. Douglas Elliott, "The Canadian Earthquake: Same-Sex Marriage in Canada," 38 New Eng. L. Rev. 591 (2004).

5. Extra-territorial Recognition of Same-sex Marriages

Because of the physical proximity of Canada and the United States, many same-sex couples from the U.S. have gone to Canada to get married since the spring of 2003. What is the potential impact of their Canadian marriages in the United States? A similar question arises for a couple married in Massachusetts. Will the marriage be recognized in other states?

Most states have specific laws that either prohibit the recognition of same-sex marriages or pronounce that such marriages are against the public policy of the state. Absent a successful constitutional challenge to the validity of these laws, recognition of same-sex marriages in these states would seem to be prohibited. But even in states with mini-DOMAs, the question arises as to whether or not the state's mini-DOMA should be applied. That is because interstate or extra-territorial recognition of marital status raises a conflict of laws question. Should the state of Iowa apply Iowa law in a same-sex marriage case if the couple was married in Massachusetts? The answer depends on the facts of the case.

Many people believe that marriages valid in one state must be recognized as valid marriages in another state because of the full faith and credit clause in the United States constitution. That clause (Article IV, § 1) provides:

> Full Faith and Credit shall be given in each State to the public Acts, Records, and Judicial Proceedings of every other state.

Marriages are not typically recognized by other states under the principles of full faith and credit because marriages, although they are *matters* of public record, are not final judgments. Instead marriages are recognized by other states under conflicts of law rules applying the broad principles of "comity." The same rules would apply to recognition of marriages from foreign countries. These principles can take into account public policy issues.

As Professor Mark Strasser explains:

> Although one might infer that the same amount of credit would be given to judicial proceedings on the one hand and public Acts and Records on the other, the Supreme Court has made clear that such an inference would be incorrect. Assuming no fraud or lack of jurisdiction, final judgments issued by a court in one state are entitled to full faith and credit in every state. However, the same "exacting" rule regarding full faith and credit is not imposed with respect to other states' acts (laws), since the forum state's public policy is a permissible

consideration in deciding whether another state's law should be applied in a particular case. Thus, as a general matter, another state's law which strongly offends local policy need not be applied if the case is being heard for the first time in the forum state.

Mark Strasser, When is a Parent not a Parent? On DOMA, Civil Unions, and Presumptions of Parenthood, 23 Cardoza L. Rev, 299 at 317–18 (2001). See also Patrick J. Borchers, The Essential Irrelevance of the Full Faith and Credit Clause to the Same-Sex Marriage Debate, 38 Creighton L. Rev. 353 (2005).

The passage of a baby DOMA by the state's legislature is good evidence that state recognition of same-sex unions is against public policy, especially if the state statute specifically states that recognition of such marriages violates the public policy of the state. State statutes differ quite a bit in how they address the issue. Compare the three statutes below and consider whether the language in the statute prevents a state court from ever recognizing a Massachusetts same-sex marriage.

Alaska Stat. § 25.05.013 — Same-sex marriages.

a. A marriage entered into by persons of the same sex, either under common law or under statute, that is recognized by another state or foreign jurisdiction is void in this state, and contractual rights granted by virtue of the marriage, including its termination, are unenforceable in this state.

b. A same-sex relationship may not be recognized by the state as being entitled to the benefits of marriage.

North Carolina Gen. Stat. § 51-1.2 — Marriages between person of the same gender not valid.

Marriages, whether created by common law, contracted, or performed outside of North Carolina, between individuals of the same gender are not valid in North Carolina.

Vermont Stat. Ann. Title 15 § 8 — Marriage definition.

Marriage is the legally recognized union of one man and one woman.

A conflict of laws question normally arises when a legal issue is being raised in the courts of one state and one of the parties is asking for the law of another state to be applied to resolve the question. For example, assume that Jane and Martha are married in Massachusetts. Some years later, assume that they find themselves in the state of North Carolina. Assume further that Jane is killed by a drunk driver, who is a resident of North Carolina. Martha attempts to sue the tortfeasor in North Carolina, making a wrongful death claim. Under North Carolina law, a wrongful death claim can be pursued by Jane's estate, but only for the benefit of her intestate heirs. See N.C.G.S §28A-18-2(a). If we assume that Jane has no surviving blood relatives, then her only intestate heir under the North Carolina statute is her spouse, Martha. Can Martha recover as Jane's spouse under North Carolina law?

The law of North Carolina does not recognize same-sex marriages. But the law of Massachusetts does. There is a clear conflict between the laws of the two states. The North Carolina court has the option of applying either North Carolina law, in which case Martha will lose, or Massachusetts law, in which case Martha will win. Choosing which law to apply requires the court to analyze North Carolina's interest in applying its own law. One important question that the court will want to consider is: why were Jane and Martha in North Carolina in the first place?

Scholars who have addressed the marriage conflict of laws question have divided the conflicts scenarios into four main fact patterns: (1) cases in which the marriage occurred in a foreign jurisdiction (Massachusetts) for the primary purpose of evading the laws of the forum jurisdiction (North Carolina); (2) cases in which the married couple was domiciled in the foreign jurisdiction at the time of the marriage, but has since moved to the forum jurisdiction; (3) cases in which the married couple wase domiciled in the foreign jurisdiction, is still domiciled in that jurisdiction, and is in the forum state only temporarily, e.g., as visitors; and (4) cases in which the married couple is domiciled and resident in the foreign state, and the legal question arises in the forum state because of some extraterritorial consideration, such as the ownership of land in the forum state. See Note, Developments in the Law—The Law of Marriage and Family: Constitutional Constraints on Interstate Same-Sex Marriage Recognition, 116 Harv. L. Rev. 2028 (2003).

Professor Andrew Koppelman, relying on these four categories, concludes that, as a matter of conflict of laws principles, in states that have a baby DOMA, the marriage should not be recognized in the first category of cases (evasive marriages), could be recognized in the second category of cases (migratory marriages), should be recognized in the third category of cases (visitor marriages), and almost always is recognized in cases that fall in the fourth category (extraterritorial marriages). See Koppelman, Interstate recognition of same-sex marriages and civil unions: a handbook for judges, 153 U. Pa. L. Rev. __ (2005). But in every case, it is up to the forum state to decide which law to apply and no legal doctrine developed to date, especially not the "full faith and credit clause," would require the state to apply any law other than its own. Koppelman, however, suggests that in appropriate cases, a married couple's constitutional right to travel might be impinged if their marital status were to change as they cross state borders.

While there is a large body of law on conflict of law principles generally, most cases raise questions of which state's tort or contract law to apply. Cases regarding marriage are less common. That is because most states agree on which marriages to recognize and generally are willing to recognize any marriage that was valid in the state of celebration. Conflicts, however, can arise when one state bans marriages within a certain degree of consanguinity and another state doesn't or when one state has minimum age requirements that differ from another state. In the past, conflicts arose between states that had miscegenation statutes and those that did not.

State v. Ross
76 N.C. 242 (1877)

[Facts: Sarah Ross, a white woman, moved from North Carolina to South Carolina, where she married Pink Ross, a black man who was a native of South Carolina. The marriage was valid under South Carolina law. The couple lived in South Carolina for three months and then moved to North Carolina, where their marriage was not valid. They were arrested for illegally cohabiting. Their defense was that they were validly married. The trial court agreed, recognized the marriage, and found the defendants not guilty.]

RODMAN, J.

The question thus presented is an important one. The State of North Carolina, with the general concurrence of its citizens of both races, has declared its conviction that marriages between them are immoral and opposed to public policy as tending to degrade them both. It has therefore declared such marriages void. It is needless to say that the members of this Court share that opinion. For that reason it becomes us to be careful not to be unduly influenced by it in ascertaining, not what the law of North Carolina is upon such marriages contracted within her limits—that is found in the Act of Assembly and is beyond doubt—but what the law of North Carolina is upon the question presented, and for that we must look beyond the statutes of the State.

If we are right in our conception of the question presented, to-wit; whether a marriage in South Carolina between a black man and a white woman *bona fide* domiciled there and valid by the law of that State, must be regarded as valid in this State when the parties afterwards migrate here? We think that the decided weight of English and American authority requires us to hold that the relation thus lawful in its inception continues to be lawful here.

We know of but two cases which appear to be to the contrary...

The general rule is admitted that a marriage between citizens of a foreign State contracted in that State and valid by its laws is valid everywhere where the parties might migrate, although not contracted with the rites required by the law of the country into which they come and between persons disqualified by such law from intermarrying....

It is contended however by the Attorney General that there is an exception to this rule as well established as the rule itself, viz; that incestuous and polygamous marriages although lawful in the country in which they are contracted, will not be recognized in other States in which such marriages are deemed immoral and are prohibited. And it is further argued that a marriage between persons of different races is as unnatural and as revolting as an incestuous one, and is declared void by the law of North Carolina.

Story [on Conflicts of Laws] (§ 113a) says, "The most prominent if not the only known exceptions to the rule are those marriages involving polygamy and incest; those positively prohibited by the public law of a country from motives of policy; and those celebrated in foreign countries by subjects entitling themselves under special circumstances to the benefit of the laws of their own country."

On examining the illustrations of these exceptions given by the author, it will be seen that they are considerably limited. Thus all Christian countries agree that marriages in the direct line and between the nearest collaterals, are incestuous, and that polygamy is unlawful, consequently such marriages will be held null everywhere, because they were null in the place of the contract. But beyond these few cases in which all States agree, there is a difference as to what marriages are incestuous, and in such cases the admitted international law leaves it to each State to say what is incestuous in respect to its own subjects. In England, a marriage with the sister of a deceased wife is held incestuous and between persons domiciled in England it will be held void wherever contracted. *Brook v. Brook,* 9 H. L. 193. But it does not follow that such a marriage contracted in a State where it was lawful, between subjects of that State, would be held void in England if the parties afterwards became domiciled there. There is no reason to think it would be. Story § 116, 116 a. Still stronger are the illustrations given in §§ 95, 96....

It is impossible to identify this case with that of an incestuous or polygamous marriage admitted to be such *jure gentium.* The law of nations is a part of the law of North Carolina. We are under obligations of comity to our sister States. We are compelled to say that this marriage being valid in the State where the parties were *bona fide* domiciled at the time of the contract must be regarded as subsisting after their immigration here.

The inconveniences which may arise from this view of the law are less than those which result from a different one. The children of such a marriage, if born in South

Carolina, could migrate here and would be considered legitimate. The only evil which could be avoided by a contrary conclusion is that the people of this State might be spared the bad example of an unnatural and immoral but lawful cohabitation....

Upon this question above all others it is desirable...that there should not be one law in Maine and another in Texas, but that the same law shall prevail at least throughout the United States.

There is no error in the judgment below. Let this opinion be certified.

READE, J. *Dissenting.*

No nation can make laws for another nation. Each is independent and makes its own laws. But by common consent of all nations, certain rules have been established for their intercourse, and these rules constitute the law of nations. And their observance is compelled by force if necessary. This is denominated public international law. Wheaton's International Law, §77.

As distinguished from *public* international law for the conduct of nations *as nations,* there are private international laws for the conduct, not of nations as nations, but of the people of different nations, by which it is tacitly agreed that rights acquired, privileges enjoyed, and relations formed in one nation, shall be recognized in another nation. But it is expressly laid down that this is only by *comity,* and is never allowed where it contravenes a prohibitory enactment. Ibid, §79.

No nation is bound to admit the laws and customs of another nation within its borders. It is independent in its Legislation and can by positive enactments refuse the operation of any law or custom of any other nation or people. I speak of the power and not of the *propriety.* If a nation should deny to the people of other nations just and reasonable privileges, it would find its punishment in having the same privileges denied to its citizens. And therefore comity, courtesy, is allowed to govern. A marriage formed in Scotland where nothing is required but the consent of the parties, we allow to be valid here, although it would be invalid if formed here; because it is a mere matter of form and we courteously recognize it. It inflicts no harm upon our people. But suppose Scotland were to allow children of ten years of age to marry, would we allow the marriage to be good here?

Probably we might allow it in the absence of a positive enactment; but we require our own people to be, the male sixteen and the female fourteen years of age; or else the marriage is void; and why may we not prohibit it in foreigners? We prohibit it among our own people, not out of caprice, but to prevent improvident marriages to the degradation and injury of the community. I give this illustration because France which has fixed ages for marriages as we have will not recognize a marriage celebrated elsewhere within the ages, although valid where celebrated. Wheat. §93. The rule is thus laid down in Wheaton, §§90-1. "A contract valid by the law of the place where it is made is generally speaking valid everywhere. The general comity and mutual convenience of nations have established the rule, that the law of that place governs in everything respecting the form, interpretation, obligation and effect of the contract wherever the authority, rights and interests of other States and their citizens are not thereby prejudiced. * * * * It cannot apply where it would injuriously conflict with the laws of another State relating to its police, its public health, its commerce, its revenue, and generally its sovereign authority and the rights and interests of its citizens."

In other words comity is secondary to the public good of any given nation, and subject to be contravened by its positive enactments. I timidly but very positively deny what a great Judge (Ruffin) has said, that a Turk with his many wives, or a Mormon, can have his rights which he has in his own country recognized here, because it is revolting to our people and against their best interests. Our law prohibits the intermarriage of whites and blacks and declares such marriages "void."

If such a marriage solemnized here between our own people is declared void, why should comity require the evil to be imported from another State? Why is not the relation severed the instant they set foot upon our soil? It is answered that we would thereby bastardize the issue and disturb the rights of property. Not at all. That does not follow. If they have issue before they come here, the status of the issue may not be changed; and by separating them we prevent issue here. Nor need their rights of property be affected. However that is not before us. And at any rate the public good is paramount. And individuals who have formed relations which are obnoxious to our laws can find their comfort in staying away from us. We give to comity all the force of a constitutional provision when we allow it to annul a statute. Indeed we put it above the Constitution itself; as I believe one of the late amendments prohibits the intermarriage of white and colored. It is inherent in every nation to prohibit whatever is an evil to its society. And it must be its own judge of what is an evil. Self-preservation requires it.

That provision in the Constitution of the United States, "The citizens of each State shall be entitled to all privileges and immunities of citizens in the several States" does not mean that a citizen of South Carolina removing here may bring with him his South Carolina privileges and immunities; but that when he comes here he may have the same privileges and immunities which our citizens have. Nothing more and nothing less. It is courteous for neighbors to visit and it is handsome to allow the visitor family privileges and even to give him the favorite seat; but if he bring his pet rattlesnake or his pet bear or spitz dog famous for hydrophobia, he must leave them outside the door. And if he bring small pox the door may be shut against him.

I am of the opinion that a prohibitory statute is paramount to what might otherwise be allowed as comity, and that the defendants are guilty.

Notes and Questions

1. Return for a moment to the case of Martha and Jane, married in Massachusetts, before Jane is hit by a North Carolina drunk driver and killed. The wrongful death claim is before the North Carolina courts. Can Martha rely on *Ross*? What arguments can you make on behalf of Martha that would address the concerns raised by the North Carolina Supreme Court in *Ross*? Can you identify the relevant harms to Martha, the state of Massachusetts, and the State of North Carolina that would result from recognition of the marriage and from nonrecognition of the marriage? Should it make any difference if Martha and Jane were current residents of North Carolina? Were in North Carolina at their "second home," a vacation retreat on the outer banks? Were merely passing through North Carolina on a trip to visit friends?

2. What result in a case in which Jane had purchased real estate in North Carolina before she moved to Massachusetts? While domiciled in Massachusetts, she marries Martha. The couple continues to live in Massachusetts and has never set foot in the state of North Carolina as a couple. Assume that Jane dies intestate and that under Massachusetts law Martha, as spouse, is entitled to inherit the entire estate. To clear up title in North Carolina, an ancillary administration is necessary. Jane's only living

relative is her brother, Bob. Bob claims that under North Carolina law, he should inherit the North Carolina realty because North Carolina law does not recognize same-sex marriages. Martha claims she should inherit as Jane's spouse. In this legal proceeding, should the North Carolina courts recognize the legitimacy of the Massachusetts marriage? See *Miller v. Lucks*, 36 So. 2d 140 (Miss. 1948), upholding the right of the white husband to inherit his black wife's Mississippi property against claims of her biological family because the couple was domiciled in Illinois where their marriage was valid. Both the Mississippi constitution and its statutes provided that such marriages "shall be unlawful and void." In ruling for the husband, the State Supreme Court explained:

> The manifest and recognized purpose of this statute was to prevent persons of Negro and white blood from living together in this state in the relationship of husband and wife. Where, as here, this did not occur, to permit one of the parties to such a marriage to inherit property in this state from the other costs no violence to the purpose of Sections 263 of our Constitution and 459 of the Code of 1942. What we are requested to do is simply to recognize this marriage to the extent only of permitting one of the parties thereto to inherit from the other property in Mississippi, and to that extent it must and will be recognized.

3. Suppose Martha and Jane were domiciled in Massachusetts and filed for bankruptcy in federal court there? Now the conflict exists between Massachusetts law and federal law. The federal DOMA clearly provides that, under federal statutes, spouses of the same sex will not be recognized as spouses. How is this situation different from a conflict between the substantive law of two states? What arguments can you make on their behalf that they should be treated as spouses under the Bankruptcy provisions of federal law? See *In re Kandu*, 315 B.R. 123 (Bankr. W.D. Wash. 2004), holding that the principles of comity did not compel the court to recognize the Canadian marriage of the spouses to allow them to file a joint bankruptcy petition and that this denial of access to the bankruptcy system and of recognition of their foreign marriage did not violate the 4th, 5th, or 10th Amendments of the U.S. Constitution.

Wilson v. Ake
354 F. Supp. 2d 1298 (M.D. Fla. 2005)

Moody, District Judge.

THIS CAUSE comes before the Court upon United States Attorney General John Ashcroft's Motion to Dismiss. The Court, having considered the Motion and Memoranda, and being otherwise fully advised, finds that the Motion should be granted.

Factual and Procedural Background

Plaintiffs Nancy Wilson and Paula Schoenwether allege that they are a lesbian couple who reside together in the Middle District of Florida. According to the Complaint, Plaintiffs were legally married in the State of Massachusetts and possess a valid marriage license from that State. Plaintiffs allege that they personally presented their Massachusetts marriage license to a Deputy Clerk at the Clerk of the Circuit Court's Office in Hillsborough County, Florida, asking for "acceptance of the valid and legal Massachusetts marriage license." (Complaint, ¶ 12). Plaintiffs allege that "[t]heir demand was refused by Defendant Ake, whose Deputy Clerk stated that according to Federal and Florida law, the Clerk is not allowed to recognize, for marriage purposes, the Massachusetts marriage license, because Federal and Florida law prohibit such recognition." (Complaint, ¶ 12).

Plaintiffs have filed a Complaint for Declaratory Judgment asking this Court to declare the Federal Defense of Marriage Act ("DOMA"), and Florida Statues § 741.212[1] unconstitutional and to enjoin their enforcement. Plaintiffs have sued, in their official capacities, Richard L. Ake, Clerk of the Circuit Court in Hillsborough County, Florida, and United States Attorney General John Ashcroft.

* * *

Plaintiffs allege that the two statutes violate the Full Faith and Credit Clause, the Due Process clause of the Fourteenth Amendment, the Equal Protection Clause of the Fourteenth Amendment, the Privileges and Immunities Clause, and the Commerce Clause of the United States Constitution.

Plaintiffs assert that Florida is required to recognize Plaintiffs' valid Massachusetts marriage license because DOMA exceeds Congress' power under the Full Faith and Credit Clause. Plaintiffs also argue that twelve United States Supreme Court cases (which Plaintiffs label "The Dynamite Dozen"), beginning with *Brown v. Board of Education*, 347 U.S. 483 (1954) and ending with *Lawrence v. Texas*, 539 U.S. 558 (2003), demonstrate a recent trend by the United States Supreme Court to expand "the fundamental liberty of personal autonomy in connection with one's intimate affairs and family relations." ... Plaintiffs urge this Court to expand on "The Dynamite Dozen" by finding that the right to enter into a same-sex marriage is protected by the Constitution.

Defendant Ashcroft has moved to dismiss Plaintiffs' Complaint pursuant to Rule 12(b)(6), Fed R. Civ. P. on the grounds that the Complaint fails to state a claim upon which relief can be granted. The United States, in a well-written Memorandum, argues that Plaintiffs' Complaint is barred as a matter of law because DOMA does not infringe on any of Plaintiffs' fundamental rights and is a legitimate exercise of the power granted to Congress by the Full Faith and Credit Clause.

* * *

---

1. Florida Statutes § 741.212, Marriages between persons of the same sex, provides:

(1) Marriages between persons of the same sex entered into in any jurisdiction, whether within or outside the State of Florida, the United States, or any other jurisdiction, either domestic or foreign, or any other place or location, or relationships between persons of the same sex which are treated as marriages in any jurisdiction, whether within or outside the State of Florida, the United States, or any other jurisdiction, either domestic or foreign, or any other place or location, are not recognized for any purpose in this state.

(2) The state, its agencies, and its political subdivisions may not give effect to any public act, record, or judicial proceeding of any state, territory, possession, or tribe of the United States or of any other jurisdiction, either domestic or foreign, or any other place or location respecting either a marriage or relationship not recognized under subsection (1) or a claim arising from such a marriage or relationship.

(3) For purposes of interpreting any state statute or rule, the term "marriage" means only a legal union between one man and one woman as husband and wife, and the term "spouse" applies only to a member of such a union.

Full Faith and Credit Clause

Plaintiffs' Complaint asserts that DOMA conflicts with the Constitution's Full Faith and Credit Clause. Article IV, Section I of the Constitution provides:

> Full Faith and Credit shall be given in each State to the public Acts, Records, and Judicial Proceedings of every other State; And the Congress may by general Laws prescribe the Manner in which such Acts, Records and Proceedings shall be proved, and the Effect thereof.

Plaintiffs argue that "[o]nce Massachusetts sanctioned legal same-gender marriage, all other states should be constitutionally required to uphold the validity of the marriage." (Complaint, ¶ 23). Plaintiffs believe that the differences in individuals' rights to enter into same-sex marriages among the States, such as Florida and Massachusetts, is exactly what the Full Faith and Credit Clause prohibits. They also assert that DOMA is beyond the scope of Congress' legislative power under the Full Faith and Credit Clause because Congress may only regulate what effect a law may have, it may not dictate that the law has no effect at all.

This Court disagrees with Plaintiff's interpretation of the Full Faith and Credit Clause. Congress' actions in adopting DOMA are exactly what the Framers envisioned when they created the Full Faith and Credit Clause. DOMA is an example of Congress exercising its powers under the Full Faith and Credit Clause to determine the effect that "any public act, record, or judicial proceeding of any other State, territory, possession, or tribe respecting a relationship between persons of the same sex that is treated as a marriage" has on the other States. 28 U.S.C.§1738C. Congress' actions are an appropriate exercise of its power to regulate conflicts between the laws of two different States, in this case, conflicts over the validity of same-sex marriages.

Adopting Plaintiffs' rigid and literal interpretation of the Full Faith and Credit Clause would create a license for a single State to create national policy. See *Nevada v. Hall*, 440 U.S. 410, 423–24 (1979) ("Full Faith and Credit does not...enable one state to legislate for the other or to project its laws across state lines so as to preclude the other from prescribing for itself the legal consequences of acts within it.")...Williams v. North Carolina, 317 U.S. 287 (1942)("Nor is there any authority which lends support to the view that the full faith and credit clause compels the courts of one state to subordinate the local policy of that state, as respects its domiciliaries, to the statutes of any other state."). The Supreme Court has clearly established that "the Full Faith and Credit Clause does not require a State to apply another State's law in violation of its own legitimate public policy." *Hall* at 422. Florida is not required to recognize or apply Massachusetts' same-sex marriage law because it clearly conflicts with Florida's legitimate public policy of opposing same-sex marriage.

Baker v. Nelson

The United States argues that this Court is bound by the United States Supreme Court's decision in *Baker v. Nelson*, 291 Minn 310, 191 N.W.2d 185 (1971), appeal dismissed, 409 U.S. 810 (1972). In *Baker v. Nelson*, two adult males' application for a marriage license was denied by the Clerk of the Hennepin County District Court because the petitioners were of the same sex. The plaintiffs, following the quashing of a writ of mandamus directing the clerk to issue a marriage license, appealed to the Minnesota Supreme Court. Plaintiffs argued that Minnesota Statute §517.08, which did not authorize marriage between persons of the same sex, violated the First, Eighth, Ninth and Fourteenth Amendments of the United States Constitution. The Minnesota Supreme

Court rejected plaintiffs' assertion that "the right to marry without regard to the sex of the parties is a fundamental right of all persons" and held that § 517.08 did not violate the Due Process Clause or Equal Protection Clause.

The plaintiffs then appealed the Minnesota Supreme Court's ruling to the United States Supreme Court pursuant to 28 U.S.C. 1257(2).[2]1 Under 28 U.S.C. 1257(2), the Supreme Court had no discretion to refuse to adjudicate the case on its merits. *Hicks v. Miranda*, 422 U.S. 332, 344 (1975). The Supreme Court dismissed the appeal "for want of a substantial federal question." *Baker*, 409 U.S. at 810.

Plaintiffs assert that *Baker v. Nelson* is not binding upon this Court because the Supreme Court did not issue a written opinion and because the case was decided thirty-two (32) years ago, before the "current civil rights revolution." This Court disagrees. A dismissal for lack of a substantial federal question constitutes an adjudication on the merits that is binding on lower federal courts. See *Hicks* at 344....

Although *Baker v. Nelson* is over thirty (30) years old, the decision addressed the same issues presented in this action and this Court is bound to follow the Supreme Court's decision....

The Supreme Court's holding in Lawrence does not alter the dispositive effect of *Baker*. See *Agostini v. Felton*, 521 U.S. 203, 207 (1997) ("The Court neither acknowledges nor holds that other courts should ever conclude that its more recent cases have, by implication, overruled an earlier precedent.")...The Supreme Court has not explicitly or implicitly overturned its holding in Baker or provided the lower courts, including this Court, with any reason to believe that the holding is invalid today. Accordingly, *Baker v. Nelson* is binding precedent upon this Court and Plaintiffs' case against Attorney General Ashcroft must be dismissed.

Due Process

Recent Eleventh Circuit precedent also constrains this Court to rule contrary to Plaintiffs' position. Plaintiffs argue that their right to marry someone of the same sex is a fundamental right that is guaranteed by the Fourteenth Amendment's Due Process Clause.[3]1 If Plaintiffs have a fundamental right to enter into a same-sex marriage, then this Court must apply a "'strict scrutiny' analysis that forbids government infringement on a fundamental liberty interest 'unless the infringement is narrowly tailored to serve a compelling state interest.'" [citations omitted] If the right to marry someone of the same sex is not a fundamental right, then the Court will apply the more liberal rational basis analysis in determining whether DOMA is constitutional.

The Supreme Court has defined fundamental rights as those liberties that are "implicit in the concept of ordered liberty, such that neither liberty nor justice would exist

---

2. At the time, 28 U.S.C. 1257(2) provided:
   Final judgments or decrees rendered by the highest court of a State in which a decision could be had, may be reviewed by the Supreme Court as follows:
   (2) [b]y appeal, where is drawn in question the validity of a statute of any state on the ground of its being repugnant to the Constitution, treaties or laws of the United States, and the decision is in favor of its validity.
   This appeal as of right was eliminated by the Supreme Court Case Selections Act (Public Law 100-352), which became law on June 27, 1988.
   3. The Court notes that the Fourteenth Amendment only applies to the states and not the federal government. Plaintiffs' claim should have been brought pursuant to the Due Process Clause of the Fifth Amendment.

if they were sacrificed."...The Court observed that the Due Process clause "specially protects those fundamental rights and liberties which are, objectively, 'deeply rooted in this Nation's history and tradition.'"...

Although the Supreme Court has held that marriage is a fundamental right,...no federal court has recognized that this right includes the right to marry a person of the same sex. See *Kandu*, 315 B.R. at 139;...Plaintiffs urge this Court to interpret the Supreme Court's decision in *Lawrence v. Texas* as establishing a fundamental right to private sexual intimacy. Plaintiffs argue that this Court should expand the fundamental right recognized in *Lawrence* to include same-sex marriages.

In *Lawrence*, the Supreme Court struck down a Texas statute that criminalized private sexual conduct between consenting adults of the same sex. The Court found that the statute could not stand under rational review because it did not further a legitimate state interest that justified the intrusion into the personal lives of homosexuals.

But the Supreme Court's decision in *Lawrence* cannot be interpreted as creating a fundamental right to same-sex marriage. First, the Eleventh Circuit disagrees with Plaintiffs' assertion that *Lawrence* created a fundamental right in private sexual intimacy and this Court must follow the holdings of the Eleventh Circuit. See *Lofton v. Sec. of Dept. of Children and Family Services*, 358 F.3d 804, 817 (11th Cir.), reh'g en banc denied by, 377 F.3d 1275 (2004), and cert. denied, 543 U.S. __ (2005) ("We conclude that it is a strained and ultimately incorrect reading of Lawrence to interpret it to announce a new fundamental right.");...The Court in *Lawrence* did not find private sexual conduct between consenting adults to be a fundamental right. Rather, the Court determined that the Texas statute failed under the rational basis analysis. *Lawrence* at 578–79.

Second, the majority in *Lawrence* was explicitly clear that its holding did not extend to the issue of same-sex marriage, stating that the case "does not involve whether the government must give formal recognition to any relationship that homosexual persons seek to enter." *Lawrence* at 578; It is disingenuous to argue that the Supreme Court's precise language in *Lawrence* established a fundamental right to enter into a same-sex marriage.

Moreover, this Court is not inclined to elevate the ability to marry someone of the same sex to a fundamental right. Although the Court recognizes the importance of a heterosexual or homosexual individual's choice of a partner, not all important decisions are protected fundamental rights....The Supreme Court has cautioned against the dangers of establishing new fundamental rights:

> By extending constitutional protection to an asserted right or liberty interest, we, to a great extent, place the matter outside the arena of public debate and legislative action. We must therefore exercise the utmost care whenever we are asked to break new ground in this field, lest the liberty protected by the Due Process Clause be subtly transformed into the policy preferences of the members of this Court. *Glucksberg*, 521 U.S. at 720.

The Eleventh Circuit has also noted that once a right is elevated to a fundamental right, it is "effectively removed from the hands of the people and placed into the guardianship of unelected judges. We are particularly mindful of this fact in the delicate area of morals legislation." *Williams*, 378 F.3d at 1250 (internal citations omitted). "Of course, the Court may in due course expand *Lawrence*'s precedent...[b]ut for us preemptively to take that step would exceed our mandate as a lower court." *Williams* at 1238. Therefore, the Court finds that the right to marry a person of the same sex is not a fundamental right under the Constitution.

Equal Protection

Plaintiffs also argue that this Court should apply strict scrutiny in determining the constitutionality of DOMA because it violates the Equal Protection Clause of the Fourteenth Amendment.[4] The Eleventh Circuit has held that homosexuality is not a suspect class that would require subjecting DOMA to strict scrutiny under the Equal Protection Clause of the Fourteenth Amendment or the equal protection component of the Fifth Amendment's Due Process Clause. See *Lofton* at 818. Moreover, DOMA does not discriminate on the basis of sex because it treats women and men equally.... Therefore this Court must apply rational basis review to its equal protection analysis of the constitutionality of DOMA.

Rational Basis Review

As the Court noted above, because Plaintiffs do not have a fundamental right to enter into a same-sex marriage and because DOMA does not create a suspect classification, the constitutionality of DOMA is reviewed under the rational basis test. Under rational basis review, this Court must determine whether the challenged legislation is rationally related to a legitimate state interest. See *Lofton* at 818.... Rational basis review is "very deferential to the legislature, and does not permit this Court to interject or substitute its own personal views of DOMA or same-sex marriage." *Kandu* at 145. This presumption of validity remains true "even if the law seems unwise or works to the disadvantage of a particular group, or if the rationale for it seems tenuous." *Lofton* at 818.

The burden is on the Plaintiffs to negate "every conceivable basis which might support [the legislation], whether or not the basis has a foundation in the record." *Id.* at 818. The United States has "no obligation to produce evidence to sustain the rationality of a statutory classification." *Id.* "A statutory classification fails rational-basis review only when it 'rests on grounds wholly irrelevant to the achievement of the State's objective.' " *Heller*, 509 U.S. at 324.

The United States asserts that DOMA is rationally related to two legitimate governmental interests. First, the government argues that DOMA fosters the development of relationships that are optimal for procreation, thereby encouraging the "stable generational continuity of the United States." DOMA allegedly furthers this interest by permitting the states to deny recognition to same-sex marriages performed elsewhere and by adopting the traditional definition of marriage for purposes of federal statutes. Second, DOMA "encourage[s] the creation of stable relationships that facilitate the rearing of children by both of their biological parents." The government argues that these stable relationships encourage the creation of stable families that are well suited to nurturing and raising children.

Plaintiffs offer little to rebut the government's argument that DOMA is rationally related to the government's proffered legitimate interests. Rather, Plaintiffs repeatedly urge the Court to apply the more rigid strict scrutiny analysis.

Although this Court does not express an opinion on the validity of the government's proffered legitimate interests, it is bound by the Eleventh Circuit's holding that encouraging the raising of children in homes consisting of a married mother and father is a le-

---

4. The Court again notes that the Fourteenth Amendment only applies to the states and that Plaintiffs' equal protection claims should have been brought pursuant to the equal protection component of the Due Process Clause of the Fifth Amendment.

gitimate state interest. See *Lofton* at 819–20. DOMA is rationally related to this interest. Moreover, Plaintiffs have failed to satisfy their burden of establishing that DOMA fails rational basis review. Accordingly, the United States' motion to dismiss is granted.

Notes and Questions

1. The *Kandu* court held that *Baker v. Nelson* was not binding precedent on the question of the constitutionality of DOMA since Baker dealt only with the constitutionality of a state statute. If *Baker* is binding precedent, as the District Court in *Wilson v. Ake* seems to hold, then why did Judge Moody separately discuss the due process and equal protection arguments? Wouldn't a cite to *Baker* have been sufficient?

2. The precedential force of Supreme Court judgments in cases like *Baker*, where no oral arguments are heard and no written opinion is handed down, has been an issue for gay rights litigators in the past. In 1976, the Court summarily affirmed a three-judge district court ruling upholding Virginia's sodomy statute against a constitutional challenge, primarily based on a right to privacy claim. *Doe v. Commonwealth's Attorney*, 425 U.S. 901 (1976), summarily affirming 403 F. Supp. 1199 (E.D. Va. 1975). In 1985, the Court of Appeals for the Fifth Circuit, relying on the summary affirmance in *Doe*, upheld the Texas sodomy statue against a similar challenge. See *Baker v. Wade*, 769 F.2d 289 (1985)(en banc). *But see Hardwick v. Bowers*, 760 F.2d 1202 (11th Cir. 1985), in which the Court of Appeals for the Eleventh Circuit refused to consider *Doe* as binding precedent on the merits because the plaintiffs in *Doe* lacked standing. A summary affirmance may approve the result below, but not necessarily the reasoning. Can a similar distinction be made as to the *Baker v. Nelson* case?

3. *Wilson v. Ake* relies heavily on *Lofton*, citing it for the point "that encouraging the raising of children in homes consisting of a married mother and father is a legitimate state interest." What exactly is the court's explanation of how DOMA rationally furthers this legitimate interest? Is it possible that the "means" of furthering the state interest that was being challenged in *Lofton* (limiting who can become adoptive parents) is rational and that the "means" being challenged in *Wilson* (i.e., limiting who can be married) is not rational?

Hennefeld v. Township of Montclair
Tax Court of New Jersey
Slip Opinion
March 15, 2005

[Facts: Louis Paul Hennefeld, a disabled veteran, was honorably discharged from the Air Force in 1968 after 15 years of service. He and his partner of 30 years, Blair William O'Dell, have jointly owned their home since 1985. New Jersey law provides a 100% tax property tax exemption for disabled veterans, provided they own their home. If the home is jointly owned, then the exemption is prorated. Because Hennefeld owned the property jointly with O'Dell, he was only allowed a 50% exemption. Had Hennefeld and O'Dell been married, the full 100% exemption would have been available. Hennefeld and O'Dell were married in Canada in 2003 and in 2004 filed a new exemption application claiming the full 100% as a married couple. In the year 2000, they had entered into a Vermont Civil Union and in July of 2004, they registered as domestic partners under the newly enacted New Jersey Domestic Partner Act. *See infra.* They claimed the 100% exemption under various theories. Below is the court's response to their claim that the state of New Jersey should recognize their Canadian marriage under principles of comity.]

I. The Plaintiffs' Marriage in Canada.

While it is undisputed that Plaintiffs were legally married under Canadian law, the court finds no basis under New Jersey law that would allow recognition of that marriage.

In urging this court to recognize their same-sex marriage in Canada, the Plaintiffs cite *Hilton v. Guyot,* 159 U.S. 113 (1895) arguing that "comity of nations" is an obligation that depends on considerations of international duty and convenience, and a preference for comity exists when the laws of the foreign nation are consistent with those of the sovereign. Id. at 163. However, "[a]s a general matter, the laws of one nation do not have force or effect beyond its borders." *In re Kandu,* 315 B.R. 123, 133 (Bankr. W.D. Wash. 2004), *citing Hilton v. Guyot, supra,* 159 *U.S.* at 163. Furthermore,

> 'Comity,' in the legal sense, is neither a matter of absolute obligation, on the one hand, nor of mere courtesy and good will, upon the other. But it is the recognition which one nation allows within its territory to the legislative, executive, or judicial acts of another nation, having due regard both to international duty and convenience.... Comity is voluntary.

[*Id., citing Hilton v. Guyot, supra,* 159 *U.S.* at 163–65.]

The Plaintiffs also rely on *Bucca v. State,* 43 N.J. Super. 315 (Ch. Div. 1957) where the court noted that the validity of marriage is determined by the law of the place where it was contracted unless it violates the state's public policy. *Ibid.* Relying on New Jersey's incest laws, the court in *Bucca v. State* denied recognition of an Italian marriage between an uncle and niece finding that "the public policy of New Jersey is opposed to such incestuous marriages." *Id.* at p. 321. The Plaintiffs contend that since New Jersey has no law specifically declaring that same-sex marriage is against the State's public policy, their Canadian marriage should therefore be recognized in New Jersey. The court rejects this argument.

Same-sex marriage has been a widely debated national issue over the past several years. Massachusetts is currently the only state that permits same-sex marriage. In 1998, Hawaii amended its constitution giving the legislature "the power to reserve marriage to opposite-sex couples," Haw. Const. art. 1 § 23, and Alaska adopted a constitutional amendment barring same-sex marriage. Alaska Const. art. I § 25. In 2004, eleven other states approved ballot measures banning same-sex marriage. Even the gay and lesbian community is divided on the issue of same-sex marriage.[1]

The Federal Government weighed in on the debate in 1996, when Congress enacted the Defense of Marriage Act ("DOMA"). DOMA has survived early constitutional challenges in the Federal Courts. *See In re Kandu, supra,* 315 B.R. at 148 (concluding that "DOMA does not violate the principles of comity, or the Fourth, Fifth, or Tenth Amendments to the U.S. Constitution."); *see Wilson v. Ake,* 2005 WL 281272 (M.D. Fla.

---

1. See Barbara J. Cox, *A (Personal) Essay on Same-Sex Marriage,* National Journal of Sexual Orientation Law, Vol. 1, Issue 1, Mary Sylla, ed., which refers to writings of several feminists who question whether seeking marriage for same-sex couples is a step toward liberation.

2005) (finding DOMA "constitutionally valid.")[2]; *but see Lawrence v. Texas*, 539 U.S. 558, 578–79 (2003) (holding that while the Due Process Clause of the Constitution protects the right of two individuals of the same sex to engage in mutually consensual private sexual conduct, the case did "not involve whether the government must give formal recognition to any relationship that homosexual persons seek to enter.")

Of these constitutional challenges to DOMA, *In re Kandu* is particularly relevant and instructive. In that case, plaintiffs sought recognition of their same-sex marriage in British Columbia, Canada to allow them to file a joint petition for bankruptcy under 11 U.S.C. §302. The United States Bankruptcy Court for the Western District of Washington found that although the plaintiffs were married according to the laws of British Columbia, Canada, the United States does not recognize same-sex marriages. The Bankruptcy Court explained that:

> DOMA states that, for federal purposes, marriage is solely the union between one man and one woman. Particularly relevant, the Supreme Court has stated that, "[a] judgment affecting the status of persons, such as a decree confirming or dissolving a marriage, is recognized as valid in every country, unless contrary to the policy of its own law."

[*In re Kandu, supra*, 315 B.R. at 133, *citing Hilton v. Guyot, supra*, 159 U.S. at 167.]

The court in *In re Kandu* concluded that "[b]ecause the British Columbia policy and the United States policy concerning marriage directly conflict, this Court must prefer its own laws finding DOMA controlling in this case."[3] *Id.* at 133–34. The court noted that "[a]ccording to the House Report [H.R.Rep. No. 104-664, at 12, *reprinted in* 1996 U.S.C.C.A.N. at 2916], the purpose of DOMA was to defend the institution of traditional, heterosexual marriage…" and concluded that "in reviewing the legislative history,…the federal government has announced a strong and clear countervailing policy concerning marriage that justifies disregarding comity." *Id.* at 133, n.3.

The debate over same-sex marriage has not eluded New Jersey.[4] In the recent decision of *Lewis v. Harris*, 2003 WL 23191114 (Law Div. 2003), the court concluded that marriage statutes in New Jersey do not permit same-sex marriages, and the right to marry does not include a fundamental right to same-sex marriage. That decision is now on appeal to the Appellate Division. It is noted, however, that recognition of same-sex marriages entered into under the laws of a foreign country was not before the court in *Lewis v. Harris*.

After the decision in *Lewis v. Harris*, the New Jersey Legislature adopted the DPA recognizing domestic partnerships and providing domestic partners with certain "rights and benefits that are accorded to married couples." N.J.S.A 26:8A-2(d). While the DPA had been adopted but was not yet effective when the Plaintiffs filed their application for a 100% disabled veteran's exemption,[6] the legislative findings and declarations set forth

---

2. "Same-sex marriage supporters in Florida announced [on January 25, 2005, six days after the U.S. District Court decision in *Wilson v. Ake*, that] they are giving up on their challenge to the federal Defense of Marriage Act (DOMA)." *See* Hunter, Melanie, *Homosexual Advocates Drop Florida DOMA Challenge*, available at http:www.cnsnews.com/ViewPrint.asp?Page=\Nation\Archive\200501\NAT20050125b.html (last visited February 17, 2005).

3. Note, however, that DOMA does not specifically address recognition of same-sex marriages legally entered into under the laws of a foreign country.

4. A bill calling for a state constitutional amendment banning same-sex marriage has been introduced. ACR-212.

6. The DPA was adopted January 12, 2004; the Plaintiffs filed for the disabled veteran's exemption on January 17, 2004. The DPA was not effective until July 10, 2004.

in the DPA, as well as the Assembly Appropriations Committee Statement (the "Committee Statement") attached to that legislation, are nevertheless pertinent and instructive to ascertain legislative intent and public policy at the time of the DPA's adoption, concerning same-sex marriage. A comprehensive analysis of the Plaintiffs rights under the DPA is found in Section VII of this opinion.

In setting forth "a clear and rational basis" for making available certain health and pension benefits to same-sex domestic partners and not to opposite sex domestic partners, the Legislature found and declared with regard to same-sex marriage that:

> ...domestic partnerships in which both persons are of the same sex...are... unable to enter into a marriage with each other that is recognized by New Jersey law, unlike persons of the opposite sex who are in a domestic partnership but have the right to enter into a marriage that is recognized by State law...

[*N.J.S.A.* 26:8A-2(e).]

The Committee Statement provides similar language:

> The bill would also make certain health and pension benefits available to dependent domestic partners in the case of domestic partnerships in which both persons are of the same sex and therefore unable to enter into a marriage with each other that is recognized by New Jersey law...

[Assemb. Appropriations Comm., Assemb. No. 3743—L. 2003, c. 246, following *N.J.S.A.* 26:8A-1.]

In the aftermath of the court's ruling in *Lewis v. Harris*, the Legislature had the opportunity to enact law permitting same-sex marriage in New Jersey. Instead, the Legislature provided certain rights and recognition to domestic partners through the enactment of the DPA, while also making it clear in that same legislation, that same-sex marriage is not recognized by New Jersey law.

Furthermore, the DPA, in recognizing certain out-of-state same-sex relationships, did not extend that recognition to out-of-state same-sex marriages. The Committee Statement is clear in providing that:

> while individuals in domestic partnerships share some of the same emotional and financial bonds and other indicia of interdependence as married couples, *domestic partnership is a status distinct from marriage.*

[Assemb. Appropriations Comm., Assemb. No. 3743—L. 2003, *c.* 246, following *N.J.S.A.* 26:8A-1 (emphasis added.)]

In view of this distinction, the Legislature, in providing that "[a] domestic partnership, civil union or reciprocal beneficiary relationship entered into outside of this State, which is valid under the laws of the jurisdiction under which the partnership was created, shall be valid in this State," N.J.S.A. 26:8A-6 (c), could not have intended to include *marriage* within the terms *domestic partnership, civil union,* or *reciprocal beneficiary relationship*, and therefore could not have intended to recognize same-sex marriages entered into outside of New Jersey.

Based on the foregoing analysis, this court finds that the marriage laws of Canada which recognize same-sex marriage are not consistent with those of New Jersey which do not recognize same-sex marriage. Moreover, the explicit legislative findings and declarations of the DPA, along with the Committee Statement, set forth the pubic policy of this state against same-sex marriage. Accordingly, the Plaintiffs' Canadian marriage cannot be afforded comity in New Jersey.

6. One Man and One Woman

Littleton v. Prange
9 S.W.3d 223 (Tex. App. 1999)

PHIL HARDBERGER, Chief Justice.

This case involves the most basic of questions. When is a man a man, and when is a woman a woman? Every schoolchild, even of tender years, is confident he or she can tell the difference, especially if the person is wearing no clothes. These are observations that each of us makes early in life and, in most cases, continue to have more than a passing interest in for the rest of our lives. It is one of the more pleasant mysteries.

The deeper philosophical (and now legal) question is: can a physician change the gender of a person with a scalpel, drugs and counseling, or is a person's gender immutably fixed by our Creator at birth? The answer to that question has definite legal implications that present themselves in this case involving a person named Christie Lee Littleton.

FACTUAL BACKGROUND

Christie is a transsexual. She was born in San Antonio in 1952, a physically healthy male, and named after her father, Lee Cavazos. At birth, she was named Lee Cavazos, Jr. (Throughout this opinion Christie will be referred to as "She." This is for grammatical simplicity's sake, and out of respect for the litigant, who wishes to be called "Christie," and referred to as "she." It has no legal implications.)

At birth, Christie had the normal male genitalia: penis, scrotum and testicles. Problems with her sexual identity developed early though. Christie testified that she considered herself female from the time she was three or four years old, the contrary physical evidence notwithstanding. Her distressed parents took her to a physician, who prescribed male hormones. These were taken, but were ineffective. Christie sought successfully to be excused from sports and physical education because of her embarrassment over changing clothes in front of the other boys.

By the time she was 17 years old, Christie was searching for a physician who would perform sex reassignment surgery. At 23, she enrolled in a program at the University of Texas Health Science Center that would lead to a sex reassignment operation. For four years Christie underwent psychological and psychiatric treatment by a number of physicians, some of whom testified in this case.

On August 31, 1977, Christie's name was legally changed to Christie Lee Cavazos. Under doctor's orders, Christie also began receiving various treatments and female hormones. Between November of 1979 and February of 1980, Christie underwent three surgical procedures, which culminated in a complete sex reassignment. Christie's penis, scrotum and testicles were surgically removed, and a vagina and labia were constructed. Christie additionally underwent breast construction surgery.

Dr. Donald Greer, a board certified plastic surgeon, served as a member of the gender dysphoria team at UTHSC in San Antonio, Texas during the time in question. Dr. Paul Mohl, a board certified psychiatrist, also served as a member of the same gender dysphoria team. Both participated in the evaluation and treatment of Christie. The gender dysphoria team was a mutli-disciplinary team that met regularly to interview and care for transsexual patients.

The parties stipulated that Dr. Greer and Dr. Mohl would testify that their background, training, education and experience is consistent with that reflected in their curriculum vitaes, which were attached to their respective affidavits in Christie's response to the motions for summary judgment. In addition, Dr. Greer and Dr. Mohl would testify that the definition of a transsexual is someone whose physical anatomy does not correspond to their sense of being or their sense of gender, and that medical science has not been able to identify the exact cause of this condition, but it is in medical probability a combination of neuro-biological, genetic and neonatal environmental factors. Dr. Greer and Dr. Mohl would further testify that in arriving at a diagnosis of transsexualism in Christie, the program at UTHSC was guided by the guidelines established by the Johns Hopkins Group and that, based on these guidelines, Christie was diagnosed psychologically and psychiatrically as a genuine male to female transsexual. Dr. Greer and Dr. Mohl also would testify that true male to female transsexuals are, in their opinion, psychologically and psychiatrically female before and after the sex reassignment surgery, and that Christie is a true male to female transsexual.

On or about November 5, 1979, Dr. Greer served as a principal member of the surgical team that performed the sex reassignment surgery on Christie. In Dr. Greer's opinion, the anatomical and genital features of Christie, following that surgery, are such that she has the capacity to function sexually as a female. Both Dr. Greer and Dr. Mohl would testify that, in their opinions, following the successful completion of Christie's participation in UTHSC's gender dysphoria program, Christie is medically a woman.

Christie married a man by the name of Jonathon Mark Littleton in Kentucky in 1989, and she lived with him until his death in 1996. Christie filed a medical malpractice suit under the Texas Wrongful Death and Survival Statute in her capacity as Jonathon's surviving spouse. The sued doctor, appellee here, filed a motion for summary judgment. The motion challenged Christie's status as a proper wrongful death beneficiary, asserting that Christie is a man and cannot be the surviving spouse of another man.

The trial court agreed and granted the summary judgment. The summary judgment notes that the trial court considered the summary judgment evidence, the stipulation, and the argument of counsel. In addition to the stipulation, Christie's affidavit was attached to her response to the motion for summary judgment. In her affidavit, Christie states that Jonathon was fully aware of her background and the fact that she had undergone sex reassignment surgery.

The Legal Issue

Can there be a valid marriage between a man and a person born as a man, but surgically altered to have the physical characteristics of a woman?

Overview of Issue

This is a case of first impression in Texas. The underlying statutory law is simple enough. Texas (and Kentucky, for that matter), like most other states, does not permit marriages between persons of the same sex. In order to have standing to sue under the wrongful death and survival statues, Christie must be Jonathon's surviving spouse. The defendant's summary judgment burden was to prove she is not the surviving spouse. Referring to the statutory law, though, does not resolve the issue. This court, as did the trial court below, must answer this question: Is Christie a man or a woman? There is no dispute that Christie and Jonathon went through a ceremonial marriage ritual. If Christie is a woman, she may bring this action. If Christie is a man, she may not.

Christie is medically termed a transsexual, a term not often heard on the streets of Texas, nor in its courtrooms. If we look at other states or even other countries to see how they treat marriages of transsexuals, we get little help. Only a handful of other states, or foreign countries, have even considered the case of the transsexual. The opposition to same-sex marriages, on the other hand, is very wide spread. Public antipathy toward same-sex marriages notwithstanding, the question remains: is a transsexual still the same sex after a sex-reassignment operation as before the operation? A transsexual, such as Christie, does not consider herself a homosexual because she does not consider herself a man. Her self-identity, from childhood, has been as a woman. Since her various operations, she does not have the outward physical characteristics of a man either. Through the intervention of surgery and drugs, Christie appears to be a woman. In her mind, she has corrected her physical features to line up with her true gender.

"Although transgenderism is often conflated with homosexuality, the characteristic, which defines transgenderism, is not sexual orientation, but sexual identity. Transgenderism describes people who experience a separation between their gender and their biological/anatomical sex." Mary Coombs, *Sexual Dis-Orientation: Transgendered People and Same-Sex Marriage,* 8 U.C.L.A. WOMEN's L. J. 219, 237 (1998).

Nor should a transsexual be confused with a transvestite, who is simply a man who attains some sexual satisfaction from wearing women's clothes. Christie does not consider herself a man wearing women's clothes; she considers herself a woman wearing women's clothes. She has been surgically and chemically altered to be a woman. She has officially changed her name and her birth certificate to reflect her new status. But the question remains whether the law will take note of these changes and treat her as if she had been born a female. To answer this question, we consider the law of those jurisdictions who have previously decided it.

CASE LAW

The English case of *Corbett v. Corbett,* 2 All E.R. 33, 1970 WL 29661 (P.1970), appears to be the first case to consider the issue, and is routinely cited in later cases, including those cases from the United States. April Ashley, like Christie Littleton, was born a male, and like Christie, had undergone a sex-reassignment operation. *Id.* at 35–36. April later married Arthur Corbett. *Id.* at 39. Arthur subsequently asked for a nullification of the marriage based upon the fact that April was a man, and the marriage had never been consummated. *Id.* at 34. April resisted the nullification of her marriage, asserting that the reason the marriage had not been consummated was the fault of her husband, not her. *Id.* at 34–35. She said she was ready, willing, and able to consummate the marriage. *Id.*

Arthur testified that he was "mesmerised" by April upon meeting her, and he dated her for three years before their marriage. *Id.* at 37. He said that she "looked like a woman, dressed like a woman and acted like a woman." *Id.* at 38. Arthur and April eventually married, but they were never successful in having sexual relations. *Id.* at 39. Several doctors testified in the case, as they did in the current case. *See id.* at 41.

Based upon the doctors' testimony, the court came up with four criteria for assessing the sexual identity of an individual. These are: (1) Chromosomal factors; (2) Gonadal factors (i.e., presence or absence of testes or ovaries); (3) Genital factors (including internal sex organs); and (4) Psychological factors. *Id.* at 44.

Chromosomes are the structures on which the genes are carried which, in turn, are the mechanism by which hereditary characteristics are transmitted from parents to offspring. *See id.* at 44. An individual normally has 23 pairs of chromosomes in his or her body cells; one of each pair being derived from each parent. *See id.* One pair of chromosomes is known to determine an individual's sex. *See id.* The English court stated that "[T]he biological sexual constitution of an individual is fixed at birth (at the latest), and cannot be changed, either by the natural development of organs of the opposite sex, or by medical or surgical means. The respondent's operation, therefore, cannot affect her true sex." *Id.* at 47. The court then reasoned that since marriage is essentially a relationship between man and woman, the validity of the marriage depends on whether April is, or is not, a woman. *Id.* at 48. The court held that the criteria for answering this question must be biological and, having so held, found that April, a transsexual, "is not a woman for the purposes of marriage but is a biological male and has been so since birth," and, therefore, the marriage between Arthur and April was void. *Id.* at 48–49. The court specifically rejected the contention that individuals could "assign" their own sex by their own volition, or by means of an operation. *Id.* at 49. In short, once a man, always a man.

The year after *Corbett* was decided in England, a case involving the validity of a marriage in which one of the partners was transsexual appeared in a United States court. This was the case of *Anonymous v. Anonymous,* 67 Misc.2d 982, 325 N.Y.S.2d 499 (N.Y.Sup.Ct.1971). This New York case had a connection with Texas. The marriage ceremony of the transsexual occurred in Belton, while the plaintiff was stationed at Fort Hood. *Id.* at 499. The purpose of the suit was to declare that no marriage could legally have taken place. *Id.* The court pointed out that this was not an annulment of a marriage because a marriage contract must be between a man and a woman. *Id.* at 501. If the ceremony itself was a nullity, there would be no marriage to annul, but the court would simply declare that no marriage could legally have taken place. *Id.* The court had no difficulty in doing so, holding: "The law makes no provision for a 'marriage' between persons of the same sex. Marriage is and always has been a contract between a man and a woman." *Id.* at 500.

Factually, the New York case was less complicated than *Corbett,* and the instant case, because there had been no sexual change operation, and the "wife" still had normal male organs. *Id.* at 499. The plaintiff made this unpleasant discovery on his wedding night. *Id.* The husband in *Anonymous* was unaware that he was marrying a transsexual. *Id.* In both *Corbett* and the instant case, the husband was fully aware of the true state of affairs, and accepted it. In fact, in the instant case, Christie and her husband were married for seven years, and, according to the testimony, had normal sexual relations. This is a much longer period of time than any of the other reported cases.

The next reported transsexual case came from New Jersey. This is the only United States case to uphold the validity of a transsexual marriage. In *M.T. v. J.T.,* 140 N.J.Super. 77, 355 A.2d 204, 205 (1976), a transsexual wife brought an action for support and maintenance growing out of her marriage. The husband interposed a defense that his wife was male, and that their marriage was void (and therefore he owed nothing). *Id.* M.T., the wife, testified she was born a male, but she always considered herself a female. *Id.* M.T. dated men all her life. *Id.* After M.T. met her husband-to-be, J.T., they decided that M.T. would have an operation so she could "be physically a woman." *Id.*

In 1971, M.T. had an operation where her male organs were removed and a vagina was constructed. *Id.* J.T. paid for the operation, and the couple were married the next year. *Id.* M.T. and J.T. lived as husband and wife and had sexual intercourse. *Id.* J.T. supported M.T. for over two years; however, in 1974, J.T. left the home, and his support of M.T. ceased. *Id.* The lawsuit for maintenance and support followed.

The doctor who had performed the sex-reassignment operation testified. *Id.* at 205–6. He described a transsexual as a person who has "a great discrepancy between the physical genital anatomy and the person's sense of self-identity as a male or as a female." *Id.* at 205. The doctor defined gender identity as "a sense, a total sense of self as being masculine or female; it pervades one's entire concept of one's place in life, of one's place in society and in point of fact the actual facts of the anatomy are really secondary." *Id.* The doctor said that after the operation his patient had no uterus or cervix, but her vagina had a "good cosmetic appearance" and was "the same as a normal female vagina after a hysterectomy." *Id.* at 206.

The trial court, in ruling for M.T. by finding the marriage valid, stated:

> It is the opinion of the court that if the psychological choice of a person is medically sound, not a mere whim, and irreversible sex reassignment surgery has been performed, society has no right to prohibit the transsexual from leading a normal life. Are we to look upon this person as an exhibit in a circus side show? What harm has said person done to society? The entire area of transsexualism is repugnant to the nature of many persons within our society. However, this should not govern the legal acceptance of a fact.

Id. at 207. The appellate court affirmed, holding:

> If such sex reassignment surgery is successful and the postoperative transsexual is, by virtue of medical treatment, thereby possessed of the full capacity to function sexually as male or female, as the case may be, we perceive no legal barrier, cognizable social taboo, or reason grounded in public policy to prevent the persons' identification at least for purposes of marriage to the sex finally indicated.

Id. at 210–11.

Ohio is the last state that has considered this issue. *See In re Ladrach,* 32 Ohio Misc.2d 6, 513 N.E.2d 828 (Ohio Probate Ct.1987). *Ladrach* was a declaratory judgment action brought to determine whether a male who became a post-operative female was permitted to marry a male. *Id.* at 829–30. The court decided she may not. *Id.* at 832.

Like Christie, Elaine Ladrach started life as a male. *Id.* at 830. Eventually, she had the transsexual operation which removed the penis, scrotum and testes and constructed a vagina. *Id.* The doctor who performed the operation testified that Elaine now had a "normal female external genitalia." *Id.* He admitted, however, that it would be "highly unlikely" that a chromosomal test would show Elaine to be a female. *Id.* The court cited a New York Academy of Medicine study of transsexuals that concluded: "…male to female transsexuals are still chromosomally males while ostensibly females." *Id.* at 831. The court stated that a person's sex is determined at birth by an anatomical examination by the birth attendant, which was done at Elaine's birth. *Id.* at 832. No allegation had been made that Elaine's birth attendant was in error. *Id.* The court reasoned that the determination of a person's sex and marital status are legal issues, and, as such, the court must look to the statutes to determine whether the marriage was permissible. *Id.* The court concluded:

> This court is charged with the responsibility of interpreting the statutes of this state and judicial interpretations of these statutes. Since the case at bar is apparently one of first impression in Ohio, it is this court's opinion that the legislature should change the statutes, if it is to be the public policy of the state of Ohio to issue marriage licenses to post-operative transsexuals.

Id. The court denied the marriage license application. *Id.*

OTHER AUTHORITIES

In an unreported case, a court in New Zealand was convinced that a fully transitioned transsexual should be permitted to marry as a member of his new sex because the alternative would be more disturbing. *See* Mary Coombs, *Sexual Dis-Orientation: Transgendered People and Same-Sex Marriage*, 8 UCLA WOMEN'S L.J. 219, 250 & n. 137 (1998) (citing *M. v. M.* (unreported) 30 May 1991, S.Ct. of NZ). That is, if a post-operative transsexual female was deemed a male, she could marry a woman, in what would to all outward appearances be a same-sex marriage. *Id.* The question would then become whether courts should approve seemingly heterosexual marriages between a post-operative transsexual female and a genetic male, rather than an apparent same-sex marriage between a post-operative transsexual female and a genetic female. *Id.*

DISCUSSION

In an appeal from a summary judgment, we must determine whether the movant has shown that no genuine issue of material facts exists and that the movant is entitled to judgment as a matter of law. As previously noted, this is a case of first impression in Texas. It involves important matters of public policy for the state of Texas. The involvement of juries in the judicial process provides an important voice of the community, but we do not ask a jury to answer questions without appropriate instructions or guidelines. In fact, cases are reversed when juries have not been provided proper instructions.

In our system of government it is for the legislature, should it choose to do so, to determine what guidelines should govern the recognition of marriages involving transsexuals. The need for legislative guidelines is particularly important in this case, where the claim being asserted is statutorily-based. The statute defines who may bring the cause of action: a surviving spouse, and if the legislature intends to recognize transsexuals as surviving spouses, the statute needs to address the guidelines by which such recognition is governed. When or whether the legislature will choose to address this issue is not within the judiciary's control.

It would be intellectually possible for this court to write a protocol for when transsexuals would be recognized as having successfully changed their sex. Littleton has suggested we do so, perhaps using the surgical removal of the male genitalia as the test. As was pointed out by Littleton's counsel, "amputation is a pretty important step." Indeed it is. But this court has no authority to fashion a new law on transsexuals, or anything else. We cannot make law when no law exists: we can only interpret the written word of our sister branch of government, the legislature. Our responsibility in this case is to determine whether, in the absence of legislatively-established guidelines, a jury can be called upon to decide the legality of such marriages. We hold they cannot. In the absence of any guidelines, it would be improper to launch a jury forth on these untested and unknown waters.

There are no significant facts that need to be decided. The parties have supplied them for us. We find the case, at this stage, presents a pure question of law and must be decided by this court. Based on the facts of this case, and the law and studies of previous cases, we conclude:

(1) Medical science recognizes that there are individuals whose sexual self-identity is in conflict with their biological and anatomical sex. Such people are termed transsexuals.

(3) Christie Littleton is a transsexual.

(4) Through surgery and hormones, a transsexual male can be made to look like a woman, including female genitalia and breasts. Transsexual medical treatment, however, does not create the internal sexual organs of a women (except for the vaginal canal). There is no womb, cervix or ovaries in the post-operative transsexual female.

(5) The male chromosomes do not change with either hormonal treatment or sex reassignment surgery. Biologically a post-operative female transsexual is still a male.

(7) Some physicians would consider Christie a female; other physicians would consider her still a male. Her female anatomy, however, is all man-made. The body that Christie inhabits is a male body in all aspects other than what the physicians have supplied.

We recognize that there are many fine metaphysical arguments lurking about here involving desire and being, the essence of life and the power of mind over physics. But courts are wise not to wander too far into the misty fields of sociological philosophy. Matters of the heart do not always fit neatly within the narrowly defined perimeters of statutes, or even existing social mores. Such matters though are beyond this court's consideration. Our mandate is, as the court recognized in *Ladrach,* to interpret the statutes of the state and prior judicial decisions. This mandate is deceptively simplistic in this case: Texas statutes do not allow same-sex marriages, and prior judicial decisions are few.

Christie was created and born a male. Her original birth certificate, an official document of Texas, clearly so states. During the pendency of this suit, Christie amended the original birth certificate to change the sex and name. Under section 191.028 of the Texas Health and Safety Code she was entitled to seek such an amendment if the record was "incomplete or proved by satisfactory evidence to be inaccurate." Tex. Health & Safety Code Ann. § 191.028 (Vernon 1992). The trial court that granted the petition to amend the birth certificate necessarily construed the term "inaccurate" to relate to the present, and having been presented with the uncontroverted affidavit of an expert stating that Christie is a female, the trial court deemed this satisfactory to prove an inaccuracy. However, the trial court's role in considering the petition was a ministerial one. It involved no fact-finding or consideration of the deeper public policy concerns presented. No one claims the information contained in Christie's original birth certificate was based on fraud or error. We believe the legislature intended the term "inaccurate" in section 191.028 to mean inaccurate as of the time the certificate was recorded; that is, at the time of birth. At the time of birth, Christie was a male, both anatomically and genetically. The facts contained in the original birth certificate were true and accurate, and the words contained in the amended certificate are not binding on this court.

There are some things we cannot will into being. They just are.

CONCLUSION

We hold, as a matter of law, that Christie Littleton is a male. As a male, Christie cannot be married to another male. Her marriage to Jonathon was invalid, and she cannot bring a cause of action as his surviving spouse. We affirm the summary judgment granted by the trial court.

Notes and Questions

1. In Texas, who can a male to female (MTF) transsexual marry? Who can a female to male (FTM) transsexual marry? How would you view such married couples—as opposite-sex or same-sex?

2. What role should a birth certificate play in the question of whether spouses are of the opposite sex? For example, was the Texas court saying that the new birth certificate indicating that Christie was female was to be ignored because it was wrongly issued or because only the original birth certificate counts? What effect would this Texas court give to birth certificates from another state, especially in those states that allow a person to change birth certificates after changing sex? See Shana Brown, Sex Change and "Opposite-Sex" Marriage: Applying the Full Faith and Credit Clause to Compel Interstate Recognition of Transgendered Persons' Amended Legal Sex for Marital Purposes, 38 San Diego L. Rev. 1113 (2001). See also *In re Marriage Licence for Nash*, 2003 WL 23097095 (Ohio App.)(slip opinion), holding that full faith and credit did not require the Ohio courts to accept a Massachusetts birth certificate that had been legally changed from female to male. The court had a copy of the original birth certificate as well as the amended one and held that they were both evidence of gender, but that the original certificate was controlling. Full faith and credit required Ohio to give only as much weight to the amended birth certificate as Massachusetts would have given. In the view of the Ohio court, the birth certificate in Massachusetts was only prima facie evidence of true gender. Thus, Ohio was not bound to accept the gender on the amended certificate. As a result, Nash, a female to male transsexual was denied the right to marry a woman. The result in Nash is criticized in Julie Greenberg, When is a Same-sex Marriage Legal? Full Faith and Credit and Sex Determination, 38 Creighton L. Rev. 289 (2005).

3. Which birth certificate should determine Christie's sex for purposes other than marriage? For example, if the military draft were in effect only as to men, could Christie be drafted?

4. Christie Littleton petitioned the United States Supreme Court to hear her case. The Court denied certiorari. The case appears to be about an interpretation of Texas state law. What federal law claim must Christie have made to support her petition for certiorari?

5. Why shouldn't Christie be treated as a "putative spouse" for purposes of this law suit, even if she was not in fact a spouse for other purposes?

> A putative marriage is one that was entered into in good faith by at least one of the parties, but which is invalid by reason of an existing impediment on the part of one or both parties. The effect of a putative marriage is to give the pu-

tative spouse, who acted in good faith, rights to property acquired during the marital relationship that are analogous to those rights given to a lawful spouse. Texas recognizes these rights for putative marriages in order to administer equity to those individuals who had a good faith belief that they were lawfully married. [In re Marriage of Sanger, 1999 WL 742607 (Tex. App—Texarkana 1999)(citations omitted).]

6. In *Estate of Gardiner*, 42 P.3d 120 (Kansas 2002), the Kansas Supreme Court held in accord with the Texas Supreme Court that a male to female transsexual was not a true spouse of her husband for inheritance purposes. But even if not a true spouse, why not a putative spouse? (Note: Kansas law is silent as to the legal recognition of putative spouses.)

7. To date, both New Jersey and California have recognized transsexual marriages of the sort denied in *Littleton* and *Gardiner*. See *M.T. v. J.T.*, 355 A.2d 204 (N.J. Super. Ct. 1976), *cert. denied*, 364 A.2d 1076 (N.J. 1976)(male to female transsexual marries a man) and *Vecchione v. Vecchione*, No. 95D003769 Minute Order 1-2 (Cal. Superior Ct. Nov. 26, 1997)(female to male transsexual marries a woman). Professor Taylor Flynn, who represented Mr. Vecchione, describes the case as follows:

> Consider, for example, the case of Vecchione v. Vecchione, in which a woman attempted to void her marriage to her husband, a female-to-male transsexual man, on the ground that he was legally female. Effectively adopting an understanding of sex that is broader than one's anatomy at birth, the court concluded that the state legislature granted legal recognition to sex reassignment when it enacted a statute permitting post-operative transsexual persons to change the sex designation on their birth certificates. After holding that the husband, Joshua Vecchione, was legally male, the court awarded him fifty percent custody of their child.

Taylor Flynn, Transforming the Debate: Why We Need to Include Transgender Rights in the Struggles for Sex and Sexual Orientation Equality, 101 Colum. L. Rev. 392, 415–16 (2001).

If the Vecchiones had remained married and moved to the state of Texas, would the state of Texas have recognized their marriage? Assume that Mrs. Vecchione, like Christie Littleton, lost her spouse as a result of medical malpractice and brought suit under the Texas wrongful death statute. Would the analysis be the same as it was in the *Littleton* case? Can Mrs. Vecchione make an additional argument relying on conflicts of law principles because her marriage was valid in California?

8. A case similar to *Vecchione* arose in Florida. Michael Kantaras was born a woman, but became a man and married Linda. He adopted her newborn child and later was listed as the father on a birth certificate of Linda's second child, born during the marriage, using the sperm of Michael's brother. At divorce, Michael claimed custody. Linda claimed they were not married because Michael was not really male. She also challenged his right to parental custody. The trial court recognized the marriage, granted the divorce, and awarded custody to Michael. A Florida appellate court has ruled that the marriage was void ab initio because Michael is not a man for purposes of the marriage statutes. But the court did not address the issue of custody, explaining: "We do not attempt to undertake a determination of the legal status of the children resulting from our conclusion that the marriage is void. The legal status of the children and the parties' property rights will be issues for the trial court to examine in the first instance on remand." See *Kantaras v. Kantaras*, 884 So.2d 155 (Fla.App 2004). What problems do you see facing Michael on remand as he argues for parental custody?

See also *In re Marriage of Simmons*, 825 N.E.2d 303, (Ill. App. 2005)(holding invalid a marriage between a woman and a transsexual male and denying transsexual male parental rights).

Case of Christine Goodwin v. the United Kingdom

European Court of Human Rights
Application No. 28957/95
July 11, 2002

[Christine Goodman, a UK national and post-operative transsexual, began her action against the United Kingdom in 1995, claiming a violation of Articles 8 and 12 of the European Convention for the Protection of Human Rights and Fundamental Freedoms. Article 8 guarantees respect for an individual's private life and Article 12 protects the right to marry. Her case was transmitted to the European Court of Human Rights in November 1999. The Court's previous cases dealing with transsexuals had not required the contracting states to provide full recognition to the sex change. In this case, the court reconsiders its earlier decisions and broadens protections for transsexuals.]

I. Alleged Violation of Article 8 of the Convention

The applicant claims a violation of Article 8 of the Convention, the relevant part of which provides as follows:

1. Everyone has the right to respect for his private...life...

2. There shall be no interference by a public authority with the exercise of this right except such as is in accordance with the law and is necessary in a democratic society in the interests of national security, public safety or the economic well-being of the country, for the prevention of disorder or crime, for the protection of health or morals, or for the protection of the rights and freedoms of others.

This case raises the issue whether or not the respondent State has failed to comply with a positive obligation to ensure the right of the applicant, a post-operative male to female transsexual, to respect for her private life, in particular through the lack of legal recognition given to her gender re-assignment.

The Court recalls that it has already examined complaints about the position of transsexuals in the United Kingdom. In those cases, it held that the refusal of the United Kingdom Government to alter the register of births or to issue birth certificates whose contents and nature differed from those of the original entries concerning the recorded gender of the individual could not be considered as an interference with the right to respect for private life.

While the Court is not formally bound to follow its previous judgments, it is in the interests of legal certainty, foreseeability and equality before the law that it should not depart, without good reason, from precedents laid down in previous cases. However, since the Convention is first and foremost a system for the protection of human rights, the Court must have regard to the changing conditions within the respondent State and within Contracting States generally and respond, for example, to any evolving convergence as to the standards to be achieved. It is of crucial importance that the Convention is interpreted and applied in a manner which renders its rights practical and effective, not theoretical and illusory....

The Court observes that the applicant, registered at birth as male, has undergone gender re-assignment surgery and lives in society as a female. Nonetheless, the applicant remains, for legal purposes, a male. This has had, and continues to have, effects on the applicant's life where sex is of legal relevance and distinctions are made between men and women.

It must also be recognised that serious interference with private life can arise where the state of domestic law conflicts with an important aspect of personal identity. The stress and alienation arising from a discordance between the position in society assumed by a post-operative transsexual and the status imposed by law which refuses to recognise the change of gender cannot, in the Court's view, be regarded as a minor inconvenience arising from a formality. A conflict between social reality and law arises which places the transsexual in an anomalous position, in which he or she may experience feelings of vulnerability, humiliation and anxiety.

In this case, as in many others, the applicant's gender re-assignment was carried out by the national health service, which recognises the condition of gender dysphoria and provides, *inter alia*, re-assignment by surgery, with a view to achieving as one of its principal purposes as close an assimilation as possible to the gender in which the transsexual perceives that he or she properly belongs.... Where a State has authorised the treatment and surgery alleviating the condition of a transsexual, financed or assisted in financing the operations...it appears illogical to refuse to recognise the legal implications of the result to which the treatment leads.

[T]he very essence of the Convention is respect for human dignity and human freedom. Under Article 8 of the Convention in particular, where the notion of personal autonomy is an important principle underlying the interpretation of its guarantees, protection is given to the personal sphere of each individual, including the right to establish details of their identity as individual human beings. In the twenty first century the right of transsexuals to personal development and to physical and moral security in the full sense enjoyed by others in society cannot be regarded as a matter of controversy requiring the lapse of time to cast clearer light on the issues involved. In short, the unsatisfactory situation in which post-operative transsexuals live in an intermediate zone as not quite one gender or the other is no longer sustainable.

The Court does not underestimate the difficulties posed or the important repercussions which any major change in the system will inevitably have, not only in the field of birth registration, but also in the areas of access to records, family law, affiliation, inheritance, criminal justice, employment, social security and insurance. However, these problems are far from insuperable. No concrete or substantial hardship or detriment to the public interest has indeed been demonstrated as likely to flow from any change to the status of transsexuals and, as regards other possible consequences, the Court considers that society may reasonably be expected to tolerate a certain inconvenience to enable individuals to live in dignity and worth in accordance with the sexual identity chosen by them at great personal cost.

Since there are no significant factors of public interest to weigh against the interest of this individual applicant in obtaining legal recognition of her gender re-assignment, it reaches the conclusion that the fair balance that is inherent in the Convention now tilts decisively in favour of the applicant. There has, accordingly, been a failure to respect her right to private life in breach of Article 8 of the Convention.

II. Alleged Violation of Article 12 of the Convention

The applicant also claimed a violation of Article 12 of the Convention, which provides as follows:

> "Men and women of marriageable age have the right to marry and to found a family, according to the national laws governing the exercise of this right."

The Court recalls that in [its previous cases] the inability of the transsexuals in those cases to marry a person of the sex opposite to their re-assigned gender was not found in breach of Article 12 of the Convention. These findings were based variously on the reasoning that the right to marry referred to traditional marriage between persons of opposite biological sex. Reference was also made to the wording of Article 12 as protecting marriage as the basis of the family.

Reviewing the situation in 2002, the Court observes that Article 12 secures the fundamental right of a man and woman to marry and to found a family. The second aspect is not however a condition of the first and the inability of any couple to conceive or parent a child cannot be regarded as *per se* removing their right to enjoy the first limb of this provision.

The exercise of the right to marry gives rise to social, personal and legal consequences. It is subject to the national laws of the Contracting States but the limitations thereby introduced must not restrict or reduce the right in such a way or to such an extent that the very essence of the right is impaired.

It is true that the first sentence refers in express terms to the right of a man and woman to marry. The Court is not persuaded that at the date of this case it can still be assumed that these terms must refer to a determination of gender by purely biological criteria. There have been major social changes in the institution of marriage since the adoption of the Convention as well as dramatic changes brought about by developments in medicine and science in the field of transsexuality. The Court has found above, under Article 8 of the Convention, that a test of congruent biological factors can no longer be decisive in denying legal recognition to the change of gender of a post-operative transsexual.

The right under Article 8 to respect for private life does not however subsume all the issues under Article 12, where conditions imposed by national laws are accorded a specific mention. The Court has therefore considered whether the allocation of sex in national law to that registered at birth is a limitation impairing the very essence of the right to marry in this case. In that regard, it finds that it is artificial to assert that post-operative transsexuals have not been deprived of the right to marry as, according to law, they remain able to marry a person of their former opposite sex. The applicant in this case lives as a woman, is in a relationship with a man and would only wish to marry a man. She has no possibility of doing so. In the Court's view, she may therefore claim that the very essence of her right to marry has been infringed.

The Court has not identified any other reason which would prevent it from reaching this conclusion. The Government have argued that in this sensitive area eligibility for marriage under national law should be left to the domestic courts within the State's margin of appreciation, adverting to the potential impact on already existing marriages in which a transsexual is a partner. It appears, however, that the domestic courts tend to the view that the matter is best handled by the legislature, while the Government have no present intention to introduce legislation.

It may be noted from the materials submitted that though there is widespread acceptance of the marriage of transsexuals, fewer countries permit the marriage of transsexuals in their assigned gender than recognise the change of gender itself. The Court is not persuaded however that this supports an argument for leaving the matter entirely to the Contracting States as being within their margin of appreciation. This would be tantamount to finding that the range of options open to a Contracting State included an effective bar on any exercise of the right to marry. The margin of appreciation cannot extend so far. While it is for the Contracting State to determine *inter alia* the conditions under which a person claiming legal recognition as a transsexual establishes that gender re-assignment has been properly effected or under which past marriages cease to be valid and the formalities applicable to future marriages (including, for example, the information to be furnished to intended spouses), the Court finds no justification for barring the transsexual from enjoying the right to marry under any circumstances.

The Court concludes that there has been a breach of Article 12 of the Convention in the present case.

Notes and Questions

1. Decisions by the European Court of Human Rights do not have quite the same kind of binding effect in Europe as United States Supreme Court decisions have in the United States. They are really declarations of the obligations of those nations that are signatories to the relevant treaties and conventions. It is then up to national governments to consider adopting or amending legislation to effectuate the court's rulings. In response to Goodwin, the British government appointed a study commission, which proposed legislation that would substantially reform British law relating to transsexuality. The resulting developments are described in the following news brief from the Summer 2004 issue of *Lesbian/Gay Law Notes*:

> Her Majesty Queen Elizabeth II has given royal assent to the Gender Recognition Act 2004, as of July 1, 2004. This was the last step to enactment of a sweeping reform of British law concerning the legal recognition of gender change, and brings to fruition the recommendations of the Interdepartmental Working Group on Transsexual People, which had been appointed by the Blair Government in response to court decisions and lobbying efforts by transgender rights advocates. The law is intended to honor the government's obligations under the Human Rights law to protect the right of transsexual persons to respect for their private lives and legal equality. Under the law, Gender Recognition Panels will be established to review applications from individuals, who are required to document that they have been diagnosed with gender dysphoria, have lived for at least two years in their acquired gender and intend to do so for the remainder of their lives. Successful applicants will receive a gender recognition certificate, according them the right of full legal recognition in their acquired gender, new birth certificates, and other legal rights accorded members of their acquired gender. They will be allowed to marry in their acquired gender. The Act will apply throughout the United Kingdom, the Scottish Parliament having voted to go along with

what the U.K. parliament decides in order to bring the U.K. into compliance with European treaty obligations. The government estimated that there are approximately 5,000 transsexual people in the U.K., and it is anticipated that the annual caseload of the Gender Recognition Panels will be about 200–300 cases.

2. Note the relative roles of the European Court and the legislative body of the United Kingdom. In the United States, if the Supreme Court finds that a right of privacy or right to marry has been violated by a state, the Court will provide a remedy. The same is true for state supreme courts and their legislatures. But recall the marriage case in Vermont, *Baker v. Vermont*. There the court held that the current state of the law, failure to allow same-sex couples to receive the benefits of marriage, violated the equality provisions of the state constitution. But, rather than provide a remedy, the *Baker* court held the legislature responsible for crafting a remedy that would remove the inequality. Why doesn't this occur more often in American law? How often do courts complain that the existing law is unfair, but unfortunately the court cannot change it? How often do courts say that change will have to come from the legislature? And how often does change then come from the legislature? See, e.g., *In re Marriage Licence for Nash*, 2003 WL 23097095 (Ohio App.)(slip opinion), holding that a female to male transsexual is still female and cannot marry a female and explaining that the question is one of public policy for the legislature to decide. What exactly is the dividing line between a protected constitutional right and public policy?

2. Can the *Goodwin* holding and rationale be stretched to include the right to same-sex marriage for lesbians and gay men?

Further Reading on the Pros and Cons of Same-Sex Marriage

Carlos A. Ball, The Positive in the Fundamental Right to Marry: Same-Sex Marriage in the Aftermath of Lawrence v. Texas, 88 Minn. L. Rev. 1184 (2004).

Mary Becker, Family Law in the Secular State and Restrictions on Same-Sex Marriage: Two are Better than One, 2001 U. Ill. L. Rev. 1.

Patricia A. Cain, Imagine There's No Marriage, 16 Quinnipiac L. Rev. 27 (1996).

David Orgon Coolidge and William C. Duncan, Reaffirming Marriage: A Presidential Priority, 24 Harv. J.L. & Pub. Pol'y 623 (2001).

Richard F. Duncan, Homosexual Marriage and the Myth of Tolerance: Is Cardinal O'-Connor a "Homophobe"? 10 Notre Dame L.J. Ethics and Pub. Pol'y 587 (1996).

Mary C. Dunlap, The Lesbian and Gay Marriage Debate: A Microcosm of Our Hopes and Troubles in the Nineties, 1 Law & Sexuality 62 (1991).

William N. Eskridge, Jr., The Case for Same-Sex Marriage (1996).

Nan D. Hunter, Marriage, Law, and Gender: A Feminist Inquiry, 1 Law & Sexuality 9 (1991).

Arthur S. Leonard, Ten Propositions About Legal Recognition of Same-Sex Partners, 30 Cap. U. L. Rev. 343 (2002).

Mark E. Wojcik, The Wedding Bells Heard Around the World: Years From Now, Will We Wonder Why We Worried About Same-sex Marriage?, 24 N. Ill. U. L. Rev. 589 (2004).

Evan Wolfson, Crossing the Threshold: Equal Marriage Rights for Lesbians and Gay Men and the Intra-Community Critique, 21 N.Y.U. Rev. L. & Soc. Change 567 (1994–95).

Evan Wolfson, Why Marriage Matters (2004).

Further Reading on the Extra-Territorial Recognition of Same-Sex Marriage

Jennifer Gerarda Brown, Extraterritorial Recognition of Same-Sex Marriage: When Theory Confronts Praxis, 16 Quinnipian L. Rev. 1 (1996).

Larry Kramer, Same-Sex Marriage, Conflict of Laws, and the Unconstitutional Public Policy Exception, 106 Yale L.J. 1965 (1997).

Andrew Koppelman, Dumb and DOMA: Why the Defense of Marriage Act is Unconstitutional, 83 Iowa L. Rev. 1 (1997).

Andrew Koppelman, Same-Sex Marriage, Choice of Law, and Public Policy, 76 Tex. L. Rev. 921 (1998).

Mark Strasser, DOMA and the Two Faces of Federalism, 32 Creighton L. Rev. 457 (1998).

Further Reading on the Rights of Transsexual Persons to Marry

Mary Coombs, Sexual Dis-Orientation: Transgendered People and Same-Sex Marriage, 8 UCLA Women's L.J. 219 (1998).

Kevin Tallant, Note, My "Dude Looks Like a Lady": The Constitutional Void of Transsexual Marriage, 36 Ga. L. Rev. 635 (2002).

B. Litigating for Spousal Status in the Absence of a Valid Marriage

1. The Putative Spouse Doctrine

State recognition of the marital relationship grants numerous benefits to the two spouses. Yet even when the state refuses to recognize the marital relationship, policy often dictates that two people who resemble a married couple ought to be treated by the state as though they were married. A common example of this situation is the case of the putative spouse. However, to claim "putative spouse" status, the person must believe in good faith that a valid marriage existed. In addition, the good faith belief in the marriage must be a reasonable belief. See, e.g., *Welch v. State*, 100 Cal. Rptr. 2d 430 (Cal. App. 2000), holding that a woman's belief that she and her male cohabitant were married was not reasonable because they had made no effort to solemnize the marriage and because she had been previously married and divorced. This prior experience with marriage meant that she should have understood the basic legal requirements for marriage. Same-sex couples have made similar claims.

Estate of Hall
707 N.E.2d 201 (Ill. App. 1998)

Justice RAKOWSKI delivered the opinion of the court:

Andrea Hall died intestate on November 16, 1996. Petitioner, Regina Pavone, Hall's life-partner, filed a petition in the probate court seeking a surviving spouse share of Hall's estate pursuant to section 2-1 of the Probate Act of 1975. Respondent, William Hall, is the administrator of Hall's estate. Respondent filed a motion to dismiss petitioner's claim contending that petitioner cannot be a surviving spouse because Illinois does not recognize same-sex marriages. The trial court granted respondent's motion to dismiss, and petitioner appeals.

On appeal, as in the trial court, petitioner challenges the constitutionality of Illinois' prohibition of same-sex marriages. Specifically, petitioner argues that the prohibition violates the equal protection provisions of the United States and Illinois Constitutions. Nevertheless, finding that this issue is not justiciable within the context of this case, we do not reach the merits of petitioner's contentions. For the reasons that follow, we affirm.

I. Background

Petitioner made the following allegations in her third amended verified complaint. Hall and petitioner met each other in February 1988. Shortly after that, they began dating exclusively and ultimately moved in together. On October 17, 1991, their relationship was solidified when Hall quitclaimed to petitioner one half interest in the property at 321 Cherry Court in Glenview, Illinois.

In September 1993, Hall and petitioner sold the 321 Cherry Court property and used the proceeds to purchase a home located at 1107 West Pratt in Chicago. The financing for this property was secured by both Hall and petitioner.

On December 23, 1995, Hall and petitioner were "married" in a private ceremony. At that ceremony, they exchanged vows and wedding bands. Although Hall and petitioner wished to formalize their union by obtaining a marriage license, they did not apply for one, reasoning that any attempt would be futile in light of Illinois' prohibition on same-sex marriages.

Nevertheless, from December 23, 1995, onward, Hall and petitioner considered themselves married. They shared the above mentioned home at 1107 West Pratt as well as a "special community of thoughts and deep emotional attachment." They also held themselves out to the world as being "married," including, but not limited to, friends and immediate family members. Moreover, they were dependent on each other for the maintenance and upkeep of their home as well as daily living expenses and necessities of life. They commingled their funds through joint bank accounts, joint lines of credit, and purchases such as boats and cars. Hall and petitioner's obligations also included the financial support of Hall's sister and Hall's minor son. In sum, petitioner contends that her relationship with Hall mirrored that of a heterosexual couple legally joined through marriage; it "exhibited all of the pertinent attributes associated with matrimony and a long term, enduring commitment between two consenting adults."

II. Justiciability of Petitioner's Constitutional Challenge

Petitioner's third amended complaint sought a surviving spouse share of Hall's estate pursuant to section 2-1 of the Probate Act. Section 2-1 provides in pertinent part:

> "The intestate real and personal estate of a resident decedent * * * descends and shall be distributed as follows:
>
> (a) If there is a surviving spouse and also a descendant of the decedent, 1/2 of the entire estate to the *surviving spouse* and 1/2 to the decedent's descendants per stirpes." (Emphasis added.)

Respondent, however, contended that petitioner cannot obtain surviving spouse status since Illinois law prohibits same-sex marriages. See 750 ILCS 5/212(a)(5) (West 1996) (prohibiting marriages between two individuals of the same sex); 750 ILCS 5/213.1 (West 1996) (declaring that "marriage between 2 individuals of the same sex is contrary to the public policy of [Illinois]"); 750 ILCS 5/201 (West 1996) (stating the formalities of a valid marriage as one that is between a man and a woman licensed, solemnized and registered). In turn, petitioner argued that the prohibition against same-sex marriages is unconstitutional. Thus, the parties redefined the issue from whether petitioner was entitled to a surviving spouse share of Hall's estate to whether Illinois' proscription on same-sex marriages is unconstitutional.

Unlike the former issue, we believe the latter issue is not justiciable in this case. Specifically, assuming we declare the proscription on same-sex marriages unconstitutional and void *ab initio*, the fact remains that petitioner and Hall were never legally married. Although the same-sex marriage prohibition explains why petitioner and Hall did not legally marry, a declaration that the same-sex marriage prohibition is unconstitutional and void *ab initio* will not change petitioner's marital status. Because Illinois law and public policy preclude us from conferring "spouse status" upon petitioner, a necessary requisite for obtaining a surviving spouse share under the Probate Act, we find that the issue is moot because it does not affect the actual controversy between the parties. We also find that petitioner lacks standing to raise the issue in this case. Thus, because an adjudication of petitioner's constitutional challenge brings her no closer to obtaining surviving spouse status, we must exercise judicial restraint and decline to address her challenge.

A. *Mootness of Petitioner's Constitutional Challenge*

To save petitioner's challenge from mootness, a declaration that the proscription is unconstitutional must have some bearing on the actual controversy of whether she is entitled to a spousal share of Hall's estate. It is axiomatic that for one to be entitled to a surviving spouse share under the Probate Act that individual must be considered a spouse of the decedent. Thus, to determine whether petitioner's constitutional challenge is a moot point, we must decide whether, assuming the prohibition on same-sex marriages is declared unconstitutional and void *ab initio,* the relationship between Hall and petitioner can be construed to be either a valid marriage or be of such nature that we can confer the rights of a "spouse" upon petitioner. See *In re Mac Harg*, 120 Ill.App.3d 753, 755, 76 Ill.Dec. 500, 458 N.E.2d 1154 (1983) ("'spouse' refers to a legal wife or husband").

It is clear from the alleged facts that the relationship did not meet the statutory requirements for a valid marriage. Under the Illinois Marriage and Dissolution of Marriage Act (Marriage Act), the formalities for a lawful marriage require "[a] marriage between a man and a woman licensed, solemnized and registered as provided in th[e] Act." 750 ILCS 5/201 (West 1996). Notwithstanding the alleged unconstitutional requirement that the couple be a man and a woman, petitioner has failed to allege sufficient facts to establish a valid marriage. Petitioner and Hall did not obtain a license nor did they register their marriage. Petitioner's pleadings also lack any allegation that the alleged solemnization was performed by someone authorized under the law. See 750 ILCS 5/209 (West 1996). Consequently, petitioner has failed to allege facts establishing a marriage that meets the requirements of the Marriage Act.

Although Illinois courts have conferred "spouse" status upon individuals where their marriages lacked compliance with one of the directory requirements of the Marriage Act, we find these cases inapplicable to the instant case. See, *e.g.*, *Haderaski v. Haderaski*, 415 Ill. 118, 119–22, 112 N.E.2d 714 (1953) (lack of license in otherwise lawful marriage did not invalidate marriage, as the statute requiring a license was directory and not mandatory). All of these cases involved situations where the party seeking enforcement of the marriage believed in good faith that he or she was lawfully married and, but for the failure to comply with a directory requirement, was otherwise lawfully married. However, in the instant case, although petitioner and Hall may have subjectively believed that the ceremony and exchange of vows and rings constituted a marriage between themselves, they nonetheless knew that the marriage was not legally recognized. This is evidenced by their failure to seek a marriage license because of their belief that any effort would have been futile under Illinois law.

The fact that petitioner knew that she was not lawfully married also precludes her from obtaining spouse status through the putative spouse provision of the Marriage Act. Section 305 of the Marriage Act provides that:

> "Any person, having gone through a marriage ceremony, who has cohabited with another to whom he is not legally married in the good faith belief that he was married to that person is a putative spouse until knowledge of the fact that he is not legally married terminates his status and prevents acquisition of further rights." 750 ILCS 5/305 (West 1996).

In this case, petitioner admits that she knew that she was not legally married to Hall. Consequently, the putative spouse provision fails to confer spouse status upon petitioner.

Because case law and the putative spouse provision fail to provide petitioner with spouse status, the only remaining option is to consider whether the relationship between petitioner and Hall is a legal equivalent to marriage. This proposition, however, must fail because treatment of their relationship as a legal equivalent to marriage would be tantamount to recognizing common law marriage, which Illinois outlawed in 1905....

[I]n this case the relationship between petitioner and Hall was, at all times, nothing more than a private contract terminable at will. Assuming *arguendo* that we were to address petitioner's issue and declare Illinois' proscription on same-sex marriages unconstitutional and void *ab initio*, the fact that petitioner and Hall never entered into a legally binding marriage would nevertheless remain. Thus, petitioner still would not be entitled to a surviving spouse share of Hall's estate. Affirmed and remanded.

Notes and Questions

1. See also *In re Estate of Cooper*, 592 N.Y.S.2d 797 (N.Y. App. Div. 1993), appeal dismissed, 624 N.E.2d 696 (N.Y. 1993), similarly holding that a surviving gay partner is not a "spouse" for purposes of the spousal election statute under New York law. The plaintiff in *Cooper*, however, argued that applying such a limited definition of "spouse" violated equal protection. The court treated the claim as a challenge to the New York marriage law and, citing *Baker v. Nelson*, the 1971 Minnesota marriage case, held that there was no constitutionally-protected right for same-sex couples to marry. Does this adequately respond to the plaintiff's argument? Might the exclusion of a surviving same-sex partner from the right of election violate equal protection, even if the equal protection is not construed to require the state to allow same-sex partners to marry? Is there a logical difference between a challenge to a state law that limits marriage to opposite-sex couples and a challenge to state laws that limit certain benefits to married couples?

2. What result in *Hall* and in *Cooper* if the same-sex couples had been married in Massachusetts after May 17, 2004? Illinois (*Hall* case) has a baby DOMA, but New York (*Cooper* case) does not. Could Hall's partner rely on the putative spouse doctrine to avoid the baby DOMA?

3. What result in *Hall* and in *Cooper* if the couples had been "married" in San Francisco or in New Paltz by public officials willing to perform marriage ceremonies for same-sex couples in the absence of licenses issued by the state? Would the putative spouse doctrine be available? See Christopher L. Blakesley, The Putative Marriage Doctrine, 60 Tulane L. Rev. 1 at 6 (1985):

> If a marriage is declared to be null or void, that declaration is retroactive to the day that the null marriage was contracted....Thus, generally, a marriage declared null produces no effects of marriage whatsoever....
>
> The putative marriage doctrine is a device developed to ameliorate or correct the injustice which would occur if civil effects were not allowed to flow to a party to a null marriage who believes in good faith that he or she is validly married. A putative marriage, therefore, is a marriage which is in reality null, but which allows the civil effects of a valid marriage to flow to the party or parties who contracted it in good faith. It is a marriage which has been solemnized in proper form and celebrated in good faith by one or both parties, but which, by reason of some legal infirmity, is either void or voidable. The doctrine developed as a canon law palliative to protect those persons who went through a marriage ceremony in the good faith belief that the marriage was valid and proper, when it was actually null due to some impediment. It provides that, notwithstanding its nullity, the civil effects of a legal marriage flow to the parties who, in good faith, contract an invalid marriage.

California Family Code

**§ 2251. Status of putative spouse; division of
community or quasi-community property**

(a) If a determination is made that a marriage is void or voidable and the court finds that either party or both parties believed in good faith that the marriage was valid, the court shall:

(1) Declare the party or parties to have the status of a putative spouse.

(2) If the division of property is in issue, divide, in accordance with Division 7 (commencing with Section 2500), that property acquired during the union which would have been community property or quasi-community property if the union had not been void or voidable. This property is known as "quasi-marital property".

2. Spousal Rights to Death Benefits

Smith v. Knoller

Superior Court, San Francisco County, California, No. 319532
(not officially published)
August 9, 2001

ROBERTSON, J.

[Summary of Facts: On January 21, 2001, Diane Whipple was brutally attacked just outside her front door by a neighbor's dogs. She was mauled to death. Her partner of seven years, Sharon Smith, with whom she had exchanged wedding rings and vows, sued the owners of the dogs for wrongful death. The defendants claimed that Smith had no standing because only a legally married spouse could bring a wrongful death claim.]

[The California wrongful death statute] provides that a "surviving spouse" may bring a cause of action for wrongful death. Plaintiff contends that the term "spouse" applies to same-sex couples or at the very least, the word is ambiguous and must be construed in a manner which effectuates the underlying purposes of the wrongful death statute. The court rejects plaintiff's argument as inconsistent with the plain meaning of the word "spouse." See Ballantine's Law Dictionary (defining "spouse" as "[a] husband or wife"); *Elden v. Sheldon* (1988) 46 Cal.3d 267; *Nieto v. City of Los Angeles* (1982) 138 Cal. App.3d 464 (unmarried heterosexual cohabitants are not "spouses" under the wrongful death statute). Plaintiff also asserts that reading the wrongful death statute to exclude her claim denies her equal protection based upon her sexual orientation in violation of Cal. Const., art I, sec. 7. The court agrees.[1]

This court has the responsibility to construe the legislation in such a manner as to save its constitutionality. An interpretation of the wrongful death statute which

---

1. Because the court concludes that interpreting the wrongful death statute to exclude homosexuals violates the rational basis test, the court need not decide whether to employ "strict scrutiny," "heightened scrutiny," or "the exacting rational basis test." It is noteworthy, however, that the rights guaranteed by the California Constitution are not dependent on those guaranteed by the United State Constitution, see *Gay Law Students Assn. v. Pacific Tel. & Tel. Co.* (1979).

would exclude such persons as plaintiff would require the court to strike down the statute as a denial of equal protection of the law; whereas to include her within the term "surviving spouse" would not, and neither would it be contrary to legislative intent nor policy. See *Hayes v. Superior Court* (1971) ("In light of the purposes and history of a particular statute or an overall statutory scheme a reviewing court may correct a discriminatory classification by invalidating the invidious exemption and thus extending statutory benefits to those whom the Legislature unconstitutionally excluded.").

Under the California Constitution, homosexuals are entitled to equal protection of the laws. "It is well established that the equal protection of the laws requires only that persons similarly situated receive like treatment…" A statute, which appears facially valid, may have a discriminatory effect in its application thereby denying equal protection of the law. *See Yick Wo v. Hopkins* (1885) 118 U.S. 356, 373. In addition, courts have not hesitated to strike down an invidious classification even though it had history and tradition on its side. *See Brown v. Board of Education* (1954).

In *Levy v. Lousiana*, (1968) 391 U.S. 68, the United States Supreme Court held that a Louisiana statute which denied illegitimate children the right to sue for the wrongful death of a natural mother created an unlawful classification. Justice Douglas explain that "[w]hen the child's claim of damage for loss of his mother is in issue, why, in terms of 'equal protection,' should the tortfeasors go free merely because the child is illegitimate?" In *Labine v. Vincent*, (1971) 401 U.S. 532, the court addressed a Louisiana statute which barred an illegitimate child, who had nevertheless been acknowledged, from sharing equally with legitimate issue in the father's estate. The high court held that there was no equal protection violation and distinguished Levy. The Labine court observed that the statute in Levy created an "insurmountable barrier" to the illegitimate child's participation while the illegitimate child in Labine encountered no such barrier (she could have inherited through a will or other means). In *Steed v. Imperial Airlines* (1974) 12 Cal.3d 115, the California Supreme Court held that the deceased's stepchild, who deceased never adopted, could not recover under the wrongful death statute as an "heir." The court noted that since the deceased could have adopted the plaintiff, "the Levy-Labine 'insurmountable barrier' test of constitutional denial is thus satisfied." *Steed…*

In this case, when one reads the wrongful death statute in conjunction with Cal. Family Code sec 308.5 ("Only marriage between a man and a woman is valid or recognized in California"), there exists an insurmountable barrier to the right of a homosexual to bring an action for the wrongful death of his or her partner. This barrier is not reasonably related to any legitimate purpose.

"The purpose behind the wrongful death statute is to provide compensation for the loss of companionship and other losses resulting from decedent's death." [cite omitted]. Here, plaintiff's sexuality has no relation to the nature of the wrong allegedly inflicted upon her and denying recovery would be a windfall for the tortfeasor. The Legislature reasonably could confine wrongful death recovery to a surviving spouse to encourage marriage. *See* Elden. However, precluding same sex partners from recovery under the wrongful death statute does not further the state's interest in promoting marriage because Cal. Family Code sec. 308.5 expressly forbids same sex marriages. Obviously, allowing plaintiff a cause of action will impose a burden on the court and intrude into plaintiff's private life. The court will need to inquire into the character of her relationship to determine whether it is sufficiently similar to the relationship between a husband and wife. Nevertheless, courts (as opposed to insurers and administrative agencies) are uniquely situated to make such a determination. Indeed, other sections of the wrongful death statute require a thorough factual analysis. Most importantly, administrative ease cannot "be made into an impenetrable barrier that works to shield otherwise invidious discrimination." *Gomez v. Perez* (1973) 409 U.S. 535, 538.

To ascertain whether plaintiff can in fact recover under the wrongful death statute, the court must make a factually intensive analysis. Such an analysis is not suitable for resolution on demurrer. Some of the factors which the court should weigh include whether the plaintiff and decedent are registered domestic partners under Cal. Family code sec 297 or if not registered, their relationship otherwise meets the standards set forth in that statute. For example, the court should examine whether a common residence exists, the degree of economic cooperation, fidelity, and the stability and duration of the relationship. While such an inquiry is intrusive, it is plaintiff's decision to bring the action. It would be untenable to deny plaintiff's claim merely because the court may need to examine her private life.

In *Hinman v. Department of Personnel Admin.*, (1985) 167 Cal.App.3d 516, the court held that denying state dental insurance coverage to a cohabitant in a homosexual relationship did not offend the equal protection clause of the state Constitution. That case is distinguishable, however. First, the cohabitant in Hinman could still obtain dental insurance. In the instant action, there exists an *insurmountable barrier* to plaintiff's recovery. Second, Hinman implicated different policy considerations, including the state coffers and a public service. Here, if the court bars plaintiff's suit, then individual tortfeasors may obtain a windfall. Third, the right to petition the court to recover for the loss of a loved one because of the misfeasance of another implicates a right and a loss far distinct from the ability to receive dental coverage.

Reading the wrongful death statute to exclude plaintiff would unduly punish her for her sexual orientation. Such a reading has no place in our system of government, which has as one of its basic tenets equal protection for all.

Notes on Wrongful Death Benefits and Similar Causes of Action

1. *History of the wrongful death cause of action*: The common law of England did not recognize a right to sue for wrongful death. At death, the victim's claim was extinguished. If the victim survived, the victim could sue the tortfeasor for damages. This situation led to the seemingly absurd result that it was cheaper to kill a person than to injure a person. England reversed this result legislatively when it passed Lord Campbell's Act in 1846, creating a statutory cause of action for certain relatives of a decedent whose death resulted from the tortious act of another. The common law rule was imported into the United States. See *Comegys v. Vasse*, 26 U.S. 193 at 213 (1828)("mere personal *torts*, which die with the party, and do not survive to his personal representative, are not capable of passing by assignment"). State by state, the common law rule was reversed by the enactment of wrongful death statutes modeled on Lord Campbell's Act. Two important points about these statutes are worth stressing: (1) Only relatives of the deceased who are named in the statute (e.g., spouses, children, parents) are entitled to sue for wrongful death, and (2) Generally these personal tort claims cannot be assigned.

2. Why should suits for wrongful death be limited to spouses and other close relatives? Would a better solution be to allow the personal representative to bring suit against the tortfeasor to recover damages for the benefit of the estate of the deceased?

3. *California's New Wrongful Death Statute:* California Code of Civil Procedure 377.60 (California's wrongful death act), was amended in 2001 to give domestic partners standing to pursue wrongful death claims. The definition of domestic partner was determined by California Family Code Section 297, which required registration with the Secretary of State. That definition was amended in 2004 to provide that for deaths occurring before January 1, 2002, registration would not be a necessary prerequisite to standing. California's domestic partnership law is discussed *infra.* at C.2.c. In Vermont, the Civil Union Act also provides that partners united in a civil union may bring lawsuits under the state's wrongful death statute. See *infra* at C.1.

4. *Common law vs. statutory law:* Courts have more leeway when applying common law principles than when applying a statute. Thus, for example, a New Jersey court ruled that an unmarried female cohabitant could bring a negligent infliction of emotional distress action against a defendant who caused the death of her fiancè. Under New Jersey common law, a plaintiff in such a situation is entitled to bring suit so long as she was within the zone of risk (she was in fact with him at the scene of the accident) and was in a close "marital or intimate familial relationship." See *Dunphy v. Gregor*, 617 A.2d. 1248 (N.J. App. Div. 1992). By contrast, the court was unwilling to allow a similar cohabitant to make a workers' compensation claim. The court explained:

> This case is fundamentally different from *Dunphy v. Gregor*, which involved the scope of the common law tort action for negligent infliction of emotional distress recognized [under New Jersey common law] if a person suffers severe emotional distress from observing the death or serious injury of a family member caused by another party's negligence. In that context, we held that parties who were engaged and living together had an "intimate, familial relationship" which could form the basis for a cause of action. In contrast, petitioner's claim is based upon a statute which limits benefits to a person who qualifies as a "wife." Petitioner did not occupy that status in relation to the decedent.

Toms v. Dee Rose Furniture, 621 A.2d 91 (N.J. App. Div. 1993).

5. *California law on suits for negligent infliction of emotional distress when partner is injured:* Unlike New Jersey, California courts have refused to extend the state's common law rule to allow unmarried cohabitants to sue for negligent infliction of emotional distress. See *Elden v. Sheldon*, 758 P.2d 582 (Cal. 1988)(citing the state's policy of fostering marriage as the justification for not extending the cause of action to cover unmarried couples). See also Dennis G. Bassi, It's all Relative: A Graphical Reasoning Model for Liberalizing Recovery of Negligent Infliction of Emotional Distress Beyond the Immediate Family, 30 Val. U. L. Rev. 913 (1996).

However, the California rule regarding who can sue for negligent infliction of emotional distress has been partially reversed by statute. Cal. Civ. Code § 1714.01 provides: "Domestic partners shall be entitled to recover damages for negligent infliction of emotional distress to the same extent that spouses are entitled to do so under California law." So long as the same-sex partners have registered as domestic partners, they are able to bring a negligent infliction of emotional distress claim for harm inflicted upon their partners.

6. *Workers' Compensation:* All states have some form of Workers' Compensation legislation that provides death benefits to the survivors of employees who are killed on the job. The benefit is not provided to the employee and it is not something that the employee can assign to someone else. Workers' Compensation laws typically provide benefits for spouses, dependent children, and, in some cases, other dependent family members. Because of this restriction, most states do not provide workers' compensation benefits to domestic partners. Challenging this exclusion, a same-sex surviving partner of a victim in the September 11, 2001, attack on the World Trade Center, joined by a partner of a victim who died in the November 12, 2001, airplane crash after take-off from Kennedy Airport, sued their partners' insurance companies for denying them spousal benefits under New York's Workers' Compensation Law. On August 20, 2002, the New York State Legislature amended the Workers' Compensation statutes at §4 to define "domestic partners" and to provide:

> 2. Death benefits. The domestic partner, at the time of the death, of any employee shall, if such employee had no spouse at the time of his or her death, be deemed to be the surviving spouse of such employee for the purposes of any death benefit, including but not limited to funeral expenses, to which a surviving spouse would be entitled upon the death of such employee, and any and all such benefits shall be paid to such domestic partner.

> 3. Applicability. The provisions of this section apply only to cases in which the employee's death occurred as a result of the terrorist attacks that occurred on September eleven, two thousand one.

The statute was deemed to be effective as of September 10, 2001. As a result, Mr. Courtney (the survivor of the partner who died on September 11) won the right to death benefits, but Mr. Valentine (the survivor of the partner who died on Nov. 12, 2001) did not. There is a bill pending in the New York legislature to strike paragraph 3 of the statute, which would thereby extend the right to benefits beyond domestic partners who lost their partners as a result of the terrorist attacks.

7. *September 11th Victim Compensation Fund:* After the terrorist attacks on September 11, 2001, Congress passed legislation creating the September 11th Victim Compensation Fund. Public Law 107-42, Sections 401–409. Section 403 of the Act provides: "It is the purpose of this title to provide compensation to any individual (or relatives of a deceased individual) who was physically injured or killed as a result of the terrorist-related aircraft crashes of September 11, 2001." Although not explicitly stated in this section, an additional purpose was to provide quick payment of damages to claimants without proof of fault in exchange for a waiver of the right to file a civil action for damages. In this way, the statute resembles workers compensation legislation, in which employees accept a lump sum payment instead of suing the employer in tort. The gain to the plaintiff in these schemes is not simply the quick payment of damages, but also the certainty of payment without having to prove fault and without the risk that, even if successful, the claim may never be paid. (E.g., the tortfeasor may be insolvent or have the judgment discharged in bankruptcy.)

The statute is quite brief. Its provisions were to be carried out by a Special Master, appointed by the Attorney General. On November 26, 2001, the Attorney General appointed Kenneth R. Feinberg as Special Master. Feinberg announced early in his tenure that he would attempt to honor the claims of same-sex partners in appropriate cases, and he had a certain amount of discretion that would allow him to do so. However, the enabling statute included legal terms such as "personal representative," which refers to the person entitled to make a claim under state law, as well as the term "relative" when describing who should benefit from the Fund. The New York statute, passed in 2002 but with retroactive effect, gave "standing" to domestic partners who resided in New York. But not every state was so clear (or so caring) about its same-sex couples. The Fund closed on June 15, 2004, and Feinberg claimed that over 98% of eligible families who lost a loved one participated in the Fund. At least 24 openly gay or lesbian survivors were identified during the Fund's operation and not all of them received equal benefits when compared to spouses of deceased victims. For more details about the position of same-sex survivors of victims of September 11, see Nancy Knauer, *The September 11 Attacks and Surviving Same-Sex Partners: Defining Family Through Tragedy*, 75 Temple L. Rev. 31 (2002).

In one case, the surviving brother of a September 11 victim refused to share Fund proceeds with the surviving lesbian partner of the victim, even though Mr. Feinberg had substantially increased the amount awarded after the surviving partner filed an affidavit about the nature of their relationship, presumably under the impression that the personal representative (the brother) would share the proceeds with the surviving partner. The partner then sued, and a New York trial court, expressing sympathy with her claim, denied the brother's motion to dismiss the case and ordered further inquiries to the Special Master to determine his intent in increasing the amount awarded, intimating that it might eventually use its equitable powers to apportion the award. *Cruz v. McAneney*, New York Law Journal, 7/16/2004, p. 18, col. 3 (N.Y.Sup.Ct., Kings Co., July 2, 2004).

8. *Hawaii's Reciprocal Beneficiary legislation*: During the same-sex marriage litigation in Hawaii, the Hawaii legislature passed a law that recognizes a new type of legal relationship known as "reciprocal beneficiaries." Same-sex couples who cannot legally marry may register with the state as reciprocal beneficiaries and receive certain rights as a result of that recognition. (See discussion of reciprocal beneficiary legislation *infra*). The Hawaii legislation provides death benefits for the surviving same-sex reciprocal beneficiary of a public safety officer who is killed in the line of duty. See Hawaii Rev. Stat. §88-163.

9. *Payment of Death Benefits under Private Pension Plans:* Marjorie Forlini and Sandra Rovira were in a committed same sex relationship for 12 years until Forlini died of cancer. Two years into the relationship, Rovira's two minor children came to live with them. Forlini supported them for 10 years, claiming them as dependents on her tax return under the provision that applies to unrelated members of the household.[2] At Forlini's death, Rovira and her sons submitted a claim to Forlini's employer, AT & T, for a death benefit payment from her pension plan. The pension plan provided for benefits only to spouses, dependent children under age 23, or other dependent relatives. Neither the partner, Rovira, nor the two sons that Forlini had supported for ten years as her own, qualified under the plan. As the AT&T Benefits Committee explained:

> The Committee determined that because Ms. Forlini and Ms. Rovira's relationship is not recognized as a valid marriage in the state in which they resided,

---

2. Under Internal Revenue Code Section 152(a)(9), a taxpayer may claim an exemption for an unrelated dependent provided the taxpayer provides over half the support for the dependent and the dependent is a member of the taxpayer's household. A person unrelated to the taxpayer satisfies this provision if the person lives with the taxpayer for the entire year as a member of the taxpayer's household and their relationship does not violate local laws. Certain temporary absences from the taxpayer's home are not taken into account. See Treas. Reg. § 1.152-1(b).

Ms. Rovira does not meet the eligibility criteria to qualify as a beneficiary under the provisions of the [Plan]. Dependent children must be either the natural or adopted children of the employee, or the natural or adopted children of the employee's legal spouse. The Committee determined that because Frank and Alfred Morales are not the natural or adopted children of Ms. Forlini or of her legal spouse, they also do not qualify as beneficiaries under the provisions of the [Plan]. The Committee also noted that the provisions of the [Plan] are administered uniformly to all employees without discrimination on the basis of race, color, religion, national origin, sex, sexual preference or orientation.

In addition to her claim that she was functionally a "spouse," Rovira argued that the plan's exclusion of her as a beneficiary conflicted with the company's own nondiscrimination policy, which prohibited discrimination on the basis of marital status or sexual orientation. She sued in federal district court because the plan was controlled by ERISA, a federal law. The court ruled against her claim, holding that the nondiscrimination policy created no third-party benefits and, under ERISA law, the nondiscrimination policy was not a "governing plan document." See *Rovira v. AT&T,* 817 F. Supp. 1062 (S.D.N.Y. 1993).

C. Statutory Alternatives to Marriage.

1. Civil Unions

In response to the *Baker* case (supra), the Vermont legislature created a new state-recognized status for same-sex couples called civil unions.

Vermont Statutes Annotated

Title Fifteen. Domestic Relations. Chapter 23. Civil Unions
15 V.S.A. § 1201 (2001)

§ 1201. Definitions

As used in this chapter:

(1) "Certificate of civil union" means a document that certifies that the persons named on the certificate have established a civil union in this state in compliance with this chapter and 18 V.S.A. chapter 106.

(2) "Civil union" means that two eligible persons have established a relationship pursuant to this chapter, and may receive the benefits and protections and be subject to the responsibilities of spouses.

(3) "Commissioner" means the commissioner of health.

(4) "Marriage" means the legally recognized union of one man and one woman.

(5) "Party to a civil union" means a person who has established a civil union pursuant to this chapter and 18 V.S.A. chapter 106.

§ 1202. Requisites of a valid civil union

For a civil union to be established in Vermont, it shall be necessary that the parties to a civil union satisfy all of the following criteria:

(1) Not be a party to another civil union or a marriage.

(2) Be of the same sex and therefore excluded from the marriage laws of this state.

(3) Meet the criteria and obligations set forth in 18 V.S.A. chapter 106.

§ 1203. Person shall not enter a civil union with a relative

(a) A woman shall not enter a civil union with her mother, grandmother, daughter, granddaughter, sister, brother's daughter, sister's daughter, father's sister or mother's sister.

(b) A man shall not enter a civil union with his father, grandfather, son, grandson, brother, brother's son, sister's son, father's brother or mother's brother.

(c) A civil union between persons prohibited from entering a civil union in subsection (a) or (b) of this section is void.

§ 1204. Benefits, protections and responsibilities of parties to a civil union

(a) Parties to a civil union shall have all the same benefits, protections and responsibilities under law, whether they derive from statute, administrative or court rule, policy, common law or any other source of civil law, as are granted to spouses in a marriage.

(b) A party to a civil union shall be included in any definition or use of the terms "spouse," "family," "immediate family," "dependent," "next of kin," and other terms that denote the spousal relationship, as those terms are used throughout the law.

(c) Parties to a civil union shall be responsible for the support of one another to the same degree and in the same manner as prescribed under law for married persons.

(d) The law of domestic relations, including annulment, separation and divorce, child custody and support, and property division and maintenance shall apply to parties to a civil union.

(e) The following is a nonexclusive list of legal benefits, protections and responsibilities of spouses, which shall apply in like manner to parties to a civil union:

(1) laws relating to title, tenure, descent and distribution, intestate succession, waiver of will, survivorship, or other incidents of the acquisition, ownership, or transfer, inter vivos or at death, of real or personal property, including eligibility to hold real and personal property as tenants by the entirety (parties to a civil union meet the common law unity of person qualification for purposes of a tenancy by the entirety);

(2) causes of action related to or dependent upon spousal status, including an action for wrongful death, emotional distress, loss of consortium, dramshop, or other torts or actions under contracts reciting, related to, or dependent upon spousal status;

(3) probate law and procedure, including nonprobate transfer;

(4) adoption law and procedure;

. . .

(9) workers' compensation benefits;

. . .

(f) The rights of parties to a civil union, with respect to a child of whom either becomes the natural parent during the term of the civil union, shall be the same as those of a married couple, with respect to a child of whom either spouse becomes the natural parent during the marriage.

§ 1205. Modification of civil union terms

Parties to a civil union may modify the terms, conditions, or effects of their civil union in the same manner and to the same extent as married persons who execute an antenuptial agreement or other agreement recognized and enforceable under the law, setting forth particular understandings with respect to their union.

§ 1206. Dissolution of civil unions

The family court shall have jurisdiction over all proceedings relating to the dissolution of civil unions. The dissolution of civil unions shall follow the same procedures and be subject to the same substantive rights and obligations that are involved in the dissolution of marriage in accordance with chapter 11 of this title, including any residency requirements.

§ 1207. Commissioner of health; duties

(a) The commissioner shall provide civil union license and certificate forms to all town and county clerks.

(b) The commissioner shall keep a record of all civil unions.

Notes and Questions

1. Mary and Susan enter into a civil union under Vermont law. One year later Mary has a child. Can Susan claim that she is also a legal parent of the child or must she first adopt the child?

2. A federal tax statute allows taxpayers to claim certain tax breaks provided they have a "qualified child." "Qualified child" is defined to include a "stepdaughter or stepson." See IRC §152(f), adopted in 2004 for tax years beginning in 2005. If Mary has a child before she enters into the civil union with Susan, will the child qualify as Susan's stepchild?

3. Vermont has a one year residency requirement for divorce and that requirement applies with equal force to dissolution of a civil union. Anthony and John entered into a civil union in 2003. They now live in Texas and want to dissolve the civil union. What do you advise them to do?

Note: Full Faith and Credit?

The question about Vermont Civil Unions that has attracted the most debate has been whether other states will recognize such unions. More specifically, will they be recognized for any purposes either by another state or by the federal government?

The passage of a baby DOMA by the state's legislature is good evidence that state recognition of same-sex unions is against public policy. Thus, it is unlikely that a Vermont same-sex couple's union will be recognized in a state that has a baby DOMA. But it is not impossible. Civil unions are not marriages. A gay-friendly judge could see the baby DOMA as literally applying only to marriage, thereby leaving the judge free to decide whether or not to recognize a civil union.

However, some states have enacted statutes that go beyond nonrecognition of same-sex marriages.

Fla. Stat. § 741.212 (1)

Marriages between persons of the same sex entered into in any jurisdiction, whether within or outside the State of Florida, the United States, or any other jurisdiction, either domestic or foreign, or any other place or location, or relationships between persons of the same sex which are treated as marriages in any jurisdiction, whether within or outside the State of Florida, the United States, or any other jurisdiction, either domestic or foreign, or any other place or location, are not recognized for any purpose in this state.

Tex. Fam. Code § 6.204

In this section, 'civil union' means any relationship status other than marriage that is intended as an alternative to marriage or applies primarily to cohabitating persons; and grants to the parties of the relationship legal protections, benefits, or responsibilities granted to the spouses of a marriage. A marriage between persons of the same sex or a civil union is contrary to the public policy of this state and is void in this state. The state or an agency or political subdivision of the state may not give effect to a: public act, record, or judicial proceeding that creates, recognizes, or validates a marriage between persons of the same sex or a civil union in this state or in any other jurisdiction; or right or claim to any legal protection, benefit, or responsibility asserted as a result of a marriage between persons of the same sex or a civil union in this state or in any other jurisdiction.

Va. Code § 20-45.3

A civil union, partnership contract or other arrangement between persons of the same sex purporting to bestow the privileges or obligations of marriage is prohibited. Any such civil union, partnership contract or other arrangement entered into by persons of the same sex in another state or jurisdiction shall be void in all respects in Virginia and any contractual rights created thereby shall be void and unenforceable.

Even if a judge outside of Vermont were willing to recognize the civil union, a claim to the benefits that accompany civil unions will raise additional problems. As of 2004, outside of Vermont there are no substantive legal consequences to apply to civil unions because the relationship is a unique relationship. Civil unions exist only in Vermont, although proposals to enact similar bills were pending in other states.

To demonstrate the problem, let's assume Joe and Gwen, a married couple from Vermont move to state X. State X becomes their domicile. If Joe and Gwen wish to divorce, they will go to the court in State X. (Note: They could go elsewhere, but most states have residency requirements that must be met before a court can entertain a petition for divorce. Marriage, by contrast, has no residency requirements.) When Joe and Gwen petition for divorce in State X, State X will recognize their Vermont marriage under conflicts of law principles. But the court will not apply Vermont divorce law. It will apply the divorce law of State X. If State X did not authorize alimony payments at divorce, for example, then the divorce court would not award alimony even though Vermont law did authorize alimony.

Change the fact pattern to Jane and Gwen, a same-sex couple who entered into a civil union in Vermont and then moved to State X. Had they stayed in Vermont and had Jane wished to terminate the relationship, she would have had to petition for dissolution of the relationship in the Vermont courts and the Vermont courts would have applied Vermont law to issues of property division and spousal support. But what should Jane do now that they are domiciled in State X?

One option would be to return to Vermont. And if they want to be certain that the Vermont rules governing civil union dissolutions are followed, returning to Vermont is their best option. But Vermont, like other states, has a residency requirement for those seeking divorce within its borders. At least one of the partners would have to move back to Vermont for one year in order to obtain a Vermont dissolution. A petition to State X might well be met with the response that since State X does not recognize civil unions, there is nothing to dissolve. This response would not help Jane if she were counting on a court's power to equitably divide property incident to the dissolution. Jane would have to argue that the relationship of civil union in Vermont carries with it the right to equitable division of property at "divorce." If State X is willing to recognize the legal consequences of the Vermont law under choice of law rules, then State X should be prepared to apply its rules of equitable division since recognition of the relationship means Jane is entitled to equitable division. On the other hand, it seems just as likely that a court in State X will say that its equitable division rules only apply in cases of marriage and divorce. Since a civil union is not a marriage, then, the equitable division rules would not apply.

A similar problem would arise if Gwen had been killed by a negligent tortfeasor. If State X says only spouses and children can sue the tortfeasor, Jane will have difficulty arguing that, as the surviving partner in a civil union, she too is entitled to sue. To recognize her right to sue, the court in State X would not only have to recognize the validity of the civil union, but would also have to import the substantive provisions of Vermont's civil union statutes into state X. Alternatively, the court might find that a civil union in Vermont is the equivalent of a marriage in state X and then the court could apply the substantive laws of state X.

Questions about the recognition of Vermont Civil Unions are beginning to arise in the courts of other states. Many couples who live outside of Vermont have traveled to the state to enter into legally recognized Civil Unions. As they return to their home states, they have begun to litigate for recognition of the relationship and some of the rights that should accompany that recognition.

Burns v. Burns

560 S.E.2d 47 (Ga. App. 2002)

MILLER, J.

The sole issue in this case is whether the trial court erred in enforcing a consent decree pursuant to a divorce between the parties in which they agreed that no child visitations would occur during any time the party being visited cohabited with or had overnight stays with any adult to whom that party was not legally married or related within the second degree. As we discern no error in enforcing this legally constituted consent order, we affirm.

Darian and Susan Burns were divorced on December 4, 1995, and Darian retained full custody of the couple's three minor children. Three years later Susan filed a motion for contempt, alleging that Darian refused to allow her visitation with the children. As a result the court issued a consent order modifying visitation rights. The modification required and the parties agreed that "[t]here shall be no visitation nor residence by the children with either party during any time where such party cohabits with or has overnight stays with any adult to which such party is not legally married or to whom party is not related within the second degree."

On July 1, 2000, the State of Vermont enacted a civil union law, and on July 3, 2000, Susan Burns and a female companion (not related to Susan) traveled to Vermont where they received a "LICENSE AND CERTIFICATE OF CIVIL UNION." Two months later Darian filed a motion for contempt, alleging that Susan violated the trial court's order by exercising visitation with the children "while cohabitating with her female lover." Susan opposed the motion for contempt, arguing that she was not in violation of the visitation requirements in that she had complied with the legally married requirement by virtue of her civil union with an adult female. No party argued that the consent decree was unenforceable.

The trial court found that the provisions of its order applied equally to both parties and to both sexes and that a "civil union" is not a marriage. The court further found that the provisions of the order were valid and enforceable.

On appeal Susan contends that she and her female companion were married in the State of Vermont and pursuant to "the full faith and credit doctrine they are married in Georgia as well." She argues further that she has a fundamental right to privacy which includes the right to define her own family and that the State of Georgia cannot place limitations on this right.

Susan's position, however, has a flawed premise: she and her female companion were not married in Vermont but instead entered into a "civil union" under 15 Vt. Stat. Ann. §1201 et seq. The definitional section of that statute expressly distinguishes between "marriage," which is defined as "the legally recognized union of one man and one woman," and "civil union," which is defined as a relationship established between two eligible persons pursuant to that chapter. The next section reemphasizes this distinction, requiring that eligible persons must "[b]e of the same sex and therefore excluded from the marriage laws of this state." Indeed, the legislative findings accompanying the enactment of the Vermont civil union statute noted that "a system of civil unions does not bestow the status of civil marriage...."

Moreover, even if Vermont had purported to legalize same-sex marriages, such would not be recognized in Georgia, the place where the consent decree was ordered and agreed to by both parties (both of whom are Georgia residents), and more importantly the place where the present action is brought. OCGA §19-3-3.1(a) clearly states that it is the public policy of Georgia "to recognize the union only of man and woman. Marriages between persons of the same sex are prohibited in this state." Additionally, under OCGA §19-3-3.1(b)

> [n]o marriage between persons of the same sex shall be recognized as entitled to the benefits of marriage. Any marriage entered into by persons of the same sex pursuant to a marriage license issued by another state or foreign jurisdiction or otherwise shall be void in this state. Any contractual rights granted by virtue of such license shall be unenforceable in the courts of this state and the courts of this state shall have no jurisdiction whatsoever under any circumstances to grant a divorce or separate maintenance with respect to such marriage or otherwise to consider or rule on any of the parties' respective rights arising as a result of or in connection with such marriage.

Moreover, Georgia is not required to give full faith and credit to same-sex marriages of other states. [Footnote cites federal Defense of Marriage Act at this point.]

What constitutes a marriage in the State of Georgia is a legislative function, not a judicial one, and as judges we are duty bound to follow the clear language of the statute. The Georgia Legislature has chosen not to recognize marriage between persons of the same sex, and any constitutional challenge to Georgia's marriage statute should be addressed to the Supreme Court of Georgia.

It is important to note that Susan's argument that her right to privacy has been infringed upon ignores her role in creating the consent decree. Although she is correct that there is a right to privacy of intimacy between persons legally able to consent, she waived that right (to the extent that right is interfered with here) when she agreed to the consent decree. That this right may be waived is clear. Indeed, if Susan wanted to ensure that her civil union would be recognized in the same manner as a marriage, she should have included language to that effect in the consent decree itself.

Simply put, the consent order signed by the presiding judge provides that visitation will not be allowed during the time that Darian or Susan cohabitates with an adult to whom he or she is not legally married, and as Susan and her companion are not legally married in the State of Vermont and clearly not legally married under Georgia law, any such activity by Susan is in violation of the court's order. Accordingly, the court did not err in its conclusion that the visitation order is valid and that such violation constitutes contempt. *Judgment affirmed.*

Langan v. St. Vincent's Hospital of N.Y.

Supreme Court, Nassau County
765 N.Y.S.2d 411 (2003)

JOHN P. DUNNE, J.

In this action for wrongful death and medical malpractice, the limited issue presented on the motion and cross-motion is whether, under principles of full faith and credit or comity, plaintiff John Langan's legal status as a spouse of Neal Spicehandler in a civil union solemnized in the State of Vermont, which union is sanctioned and affords all benefits and obligations of marriage under the laws of Vermont, entitles him to recognition as a "spouse" under New York's wrongful death statute. Plaintiff does not raise any derivative claim for loss of consortium.

Neal Conrad Spicehandler and John Langan met on November 1, 1986 when Spicehandler was 26 and Langan was 25. They moved in together eight months later and lived together until Spicehandler's death at age 41. They provided each other with health care proxies, each was the sole beneficiary on the other's life insurance policy, they were joint owners on homeowner's insurance, and were the sole legatees under each other wills.

In the year 2000 Vermont enacted a statute which legally sanctioned homosexual unions in the same manner as a marriage. The civil union required the same solemnization as a marriage and created spouses for all purposes under Vermont state law. Within four months of its passage, Spicehandler and Langan, in a formal ceremony with approximately forty family members and friends attending, were joined in a union solemnized by a Justice of the Peace. Their vows included taking each other "to be my spouse". They exchanged wedding bands; they planned to adopt children, and finally purchased a house in Massapequa, Long Island. Within hours of the closing Neal Spicehandler was struck by the automobile driven by Ronald Popadich who ran down and injured 18 people in Manhattan. He was taken to St. Vincent's Hospital with a broken leg, and underwent two surgeries. He died while in the hospital from an embolus of "unknown origin."

Neal Conrad Spicehandler was known as both Neal and Conrad. He is referred to as both by different family members and friends as they describe the nature of his relationship with plaintiff. Their words are telling. First, the parents. Ruth Spicehandler, Neal's mother knew John Langan as her son's partner for 16 years, and even her grandchildren know John as an uncle. She explains, "John has been Neal's partner in all aspects of life". They participated together "in all family functions" including "birthdays, anniversaries, religious events, holidays, dinners, and vacations". Plaintiff's parents, Daniel and Barbara Langan, worried that their son would face "prejudice, hostility and other difficulties" and initially did not accept his relationship with Spicehandler. But they changed, stating "John has always loved life, but we believe he loved Conrad even more. It is as if a part of him died when Conrad died."

Jeremy Spicehandler, Neal's brother says of plaintiff, "I…think of him and care for him as a family member…" He relates how John had been a source of strength when his father died, and how he and Neal, knowing it would be difficult for his mother, held the holiday Seders at their home in Massapequa, Long Island. "It was a difficult time for everyone, made easier by being in their loving home." Elliot Spicehandler, another brother, states that the civil union was important to Neal because of his "interest in adopting children".

There are additional affidavits from family, a sister-in-law Laura Spicehandler stated, "There was never a time in all those 16 years when it was just Neal, or just John. It was always Neal and John, together, spouses…as inseparable as any married couple could possibly be." The affidavits of other family members, cousins, aunts, godmother, echo these sentiments. Cousin Kim Marie Merritt sums up their loss, stating that since Neal's loss John "is still working to put one foot in front of the other…We are all working to put our lives back together after losing a beloved family member so young, so suddenly". Friends of the Langan and Spicehandler have come forward to provide evidence of their relationship. Alan Matzkin tells of Neal's sacrifice for John in the Spring of 1998 when Neal temporarily set aside his legal career ambitions "to help John improve his career prospects and the value of his business". Nancy M. Starznski, one of the many friends and business associates submitting affidavits, and a college friend who often celebrated family events and holidays together with John and Neal says, "David and I are heartbroken that this affidavit is necessary to quantify the union between these two wonderful people. Their love for each other was so strong…"

New York does not compensate a spouse for spiritual or emotional loss, but it may compensate Langan for his pecuniary loss if it is determined that he is a spouse for purposes of the wrongful death statute. There is no infirmity of proof on the factual issues. The evidence offered establishes that John Langan and Neal Conrad Spicehandler lived together as spouses from shortly after they met in 1985 until the year 2000, when they took the first opportunity to secure legal recognition of their union in the State of Vermont, and were joined legally as lawful spouses.

Under New York law as it now stands, if Langan were a registered domestic partner, he would be able to succeed to a rent controlled apartment as a "family member", would be able to recover had his partner been lost in the September 11 tragedy, would be eligible for the derivative employment benefits of a city or state employed partner, including death benefits, would be eligible to adopt his partner's biological child, and would be entitled to be free from discrimination on the basis of sexual orientation under the civil rights and executive law. He would not, however, be able to recover as a spouse under the wrongful death statute based upon the holding of *Raum v. Restaurant Assoc.*, 252 A.D.2d 369, 675 N.Y.S.2d 343, *app. dsmd.* 92 N.Y.2d 946, 681 N.Y.S.2d 476, 704 N.E.2d 229.

At the time *Raum* was decided however, there was no state sanctioned union equivalent to marriage. Passage of the Vermont civil union statute provides a basis to distinguish *Raum,* and an earlier case, *Matter of Cooper,* which withheld recognition of a right of election under the EPTL for same-sex couples. The laws regarding recognition of sister state marriages, such as a common law marriage, provide a legal ground to revisit the meaning of the term spouse as used in the EPTL, and to distinguish the holdings in *Raum* and *Cooper.*

With respect to marriages entered into in sister states, New York adheres to the general rule that "marriage contracts, valid where made, are valid everywhere, unless contrary to natural laws or statutes" (*Shea v. Shea,* 294 N.Y. 909, 63 N.E.2d 113) [holding that a valid common law marriage from another state would be recognized in New York despite New York's statutory ban on common law marriages]. This is true for purposes of descent in the Surrogate's court (*Matter of Watts,* 31 N.Y.2d 491, 495, 341 N.Y.S.2d 609, 294 N.E.2d 195), and for purposes of the wrongful death statute (*Black v. Moody,* 276 A.D.2d 303, 714 N.Y.S.2d 30). Thus, notwithstanding the premise in *Raum v. Restaurants Assoc.,* supra that unmarried heterosexual and homosexual couples are treated equally under the wrongful death statutes in New York, a common law marriage may be established for an unmarried heterosexual couple under the jurisdiction of a sister state and the survivor becomes a "spouse" under the EPTL (*Black v. Moody,* supra). It follows that, if plaintiff has a validly contracted marriage in the State of Vermont, and if the Vermont civil union does not offend public policy as would an incestuous or polygamous union, it will be recognized in the State of New York for purposes of the wrongful death statute.

Initially, the court acknowledges the precept which calls for a court not to decide issues unnecessary to the resolution of a case. Thus the court will not determine whether plaintiff has a valid marriage in the State of New York for all purposes, but only whether he may be considered a spouse for purposes of the wrongful death statute, much as the Court of Appeals has held that a same sex domestic partner is a "family" member for the limited purposes of the New York City's rent control laws (*see, Braschi v. Stahl Assoc.,* 74 N.Y.2d 201, 544 N.Y.S.2d 784, 543 N.E.2d 49). Although the court must examine the nature of the Vermont civil union, and whether it can be distinguished from the honored state of marriage, the purpose of doing so is thus limited. To resolve the statutory spouse issue, discussion must primarily focus upon what a Vermont civil union is, and is not, and compare it to a marriage, and determine whether New York's public policy precludes recognition under full faith and credit, as "there are some limitations upon the extent to which a state may be required by the full faith and credit clause to enforce even the judgment of another state in contravention of its own statutes or policy"

Addressing the issue of policy first, New York has not enacted a mini DOMA. This acronym refers to the federal Defense of Marriage Act, which in response to Vermont's civil union statute, declares that a marriage is a union between a man and a woman, and that no State shall be "required to give effect" to a same-sex union. It is unclear by what authority the Congress may suspend or limit the full faith and credit clause of the Constitution, and the constitutionality of DOMA has been put in doubt (see, e.g. Mark Strasser, Baker and Some Recipes for Disaster: on DOMA, Covenant Marriages, and Full Faith and Credit Jurisprudence, 64 Brook. L.Rev. 307). Nevertheless, thirty five states have passed mini DOMAs (*see, e.g., Burns v. Burns,* 253 Ga.App. 600, 601, 560 S.E.2d 47 [statute declares that no "marriage between persons of the same sex" shall be recognized as entitled to the benefits of marriage]; New York is not among them.

Both the State of New York, and the City of New York, recognize same sex domestic partnerships for employment benefits. New York's public policy is also revealed in the decision in *Braschi v. Stahl Assoc. Co.,* 74 N.Y.2d 201, 544 N.Y.S.2d 784, 543 N.E.2d 49, supra, which was "the first appellate decision in the United States to accord legal recognition to a same-sex couple" (Arthur S. Leonard, Symposium on Same-Sex Marriage, Civil Unions, and Domestic Partnerships, Ten Propositions about Legal Recognition of Same-Sex Partners, 30 Cap. U.L.Rev. 343, 354). The *Braschi* court stated that a "realistic and valid" view of family "includes two adult lifetime partners whose relationship is long term and characterized by an emotional and financial commitment and interdependence." As a guide to assessing whether one is a "family" member eligible for succession to a rent controlled apartment, and revealing the evolving attitudes toward same-sex couples, the court stated:

> In making this assessment, the lower courts of this State have looked to a number of factors, including the exclusivity and longevity of the relationship, the level of emotional and financial commitment, the manner in which the parties have conducted their everyday lives and held themselves out to society, and the reliance placed upon one another for daily family services * * * These factors are most helpful, although it should be emphasized that the presence or absence of one or more of them is not dispositive since it is the totality of the relationship as evidenced by the dedication, caring and self-sacrifice of the parties which should, in the final analysis, control.

(*Braschi v. Stahl Assoc. Co.,* supra at p. 213, 544 N.Y.S.2d 784, 543 N.E.2d 49).

New York has also interpreted adoption laws to allow what has been termed "second parent adoption", i.e., to allow the biological parent's live-in homosexual life partner to adopt the child, rejecting a literal reading of the statute that would have forced the biological parent to relinquish parental rights (*see Matter of Jacob,* 86 N.Y.2d 651, 668, 636 N.Y.S.2d 716, 660 N.E.2d 397).

Finally, and without being exhaustive as to the rights of gays and lesbians under New York law, same-sex partners are entitled to recompense as those aggrieved by the tragic loss of life on September 11, New York City has amended its Domestic Partner Registry "to extend New York City's commitment to recognizing rights of same sex partners by revising the definition of 'domestic partners' in the administrative code to include persons who have...entered civil unions or marriages not explicitly recognized by New York State in other jurisdictions," and, while other jurisdictions were enacting mini-DOMAs, New York State amended Civil Rights Law §40-c regarding equal protection to prohibit discrimination on the basis of sexual orientation, and Executive Law §291 to prohibit discrimination in employment, education and housing accommodations.

Concluding that New York's public policy does not preclude recognition of a same-sex union entered into in a sister state, the next issue is Vermont's civil union statute. Passage of Vermont's historic civil union statute was compelled by a decision of the Vermont Supreme Court which, acknowledging that the question before it "arouses deeply-felt religious, moral, and political beliefs", and framing the question to focus "on the statutory and constitutional basis for the exclusion of same-sex couples from the secular benefits and protections offered married couples", held that all Vermont citizens, both heterosexual and homosexual, are entitled to the benefits and protections of a state-sanctioned union under the Common Benefits Clause of the Vermont Constitution (*Baker v. State,* 170 Vt. 194, 197, 744 A.2d 864)....

The Vermont statute, effective July 1, 2000, requires that plaintiff be entitled to "the benefits and protections" and "be subject to the rights and responsibilities" of "spouses" (15 VSA § 1201[2]), and "gives same-sex couples access to more than 300 rights derived from Vermont state law." ... A civil union under Vermont law is distinguishable from marriage only in title, as it defines marriage as "the legally recognized union of one man and one woman" (15 VSA § 1201[4]). Yet it goes so far as to include a presumption of legitimacy for either party's natural child born during the union, giving new meaning to the well established legal fiction intended to protect innocent children "ensuring their financial and emotional security, and ultimately preserving the stability of the family unit" (15 VSA § 1204[f]; *see, Godin v. Godin,* 168 Vt. 514, 521, 522, 725 A.2d 904). The presumption of legitimacy, when extended to a same-sex couple, together with the obligations of support and requirement for a divorce, indicate that the civil union is indistinguishable from marriage, notwithstanding that the Vermont legislature withheld the title of marriage from application to the union....

Under principles of full faith and credit and comity, and following authority which advances the concept that citizens ought to be able to move from one state to another without concern for the validity or recognition of their marital status, New York will recognize a marriage sanctioned and contracted in a sister state and there appears to be no valid legal basis to distinguish one between a same-sex couple. And, unlike a non-ceremonial common law marriage contracted in a sister state which may be dissolved at will, yet is recognized in New York, the Vermont civil union requires a sanctioned civil ceremony, a license, and, significantly, a divorce to end the union.

Thus the Vermont Civil Union, which is subject to legislative control conforms in all respects to the requirements for a marriage. Although it explicitly reserves the title "marriage" for a union between a man and a woman, it does not so reserve the title "spouse", as a civil union partner, like a husband or a wife, is a spouse for all purposes under Vermont law, and the meaning of the term spouse is the only issue here....

Turning to legislative purpose, the wrongful death statute is intended to "promote the public welfare", and its goals "are to compensate the victim's dependents, to punish and deter tortfeasors and to reduce welfare dependency by providing for the families of those who have lost their means of support." Thus the wrongful death statute is intended to compensate the pecuniary losses first and foremost of the decedent's immediate family, that is, his or her spouse and children, those most likely to have expected support and to have suffered pecuniary injury (*see generally, Loucks v. Standard Oil Co. of New York,* 224 N.Y. 99, 104, 120 N.E. 198 [Cardozo, J.]). The person most likely to have expected support and to have suffered pecuniary injury here is plaintiff, Spicehandler's immediate family and spouse under the Vermont statute, and the only legatee under his will....

The court acknowledges that at the time the wrongful death statutes were written, the use of the term spouse did not envision inclusion of a same-sex marital partner. But as the concepts of marriage evolve over time, leaving behind the common law doctrine that "a woman was the property of her husband" and her "legal existence" was " 'incorporated and consolidated into that of the husband' " (*see People v. Liberta,* 64 N.Y.2d 152, 164, 485 N.Y.S.2d 207, 474 N.E.2d 567), so too public opinion regarding same-sex unions is evolving. At the time the statute was written, there were no sanctioned same-sex couples, much less domestic partnerships, civil unions, reciprocal beneficiaries, and, as in the Netherlands, full fledged same-sex marriage.

The words of the statute, referring to a spouse as a husband or wife, operate to clarify that the intended primary beneficiaries are the members of the legally sanctioned family unit which is still intact.

There is a compelling reason to construe the EPTL to include a Vermont spouse under the fundamental tenet of construction that "a statute ought normally to be saved by construing it in accord with constitutional requirements." That "the very language of the statute must be fairly susceptible of such an interpretation" is not an obstacle here, and the court " 'may reasonably find implicit' in the words used by the Legislature" that all spouses were to be included (*see, People v. Dietze*, 75 N.Y.2d 47, 52, 550 N.Y.S.2d 595, 549 N.E.2d 1166). Spouse is a gender neutral word, it applies to a man or a woman, and is applied to plaintiff under the Vermont civil union. As the EPTL is construed to apply to a common law couple who have not been joined by a civil ceremony and may separate at will, it is impossible to justify, under equal protection principles, withholding the same recognition from a union which meets all the requirements of a marriage in New York but for the sexual orientation of its partners. The state "may not draw distinctions between individuals based solely on differences that are irrelevant to a legitimate governmental objective" (*Under 21 v. City of New York*, 488 N.Y.S.2d 669...). For example, with respect to wrongful death statutes, the Supreme Court has held that a distinction between illegitimate and legitimate children for purposes of recovery is an irrational one (*Glona v. American Guar. & Liab. Ins. Co.*, 391 U.S. 73, 88 S.Ct. 1515, 20 L.Ed.2d 441).

Although discrimination on the basis of sexual orientation constitutes a violation of equal protection under the United States and New York Constitutions, a heightened level of scrutiny to classifications based on "sexual orientation" has not been applied. Thus the constitutional question to be answered is whether a refusal to recognize plaintiff as a surviving spouse under the EPTL is supported by a "rational basis."

This court is mindful that it must pay due respect to the legal wisdom of the rule that a court should be "certain of its ground before making a categorical finding that there is no permissible objective served by a state statute or that there is utterly no sensible of discernible relation between the legislature's classification and a legitimate end." But where a statute draws a distinction based upon marital status the distinction "must be based upon 'some ground of difference that rationally explains the different treatment' " (*People v. Liberta*, 64 N.Y.2d 152, 163, 485 N.Y.S.2d 207, 474 N.E.2d 567). Here there is no difference for state purposes between a married person and a person joined in civil union under the laws of Vermont *except* sexual orientation. Upon examination of the rejection of homosexual unions in the past, the reasons propounded for supporting distinctions, such as the at will nature of homosexual relationships and the absence of children, society's future, from their unions, simply do not apply, in light of the Vermont civil union and New York's and Vermont's rules regarding adoption. The civil union is indistinguishable for societal purposes from the nuclear family and marriage.

Accordingly, this court finds, as have other courts addressing the issue of wrongful death benefits for a same-sex partner in the Superior Court of California (*Smith v. Knoller*, n.o.r., Index No. 319532, Superior Court, San Francisco, August 9, 2001), that plaintiff, a surviving spouse under the laws of Vermont, is included within the meaning of spouse as it is used under section 4-1.1 of the EPTL, and has standing to recover for the wrongful death of Neal Conrad Spicehandler.

Hennefeld v. Township of Montclair

Tax Court of New Jersey
2005
(see summary of facts at pages [251–52])

IV. The Plaintiffs' Civil Union in Vermont.

As with their Canadian marriage, it is undisputed that Plaintiffs legally entered into a civil union in Vermont on July 6, 2000.

Vermont's Civil Union Statute provides that:

[a] party to a civil union shall be included in any definition or use of the terms "spouse", "family," "immediate family," "dependent," "next of kin," and other terms that denote the spousal relationship, as those terms are used throughout the law.

[15 *Vt. Stat. Ann.* § 1204(b).]

In Vermont, same-sex partners in "a civil union have all the same benefits, protections, and responsibilities under law…as are granted to spouses in a marriage" [15 Vt. Stat. Ann. § 1204(a)], including the "eligibility to hold real and personal property as tenants by the entirety…," [15 Vt. Stat. Ann. § 1204(e)(1)], a form of property ownership that has traditionally been reserved for married persons. *See Wyckoff v. Young Women's Christian Ass'n*, 37 N.J. Super. 274, 281 (Ch. Div. 1955). It is on the basis of Vermont law and their marriage in Canada that Plaintiffs have re-conveyed to themselves title to the subject property in New Jersey as tenants by the entirety. This is discussed more fully in Section V of this opinion.

It has been observed that:

Vermont [same-sex] couples who [enter into civil unions and] remain in Vermont immediately obtain numerous benefits, protections, and responsibilities that same-sex couples have never before received from state government….

But should they…leave Vermont,…their status as a couple protected by the government will immediately become uncertain.

This uncertainty is even greater for non-Vermont couples [like the Plaintiffs] who travel to Vermont, enter into civil unions, and then return to their domiciles.

[Cox, Barbara J., *But Why Not Marriage: An Essay on Vermont's Civil Unions Law, Same-Sex Marriage, and Separate But (Un)Equal*, 25 Vt. L. Rev. 113, 137 (2000).]

The Plaintiffs contend that since they were joined in a lawful civil union and are considered "spouses" under Vermont law, and since that civil union is valid in New Jersey pursuant to the [Domestic Partnership Act] (N.J.S.A. 26:8A-6(c)), then they must be included in any definition or use of the term "spouse", under New Jersey Law. The Plaintiffs' argument, however, ignores the fact that the DPA was not effective until July 10, 2004 (as discussed in Section VIII of this opinion), and would therefore not mandate recognition of out-of-state same-sex unions before that date.

Alternatively, even assuming the DPA is applicable, the court finds that the Plaintiffs' argument is no more persuasive. It is clear that under the DPA the Plaintiffs' civil union in Vermont would be valid in New Jersey. N.J.S.A. 26:8A-6(c). Under the doctrine of state comity, "[t]here is no question...that where the laws of a foreign state do not conflict with the laws of our state or the public policy of this state, it is the duty of our Courts to recognize and enforce the laws of said sister state." *Liberty Mut. Ins. Co. v. Mahieu Const. Co.*, 26 N.J. Misc. 12, 13 (Dist. Ct. 1947); *see also Zurich General Accident & Liability Ins. Co. v. Ackerman Bros.*, 124 N.J.L. 187 (E. & A. 1940); *Giardini v. McAdoo*, 93 N.J.L. 138 (E. & A. 1919); *but see In re Winter's Estate*, 24 N.J. Misc. 167, 169 (Orph. 1946) (finding that "[t]here is no principle of interstate comity which can effect the disposition of New Jersey real estate, either by wills not according to our laws..., or by foreign statutes.) (Citations omitted)....

As discussed in Section III above, DOMA protects any "State...[from being] required to give effect to any public act, record, or judicial proceeding of any other State...respecting a relationship between persons of the same sex that is treated as a marriage under the laws of such other State." 28 U.S.C.A. § 1738C....

Vermont's Civil Union Statute is clearly more expansive than New Jersey's DPA. New Jersey does not extend the rights of married persons to same-sex couples to the same degree that Vermont does. The Full Faith and Credit Clause does not require a State to apply another State's law where it violates its own legitimate public policy. *Wilson v. Ake*....Accordingly, New Jersey cannot be mandated to accept more of another state's law, with regard to same-sex relationships, than New Jersey's Legislature intended. To hold otherwise would offend the spirit, intent, and substance of DOMA.

Notes and Questions

1. The New Jersey legislature passed the Domestic Partnership Act (DPA), referred to by the Tax Court in *Hennefeld*, in response to litigation seeking the right to same-sex marriage in New Jersey. The rights accorded domestic partners under the DPA are minimal. The only rights mentioned in the statute are "statutory protection against various forms of discrimination against domestic partners; certain visitation and decision-making rights in a health care setting; and certain tax-related benefits; and, in some cases, health and pension benefits that are provided in the same manner as for spouses." N.J.S.A. §26:8A-2(c). The tax benefits appear to be limited to the ability to claim a spousal exemption for income tax purposes and the tax free transfer of property at death, which is available to a spouse. Section 26:8A-6(c) provides as follows: "A domestic partnership, civil union or reciprocal beneficiary relationship entered into outside of this State, which is valid under the laws of the jurisdiction under which the partnership was created, shall be valid in this State." How did the court in *Hennefeld* interpret this language in determining how to honor the validity of the civil union?

2. Ultimately the court awarded Hennefeld the 100% exemption on a par with spouses, holding that the exemption was authorized by a liberal reading of the DPA. The DPA granted certain tax benefits to domestic partners on a par with spouses. The court was willing to construe the statute to include this particular tax benefit even though the only specific tax benefits mentioned were the spousal exemption under the state income tax and the exemption from state inheritance taxes. The two men had become registered domestic partners in New Jersey in July of 2004. Thus, the 100% exemption became available to them as of that date.

Note

Dissolution of civil unions has been the subject of litigation in a number of states. Many couples flocked to Vermont to experience the "high" of legal recognition after so many years of discrimination. Then they returned to their own states. Within time, some couples drifted apart and have paid little attention to the legal status of their relationships. Others, understanding that the state sanction had meaning (e.g., a right to equitable division upon "divorce") have sued in their home states to dissolve their unions. As of summer 2004, there were only two reported opinions on this issue: (1) Massachusetts—*Salucco v. Alldredge*, 17 Mass.L.Rptr. 498, 2004 WL 864459 (dissolution granted); (2) Connecticut—*Rosengarten v. Downes*, 802 A.2d 170 (Conn. App. 2002)(holding no jurisdiction to grant dissolution).

But there are at least three additional unreported opinions: (1) A dissolution was granted in December 2002 in Marion County, West Virginia; (2) A "divorce" was initially granted to a civil union couple by a judge in Beaumont, Texas, then challenged by the State Attorney General, at which time the parties withdrew the petition; (3) A "divorce" was initially granted in Woodbury County, Iowa, then when challenged because there was no "marriage," the Iowa judge stood by the dissolution ruling.

The lack of legal certainty regarding the effect of these unions in other states could prove to be a huge problem for couples who separate with no formal dissolution and begin new relationships.

2. Domestic Partnerships

a. In general

Domestic partnership is a term that was coined in San Francisco in the early 1980s. It has no fixed meaning as a legal term. It is a recognized relationship in numerous cities and counties, where ordinances set forth definitions and the accompanying benefits and obligations.

Domestic partnerships have recently been recognized at the state level in California and in New Jersey. The status entitles the partners to certain benefits set forth in the domestic partner statutes. Some people refer to the Vermont Civil Union Act as creating "domestic partnerships," reflecting the common understanding that a "domestic partnership" is any spousal-like relationship other than marriage.

The earliest attempts to establish a legally recognized relationship for same-sex couples were in California and Wisconsin. See Barbara J. Cox, "The Little Project:" From Alternative Families to Domestic Partnerships to Same-Sex Marriage, 15 Wisc. Women's L. J. 77 (2000). These early attempts were always at the local level where lesbian and gay rights activists sometimes held some political influence with elected municipal officials. Civil rights movements have often met with success at the local level before gaining rights at the state or national level. For example, the first law banning racial discrimination in employment was enacted by the City of Chicago in

1945. Milwaukee, Minneapolis, and New York City soon followed. In the ensuing decades twenty states adopted state-wide laws banning race discrimination in employment, followed finally by the U. S Congress when it adopted Title VII of the Civil Rights Act in 1964. The lesbian and gay civil rights movement has similarly worked at a grassroots level to gain many important victories at the city and county level, before gaining success at the state level. The story of domestic partnership legislation follows this trend.

> The first move toward a formally recognized new status for the unmarried occurred in the 1980s, when several politically liberal cities adopted ordinances that permitted same-sex couples and sometimes opposite-sex unmarried couples to register as "domestic partners." To register, the couple typically was required to affirm that they were in a relationship of love and mutuality and that they lived together and shared expenses. In many cities, no benefits attached to the registration except the psychic benefit of the public affirmation of their relationship. A few cities, within the limited range of their municipal powers, did attach some legal consequences to the registration, such as rights of hospital visitation and access to health insurance for the partners of municipal employees.

David L. Chambers, For the Best of Friends and for Lovers of all Sorts, a Status Other Than Marriage, 76 Notre Dame L. Rev. 1347 at (2001)

b. Domestic Partnerships at the city and county level

Today more than 130 municipalities and counties have enacted some form of domestic partner law. As of 2004, the Human Rights Campaign reported that over 7400 employers, both public and private, offer domestic partner benefits. Yet there is no standard definition of domestic "partner." An employer may or may not use the same definition as the municipality in which the employee works.

> Over half of the jurisdictions include some sort of requirement that the parties be engaged in an intimate relationship. This is generally designated as a relationship of "mutual support, caring and commitment." Another common description is a "close and committed personal relationship" or some variation of that theme. It is not clear whether this "intimacy" requirement means a sexual relationship, although that seems to be the implication. Some describe the relationship by reference to marriage. For instance, Albuquerque requires a "mutual commitment similar to marriage." The requirement in Minneapolis is that the parties be "committed to one another to the same extent as married persons are to each other, except for the traditional marital status and solemnities." Northampton requires an "exclusive mutual commitment similar to that of marriage." Los Angeles County's law describes an "intimate and committed relationship of mutual caring," and Santa Monica's law is substantially the same. San Francisco's law states that the parties will have "chosen to share one another's lives in an intimate and committed relationship of mutual caring...." Two cities reference "family": Cambridge requires that the parties "consider themselves to be a family"; Key West is similar in requiring that the partners "consider themselves to be members of each other's immediate family" and that they have "chosen to share one another's lives in a family relationship." Madison's description employs both positive ("relationship is of a permanent and distinct domestic character") and negative ("not in a relationship that is merely temporary, social, politi-

cal, commercial or economic in nature") elements. Rochester wants the partners to be "committed to the physical, emotional and financial care and support of each other."

Willliam C. Duncan, Domestic Partnership Laws in the United States: A Review and Critique, 2001 B.Y.U. L. Rev. 961.

Usually the partners sign an affidavit attesting to the nature of their relationship. But some municipalities want further proof of the financial interdependence of the parties. For example, some cities may require the partners to live together or to share checking accounts. Almost all municipal domestic partner ordinances require the parties to meet the following requirements:

- the parties be at least 18 years old.

- only two persons can enter the relationship of domestic partnership.

- neither party can be married or in another domestic partnership relationship.

- the parties share joint responsibility for expenses or agree to support each other.

- the parties are not related in a way that would prevent them from being married.

Iowa City Code
Chapter 6
Domestic Partnership
November 8, 1994

2-6-1: PURPOSE

A. The City recognizes that nationwide debate has advanced an expanded concept of familial relationships beyond traditional marital and blood relationships. This expanded concept recognizes the relationship of two (2) non-married but committed adult partners. Recognizing this, the City hereby adopts a process to provide persons to declare themselves as domestic partners, thus enabling employers to voluntarily provide equal treatment in employment benefits for such partners and their dependents.

B. This Chapter establishes a mechanism for the public expression and documentation of the commitment reflected by the domestic partnership whose members cannot or choose not to marry.

C. It is appropriate and fair that certain of the societal privileges and benefits now accorded to members of a marriage be extended to those who meet the qualifications of a domestic partnership. The mechanism established by this Chapter will facilitate the definition of those entitled to such privileges.

2-6-2: REQUIREMENTS AND ELIGIBILITY:

A domestic partnership shall exist between two (2) adults if all of the following are true:

A. The persons are not related by blood closer than permitted under the marriage laws of the State.

B. Neither person is married.

C. The persons are competent to enter into a contract.

D. The persons declare that they are each other's sole domestic partner.

E. The persons declare that they are in a relationship of mutual support, caring and commitment and are responsible for each other's welfare. For these purposes, "mutual support" means that they contribute mutually to each other's maintenance and support.

F. The persons file a statement of domestic partnership as set forth in this Chapter.

G. The persons agree to notify the City of the termination of their domestic partnership, or a change in their employment or residence which would render them ineligible to register as domestic partners under this Chapter.

2-6-3: Statements of Domestic Partnership; Registration:

A. The City Clerk shall accept an application to register as domestic partners from persons who state in such application that they meet the definition of "domestic partners" in this Chapter. The City Clerk shall provide forms as necessary to interested individuals.

B. The City Clerk shall only accept applications for registration of domestic partnership from those persons:

1. In a partnership where at least one person resides in Iowa City; or

2. In a partnership in which at least one person is employed in Iowa City.

C. The City Clerk shall charge an application fee as set by resolution of the City Council for the registration of a domestic partnership. The payment of this fee entitles the person filing a statement on behalf of the domestic partnership to two (2) copies of the statement certified by the City Clerk. Additional certified copies may be purchased by the person. These copies of the certified statement shall not be issued prior to the third working day after the date of application.

D. The application and certified statement may be used as evidence of the existence of a domestic partners relationship.

2-6-4: Termination:

A. Either person in a domestic partnership may initiate termination of the domestic partnership by written notification to the City Clerk. The person filing the termination statement must declare that:

1. The domestic partnership is terminated; and

2. A copy of the termination statement has been mailed to the other domestic partner by certified mail, return receipt requested.

B. A domestic partnership terminates when the earlier of the following occurs:

1. One of the persons in the domestic partnership dies; or

2. Ninety (90) days elapse after both partners file a notice of termination of domestic partnership; or

3. Ninety (90) days elapse after one partner files a notice of termination of domestic partnership and provides the City Clerk proof that the notice of termination of partnership has been mailed to the other partner at the last known address, or that the partner cannot be located or refuses to accept the mailed notice. A properly mailed notice which is returned as refused or undeliverable shall be adequate proof.

C. If any of the criteria under Section 2-6-2 cease to exist, the parties shall be ineligible for any benefits based upon the domestic partnership unless otherwise provided by law or the employer.

D. When an employer permits or provides benefits to the domestic partner of an employee, the domestic partner may be eligible to continue to receive benefits for a period of sixty (60) days after the death of the employee. The employer shall give the domestic partner written notice by U.S. mail, postage prepaid, at the address provided by the employee stating whether such benefits are available to the partner. Said notice shall state the date on which group benefit coverage, if any, terminates, and shall state the right, if any, of the domestic partner to transfer benefit coverage to a nongroup plan without lapse of coverage and without providing evidence of good health.

E. No person who has registered as a domestic partner pursuant to Section 2-6-3 of this Chapter shall be eligible to file a new application for registration as a domestic partner until ninety (90) days have elapsed after the domestic partnership has terminated.

Notes and Questions

1. The three key issues for drafters of ordinances appear to be: (1) who can qualify as a domestic partner, (2) what benefits and burdens shall be extended to domestic partners, and (3) how to terminate a domestic partnership relationship. There are numerous debatable points under each issue. Determine whether you agree or disagree with the following positions:

> Domestic partnerships should be limited to same-sex couples since opposite-sex couples have the option to marry.

> Domestic partners should be required to share a household and prove financial interdependence (e.g., joint ownership of a residence or joint liability as lessees).

> If benefits are to be extended (e.g., health insurance by the employer) then it is only fair to require financial interdependence such as a contractual obligation to support each other.

> It is not fair to require domestic partners to wait for a specified length of time after terminating one relationship before they can enter into another relationship.

2. Hal and Sam live together and qualify as domestic partners under the Iowa City ordinance. Neither one of them works for the city and thus the couple would not be entitled to the domestic partner fringe benefits that the city provides to its employees. What is to be gained by registering as a domestic partner? What is the downside? For example, if they sign an affidavit attesting to the fact that they are in a relationship of "mutual support," are they contracting to support each other? Can Hal enforce the contract against Sam? Can a support creditor of Hal's (e.g., a doctor) enforce the agreement against Sam?

3. Assume Hal and Sam have registered as domestic partners under the Iowa City ordinance. Two years later they move to Ames, Iowa, which also has a domestic partner ordinance very similar to the one in Iowa City. Should Hal and Sam register anew in Ames or should they be able to rely on their registration in Iowa City? (Remember that spouses do not need to get remarried whenever they move to a new location.)

––––––––––

Tyma v. Montgomery County
801 A.2d 148 (Md. App. 2002)

Bell, Chief Justice.

The question this case presents is whether Montgomery County, Maryland, ("the appellee" or "the County"), exceeded its authority under, or otherwise contravened, State and federal law by enacting an ordinance that extends employment benefits to the domestic partners of county employees. The trial court, the Circuit Court for Montgomery County, concluded that the Montgomery County Council had authority under the Maryland Constitution and laws to enact such benefits legislation and further, that the ordinance was a local law that did not conflict with, and, therefore, was not preempted by, State or federal law. We agree. Accordingly, we shall affirm the judgment of the trial court.

On November 30, 1999, the Montgomery County Council (the "Council") enacted and the County Executive signed, Montgomery County Bill No. 29-99, the "Employee Benefits Equity Act of 1999 (the "Act")." Generally, the Act, which became effective March 3, 2000 and applies to all active and retired County employees, extends benefits, such as health, leave, and survivor benefits comparable to those afforded the spouses of County employees, to the domestic partners of County employees. In enacting the ordinance, the Council noted the County's "longstanding policy, in law and practice, against employment discrimination based on sexual orientation," as well as its belief that "it is unfair to treat employees differently based solely on whether the employee's partner is legally recognized as a spouse." *See* §33-22(a). In addition, the Council found that "many private and public employers provide or plan to provide benefits for the domestic partners of their employees" and that "[p]roviding domestic partner benefits will significantly enhance the County's ability to recruit and retain highly qualified employees and will promote employee loyalty and workplace diversity." *Id.*

The Act amended the definitions of "immediate family" and "relative" in Chapter 19A, Ethics, of the County Code, expanding them to include domestic partners, *see id.* at §§19A-4(i) and (n), thus, extending to domestic partners "benefits equivalent to those available for an employee's spouse or spouse's dependent," including those benefits available " under the Consolidated Omnibus Budget Reconciliation Act of 1985 ("COBRA"), the federal Family and Medical Leave Act ("FMLA"), and other federal laws that apply to County employment benefits." *Id.* at §33-22(b). To qualify as a domestic partner for purposes of the Act, the County employee and his or her partner must satisfy all of a number of specific requirements or, in the event a domestic partnership registration system exists in the jurisdiction in which the employee resides and the County's Director of Human Resources determines that the legal requirements for registration are substantially similar, legally register the domestic partnership. *See* §33-22(c).[1] A domestic partnership terminates, §33-22(e) instructs, by the death of a

---

1. Section 33-22(c)(1) of the County Code provides:
   "(c) Requirements for domestic partnership. To establish a domestic partnership, the employee and the employee's partner must...
   "(1) satisfy all of the following requirements:
   "(A) be the same sex;
   "(B) share a close personal relationship and be responsible for each other's welfare;
   "(C) have shared the same legal residence for at least 12 months; "(D) be at least 18 years old;
   "(E) have voluntarily consented to the relationship, without fraud or duress

partner or its dissolution, *see* subsection (e)(1), or the occurrence of "any other change in circumstances that disqualifies the relationship as a domestic partnership," *see* subsection (e)(2), either of which the employee is required to notify the County of within 30 days.

The appellants, employees and residents of Montgomery County, filed an action in the Circuit Court for Montgomery County, in which they requested the court to enter a declaratory judgment that the Act is invalid and an order enjoining its implementation. In their complaint, the appellants alleged, as they would later argue, that the Act exceeded the County's authority to enact local laws, conflicted with State law, was preempted by federal law, and was unconstitutionally vague. The Circuit Court rejected all of these arguments. Thus, it granted the County's motion for summary judgment, denied the appellants' cross-motion, and declared the Act constitutional. As indicated, we shall affirm the judgment of the Circuit Court, holding that, despite the challenges presented by the appellants, the County's action in passing the Act is authorized under the constitution and laws of this State and that it conflicts with neither State nor federal law.

Article XI-A of the State Constitution, known as the "Home Rule Amendment," enabled counties, like Montgomery County, which chose to adopt a home rule charter, to achieve a significant degree of political self-determination. "Its purpose was to [ ] transfer the General Assembly's power to enact many types of county public local laws to the Art. XI-A home rule counties."

Section 3 [of Article XI-A] empowers any county adopting a charter form of government, "[f]rom and after the adoption of a charter," to enact local laws upon all matters covered by the express powers the General Assembly was authorized to grant, "except that in the case of any conflict between said local law and any General Public Law now or hereafter enacted the General Public Law shall control." ...

The appellants start with the premise that "Maryland law expressly prohibits recognition of same-sex and common law 'marriages,' a fortiori, it expressly prohibits the granting of the rights of same-sex, common law marriage to same-sex partners of Montgomery County employees disguised as a domestic partners benefits ordinance." In support of that premise, they rely on Maryland Comm'n on Human Relations v. Greenbelt Homes, 475 A.2d 1192 (1984), in which this Court observed:

> "Only marriage as prescribed by law can change the marital status of an individual to a new legal entity of husband and wife. The law of Maryland does not recognize common law marriages or other unions of two or more persons — such as concubinage, syneisaktism, relationships of homosexuals or lesbians — as legally bestowing upon two people a legally cognizable marital status. Such relationships are simply illegitimate unions unrecognized, or in some instances condemned, by the law."

"(F) not be married to, or in a domestic partnership with, any other person;

"(G) not be related by blood or affinity in a way that would disqualify them from marriage under State law if the employee and partner were opposite sexes;

"(H) be legally competent to contract; and

"(I) share sufficient financial and legal obligations to satisfy subsection (d)(2)."

Section (d) addresses the acceptable evidence of domestic partnership. Pursuant to subsection (d)(1), such evidence consists of either "an affidavit signed by both the employee and the employee's partner under penalty of perjury" or an official copy of the domestic partner registration, and under subsection (d)(2), evidence that the employee and partner share certain of several enumerated items, such as a joint lease, *see* §(d)(2)(A), or checking account, *see* §(d)(2)(C), that may document a domestic partnership.

Thus, the appellants assert that the County exceeded its authority under the constitution and laws of Maryland by extending employment benefits to the domestic partners of its employees because Maryland does not recognize either same-sex or common law marriages. They argue that "[t]he County's actions are an unlawful, back-door attempt to circumvent State law which disallows same-sex unions" and "an attempt to legitimize illegitimate relationships under Maryland law by attempting to create, in the guise of a benefits ordinance, a legal equivalency between lawful spouses and same-sex domestic partners." They further assert that the recognition of domestic partnerships, an *ultra vires* act, "affects the interests of the whole State as well as interests outside of the state" and, in addition, requires the expenditure of state funds. They conclude that the provision of such benefits to domestic partners is inconsistent with federal benefits laws that do not include domestic partners among the enumerated "qualified beneficiaries."[2]

Contrary to the appellants' position, the County maintains that "the Act does not create a marital relationship between domestic partners;" rather, "it merely extends to domestic partners many of the employment benefits currently available to County employees' spouses." Relying upon the Home Rule Amendment and the general welfare clause,...the County argues that it clearly is authorized to extend employment benefits "where those benefits serve a valid public purpose," in this case, "recruiting and retaining qualified employees and promoting employee loyalty." Citing decisions from other jurisdictions reviewing similar laws and rejecting the argument that such laws implicate the State's interest in marriage, *see, e.g., Slattery v. New York*, 697 N.Y.S.2d 603 (1999), *appeal dismissed,*727 N.E.2d 1253 (2000) ("there are enormous differences between marriage and domestic partnership, and, in light of those very substantial differences, the DPL cannot reasonably be construed as impinging upon the State's exclusive right to regulate the institution of marriage"); *Crawford v. Chicago*, 710 N.E.2d 91, *petition to appeal denied*, 720 N.E.2d 1090 (1999)("Nothing in the DPO purports to create a marital status or marriage as those terms are commonly defined. Rather, the DPO addresses only health benefits extended to City employees and those residing with them"); *Schaefer v. City and County of Denver*, 973 P.2d 717 (Colo. Ct. A00. 1998), *cert. denied* (April 12, 1999) ("The ordinance qualifies a separate and distinct group of people who are not eligible to contract a state-sanctioned marriage to receive health and dental insurance benefits from the City. Therefore, the ordinance does not adversely impact the integrity and importance of the institution of marriage"); *Lowe v. Broward County*, 766 So.2d 1199 (Fla. Dist.Ct. App. 2000) *review denied*, ("The Act does not create a legal relationship that, because of the interest of the state, gives rise to rights and obligations that survive the termination of the relationship. Unlike a traditional marriage, a domestic partnership is purely contractual, based on the mutual agreement of the parties"), it argues that because it "does not interfere with State interests," the Act is a local law. The out-of-State cases have upheld these similar laws on the basis that the applicable constitutional provisions, as is the case here, delegate broad law-making authority to local governments. Only when "the enabling statute expressly limits a local government's ability to grant employment benefits to 'its employees and dependents,' " the County asserts, "have courts in some jurisdictions invalidated similar laws." *See, e.g., Arlington County v. White*, 259 Va. 708, 528 S.E.2d 706 (2000); *Lilly v. Minneapolis*, 527 N.W.2d 107 (Minn. App. 1995).

---

2. The appellants cite, for example, sections of the Internal Revenue Code, pertaining to COBRA, that define "qualified beneficiaries" as the plan participant's spouse and dependent children. *See generally* I.R.C.§152.

The county also asserts that it is authorized to fund the Act with State monies, which the State generally provides for any valid public purpose. It further argues that federal benefits laws do not preempt the Act because "these laws represent federal minimum standards that the County is free to exceed at its choosing."

We agree with the Circuit Court that the County had the authority, and clearly so, to enact the subject benefits legislation and that the Act is a local law that does not infringe upon the Legislature's ability to regulate marriage on a statewide basis.…

The Act at issue in this case does not, and does not purport to, define, redefine or regulate marriage in Maryland. Indeed, the Act itself includes the purpose for which the County enacted it, setting out the County's specific findings that "many private and public employers provide or plan to provide benefits for the domestic partners of their employees" and that "[p]roviding domestic partner benefits will significantly enhance the County's ability to recruit and retain highly qualified employees and will promote employee loyalty and workplace diversity."…

The determination that the County has the authority to pass the subject Act…also disposes of the appellants' argument that the Act is general, or non-local, legislation. Such benefits legislation, moreover, does not infringe upon the State's interest in marriage. This Court has invalidated ordinances passed by Home Rule counties only when they have intruded on some well defined State interest.…

To be sure, in the Act, the requirements for domestic partnership generally parallel those for marriage. On the other hand, the Act does not create "a legal equivalency between lawful spouses and same-sex domestic partners" or otherwise impinge upon the State's interest in marriage. It simply provides that "[a]ny benefit the County provides for the spouse…of a County employee or the spouse's dependent must be provided, in the same manner and to the same extent, for the domestic partner of a County employee and the partner's dependents, respectively." And that essentially is all that it does. Nothing in the Act purports to, or can be construed to, create an alternate form of marriage, authorize common law marriage or create any legal relationship. Nor does the Act, by its terms or implication, restrict, modify or alter any rights incident to a marriage recognized in this State or give one domestic partner rights, beyond the employment benefits enumerated, against the other. And, as the State of Maryland, as amicus curiae, points out:

> "The partners gain no rights in property and income of the other that are earned during the marriage and have no legally protected share in each other's estates. Termination of the relationship requires no legal process or judicial intervention, and can be done unilaterally by the filing of a notice with the county."

As a matter of fact, therefore and in sum, the Act affects only the personnel policies of Montgomery County and does not implicate the State's interest in marriage or affect the State's ability to regulate marriage on a statewide basis. Moreover, the only employer the ordinance impacts is the County; it has no effect outside the County and, therefore, no statewide interests are affected. The ordinance simply has no resemblance to other enactments that we have held were not local laws.

This conclusion is consistent with the results reached by our sister courts that have addressed the issue. *See, e.g., Schaefer v. City and County of Denver, supra* ("the ordinance does not adversely impact the integrity and importance of the institution of marriage"); *Lowe v. Broward County, supra* ("We disagree with Lowe's contention that the Act has created a 'new marriage-like relationship' "); *Crawford v. Chicago supra* (the DPO "does not address the panoply of statutory rights and obligations exclusive to the traditional marriage," "is purely contractual, based on the mutual agreement of the parties," and does not "purport[ ] to create a marital status or marriage as those terms are commonly defined, and addresses only health benefits extended to City employees and those residing with them")...

Finally,...the appellants contend that "[t]he Act provides for the 'equivalent of' Consolidated Omnibus Budget Reconciliation Act benefits, federal Family and Medical Leave Act benefits, as well as 'other federal laws that apply to County employment benefits," specifically, the Public Health Services Act, and that because these "equivalents" are neither federally funded nor the result of the amendment of the federal programs, the Act "is an ultra vires legislative enactment to State funded benefits plans and implicates use of State monies without State legislative warrant." We agree with the County and the Circuit Court that these laws represent minimum standards, which the County is permitted, and in this case elected, to exceed. Similarly, the regulations implementing the FMLA state, "an employer must observe any employment benefit program or plan that provides greater family or medical leave rights to employees than the rights established by the FMLA."

A similar position has been taken by other courts that have considered the issue; they have overwhelmingly concluded that local domestic partnership legislation is not preempted by federal law. [citations omitted]

Thus, to the extent that its power to do so is challenged, we hold that a home rule county that provides benefits to the domestic partners of its employees does not exceed its local lawmaking authority or otherwise undermine State and federal law.

Notes and Questions

1. Article I, Section 29 of the Nebraska constitution provides: "Only marriage between a man and a woman shall be valid or recognized in Nebraska. The uniting of two persons of the same sex in a civil union, domestic partnership, or other similar same-sex relationship shall not be valid or recognized in Nebraska." How should this provision affect employers who want to provide domestic partnership benefits? How should it affect city or county governments that wish to enact a domestic partner registry and extend certain limited rights to domestic partners?

On March 10, 2003, the Nebraska attorney general responded to a request submitted by a state senator, who had asked the following question: "If the legislature were to grant rights to a domestic partner to donate organs of a decedent and control the disposition of a decedent's remains, would such law be constitutional?" The attorney general reasoned that such a law would violate Section 29 because it would accord spousal rights (i.e., the right to direct burial) to a domestic partner.

Several other states have enacted statutes and constitutional provisions that, like Nebraska's, might be applied to invalidate domestic partner registries or grants of domestic partner benefits. See, e.g., the 2004 amendment to the Michigan constitution, which says, "..., the union of one man and one woman in marriage shall be the only agreement recognized as a marriage or *similar union for any purpose*." (emphasis added). See also Virginia Code §20-45.3, which provides, "A civil union, partnership contract or other arrangement between persons of the same sex purporting to bestow the privileges or obligations of marriage is prohibited."

c. Domestic Partnerships at the state level

California was the first state to create a statewide domestic partner registry that carried with it significant rights. In its earliest version, however, only a handful of marital-type rights were accorded California domestic partners. In its original version, enacted in 1999 and effective as of January 1, 2000, only two rights were available: (1) the right of hospital visitation, and (2) health insurance benefits for state employees. See David Chambers, For the Best of Friends and for Lovers of all Sorts, a Status other than Marriage, 76 Notre Dame L. Rev. 1347 (2001), describing these early California efforts, as well as the reciprocal beneficiary legislation in Hawaii.

In 2003, California substantially increased the rights of domestic partners when it enacted the Domestic Partner Rights and Responsibilities Act, also known as AB 205 (Assembly Bill 205). The law took full effect on January 1, 2005, at which time California domestic partners began enjoying most of the same rights and responsibilities as married couples.

CALIFORNIA FAMILY CODE

§ 297. Domestic Partner Registration

(a) Domestic partners are two adults who have chosen to share one another's lives in an intimate and committed relationship of mutual caring.

(b) A domestic partnership shall be established in California when both persons file a Declaration of Domestic Partnership with the Secretary of State pursuant to this division, and, at the time of filing, all of the following requirements are met:

(1) Both persons have a common residence.

(2) Neither person is married to someone else or is a member of another domestic partnership with someone else that has not been terminated, dissolved, or adjudged a nullity.

(3) The two persons are not related by blood in a way that would prevent them from being married to each other in this state.

(4) Both persons are at least 18 years of age.

(5) Either of the following:

(A) Both persons are members of the same sex.

(B) One or both of the persons meet the eligibility criteria under Title II of the Social Security Act as defined in 42 U.S.C. Section 402(a) for old-age insurance benefits or Title XVI of the Social Security Act as defined in 42 U.S.C. Section 1381 for aged individuals. Notwithstanding any other provision of this section, persons of opposite sexes may not constitute a domestic partnership unless one or both of the persons are over the age of 62.

(6) Both persons are capable of consenting to the domestic partnership.

(c) "Have a common residence" means that both domestic partners share the same residence. It is not necessary that the legal right to possess the common residence be in both of their names. Two people have a common residence even if one or both have additional residences. Domestic partners do not cease to have a common residence if one leaves the common residence but intends to return.

§ 297.5. Rights, protections and benefits; responsibilities, obligations and duties under law

(a) Registered domestic partners shall have the same rights, protections, and benefits, and shall be subject to the same responsibilities, obligations, and duties under law, whether they derive from statutes, administrative regulations, court rules, government policies, common law, or any other provisions or sources of law, as are granted to and imposed upon spouses.

(b) Former registered domestic partners shall have the same rights, protections, and benefits, and shall be subject to the same responsibilities, obligations, and duties under law, whether they derive from statutes, administrative regulations, court rules, government policies, common law, or any other provisions or sources of law, as are granted to and imposed upon former spouses.

(c) A surviving registered domestic partner, following the death of the other partner, shall have the same rights, protections, and benefits, and shall be subject to the same responsibilities, obligations, and duties under law, whether they derive from statutes, administrative regulations, court rules, government policies, common law, or any other provisions or sources of law, as are granted to and imposed upon a widow or a widower.

(d) The rights and obligations of registered domestic partners with respect to a child of either of them shall be the same as those of spouses. The rights and obligations of former or surviving registered domestic partners with respect to a child of either of them shall be the same as those of former or surviving spouses.

(e) To the extent that provisions of California law adopt, refer to, or rely upon, provisions of federal law in a way that otherwise would cause registered domestic partners to be treated differently than spouses, registered domestic partners shall be treated by California law as if federal law recognized a domestic partnership in the same manner as California law.

(f) Registered domestic partners shall have the same rights regarding nondiscrimination as those provided to spouses.

(g) Notwithstanding this section, in filing their state income tax returns, domestic partners shall use the same filing status as is used on their federal income tax returns, or that would have been used had they filed federal income tax returns. Earned income may not be treated as community property for state income tax purposes.

(h) No public agency in this state may discriminate against any person or couple on the ground that the person is a registered domestic partner rather than a spouse or that the couple are registered domestic partners rather than spouses, except that nothing in this section applies to modify eligibility for long-term care plans.…

(i) This act does not preclude any state or local agency from exercising its regulatory authority to implement statutes providing rights to, or imposing responsibilities upon, domestic partners.

(j) This section does not amend or modify any provision of the California Constitution or any provision of any statute that was adopted by initiative.

(k) This section does not amend or modify federal laws or the benefits, protections, and responsibilities provided by those laws.

(l) Where necessary to implement the rights of registered domestic partners under this act, gender-specific terms referring to spouses shall be construed to include domestic partners.

(m)(1) For purposes of the statutes, administrative regulations, court rules, government policies, common law, and any other provision or source of law governing the rights, protections, and benefits, and the responsibilities, obligations, and duties of registered domestic partners in this state, as effectuated by this section, with respect to community property, mutual responsibility for debts to third parties, the right in particular circumstances of either partner to seek financial support from the other following the dissolution of the partnership, and other rights and duties as between the partners concerning ownership of property, any reference to the date of a marriage shall be deemed to refer to the date of registration of a domestic partnership with the state.

(2) Notwithstanding paragraph (1), for domestic partnerships registered with the state before January 1, 2005, an agreement between the domestic partners that the partners intend to be governed by the requirements set forth in Sections 1600 to 1620, inclusive, and which complies with those sections, except for the agreement's effective date, shall be enforceable as provided by Sections 1600 to 1620, inclusive, if that agreement was fully executed and in force as of June 30, 2005.

§ 298.5. Filing of Declaration of Domestic Partnership forms; registration

(a) Two persons desiring to become domestic partners may complete and file a Declaration of Domestic Partnership with the Secretary of State.

(b) The Secretary of State shall register the Declaration of Domestic Partnership in a registry for those partnerships, and shall return a copy of the registered form and a Certificate of Registered Domestic Partnership to the domestic partners at the mailing address provided by the domestic partners .

(c) No person who has filed a Declaration of Domestic Partnership may file a new Declaration of Domestic Partnership or enter a civil marriage with someone other than their registered domestic partner unless the most recent domestic partnership has been terminated or a final judgment of dissolution or nullity of the most recent domestic partnership has been entered. This prohibition does not apply if the previous domestic partnership ended because one of the partners died.

§ 299. Termination of domestic partnership; filing of Notice of Termination of Domestic Partnership; conditions; effective date; setting aside termination; jurisdiction

(a) A domestic partnership may be terminated without filing a proceeding for dissolution of domestic partnership by the filing of a Notice of Termination of Domestic Partnership with the Secretary of State pursuant to this section, provided that all of the following conditions exist at the time of the filing:

(1) The Notice of Termination of Domestic Partnership is signed by both domestic partners.

(2) There are no children of the relationship of the parties born before or after registration of the domestic partnership or adopted by the parties after registration of the domestic partnership, and neither of the domestic partners, to their knowledge, is pregnant.

(3) The domestic partnership is not more than five years in duration.

(4) Neither party has any interest in real property wherever situated, with the exception of the lease of a residence occupied by either party which satisfies the following requirements:

(A) The lease does not include an option to purchase.

(B) The lease terminates within one year from the date of filing of the Notice of Termination of Domestic Partnership.

(5) There are no unpaid obligations in excess of the amount described in paragraph (6) of subdivision (a) of Section 2400, as adjusted by subdivision (b) of Section 2400, incurred by either or both of the parties after registration of the domestic partnership, excluding the amount of any unpaid obligation with respect to an automobile.

(6) The total fair market value of community property assets, excluding all encumbrances and automobiles, including any deferred compensation or retirement plan, is less than the amount described in paragraph (7) of subdivision (a) of Section 2400, as adjusted by subdivision (b) of Section 2400, and neither party has separate property assets, excluding all encumbrances and automobiles, in excess of that amount.

(7) The parties have executed an agreement setting forth the division of assets and the assumption of liabilities of the community property, and have executed any documents, title certificates, bills of sale, or other evidence of transfer necessary to effectuate the agreement.

(8) The parties waive any rights to support by the other domestic partner.

(9) The parties have read and understand a brochure prepared by the Secretary of State describing the requirements, nature, and effect of terminating a domestic partnership.

(10) Both parties desire that the domestic partnership be terminated.

(b) The domestic partnership shall be terminated effective six months after the date of filing of the Notice of Termination of Domestic Partnership with the Secretary of State pursuant to this section, provided that neither party has, before that date, filed with the Secretary of State a notice of revocation of the termination of domestic partnership, in the form and content as shall be prescribed by the Secretary of State, and sent to the other party a copy of the notice of revocation by first-class mail, postage prepaid, at the other party's last known address. The effect of termination of a domestic partnership pursuant to this section shall be the same as, and shall be treated for all purposes as, the entry of a judgment of dissolution of a domestic partnership.

(c) The termination of a domestic partnership pursuant to subdivision (b) does not prejudice nor bar the rights of either of the parties to institute an action in the superior court to set aside the termination for fraud, duress, mistake, or any other ground recognized at law or in equity. A court may set aside the termination of domestic partnership and declare the termination of the domestic partnership null and void upon proof that the parties did not meet the requirements of subdivision (a) at the time of the filing of the Notice of Termination of Domestic Partnership with the Secretary of State.

(d) The superior courts shall have jurisdiction over all proceedings relating to the dissolution of domestic partnerships, nullity of domestic partnerships, and legal separation of partners in a domestic partnership. The dissolution of a domestic partnership, nullity of a domestic partnership, and legal separation of partners in a domestic partnership shall follow the same procedures, and the partners shall possess the same rights, protections, and benefits, and be subject to the same responsibilities, obligations, and duties, as apply to the dissolution of marriage, nullity of marriage, and legal separation of spouses in a marriage, respectively, except as provided in subdivision (a), and except that, in accordance with the consent acknowledged by domestic partners in the Declaration of Domestic Partnership form, proceedings for dissolution, nullity, or legal separation of a domestic partnership registered in this state may be filed in the superior courts of this state even if neither domestic partner is a resident of, or maintains a domicile in, the state at the time the proceedings are filed.

§ 299.2. Recognizing same sex unions from another jurisdiction as a valid domestic partnership

A legal union of two persons of the same sex, other than a marriage, that was validly formed in another jurisdiction, and that is substantially equivalent to a domestic partnership as defined in this part, shall be recognized as a valid domestic partnership in this state regardless of whether it bears the name domestic partnership.

§ 299.6. Preemption of local ordinances or laws

(a) Any local ordinance or law that provides for the creation of a "domestic partnership" shall be preempted on and after July 1, 2000, except as provided in subdivision (c).

(b) Domestic partnerships created under any local domestic partnership ordinance or law before July 1, 2000, shall remain valid. On and after July 1, 2000, domestic partnerships previously established under a local ordinance or law shall be governed by this division and the rights and duties of the partners shall be those set out in this division, except as provided in subdivision (c), provided a Declaration of Domestic Partnership is filed by the domestic partners under Section 298.5.

(c) Any local jurisdiction may retain or adopt ordinances, policies, or laws that offer rights within that jurisdiction to domestic partners as defined by Section 297 or as more broadly defined by the local jurisdiction's ordinances, policies, or laws, or that impose duties upon third parties regarding domestic partners as defined by Section 297 or as more broadly defined by the local jurisdiction's ordinances, policies, or laws, that are in addition to the rights and duties set out in this division, and the local rights may be conditioned upon the agreement of the domestic partners to assume the additional obligations set forth in this division.

Knight v. Superior Court
26 Cal. Rptr. 3d 687 (Cal. App. 2005)

SCOTLAND, P.J.

In March 2000, a majority of California's voters approved Proposition 22, codified in Family Code section 308.5, which states: "Only marriage between a man and a woman is valid or recognized in California." (We shall refer to this as the defense of marriage initiative or Proposition 22.)

Thereafter, the Legislature enacted Family Code section 297.5, effective on January 1, 2005, which states in part: "(a) Registered domestic partners shall have the same rights, protections, and benefits, and shall be subject to the same responsibilities, obligations, and duties under law,...as are granted to and imposed upon spouses." (We shall refer to this as the domestic partners act.)

Petitioners filed a complaint for declaratory and injunctive relief, seeking a determination that the Legislature's enactment of the domestic partners act is void because, they argued, it in effect amends Proposition 22, the defense of marriage initiative, without obtaining separate approval of the voters, which petitioners believe was required by article II, section 10, subdivision (c), of the California Constitution. This constitutional provision states that a legislative amendment of an initiative statute "becomes effective only when approved by the electors unless the initiative statute permits amendment or repeal without their approval." As petitioners point out, Proposition 22 did not contain a clause permitting such a result.

Ruling on the parties' motions for summary judgment, the trial judge held that (1) the domestic partners act does not amend the defense of marriage initiative and, therefore, its enactment without subsequent voter approval does not violate California's Constitution, and (2) in any event, interpreting the initiative in the manner urged by petitioners would likely violate the equal protection guarantees of our state's Constitution. Consequently, a judgment was entered denying petitioners' request to declare the domestic partners act to be void.

In December 2004, petitioners filed in this court a petition for writ of mandate, challenging the trial judge's ruling. Since the legislation would become effective on January 1, 2005, they asked us to issue an interim stay to prohibit enforcement of the contested provisions of the domestic partners act pending our decision on the merits of petitioners' writ petition. We denied the request for a stay but issued an alternative writ of mandate to address petitioners' legal challenge to the domestic partners act.

We conclude the trial judge was correct in ruling that the Legislature's enactment of the domestic partners act did not constitute an amendment of the defense of marriage initiative and, thus, that the Legislature's action without separate voter approval did not violate article II, section 10, subdivision (c) of the California Constitution.

As we will explain, the plain and unambiguous language of Proposition 22 shows that the initiative was intended only to limit the status of marriage to heterosexual couples and to prevent the recognition in California of homosexual marriages that have been, or may in the future be, legitimized by laws of other jurisdictions. The words of Proposition 22, and also its ballot pamphlet materials, do not express an intent to repeal our state's then-existing domestic partners laws or to limit the Legislature's authority to enact other legislation regulating such unions. If this were the intention of proponents of Proposition 22, the electorate was not given the opportunity to vote on that undisclosed objective, and courts are precluded from interpreting Proposition 22 in a manner that was not presented to the voters.

Contrary to petitioners' suggestion, the Legislature has not created a "marriage" by another name or granted domestic partners a status equivalent to married spouses. We shall recount in the discussion, *post,* the numerous statutory dissimilarities between the two types of unions, which disclose that the Legislature has not created a "same-sex marriage" under the guise of another name.

In sum, it is the role of the Legislature, not the courts, to make such public policy. Here, the trial judge did not make public policy; rather, Judge Loren McMaster conscientiously applied well-established rules of statutory construction to reach a decision compelled by the law. As he was required to do, Judge McMaster correctly ruled that the Legislature's enactment of section 297.5 did not constitute an amendment of Proposition 22; that the statute thus became effective without separate approval by the electorate; and, therefore, that section 297.5 is not void.

Accordingly, we shall deny the petition for writ of mandate, without need to address the merits of Judge McMaster's alternate reason for denying petitioners' request for relief. If they feel that the statutory scheme is not wise public policy, petitioners must turn to the Legislature or to the electorate, not the courts, to correct it.

DISCUSSION

I

Family Code section 300 defines a valid marriage as follows: "Marriage is a personal relation arising out of a civil contract between a man and a woman, to which the consent of the parties capable of making that contract is necessary. Consent alone does not constitute marriage. Consent must be followed by the issuance of a license and solemnization as authorized by this division...." (Further section references are to the Family Code unless otherwise specified.)

Section 308 expands upon this definition by providing that "[a] marriage contracted outside this state that would be valid by the laws of the jurisdiction in which the marriage was contracted is valid in this state." Thus, although common law marriage has been abolished in California, California recognizes the validity of a common law marriage contracted in another state which would be valid under the laws of that state. And under the plain language of section 308, if another state legalizes same-sex marriage, such marriages would be recognized as valid in California; however, this outcome has been prevented by subsequent legislation.

In 1996, in anticipation of the possible legalization of same-sex marriages in Hawaii, Congress enacted the Defense of Marriage Act....

In March 2000, the California electorate passed its own defense of marriage initiative, which states: "Only marriage between a man and a woman is valid or recognized in California." Section 308.5. Pursuant to section 308.5, California will not recognize same-sex marriages even if those marriages are validly formed in other jurisdictions. In other words, section 308.5 supplants the directive of section 308 in the case of same-sex marriages.

Prior to the passage of Proposition 22, the Legislature enacted section 297, establishing domestic partnership as a recognized legal relationship. (Stats.1999, ch. 588 (Assem. Bill No. 26), §2.) That section authorized two persons to register as domestic partners if they were adults sharing a common residence, they agreed to be jointly responsible for each other's basic living expenses, and they were either (1) both persons of the same sex, or (2) persons of the opposite sex, who were both over the age of 62 and eligible to receive social security. (Former §297, subd. (b).) Domestic partners were entitled to certain limited rights concerning hospital visitation, and to health benefits if one of the partners was a state employee.

Thereafter, the Legislature amended the domestic partnership statutes to expand the rights and obligations of domestic partners (Stats.2001, ch. 893 (Assem. Bill No. 25), §§1-61; Stats.2002, ch. 447 (Assem. Bill No. 2216), §§1-3) and to provide that for heterosexual domestic partnerships only one of the partners need be over the age of 62. (Stats.2001, ch. 893 (Assem. Bill No. 25), §3.)

In 2003, the Legislature amended the domestic partnership laws again in The California Domestic Partner Rights and Responsibilities Act of 2003 (the Act). (Stats.2003, ch. 421 (Assem. Bill No. 205), §4, eff. Jan. 1, 2005.) Section 297.5, subdivision (a) of the Act states: "Registered domestic partners shall have the same rights, protections, and benefits, and shall be subject to the same responsibilities, obligations, and duties under law, whether they derive from statutes, administrative regulations, court rules, government policies, common law, or any other provisions or sources of law, as are granted to and imposed upon spouses."

However, the statute goes on to provide that domestic partners may not file joint tax returns and their earned income is not treated as community property for the purposes of state income tax and that they are not entitled to many of the benefits the federal government provides to married couples, such as marital benefits relating to social security, Medicare, federal housing, food stamps, veterans' benefits, military benefits, and federal employment benefit laws.

Section 299.2 of the Act states: "A legal union of two persons of the same sex, other than a marriage, that was validly formed in another jurisdiction, and that is substantially equivalent to a domestic partnership as defined in this part, shall be recognized as a valid domestic partnership in this state regardless of whether it bears the name domestic partnership." Thus, a same-sex legal union that is valid in another jurisdiction will be recognized by California as a domestic partnership (§299.2), but not as a marriage (§308.5).

The Legislature specified that the Act "is not intended to repeal or adversely affect any other ways in which relationships between adults may be recognized or given effect in California, or the legal consequences of those relationships, including, among other things, civil marriage" (Stats.2003, ch. 421 (Assem. Bill No. 205), §1(c)), and it "does not amend or modify any provision of the California Constitution or any provision of any statute that was adopted by initiative."

II

According to petitioners, Proposition 22 did more than prevent California from recognizing same-sex marriages from other states; it was designed to protect the institution of marriage by precluding the Legislature from giving the rights and benefits of marriage to alternative relationships.

Therefore, petitioners argue, section 297.5 in effect amended Proposition 22. Citing article II, section 10, subdivision (c), of California's Constitution, petitioners claim that is void because it has not been approved by the voters.

The parties disagree as to whether section 297.5 constitutes an amendment of Proposition 22. There are no disputed material facts; the parties simply dispute the legal significance of the relevant facts and reach different conclusions as to whether section 297.5 adds to or takes away from Proposition 22, as codified in section 308.5. Since the answer to this question turns on an interpretation of the two statutes, it is an issue of law that a court may resolve in a summary judgment motion.

In interpreting a voter initiative such as Proposition 22, courts apply the same principles governing the construction of a statute. We begin by examining the language of the initiative statute, giving the words their usual and ordinary meaning, viewed in the context of the statute as a whole and the overall statutory scheme. If the terms of the statute are unambiguous, we presume the lawmakers meant what they said, and the plain meaning of the language governs.

At the time the voters passed Proposition 22, existing statutes defined marriage and domestic partnerships in a manner that indicates they are different legal relationships. Section 300 defines a valid marriage as "a personal relation arising out of a civil contract between a man and a woman, to which the consent of the parties capable of making that contract is necessary... followed by the issuance of a license and [a solemnizing ceremony]." In contrast, section 297 stated that domestic partners were "two adults who have chosen to share one another's lives in an intimate and committed relationship of mutual caring," and were both of the same sex, or of the opposite sex as long as they were both over the age of 62. (Former § 297; Stats.1999, ch. 588, § 2 (Assem. Bill No. 26).) Then-existing statutes also granted rights and imposed obligations upon both types of relationships.

The plain language of Proposition 22 and its initiative statute, section 308.5, reaffirms the definition of marriage in section 300 by stating that only marriage between a man and a woman shall be valid and recognized in California. This limitation ensures that California will not legitimize or recognize same-sex marriages from other jurisdictions, as it otherwise would be required to do pursuant to section 308, and that California will not permit same-sex partners to validly marry within the state.

Without submitting the matter to the voters, the Legislature cannot change this absolute refusal to recognize *marriages* between persons of the same sex. But the same is not true for enactment of legislation concerning domestic partnerships, a relationship other than marriage. This is so because the plain, unambiguous language of section 308.5 does not state an intent to repeal existing domestic partnership laws or to limit the Legislature's authority to regulate such unions. Section 308.5 does not state that the Legislature is precluded from expanding the rights and obligations of domestic partnerships or that, henceforth, such relationships will not be recognized or fostered in any fashion.

If that had been its purpose, the initiative easily and effectively could have accomplished that goal by using language akin to words used in laws from other states. For example, article I, section 29 of the Nebraska Constitution provides: "Only marriage between a man and a woman shall be valid or recognized in Nebraska. *The uniting of two persons of the same sex in a civil union, domestic partnership, or other similar same-sex relationship shall not be valid or recognized in Nebraska.*" (Italics added.) (See also, Ark. Const. Amend. 83 §2 ["Legal status for unmarried persons which is identical or substantially similar to marital status shall not be valid or recognized in Arkansas, except that the Legislature may recognize a common law marriage from another state between a man and a woman"]; Ga. Const., art. 1, 4, I(b) ["No union between persons of the same sex shall be recognized by this state as entitled to the benefits of marriage"]; Ky. Const. § 233A ["Only a marriage between one man and one woman shall be valid or recognized as a marriage in Kentucky. A legal status identical or substantially similar to that of marriage for unmarried individuals shall not be valid or recognized"]; La. Const., art. 12 §15 ["No official or court of the state of Louisiana shall construe this constitution or any state law to require that marriage or the legal incidents thereof be conferred upon any member of a union other than the union of one man and one woman. A legal status identical or substantially similar to that of marriage for unmarried individuals shall not be valid or recognized"]; Ohio Const., art. XV, § 11 ["Only a union between one man and one woman may be a marriage valid in or recognized by this state and its political subdivisions. This state and its political subdivisions shall not create or recognize a legal status for relationships of unmarried individuals that intends to approximate the design, qualities, significance or effect of marriage"]; Tex. Fam. Code § 6.204 [a marriage between persons of the same sex or a civil union granting to the parties of the relationship the legal protections, benefits, or responsibilities granted to the spouses of a marriage is contrary to public policy and void].)

The plain language of the above-cited laws of other states demonstrates an indisputable intent (1) to limit the benefits associated with marriage to marriages between men and women, and (2) to prohibit the recognition of other types of domestic unions or partnerships. Proposition 22 contains no similar language. Given the existence of domestic partnership statutes in California when the initiative was put on the ballot, Proposition 22 needed such language if it was intended to supplant the Legislature's authority to enact and to amend legislation regarding domestic partnerships. Instead, Proposition 22 unambiguously limits its scope to whether California will recognize the validity of *marriages* between persons of the same sex; it says nothing about whether other types of relationships may be permitted to enjoy the rights typically conferred upon married couples.

Because the plain, unambiguous language of Proposition 22 is concerned only with who is entitled to obtain the status of marriage, and not with the rights and obligations associated with marriage, section 297.5 (which does not grant the legal status of marriage to registered domestic partners) does not add to, or take away from, Proposition 22.

III

Despite the plain, unambiguous language of Proposition 22, and its intent as evidenced in the ballot materials, petitioners persist in contending that the initiative did more than simply preserve the status of marriage for partners of the opposite sex. They argue that Proposition 22 protects the institution of marriage itself, which they contend requires that the myriad of rights, benefits, and obligations associated therewith must be reserved only for married persons.

Petitioners point to *Elden v. Sheldon*, 46 Cal.3d 267 (hereafter *Elden*), in which the California Supreme Court said: "[T]he state has a strong interest in the marriage relationship; to the extent unmarried cohabitants are granted the same rights as married persons, the state's interest in promoting marriage is inhibited.... 'Spouses receive special consideration from the state, for marriage is a civil contract "of so solemn and binding a nature...that the consent of the parties alone will not constitute marriage... the consent of the state is also required." [Citation.] Marriage is accorded this degree of dignity in recognition that "[t]he joining of the man and woman in marriage is at once the most socially productive and individually fulfilling relationship that one can enjoy in the course of a lifetime." [Citation.] Consonant therewith, the state is most solicitous of the rights of spouses. [Citation.] The state affords similar protection to certain putative relationships in recognition of the good faith in which the innocent party undertook to marry. [Citation.] Unmarried cohabitants receive no similar solicitous statutory protection, nor should they; such would impede the state's substantial interest in promoting and protecting marriage.' [Citation.]" (*Id.* at pp. 274–75.)

According to petitioners, because *Elden* tied the conferral of marital rights to the state's interest in promoting marriage, Proposition 22 necessarily was intended to withhold those rights from alternative relationships. They contend that the conferral of those rights on domestic partnerships is the equivalent of permitting homosexuals to marry, which they say is an absurd result and conflicts with fundamental public policy.

Petitioners misinterpret *Elden*, which involved a male plaintiff's causes of action for loss of consortium and negligent infliction of emotional distress, based on witnessing his female cohabitant's tortious injury and death. Holding that neither cause of action can be extended to unmarried cohabiting couples, *Elden* explained: "Our emphasis on the state's interest in promoting the marriage relationship is not based on anachronistic notions of morality. The policy favoring marriage is 'rooted in the necessity of providing an institutional basis for defining the fundamental relational rights and responsibilities of persons in organized society.' [Citation.] ... Plaintiff does not suggest a convincing reason why cohabiting unmarried couples, who do not bear such legal obligations toward one another, should be permitted to recover for injuries to their partners to the same extent as those who undertake these responsibilities." (*Id.* at p. 275.)

Thus, *Elden* was concerned with granting rights associated with marriage to cohabitants who had the ability to marry but chose not to do so, and therefore had not taken on any of the responsibilities and burdens of marriage. That is a very different situation than the one presented here. Unlike heterosexuals who cohabitate, homosexuals are precluded from marrying their cohabiting partners; but by registering as domestic partners, they agree to accept the responsibilities imposed on a spouse in exchange for receiving the associated benefits. Granting such rights to domestic partners of the same sex will not impede the state's interest in promoting and protecting marriage because the voters have decided that homosexual couples cannot marry. Stated another way, unlike the withholding of benefits from same-sex cohabitants in order to promote and protect marriage by encouraging them to marry, the withholding of statutory benefits for homosexual domestic partners will not, indeed cannot, encourage them to marry.

Furthermore, California's societal interest in " 'providing an institutional basis for defining the fundamental relational rights and responsibilities of persons in organized society' " applies equally to domestic partners. This is so because although homosexual domestic partners cannot marry, they are not precluded from creating families using the same methods utilized by many heterosexual couples, i.e., adoption, artificial insemination, and surrogacy. The children of such unions are no less deserving of the protections afforded the children of heterosexual marriages. For this reason, the Legislature has directed in the law challenged by petitioners that "[t]he rights and obligations of registered domestic partners with respect to a child of either of them shall be the same as those of spouses," both during the domestic partnership and after its termination.

Thus, the Legislature was entitled to conclude that enactment of a statute encouraging same-sex couples to register as domestic partners is beneficial to society in the same way as is encouraging heterosexual couples to marry. It provides an institutional basis for defining their fundamental rights and responsibilities, which is essential to an organized and civilized society and to promote family stability. In the words of the Legislature while enacting section 297.5: "Expanding the rights and creating responsibilities of registered domestic partners would further California's interests in promoting family relationships and protecting family members during life crises, and would reduce discrimination on the bases of sex and sexual orientation in a manner consistent with the requirements of the California Constitution...." (Stats.2003, ch. 421 (Assem. Bill No. 205), § 1.)

We cannot say, as petitioners would like us to do, that this public policy decision by the Legislature to grant to registered domestic partners some of the benefits, and to impose upon them the responsibilities, associated with spouses is an absurd violation of public policy. Indeed, it is the role of the Legislature, not the courts, to make public policy.

Contrary to petitioners' suggestion, the Legislature has not created a "marriage" by another name or granted domestic partners a status equivalent to married spouses. In fact, domestic partners do not receive a number of marital rights and benefits. For example, they may not file joint tax returns and their earned income is not treated as community property for state income tax purposes and they are not entitled to numerous benefits provided to married couples by the federal government...

And prerequisites for the formation of domestic partnerships differ from marriage. Persons under the age of 18 who wish to marry may do so with parental consent (§ 302); however, there is no similar provision for minors to register as domestic partners. In addition, homosexuals must share a common residence before they can register as domestic partners (§ 297, subd. (b)(1)), but there is no similar limitation for persons who wish to marry. Thus, prison inmates have the right and ability to marry despite the fact they are incarcerated, do not currently reside with their intended spouse, and might never reside with their spouse; however, similarly situated homosexual inmates cannot register as domestic partners.

In addition, the mechanisms for forming and terminating the relationships are different. Domestic partners simply file with the Secretary of State a Declaration of Domestic Partnership to form their legal union (§ 298.5); but couples who want to marry must obtain a license and participate in some form of ceremony solemnizing their marriage. Another difference is the method for terminating a domestic partnership. If there are no children of the union, if the partnership is not more than five years in duration, and if the partners meet certain conditions relating to property and debts, they may terminate the relationship simply by filing with the Secretary of State a Notice of Termination of Domestic Partnership (§ 299.) The dissolution of a marriage under similar circumstances requires judicial intervention. (§§ 2400-2403.) These factors indicate marriage is considered a more substantial relationship and is accorded a greater stature than a domestic partnership. More than the mere filing of documents with the Secretary of State is required to form or dissolve a marriage.

Where the domestic partnership is long term, involves children, or involves substantial property, the procedure for terminating the partnership shares more similarities to dissolution of a marriage and does require judicial intervention. (§§ 299, subd. (d), 2330.) Differences remain, however, such as the fact there is no California residency requirement for termination of a domestic partnership, unlike a marital dissolution. (§§ 299, subd. (d), 2320.)

Furthermore, unlike a marriage, a domestic partnership will not automatically be recognized by other states. Therefore, if the domestic partners move out of California, the rights bestowed by our state's domestic partnership law may well become illusory. For example, domestic partners may find it difficult to terminate their relationship in other jurisdictions. (See, e.g., Rosengarten v. Downes, (Conn. 2002) And many of the rights bestowed upon domestic partners, such as the right to visit their hospitalized partner and to make medical decisions for him or her, may not be acknowledged by other states. Consequently, domestic partners do not have the same freedom to travel and retain the benefits associated with their union as do married persons.

The numerous dissimilarities between the two types of unions disclose that the Legislature has not created a "same-sex marriage" under the guise of another name.

For all of the reasons stated above, we conclude the trial judge correctly ruled that the Legislature's enactment of section 297.5 did not constitute an amendment of Proposition 22; that the statute thus became effective without separate approval by the electorate; and, therefore, that section 297.5 is not void.

Notes and Questions

1. What do you think should happen if a couple from Vermont, who have entered into a civil union, move to California? Suppose for example that six months after establishing residence, one of the partners is killed in an automobile accident. Should the survivor be able to sue for wrongful death even though the couple did not register with the California Secretary of State?

2. Could Sharon Smith, the surviving lesbian partner of Diane Whipple, the woman who was mauled to death by a neighbor's dogs in San Francisco, benefit from the domestic partnership act in her suit against the neighbors? The death occurred on January 26, 2001. While registration with the Secretary of State was possible by then, domestic partners were given very few rights. Thus, there was little reason to register. California statutes did not give standing to domestic partners in wrongful death cases until January 1, 2002. Even if the amendment to the wrongful death statute was applied retroactively, it would have been impossible for a couple like Sharon Smith and Diane Whipple to know that they had good reason to register as domestic partners because it wasn't until after Whipple's death that the status of domestic partner carried with it any meaningful benefits. See *Armijo v. Miles*, 2005 WL 714211 (Cal. App. 2005)(explaining the piecemeal enactment of California's domestic partner laws and how they applied to cases of wrongful death). The court in *Armijo* upheld the right of a lesbian to bring a wrongful death action against the hospital and doctors allegedly responsible for her partner's death on August 6, 2001. Her case was initially dismissed on standing grounds because at the time she filed in 2002 only registered domestic partners were granted standing by the wrongful death statute. In 2004, while her case was on appeal, the statute was amended to provide standing to non-registered partners who otherwise met the statutory definition of domestic partner.

3. Do you agree with the California court in *Knight* that the domestic partner statute is not the equivalent of marriage? Could you rely on the analysis in *Knight* to argue in favor of domestic partner legislation in those states, like Nebraska, that have laws that go further than limiting marriage to opposite sex couples?

4. In 2002, the Connecticut legislature added a provision to the general statutes that would allow an adult to designate another adult for limited purposes, primarily involving issues that occur as a result of tragedy or death. But the statute did not create standing to bring wrongful death claims. In early 2005, the Connecticut legislature was very close to passing a statewide civil union bill.

5. Hawaii's "Reciprocal Beneficiary" legislation provides a significant number of rights and benefits. Among the benefits available to a reciprocal beneficiary are: (1) the right to pension and related insurance benefits of a government employee, (2) right to hospital visitation, (3) rights at death of partner under workers' compensation or crime victims' fund, (4) right to death benefits if partner is public safety officer killed on duty, (5) intestate heir, (6) right to elective share under probate code, (7) included in family leave rules, and (8) right to hold land as tenants by the entirety (which in Hawaii gives added protection from creditors).

6. New Jersey's statewide Domestic Partner Act became effective in July, 2004. Its benefits are limited and do not expressly include the right to sue for wrongful death. What result if New Jersey domestic partners are visiting in California and one of the partners is the victim of a negligent homicide? Should the surviving partner be able to sue in California?

7. The state of Maine has statutes mandating insurance carriers to provide coverage plans that include domestic partners.

3. Adult Adoption

In 1971, the Minnesota Supreme Court ruled against Jack Baker and Mike Mc-Connell, who had sued for the right to marry each other. Unable to form a marital relationship, the couple sought alternatives. McConnell, the older of the two, petitioned to adopt Baker, thereby creating a family relationship of father and son. According to press reports at the time, the adoption was one of the first of its kind. While parent-child relationships do not carry many legal rights and responsibilities once the child becomes an adult, there are a few rights that are worth mentioning. First of all, in the absence of any other children [or spouses], a father and son inherit from each other as the nearest living heir. Ideally, one would have a duly executed will bequeathing one's property to one's partner. But wills can always be challenged by the nearest living heir. If Jack and Mike are each other's nearest living heir after the adoption, then family members arguably lose their standing to contest the will. Second, some housing statutes and ordinances protect families more than they protect an unrelated couple. Third, some states have an inheritance tax separate from the estate tax that will apply to any wealth that is inherited by someone other than a spouse or child or parent. These tax rates run from 10% to 15% depending on the state. Establishing a valid parent-child relationship would enable the couple to avoid the tax, no matter which partner died first. Finally, a parent-child relationship is sufficient in some states to bring a wrongful death claim, while unrelated persons are generally not entitled to bring such claims.

In Re Adoption of Robert Paul P.
471 N.E.2d 424 (N.Y. 1984)

JASEN, Judge.

We are asked to decide whether it was error for Family Court to deny the petition of a 57-year-old male to adopt a 50-year-old male with whom he shares a homosexual relationship. Appellants are two adult males who have resided together continuously for more than 25 years. The older of the two, who was 57 years of age when this proceeding was commenced, submitted a petition to adopt the younger, aged 50 at the time. The two share a homosexual relationship and desire an adoption for social, financial and emotional reasons.[1]...Family Court denied the petition. That court concluded that the

---

1. The parties' affidavit, attached to the petition, states the following reasons for the proposed adoption:

"2. The two of us have lived together for a period of over 25 years. We consider ourselves to be a family, though this might not be true in the traditional sense. Though not the only reason for our petition, our present living arrangements, in a leased apartment, are not formalized and we fear the possibility of eviction; our financial and personal lives are entwined together and though it is not expected, we are concerned about the disposition of our estates upon death and lastly, though not least, we expect to live out our lives together and are concerned about the ability and right under the law for each of us to take care of the other should unexpected events occur.

"3. Though the above reasons indicate financial, economic and practical considerations for our petition, not of any lesser extent and perhaps of more importance, are the many

parties were attempting to utilize an adoption for the purposes properly served by marriage, wills and business contracts and that the parties lacked any semblance of a parent-child relationship.... We now affirm for the reasons that follow.

Our adoption statute embodies the fundamental social concept that the relationship of parent and child may be established by operation of law. Despite the absence of any blood ties, in the eyes of the law an adopted child becomes "the natural child of the adoptive parent" with all the attendant personal and proprietary incidents to that relationship. Indeed, the adoption laws of New York, as well as those of most of the States, reflect the general acceptance of the ancient principle of adoptio naturam imitatur—i.e., adoption imitates nature, which originated in Roman jurisprudence, which, in turn, served as a guide for the development of adoption statutes in this country.

In imitating nature, adoption in New York, as explicitly defined in § 110 of the Domestic Relations Law, is "the legal proceeding whereby a person takes another person into the relation of child and thereby acquires the rights and incurs the responsibilities of parent." It is plainly not a quasi-matrimonial vehicle to provide nonmarried partners with a legal imprimatur for their sexual relationship, be it heterosexual or homosexual. Moreover, any such sexual intimacy is utterly repugnant to the relationship between child and parent in our society, and only a patently incongruous application of our adoption laws—wholly inconsistent with the underlying public policy of providing a parent-child relationship for the welfare of the child—would permit the employment of adoption as the legal formalization of an adult relationship between sexual partners under the guise of parent and child.

While the adoption of an adult has long been permitted under the Domestic Relations Law, there is no exception made in such adoptions to the expressed purpose of legally formalizing a parent-child relationship. Adoption laws in this State, first enacted in 1873, initially only provided for the "adoption of minor children by adult persons." As early as 1915, however, the statute was amended to allow adoption of "a person of the age of twenty-one years and upwards" and presently the law simply provides that an unmarried adult or married adults together "may adopt another person" without any restriction on the age of the "adoptive child" or "adoptee". Despite these and other statutory changes since adoption came into existence in New York, the basic function of giving legal effect to a parent-child relationship has remained unaltered.

Indeed, although the statutory prerequisites may be less compelling than in the case of the adoption of a minor, an adult adoption must still be "in the best interests of the [adoptive] child" and "the familial, social, religious, emotional and financial circumstances of the adoptive parents which may be relevant" must still be investigated. Neither the explicit statutory purpose nor criteria have been diluted for adult adoptions, and this court has no basis for undoing what the Legislature has left intact.

Moreover, deference to the narrow legislative purpose is especially warranted with adoption, a legal relationship unknown at common law. It exists only by virtue of the legislative acts that authorize it. Although adoption was widely practiced by the Egyptians, Greeks and Romans, it was unknown in England until the Adoption of Children Act of 1926, more than 50 years subsequent to the enactment of adoption laws in New York. Adoption in this State is "solely the creature of, and regulated by, statute law" and

---

personal, emotional and sentimental reasons for which we present our petition. Simply
stated we are a family and seek to formalize such."

"'[t]he Legislature has supreme control of the subject.'" Consequently, because adoption is entirely statutory and is in derogation of common law, the legislative purposes and mandates must be strictly observed.

Here, where the appellants are living together in a homosexual relationship and where no incidents of a parent-child relationship are evidenced or even remotely within the parties' intentions, no fair interpretation of our adoption laws can permit a granting of the petition. Adoption is not a means of obtaining a legal status for a nonmarital sexual relationship—whether homosexual or heterosexual. Such would be a "cynical distortion of the function of adoption." (Matter of Adult Anonymous II, 88 A.D.2d 30, 38 [Sullivan, J.P., dissenting].) Nor is it a procedure by which to legitimize an emotional attachment, however sincere, but wholly devoid of the filial relationship that is fundamental to the concept of adoption.

While there are no special restrictions on adult adoptions under the provisions of the Domestic Relations Law, the Legislature could not have intended that the statute be employed "to arrive at an unreasonable or absurd result." Such would be the result if the Domestic Relations Law were interpreted to permit one lover, homosexual or heterosexual, to adopt the other and enjoy the sanction of the law on their feigned union as parent and child.

There are many reasons why one adult might wish to adopt another that would be entirely consistent with the basic nature of adoption, including the following: a childless individual might wish to perpetuate a family name; two individuals might develop a strong filial affection for one another; a stepparent might wish to adopt the spouse's adult children; or adoption may have been forgone, for whatever reason, at an earlier date. But where the relationship between the adult parties is utterly incompatible with the creation of a parent-child relationship between them, the adoption process is certainly not the proper vehicle by which to formalize their partnership in the eyes of the law. Indeed, it would be unreasonable and disingenuous for us to attribute a contrary intent to the Legislature.[2]

If the adoption laws are to be changed so as to permit sexual lovers, homosexual or heterosexual, to adopt one another for the purpose of giving a nonmatrimonial legal status to their relationship, or if a separate institution is to be established for the same purpose, it is for the Legislature, as a matter of State public policy, to do so. Absent any such recognition of that relationship coming from the Legislature, however, the courts ought not to create the same under the rubric of adoption.

MEYER, Judge (dissenting).

Having concluded in People v. Onofre that government interference with a private consensual homosexual relationship was unconstitutional because it would not "do anything other than restrict individual conduct and impose a concept of private morality chosen by the State," the court now inconsistently refuses to "permit the employment of adoption as the legal formalization of an adult relationship between sexual

---

2. The dissent's reliance on People v. Onofre, 51 N.Y.2d 476, is misplaced. The issue in this case is not whether private consensual homosexual conduct is legally proscribable—this court has already answered that question in the negative and the decision today in no way affects or conflicts with that holding. The sole issue addressed today is whether adoption under the Domestic Relations Law is an appropriate means to legally formalize an indisputably and entirely nonfilial relationship between sexual partners—regardless of whether their relationship is homosexual or heterosexual. The decision today in no way imposes or chooses a "concept of private morality" nor in any way judges the propriety or morality of the parties' "individual conduct."

partners under the guise of parent and child." I write…essentially to emphasize the extent to which, in my view, the majority misconceives the meaning and purpose of article 7 of the Domestic Relations Law.

Under that article the relationship of parent and child is not a condition precedent to adoption; it is rather the result of the adoption proceeding. This is clear from the provisions of §§ 110 and 117. The second unnumbered paragraph of § 110 defines "adoption" as "the legal proceeding whereby a person takes another person into the relation of child and thereby acquires the rights and incurs the responsibilities of parent in respect of such other person," and § 117, which spells out the "effect of adoption," provides in the third unnumbered paragraph of subdivision 1 that, "The adoptive parents or parent and the adoptive child shall sustain toward each other the legal relation of parent and child and shall have all the rights and be subject to all the duties of that relation including the rights of inheritance from and through each other and the natural and adopted kindred of the adoptive parents or parent." From those provisions and the statement in the opening sentence of § 110 that, "An adult unmarried person * * * may adopt another person," no other conclusion is possible than that the Legislature has not conditioned adult adoption upon there being a parent-child relationship, but rather has stated that relationship to be the result of adoption. Indeed, had it intended to impose limitations of age, consent of others, sexual orientation, or other such condition upon adult adoption, it could easily have done so.

Nor will it do to argue…that because the Legislature that provided for adoption of adults continued the proscription against homosexuality, it did not envision adoption as a means of formalizing a homosexual relationship. The wording of § 110 being sufficiently broad to permit such formalization once the prior criminal proscription has been declared unconstitutional, to deny it that effect is to ignore the rule that a court is "not at liberty to restrict by conjecture, or under the guise or pretext of interpretation, the meaning of" the language chosen by the Legislature. It is "incumbent upon the courts to give effect to legislation as it is written, and not as they or others might think it should be written."

Contrary to the suggestion of the majority that the adoption statute must be strictly construed, it "has been most liberally and beneficently applied."…[T]here is no suggestion of undue influence and the relationship, which by the present decision is excised from the adoption statute's broad wording, has, since the Onofre decision, been subject to no legal impediment. That it remains morally offensive to many cannot justify imposing upon the statute a limitation not imposed by the Legislature.

What leads to the majority's conclusion that the relationship of the parties "is utterly incompatible with the creation of a parent-child relationship between them" is that it involves a "nonmarital sexual relationship." But nothing in the statute requires an inquiry into or evaluation of the sexual habits of the parties to an adult adoption or the nature of the current relationship between them. It is enough that they are two adults who freely desire the legal status of parent and child. The more particularly is this so in light of the absence from the statute of any requirement that the adoptor be older than the adoptee, for that, if nothing else, belies the majority's concept that adoption under New York statute imitates nature, inexorably and in every last detail.

Under the statute "the relationship of parent and child, with all the personal and property rights incident to it, may be established, independently of blood ties, by operation of law"; existence of a parent-child relationship is not a condition of, but a result of, adoption. The motives which prompt the present application are in no way contrary to public policy…Absent any contravention of public policy, we should be "concerned only with the clear, unqualified statutory authorization of adoption;" and should, therefore, reverse the Appellate Division's order.

In re Adoption of James A. Swanson
623 A.2d 1059 (Delaware 1993)

Moore, J.

Richard Sorrels appeals the denial of his petition in the Family Court to adopt James A. Swanson, a consenting adult. We confront an issue of first impression: Is a pre-existing parent-child relationship required under our adult adoption statutes in order for one adult to adopt another? Although the statutes do not contain that requirement, the Family Court implied such a condition in our law, and denied the adoption petition. Based on principles of statutory construction, and in the absence of any countervailing public policy, we conclude that it was an error of law to have appended the foregoing condition to an adult adoption. Accordingly, we reverse.

When Richard Sorrels sought to adopt, James Swanson, his companion of 17 years, they were, respectively, 66 and 51 years of age. The adoption had two purposes—to formalize the close emotional relationship that had existed between them for many years and to facilitate their estate planning. Apparently, they sought to prevent collateral claims on their respective estates from remote family members, and to obtain the reduced inheritance tax rate which natural and adopted children enjoy under Delaware law. Admittedly, there was no pre-existing parent-child relationship between them, and on that basis the Family Court denied the petition.

Adult adoptions in Delaware are governed by our Domestic Relations Law, 13 Del. C. §§ 951 through 956. Section 943 provides that "[i]lf the petition complies with the requirements of §§ 951 and 952 of this title, and if the person or persons to be adopted appear in court and consent to the adoption, the Family Court may render a decree ordering the issuance of a certificate of adoption to the petitioner."[1] Although the statute mentions no other requirements beyond those listed in §§ 951-952, the Family Court sua sponte concluded that approval of an adult adoption was contingent upon a pre-existing family relationship:

> Indisputably, the legislature, by providing for adoption of minors, intended to allow for the creation and formalization of parent-child relationships between nonrelated adults and children. It is reasonable to infer that the legislature, by providing for adult adoptions, sought to extend this principle to those situations where no adoption occurred before the age of majority or where the parent-child relationship developed during adulthood. It is reasonable to infer that the legislature, by providing for adult adoptions, intended to allow for the formalization of the parent-child relationship where there is an existing parent-child relationship between nonrelated individuals.... It is simply illogical that the legislature enacted the adult adoption statute to make familial inheri-

---

1. 13 Del. C. § 951 provides that: Any person, or any husband and wife jointly, desiring to adopt any person or persons upwards of 18 years of age, shall file a petition in the Family Court of the county in which the petitioner or the person to be adopted resides. 13 Del. C. § 952 describes the contents of the petition: The petition shall state the name, sex and date of be of the person or persons whose adoption is sought and that the petitioner or petitioners desire to adopt such person or persons. The petition shall be signed by the petitioner or petitioners.

tance rights available to all. Furthermore, it is unlikely that the legislature intended to extend adoption to all other kinds of relationships, including friendships and sexual relationships. Petitioner's interpretation of the statute would lead to these results.

Thus, the Family Court implied a new requirement into the adult adoption process. As a result, we are faced with a simple question of statutory construction—did the Family Court err as a matter of law in formulating or applying legal principles when it interpreted § 953 to require a preexisting parent-child relationship?

We begin with the basic rule of statutory construction that requires a court to ascertain and give effect to the intent of the legislature. If the statute as a whole is unambiguous and there is no reasonable doubt as to the meaning of the words used, the court's role is limited to an application of the literal meaning of those words. However, where, as here, the Court is faced with a novel question of statutory construction, it must seek to ascertain and give effect to the intention of the General Assembly as expressed by the statute itself.

There is no reference in § 953 to any condition of a pre-existing parent-child relationship. Instead, the statute only compels a person seeking an adult adoption to sign and file a petition containing certain basic personal data. If, after having done so, the adoptee appears in court and consents to the adoption, the Family Court may grant the petition for adoption. When statutory language is clear, unambiguous, and consistent with other provisions of the same legislation, the court must give effect to its intent. Moreover, 13 Del C. § 953, the relevant adult adoption statute, has existed in equivalent form since 1915, without any material change by the General Assembly. That is indicative of legislative satisfaction with the provisions of the statute.

Regardless of one's views as to the wisdom of the statute, our role as judges is limited to applying the statute objectively and not revising it. A court may not engraft upon a statute language which has been clearly excluded therefrom. Thus, where, as here, provisions are expressly included in one part of a statute, but omitted from another, it is reasonable to conclude that the legislature was aware of the omission and intended it. As a result, the omission from the adult adoption procedure for investigation and supervision of prospective placements, found in the requirements for adopting minors, persuades us that it was not the result of an accident. If anything, it is the best evidence of a legislative policy against imposing unnecessary conditions upon the adult adoption process.

Many jurisdictions limit inquiry into the motives or purposes of an adult adoption. However, most recognize that adult adoptions for the purpose of creating inheritance rights are valid. In one of the earliest cases, the Supreme Judicial Court of Massachusetts upheld an adoption of three adults, aged 43, 39 and 25 respectively, by a 70 year old person who intended the adoption to operate in lieu of a will. Collamore v. Learned, 50 N.E. 518 (Mass. 1898). The court ruled that motive, although proper in that case, had no effect on the validity of the adoption....Likewise, in Ex parte Libertini, 224 A.2d 443 (Md. 1966), the Maryland Court of Appeals permitted the adoption of an unmarried thirty-five year old woman by an unmarried fifty-six year old woman, initiated for reasons of inheritance and maternal feelings. The court rejected outright the lower court's conclusion that granting the adoption would pervert the entire adoptive process. The court noted that an adoption for the purpose of inheritance does not change the social or domestic relationship of the parties. Rather, its purpose and effect bestows on the adoptee the right of a natural heir to inherit property. This motive was not improper, the court concluded, and therefore had no bearing on a determination of the adoption's propriety. Cases upholding adoptions for the purpose of inproving the adoptee's inheritance rights continue to grow....

The general disinclination to examine the motives of the petitioner has been extended beyond the area of inheritance rights. In 333 East 53rd Street Associates v. Mann, 503 N.Y.S.2d 752 (App.Div., 1st Dept. 1986), a petitioner adopted an adult woman in order to ensure that she would succeed to the tenancy of a rent controlled apartment. The building's owner sought a declaratory judgment that the adoptee had no rights in the apartment. The appellate court found nothing inherently wrong with an adoption intended to confer an economic benefit on the adopted person.

On the other hand, the New York Court of Appeals ruled that a fifty-seven year old man could not adopt a fifty year old male with whom he shared a homosexual relationship. Matter of Adoption of Robert Paul P., 481 N.Y.S.2d 652 (N.Y. 1984). The court reasoned that adoption is not a quasi-matrimonial device to provide unmarried partners with a legal imprimatur for their sexual relationship. The court also determined that New York's adult adoption process requires the adoption to be in the best interests of the adoptee, and thus, the financial and emotional condition of the petitioner must still be investigated. Delaware's adult adoption process clearly abandons the requirement for such an investigation. It suggests no corresponding need to determine that an adult adoption be in the best interests of the adoptee. We also note the compelling dissent in Matter of Adoption of Robert Paul P., 481 N.Y.S.2d at 656 (Meyer, J. dissenting), taking the majority to task for imposing limitations on the process that are not found in New York's adult adoption statute.

There are, of course, common sense limitations on any adult adoption. That is why our statute appears to confer reasonable discretion upon the Family Court's approval of an adult adoption. Solely by way of example, no court should countenance an adoption to effect a fraudulent, illegal or patently frivolous purpose. See, e.g., In re Jones, 411 A.2d 910 (R.I.Supr. 1980), where an older married man sought to adopt his 20 year old paramour to the economic detriment of his wife and family. Delaware law is not necessarily inconsistent with the results in Adoption of Robert Paul P. and In re Jones. Adult adoptions intended to foster a sexual relationship would be against public policy as violative of the incest statute. See 11 Del. C. § 766(b), which defines the crime of incest to include sexual intercourse between a parent and child "without regard to...relationships by adoption."

A statute cannot be construed to produce an absurd, meaningless or patently inane result. However, where, as here, the petition contemplates an adoption that is not only within the scope of the statute, but which is also widely recognized as a proper exercise of the authority granted by the statute, we can divine no reason why this petition should be denied.... We have long held that our courts do not sit as a superlegislature to eviscerate proper legislative enactments. It is beyond the province of courts to question the policy or wisdom of an otherwise valid law. Instead, each judge must take and apply the law as they find it, leaving any changes to the duly elected representatives of the people. Accordingly, the order of the Family Court dismissing the petition is REVERSED. The Family Court is directed to issue an appropriate decree of adoption.

Notes and Questions

1. Attorneys practicing in the Family Court in New York City reported that sympathetic judges continued to grant adoptions for same-sex adult couples after the Court of

Appeals' decision in Robert Paul P., in cases where papers were drafted without reference to sexual relationships between the parties and emphasized the desire to create family ties for other purposes.

2. Are there reasons why an adult adoption proceeding is not a desirable alternative in the absence of the ability to formalize a relationship in any other manner? What are the possible downside consequences of adoption?

3. Many adult adoptions took place in California in the 1980s. Consider the case of Bill and Bo, a gay couple who through adoption became father and son. What do you advise them when they ask you about registering as domestic partners under the new California law?

4. Legal Guardianship

Another context in which non-traditional families may seek legal recognition is the situation where one person in the relationship becomes incapacitated and incapable of making decisions or taking care of himself or herself. In such circumstances, a spouse would naturally act as guardian of the incapacitated person. What if this situation befalls an unmarried couple? Would parents necessarily take priority? Could the situation be affected by advanced planning, through the execution of contingent guardianship or power of attorney papers? Consider the following case:

In re Guardianship of Sharon Kowalski
478 N.W.2d 790 (Minn. Ct. App. 1991)
Review Denied Feb. 10, 1992.

DAVIES, Judge.

Appellant Karen Thompson challenges the trial court's denial of her petition for guardianship of Sharon Kowalski, and the court's award of guardianship to Karen Tomberlin. We reverse and remand for appointment of Karen Thompson as guardian.

FACTS

Sharon Kowalski is 35 years old. On November 13, 1983, she suffered severe brain injuries in an automobile accident which left her in a wheelchair, impaired her ability to speak, and caused severe loss of short-term memory. At the time of the accident, Sharon was sharing a home in St. Cloud with her lesbian partner, appellant Karen Thompson. They had exchanged rings, named each other as insurance beneficiaries, and had been living together as a couple for four years. Sharon's parents were not aware of the lesbian relationship at the time of the accident. Sharon's parents and siblings live on the Iron Range, where Sharon was raised.

In March of 1984, both Thompson and Sharon's father, Donald Kowalski, cross-petitioned for guardianship. Thompson, expecting that she would have certain visitation rights and input into medical decisions, agreed to the appointment of Mr. Kowalski as Sharon's guardian. The guardianship order, however, gave complete control of visitation to Kowalski, who subsequently received court approval to terminate Thompson's visitation rights on July 25, 1985. Kowalski immediately relocated Sharon from a nursing home in Duluth to one in Hibbing.

In May of 1988, Judge Robert Campbell ordered specialists at Miller-Dwan Medical Center to examine Sharon to determine her level of functioning and whether Sharon could express her wishes on visitation. The doctors concluded that Sharon wished to see Thompson, and the court permitted Thompson to reestablish visitation in January of 1989. The doctors also recommended in 1989 that Sharon be relocated to Trevilla at Robbinsdale, where she currently resides. After Sharon's move, Thompson was permitted to bring Sharon to her St. Cloud home for semi-monthly weekend visits.

In late 1988, Kowalski notified the court that, due to his own medical problems, he wished to be removed as Sharon's guardian. The court granted his request effective May 1990. After being notified of Kowalski's request to relinquish guardianship, Thompson, on August 7, 1989, filed a petition for appointment as successor guardian of Sharon's person and estate. No competing petition was filed. The court held a hearing on Thompson's petition on August 2, 1990. The court wished to conduct further evidentiary hearings, and evidence was taken in both Duluth and Minneapolis over the next several months.

Karen Tomberlin is a friend of the Kowalski family. She did not file a petition for guardianship. Rather, she contacted Sharon's attorney indicating that she wished to testify in opposition to Thompson's petition and submitted a letter to the court suggesting that she be considered as an alternative guardian. Sharon's attorney, in a letter to the trial court prior to the initial August 2, 1990, hearing on Thompson's petition, also included Tomberlin's name as a possibility for guardianship.

The evidentiary hearings in Minneapolis and Duluth were directed toward evaluating Thompson's petition. Thompson called approximately 16 medical witnesses, all of whom had treated Sharon and had firsthand knowledge of her condition and care. Thompson thus exercised little choice as to which medical witnesses were called from Miller-Dwan and Trevilla. The trial court appointed the Miller-Dwan evaluation team, and it was that team which recommended Sharon's transfer to Trevilla. The court also appointed the social worker who testified at the hearing. These witnesses testified about Thompson's interaction with Sharon and the medical staff, Sharon's recovery progress, and Sharon's ability reliably to express her preference in this matter.

The court also heard testimony from three witnesses in opposition to Thompson's petition: Debra Kowalski, Sharon's sister; Kathy Schroeder, a friend of Sharon and the Kowalskis; and Tomberlin. These witnesses had no medical training, each had visited Sharon infrequently in recent years, and none had accompanied Sharon on any outings from the institution. Sharon's parents chose not to attend the hearing.

On April 23, 1991, the trial court denied Thompson's petition for guardianship and simultaneously appointed Tomberlin as guardian without conducting a separate hearing into her qualifications. Thompson appeals to this court.

Issue

Did the trial court abuse its discretion in denying appellant's petition for guardianship of Sharon Kowalski?

Analysis

The appointment of a guardian is a matter peculiarly within the discretion of the probate court. The reviewing court shall not interfere with the exercise of this discretion except in the case of clear abuse. In 1980, the legislature, to protect the rights and best interests of the ward, rewrote the guardianship statutes to require the probate court to make specific findings detailing both the necessity for the proposed guardianship of the ward and the qualifications of the proposed guardian. Minn.Stat. §525.551, subd. 5 (1990). The only issue on appeal is the court's choice of guardian and its findings and conclusions on the comparative qualifications of Thompson and Tomberlin.

Guardianship proceedings are governed by Minn.Stat. §§525.539—525.6198 (1990). Minn.Stat. §525.551, subd. 5, provides that after a hearing on a petition for guardianship, [t]he court shall make a finding that appointment of the person chosen as guardian or conservator is in the best interests of the ward. The statute defines the "best interests of the ward" to be:

> [A]ll relevant factors to be considered or evaluated by the court in nominating a guardian or conservator, including but not limited to: (1) the reasonable preference of the ward or conservatee, if the court determines the ward or conservatee has sufficient capacity to express a preference; (2) the interaction between the proposed guardian or conservator and the ward or conservatee; and (3) the interest and commitment of the proposed guardian or conservator in promoting the welfare of the ward or conservatee and the proposed guardian's or conservator's ability to maintain a current understanding of the ward's or conservatee's physical and mental status and needs.

In the case of a ward or conservatorship of the person, welfare includes: (i) food, clothing, shelter, and appropriate medical care; (ii) social, emotional, religious, and recreational requirements; and (iii) training, education, and rehabilitation. Kinship is not a conclusive factor in determining the best interests of the ward or conservatee but should be considered to the extent that it is relevant to the other factors contained in this subdivision. Minn.Stat. §525.539, subd. 7.

There is no language in the statute specifically directing that a guardian be a neutral, detached party. To the contrary, when taken as a whole, the statute's enumerated factors direct that a guardian be someone who is preferred by the ward if possible, has a positive interaction with the ward, and has high involvement with, and commitment to, promoting the ward's welfare. This necessarily entails a guardian with demonstrated understanding and knowledge of the ward's physical and emotional needs.

1. The Ward's Expressed Preference

The court heard testimony from its appointed evaluation team[1] at Miller-Dwan about Sharon's ability to express a reliable preference as to where and with whom she wanted to be. After a four-month evaluation, the doctor overseeing the evaluation submitted the following recommendation to the court:

> We believe Sharon Kowalski has shown areas of potential and ability to make rational choices in many areas of her life and she has consistently indicated a desire to return home. And by that, she means to St. Cloud to live with Karen Thompson again. Whether that is possible is still uncertain as her care will be difficult and burdensome. We think she deserves the opportunity to try. All the professional witnesses concurred in this conclusion, including Sharon's current treating physician. No contradictory evidence was provided from any professionals who worked with Sharon.

---

1. The evaluation team included personnel in physical therapy, occupational therapy, speech and language pathology, social work, psychology, and nursing.

The three lay witnesses who opposed Thompson's petition were skeptical that Sharon could reliably express her wishes, saying that Sharon changed her mind too often to believe what she said, given her impaired short-term memory. Despite the uncontradicted medical testimony about Sharon's capability to make choices in her life, the trial court concluded that Sharon could not express a reliable preference for guardianship. This court finds that, in the absence of contradictory evidence about Sharon's decision-making capacity from a professional or anyone in daily contact with her, the trial court's conclusion was clearly erroneous.

A ward with sufficient capacity may express a wish as to a guardian under Minn.Stat. §525.539, subd. 7, and may also nominate a successor guardian under Minn.Stat. §525.59. If the ward has sufficient capacity, the ward's choices may only be denied by the court if found not to be in the ward's best interests. It is clear that Sharon's expressed preference to live with Thompson and to return home to St. Cloud is a significant factor that must be considered in the guardianship proceeding.

2. Petitioner's Qualifications

The medical professionals were all asked about Thompson's qualifications with respect to the statutory criteria. The testimony was consistent that Thompson: (1) achieves outstanding interaction with Sharon; (2) has extreme interest and commitment in promoting Sharon's welfare; (3) has an exceptional current understanding of Sharon's physical and mental status and needs, including appropriate rehabilitation; and (4) is strongly equipped to attend to Sharon's social and emotional needs. Sharon's caretakers described how Thompson has been with Sharon three or more days per week, actively working with her in therapy and daily care. They described Thompson's detailed knowledge of Sharon's condition, changes, and needs. The doctors unanimously testified that their long-term goal for Sharon's recovery is to assist her in returning to life outside an institution. It is undisputed that Thompson is the only person willing or able to care for Sharon outside an institution. In fact, Thompson has built a fully handicap-accessible home near St. Cloud in the hope that Sharon will be able to live there. On the other hand, Sharon's sister testified that none of her relatives is able to care for Sharon at home, and that her parents can no longer take Sharon for overnight visits. Tomberlin testified that she is not willing or able to care for Sharon at home and is in a position only to supervise Sharon's needs in an institution. Sharon's doctors and therapists testified that care for Sharon on an outing and in a home setting could be provided by a person acting alone. While Thompson would certainly need assistance for bathing, therapy, and medical care, the doctors testified that this can be accomplished with the assistance of a home health care organization.

The medical witnesses also testified about Thompson's effectiveness with Sharon's rehabilitation. They all agreed that Sharon can be stubborn and will often refuse to cooperate in therapy. They testified, however, that Thompson is best able to get Sharon motivated to work through the sometimes painful therapy. Moreover, Thompson is oftentimes the only one who can clean Sharon's mouth and teeth, since Sharon is apparently highly sensitive to invasion of her mouth. Oral hygiene is crucial to prevent recurrence of a mouth fungus which can contribute to pain and tooth loss, further inhibiting Sharon's communication skills and her ability to eat solid foods.

Finally, the medical witnesses were asked how Thompson interacted with the staff and whether she was troublesome or overbearing in her demands for Sharon. No witness responded that Thompson caused trouble, but rather each said she is highly cooperative and exceptionally attentive to what treatments and activities are in Sharon's best interests. The court-appointed social worker also testified that Thompson was attentive to Sharon's needs, and would be a forceful advocate for Sharon's rehabilitation.

The trial court concluded that "[c]onstant, long-term medical supervision in a neutral setting, such as a nursing home * * * is the ideal for Sharon's long-term care," and that "Ms. Thompson is incapable of providing, as a single caretaker, the necessary health care to Sharon at Thompson's home in St. Cloud." These conclusions are without evidentiary support and clearly erroneous as they are directly contradicted by the testimony of Sharon's doctors and other care providers. The court is not in a position to make independent medical determinations without support in the record.

3. The Court's Choice of a "Neutral" Guardian

The trial court recognized Thompson and Sharon as a "family of affinity" and acknowledged that Thompson's continued presence in Sharon's life was important. In its guardianship decision, however, the court responded to the Kowalski family's steadfast opposition to Thompson being named guardian. Debra Kowalski testified that her parents would refuse ever to visit Sharon if Thompson is named guardian. The trial court likened the situation to a "family torn asunder into opposing camps," and concluded that a neutral third party was needed as guardian.

The record does not support the trial court's conclusion that choosing a "neutral" third party is now necessary. Thompson testified that she is committed to reaching an accommodation with the Kowalskis whereby they could visit with Sharon in a neutral setting or in their own home. While acknowledging Thompson's demonstrated willingness to facilitate all parties' involvement with Sharon, the trial court failed to address any alternative visitation arrangements for the Kowalskis such as Thompson's suggestion that Tomberlin be a neutral driver for Sharon on regular visits to the Iron Range. Thompson's appointment as guardian would not, of itself, result in the family ceasing to visit Sharon. The Kowalskis are free to visit their daughter if they wish. It is not the court's role to accommodate one side's threatened intransigence, where to do so would deprive the ward of an otherwise suitable and preferred guardian.

The court seized upon Tomberlin as a neutral party in this case. This decision, however, is not supported by sufficient evidence in the record as to either Tomberlin's suitability for guardianship or her neutrality. The record is clear that at all times, the focus of the evidentiary hearing was to evaluate Thompson's qualifications to be guardian, not to evaluate the qualifications of Tomberlin. The medical and therapy staff were not questioned about Tomberlin's interaction with Sharon, her knowledge and current understanding of Sharon's medical and physical needs, or her ability to attend to Sharon's other social and emotional needs. Sharon's current treating physician testified that she had had no interaction with Tomberlin, and she was not asked to evaluate Tomberlin's knowledge of, or interaction with, Sharon. In fact, given that Tomberlin rarely visited Sharon, it is unlikely that these witnesses would have been able to comment knowledgeably on Tomberlin's qualifications.

The trial court's written findings on Tomberlin's qualifications are merely a recitation of the statutory criteria without reference to any evidence presented in court. Given that none of the witnesses except Debra Kowalski and Schroeder were questioned about Tomberlin, there was no substantive basis on which the court could make a reasoned determination that she is superior to Thompson.

There was equally little evidence establishing Tomberlin's neutrality in this case. Tomberlin testified that all her information about Sharon's situation has come directly from the Kowalskis and that she talks with them weekly. Tomberlin lives near the Kowalskis and helped facilitate the appearance at the hearing of Schroeder and Debra Kowalski in opposition to Thompson. Both in her deposition and at the hearing, Tomberlin testified that her first and primary goal as guardian was to relocate Sharon to the Iron Range, close to her family. This testimony undermines the one "qualification" relied on by the trial court in appointing Tomberlin—her role as an impartial mediator.

4. Court-Identified Deficiencies in Appellant's Petition

Part of the court's attempt to find a third party to act as Sharon's guardian apparently stemmed from certain past decisions and actions of the parties. The court found fault with Thompson on several issues the court viewed as contrary to Sharon's best interest. Specifically, the court suggested that Thompson's statement to the family and to the media that she and Sharon are lesbians was an invasion of privacy, perhaps rising to the level of an actionable tort. The court also took issue with Thompson taking Sharon to public events, including some gay and lesbian-oriented gatherings and other community events where Thompson and Sharon were featured guests. Finally, the court concluded that Thompson's solicitation of legal defense funds and her testimony that she had been involved in other relationships since Sharon's accident raised questions of conflicts of interest with Sharon's welfare.

The record does not support the trial court's concern on any of these issues. First, while the extent to which Sharon had publicly acknowledged her sexual preference at the time of the accident is unclear, this is no longer relevant. Since the accident, Sharon's doctors and therapists testified that Sharon has voluntarily told them of her relationship with Thompson. Moreover, Sharon's doctor testified that it was in Sharon's best interest for Thompson to reveal the nature of their relationship promptly after the accident because it is crucial for doctors to understand who their patient was prior to the accident, including that patient's sexuality.

Second, there was no evidence offered at the hearing to suggest that Sharon is harmed or exploited by her attendance at public events. In fact, the court authorized Sharon to travel with Thompson to receive an award at the National Organization for Women's annual convention. A staff person who accompanied Sharon to one of these events testified that Sharon "had a great time" and interacted well with other people. A doctor who observed Sharon at two different events testified that Sharon enjoyed herself and was happy to be in attendance. The only negative testimony about these outings consisted of speculation from Schroeder and Debra Kowalski that they did not think Sharon would enjoy the events, particularly those that were gay and lesbian-oriented in nature. They were, however, never in attendance and had no opportunity to evaluate Sharon's reaction firsthand.

Finally, there is no evidence in the record about a conflict of interest over Thompson's collection of defense funds or her other personal relationships. The evidence showed the money was raised in Thompson's own name to help defray the cost of years of litigation and that none of it was used for her personal expenses. Thompson testified that whatever extra money raised was used to purchase special equipment for Sharon, such as her voice machine, motorized wheelchair, hospital bed, and a special lift for transfers.

Only one doctor was questioned about the issue of Thompson's social life. The doctor routinely deals with families of brain-injured patients, and testified that each family deals with such a crisis in its own way. She said it is not uncommon for spouses to make changes in their personal lives while maintaining their commitment to the injured person. Thompson testified that anyone who is involved in her life understands that she and Sharon are "a package deal," and that nothing would interfere with her commitment to Sharon's well-being. The other witnesses who testified about Thompson's interaction with Sharon over the past seven years could find no reason to question Thompson's commitment to Sharon's best interests....

CONCLUSION

While the trial court has wide discretion in guardianship matters, this discretion is not boundless. The Minnesota guardianship statutes are specific in their requirement that factual findings be made on a guardian's qualifications. The statutes also consistently require the input of the ward where possible. Upon review of the record, it appears the trial court clearly abused its discretion in denying Thompson's petition and naming Tomberlin guardian instead.

All the medical testimony established that Sharon has the capacity reliably to express a preference in this case, and she has clearly chosen to return home with Thompson if possible. This choice is further supported by the fact that Thompson and Sharon are a family of affinity, which ought to be accorded respect. Thompson's suitability for guardianship was overwhelmingly clear from the testimony of Sharon's doctors and caretakers. At the same time, evidence of Tomberlin's qualifications was not in the record. Moreover, Tomberlin's status as a neutral party was undermined by evidence of her close ties to the Kowalskis and her expressed intention to relocate Sharon, contrary to the doctors' recommendations that Sharon have a less-restrictive environment near Thompson.

We reverse the trial court and grant Thompson's petition. While under Minn.Stat. §525.56, subd. 1, a guardian always remains subject to court control, it should be made clear that this court is also reversing specific restrictions on the guardian's decision-making power that might be read into the trial court order. She is free to make whatever decisions she and the doctors feel are necessary to achieve Sharon's best interests, including decisions regarding Sharon's location. Thompson is, however, directed to continue efforts at accommodating visitation between Sharon and the Kowalskis, without unreasonable restrictions....

Notes and Questions

1. The *Kowalski* case presents the situation of a lesbian couple who were not open about their sexuality or the nature of their relationship with other people, including their family members. Consequently, when it became necessary to prove the nature of the relationship in court, solid evidence was lacking. What steps might a couple take to create such evidence? Is it possible to do so without "coming out" to relatives, business associates, or neighbors?

2. Karen's legal battle to gain the right to see Sharon lasted over 8 years. During some of that period, Sharon's father, as guardian, prevented Karen from having any contact with Sharon. Many lawyers advise clients who are in committed same-sex relationships to execute a durable power of attorney for health care (sometimes called a health care proxy) naming the partner as the "attorney-in-fact," who is empowered to make med-

ical decisions for a disabled partner. These durable power of attorney statutes co-exist in a state statutory scheme that continues to authorize a court to appoint a guardian for anyone who is incompetent. In other words, merely having a durable power of attorney will not prevent a court from appointing a guardian for an incapacitated person. What if Sharon had named Karen as her attorney in fact in a valid durable power of attorney for health care? Would that have prevented Sharon's father from asserting his rights over Karen's? What legal issue would need to be resolved to answer this question? See Minn. Stat. §524.5-315(c), which provides: "If a health care directive is in effect, absent an order of the court to the contrary, a health care decision of the guardian takes precedence over that of an agent."

As a matter of policy, once someone is incompetent, should their earlier choices regarding durable powers of attorney (for health care or for financial matters) be irreversible? If you were drafting a power of attorney statute, what provisions would you include to balance the interest of the principal in having the named attorney continue in office despite protests from family members, as against the interest in providing checks on attorneys who might abuse their incapacitated principals?

3. California's domestic partnership legislation, in its early phases, dictated a revision of standard forms used in California for guardian designation purposes, to make clear that same-sex partners can be designated as potential guardians.

D. Litigating for Recognition of Same-Sex Relationships, But Not Claiming Spousal Status

1. Same-sex Partners as "Family"

Braschi v. Stahl Assoc. Co.
543 N.E.2d 49 (N.Y. 1989)

TITONE, Judge.

Appellant, Miguel Braschi, was living with Leslie Blanchard in a rent-controlled apartment located at 405 East 54th Street from the summer of 1975 until Blanchard's death in September of 1986. In November of 1986, respondent, Stahl Associates Company, the owner of the apartment building, served a notice to cure on appellant contending that he was a mere licensee with no right to occupy the apartment since only Blanchard was the tenant of record. In December of 1986 respondent served appellant with a notice to terminate informing appellant that he had one month to vacate the apartment and that, if the apartment was not vacated, respondent would commence summary proceedings to evict him.

Appellant then initiated an action seeking a permanent injunction and a declaration of entitlement to occupy the apartment. After examining the nature of the relationship between the two men, Supreme Court concluded that appellant was a "family member" within the meaning of the regulation and, accordingly, that a preliminary injunction should be issued. The court based the decision on its finding that the long-term interdependent nature of the 10-year relationship between appellant and Blanchard "fulfills any definitional criteria of the term 'family.'" The Appellate Division reversed, concluding that § 2204.6(d) provides noneviction protection only to "family members within traditional, legally recognized familial relationships."

It is fundamental that in construing the words of a statute "[t]he legislative intent is the great and controlling principle." Statutes are ordinarily interpreted so as to avoid objectionable consequences and to prevent hardship or injustice. Hence, where doubt exists as to the meaning of a term, and a choice between two constructions is afforded, the consequences that may result from the different interpretations should be considered. In addition, since rent-control laws are remedial in nature and designed to promote the public good, their provisions should be interpreted broadly to effectuate their purposes. Finally, where a problem as to the meaning of a given term arises, a court's role is not to delve into the minds of legislators, but rather to effectuate the statute by carrying out the purpose of the statute as it is embodied in the words chosen by the Legislature. The present dispute arises because the term "family" is not defined in the rent-control code and the legislative history is devoid of any specific reference to the noneviction provision. All that is known is the legislative purpose underlying the enactment of the rent-control laws as a whole.

Rent control was enacted to address a "serious public emergency" created by "an acute shortage in dwellings," which resulted in "speculative, unwarranted and abnormal increases in rents." These measures were designed to regulate and control the housing market so as to "prevent exactions of unjust, unreasonable and oppressive rents and rental agreements and to forestall profiteering, speculation and other disruptive practices tending to produce threats to the public health * * * [and] to prevent uncertainty, hardship and dislocation."

To accomplish its goals, the Legislature recognized that not only would rents have to be controlled, but that evictions would have to be regulated and controlled as well. Hence, section 2204.6 of the New York City Rent and Eviction Regulations (9 NYCRR 2204.6), which authorizes the issuance of a certificate for the eviction of persons occupying a rent-controlled apartment after the death of the named tenant, provides, in subdivision (d), noneviction protection to those occupants who are either the "surviving spouse of the deceased tenant or some other member of the deceased tenant's family who has been living with the tenant [of record]." The manifest intent of this section is to restrict the landowners' ability to evict a narrow class of occupants other than the tenant of record. The question presented here concerns the scope of the protections provided. Juxtaposed against this intent favoring the protection of tenants, is the over-all objective of a gradual "transition from regulation to a normal market of free bargaining between landlord and tenant."

Emphasizing the latter object, respondent argues that the term "family member" as used in 9 NYCRR 2204.6(d) should be construed, consistent with this State's intestacy laws, to mean relationships of blood, consanguinity and adoption in order to effectuate the over-all goal of orderly succession to real property. Under this interpretation, only those entitled to inherit under the laws of intestacy would be afforded noneviction protection. Further, as did the Appellate Division, respondent relies on our decision in *Matter of Robert Paul P.*, 63 N.Y.2d 233, arguing that since the relationship between appellant and Blanchard has not been accorded legal status by the Legislature, it is not entitled to the protections of section 2204.6(d), which, according to the Appellate Division, applies only to "family members within traditional, legally recognized familial relationships."

Respondent's reliance on *Matter of Robert Paul P.* is misplaced, since that case, which held that one adult cannot adopt another where none of the incidents of a filial relationship is evidenced or even remotely intended, was based solely on the purposes of the adoption laws and has no bearing on the proper interpretation of a provision in the rent-control laws.

We also reject respondent's argument that the purpose of the noneviction provision of the rent-control laws is to control the orderly succession to real property in a manner similar to that which occurs under our State's intestacy laws. The noneviction provision does not concern succession to real property but rather is a means of protecting a certain class of occupants from the sudden loss of their homes. [S]uch a construction would be inconsistent with the purposes of the rent-control system as a whole, since it would afford protection to distant blood relatives who actually had but a superficial relationship with the deceased tenant while denying that protection to unmarried lifetime partners.

Contrary to all of these arguments, we conclude that the term family, as used in 9 NYCRR 2204.6(d), should not be rigidly restricted to those people who have formalized their relationship by obtaining, for instance, a marriage certificate or an adoption order. The intended protection against sudden eviction should not rest on fictitious legal distinctions or genetic history, but instead should find its foundation in the reality of family life. In the context of eviction, a more realistic, and certainly equally valid, view of a family includes two adult lifetime partners whose relationship is long term and characterized by an emotional and financial commitment and interdependence. This view comports both with our society's traditional concept of "family" and with the expectations of individuals who live in such nuclear units.

In fact, Webster's Dictionary defines "family" first as "a group of people united by certain convictions or common affiliation" (Webster's Ninth New Collegiate Dictionary 448 [1984]; see, Ballantine's Law Dictionary 456 [3d ed. 1969] ["family" defined as "(p)rimarily, the collective body of persons who live in one house and under one head or management"]; Black's Law Dictionary 543 [Special Deluxe 5th ed. 1979]). Hence, it is reasonable to conclude that, in using the term "family," the Legislature intended to extend protection to those who reside in households having all of the normal familial characteristics. Appellant Braschi should therefore be afforded the opportunity to prove that he and Blanchard had such a household.

Family members, whether or not related by blood or law, who have always treated the apartment as their family home will be protected against the hardship of eviction following the death of the named tenant, thereby furthering the Legislature's goals of preventing dislocation and preserving family units which might otherwise be broken apart upon eviction. This approach will foster the transition from rent control to rent stabilization by drawing a distinction between those individuals who are, in fact, genuine family members, and those who are mere roommates or newly discovered relatives hoping to inherit the rent-controlled apartment after the existing tenant's death.

The determination as to whether an individual is entitled to noneviction protection should be based upon an objective examination of the relationship of the parties. In making this assessment, the lower courts of this State have looked to a number of factors, including the exclusivity and longevity of the relationship, the level of emotional and financial commitment, the manner in which the parties have conducted their everyday lives and held themselves out to society, and the reliance placed upon one another for daily family services. These factors are most helpful, although it should be emphasized that the presence or absence of one or more of them is not dispositive since it is the totality of the relationship as evidenced by the dedication, caring and self-sacrifice of the parties which should, in the final analysis, control. Appellant's situation provides an example of how the rule should be applied.

Appellant and Blanchard lived together as permanent life partners for more than 10 years. They regarded one another, and were regarded by friends and family, as spouses. The two men's families were aware of the nature of the relationship, and they regularly visited each other's families and attended family functions together, as a couple. Even today, appellant continues to maintain a relationship with Blanchard's niece, who considers him an uncle. In addition to their interwoven social lives, appellant clearly considered the apartment his home. He lists the apartment as his address on his driver's license and passport, and receives all his mail at the apartment address. Moreover, appellant's tenancy was known to the building's superintendent and doormen, who viewed the two men as a couple. Financially, the two men shared all obligations including a household budget. The two were authorized signatories of three safe-deposit boxes, they maintained joint checking and savings accounts, and joint credit cards. In fact, rent was often paid with a check from their joint checking account. Additionally, Blanchard executed a power of attorney in appellant's favor so that appellant could make necessary decisions—financial, medical and personal—for him during his illness. Finally, appellant was the named beneficiary of Blanchard's life insurance policy, as well as the primary legatee and coexecutor of Blanchard's estate. Hence, a court examining these facts could reasonably conclude that these men were much more than mere roommates.

[W]e conclude only that appellant has demonstrated a likelihood of success on the merits, in that he is not excluded, as a matter of law, from seeking noneviction protection. Since all remaining issues are beyond this court's scope of review, we remit this case to the Appellate Division so that it may exercise its discretionary powers in accordance with this decision.

[Concurring Opinion of Judge Bellacosa omitted]

SIMONS, Judge (dissenting).

I would affirm. The plurality has adopted a definition of family which extends the language of the regulation well beyond the implication of the words used in it. In doing so, it has expanded the class indefinitely to include anyone who can satisfy an administrator that he or she had an emotional and financial "commitment" to the statutory tenant. Its interpretation is inconsistent with the legislative scheme underlying rent regulation, goes well beyond the intended purposes of 9 NYCRR 2204.6(d), and produces an unworkable test that is subject to abuse. The concurring opinion fails to address the problem. It merely decides, ipse dixit, that plaintiff should win.

A limited exception to the general rule that rent-controlled properties, when vacated, become subject to rent stabilization provides that: "(d) No occupant of housing accommodations shall be evicted under this section where the occupant is either the surviving spouse of the deceased tenant or some other member of the deceased tenant's family who has been living with the tenant." Occupants who come within the terms of the section obtain a new statutory rent-controlled tenancy. Nowhere in the regulations or in the rent-control statutes is the phrase or the word "family" defined. Notably, however, family is linked with spouse, a word of clearly defined legal content. Thus, one would assume that the draftsman intended family to be given its ordinary and commonly accepted meaning related in some way to customary legal relationships established by birth, marriage or adoption.

Analysis starts with the familiar rule that a validly enacted regulation has "the force and effect of law"; it should be interpreted no differently than a statute. As such, the regulation should not be extended by construction beyond its express terms or the reasonable implications of its language and absent further definition in the regulation or enabling statutes, the words of the section are to be construed according to their ordinary and popular significance.

Central to any interpretation of the regulatory language is a determination of its purpose. There can be little doubt that the purpose of § 2204.6(d) was to create succession rights to a possessory interest in real property where the tenant of record has died or vacated the apartment. It creates a new tenancy for every surviving family member living with decedent at the time of death who then becomes a new statutory tenant until death or until he or she vacates the apartment. The State concerns underlying this provision include the orderly and just succession of property interests (which includes protecting a deceased's spouse and family from loss of their longtime home) and the professed State objective that there be a gradual transition from government regulation to a normal market of free bargaining between landlord and tenant. Those objectives require a weighing of the interests of certain individuals living with the tenant of record at his or her death and the interests of the landlord in regaining possession of its property and rerenting it under the less onerous rent-stabilization laws.

The interests are properly balanced if the regulation's exception is applied by using objectively verifiable relationships based on blood, marriage and adoption, as the State has historically done in the estate succession laws, family court acts and similar legislation. The distinction is warranted because members of families, so defined, assume certain legal obligations to each other and to third persons, such as creditors, which are not imposed on unrelated individuals and this legal interdependency is worthy of consideration in determining which individuals are entitled to succeed to the interest of the statutory tenant in rent-controlled premises. Moreover, such an interpretation promotes certainty and consistency in the law and obviates the need for drawn out hearings and litigation focusing on such intangibles as the strength and duration of the relationship and the extent of the emotional and financial interdependency. So limited, the regulation may be viewed as a tempered response, balancing the rights of landlords with those of the tenant. To come within that protected class, individuals must comply with State laws relating to marriage or adoption. Plaintiff cannot avail himself of these institutions, of course, but that only points up the need for a legislative solution, not a judicial one.

Notes and Questions

1. The *Braschi* case arose in the context of the AIDS epidemic. In New York City, large numbers of gay men were threatened with eviction from rent-regulated apartments when their youthful or middle-aged lovers died. Because the number of apartments covered by the rent stabilization system was ten times as many as the number covered by the rent control system, most of the litigation arose under the rent stabilization code, which included an explicit listing of the categories of persons protected from eviction upon the death of a tenant. The Code, unlike the Rent Control regulations at issue in *Braschi*, did not use the vague term "family." If a case arose after the *Braschi* de-

cision presenting the same facts except that the apartment involved was governed by rent stabilization rather than rent control, how do you think the case would be decided?

2. Four months after the *Braschi* decision was issued, the New York State Division of Housing and Community Renewal proposed amendments to the rent stabilization code and to the rent control regulations, extending protection against eviction when a tenant dies or otherwise permanently vacates an apartment, to all other persons who had resided with the tenant for at least two years (one year in the case of elderly or disabled persons) who met the following qualifications:

> "Any other person residing with the tenant or permanent tenant in the housing accommodation as a primary or principal residence, respectively, who can prove emotional and financial commitment, and interdependence between such person and the tenant or permanent tenant. Although no single factor shall be solely determinative, evidence which is to be considered in determining whether such emotional and financial commitment and interdependence existed, may include without limitation, such factors as listed below. In no event would evidence of a sexual relationship between such persons be required or considered.
>
> (i) longevity of the relationship;
>
> (ii) sharing of or relying upon each other for payment of household or family expenses, and/or other common necessities of life;
>
> (iii) intermingling of finances as evidence by, among other things, joint ownership of bank accounts, personal and real property, credit cards, loan obligations, sharing a household budget for purposes of receiving government benefits, etc.;
>
> (iv) engaging in family-type activities by jointly attending family functions, holidays and celebrations, social and recreational activities, etc.;
>
> (v) formalizing of legal obligations, intentions, and responsibilities to each other by such mean as executing wills naming each other as executor and/or beneficiary, granting each other a power of attorney and/or conferring upon each other authority to make health care decisions each for the other, entering into a personal relationship contract, making a domestic partnership declaration, or serving as a representative payee for the purpose of public benefits, etc.;
>
> (vi) holding themselves out as family members to other family members, friends, members of the community or religious institutions, or society in general, through their words or actions;
>
> (vii) regularly performing family functions, such as caring for each other or each other's extended family members, and/or relying upon each other for daily family services;
>
> (viii) engaging in any other pattern of behavior, agreement, or other action which evidences the intention of creating a long-term, emotionally committed relationship.

See 9 N.Y.C.R.R. sections 2520.6 and 2523.5.

Is this regulation more or less protective than the *Braschi* opinion itself with regard to rent controlled tenants?

2. Quasi-marriage

In a 1995 case involving an unmarried opposite-sex couple, the Supreme Court of Washington crafted a judicial rule recognizing the relationship. If a partner can prove the existence of a "meretricious" relationship, then certain property rights, similar to the rights spouses have in community property, arise. According to the court, a relationship must satisfy three elements to be meretricious: (1) it must be "stable," (2) it must be "marital-like," and (3) the parties must "cohabit with knowledge that a lawful marriage between them does not exist." See *Connell v. Francisco*, 898 P.2d 831 (Wash. 1995). In *Connell*, and subsequent cases, proof of a meretricious relationship meant that all property acquired during the relationship was presumed to be jointly owned and subject to equitable division when the parties separated. Although the presumption of joint ownership can be rebutted, the fact that legal title to the property is in one party's name is not sufficient to rebut the presumption.

In *Vasquez v. Hawthorne*, the question facing the court of appeals was whether the surviving partner in a same-sex couple could claim the rights accorded opposite-sex couples found to be in a meretricious relationship. The intermediate appellate court held that the surviving partner had no property rights, explaining:

> We deduce from *Connell* and its predecessors that a "meretricious relationship" is one where the parties may legally marry. And it is clear that these courts implicitly assumed that a meretricious relationship can only exist between a man and a woman. In Washington, there are statutory limitations on who may marry. We hold that these limitations are relevant in determining whether a relationship is sufficiently "marital-like" to be meretricious. To marry, parties must be over the age of 18 and mentally competent. Further, neither party may be married to another person, the parties must be of the opposite sex, and the parties must not be nearer of kin than second cousins.

994 P.2d 240 at 242–43 (Wash. App. 2000).

Vasquez asked the Supreme Court of Washington to reverse the holding of the court of appeals.

Vasquez v. Hawthorne
33 P.3d 735 (Wash. 2001)

JOHNSON, J.

The issue in this case is whether the facts were sufficient to grant summary judgment based on the equitable doctrine of meretricious relationship. Granting summary judgment for the plaintiff, the trial court held Frank Vasquez (Vasquez) had proved he was involved in a long term, stable, cohabiting relationship with the decedent, Robert Schwerzler (Schwerzler). The trial court further found the property acquired during the relationship was the joint property of Vasquez and Schwerzler, and that it passed to Vasquez upon Schwerzler's death and was not part of the estate. Since Schwerzler died without a will, the trial court drew an analogy to community property laws and the probate statute governing intestate distribution in awarding property. The Court of Appeals reversed, reasoning that because meretricious relationships are marital-like and persons of the same sex cannot be legally married, a meretricious relationship cannot exist between members of the same sex. The Court of Appeals, however, remanded for trial on other equitable theories. We granted review.

We hold the trial court erred in resolving this case on summary judgment. The record on summary judgment is inadequate to reach the legal issue presented. It was further error for the Court of Appeals to reach the merits of the case. We vacate the decision of the Court of Appeals and remand this case to the superior court for trial.

FACTS

Upon Schwerzler's death, Vasquez filed a claim against the estate asserting he and Schwerzler had formed an economic community and he was entitled to an equitable share of the property. Joseph Hawthorne (Hawthorne), who was appointed personal representative of the estate, denied the claim. Vasquez filed suit in superior court, asserting his claim under several equitable theories. Vasquez made a motion for partial summary judgment requesting relief under the meretricious relationship doctrine. To decide the motion, the trial court considered several conflicting affidavits of the parties. The trial court made two rulings relevant to this case. First, the trial court determined Vasquez and Schwerzler had a meretricious relationship and the property acquired during the course of their relationship was presumed jointly owned. Second, the trial court awarded some of the property to Vasquez by analogizing to our probate laws (i.e., community-like property goes to the survivor). Hawthorne appealed. The Court of Appeals reversed and remanded the case for trial on the theories of implied partnership and equitable trust, which had not been decided by the trial court. We granted Vasquez's petition for review.

ANALYSIS

A summary judgment motion can be granted only if the pleadings, affidavits, depositions, and admissions on file demonstrate no genuine issues of material fact, and that the moving party is entitled to judgment as a matter of law. The court must consider all facts submitted and all reasonable inferences from those facts in the light most favorable to the nonmoving party. The motion should be granted only if, from all the evidence, reasonable persons could reach but one conclusion.

The facts of this case are contested through the affidavits of the parties. First, the nature of the relationship between Vasquez and Schwerzler is disputed. Vasquez presents affidavits asserting he and Schwerzler were a same sex couple. The estate offers affidavits contending Vasquez and Schwerzler were not a same sex couple and did not hold themselves out as such. Vasquez offers as proof of their relationship that he and Schwerzler lived together from April 1967 until October 1995, with the exception of two years in the early 1970s during which they lived in different apartments in the same building. The estate counters that no such relationship existed. Although they lived together, Vasquez and Schwerzler did not travel together on vacation and each had his own bedroom.

Similarly, the nature of Vasquez's and Schwerzler's business relationship is disputed. On the one hand, Vasquez contends the couple made their living recycling boxes and bags. Schwerzler managed their financial affairs and any remuneration Vasquez earned was contributed to their economic community. On the other hand, the estate argues that Schwerzler inherited the bag business from his father and any property he owned was derived from either his inherited wealth or through his separate businesses. Schwerzler placed all property acquired during their 28 years together in his own name, including the house he and Vasquez shared, a life insurance policy, two automobiles, and a checking account. The estate argues Vasquez was merely a handyman and any property found in Schwerzler's home should be included in his estate and pass to his legal heirs.

On review, we conclude the trial court did not have sufficient undisputed factual information to resolve this case on its merits. From the affidavits, the trial court could not determine what type of relationship existed between Vasquez and Schwerzler. Nor could it conclude what property acquired during the course of their relationship could be subject to equitable division. Without proof of the facts asserted, it was not possible for the trial court to know the character of the relationship between Schwerzler and Vasquez, the nature and extent of contribution to any property acquired by the parties, and what equitable theories are most appropriate. Therefore, we must remand this case for the trial court to review under the various theories Vasquez asserts.

Vasquez presented claims for equitable relief under several theories, including meretricious relationship, implied partnership, and equitable trust. When equitable claims are brought, the focus remains on the equities involved between the parties. Equitable claims are not dependent on the "legality" of the relationship between the parties, nor are they limited by the gender or sexual orientation of the parties. For example, the use of the term "marital-like" in prior meretricious relationship cases is a mere analogy because defining these relationships as related to marriage would create a de facto common-law marriage, which this court has refused to do. Rather than relying on analogy, equitable claims must be analyzed under the specific facts presented in each case. Even when we recognize "factors" to guide the court's determination of the equitable issues presented, these considerations are not exclusive, but are intended to reach all relevant evidence. In a situation where the relationship between the parties is both complicated and contested, the determination of which equitable theories apply should seldom be decided by the court on summary judgment. In this case, the trial court must weigh the evidence to determine whether Vasquez has established his claim for equitable relief.

Because we remand this case for trial, we need not resolve the evidentiary issues raised by the estate concerning the deadman's statute. Any objection to specific testimony will be resolved at trial.

Conclusion

We vacate the decision of the Court of Appeals, reverse the trial court's granting of the motion for partial summary judgment, and remand this case for trial.

Alexander, C.J. (concurring).

I agree with the majority that we should remand this case to the trial court so that it may consider whether Frank Vasquez can establish any of his claims for relief under the equitable doctrines of implied partnership and equitable trust. I write separately simply to indicate my agreement with Justice Sanders' view that the meretricious relationship doctrine is unavailable to a party who seeks relief when, as is the case here, one party to the alleged meretricious relationship is deceased. I reach that conclusion because the meretricious relationship doctrine is limited in that the trial court is to apply, by analogy, the provisions of [Washington's equitable division at divorce statutes] when it distributes the property of persons who have been living in a "marital-like relationship." Indeed, we developed this equitable doctrine because the legis-

lature has not provided a statutory means of resolving the property distribution issues that arise when unmarried persons, who have lived in a marital-like relationship
and acquire what would have been community property had they been married, separate.

On the other hand, the laws of intestacy, RCW 11.04.015.290, dictate how property
is to be distributed when an individual dies without leaving a will. Accordingly, we have
held that the meretricious relationship doctrine does not apply when a relationship between unmarried cohabitants is terminated by death of one cohabitant. Thus, under the
circumstances of this case, I would hold that the meretricious relationship doctrine is
not an available form of equitable relief. The question of whether the doctrine has application when parties of the same sex separate after having lived together in a long-
term stable relationship, we should leave to another day when that issue is properly before us.

SANDERS, J. (concurring)

For Vasquez to prevail on summary judgment it is necessary to establish, without
material factual dispute, the existence of a meretricious relationship. This requires the
prima facie presence of several factors:

> Relevant factors establishing a meretricious relationship include, but are not
> limited to: continuous cohabitation, duration of the relationship, purpose of
> the relationship, pooling of resources and services for joint projects, and the
> intent of the parties.

I agree with the majority that many of the traditional factors associated with the existence of a meretricious relationship, at least when considered in isolation, are certainly
subject to material factual dispute in the record before us.

However there is one fact, that these individuals are of the same sex, which distinguishes this case from others preceding it. The legal consequence of this undisputed fact
is central to the briefing of the parties as well as amici Northwest Women's Law Center
and Lambda Legal Defense and Education Fund. Moreover, it is that fact which the
Court of Appeals cited as determinative, prompting our review. Therefore the majority
opinion, which avoids meaningful discussion of this issue, provides somewhat less satisfaction than can be obtained from kissing one's sister: the majority reverses the summary judgment in favor of Vasquez, remands for further proceedings consistent with its
opinion, but fails to articulate potentially dispositive legal criteria to aid the trial court
in its task.

As to the merits of the meretricious relationship claim, I can do no better than defer
to the unanimous and thoughtful opinion of the Court of Appeals.

For any claim to be premised upon a meretricious relationship, there must first of
course be such a relationship. Our previous case law, little of which is cited in the majority opinion, makes it abundantly clear that whether even uncontested facts satisfy the
necessary requirements to establish such a relationship is a question of law subject to de
novo review.

The necessary but not sufficient requirement that the cohabitating couple possess the
requisite legal ability to wed is quite pronounced. No case holds that even a cohabiting
heterosexual couple can successfully establish a meretricious relationship where either
lacks the legal entitlement to marry. I therefore posit if that is the requirement for a heterosexual couple, it must equally be the requirement for a homosexual couple....

Notes and Questions

1. Rather than return to court, the parties, Vasquez and Hawthorne, entered into a settlement under which Vasquez was given the right to continue living in the home owned by the deceased until his own death.

2. If a same-sex couple is "breaking up," do you think they can rely on the *Vasquez* opinion to claim the right to equitable division? If so, what exactly would they have to prove in order to qualify as a meretricious relationship? What if one of the partners asserts that, although they have lived together for over 20 years, they have not had a sexual relationship for the past 17 years, did not share the same bedroom, but merely continued to live together out of convenience?

Gormley v. Robertson
83 P.3d 1042 (Wash. App. 2004)

KATO, J.

This appeal involves the division of property after the intimate domestic relationship ended between two single women, Lynn Gormley and Julia Robertson, who had cohabitated for some 10 years. The trial court applied the meretricious relationship doctrine to this same-sex couple in dividing their assets and liabilities. We affirm.

Between July 1988 and August 1998, Ms. Gormley and Dr. Robertson lived together. Both were lieutenant commanders in the Navy when they met. Dr. Robertson is a physician; Ms. Gormley is a nurse and administrator. They began their relationship having nearly equal incomes, but Dr. Robertson earned significantly more by the time it ended. They pooled their resources and acquired property as well as debt. They had a joint banking account that was used to pay all monthly obligations, whether pre-existing or incurred separately or jointly. In 1992, the couple borrowed $20,000 from Ms. Gormley's father. The money was used to consolidate debts, including paying off a debt of Dr. Robertson's that was incurred before their relationship began. The balance at separation was $7,188. The last joint payment on the loan was made on September 17, 1998. In 1993, Ms. Gormley and Dr. Robertson bought a Yakima home that was put only in the doctor's name for convenience and financing. Payments were made from the joint account into which they both deposited their incomes. They used joint funds to improve, decorate, and furnish the home. The net equity in the home at the time of separation was $35,255. They spent at least $38,704 on improvements.

When they separated in 1998, a dispute over property arose. Seeking equitable relief based on constructive trust, implied partnership, joint tenancy, joint venture, conversion, implied contract, and joint acquisition, Ms. Gormley sued Dr. Robertson. Ms. Gormley was later permitted to add partition as another theory of recovery.

Judge F. James Gavin dismissed on summary judgment the implied partnership and joint venture claims. Based on the Court of Appeals decision in *Vasquez v. Hawthorne*, 99 Wash.App. 363, 994 P.2d 240 (2000), Judge Gavin also dismissed any claims based on the theories of marriage and meretricious relationship "because these theories do not apply in Washington to a same sex, life partnership relationship." After the summary judgment order but before trial, our Supreme Court, at 145 Wash.2d 103, 33 P.3d 735 (2001), reversed and vacated the Court of Appeals' decision. After additional briefing, the trial judge, Heather K. Van Nuys, determined she was not bound by Judge Gavin's decision and agreed with Ms. Gormley's position that the meretricious relationship doctrine applied to same-sex relationships.

Dr. Robertson contends the court erred by concluding the meretricious relationship doctrine was applicable to this same-sex couple.

The court's findings of fact are entitled to deference while conclusions of law are reviewed de novo. Here, Dr. Robertson assigns no error to any of the court's findings of fact relating to the factors it considered in determining whether a meretricious relationship existed. They are thus verities on appeal.

In *Connell v. Francisco*, 127 Wash.2d 339, 346, 898 P.2d 831 (1995), the court stated that "[a] meretricious relationship is a stable, marital-like relationship where both parties cohabit with knowledge that a lawful marriage between them does not exist." Non-exclusive factors establishing a meretricious relationship include "continuous cohabitation, duration of the relationship, purpose of the relationship, pooling of resources and services for joint projects, and the intent of the parties."

The trial court made detailed findings of fact reflecting its consideration of these factors. Each weighs in favor of finding a meretricious relationship. Since these findings are unchallenged, the next inquiry is whether the court's conclusion that a meretricious relationship existed is supported by them. *Dumas v. Gagner*, 137 Wash.2d 268, 280, 971 P.2d 17 (1999). Had Ms. Gormley and Dr. Robertson not been a same-sex couple, the trial court could only conclude that a meretricious relationship existed between them. But because they were not, the issue squarely presented, and undecided by our Supreme Court in *Vasquez*, is whether the meretricious relationship doctrine applies to same-sex couples.

Division Two of this court has held that "a same-sex relationship cannot be a meretricious relationship because such persons do not have a 'quasi-marital' relationship." *Vasquez*, 99 Wash.App. at 369, 994 P.2d 240. Because persons of the same sex cannot legally marry, they are "not entitled to the rights and protections of a quasi-marriage, such as community property-like treatment." But it is of no consequence to the cohabitating couple, same-sex or otherwise, whether they can legally marry. Indeed, one of the key elements of a meretricious relationship is knowledge by the partners that a *lawful* marriage between them does not exist.

Moreover, Division Two's reliance on "*Connell* and its predecessors," as indicating that a meretricious relationship can exist only between a man and a woman, is misplaced. *Id.* at 367–68, 994 P.2d 240. Those cases all addressed relationships between men and women simply because same-sex couples were not involved. Relying on this historical perspective not only ignores the present, but also makes too much of the past.

In refusing to find a meretricious relationship, Division Two also stated: "We find no legal basis for judicially extending the rights and protections of marriage to same-sex relationships. Such an extension of the law is for the Legislature to decide, not the courts." *Vasquez*, 99 Wash.App. at 368–69, 994 P.2d 240.

Whether same-sex couples can legally marry is for the legislature to decide. But the rule that courts must "'examine the [meretricious] relationship and the property accumulations and make a just and equitable disposition of the property'" is a judicial, not a legislative, extension of the rights and protections of marriage to intimate, unmarried cohabitants. *See In re Marriage of Lindsey*, 101 Wash.2d 299, 304, 678 P.2d 328 (1984) (quoting *Latham v. Hennessey*, 87 Wash.2d 550, 554, 554 P.2d 1057 (1976)); *Vasquez*,

145 Wash.2d at 109, 33 P.3d 735 (Alexander, C.J., concurring). We hold that the meretricious relationship doctrine should be extended to same-sex couples. The trial court is affirmed.

BROWN, C.J. (concurring).

I disagree with the meretricious relationship rationale as the basis for the majority's decision. This case is best viewed as a property dispute filed as a civil suit, which it was, and decided in equity, not a domestic relations case. The parties were involved in a conceded 10-year, same-sex cohabitation relationship. With compassion for the parties and with the respect and dignity deserved by and accorded to all persons coming to courts for judicial dispute resolution, our duty remains to competently apply existing law to the facts presented and not venture into policy making best left to the legislature. In my view, based upon existing law, we should affirm based solely upon the facts and resulting equities between the parties, not the legal status of their relationship.

Our Supreme Court, *Vasquez v. Hawthorne*, 145 Wash.2d 103, 107, 33 P.3d 735 (2001) (*Vasquez* II), held the court in *Vasquez v. Hawthorne*, 99 Wash.App. 363, 994 P.2d 240 (2000) (*Vasquez* I) erred in reaching the merits of deciding whether a meretricious relationship existed in a same-sex couple context. But, the *Vasquez* II majority did not approve or disapprove the meretricious relationship rationale of *Vasquez* I. It left that decision for another time. For now, I would follow the existing guidance from *Vasquez* II, use a fact-equity analysis, and reject the meretricious relationship rationale for same-sex couples.

The *Vasquez* I court extensively analyzed the history of the meretricious relationship doctrine before deducing that a meretricious relationship is one where the parties can legally marry. *Vasquez* I, 99 Wash.App. at 367, 994 P.2d 240. Our legislature has defined a marriage as a civil union between a man and woman. RCW 26.04.010(1). The *Vasquez* I court held a meretricious relationship is a "quasi-marital" relationship; as such "we accord some of the protections of marriages and community property law." *Vasquez* I, 99 Wash.App. at 368, 994 P.2d 240. RCW 26.16.030 clearly limits the application of community property laws to opposite-sex relationships. No precedent exists for applying marital concepts, either rights or protections, to same-sex relationships. *Id.* "Such an extension of the law is for the Legislature to decide, not the courts." *Id.* at 369, 994 P.2d 240.

Here, Judge F. James Gavin summarily, and in my view correctly, rejected Ms. Gormley's meretricious relationship theories based upon the reasoning of *Vasquez* I. Judge Heather K. Van Nuys, the trial judge, incorrectly interpreted *Vasquez* II as giving her the authority to ignore Judge Gavin's ruling before she decided a meretricious relationship can and did exist for this same-sex couple.

Significantly, the *Vasquez* II court vacated the court of appeals decision, but also reversed the trial court, concluding "the trial court did not have sufficient undisputed factual information to resolve this case on its merits." *Vasquez* II, 145 Wash.2d at 107, 33 P.3d 735. However, the Supreme Court provided specific, pertinent guidance for us now:

> When equitable claims are brought, the focus remains on the equities involved between the parties. Equitable claims are not dependent on the 'legality' of the relationship between the parties, nor are they limited by the gender or sexual orientation of the parties. For example, the use of the term 'marital-like' in

prior meretricious relationship cases is a mere analogy because defining these relationships as related to marriage would create a de facto common-law marriage, which this court has refused to do. *In re Marriage of Pennington*, 142 Wash.2d 592, 601, 14 P.3d 764 (2000). Rather than relying on analogy, equitable claims must be analyzed under the specific facts presented in each case. Even when we recognize 'factors' to guide the court's determination of the equitable issues presented, these considerations are not exclusive, but are intended to reach all relevant evidence.

Id. at 107–8, 33 P.3d 735.

Chief Justice Alexander, concurring, noted the question of whether the meretricious relationship doctrine applies after a same-sex couple separates should be left "to another day." Justice Sanders, in his concurrence, agreed with the *Vasquez* I rationale regarding the merits of the meretricious relationship claim and observed the majority "fails to articulate potentially dispositive legal criteria" on the subject.

Considering the *Vasquez* II majority guidance, together with the concurrences noted, and the persuasive reasoning of *Vasquez* I, I would hold the meretricious relationship doctrine does not directly or by analogy apply to same-sex couples. Thus, the other phrases coined by the trial court, "intimate domestic union" or "intimate domestic partnership," to the extent they are meant by analogy to embody quasi-marital relationships, are equally inapt.

Although I reject an application of the meretricious relationship rationale here, the trial court properly acted within its fact-finding discretion and inherent equitable power by alternatively focusing upon the equities between the parties when resolving this civil property dispute; therefore, it did not err in this respect. Accordingly, I concur in the result.

3. Creating a Family Name

In re Bicknell
771 N.E.2d 846 (Ohio 2002)

Alice Robie Resnick, J.

In January 2000, appellants, Jennifer Lane Bicknell and Belinda Lou Priddy, filed individual applications with the Butler County Probate Court to have their surnames changed to "Rylen," which is a combination of letters from both of their last names. The reason given on both applications was: "Applicant desires to legally have the same last name as her long-term partner of nine (9) years. This name change will only add to the level of commitment they have for each other, as well as that of their unborn child. Also, so that this tender and new family will have a unified name in the eyes of the law." At the time of the hearing on the applications, Ms. Bicknell was pregnant by artificial insemination.

A magistrate issued a decision denying both applications, writing, "To grant their petitions would be contrary to the public good, contrary to encoded public policy, and contrary to natural law." Although the probate court rejected the magistrate's conclusions of law, it also denied the applications, concluding, "It is not reasonable and proper to change the surnames of cohabiting couples, because to do so would be to give an aura of propriety and official sanction to their cohabitation and would under-mine the public policy of this state which promotes legal marriages and withholds offi-cial sanction from non-marital cohabitation."

The court of appeals affirmed the decision of the trial court, holding: "We find that there is support for the trial court's determination that Ohio law favors solem-nized marriages and that cohabitation contravenes this policy. Accordingly, the trial court did not abuse its discretion by finding that court sanctioning of the use of the same surname by two unmarried cohabitants is against Ohio's public policy promot-ing marriage." The cause is now before this court on the allowance of a discretionary appeal.

This is a case of first impression in Ohio, and in spite of the unique circumstances involved, the only issue before us is whether the appellants' request to change their sur-names is reasonable and proper under R.C. 2717.01. We hold today that it is and there-fore reverse the judgment of the court of appeals.

R.C. 2717.01(A) states:

> A person desiring a change of name may file an application in the probate court of the county in which the person resides. The application shall set forth that the applicant has been a bona fide resident of that county for at least one year prior to the filing of the application, the cause for which the change of name is sought, and the requested new name. ***

> Upon proof that proper notice was given and that the facts set forth in the ap-plication show *reasonable and proper cause* for changing the name of the appli-cant, the court may order the change of name. (Emphasis added.)

Moreover, in *Pierce v. Brushart* (1950), 402, 92 N.E.2d 4, 8, this court noted, "It is universally recognized that a person may adopt any name he may choose so long as such change is not made for fraudulent purposes." Thus, we must determine whether appel-lants meet the requirements of R.C. 2717.01(A).

It is undisputed that appellants filed the applications in the Butler County Probate Court, that they lived in Butler County for more than one year, that they stated the rea-son for which the name changes were sought, and that they identified the requested new name. Thus, this court must decide whether appellants show reasonable and proper cause for changing their names.

Other jurisdictions have considered this issue. In *In re Bacharach* (2001), 344 N.J.Super. 126, 780 A.2d 579, the Superior Court of New Jersey, Appellate Division, was asked to consider whether the plaintiff would be able to adopt a hyphenated surname to include the name of her same-sex partner. The court began its analysis by observing, "It has been held that names should not be changed for trivial, capricious, or vainglorious reasons, that a change of name will be refused if the court entertains a serious doubt as to the propriety of granting it. * * * [M]oreover, a judge may deny such requests if it is based upon an 'unworthy motive,' the possibility of fraud on the public, fraudulent or criminal purposes or that there is an overriding social policy, which militates against the change * * *." Id. at 129, 780 A.2d 579.

The court reversed the judgment of the lower court, holding, "There is no fraudu-lent or criminal purpose or any other substantial reason to deny appellant the relief she seeks. We hold that the denial of her request was a misapplication of judicial discretion, and we direct that the hearing judge execute an order granting the application * * *." Id. at 136, 780 A.2d 579. The court further stated:

We underscore that the hearing judge did not base his decision on any disapproval of appellant or her same-sex relationship. Rather he found that there was an inappropriate purpose to the application and a potential fraud upon the public because the name change might give the misperception that New Jersey recognizes same-sex marriages as lawful.

This concern is misconceived. Appellant and her partner can exchange rings, proclaim devotion in a public or private ceremony, call their relationship a marriage, use the same surname, adopt and rear children. All these actions may be taken in full public view. None are offensive to the laws or stated policies of this state. To deny the applicant a statutory change of a portion of her surname to that of her same-sex partner on the hypothesis that some members of the public may be misled about the legal status of same-sex marriages in New Jersey is far-fetched and inherently discriminatory."

Id., 344 N.J.Super. at 135–36, 780 A.2d 579.

In the case at bar, appellants' only stated purpose for changing their names is to carry the same surname to demonstrate their level of commitment to each other and to the children that they planned to have. Both acknowledge that same-sex marriages are illegal in Ohio, and it is not their intention to have this court validate a same-sex union by virtue of granting the name-change applications. Any discussion, then, on the sanctity of marriage, the well-being of society, or the state's endorsement of nonmarital cohabitation is wholly inappropriate and without any basis in law or fact.

In summarizing her rationale for the name change, Ms. Bicknell stated, "[W]e just want to share a name so that when we do have kids, when this child is born seven or eight months from now, the three of us will share the same name and we'll be a family."

Similarly, in *In re Application of Ferner* (1996), 295 N.J.Super. 409, 415, 685 A.2d 78, in which the applicants petitioned to assume a single name, the Superior Court of New Jersey stated that "a properly presented request should not be denied because of an individual judge's preferences or speculation about whether the applicant has made a wise decision."

Finally, in *In re McIntyre* (1998), 552 Pa. 324, 330, 715 A.2d 400, the Supreme Court of Pennsylvania reasoned, "As the name change statute and the procedures thereunder indicate a liberal policy regarding change of name requests, * * * we see no reason to impose restrictions which the legislature has not."

It is clear that appellants have no criminal or fraudulent purpose for wanting to change their names. They are not attempting to evade creditors or to create the appearance of a state-sanctioned marriage. Accordingly, we hold that appellants' name change applications are reasonable and proper under R.C. 2717.01(A) and, therefore, reverse the judgment of the court of appeals. Judgment reversed.

LUNDBERG STRATTON, J., dissenting.

By our decision today, we have judicially read into a statute an interpretation that I do not believe the General Assembly intended. Allowing unmarried couples, whether homosexual or heterosexual, to legally assume the same last name with the stamp of state approval is directly contrary to the state's position against same-sex and common-law marriages, neither of which Ohio recognizes. This is a social policy decision that should clearly be made by the General Assembly after full public debate and discourse, not by judicial legislation. Therefore, I respectfully dissent and would affirm the judgment of the court of appeals.

Note

Ohio is not the only state to have struggled with requests by unmarried couples to share the same last name. See, e.g., *In re Nadine Ann Miller*, 824 A.2d 1207 (Pa. Super. 2003) (reversing trial court's denial of name change petition in fact situation similar to *Bicknell*) and *In re Application of Gena Michele Daniels*, 773 N.Y.S.2d 220 (Civ. Ct., City of N.Y. 2003)(holding that absent intent to defraud, applicant could change last name to that of her partner).

E. Relationship by Contract

When two people marry, they enter into a relationship that has legal consequences. Although there is no official civil "marriage contract" as such, being married is very like entering into a contractual relationship in which the state has provided all the terms. In effect, the "marriage contract" provides a set of default rules for married couples. Sometimes one can opt out of the state's terms, sometimes one cannot. If the couple does not opt out of the intestacy statutes by executing wills, for example, the default rule will control and spouses will inherit from each other under the intestacy provisions of state law. But if one spouse opts out of the intestacy statutes by executing a will that totally disinherits a spouse, most states have default rules that will protect the disinherited spouse from complete loss. See *Estate of Hall*, *supra* (denying the elective share to a same-sex cohabitant). Similarly, when spouses divorce, absent a prenuptial agreement, the state's default rules will determine such issues as division of property.

Unmarried couples experience the same changes in their relationships as married couples do. One partner might die unexpectedly, or become disabled. Alternatively, the relationship might turn sour and the partners might decide it is best for them to terminate their cohabitation. In that case, the single household that they shared as one economic unit will need to be transformed into two economic units. Issues of property ownership or use, and issues of child custody (covered in the following chapter) will arise in the same manner that such issues arise in the case of divorce. But for unmarried couples, the state provides no useful default rules.

To deal with these issues responsibly, committed couples are advised to execute legal documents in the form of contracts, directives, and wills that will take care of the tragedies of death, disability, and "divorce." A typical set of documents for a couple who wants to create a committed relationship by contract include: (1) A relationship, or living together, agreement, (2) A will, or a revocable living trust and pourover will, (3) A durable power of attorney for health care (health care proxy), (4) A durable general power of attorney (for financial arrangements and property management), (5) Burial directives. In addition, some partners, when it is possible to do so under state law, nominate each other as a "standby" guardian or conservator. The advance nomination helps to ensure that the partner will be named as guardian of the person or conservator of the property if the nominator becomes disabled. When there are children living in the household, additional documents may be needed to ensure that each partner has a legal right to make decisions regarding the child.

Even though these documents may be executed by the parties, there is no guarantee that third parties will honor the documents. Most states do not have statutory remedies for failure to honor powers of attorney. But see Florida Stat. s. 709.08(11), providing:

> In any action under this section, including, but not limited to, the unreasonable refusal of the third party to allow an attorney in fact to act pursuant to the power, and challenges to the proper exercise if authority by the attorney in fact, the prevailing party is entitled to damages and costs, including reasonable attorney's fees.

Written contracts dealing with property ownership and support are generally enforceable under contract law. The same is true for express oral contracts, which are generally enforceable, subject to the Statute of Frauds. Some states will also enforce implied contracts. Unmarried couples have often had to contend with the common law rule that a court could refuse to enforce the terms of a contract if the terms violated clearly established public policy. Contracts that were the product of a meretricious relationship have sometimes been held unenforceable, because cohabitation outside the bonds of marriage was against public policy. These cases generally involved opposite-sex couples.

In most situations, cohabitants did not bother to execute written contracts spelling out their understanding of the relationship. When a long-term cohabitation ended, the less powerful and poorer partner would have a difficult time proving any right to continued support, or to property rights, including the right to remain in the homestead if it was owned by the other partner. In 1976, the California Supreme Court, handed down a significant opinion that instituted a sea change in the enforcement of contracts between unmarried cohabitants. The case stemmed from a claim by Michelle Triola Marvin against the actor Lee Marvin.

Marvin v. Marvin
557 P.2d 106 (Cal. 1976)

TOBRINER, Justice.

During the past 15 years, there has been a substantial increase in the number of couples living together without marrying.[1] Such nonmarital relationships lead to legal controversy when one partner dies or the couple separates. Courts of Appeal, faced with the task of determining property rights in such cases, have arrived at conflicting positions: two cases have held that the Family Law Act requires division of the property according to community property principles, and one decision has rejected that holding. We take this opportunity to resolve that controversy and to declare the principles which should govern distribution of property acquired in a nonmarital relationship.

We conclude: (1) The provisions of the Family Law Act do not govern the distribution of property acquired during a nonmarital relationship; such a relationship remains subject solely to judicial decision. (2) The courts should enforce express contracts between nonmarital partners except to the extent that the contract is explicitly founded on the consideration of meretricious sexual services. (3) In the absence of an express con-

---

1. "The 1970 census figures indicate that today perhaps eight times as many couples are living together without being married as cohabited ten years ago." (Comment, In re Cary: A Judicial Recognition of Illicit Cohabitation (1974) 25 Hastings L.J. 1226.)

tract, the courts should inquire into the conduct of the parties to determine whether that conduct demonstrates an implied contract, agreement of partnership or joint venture, or some other tacit understanding between the parties. The courts may also employ the doctrine of quantum meruit, or equitable remedies such as constructive or resulting trusts, when warranted by the facts of the case.

In the instant case plaintiff and defendant lived together for seven years without marrying; all property acquired during this period was taken in defendant's name. When plaintiff sued to enforce a contract under which she was entitled to half the property and to support payments, the trial court granted judgment on the pleadings for defendant, thus leaving him with all property accumulated by the couple during their relationship. Since the trial court denied plaintiff a trial on the merits of her claim, its decision conflicts with the principles stated above, and must be reversed. * * *

Note

On remand, the trial court ordered Lee to pay Michelle $104,000, which the court determined she needed as a form of rehabilitative support. Lee appealed and the appellate court reversed the trial court, explaining that it had not found for Michelle on any of the grounds approved by the Supreme Court, i.e., implied contract, quantum meruit, or any other equitable theory. The appellate court noted that Lee had supported Michelle and she had benefited from the relationship so that there was no resulting unjust enrichment to support the award of damages. *Marvin v. Marvin*, 176 Cal. Rptr. 555 (Cal. App. 1981).

Hewitt v. Hewitt
394 N.E.2d 1204 (Ill. 1979)

UNDERWOOD, Justice:

The issue in this case is whether plaintiff Victoria Hewitt, whose complaint alleges she lived with defendant Robert Hewitt from 1960 to 1975 in an unmarried, family-like relationship to which three children have been born, may recover from him "an equal share of the profits and properties accumulated by the parties" during that period. * * *

Plaintiff [alleged] the following bases for her claim: (1) that because defendant promised he would "share his life, his future, his earnings and his property" with her and all of defendant's property resulted from the parties' joint endeavors, plaintiff is entitled in equity to a one-half share; (2) that the conduct of the parties evinced an implied contract entitling plaintiff to one-half the property accumulated during their "family relationship"; (3) that because defendant fraudulently assured plaintiff she was his wife in order to secure her services, although he knew they were not legally married, defendant's property should be impressed with a trust for plaintiff's benefit; (4) that because plaintiff has relied to her detriment on defendant's promises and devoted her entire life to him, defendant has been unjustly enriched.

The factual background alleged or testified to is that in June 1960, when she and defendant were students at Grinnell College in Iowa, plaintiff became pregnant; that defendant thereafter told her that they were husband and wife and would live as such, no formal ceremony being necessary, and that he would "share his life, his future, his earnings and his property" with her; that the parties immediately announced to their respective parents that they were married and thereafter held themselves out as husband and wife; that in reliance on defendant's promises she devoted her efforts to his professional education and his establishment in the practice of pedodontia, obtaining financial assistance from her parents for this purpose; that she assisted defendant in his career with her own special skills and although she was given payroll checks for these services she placed them in a common fund; that defendant, who was without funds at the time of the marriage, as a result of her efforts now earns over $80,000 a year and has accumulated large amounts of property, owned either jointly with her or separately; that she has given him every assistance a wife and mother could give, including social activities designed to enhance his social and professional reputation.

The...complaint was...dismissed, the trial court finding that Illinois law and public policy require such claims to be based on a valid marriage. The appellate court reversed, stating that because the parties had outwardly lived a conventional married life, plaintiff's conduct had not "so affronted public policy that she should be denied any and all relief"...and that plaintiff's complaint stated a cause of action on an express oral contract. We granted leave to appeal. Defendant apparently does not contest his obligation to support the children, and that question is not before us.

The appellate court, in reversing, gave considerable weight to the fact that the parties had held themselves out as husband and wife for over 15 years. The court noted that they lived "a most conventional, respectable and ordinary family life"...that did not openly flout accepted standards, the "single flaw" being the lack of a valid marriage.... Noting that the Illinois Marriage and Dissolution of Marriage Act does not prohibit nonmarital cohabitation and that the Criminal Code of 1961 makes fornication an offense only if the behavior is open and notorious, the appellate court concluded that plaintiff should not be denied relief on public policy grounds.

In finding that plaintiff's complaint stated a cause of action on an express oral contract, the appellate court adopted the reasoning of the California Supreme Court in the widely publicized case of *Marvin v. Marvin* (1976). In *Marvin*, Michelle Triola and defendant Lee Marvin lived together for 7 years pursuant to an alleged oral agreement that while "the parties lived together they would combine their efforts and earnings and would share equally any and all property accumulated as a result of their efforts whether individual or combined." In her complaint she alleged that, in reliance on this agreement, she gave up her career as a singer to devote herself full time to defendant as "companion, homemaker, housekeeper and cook." In resolving her claim for one-half the property accumulated in defendant's name during that period the California court held that "The courts should enforce express contracts between nonmarital partners except to the extent that the contract is explicitly founded on the consideration of meretricious sexual services" and that "In the absence of an express contract, the courts should inquire into the conduct of the parties to determine whether that conduct demonstrates an implied contract, agreement of partnership or joint venture, or some other tacit understanding between the parties. The courts may also employ the doctrine of quantum meruit, or equitable remedies such as constructive or resulting trusts, when warranted by the facts of the case." The court reached its conclusions because:

> "In summary, we believe that the prevalence of nonmarital relationships in modern society and the social acceptance of them, marks this as a time when

our courts should by no means apply the doctrine of the unlawfulness of the so-called meretricious relationship to the instant case. * * *

The mores of the society have indeed changed so radically in regard to cohabitation that we cannot impose a standard based on alleged moral considerations that have apparently been so widely abandoned by so many."

It is apparent that the *Marvin* court adopted a pure contract theory, under which, if the intent of the parties and the terms of their agreement are proved, the pseudo-conventional family relationship which impressed the appellate court here is irrelevant; recovery may be had unless the implicit sexual relationship is made the explicit consideration for the agreement. In contrast, the appellate court here, as we understand its opinion, would apply contract principles only in a setting where the relationship of the parties outwardly resembled that of a traditional family. It seems apparent that the plaintiff in *Marvin* would not have been entitled to recover in our appellate court because of the absence of that outwardly appearing conventional family relationship.

The issue of whether property rights accrue to unmarried cohabitants can not, however, be regarded realistically as merely a problem in the law of express contracts. Plaintiff argues that because her action is founded on an express contract, her recovery would in no way imply that unmarried cohabitants acquire property rights merely by cohabitation and subsequent separation. However, the *Marvin* court expressly recognized and the appellate court here seems to agree that if common law principles of express contract govern express agreements between unmarried cohabitants, common law principles of implied contract, equitable relief and constructive trust must govern the parties' relations in the absence of such an agreement. In all probability the latter case will be much the more common, since it is unlikely that most couples who live together will enter into express agreements regulating their property rights. The increasing incidence of nonmarital cohabitation referred to in *Marvin* and the variety of legal remedies therein sanctioned seem certain to result in substantial amounts of litigation, in which, whatever the allegations regarding an oral contract, the proof will necessarily involve details of the parties' living arrangements.

Apart, however, from the appellate court's reliance upon *Marvin* to reach what appears to us to be a significantly different result, we believe there is a more fundamental problem. We are aware, of course, of the increasing judicial attention given the individual claims of unmarried cohabitants to jointly accumulated property, and the fact that the majority of courts considering the question have recognized an equitable or contractual basis for implementing the reasonable expectations of the parties unless sexual services were the explicit consideration. The issue of unmarried cohabitants' mutual property rights, however, as we earlier noted, cannot appropriately be characterized solely in terms of contract law, nor is it limited to considerations of equity or fairness as between the parties to such relationships. There are major public policy questions involved in determining whether, under what circumstances, and to what extent it is desirable to accord some type of legal status to claims arising from such relationships. Of substantially greater importance than the rights of the immediate parties is the impact of such recognition upon our society and the institution of marriage. Will the fact that legal rights closely resembling those arising from conventional marriages can be acquired by those who deliberately choose to enter into what have heretofore been commonly referred to as "illicit" or "meretricious" relationships encourage formation of such relationships and weaken marriage as the foundation of our family-based society? In the event of death shall the survivor have the status of a surviving spouse for purposes of inheritance, wrongful death actions, workmen's compensation, etc.? And still more importantly: what of the children born of such relationships? What are their support and inheritance rights and by what standards are custody questions resolved? What of the sociological and psychological effects upon them of that type of environment? Does not the recognition of legally enforceable property and custody rights emanating from nonmarital cohabitation in practical effect equate with the legalization of common law marriage at least in the circumstances of this case? And, in summary, have the increasing numbers of unmarried cohabitants and changing mores of our society...reached the point at which the general welfare of the citizens of this State is best served by a return to something resembling the judicially created common law marriage our legislature outlawed in 1905?

Illinois' public policy regarding agreements such as the one alleged here was implemented long ago in *Wallace v. Rappleye* (1882), 103 Ill. 229, 249, where this court said: "An agreement in consideration of future illicit cohabitation between the plaintiffs is void." This is the traditional rule, in force until recent years in all jurisdictions....Section 589 of the Restatement of Contracts (1932) states, "A bargain in whole or in part for or in consideration of illicit sexual intercourse or of a promise thereof is illegal." See also 6A Corbin, Contracts sec. 1476 (1962), and cases cited therein.

It is true, of course, that cohabitation by the parties may not prevent them from forming valid contracts about independent matters, for which it is said the sexual relations do not form part of the consideration. (Restatement of Contracts secs. 589, 597 (1932); 6A Corbin, Contracts sec. 1476 (1962).) Those courts which allow recovery generally have relied on this principle to reduce the scope of the rule of illegality. Thus, California courts long prior to *Marvin* held that an express agreement to pool earnings is supported by independent consideration and is not invalidated by cohabitation of the parties, the agreements being regarded as simultaneous but separate. More recently, several courts have reasoned that the rendition of housekeeping and homemaking services such as plaintiff alleges here could be regarded as the consideration for a separate contract between the parties, severable from the illegal contract founded on sexual relations.

The real thrust of plaintiff's argument here is that we should abandon the rule of illegality because of certain changes in societal norms and attitudes. It is urged that social mores have changed radically in recent years, rendering this principle of law archaic. It is said that because there are so many unmarried cohabitants today the courts must confer a legal status on such relationships. If this is to be the result, however, it would seem more candid to acknowledge the return of varying forms of common law marriage than to continue displaying the naivete we believe involved in the assertion that there are involved in these relationships contracts separate and independent from the sexual activity, and the assumption that those contracts would have been entered into or would continue without that activity....

In our judgment the fault in the appellate court holding in this case is that its practical effect is the reinstatement of common law marriage, as we earlier indicated, for there is no doubt that the alleged facts would, if proved, establish such a marriage under our pre-1905 law. "(T)he effect of these cases is to reinstitute common-law marriage in California after it has been abolished by the legislature." (Clark, The New Marriage, Williamette L.J. 441, 449 (1976).) "(*Hewitt*) is, if not a direct resurrection of common-law marriage contract principles, at least a large step in that direction." Reiland, *Hewitt v. Hewitt*: Middle America, *Marvin* and Common-Law Marriage, 60 Chi.B.Rec. 84, 88–90 (1978).

We do not intend to suggest that plaintiff's claims are totally devoid of merit. Rather, we believe that our statement in *Mogged v. Mogged* (1973), 55 Ill.2d 221, 225, 302

N.E.2d 293, 295, made in deciding whether to abolish a judicially created defense to divorce, is appropriate here:

> "Whether or not the defense of recrimination should be abolished or modified in Illinois is a question involving complex public-policy considerations as to which compelling arguments may be made on both sides. For the reasons stated hereafter, we believe that these questions are appropriately within the province of the legislature, and that, if there is to be a change in the law of this State on this matter, it is for the legislature and not the courts to bring about that change."

We accordingly hold that plaintiff's claims are unenforceable for the reason that they contravene the public policy, implicit in the statutory scheme of the Illinois Marriage and Dissolution of Marriage Act, disfavoring the grant of mutually enforceable property rights to knowingly unmarried cohabitants. The judgment of the appellate court is reversed and the judgment of the circuit court of Champaign County is affirmed.

Notes and Questions

1. Ms. Hewitt originally filed for a divorce, but when Mr. Hewitt averred they had never gone through a marriage ceremony or obtained a license, she changed her pleadings. While it is true that Illinois has abolished common law marriages, Iowa has not. '[W]here the parties reside in another state at the time of contracting a common law marriage that was valid in that state, such marriage will be considered valid here upon their removal to Illinois." *Peirce v. Peirce*, 379 Ill. 185, 39 N.E.2d 990 (Ill. 1942). Is it possible that Ms. Hewitt was too quick to change her claim to one based on *Marvin* rather than developing the common law marriage argument? A common law marriage exists if the parties agreed to be husband and wife and held themselves out to others as husband and wife. The facts suggest that Ms. Hewitt could have met the test for a common law marriage under Iowa law.

2. Should the court's reasoning apply to a same-sex couple who have agreed to live as though they were married and share income and property? Why or why not?

3. New York courts will enforce express contracts between unmarried cohabitants, but view claims based on implied contract as violations of public policy. See *Soderholm v. Kosty*, 676 N.Y.S.2d 850 (Justice Court, Village of Horseheads 1998)("Such a claim in the surrounding of a cohabiting relationship is not only against New York's public policy (as evidenced by the 1933 abolition of common-law marriages) but runs in to too great a risk of error for a court, in hindsight, ... to sort out the intentions of the parties and to fix jural significance to conduct carried out within an essentially private and generally noncontractual relationship ..., " citing *Morone v. Morone*, 413 N.E.2d 1154 (N.Y. 1980).

Posik v. Layton
695 So.2d 759 (Fla. App. 1997)
review denied, 699 So.2d 1374 (Fla. 1997)

HARRIS, Judge.

Emma Posik and Nancy L.R. Layton were close friends and more. They entered into a support agreement much like a prenuptial agreement. The trial court found that the agreement was unenforceable because of waiver. We reverse.

Nancy Layton was a doctor practicing at the Halifax Hospital in Volusia County and Emma Posik was a nurse working at the same facility when Dr. Layton decided to remove her practice to Brevard County. In order to induce Ms. Posik to give up her job and sell her home in Volusia County, to accompany her to Brevard County, and to reside with her "for the remainder of Emma Posik's life to maintain and care for the home," Dr. Layton agreed that she would provide essentially all of the support for the two, would make a will leaving her entire estate to Ms. Posik, and would "maintain bank accounts and other investments which constitute non-probatable assets in Emma Posik's name to the extent of 100% of her entire non-probatable assets." Also, as part of the agreement, Ms. Posik agreed to loan Dr. Layton $20,000 which was evidenced by a note. The agreement provided that Ms. Posik could cease residing with Dr. Layton if Layton failed to provide adequate support, if she requested in writing that Ms. Posik leave for any reason, if she brought a third person into the home for a period greater than four weeks without Ms. Posik's consent, or if her abuse, harassment or abnormal behavior made Ms. Posik's continued residence intolerable. In any such event, Dr. Layton agreed to pay as liquidated damages the sum of $2,500 per month for the remainder of Ms. Posik's life.

It is apparent that Ms. Posik required this agreement as a condition of accompanying Dr. Layton to Brevard. The agreement was drawn by a lawyer and properly witnessed. Ms. Posik, fifty-five years old at the time of the agreement, testified that she required the agreement because she feared that Dr. Layton might become interested in a younger companion. Her fears were well founded. Some four years after the parties moved to Brevard County and without Ms. Posik's consent, Dr. Layton announced that she wished to move another woman into the house. When Ms. Posik expressed strong displeasure with this idea, Dr. Layton moved out and took up residence with the other woman.

Dr. Layton served a three-day eviction notice on Ms. Posik. Ms. Posik later moved from the home and sued to enforce the terms of the agreement and to collect on the note evidencing the loan made in conjunction with the agreement. Dr. Layton defended on the basis that Ms. Posik first breached the agreement. Dr. Layton counterclaimed for a declaratory judgment as to whether the liquidated damages portion of the agreement was enforceable.

The trial judge found that because Ms. Posik's economic losses were reasonably ascertainable as to her employment and relocation costs, the $2,500 a month payment upon breach amounted to a penalty and was therefore unenforceable. The court further found that although Dr. Layton had materially breached the contract within a year or so of its creation, Ms. Posik waived the breach by acquiescence. Finally, the court found that Ms. Posik breached the agreement by refusing to continue to perform the house work, yard work and cooking for the parties and by her hostile attitude which required Dr. Layton to move from the house. Although the trial court determined that Ms. Posik was entitled to quantum meruit, it also determined that those damages were off-set by the benefits Ms. Posik received by being permitted to live with Dr. Layton. The court did award Ms. Posik a judgment on the note executed by Dr. Layton.

Although neither party urged that this agreement was void as against public policy, Dr. Layton's counsel on more than one occasion reminded us that the parties had a sexual relationship. Certainly, even though the agreement was couched in terms of a personal services contract, it was intended to be much more. It was a nuptial agreement entered into by two parties that the state prohibits from marrying. But even though the state has prohibited same-sex marriages and same-sex adoptions, it has not prohibited this type of agreement. By prohibiting same-sex marriages, the state has merely denied homosexuals the rights granted to married partners that flow naturally from the marital relationship. In short, "the law of Florida creates no legal rights or duties between live-ins." *Lowry v. Lowry*, 512 So.2d 1142 (Fla. 5th DCA 1987). (Sharp, J., concurring specially). This lack of recognition of the rights which flow naturally from the break-up of a marital relationship applies to unmarried heterosexuals as well as homosexuals. But the State has not denied these individuals their right to either will their property as they see fit nor to privately commit by contract to spend their money as they choose. The State is not thusly condoning the lifestyles of homosexuals or unmarried live-ins; it is merely recognizing their constitutional private property and contract rights.

Even though no legal rights or obligations flow as a matter of law from a non-marital relationship, we see no impediment to the parties to such a relationship agreeing between themselves to provide certain rights and obligations. Other states have approved such individual agreements. In *Marvin v. Marvin*, 18 Cal.3d 660, 134 Cal.Rptr. 815, 557 P.2d 106 (1976), the California Supreme Court held:

> [W]e base our opinion on the principle that adults who voluntarily live together and engage in sexual relations are nonetheless as competent as any other persons to contract respecting their earnings and property rights. . . . So long as the agreement does not rest upon illicit meretricious consideration, the parties may order their economic affairs as they choose. . . .

In *Whorton v. Dillingham*, 202 Cal.App.3d 447, 248 Cal.Rptr. 405 (1988), the California Fourth District Court of Appeal extended this principle to same-sex partners. We also see no reason for a distinction. . . .

Addressing the invited issue, we find that an agreement for support between unmarried adults is valid unless the agreement is inseparably based upon illicit consideration of sexual services. Certainly prostitution, heterosexual or homosexual, cannot be condoned merely because it is performed within the confines of a written agreement. The parties, represented by counsel, were well aware of this prohibition and took pains to assure that sexual services were not even mentioned in the agreement. That factor would not be decisive, however, if it could be determined from the contract or from the conduct of the parties that the primary reason for the agreement was to deliver and be paid for sexual services. See *Bergen v. Wood*, 14 Cal.App.4th 854, 18 Cal.Rptr.2d 75 (1993). This contract and the parties' testimony show that such was not the case here. Because of the potential abuse in marital-type relationships, we find that such agreements must be in writing. The Statute of Frauds (section 725.01, Florida Statutes) requires that contracts made upon consideration of marriage must be in writing. This same requirement should apply to non-marital, nuptial-like agreements. In this case, there is (and can be) no dispute that the agreement exists.

The obligations imposed on Ms. Posik by the agreement include the obligation "to immediately commence residing with Nancy L.R. Layton at her said residence for the remainder of Emma Posik's life. . . ." This is very similar to a "until death do us part" commitment. And although the parties undoubtedly expected a sexual relationship, this record shows that they contemplated much more. They contracted for a permanent sharing of, and participating in, one another's lives. We find the contract enforceable.

We disagree with the trial court that waiver was proved in this case. Ms. Posik consistently urged Dr. Layton to make the will as required by the agreement and her failure to do so was sufficient grounds to declare default. And even more important to Ms. Posik was the implied agreement that her lifetime commitment would be reciprocated by a lifetime commitment by Dr. Layton—and that this mutual commitment would be monogamous. When Dr. Layton introduced a third person into the relationship, although it was not an express breach of the written agreement, it explains why Ms. Posik took that opportunity to hold Dr. Layton to her express obligations and to consider the agreement in default.

We also disagree with the trial court that Ms. Posik breached the agreement by refusing to perform housework, yard work, provisioning the house, and cooking for the parties. This conduct did not occur until after Dr. Layton had first breached the agreement. One need not continue to perform a contract when the other party has first breached. *City of Miami Beach v. Carner*, 579 So.2d 248 (Fla. 3d DCA 1991). Therefore, this conduct did not authorize Dr. Layton to send the three-day notice of eviction which constituted a separate default under the agreement.

We also disagree that the commitment to pay $2,500 per month upon termination of the agreement is unenforceable as a penalty. We agree with Ms. Posik that her damages, which would include more than mere lost wages and moving expenses, were not readily ascertainable at the time the contract was created. Further, the agreed sum is reasonable under the circumstances of this case. It is less than Ms. Posik was earning some four years earlier when she entered into this arrangement. It is also less than Ms. Posik would have received had the long-term provisions of the contract been performed. She is now in her sixties and her working opportunities are greatly reduced.

We recognize that this contract, insisted on by Ms. Posik before she would relocate with Dr. Layton, is extremely favorable to her. But there is no allegation of fraud or overreaching on Ms. Posik's part. This court faced an extremely generous agreement in *Carnell v. Carnell*, 398 So.2d 503 (Fla. 5th DCA 1981). In *Carnell*, a lawyer, in order to induce a woman to become his wife, agreed that upon divorce the wife would receive his home owned by him prior to marriage, one-half of his disposable income and one-half of his retirement as alimony until she remarried. Two years after the marriage, she tested his commitment. We held:

> The husband also contends that the agreement is so unfair and unreasonable that it must be set aside…."The freedom to contract includes the right to make a bad bargain." (Citation omitted). The controlling question here is whether there was overreaching and not whether the bargain was good or bad.

398 So.2d at 506.

Contracts can be dangerous to one's well-being. That is why they are kept away from children. Perhaps warning labels should be attached. In any event, contracts should be taken seriously. Dr. Layton's comment that she considered the agreement a sham and never intended to be bound by it shows that she did not take it seriously. That is regrettable.

We affirm that portion of the judgment below which addresses the promissory note and attorney's fees and costs associated therewith. We reverse that portion of the judgment that fails to enforce the parties' agreement.

Notes and Questions

1. The *Posik* courts says that "[t]he Statute of Frauds (section 725.01, Florida Statutes) requires that contracts made upon consideration of marriage must be in writ-

ing. This same requirement should apply to non-marital, nuptial-like agreements." The court's statement is dictum since the validity of an oral agreement was not at issue in the case. Do you think the Florida statute should be applied to contractual claims by unmarried cohabitants? See *Brodie v. All Corporation of USA*, 876 So.2d 577 (Fla. App. 2004)(oral contract between opposite-sex cohabitants enforced and no Statute of Frauds issue raised).

2. Minnesota Statutes §513.075 provides:

> If sexual relations between the parties are contemplated, a contract between a man and a woman who are living together in this state out of wedlock, or who are about to commence living together in this state out of wedlock, is enforceable as to terms concerning the property and financial relations of the parties only if:
>
> > (1) the contract is written and signed by the parties, and
> >
> > (2) enforcement is sought after termination of the relationship.

What result in Minnesota if a same-sex couple splits up and one partner brings a *Marvin*-type claim, based on an oral contract?

3. The Texas Business and Commerce Code §26.01 provides:

> (a) A promise or agreement described in Subsection (b) of this section is not enforceable unless the promise or agreement, or a memorandum of it, is
>
> > (1) in writing; and
> >
> > (2) signed by the person to be charged with the promise or agreement or by someone lawfully authorized to sign for him.
>
> (b) Subsection (a) of this section applies to:
>
> ...
>
> > (3) an agreement made on consideration of marriage or on consideration of nonmarital conjugal cohabitation;

F. Equitable Property Rights of Same-Sex Partners

Marvin stands for the proposition that cohabitants may have rights in each other's property under theories other than express or implied contract. Equitable doctrines such as constructive or resulting trusts, quantum meruit, and unjust enrichment are all possible.

1. Constructive Trust

Bramlett v. Selman
597 S.W.2d 80 (Ark. 1980)

STROUD, Justice.

Appellee filed suit against his homosexual companion to require appellant to convey the title to a residence purchased with funds furnished by appellee. Appellant contended the purchase money was a gift from his paramour, but the trial court accepted appellee's position that the title was held by appellant as constructive trustee for appellee. We agree with the Chancellor.

In early 1977 appellant and appellee became involved in a homosexual relationship and appellee left his wife and children and moved in with appellant in his apartment. Shortly thereafter divorce proceedings were instituted between appellee and his wife. In April of 1977 appellee opened an account in a local savings and loan institution in appellant's name and deposited a total of $7,000.00. These are the only material facts on which the parties agree. Appellant asserts that the appellee "lavished" him with a variety of gifts, including the $7,000.00 used to purchase a residence on Spring Street which both parties occupied after the purchase was closed. However, appellee claims the money was not a gift, but was put into appellant's account for the sole purpose of having appellant purchase the Spring Street property in his name for the benefit of appellee. Appellee testified that there was a clear understanding of the scheme to conceal the acquisition of the property from his wife due to their pending divorce action. According to appellee, appellant had orally agreed to convey title to the property to him once the divorce was concluded. Various improvements were made by both parties to the structure on the property, although the evidence tended to show that the vast majority of them were either paid for by appellee and his father or were performed by appellee and his parents.

Appellee testified that he eventually felt guilty about hiding the property from his wife and, after discussing it with his attorney, had his attorney inform her of the situation. His testimony is uncontroverted that by way of settlement, he paid his wife $2,000 for her dower interest in the Spring Street property. Near the end of December of 1977, appellant and appellee had a falling out and a dispute ensued over the ownership of the property. Appellant claimed they "separated" because of appellee's jealousy, but appellee said the quarrel was over appellant's refusal to convey the property to him as previously agreed. At any rate, appellee moved out of the Spring Street residence, and on March 1, 1978, brought this action requesting the court to settle the ownership of certain personal property, to require appellant to vacate the Spring Street property, and compel appellant to convey the property to him. After hearing all the arguments and evidence offered by each party, the chancellor found that appellant held title to the property as constructive trustee for appellee, ordered appellant to vacate the premises, and ordered him to convey title to the property to appellee. The chancellor also settled the ownership of certain personal property, but ordered appellee to reimburse appellant in the amount of $1,624.48 for his expenses incurred as constructive trustee. From the decision of the chancellor appellant brings this appeal...

Appellant alleges that the trial court erred in finding the existence of a constructive trust. He contends that the evidence was insufficient as there was no proof of positive fraud which appellant contends is required for a constructive trust. Such is not the case, as proof of fraud is not necessary for the imposition of a constructive trust. This court has often held that although a grantee's oral promise to hold the title to land for a third person is unenforceable, a constructive trust will be imposed if it is shown by clear, cogent and convincing evidence that the grantee's promise was intentionally fraudulent or that the parties were in a confidential relationship. The evidence in this case is not supportive of a finding that appellant took title to the property with an intent to permanently deprive appellee of the property. To the contrary, the evidence indicates that no such intent was evident until several months after the deed to appellant had been executed. The trial court undoubtedly believed the testimony of appellee that the dispute arose in December of 1977 when appellant refused to convey the property to appellee pursuant to their oral agreement. Therefore, for a constructive trust to be imposed by the court of equity in this case, it must rest not upon fraud but upon the existence of a confidential relationship.

Appellant claims that the trial court erred in holding as a matter of law that a fiduciary relationship existed between the parties based on their homosexual involvement. The trial court did not hold that all homosexual relationships as a matter of law involve a confidential relationship. Whether or not a confidential relationship exists depends upon the actual relationship between the parties. It is not surprising that this court held in Walker v. Biddle, that "The relation between brother and sister is, in the absence of estrangement or other unusual circumstances, one of confidence;..." The relation between aunt and niece would usually be less close, but in Henry & Mullen v. Goodwin & Attaway, a confidential relationship was found to exist when the niece lived near her aunt and visited with her on a daily basis. There the court adopted a definition of the term from the Restatement Second, Trusts, "A confidential relation exists between two persons when one has gained the confidence of the other and purports to act or advise (with) the other's interest in mind." In the case on appeal, appellee clearly demonstrated confidence in appellant, and appellant certainly purported to act with appellee's interest in mind at the time he purchased the property. A kinship is not necessary for a confidential relationship, as is apparent in *Kingrey v. Wilson*, 227 Ark. 690, 301 S.W.2d 23 (1957). There, a constructive trust was imposed when grantee was not related to the grantor, but was merely a friend and neighbor.

In the case now on appeal, the facts were sufficiently clear, cogent and convincing for the chancellor to find that a confidential relation existed between appellant and appellee when the undisputed testimony indicated they had been homosexual lovers for approximately a year and had lived together for most of that year....

All homosexual involvements are not as a matter of law confidential relationships sufficient to support a constructive trust, but a court of equity should not deny relief to a person merely because he is a homosexual. This is the view adopted by the Georgia Supreme Court in 1979 in *Weekes v. Gay*, 243 Ga. 784, 256 S.E.2d 901 (1979). There, a house shared by homosexuals was destroyed by fire and the court imposed an implied trust on the proceeds. The proceeds were deemed held for the benefit of the party who furnished the purchase money, even though his name did not appear on the deed nor was he an insured under the insurance policy. Irrespective of the homosexual relationship, the court noted that equity will not allow a windfall to one party when the beneficial interest should flow to the other party. It can be said no clearer than it was said last year by this court in Henry, supra:

> Equity, however, will impose a constructive trust when a grantee standing in a confidential relation to the grantor orally promises to hold land for the grantor and later refuses to perform his promise.

Affirmed.

Note

In *Spafford v. Coats*, an Illinois appellate court was faced with the question of whether the *Hewitt* decision prevented the recognition of all equitable claims to property that arise within the context of a cohabitation. Donna Spafford, like the appellee in *Bramlett*, had contributed her own funds to help purchase vehicles in her opposite-sex partner's name. In finding for Spafford on the constructive trust claim, the Illinois court explained:

> We perceive the real and underlying concern of the supreme court in *Hewitt* was that judicial recognition of mutual property rights between knowingly un-married cohabitants—where the claim is based upon or intimately related to the cohabitation of the parties—would in effect grant to unmarried cohabi-tants substantially the same marital rights enjoyed by married persons, resur-rect the doctrine of common law marriage, and contravene the public policy enunciated by the Illinois legislature to strengthen and preserve the integrity of marriage. The plaintiff's claims in *Hewitt* for one-half of defendant's property were based primarily upon her services as housekeeper and homemaker and obviously fell afoul of the court's concerns. However, where the claims do not arise from the relationship between the parties and are not rights closely re-sembling those arising from conventional marriages, we conclude that the public policy expressed in *Hewitt* does not bar judicial recognition of such claims.
>
> Unlike the plaintiff's claims in *Hewitt,* the claims of Donna Spafford are based on evidence that she furnished substantially all of the consideration for the pur-chase of several vehicles and that under the circumstances shown by the evi-dence adduced by the plaintiff, permitting the defendant to retain all of the ve-hicles would constitute an unjust enrichment which equity should not permit.

455 N.E.2d 241 at 245 (Ill.App. 1983).

2. Resulting Trust

Scott v. Commissioner of Internal Revenue
226 F.3d 871 (7th Cir. 2000)

WILLIAMS, Circuit Judge.

The decedent, Lucille M. Horstmeier and petitioner Mary E. Scott lived together as a couple from 1974 to 1993. Throughout their relationship, Scott handled household maintenance and Horstmeier worked as a successful business owner, providing signifi-cant financial support to Scott. At issue in this appeal is the ownership of the Glenview, Illinois, home where the two lived but that Horstmeier alone purchased.

When Horstmeier died, Scott was appointed executor of Horstmeier's estate. In filing taxes for the estate, Scott included only 50 percent of the Glenview property's value, claiming that she personally had a resulting trust in the property that gave her a 50 per-cent ownership stake. The IRS disagreed and found that Horstmeier owned 100 percent of the property at the time of her death and, consequently, ruled that 100 percent of the property's value should have been included in the estate...Scott then took the matter to federal tax court. The tax court found that Scott presented insufficient evidence to prove that a resulting trust existed at the time of Horstmeier's death and agreed with the IRS's tax deficiency determination. Scott now appeals. Because we find that the tax court's findings were not clearly erroneous, we affirm.

During the nearly 20 years that Horstmeier and Scott lived together, they shared three different homes. First, they lived in a Skokie condominium, which Horstmeier purchased and held in her name. Next, they moved to the Glenview home at issue here. To purchase this home, Horstmeier put $50,000 down and took out a mortgage for $55,000 in her name alone. Scott's name does not show up on any documents relating to this property. The two lived in the Glenview home until Horstmeier's death on January 25, 1993. During that time, as in the Skokie home, Scott did all the housework, performed household maintenance, and managed the couple's finances. Horstmeier deducted 100 percent of the mortgage interest and real estate taxes from the Glenview home on her own federal taxes from 1975 to 1992.

According to Scott, the two agreed that Horstmeier would serve as the nominee for the couple as joint owners of both the Skokie and Glenview homes. They did this because Horstmeier was a prominent business person in the Chicago community, and at that time, their same-sex relationship would have been condemned and could have caused controversy. At the time that the Glenview home was purchased, Scott had no assets to contribute to the purchase and had no regular source of income. She received some support from her parents and took a few low-paying jobs from time to time. In 1979, Scott began working as a full-time employee at the school that Horstmeier managed. Scott initially earned about $200 per week and eventually made about $21,000 per year. Still, the record contains no evidence that Scott ever made any mortgage payments to the bank or cash payments to Horstmeier specifically for her share of the down payment on the Glenview home. In fact, at one point, Horstmeier took out a second mortgage on the Glenview home in order to get money for her business. Scott objected, but Horstmeier took the loan out anyway.

The couple purchased a third home in Wisconsin in 1979. This time, both Horstmeier and Scott contributed to the down payment of approximately $4000, and originally, the property was titled in both their names. After Scott made all 36 monthly mortgage payments, she ultimately took title to the property in her name alone.

When Horstmeier died in early 1993, Scott was appointed the executor of Horstmeier's estate. In her will, Horstmeier did not provide instructions concerning the Glenview home. Instead, the property passed to Scott as the residuary beneficiary of a trust to which Horstmeier bequeathed her assets that were not required for estate administration.

In 1993, Scott filed a claim in probate court seeking a 50 percent tenancy-in-common interest in the Glenview home. She filed this claim in response to an investigation into Horstmeier's business's finances. Scott was concerned that the Glenview property might be vulnerable to attack by creditors. In support of her claim, Scott maintained that (1) she and Horstmeier agreed they would share expenses concerning the home and (2) Horstmeier required Scott to pay $3000 per year until she paid a total of $25,000, which equaled one-half the down payment made when the home was originally purchased. In addition, Scott and Horstmeier shared expenses as agreed, but Horstmeier actually forgave the required payment and made an annual $3000 gift to Scott. The court approved Scott's claim without reaching the merits or the underlying facts of the claim.

When she filed the federal taxes for the Horstmeier estate, Scott included only 50 percent of the value of the Glenview home in the gross estate and deducted only 50 percent of the remaining note balance. She did so on the theory that she personally owned 50 percent of the home, while the Horstmeier estate owned the other 50 percent. The IRS determined otherwise and concluded that Horstmeier alone owned the home. As a result, the IRS found that 100 percent of the value of the home should have been included and 100 percent of the mortgage note balance should have been deducted on the Horstmeier estate tax return. The result was a $157,404 tax deficiency.

As executor of the Horstmeier estate, Scott challenged the IRS ruling in tax court. The court agreed with the IRS. It ruled that Scott failed to present sufficient evidence that a resulting trust had been created. Specifically, the court concluded that there was not enough evidence to show that an agreement existed between Scott and Horstmeier for the joint purchase of the Glenview home. The judge cited a number of issues as problematic: (1) the lack of clarity concerning how Scott's share of the down payment was to be repaid; (2) the securing of a second mortgage on the property by Horstmeier, over Scott's disapproval; and (3) the couple's willingness to take joint title to the Wisconsin property when both contributed to the initial down payment. The judge concluded that "[t]he infirmities in petitioner's theory are cumulative and, considered together, cast doubt on the factual support for a resulting trust in this case."

We review the tax court's judgment using the same standards that apply when examining a district court's decisions in a civil bench trial. Therefore, we review the tax court's findings of fact for clear error. Scott's principal argument is that the tax court erred in concluding that she failed to prove she had a 50 percent interest in the Glenview home, obtained through a resulting trust. To decide whether a resulting trust arose, we apply the law of the State of Illinois. *See Estate of Young v. Commissioner,* 110 T.C. 297, 300, 1998 WL 235975 (1998) (citing *Fernandez v. Wiener,* 326 U.S. 340, 355–57, 66 S.Ct. 178, 90 L.Ed. 116 (1945)) ("[W]hat constitutes an interest in property held by a person within a State is a matter of State law.").

Under Illinois law, a court may impose a trust when none exists to effectuate the parties' intent. *See In re Estate of Wilson,* 410 N.E.2d 23, 26 (1980). Accordingly, a resulting trust is established when one person furnishes consideration for property and title is taken in the name of someone else with the intent that the person furnishing consideration retains beneficial ownership of the property. The pivotal question in determining whether a resulting trust has been created is "whether the nominal purchaser intended the actual payor to have an ownership interest in the good." Because Scott is rebutting recorded legal title, she "must demonstrate the requisite intent to create a [resulting] trust through 'clear and convincing evidence' that is 'unequivocal both as to its existence and to its terms and conditions.'" Furthermore, she must present facts that suggest a resulting trust is the only reasonable remedy. "If the evidence is doubtful or capable of reasonable explanation upon any theory other than the existence of a trust, it is insufficient." *Kohlhaas v. Smith,* 408 Ill. 535, 97 N.E.2d 774, 776 (1951).

Once we review the facts in light of this high burden of proof and the required deferential standard of review, it becomes clear that Scott loses. Scott claims that at the time Horstmeier paid for the Glenview home, they agreed that Scott would repay her half of the down payment in installments and would contribute her share of the monthly mortgage payments and property taxes by providing all services required for upkeep of the home. In our view, Scott failed to establish that (1) Horstmeier actually expected consideration in return for Scott's share of the Glenview home; (2) she actually paid the consideration Horstmeier allegedly expected; and (3) she and Horstmeier actually intended to create a resulting trust.

With regard to Horstmeier's expectations, testimony indicated that even though Scott wanted to "pay her fair share," Horstmeier did not really expect Scott to pay her for the down payment or for living expenses. A resulting trust arises, "if at all, at the instant legal title is taken and vests." *Hanley v. Hanley,* 152 N.E.2d 879, 882 (1958). Therefore, the question is whether a trust was created at the time Horstmeier purchased the Glenview home. When Horstmeier purchased the home, Scott had very few resources to actually pay consideration. She paid no household expenses until 1979, and even then, she never specified what those payments were for beyond reimbursement for "bills." These facts refute Scott's claim that they made any arrangement for Horstmeier advancing Scott her portion of the purchase price in exchange for deferred consideration furnished by Scott.

While "[a]cts of the alleged trustee or equitable owner subsequent to the taking of title have no bearing upon the question of whether a resulting trust was raised," these subsequent acts may be considered as evidence of intent. *Id.* "Intention is the key to the doctrine of resulting trusts." *Wilson,* 410 N.E.2d at 27. The tax court highlighted several aspects of Scott's story that work against evincing Horstmeier's intent to convey Scott a 50 percent interest in the Glenview home. We find the reasoning of the tax court compelling. If Horstmeier really expected repayment of Scott's share of the down payment and mortgage, Horstmeier probably would have been more vigilant about ensuring that Scott actually made the payments. Instead, Scott's own testimony suggests that Horstmeier did not really care if Scott paid her share or not. Consequently, sufficient doubt was created whether Horstmeier had agreed to lend Scott one-half of the down payment, with an expectation that she repay it.

Additionally, if Scott was really expected to reimburse Horstmeier for her share of the down payment, she probably would not have spent her meager earnings on luxuries like a Porsche, a motorcycle, or the Wisconsin home. While Scott offers reasonable explanations for permitting Horstmeier to take out the second mortgage and for holding joint title in the Wisconsin home, we also find the tax court's interpretation of these events reasonable. The court surmised that while the couple agreed to own the Wisconsin home jointly, they never came to a similar agreement to jointly own the Glenview home.

Because Scott cannot set forth facts precluding all reasonable explanations except a resulting trust, her claim must fail. While Scott provided valuable services to Horstmeier and the two shared the Glenview home, these facts do not necessarily mean that Scott was a co-owner. It is equally plausible that Scott performed those services as reimbursement for the rent and living expenses Horstmeier paid on Scott's behalf. This reasonable, alternative explanation is in itself sufficient to defeat Scott's claim.

The vehicle Scott chose to establish that she had an interest in the Glenview home, a resulting trust, is one that requires clear, convincing, and unmistakable proof. The tax court judge reviewed the evidence and concluded that Scott could not meet that standard of proof. His ultimate determination was a reasonable one.

Notes and Questions

1. What is at stake in this litigation? Note this is not a contest about who owns the property at Ms. Hortmeier's death. Her will clearly devised the property to Ms. Scott through the residuary bequest. The key problem, from Ms. Scott's point of view, is that when she inherited the residence she had lived in for almost 20 years, a residence she no

doubt thought of as "hers" at least in part, it turns out that she had to pay an estate tax on its full value.

2. The home was worth $459,000 at the time of Ms. Horstmeier's death in 1993 and was subject to a remaining mortgage balance of $29,000. Thus the issue for Ms. Scott, when she inherited the home, was whether she would have to pay estate taxes on 50% of the net value ($215,000) or on 100% of the net value ($430,000). Apparently, this was a large estate. Horstmeier's salary at the time they purchased the Glenview home was $90,000 a year. Including this additional $215,000 in the taxable estate probably cost the estate an additional $107,500 in estate taxes. The top estate tax bracket in 1993 imposed a tax at 50% on all transfers above $2.5 million. The court says the total deficiency was $157,404, which may have included an addition for interest on the outstanding deficiency. If Ms. Scott and Ms. Horstmeier had been married, no tax would have been payable on any portion of the estate willed to Ms. Scott because spouses are entitled to a 100% marital deduction. Is the difference in treatment justified? Why or why not?

3. Could Scott have relied on the doctrine of constructive trust to claim 50% ownership in the home since she and Horstmeier were in a confidential relationship? Why or why not?

4. Could Scott have relied on the doctrine of implied contract? Why or why not? (Remember this case occurred in the state of Illinois.)

5. Ms. Horstmeier was diagnosed with pancreatic cancer in March of 1992 and knew she had less than a year to live. She died in January of 1993. If she had consulted an estate planner before her death and transferred title to Ms. Scott, could they have avoided an estate tax payable on this home? To answer this, you will need to know that "gifts" made during lifetime are subject to the estate tax at their date of gift value. So the only way to avoid the tax would be to characterize the transaction as something other than a gift. Is that possible?

6. Some tax observations: The fact that Horstmeier paid the interest on the mortgage and claimed the interest deduction should not defeat Scott's claim to 50% ownership. The house was purchased in 1975 for $105,000. Horstmeier made a $50,000 down payment. For Scott to "purchase" a 50% interest in the home, she would have to pay Horstemier $52,500 over some period of time. Either at time of purchase or sometime shortly thereafter, the couple could have agreed that Scott would make these payments at the rate of $3,000 per year and Horstmeier could have forgiven that $3,000 debt each year, just as Scott claimed. If the form of the transaction were honored for tax purposes, then Scott would be purchasing the home by paying off an interest-free loan in the amount of $52,500, which, at the rate of $3,000 per year would take 17.5 years. It would have been paid in full by 1993. And during this time, Horstmeier would have been making the mortgage payments and properly deducting the interest. The reason for structuring the loan between Horstmeier and Scott as one requiring an annual payment of $3,000 is that the forgiveness of that amount, which is in substance a gift, would not have been subjected to the gift tax. In 1975, the maximum amount that a donor could give away without any gift tax consequences whatsoever was $3,000 per donee per year. This exemption from tax is known as the annual exclusion. The amount was increased to $10,000 in 1981 and can now be increased to reflect inflation. As of 2004, the adjusted exclusion amounted to $11,000 per donee per year. See IRC §2503(b).

7. Assuming the agreement that Scott described actually existed, Horstmeier and Scott should have provided some written evidence of the agreement. Transferring title to Scott (50% or 100%) would be some evidence. But an additional writing explaining

the ways in which Scott had contributed to the purchase price of the property would also be advisable.

8. The agreement, as described by Scott, raises a couple of additional tax questions. Did the annual payment remain at $3,000 or did they intend to increase it to $10,000 when the annual exclusion amount was increased in 1981? If Horstmeier had intended from the beginning to forgive all of the annual payments, then should the transaction be considered a completed gift of a half interest in the property from the beginning? In 1975, making an interest-free loan caused no adverse tax consequences, but in 1984, Section 7872 of the Internal Revenue Code was enacted. For "gift" loans in excess of $10,000, interest will normally be imputed if not charged. How might this affect the transaction? Finally, if the agreement was for Scott to provide household services in exchange for Horstmeier's payment of the mortgage, then would Scott have taxable income to the extent she received something of value in exchange for services rendered? See I.R.C. §83.

9. What tax result in *Scott* if the couple had a valid Civil Union in Vermont, and Ms. Horstmeier had died there, with title to the home in her name?

10. What tax result if the couple had a valid marriage in Massachusetts, and Ms. Horstmeier had died there with title to the home in her name?

12. What tax result if the couple had resided in Washington and could take advantage of the meretricious relationship doctrine?

13. What tax result if the couple resided in California, had a valid California domestic partnership, and the death occurs after January 1, 2005? [After January 1, 2005 any property acquired during the term of the partnership, even if acquired before January 1, 2005, is community property.] Assume the couple registered as domestic partners on January 1, 2000, when the statewide registry first became available and assume that Horstmeier purchased the home in her own name on January 2, 2000. At her death, how much of the value of the home should be included in her estate for estate tax purposes. Recall the quote in *Scott* from the U.S. Supreme Court: "[W]hat constitutes an interest in property held by a person within a State is a matter of State law."

14. Before answering questions 8—13, you might want to consult Subpart G of this Chapter, Federal Tax Considerations. See *infra*.

3. Unjust Enrichment

Mitchell v. Moore
729 A.2d 1200 (Penn. Superior Ct. 1999)
appeal denied, 751 A.2d 192 (Penn. 2000)

CIRILLO, President Judge Emeritus:

William Moore, III (Moore), appeals from the order entered in the Court of Common Pleas of Chester County denying his post-trial motions and entering judgment on a jury verdict of $130,000.00 awarded to Appellee, Thomas Mitchell (Mitchell). We affirm in part and reverse in part.

Thomas Mitchell and William Moore first met in 1980; the two men quickly developed a romantic relationship. Moore resided in Elverson, Pennsylvania and Mitchell in

South Carolina. In the spring of 1981, Mitchell accepted Moore's invitation to spend his "off season"[1] at Moore's Chester County farm. By 1985, Mitchell had permanently moved to Elverson, where he resided at Moore's farm without paying rent, worked a full-time job with a company located in Lancaster, Pennsylvania, and assisted Moore in maintaining his house and farm. Among other things, Mitchell took care of the farm animals, which included aiding in the breeding of sheep and birds. In 1990, Mitchell enrolled at Penn State University for graduate studies. As a result of his academic schedule, he was unable to run the sheep and bird businesses or maintain the farm. Soon thereafter, the parties' relationship soured; Mitchell moved out of Moore's residence in June of 1994.

In 1995, Mitchell brought an action against Moore sounding in fraud, *quantum meruit*, and implied contract. Specifically, Mitchell sought compensation, in the form of restitution, for the services he rendered to Moore throughout the thirteen years the two men lived together on the farm. In his complaint, Mitchell alleged that Moore had: promised him compensation for his services rendered to maintain and operate his farm; agreed to compensate him for his help in running an antique cooperative (co-op) that Mitchell had purchased; promised him future compensation and the devise of property in a will and codicil; and failed to compensate him for monetary contributions he had made towards Moore's purchase of real estate on Amelia Island, Florida.

In response to Mitchell's action, Moore filed preliminary objections seeking a demurrer. The court granted the objections in part and denied the objections in part, striking Mitchell's claim of fraud for lack of specificity,…but granting Mitchell leave to file an amended complaint. Mitchell filed an amended complaint, now including only counts for quantum meruit /unjust enrichment[2] and implied contract. Moore filed a counterclaim seeking $139,300.00 representing reasonable rent for the 139 months Mitchell lived on his farm rent-free and as compensation for various utility and telephone bills, taxes, car payments, and other miscellaneous expenses paid by Moore on Mitchell's behalf.

After a jury trial, a verdict was rendered in favor of Mitchell on the basis of unjust enrichment and against Moore on the counterclaim. [Moore appeals.]

"Unjust enrichment" is essentially an equitable doctrine. Where unjust enrichment is found, the law implies a contract, which requires the defendant to pay to the plaintiff the value of the benefit conferred.

The elements necessary to prove unjust enrichment are:

(1) benefits conferred on defendant by plaintiff;

(2) appreciation of such benefits by defendant; and

(3) acceptance and retention of such benefits under such circumstances that it would be inequitable for defendant to retain the benefit without payment of value.

---

1. Mitchell was a tobacco broker in South Carolina. He did not work during the winter months.

2. A cause of action in quasi-contract for quantum meruit, a form of restitution, is made out where one person has been unjustly enriched at the expense of another. *Feingold v. Pucello,* 439 Pa.Super. 509, 654 A.2d 1093, 1095 (1995) (Beck, J., concurring) (citation omitted). Therefore, a claim of quantum meruit raises the issue of whether a party has been unjustly enriched, and in order to prove such claim a party must successfully prove the elements of unjust enrichment discussed infra.

The application of the doctrine depends on the particular factual circumstances of the case at issue. In determining if the doctrine applies, our focus is not on the intention of the parties, but rather on whether the defendant has been unjustly enriched.

In its opinion, the trial court clearly determines that a benefit was conferred upon Moore as a result of the extensive labor and services Mitchell provided him on his farm and in his home. The critical question, with regard to whether as a result of this benefit Moore was unjustly enriched, was answered in the positive by the court as follows:

> Assuming the jury established that a benefit had been conferred by Plaintiff [Mitchell] and received by Defendant [Moore], they only had to determine that Defendant's acceptance of these benefits and failure to compensate Plaintiff resulted in an unconscionable bargain. The jury was aware that Defendant [sic] moved hundreds of miles away from his job, house, friends and family to a different region of the country where he took on a new job and did work on Defendant's [Moore's] farm. It is not unreasonable to suggest that the jury believed Plaintiff [Mitchell] in that he made that life-altering change based on something besides his desire to develop his relationship with Defendant [Moore]. Given this potential scenario, it is likely that the jury could have found that the lack of compensation Plaintiff [Mitchell] received amounted to an unconscionable bargain and therefore, Defendant's [Moore's] unjust enrichment.

"It has been said, an intention to pay for work done will be assumed, except in the case of parent and child. Where, however, it is apparent that the parties, though not so related by blood, in reality bore like connection to each other, the implication does not arise." *Brown v. McCurdy*, 278 Pa. 19, 22, 122 A. 169, 170 (1923). While it has been held that the presumption of gratuitous services does not automatically arise in a daughter-in-law/mother-in-law context, where a claimant has become "part of the family" the contrary is true. *Id.*

Both parties concur that when Mitchell moved into Moore's home on a full-time basis, Moore paid many of Mitchell's bills, including car payments, VISA and SEARS card charges, and phone bills. Moreover, Moore claims that Mitchell became part of his own family; Mitchell, himself, admits to having celebrated all the major holidays with Moore's immediate family and received gifts from them on special occasions.

In *Brown, supra*, the law and facts centered around the issue of whether a presumption of payment, based upon an express contract to pay for services rendered by a daughter-in-law to her mother-in-law, had been successfully established based upon the evidence at trial. The court demanded strict proof of an express contract in order to overcome any presumption that the services were gratuitous. Although the instant case is not based upon either an express contract or written agreement, we find the principles espoused in Brown equally applicable, namely, in order to prove that the defendant in the present case had been unjustly enriched by plaintiff's actions and services, there must be some convincing evidence establishing that plaintiff's services were not gratuitous.

We first note that Mitchell had complete access to a large farm house where he lived rent-free and virtually unencumbered by any utility expenses. The nature and amount of benefits that plaintiff received from living at Moore's farm rebuts any presumption that the benefit conferred upon Moore was unjust. In fact, the advantages plaintiff obtained were compensation enough for all the work he offered to do on the farm; further,

Mitchell derived an obvious personal benefit by living with the defendant, his partner for thirteen years, at his farm.

Having found no evidence which would imply that Moore's services were anything but gratuitous, we cannot agree with the trial court that a theory of unjust enrichment has been proved. While defendant indisputably bequeathed plaintiff his farm (found within the provisions of two wills that were later supplanted by a codicil), the gift was exactly that, an intention to reward the plaintiff through a testamentary provision.... Such bequest is not equivalent to a finding that the defendant intended to compensate the plaintiff for his services and that upon failure to remit such monies the defendant became unjustly enriched.

Furthermore, the defendant testified that the plaintiff himself suggested that he move in with the defendant because he could not afford to rent an apartment on his own at the time. He, as well as the defendant, thought such potential living arrangement would give the two men more time to foster their relationship. In fact, upon learning of plaintiff's potential job opportunity in nearby Lancaster, Pennsylvania, the defendant anticipated that the two parties would be able to grow closer in a permanent "live-in" situation—another indication that there existed no expectation of payment for plaintiff's voluntary work on the defendant's farm. Moreover, plaintiff testified that he never asked the defendant for compensation for his services and that the defendant never told him he would pay him for his help around the house and the farm.

To solidify the fact that the plaintiff's actions were gratuitous services rendered during a "close, personal" relationship, the plaintiff testified at trial that after he moved in and began to help around the farm, the defendant told him he "did a great job, that he appreciated what I [plaintiff] did, and it was for—it made the house much better looking, it kept it stable, and that we were building a future together and some day it would all be worth it for me [plaintiff]." While Mitchell would characterize the nature of the parties' relationship as a type of business venture between partners, the evidence at trial indicates a very different aspect of their lives. As Mitchell, himself, testified, he had a "romantic or sexual aspect to his relationship with Dr. Moore." Furthermore, the parties conducted themselves around the home like parties in a loving relationship; they shared household chores, cooked dinners for each other, bestowed gifts upon one another, attended events together, and shared holidays and special occasions with Moore's family. Most potent, however, is the following language used in a letter written by Mitchell to Moore sometime in 1993, "The time I have given you breaking my back with the house and grounds were just that, a gift to our relationship." Moore testified that Mitchell was "his lover and we were living together as partners, and I felt like anything I could do for him, you know, gave me pleasure." To find restitution (compensation) proper for services performed in such a relationship, we would curtail the freedom associated in forming new personal bonds based upon the important facet of mutual dependence.

After a review of the record in this case, including the pivotal testimony of both Mitchell and Moore, we cannot find that the defendant benefited unjustly from plaintiff's services. While we do not attempt to characterize the services rendered in all unmarried couple's relationships as gratuitous, we do believe that such a presumption exists and that in order to recover restitution for services rendered, the presumption must be rebutted by clear and convincing evidence. The basis of this presumption rests on the fact that services provided by plaintiff to the defendant are not of the type for which one would normally expect to be paid, nor did they confer upon the defendant a benefit that is unconscionable for him to retain without making restitution to the plaintiff. See *Feingold, supra* (Beck, J., concurring).

The circumstances of this case do not require the law to imply a contract in order to avoid an injustice. See *Feingold*, 654 A.2d at 1095 (Beck, J., concurring) ("unlike true contracts, quasi-contracts are not based on the apparent intention of the parties to undertake the performances in question, nor are they promises. They are obligations created by law for reasons of justice.") Accordingly, we reverse the trial court's verdict in favor of plaintiff; the plaintiff did not "wrongfully secure a benefit that is unconscionable for him to retain."

Note

Other similar cases involving same-sex partners include: (1) *Ireland v. Flanagan*, 672 Ore Ct. App. 1981)(upholding oral agreement between lesbians to share property despite fact that property was held in sole name of one partner); *Jones v. Daly*, 176 Cal. Rptr 130 (Cal. App. 1981)(contract held to be unenforceable because the consideration for the contract was sexual services); *Whorton v. Dillingham*, 248 Cal. Rptr. 405 (Cal. App. 1988)(contract enforceable because sexual services were severable from independent consideration); *Small v. Harper*, 638 S.W.2d 24 (Tex. Ct. App. 1982)(contract between lesbians to share property can be enforced if proved; public policy exception will not apply); *Crooke v. Gilden*, 414 S.E.2d 645 (Ga. 1992)(written contract between lesbians to split proceeds on sale of home upheld, reversing court below that had held public policy considerations would prevent enforcement because the contract related to the home where presumably illegal sodomy took place); *Seward v. Metrup*, 622 N,E.2d 756 (Ohio App. 1993)(absent express agreement, lesbian partner has no claim to division of property at end of 9 year relationship).

G. Federal Tax Considerations

The Internal Revenue Code ("Code") treats spouses differently from unmarried life partners. This is true no matter how financially and emotionally intertwined the unmarried partners are. Sometimes this disparate treatment creates tax burdens for unmarried couples. Sometime the difference creates a benefit, such as avoiding the "marriage tax penalty," which usually arises when both spouses have income. However, the difference in treatment between married and unmarried couples, whether the economic effect is beneficial to one class or the other, always carries stigmatic harm to the extent that the message heard by gay and lesbian taxpayers is that their relationships do not count. Closely related to this stigmatic harm is another hidden burden the Code has created in its privileging of heterosexual marriage. The Code presumes that persons are either married or live their lives financially separated from others. The reality is that many same-sex, committed couples do not live in a world of financial separation. The tax laws, in effect, force them into a reporting stance that is not reflective of their day-to-day lives. See generally Patricia A. Cain, Heterosexual Privilege and the Internal Revenue Code, 34 U.S.F. Law Rev 465 (2000).

1. Income Tax Issues

Massachusetts recognizes same-sex marriages. In Vermont, partners in a civil union are accorded the same rights and responsibilities as spouses. And, in California, registered domestic partners are treated virtually the same as spouses. The laws of these states create legally recognized familial relationships and vest in the partners certain property rights that are generally unavailable to unmarried partners in other states. In Massachusetts and Vermont, for example, spouses (and partners in a civil union) can own property as tenants by the entirety. In California, domestic partners can own community property in the same manner as spouses. Spousal obligations of support are imposed by state law in all three states. And, when the relationship is terminated, divisions of property follow the same general rules that are applied in heterosexual marriages. What impact should these state laws have on the application of federal income tax rules? See generally Patricia A. Cain, Federal Tax Consequences of Civil Unions, 30 Cap. U. L. Rev. 387 (2002).

a. Filing status

Marital status affects filing status. Married individuals can file joint returns. Unmarried individuals file separately as "unmarried" or as "head of household." Before the enactment of DOMA in 1996, there was no federal tax law definition of "marriage" or "spouse." Marital status was determined under the relevant state law. If a state recognized common law marriage, then the federal tax law viewed couples who were common law spouses as married.

DOMA provides, in part: "In determining the meaning of any Act of Congress, or of any ruling, regulation, or interpretation of the various administrative bureaus and agencies of the United States, the word "marriage" means only a legal union between one man and one woman as husband and wife, and the word "spouse" refers only to a person of the opposite sex who is a husband or a wife." Absent a determination that this part of DOMA is unconstitutional, the law as to filing status should be clear. Same-sex spouses in Massachusetts and same-sex marriages that are imported from Canada will not be recognized by the federal tax code. Married couples will have to file separate returns as single taxpayers or as "head of household" taxpayers.

Some couples complain that the IRS has not yet adjusted the 1040 tax return form to reflect this new reality. On this form, taxpayers in a same-sex marriage are expected to check a box that says they are single rather than married, even though they are validly married and that marriage is recognized by their state of domicile. Several tax preparers have suggested that persons who feel they should not sign such a false representation under penalties of perjury should attach a "rider" to the return stating that they are married, but are checking the single box because of DOMA. As of tax filing time in April of 2005, the IRS had issued no guidance on this question.

b. Payment of support

Under the income tax law, payments of support do not create income for the recipient. There is no express code provision stating this rule and the only reported cases on taxation of support payments are concerned with payments made after divorce. One might argue that support payments made during the relationship are excluded from income because they are gifts. See §102 IRC. While that characterization might be correct for support payments that are made voluntarily, spousal support payments, as well as support payments for the benefit of minor children, are required under state law, and so do not readily fit into the accepted definition of "gift" for income tax purposes, i.e., a transfer made with "detached and disinterested generosity." See *Commissioner v. Duberstein*, 363 U.S. 278 (1960). In any event, the IRS has never attempted to tax support payments made during a marriage to the recipient spouse, even when spouses used to file separate tax returns. [Note: The modern joint return was not part of our income tax system until 1948.]

The more interesting income tax question is how to treat support payments that may be made after the relationship is dissolved. Sections 71 and 215 of the Internal Revenue Code set the rules for alimony when it is paid by ex-spouses. But same-sex couples, even if married, cannot take advantage of these rules because of DOMA. However, before these code provisions existed, the Supreme Court announced the rule that should be applied to alimony payments in the absence of a controlling statute. In *Gould v. Gould*, the Court ruled that alimony payments from the ex-husband to the ex-wife were not taxable income to the ex-wife. 245 U.S. 151 (1917). While this decision is unclear as to the reason such payments are not income, it is possible that the case stands for the proposition that payments received in lieu of something that would have otherwise been nontaxable (i.e., support payments during the marital relationship) should not be treated as taxable income. Same-sex couples who divorce or otherwise terminate a relationship and negotiate ongoing support payments from one partner to the other ought to be able to cite *Gould* and claim that the payments are not income to the recipient. Nor can the payments be deducted by the payor, as there is no section authorizing such a deduction other than §215, which by its terms applies only to spouses.

The larger question in most of these arrangements is whether the payments constitute a taxable gift by the payor. If the payment exceeds $11,000 a year, the gift tax rules might well be triggered. The definition of gift for gift tax purposes is different from the definition for income tax purposes. Further discussion of the gift tax issues is included in Part 2 below.

c. *Dependency exemptions and tax credits*

Taxpayers can claim dependency exemptions for any "qualifying child" and for any "qualifying relative." The definitions of "qualifying child" and "qualifying relative" are new for tax year 2005, but are derived from earlier code provisions.

§ 152. Dependent defined.

(a) In general. For purposes of this subtitle, the term "dependent" means—

(1) a qualifying child, or

(2) a qualifying relative.

(c) Qualifying child. For purposes of this section—

(1) In general. The term "qualifying child" means, with respect to any taxpayer for any taxable year, an individual—

(A) who bears a relationship to the taxpayer described in paragraph (2),

(B) who has the same principal place of abode as the taxpayer for more than one-half of such taxable year,

(C) who meets the age requirements of paragraph (3), and

(D) who has not provided over one-half of such individual's own support for the calendar year in which the taxable year of the taxpayer begins.

(2) Relationship. For purposes of paragraph (1)(A), an individual bears a relationship to the taxpayer described in this paragraph if such individual is—

(A) a child of the taxpayer or a descendant of such a child, or

(B) a brother, sister, stepbrother, or stepsister of the taxpayer or a descendant of any such relative

(3) Age requirements.

(A) In general. For purposes of paragraph (1)(C), an individual meets the requirements of this paragraph if such individual—

(i) has not attained the age of 19 as of the close of the calendar year in which the taxable year of the taxpayer begins, or

(ii) is a student who has not attained the age of 24 as of the close of such calendar year.

(d) Qualifying relative. For purposes of this section—

(1) In general. The term "qualifying relative" means, with respect to any taxpayer for any taxable year, an individual—

(A) who bears a relationship to the taxpayer described in paragraph (2),

(B) whose gross income for the calendar year in which such taxable year begins is less than the exemption amount (as defined in section 151(d)),

(C) with respect to whom the taxpayer provides over one-half of the individual's support for the calendar year in which such taxable year begins, and

(D) who is not a qualifying child of such taxpayer or of any other taxpayer for any taxable year beginning in the calendar year in which such taxable year begins.

(2) Relationship. For purposes of paragraph (1)(A), an individual bears a relationship to the taxpayer described in this paragraph if the individual is any of the following with respect to the taxpayer:

(A) A child or a descendant of a child.

(B) A brother, sister, stepbrother, or stepsister.

(C) The father or mother, or an ancestor of either.

(D) A stepfather or stepmother.

(E) A son or daughter of a brother or sister of the taxpayer.

(F) A brother or sister of the father or mother of the taxpayer.

(G) A son-in-law, daughter-in-law, father-in-law, mother-in-law, brother-in-law, or sister-in-law.

(H) An individual (other than an individual who at any time during the taxable year was the spouse, determined without regard to section 7703, of the taxpayer) who, for the taxable year of the taxpayer, has the same principal place of abode as the taxpayer and is a member of the taxpayer's household.

(f) Other definitions and rules. For purposes of this section—

(1) Child defined.

(A) In general. The term "child" means an individual who is—

(i) a son, daughter, stepson, or stepdaughter of the taxpayer, or

(ii) an eligible foster child of the taxpayer.

(B) Adopted child. In determining whether any of the relationships specified in subparagraph (A)(i) or paragraph (4) exists, a legally adopted individual of the taxpayer, or an individual who is lawfully placed with the taxpayer for legal adoption by the taxpayer, shall be treated as a child of such individual by blood.

(C) Eligible foster child. For purposes of subparagraph (A)(ii), the term "eligible foster child" means an individual who is placed with the taxpayer by an authorized placement agency or by judgment, decree, or other order of any court of competent jurisdiction.

(3) Determination of household status. An individual shall not be treated as a member of the taxpayer's household if at any time during the taxable year of the taxpayer the relationship between such individual and the taxpayer is in violation of local law.

In addition to the dependency exemption, a taxpayer who has a "qualifying child" in the household may claim the child tax credit (§24 IRC), the earned income credit (§32 IRC) and may also be able to file as "head of household," a tax rate schedule that is slightly lower than that for single taxpayers. See §1(b) and §2(b) IRC. Note that the definition of "child" in §152 includes stepchildren, but that there is no definition of "stepchild."

Notes and Questions

1. If Ann and Beth are married in Massachusetts, or civil unioned in Vermont, or domestic partnered in California, can Ann claim that she is the stepmother of Beth's children? [Note: If Ann is the partner with the higher income, the household is likely to benefit if she is the one to claim the dependency exemption and head of household filing status because deductions and reduced rates are of greater benefit to taxpayers in higher brackets.]

2. If Ann supports Beth during the tax year because Beth is a full-time student and has no income of her own, can Ann claim Beth as a dependent? Section 151 IRC allows a deduction for each dependent as defined in §152. Should it matter whether Ann and Beth are married? What if they were married in Canada and are now living in Virginia, which has a statute that says same-sex marriages are "prohibited?"

d. Taxation of domestic partner benefits

When an employer pays for the health care of an employee or an employee's family, the employer is in effect paying the employee a higher salary. The benefit to the employee is taxable income. However, the Internal Revenue Code explicitly excludes from income certain health care benefits, paid pursuant to a plan, so long as the benefits are paid to employees, their spouses and dependents. See Sections 105 and 106 I.R.C. Since most domestic partners do not qualify as dependents under Section 152 and since federal tax law does not recognize domestic partners (or even same-sex spouses) as spouses, the value of the domestic partner benefit must be reported as taxable income to the employee.

Question: Can you put together a good equal protection challenge to this particular tax rule? Can you, on behalf of the government, justify this distinction on rational basis grounds?

e. Income from community property

Community property is viewed for tax purposes as owned equally between the spouses. In California, domestic partners can own community property and presumably the same tax rule would apply to them that applies to spouses. DOMA should not apply to prevent the income splitting because income splitting is not a rule contained in a federal tax statute and it is not specifically restricted to spouses. The income tax rules for community property have been established by case law based on an analysis of the ownership rights created by the community property regime. See *Poe v. Seaborn*, 282 U.S. 101 (1930)(husband and wife equally owned community property and thus each was taxed on half of the income produced by the property). It is the vested property right that causes the income to be split between the two property owners. This result should not be surprising. All jointly owned property, whether owned as tenants in common, as joint tenants, as tenants by the entirety, or as community property, produces the same tax consequences. Income from jointly owned property is taxed to the joint owners in proportion to their ownership interests. That is a marriage neutral rule.

But there is another aspect to the *Poe v. Seaborn* decision that requires closer analysis. The Court also held that earnings of the husband were community earnings and thus should be taxed half to the wife since she effectively owned half the earnings. This rule continues to apply to spouses who file separate returns. And, even though most of the income-splitting value of *Seaborn* has been obliterated by the joint return, no one has ever suggested that *Seaborn* is not still good law as to the underlying principle: community earnings are split for tax purposes, whether the earnings are from property or the labor of the spouses.

A very interesting question arises for domestic partners in California. Since they cannot file jointly, can they take advantage of the income splitting aspect of the *Seaborn* decision? The tax savings could be significant. In a situation in which only one of the partners is earning a salary, the ability to report half of that salary as the income of the other partner shifts income dollars that would have been taxed at the top marginal bracket of the earning partner to the lower bracket of the non-earning partner. There is absolutely nothing in the analysis in *Seaborn* and cases following it that would restrict the income splitting potential to spouses. After all, the domestic partner "owns" half of the salary earned by her partner just as much as Mrs. Seaborn "owned" half of Mr. Seaborn's salary. The IRS, however, has yet to speak publicly about this issue. Some tax lawyers predict that when the IRS does speak, it will be to deny the application of *Seaborn* to same-sex partners. If you were assigned to write a draft of a Revenue Ruling on this question, what would you say?

f. Property divisions at divorce

In 1962, the United States Supreme Court ruled that property divisions at divorce could trigger taxable gain to the spouse who transferred appreciated property to the other spouse in exchange for inchoate marital rights. *United States v. Davis*, 370 U.S. 65 (1962). In 1984, Congress added §1041 to the Internal Revenue Code, essentially reversing *Davis* and providing that property transfers incident to a divorce would not be treated as taxable exchanges of property. Section 1041 only applies to spouses and ex-spouses. Same-sex couples would not be able to rely on this provision to claim that property divisions at "divorce" are not taxable. Thus, for example, if Ann were to transfer to Beth real estate with a cost basis of $10x and a fair market value of $100x in a property settlement incident to a Massachusetts divorce (or termination of a Vermont Civil Union), the *Davis* rule would tax Ann on a gain of $90x.

However, equal divisions of jointly owned property are generally not taxable. This result seems exactly right when two co-owners of property decide to partition the property into two tracts and each take sole ownership of one of the two tracts. The transaction is a mere change in the form of ownership and the resulting ownership rights do not seem sufficiently different from what they were before the partition to warrant the triggering of a tax payment. In the tax world, we say that this is not a "realization" event. The owners merely carry their old historical cost basis in the whole property over into their new ownership of the partitioned property. Gain will be recognized when a sale or some other realization event occurs.

Relying on this basic rule regarding realization, courts established exceptions to the *Davis* rule well before §1041 was enacted. For example, a division of community property between husband and wife seemed as much of a non-realization event as two co-owners partitioning a single tract of land. Eventually the rule was expanded to include any substantially equal division of community property, even if husband claimed all the stocks and bonds and wife claimed all the real estate. The IRS agreed with the courts. See Rev. Rul. 76-83, 1976-1 C.B. 213. Ultimately other courts followed suit and ruled that even in non-community property states, so long as the non-titled spouse had a strong equitable claim under state law to an ownership interest in the property being divided at divorce, the division would not trigger taxable gain. See *Imel v. United States*, 375 F. Supp. 1102 (D. Col. 1974)(split of marital property under equitable division rules of Colorado is a nontaxable division of jointly owned property). If this latter case is applied to Ann and Beth and if they are dividing their property under the state law of Vermont or Massachusetts, should the division be taxable?

2. Gift and Estate Tax

Gratuitous transfers to spouses, whether made during lifetime or at death, are not taxable. There is a 100% marital deduction under both the gift tax and the estate tax for all such transfers. Thus, the surviving spouse can enjoy the couple's lifetime accumulation of property without any reduction in the form of a tax payment at the time of death of the first spouse. Same-sex couples, whether married or otherwise committed to each other, cannot enjoy this benefit.

a. Gift tax issues

Absent a marital deduction, a transfer of property from one partner to the other for "less than full and adequate consideration" will be treated as a gift for gift tax purposes, even if it is not treated as a gift for income tax purposes. Gifts in excess of the annual exclusion (currently $11,000, but subject to adjustment for inflation) are "taxable gifts" and must be reported in a gift tax return. There is a lifetime exclusion from tax for the first $1.0 million of taxable gifts (i.e., counting only those gifts that exceed the annual exclusion). Once cumulative "taxable gifts" exceed the $1.0 million amount, gift taxes will be payable, starting at approximately 40% on any amount of $1.0 million.

Given the lifetime exclusion, gift tax problems are not relevant for most couples. But there are a sufficient number of same-sex couples who are affected by these rules. Assume Harry owns a home in San Francisco worth $2.0 million and a vacation home up the coast valued at $2.0 million. Then Harry meets Sam and before long they decide to register as domestic partners. Harry would like Sam to co-own the real property with him. If he transfers a fifty percent ownership interest to Sam, the transfer will trigger some gift tax liability.

So, Harry elects, for tax reasons, not to make the transfer. However, he does expect Sam to live with him in the San Francisco home and to accompany him when he visits his second home up the coast. And, since Harry has sufficient income, he encourages Sam to stay home and take care of domestic things. Harry's income pays for everything, including Sam's clothes, his car, and several trips to Europe each year. Is Harry making a taxable gift to Sam in each year that the value of these benefits exceeds $11,000? Most commentators in the past have said yes. The clearly established rule is that when A supports B, but has no legal obligation to do so, the support payment is a gift, reachable by the gift tax to the extent it exceeds $11,000 a year. [But no tax will be payable on these cumulative annual gifts until they total $1.0 million, when aggregated with all other taxable gifts.] See, e.g., Rev. Rul 54-343, 1954-2 C.B. 318 (father's payments of hospital bills and living expenses of son and son's family held as taxable gifts); Rev. Rul. 82-98, 1982-1 C.B. 141 (parental support of adult disabled child held as taxable gifts). See Robert G. Popovich, Support Your Family, but Leave out Uncle Sam: A Call for Federal Gift Tax Reform, 55 Md. L. Rev. 343 (1996); see also Patricia A. Cain, Same-Sex Couples and the Federal Tax Laws, 1 Law. & Sexuality 97 (1991) (arguing that support payments by one partner for the joint consumption of both partners should not be viewed as taxable gifts because they are not transfers of property and such payments do not constitute the sort of estate depleting transfers that the gift tax was intended to cover).

Domestic partners in California should be able to avoid this gift tax trap. Once they become registered domestic partners, all of the property they acquire and all of the income they earn is community property. Under the California community property regime, Harry and Sam are viewed as owning property and current income fifty-fifty. So, if current income is used for their joint support and if they both use the jointly owned property, Sam should be viewed as contributing to his own support and Harry only to his own support.

Same-sex spouses in Massachusetts and partners in a Vermont civil union should also be able to avoid this gift tax trap because, under state law, such spouses and partners are required to support each other. The same is true for domestic partners in California. So if Harry supports Sam out of his separate funds, the state-imposed obligation should prevent the support from being a taxable gift. Support payments that are required by state law, rather than by choice of the payor, have never been considered taxable gifts. This should be true both for support payments made during the marriage or partnership and for support payments made in the event of a divorce or termination. See Rev. Rul. 68-379, 1968-2 C.B. 414, ruling that property transferred to wife to satisfy her claim for support was not a taxable gift because it was a payment of a legal obligation.

Conceptually, one might argue that the acquisition of community property during the existence of the domestic partnership in California, especially when the funds for purchase are provided solely from the earnings of one partner, constitute taxable gifts as a sort of constructive transfer of property rights to the non-earning partner. However, no one has ever seriously argued that the creation of marital rights during marriage, including community property rights, are taxable gifts. The 100% marital deduction did not exist for the first 50 to 60 years of the gift tax. Yet no one argued that when a poor person married a rich person and thereby acquired certain rights in the rich person's current and future property, that a taxable gift occurred. It should be noted, however, that a spouse (or partner) who transmutes separate property into community property, which is possible under California law, does in fact make a gift of 50% of the property's value.

In California, when domestic partners terminate a relationship and divide the community property, presumably no taxable gift occurs. Each partner is merely receiving what is his.

Property divisions in Massachusetts and Vermont are somewhat different. While the non-titled spouse or partner has an equitable interest in the property of the other spouse (or partner), that interest is less firmly vested than the community property interests of spouses and partners in California. Whether property divisions at divorce are taxable as gifts in common law states, as opposed to community property states, is a complex question. For spouses the answer is covered by §2516, which provides that such transfers are not gifts. But same-sex couples, whether married or not, cannot rely on §2516. They can, however, rely on Rev. Rul. 68-369, *supra*, if the property transferred is to settle the obligation of support. In addition, they can rely on *Estate of Glen v. Commissioner*, 45 T.C. 323 (1966), which held that a property transfer from husband to wife, incident to a divorce but not covered by §2516, was not a taxable gift so long as the wife had a presently enforceable claim to an ownership interest in the property at the time of divorce. Apparently, the only transfers that continue to be covered by §2516 are transfers incident to divorce that are made in satisfaction of inchoate marital rights, such as the right to share in the spouse's estate at death.

b. Estate tax issues

While there is talk of a permanent repeal of the estate tax, that repeal has not yet occurred. The exemption amount, however, has been increased (in 2005 it is $1.5 million), and will continue to increase until 2009, when it becomes $3.5 million. It should be noted that, even if the estate tax is repealed, there is currently no plan to repeal the gift tax, and the exemption will remain at $1.0 million.

For same-sex couples with significant property, the estate tax remains a problem. A common practice is for one partner to own a life insurance policy on the other partner in an amount sufficient to pay the tax. Life insurance is usually included in the estate of the insured, but not if it is totally owned by someone other than the insured. See §2042.

California domestic partners have a clear advantage under the estate tax because they can own community property. At death, community property is in essence divided in half. One half is considered owned by the decedent with the other half owned by the surviving partner. Only the half owned by the decedent will be included in the gross estate for tax purposes.

Of course, couples in other states can achieve the same result by co-owning property. Only the portion of the property owned by the decedent will be included in the estate at death. [But see §2040 which sets forth a tax trap for those who own property as joint tenants with right of survivorship. The survivor will need to prove that he or she actually contributed funds to the purchase of the interest owned by the survivor.] The real advantage for community property partners is that as property is acquired during the relationship it is characterized as community property, presumably with no gift tax consequences. In common law property states, if one partner pays for the property and takes title as a co-owner with the other partner, the transaction appears to be a gift.

The controlling statute for what property is included in the gross estate is §2033 of the Internal Revenue Code, which provides: "The value of the gross estate shall include the value of all property to the extent of the interest therein of the decedent at the time of his death." At the time of death, the decedent's interest in community property is 50%. The decedent's interest in property owned as co-tenants with a partner is presumptively 50%. Property owned as joint tenants and as tenants by the entirety are separately covered by §2040. Only 50% will be included in the decedent's estate if the surviving partner can prove original contribution toward the purchase of the other 50% interest.

Notes and Questions

In common law states, spouses are often given an interest in the other spouse's property at death. At common law, that interest was known as dower for a wife and curtesy for a husband. Most states now provide for a statutory share in lieu of dower or curtesy. For example, in Hawaii, spouses and reciprocal beneficiaries who have been in the relevant relationship with the decedent for 15 years or more are entitled to a 50% share of the decedent's estate at death, regardless of what the decedent may have provided in a will. See Hawaii Stat. §560:2-202. Massachusetts and Vermont have similar provisions for same-sex couples in marriages or civil unions, although the share is smaller, basically one-third. If Harry and Sam are Hawaii residents and have been registered as reciprocal beneficiaries for 15 years, do you think they can claim that only half of Harry's estate is included in his gross estate at death?

See I.R.C. §2034, which provides: "The value of the gross estate shall include the value of all property to the extent of any interest therein of the surviving spouse, existing at the time of the decedent's death as dower or curtesy, or by virtue of a statute creating an estate in lieu of dower or curtesy."

Advance Tax Problem for Discussion

Marjorie and Judy have lived together in a committed lesbian relationship for ten years. They have raised two children together. Judy has been a stay-at-home Mom, while Marjorie has worked hard at her career as a Hollywood screen star. All assets acquired during the relationship have been titled in Marjorie's name. The assets include a personal residence worth over $1 million with a cost basis of $900,000, a vacation home worth $1.5 million with a cost basis of $800,000, and stocks and bonds worth $750,000, with a cost basis of $700,000. The two women have decided to end their relationship and agree that the property acquired during the marriage should be treated as "marital property" and evenly divided. In addition, Marjorie intends to live up to her promise that if they did split-up, she would pay Judy $100,000 per year in support for three years. The couple currently resides in California. They have never registered at domestic partners.

How do you think the property division and support payments *should* be treated for tax purposes? For the tax buffs, how do you think the property division and support payments *will* be treated for tax purposes? What steps might you take to ensure the most positive outcome?

Further Reading on Tax Issues of Same-Sex Partners

Jarrett Tomas Barrios, Growing Pains in the Workplace: Tax Consequences of Health Plans for Domestic Partners, 47 Tax. Law. 845 (1994).

Patricia A. Cain, "Dependency, Taxes, and Alternative Families," 5 Iowa Journal of Gender Race & Justice 267 (2002).

_____Cain, "Death Taxes: A Critique from the Margin," 48 Cleveland Marshall Law Rev. 677 (2000).

_____Cain, "Taxing Lesbians,"6 So. Calif. Rev. of Law and Women's Studies 471 (1997).

_____Cain, "Same-Sex Couples and the Federal Tax Laws," 1 Law & Sexuality 97 (1991).

Adam Chase, Tax Planning for Same-Sex Couples, 72 Denv. L. Rev. 359 (1995).

Anthony C. Infanti, Tax Protest, "A Homosexual," and Frivolity: A Deconstructionist Meditation, 24 St. Louis U. Pub. L. Rev. 21 (2005).

Nancy J. Knauer, Heteronormativity and Federal Tax Policy, 101 W. Va. L. Rev. 129 (1998).

Christopher T. Nixon, Should Congress Revise the Tax Code to Extend the Same Tax Benefits to Same-sex Couples as are Currently Granted to Married Couples?: An Analysis in Light of Horizontal Equity, 23 S. Ill. U. L.J. 41 (1998).

Chapter Five

Recognition of the Parent-Child Relationship

A. Constitutional Foundations

Family law has historically been a matter of state, rather than federal, concern. State law defines who is or is not a parent and spells out parental responsibilities for children. State law regulates marriage and divorce. And, as we saw in Chapter Four, state law is responsible for expanding the definitions of family by extending legal recognition to couples outside of marriage. How children fare in these state schemes of regulation can vary from state to state, although all states claim to interpret their statutes so as to be "in the best interest" of the child.

But family law is not just a matter for state legislatures. State law is subject to the overriding requirements of due process and equal protection pronounced in the Fourteenth Amendment of the Federal Constitution. Two of the early key cases upon which the modern constitutional right of privacy is based involved the right of parents to control the raising and education of their children. *Meyer v. Nebraska*, 262 U.S. 390 (1923); *Pierce v. Society of Sisters*, 268 U.S. 510 (1925). These cases were decided in the heyday of the *Lochner* doctrine, which gave strong constitutional protection to "liberty" interests under the due process clause, including liberty of contract. Protecting individual liberty by striking down legislative infringements on that liberty is often referred to as "substantive due process." The *Lochner* era ended in 1937, and the Supreme Court began to defer more readily to legislative decisions, regardless of whether they interfered with individual liberty interests. In 1965, *Griswold v. Connecticut* ushered in a new era of constitutional protection for certain liberty interests under the due process clause. The Court remained unwilling to strike down legislation that restricted economic liberty interests, but began to scrutinize more closely legislation that infringed on personal liberty interests. Concern for family relationships was at the center of this new "substantive due process doctrine."

1. Who is a Parent?

Stanley v. Illinois
405 U.S. 645 (1972)

WHITE, J.

Joan Stanley lived with Peter Stanley intermittently for 18 years, during which time they had three children. When Joan Stanley died, Peter Stanley lost not only her but also his children. Under Illinois law, the children of unwed fathers become wards of the State upon the death of the mother. Accordingly, upon Joan Stanley's death, in a dependency proceeding instituted by the State of Illinois, Stanley's children were declared wards of the State and placed with court-appointed guardians. Stanley appealed, claiming that he had never been shown to be an unfit parent and that since married fathers and unwed mothers could not be deprived of their children without such a showing, he had been deprived of the equal protection of the laws guaranteed him by the Fourteenth Amendment. The Illinois Supreme Court accepted the fact that Stanley's own unfitness had not been established but rejected the equal protection claim, holding that Stanley could properly be separated from his children upon proof of the single fact that he and the dead mother had not been married. Stanley's actual fitness as a father was irrelevant. Stanley presses his equal protection claim here.

We conclude that, as a matter of due process of law, Stanley was entitled to a hearing on his fitness as a parent before his children were taken from him and that, by denying him a hearing and extending it to all other parents whose custody of their children is challenged, the State denied Stanley the equal protection of the laws guaranteed by the Fourteenth Amendment.

The private interest here, that of a man in the children he has sired and raised, undeniably warrants deference and, absent a powerful countervailing interest, protection. It is plain that the interest of a parent in the companionship, care, custody, and management of his or her children "come(s) to this Court with a momentum for respect lacking when appeal is made to liberties which derive merely from shifting economic arrangements."

The Court has frequently emphasized the importance of the family. The rights to conceive and to raise one's children have been deemed "essential," *Meyer v. Nebraska*, 262 U.S. 390, 399 (1923), "basic civil rights of man," *Skinner v. Oklahoma*, 316 U.S. 535, 541 (1942), and "(r)ights far more precious...than property rights," *May v. Anderson*, 345 U.S. 528, 533 (1953). "It is cardinal with us that the custody, care and nurture of the child reside first in the parents, whose primary function and freedom include preparation for obligations the state can neither supply nor hinder." *Prince v. Massachusetts*, 321 U.S. 158, 166 (1944). The integrity of the family unit has found protection in the Due Process Clause of the Fourteenth Amendment, the Equal Protection Clause of the Fourteenth Amendment, and the Ninth Amendment.

Nor has the law refused to recognize those family relationships unlegitimized by a marriage ceremony. The Court has declared unconstitutional a state statute denying natural, but illegitimate, children a wrongful-death action for the death of their mother, emphasizing that such children cannot be denied the right of other children because familial bonds in such cases were often as warm, enduring, and important as those arising within a more formally organized family unit. *Levy v. Louisiana*, 391

U.S. 68, 71–72 (1968). "To say that the test of equal protection should be the 'legal' rather than the biological relationship is to avoid the issue. For the Equal Protection Clause necessarily limits the authority of a State to draw such 'legal' lines as it chooses." *Glona v. American Guarantee & Liability Ins. Co.*, 391 U.S. 73, 75–76 (1968).

These authorities make it clear that, at the least, Stanley's interest in retaining custody of his children is cognizable and substantial.

Notes and Questions

1. Stanley's only legal theory was equal protection. But Justice White, writing for the majority, finds a due process violation, a fact that concerned Justices Burger and Blackmun in dissenting opinions, omitted here. By focusing on Stanley's "interest" in retaining custody of his children, the Court's ruling offers greater protection for this "personal liberty" interest than it would offer for "liberties which derive merely from shifting economic arrangements."

2. How would you describe the liberty interest in *Stanley* and who do you think is entitled to this liberty interest? And, what protection does the Court offer this liberty interest? E.g., does *Stanley* merely stand for the proposition that parental rights cannot be terminated without sufficient procedural due process, or does it stand for the broader principle that parental rights are fundamental and thus subject to heightened scrutiny whenever the state infringes those rights?

3. Three key unwed father cases followed *Stanley*:

(a) In *Quilloin v. Walcott*, 434 U.S. 246 (1978), the biological father asserted his parental rights in an attempt to block the adoption of his child by the mother's husband, who had been raising the child for some time. He also asked for visitation rights. The Court denied his claim, emphasizing that he had had eleven years to establish his parental rights and had failed to do so. The Court allowed the adoption to proceed, which necessitated the termination of the biological father's parental rights.

(b) Next came *Caban v. Mohammed*, 441 U.S. 380 (1979). Here, too, the biological father asserted his parental rights to block the adoption of his children by the mother's husband. He also petitioned to adopt the children himself. The Court distinguished *Quilloin* in two ways. First, the father in this case had developed a relationship with the children, unlike the father in *Quilloin*. Second, the case was decided on equal protection grounds, with the Court holding that the state could not prefer mothers over fathers with respect to parental rights of their nonmarital children. The Court did not reach the due process claim. However, the dissent did. Four Justices held that the New York Statute allowing mothers, but not fathers, of nonmarital children to veto adoptions was constitutional under both equal protection and due process analysis. The dissenting Justices did not deny the existence of a constitutional parental right in the father. Instead they felt that the state's interest in facilitating adoption and the legitimation of the children was sufficiently compelling to justify the infringement of an unwed father's rights, especially since he had never legitimated the children himself.

(c) In the third case, *Lehr v. Robertson*, 463 U.S. 248 (1983), again a biological father asserted his parental rights to block the adoption of his child. While the court ruled against the father, it announced the following legal principle:

> "When an unwed father demonstrates a full commitment to the responsibilities of parenthood by 'com(ing) forward to participate in the rearing of his child,' his interest in personal contact with his child acquires substantial protection under the Due Process Clause."

Read together, these cases appear to stand for the principle that a biological parent, regardless of gender, who has established a relationship with his or her child, has a strong liberty interest, perhaps even a "fundamental right" that can only be infringed for compelling reasons.

The next case, *Michael H. v. Gerald D.*, challenged this understanding of the law.

Michael H. v. Gerald D.
491 U.S. 110 (1989)

SCALIA, J.

Under California law, a child born to a married woman living with her husband is presumed to be a child of the marriage. Cal.Evid.Code Ann. Sec. 621 (West Supp.1989). The presumption of legitimacy may be rebutted only by the husband or wife, and then only in limited circumstances. The instant appeal presents the claim that this presumption infringes upon the due process rights of a man who wishes to establish his paternity of a child born to the wife of another man, and the claim that it infringes upon the constitutional right of the child to maintain a relationship with her natural father.

The facts of this case are, we must hope, extraordinary. On May 9, 1976, in Las Vegas, Nevada, Carole D., an international model, and Gerald D., a top executive in a French oil company, were married. The couple established a home in Playa del Rey, California, in which they resided as husband and wife when one or the other was not out of the country on business. In the summer of 1978, Carole became involved in an adulterous affair with a neighbor, Michael H. In September 1980, she conceived a child, Victoria D., who was born on May 11, 1981. Gerald was listed as father on the birth certificate and has always held Victoria out to the world as his daughter. Soon after delivery of the child, however, Carole informed Michael that she believed he might be the father.

In the first three years of her life, Victoria remained always with Carole, but found herself within a variety of quasi-family units. In October 1981, Gerald moved to New York City to pursue his business interests, but Carole chose to remain in California. At the end of that month, Carole and Michael had blood tests of themselves and Victoria, which showed a 98.07% probability that Michael was Victoria's father. In January 1982, Carole visited Michael in St. Thomas, where his primary business interests were based. There Michael held Victoria out as his child. In March, however, Carole left Michael and returned to California, where she took up residence with yet another man, Scott K. Later that spring, and again in the summer, Carole and Victoria spent time with Gerald in New York City, as well as on vacation in Europe. In the fall, they returned to Scott in California.

In November 1982, rebuffed in his attempts to visit Victoria, Michael filed a filiation action in California Superior Court to establish his paternity and right to visitation. In March 1983, the court appointed an attorney and guardian ad litem to represent Victoria's interests. Victoria then filed a cross-complaint asserting that if she had more than one psychological or *de facto* father, she was entitled to maintain her filial relationship, with all of the attendant rights, duties, and obligations, with both. In May 1983, Carole filed a motion for summary judgment. During this period, from March through July 1983, Carole was again living with Gerald in New York. In August, however, she returned to California, became involved once again with Michael, and instructed her attorneys to remove the summary judgment motion from the calendar.

For the ensuing eight months, when Michael was not in St. Thomas he lived with Carole and Victoria in Carole's apartment in Los Angeles and held Victoria out as his daughter. In April 1984, Carole and Michael signed a stipulation that Michael was Victoria's natural father. Carole left Michael the next month, however, and instructed her attorneys not to file the stipulation. In June 1984, Carole reconciled with Gerald and joined him in New York, where they now live with Victoria and two other children since born into the marriage.

In May 1984, Michael and Victoria, through her guardian ad litem, sought visitation rights for Michael *pendente lite.* To assist in determining whether visitation would be in Victoria's best interests, the Superior Court appointed a psychologist to evaluate Victoria, Gerald, Michael, and Carole. The psychologist recommended that Carole retain sole custody, but that Michael be allowed continued contact with Victoria pursuant to a restricted visitation schedule....

On October 19, 1984, Gerald, who had intervened in the action, moved for summary judgment on the ground that under Cal.Evid.Code § 621 there were no triable issues of fact as to Victoria's paternity. This law provides that "the issue of a wife cohabiting with her husband, who is not impotent or sterile, is conclusively presumed to be a child of the marriage." Cal.Evid.Code Ann. § 621(a) (West Supp.1989). The presumption may be rebutted by blood tests, but only if a motion for such tests is made, within two years from the date of the child's birth, either by the husband or, if the natural father has filed an affidavit acknowledging paternity, by the wife. §§ 621(c) and (d).

On January 28, 1985, having found that affidavits submitted by Carole and Gerald sufficed to demonstrate that the two were cohabiting at conception and birth and that Gerald was neither sterile nor impotent, the Superior Court granted Gerald's motion for summary judgment, rejecting Michael's and Victoria's challenges to the constitutionality of § 621.

On appeal, Michael asserted, *inter alia,* that the Superior Court's application of sec. 621 had violated his substantive due process rights. Victoria also raised a due process challenge to the statute, seeking to preserve her *de facto* relationship with Michael as well as with Gerald. She contended, in addition, that as sec. 621 allows the husband and, at least to a limited extent, the mother, but not the child, to rebut the presumption of legitimacy, it violates the child's right to equal protection. Finally, she asserted a right to continued visitation with Michael under sec. 4601. After submission of briefs and a hearing, the California Court of Appeal affirmed the judgment of the Superior Court and upheld the constitutionality of the statute.

We address first the claims of Michael. At the outset, it is necessary to clarify what he sought and what he was denied. California law, like nature itself, makes no provision for dual fatherhood. Michael was seeking to be declared *the* father of Victoria. The immediate benefit he evidently sought to obtain from that status was visitation rights. But if Michael were successful in being declared the father, other rights would follow—most importantly, the right to be considered as the parent who should have custody,

Cal.Civ.Code Ann. § 4600 (West 1983), a status which "embrace[s] the sum of parental rights with respect to the rearing of a child, including the child's care; the right to the child's services and earnings; the right to direct the child's activities; the right to make decisions regarding the control, education, and health of the child; and the right, as well as the duty, to prepare the child for additional obligations, which includes the teaching of moral standards, religious beliefs, and elements of good citizenship." All parental rights, including visitation, were automatically denied by denying Michael status as the father. While Cal.Civ.Code Ann. Sec. 4601 places it within the discretionary power of a court to award visitation rights to a nonparent, the Superior Court here, affirmed by the Court of Appeal, held that California law denies visitation, against the wishes of the mother, to a putative father who has been prevented by sec. 621 from establishing his paternity.

Michael contends as a matter of substantive due process that, because he has established a parental relationship with Victoria, protection of Gerald's and Carole's marital union is an insufficient state interest to support termination of that relationship. This argument is, of course, predicated on the assertion that Michael has a constitutionally protected liberty interest in his relationship with Victoria.

It is an established part of our constitutional jurisprudence that the term "liberty" in the Due Process Clause extends beyond freedom from physical restraint. See, e.g., *Pierce v. Society of Sisters*, 268 U.S. 510 (1925); *Meyer v. Nebraska*, 262 U.S. 390 (1923).

In an attempt to limit and guide interpretation of the Clause, we have insisted not merely that the interest denominated as a "liberty" be "fundamental" (a concept that, in isolation, is hard to objectify), but also that it be an interest traditionally protected by our society. As we have put it, the Due Process Clause affords only those protections "so rooted in the traditions and conscience of our people as to be ranked as fundamental."

This insistence that the asserted liberty interest be rooted in history and tradition is evident, as elsewhere, in our cases according constitutional protection to certain parental rights. Michael reads the landmark case of *Stanley v. Illinois*, 405 U.S. 645 (1972) [and subsequent cases] as establishing that a liberty interest is created by biological fatherhood plus an established parental relationship—factors that exist in the present case as well. We think that distorts the rationale of those cases. As we view them, they rest not upon such isolated factors but upon the historic respect—indeed, sanctity would not be too strong a term— traditionally accorded to the relationships that develop within the unitary family. In *Stanley*, for example, we forbade the destruction of such a family when, upon the death of the mother, the State had sought to remove children from the custody of a father who had lived with and supported them and their mother for 18 years.

Thus, the legal issue in the present case reduces to whether the relationship between persons in the situation of Michael and Victoria has been treated as a protected family unit under the historic practices of our society, or whether on any other basis it has been accorded special protection. We think it impossible to find that it has. In fact, quite to the contrary, our traditions have protected the marital family (Gerald, Carole, and the child they acknowledge to be theirs) against the sort of claim Michael asserts.

The presumption of legitimacy was a fundamental principle of the common law. Traditionally, that presumption could be rebutted only by proof that a husband was incapable of procreation or had had no access to his wife during the relevant period. The primary policy rationale underlying the common law's severe restrictions on rebuttal of the presumption appears to have been an aversion to declaring children illegitimate, thereby depriving them of rights of inheritance and succession, and likely making them wards of the state. A secondary policy concern was the interest in promoting the "peace and tranquillity of States and families," a goal that is obviously impaired by facilitating suits against husband and wife asserting that their children are illegitimate.

We have found nothing in the older sources, nor in the older cases, addressing specifically the power of the natural father to assert parental rights over a child born into a woman's existing marriage with another man. What Michael asserts here is a right to have himself declared the natural father *and thereby to obtain parental prerogatives.* What he must establish, therefore, is not that our society has traditionally allowed a natural father in his circumstances to establish paternity, but that it has traditionally accorded such a father parental rights, or at least has not traditionally denied them.

We have never had occasion to decide whether a child has a liberty interest, symmetrical with that of her parent, in maintaining her filial relationship. We need not do so here because, even assuming that such a right exists, Victoria's claim must fail. Victoria's due process challenge is, if anything, weaker than Michael's. Her basic claim is not that California has erred in preventing her from establishing that Michael, not Gerald, should stand as her legal father. Rather, she claims a due process right to maintain filial relationships with both Michael and Gerald. This assertion merits little discussion, for, whatever the merits of the guardian ad litem's belief that such an arrangement can be of great psychological benefit to a child, the claim that a State must recognize multiple fatherhood has no support in the history or traditions of this country. Moreover, even if we were to construe Victoria's argument as forwarding the lesser proposition that, whatever her status vis-a-vis Gerald, she has a liberty interest in maintaining a filial relationship with her natural father, Michael, we find that, at best, her claim is the obverse of Michael's and fails for the same reasons. *Affirmed.*

Justice STEVENS, concurring in the judgment.

As I understand this case, it raises two different questions about the validity of California's statutory scheme. First, is Cal. Evid. Code Ann. Sec. 621 (West Supp.1989) unconstitutional because it prevents Michael and Victoria from obtaining a judicial determination that he is her biological father—even if no legal rights would be affected by that determination? Second, does the California statute deny appellants a fair opportunity to prove that Victoria's best interests would be served by granting Michael visitation rights?

On the first issue I agree with Justice Scalia that the Federal Constitution imposes no obligation upon a State to "declare facts unless some legal consequence hinges upon the requested declaration." *Ante,* at 2343. "The actions of judges neither create nor sever genetic bonds." *Lehr v. Robertson,* 463 U.S. 248, 261 (1983).

On the second issue I do not agree with Justice Scalia's analysis. He seems to reject the possibility that a natural father might ever have a constitutionally protected interest in his relationship with a child whose mother was married to, and cohabiting with, another man at the time of the child's conception and birth. I think cases like *Stanley v. Illinois,* 405 U.S. 645, 92 S.Ct. 1208, 31 L.Ed.2d 551 (1972), and *Caban v. Mohammed,* 441 U.S. 380 (1979), demonstrate that enduring "family" relationships may develop in unconventional settings. I therefore would not foreclose the possibility that a constitutionally protected relationship between a natural father and his child might exist in a case like this. Indeed, I am willing to assume for the purpose of deciding this case that Michael's relationship with Victoria is strong enough to give him a constitutional right to try to convince a trial judge that Victoria's best interest would be served by granting him visitation rights. I am satisfied, however, that the California statute, as applied in this case, gave him that opportunity.

Section 4601 of the California Civil Code Annotated (West Supp.1989) provides:

"[R]easonable visitation rights [shall be awarded] to a parent unless it is shown that the visitation would be detrimental to the best interests of the child. In the discretion of the court, reasonable visitation rights may be granted *to any other person having an interest in the welfare of the child*." (Emphasis added.)

The presumption established by § 621 denied Michael the benefit of the first sentence of § 4601 because, as a matter of law, he is not a "parent." It does not, however, prevent him from proving that he is an "other person having an interest in the welfare of the child." On its face, therefore, the statute plainly gave the trial judge the authority to grant Michael "reasonable visitation rights."

I recognize that my colleagues have interpreted sec. 21 as creating an absolute bar that would prevent a California trial judge from regarding the natural father as either a "parent" within the meaning of the first sentence of § 4601or as "any other person" within the meaning of the second sentence.... That is not only an unnatural reading of the statute's plain language, but it is also not consistent with the California courts' reading of the statute. [See] *Vincent B. v. Joan R.*, 126 Cal.App.3d 619, 179 Cal.Rptr. 9 (1981), appeal dism'd, 459 U.S. 807 (1982).

Under the circumstances of the case before us, Michael was given a fair opportunity to show that he is Victoria's natural father, that he had developed a relationship with her, and that her interests would be served by granting him visitation rights. On the other hand, the record also shows that after its rather shaky start, the marriage between Carole and Gerald developed a stability that now provides Victoria with a loving and harmonious family home. In the circumstances of this case, I find nothing fundamentally unfair about the exercise of a judge's discretion that, in the end, allows the mother to decide whether her child's best interests would be served by allowing the natural father visitation privileges. Because I am convinced that the trial judge had the authority under state law both to hear Michael's plea for visitation rights and to grant him such rights if Victoria's best interests so warranted, I am satisfied that the California statutory scheme is consistent with the Due Process Clause of the Fourteenth Amendment.

Notes and Questions

1. How would you describe the fundamental right to exercise parental rights after the decision in *Michael H.*? Note that the initial issue here was one of parental identity, i.e., who will be recognized as a parent. Does Michael lose because he is unable to establish that he is a parent or because his liberty interest as a parent is trumped by competing liberty interests?

Justice Scalia recognized the competing liberty interests when he said:

Here, to *provide* protection to an adulterous natural father is to *deny* protection to a marital father, and vice versa. If Michael has a "freedom not to conform" (whatever that means), Gerald must equivalently have a "freedom to conform." One of them will pay a price for asserting that "freedom"— Michael by being unable to act as father of the child he has adulterously begotten, or Gerald by being unable to preserve the integrity of the traditional family unit he and Victoria have established. Our disposition does not choose between these two "freedoms," but leaves that to the people of California.

In *Stanley*, by contrast, there were no competing interests between persons claiming parental rights.

2. Is there any way to protect both Michael's and Gerald's interests?

3. The decision in *Michael H.* was 5-4. Scalia's opinion was a plurality opinion. Justice Stevens concurred, but disagreed with Scalia's opinion to the extent it stood as an absolute bar for unwed fathers to seek visitation with a child conceived while the mother was married to someone else. Does this mean that the Court recognized a substantive due process right in Michael, but disagreed as to whether the state had justified its infringement? Does the Stevens opinion make sense to you? I.e., if a biological father who has established a relationship with his child has a constitutionally protected right in that relationship, shouldn't that right be exercised as a *"father"* rather than as *"any other person having an interest in the welfare of the child?"*

4. In *Michael M. v. Giovanni F.*, 7 Cal. Rptr. 2d 460 (Cal. App. 1992), the court ruled in favor of a biological father's right to establish paternity and seek visitation and custody rights for his child, who was born to a mother, married to another man at the time of birth, but not at the time of conception. *Michael H.* was distinguished.

2. The Competing Interests of Parents and Nonparents

Troxel v. Granville
530 U.S. 57 (2000)

O'CONNOR, J. (joined by Chief Justice Rehnquist and Justices Ginsburg and Breyer):

Section 26.10.160(3) of the Revised Code of Washington permits "[a]ny person" to petition a superior court for visitation rights "at any time," and authorizes that court to grant such visitation rights whenever "visitation may serve the best interest of the child." Petitioners Jenifer and Gary Troxel petitioned a Washington Superior Court for the right to visit their grandchildren, Isabelle and Natalie Troxel. Respondent Tommie Granville, the mother of Isabelle and Natalie, opposed the petition. The case ultimately reached the Washington Supreme Court, which held that §26.10.160(3) unconstitutionally interferes with the fundamental right of parents to rear their children.

Tommie Granville and Brad Troxel shared a relationship that ended in June 1991. The two never married, but they had two daughters, Isabelle and Natalie. Jenifer and Gary Troxel are Brad's parents, and thus the paternal grandparents of Isabelle and Natalie. After Tommie and Brad separated in 1991, Brad lived with his parents and regularly brought his daughters to his parents' home for weekend visitation. Brad committed suicide in May 1993. Although the Troxels at first continued to see Isabelle and Natalie on a regular basis after their son's death, Tommie Granville informed the Troxels in October 1993 that she wished to limit their visitation with her daughters to one short visit per month.

In December 1993, the Troxels commenced the present action by filing, in the Washington Superior Court for Skagit County, a petition to obtain visitation rights with Isabelle and Natalie. Section 26.10.160(3) provides: "Any person may petition the court for visitation rights at any time including, but not limited to, custody proceedings. The court may order visitation rights for any person when visitation may serve the best interest of the child whether or not there has been any change of circumstances." At trial, the Troxels requested two weekends of overnight visitation per month and two weeks of visitation each summer. Granville did not oppose visitation altogether, but instead asked the court to order one day of visitation per month with no overnight stay. In 1995, the Superior Court issued an oral ruling and entered a visitation decree ordering visitation one weekend per month, one week during the summer, and four hours on both of the petitioning grandparents' birthdays.

Granville appealed, during which time she married Kelly Wynn. The Superior Court found that visitation was in Isabelle's and Natalie's best interests:

> "The Petitioners [the Troxels] are part of a large, central, loving family, all located in this area, and the Petitioners can provide opportunities for the children in the areas of cousins and music.

> "...The court took into consideration all factors regarding the best interest of the children and considered all the testimony before it. The children would be benefitted from spending quality time with the Petitioners, provided that that time is balanced with time with the childrens' [sic] nuclear family. The court finds that the childrens' [sic] best interests are served by spending time with their mother and stepfather's other six children."

Approximately nine months after the Superior Court entered its order on remand, Granville's husband formally adopted Isabelle and Natalie.

The Washington Court of Appeals reversed the lower court's visitation order and dismissed the Troxels' petition for visitation, holding that nonparents lack standing to seek visitation under §26.10.160(3) unless a custody action is pending. In the Court of Appeals' view, that limitation on nonparental visitation actions was "consistent with the constitutional restrictions on state interference with parents' fundamental liberty interest in the care, custody, and management of their children." Having resolved the case on the statutory ground, however, the Court of Appeals did not expressly pass on Granville's constitutional challenge to the visitation statute.

The Washington Supreme Court granted the Troxels' petition for review and, after consolidating their case with two other visitation cases, affirmed. The court disagreed with the Court of Appeals' decision on the statutory issue and found that the plain language of §26.10.160(3) gave the Troxels standing to seek visitation, irrespective of whether a custody action was pending. The Washington Supreme Court nevertheless agreed with the Court of Appeals' ultimate conclusion that the Troxels could not obtain visitation of Isabelle and Natalie pursuant to §26.10.160(3). The court rested its decision on the Federal Constitution, holding that §26.10.160(3) unconstitutionally infringes on the fundamental right of parents to rear their children. In the court's view, there were at least two problems with the nonparental visitation statute. First, according to the Washington Supreme Court, the Constitution permits a State to interfere with the right of parents to rear their children only to prevent harm or potential harm to a child. Section 26.10.160(3) fails that standard because it requires no threshold showing of harm. Second, by allowing " 'any person' to petition for forced visitation of a child at 'any time' with the only requirement being that the visitation serve the best interest of the child," the Washington visitation statute sweeps too broadly. "It is not within the province of the state to make significant decisions concerning the custody of children merely because it could make a 'better' decision." The Washington Supreme Court held that "[p]arents have a right to limit visitation of their children with third persons," and that between parents and judges, "the parents should be the ones to choose whether to expose their children to certain people or ideas." Four justices dissented from the Washington Supreme Court's holding on the constitutionality of the statute.

We granted certiorari, and now affirm the judgment.

The demographic changes of the past century make it difficult to speak of an average American family. The composition of families varies greatly from household to household. While many children may have two married parents and grandparents who visit regularly, many other children are raised in single-parent households. In 1996, children living with only one parent accounted for 28 percent of all children under age 18 in the United States. U.S. Dept. of Commerce, Bureau of Census, Current Population Reports, 1997 Population Profile of the United States 27 (1998). Understandably, in these single-parent households, persons outside the nuclear family are called upon with increasing frequency to assist in the everyday tasks of child rearing. In many cases, grandparents play an important role.

The Fourteenth Amendment provides that no State shall "deprive any person of life, liberty, or property, without due process of law." We have long recognized that the Amendment's Due Process Clause, like its Fifth Amendment counterpart, "guarantees more than fair process." The Clause also includes a substantive component that "provides heightened protection against government interference with certain fundamental rights and liberty interests."

The liberty interest at issue in this case—the interest of parents in the care, custody, and control of their children—is perhaps the oldest of the fundamental liberty interests recognized by this Court. More than 75 years ago, in *Meyer v. Nebraska*, 262 U.S. 390, 399, 401 (1923), we held that the "liberty" protected by the Due Process Clause includes the right of parents to "establish a home and bring up children" and "to control the education of their own." Two years later, in *Pierce v. Society of Sisters*, 268 U.S. 510, 534–35 (1925), we again held that the "liberty of parents and guardians" includes the right "to direct the upbringing and education of children under their control."

In subsequent cases also, we have recognized the fundamental right of parents to make decisions concerning the care, custody, and control of their children. See, *e.g., Stanley v. Illinois,* 405 U.S. 645, 651 (1972) ("It is plain that the interest of a parent in the companionship, care, custody, and management of his or her children 'come[s] to this Court with a momentum for respect lacking when appeal is made to liberties which derive merely from shifting economic arrangements'" (citation omitted)); *Wisconsin v. Yoder*, 406 U.S. 205, 232 (1972) ("The history and culture of Western civilization reflect a strong tradition of parental concern for the nurture and upbringing of their children. This primary role of the parents in the upbringing of their children is now established beyond debate as an enduring American tradition"); *Quilloin v. Walcott*, 434 U.S. 246, 255 (1978) ("We have recognized on numerous occasions that the relationship between parent and child is constitutionally protected");...*Santosky v. Kramer*, 455 U.S. 745, 753 (1982) (discussing "[t]he fundamental liberty interest of natural parents in the care, custody, and management of their child")...In light of this extensive precedent, it cannot now be doubted that the Due Process Clause of the Fourteenth Amendment protects the fundamental right of parents to make decisions concerning the care, custody, and control of their children.

Section 26.10.160(3), as applied to Granville and her family in this case, unconstitutionally infringes on that fundamental parental right. The Washington nonparental visitation statute is breathtakingly broad. According to the statute's text, "*[a]ny person* may petition the court for visitation rights *at any time,*" and the court may grant such visitation rights whenever "visitation may serve *the best interest of the child.*" That language effectively permits any third party seeking visitation to subject any decision by a parent concerning visitation of the parent's children to state-court review. Once the visitation petition has been filed in court and the matter is placed before a judge, a parent's decision that visitation would not be in the child's best interest is accorded no deference. Section 26.10.160(3) contains no requirement that a court accord the parent's decision any presumption of validity or any weight whatsoever. Instead, the Washington statute places the best-interest determination solely in the hands of the judge. Should the judge disagree with the parent's estimation of the child's best interests, the judge's view necessarily prevails. Thus, in practical effect, in the State of Washington a court can disregard and overturn *any* decision by a fit custodial parent concerning visitation whenever a third party affected by the decision files a visitation petition, based solely on the judge's determination of the child's best interests.

Turning to the facts of this case, the record reveals that the Superior Court's order was based on precisely the type of mere disagreement we have just described and nothing more. The Superior Court's order was not founded on any special factors that might justify the State's interference with Granville's fundamental right to make decisions concerning the rearing of her two daughters. To be sure, this case involves a visitation petition filed by grandparents soon after the death of their son—the father of Isabelle and Natalie—but the combination of several factors here compels our conclusion that § 26.10.160(3), as applied, exceeded the bounds of the Due Process Clause.

The decisional framework employed by the Superior Court directly contravened the traditional presumption that a fit parent will act in the best interest of his or her child. See *Parham, supra,* at 602. In this respect, the court's presumption failed to provide any protection for Granville's fundamental constitutional right to make decisions concerning the rearing of her own daughters. And, if a fit parent's decision of the kind at issue here becomes subject to judicial review, the court must accord at least some special weight to the parent's own determination.

Finally, we note that there is no allegation that Granville ever sought to cut off visitation entirely. Rather, the present dispute originated when Granville informed the Troxels that she would prefer to restrict their visitation with Isabelle and Natalie to one short visit per month and special holidays. In the Superior Court proceedings Granville did not oppose visitation but instead asked that the duration of any visitation order be shorter than that requested by the Troxels. While the Troxels requested two weekends per month and two full weeks in the summer, Granville asked the Superior Court to order only one day of visitation per month (with no overnight stay) and participation in the Granville family's holiday celebrations. The Superior Court gave no weight to Granville's having assented to visitation even before the filing of any visitation petition or subsequent court intervention. The court instead rejected Granville's proposal and settled on a middle ground, ordering one weekend of visitation per month, one week in the summer, and time on both of the petitioning grandparents' birthdays. Significantly, many other

States expressly provide by statute that courts may not award visitation unless a parent has denied (or unreasonably denied) visitation to the concerned third party.

Considered together with the Superior Court's reasons for awarding visitation to the Troxels, the combination of these factors demonstrates that the visitation order in this case was an unconstitutional infringement on Granville's fundamental right to make decisions concerning the care, custody, and control of her two daughters. Accordingly, we hold that § 26.10.160(3), as applied in this case, is unconstitutional.

Notes and Questions

1. Does the *Troxel* holding mean that the rights of biological parents will always trump the rights of others who claim a protected interest in continuing a relationship with the child?

2. Were the grandparents in *Troxel* accorded more or less protection than Michael H?

3. Can *Troxel* be used to benefit biological or adoptive parents who want their wishes regarding a partner's role in childrearing to be honored by the courts? See cases *infra* at Part C (Who can Become a Parent) and Part D (Rights of the "Second Parent" Who Has Not Adopted).

3. Equal Protection and Child Custody

Palmore v. Sidoti
466 U.S. 429 (1984)

BURGER, C.J.

When petitioner Linda Sidoti Palmore and respondent Anthony J. Sidoti, both Caucasians, were divorced in May 1980 in Florida, the mother was awarded custody of their 3-year-old daughter. In September 1981 the father sought custody of the child by filing a petition to modify the prior judgment because of changed conditions. The change was that the child's mother was then cohabiting with a Negro, Clarence Palmore, Jr., whom she married two months later.

[The Florida court heard a] counselor's recommendation for a change in custody because "[t]he wife [petitioner] has chosen for herself and for her child, a life-style unacceptable to the father and to society.... The child...is, or at school age will be, subject to environmental pressures not of choice." The court then concluded that the best interests of the child would be served by awarding custody to the father. The court's rationale is contained in the following:

> The father's evident resentment of the mother's choice of a black partner is not sufficient to wrest custody from the mother. It is of some significance, however, that the mother did see fit to bring a man into her home and carry on a sexual relationship with him without being married to him. Such action tended to place gratification of her own desires ahead of her concern for the child's future

welfare. This Court feels that despite the strides that have been made in bettering relations between the races in this country, it is inevitable that Melanie will, if allowed to remain in her present situation and attains school age and thus more vulnerable to peer pressures, suffer from the social stigmatization that is sure to come.

The Second District Court of Appeal affirmed without opinion, thus denying the Florida Supreme Court jurisdiction to review the case. We granted certiorari, and we reverse.

The judgment of a state court determining or reviewing a child custody decision is not ordinarily a likely candidate for review by this Court. However, the court's opinion, after stating that the "father's evident resentment of the mother's choice of a black partner is not sufficient" to deprive her of custody, then turns to what it regarded as the damaging impact on the child from remaining in a racially mixed household. This raises important federal concerns arising from the Constitution's commitment to eradicating discrimination based on race.

A core purpose of the Fourteenth Amendment was to do away with all governmentally-imposed discrimination based on race. Classifying persons according to their race is more likely to reflect racial prejudice than legitimate public concerns; the race, not the person, dictates the category. Such classifications are subject to the most exacting scrutiny; to pass constitutional muster, they must be justified by a compelling governmental interest and must be "necessary...to the accomplishment" of its legitimate purpose.

It would ignore reality to suggest that racial and ethnic prejudices do not exist or that all manifestations of those prejudices have been eliminated. There is a risk that a child living with a step-parent of a different race may be subject to a variety of pressures and stresses not present if the child were living with parents of the same racial or ethnic origin.

The question, however, is whether the reality of private biases and the possible injury they might inflict are permissible considerations for removal of an infant child from the custody of its natural mother. We have little difficulty concluding that they are not. The Constitution cannot control such prejudices but neither can it tolerate them. Private biases may be outside the reach of the law, but the law cannot, directly or indirectly, give them effect. "Public officials sworn to uphold the Constitution may not avoid a constitutional duty by bowing to the hypothetical effects of private racial prejudice that they assume to be both widely and deeply held."

B. State Regulation of the Parent-Child Relationship

The state regulates the parent-child relationship as heavily as it regulates the marital relationship. As the previous section demonstrates, however, state regulation must comply with equal protection and due process principles contained in the Fourteenth Amendment. Some scholars have opined that based on the *Caban* line of cases, which protects a biological parent's right to develop and enjoy a relationship with nonmarital children, the Court has created a fundamental right in parents that must be honored in all cases involving child custody and visitation. So long as the parent can prove that he or she is a parent (i.e., the parental identification issue, which was at issue in *Michael H.*), then the courts must apply heightened scrutiny and the compelling state interest test when determining the relative rights of parents.

1. Child Custody Decisions at Divorce

If divorcing parents cannot decide how to handle child custody, a court will be asked to make the decision, exercising its equity jurisdiction. Traditionally, courts in this country have had to decide between one deserving parent and another. Gender discrimination permeated the early history of child custody law. Under English common law, custody was automatically awarded to fathers. When that doctrine was rejected in America, it was replaced with a maternal preference. See Rena K. Uviller, Fathers' Rights and Feminism: The Maternal Presumption Revisited, 1 Harv. Women's L.J. 107 (1978). Today, to provide gender equity, states apply gender neutral rules when required to decide between a mother and a father. Thus, states have adopted the "primary caretaker" preference to replace the maternal preference.

The guiding principle in all custody decisions is "the best interest of the child." While the principle offers a certain amount of rhetorical appeal, it is in practice a very indeterminate standard. Judges have relied upon the "best interest" standard to justify preferring a father over a mother when the mother had decided to attend law school, finding that her pursuit of a legal education would be detrimental to her children. See *Marriage of Tresnak*, 297 N.W.2d 109 (Iowa 1980), reversing the custody decision made at trial and awarding custody to the mother despite her desire to attend law school. See also *Ireland v. Smith*, 214 Mich. App. 235, 542 N.W.2d 344 (1996)(reversing a lower court decision that awarded custody to the father because the mother had decided to attend college and put her child in child care, whereas the father, also attending college, could provide child care through his mother, the child's paternal grandmother).

One scholar has argued that if parents have a fundamental right in the continued custody of their children, then they have a right to joint custody at divorce, absent some compelling reason to deny joint custody. See Holly L. Robinson, Joint Custody: Constitutional Imperatives, 54 U. Cin. L. Rev. 27 (1985). Joint custody is of recently relative vintage. In 1975, it was available in only one state. See Jana B. Singer and William L. Reynolds, A Dissent on Joint Custody, 47 Md. L. Rev. 497 (1988)(raising serious questions about the workability of joint custody, especially when it is court imposed over the opposition of one parent). When imposed by a court, it usually means that the parents have joint legal custody and thus the right to make joint decisions about the child's upbringing. Joint physical custody, meaning equal physical custody, is rarely possible as a practical matter. Normally one parent has primary physical custody and the other parent has liberal visitation rights.

Disputes over physical custody and visitation rights have plagued lesbian moms and gay dads for ages. The difficulty is that trial courts, exercising their equity jurisdiction, have great latitude in making decisions about custody. Usually these decisions are only overturned on appeal if they are arbitrary or an abuse of discretion.

A different standard applies when a change in custody is requested by one parent. Stability is in the child's best interest. Finality of a custody decision is thus in the child's interest.

Christian v. Randall

516 P.2d 132 (Col. App. 1973)

SILVERSTEIN, Chief Judge.

Duane Christian filed a petition in the District Court of Delta County seeking custody of his four daughters who were then in the custody of respondent, his former wife, pursuant to a 1964 Nevada divorce decree. The trial court granted the petition, and the respondent appeals from that judgment. We reverse.

The parties to this action were married in 1953, and four daughters were born of the marriage. The children lived with the respondent continuously following the divorce, having resided in Colorado for six years at the time this action was brought. On September 27, 1972, after a hearing upon the petition, the trial court awarded custody of the girls to the petitioner, a Nevada resident.

The issues in this appeal are whether there was sufficient evidence before the trial court to support its conclusion that it would be in the best interests of the children to transfer custody from the respondent to the petitioner and whether in so doing the trial court abused its discretion.

In reviewing an order affecting the custody of a child, appellate courts will make every reasonable presumption in favor of the action of the trial court. *Searle v. Searle*, 115 Colo. 266, 172 P.2d 837. We are always reluctant to disturb rulings of the trial court in custody matters, absent circumstances clearly disclosing an abuse of discretion. In the present case, however, our review of the record persuades us that, there being no evidence to support its conclusion, the trial court clearly abused its discretion. Under such circumstances the order cannot be allowed to stand.

The applicable statute, 1971 Perm.Supp., C.R.S.1963, 46—1— 31(2)(a), provides, 'The court shall not modify a prior custody decree unless it finds...that a change has occurred in the circumstances of the child or his custodian and that the modification is necessary to serve the best interests of the child.' Thus, a mere change of circumstances alone is insufficient to justify a change of custody.

Section 46—1—31(2)(a) further dictates that, in applying the above standards:

'(T)he court *shall retain* the custodian established by the prior decree *unless:*...
(d) The child's present environment endangers his physical health or significantly impairs his emotional development and the harm likely to be caused by a change of environment is outweighed by the advantage of a change to the child.' (emphasis supplied)

Further, 1971 Perm.Supp., C.R.S.1963, 46—1—24(1), provides:

'(a)...In determining the best interests of the child, the court shall consider all relevant factors including:

(b) The wishes of the child's parent or parents as to his custody;

(c) The wishes of the child as to his custodian;

(d) The interaction and interrelationship of the child with his parent or parents, his siblings, and any other person who may significantly affect the child's best interests;

(e) The child's adjustment to his home, school, and community; and

(f) The mental and physical health of all individuals involved.'

The record contains no evidence that the environment of respondent's home in Colorado endangered the children's physical health or impaired their emotional development. On the contrary, the evidence shows that the children were happy, healthy, well-adjusted children who were doing well in school and who were active in community activities.

The evidence included a letter from the school principal to the petitioner stating that he was well acquainted with the children and that he thought they were 'wonderful' and that the older three girls (ages 11, 13 and 16) who were in his school ranked 'very high on our Iowa Tests of Basic Skills.'

The investigative report prepared for the court by the Delta County Family and Children's Services stated:

> 'All of the girls have good report cards. Also each one has various special achievement awards such as art, music, etc. The oldest girl, Lou Ann, was elected Cherry Queen. All of the girls have many friends and enjoy school immensely.'

* * *

'Conclusions

From my interview with this family it would appear that all of the girls are being well cared for and provided with the necessities of life. Also there are no indications of any emotional or social retardation as a result of their home life for any of the children in this family. There appears to be a close and warm relationship between all of the children and between the children and the adults.' 1971 Perm.Supp., C.R.S.1963, 46—1—31(2)(d) recognizes that a modification of custody is likely to result in some harm to the child involved. At the hearing two experts testified that it would be traumatic for the children to leave a happy home where they were well adjusted. The evidence failed to show that the anxiety and confusion created by a change of custody would be outweighed by any advantages to the children resulting from such a change.

In its order at the close of the hearing the court found that respondent was 'going through a transsexual change' and based its conclusion that a change of custody would be to the best interest of the children solely on that ground. The evidence shows that, subsequent to the 1964 divorce, the respondent has been going through a transsexual change from female to male, that the respondent's name was legally changed from Gay Christensen Christian to Mark Avle Randall, and that subsequent to the filing of the petition respondent married a woman. 1971 Perm.Supp., C.R.S.1963, 46—1— 24(2), specifically directs that, in determining best interests, 'The court *shall not* consider conduct of a proposed custodian that does not affect his relationship with the child.' (emphasis supplied) The record discloses that the above circumstances did not adversely affect respondent's relationship with the children nor impair their emotional development.

In expanded findings made after a hearing on respondent's motion for new trial the court found that respondent had suffered financial reverses. There was no showing, however, that respondent's income from earnings and support was inadequate to provide for the children.

The earlier financial reverses and the status of the respondent are not sufficient grounds for changing custody in view of the uncontradicted evidence of the high quality of the environment and home life of respondent and the children. 'Ordinarily, if findings are supported by competent evidence, they will not be disturbed by the reviewing court, but if erroneous principles of law were applied to the facts, judgment rendered on such facts will not be upheld on review.' *American National Bank of Denver v. Christensen*, 28 Colo.App. 501, 476 P.2d 281.

The court further stated that, from testimony of the children in the courtroom and separate interviews in chambers, it was concerned because there was an indication that the older two girls were mentally disturbed. This concern of the court is not justified by the record. First, the record does not disclose that any testimony by the children was taken in the courtroom. Second, the interviews with the four girls indicate no abnormality whatsoever, but only a sincere desire to remain with respondent, on lucid, logical bases.

We recognize that a trial court need not accept at face value all of the evidence introduced in a proceeding; however, when there is no evidence to support a finding or conclusion and such finding or conclusion is manifestly against the weight of the evidence, it cannot be permitted to stand.

In *Anderson v. Cold Spring Tungsten, Inc.*, 170 Colo. 7, 458 P.2d 756, the Supreme Court said,

> 'In reviewing such issues of fact, this Court has taken the position that it will not set aside the findings of the trial judge where they are sustained by competent and adequate evidence, *amply appearing from the record....* But such restraint in no way limits the power of this Court to reject the findings and conclusions of the trial judge where they are not supported by any evidence in the record or where the law has not been applied correctly.'

The judgment of the trial court is reversed, and the cause is remanded with directions to enter an order denying the petition for modification of custody.

Schuster v. Schuster
585 P.2d 130 (Wash. 1978)

BRACHTENBACH, Justice.

These consolidated cases involve factually related divorces. The respondent women separated from their husbands and lived together in a lesbian relationship with their children of their marriages. The appellant fathers filed for divorces from their respective spouses. Each mother was given custody of her children. However, the mothers were ordered to live separate and apart and were prohibited from removing the children from the state. Those decrees were not appealed.

Later, each of the fathers filed modification petitions seeking custody of their children. Subsequently, motions for contempt were filed charging violations of the original decrees. The alleged violations by the mothers were: (1) renting separate apartments in the same building but in fact living together along with all the children; and (2) taking the children out of state. The mothers filed counter petitions seeking modification of the original decrees by deleting the prohibition against their living together.

The two modification proceedings were joined for hearing. An attorney was appointed to represent the children's interests. The findings and conclusions resulted in the custody of the children remaining with the mothers and the deletion of the prohibition against the mothers living together in an open and publicized lesbian relationship. We affirm in part and reverse in part.

At the outset we emphasize that these cases do not involve the question of whether it was proper to award custody of the children to lesbian mothers. That question was litigated in the original divorce actions. No appeal was taken by any party. There being no appeal, the original award of custody with all limitations contained therein is binding on all parties and upon this court. The issue is simply not before us.

The only question presented by this appeal is whether any modification of the original decrees was proper. When is a modification of the custody provisions of an original divorce decree justified? We have long held that a modification will not be granted unless there has been a subsequent substantial change in circumstances which requires a modification of custody in the best interests of the children. *Peugh v. Peugh*, 67 Wash.2d 469, 408 P.2d 10 (1965).

The policy is obvious. Children and their parents should not be subjected to repeated relitigation of the custody issues determined in the original action. Stability of the child's environment is of utmost concern. If an error was allegedly made in the original custody award, the remedy is by appeal. We repeat that the fathers did not appeal from the award of custody to the mothers; the mothers did not appeal from the prohibition against their living together.

This philosophy of stability in custody matters has been adopted by the legislature. In the marriage dissolution act of 1973, it prohibited a modification of a prior custody decree unless the court finds, upon the basis of facts that have arisen since the prior decree or that were unknown to the court at the time of the prior decree, that a change has occurred in the circumstances of the child or his custodian and that a modification is necessary to serve the best interests of the child. RCW 26.09.260(1).

Under these guidelines, the fathers must lose their modification petitions. Their circumstances have changed; each has remarried. They were found by the trial court to be good and capable fathers, vitally interested in their children. But the statute requires a change in the circumstances of either the child or the custodian, the mothers in this case.

Has there been any change in the circumstances of the mothers to warrant a modification of the custody decree to allow them to live together?

In their modification petitions, the respondent mothers did not allege any change of circumstances and the findings and conclusions evidence absolutely none. At best the respondents established that it was preferable for their own personal circumstances, both financially and in pursuit of their relationship, to live together. That issue had been tried, they lost and did not appeal. They did not meet the judicial or statutory standards to change it. Therefore it was error to modify that aspect of the decrees.

Respondents make a belated effort to raise constitutional questions of freedom of association, equal protection and due process from the requirement that they live separate and apart. First, there is more involved than the rights of these two women. The lives of six children are at stake. Second, neither side has briefed nor argued the constitutional issues as they relate to this requirement. Though the amicus curiae brief did discuss the issue, appellate courts will not pass upon points raised only by amicus. *Long v. Odell*, 60 Wash.2d 151, 372 P.2d 548 (1962).

The trial court is affirmed except for its deletion of the requirement that the respondent mothers live separate and apart. As to that, it is reversed. The matter is remanded for entry of decrees in accordance with this opinion.

STAFFORD, HOROWITZ AND HICKS, J.J., concur.

DOLLIVER, Justice (concurring in part; dissenting in part).

I concur with the reasoning of the majority in its affirmance of the award of custody to the [mothers]. I dissent on the modification of the decree relating to the defendants' living arrangements.

The controlling statute on modification of custody awards states, in relevant part:

> The court shall not modify a prior custody decree unless it finds, upon the basis of facts that have arisen since the prior decree or that were unknown to the court at the time of the prior decree, that a change has occurred in the circumstances of the child or his custodian and that the modification is necessary to serve the best interests of the child. RCW 26.09.260(1).

In the findings at the time of the dissolutions, the trial court specifically found Sandra Schuster and Madeleine Isaacson were cohabiting and that "such living arrangements are not in the best interest of the children." However, the court in the modification proceedings which are now before us found:

> That since the time of the Divorce Decree the respondents at first lived separate and apart and then moved into adjoining apartments where they in fact lived together as one household and that the living arrangement did not prove to be against the best interests of the children, except it added a financial burden.

Thus, contrary to the assertion of the majority, a change of circumstances is contained in the findings. This change went far beyond the personal convenience of the defendants and was not to be found against the best interests of the children. The crucial question, then, is not whether the trial court made a finding of changed circumstances but whether there is evidence in the record to support the findings.

During the trial, voluminous testimony was taken on the living environment in which the children of the parties were being raised. According to expert testimony, since the divorce decrees the Isaacsons and Schusters had come to regard themselves as a family of eight; the Isaacson and Schuster children would refer to one another as brother or sister. Testimony established that there was a "cross-over of the parent roles" between Ms. Isaacson and Ms. Schuster for the nurturing and assistance of the children. This development of a family unit and the strengthening of the relationships among the eight family members presents a significant change of circumstances which may appropriately be recognized and was recognized by the trial court in its findings.

Furthermore, in its oral opinion, the trial court stated that living apart for the sake of appearances was imposing a financial burden on the parties and their children. This circumstance was also recognized in the findings. Where the funds of the parties are limited, the children would naturally be affected adversely by an unnecessary expenditure of household resources.

The trial court should be given broad discretion in matters dealing with the welfare of the children. A finding was made of changed circumstances. Substantial evidence is in the record to support this finding. The disposition of this case should not be disturbed except for a manifest abuse of discretion. *Lambert v. Lambert*, 66 Wash.2d 503, 403 P.2d 664 (1965); *Selivanoff v. Selivanoff*, 12 Wash.App. 263, 266, 529 P.2d 486 (1974). No abuse has been shown.

The change of circumstances which occurred here may have developed while Ms. Schuster and Ms. Isaacson were in violation of the original decree, an act which this court need not approve. Nevertheless, it occurred. The trial court chose not to punish the parties for contempt and, finding no abuse of discretion, we have agreed. The majority rightly states that "Punishment of the parent for contempt may not be visited upon the child in custody cases. The custody of the child is not to be used as a reward or punishment for the conduct of the parents." This is a salutary rule. Having so held, we should not now punish the parties backhandedly by refusing to recognize an unquestionable change of circumstances found by the trial court and established by ample evidence.

UTTER, J., concurs

ROSELLINI, Justice (dissenting).

In awarding custody of children, the primary or paramount consideration is the welfare of the children. *Pierce v. Pierce*, 52 Wash. 679, 101 P. 358 (1909); *Thompson v. Thompson*, 56 Wash.2d 244, 352 P.2d 179 (1960).

Granting that a change of circumstances needs to be found to modify a custody decree, such change of circumstances exists. In the finding at the time of the dissolution, the trial court specifically found that Sandra Schuster and Madeleine Isaacson were cohabiting and that such living arrangements were not in the best interest of the children.

This finding was made to insulate the children from the harmful atmosphere of living together in the same household where evidence of cohabitation would be apparent.

Since that time the respondents have in fact lived together in one household and have publicly espoused on radio, television and in lectures the superiority of the homosexual lifestyle. They have involved their children in these activities. This is a change of circumstances that requires the court to reexamine the correctness of its previous custody order.

In *Gaylord v. Tacoma School Dist.* 10, 88 Wash.2d 286, 559 P.2d 1340 (1977), this court held that a teacher was "guilty" of immorality because of his status of being a homosexual. Also, the evidence in the case did not involve any known homosexual acts. Nevertheless, this court assumed that his effectiveness as a teacher would be impaired. Mr. Gaylord was an excellent teacher. His superior's evaluation of his teaching effectiveness stated: "Mr. Gaylord continues his high standards and thorough teaching performance. He is both a teacher and student in his field."

In regard to the effect of Mr. Gaylord's status as a homosexual, the opinion stated at pages 298–99, 559 P.2d at 1347:

> It is important to remember that Gaylord's homosexual conduct must be considered in the context of his position of teaching high school students. Such students could treat the retention of the high school teacher by the school board as indicating adult approval of his homosexuality. It would be unreasonable to assume as a matter of law a teacher's ability to perform as a teacher required to teach principles of morality (RCW 28A.67.110) is not impaired and creates no danger of encouraging expression of approval and of imitation. Likewise to say that school directors must wait for prior specific overt expression of homosexual conduct before they act to prevent harm from one who chooses to remain "erotically attracted to a notable degree towards persons of his own sex and is psychologically, if not actually disposed to engage in sexual

activity prompted by this attraction" is to ask the school directors to take an unacceptable risk in discharging their fiduciary responsibility of managing the affairs of the school district.

In the instant case, Sandra Schuster and Madeleine Isaacson were and are living together in a homosexual relationship. The respondents are living together with their children as a family unit.

The respondents have been engaged in publicizing the homosexual cause in general and their lesbian relationship. They have given a series of lectures and granted interviews where they discussed their own homosexual lifestyle. The children have accompanied respondents at some of these engagements, and the respondents and their children participated in making a movie which depicts the lifestyle of two families bound together by homosexual parents.

They have advertised in a brochure entitled "The Gay Family A Valid Life-Style?" in which they offered interested persons a booklet, "Love is for All", and information about a film entitled "Sandy and Madeleine's Family", and also offer to make personal appearances. An article in the San Francisco Chronicle with the headline "The Lesbian Love of Two Mothers" explained the appearance of the two women visiting in the Bay Area publicizing their film.

From such publicizing it can be readily seen that they are not content to pursue their lifestyle but are also using their children for the purpose of advocating and proselytizing that style.

I am unable to understand how the court can declare that a school teacher who only admitted to his preference as a homosexual and did not engage in any overt act, is guilty of immorality, and yet, in the instant case, can find perfectly moral the conduct of the respondents.

The State does have an interest in the matter of heterosexual acts versus homosexual acts. Professors J. Harvie Wilkinson III and G. Edward White, writing in 62 Cornell L.Rev. 563, 595–96 (1977), in an article entitled "Constitutional Protection for Personal Lifestyles", state that

> (t)he most threatening aspect of homosexuality is its potential to become a viable alternative to heterosexual intimacy. This argument is premised upon the belief that the practice of an alternative mode of sexual relations will inimically affect the predominant mode. Thus, any recognition of a constitutional right to practice homosexuality would undermine the value of heterosexuality and the institutions and practices—conventional marriage and childrearing—associated with it.

> This state concern, in our view, should not be minimized. The nuclear, heterosexual family is charged with several of society's most essential functions. It has served as an important means of educating the young; it has often provided economic support and psychological comfort to family members; and it has operated as the unit upon which basic governmental policies in such matters as taxation, conscription, and inheritance have been based. Family life has been a central unifying experience throughout American society. Preserving the strength of this basic, organic unit is a central and legitimate end of the police power. The state ought to be concerned that if allegiance to traditional family arrangements declines, society as a whole may well suffer.

The Superior Court of New Jersey held in *In the Matter of J. S. & C.*, 129 N.J.Super. 486, 324 A.2d 90 (1974), that granting a father, who was deeply involved in the movement to further homosexuality, the right to unrestricted visitation would not be in the best interest of the children, and that such visitation right should extend to the daytime hours only. And in *Chaffin v. Frye*, 45 Cal.App.3d 39, 119 Cal.Rptr. 22 (1975), where a mother was a homosexual living with a female companion in the same apartment that the children would occupy, the trial court's implied finding that an award of custody to the mother would be detrimental to the children was sustained.

In this case the trial court found, in the original trial, that both parents were fit and proper persons to have the custody of the children. The fathers have since remarried and have established good homes. Where should the scale of justice be tipped? In favor of the mothers who are living in a lesbian relationship? Or on the side of the fathers whose lifestyles and relationships are considered normal and moral?

On the state of this record, the primary and paramount consideration in awarding the children to a parent is the welfare of the children. I would hold that the mothers are not morally fit to have the custody of the children, and I would award the children to the fathers.

WRIGHT, C. J., AND HAMILTON, J., concur.

Notes and Questions

1. This divided opinion raises many issues. First, the court readily endorsed the initial custody decision and agreed that custody should remain with the lesbian mothers. It appears from the facts that the husbands were aware of the lesbian relationship at the time of divorce. Do you think it would have made any difference to this court if the lesbian relationship had been closeted at the time of divorce and only come to light recently?

2. The dissent analogizes a gay school teacher's dismissal with a gay parent's claim to custody. Is that a fair analogy? Why or why not?

3. The majority opinion reinstated the original condition that that the mothers not live together, holding that they had not presented sufficient evidence of change. The concurring judge disagrees. Conditions such as this are often imposed on divorced parents, gay and non-gay. The assumption is that evidence of a non-marital relationship is bad for the children. Assuming that the initial condition is valid, what legal test do you think a court ought to apply to consider removing such a condition?

4. Constitutional arguments were raised in the appeal, but the court refused to consider them because they had not been raised at trial. What constitutional arguments would you have developed in this case?

Jarrett v. Jarrett
400 N.E.2d 421 (Ill. 1980)

UNDERWOOD, Justice:

On December 6, 1976, Jacqueline Jarrett received a divorce from Walter Jarrett in the circuit court of Cook County on grounds of extreme and repeated mental cruelty. The divorce decree, by agreement, also awarded Jacqueline custody of the three Jarrett children subject to the father's right of visitation at reasonable times. Seven months later, alleging changed conditions, Walter petitioned the circuit court to modify the divorce decree and award him custody of the children. The circuit court granted his petition subject to the mother's right of visitation at reasonable times, but a majority of the appellate court reversed, and we granted leave to appeal.

During their marriage, Walter and Jacqueline had three daughters, who, at the time of the divorce, were 12, 10 and 7 years old. In addition to custody of the children, the divorce decree also awarded Jacqueline the use of the family home, and child support; Walter received visitation rights at all reasonable times and usually had the children from Saturday evening to Sunday evening. In April 1977, five months after the divorce, Jacqueline informed Walter that she planned to have her boyfriend, Wayne Hammon, move into the family home with her. Walter protested, but Hammon moved in on May 1, 1977. Jacqueline and Hammon thereafter cohabited in the Jarrett home but did not marry.

The children, who were not "overly enthused" when they first learned that Hammon would move into the family home with them, asked Jacqueline if she intended to marry Hammon, but Jacqueline responded that she did not know. At the modification hearing Jacqueline testified that she did not want to remarry because it was too soon after her divorce; because she did not believe that a marriage license makes a relationship; and because the divorce decree required her to sell the family home within six months after remarriage. She did not want to sell the house because the children did not want to move and she could not afford to do so. Jacqueline explained to the children that some people thought it was wrong for an unmarried man and woman to live together but she thought that what mattered was that they loved each other. Jacqueline testified that she told some neighbors that Hammon would move in with her but that she had not received any adverse comments. Jacqueline further testified that the children seemed to develop an affectionate relationship with Hammon, who played with them, helped them with their homework, and verbally disciplined them. Both Jacqueline and Hammon testified at the hearing that they did not at that time have any plans to marry. In oral argument before this court Jacqueline's counsel conceded that she and Hammon were still living together unmarried.

Walter Jarrett testified that he thought Jacqueline's living arrangements created a moral environment which was not a proper one in which to raise three young girls. He also testified that the children were always clean, healthy, well dressed and well nourished when he picked them up, and that when he talked with his oldest daughter, Kathleen, she did not object to Jacqueline's living arrangement.

The circuit court found that it was "necessary for the moral and spiritual well-being and development" of the children that Walter receive custody. In reversing, the appellate court reasoned that the record did not reveal any negative effects on the children caused by Jacqueline's cohabitation with Hammon, and that the circuit court had not found Jacqueline unfit. It declined to consider potential future harmful effects of the cohabitation on the children.

The chief issue in this case is whether a change of custody predicated upon the open and continuing cohabitation of the custodial parent with a member of the opposite sex is contrary to the manifest weight of the evidence in the absence of any tangible evidence of contemporaneous adverse effect upon the minor children. We conclude that under the facts in this case the trial court properly transferred custody of the Jarrett children from Jacqueline to Walter Jarrett.

The relevant standards of conduct are expressed in the statutes of this State: Section 11-8 of the Criminal Code of 1961 provides that "(a)ny person who cohabits or has sexual intercourse with another not his spouse commits fornication if the behavior is open and notorious." In *Hewitt v. Hewitt* (1979), 394 N.E.2d 1204, we emphasized the refusal of the General Assembly in enacting the new Illinois Marriage and Dissolution of Marriage Act to sanction any nonmarital relationships and its declaration of the purpose to "strengthen and preserve the integrity of marriage and safeguard family relationships."

Jacqueline argues, however, that her conduct does not affront public morality because such conduct is now widely accepted, and cites 1978 Census Bureau statistics that show 1.1 million households composed of an unmarried man and woman, close to a quarter of which also include at least one child. This is essentially the same argument we rejected last term in *Hewitt v. Hewitt* (1979), 394 N.E.2d 1204, and it is equally unpersuasive here. The number of people living in such households forms only a small percentage of the adult population, but more to the point, the statutory interpretation urged upon us by Jacqueline simply nullifies the fornication statute. The logical conclusion of her argument is that the statutory prohibitions are void as to those who believe the proscribed acts are not immoral, or, for one reason or another, need not be heeded. So stated, of course, the argument defeats itself. The rules which our society enacts for the governance of its members are not limited to those who agree with those rules they are equally binding on the dissenters. The fornication statute and the Illinois Marriage and Dissolution of Marriage Act evidence the relevant moral standards of this State, as declared by our legislature. The open and notorious limitation on the former's prohibitions reflects both a disinclination to criminalize purely private relationships and a recognition that open fornication represents a graver threat to public morality than private violations. Conduct of that nature, when it is open, not only violates the statutorily expressed moral standards of the State, but also encourages others to violate those standards, and debases public morality. While we agree that the statute does not penalize conduct which is essentially private and discreet, Jacqueline's conduct has been neither, for she has discussed this relationship and her rationalization of it with at least her children, her former husband and her neighbors. It is, in our judgment, clear that her conduct offends prevailing public policy.

Finally, we do not believe that the United States Supreme Court's opinion in *Stanley v. Illinois* (1972), 405 U.S. 645, requires a different result. In *Stanley* the Supreme Court found that Illinois statutes created a presumption that an unwed father is unfit to exercise custody over his children. The court held that depriving an unwed father of his illegitimate children without a prior hearing to determine his actual rather than presumptive unfitness, when the State accords that protection to other parents, deprives him of equal protection of the law.

The case before us is fundamentally different. The trial court did not presume that Jacqueline was not an adequate parent, as the juvenile court in effect did in *Stanley*. Rather the trial court recognized that the affection and care of a parent do not alone assure the welfare of the child if other conduct of the parent threatens the child's moral development. Since the evidence indicated that Jacqueline had not terminated the troublesome relationship and would probably continue it in the future, the trial court transferred custody to Walter Jarrett, an equally caring and affectionate parent whose conduct did not contravene the standards established by the General Assembly and earlier judicial decisions. Its action in doing so was not contrary to the manifest weight of the evidence. Accordingly, we reverse the judgment of the appellate court.

GOLDENHERSH, Chief Justice, with whom THOMAS J. MORAN, Justice, joins, dissenting:

The effect of the decision is that the plaintiff's cohabitation with Hammon per se was sufficient grounds for changing the custody order previously entered. As a legal matter, simply stated, the majority has held that on the basis of her presumptive guilt of fornication, a Class B misdemeanor, plaintiff, although not declared to be an unfit mother, has forfeited the right to have the custody of her children. This finding flies in the face of the established rule that, in order to modify or amend an award of custody, the evidence must show that the parent to whom custody of the children was originally awarded is unfit to retain custody, or that a change of conditions makes a change of custody in their best interests. This record fails to show either. Mr. Justice Moran and I dissent and would affirm the decision of the appellate court.

MORAN, Justice, with whom GOLDENHERSH, Chief Justice, joins, dissenting:

I join in the dissent of the chief justice, but also dissent separately. My primary disagreement with the majority lies with its countenancing a change of custody based solely on a conclusive presumption that harm to the Jarrett children stemmed from Jacqueline's living arrangements. The majority purports to follow the Illinois Marriage and Dissolution of Marriage Act. Yet, under that act, only on the basis of fact can there be a finding that a change in circumstances has occurred and that modification of the prior custody judgment is necessary to serve the best interest of the children. The court is not to consider conduct of a custodian if that conduct does not affect his relationship to the child. In this case, not one scintilla of actual or statistical evidence of harm or danger to the children has been presented. To the contrary, all of the evidence of record, as related by the majority, indicates that under Jacqueline's custodianship the children's welfare and needs were met. Also, the trial court expressly declined to find Jacqueline unfit. Nevertheless, the majority's finding of a violation of the seldom-enforced fornication statute effectively foreclosed any further consideration of the custody issue. Instead of focusing solely on the best interest of the children—the "guiding star—the majority has utilized child custody as a vehicle to punish Jacqueline for her "misconduct." Such selective enforcement of a statute is inappropriate and, especially in the child-custody context, unfortunate.

The majority decision also is at odds with the principle of *Stanley v. Illinois* (1972), 405 U.S. 645. The constitutional infirmity of the statutory presumption in Stanley casts doubt on the validity of the judicially created conclusive presumption in this case. After Stanley, an unwed father may not be deprived of his illegitimate children without a prior hearing to determine his actual fitness. Similarly, Jacqueline should not be deprived of the children in the absence of evidence that a change is necessary to serve the best interest of the children. A hearing at which custody is determined on the basis of the conclusive presumption sanctioned by the majority amounts to no hearing at all.

Notes and Questions

1. Is the court correct in asserting that *Stanley v. Illinois* is not relevant to the decision of this case? Has the court adopted a presumption that parents who cohabit with persons of the opposite sex are unfit for custody of their natural children?

2. Some lower Illinois appellate courts have taken pains to distinguish *Jarrett v. Jarrett* on its facts in later cases. See, e.g., *Blonsky v. Blonsky*, 84 Ill.App.3d 810, 405 N.E.2d 1112 (1980)(*Jarrett* distinguished in part because it involved illegal cohabitation under Illinois law, whereas husband in *Blonsky* had sexual relationship with woman in California which was not illegal under California law).

3. To what extent can the decision in *Jarrett v. Jarrett* be attributed to the existence of a fornication law in Illinois at the time of the events in question? Would the Illinois Supreme Court distinguish between behavior which the law permits and behavior which the law prohibits in deciding whether such conduct endangers the "morality" of the children? Knowing that Illinois does not penalize consensual sodomy between adults, how do you think an Illinois court would have handled the Jarrett case had Mrs. Jarrett been cohabiting with a woman rather than a man?

In re Marriage of R.S.
677 N.E.2d 1297 (Ill. App. 1996)

Presiding Justice BRESLIN delivered the opinion of the court:

We are asked in this appeal to determine whether the trial court erred when it modified a prior custody arrangement based on the custodial parent's homosexual relationship and the possibility that the children could experience social condemnation as a result of this relationship. We hold that the potential for social condemnation, standing alone, cannot justify a change in custody. Moreover, we find that the non-custodial parent failed to meet the burden of proof required to justify a modification of custody. Thus, for the reasons which follow, we reverse the trial court's judgment.

R.S. and S.S. married in 1983 and subsequently had two children. When the parties divorced in July 1991, they agreed that the mother should have sole custody of the children.

The father remarried in 1993. In August of that year he filed the instant petition for modification of custody. In his petition, the father alleged that a substantial change in circumstances had occurred because he had remarried and the mother had embraced an openly homosexual lifestyle, placing her sexual desires ahead of the emotional, moral and educational needs of the children by residing with her homosexual partner. He further alleged that her live-in partner had contracted mononucleosis and hepatitis and that it would be detrimental to the children's emotional, physical and moral well-being to have them remain in the mother's home.

The following facts were adduced at the hearings on the father's petition. The mother and her partner, J.S., who are both bisexual, met in 1993 at the hospital where they work. J.S. moved into the mother's home later that year. Soon after she moved in, J.S. contracted mononucleosis and hepatitis from one of the children, who had a virus. However, J.S. took several precautions and avoided infecting the remaining members of the household. She recuperated fully from this illness. In June 1994, the mother sold her home and moved with the children into J.S.'s home in a nearby town.

All of the parties, including the father, agreed that the children were well-adjusted and were not experiencing any problems. The father testified that the children have been reluctant to return to the mother following visitation. Likewise, the mother testified that the children have been reluctant to visit with the father.

The father testified that the children were doing well in school and extra-curricular activities and were getting a good education. He also testified that the children looked healthy, dressed appropriately and ate regularly. He testified that he believed the children were afraid of him. He was concerned that J.S. showed affection toward his daughter by hugging and kissing her. He stated that if he gained custody of the children, he would ask the court to restrict her contact with them.

The children's paternal grandmother testified that before they moved out of town, she babysat the children three to four days a week after school. She stated that both parents had told her that she would have less contact with the children as they grew older. However, she spent less time with the children after they moved. She testified that the mother told her she was free to visit the children, but she took the children only when the mother asked her to take them. She made it a practice, however, to speak to the children each night on the telephone.

The mother testified that, after returning from a visit with their father, her daughter informed her that her father and grandmother had asked questions about the mother's relationship with J.S. As a consequence, the mother explained the nature of her relationship with J.S. to her daughter in general terms while her son was present. She also acknowledged her relationship with J.S. to her daughter's teacher when the teacher asked about her daughter's relationship to J.S. The mother testified that she and J.S. sleep in the same room, but the children have never seen them involved in any sexual relations. The father expressed disapproval of the mother's openness to the children about her homosexual relationship and argued that the mother should not have revealed the nature of her relationship with J.S. to the children.

The son's teacher testified that he was an A student and had no discipline problems. She stated that he got along well with other students and had adjusted well to the move. The daughter's teacher testified that she was an excellent student and that the mother actively participated in school activities.

The trial court appointed T.W. Mathews, a clinical psychologist, to perform a psychological home study and evaluation of the parties and the children. According to Mathews' report, the psychological and emotional needs of the children were being served by the existing custodial arrangement. He found nothing that would lead him to conclude that a change in custody would serve the best interests of the children. Mathews testified that there were no psychological problems evident in the children and that all adults on both sides agreed that the children were developing satisfactorily. He believed that all of the parties involved were "perfectly capable of meeting the array of psychological concerns that are necessary to look out for the well-being of the children."

Mathews also testified that there was no empirical evidence which suggested that children growing up in a homosexual environment would experience increased psychological problems. He raised the concern that the children could be harassed because of the mother's relationship with J.S., but there was no evidence that the children had experienced any such harassment. Although he recognized that a change in custody would not insulate the children from possible social disapproval of their mother's sexuality, Mathews thought that there was slight weight in favor of the father being the primary custodian because of the possibility that the children will be harassed. He also testified that he had some concern about empirical evidence regarding male role modeling, but the information he had seen was ambiguous.

Mathews believed that the children's paternal grandmother was a positive influence on them and that she should continue to have contact with the children. He reported that she was primarily responsible for the children's stability throughout the divorce.

After the testimony of the witnesses, the trial court found three factors which, together, amounted to a substantial change in circumstances: (1) the father's remarriage and the children's familial relationship with the father's wife and children; (2) the mother's involvement in a conjugal homosexual relationship; and (3) the mother's reduction in the children's contact with their paternal grandmother. Based on these circumstances, the court found held it was in the best interests of the children to modify custody by awarding custody to the father.

The sole issue on appeal is whether the father presented clear and convincing evidence at trial to show that a change in custody was necessary to serve the best interests of the children.

Two elements must be proved to succeed in a petition to modify custody. First, there must be a change in the circumstances of the child or the custodial parent. Second, a modification must be necessary to serve the best interests of the child. The burden of proof rests upon the party requesting modification, and that party must prove its case by clear and convincing evidence. Changed conditions alone will not justify a modification of custody unless such conditions adversely affect the welfare of the child. While a court may consider the custodial parent's homosexual relationship when making a custody determination, the trial court's function is limited to determining the effect of the parent's conduct upon the children.

Neither the father nor the trial court could point to any negative consequences that had befallen the children as a result of the mother's sexual orientation or conjugal relationship. Instead, each theorized that the children might suffer some future social condemnation. The trial court noted that in *Bottoms v. Bottoms*, 249 Va. 410, 457 S.E.2d 102 (1995), the Virginia Supreme Court held that the potential for such social condemnation is a factor to be considered when making a custody determination. However, the *Bottoms* court also noted that a lesbian mother is not presumed to be an unfit parent. 249 Va. at 419, 457 S.E.2d at 108. Rather, the court held that custody determinations must be made by considering several factors, including "misconduct that affects the child." 249 Va. at 419, 457 S.E.2d at 107. In this regard, the *Bottoms* case is in accord with Illinois law, which requires custody determinations to be made by considering all of the circumstances that affect the best interests of the child rather than by applying *per se* rules.

Illinois and Virginia share this position with many other states. See *D.H. v. J.H.*, 418 N.E.2d 286 (Ind.Ct.App.1981) (homosexuality, standing alone, is not grounds for denial of custody in the absence of showing that sexual misconduct had an adverse effect upon welfare of children); *Hall v. Hall*, 95 Mich.App. 614, 291 N.W.2d 143 (Mich.Ct.App.1980) (homosexuality is only one of many factors court should consider when making custody determination); *Nadler v. Superior Court*, 255 Cal.App.2d 523, 63 Cal.Rptr. 352 (1967) (trial court erred by holding as a matter of law that mother was unfit on the basis that she is a homosexual); *Paul C. v. Tracy C.*, 622 N.Y.S.2d 159, 209 A.D.2d 955 (1994) (sexual preference is not determinative in child custody dispute unless it adversely affects children).

In the end, the *Bottoms* court changed the custody of the child to the maternal grandmother. The court, however, found that there was proof that the child had been harmed as a result of living with his mother. 249 Va. at 420, 457 S.E.2d at 108. Several factors, including incidents of significant abuse, neglect and abandonment supported this finding. 249 Va. at 414–20, 457 S.E.2d at 105–8.

Nevertheless, the father argues that he was entitled to a change in custody based solely on the immorality of the mother's relationship with J.S. Citing *Jarrett v. Jarrett*, 78 Ill.2d 337, 36 Ill.Dec. 1, 400 N.E.2d 421 (1979), he claims that the open and notorious nature of the mother's relationship endangered the moral well-being of the children and required a change in custody. Moreover, the father claims that under *Jarrett*, he did not need to show that the mother's relationship had any tangible adverse affects on the children in order to meet his burden of proof.

In *Jarrett*, the supreme court held that open and notorious cohabitation by a custodial parent, standing alone, justified a change in custody. 78 Ill.2d at 345–48, 36 Ill.Dec. at 4, 400 N.E.2d at 424–25. According to the court, cohabitation was an affront to the statutorily expressed moral standards of the State and was thus injurious to the moral well-being of the children who were being raised in such an environment. Four years later, however, the supreme court made the following comment on its holding in *Jarrett*:

> "The *Jarrett* case does not establish a conclusive presumption that, because a custodial parent cohabits with a member of the opposite sex, the child is harmed. No such presumption exists in this State. The court in *Jarrett* indicated that a custody award is not arrived at by pressing one lever and mechanically denying custody to one parent; rather all of the circumstances must be considered that affect the best interests of the child. [Citations.]" *In re Marriage of Thompson*, 96 Ill.2d 67, 78, 70 Ill.Dec. 214, 219, 449 N.E.2d 88, 93 (1983).

Therefore, to the extent that *Jarrett* held that open and notorious cohabitation necessarily requires a change in custody, that holding was effectively reversed by the *Thompson* court. Further, *Thompson* makes it clear that Illinois courts cannot presume that a custodial parent's cohabitation is harmful to a child.

The Illinois Marriage and Dissolution of Marriage Act clearly places great emphasis upon stability and continuity in custody arrangements. See *In re Marriage of Wycoff*, 266 Ill.App.3d 408, 203 Ill.Dec. 338, 639 N.E.2d 897 (1994). Thus, the Act requires that a petitioner present clear and convincing evidence to support a modification of custody. In this case, the evidence established that the children were thriving in their mother's care. The only evidence that the children would be better off with their father was Mathews' opinion that there was a "slight" advantage to him having custody. The applicable standard, however, is not whether one arrangement is slightly better than another. The proposed arrangement must be shown by clear and convincing evidence to be necessary to serve the best interests of the children. Thus, the father has failed to meet his burden of proof.

For the foregoing reasons, the judgment of the circuit court of Tazewell County is reversed.

Notes and Questions

1. In a similar fact situation in Alabama, the trial court ruled against the lesbian mother and transferred custody to the recently married father. The trial court granted visitation rights to the mother on condition that she not exercise her right of visitation with the minor child in the presence of her female companion. The court of appeals reversed, finding that there was no evidence that the mother's relationship had

harmed the child, who by this time was seven years old and had been with her mother as primary caretaker since birth. The mother and mother's partner had been together and the child had been living with them from the time of the divorce four years earlier. The Supreme Court of Alabama reversed and reinstated the change of custody decision of the trial court. In its decision, the court stressed that "the mother and G.S. have established a two-parent home environment where their homosexual relationship is openly practiced and presented to the child as the social and moral equivalent of a heterosexual marriage." It then cited to Alabama's version of DOMA. By contrast, "the father and the stepmother have established a two-parent home environment where heterosexual marriage is presented as the moral and societal norm." Ultimately the court concluded:

> After carefully considering all of the evidence, we simply cannot hold that the trial court abused its discretion in determining that the positive good brought about by placing the child in the custody of her father would more than offset the inherent disruption brought about by uprooting the child from her mother's custody. While the evidence shows that the mother loves the child and has provided her with good care, it also shows that she has chosen to expose the child continuously to a lifestyle that is "neither legal in this state, nor moral in the eyes of most of its citizens."[1] The record contains evidence from which the trial court could have concluded that "[a] child raised by two women or two men is deprived of extremely valuable developmental experience and the opportunity for optimal individual growth and interpersonal development" and that "the degree of harm to children from the homosexual conduct of a parent is uncertain...and the range of potential harm is enormous." Lynn D. Wardle, The Potential Impact of Homosexual Parenting on Children, 1997 U. Ill. L.Rev. 833, 895 (1997).

> While much study, and even more controversy, continue to center upon the effects of homosexual parenting, the inestimable developmental benefit of a loving home environment that is anchored by a successful marriage is undisputed. The father's circumstances have changed, and he is now able to provide this benefit to the child. The mother's circumstances have also changed, in that she is unable, while choosing to conduct an open cohabitation with her lesbian life partner, to provide this benefit. The trial court's change of custody based upon the changed circumstances of the parties was not an abuse of discretion; thus, the Court of Civil Appeals erred in reversing the trial court's judgment....

Ex Parte J.M.F., 730 So.2d 1190 (Ala. 1998).

2. In a 1985 Alaska case, in which the father requested a change in custody based on the mother's lesbian status, the court responded:

> In marked contrast to the wealth of testimony that Mother is a lesbian, there is no suggestion that this has or is likely to affect the child adversely. The

---

1. Under Ala.Code 1975, § 13A-6-65, it is a Class A misdemeanor to engage in consensual "deviate sexual intercourse with another person"; this statute was specifically altered by the legislature from the original draft of the "Alabama Criminal Code" proposed to the legislature, so as "to make all homosexual conduct criminal." See Commentary to § 13A-6-65 and § 13A-1-1.

In addition, Alabama has established that "[c]ourse materials and instruction" in the public schools "that relate to [sex] education" shall emphasize, "in a factual manner and from a public health perspective, that homosexuality is not a lifestyle acceptable to the general public and that homosexual conduct is a criminal offense under the laws of the state." Ala.Code 1975, § 16-40A-2(c))(8).

record contains evidence showing that the child's development to date has been excellent, that Mother has not neglected him, and that there is no increased likelihood that a male child raised by a lesbian would be homosexual. Simply put, it is impermissible to rely on any real or imagined social stigma attaching to Mother's status as a lesbian. *Cf. Palmore v. Sidoti*, 466 U.S. 429 (1984).

S.N.E. v. v. R.L.B., 699 P.2d 875 (Alaska 1985).

3. Was the mother's sexual orientation determinative in the Alabama case? If not, what was? Would the court have ordered a change in custody if the mother had been a single mom, living alone?

4. Would you advise the mother in the Alabama case to petition the Supreme Court, relying on *Palmore v. Sidoti* and *Romer v. Evans*? What, exactly, would be her constitutional claim? Is there any way she can get heightened scrutiny of the Alabama court's decision?

5. *Lawrence v. Texas* was decided after this case. Had it been decided before this case, what impact would it have had?

6. What does the Alabama court do to protect the mother's fundamental right to parent? To protect the father's fundamental right to parent? Is it possible to fashion a legal rule that would protect both interests? Does the statutory scheme in Alabama adequately protect the constitutional interests in family integrity?

7. No state currently applies a rule that denies custody or visitation to a parent solely because of that parent's sexuality. But when you read the cases carefully, you will find that a parent's sexuality, combined with conduct, is often determinative in custody battles. See, e.g., *J.A.D v. E.J.D.*, 978 S.W.2d 336 (Mo. 1998)("A homosexual parent is not *ipso facto* unfit for custody of his or her child, and no reported Missouri case has held otherwise. It is not error, however, to consider the impact of homosexual or heterosexual misconduct upon the children in making a custody determination.") Conduct, in many cases, is nothing more than having a relationship with a person of the same sex and being honest about it, holding hands, kissing, and participating in gay rights activities. See, e.g., *Pulliam v. Smith*, 301 S.E.2d 898 (N.C. 1998), in which the court took custody away from a gay male father who had raised his two sons from birth solely because the ex-wife complained once she learned he was gay. The offensive conduct was public expression of affection between the two men and the fact that they carried on a sexual relationship behind closed doors.

2. Restrictions on Retaining Custody and Visitation Rights

Taylor v. Taylor
47 S.W. 3d 222 (Ark. 2001)

Tom Glaze, Justice.

This custody case began in 1998, when Linda Taylor was granted a divorce from Chris Taylor. Originally, the chancery court awarded the Taylors joint custody of their two minor children, Jessica and Megan. Megan is the youngest child, and suffers from a developmental disability that appears to be either a form of autism or attention deficit disorder. In 1999, Chris Taylor petitioned for custody of the girls. He alleged that Linda was engaged in a romantic relationship and cohabitating with Christina Richards. Apparently, Linda had been romantically involved with Richards since the divorce, and the two had purchased a home together.

On August 5, 1999, the chancery court issued a temporary custody order, which contained a non-cohabitation clause that ordered Linda not to permit Christina Richards to remain in residence or to be an overnight guest in the home when the children were present. After the temporary custody order issued, Linda made arrangements for Christina to continue to live in the home and provide care for the children on the nights that Linda worked overnight shifts.

Before the hearing on Chris Taylor's petition for custody, he also moved for the chancellor to hold Linda in contempt of the temporary order. Linda filed a petition for custody to remain with her and moved for a modification of the temporary order to allow Christina Richards to live in the home with her and the children, and continue in her role as a secondary caregiver. Linda also filed a motion for a continuance to allow time for further testing of Megan's developmental disorder to determine whether it was a form of autism. No continuance was granted.

On April 10, 2000, at a hearing on the motions and custody petitions, the court heard evidence from each party, as well as the expert testimony of Dr. Deyoub, a clinical psychologist appointed by the court at Linda's request. Linda attempted to present evidence from two other experts, Dr. Cheralyn Powers, a clinical psychologist, and Anna Vollers, an expert in the care of autistic children. Powers's and Vollers's testimonies were largely foreclosed by the chancellor's rulings on objections from opposing counsel, but Linda proffered her experts' testimonies.

At the conclusion of the hearing, the chancellor adopted Dr. Deyoub's recommendation that primary custody remain with Linda, conditioned upon Christina Richards's removal from the household. Although the court ruled from the bench that Christina must move out immediately, the court modified that ruling, upon Linda's request, to allow an additional thirty days for compliance. The court held Linda in contempt for violating the non-cohabitation clause in its temporary custody order, but withheld punishment pending her compliance with the final order. Despite the grant of custody in her favor, Linda appealed the custody order, including procedural and evidentiary rulings of the chancellor and his finding of contempt. Linda's arguments are the only ones submitted for review, since Chris Taylor chose not to respond or participate in this appeal.

First, it is important to note the level of deference that a reviewing court will give a chancery court in its *de novo* review of child custody cases. The chancellor's findings will not be reversed unless they are clearly erroneous. *See Campbell v. Campbell,* 336 Ark. 379, 985 S.W.2d 724 (1999). This court has held that there is no other case in which the superior position, ability, and opportunity of the chancellor to observe the parties carries a greater weight than one involving the custody of minor children. *See, e.g., Jones v. Strauser,* 266 Ark. 441, 585 S.W.2d 931 (1979). The best interest of the child is the polestar in every child-custody case; all other considerations are secondary.

On appeal, Linda argues that Christina's presence in the household is in the best interests of the children. However, this argument appears largely moot because the custody order allows Christina to remain as a caretaker for the children on the nights that Linda has to work, conditioned upon the approval of Dr. Deyoub and Chris Taylor. The circumstance with which the chancellor took issue was Christina's continued presence as a resident in the household, not Christina's caretaker abilities. Arkansas's appellate courts have steadfastly upheld chancery court orders that prohibit parents from allowing romantic partners to stay or reside in the home when the children are present. *See Campbell*, 336 Ark. at 389, 985 S.W.2d 724 (this court and the court of appeals have never condoned a parent's promiscuous conduct or lifestyle when such conduct has been in the presence of a child);... The *Campbell* court stated that the purpose of the overnight-guest order is to promote a stable environment for the children and is not imposed merely to monitor a parent's sexual conduct. 336 Ark. at 389, 985 S.W.2d 724. Linda does not seek to overturn these decisions, but instead tries to distinguish them from the facts here. For example, Linda asserts no evidence has been presented that she has engaged in promiscuous or illicit behavior with Christina Richards in the presence of the children. Linda's argument, however, misses the point. As emphasized by our court's earlier decisions, the trial court's use of the non-cohabitation restriction is a material factor to consider when determining custody issues. Such a restriction or prohibition aids in structuring the home place so as to reduce the possibilities (or opportunities) where children may be present and subjected to a single parent's sexual encounters, whether they be heterosexual or homosexual.

Linda has failed to demonstrate how the chancellor erred in finding that it was against the children's best interests for her to remain living in an admittedly romantic relationship with Christina while residing in the home with the children present. Once again, Arkansas case law simply has never condoned a parent's unmarried cohabitation, or a parent's promiscuous conduct or lifestyle, when such conduct is in the presence of a child. *See Campbell, supra,* and the cases cited therein. The chancellor here acted within his authority and was not clearly erroneous in determining that it was not in the children's best interests for their primary custodian to continue cohabitating with another adult with whom she admitted being romantically involved.

Finally, Linda argues that the chancellor's finding of contempt was in error because she had complied with the non-cohabitation clause contained in the temporary custody order by making arrangements so that she and Richards never slept in the home on the same night. From Linda's and Christina's own admissions at the final hearing, and despite the living arrangements that she devised in reaction to the non-cohabitation order, Linda still considered Christina to be a resident of the household and allowed her to remain living there overnight in the presence of the children, three nights a week when Linda worked overnight shifts.

As the chancellor noted in finding Linda in contempt of his order, the temporary order clearly mandated that Christina be removed from the same household as the children and forbade Linda from sharing the residence and living arrangements with Christina when the children were present. Christina's continued residence in the home was a violation of the express terms of the non-cohabitation clause, and the chancellor did not err in holding Linda in contempt. It is important to note that the custody order conditions Linda's continued custody on compliance with this provision and allows custody to revert to Chris Taylor should he demonstrate that Linda has failed to comply with the non-cohabitation order.

Notes and Questions

Courts in other states regularly impose restrictions on the custodial parent, which deny the custodial parent the right to cohabit with a sexual partner outside of marriage.

As we saw in the *Burns* case from Georgia, engaging in a civil union with the partner is not sufficient to remove the ban on cohabitation. In the case of a gay or lesbian parent, who is not able to marry a same-sex partner, the result is a Sophie's Choice: my children or my partner. What legal arguments are available to lesbian and gay parents who are faced with such choices? Can *Lawrence v. Texas* be cited in support of such parents?

In re Marriage of Dorworth
33 P.3d 1260 (Col. App. 2001)

Opinion by Judge METZGER

Edward E. Dorworth (father) appeals the portion of the permanent orders imposing restrictions upon the exercise of parenting time with his daughter, who resides primarily with Sheri J. Dorworth (mother). We affirm in part and vacate in part.

As part of the dissolution of their marriage, the parties reached a partial separation agreement and parenting plan, which the court determined was in the best interests of the child. Under that agreement, the child legally resides with mother, and father has parenting time on alternate weekends from Thursday after school until 10:00 a.m. Sunday morning. The parties share major decisionmaking responsibility for their daughter's education, as well as for her medical, dental, and mental health care issues. They reserved allocation of religious decisionmaking authority.

Mother sought to restrict father, who describes himself as "bisexual," from exercising parenting time when he was in the company of gays or lesbians and to preclude him from taking the child to his church, which has a congregation with a gay orientation. After a hearing, the trial court found that the child was of tender years, that she had not been exposed to any type of education regarding sex and relationships, and that the parties had held themselves out as husband and wife and had raised the child in that environment. The court also found that the child had not been exposed to father's gay lifestyle during the marriage, that father "came out" after the parties separated, and that the parties had not discussed father's sexual orientation with the child.

The court determined it was not in the best interests of the child to be exposed to father's gay lifestyle, especially because the parties had not talked with her about his sexual orientation. For the same reason, the court determined it was not in the child's best interests to see her father having an intimate relationship with a male. The court also found that it would be confusing for the child to be exposed to the gay environment of father's church.

Based on these findings, the court precluded father from having any other person spend the night at his home during parenting time and from taking the child to his church.

Father contends the trial court erred in restricting his parenting time without a finding that, absent such restriction, the child would have been physically endangered or her emotional development would have been significantly impaired. Additionally, father asserts the record contains no evidence that would support such a finding. We agree with both contentions.

The court may make provisions for parenting time that the court finds are in the child's best interests unless it finds, after a hearing, that parenting time by the party would endanger the child's physical health or significantly impair the child's emotional development. Section 14-10-124(1.5)(a), C.R.S.2000, lists eleven factors for the court to consider, at a minimum, in making that determination. Section 14-10-129(1), C.R.S.2000, similarly provides that:

> The court may make or modify an order granting or denying parenting time rights whenever such order or modification would serve the best interests of the child; but the court shall not restrict a parent's parenting time rights unless it finds that the parenting time would endanger the child's physical health or significantly impair the child's emotional development.

Thus, the General Assembly has directed that, in determining parenting time or decisionmaking responsibilities, trial courts shall not consider conduct of a proposed custodian that does not affect that party's relationship to the child.

Additionally, a trial court has no authority to intervene in the custodian's determination of the child's religious training unless it finds that the child's physical health would be endangered or that the child's emotional development would be significantly impaired.

Here, the record shows that father had been the primary caretaker of the child for the first six years of her life. She was a happy and secure nine-year-old. Father denied ever exposing the child to any sexual or inappropriate behavior, and the record contains no evidence to the contrary.

Mother was concerned that the child would be confused because she had been reared in a conservative religious environment and perceived a family as being comprised only of a mother, father, and child. Mother also testified that the child had not yet been exposed to sex education, and asserted that, for that reason, the parties had agreed no one should presently spend the night at either parent's home. Finally, mother believed there was a risk that father would expose the child to inappropriate conduct and that she would be harmed by exposure to either homosexual or heterosexual strangers. Mother thought a restriction until the child reached the age of fourteen was appropriate, at which time the child would learn of her own sexuality.

Father agreed it would be harmful to disclose his sexuality to the child at this time because she already was experiencing turmoil from the dissolution. He believed, however, that disclosure should not be delayed for five or ten years, because the child would feel that he had lied to her regarding the circumstances of the dissolution of the marriage.

The trial court made no finding that father's conduct endangered the child physically or impaired her emotional development. Nor does the evidence support such a finding. Therefore, the portion of the judgment that precludes father from having overnight guests during parenting time cannot be sustained. *See In re Marriage of Jarman*, 752 P.2d 1068 (Colo.App.1988); *Christian v. Randall, supra.*

Other jurisdictions that have adopted the Uniform Dissolution of Marriage Act are in accord with the result we have reached here, i.e., that the court may not restrict parenting time merely because of a parent's sexual orientation. *See, e.g., In re Marriage of Pleasant*, 256 Ill.App.3d 742, 195 Ill.Dec. 169, 628 N.E.2d 633 (1993)(parent's open involvement in lesbian relationship not grounds to restrict visitation in the absence of evidence of inappropriate behavior in child's presence); *In re Marriage of Wicklund*, 84 Wash.App. 763, 932 P.2d 652 (1996)(parental conduct may be restricted only if child's physical, mental, or emotional health would be endangered).

Courts in states that have not adopted the Uniform Act have also reached the same conclusion. *See, e.g., In re Marriage of Birdsall*, 197 Cal.App.3d 1024, 243 Cal.Rptr. 287

(1988); *Boswell v. Boswell,* 352 Md. 204, 721 A.2d 662 (1998); *Weigand v. Houghton,* 730 So.2d 581 (Miss.1999); *Conkel v. Conkel,* 31 Ohio App.3d 169, 509 N.E.2d 983 (1987); *In re Marriage of Ashling,* 42 Or.App. 47, 599 P.2d 475 (1979); *Blew v. Verta,* 420 Pa.Super. 528, 617 A.2d 31 (1992).

For the same reasons, the portion of the judgment that restricted father from taking the child to his church cannot stand. Finally, because we have resolved the issues by applying the standards in §§ 14-10-124(1.5)(a) and 14-10-129(1), we need not address the constitutional arguments raised by father and amici curiae.

Those portions of the judgment that preclude father from having overnight guests during parenting time and from taking the child to his church are vacated. In all other respects, the judgment is affirmed.

Notes and Questions

1. The court cites the best interest of the child standard as the appropriate standard for custody modifications, but then says that parenting time should not be restricted unless it finds that visitation "would endanger the child's physical health or significantly impair the child's emotional development." Is the latter a different standard from "best interest?"

2. Professor Eric Andersen had identified three interests that are at stake in disputes involving child custody and visitation and suggests that these three interests should be "the source of legal standards courts apply in constests between adults over legally enforceable relationships with children." The three interests are: (1) the interest of the child, which is reflected in the "best interests" standard, (2) the interest of the parent, which is protected whenever a standard requires proof of harm before the state can intervene, e.g., the "unfitness standard,"which must be met before parental rights are terminated, and (3) the interest of society, which is served by the "unfitness standard" because it authorizes intervention to protect the child when needed, while at the same time preserving family privacy by restraining intervention. The societal interest at stake is the interest in having parents raise their own children requiring both of these standards. If the child's interest were paramount, then the "best interests" standard would always be applied. See Andersen, Children, Parents, and Nonparents: Protected Interests and Legal Standards. 1998 B.Y.U. L. Rev. 935 (1998).

C. Who Can Become a Parent?

1. Adoption by Gay and Lesbian People

Some litigants have argued that the right to family integrity recognized by the courts in parent-child relationships should be extended to nontraditional families. To date, the Supreme Court has not ruled directly on this question. It has suggested that there may be constitutional protection for some nontraditional families. See *Moore v.*

City of East Cleveland, 431 U.S. 494 (1977)(holding zoning ordinance that only allowed certain types of families to live in single family zone was unconstitutional as applied to a grandmother and grandson)(plurality opinion). But *Moore* has not been
generally extended to provide grandparents with constitutionally protected rights in
other fact situations where they have sought a legal relationship with the child, e.g., by
adoption. See *Mullins v. Oregon*, 57 F.3d 789 (9th Cir. 1995)(refusing to extend *Moore*
to recognize a constitutional right for grandparents to adopt grandchildren after
parental rights had been terminated). *Accord, Miller v. California*, 355 F.3d 1172 (9th
Cir. 2004). See also *In re Richard G., Jr.*, 770 A.2d 625 (Maine 2001)(rejecting grandmother's claim that she had a constitutionally protected right to custody of grandchild
as against foster parents who were given custody after natural parents' rights were terminated).

Nor has *Moore* been extended to give constitutional protection to unrelated persons
who act as functional parents. As one commentator put it: "For a parent-child relationship to be legally recognized as a family, either biological or legal consanguinity is required." See Richard F. Storrow, The Policy of Family Privacy: Uncovering the Bias in
Favor of Nuclear Families in American Constitutional Law and Policy Reform, 66 Mo. L.
Rev. 527 (2001).

Thus, as a general rule, before one can enjoy parental rights and their constitutional protection one must first become a parent. Each state has its own rules about
who is a parent. For same-sex couples, becoming joint parents through reproductive
sex is not an option. The most common method for establishing joint parenthood is
through adoption. Single lesbians and gay men also use adoption to establish parenthood. Does a state law that forbids adoptions by gay people violate the constitutional
guarantees of due process and equal protection? In *Lofton v. Secretary of the Department of Children and Family Services*, which is the focus of Chapter Two, above, that
question was answered in the negative. Review that decision before answering the following questions.

Notes and Questions

1. A lesbian biological mom, living and raising her child in Florida, enters into a long-
term committed relationship with another woman. The mom desperately wants her
child to have the stability and support of two parents and has asked her partner to adopt
the child. The partner wants to adopt the child. What result under Florida law and
Lofton?

2. A lesbian mom and her child live in Connecticut. She enters into a long-term committed relationship with another woman and the woman adopts the child under Connecticut law, which recognizes such adoptions. When the couple moves to Florida, will
the adoption be recognized? For example, assume the adoptive Mom dies in an automobile accident. The adopted child sues the tortfeasor for wrongful death. Can the tortfeasor challenge the adoption under Florida law, claiming that it is not valid in Florida? See
Russell v. Bridgens, 647 N.W.2d 56 (Neb. 2002), *infra*, raising full faith and credit issue
for a Pennsylvania adoption that would not have been possible under Nebraska law.

3. Jim and Jane Greenleaf, residents of New York, have a daughter named Tabatha. In
their wills they express the desire to have Jane's sister, Terra, become Tabatha's guardian

should anything happen to Jim and Jane. Jim and Jane die in an airplane accident in New York. Terra, who lives in Florida and is an open lesbian, wants to adopt Tabatha. Does *Lofton* apply? How might you distinguish *Lofton*?

Note

Florida is the only state that has a statutory ban on "homosexuals" adopting children. Some other states specifically ban adoptions by unmarried adult couples, regardless of gender, and a few restrict adoptions by same-sex couples (without restricting adoptions by individual gay people, at least by statute). See, e.g., Miss. Code §93-17-3(2), which prohibits adoption by couples of the same gender; Utah Code §78-30-1(3)(b), which prohibits an individual from adopting if that individual is cohabiting with someone outside of a legal marriage. The overwhelming majority of U.S. jurisdictions place no statutory restriction on adoptions by gay people, and some actively encourage such adoptions when the child in question has special needs or is otherwise difficult to place due to age, previous history, or medical condition. Gay parents in many jurisdictions have been particularly successful in adopting HIV-positive infants, in some cases whose parents had died from AIDS. In at least one case, a state's highest court has overruled lower court rulings against adoptions by gay parents, finding that sexual orientation was not, standing alone, a reason to reject otherwise qualified adoptive parents. See *In re Adoption of Charles B.*, 50 Ohio St. 3d 88, 552 N.E.2d 884 (1990).

2. Second Parent Adoptions

A second parent adoption occurs when the unmarried partner of a person who is already a parent wishes to establish a legal parental relationship with the child while allowing the existing parent-child relationship to continue. For lesbian and gay couples, the closest analogy would be a stepparent adoption, where the spouse of the existing parent wishes to adopt. Only three states, Vermont, Connecticut, and California, have statutes that address the question of second parent adoption directly, and these statutes are of very recent vintage. In Massachusetts, where same-sex marriage is possible, married couples can rely on stepparent adoption statutes. Massachusetts was also one of the early states to judicially recognize the validity of second parent adoption. See *In re Adoption of Tammy*, 619 N.E.2d 315 (Mass. 1993), *infra*.

The difficulty in obtaining a second parent adoption stems from the specific wording of most adoption statutes, which typically provide that the natural or existing parent must relinquish his or her parental rights as a result of adoption of the child by anyone other than a spouse. While the language is slightly different in the various state statutes, it is clear that these statutes were all drafted with one primary adoption scenario in mind: a child is removed from the existing family of birth and is adopted by a new family, in which case all legal connections with the original family should be terminated. States then created an exception to this rule in the case of a stepparent adoption. In such cases, if a new husband were to adopt his wife's child, then the wife's parental status would not have to be terminated. However, as a general rule, the biological father's parental status would have to be terminated when a new father adopts. These statutes were clearly adopted by legislatures who viewed nuclear families, whether a family of origin, or a later reformulated family through adoption, as ones that consisted of one mother and one father.

There is another way for a same-sex partner to become a co-parent with the biological or pre-existing adoptive parent. The partners could petition for joint adoption of the child, which would terminate the existing parental-child legal bond, but at the same time would recognize both parents as the new adoptive parents. Once again, the language of the state adoption statute is likely to become a problem. Most statutes only anticipated joint adoption by a husband and wife and some expressly limit co-adoption to a married couple. In other states, the statute is less clear. While adoption by a single person is permitted in almost every state, a joint adoption by two single persons is generally not addressed in the statute.

In states that have considered and approved adoptions that create two-mother or two-father families, the courts have had to engage in creative statutory construction to reach the desired result. In cases involving a second parent adoption that would otherwise cut-off the parental rights of the existing parent, the court will have to find a way to construe the "relinquishment of parental rights" provision out of the statute. And in cases that involve joint adoptions by unmarried persons (two women or two men), the court will have to interpret statutes that permit adoptions by a single person to mean that two single persons can adopt jointly.

The canon of statutory construction that is most troubling in these cases is the canon that provides that statutes in derogation of the common law must be construed narrowly. Adoption does not exist at common law. All adoption statutes are thus in derogation of common law. At the same time, a counter statutory construction principle is found in the adoption provisions of most family law codes. Such statutes usually include a directive that they are to be construed liberally in the best interest of the child.

In re Adoption of Tammy
619 N.E.2d 315 (Mass. 1993)

Greaney, Justice.

In this case, two unmarried women, Susan and Helen, filed a joint petition in the Probate and Family Court Department under G.L. c. 210, §1 (1992 ed.) to adopt as their child Tammy, a minor, who is Susan's biological daughter. Following an evidentiary hearing, a judge of the Probate and Family Court entered a memorandum of decision containing findings of fact and conclusions of law. Based on her finding that Helen and Susan "are each functioning, separately and together, as the custodial and psychological parents of [Tammy]," and that "it is the best interest of said [Tammy] that she be adopted by both," the judge entered a decree allowing the adoption. Simultaneously, the judge reserved and reported to the Appeals Court the evidence and all questions of law, in an effort to "secure [the] decree from any attack in the future on jurisdictional grounds." See G.L. c. 215, §13 (1992 ed.). See also *Adoption of Thomas*, 408 Mass. 446, 559 N.E.2d 1230 (1990). We transferred the case to this court on our own motion. We conclude that the adoption was properly allowed under G.L. c. 210.[1]

---

1. The judge also decreed, as an alternative to the adoption ordered under G.L. c. 210, "[I]t would be in the best interest of the child to permit [Helen] to adopt [Tammy] and [Susan] to retain postadoptive parental rights of custody and visitation pursuant to its equitable powers, under G.L.

We summarize the relevant facts as found by the judge. Helen and Susan have lived together in a committed relationship, which they consider to be permanent, for more than ten years. In June, 1983, they jointly purchased a house in Cambridge. Both women are physicians specializing in surgery. At the time the petition was filed, Helen maintained a private practice in general surgery at Mount Auburn Hospital and Susan, a nationally recognized expert in the field of breast cancer, was director of the Faulkner Breast Center and a surgical oncologist at the Dana Farber Cancer Institute. Both women also held positions on the faculty of Harvard Medical School.

For several years prior to the birth of Tammy, Helen and Susan planned to have a child, biologically related to both of them, whom they would jointly parent. Helen first attempted to conceive a child through artificial insemination by Susan's brother. When those efforts failed, Susan successfully conceived a child through artificial insemination by Helen's biological cousin, Francis. The women attended childbirth classes together and Helen was present when Susan gave birth to Tammy on April 30, 1988. Although Tammy's birth certificate reflects Francis as her biological father, she was given a hyphenated surname using Susan and Helen's last names.

Since her birth, Tammy has lived with, and been raised and supported by, Helen and Susan. Tammy views both women as her parents, calling Helen "mama" and Susan "mommy." Tammy has strong emotional and psychological bonds with both Helen and Susan. Together, Helen and Susan have provided Tammy with a comfortable home, and have created a warm and stable environment which is supportive of Tammy's growth and over-all well being. Both women jointly and equally participate in parenting Tammy, and both have a strong financial commitment to her. During the work week, Helen usually has lunch at home with Tammy, and on weekends both women spend time together with Tammy at special events or running errands. When Helen and Susan are working, Tammy is cared for by a nanny. The three vacation together at least ten days every three to four months, frequently spending time with Helen's and Susan's respective extended families in California and Mexico. Francis does not participate in parenting Tammy and does not support her. His intention was to assist Helen and Susan in having a child, and he does not intend to be involved with Tammy, except as a distant relative. Francis signed an adoption surrender and supports the joint adoption by both women.

Helen and Susan, recognizing that the laws of the Commonwealth do not permit them to enter into a legally cognizable marriage, believe that the best interests of Tammy require legal recognition of her identical emotional relationship to both women. Susan expressed her understanding that it may not be in her own long-term interest to permit Helen to adopt Tammy because, in the event that Helen and Susan separate, Helen would have equal rights to primary custody. Susan indicated, however, that she has no reservation about allowing Helen to adopt. Apart from the emotional security and current practical ramifications which legal recognition of the reality of her parental relationships will provide Tammy, Susan indicated that the adoption is important for Tammy in terms of potential inheritance from Helen. Helen and her living issue are the beneficiaries of three irrevocable family trusts. Unless Tammy is adopted, Helen's share of the trusts may pass to others. Although Susan and Helen have estab-

---

c. 215." Because we conclude that the adoption was properly allowed under G.L. c. 210, we need not consider the alternative equitable ground relied on by the judge in permitting Helen to adopt Tammy and Susan to maintain postadoptive rights.

lished a substantial trust fund for Tammy, it is comparatively small in relation to Tammy's potential inheritance under Helen's family trusts.

Over a dozen witnesses, including mental health professionals, teachers, colleagues, neighbors, blood relatives and a priest and nun, testified to the fact that Helen and Susan participate equally in raising Tammy, that Tammy relates to both women as her parents, and that the three form a healthy, happy, and stable family unit. Educators familiar with Tammy testified that she is an extremely well-adjusted, bright, creative, cheerful child who interacts well with other children and adults. A priest and nun from the parties' church testified that Helen and Susan are active parishioners, that they routinely take Tammy to church and church-related activities, and that they attend to the spiritual and moral development of Tammy in an exemplary fashion. Teachers from Tammy's school testified that Helen and Susan both actively participate as volunteers in the school community and communicate frequently with school officials. Neighbors testified that they would have no hesitation in leaving their own children in the care of Helen or Susan. Susan's father, brother, and maternal aunt, and Helen's cousin testified in favor of the joint adoption. Members of both women's extended families attested to the fact that they consider Helen and Susan to be equal parents of Tammy. Both families unreservedly endorsed the adoption petition.

The Department of Social Services (department) conducted a home study in connection with the adoption petition which recommended the adoption, concluding that "the petitioners and their home are suitable for the proper rearing of this child." Tammy's pediatrician reported to the department that Tammy receives regular pediatric care and that she "could not have more excellent parents than Helen and Susan." A court-appointed guardian ad litem, Dr. Steven Nickman, assistant clinical professor of psychiatry at Harvard Medical School, conducted a clinical assessment of Tammy and her family with a view toward determining whether or not it would be in Tammy's best interests to be adopted by Helen and Susan. Dr. Nickman considered the ramifications of the fact that Tammy will be brought up in a "non-standard" family. As part of his report, he reviewed and referenced literature on child psychiatry and child psychology which supports the conclusion that children raised by lesbian parents develop normally. In sum, he stated that "the fact that this parent-child constellation came into being as a result of thoughtful planning and a strong desire on the part of these women to be parents to a child and to give that child the love, the wisdom and the knowledge that they possess...[needs to be taken into account].... The maturity of these women, their status in the community, and their seriousness of purpose stands in contrast to the caretaking environments of a vast number of children who are born to heterosexual parents but who are variously abused, neglected and otherwise deprived of security and happiness." Dr. Nickman concluded that "there is every reason for [Helen] to become a legal parent to Tammy just as [Susan] is," and he recommended that the court so order. An attorney appointed to represent Tammy's interests also strongly recommended that the joint petition be granted.

Despite the overwhelming support for the joint adoption and the judge's conclusion that joint adoption is clearly in Tammy's best interests, the question remains whether there is anything in the law of the Commonwealth that would prevent this adoption. The law of adoption is purely statutory, and the governing statute, G.L. c. 210 (1992 ed.), is to be strictly followed in all its essential particulars. *Purinton v. Jamrock*, 80 N.E. 802 (1907). To the extent that any ambiguity or vagueness exists in the statute, judicial construction should enhance, rather than defeat, its purpose. *Hayon v. Coca Cola Bottling Co. of New England*, 378 N.E.2d 442 (1978). The primary purpose of the adoption statute, particularly with regard to children under the age of fourteen, is undoubtedly the advancement of the best interests of the subject child. See G.L. c.

210, §§ 3, 4A, 5A, 5B, 6. *See also…Purinton v. Jamrock, supra,* 195 Mass. at 199, 80 N.E. 802 ("[I]t is the right of the children that is protected by this statute…. The first and paramount duty is to consult the welfare of the child"). With these considerations in mind, we examine the statute to determine whether adoption in the circumstances of this case is permitted.

1. The initial question is whether the Probate Court judge had jurisdiction under G.L. c. 210 to enter a judgment on a joint petition for adoption brought by two unmarried cohabitants in the petitioners' circumstances. We answer this question in the affirmative.

There is nothing on the face of the statute which precludes the joint adoption of a child by two unmarried cohabitants such as the petitioners. Chapter 210, § 1, provides that "[a] person of full age may petition the probate court in the county where he resides for leave to adopt as his child another person younger than himself, unless such other person is his or her wife or husband, or brother, sister, uncle or aunt, of the whole or half blood."[2] Other than requiring that a spouse join in the petition, if the petitioner is married and the spouse is competent to join therein, the statute does not expressly prohibit or require joinder by any person. Although the singular "a person" is used, it is a legislatively mandated rule of statutory construction that "[w]ords importing the singular number may extend and be applied to several persons" unless the resulting construction is "inconsistent with the manifest intent of the law-making body or repugnant to the context of the same statute." G.L. c. 4, § 6 (1992 ed.). In the context of adoption, where the legislative intent to promote the best interests of the child is evidenced throughout the governing statute, and the adoption of a child by two unmarried individuals accomplishes that goal, construing the term "person" as "persons" clearly enhances, rather than defeats, the purpose of the statute. Furthermore, it is apparent from the first sentence of G.L. c. 210, § 1, that the Legislature considered and defined those combinations of persons which would lead to adoptions in violation of public policy. Clearly absent is any prohibition of adoption by two unmarried individuals like the petitioners.

While the Legislature may not have envisioned adoption by same-sex partners, there is no indication that it attempted to define all possible categories of persons leading to adoptions in the best interests of children. Rather than limit the potential categories of persons entitled to adopt (other than those described in the first sentence of § 1), the Legislature used general language to define who may adopt and who may be adopted.

In this case all requirements in §§ 2 and 2A are met, and there is no question that the judge's findings demonstrate that the directives set forth in §§ 5B and 6, and in case law, have been satisfied. Adoption will not result in any tangible change in Tammy's daily life; it will, however, serve to provide her with a significant legal relationship which may be important in her future. At the most practical level, adoption will entitle Tammy to inherit from Helen's family trusts and from Helen and her family under the law of intestate succession (G.L. c. 210, § 6), to receive support from Helen, who will be legally ob-

---

2. There is no question that Helen and Susan each individually satisfy the identity requirements of G.L. c. 210, § 1. Although the adoption statute, as it first appeared (St. 1851, c. 324) precluded a person from adopting his or her own child by birth, the statute was amended to permit adoption by the child's natural parents. *Curran, Petition of,* 314 Mass. 91, 49 N.E.2d 432 (1943) (natural mother of child born out of wedlock proper party to adoption petition). None of the prohibitions to adoption set forth in § 1 is applicable. Furthermore, there is nothing in the statute that prohibits adoption based on gender or sexual orientation. Contrast Fla.Stat. § 63.042(3) (1991) (prohibiting homosexuals from adopting); N.H.Rev.Stat.Ann. § 170-B:4 (1990) (same). 381 Mass. 563, 579, 410 N.E.2d 1207 (1980).

ligated to provide such support, to be eligible for coverage under Helen's health insurance policies, and to be eligible for social security benefits in the event of Helen's disability or death (42 U.S.C. §402[d] [1988]).

Of equal, if not greater significance, adoption will enable Tammy to preserve her unique filial ties to Helen in the event that Helen and Susan separate, or Susan predeceases Helen.[3] As the case law and commentary on the subject illustrate, when the functional parents of children born in circumstances similar to Tammy separate or one dies, the children often remain in legal limbo for years while their future is disputed in the courts. Polikoff, This Child Does Have Two Mothers: Redefining Parenthood to Meet the Needs of Children in Lesbian-Mother and Other Nontraditional Families, 78 Geo.J.L. 459, 508–22 (1990); Comment, Second Parent Adoption for Lesbian-Parented Families: Legal Recognition of the Other Mother, 19 U.C.Davis L.Rev. 729, 741–45 (1986). In some cases, children have been denied the affection of a functional parent who has been with them since birth, even when it is apparent that this outcome is contrary to the children's best interests.[4] Adoption serves to establish legal rights and responsibilities so that, in the event that problems arise in the future, issues of custody and visitation may be promptly resolved by reference to the best interests of the child within the recognized framework of the law. See G.L. c. 209C, §10. See also *Adoption of B.L.V.B.*, 628 A.2d 1271 (Vt.1993). There is no jurisdictional bar in the statute to the judge's consideration of this joint petition. The conclusion that the adoption is in the best interests of Tammy is also well warranted.

2. The judge also posed the question whether, pursuant to G.L. c. 210, §6 (1992 ed.), Susan's legal relationship to Tammy must be terminated if Tammy is adopted. Section 6 provides that, on entry of an adoption decree, "all rights, duties and other legal consequences of the natural relation of child and parent shall…except as regards marriage, incest or cohabitation, terminate between the child so adopted and his natural parents and kindred." Although G.L. c. 210, §2, clearly permits a child's natural parent to be an adoptive parent, §6 does not contain any express exceptions to its termination provision. The Legislature obviously did not intend that a natural parent's legal relationship to its child be terminated when the natural parent is a party to the adoption petition.

Section 6 clearly is directed to the more usual circumstances of adoption, where the child is adopted by persons who are not the child's natural parents (either because the natural parents have elected to relinquish the child for adoption or their parental rights have been involuntarily terminated). The purpose of the termination provision is to protect the security of the child's newly-created family unit by eliminating in-

---

3. Although Susan has designated Helen guardian of Tammy in her will, Helen's custody of Tammy could conceivably be contested in the event of Susan's death, particularly by Francis, members of his family or members of Susan's family. Absent adoption, Helen would not have a dispositive legal right to retain custody of Tammy, because she would be a "legal stranger" to the child.

4. Cases from other jurisdictions demonstrate the difficulties resulting from the lack of an established legal relationship between a child and its second functional parent. See,…*In re Pearlman*, 15 Fam.L.Rep. (BNA) 1355 (Fla.Cir.Ct.1989) (unreported) (custody of child conceived by artificial insemination during lesbian couple's relationship awarded to "de facto" parent after four years of litigation with child's maternal grandparents following death of natural mother; child, who had been separated from her functional parent and suffered anxiety as a result, told the court "for Christmas I don't really want a present. All I want is to live with Neenie ["de facto" parent]").

volvement with the child's natural parents. Although it is not uncommon for a natural parent to join in the adoption petition of a spouse who is not the child's natural parent, see, e.g., *Adoption of a Minor (No. 1)*, 367 Mass. 907, 327 N.E.2d 735 (1975)..., the statute has never been construed to require the termination of the natural parent's legal relationship to the child in these circumstances. Nor has §6 been construed to apply when the natural mother petitions alone to adopt her child born out of wedlock. See *Curran, petitioner,* 314 Mass. 91, 49 N.E.2d 432 (1943). Reading the adoption statute as a whole, we conclude that the termination provision contained in §6 was intended to apply only when the natural parents (or parent) are not parties to the adoption petition.[5]

3. We conclude that the Probate Court has jurisdiction to enter a decree on a joint adoption petition brought by the two petitioners when the judge has found that joint adoption is in the subject child's best interests. We further conclude that, when a natural parent is a party to a joint adoption petition, that parent's legal relationship to the child does not terminate on entry of the adoption decree.

4. So much of the decree as allows the adoption of Tammy by both petitioners is affirmed. So much of the decree as provides in the alternative for the adoption of Tammy by Helen and the retention of rights of custody and visitation by Susan is vacated.

So ordered.

[Dissenting opinions omitted, holding that statute should not be construed to allow joint adoption, but might be construed to permit "Helen to adopt Tammy while allowing Susan to retain all her parental rights and obligations."]

In re Adoption of Jane Doe

719 N.E.2d 1071 (Ohio App. 1998)

SHEILA G. FARMER, Judge.

Jane Doe was born on July 28, 1990. Jane Doe's biological mother and appellant, the biological mother's lesbian partner, have been together since 1981.

On October 16, 1996, appellant filed a complaint for declaratory judgment seeking to adopt Jane Doe while continuing the parental rights of the biological mother. After extensive briefing, the trial court found appellant to be a suitable person to adopt under R.C. 3107.03, but denied the requested relief because the biological mother could not retain her parental rights if appellant or appellant and the biological mother together were to adopt Jane Doe.

Appellant filed a notice of appeal, and this matter is now before this court for consideration. Assignments of error are as follows:

---

5. In interpreting a provision similar to G.L. c. 210, §6, the Vermont Supreme Court, citing support from trial courts in other jurisdictions, likewise concluded that the natural or prior adoptive parent's legal relationship to the child does not terminate when the child is adopted by the same-sex partner of the child's legal parent. See *Adoption of B.L.V.B.,* 628 A.2d 1271 (Vt.1993), citing *Matter of Evan,* 153 Misc.2d 844, 583 N.Y.S.2d 997 (N.Y.Sur. 1992), and *In re Adoption of Minor (T.),* 60 U.S.L.W. 2191, 1991 WL 291598 (D.C.Super.Ct. Sept. 24, 1991) (unreported).

I

"The trial court erred in ruling that it had no authority to grant an adoption of a child by her lifelong second parent without terminating the biological mother's parental rights under R.C. 3107.15(A)(1), and in denying declaratory relief and dismissing the adoption petition."

II

"The trial court erred by not declaring that it had authority to allow a legal parent to relinquish her parental rights and immediately adopt her biological child jointly with the child's second parent, and in denying declaratory relief and dismissing the adoption petition."

I

Appellant claims that the trial court erred in denying the petition for declaratory relief. Specifically, appellant claims that the trial court erred in finding that R.C. 3107.15(A)(1) would terminate the biological mother's parental rights upon adoption of Jane Doe by appellant, a nonstepparent. We disagree.

The complaint for declaratory judgment requested a judgment granting the biological mother continued parental rights to Jane Doe, a judgment allowing the filing of the adoption petition by appellant and a judgment approving the adoption of Jane Doe by appellant.

As noted by the trial court, there is no impediment for the proposed adoption because appellant fulfills the requirements of R.C. 3107.03(B) to adopt as appellant is "[a]n ummarried adult." The gravamen of this appeal is what is the effect of an adoption by appellant, "an unmarried adult," on the parental rights of the biological mother.

By opinion and order filed March 4, 1998, the trial court strictly construed R.C. 3107.15(A)(1) and found that an adoption by appellant would terminate the parental rights of the biological parent. The trial court reached this conclusion by finding that the unambiguous language and meaning of the statute required strict construction. We concur with this reasoning based upon the following analysis.

R.C. 3107.15(A)(1) states:

> "A final decree of adoption * * * shall have the following effects as to all matters within the jurisdiction or before a court of this state * * *:

> "(1) Except with respect to a spouse of the petitioner and relatives of the spouse, to relieve the biological or other legal parents of the adopted person of all parental rights and responsibilities, and to terminate all legal relationships between the adopted person and the adopted person's relatives, including the adopted person's biological or other legal parents, so that the adopted person thereafter is a stranger to the adopted person's former relatives for all purposes * * *."

Adoption in Ohio is a creature of statute. Therefore, the general rule that issues not available at common law but subject to statutory creation must be strictly construed must be applied.

In *State ex rel. Kaylor v. Bruening* (1997), the Supreme Court of Ohio recognized the nature of the language in R.C. 3107.15(A)(1) and its effect on a biological parent:

" R.C. 3107.15(A)(1) provides that a final decree of adoption issued by an Ohio court has the effect of terminating all parental rights of biological parents and creating parental rights in adoptive parents." *State ex rel. Smith v. Smith.* . . .

Appellant and *amicus* argue that the precedent set forth in other Ohio cases indicates that the Supreme Court of Ohio understands that the granting of an adoption relies on a case-by-case analysis:

> "Pursuant to R.C. 3107.14, adoption matters must be decided on a case-by-case basis through the able exercise of discretion by the trial court giving due consideration to all known factors in determining what is in the best interest of the person to be adopted." *In re Adoption of Charles B. (1990).* . . .

We find the cases cited by appellant to be distinguishable from the case *sub judice.* In the cited cases, the Supreme Court of Ohio emphasized the trial court's discretion in determining eligibility to adopt. The case *sub judice* involves not eligibility to adopt but the effects of adoption.

We find this "tremendous trifle" to be the linchpin of this case. By strictly construing the statute that involves the termination of parental rights in favor of adoption, we are adhering to the maxim "adoption statutes are in derogation of common law and therefore must be strictly construed * * *."

Although we are mindful of the dilemma facing the parties and are sympathetic to their plight, it is not within the constitutional scope of judicial power to change the face and effect of the plain meaning of R.C. 3107.15. This case is not about alternative lifestyles but about statutory construction. When we balance the spirit and motivation of the adoption laws (as appellant argues) against the plain meaning of the statutory language created by the state legislature, we are not empowered to find that the "spirit" includes the issue presented *sub judice.*

Appellant argues that we should use the best interest of the child test in interpreting the statute. We find that to do so would place the "cart before the horse." Best interest pertains to the adoption process, not to the legal effects of the adoption. Based upon the clear meaning of R.C. 3107.15(A), we find that the trial court did not err in finding that the biological mother's parental rights would terminate upon adoption of the child by appellant, a nonstepparent.

Assignment of Error I is denied.

II

Based upon our decision in Assignment of Error I, we find Assignment of Error II to be moot.

The judgment of the Court of Common Pleas of Summit County, Ohio, Probate Division, is hereby affirmed.

Judgment affirmed.

John W. Wise, Judge, concurring.

I concur in the majority opinion and write separately on Assignment of Error I only to emphasize my belief that this is a legislative issue for the General Assembly. Inherent but unspoken in this case is the legal reality that two individuals of the same sex cannot marry under existing Ohio law and therefore cannot be spouses to each other. Until such time as the General Assembly of Ohio changes the law pertaining to same-sex marriages or rewrites the adoption statutes to specifically allow the requested legal relationship, I cannot interpret the existing adoption statute as contemplating a spousal relationship between two individuals of the same sex such as to create a stepparent relationship in a legal context.

Notes and Questions

1. Do you agree with the majority opinion in *Adoption of Tammy*? The legislature may not have contemplated adoptions by a committed lesbian couple, but what might the legislature have thought about an unmarried opposite-sex couple adopting? See *In re Jason C.*, 533 A.2d 32 (N.H. 1987), construing similar statute in New Hampshire and holding that it would not allow a divorced husband and wife to co-adopt.

2. Lawyers in the *Jane Doe* case asked the Supreme Court of Ohio to grant discretionary review in the case and reverse. The Supreme Court declined jurisdiction to review the case. 709 N.E.2d 173 (Ohio 1999). Under the Ohio constitution, the Supreme Court of Ohio has appellate jurisdiction "in cases of public or great general interest." Ohio Const. art IV, §2(B)(2)(d). Addressing that question, the MEMORANDUM IN SUPPORT OF JURISDICTION OF APPELLANTS argued as follows:

EXPLANATION OF WHY THE CASE IS OF
PUBLIC AND GREAT GENERAL INTEREST

In this adoption case, appellants "Trish Smith" and "Marcia Jones" ask the Court to allow their daughter "Jane Doe" the sane legal, financial and emotional security that other Ohio children take for granted by securing her legal relationships with each of them. [Note: the names are pseudonyms] Because appellants are an unmarried, lesbian couple, however, the Court of Appeals held that it was impossible under the Ohio Adoption Act ("Act"), to extend these protections to Jane through legal recognition of her relationship with Trish without terminating the rights of her biological mother, Marcia. Instead, her two lifelong parents are compelled by the decision below to choose which one of them will be Jane's sole, legally recognized parent and to hope that life fortuitously spares their daughter from any ensuing harm.

Such a result is unjust, unreasonable and grossly contrary to Jane's best interests. The sane is true for countless other Ohio children who are comparably situated and put in harm's way by the decision below. Without the security that adoption would afford, Jane faces devastating loss and insecurity if she loses either parent, beyond that any child would suffer, and great physical harm if she needs any treatment for her chronic medical condition and Trish cannot legally consent. Jane also must plan to get by without Trish's child support, health care coverage, social security or other benefits. While Marcia and Trish can take certain measures to protect Jane under Ohio law, all are subject to revocation and their enforcement cannot be assumed. None provides the security of adoption. It is a matter of substantial public interest that the calamities that may befall children like Jane—and their attendant social costs—be avoided by granting jurisdiction to review the decision below.

It is also very much in the public interest that this Court restore the probate courts to their paramount position as protectors of children in adoption proceedings. The decision below dislodges the probate courts from their rightful post in favor of a method of statutory construction that no legislative act demands and no decision of this Court approves. The Court already has recognized that "[m]atters of adoption are of such compelling public interest that any statutory incroachment upon the power of the courts to exercise the discretion granted them by statutory and constitutional provisions must be carefully scrutinized." *State ex rel. Portage County Welfare Dept. v. Summers* (1974). The decision below amounts to a judicial abdication of duty—and particularly the paramount statutory duty to act in the best interests of the child—in interpreting the Act. In ruling that a statutory provision drafted for other circumstances must be construed to Jane's detriment here, without regard to the consequences for her, the courts below surrendered their role without serving any policy underlying the Act.

The important issues presented by this case are matters of first impression in Ohio, but the legal and policy principles appellants rely upon are well-established in the Court's precedents. Numerous other state courts of appeal have allowed so-called "second-parent adoptions" under statutes and precedents essentially identical to Ohio's. The highest courts of Vermont, Massachusetts and New York have done so, as have appellate courts in New Jersey, Illinois and the District of Columbia. Trial courts in at least sixteen other states are known to have approved such adoptions, and many thousands of couples nationally have secured their children's best interests through this mechanism. Ohio children are no less in need of this vital legal safeguard.

Further, the lower courts' construction of R.C. 3107.15(A)(1) to prohibit second-parent adoptions should logically have had no bearing on appellants' alternative request for a joint adoption. This second approach assumed that Marcia's rights would have to be terminated, to be followed immediate by a joint adoption of Jane with Trish that would restore Marcia's and Jane's full legal rights. However, neither court engaged the merits of appellants' joint adoption request. The trial court entered its judgment without discussion of the merits. The Court of Appeals inexplicably declared the issue moot. This argument plainly was not moot and should be reviewed, not only to serve the many public interests identified above, but also the interest of every citizen in a full and fair hearing on properly raised, justiciable issues.

Finally, the issues presented in this case also are of great general interest. American society is awash in discussion of the needs of changing families and the rights of its gay and lesbian citizens. This Court has set an enviable standard in past cases for deciding these issues dispassionately, in light of the best interests of the children before it, proven facts and the application of settled law. That is all appellants ask here. The decision below, by elevating form over substance in its first section and tidily declaring the second issue moot, deprives Jane of a true judicial interpretation of law and of the fulfillment of her best interests to which every child is entitled.

3. There are twelve courts of appeal in Ohio. Only one has ruled that second parent adoptions are not possible. Probate courts in other parts of the state are free to grant

second parent adoptions so long as they construe the statutes to allow them. As a result, legal protections for children in same-sex couple households vary greatly throughout the state. What do you think some of the most important differences are? Are there alternative ways to gain some of the legal protections for children living in those parts of the state where second parent adoption is not permitted? See *In re Bonfield*, 780 N.E.2d 241 (Ohio 2002). In this case the lesbian couple petitioned the court for "allocation of parental rights and responsibilities" by filing their co-parenting agreement with the court. The court dismissed the petition on jurisdictional grounds, holding that it could only approve co-*parenting* rights when both parties were actually *parents*. The court of appeals agreed and held further that the court also had no jurisdiction to approve a similar allocation of *custodial* rights and responsibilities because that too would require that both parties be parents. This time the Supreme Court granted the appeal. The Court affirmed on the issue regarding co-parenting but reversed on the issue of custodial rights and remanded to the trial court to determine how to allocate custodial rights and responsibilities in the best interest of the child.

An interesting aspect of the Supreme Court's opinion is that in its initial version, it included the following explanation: ""However, because second parent adoption is not available in Ohio, Shelly cannot adopt the children. Instead, if Shelly were to adopt the children herself, the effect would be to terminate Teri [Bonfield]'s rights and responsibilities as an adoptive parent. See R.C. 3107.15(A). Therefore, because Teri wishes to retain her rights as a parent, adoption of the children by Shelly is not a viable option." The adoption issue was not before the court and so this language is clearly dictum. The lawyers in the case had maintained all along that the appellate decision in the *Jane Doe* case was wrong and that probate courts elsewhere in Ohio were granting second parent adoptions. On motion for reconsideration, the Supreme Court agreed to remove the dictum from its final published opinion.

4. The *In re Bonfield* attorneys also argued on appeal, citing to *Troxel v. Granville*, that the mother's constitutional rights had been infringed by the court's refusal to grant her wishes regarding her child's upbringing. The Supreme Court responded as follows:

> Appellants argue that a biological or adoptive parent has the fundamental constitutional right, which may not be restricted by statute, to voluntarily enter into a court-approved shared parenting plan with a "psychological" or "second" parent. The fundamental due process right to make decisions concerning the care, custody, and control of one's children has been upheld in *Troxel v. Granville* (200), 530 U.S. 45, 66. However, this right does not embrace the right to have all decisions recognized or approved in law. In other words, although Teri's decision to co-parent her children with Shelly may be protected from interference by the state, Teri is not entitled to the benefit of statutes that are clearly inapplicable to such a familial arrangement.

5. In 2004, the following provision was added to the Ohio Constitution:

> Only a union between one man and one woman may be a marriage valid in or recognized by this state and its political subdivisions. This state and its political subdivisions shall not create or recognize a legal status for relationships of unmarried individuals that intends to approximate the design, qualities, significance or effect of marriage.

Should this provision have any effect on a court's ability to recognize joint adoptions in the future? To approve joint custodial agreements?

6. In addition to the Court of Appeals in Ohio, appellate courts in Colorado, Nebraska and Wisconsin have also ruled against second parent adoption. See *In re Adoption of T.K.J.*, 931 P.2d 488 (Colo. Ct. App. 1996); *In re Adoption of Luke*, 640 N.W.2d 374 (Neb. 2002); *In re Angel Lace M.*, 516 N.W.2d 678 (Wis. 1994). The Connecticut courts also ruled against second parent adoptions (*In re Adoption of Baby Z.*, 724 A.2d 1035 (Conn. 1999)), but that result has been reversed by statute.

7. Second-parent adoptions have been approved by the highest courts in California, *Sharon S. v. Superior Court*, 73 P.3d 554 (Calif. 2003), cert. denied, 540 U.S. 1220 (2004), New York, *Matter of Jacob*, 660 N.E. 2d 651 (N.Y. 1995), Pennsylvania, *Adoption of R.B.F. and R.C.F.*, 803 A.2d 1195 (Pa. 2002), and Vermont, *Adoptions of B.L.V.B. and E.L.V.B.*, 628 A.2d 1271 (Vt. 1993).

8. Should adoption be limited to a "second" parent? Suppose Alice and Fred have a child, Clarissa. They get divorced and Alice is awarded primary custody. Fred supports Clarissa and has occasional visitation. Alice then becomes involved in a new relationship with Sandy and Sandy develops a strong relationship with Clarissa. What are the pros and cons of allowing Sandy to adopt Clarissa while maintaining both Alice and Fred as biological parents? Should it matter whether Sandy is a new husband to Alice or a lesbian partner in a committed long term relationship? See Pamela Gatos, Note, Third-Parent Adoption in Lesbian and Gay Families, 26 Vt. L. Rev. 195 (2001).

3. Interstate Recognition of Adoptions

Russell v. Bridgens
647 N.W.2d 56 (Neb. 2002)

STEPHAN, J.

Appellant, Serenna D. Russell, appeals from an order of the district court for Douglas County granting the summary judgment motion of appellee, Joan C. Bridgens, and a further order overruling Russell's motion for reconsideration. We conclude that the district court erred in granting the summary judgment motion, and reverse, and remand for further proceedings.

FACTS

Bridgens adopted a minor child in Pennsylvania in September 1996. In December 1997, both Bridgens and Russell adopted the same minor child in what is referred to in the record as a "coparent" adoption. Although a certified copy of the 1997 adoption decree is a part of the record, the petition requesting such adoption is not. The certified decree expressly states that "[a]ll requirements of the Acts of Assembly have been fulfilled and complied with."

Bridgens and Russell are unmarried and of the same sex. They lived together and raised the child until August 1999. At that time, Russell and the minor child, who both had been residing with Bridgens in Germany, returned to the United States while Bridgens remained in Germany. On November 21, 2000, Russell filed a petition to establish custody and support for the minor child in the district court for Douglas County, Nebraska. After answering and cross-petitioning for custody and support, Bridgens filed a motion for summary judgment on May 16, 2001. The motion alleged that the 1997 adoption was invalid under Pennsylvania law. On July 23, 2001, the district court granted Bridgens' motion for summary judgment. The court reasoned that Pennsylvania law required Bridgens to terminate her parental rights prior to the 1997 adoption and found that "[i]t appears to the Court this was not done and [Russell] has not offered evidence to the contrary." In a subsequent order denying Russell's motion for reconsideration, the district court clarified that because the Pennsylvania statutory requirements for adoption were not met, the Pennsylvania court lacked subject matter jurisdiction to grant the adoption and that therefore, the adoption was not entitled to full faith and credit under the U.S. Constitution. Russell timely appealed, and we moved the case to our docket on our own motion pursuant to our authority to regulate the dockets of the appellate courts of this state.

Assignments of Error

Russell assigns that the district court erred in (1) failing to apply the Full Faith and Credit Clause of the U.S. Constitution, (2) failing to recognize that res judicata bars an attack on the Pennsylvania decree, (3) not admitting Russell's affidavit in evidence, (4) failing to consider and find equitable estoppel as a bar to Bridgens' motion for summary judgment, and (5) failing to address Russell's status as a parent under the in loco parentis doctrine and failing to consider the minor's best interests.

Analysis

The dispositive issue in this appeal is whether the record demonstrates as a matter of law that the 1997 Pennsylvania adoption decree was not entitled to full faith and credit under the U.S. Constitution. A judgment rendered in a sister state court which had jurisdiction is to be given full faith and credit and has the same validity and effect in Nebraska as in the state rendering judgment. The Full Faith and Credit Clause of the U.S. Constitution prohibits a Nebraska court from reviewing the merits of a judgment rendered in a sister state, but a foreign judgment can be collaterally attacked by evidence that the rendering court was without jurisdiction over the parties or the subject matter. In the instant case, Bridgens seeks to collaterally attack the judgment on the basis that the Pennsylvania court lacked subject matter jurisdiction to grant the adoption.

Whether the Pennsylvania court had subject matter jurisdiction is dependent upon Pennsylvania law. Bridgens' argument is based upon the contention that the Pennsylvania court lacked subject matter jurisdiction because Bridgens and Russell did not comply with the requirements of the Pennsylvania adoption statutes at the time of the 1997 decree. Specifically, Bridgens argues that the extrinsic evidence in the record establishes that she had not relinquished her parental rights prior to the 1997 "coparent" adoption and that the requisite parental consents were not included in the adoption petition. In this regard, 23 Pa. Cons. Stat. Ann §2701(7) provides that a petition for adoption shall state that "all consents required by section 2711 (relating to consents necessary to adoption) are attached as exhibits or the basis upon which such consents are not required." Further, §2711(a)(3) requires consent from "[t]he parents or surviving parent of an adoptee who has not reached the age of 18 years." In particular, the consenting parent must state, in part, "I hereby voluntarily and unconditionally consent to the adoption of the [minor] child. I understand that by signing this consent I indicate my intent to permanently give up all rights to this child." An exception to the unqualified consent requirement is found in §2903, which provides that "[w]henever a parent consents to the adoption of his child by his spouse, the parent-child relationship between him and his child shall remain whether or not he is one of the petitioners in the adoption proceeding." In addition, §2901 provides that "[u]nless the court for cause shown determines otherwise, no decree of adoption shall be entered unless...all other legal requirements have been met."

A party moving for summary judgment must make a prima facie case by producing enough evidence to demonstrate that the movant is entitled to judgment if the evidence were uncontroverted at trial. Once the moving party makes a prima facie case, the burden to produce evidence showing the existence of a material issue of fact that prevents judgment as a matter of law shifts to the party opposing the motion. *Id.* As the party moving for summary judgment, it was Bridgens' burden to demonstrate that the Pennsylvania court lacked subject matter jurisdiction due to lack of compliance with the requirements of the adoption statutes. The record before us, however, contains only the 1997 Pennsylvania adoption decree which affirmatively alleges on its face that it was decreed in conformance with Pennsylvania law. There is no evidence in the record establishing that the necessary consents were not included with the petition for adoption or that Bridgens did not, in fact, relinquish her parental rights prior to the 1997 "coparent" adoption. Contrary to the finding of the district court, based upon this evidence the burden did not shift to Russell to affirmatively demonstrate that the requirements of the adoption statutes were met prior to the 1997 decree. On the record before us, Bridgens failed to meet her burden entitling her to summary judgment, and the district court erred in granting the motion.

Because this error requires reversal and remand for further proceedings, we do not reach Russell's remaining assignments of error.

Conclusion

For the foregoing reasons, the judgment of the district court is reversed and the cause is remanded for further proceedings. For the benefit of the parties and the district court, we note that the legal issue of whether compliance with the statutory requirements of the Pennsylvania adoption act is an aspect of subject matter jurisdiction is an issue we view to be significantly dependent upon the Supreme Court of Pennsylvania's resolution of the pending appeals in *In re Adoption of B.B.F.*, 762 A.2d 739 (Pa. Super 2000) and *In re Adoption of C.C.G.*, 762 A.2d 724 (Pa. Super 2000).

Gerrard, J., concurring.

I agree with the majority's disposition of this appeal insofar as the court concludes that Pennsylvania law controls the question whether the Pennsylvania adoption decree is valid and that on the record presented, the district court erred in entering summary judgment for Joan C. Bridgens. I would, however, reverse the judgment of the district court based on my view that the Pennsylvania adoption decree was entered by a court with subject matter jurisdiction and is entitled to full faith and credit in Nebraska. I write separately, not because of a petty disagreement with the rationale of the majority opinion or as a mere intellectual exercise, but because the record reflects that the minor child's best interests have needlessly remained unaddressed while these proceedings continue on. The minor child affected by these proceedings has not had court-ordered visitation with Serenna D. Russell (a primary caregiver in his life) for several months, nor have the custody or visitation issues been addressed as they should have.

Significantly, for the reasons that follow, I would also conclude that even if the Pennsylvania Court of Common Pleas erred in concluding that it had subject matter jurisdiction, under Pennsylvania law, the Court of Common Pleas' determination that all jurisdictional requirements had been satisfied is res judicata as to the parties to the adoption. Finally, I believe that the district court erred in excluding Russell's affidavit concerning her relationship with the minor child and in not considering the doctrine of in loco parentis at the summary judgment proceeding, as that doctrine provides a basis for Russell to proceed with this action regardless of the validity of the Pennsylvania adoption decree.

SUBJECT MATTER JURISDICTION

U.S. Const. art. IV, §1 provides that "Full Faith and Credit shall be given in each State to the Public Acts, Records, and judicial Proceedings of every other State." In order to fulfill this constitutional mandate, the judgment of a state court should have the same credit, validity, and effect in every other court of the United States, which it had in the state where it was pronounced.

There are, however, basic limitations on the principles of full faith and credit. *Id.* Chief among these limitations is the caveat that " 'a judgment of a court in one State is conclusive upon the merits in a court in another State only if the court in the first State had power to pass on the merits—had jurisdiction, that is, to render the judgment.' " Consequently, before a court is bound by the judgment rendered in another state, it may inquire into the jurisdictional basis of the foreign court's decree. *Id.* If that court did not have jurisdiction over the subject matter or the relevant parties, full faith and credit need not be given. *Id.*

For purposes of argument, I am assuming that under Pennsylvania law—at least, as that law currently stands—the Court of Common Pleas may have erred in entering the adoption decree at issue in this case. See, *In re Adoption of R.B.F and In re Adoption of C.C.G.* (appeals granted at 566 Pa. 684, 784 A.2d 119 (2001)). However, the dispositive question in this appeal is whether Bridgens' failure to relinquish her parental rights prior to the purported adoption was fatal to the subject matter jurisdiction of the Pennsylvania court.

Jurisdiction of subject matter relates to the competence of a court to hear and determine controversies of the general nature of the action before the court. The test of whether a court has jurisdiction over a particular controversy depends upon the competency of the court to determine controversies of the general class to which the case presented for consideration belonged—whether the court had power to enter upon the inquiry, not whether it might ultimately decide that it was unable to grant the relief sought in a particular case. The thing of chief importance on a question of jurisdiction over the subject matter is not whether the petitioner may recover in the particular forum on the cause of action pleaded but whether the court is empowered to hear and determine a controversy of the character involved. [citations to Pennsylvania cases omitted]

It is plain that pursuant to the foregoing propositions, the Court of Common Pleas had subject matter jurisdiction to enter the adoption decree at issue. "The court of common pleas of each county shall exercise... original jurisdiction over voluntary relinquishment, involuntary termination and adoption proceedings."

The Superior Court's decisions of *In re Adoption of R.B.F., supra,* and *In re Adoption of C.C.G., supra,* are not to the contrary. Those cases were presented to the Superior Court as direct appeals from the Court of Common Pleas from denials of petitions for adoption. The Superior Court was not confronted with a collateral attack on a final adoption decree. In this case, the Court of Common Pleas had jurisdiction over adoption cases generally and entered a decree of adoption and that decree became a final judgment not subject to collateral attack on the ground of subject matter jurisdiction....

Because the record is sufficient to conclude, as a matter of law, that the Court of Common Pleas had subject matter jurisdiction to enter the adoption decree at issue, I would reverse the district court's order of summary judgment on that basis, and remand the cause to the district court for a determination of the merits of Russell's petition.

Res Judicata

Even assuming that the Court of Common Pleas lacked subject matter jurisdiction because of the parties' failure to strictly comply with the Pennsylvania adoption statutes, Bridgens cannot assert that argument in this proceeding. Under Pennsylvania law, jurisdictional determinations made in a prior proceeding are res judicata in a subsequent proceeding involving the same litigants.

Although a court may have no jurisdiction over a particular subject matter, it may have jurisdiction to determine the question of its own jurisdiction, and an unappealed final determination of its subject matter jurisdiction—albeit erroneous—is res judicata as to those litigants. [citations to Pennsylvania cases omitted]

This principle, long recognized in the Commonwealth of Pennsylvania and other forums, reflects judicial concern for finality of judgments, even when said judgments have been rendered by a court without jurisdiction of the subject matter.

Thus, even if we were to assume that subject matter jurisdiction was wanting, the Court of Common Pleas made a jurisdictional determination regarding compliance with the requirements of the "Acts of Assembly" and specifically foreclosed the argument Bridgens now seeks to advance. Under established principles of Pennsylvania law, the court's determination is res judicata, even if erroneous, and entitled to full faith and credit in the State of Nebraska.

In Loco Parentis

Russell also assigned that the district court erred by not considering Russell's affidavit concerning her relationship with the minor child and in not discussing the doctrine of in loco parentis. Russell's assigned error has merit and should be considered on appeal. Discussion of this issue is essential because under the in loco parentis doctrine, as established by both Nebraska and Pennsylvania law, Russell can maintain her petition for custody even if the Pennsylvania adoption decree is not entitled to full faith and credit. The district court's order of summary judgment was premised on the assumption that the adoption issue was dispositive of the action. However, we have stated that

> "a person standing in loco parentis to a child is one who has put himself or herself in the situation of a lawful parent by assuming the obligations incident to the parental relationship, without going through the formalities necessary to a legal adoption, and *the rights, duties, and liabilities of such person are the same as those of the lawful parent.*" (Emphasis in original) Weinand v. Weinand, 616 N.W.2d 1, 6 (2000). Accord T.B. v. L.R.M., 786 A.2d 913 (2001) (lesbian former partner of biological mother had standing, in loco parentis, to maintain complaint for custody and visitation against biological mother).

The term "in loco parentis" refers to a person who has fully put himself or herself in the situation of a lawful parent by assuming *all* the obligations incident to the parental relationship and who actually discharges those obligations. *Weinand, supra.* Accord *T.B., supra.* The assumption of the parental relationship is largely a question of fact which should not lightly or hastily be inferred. *Weinand, supra.* The parental relationship should be found to exist only if the facts and circumstances show that the stepparent *means* to take the place of the lawful father or mother not only in providing support but also with reference to the natural parent's office of educating and instructing and caring for the general welfare of the child. *Id.* Once established, "[t]he rights and liabilities arising out of an *in loco parentis* relationship are, as the words imply, exactly the same as between parent and child."

Based on the foregoing principles, it is clear that resolution of the validity of the Pennsylvania adoption is not dispositive of Russell's petition. Russell can maintain her petition regardless of whether the Pennsylvania adoption decree is given full faith and credit, if Russell can demonstrate an in loco parentis relationship with the minor child. The fact that Russell affected an adoption of the minor child is, standing alone, persuasive evidence supporting the existence of an in loco parentis relationship between Russell and the minor child. Furthermore, Russell proffered evidence to support such a finding. Russell offered an affidavit which describes, in detail, Russell's activities in the role of "primary care provider for [the minor child] since [the minor child] was adopted at age 9 months." The district court determined that this affidavit was irrelevant because of the district court's resolution of the adoption issue.

Moreover, in my view, the record establishes conclusively that there exists a material issue of fact with respect to Russell's in loco parentis relationship with the minor child. On a motion for summary judgment, the question is not how a factual issue is to be decided, but whether any real issue of material fact exists.... Even if the Pennsylvania adoption decree is not entitled to full faith and credit, Russell is entitled to proceed to trial standing in loco parentis. This does not necessarily mean that Russell will prevail in seeking custody—but she at least has standing to fully litigate the issue.

At the very least, Russell's opportunity to litigate the issues of custody and visitation, pursuant to the doctrine of in loco parentis, should suggest to the district court that interim arrangements be made for the minor child's visitation with whichever party does not have temporary custody. So long as the ultimate disposition of this case remains uncertain, a temporary order of visitation should be entered that is consistent with the best interests of the child.

Conclusion

Therefore, for substantially different reasons than the majority—in both import and impact on the best interests of the minor child—I concur only with the result (i.e., reversal of summary judgment).

Notes and Questions

1. The majority opinion appears to conclude that the Pennsylvania adoption will only be accorded full faith and credit if it turns out that second parent adoptions are valid in Pennsylvania. The two cases cited, *In re Adoption of R.B.F.* and *In re Adoption of R.C.F.*, both involved a same sex partner (male in one case and female in the other) who wanted to adopt the partner's child. The Superior Courts in each case upheld the denial of the adoption petition, holding that the couples were not entitled to the benefit of stepparent adoption, which would allow the existing parent to maintain the legal

parental tie to the child. The Pennsylvania Supreme Court handed down its decision two months after *Russell v. Bridges* was decided. The Pennsylvania court held that the same-sex partners should be accorded an opportunity to demonstrate cause as to whether relinquishment of parental rights was proper in their cases. See 803 A.2d 1195 (Penn. 2002). How should this holding affect the outcome in the Nebraska case? What if the Pennsylvania case had decided that second parent adoptions are not possible in Pennsylvania? How would that have affected the Nebraska case? How would that have affected earlier Pennsylvania cases?

2. In a much publicized California case, *Sharon S. v. Superior Court*, the California Court of Appeals, District 4, in 2001, issued a ruling declaring second parent adoptions invalid under California law. The breadth of the holding sent waves of fear throughout the state to the more than 10,000 couples that had formalized their family relationships by having one partner adopt while the other partner retained parental rights. In some cases these adoptions were more than 20 years old. The California Supreme Court reversed, upholding the practice of and validating the numerous second parent adoptions that had occurred in California. 73 P.3d 554 (Cal. 2003). But even the dissenter, who believed the question was one for the legislature, would have validated all prior adoptions in the interest of not disturbing "settled familial relationships." Is this the same thing as *res judicata*? Can you think of any situations in which a collateral attack on an otherwise final adoption should be allowed?

Mariga v. Flint
822 N.E.2d 620 (Ind. App. 2005)

BAKER, Judge

This case requires us to examine the nature of parenthood. Whether a parent is a man or a woman, homosexual or heterosexual, or adoptive or biological, in assuming that role, a person also assumes certain responsibilities, obligations, and duties. That person may not simply choose to shed the parental mantle because it becomes inconvenient, seems ill-advised in retrospect, or becomes burdensome because of a deterioration in the relationship with the children's other parent. To the contrary, of key importance is the relationship between parent and children, not between parent and parent. What we must focus on is the duties owed by a parent to her children, and those duties do not evaporate along with the relationship between the parents—indeed, those duties do not evaporate even if the relationship between parent and children deteriorates.

Appellant-respondent Julie Mariga appeals from two orders: the Tippecanoe County Superior Court's (Superior Court) order granting appellee-petitioner Lori Flint's Petition for Child Support and the Tippecanoe County Circuit Court's (Circuit Court) order denying Julie's Petition to Vacate Adoption.

Julie argues that the Circuit Court erred in denying her petition to vacate the adoption. Specifically, Julie raises the following arguments with respect to the Adoption Order: (1) the Circuit Court did not have the authority to grant Julie's Petition for Adoption because the same-sex partner of a biological parent cannot be a stepparent pursuant to the stepparent adoption statute; and (2) the adoption was procured by fraud because Lori never intended for her relationship with Julie to be a lifelong commitment.

Finding that this court has previously determined that a person may validly adopt the children of her same-sex partner without divesting the partner of any parental rights, that as a result Julie is a parent to Lori's children, and that the adoption was not procured by fraud, we affirm the judgment of the Circuit Court.

FACTS

Lori is the biological mother of a 16-year-old daughter and a 13-year-old son. In 1992, Lori and the children's biological father divorced, and, shortly thereafter, Lori and Julie began a romantic relationship. During the course of their relationship, Julie played an active role in the children's lives, attending their sporting events and school conferences.

In 1996, Julie sought to adopt the children pursuant to Indiana's stepparent adoption statute. Julie and Lori decided that Julie should adopt the children for a variety of reasons, among them Julie's desire to provide financially for the children via life insurance, college assistance, and health insurance, and a hope to solidify their family unit. Lori informed the court that Julie was her "life-time companion" and that she wished to "co-parent" the children with Julie. The children's biological father agreed to terminate his parental rights to permit Julie to adopt the children without terminating Lori's parental rights. The Tippecanoe County Circuit Court granted her petition for adoption on July 10, 1997, and the children's last names were officially changed to "Mariga-Morris." In November 1998, Lori and Julie separated, and since that time both children have remained with Lori.

In June 1999, Lori married a man, and, in January 2000, Lori had a third child with her new husband. On February 8, 2001, Lori filed a Petition to Establish Custody, Visitation, and Support (the "First Petition") in the Tippecanoe County Circuit Court. In June 2001, Lori moved to Georgia with her husband and children because her husband was promoted by his employer and transferred to Georgia. Julie did not challenge Lori's relocation with the children.

After her relationship with Lori ended, Julie visited regularly with the children. But, the visits became sporadic, and she began attending their school activities less frequently. After Lori and the children moved to Georgia, they rarely, if ever, communicated with Julie, and she did not visit them at all during that period of time. Furthermore, while Julie initially paid child support, pursuant to an informal agreement between the parties, she stopped making payments after Lori filed the First Petition. She continues to carry the children on her health insurance plan.

In October 2003, Lori and her second husband divorced and she moved back to Indiana with her three children. In December 2003, Lori filed a Petition to Re-Open in the Superior Court in light of the fact that Indiana had again become the "home state" for Lori and her children. The Superior Court granted her petition to re-open. On June 25, 2004, Julie filed an Amended Motion to Dismiss or Stay Proceedings. On June 28, 2004, the Superior Court denied Julie's motion and granted Lori's Petition to Establish Custody, Visitation, and Support. Among other things, the order requires Julie to pay child support in the amount of $290 per week and renders Julie responsible for 75% of the children's uninsured medical, optical, and dental expenses.

While Lori's petition to establish custody, support, and visitation was pending in Superior Court, Julie filed a Petition to Vacate Adoption in the Circuit Court on April 2, 2004. On June 25, 2004, Julie filed an Amended Petition to Vacate Adoption. After a hearing on September 1, 2004, approximately two months after the Superior Court entered its order requiring Julie to pay child support, the Circuit Court denied Julie's petition to vacate the adoptions.

Julie now appeals the Circuit Court's order denying Julie's petition to vacate the adoptions and the Superior Court's order granting Lori's petition for child custody, support and visitation, and denying Julie's motion to dismiss.

DISCUSSION AND DECISION

I. Adoption Order

Julie argues that the Circuit Court erred in denying her petition to vacate the adoption. Specifically, Julie contends that: (1) the Circuit Court did not have the authority to grant Julie's Petition for Adoption because the same-sex partner of a biological parent cannot be a stepparent pursuant to the stepparent adoption statute; and (2) the adoption was procured by fraud because Lori never intended for her relationship with Julie to be a life-long commitment.

A. Circuit Court's Authority

This court has recently decided several cases that are adverse to Julie's contention that the Circuit Court did not have authority to grant her adoption of Lori's biological children. In *In re Adoption of K.S.P.*, 804 N.E.2d 1253 (Ind. Ct. App. 2004), we held that a same-sex domestic partner may adopt the biological children of her partner without divesting the parental rights of the biological parent....

The facts of *K.S.P.* are remarkably similar to this case. The children are the product of a failed marriage, and their biological father had little involvement in their lives, ultimately agreeing to terminate his parental rights and not objecting to the adoption. The children experienced the majority of their formative years with their biological mother's same-sex partner living in their home, acting as partner to their mother and parent to them. The adoptive parent was significantly involved in the children's day-to-day lives, and it was because of her close relationship to them and to their mother that she chose to adopt them.

Julie...argues that even if *K.S.P.* applies to this case, we should not apply the decision retroactively because it announced a change in the common law. Generally, "pronouncements of common law made in rendering judicial opinions of civil cases have retroactive effect unless such pronouncements impair contracts made or vested rights acquired in reliance on an earlier decision." Here, there is no contract that was impaired, nor did Julie acquire vested rights in reliance on pre-*K.S.P.* law of which she might now be divested. To the contrary, *K.S.P.* merely validated that which she had already asked for and received— the right to adopt Lori's children. Thus, we will apply *K.S.P.* retroactively.

B. Fraud

Julie also contends that the adoption was invalid because it was procured by fraud. Specifically, she contends that Lori was dishonest when she told the Circuit Court that Julie was her life-long partner, that in fact Lori is heterosexual, and that Lori merely desired the financial benefits she and the children would receive if Julie became the children's adoptive parent.

As we consider this argument, we note that the decision in this case was the result of a bench trial, and, as such, we will set aside the trial court's findings and conclusions only if they are clearly erroneous. To vacate a decree of adoption based on fraud, there must have been a material misrepresentation of past or existing fact made with knowledge or reckless disregard for the falsity of the statement, and the misrepresentation must have been relied upon to the detriment of the relying party.

The only evidence to which Julie cites to support her claim of fraud is Lori's statement at the hearing on the petition to vacate adoption that she is heterosexual. Julie also points to the fact that after her relationship with Lori ended, Lori began dating—and ultimately married—a man. From these two facts, Julie deduces that "[i]t seems only logical that at the time of the adoption, [Lori] knew that she really wanted true companionship with a man."

Our review of the record reveals that at the time that Julie sought to adopt Lori's children, Lori stated that it was her intention to "co-parent" with Julie, her "life-time companion." Lori also testified that Julie adopted the children to "solidify the family unit that [they] already had." That Lori and Julie's relationship later deteriorated, and that Lori may have subsequently rediscovered her heterosexuality, is of no moment. A claim of fraud cannot be premised upon future conduct.

At the time of the adoption, Lori and Julie had been in a committed relationship for five years. By way of comparison, Lori's marriage to the children's biological father lasted only four years, as did Lori's marriage that she entered into after her relationship with Julie ended. There is no evidence that Lori made any knowing or reckless material misrepresentations of a past or existing fact to Julie or to the Circuit Court at the time that Julie petitioned to adopt Lori's children. Accordingly, the Circuit Court's conclusions of law were not clearly erroneous, and it properly denied Julie's petition to vacate the adoption.

[The court also upheld the order that Julie pay child support.]

Further Reading on Second Parent Adoption

Barbara J. Cox, Adoptions by Lesbian and Gay Parents Must be Recognized by Sister States Under Full Faith and Credit Clause Despite Anti-Marriage Statutes that Discriminate Against Same-Sex Couples, 31 Cap. U. L. Rev. 751 (2003)

Patricia M. Logue, The Rights of Lesbian and Gay Parents and Their Children, 18 J Am. Acad. Matrim. Law 95 (2002).

Jane S. Schacter, Contructing Families in a Democracy: Courts, Legislatures and Second-Parent Adoption, 75 Chicago-Kent Law Rev. 933 (2000).

D. Rights of the "Second Parent" Who Has Not Adopted

Family law principles have long embraced the nuclear family of one father and one mother, preferably married to each other. *Gerald D. v. Michael M.* is illustrative of the commitment to that model. Traditionally the only way to become a parent was through biology, marriage or adoption. In the modern world, even biological parenthood has become contested. A child can easily have two biological mothers, for example, if one contributes the genetic material (the egg) and the other carries the child. Tradition has proved not to be very helpful in the modern world of alternative families and new reproductive technology.

Nonetheless, traditional rules retain much force in this contested arena. Parental rights, including rights of visitation and custody, are normally only granted to parents. While some states have enacted statutes that provide limited rights to visitation for other family members, typically grandparents, those statutes usually require some recognized familial connection. In addition, rights granted under these statutes are limited by the parent's constitutionally protected interest in childrearing. See *Troxel*.

Partners of parents, who function as parents themselves, think of themselves as parents. The children also often think of the partner as a "second parent." But the law, often slow to follow social change, has proved to be a barrier to recognizing the reality of the lives of these alternative families. "Second parent adoptions" were occurring in communities long before there was ever a reported court decision validating the process. To learn of the possibility, a lesbian couple would have had to consult a lawyer who was knowledgeable about the practice. Even with knowledge, "second parent adoptions" were not readily available to everyone. Lawyers had to be hired, home studies had to be completed, and judges needed to be convinced. Working class moms with little time or money and no experience with the legal system were unlikely to realize the need for adoption until it was too late. Issues regarding the standing of these "second parents" to claim visitation or custody, or even to make medical decisions for their children, usually arise when the relationship between the parent and the partner ends. If the relationship has ended and the parent is still alive and wants the status of sole parent, then she will claim that her "parenthood" not only trumps the interest of the "second parent," but that it gives her the right to exclude the "second parent" under *Troxel*-type arguments. If the relationship has ended with the death of the parent, then family members may step in and claim custody of the child, and, if they win, they can exclude the "second parent."

The standing of "second parents" to litigate for these important rights after relationships have terminated and mutual agreements are no longer controlling became a pressing issue in litigation in the early 1990s. For background on the social and legal history at this time, and a thorough and insightful discussion of the issues, see Nancy Polikoff, This Child Does Have Two Mothers: Redefining Motherhood to Meet the Needs of Children in Lesbian-Mother Families and Other Nontraditional Families, 78 Georgetown L. J. 459 (1990).

1. Common Law Theories that Can Help Establish Parenthood

Nancy S. v. Michele G.

279 Cal.Rptr. 212 (Cal. App. 1991)

Stein, Associate Justice

Appellant, Michele G., appeals from a judgment under the Uniform Parentage Act determining that respondent, Nancy S., is the only parent of the two minor children that respondent conceived by artificial insemination during her relationship with appellant. The judgment further provided that respondent, as the only legal parent of the two minor children, is entitled to sole legal and physical custody and that any further contact between appellant and the children shall only be by respondent's consent.

The issue presented is whether the court erred in determining, as a matter of law, that appellant has no right to an award of custody or visitation under the Uniform Parentage Act.

FACTS

In August of 1969, appellant and respondent began living together, and in November of that year they had a private "marriage" ceremony. Eventually they decided to have children by artificially inseminating respondent. In June of 1980, respondent gave birth to a daughter, K. Appellant was listed on the birth certificate as the father, and K. was given appellant's family name. On June 13, 1984, respondent gave birth to a son, S. Again appellant was listed as the father on the birth certificate, and S. was given appellant's family name. Both children refer to appellant and respondent as "Mom." Although the parties considered arranging for appellant to adopt the children, they never initiated formal adoption proceedings.

In January of 1985 appellant and respondent separated. They agreed that K. would live with appellant and that S. would live with respondent. They arranged visitation so that appellant would have K. five days a week and respondent would have S. five days a week, but the children would be together, either at appellant's or respondent's home for four days a week. After approximately three years, respondent wanted to change the custody arrangement so that each had custody of both children 50 percent of the time. Appellant opposed any change, and attempts to mediate the dispute failed.

Respondent then commenced this Uniform Parentage Act proceeding. Her complaint sought a declaration that appellant is not a parent of either child, that respondent is entitled to sole legal and physical custody and that appellant is entitled to visitation only with respondent's consent. The court issued a temporary restraining order and granted temporary custody to respondent. Appellant answered the complaint and admitted that respondent is the biological mother of the children. She denied, however, the allegations that she was not also a parent of the children. She sought an order for custody and visitation in accordance with their original custody agreement.

A hearing was held on respondent's order to show cause and appellant's cross-motion for custody and visitation. The parties fully briefed and argued the issue whether appellant could qualify as a parent and seek custody and visitation under the Uniform Parentage Act. Appellant admitted that she was not the biological mother and had not adopted the children. Nonetheless, she argued that she had attained the status of a de facto parent, or that respondent should be estopped to deny appellant's status as a parent. The court determined that appellant was not a parent under the Uniform Parentage Act, and that even if she could prove that she had the status of a de facto parent, that it could not award her custody over the objections of respondent, the natural mother, who did qualify as a parent under the act. The court therefore awarded sole physical and legal custody to respondent.[1]

---

1. By denying appellant any relief, the court also impliedly found as a matter of law that appellant could not attain the status of a parent by equitable estoppel.

ANALYSIS

Civil Code section 4600, subdivision (c) provides that, in any proceeding where there is at issue the custody of a minor child, "Before the court makes any order awarding custody to a person...other than a parent, without the consent of the parents, it shall make a finding that an award of custody to a parent would be detrimental to the child and the award to a nonparent is required to serve the best interests of the child." Appellant acknowledges that, regardless of the statutory basis of the underlying proceeding, i.e., whether it was brought under the Uniform Parentage Act, or as a guardianship, dependency, or dissolution proceeding, she is entitled to seek custody and visitation over the objections of the children's natural mother, based on the "best interests" of the children, only if she has alleged facts upon which the court could determine that she is a parent of the children.

The Uniform Parentage Act defines a parent as one who is the natural or adoptive parent of a child. The existence of the relationship of parent and child may be proved between a child and its natural mother by proof of her having given birth to the child, between a child and an adoptive parent by proof of adoption, and between a natural father and a child as provided in the act [at Civ. Code § 7003, subd (2)].[2]

It is undisputed that appellant is not the natural mother of K. and S., and that she has not adopted either child. She does not contend that she and respondent had a legally recognized marriage when the children were born. Based on these undisputed facts, the court correctly determined that appellant could not establish the existence of a parent-child relationship under the Uniform Parentage Act.

Appellant nonetheless asserts that the Uniform Parentage Act does not provide the exclusive definition of a parent. She asserts that her allegations of a long-term relationship in which she has become a "psychological parent" of the children would, if proved, entitle her to seek custody and visitation as if the dispute were between two legally recognized parents. She advances several legal theories to support her assertion that she has acquired "parental rights," i.e, the right to seek custody and visitation on an equal footing with the children's natural mother and over their natural mother's objections. First, she argues that she is either a "de facto" parent, or that she stands "in loco parentis."

A. De Facto Parenthood

A de facto parent is "that person who, on a day-to-day basis, assumes the role of parent, seeking to fulfill both the child's physical needs and his psychological need for affection and care." (*In re B.G.* (1974) 11 Cal.3d 679, 692, fn. 18, 114 Cal.Rptr. 444, 523 P.2d 244.) Appellant alleged that she helped facilitate the conception and birth of both children and immediately after their birth assumed all the responsibilities of a parent. K. lived with appellant until the underlying dispute arose, and S. also lived with appellant until appellant and respondent separated, and thereafter S. visited with appellant on a regular basis. These facts may well entitle appellant to the status of a "de facto" parent. It does not, however, follow that as a "de facto" parent appellant has the same rights as a parent to seek custody and visitation over the objection of the children's natural mother. In *In re B.G., supra,* the court ac-

---

2. The Uniform Parentage Act also creates a presumption that a man is the natural father if he meets the conditions set forth in section 621 of the Evidence Code, or the child is born during a valid marriage or a marriage that apparently complies with the law. A man may also be presumed to be a natural father if after the child is born, he and the child's mother marry or attempt to marry and he engages in conduct holding the child out as his own by, for example, permitting his name to be put on the birth certificate. The Uniform Parentage Act also establishes that the husband of a woman who bears a child through artificial insemination is deemed to be the child's natural father.

knowledged that the concept of "de facto" parenthood could apply to long-term foster parents for the purpose of permitting them to intervene in a dependency proceeding. The court went on to hold that, nonetheless, *custody* could not be awarded to the foster parents over the objections of the natural mother without a finding that parental custody would be detrimental to the children. The court also specifically stated that, "[w]e do not hold that a de facto parent is a 'parent' or 'guardian' as those terms are used in the Juvenile Court Law."

No cases support appellant's contention that if she could prove her status as a de facto parent, she would be entitled to seek custody of respondent's children according to the same standards applied in a dispute between two parents. To the contrary, the cases establish that nonparents, even if they qualify as "de facto parents," may be recognized in guardianship or dependency proceedings and may even obtain custody over children with whom they have established a de facto parent-child relationship, but that custody can be awarded to a de facto parent *only* if it is established by clear and convincing evidence that parental custody is detrimental to the children.

Appellant argues that, in this case, the "detriment" standard should not apply because appellant is not an "outsider" and does not seek to exclude the parent but wants to share custody. In *all* of the cases involving a "de facto" parent, the individual claiming such status necessarily is not an "outsider" and, like appellant, has undoubtedly developed deep psychological and emotional bonds with the child. Nonetheless, the courts and our Legislature have chosen to place paramount importance upon the relationship between the natural or adoptive parent and the child. Even the discretionary visitation provided nonparents by Civil Code section 4601 "must give way to the paramount right to parent if the visitation creates conflicts and problems.... The critical importance in California of the right to parent has been affirmed and reaffirmed. It only gives way upon a showing of parental unfitness, detrimental to the child's welfare." *In re Marriage of Jenkins* (1981).

B. In Loco Parentis

Appellant next advances the theory that the common law doctrine of "in loco parentis" could be applied to confer upon her the same rights as a parent to seek custody and visitation of S. and K. In the context of torts, the concept of in loco parentis has been used to impose upon persons standing "in loco parentis" the same rights and obligations imposed by statutory and common law upon parents. It has also been applied to confer certain benefits upon a child, such as more favorable inheritance tax treatment, or workers' compensation benefits. The concept of "in loco parentis," however, has never been applied in a custody dispute to give a nonparent the same rights as a parent, and we are unpersuaded that the concept should be so extended.

In *Perry v. Superior Court*, (1980) 108 Cal.App.3d 480, 166 Cal.Rptr. 583, the court referred to the concept of in loco parentis in the context of a custody dispute. The trial court awarded the mother's husband of six years visitation rights to her child by a former marriage. The trial court found that the husband had performed the role of father to the child and the fact that there was no blood relationship was inconsequential because visitation was in the best interests of the child. The court of appeal reversed holding that the trial court had no authority to award custody or visitation unless the minor was a "child of the marriage." Noting that the result was "not particularly palatable," the court invited the Legislature to address the problem of visitation rights for stepparents. The Legislature responded by enacting Civil Code § 4351.5 in 1982. Although that section creates discretion to award a limited form of visitation rights to stepparents in a dissolution proceeding, the Legislature again acknowledged the importance of parental autonomy by cautioning that even an award of visitation to a stepparent "shall not conflict with any visitation or custodial right of a natural or adoptive parent who is not a party to the proceeding." Courts have consistently refused to expand §4351.5 to cover factual situations not specifically addressed by that section. [citations omitted]

C. Parenthood by Equitable Estoppel

Appellant argues that the court could apply the doctrine of equitable estoppel to prevent respondent from denying the existence of a parent-child relationship that she allegedly encouraged and supported for many years and which she now denies for the sole purpose of obtaining unfettered control over the custody of the children.

In California, equitable estoppel has been invoked for the purpose of imposing support obligations on a husband who has represented to his wife's children that he is their natural father and subsequently seeks to deny paternity for the purpose of avoiding support obligations. Equitable estoppel has never been invoked in California against a natural parent for the purpose of awarding custody and visitation to a nonparent.

Other states, however, have begun to use the doctrine of equitable estoppel to prevent a wife from denying the paternity of her husband. For example, in *In re Paternity*, of D.L.H. (Ct.App.1987) 142 Wis.2d 606, 419 N.W.2d 283, the court held that a wife could be estopped to deny the paternity of her husband, even where human leukocyte antigen (HLA) tests had excluded the husband as the natural father. The husband knew, even before the child's birth, that he was not the biological father but promised to raise the child as his own. He had developed a strong relationship with the child and had paid support to the mother after the couple separated. The court held it was error to dismiss the husband from the paternity proceedings after the HLA tests excluded him as the natural father, and remanded to permit him to prove the elements of equitable estoppel. The court, however, specifically reserved the question whether, even if the wife were estopped to deny paternity, the husband would have the status of a parent in a custody dispute and could thereby invoke the standard of the best interests of the child. Even if the doctrine of equitable estoppel could be used against a wife and in favor of a husband to award custody as if the dispute were between two natural parents, we note that the use of the doctrine of equitable estoppel, in these out-of-state cases, is rooted in "[o]ne of the strongest presumptions in law [i.e.] that a child born to a married woman is the legitimate child of her husband." No similar presumption applies in this case.

It is important not to confuse appellant's argument regarding equitable estoppel with the concept of an "equitable parent." The concept of an "equitable parent" has been recognized by the Michigan Court of Appeals in a divorce proceeding to permit a husband, who is not the biological father of a child born during the marriage, to obtain the status of a parent in a custody dispute with the natural mother, and to have the custody dispute settled as if it were between two natural parents, according to the child's best interests. (*Atkinson v. Atkinson* (1987), 408 N.W.2d 516, 517–20.) The primary difference between the concept of an "equitable parent" and the equitable estoppel theory advanced by appellant is that the "equitable parent" theory is rooted in a statutory recognition of "equitable adoption" for purposes of inheritance and may require proof of an express or implied contract to adopt. At least one California court has already declined to adopt the concept of an "equitable parent" for the purpose of awarding joint custody to a stepfather over the objections of the child's natural mother despite the fact that California, like Michigan, recognizes the doctrine of "equitable adoption" for purposes of inheritance.... The court stressed that given the "complex practical, social and constitutional ramifications" of expanding the class of persons entitled to assert parental rights, the decision was better left to the Legislature.

D. Functional Definition of Parenthood

Finally, appellant urges us to adopt what she describes as a "functional" definition of parenthood in order to protect on-going relationships between children and those who function as their parents. In accordance with this new definition, the class of persons entitled to seek custody and visitation according to the same standards as a natural parent would include "anyone who maintains a functional parental relationship with a child when a legally recognized parent created that relationship with the intent that the relationship be parental in nature." (See Polikoff, This Child Does Have Two Mothers: Redefining Parenthood to Meet the Needs of Children in Lesbian-Mother and Other Nontraditional Families (1990) 78 Georgetown L.J. 459, 464.)

We agree with appellant that the absence of any legal formalization of her relationship to the children has resulted in a tragic situation. As is always the case, it is the children who will suffer the most as a result of the inability of the adults, who they love and need, to reach an agreement. We do not, however, agree that the only way to avoid such an unfortunate situation is for the courts to adopt appellant's novel theory by which a nonparent can acquire the rights of a parent, and then face years of unraveling the complex practical, social, and constitutional ramifications of this expansion of the definition of parent.

CONCLUSION

Although the facts in this case are relatively straightforward regarding the intent of the natural mother to create a parental relationship between appellant and her children, expanding the definition of a "parent" in the manner advocated by appellant could expose other natural parents to litigation brought by child-care providers of long standing, relatives, successive sets of stepparents or other close friends of the family. No matter how narrowly we might attempt to draft the definition, the fact remains that the status of individuals claiming to be parents would have to be litigated and resolution of these claims would turn on elusive factual determinations of the intent of the natural mother, the perceptions of the children, and the course of conduct of the party claiming parental status. By deferring to the Legislature in matters involving complex social and policy ramifications far beyond the facts of the particular case, we are not telling the parties that the issues they raise are unworthy of legal recognition. To the contrary, we intend only to illustrate the limitations of the courts in fashioning a comprehensive solution to such a complex and socially significant issue.

The judgment is affirmed.

Notes and Questions

1. Was Michele G. completely denied the opportunity to request visitation? Under what circumstances might she have been granted visitation rights?

2. This decision was handed down two years after the United States Supreme Court decision in *Michael H. v. Gerald D.*, similarly holding under California law that a biological parent cannot be granted visitation rights over the objection of the biological

mother when the mother's husband is presumed to be the child's father. Is Michele G. in the same legal position as Michael H.?

3. The court was concerned that if it granted standing to Michele G., claims by nannies and babysitters would follow close behind. Do you think this is a valid concern? Do you think any of the legal theories set forth by Michele G. could be used to support Michele's rights while at the same time protecting the rights of Nancy S.?

Alison D. v. Virginia M.
572 N.E.2d 27 (N.Y. 1991)

[Just 43 days after Nancy S. was decided, the New York Court of Appeals reached the same conclusion under New York law. Alison D., the "second parent," sought only visitation rights with the child. Alison and Virginia raised the child together for the first two years of his life. After their relationship ended, Virginia allowed Alison to spend time with the child and Alison contributed to household expenses. Four years later, Virginia changed her mind and refused to let Alison see the child any more. The New York Court of Appeals held that since Alison was not a parent, she had no right to seek visitation. Judge Kaye dissented.]

Dissenting Opinion of Judge KAYE:

The Court's decision, fixing biology as the key to visitation rights, has impact far beyond this particular controversy, one that may affect a wide spectrum of relationships— including those of longtime heterosexual stepparents, "common-law" and nonheterosexual partners such as involved here, and even participants in scientific reproduction procedures. Estimates that more than 15.5 million children do not live with two biological parents, and that as many as 8 to 10 million children are born into families with a gay or lesbian parent, suggest just how widespread the impact may be.

But the impact of today's decision falls hardest on the children of those relationships, limiting their opportunity to maintain bonds that may be crucial to their development. The majority's retreat from the courts' proper role— its tightening of rules that should in visitation petitions, above all, retain the capacity to take the children's interests into account—compels this dissent.

In focusing the difference, it is perhaps helpful to begin with what is *not* at issue. This is not a custody case, but solely a visitation petition. The issue on this appeal is not whether petitioner should actually have visitation rights. Nor is the issue the relationship between Alison D. and Virginia M. Rather, the sole issue is the relationship between Alison D. and A.D.M., in particular whether Alison D.'s petition for visitation should even be considered on its merits. I would conclude that the trial court had jurisdiction to hear the merits of this petition.

The relevant facts are amply described in the Court's opinion. Most significantly, Virginia M. agrees that, after long cohabitation with Alison D. and before A.D.M.'s conception, it was "explicitly planned that the child would be theirs to raise together." It is also uncontested that the two shared "financial and emotional preparations" for the birth, and that for several years Alison D. actually filled the role of coparent to A.D.M., both tangibly and intangibly. In all, a parent-child relationship—encouraged or at least condoned by Virginia M.—apparently existed between A.D.M. and Alison D. during the first six years of the child's life.

While acknowledging that relationship, the Court nonetheless proclaims powerlessness to consider the child's interest at all, because the word "parent" in the statute imposes an absolute barrier to Alison D.'s petition for visitation. That same conclusion would follow, as the Appellate Division dissenter noted, were the coparenting relationship one of 10 or more years, and irrespective of how close or deep the emotional ties might be between petitioner and child, or how devastating isolation might be to the child. I cannot agree that such a result is mandated by section 70, or any other law.

Domestic Relations Law §70 provides a mechanism for "either parent" to bring a habeas corpus proceeding to determine a child's custody. Other State Legislatures, in comparable statutes, have defined "parent" specifically (see, e.g., Cal. Civ. Code §700 [defining parent-child relationship as between "a child and his natural or adoptive parents"]), and that definition has of course bound the courts (see, Nancy S.v. Michele G., [applying the statutory definition]). Significantly, the Domestic Relations Law contains no such limitation. Indeed, it does not define the term "parent" at all. That remains for the courts to do, as often happens when statutory terms are undefined.

The majority insists, however, that, the word "parent" in this case can only be read to mean biological parent; the response "one fit parent" now forecloses all inquiry into the child's best interest, even in visitation proceedings. We have not previously taken such a hard line in these matters, but in the absence of express legislative direction have attempted to read otherwise undefined words of the statute so as to effectuate the legislative purposes. The Legislature has made plain an objective in section 70 to promote "the best interest of the child" and the child's "welfare and happiness." Those words should not be ignored by us in defining standing for visitation purposes—they have not been in prior case law.

Apart from imposing upon itself an unnecessarily restrictive definition of "parent,"...the Court also overlooks the significant distinction between visitation and custody proceedings.

While both are of special concern to the State, custody and visitation are significantly different. Custody disputes implicate a parent's right to rear a child—with the child's corresponding right to be raised by a parent. Infringement of that right must be based on the fitness—more precisely the lack of fitness—of the custodial parent.

Visitation rights also implicate a right of the custodial parent, but it is the right to choose with whom the child associates. Any burden on the exercise of that right must be based on the child's overriding need to maintain a particular relationship. Logically, the fitness concern present in custody disputes is irrelevant in visitation petitions, where continuing contact with the child rather than severing of a parental tie is in issue.....

Of course there must be some limitation on who can petition for visitation. Domestic Relations Law §70 specifies that the person must be the child's "parent," and the law additionally recognizes certain rights of biological and legal parents. Arguments that every dedicated caretaker could sue for visitation if the term "parent" were broadened, or that such action would necessarily effect sweeping change throughout the law, overlook and misportray the Court's role in defining otherwise undefined statutory terms to effect particular statutory purposes, and to do so narrowly, for those purposes only.

Countless examples of that process may be found in our case law...Only recently, we defined the term "family" in the eviction provisions of the rent stabilization laws so as to advance the legislative objective, making abundantly clear that the definition was limited to the statute in issue and did not effect a wholesale change in the law (see, Braschi v. Stahl Assocs. Co., 74 N.Y.2d 201, 211–13, 544 N.Y.S.2d 784, 543 N.E.2d 49)....

It is not my intention to spell out a definition but only to point out that it is surely within our competence to do so. It is indeed regrettable that we decline to exercise that authority in this visitation matter, given the explicit statutory objectives, the courts' power, and the fact that all consideration of the child's interest is, for the future, otherwise absolutely foreclosed.

I would remand the case to Supreme Court for an exercise of its discretion in determining whether Alison D. stands in loco parentis to A.D.M. and, if so, whether it is in the child's best interest to allow her the visitation rights she claims.

Notes and Questions

1. Both the California court and the New York court were concerned about construing the word "parent" in the statute too broadly. Judge Kaye thought otherwise. Courts often construe words in statutes to carry out the intent of the statute. If you were asked to draft a legislative definition of "parent" to cover second parents such as Michele G. and Alison D., what language would you include?

2. Many of the cases in this chapter have identified a tension between legislatures and courts, often suggesting that legislatures are better equipped as a matter of institutional competence to make decisions about alternative families. What do you think of this argument? What is the role of a common law court in this age of so many statutory provisions?

3. During oral argument, the lawyer for Alison D. was asked why Alison had not adopted the child. At the time, second parent adoption had not been approved by the New York courts. The first reported case that endorsed second parent adoption was in the Surrogate's Court in 1992, See *Matter of Adoption of Evan*, 583 N.Y.S.2d 997. Several years later, conflicting opinions were handed down by the Appellate Division. Ultimately, the New York Court of Appeals upheld the right of second parents, whether in a same-sex or opposite-sex couple, to adopt without forcing the existing parent to give up her parental rights. See *Matter of Jacob*, 660 N.E.2d 397 (N.Y. 1995). What effect, if any, do you think the right to adopt should have on the question of whether the second parent ought to be accorded custody or visitation rights?

Titchenal v. Dexter
693 A.2d 682 (Vt. 1997)

ALLEN, Chief Justice.

The issue in this case is whether the superior court may apply its equitable powers to adjudicate a visitation dispute that cannot be brought in statutory proceedings within the family court's jurisdiction. We affirm the superior court's decision that it does not possess the authority to adjudicate such matters.

The dispute arose after the breakup of a relationship between two women who had both participated in raising a child adopted by only one of them. Plaintiff alleges the following facts, which are disputed but accepted as true for purposes of reviewing the trial court's dismissal of the case. In 1985, plaintiff Chris Titchenal and defendant Diane

Dexter began an intimate relationship. They purchased a home together, held joint bank accounts, and jointly owned their automobiles. They both contributed financially to their household, and each regarded the other as a life partner.

At some point, the parties decided to have a child. When their attempts to conceive via a sperm donor failed, they decided to adopt a child. In July 1991, defendant adopted a newborn baby girl, who was named Sarah Ruth Dexter-Titchenal. The parties held themselves out to Sarah and all others as her parents. The child called one parent "Mama Chris" and the other parent "Mama Di." For the first three and one-half years of Sarah's life, until the parties' separation, plaintiff cared for the child approximately 65% of the time. Plaintiff did not seek to adopt Sarah because the parties believed that the then-current adoption statute would not allow both of them to do so.

Eventually, the parties' relationship faltered, and by November 1994 defendant had moved out of the couple's home, taking Sarah with her. For the first five months following the parties' separation, Sarah stayed with plaintiff between Wednesday afternoons and Friday evenings. By the spring of 1995, however, defendant had severely curtailed plaintiff's contact with Sarah and had refused plaintiff's offer of financial assistance.

In October 1995, plaintiff filed a complaint requesting that the superior court exercise its equitable jurisdiction to establish and enforce regular, unsupervised parent-child contact between her and Sarah. The court granted defendant's motion to dismiss, refusing to recognize a cause of action for parent-child contact absent a common-law or statutory basis for the claim. On appeal, plaintiff argues that the superior court has equitable jurisdiction under the state's parens patriae authority to consider her complaint, and that both public policy and the doctrines of in loco parentis and de facto parenthood allow the court to exercise its equitable authority in cases such as this. An organization called the Gay & Lesbian Advocates & Defenders (GLAD) makes essentially the same arguments in its amicus curiae brief.

Plaintiff urges us to grant "nontraditional" family members access to the courts by recognizing the legal rights of de facto parents. According to plaintiff, the state's parens patriae power to protect the best interests of children permits the superior court to adjudicate disputes over parent-child contact outside the context of a statutory proceeding.....

We find no legal basis for plaintiff's proposal. Courts cannot exert equitable powers unless they first have jurisdiction over the subject matter and parties. Equity generally has no jurisdiction over imperfect rights arising from moral rather than legal obligations; not every perceived injustice is actionable in equity—only those violating a recognized legal right. *In re E.C.*, 130 Wis.2d 376, 387 N.W.2d 72, 77 (1986). A court of equity does not create rights, but rather determines whether legal rights exist and, if so, whether it is proper and just to enforce those rights. In short, a court may exert its equitable powers to grant appropriate relief only when a judicially cognizable right exists, and no adequate legal remedy is available. See *Chapman v. Sheridan-Wyoming Coal Co.*, 338 U.S. 621, 630–31, 70 S.Ct. 392, 397, 94 L.Ed. 393 (1950) (courts applying their equitable powers "can intervene only where legal rights are invaded or the law violated").

The issue, then, is whether there is any underlying legal basis for plaintiff's cause of action that would allow the superior court to apply its equitable powers to adjudicate her claim. Courts may exert equitable powers based upon common-law, statutory, or constitutional rights, or upon judicial acknowledgment of public-policy considerations establishing an as-yet-unrecognized legal right.

Here, we find no legal basis from any of the above sources for plaintiff's claimed right to parent-child contact in her capacity as an equitable or de facto parent. Notwithstanding plaintiff's claims to the contrary, there is no common-law history of Vermont courts interfering with the rights and responsibilities of fit parents absent statutory authority to do so....

With one possible minor exception, the custody-related cases cited by plaintiff and amicus curiae involve decisions made within the context of statutory proceedings. See *In re B.L.V.B.*, 160 Vt. 368, 371–73, 628 A.2d 1271, 1273–74 (1993) (construing provisions of adoption statute); *Bissonette v. Gambrel*, 152 Vt. 67, 69, 564 A.2d 600, 601 (1989) (action brought under statutory parentage proceeding); *S.B.L.*, 150 Vt. at 306, 311, 553 A.2d at 1086, 1089 (construing guardianship and grandparent visitation statutes); *Paquette v. Paquette*, 146 Vt. 83, 85, 499 A.2d 23, 25 (1985) (construing divorce and separation statutes); *Bioni*, 99 Vt. at 456, 134 A. at 607 (petition brought under statutory guardianship proceeding). From early on, Vermont courts intervened in custody matters concerning fit parents only under the authority of divorce statutes originating from the eighteenth century, and later nonsupport and separation statutes. See *Ward v. Ward*, 70 Vt. 430, 431, 41 A. 435, 435 (1898) (petition for custody under separation statute); *Buckminster v. Buckminster*, 38 Vt. 248, 249–50 (1865) (construing divorce statutes).

In 1984, the Legislature enacted both a parentage act that gave putative fathers the right to bring an action to establish paternity (and thus seek custody or visitation), 15 V.S.A. §§ 301–306, and an act allowing grandparents to request visitation under limited circumstances, 15 V.S.A. §§ 1011–1016. Until then, visitation rights in Vermont had been restricted to married biological parents. Since then, this Court has continued to refuse to allow courts to adjudicate disputes over parent-child contact outside the context of statutory proceedings. See *Rivers v. Gadwah*, 165 Vt. ——, ——, 679 A.2d 891, 891 (1996) (dismissing grandparents' visitation petition because it failed to fit within statutory jurisdictional constraints).

Plaintiff acknowledges that no specific statutory or constitutional provisions require the superior court to assume jurisdiction over her claim, but she argues that public policy compels such a result, given her status as Sarah's de facto parent. We do not agree. The superior court's refusal to extend its jurisdiction here does not create circumstances "cruel or shocking to the average [person's] conception of justice." *Payne*, 147 Vt. at 493, 520 A.2d at 588. Persons affected by this decision can protect their interests. Through marriage or adoption, heterosexual couples may assure that nonbiological partners will be able to petition the court regarding parental rights and responsibilities or parent-child contact in the event a relationship ends. Nonbiological partners in same-sex relationships can gain similar assurances through adoption.

In this case, plaintiff contends that she did not attempt to adopt Sarah at the time defendant did because the parties believed that Vermont's then-current adoption laws would not permit it. See 15 V.S.A. § 431 (repealed 1996) ("A person or husband and wife together...may adopt any other person...."). The language of the statute, however, certainly did not preclude plaintiff from seeking to adopt Sarah; indeed, as of December 1991, when Sarah was only five months old, at least one Vermont probate court had allowed the female partner of a child's adoptive mother to adopt the child as a second parent. See *B.L.V.B.*, 160 Vt. at 373 n. 3, 628 A.2d at 1274 n. 3. Further, in June 1993, more than a year before plaintiff alleges that the parties' relationship ended, this Court construed the earlier adoption statute as allowing a biological mother's female partner to adopt the mother's child without the mother having to terminate her parental rights. *Id.* at 369, 628 A.2d at 1272.

In 1996, the Legislature enacted a new adoption statute embracing our holding in *B.L.V.B.* and allowing unmarried adoptive partners to petition the family court regarding parental rights and responsibilities or parent-child contact. See 15A V.S.A. § 1-102(b) (if family unit consists of parent and parent's partner, and adoption is in child's best interest, partner of parent may adopt child without terminating parent's rights); 15A V.S.A. § 1-112 (family court shall have jurisdiction to hear and dispose of issues pertaining to parental rights and responsibilities and parent-child contact in accordance with statutory divorce proceedings when two unmarried persons who have adopted minor child terminate their domestic relationship); see also 15 V.S.A. § 293(a) (amended version allows parents and stepparents, *whether married or unmarried,* to petition family court regarding parental rights and responsibilities and parent-child contact). Thus, same-sex couples may participate in child-rearing and have recourse to the courts in the event a custody or visitation dispute results from the breakup of a relationship.

... [T]he dissent suggests that we employ the doctrine of equitable adoption. The dissent would have the family court determine on remand whether plaintiff would have adopted Sarah except for the perceived legal impediment; if so, plaintiff would be deemed the equitable adoptive mother, and the court presumably could accord her all the rights of a legal adoptive parent. Even if we ignore its inherent jurisdictional problems, the dissent's position does not withstand scrutiny.

Though the dissent disavows extending the doctrine of equitable adoption into the realm of equitable parentage, that is precisely what it is doing. As we stated in *Whitchurch v. Perry,* 137 Vt. 464, 470–71, 408 A.2d 627, 631 (1979):

> Courts generally apply the doctrine of equitable adoption *in cases of intestate succession* to permit participation in the estate by a foster child who was never legally, *i.e.,* statutorily, adopted by the decedent. Typically the decedent obtained custody by expressly or implicitly promising the child, the child's natural parents, or someone *in loco parentis* that an adoption would occur. Custody is transferred and the child lives with the foster parent as would a natural child, but, *for one reason or another* (usually the promisor's neglect), an adoption never occurs. Upon the foster parent's death, a court, applying the maxim that "equity regards that as done which ought to be done," declares that the child is entitled to share in the estate as if he were a legally adopted child. (Emphasis added.)

For the doctrine to apply, there must either be an *agreement to adopt* or an *undertaking* to effect a statutory adoption, *id.* at 471, 408 A.2d at 631, neither of which took place here. In *Whitchurch,* we declined to expand the doctrine to confer on the plaintiffs a "next of kin" status to provide standing for them to bring a wrongful death action, stating that the doctrine of equitable adoption "permits enforcement of the promise of inheritance implied from the agreement to adopt, but it does not alter the *status* of the parties." ... It is obvious from the discussion in *Whitchurch* that in this case the dissent would not be employing the doctrine of equitable adoption, but rather a much more expansive variant thereof aimed at allowing "equitable parents" to interfere with the custodial rights of legal parents. See *Pierce v. Pierce,* 198 Mont. 255, 645 P.2d 1353, 1355

(1982) (doctrine of equitable adoption had no application to proceeding where stepfather was seeking to establish custodial rights over his former stepchild against wishes of biological mother).

Ironically, after stretching the doctrine of equitable adoption beyond recognition in an effort to provide relief to this particular plaintiff, the dissent would then let it snap back into place to prevent any future plaintiffs from taking advantage of its expanded form. But there is no principled way to adopt the equitable-parent doctrine for this one case. Indeed, the dissent's avowed purpose for affording plaintiff relief—to achieve an equitable and just result—contradicts its desire to limit the application of that doctrine. If achieving an equitable result is the goal, then a wide variety of reasons for failing to adopt—lack of funds or fear of discrimination by the adopting agency, for example— could form the basis for the family court's jurisdiction to resolve factual disputes concerning whether a nonparent equitably adopted a legal parent's child. We decline to join the dissent's expansion of a judicial doctrine for the sole purpose of creating jurisdiction in the family court to benefit this particular plaintiff, only to foreclose all others having legitimate reasons for failing to adopt from seeking such equitable relief....

We recognize that, in this age of the disintegrating nuclear family, there are public-policy considerations that favor allowing third parties claiming a parent-like relationship to seek court-compelled parent-child contact. In our view, however, these considerations are not so clear and compelling that they require us to acknowledge that de facto parents have a legally cognizable right to parent-child contact, thereby allowing the superior court to employ its equitable powers to adjudicate their claims. Given the complex social and practical ramifications of expanding the classes of persons entitled to assert parental rights by seeking custody or visitation, the Legislature is better equipped to deal with the problem.... Deference to the Legislature is particularly appropriate in this arena because the laws pertaining to parental rights and responsibilities and parent-child contact have been developed over time solely through legislative enactment or judicial construction of legislative enactments.

For the reasons stated, we concur with the superior court's conclusion that it was without authority to consider plaintiff's petition for visitation.... We decline to judicially create a right of unrelated third-party visitation actionable in superior court pursuant to the court's equitable powers and subject only to the court's discretion—a right that would exist above and beyond the circumscribed rights granted by the Legislature. Were we to do so, we would establish, in effect, a two-tiered system in which persons who could not bring their visitation and custody petitions in statutory proceedings before the family court would turn to the superior court for relief. The Legislature did not contemplate such a system, and the law does not compel it.

Affirmed.

MORSE, Justice, dissenting.

I respectfully dissent. The Court rejects plaintiff's effort to establish visitation with the minor child on the ground that there is no legal right by which the court might fashion an equitable remedy, and the Court is unwilling to create a new legal right of "equitable parentage." Although other courts have embraced the concept, see, e.g., *In re Custody of H.S.H.-K.,* 193 Wis.2d 649, 533 N.W.2d 419, *cert. denied, Knott v. Holtzman,* 516 U.S. 975, 116 S.Ct. 475, 133 L.Ed.2d 404 (1995) (court may grant visitation to former lesbian partner if petitioner proves parent-like relationship with minor child), I agree with the Court that the social implications of the equitable-parent doctrine are sufficiently complex that any major policy decision in this area properly rests with the Legislature. That is not, however, the only avenue of relief available to plaintiff.

As explained more fully below, the doctrine of "equitable adoption" provides an alternative, well-established remedy that is well suited to the factual circumstances of this case. Based on the law as it was reasonably understood at the time, plaintiff was compelled to forego the opportunity, together with her partner, to adopt the minor child as any other married couple could have done. That law subsequently changed, and so, unfortunately, did plaintiff's domestic circumstances. It is too late apparently for the parties to cooperate, but not for the law to provide a just remedy, by permitting plaintiff to establish an *intent* to adopt and thus preserve the critically important parent-child relationship.

The Court dismisses this approach out of hand. Apart from a rather unrestrained accusation of unprincipled special pleading on behalf of plaintiff, the actual reasons offered by the Court unravel upon detached analysis. This is not a particularly difficult case. Although the context is novel, the legal principle is settled and the facts are compelling....

Although courts have traditionally characterized the concept as an equitable remedy for an unperformed "contract" to adopt, in reality the agreement "to adopt is found when a close relationship, similar to parent-child, exists between a child and the deceased." An agreement to adopt may be inferred from the "acts, conduct and admissions of the parties and other relevant facts and circumstances," *Cavanaugh v. Davis*, 149 Tex. 573, 235 S.W.2d 972, 975 (1951), which might include such evidentiary facts as an assumption by the child of the deceased's surname, identification of the deceased as the child's parent on school and other formal records, and, most significantly, evidence of a relationship of love and affection between the deceased and the child. The concept of equitable adoption has been recognized both in Vermont, *Whitchurch*, 137 Vt. at 470–71, 408 A.2d at 631, and broadly across the country. See Annotation, *Modern Status of Law as to Equitable Adoption or Adoption by Estoppel*, 97 A.L.R.3d 347 (1980) (collecting cases).

While equitable adoption most commonly involves a child's effort to share in the intestate estate of a foster parent who had intended to adopt, it has been applied in a variety of other contexts. It has been invoked, for example, to entitle a child to maintain an action for the wrongful death of a foster parent where the evidence disclosed an unconsummated intent to adopt. See *Holt v. Burlington Northern RR.*, 685 S.W.2d 851, 857 (Mo.Ct.App.1984); *Bower v. Landa*, 78 Nev. 246, 371 P.2d 657, 661 (1962). It has also been extended to allow a parent to obtain the death benefits of a child under a workers' compensation statute where the evidence disclosed an unfulfilled intent to adopt the deceased child. *Jones v. Loving*, 363 P.2d 512, 515 (Okla.1961). And in a recent Michigan case, the doctrine was invoked to support the parental rights of a nonbiological father to the daughter born while he was married to the mother. *Atkinson*, 408 N.W.2d at 520.

We need not go as far as the Michigan court, which adopted the broader doctrine of equitable parentage, *id.* at 519, to recognize that the principle of equitable adoption has valid applications outside the context of inheritance law. Here I propose an application much closer to the original equitable-adoption concept. The purpose of the doctrine, as noted, is to allow a court to find, in retrospect, an intent to adopt by a person who had never formally done so, for the purpose of achieving a just result. Plaintiff in this matter contends that she would have adopted the minor child when she was born in 1991, but that the adoption statute then appeared to allow only one nonmarried person to adopt, and defendant was designated as the adoptive parent. The rules of adoption were liberalized in 1993, when the Court recognized the right of a nonmarried parental partner to adopt, see *In re B.L.V.B.*, 160 Vt. 368, 369–73, 628 A.2d 1271, 1272–74 (1993), and substantially revised in 1996, when the Legislature enacted a new adoption statute formally recognizing the right of nonmarried cohabitants to freely adopt....

Given these subsequent rule changes, plaintiff, in my view, should be accorded the opportunity to demonstrate on remand that, except for the perceived legal impediment in light of her personal circumstances at that time, she would have adopted the minor child as did defendant. Plaintiff should be allowed to prove, in other words, an intent to establish an adoptive relationship with the child that was never formally consummated because of the then current state of the law. All that this amounts to, in effect, is application of the principle of equitable adoption in a novel factual context—a retrospective inquiry by the court into whether plaintiff intended, but because of the then-current adoption statute failed, to effectuate an adoption of the minor child, to the end of achieving a fair result.

In such a proceeding, plaintiff would be allowed to adduce evidence identical to that generally considered to be material in the equitable-adoption context— reciprocal love and affection between parent and child, holding-out as the parent, "parental" designation on official forms, and the like. Indeed, without purporting to prejudge the issue, I would note in this regard that plaintiff alleges she was the minor child's primary caretaker: she dressed and fed the minor every morning before driving her to daycare, spent extensive time with the minor playing, talking and reading, and exercised primary responsibility for the minor during the evening. Plaintiff also allegedly shares a surname with the minor ("Dexter-Titchenal") and is listed as the minor's parent on her daycare enrollment form, probate records, and baptismal papers. Defendant's last will and testament further states that plaintiff has "shared in the parenting of [the minor] since the day [she] came into [their] lives." Should plaintiff establish these allegations at trial and persuade the court of her intent to adopt, she would be accorded the legal status of an adoptive parent, and the family court could then resolve the visitation issue as though it were a regular dissolution proceeding, determining what is in the best interests of the child.

In adopting this approach, the court would not be "creating" any new legal rights; adoptive parents have all of the rights and responsibilities of a natural parent, including the right, upon termination of the parents' relationship, to seek visitation. 15A V.S.A. §§ 1-104, 1-112. We merely apply a settled equitable remedy—equitable adoption—to recognize retrospectively the adoptive relationship between plaintiff and the minor in order to achieve an equitable result.

A decision along these lines would present none of the drawbacks of a broader holding recognizing the rights of "equitable parents." It would apply only to this case, and any other in which a party allegedly failed to adopt because it was not a reasonable legal option. It is safe to assume that the courts will not be flooded with similar claims. Indeed, the number of potential claimants is finite by definition, since the holding would apply only to those who, like plaintiff, allegedly failed to adopt prior to the 1996 statutory changes in the adoption law. This approach also shields the family courts from the most common and problematic situation in which a cohabitant lives with the natural parent and child for some period of time, separates, and then seeks parental rights. Since the parties could have married and the cohabitant could have adopted, our holding would plainly not extend to them. In sum, a holding along the lines outlined above holds the promise of fairness, yet avoids the real risks, identified by the Court, of a broader-based holding recognizing the rights of equitable parents.

The Court, nevertheless, rejects this approach on three grounds. First, it claims the family court lacks jurisdiction to adjudicate such a matter.....

Second, the Court rather colorfully chides the dissent for "stretching the doctrine... beyond recognition in an effort to provide relief to this particular plaintiff" while providing no "principled" justification or limitation....

Finally, the Court advances the remarkable proposition that plaintiff somehow could, and should, have attempted to adopt the minor child prior to the couple's separation in 1994. The Court observes that one probate court in 1991 had allowed an adoption in similar circumstances, and that in 1993 we issued our decision in *B.L.V.B.* broadening the right of nonmarried cohabitants to adopt. It is one thing to presume that parties are aware of, and bound by, general enactments of the Legislature that amend the law; it is quite another, however, to impute to a nonattorney specific knowledge of one probate decision and a later, confirming appellate court decision. The rule that everyone is presumed to know the law, and the corollary that ignorance of the law is no excuse, is a rule of necessity designed to ensure that mere ignorance does not immunize one who commits a crime from its penal consequences.... It would be contrary to common sense and fairness to conclude that plaintiff, or anyone similarly situated, should have known that she had the legal right to adopt prior to the effective date of 15A V.S.A. § 1-102.

It is especially unfair in this case to assert, as the Court does, that plaintiff somehow "slumbered" and was less than vigilant. Plaintiff and defendant wanted a child to raise together as their own. They were not seeking to become a "test case" for the rights of gay and lesbian parents, nor should they have been expected to do so. They obeyed the law as it was then reasonably understood, and they had no cause to challenge it. They could not anticipate that the law would change, any more than they could anticipate that their relationship would change. But change they did, and by then it was too late to obtain the cooperation from defendant that would have avoided this dispute. It is wrong to suggest that plaintiff somehow brought this problem upon herself.

For all of the foregoing reasons, I would remand the matter to the family court for further proceedings consistent with the views expressed herein. Justice Johnson joins in the dissent.

Notes and Questions

1. Is the dissent arguing that the plaintiff should be considered a parent solely for purposes of establishing whether she should be granted visitation rights? Or, would his equitable adoption theory carry with it additional rights and responsibilities of parenthood? I.e., could the theory be used to support a claim by the child for child support?

2. Would a possible solution be for the plaintiff to adopt the child now? The Vermont statute provides:

§ 1-102 Who may adopt or be adopted

(a) Subject to this title, any person may adopt or be adopted by another person for the purpose of creating the relationship of parent and child between them.

(b) If a family unit consists of a parent and the parent's partner, and adoption is in the best interest of the child, the partner of a parent may adopt a child of the parent. Termination of the parent's parental rights is unnecessary in an adoption under this subsection.

3. What should the result be in a case in which the partner has begun the adoption proceedings by filing papers, but then the biological parent terminates the relationship before the adoption is completed?

In re the Parentage of A.B
818 N.E.2d 126 (Ind. App. 2004)

FRIEDLANDER, Judge

Dawn King, on her own behalf and as next friend of A.B., a minor, initiated the instant declaratory judgment action against A.B.'s biological mother, Stephanie Benham, seeking to establish her (Dawn's) co-parentage of A.B., a child conceived by artificial insemination during Dawn and Stephanie's intimate domestic relationship. Dawn appeals the trial court's dismissal of her complaint for failure to state a claim upon which relief may be granted. We reverse and remand.

The complaint reveals the following relevant facts. Dawn and Stephanie shared their home and their lives for nearly nine years, beginning in 1993. During their relationship, the couple shared joint finances and held themselves out to their families, friends, and community as a couple in a committed, loving relationship. Dawn and Stephanie even participated in a commitment ceremony at which they proclaimed themselves to be committed domestic partners before family and friends.

After several years together, the couple jointly decided to bear and raise a child together. They mutually determined that Stephanie would be impregnated by artificial insemination and that Dawn's brother would be the semen donor. Stephanie suggested using Dawn's brother as the semen donor because she wanted both herself and Dawn to be genetically related to the child. Dawn's brother agreed to be the semen donor. All parties involved (Dawn, Stephanie, and the brother) intended for Dawn and Stephanie to be co-parents of the resulting child, assuming equal parental roles in the child's care and support. Stephanie was artificially inseminated with semen donated by Dawn's brother in August 1998, and A.B. was born on May 15, 1999. Dawn was present for and participated in A.B.'s birth. Further, all expenses associated with the pregnancy and birth that were not covered by insurance were paid from the couple's joint bank account.

At some point following A.B.'s birth, Dawn, with Stephanie's consent, filed a co-parent petition to adopt A.B. While the adoption was pending, the parties separated for approximately three months, and Stephanie withdrew her consent to the adoption. During this brief period of separation, Dawn paid child support for A.B.'s benefit and enjoyed regular visitation. For reasons not apparent in the record, the adoption was not pursued any further after Dawn and Stephanie reconciled and resumed living together as a family. The relationship between Dawn and Stephanie eventually ended in January 2002. Thereafter, Dawn paid monthly child support and continued to have regular and liberal visitation with A.B. until late July 2003. At that point, Stephanie unilaterally terminated visitation and began rejecting Dawn's support payments.

From A.B.'s birth until July 2003, Dawn and Stephanie acted as co-parents, with important decisions concerning A.B. being determined by them in concert. Dawn has cared for A.B. as a parent, feeding and bathing her, attending doctor's appointments, providing health insurance coverage, and generally providing the financial and emotional support of a parent. She held A.B. out to family, friends, and the community as her daughter. Stephanie consented to and encouraged the formation of a parent-child relationship between Dawn and A.B. Dawn and A.B. have established a bonded, dependent parent-child relationship, and A.B. knows Dawn as her mother in the same manner that she knows Stephanie as her mother. A.B. calls Dawn Momma.

On October 31, 2003, Dawn filed the instant declaratory judgment action, seeking to be recognized as A.B.'s legal second parent with all of the attendant rights and obligations of a biological parent. Alternatively, the complaint asserted that, even if Dawn is not A.B.'s legal second parent, she nonetheless acted in loco parentis and in a custodial and parental capacity entitling her to, at a minimum, continued visitation with A.B. Stephanie moved to dismiss the complaint for failure to state a claim upon which relief may be granted. The trial court heard argument on the motion to dismiss on March 8, 2004. Thereafter, on June 1, 2004, the trial court, with apparent reluctance, dismissed the complaint for failure to state a claim. The trial court concluded in part:

> The State of Indiana has recognized four sources of parentage: heterosexual marriages and biological paternity, the limited circumstance of children conceived by artificial fertilization within a marital relationship with the assistance of an anonymous semen donor, [see *Levin v. Levin*] and adoption. Only adoption has provided a vehicle by which gay-lesbian couples in Indiana who wish to co-parent children may avoid public policy issues and biologically-related sub-issues related to same-sex relationships. For reasons not known to the Court, Dawn did not pursue to conclusion her petition to adopt A.B. in the four years which elapsed between A.B.'s birth and the date the parties separated. Dawn's claim could be granted only if the Court were to create by its order a relationship for which there is no statutory or judicial authority in the State of Indiana. It is not within the province of the trial court to do so.

* * *

Dawn asserts that the trial court interpreted *Levin v. Levin* too narrowly and that the reasoning of that case should apply here. In particular, she claims that when a committed same-sex couple makes a joint decision to bear a child through artificial insemination and raise the child together as co-parents, Indiana law should protect the relationship between the child and her second parent in the same manner it protects the relationship between a nonbiological parent and his child born within the marriage under similar circumstances.

In *Levin v. Levin,* our supreme court decided an issue of first impression brought on by advancing reproductive technology, an area that our legislature has been slow to address. In particular, the court was asked to determine whether a husband who consents to artificial insemination of his wife with the sperm of a third-party donor is the legal father of the resulting child. In that case, Donald Levin sought to vacate a child support order on the basis that the child was not his biological son. The supreme court held, in part, that Donald was equitably estopped from denying his child support obligation (i.e., he was legally responsible for the child), explaining as follows:

> The doctrine of estoppel springs from equitable principles, and it is designed to aid in the administration of justice where, without its aid, injustice might result. Our use of this doctrine is not limited to circumstances involving an actual or false representation or concealment of an existing material fact. Rather, equitable estoppel is an [sic] remedy available if one party through his course

of conduct knowingly misleads or induces another party to believe and act upon his conduct in good faith without knowledge of the facts.

The trial court found that Donald induced Barbara to go forward with the artificial insemination. He consented both orally and in writing to the procedure. This consent constituted Donald's promise to become the father of the resulting child and to assume his support. Moreover, Donald held the child out as his own for fifteen years. He made no objection to declaring the child a child of the marriage in the dissolution decree in 1987. Barbara relied in good faith upon Donald's actions and consequently bore a child for which she believed both she and Donald would be responsible. Accordingly, Donald is now estopped from denying his obligations toward this child. To hold otherwise would be unjust.

Levin v. Levin at 604–5

While *Levin v. Levin* was certainly presented in the context of a marriage, the supreme court's analysis as set forth above does not expressly hinge on the marital status of the parties and is equally applicable to the case at hand. Moreover, we agree with Dawn that "no [legitimate] reason exists to provide the children born to lesbian parents through the use of reproductive technology with less security and protection than that given to children born to heterosexual parents through artificial insemination." *Appellant's Brief* at 11. As we have recently observed in the context of same-sex adoptions, we cannot close our eyes to the legal and social needs of our society; the strength and genius of the common law lies in its ability to adapt to the changing needs of the society it governs.

> "[O]ur paramount concern should be with the effect of our laws on the reality of children's lives. It is not the courts that have engendered the diverse composition of today's families. It is the advancement of reproductive technologies and society's recognition of alternative lifestyles that have produced families in which a biological, and therefore a legal, connection is no longer the sole organizing principle. But it is the courts that are required to define, declare and protect the rights of children raised in these families, usually upon their dissolution. At that point, courts are left to vindicate the public interest in the children's financial support and emotional well-being by developing theories of parenthood, so that "legal strangers" who are de facto parents may be awarded custody or visitation or reached for support. Case law and commentary on the subject detail the years of litigation spent in settling these difficult issues while the children remain in limbo, sometimes denied the affection of a "parent" who has been with them from birth."

Adoption of K.S.P., 804 N.E.2d at 1259 (quoting Adoptions of B.L.B.V. & E.L.V.B., 628 A.2d 1271 (1993)

We encourage the Indiana legislature to help us address this current social reality by enacting laws to protect children who, through no choice of their own, find themselves born into unconventional familial settings. Until the legislature enters this arena, however, we are left to fashion the common law to define, declare, and protect the rights of these children. *See* Ind. Const. art. I, § 12 (providing in part, "[a]ll courts shall be open; and every person, for injury done to him...shall have remedy by due course of law"). We, therefore, hold that when two women involved in a domestic relationship agree to bear and raise a child together by artificial insemination of one of the partners with donor semen, both women are the legal parents of the resulting child.

Assuming the facts alleged in the complaint to be true, as we must at this stage, it is apparent that A.B. would not have been born if Dawn and Stephanie had not agreed to be co-parents to the resulting child. Dawn, as well as her brother who acted as the semen donor, relied in good faith on Stephanie's representations in this regard. Dawn and Stephanie, as a committed couple who could not marry, determined to bear and raise a child together. With the help of reproductive technology and the donation from Dawn's brother, they engaged in a nontraditional procreative act and achieved their goal of having a child who is genetically related to both women. Dawn and Stephanie proceeded, as agreed and intended, to raise the child together, both financially and emotionally, and to hold A.B. out as the daughter of both women for several years. Even after the couple's relationship ended, Dawn continued to share in the parenting of A.B., enjoying liberal visitation with A.B. and paying monthly child support for well over a year. For the first four years of A.B.'s life, Stephanie consented to and encouraged the formation of a parent-child relationship between Dawn and A.B. A bonded, dependent parent-child relationship was, in fact, established between Dawn and A.B., and A.B. has grown up knowing Dawn as her mother in the same manner that she knows Stephanie as her mother.

Stephanie asserts, with little analysis, that establishing Dawn as a parent, over Stephanie's objection as the child's biological parent, would violate her constitutional right to make decisions concerning the custody and control of her daughter. We do not dispute that the Due Process Clause of the Fourteenth Amendment of the United States Constitution protects the fundamental right of parents to make decisions concerning the care, custody, and control of their children. *See Troxel v. Granville,* 530 U.S. 57, 120 S.Ct. 2054, 147 L.Ed.2d 49 (2000) (plurality); In the instant case, however, we have determined that both Stephanie and Dawn are the legal parents of A.B. and stand on equal footing with respect to the child. When Stephanie agreed to bear and raise a child with Dawn and, thereafter, consented to and actively fostered a parent-child relationship between Dawn and A.B., she presumptively made decisions in the best interest of her child and effectively waived the right to unilaterally sever that relationship when her romantic relationship with Dawn ended. *Cf. T.B. v. L.R.M.,* 567 Pa. 222, 786 A.2d 913 (2001) (observing, under similar circumstances, that biological mother's rights do not extend to erasing a relationship between her partner and her child which she voluntarily created and actively fostered simply because after the parties' separation she regretted having done so); *Parentage of L.B.,* 121 Wash. App. 460, 484, 89 P.3d 271 283 (2004)("de facto parentage rule recognized by other states *emphasizes the original consent of the legal parent to the relationship* ") (emphasis in original).

We conclude that the facts alleged in the complaint, including the reasonable inferences that can be drawn from those facts, are capable of supporting the relief sought by Dawn in her claim for declaratory judgment. Therefore, the trial court erroneously granted the motion to dismiss. We remand for further proceedings consistent with this opinion.

Questions

What is the theory of parenthood in the Indiana case? Could the theory be used to establish parenthood for Dawn if Stephanie had adopted the child rather than given birth? What if Stephanie had adopted the child before the relationship with Dawn had started, but then once they were in the relationship, Stephanie and Dawn had agreed to co-parent the child?

2. Intentional parenthood

In the Matter of the Appeal of Helmi A. Hisserich
State Board of Equalization
State of California
No. 99A-0341
Case No. 89002469560
November 1, 2000

JOHN KLEHS, JOHN CHIANG, KATHLEEN CONNELL, members of the Board:

This appeal is made pursuant to section 19045 of the Revenue and Taxation Code from the action of the Franchise Tax Board on the protest of Helmi A. Hisserich against a proposed assessment of additional personal income tax in the amount of $1,158 for the year 1997. The issue presented by this appeal is whether appellant may claim as the qualifying individual for her head of household filing status the minor child born to her domestic partner and which child was jointly planned by appellant and her domestic partner and conceived through alternative reproductive technology, and which child otherwise satisfies all of the requirements as a qualifying individual under Internal Revenue Code (IRC) sections 2 and 152.

A. Background

Appellant and her domestic partner, Tori Patterson, have lived together since 1986, and, not having the option to marry under California law, have registered as domestic partners with the State of California, the County of Los Angeles, and the cities of Los Angeles and Santa Monica. After approximately 10 years together and thoughtful consideration concerning their relationship, appellant and Ms. Patterson decided to have and rear a child together. The couple decided that appellant would continue to work and support the family, while Ms. Patterson, utilizing alternative reproductive technology (specifically, anonymous donor insemination), would attempt to become pregnant. Together, they consulted a licensed California sperm bank, Pacific Reproductive Services, wherein the insemination occurred under the direction of a licensed physician. Appellant's decision to have a child was made jointly with her partner and neither would have attempted to have a child without the involvement of the other.

Following the birth of the child (Madeline) on April 18, 1997, appellant and Ms. Patterson initiated adoption proceedings to formalize appellant's parental status. No court order of adoption had been obtained as of the end of 1997. Appellant's employer provides health insurance coverage for Ms. Patterson and Madeline; appellant and Ms. Patterson hold assets jointly; they each name the other as beneficiary on their respective life insurance policies; and, they are recognized as a family unit by their church, Madeline's preschool, and their respective families.

Appellant claimed head of household filing status on her 1997 personal income tax return, identifying "Madeline Tess Hisserich-Patterson, child," as her dependent. In order to verify appellant's filing status, respondent sent appellant a Head of Household

Audit Letter for 1997. Appellant responded under penalty of perjury that she was single and had not been married prior to January 1, 1998. Appellant indicated that Madeline had lived with her for nine months during 1997, beginning on April 18, 1997 (Madeline's date of birth), through December 31, 1997. Appellant attached correspondence, dated July 24, 1998, stating that Madeline was the natural child of her domestic partner, and that she had not formally adopted Madeline during 1997. Appellant stated that she was financially responsible for Madeline and considered the child to be her own daughter.

Respondent issued a Notice of Proposed Assessment (NPA) denying appellant's head of household filing status. The NPA stated that a child living in the same household with a parent and an unrelated nonparent did not qualify the nonparent for head of household filing status. Respondent revised appellant's filing status to single and reduced appellant's standard deduction to reflect the change in filing status, resulting in a proposed assessment of additional tax in the amount of $1,158. This appeal resulted.

California Revenue and Taxation Code section 17042 sets forth the requirements for head of household filing status by reference to IRC sections 2(b) and 2(c). IRC section 2(b) provides that the taxpayer must be unmarried (at the close of the taxable year), and must maintain as his or her home a household which constitutes the principal place of abode, as a member of such household, of a qualifying individual for more than one-half of the year. The list of potential qualifying individuals includes unmarried sons, daughters, stepsons, and stepdaughters of the taxpayer; closely related dependents of the taxpayer, as listed in IRC section 152, subsections (a)(1) through (a)(8); a legally adopted child of the taxpayer; and a foster child of the taxpayer. (Int.Rev. Code, 2(b), 152(b).) However, those individuals who qualify as the taxpayer's dependents based solely on having as a principal place of abode the home of the taxpayer and living as a member of the taxpayer's household are not included in the list of potential qualifying individuals. (Int.Rev. Code, 2(b)(3)(B)(i); 152(A)(9).)

Appellant sets forth a number of contentions in support of her claimed head of household filing status. At the heart of appellant's contentions is her claim that Madeline is her daughter, and thus Madeline is a qualifying dependent under the head of household rules in IRC section 2(b). Appellant asserts that in every aspect of her life she is treated as Madeline's parent.

Appellant contends that the facts of this matter support the conclusion that Madeline is her daughter under the "doctrine of intentional parenthood," enunciated in the California Supreme Court's opinion in Johnson v. Calvert (1993) 5 Cal.4th 84, and as applied in *Buzzanca v. Buzzanca* (1998) 61 Cal.App.4th 1410.[1]

Respondent contends that neither the IRC nor its regulations include provisions allowing appellant to claim Madeline as her qualifying individual for head of household filing status, as Madeline does not fall within any of the classes of individuals identified in statute who qualify appellant for head of household filing status. In support of this contention, respondent notes that IRC section 2(b)(1)(A)(i) allows a taxpayer to claim a son, stepson, daughter, or stepdaughter as the qualifying individual for head of household filing status. Respondent further notes that the word "child" is defined in IRC section 151(c)(3) as an individual who is the son, stepson, daughter, or step-

---

1. This argument was first proposed in an amicus brief filed in this matter by Patricia A. Cain, Professor of Law, University of Iowa, College of Law.

daughter of the taxpayer. Finally, respondent states that IRC section 152(b)(2) provides that a taxpayer may claim a legally adopted child or foster child as the qualifying individual. Respondent argues that other than these identified sections, the IRC contains no other provisions for claiming a child as a qualifying individual for head of household purposes.

B. Applicable Law

The words "son" and "daughter" traditionally have been construed to include only lineal descendants of the first degree by blood, as well as through marriage, legal adoption, or a foster arrangement. We conclude that, at least in this state, the words "son" and "daughter" are invested with additional meaning beyond the traditional construction as a result of the California Supreme Court's decision in *Johnson v. Calvert* and the subsequent application of this decision by the court of appeal in *Buzzanca v. Buzzanca*, supra.

Initially, we note that as a general proposition "where a California tax statute uses the same language as a federal statute, federal case law is persuasive on the proper interpretation to be given to the California statute." (Rihn v. Franchise Tax Board (1955) 131 Cal.App.2d 356, 360.) However, the United States Supreme Court in De Sylva v. Ballentine (1956) 351 U.S. 570, applied California state law to define the word "children" in application of the federal copyright laws to residents of California. The Supreme Court stated that "there is no federal law of domestic relations, which is primarily a matter of state concern." (De Sylva v. Ballentine, supra, 351 U.S. at pp. 351–52.) The Supreme Court also observed in United States v. Yazell (1966) 382 U.S. 341, 352, that the "theory and the precedents of this Court teach us solicitude for state interests, particularly in the field of family and family-property arrangements." It is apparent from these decisions that California law is controlling in a matter such as the issue at hand, namely, a determination of a familial relationship.

In the Johnson case, the court addressed legal issues raised by advances in reproductive technology. Specifically, the court addressed the question of parentage of a child conceived from the egg of the wife fertilized by the sperm of the husband, and gestated in another woman pursuant to a surrogacy agreement. The genetic parents and the gestational surrogate both claimed rights as parents of the child. After reviewing the provisions of the Uniform Parentage Act (UPA), the court concluded that the purpose of the legislation was to eliminate the legal distinction between legitimate and illegitimate children by basing parent and child rights on the parent and child relationship, rather than on the marital status of the parents. (Johnson v. Calvert, supra, 5 Cal.4th at p. 89.) The court also concluded that due to ambiguities arising from artificial reproductive techniques it could not reach a conclusion under the UPA without inquiring into the parties' intentions as manifested in the surrogacy agreement. (Id. at p. 93.) Upon review of the intentions of each of the parties, the court found that the genetic parents had the requisite intention to bring the child into existence and act as the child's parents. (Id.) They, therefore, were determined to be the child's lawful parents. (Id.)

The Johnson court found that the couple desired to have a child, but were physically unable to do so without the aid of reproductive technology, and they therefore took the necessary affirmative steps to effect the birth of the child. (Id.) As stated by the court, "[b]ut for their acted-on intention, the child would not exist." (Id.) In support of its finding of a parent and child relationship based on other than a gestational relationship, the court adopted the ideas of several legal commentators writing on parentage and artificial reproductive technology, and quoted therefrom. (Id. at pp. 93–94.) In summary, these commentators proposed that developments in reproductive technology allowed individuals to intentionally bring into existence a child that could not otherwise have been conceived, and that the individuals who conceived of the idea of the child and intentionally took affirmative steps to achieve the birth of the child should be presumed to be the parents of the child. (Id.) Further, by honoring the intentions of the individuals who take affirmative steps to bring the child into being, we honor the plans and expectations of those individuals with regard to parenting the child, as well as societal expectations for proper care of the child. (Id. at p. 94.)

In Buzzanca v. Buzzanca, supra, the court of appeal confronted a case wherein a child was born because Luanne and John Buzzanca agreed to have an embryo genetically unrelated to either of them implanted in a woman who would carry and give birth to the child for them. Luanne and John separated after the fertilization, implantation, and pregnancy, leaving for the court to decide the identity of the child's lawful parents. John and the surrogate mother both disclaimed any responsibility for the child. The court held Luanne and John to be the lawful parents of the genetically unrelated child because they initiated and consented to the medical procedure resulting in the conception and birth of the child. The court explained that in Johnson the California Supreme Court "looked to intent to parent as the ultimate basis for its decision" and concluded that the court "employed a legal idea that was unrelated to any necessary biological connection." (Id. at p. 1428, original italics.)

C. Application of Law

We find the reasoning of the California Supreme Court and the court of appeal persuasive and applicable to the question of parentage in the matter before us. We also find persuasive the fact that no other individuals claim or may claim Madeline as a child or qualifying individual for head of household filing status. Appellant and her domestic partner, unable to marry under California law, registered as domestic partners with the city, county, and state in which they lived; they maintained a committed relationship for a substantial period of time prior to the decision to have a child; they decided to have a child together with the specific intent to rear the child together; they voluntarily and knowingly consented to the artificial insemination of Ms. Patterson with a licensed California sperm bank under the direction of a licensed California physician; appellant further exhibited her intent to be Madeline's parent by initiating adoption proceedings following Madeline's birth; and they lived together, conducted themselves, and held themselves out to the community as a family following the birth of Madeline.

We therefore conclude that but for the acted-on intention of appellant and Ms. Patterson to conceive and parent a child, Madeline would not exist. It is essential to our conclusion that appellant and Ms. Patterson, each of whom voluntarily and knowingly consented to the use of alternative reproductive technology as a necessary surrogate for procreative intercourse for the conception of the child, are an unmarried couple who maintained a committed relationship, that their aim was to bring Madeline into the world and to provide a home for her and assume responsibility for her care, that appellant intended from the outset to be Madeline's parent and continued to exhibit her intent to parent after Madeline's birth, that Madeline otherwise qualifies as a qualified individual under the head of household rules, and that no one else can claim Madeline as a dependent.

To find that Madeline is not appellant's child would be to ignore the fact that in today's society families are created in many different ways, including means of in vitro and artificial insemination. The tax code should be interpreted in a manner which encourages and supports parental responsibility. Under the circumstances, therefore, there does not appear to be any logical, let alone legal, reason to deny appellant head of household status. We conclude that the requisite intent to parent has been exhibited by appellant, and that Madeline is appellant's "daughter" for purposes of claiming head of household filing status under California income tax law.

DISSENTING OPINION [Dean Andal, Chairman, and Claude Parrish, Vice Chairman]

We dissent. The Board should reject the head of household filing status claimed by the taxpayer because it does not comply with the clear and long-established law. There are only two ways which head of household filing status could be allowed in situations similar to this case. First, the California Legislature or Congress could amend the law to provide for filing as head of household when the person claiming the status is not related by blood or law to the qualifying dependent child. Second, the taxpayer could complete the adoption process of the child, which she has apparently abandoned. Absent such a change in law by the Legislature or Congress or legal action by the taxpayer, the filing status of head of household must be denied.

An amicus brief filed on behalf of petitioner applies abstract and controversial family and contract law cases to come to the conclusion that petitioner is a parent in this case. These family and contract law cases involve entirely different public policy issues such as custody and visitation rights and contractual obligations to provide support. With almost 50 years of established interpretation in the area of tax law, there is no need to look outside tax law to resolve this dispute.

Furthermore, when the language of a statute is clear, a court interpreting it should follow its plain meaning. Lennand v. Franchise Tax Board (1994) 9 Cal.4th 263, 268. The words of a statute are to be given its ordinary meaning unless a different meaning is clearly intended. Sec. 1861 C.C.P., Hazelwood v. Hazelwood, 57 Cal.App.3d 693, 698. Statutory terms should be construed in accordance with the usual or ordinary meaning of the words used. See Schmidt v. Superior Court, 48 Cal.3d 370, 379–80.

In this case, the pertinent part of the statute uses the term "daughter." The meaning of the word "daughter" is so ordinary that we need not refer to a dictionary, never mind complicated and controversial family law cases that have completely different public policies at stake, in order to determine its meaning. A change in the law would be required to change the clear meaning of the term provided in the statute. That is exactly what was required and done in the case of foster children....

The case currently before us involves a lesbian petitioner that is claiming head of household filing status. The qualifying dependent is the daughter of petitioner's partner. Petitioner and her partner planned the conception and birth through artificial insemination. There are very broad unintended consequences resulting from the majority decision. For example, nothing in the majority decision would limit the right of an unmarried heterosexual partner to claim head of household status in a similar situation. The decision would apply equally to the male partner of an unmarried heterosexual couple that planned the conception and birth of a child through artificial insemination using the sperm of an unrelated or anonymous donor.

The majority decision promotes a public policy that discourages marriage and legal adoption. In the case before us, the decision removes an incentive to legally adopt the child. In the above example of a similarly situated heterosexual couple, the decision removes an incentive for the couple to marry or for the male partner to legally adopt the child.

For these reasons, we dissent.

Notes and Questions

1. The Franchise Tax Board did not appeal the *Hisserich* decision. When it issued its written opinion, the Board of Equalization indicated that the decision was to be considered precedential and that similarly situated California taxpayers would be entitled to Head of Household filing status. The Internal Revenue Service never investigated Hisserich's federal filing status and the statute of limitations has run on those years.

2. A nonprofit anti-gay public interest litigation group, the Proposition 22 Legal Defense and Education Fund, expressed its displeasure with the *Hisserich* opinion by bringing a collateral challenge under California statutes that grant taxpayers standing to challenge tax rules by administrative agencies. The Prop 22 Legal Defense Fund brought suit against the California Board of Equalization and Franchise Tax Board, claiming that the tax administrative agencies had exceeded their limited abilities to interpret tax statutes and had applied an interpretation that was not supported by existing statutes and cases. The Superior Court of Sacramento County agreed and issued an order that the Board of Equalization stop applying the *Hisserich* decision as precedent. No one appealed that decision. Hisserich was not a party to that decision because the earlier Board of Equalization ruling was, as to her, res judicata. And, any taxpayer, who had relied on *Hisserich* as precedent, should have been similarly protected. Indeed, since no lesbian or gay parent was a party in the Prop 22 challenge, no such parent should be bound by the superior court's opinion. Lesbian and gay taxpayers in the future could argue, as Helmi Hisserich argued, that under California law, they should be recognized as "intentional parents" for purposes of state tax laws.

3. As a practical matter, the problem that faced parents like Helmi Hisserich has been resolved by statute. In 2001, the California legislature amended the stepparent adoption statutes in the California Family Code to include adoptions by domestic partners of the legal parent. See California Family Code §9000(f). Thus, a parent in Helmi's position can now adopt without the need for costly and timely home studies and without the risk that the adoption might be delayed by a homophobic clerk.

4. Is "psychological parenthood" the same as "intentional parenthood?"

5. Can psychological parents be held liable for child support? Can intentional parents be held liable for child support? See e.g., *Elisa Maria B v. Superior Court*, 13 Cal. Rptr. 3d 494 (Cal. Ct. App., 3rd Dist., May 20, 2004), which addressed the issue of whether "a person in a same-sex relationship, who encourages her partner to give birth to a child via artificial insemination and who then holds out the child as her own, can be required to pay child support after she and her partner split up." The court answered the question in the negative, holding that the partner was not a parent. However, the California Supreme Court has vacated the opinion and will ultimately decide the issue itself.

6. Should the same substantive tests for parenthood apply in all of the following circumstances:

(1) Second parent is challenging biological parent for custody and visitation;

(2) Second parent is being asked to honor parental support obligations;

(3) Second parent wants to claim Head of Household status or other tax benefits (e.g., child credits) which are intended to provide some financial assistant to families who have children.

3. Genetic Mom and Gestational Mom

What should be the outcome when a lesbian couple elects to have one partner donate the egg and the other partner carry the child to term? Does this arrangement create two legal mothers?

In *K.M. v. E.G.*, 13 Cal. Rptr. 3d 136 (Cal. Ct. App., 1st Dist., May 10, 2004), the genetic mother had signed a waiver before the birth of the children agreeing that the birth mother would be the only legal parent. The appellate court held the waiver binding and refused to recognize her as a parent. The couple had split up several years after the birth of twins and the genetic mother was seeking parental status. The decision has been vacated and is under consideration by the California Supreme Court.

4. Parenthood by Declaration

The following case has also been vacated by the California Supreme Court and will be decided on appeal in tandem with *K.M. v. E.G.*, *supra* and *Elisa Maria B. v. Superior Court of El Dorado County, supra*.

Kristine Renee H. v. Lisa Ann R.
16 Cal. Rptr. 3d 123 (Cal. Ct. App., 2nd Dist., June 30, 2004)

CROSKEY, J.

Two women in a long-term relationship decided to have a child. They arranged for one of them to conceive a child through artificial insemination. One month before the child's birth, the women obtained a prebirth judgment (judgment) based on their stipulation in which they declared themselves to be the "joint intended legal parents" of the unborn child. Following the child's birth, they raised her together for almost two years. Thereafter, the women separated and the natural mother brought a motion to vacate the judgment on the ground that the family court lacked jurisdiction under California's version of the Uniform Parentage Act (the Act) (Fam.Code, § 7600, et seq.) to determine that her partner was the child's second parent. The family court denied the motion, and the natural mother appealed. Under these circumstances, we must first determine whether the judgment entered before the child was born is void. If so, we must then consider whether the natural mother's former partner can establish parentage under the Act....

As we will explain, we first conclude that the judgment is void. The family court could not accept the parties' stipulation as a basis for entering the judgment of parentage. A determination of parentage cannot rest simply on the parties' agreement. Rather, because the partner did not adopt the child, the sole basis upon which the family court could determine parentage is under the Act. Therefore, the judgment based on the parties' stipulation was in excess of the family court's jurisdiction and of no legal effect.

We answer the second question in the affirmative, concluding that the partner may be able to establish parentage under the Act. Our conclusion on this question differs from the one reached by the *Elisa B.* court. We conclude that the Act does provide a basis upon which the former partner can establish parentage. While such a conclusion under the Act may not be a result that the Legislature *expressly* contemplated, the Act does mandate that we read the provisions in a gender-neutral manner and that mandate compels our conclusion. The Act states that insofar as *practicable, the provisions that are applicable to establishing a father and child relationship apply to determine the existence of a mother and child relationship.* (§ 7650 [emphasis added].) Because the former partner is neither a natural mother nor an adoptive mother, we may look to the provisions of the Act establishing the father-child relationship to determine whether the former partner can establish parentage.

Section 7611, subdivision (d), commonly referred to as the *presumed father* statute, provides a basis upon which the partner can establish parentage. That statute, *when read in a gender-neutral manner,* provides that a woman is presumed to be a parent of a child if "[s]he receives the child into [her] home and openly holds out the child as h[er] natural child." We see no prohibition in the Act that prevents us from concluding that a child has two parents of the same sex, especially here when no one other than the partner is vying to become the child's *second parent.* We, therefore, reverse the order denying the motion to vacate and remand to the family court to make the predicate determination of parentage before addressing the permanent custody and visitation issues presently before that court.

Notes and Questions

Whatever the outcome on appeal of these three consolidated cases, do you think this court's decision would be the same if the Judicial declaration had been based not only on the contract between the two parties, but also on the fact that one partner was the gestational mother and the other was the genetic mother?

5. Asserting Rights as a Nonparent

As a general rule, the second parent must prove that he or she is a parent before a court will entertain a claim for visitation or custody. But, some states have statutes that may apply to grant interested parties, other than parents, standing to claim visitation rights. We saw such a statute in *Troxel v. Granville*, the grandparent visitation case decided by the United States Supreme Court. Because the parent's right to make decisions regarding childrearing is protected by the constitution, it will usually be difficult for a nonparent to assert visitation rights over the objection of a parent. Nonetheless, such assertions are not impossible.

In re Guardianship of Olivia
101 Cal. Rptr. 2d 364 (Cal. App. 2000)

STEIN, J.

Karen B. (appellant), the former domestic partner of Jennifer J. (respondent), appeals from a judgment dismissing her petition for guardianship of the minor, Olivia J., born to respondent while she and appellant were living in the same household as a couple. Appellant alleged that, with respondent's encouragement, she loved and supported Olivia as her daughter, and Olivia called her "Mama," and respondent, "Mommy." Before the child was two years old, the relationship between appellant and respondent ended. When respondent moved out of house, with Olivia, she told appellant that she would never see Olivia again. After consulting with several lawyers, including Carol Amyx, who ultimately represented respondent, appellant filed a petition for guardianship.

Appellant contends that the court erred by dismissing her petition without an evidentiary hearing to determine the merits of her allegation that parental custody is detrimental to the minor.

We shall reverse the judgment dismissing the guardianship petition, and remand for further proceedings.

ANALYSIS

I.

Dismissal of the Petition for Guardianship

In *Nancy S. v. Michele G* (1991), this court addressed the question whether a trial court had erred in finding a former domestic partner of the natural mother of two children was not a "parent" under the Uniform Parentage Act. In that case, we rejected the argument of Michele G., who was neither the natural, nor the adoptive mother of the children, that the statutory definition of a "parent" should be judicially expanded, to include a person such as herself, who had lived in the same household with the children and performed the role of a parent, fulfilling the child's physical and emotional needs.

This court observed that "the absence of any legal formalization of [Michele G.'s] relationship to the children" had "resulted in a tragic situation." Nevertheless, we held that "expanding the definition of a 'parent' in the manner advocated by appellant could expose other natural parents to litigation brought by child-care providers of long standing, relatives, successive sets of stepparents, or other close friends of the family. No matter how narrowly we might attempt to draft the definition, the fact remains that the status of individuals claiming to be parents would have to be litigated and resolution of these claims would turn on elusive factual determinations of the intent of the natural mother, the perceptions of the child and the course of conduct of the person claiming parental status."

Although the *facts* in *Nancy S.* concerning the relationship between appellant and the respondent, the intent of respondent to create and support a relationship between her former partner and the minor similar to the relationship between parent and child, and the perceptions of the child are very similar to the facts asserted by appellant in several declarations below, the *legal issues* presented in this appeal are quite different. Appellant has filed a petition for guardianship pursuant to Probate Code § 1510 for appointment of a guardian for a minor, and has alleged that *parental custody is detrimental to the child.* (See Fam. Code § 3041 [the court may not grant custody to a nonparent over the objections of a parent unless it finds that parental custody is detrimental to the child and that granting to a nonparent is required to serve the best interests of the child].) Although appellant describes her relationship with the minor as a parent-child relationship, she *does not* seek a declaration of the existence of a parent-child relationship under the Uniform Parentage Act, and concedes, for the purpose of this proceeding, that *she does not have the legal status of a parent.* She therefore is not entitled to have the court decide whether to appoint her as guardian based upon the best interests of the child. On appeal, she contends only that the court erred by dismissing her petition, without allowing her an opportunity to prove that parental custody is detrimental to the child and that an award of custody to a nonparent is required to serve the best interests of the child.

Although we emphasize that appellant's burden, on remand, to establish that parental custody is detrimental to the child will be difficult to meet, we shall reverse the dismissal of her petition, because the court: (1) applied the wrong legal standard by ruling that appellant, as a nonparent, could not establish parental custody is detrimental to the child in the absence of an allegation of "serious abuse, neglect, or abandonment by the parent"; and (2) erroneously interpreted *Guardianship of Z.C.W.*, as standing for the proposition that loss or termination of a child's relationship with a nonparent cannot, *as a matter of law,* be a basis for finding parental custody to be detrimental to the child.

1. A Nonparent Petitioning for Guardianship Need Not Allege Serious Abuse, Neglect or Abandonment.

Probate Code § 1510 provides that a relative, "or other person on behalf of the minor,...may file a petition for the appointment of a guardian of the minor." Therefore, appellant's status as a nonparent does not preclude her from filing the petition. However, her status as a nonparent does require that she meet a heavy burden before the court may grant her petition. As this court explained, in *Guardianship of Phillip B.* (1983): "Courts generally may appoint a guardian over the person or estate of a minor 'if it appears necessary or convenient.' (Prob. Code § 1514 subd. (a).) But the right of parents to retain custody of a child is fundamental and may be disturbed ' "...only in extreme cases of persons acting in a fashion incompatible with parenthood." ' Accordingly, the Legislature has imposed the stringent requirement that before a court may make an order awarding custody of a child to a nonparent without consent of the parents, 'it shall make a finding that an award of custody to a parent would be detrimental to the child and the award to a nonparent is required to serve the best interests of the child.' (Civ Code § 4600 subd. (c))...

The trial court's imposition of the requirement that, in addition to alleging that parental custody is detrimental to the child, appellant must allege "serious abuse, neglect, or abandonment by the parent" apparently is derived from the standard set forth in former Welfare and Institutions Code section 361, subdivision (b), which required a court, in juvenile dependency proceedings, to find by clear and convincing evidence, "physical abuse, psychological abuse, sexual abuse, and the absence of a parent willing to have physical custody," before the state may remove a child from the physical custody of a parent and declare the child a dependent of the court. Probate Code § 1514, subdivision (b) specifies that in deciding whether to appoint a guardian, the court, instead, is governed by Family Code § 3041, which requires that, in a dispute between a parent and a nonparent, before awarding custody to a nonparent, the court must make an express finding that parental custody is detrimental to the child. Although evidence of the specific abuses necessary for a juvenile court in a dependency proceeding to remove a child from the custody of a parent, would no doubt support a finding of detriment, we find nothing in Probate Code § 1514, subdivision (b), or Family Code § 3041 that *limits* the court to those circumstances.

...[W]e decline to judicially engraft a requirement that the petition specifically plead, abuse, neglect, or abandonment. The question whether parental custody is detrimental to the child is highly dependent upon facts unique to each child and parent. To attempt to define the circumstances that might qualify as an "unusual and extreme [case]" warranting appointment of a nonparent as guardian, over the objections of a parent, would deprive the court of the flexibility essential to its equitable jurisdiction.... The preference for parental custody is adequately protected by requiring that the petitioner demonstrate by clear and convincing evidence that parental custody is detrimental to the child, without attempting to enumerate, by judicial gloss on the statutory language, what categories of factual circumstances may or may not be recognized as detrimental to the child.

2. Loss of a Relationship with a Nonparent may be Factor Supporting a Finding of Detriment

In addition to finding the allegation of detriment inadequate as a matter of law. because of the absence of an allegation of abuse, neglect or abandonment, the court also ruled that the psychological harm caused by the loss of a relationship with a nonparent is not, as a matter of law, a basis for a finding that parental custody is detrimental to the child.

Our review of the relevant authority satisfies us that the loss of a relationship with a nonparent who has acted as a de facto, or psychological parent, is a factor the court may consider in determining whether parental custody is detrimental to the child. The court in *Guardianship of Zachary H* explicitly rejected the contention of the natural father that the "detriment prong [of Family Code § 3041] cannot be satisfied by a showing that removal from a nonparent will be detrimental." That court relied on evidence that termination of the child's relationship with the petitioners, who were not Zachary's legal parents, would result in permanent psychological harm as a basis for finding that parental custody would be detrimental to the child.

Nor is the recognition of the loss of such a relationship as a factor supporting a finding of detriment limited to cases of failed adoptions. In *Guardianship of Phillip B* this court held the finding that parental custody was detrimental to the child was supported, in part, by evidence of the emotional harm that would result if the parents retained custody, and prevented Phillip B. from visiting petitioners, with whom Phillip B. had formed a close psychological and emotional bond.

Respondent correctly observes that in *Zachary H.* and *Phillip B.* the children did not live, and never had lived with their natural parents. In the case of *Zachary H*, the only parent-child like bond was between the child and the intended adoptive parents, and the natural father was a virtual stranger to the child. In the case of *Phillip* , the parents had purposefully emotionally detached themselves, and their other children, from Phillip B. Respondent also demonstrates that, in nearly every other case appointing a nonparent as guardian, the parents were either dead, or did not reside with the child, or had intentionally relinquished, or passively transferred, responsibility for the care of the child to the nonparent seeking guardianship. Respondent's analysis of these cases illustrates that the absence of a meaningful parent-child relationship is a significant *fact* weighing in support of a court's ultimate conclusion that the loss of a relationship with a nonparent is sufficiently detrimental to the child to warrant an award of custody to a nonparent. In each of these cases, however, the court heard and weighed all of the relevant evidence, and the Court of Appeal reviewed the *factual* finding that parental custody is detrimental to the child, or in some of the older decisions, a determination that the parent was "unfit." They do not stand for the proposition that detriment can be found *only* when the child has been relinquished to others or the parents are deceased.

We conclude that the court erred in granting the motion to dismiss because it cannot be said on the face of the pleadings that appellant is not entitled to any relief....

Our holding is very limited, based upon the procedural posture of the case when it was disposed of in the trial court. It should not be construed as an expression of an opinion on the merits of appellant's petition, because we hold only that the court erred by finding as a matter of law that appellant could not establish parental custody is detrimental to the child. Nor should it be construed as an endorsement of the use of a petition for guardianship as a forum for a nonparent to obtain visitation rights over the objection of the parent, because we do not reach the issue of whether, when, and in accordance with what legal standard, visitation may be awarded in such a proceeding.[1]

We also caution that because of the strong preference for parental custody, and the heavy burden a nonparent must carry of demonstrating that parental custody is detrimental to the child, a petition for guardianship is an intrusive and limited remedy not easily adapted to achieving appellant's goal, i.e., to protect the child from psychological harm, and to maintain her relationship with the child. As we observed in *Nancy S v. Michele G, supra,* the underlying problem is that, in the absence of a lawful marriage, or legal status as a parent, or some other statutory recognition of her role as a member of the child's family, we know of no principled way, under existing law, to distinguish appellant's status from that of any unmarried member of a household who forms a close attachment with another person's child. At the same time, we recognize that the facts may well bear out appellant's contention that, from the minor's point of view, she does indeed have "two mothers."...Perhaps the repetition of this unfortunate scenario, in case after case, in which the appellant unsuccessfully avails herself of legal remedies not designed to suit the factual circumstances, will eventually lead to a legislative solution, if for no other reason than to protect the children involved from becoming pawns in the conflict of the adults who care for them.

Notes and Questions

1. The California legislature has responded. The newly effective Domestic Partnership Law would treat Karen B. and Nancy S. as legal parents so long as the children were born after the couple had registered as domestic partners. Registered domestic partners are treated the same as spouses. Thus if a stepparent has a right to visitation, even though not a parent, a domestic partner would similarly have a right to visitation.

2. Questions can still arise, even in California, when the children being raised by the couple were not born during the relationship but were brought into the relationship by one of the partners. In a case in Michigan, the surviving partner in an eight year committed relationship, lost custody of the children she and her partner had been raising despite the fact that the mother had executed a power of attorney delegating parental powers to her partner and had executed a will that named the partner the guardian of

---

1. Awarding visitation to a nonparent, over the objection of a parent, may be subject to constitutional limitations. [See *Troxel v. Granville.*]

the children. The will specifically explained that the father should not be guardian because he had failed to establish a relationship with the children. At the time of the mother's death, the father's support obligation was nearly $20,000 in arrears. Immediately after the death of the mother, the partner filed a petition for guardianship and was required to give notice to the father. Before the petition could be heard, the father obtained an ex parte order for custody and claimed physical custody by picking the children up from school and taking them home with him. The partner challenged his claim to custody, but the court held she had no standing because she was neither a parent nor a guardian. The court noted that if she was successful in her claim for guardianship, then she would have standing to challenge custody. See *McGuffin v. Overton*, 542 N.W.2d 288 (Mich. App. 1995).

3. Provisions in a will naming a partner as guardian have little force if there is a surviving biological parent who can challenge the partner. Even in cases where there is no surviving biological parent, such provisions are not binding. A court could always find that some other custodial arrangement is in the child's best interest. But there is one additional bit of planning a biological parent can do to ensure that the child will continue to have contact with the partner. Rather than leave property directly to the child, the parent could transfer property into a trust for the benefit of the child and name the partner as trustee. While the other parent might seek guardianship and custody, the partner will control the child's property in the trust.

4. What effect should an agreement to co-parent have when it is a contract between a parent and a non-parent? The New York Court of Appeals ignored the agreement between Alison D. and Virginia M. when it held that Alison D. had no standing. *See Alison D v. Virginia M., supra*. In a similar case in New Mexico involving a settlement agreement between the two parents agreeing to shared custody and visitation that was entered into when the dispute arose, the New Mexico Court of Appeals ruled that the agreement might be enforceable, reversing the trial court, which had appeared to rule that such contracts between a parent and non-parent were not in the best interest of the child as a matter of law. The appellate court directed the trial court to consider all the evidence before determining what might be in the best interest of the child. *See A.C. v. C.B.*, 829 P.2d 660 (N.M. Ct. App. 1992). How do you think *Troxel* might be applied to the holding of the New Mexico court?

E. The Role of Assisted Reproductive Technologies in Creating Gay and Lesbian Families

1. Overview

"The first generation of gay fathers to come to the consciousness of the American public fathered their children in a heterosexual marriage." See E. Gary Spitko, From Queer to Paternity: How Primary Gay Fathers are Changing Fatherhood and Gay Identity, 24 St. Louis U. Pub. L. Rev. 195 (2005). These fathers can share custody and parental rights, where legally possible, with their male partners through second parent adoption or shared custodial arrangements. But to bring a child into an existing gay male partnership, there are really only two possibilities: (1) joint adoption of a new child, or (2) surrogacy arrangements with a woman who is willing to bear the child of one of the gay male partners. In a surrogacy arrangement, only one partner can be the biological partner. The other partner usually becomes a parent through adoption.

For lesbian couples, joint parenthood can be established either through joint adoption or second parent adoption of the biological child of one of the partners. When a lesbian couple desires to have a child together, they can use artificial insemination of a known or unknown donor.

Use of "assisted reproductive technologies," often referred to as ARTs, raise a number of legal questions. Should adoption law principles be applied (e.g., best interest of the child) since ARTs are intended to result in a parent-child relationship similar to the process of adoption? Is there a constitutionally protected right or liberty interest in using ARTs to procreate? Does a surrogacy contract which provides for the birth mother to relinquish parental rights in exchange for a fee constitute illegal baby selling?

Notes and Questions

1. Developments in the Law—The Law of Marriage and Family: Changing Realities of Parenthood: The Law's Response to the Evolving American Family and Emerging Reproductive Technologies, 116 Harv. L. Rev. 2052 (2003) raises the following issues:

> The development of artificial insemination and in vitro fertilization and the practices of sperm donation, ova donation, and surrogate motherhood raise profound questions about—and lead to complex conflicts involving—the meaning of parenthood. Can parental rights be acquired by contract? Can parental rights be forfeited through contract? To what extent does a genetic relationship determine parental status? Can one sell an embryo? In the absence of contract, as medical techniques and complex relationships press our legal definitions of parenthood, how should legislatures define, and courts adjudge, parental status?

> The resolution of these questions remains, for the most part, incomplete. Legislatures have left the field of medical reproductive technologies largely unregulated, and courts are reluctant to act on their own. The proliferation of these technologies and surrounding transactions forces us to reevaluate the assumptions about parenting with which they conflict. Many of these conflicting assumptions underlie the current law of adoption. The inconsistency between these assumptions and modern reproductive technologies— and the social arrangements associated with these technologies—is cause for a reexamination of the assumptions generally. The significance of these emerging transactions and arrangements lies in their implications for our existing social and legal institutions. As Professor Elizabeth Bartholet argues, "what is so interesting about [these new procreative arrangements] is that although they result in the social equivalent of adoption, they are generally not subject to any of the legal requirements involved in traditional adoption."

2. Professor John Robertson argues that courts should recognize a procreative liberty interest and accord it constitutional protection. See John A. Robertson, Procreative Liberty and Harm to Offspring in Assisted Reproduction, 30 Am. J. L. & Med. 7 (2004). With respect to gay and lesbian families, he opines:

Many persons have also objected to ARTs when they are used to create non-nuclear families. Objections have been made to the complete range of novel families—from the use of donor gametes and surrogacy for married couples to artificial insemination and IVF for single women, women who have been widowed, and gay and lesbian persons or couples. Opponents of such arrangements argue, among other things, that the well-being of children is affected by being reared without two heterosexual, married partners.

... Yet there appears to be ample evidence that gay or straight single persons and gay and lesbian couples are excellent child-rearers, and should not be denied the right to reproduce and rear on that ground alone. Indeed, as we have seen, the children in question could not have been born other than in the rearing situation of concern. The gay persons seeking to have them are seeking the traditional reproductive experience of genetic connection and rearing of their own children. Even if later evidence shows that children reared by heterosexual couple fare somewhat better, the difference is unlikely to be so significant to justify denying gay males and lesbians the opportunity to reproduce.

The question remains, however, whether the right of gays to reproduce should be deemed so important that they should be protected against discrimination by ART providers who object to gay reproduction and rearing. A cogent case can be made that gays, just like persons with disabilities, have the same interests in reproducing—in gene transmission and companionship—that non-gays have, and should not be denied access to reproductive or other services because of their status as gays or persons with disabilities. If bans on anti-gay discrimination are enacted into law, ART providers could not withhold services from gay persons.

3. See also John Lawrence Hill, What Does It Mean To Be A Parent? The Claims of Biology as the Basis of Parental Rights, 66 N.Y.U. L. Rev. 353 (1991) (arguing in favor of a right to procreative liberty). Do you think that current constitutional jurisprudence supports the recognition of procreative liberty? Do you think courts ought to recognize such a right? What should be the contours of it? Should a state be required to assist in producing children using assisted reproductive technology or merely be required not to discriminate? Under what conditions would a provider be justified in withholding reproductive assistance?

2. Lesbian Couples and Sperm Donors

Tripp v. Hinckley
736 N.Y.S.2d 506 (App. Div. 2002)

ROSE, J.

Appeal from an order of the Family Court of Albany County (Maney, J.), entered September 5, 2001, which, *inter alia,* granted petitioner's application, in a proceeding pursuant to Family Court Act article 6, for visitation with the parties' children.

Pursuant to respondent's plan to form a family with her lesbian partner, petitioner agreed that he would donate his sperm to artificially inseminate respondent, and that respondent and her partner would be the children's custodial parents while petitioner and his gay partner would have regular contact with the children. Accordingly, respondent bore two children, one in 1994 and the other in 1996, and signed acknowledgments of paternity authorizing the entry of petitioner's name as father on each child's birth certificate (*see*, Public Health Law §4135-b). After the second child's birth, the parties and their partners executed a "visitation agreement" providing that, *inter alia*, petitioner could visit with the children one day per week, one weekend per month, and one week during the summer.

Respondent and her partner later ended their relationship, leading petitioner to commence this proceeding seeking, *inter alia*, more frequent visitation. The parties stipulated to respondent's retention of physical custody of the children and petitioner's access to their school and medical records, and Family Court then heard undisputed testimony that petitioner has been consistently involved with the children since their births, the children want to have visitation with him and they enjoy their visits. Respondent conceded that the children love petitioner, refer to him as Daddy and view him as their father. No concerns were raised about his parenting skills, and the Law Guardian supported the court-appointed psychologist's opinion that petitioner should have a more traditional, expanded schedule of visitation. Finding expanded visitation to be in the best interests of the children, Family Court granted petitioner visitation one evening per week, alternate weekends and holidays, and two weeks each summer. Respondent appeals, contending that petitioner is merely a sperm donor who should be restricted to the terms of the parties' written agreement. We cannot agree.

Respondent's claim that petitioner should not be treated as the children's parent is belied by the undisputed evidence of paternity and his regular contacts with the children since their births, as well as respondent's own testimony that the children view petitioner as their father and love him. As to the effect of the parties' written visitation agreement, we note that while the courts have recognized such agreements, they are not binding and will be enforced only when the prescribed visitation schedule is found to be in the best interests of the children. "It is fundamental that the best interests of the children are the paramount concern in determining a visitation schedule" (*Matter of La Scola v. Litz*, 258 A.D.2d 792, 792, 685 N.Y.S.2d 862, *lv. denied* 93 N.Y.2d 809, 694 N.Y.S.2d 631, 716 N.E.2d 696), and visitation must be frequent and regular to be meaningful (*see, Matter of Haran-Buckner v. Buckner, supra*, at 707, 590 N.Y.S.2d 582; *Matter of Dervay v. Dervay*, 111 A.D.2d 462, 463, 488 N.Y.S.2d 518).

We also find no merit in respondent's claim that the circumstances here give rise to either a waiver or an estoppel precluding petitioner from obtaining increased visitation. As petitioner has been actively exercising the parental rights permitted under the agreement throughout the children's lives (*compare, Matter of Thomas S. v. Robin Y.*, 209 A.D.2d 298, 618 N.Y.S.2d 356, *appeal dismissed* 86 N.Y.2d 779, 631 N.Y.S.2d 611, 655 N.E.2d 708), and the court-appointed professionals believe expanded visitation would be in the children's best interests, we find a sound and substantial basis in the record for the visitation ordered by Family Court (*see, Matter of Donato v. McLaughlin*, 249 A.D.2d 859, 672 N.Y.S.2d 467; *Colley v. Colley*, 200 A.D.2d 839, 840, 606 N.Y.S.2d 796). ORDERED that the order is affirmed, without costs.

Notes and Questions

1. New York statutes are silent regarding the parental status of sperm donors, although McKinney's Domestic Relations Law §73 does provide that when a child is born

to a married woman using artificial insemination, with the aid of a physician, the woman's husband will be presumed to be the father of the child, provided the spouses so agree.

2. California Family Code provides:

Sec. 7613. Natural father of child conceived by artificial insemination; conditions

(a) If, under the supervision of a licensed physician and surgeon and with the consent of her husband, a wife is inseminated artificially with semen donated by a man not her husband, the husband is treated in law as if he were the natural father of a child thereby conceived. The husband's consent must be in writing and signed by him and his wife. The physician and surgeon shall certify their signatures and the date of the insemination, and retain the husband's consent as part of the medical record, where it shall be kept confidential and in a sealed file. However, the physician and surgeon's failure to do so does not affect the father and child relationship. All papers and records pertaining to the insemination, whether part of the permanent record of a court or of a file held by the supervising physician and surgeon or elsewhere, are subject to inspection only upon an order of the court for good cause shown.

(b) The donor of semen provided to a licensed physician and surgeon for use in artificial insemination of a woman other than the donor's wife is treated in law as if he were not the natural father of a child thereby conceived.

Thus, if a lesbian couple in California wants to use a known donor, and if the donor consents to provide the semen to a licensed physician, the sperm donor will not be accorded parental rights.

3. Why should it matter whether the semen is provided to a licensed physician? If two women want to have a child and do the insemination themselves with semen provided by a friend or relative, should they draft a contract that provides what the relative rights and responsibilities vis-a-vis the child are? Do you think the contract would be enforceable? Even if it were not enforceable, would you advise the parties to execute such a contract?

4. How do you advise your lesbian client in New York who wants to have a child via artificial insemination and does not want the sperm donor to claim parental rights? See *Thomas S. v. Robin Y.*, 618 N.Y.S.2d 356 (App Div. 1994)(holding sperm donor entitled to filiation order despite oral agreement between the parties that he would not seek to be a father to the child), appeal dismissed 655 N.E.2d 708 (N.Y. 1995); See also Fred A. Bernstein, This Child Does have Two Mothers... and a Sperm Donor with Visitation, 22 N.Y.U. Rev. Law & Soc. Change 1 (1996).

3. Gay Male Couples and Surrogates

A gay male couple will need a gestational mother to agree to carry any child that the two men want to have together. The gestational mother need not be the same person as the genetic mother. In any event the gestational mother will usually want compensation for her efforts. Some people argue that it is against public policy to pay a woman to have a baby for someone else and that there ought to be a ban on such arrangements. Others argue that a woman has a liberty interest in her own body and ought to be able to use it in any way she wants.

State law varies quite a bit on the legality of surrogacy contracts. Some states statutorily prohibit such contracts altogether, some states regulate them very heavily by statute, and other states have no statutory provisions. In the latter case, the legality of surrogacy contracts has, in some states, been tested in the courts, and in other states, has yet to be tested. See e.g., *In re Baby M.*, 537 A.2d 1227 (N.J. 1988)(holding surrogacy contract void as against public policy).

New York Domestic Relations Law

§ 123. Prohibitions and Penalties

1. No person or other entity shall knowingly request, accept, receive, pay or give any fee, compensation or other remuneration, directly or indirectly, in connection with any surrogate parenting contract, or induce, arrange or otherwise assist in arranging a surrogate parenting contract for a fee, compensation or other remuneration, except for:

(a) payments in connection with the adoption of a child... or

(b) payments for reasonable and actual medical fees and hospital expenses for artificial insemination or in vitro fertilization services incurred by the mother in connection with the birth of the child.

2. (a) A birth mother or her husband, a genetic father and his wife, and, if the genetic mother is not the birth mother, the genetic mother and her husband who violate this section shall be subject to a civil penalty not to exceed five hundred dollars.

(b) Any other person or entity who or which induces, arranges or otherwise assists in the formation of a surrogate parenting contract for a fee, compensation or other remuneration or otherwise violates this section shall be subject to a civil penalty not to exceed ten thousand dollars and forfeiture to the state of any such fee, compensation or remuneration..., for the first such offense. Any person or entity who or which induces, arranges or otherwise assists in the formation of a surrogate parenting contract for a fee, compensation or other remuneration or otherwise violates this section, after having been once subject to a civil penalty for violating this section, shall be guilty of a felony.

§ 124. Proceedings regarding parental rights, status or obligations

In any action or proceeding involving a dispute between the birth mother and (i) the genetic father, (ii) the genetic mother, (iii) both the genetic father and genetic mother, or (iv) the parent or parents of the genetic father or genetic mother, regarding parental rights, status or obligations with respect to a child born pursuant to a surrogate parenting contract:

1. the court shall not consider the birth mother's participation in a surrogate parenting contract as adverse to her parental rights, status, or obligations;...

Professor Martha Ertman, commenting on the New York law, says:

A surrogate's fee typically ranges from about $10,000 to $20,000, in addition to payment for her expenses, though the parties may negotiate some other fee. Due to the Baby M case, surrogacy has received more media and legal attention than other reproductive technologies and thus is more highly regulated than either in vitro fertilization or alternative insemination. Almost half the states have statutes regulating surrogacy arrangements, and most of these ban commercial surrogacy contracts.

Like adoption, commodification of parenthood through surrogacy is only selectively controversial. New York, for example, forbids payments to the gestational/genetic mother in surrogacy arrangements. But, as is the case with adoption, both law and culture allow professionals such as doctors and lawyers to receive monetary compensation and sometimes allow the broker of the surrogacy arrangement to get paid as well. Each of these intermediaries spends a few hours working for their money, yet the mother spends a minimum of nine months, is on task twenty-four hours a day altering her nutrition and other behaviors, risking physical injury, undergoing profound emotional and hormonal changes, and also enduring extraordinary physical pain and hardship while giving birth. In both adoption and surrogacy, despite the fact that it is the birth mother doing the most work in the transaction—indeed the most dangerous, life-altering work—public policy paradoxically forbids only her from receiving payment....

Martha M. Ertman, What's Wrong with a Parenthood Market? A New and Improved Theory of Commodification, 82 N.C. L. Rev. 1 (2003).

Questions

A gay male couple in New York come to you for advice in drafting a surrogacy contract. What do you tell them? Would it be advisable for them to seek out an egg donor who is unknown and use the surrogate only for gestation? Does the New York statute determine whether the birth mother or the genetic mother is the child's mother, or, does it presume that both are?

A.H.W. v. G.H.B.
722 A.2d 948 (N.J. Super. 2000)

Koblitz, P.J.F.P.

The novel issue presented in this surrogacy matter is whether or not a court may issue a pre-birth order directing a delivering physician to list the man and woman who provided the embryo carried by a third party as legal parents on a child's birth certificate. Both the petitioning biological parents and the defendant surrogate who carried the baby agree that petitioners should be listed as the legal parents on the baby's birth certificate. However, the Attorney General's Office opposes the request of the biological parents for a pre-birth order claiming the relief is contrary to the law prohibiting surrender of a birth mother's rights until seventy-two hours after birth, and the public policy of the State of New Jersey as expressed by the New Jersey Supreme Court in *In re Baby M* (1988). After considering case law and statutes in other states as well as New Jersey, this Court denies plaintiffs and the defendant surrogate's request for a pre-birth order, but will issue an order which allows the petitioning biological parents' names to be placed on the birth certificate after the seventy-two hour statutory waiting period has expired but before the birth certificate must be filed. To understand this unusual relief, the facts of this case must be explored, then a review of other states' law in this area, followed by a consideration of New Jersey case law, public policy implications and statutes.

FACTS

G.H.B., hereinafter "Gina," is the unmarried sister of plaintiff A.H.W., "Andrea," and the sister-in-law of P.W., "Peter." The biological parents, Andrea and Peter, entered into a gestational surrogacy contract with Gina. Gina, without financial compensation, agreed to have embryos implanted into her uterus that were created from the sperm of her brother-in-law, Peter, and the ova of her sister, Andrea. This medical procedure is commonly referred to as "ovum implantation," and permits a woman who is incapable of carrying a baby to term to have a child who is genetically related to her. The child is due to be born in about two weeks at a Bergen County hospital.

Plaintiffs filed a complaint to declare the maternity and paternity of unborn Baby A. Plaintiffs seek a pre-birth order establishing them as the legal mother and father of unborn Baby A, and placing their names on the child's birth certificate. They argue that a pre-birth order is appropriate with a gestational surrogacy.

Gestational surrogacy and surrogate motherhood are the two currently recognized forms of surrogacy arrangements. A "surrogate mother" is the genetic mother and gives birth to a child formed from her ova and either the sperm of the husband of an infertile couple, or that of a sperm donor. The husband has a biological link with the child if his sperm is used, and his wife has the opportunity to adopt and raise the child. The wife has no genetic relationship to the baby. In contrast, a surrogacy arrangement involving a "gestational carrier" is one where there is no genetic relationship between the woman giving birth and the fetus. *R.R. v. M.H., D.H.* 689 N.E.2d 790, 795 (Mass. 1998).

Rather, the gestational surrogate carries embryos fertilized by both the husband and wife of an infertile couple. *See id.* Gestational surrogacy, unlike surrogate motherhood, gives the wife of an infertile couple the opportunity to be biologically related to the baby and ensures that the woman who gives birth is not genetically linked to the child.

LAW FROM OTHER STATES

Plaintiffs argue that an order should be issued pre-birth as requested because the gestational carrier has no biological link or legal rights to the fetus. In support of their position, plaintiffs cite to surrogacy procedures authorizing pre-birth orders utilized in California and Massachusetts, where the courts have dealt with the issue and in Florida, where gestational surrogacy is governed by statute.

The first case in California regarding gestational surrogacy contracts is *Johnson v. Calvert*, 851 P.2d 776, *cert denied* 510 U.S. 874, *cert. dismissed* 510 U.S. 938 (1993). In that case, Mr. and Mrs. Calvert were approached by Ms. Johnson who volunteered to act as a surrogate after learning from a mutual acquaintance of Mrs. Calvert's inability to carry a baby. The parties entered into a contract which provided that Ms. Johnson would carry to term an embryo fertilized with Mr. Calvert's sperm and Mrs. Calvert's egg. *Id.* Ms. Johnson agreed to relinquish all parental rights to the couple who in turn would raise the child. As consideration, the Calverts agreed to pay Johnson $10,000 and to obtain and pay for a $200,000 insurance policy on Ms. Johnson's life. *Id.* Relations between the parties deteriorated when the Calverts learned of Ms. Johnson's previous miscarriages and still births, and Ms. Johnson discovered that the Calverts never obtained the life insurance policy. Ms. Johnson demanded payment of the $10,000 and threatened to keep the baby if the Calvert's did not pay. Both parties filed petitions with the court seeking to be declared the legal parents of the unborn child. *Id.* Mrs. Calvert and Ms. Johnson both claimed to be the baby's natural mother. The baby was born while the litigation was still pending and blood tests conclusively showed that Mrs. Calvert and not Ms. Johnson was the baby's mother.

The California Supreme Court ruled that a gestational surrogate has no parental rights to the child she carries because the infant is not genetically linked to her. The Court gave substantial weight to the fact that the parties intended to bring about the birth of an infant by means of a surrogacy arrangement, and not to donate an embryo to Ms. Johnson. The Calverts "affirmatively intended the birth of the child, and took the steps necessary to effect in vitro fertilization. But for their acted-on intention, the child would not exist." *Id.* Though Ms. Johnson's decision to carry the baby was necessary to facilitate the Calverts' intent, she would not have had the opportunity to gestate the embryo had she manifested an intent to keep the baby. *Id.* The Court concluded that the legal mother is the woman who intended to bring about the conception of the baby with the intent to raise him/her. *Id.* The issue of a pre-birth order was moot in *Calvert* as the litigation concluded after the birth of the child.

Like California and New Jersey, Massachusetts has no statute directly addressing the issuance of pre-birth orders. Only two reported Massachusetts cases address gestational surrogacy, and while neither case is completely on point with the situation presented here, at least one of the decisions implicitly permitted the issuance of a pre-birth order. In *R.R. v. M.H. & another*, 689 N.E.2d 790 (1998), the Supreme Judicial Court of Massachusetts held that the parties' surrogate contract was invalid because it forced the mother to give up custody of the baby prior to its birth. In a footnote, the Court distinguished traditional surrogacy from gestational surrogacy, stating that the two involved different considerations and noted that the gestational surrogate is not the mother of the child she carries.

One year later in *Smith v. Brown*, 718 N.E.2d 844 (1999), the Supreme Judicial Court of Massachusetts permitted the Probate and Family Court's decision to issue a pre-birth order in a gestational surrogacy situation to stand. *Id.* While not addressing the issue of pre-birth orders directly, the Court did comment that the procedure used by the Probate and Family Court to enter the pre-birth order was technically incorrect and so implicitly ratified the entry of the pre-birth order while not endorsing the method of entry.

Unlike Massachusetts, California and New Jersey, in Florida gestational surrogacy is governed by statute. A valid gestational surrogacy contract must comply with the statute's stringent procedural requirements. Valid contracts must include a provision stating that either the commissioning mother is unable physically to gestate a pregnancy to term; or that gestation will cause a risk to the health of the commissioning mother or fetus. F.S.A. §742.15(2)(a)(b)&(c). The contract must recite that the gestational surrogate will be the only one with the power to consent to clinical intervention in the pregnancy, but that she will agree to submit to reasonable medical evaluation and treatment. F.S.A. §742.15(3)(a)&(b). The commissioning couple must also agree to accept responsibility for the child after birth even if the baby is born with impairments so long as one of the commissioning parents is the genetic parent. If neither commissioning parent is the genetic parent of the infant, the gestational carrier must accept responsibility for the baby. The surrogate mother may receive reasonable living, legal and medical expenses. F.S.A. §742.15(4).

F.S.A. §742.16 governs the procedure for affirming the genetic parents' status and requires the commissioning couple to file a petition with the court within three days after the birth of a child for an expedited affirmation of parental status. A hearing is held after noticing the woman who carried the baby, any person claiming paternity and the treating doctor from the assisted reproductive technology facility. The primary purpose of the hearing is to determine the validity of the gestational surrogacy contract, and to ensure that at least one member of the commissioning couple is the genetic parent of the baby. Once the court determines that the contract is valid and one commissioning parent is the genetic parent, the court must issue an order naming the commissioning parents as the baby's legal parents. The Court then issues a second order directing the Department of Health to seal the original birth certificate and issue a new one listing the genetic parents as the legal parents of the infant. Thus, Florida's statutory scheme does not permit the issuance of pre-birth orders although it does permit gestational surrogacy.

Several states ban surrogacy contracts as contrary to public policy regardless of whether the woman carrying the baby is compensated or not. These include New York, Utah, Michigan and Arizona. *See,N.Y. Dom. Rel. Law* §123, *Utah Code Ann.* §76-7-204(1)(d), *Mich. Comp. Laws Ann.* §722.855, *Ariz. Rev. Stat. Ann.* §25-218(A). Washington, Louisiana, Nebraska and Kentucky prohibit by statute surrogacy contracts which include a compensation element. *Wash. Rev. Code Ann* §§ 26.26.230-26.26.240, *La. Rev. Stat. Ann.* §9:2713, *Neb. Rev. Stat.* §§ 25-21, 200, *Ky. Rev. Stat. Ann.* § 199.590. However, courts in these states may in the future permit gestational surrogacy agreements where, as is the case here, there is no compensation given to the woman carrying the baby.

New Jersey Case Law

The New Jersey Supreme Court dealt with the issue of surrogate motherhood agreements in the landmark case of *In re Baby M, supra.* In *Baby M,* Mr. and Mrs. Stern entered into a contract with Mrs. Whitehead who agreed, for a fee of $10,000, to be artificially inseminated with Mr. Stern's sperm and, upon giving birth, terminate her parental rights so that Mrs. Stern could adopt the child. Litigation ensued when Mrs. Whitehead refused to give up the baby.

The Court, in an opinion written by Chief Justice Wilentz, ruled that the surrogacy contract was void because it was contrary to public policy and in direct conflict with then existing laws. The Court found that there was "coercion of contract" because Mrs. Whitehead was forced to give up her child irrevocably prior to conception. Justice Wilentz wrote that "(t)he whole purpose and effect of the surrogacy contract was to give the father the exclusive right to the child by destroying the rights of the mother."

Perhaps most troubling to the Court was that Mrs. Whitehead was to be paid a $10,000 fee by the Sterns for providing the ova and carrying the baby to term. Likening the parties' contract to "baby-bartering," the Court expressed its doubt that surrogacy arrangements would continue in the absence of compensation. Chief Justice Wilentz opined that paid surrogacy contracts exploit a woman's financial need by providing her with economic aid in exchange for her child. "Whatever idealism may have motivated any of the participants, the profit motive predominates, permeates, and ultimately governs the transaction." *Id.* The Court emphasized that it found "no offense to our present laws where a woman voluntarily and without payment agrees to act as a surrogate mother, provided that she is not subject to a binding agreement to surrender her child." Here a pre-birth order would bind Gina to surrendering the baby upon its birth.

Public Policy and Statutes

The biological parents, Andrea and Peter, and the gestational surrogate, Gina, argue that Gina has no biological ties to the unborn child and liken the gestational carrier's role to that of an incubator. They argue that *Baby M* is distinguishable because the surrogate mother in that case was also the biological mother. While Andrea, Peter and Gina are correct that Gina will have no biological ties to the baby, their simplistic comparison to an incubator disregards the fact that there are human emotions and biological changes involved in pregnancy.

A bond is created between a gestational mother and the baby she carries in her womb for nine months. During the pregnancy, the fetus relies on the gestational mother for a myriad of contributions. A gestational mother's endocrine system determines the timing, amount and components of hormones that affect the fetus. The absence of any component at its appropriate time will irreversibly alter the life, mental capacity, appearance, susceptibility to disease and structure of the fetus forever. The gestational mother contributes an endocrine cascade that determines how the child will grow, when its cells will divide and differentiate in the womb, and how the child will appear and function for the rest of its life.

In this case, Gina has previously had one child and therefore had an understanding of what is involved in carrying a pregnancy to term at the time she signed the contract. The problem case will present itself when a gestational mother changes her mind and wishes to keep the newborn. This may be more likely where a gestational mother has never had a child and is unfamiliar with the emotions and biological changes involved in a pregnancy. She will not be able to predict what her feelings will be towards the child she bears. Her body will undergo significant changes and she will continue to react biologically as any other birth mother. In this case, it seems likely that the transfer of the child will occur without incident due to the close family ties of the parties and Gina's previous experience with childbirth. However, although Gina is extremely likely to surrender her rights as planned, she must not be compelled to do so in a pre-birth order.

New Jersey regulations governing the creation of birth records state that the woman who gives birth must be recorded as a parent on the birth certificate. N.J.A.C. 8:2-1.4(a). This regulation would normally necessitate that Gina's name be placed on the birth certificate along with her brother-in-law, Peter, as the father. However, all parties have agreed by written contract that Andrea and Peter's names should be placed on the birth certificate.

In New Jersey, a birth certificate must be issued and filed within five days of birth with the local registrar of the district in which the birth occurred. Pursuant to N.J.S.A. 26:8-30, "the attending physician, midwife or person acting as the agent of the physician or midwife, who was in attendance upon the birth shall be responsible for the proper execution and return of a certificate of birth."

In recognition of the emotional and physical changes in the mother which occur at birth, voluntary surrenders are not valid if taken within seventy-two hours after the birth of the child. Thus after seventy-two hours have elapsed, Gina will be able to lawfully surrender her parental rights. She will have the responsibility of making decisions for the child during this seventy-two hour period, even if her ultimate decision is to surrender her parental rights.

It is not necessary now to determine what parental rights, if any, the gestational mother may have vis-a-vis the newborn infant. That decision will have to be made if and when a gestational mother attempts to keep the infant after birth in violation of the prior agreement. Here, Gina, Peter and Andrea are closely related. The parties' detailed fifteen page agreement clearly reflects their shared intent and desired outcome for this case. Further, Gina, as Andrea's sister and Peter's sister-in-law knows the biological parents intimately and is in an excellent position to know the type of home they will provide for the child. Thus almost certainly Gina will honor the contract and surrender her rights.

CONCLUSION

The Legislature may well choose to clarify the rights and responsibilities of parties in a gestational surrogacy. The most prudent course, prior to legislative action, is to follow the current statutes as closely as possible while allowing the parties, to the maximum extent possible, the relief requested. A court order for the pre-birth termination of the pregnant defendant's parental rights is the equivalent of making her subject to a binding agreement to surrender the child and is contrary to New Jersey statutes and *Baby M*. Therefore, the gestational mother may surrender the child seventy-two hours after giving birth, which is forty-eight hours before the birth certificate must be prepared. If Gina does choose to surrender the infant, and she certifies that she wishes to relinquish all rights, then the original birth certificate will list the two biological parents, Andrea and Peter, as the baby's parents. If Gina changes her mind once the baby is born, she will have a chance to litigate for parental rights to the child.

The attending physician who delivers Baby A should prepare a Certificate of Parentage four days after the birth of the child. This waiting period will allow Gina to surrender her parental rights after seventy-two hours and also allow a birth certificate to be issued within five days of birth. After Gina surrenders any parental rights she might have, the Certificate of Parentage shall be completed with Peter as the legal father and Andrea the legal mother. This solution represents a modification of the agreement between the parties to the least extent necessary to comply with current New Jersey statutes and the public policy concerns expressed by the Supreme Court in *Baby M*.

Questions

1. Is the New Jersey court holding that, at the time of birth, this child will have two mothers?

2. If you are a lawyer in New Jersey and a gay couple from New York comes to see you about drafting a surrogacy contract, will you take the case? What sort of terms would you put in the contract? See Susan French Appleton, Surrogacy Arrangements and the Conflict of Laws, 1990 Wis. L. Rev. 399.

3. If a gay male couple from New York comes to your New York office, can you refer them to a lawyer in New Jersey?

Further Reading on Reproductive Technology

Lori B. Andrews, The Clone Age: Adventures in the New World of Reproductive Technology (Henry Holt 2000).

Susan French Appleton, Adoption in the Age of Reproductive Technology, 2004 U. Chi. Legal F. 393.

Janet L. Dolgin, An Emerging Consensus: Reproductive Technology and the Law, 23 Vt. L. Rev. 225 (1998).

Marsha Garrison, Law Making for Baby Making: An Interpretive Approach to the Determination of Legal Parentage, 113 Harv. L. Rev. 835 (2000).

Nancy G. Maxwell and Caroline J. Forder, The Inadequacies in U.S. and Dutch Adoption Law to Establish Same-Sex Couples as Legal Parents: A Call for Recognizing Intentional Parenthood, 38 Fam. L. Q. 623 (2004).

John A. Robertson, Children of Choice: Freedom and the New Reproductive Technologies (Princeton 1994).

Marjorie Maguire Shultz, Reproductive Technology and Intent-Based Parenthood: An Opportunity for Gender Neutrality, 1990 Wis. L. Rev. 297.

Chapter Six

Discrimination, Fairness & Equality

A. Introduction

This chapter is concerned with legal principles governing the participation of members of sexual minorities in society. Chapter III dealt with a portion of this subject, focusing on issues of conduct and the limits of criminal law in its application to sexual behavior. Chapters IV and V dealt with another aspect of this subject, focusing on the domestic relations sphere of family relationships, both in the context of legal recognition for couples in Chapter IV and of the relationships between adults and children in Chapter V. This chapter extends the inquiry into the public sphere, with a particular emphasis on legal entitlement to formal equality and non-discrimination in the context of the workplace—governmental, military, and private sector—and other aspects of participation by sexual minorities in civil society.

The United States Constitution's 14th Amendment contains a promise of formal equality that is binding on the state and local governments under the Equal Protection Clause. By interpretation of the substantive content of the Due Process Clause of the 5th Amendment, the Supreme Court has found a similar promise of formal equality that is binding on the federal government. The meaning of the promise of Equal Protection of the Laws has already been addressed in several contexts in previous chapters. In this chapter, it will be addressed mainly by looking at the public workplace, both civilian and military, and at other situations where government policies threaten the ability of sexual minorities to participate fully in the public sphere. During the last quarter of the 20th century, the Supreme Court began to construe the Equal Protection requirement to include unequal treatment on the basis of sex or gender. The degree to which this promise extends to sexual minorities is a matter of continuing debate, as is the extent of protection against discrimination that is specifically grounded in the sexual orientation or the gender identity of the victim. First Amendment issues are also raised in some of these cases about public participation.

The federal Congress has undertaken to enforce constitutional guarantees of formal equality by passing statutes that purport to bind itself and the states and local governments (both as employers and as protectors and providers of public benefits and fora) not to discriminate in various kinds of activities on the basis of specified personal characteristics. In cases decided beginning in the last decade of the 20th century, the Supreme Court found that 11th Amendment concerns about federalism and state sovereignty stood in the way of attempts by individuals to enforce some civil rights statutory protections against their state government employers.

Congress has extended non-discrimination requirements into the private sector by virtue of its power to regulate commerce between the states, by passing a series of Civil Rights Acts, beginning shortly after the Civil War (1860–65) and continuing to recent times. The federal statute of most importance today in considering the legal rights of sexual minorities is the Civil Rights Act of 1964, which prohibits discrimination on the basis of sex in employment and various other activities. Other federal laws dealing with sex discrimination include the Housing Rights Act, the Equal Pay Act, the Violence Against Women Act, the Family and Medical Leave Act, and various statutes dealing with federal financial assistance to educational and other non-profit institutions. In some cases, the ban on discrimination is indirect, by disqualifying discriminatory institutions from being recipients of continued federal financial assistance.

Congress has yet to pass legislation expressly extending protection against discrimination on the basis of sexual orientation or gender identity, although some of the lower federal courts have found a certain degree of protection for sexual minorities under certain circumstances. By contrast, about a dozen states and scores of counties and municipal governments, together covering a substantial portion of the U.S. population, have specifically included "sexual orientation" in their civil rights laws regulating state and local government and, in many cases, private sector activities, including employment. A smaller number of state and local governments have also included "gender identity" or some equivalent term in their civil rights laws, intending to provide protection for transsexuals. These state and local laws are not, of course, binding on the federal government.

One recurring theme in this chapter is to explore the meaning of "discrimination because of sex" and to ask whether, when, and under what circumstances constitutional principles or statutory law forbidding such discrimination can be applied to the equality claims of sexual minorities. A second issue involves the interpretation of express promises of equality to sexual minorities embodied in the state and local laws mentioned above.

B. Constitutional Equality — Sexual Orientation Discrimination

The Supreme Court's first consideration on the merits of an equal protection claim raised on behalf of lesbian and gay litigants was the challenge to Colorado Amendment 2 in *Romer v. Evans*. That opinion is found in Chapter 1, and should be reviewed again at the end of Part 1 of this section. The meaning of *Romer v. Evans* remains contested ground a decade later, and even more contested is the meaning of *Romer* in light of the Supreme Court's 2003 decision in *Lawrence v. Texas*. In Chapter 2, we explored the reaction of the 11th Circuit Court of Appeals to an equal protection claim in a challenge to Florida's statutory ban on the adoption of children by "homosexuals" in the *Lofton* case. In Chapter 3, we considered the Kansas Court of Appeals' consideration of an equality claim by a teenager who asserted that his sentence for sexual misbehavior was unfair, in the *Limon* case. In both cases, the courts asserted that the correct standard for evaluating government action that discriminates on the basis of sexual orientation is the rationality test, the test that is used when discrimination does not involve a suspect classification or a fundamental right. Thus, the questions whether "sexual orientation" or "gender identity" should be considered suspect classifications, which the Supreme Court did not explicitly address in *Romer*, or whether discrimination claims by sexual minorities are entitled to some form of "heightened scrutiny" in the judicial review process, remain important questions, not yet definitively answered by the high court.

In its most revealing discussion of the criteria for determining that a particular classification is "suspect" or otherwise subject to "heightened scrutiny," the Supreme Court was considering whether a municipality could adopt a special zoning permit requirement applicable only to group homes for mentally retarded adults. The Court decided in *City of Cleburne v. Cleburne Living Center*, 473 U.S. 432 (1985), that mental disability was not a suspect classification, but nonetheless struck down the special zoning requirement, finding that the city's sole justification for it was fear and dislike for persons with mental disabilities. The Court had this to say on the general question of how to determine whether a classification is suspect:

> The Equal Protection Clause of the Fourteenth Amendment commands that no State shall "deny to any person within its jurisdiction the equal protection of the laws," which is essentially a direction that all persons similarly situated should be treated alike. Section 5 of the Amendment empowers Congress to enforce this mandate, but absent controlling congressional direction, the courts have themselves devised standards for determining the validity of state legislation or other official action that is challenged as denying equal protection. The general rule is that legislation is presumed to be valid and will be sustained if the classification drawn by the statute is rationally related to a legitimate state interest. When social or economic legislation is at issue, the Equal Protection Clause allows the States wide latitude, and the Constitution presumes that even improvident decisions will eventually be rectified by the democratic processes.

> The general rule gives way, however, when a statute classifies by race, alienage, or national origin. These factors are so seldom relevant to the achievement of any legitimate state interest that laws grounded in such considerations are deemed to reflect prejudice and antipathy—a view that those in the burdened class are not as worthy or deserving as others. For these reasons and because such discrimination is unlikely to be soon rectified by legislative means, these laws are subjected to strict scrutiny and will be sustained only if they are suitably tailored to serve a compelling state interest. Similar oversight by the courts is due when state laws impinge on personal rights protected by the Constitution.

> Legislative classifications based on gender also call for a heightened standard of review. That factor generally provides no sensible ground for differential treatment. "[W]hat differentiates sex from such nonsuspect statuses as intelligence or physical disability...is that the sex characteristic frequently bears no relation to ability to perform or contribute to society." Rather than resting on meaningful considerations, statutes distributing benefits and burdens between the sexes in different ways very likely reflect outmoded notions of the relative capabilities of men and women. A gender classification fails unless it is substantially related to a sufficiently important governmental interest. Because illegitimacy is beyond the individual's control and bears "no relation to the individual's ability to participate in and contribute to society," official discriminations resting on that characteristic are also subject to somewhat

heightened review. Those restrictions "will survive equal protection scrutiny to the extent they are substantially related to a legitimate state interest."

We have declined, however, to extend heightened review to differential treatment based on age:

> "While the treatment of the aged in this Nation has not been wholly free of discrimination, such persons, unlike, say, those who have been discriminated against on the basis of race or national origin, have not experienced a 'history of purposeful unequal treatment' or been subjected to unique disabilities on the basis of stereotyped characteristics not truly indicative of their abilities."

> The lesson…is that where individuals in the group affected by a law have distinguishing characteristics relevant to interests the State has the authority to implement, the courts have been very reluctant, as they should be in our federal system and with our respect for the separation of powers, to closely scrutinize legislative choices as to whether, how, and to what extent those interests should be pursued. In such cases, the Equal Protection Clause requires only a rational means to serve a legitimate end.

The Court went on to find that "mental disability" was not a suspect classification, but that fears and misconceptions about people with mental disabilities could not serve as legitimate justifications for the special zoning permit requirement, and that the city had articulated no other plausible reasons for the requirement. Some commentators questioned whether this was a traditional application of rationality review, inasmuch as the city had articulated concerns about locating a home for the mentally disabled on a flood plain for safety reasons, and such a justification would probably be sufficient to sustain the unequal treatment under traditional notions of rationality review. As a result, some characterized this ruling as a new variety of rationality review "with teeth" and speculated about whether other classifications could merit similarly somewhat heightened scrutiny.

1. The pre-*Romer* cases

Many of the federal appellate opinions containing extensive discussion of what level of scrutiny to give to official anti-gay policies were decided before *Romer v. Evans*. Following are excerpts from the leading opinions.

Padula v. Webster
822 F.2d 97 (D.C.Cir. 1987)

SILBERMAN, Circuit Judge:

[The case involves a lesbian, Margaret A. Padula, who had applied for a position as an agent with the Federal Bureau of Investigation (FBI), a law enforcement agency within the U.S. Department of Justice. Padula's application was rejected after the FBI's investigation of her background yielded evidence that she was a lesbian who lived with a same-sex partner. Padula was apparently otherwise qualified for employment in this position under the standards then being applied by the agency. She sued, claiming that rejection of her application on this ground violated her right to Equal Protection under the 5th Amendment. In an opinion issued one year after the Supreme Court's ruling in *Bowers v. Hardwick*, the court analyzed Padula's equal protection claim as follows:]

III.

…We perceive ostensible disagreement between the parties as to the description of the class in question. The government insists the FBI's hiring policy focuses only on homosexual conduct, not homosexual status. By that, we understand the government to be saying that it would not consider relevant for employment purposes homosexual orientation that did not result in homosexual conduct. Plaintiff rejects that distinction, suggesting that "homosexual status is accorded to people who engage in homosexual conduct, and people who engage in homosexual conduct are accorded homosexual status." But whether or not homosexual status attaches to someone who does not—for whatever reason—engage in homosexual conduct, appellant does not claim those circumstances apply to her. The parties' definitional disagreement is therefore irrelevant.

The Supreme Court has used several explicit criteria to identify suspect and quasi-suspect classifications. In *San Antonio School Dist. v. Rodriguez*, the Court stated that a suspect class is one "saddled with such disabilities, or subjected to such a history of purposeful unequal treatment, or relegated to such a position of political powerlessness as to command extraordinary protection from the majoritarian political process." The immutability of the group's identifying trait is also a factor to be considered. See *Frontiero v. Richardson*, 411 U.S. 677, 686 (1973). However, the Supreme Court has recognized only three classifications as suspect: race, alienage, and national origin; and two others as quasi-suspect: gender, and illegitimacy. Appellant, asserting that homosexuals meet all the requisite criteria, would have us add homosexuality to that list. Appellees, on the other hand, contend that two recent cases, *Bowers v. Hardwick*, 106 S.Ct. 2841 (1986) and *Dronenburg v. Zech*, 741 F.2d 1388 (D.C.Cir.1984), are insurmountable barriers to appellant's claim. We agree.

In Dronenburg, a naval petty officer claimed violation of his constitutional rights to privacy and to equal protection of the laws because he was discharged from the Navy for engaging in homosexual conduct. A panel of this court rejected the claim, holding that "we can find no constitutional right to engage in homosexual conduct and, as judges, we have no warrant to create one." Although the court's opinion focused primarily on whether the constitutional right to privacy protected homosexual conduct, the court reasoned that if the right to privacy did not provide protection "then appellant's right to equal protection is not infringed unless the Navy's policy is not rationally related to a permissible end." The unique needs of the military, the court concluded, justified discharge for homosexual conduct. Dronenburg anticipated by two years the Supreme Court's decision in *Hardwick*.

Padula argues that both *Dronenburg* and *Hardwick* are inapposite because they addressed only the scope of the privacy right, not what level of scrutiny is appropriate under equal protection analysis. But as we have noted, Dronenburg did involve an equal protection claim. Although the court did not explicitly consider whether homosexuals should be treated as a suspect class, it seemed to regard that question settled by its conclusion that the Constitution does not afford a privacy right to engage in homosexual conduct. In *Hardwick*, to be sure, plaintiffs did not rely on the equal protection clause, but after the Court rejected an extension of the right to privacy, it responded to plaintiffs' alternate argument that the Georgia law should be struck down as without rational basis (under the due process clause) since it was predicated merely on the moral judg-ment of a majority of the Georgia electorate. The Court summarily rejected that posi-tion, refusing to declare the Georgian majoritarian view "inadequate" to meet a rational basis test. We therefore think the courts' reasoning in *Hardwick* and *Dronenburg* fore-closes appellant's efforts to gain suspect class status for practicing homosexuals. It would be quite anomalous, on its face, to declare status defined by conduct that states may constitutionally criminalize as deserving of strict scrutiny under the equal protec-tion clause. More importantly, in all those cases in which the Supreme Court has ac-corded suspect or quasi-suspect status to a class, the Court's holding was predicated on an unarticulated, but necessarily implicit, notion that it is plainly unjustifiable (in ac-cordance with standards not altogether clear to us) to discriminate invidiously against the particular class. If the Court was unwilling to object to state laws that criminalize the behavior that defines the class, it is hardly open to a lower court to conclude that state sponsored discrimination against the class is invidious. After all, there can hardly be more palpable discrimination against a class than making the conduct that defines the class criminal.

That does not mean, however, that any kind of negative state action against homo-sexuals would be constitutionally authorized. Laws or government practices must still, if challenged, pass the rational basis test.

The FBI, as the Bureau points out, is a national law enforcement agency whose agents must be able to work in all the states of the nation. To have agents who engage in conduct criminalized in roughly one-half of the states would undermine the law en-forcement credibility of the Bureau. Perhaps more important, FBI agents perform counterintelligence duties that involve highly classified matters relating to national secu-rity. It is not irrational for the Bureau to conclude that the criminalization of homosex-ual conduct coupled with the general public opprobrium toward homosexuality ex-poses many homosexuals, even "open" homosexuals, to the risk of possible blackmail to protect their partners, if not themselves. We therefore conclude the Bureau's specialized functions, like the Navy's in Dronenburg, rationally justify consideration of homosex-ual conduct that could adversely affect that agency's responsibilities.

High Tech Gays v. Defense Industrial Security Clearance Office
895 F.2d 563 (9th Cir. 1990)

[The case involved a challenge by an organization of professional and technical employ-ees to the procedures used by the defendant, an agency within the U.S. Department of Defense, to determine whether security clearances should be issued to prospective em-ployees of defense contractors. If the agency's investigation of a security clearance appli-cant revealed evidence of homosexuality, the application would trigger a second, much more prolonged investigation to determine whether the individual's conduct raised is-sues relevant to national security. The agency's purported main concern was about the possibility that gay employees could be blackmailed by agents of foreign powers. Re-member that these policies were devised during the Cold War when concerns about for-eign spying and espionage, especially in defense industries, were quite real. By the time the 9th Circuit issued its opinion in this case, the Soviet Union had collapsed and the Cold War was drawing to a close, but the concerns about spying and espionage re-mained real. The acronym generally used to refer to the defendant, DISCO, results in the amusing, and somewhat bizarre name by which this case is generally known: *High Tech Gays v. DISCO.*]

BRUNETTI, Circuit Judge:

...In analyzing the equal protection challenge, the district court concluded that "gay people are a 'quasi-suspect class' entitled to heightened scrutiny," and that the DoD security clearance regulations "must withstand strict scrutiny because they impinge upon the right of lesbians and gay men to engage in any homosexual activity, not merely sodomy, and thus impinge upon their exercise of a fundamental right." The district court rejected the reasons proffered by the DoD to justify its policies and found the absence of even a "rational basis for defendants' subjecting all gay applicants to expanded investigations and mandatory adjudications while not doing the same for all straight applicants." The district court therefore concluded that the DoD policy violates the Constitution and granted summary judgment to the plaintiffs...

III.

Equal Protection

In *Bolling v. Sharpe*, 347 U.S. 497 (1954), the Supreme Court held that while the Equal Protection Clause of the Fourteenth Amendment prohibited states from maintaining racially segregated public schools, only the Fifth Amendment, not the Fourteenth, was applicable in the District of Columbia. The Court noted that the Fifth Amendment "does not contain an equal protection clause as does the Fourteenth Amendment which applies only to the states," and held that racial segregation in the District of Columbia public schools violated the Due Process Clause of the Fifth Amendment. The Court believed that in light of their decision in *Brown* that the Constitution prohibits states from maintaining racially segregated schools, "it would be unthinkable that the same Constitution would impose a lesser duty on the Federal Government." The Court also noted that

> the concepts of equal protection and due process, both stemming from our American ideal of fairness, are not mutually exclusive. The "equal protection of the laws" is a more explicit safeguard of prohibited unfairness than "due process of law," and, therefore, we do not imply that the two are always interchangeable phrases. [However], discrimination may be so unjustifiable as to be violative of due process.

It is thus clear that there is an equal protection component of the Due Process Clause of the Fifth Amendment which applies to the federal government.

In this case, the plaintiffs challenge the validity of the DoD Security Clearance Regulations under the equal protection component of the Fifth Amendment; specifically, that the DoD security clearance regulations discriminate against gay people. In considering such Fifth Amendment claims, the Supreme Court has held:

> While the Fifth Amendment contains no equal protection clause, it does forbid discrimination that is so unjustifiable as to be violative of due process. This Court's approach to Fifth Amendment equal protection claims has always been precisely the same as to equal protection claims under the Fourteenth Amendment.

It is well established that there are three standards we may apply in reviewing the plaintiffs' equal protection challenge to the DoD Security Clearance Regulations: strict scrutiny, heightened scrutiny, and rational basis review. The plaintiffs assert that homosexuality should be added to the list of suspect or quasi-suspect classifications requiring strict or heightened scrutiny. We disagree and hold that the district court erred in applying heightened scrutiny to the regulations at issue and that the proper standard is rational basis review.

The Supreme Court has ruled that homosexual activity is not a fundamental right protected by substantive due process and that the proper standard of review under the Fifth Amendment is rational basis review. *Bowers v. Hardwick,* 478 U.S. 186, 194–96 (1986)...In holding that the Constitution does not confer a fundamental right upon homosexuals to engage in consensual sodomy, the Court stated:

> There should be, therefore, great resistance to expand the substantive reach of [the Due Process Clauses of the Fifth and Fourteenth Amendments], particularly if it requires redefining the category of rights deemed to be fundamental. Otherwise, the Judiciary necessarily takes to itself further authority to govern the country without express constitutional authority.

There has been a repudiation of much of the substantive gloss that the Court has placed on the Due Process Clauses of the Fifth and Fourteenth Amendments. If for federal analysis we must reach equal protection of the Fourteenth Amendment by the Due Process Clause of the Fifth Amendment, and if there is no fundamental right to engage in homosexual sodomy under the Due Process Clause of the Fifth Amendment, it would be incongruous to expand the reach of equal protection to find a fundamental right of homosexual conduct under the equal protection component of the Due Process Clause of the Fifth Amendment.

Other circuits are in accord and have held that although the Court in *Hardwick* analyzed the constitutionality of the sodomy statute on a due process rather than equal protection basis, by the *Hardwick* majority holding that the Constitution confers no fundamental right upon homosexuals to engage in sodomy, and because homosexual conduct can thus be criminalized, homosexuals cannot constitute a suspect or quasi-suspect class entitled to greater than rational basis review for equal protection purposes.

This court first considered equal protection and governmental classifications based on homosexuality in *Hatheway v. Secretary of Army,* 641 F.2d 1376 (9th Cir.), *cert. denied,* 454 U.S. 864 (1981). In *Hatheway,* an Army lieutenant challenged his court-martial conviction for sodomy under Article 125 of the Uniform Code of Military Justice (U.C.M.J.), which makes it a crime for a service person to engage in "unnatural carnal copulation with another person of the same or opposite sex." (quoting U.C.M.J., 10 U.S.C. §925 (1976)). Hatheway contended that the convening authority prosecuted only homosexual sodomy cases, would not prosecute any cases involving heterosexual sodomy, and thus violated his constitutional rights.

We understood Hatheway's claim to be an equal protection argument, but did not reach the question whether homosexuals were a suspect or quasi-suspect class. However, we noted that "heightened scrutiny is independently required where a classification penalizes the exercise of a fundamental right," and we applied an intermediate level of review based upon "the similarity of the interests at stake" in *Hatheway* and an earlier Fifth Amendment substantive due process case, *Beller v. Middendorf,* 632 F.2d 788 (9th Cir.1980).

> In *Beller,* in deciding whether the Navy's regulations, which provided for discharge of persons in the service engaging in homosexual activities, violated the substantive due process guarantees of the Fifth Amendment, we stated

that the case was "somewhere between" the lowest tier of equal protection scrutiny—a rational relation to a legitimate government interest—and where the government seriously intrudes into matters which deserve due process protection. We stated that in light of the authorities reviewed (at that time), the reasons which led the Supreme Court to protect certain private decisions intimately linked with one's personality suggest that some kind of government regulation of private consensual homosexual behavior may face substantial constitutional challenge. We further noted that certain cases may require resolution of whether there is a right to engage in consensual homosexual behavior, but that in the instant case (*Beller*) involving a military regulation which prohibited homosexual conduct of persons in the service, "the importance of the government interests furthered, and to some extent the relative impracticality at this time of achieving the Government's goals by regulations which turn more precisely on the facts of an individual case, outweigh whatever heightened solicitude is appropriate for consensual private homosexual conduct."

Beller has since been overruled by *Hardwick*. Because *Beller* is no longer good law, *Hatheway*'s holding that homosexual conduct is a protected fundamental right for equal protection purposes is no longer valid. Neither *Beller* nor *Hatheway* is binding authority on us regarding heightened scrutiny for classifications based on homosexuality.

There is further support for our holding that homosexuals are not a suspect or quasi-suspect class as specifically applied to the plaintiffs' challenge to the DoD Security Clearance Regulations.

The general rule is that legislation is presumed to be valid and will be sustained if the classification drawn by the statute is rationally related to a legitimate [governmental] interest....

The general rule gives way, however, when a statute classifies by race, alienage, or national origin....[B]ecause such discrimination is unlikely to be soon rectified by legislative means, these laws are subjected to strict scrutiny....

[C]lassifications based on gender also call for heightened standard of review [as do classifications based on] illegitimacy.

Cleburne, 473 U.S. at 440–41(quotation omitted).

It is apparent that while the Supreme Court has identified that legislative classifications based on race, alienage, or national origin are subject to strict scrutiny and that classifications based upon gender or illegitimacy call for a heightened standard, the Court has never held homosexuality to a heightened standard of review.

To be a "suspect" or "quasi-suspect" class, homosexuals must 1) have suffered a history of discrimination; 2) exhibit obvious, immutable, or distinguishing characteristics that define them as a discrete group; and 3) show that they are a minority or politically powerless, or alternatively show that the statutory classification at issue burdens a fundamental right. *Bowen v. Gilliard*, 483 U.S. 587, 602–3 (1987) (due to a lack of these characteristics, the statutory classifications of the Federal Aid to Families with Dependent Children Program were subject to only a rational basis review) (citing *Lyng v. Castillo*, 477 U.S. 635, 638 (1986) (due to a lack of these characteristics, the statutory classifications of the Federal Food Stamp Program were subject to only a rational basis review)).

While we do agree that homosexuals have suffered a history of discrimination, we do not believe that they meet the other criteria. Homosexuality is not an immutable characteristic; it is behavioral and hence is fundamentally different from traits such as race, gender, or alienage, which define already existing suspect and quasi-suspect classes. The behavior or conduct of such already recognized classes is irrelevant to their identification.

Moreover, legislatures have addressed and continue to address the discrimination suffered by homosexuals on account of their sexual orientation through the passage of anti-discrimination legislation. Thus, homosexuals are not without political power; they have the ability to and do "attract the attention of the lawmakers," as evidenced by such legislation. Lastly, as previously noted, homosexual conduct is not a fundamental right.

Our review compels us to agree with the other circuits that have ruled on this issue and to hold that homosexuals do not constitute a suspect or quasi-suspect class entitled to greater than rational basis scrutiny under the equal protection component of the Due Process Clause of the Fifth Amendment.

Because the district court erred in granting the plaintiffs' motion for summary judgment by applying heightened scrutiny in its equal protection analysis, we now review the plaintiffs' and defendants' cross-motions for summary judgment applying rational basis scrutiny. [The court concluded that the government's national security concerns provided a rational basis for undertaking a more probing security investigation if a clearance applicant's initial investigation revealed evidence of homosexuality. The main evidence upon which the court relied was then-recent hearing testimony in a Congressional investigation about attempts by female foreign agents to seduce male American service personnel providing security at U.S. embassies in Europe.]

Watkins v. United States Army
875 F.2d 699 (9th Cir. en banc, 1989),
cert. denied, 498 U.S. 957 (1990).

[The case involved Perry Watkins, who enlisted in the U.S. Army during the Vietnam War, decided to remain in the peacetime Army as a career officer, and was denied re-enlistment on grounds of homosexuality twice during the 1980s. Watkins had a sterling record of performance as an Army supply clerk, winning numerous commendations, and was also renowned throughout the service as a premiere "drag" performer at Army talent shows. Watkins in a dress was, reportedly, something quite special, and his commanding officers commended his performances. When he first enlisted, he checked "yes" on the recruitment form in response to the question whether he had any "homosexual tendencies" but such a response without supporting documentation from a psychiatrist would not prevent enlistment during the Vietnam War years, and only became an issue later on when certain commanders felt duty-bound to enforce military regulations, which had changed substantially in 1980 to eliminate discretion to retain highly valued "homosexual" service members. Watkins' case was considered numerous times by the district court and the court of appeals. After a three-judge panel had ruled that the Army's anti-gay policies violated the Equal Protection Clause, the government's petition for en banc rehearing was granted and an eleven-judge panel of the 9th Circuit was convened. The en banc panel affirmed the three-judge panel's order to allow Watkins to re-enlist, but on grounds that the Army was equitably estopped by its prior conduct in allowing Watkins to serve for many years. The court was undoubtedly swayed by the fact that Watkins needed just a few more years of service to qualify for a full military pension, and by the likelihood that the Army would settled the case by offering cash to Watkins in order to get him to withdraw his re-enlistment papers, as actually happened. Judge William Norris, who was the author of the three-judge panel opinion, filed a concurrence, reiterating his view that sexual orientation classifications are suspect and that the military policy was unconstitutional.]

Norris, J., concurring in the result:

... The Supreme Court has identified several factors that guide our suspect class inquiry. The first factor the Supreme Court generally considers is whether the group at issue has suffered a history of purposeful discrimination. As the Army concedes, it is indisputable that "homosexuals have historically been the object of pernicious and sustained hostility." Discrimination against homosexuals has been pervasive in both the public and private sectors. Legislative bodies have excluded homosexuals from certain jobs and schools, and have prevented homosexual marriage. In the private sphere, homosexuals continue to face discrimination in jobs, housing and churches. Moreover, reports of violence against homosexuals have become commonplace in our society. In sum, the discrimination faced by homosexuals is plainly no less pernicious or intense than the discrimination faced by other groups already treated as suspect classes.

The second factor that the Supreme Court considers in suspect class analysis is difficult to capsulize and may in fact represent a cluster of factors grouped around a central idea — whether the discrimination embodies a gross unfairness that is sufficiently inconsistent with the ideals of equal protection to term it "invidious." Consideration of this additional factor makes sense. After all, discrimination exists against some groups because the animus is warranted — no one could seriously argue that burglars form a suspect class. In giving content to this concept of gross unfairness, the Court has considered (1) whether the disadvantaged class is defined by a trait that "frequently bears no relation to ability to perform or contribute to society," (2) whether the class has been saddled with unique disabilities because of prejudice or inaccurate stereotypes; and (3) whether the trait defining the class is immutable.

Sexual orientation plainly has no relevance to a person's "ability to perform or contribute to society." Sergeant Watkins' exemplary record of military service stands as a testament to quite the opposite. This irrelevance of sexual orientation to the quality of a person's contribution to society also suggests that classifications based on sexual orientation reflect prejudice and inaccurate stereotypes — the second indicium of a classification's gross unfairness. I agree with Justice Brennan that "discrimination against homosexuals is 'likely... to reflect deep-seated prejudice rather than... rationality.'" *Rowland*, 470 U.S. at 1014 (Brennan, J., dissenting from denial of cert.).

The Army suggests that the opprobrium directed towards gays does not constitute prejudice in the pejorative sense of the word, but rather is simply appropriate public disapproval of persons who engage in immoral behavior. The Army equates homosexuals with sodomists and justifies its regulations as simply reflecting a rational bias against a class of persons who engage in criminal acts of sodomy. In essence, the Army argues that homosexuals, like burglars, cannot form a suspect class because they are criminals. The Army's argument rests on two false premises. First, as I have noted throughout this opinion, the class burdened by the regulations at issue in this case is defined by the sexual orientation of its members, not by their sexual conduct. Any attempt to criminalize the status of an individual's sexual orientation would present grave constitutional problems. See generally *Robinson v. California*, 370 U.S. 660 (1962).

Second, little of the homosexual conduct covered by the regulations is criminal. The regulations reach many forms of homosexual conduct other than sodomy such as kissing, hand-holding, caressing, and hand-genital contact. Yet, sodomy is the only consensual adult sexual conduct that Congress has criminalized. Indeed, the Army points to no law, federal or state, which criminalizes any form of private consensual homosexual behavior other than sodomy. The Army's argument that its regulations merely ban a class of criminals might be relevant, although not necessarily persuasive, if the class at issue were limited to sodomists. But the class banned from Army service is not comprised of sodomists.

Finally, I turn to immutability as an indicator of gross unfairness. The Supreme Court has never held that only classes with immutable traits can be deemed suspect. I nonetheless consider immutability because the Supreme Court has often focused on immutability, and has sometimes described the recognized suspect classes as having immutable traits. It is clear that by "immutability" the Court has never meant strict immutability in the sense that members of the class must be physically unable to change or mask the trait defining their class. People can have operations to change their sex. Aliens can ordinarily become naturalized citizens. The status of illegitimate children can be changed. People can frequently hide their national origin by changing their customs, their names, or their associations. Lighter skinned blacks can sometimes "pass" for white, as can Latinos for Anglos, and some people can even change their racial appearance with pigment injections. At a minimum, then, the Supreme Court is willing to treat a trait as effectively immutable if changing it would involve great difficulty, such as requiring a major physical change or a traumatic change of identity. "Immutability" may describe those traits that are so central to a person's identity that it would be abhorrent for government to penalize a person for refusing to change them, regardless of how easy that change might be physically. Racial discrimination, for example, would not suddenly become constitutional if medical science developed an easy, cheap, and painless method of changing one's skin pigment.

With these principles in mind, I have no trouble concluding that sexual orientation is immutable for the purposes of equal protection doctrine. Although the causes of homosexuality are not fully understood, scientific research indicates that we have little control over our sexual orientation and that, once acquired, our sexual orientation is largely impervious to change. Scientific proof aside, it seems appropriate to ask whether heterosexuals feel capable of changing their sexual orientation. Would heterosexuals living in a city that passed an ordinance burdening those who engaged in or desired to engage in sex with persons of the opposite sex find it easy not only to abstain from heterosexual activity but also to shift the object of their sexual desires to persons of the same sex? It may be that some heterosexuals and homosexuals can change their sexual orientation through extensive therapy, neurosurgery or shock treatment. But the possibility of such a difficult and traumatic change does not make sexual orientation "mutable" for equal protection purposes. I conclude that allowing the government to penalize the failure to change such a central aspect of individual and group identity would be abhorrent to the values animating the constitutional ideal of equal protection.

The final factor the Supreme Court considers in suspect class analysis is whether the group burdened by official discrimination lacks the political power necessary to obtain redress from the political branches. The very fact that homosexuals have historically been underrepresented in and victimized by political bodies is itself strong evidence that they lack the political power necessary to ensure fair treatment. In addition, homosexuals as a group are handicapped by structural barriers that operate to make effective political participation unlikely if not impossible.

First, the social, economic, and political pressures to conceal one's homosexuality operate to discourage gays from openly protesting anti-homosexual governmental action. Ironically, by "coming out of the closet" to protest against discriminatory legislation and practices, homosexuals expose themselves to the very discrimination they seek to eliminate. As a result, the voices of many homosexuals are not even heard, let alone counted.

Even when gays do come out of the closet to participate openly in politics, the general animus towards homosexuality may render this participation ineffective. Many heterosexuals, including elected officials, find it difficult to empathize with and take seriously the arguments advanced by homosexuals, in large part because of the lack of meaningful interaction between the heterosexual majority and the homosexual minority. Most people have little exposure to gays, both because they rarely encounter gays and because—as I noted above—homosexuals are often pressured into concealing their sexual identity. Thus, elected officials sensitive to public prejudice and ignorance, and insensitive to the needs of the homosexual constituency, may refuse to even consider legislation that even appears to be pro-homosexual. Indeed, the Army itself argues that its regulations are justified by the need to "maintain the public acceptability of military service," AR 635-200, P 15-2(a), because "toleration of homosexual conduct... might be understood as tacit approval" and "the existence of homosexual units might well be a source of ridicule and notoriety." These barriers to the exercise of political power both reinforce and are reinforced by the underrepresentation of avowed homosexuals in the decisionmaking bodies of government and the inability of homosexuals to prevent legislation hostile to their group interests.

In sum, all of the relevant factors drive me to the conclusion that homosexuals constitute a suspect class for equal protection purposes.

Notes and Questions

1. These three decisions set out the range of discussion about the question whether sexual orientation classifications should receive heightened or strict scrutiny prior to the Supreme Court's decision in *Romer v. Evans.* Did *Bowers v. Hardwick* require the lower federal courts to refrain from affording heightened or strict scrutiny to anti-gay governmental policies? Have the courts correctly conflated status and conduct in considering this issue?

2. It is noteworthy that Justice Anthony M. Kennedy, author of the Supreme Court's opinions in *Romer* and *Lawrence,* was serving as a judge of the 9th Circuit when he wrote the panel decision in *Beller v. Middendorf* that is referred to by the court in *High Tech Gays.* In *Beller,* a pre-*Hardwick* case, then-Judge Kennedy expressed the view that

in light of the Supreme Court's sexual privacy cases, it was possible that laws against sodomy were unconstitutional. Those who might assert that Kennedy had "changed" his views on gay rights after coming to serve on the Supreme Court might well be directed back to his opinion in *Beller*, which suggests that his opinions on these issues have been consistent over time.

3. In his dissent in *Romer v. Evans*, Justice Scalia argued that the Court's decision was inconsistent with *Hardwick* and had, in effect, overruled the earlier decision. If that was so, how should a court approach an equal protection claim by a gay litigant after *Romer* (but before *Lawrence*)? Following are the responses of two federal appellate courts.

* * *

At this point, you should review the Supreme Court's decision in *Romer v. Evans*, found in Chapter 1. Read the majority and dissenting opinions in light of the arguments made by the judges in the preceding cases. Has the majority dealt with the issues raised in these cases? Is the dissent correct in arguing that the Court is departing from settled precedent by adopting a new approach to equal protection without distinguishing or overruling *Bowers v. Hardwick*?

2. Post-*Romer* decisions

Nabozny v. Podlesny
92 F.3d 446 (7th Cir. 1996)

ESCHBACH, Circuit Judge.

From his birth in 1975, Jamie Nabozny lived in Ashland, Wisconsin. Throughout his childhood, adolescence, and teenaged years he attended schools owned and operated by the Ashland Public School District. In elementary school, Nabozny proved to be a good student and enjoyed a positive educational experience.

When Nabozny graduated to the Ashland Middle School in 1988, his life changed. Around the time that Nabozny entered the seventh grade, Nabozny realized that he is gay. Many of Nabozny's fellow classmates soon realized it too. Nabozny decided not to "closet" his sexuality, and considerable harassment from his fellow students ensued. Nabozny's classmates regularly referred to him as "faggot," and subjected him to various forms of physical abuse, including striking and spitting on him. Nabozny spoke to the school's guidance counselor, Ms. Peterson, about the abuse, informing Peterson that he is gay. Peterson took action, ordering the offending students to stop the harassment and placing two of them in detention. However, the students' abusive behavior toward Nabozny stopped only briefly. Meanwhile, Peterson was replaced as guidance counselor by Mr. Nowakowski. Nabozny similarly informed Nowakowski that he is gay, and asked for protection from the student harassment. Nowakowski, in turn, referred the matter to school Principal Mary Podlesny; Podlesny was responsible for school discipline.

Just before the 1988 Winter holiday, Nabozny met with Nowakowski and Podlesny to discuss the harassment. During the meeting, Nabozny explained the nature of the harassment and again revealed his homosexuality. Podlesny promised to protect Nabozny, but took no action. Following the holiday season, student harassment of

Nabozny worsened, especially at the hands of students Jason Welty and Roy Grande. Nabozny complained to Nowakowski, and school administrators spoke to the students. The harassment, however, only intensified. A short time later, in a science classroom, Welty grabbed Nabozny and pushed him to the floor. Welty and Grande held Nabozny down and performed a mock rape on Nabozny, exclaiming that Nabozny should enjoy it. The boys carried out the mock rape as twenty other students looked on and laughed. Nabozny escaped and fled to Podlesny's office. Podlesny's alleged response is somewhat astonishing; she said that "boys will be boys" and told Nabozny that if he was "going to be so openly gay," he should "expect" such behavior from his fellow students. In the wake of Podlesny's comments, Nabozny ran home. The next day Nabozny was forced to speak with a counselor, not because he was subjected to a mock rape in a classroom, but because he left the school without obtaining the proper permission. No action was taken against the students involved. Nabozny was forced to return to his regular schedule. Understandably, Nabozny was "petrified" to attend school; he was subjected to abuse throughout the duration of the school year.

The situation hardly improved when Nabozny entered the eighth grade. Shortly after the school year began, several boys attacked Nabozny in a school bathroom, hitting him and pushing his books from his hands. This time Nabozny's parents met with Podlesny and the alleged perpetrators. The offending boys denied that the incident occurred, and no action was taken. Podlesny told both Nabozny and his parents that Nabozny should expect such incidents because he is "openly" gay. Several similar meetings between Nabozny's parents and Podlesny followed subsequent incidents involving Nabozny. Each time perpetrators were identified to Podlesny. Each time Podlesny pledged to take action. And, each time nothing was done. Toward the end of the school year, the harassment against Nabozny intensified to the point that a district attorney purportedly advised Nabozny to take time off from school. Nabozny took one and a half weeks off from school. When he returned, the harassment resumed, driving Nabozny to attempt suicide. After a stint in a hospital, Nabozny finished his eighth grade year in a Catholic school.

The Catholic school attended by Nabozny did not offer classes beyond the eighth grade. Therefore, to attend the ninth grade, Nabozny enrolled in Ashland High School. Almost immediately Nabozny's fellow students sang an all too familiar tune. Early in the year, while Nabozny was using a urinal in the restroom, Nabozny was assaulted. Student Stephen Huntley struck Nabozny in the back of the knee, forcing him to fall into the urinal. Roy Grande then urinated on Nabozny. Nabozny immediately reported the incident to the principal's office. Nabozny recounted the incident to the office secretary, who in turn relayed the story to Principal William Davis. Davis ordered Nabozny to go home and change clothes. Nabozny's parents scheduled a meeting with Davis and Assistant Principal Thomas Blauert. At the meeting, the parties discussed numerous instances of harassment against Nabozny, including the restroom incident.

Rather than taking action against the perpetrators, Davis and Blauert referred Nabozny to Mr. Reeder, a school guidance counselor. Reeder was supposed to change Nabozny's schedule so as to minimize Nabozny's exposure to the offending students. Eventually the school placed Nabozny in a special education class; Stephen Huntley and Roy Grande were special education students. Nabozny's parents continued to insist that the school take action, repeatedly meeting with Davis and Blauert among others. Nabozny's parents' efforts were futile; no action was taken. In the middle of his ninth grade year, Nabozny again attempted suicide. Following another hospital stay and a period living with relatives, Nabozny ran away to Minneapolis. His parents convinced him to return to Ashland by promising that Nabozny would not have to attend Ashland High. Because Nabozny's parents were unable to afford private schooling, however, the Department of Social Services ordered Nabozny to return to Ashland High.

In tenth grade, Nabozny fared no better. Nabozny's parents moved, forcing Nabozny to rely on the school bus to take him to school. Students on the bus regularly used epithets, such as "fag" and "queer," to refer to Nabozny. Some students even pelted Nabozny with dangerous objects such as steel nuts and bolts. When Nabozny's parents complained to the school, school officials changed Nabozny's assigned seat and moved him to the front of the bus. The harassment continued. Ms. Hanson, a school guidance counselor, lobbied the school's administration to take more aggressive action to no avail. The worst was yet to come, however. One morning when Nabozny arrived early to school, he went to the library to study. The library was not yet open, so Nabozny sat down in the hallway. Minutes later he was met by a group of eight boys led by Stephen Huntley. Huntley began kicking Nabozny in the stomach, and continued to do so for five to ten minutes while the other students looked on laughing. Nabozny reported the incident to Hanson, who referred him to the school's "police liaison" Dan Crawford. Nabozny told Crawford that he wanted to press charges, but Crawford dissuaded him. Crawford promised to speak to the offending boys instead. Meanwhile, at Crawford's behest, Nabozny reported the incident to Blauert. Blauert, the school official supposedly in charge of disciplining, laughed and told Nabozny that Nabozny deserved such treatment because he is gay. Weeks later Nabozny collapsed from internal bleeding that resulted from Huntley's beating. Nabozny's parents and counselor Hanson repeatedly urged Davis and Blauert to take action to protect Nabozny. Each time aggressive action was promised. And, each time nothing was done.

Finally, in his eleventh grade year, Nabozny withdrew from Ashland High School. Hanson told Nabozny and his parents that school administrators were unwilling to help him and that he should seek educational opportunities elsewhere. Nabozny left Ashland and moved to Minneapolis where he was diagnosed with Post Traumatic Stress Disorder. In addition to seeking medical help, Nabozny sought legal advice.

On February 6, 1995, Nabozny filed the instant suit pursuant to 42 U.S.C. § 1983 against Mary Podlesny, William Davis, Thomas Blauert, and the District alleging, among other things, that the defendants violated his Fourteenth Amendment rights to equal protection and due process. The defendants moved for summary judgment. The district court ruled in favor of the defendants. The court dispensed with Nabozny's gender equal protection claim, holding that Nabozny failed to produce evidence to establish that the defendants discriminated against him based on his gender. The court did not specify its basis for deciding Nabozny's sexual orientation equal protection claim. It appears from the order, however, that the court intended the reasoning that it applied to Nabozny's gender claim to apply to the sexual orientation claim as well. Regarding Nabozny's due process claims, the court concluded that Nabozny failed to produce evidence to establish that the defendants either created or exacerbated the risk of harm to Nabozny posed by other students. The court also concluded that Nabozny could not prevail on his claim that the defendants' policies encouraged a climate in which Nabozny suffered harm because none of Nabozny's assailants were state actors. In the alternative, the court granted qualified immunity to all of the defendants against all of Nabozny's claims. Nabozny now brings this timely appeal. We have jurisdiction pursuant to 28 U.S.C. § 1291.

We will begin our analysis by considering Nabozny's equal protection claims. Wisconsin has elected to protect the students in its schools from discrimination. Wisconsin statute section 118.13(1), regulating general school operations, provides that:

> No person may be denied…participation in, be denied the benefits of or be discriminated against in any curricular, extracurricular, pupil services, recreational or other program or activity because of the person's sex, race, religion, national origin, ancestry, creed, pregnancy, marital or parental status, sexual orientation or physical, mental, emotional or learning disability.

Since at least 1988, in compliance with the state statute, the Ashland Public School District has had a policy of prohibiting discrimination against students on the basis of gender or sexual orientation. The District's policy and practice includes protecting students from student-on-student sexual harassment and battery. Nabozny maintains that the defendants denied him the equal protection of the law by denying him the protection extended to other students, based on his gender and sexual orientation.

The Equal Protection Clause grants to all Americans "the right to be free from invidious discrimination in statutory classifications and other governmental activity." *Harris v. McRae,* 448 U.S. 297, 322 (1980). When a state actor turns a blind eye to the Clause's command, aggrieved parties such as Nabozny can seek relief pursuant to 42 U.S.C. § 1983. In order to establish liability under § 1983, Nabozny must show that the defendants acted with a nefarious discriminatory purpose and discriminated against him based on his membership in a definable class. As we explained in *Shango v. Jurich,* 681 F.2d 1091 (7th Cir.1982):

> The gravamen of equal protection lies not in the fact of deprivation of a right but in the invidious classification of persons aggrieved by the state's action. A plaintiff must demonstrate intentional or purposeful discrimination to show an equal protection violation. Discriminatory purpose, however, implies more than intent as volition or intent as awareness of consequences. It implies that a decision-maker singled out a particular group for disparate treatment and selected his course of action at least in part for the purpose of causing its adverse effects on the identifiable group.

A showing that the defendants were negligent will not suffice. Nabozny must show that the defendants acted either intentionally or with deliberate indifference. To escape liability, the defendants either must prove that they did not discriminate against Nabozny, or at a bare minimum, the defendants' discriminatory conduct must satisfy one of two well-established standards of review: heightened scrutiny in the case of gender discrimination, or rational basis in the case of sexual orientation.

The district court found that Nabozny had proffered no evidence to support his equal protection claims. In the alternative, the court granted to the defendants qualified immunity. Considering the facts in the light most favorable to Nabozny, we respectfully disagree with the district court's conclusions.

A. Gender and Equal Protection.

The district court disposed of Nabozny's equal protection claims in two brief paragraphs. Regarding the merits of Nabozny's gender claim, the court concluded that "[t]here is absolutely nothing in the record to indicate that plaintiff was treated differently because of his gender." The district court's conclusion affords two interpretations:

1) there is no evidence that the defendants treated Nabozny differently from other students; or, 2) there is no evidence that the discriminatory treatment was based on Nabozny's gender. We will examine each in turn.

The record viewed in the light most favorable to Nabozny, combined with the defendants' own admissions, suggests that Nabozny was treated differently from other students. The defendants stipulate that they had a commendable record of enforcing their anti-harassment policies. Yet Nabozny has presented evidence that his classmates harassed and battered him for years and that school administrators failed to enforce their anti-harassment policies, despite his repeated pleas for them to do so. If the defendants otherwise enforced their anti-harassment policies, as they contend, then Nabozny's evidence strongly suggests that they made an exception to their normal practice in Nabozny's case.

Therefore, the question becomes whether Nabozny can show that he received different treatment because of his gender. Nabozny's evidence regarding the defendants' punishment of male-on-female battery and harassment is not overwhelming. Nabozny contends that a male student that struck his girlfriend was immediately expelled, that males were reprimanded for striking girls, and that when pregnant girls were called "slut" or "whore," the school took action. Nabozny's evidence does not include specific facts, such as the names and dates of the individuals involved. Nabozny does allege, however, that when he was subjected to a mock rape Podlesny responded by saying "boys will be boys," apparently dismissing the incident because both the perpetrators and the victim were males. We find it impossible to believe that a female lodging a similar complaint would have received the same response.

More important, the defendants do not deny that they aggressively punished male-on-female battery and harassment. The defendants argue that they investigated and punished all complaints of battery and harassment, regardless of the victim's gender. According to the defendants, contrary to the evidence presented by Nabozny, they aggressively pursued each of Nabozny's complaints and punished the alleged perpetrators whenever possible. Like Nabozny, the defendants presented evidence to support their claim. Whether to believe the defendants or Nabozny is, of course, a question of credibility for the fact-finder. In the context of considering the defendants' summary judgment motion, we must assume that Nabozny's version is the credible one. If Nabozny's evidence is considered credible, the record taken in conjunction with the defendants' admissions demonstrates that the defendants treated male and female victims differently.

The defendants also argue that there is no evidence that they either intentionally discriminated against Nabozny, or were deliberately indifferent to his complaints. The defendants concede that they had a policy and practice of punishing perpetrators of battery and harassment. It is well settled law that departures from established practices may evince discriminatory intent. Moreover, Nabozny introduced evidence to suggest that the defendants literally laughed at Nabozny's pleas for help. The defendants' argument, considered against Nabozny's evidence, is simply indefensible.

Our inquiry into Nabozny's gender equal protection claim does not end here, because the district court granted to the defendants qualified immunity. [Qualified immunity is a doctrine that protects public officials from liability for performing discretionary functions if it was not "clearly established" at the relevant time that their actions would be considered unlawful. The district judge evidently believed that as of 1988 it was not clearly established that unequal application of a sexual harassment policy based on the gender of the victim could violate the Equal Protection clause. The court of appeals found that by 1988 it was well established in federal law that the Equal Protection clause required the government not to discriminate on the basis of sex without a substantial non-discriminatory justification, and thus that school officials should not be shielded by immunity on the sex discrimination charge.]

B. Sexual Orientation and Equal Protection.

On the face of the summary judgment order, the fate of Nabozny's sexual orientation equal protection claim is unclear. In the interest of judicial economy, we will assume that the court's disposition of Nabozny's sexual orientation claim was synonymous with, and on the same grounds as, the court's disposition of Nabozny's gender claim.

First we must consider whether Nabozny proffered a sufficient evidentiary basis to support his claim. As we noted above, Nabozny's evidence, combined with the defendants' admissions, demonstrates that Nabozny was treated differently. What is more, Nabozny introduced sufficient evidence to show that the discriminatory treatment was motivated by the defendants' disapproval of Nabozny's sexual orientation, including statements by the defendants that Nabozny should expect to be harassed because he is gay.

Next we must consider whether the defendants are entitled to qualified immunity. In other words, we must determine whether reasonable persons in the defendants' positions would have known that discrimination against Nabozny based on his sexual orientation, viewed in the light of the law at the time, was unlawful.

Our discussion of equal protection analysis thus far has revealed a well established principle: the Constitution prohibits intentional invidious discrimination between otherwise similarly situated persons based on one's membership in a definable minority, absent at least a rational basis for the discrimination. There can be little doubt that homosexuals are an identifiable minority subjected to discrimination in our society. Given the legislation across the country both positing and prohibiting homosexual rights, that proposition was as self-evident in 1988 as it is today. In addition, the Wisconsin statute expressly prohibits discrimination on the basis of sexual orientation. Obviously that language was included because the Wisconsin legislature both recognized that homosexuals are discriminated against, and sought to prohibit such discrimination in Wisconsin schools. The defendants stipulate that they knew about the Wisconsin law, and enforced it to protect homosexuals. Therefore, it appears that the defendants concede that they knew that homosexuals are a definable minority and treated them as such.

In this case we need not consider whether homosexuals are a suspect or quasi-suspect class, which would subject the defendants' conduct to either strict or heightened scrutiny. Our court has already ruled that, in the context of the military, discrimination on the basis of sexual orientation is subject to rational basis review. *See Ben-Shalom v. Marsh,* 881 F.2d 454, 464 (7th Cir.1989), *cert. denied,* 494 U.S. 1004 (1990). The rational basis standard is sufficient for our purposes herein.

Under rational basis review there is no constitutional violation if "there is any reasonably conceivable state of facts" that would provide a rational basis for the government's conduct. We are unable to garner any rational basis for permitting one student to assault another based on the victim's sexual orientation, and the defendants do not offer us one. Like Nabozny's gender claim, the defendants argue that they did not discriminate against Nabozny.

Absent any rational basis for their alleged discrimination, the defendants are left to argue that the principle that the Constitution prohibits discrimination between similarly situated persons based on membership in a delineable class was somehow unclear back in 1988. We find that suggestion unacceptable. As early as 1886 the Supreme Court held that if the law "is applied and administered by public authority with an evil eye and an unequal hand, so as practically to make unjust and illegal discriminations between persons in similar circumstances, material to their rights, the denial of equal justice is still within the prohibition of the Constitution." *Yick Wo v. Hopkins,* 118 U.S. 356, 373–74 (1886). Further, almost every case that we have cited thus far was decided prior to the events giving rise to this litigation.

Our discussion of qualified immunity cannot end without mentioning one case in the area of "homosexual rights" commonly cited during the period in question: *Bowers v. Hardwick,* 478 U.S. 186 (1986). In *Bowers,* the Supreme Court ruled that state sodomy statutes that prohibit sodomy performed in private between two consenting adults do not run afoul of an individual's Fourteenth Amendment right to substantive due process. We will address Nabozny's due process arguments below. However, reliance on *Bowers* by the defendants in this case is misplaced. *Bowers* addressed the criminalization of sodomy. The defendants make no mention of sodomy as a motive for their discrimination. To the contrary, the defendants offer us no rational basis for their alleged conduct. The defendants certainly cannot rely on *Bowers*'s rational basis analysis to establish qualified immunity when they do not assert a rational basis for their alleged conduct, and expressly maintain that they did not discriminate on the basis of sexual orientation. [Footnote: Of course, *Bowers* will soon be eclipsed in the area of equal protection by the Supreme Court's holding in *Romer v. Evans,* 517U.S. 620 (1996). *Romer,* which was decided following the oral argument in this case, struck down on equal protection grounds a Colorado constitutional amendment that discriminated against homosexuals. Although *Romer* bolsters our analysis in this case to some extent, we do not rely on it. To do so would be especially inappropriate in the context of rejecting the defendants' qualified immunity argument.] Therefore, although it presents a closer question than does Nabozny's gender claim, we hold that reasonable persons in the defendants' positions in 1988 would have concluded that discrimination against Nabozny based on his sexual orientation was unconstitutional.

[The court then rejected Nabozny's due process arguments, finding that there was no evidence that the school's failure to take action against his student assailants had increased the danger to him. The result was an inevitable consequence of a then-recent U.S. Supreme Court decision, ruling that public officials do not have an affirmative obligation to protect individual citizens from harm, although they do have a duty to avoid contributing to the harm or exacerbating it.]

We conclude that, based on the record as a whole, a reasonable fact-finder could find that the District and defendants Podlesny, Davis, and Blauert violated Nabozny's Fourteenth Amendment right to equal protection by discriminating against him based on his gender or sexual orientation. Further, the law establishing the defendants' liability was sufficiently clear to inform the defendants at the time that their conduct was unconstitutional. Nabozny's equal protection claims against the District, Podlesny, Davis, and Blauert are reinstated in toto. We further conclude that Nabozny has failed to produce sufficient evidence to permit a reasonable fact-finder to find that the defendants violated Nabozny's Fourteenth Amendment right to due process either by enhancing his risk of harm or by encouraging a climate to flourish in which he suffered harm. Our disposition of Nabozny's due process claims renders the district court's award of qualified immunity as to those claims moot.

Notes and Questions

1. After this opinion was issued, the case went to trial, and a jury found that the defendants had violated Nabozny's constitutional rights. The trial then recessed for settlement negotiations, and the school district agreed to pay Nabozny compensation totaling almost $1 million to settle the case, so the issue of damages was never submitted to the jury.

2. This case might be seen as a pre-*Romer* case, because of the court's finding that it would be inappropriate to base its ruling on *Romer* in light of the qualified immunity issue, as the defendant's exposure to liability had to be evaluated as of the time the events occurred, many years before *Romer* was decided. On the other hand, the opinion is significant both for the way in which the court treats the precedent of *Bowers v. Hardwick* and for its comment about the potential impact of *Romer* for future Equal Protection claims.

3. The problem of harassment of sexual minority students is significant and nationwide in scope. The ruling in *Nabozny*, and the subsequent substantial monetary settlement, attracted significant attention from school administrators and school board associations, leading many districts to adopt new policies or improve existing ones. The case has been cited as precedent in numerous subsequent lawsuits by students who were either gay or gender-non-conforming in a way that attracted homophobic harassment. For recent examples, see *Flores v. Morgan Hill Unified School Dist.*, 324 F.3d 1130 (9th Cir. 2003); *Doe v. Perry Community School Dist.*, 316 F.Supp.2d 809 (S.D.Iowa 2004).

* * *

The most heavily contested area of equal protection litigation against the federal government on behalf of gay and lesbian plaintiffs, beginning during the 1970s, has concerned military personnel policy.

Since early in our history, statutes and regulations governing military conduct have made it illegal for uniformed personnel to engage in "sodomy," but prior to the 20th century there was no systematic effort to exclude "homosexuals" from the armed forces, mainly because the very concept of "homosexuals" did not emerge until late in the 19th century. By the period immediately prior to World War II, psychiatrists employed by the Department of the Army, embracing views then prevalent in the psychiatric profession, had concluded that "homosexuals" possessed personality traits that were undesirable from the point of view of military service, and prevailed on the heads of the military services to authorize a screening program to attempt to detect homosexuals among those who might try to enlist or respond to the military draft and exclude them from the service. Although large numbers of sexual minorities served without incident in the armed forces during World War II, many individuals were "screened" out during the intake process, and some active duty military personnel were dismissed from the service for "homosexuality." In cases where "homosexual behavior" was involved, criminal prosecution might follow, and in all cases of exclusion, the discharge from service was characterized in a pejorative sense that would follow the individual into civilian life with adverse effects.

The policy in effect from the Korean War (early 1950s) through the Vietnam War period (mid-1960s through 1974) and immediately thereafter was expressed in regulations declaring that homosexuality was incompatible with military service and authorizing the discharge of service members found to be gay, regardless whether they had engaged in any conduct prohibited by military law. However, discharge was not expressly mandated, and commanders had discretion to decline to move against valued personnel. The application of such discretion varied widely, however, and the Defense Department was embarrassed when the U.S. Court of Appeals for the District of Columbia ruled in a pair of cases involving the Air Force and the Navy that the Department's failure to explain why two highly-esteemed gay members were not retained raised constitutional issues. *Matlovitch v. Secretary of the Air Force*, 591 F.2d 852 (D.C. Cir. 1978); *Berg v. Claytor*, 591 F.2d 849 (D.C. Cir. 1978). Even though the Carter Administration had implemented regulatory changes ending the practice of characterizing discharges for "homosexuality" in stigmatizing terms, the Department's reaction to these cases was to adopt new regulations, going into force as the Reagan Administration was coming into power, under which the discretion of commanders was ended and discharge was mandated for all "homosexuals" found in the service.

Numerous cases were litigated challenging this policy, none ultimately successfully, prior to the Supreme Court's decision in *Romer v. Evans*. Along the way, President Bill Clinton, who had campaigned for office in 1992 with a promise to end the ban on military service by gay people, agreed with Congressional leaders in 1993 to the notorious "don't ask, don't tell" policy, codified at 10 U.S.C. sec. 654, under which gay people could serve in the military provided that they kept their sexual orientation completely secret. Prior Defense Department policies on homosexuality had been a matter of regulation. The 1993 statute was the first Congressional enactment to address the question. Part of the supposed "bargain" was that the military would abandon its practice of energetic investigation to uncover gay servicemembers, and that new recruits to the all-volunteer forces would not be specifically questioned about their sexual orientation. However, old practices die hard, and there were indications that the military continued some of its old investigative practices. Indeed, the number of discharges for "homosexuality" actually increased through the 1990s, even as the size of the military was shrinking after the end of the Cold War.

Lesbian and gay litigation groups put together a class-action to take on the new policy, filing suit in the U.S. District Court for the Eastern District of New York in Brooklyn, N.Y. During the course of the litigation, the Supreme Court decided *Romer v. Evans*. Although a senior federal district judge twice found the policy unconstitutional, ultimately the 2nd Circuit Court of Appeals refused to strike it down:

Able v. United States
155 F.3d 628 (2nd Cir. 1998)

JOHN M. WALKER, JR., Circuit Judge:

Defendants appeal from the July 2, 1997 Memorandum and Order of the United States District Court for the Eastern District of New York (Eugene H. Nickerson, *Senior District Judge*), which found that §571(b) of the National Defense Authorization Act for the Fiscal Year 1994, *codified at* 10 U.S.C. §654(b), which mandates the termination of a service member of the armed forces for engaging in homosexual conduct, violates the Equal Protection Clause of the Fifth Amendment.

BACKGROUND

The "don't ask, don't tell" policy is embodied in §654(b) as well as various Department of Defense (DoD) directives. Section 654(b) provides for a service member's separation from the armed services if he or she has: (1) "engaged in, attempted to engage in, or solicited another to engage in a homosexual act;" (2) "stated that he or she is a homosexual or bisexual,...unless...the member has demonstrated that he or she is not a person who engages in, attempts to engage in, has a propensity to engage in, or intends to engage in homosexual acts;" (3) or has "married or attempted to marry a person known to be of the same biological sex." 10 U.S.C. §§654(b)(1), (2), (3). The statute defines "homosexual act" as "(A) any bodily contact, actively undertaken or passively permitted, between members of the same sex for the purpose of satisfying sexual desires; and (B) any bodily contact which a reasonable person would understand to demonstrate a propensity or intent to engage in an act described in subparagraph (A)." 10 U.S.C. §654(f)(3). DoD Directive 1332.14(H)(1)(a) (Dec. 21, 1993), which implements the statute, provides that:

> Homosexual conduct is grounds for separation from the Military Services.... Homosexual conduct includes homosexual acts, a statement by a member that demonstrates a propensity or intent to engage in homosexual acts, or a homosexual marriage or attempted marriage. A statement by a member that demonstrates a propensity or intent to engage in homosexual acts is grounds for separation not because it reflects the member's sexual orientation, but because the statement indicates a likelihood that the member engages in or will engage in homosexual acts. A member's sexual orientation is considered a personal and private matter, and is not a bar to continued service under this section unless manifested by homosexual conduct.

A service member who has stated that he or she is gay is given the opportunity to rebut the presumption that he or she has a propensity to commit homosexual acts by presenting evidence to an administrative board that he or she "is not a person who engages in, attempts to engage in, has a propensity to engage in, or intends to engage in homosexual acts." Directive 1332.14(H)(1)(b)(2).

Plaintiffs filed the instant action on March 7, 1994, in the Eastern District of New York claiming that the Act and the DoD Directives violate their rights under the First and Fifth Amendments to free speech, equal protection, and expressive and intimate association, and violate due process by failing to give adequate notice of what speech or behavior is proscribed.

DISCUSSION

The Due Process Clause of the Fifth Amendment assures every person the equal protection of the laws, "which is essentially a direction that all persons similarly situated should be treated alike." Of course, the government can treat persons differently if they are not "similarly situated." As a general rule, the equal protection guarantee of the Constitution is satisfied when the government differentiates between persons for a reason that bears a rational relationship to an appropriate governmental interest. However, in limited circumstances when the subject of the different treatment is a member of a class that historically has been the object of discrimination, the Supreme Court has required a higher degree of justification than a rational basis, either strict or intermediate scrutiny. Under the strict scrutiny test the government must demonstrate a compelling need for the different treatment and that the provision in question is narrowly tailored to achieve its objective. Under intermediate scrutiny, the government must at least demonstrate that the classification is substantially related to an important governmental objective. The suspect or quasi-suspect classes that are entitled to heightened scrutiny have been limited to groups generally defined by their status, such as race, national ancestry or ethnic origin, alienage, gender and illegitimacy, and not by the conduct in which they engage.

The government argues that the Act in this case proscribes homosexual conduct and that, since any governmental differentiation is based on conduct, not status, no heightened scrutiny is required. The government adds, moreover, that even if, as plaintiffs contend, the Act targets homosexuals based on status, heightened scrutiny still would not be appropriate because other circuits reviewing the Act have not recognized homosexuals as a suspect class and have applied a rational basis test.

In striking down the Act as failing to bear even a rational relationship to a legitimate governmental interest, the district court strongly suggested that in reviewing statutes that discriminate on the basis of homosexuality heightened scrutiny would be appropriate. We need not decide this question because at oral argument plaintiffs asserted that they were not seeking any more onerous standard than the rational basis test. Accordingly, the sole question before us is whether the Act survives rational basis review.

In a long series of cases, the Supreme Court has narrowly defined the concept of rational basis review. In *Heller,* 509 U.S. at 319 (1993), the Supreme Court held that "rational-basis review in equal protection analysis 'is not a license for courts to judge the wisdom, fairness, or logic of legislative choices.'" Rather, "a classification neither involving fundamental rights nor proceeding along suspect lines is accorded a strong presumption of validity," which "'must be upheld against equal protection challenge if there is any reasonably conceivable state of facts that could provide a rational basis for the classification.'" Under the rational basis test, the government "has no obligation to produce evidence to sustain the rationality of a statutory classification." We will assume that a statute is constitutional and "the burden is on the one attacking the legislative arrangement to negative every conceivable basis which might support it, whether or not the basis has a foundation in the record."

In the military setting, the Supreme Court has narrowed our review in a further respect. As we discussed in our previous opinion, we are required to give great deference to Congressional judgments in matters affecting the military. The Supreme Court has instructed that "'judicial deference is at its apogee when legislative action under the congressional authority to raise and support armies and make rules and regulations for their governance is challenged.'" *Goldman v. Weinberger,* 475 U.S. 503, 508 (1986). This is especially the case where, as here, the challenged restriction was the result of exhaustive inquiry by Congress in hearings, committee and floor debate.

Moreover, in the military context, the Court has recognized that "[t]he essence of military service 'is the subordination of the desires and interests of the individual to the needs of the service.'" *Goldman,* 475 U.S. at 507. Courts are to "give great deference to the professional judgment of military authorities concerning the relative importance of a particular military interest." The framers did not view the federal judiciary—appointed with life tenure—as the appropriate body to exercise military authority and therefore gave the judiciary "no influence over either the sword or the purse." THE FEDERALIST No. 78, at 520 (Alexander Hamilton) (Heritage Press ed., 1945). In these circumstances, we "must be particularly careful not to substitute our judgment of what is desirable for that of Congress, or our own evaluation of evidence for a reasonable evaluation by the Legislative Branch."

Deference by the courts to military-related judgments by Congress and the Executive is deeply recurrent in Supreme Court case law and repeatedly has been the basis for rejections to a variety of challenges to Congressional and Executive decisions in the military domain. In full recognition that within the military individual rights must of necessity be curtailed lest the military's mission be impaired, courts have applied less stringent standards to constitutional challenges to military rules, regulations and procedures than they have in the civilian context. Thus, "our review of military regulations is far more deferential than constitutional review of similar laws or regulations designed for civilian society." *Goldman*, 475 U.S. at 507.

Justice is afforded on different terms than is found in civilian life because the military is a "specialized community governed by a separate discipline." Before a military tribunal, a defendant's constitutional rights are diminished. There is no right to a trial by a jury of one's peers. The right of appeal from a criminal conviction is restricted. Habeas corpus relief is circumscribed. Fourth Amendment protections are less available. Furthermore, courts have deferred to military judgments that restrict First Amendment privileges including requiring members of the Air Force to obtain approval before circulating petitions on air force bases, *see Brown v. Glines*, 444 U.S. 348, 357 (1980), and restricting political speeches and distribution of political leaflets on military bases, *see Greer v. Spock*, 424 U.S. 828, 838 (1976).

The free exercise of religion is also limited in the military setting. In employing its power to raise troops, Congress has been given considerable freedom to exempt some citizens from military service for religious reasons while denying exemption or discharge from service to others who invoke the free exercise clause of the Constitution. *See, e.g., Gillette v. United States*, 401 U.S. 437, 462 (1971). Regulations regarding the dress code in the military have been held to override a religious practice dictated by Orthodox Judaism, so that a member of the service can be discharged from service if he conscientiously obeys a principle of his religion in direct contravention of a military order. *See Goldman*, 475 U.S. at 509.

The conclusion that we draw from these pronouncements is that, while we are not free to disregard the Constitution in the military context, we owe great deference to Congress in military matters. Although deference does not equate to abdication of our constitutional role, in considering whether there is substance to the government's justification for its action, courts are ill-suited to second-guess military judgments that bear upon military capability or readiness.

In this litigation, the United States has justified § 654's prohibition on homosexual conduct on the basis that it promotes unit cohesion, enhances privacy and reduces sexual tension. The plaintiffs have attacked each of these rationales as simply masking irrational prejudice against homosexuals. The plaintiffs argue that an illegitimate purpose can never support the different treatment accorded to homosexual as compared to heterosexual conduct, *see Cleburne Living Ctr.*, 473 U.S. at 448, and that the Act violates the Fifth Amendment's equal protection guarantee. Moreover, plaintiffs contend that the government's proffered reasons, unit cohesion, privacy and the reduction in sexual tensions, are not rationally related to the Act's prohibition on homosexual conduct. In this case, we believe that the rationales provided by the United States, grounded in the extensive findings set forth in the Act itself, are sufficient to withstand both aspects of plaintiffs' equal protection challenge.

First, plaintiffs rely on *Romer v. Evans*, 517 U.S. 620 (1996); *Cleburne Living Ctr.*, 473 U.S. at 448; and *Palmore v. Sidoti*, 466 U.S. 429 (1984), for the proposition that the Act cannot survive even rational basis review because it is motivated by irrational fear and prejudice toward homosexuals. In these cases, the Supreme Court held that the accommodation of an individual's bias or animosity can never serve as a legitimate government interest; "mere negative attitudes, or fear, unsubstantiated by factors which are properly cognizable in the circumstances, are not permissible bases" for differential treatment by the government. *Cleburne Living Ctr.*, 473 U.S. at 448.

The analysis set forth in *Romer, Cleburne Living Ctr.,* and *Palmore* differed from traditional rational basis review because it forced the government to justify its discrimination. Moreover, the Court did not simply defer to the government; it scrutinized the justifications offered by the government to determine whether they were rational. In this case, plaintiffs' reliance on *Romer, Cleburne Living Ctr.* and *Palmore* is misplaced. Those cases did not arise in the military setting. In the civilian context, the Court was willing to examine the benign reasons advanced by the government to consider whether they masked an impermissible underlying purpose. In the military setting, however, constitutionally-mandated deference to military assessments and judgments gives the judiciary far less scope to scrutinize the reasons, legitimate on their face, that the military has advanced to justify its actions.

Moreover, in this case the military's justifications are based on factors which are unique to military life. The military argues that the prohibition on homosexual conduct is necessary for military effectiveness because it maintains unit cohesion, reduces sexual tension and promotes personal privacy. These concerns distinguish the military from civilian life and go directly to the military's need to foster "instinctive obedience, unity, commitment, and esprit de corps." *Goldman,* 475 U.S. at 507.

Romer and *Cleburne Living Ctr.* also differ from this case because they involved restrictions based on status. In our previous opinion, we rejected plaintiffs' argument that the Act was only a status-based prohibition and held that the Act targets conduct. *See Able,* 88 F.3d at 1297–99; *see also* DoD Directive 1332.14(H)(1)(a) (a service member's "sexual orientation... is not a bar to continued service").

Plaintiffs also contend that the government's proffered reasons, unit cohesion, privacy and the reduction in sexual tensions, are not rationally related to the Act's prohibition on homosexual conduct. As discussed above, our review of this question is circumscribed both by the nature of rational basis review and our recognition of the special status of the military. In these circumstances, in evaluating whether the government's announced purposes are rationally related to the Act's prohibition of conduct, we defer to the judgment of Congress. The Act is entitled to "a strong presumption of validity," and must be sustained if "there is any reasonably conceivable state of facts that could provide a rational basis for the classification." *Heller,* 509 U.S. at 319–20. Under this standard, the Act does not violate the Equal Protection Clause.

The Act is supported by extensive Congressional hearings and deliberation. In reaching its decision, Congress relied on testimony from military officers, defense experts, gay rights advocates, and other military personnel as well as reports by both houses explaining their conclusions. After this extensive legislative examination, embodied in numerous findings, *see* § 654(a), we cannot say that the reliance by Congress on the professional judgment and testimony of military experts and personnel that those who engage in homosexual acts would compromise the effectiveness of the military was irrational.

Numerous military leaders testified that regulation of homosexual conduct is necessary to unit cohesion and the military mission. It was rational for Congress to credit the testimony of these military officers and defense experts. As we described in our previous decision, after Congress and the Executive reviewed the policies regarding homosexuals in the military, Congress made detailed findings in support of § 654 which were embodied in the Act itself. Congress justified its decision to enact §654 in fifteen separate findings including the following:

> Military life is fundamentally different from civilian life in that...the extraordinary responsibilities of the armed forces, the unique conditions of military service, and the critical role of unit cohesion, require that the military community, while subject to civilian control, exist as a specialized society; and...the military society is characterized by its own laws, rules, customs, and traditions, including numerous restrictions on personal behavior, that would not be acceptable in civilian society.

> The pervasive application of the standards of conduct is necessary because members of the armed forces must be ready at all times for worldwide deployment to a combat environment.

> The worldwide deployment of United States military forces, the international responsibilities of the United States, and the potential for involvement of the armed forces in actual combat routinely make it necessary for members of the armed forces involuntarily to accept living conditions and working conditions that are often spartan, primitive, and characterized by forced intimacy with little or no privacy.

> The prohibition against homosexual conduct is a longstanding element of military law that continues to be necessary in the unique circumstances of military service.

> The armed forces must maintain personnel policies that exclude persons whose presence in the armed forces would create an unacceptable risk to the armed forces' high standards of morale, good order and discipline, and unit cohesion that are the essence of military capability.

> The presence in the armed forces of persons who demonstrate a propensity or intent to engage in homosexual acts would create an unacceptable risk to the high standards of morale, good order and discipline, and unit cohesion that are the essence of military capability.

Given the strong presumption of validity we give to classifications under rational basis review and the special respect accorded to Congress's decisions regarding military matters, we will not substitute our judgment for that of Congress. We find that Congress has proffered adequate justifications for the Act.

In our previous opinion, we held that the statements provision §654(b)(2) "substantially furthers the government's interest in preventing the occurrence of homosexual acts in the military," and concluded that "if the acts prohibition of subsection (b)(1) is constitutional the statements presumption of subsection (b)(2) does not violate the First Amendment." Because we now hold that the acts prohibition, §654(b)(1), is constitutional, we therefore conclude that the prohibition on statements, §654(b)(2), is constitutional as well.

Notes and Questions

1. In light of the *Able* court's refusal to use *Romer v. Evans* to overturn the military ban, lesbian and gay litigation groups largely abandoned the idea of seeking a change in military policy through litigation in the short term. However, after *Lawrence v. Texas*

was decided, new challenges were filed by individuals who had been excluded from the military, arguing that the policy was now subject to more searching scrutiny. They were still pending in the lower federal courts when this book was being prepared. In addition to the decision in *Lawrence*, another major change that has occurred since *Able* is that the number of U.S. military allies who also exclude gay people from their armed forces has dropped precipitously, and the United Kingdom, America's principal ally in the war in Iraq begun by the Bush Administration in 2003, had dropped its ban without incident in response to a ruling by the European Court of Human Rights. Consider whether this combination of factors might lead to a different judicial outcome in reviewing the military policy for constitutionality.

Quinn v. Nassau County Police Department
53 F.Supp.2d 347 (E.D.N.Y. 1999)

SPATT, District Judge.

The plaintiff, a homosexual man and a former Nassau County police officer, claims that his fellow police officers and supervisors embarked on a vicious campaign of harassment against him because of his sexual orientation, in violation of 42 U.S.C. Sections 1983 and 1985. During a three-week jury trial, the plaintiff testified that approximately a year after he joined the police force in 1986, other officers learned he was gay and over a nine-year period, tormented him with pornographic cartoons and photographs, anti-gay remarks, and barbaric "pranks." The plaintiff further testified that his supervisors at the police department knew of the harassment but did nothing to stop it, and that some supervisors even joined in the harassment. The jury awarded him the total sum of $380,000 in compensatory and punitive damages.

The central question confronting the Court is whether government employees who are homosexual may be singled out for discrimination and abuse in the workplace because of their sexual orientation. In the Court's view, the United States Constitution and the provisions of 42 U.S.C. § 1983, combined with logic, common sense and fairness dictate the answer: individuals have a constitutional right under the Equal Protection Clause to be free from sexual orientation discrimination causing a hostile work environment in public employment.

42 U.S.C. section 1983 provides, in relevant part:

> Every person who, under color [of law]...subjects, or causes to be subjected, any citizen of the United States...to the deprivation of any rights, privileges, or immunities secured by the Constitution and laws, shall be liable to the party injured in an action at law, suit in equity, or other proper proceeding for redress.

This statute furnishes a cause of action for the violation of federal rights created by the Constitution. Therefore, a Section 1983 claim has two essential elements: (1) the defendant acted under color of state law; and (2) as a result of the defendant's actions, the plaintiff suffered a denial of his federal statutory rights, or his constitutional rights or privileges. Here, the plaintiff asserts that the defendants, acting under color of state law, violated his constitutional right to Equal Protection.

1. *"Under Color of State Law" Element of a Section 1983 Claim*

In the Court's view, "[t]here can be no question that defendants [Donald Kane, the Commissioner of the Nassau County Police Department; Lieutenant Edward Gonzalez; Deputy Chief Daniel Lishansky; Sergeant John Ryan; and Lieutenant Joseph Allen] are, in their personal capacities, amenable to suit under [§ 1983], inasmuch as they were conducting themselves as supervisors for a public employer and thus were acting under color of state law." *Annis v. County of Westchester*, 36 F.3d 251, 253–55 (2d Cir.1994) (citing *Carrero v. New York City Hous. Auth.*, 890 F.2d 569, 577 [2d Cir.1989]).

2. Denial of Equal Protection Element of a Section 1983 Claim

a. Elements of an Equal Protection Violation

Generally speaking, the Equal Protection Clause of the Fourteenth Amendment directs state actors to treat similarly situated people alike. To establish an Equal Protection violation, a plaintiff must prove purposeful discrimination directed at an identifiable or suspect class. As the Second Circuit explained in *FSK Drug Corp. v. Perales*, 960 F.2d 6, 10 (2d Cir.1992) ("*FSK*"), an Equal Protection violation based upon selective application of a facially lawful state regulation is properly found when: (1) the person, compared with others similarly situated, was selectively treated; and (2) the selective treatment was motivated by an intention to discriminate on the basis of impermissible considerations, such as race or religion, to punish or inhibit the exercise of constitutional rights, or by a malicious or bad faith intent to injure the person.

b. Harassment in the Public Workplace as an Equal Protection Violation

One manifestation of impermissible selective treatment is employment discrimination in the public workplace. In fact, the Supreme Court declared two decades ago that individuals have a constitutional right under the Equal Protection Clause to be free from sex discrimination in public employment. *See Davis v. Passman*, 442 U.S. 228, 234–35 (1979). In refining this declaration, the Second Circuit has explained that sexual harassment can, under certain circumstances, amount to a constitutional tort. *Annis*, 36 F.3d at 253–55 (citing *Gierlinger v. New York State Police*, 15 F.3d 32, 34 [2d Cir.1994]) ("[I]n some circumstances a § 1983 claim may be properly grounded on a violation of the Equal Protection Clause of the Fourteenth Amendment based on sexual harassment in the workplace."). "Such unjustified unequal treatment is exactly the type of behavior prohibited by the Equal Protection clause as interpreted in *Davis v. Passman*, 442 U.S. 228, 234–35 (1979)." *Bohen v. City of East Chicago, Ind.*, 799 F.2d 1180, 1186 (7th Cir.1986).

With respect to sexual harassment, a District Court in this Circuit has noted that "[c]reating abusive conditions for female employees and not for male employees is discrimination [under § 1983.]" *Osier v. Broome County*, 47 F.Supp.2d 311, 328 (N.D.N.Y. 1999) (quoting *Bohen v. City of East Chicago, Indiana*, 799 F.2d at 1185). The District Court remarked that "a plaintiff can make an ultimate showing of sex discrimination either by showing that sexual harassment that is attributable to the employer under § 1983 amounted to intentional sex discrimination or by showing that the conscious failure of the employer to protect the plaintiff from the abusive conditions created by fellow employees amounted to intentional discrimination." In this context, "Section 1983 liability can be imposed upon individual employers, or responsible supervisors, for failing properly to investigate and address allegations of sexual harassment when through this failure, the conduct becomes an accepted custom or practice of the employer." *Gierlinger v. New York State Police*, 15 F.3d at 34 (citing *Bohen v. City of East Chicago, Ind.*, 799 F.2d at 1189).

c. *Sexual Orientation Harassment as an Equal Protection Violation*

In the Court's view, harassment in the public workplace against homosexuals based on their sexual orientation falls within the ambit of *Annis* and its progeny. Just as *Annis* recognized that harassment of women in the public workplace that transcends coarse, hostile and boorish behavior can rise to the level of a constitutional tort, so too, in the Court's view, does a hostile work environment directed against homosexuals based on their sexual orientation constitute an Equal Protection violation.

In so finding, the Court notes that in 1996, the Supreme Court struck down, on Equal Protection Clause grounds, a state constitutional amendment categorically prohibiting gay men and lesbians from obtaining state or local legal protection from discrimination based on their sexual orientation. *See Romer v. Evans,* 517 U.S. 620 (1996). The *Romer* Court established that government discrimination against homosexuals, in and of itself, violates the Equal Protection Clause.

In *Romer,* the issue before the Supreme Court was whether an amendment to Colorado's state constitution, which prohibited any legislation or judicial action designed to protect the status of a person based on sexual orientation, violated the Fourteenth Amendment's Equal Protection Clause. The Supreme Court had little difficulty finding that it did. The Court noted that under the ordinary deferential Equal Protection standard—that is, the "rational basis standard"—the Court would "insist on knowing the relation between the classification adopted and the object to be obtained." The Court explained that this "link" between classification and the objective "gives substance to the Equal Protection Clause." This "link" was lacking in *Romer.* In reaching its conclusion, the Court observed that the "inevitable inference" from a law of this sort is that it is "born of animosity toward the class of persons affected." The Court characterized the amendment as "a status-based enactment divorced from any factual context from which we could discern a relationship to legitimate state interests."

Several Courts have recently considered the question of Equal Protection and sexual orientation and applied the "rational basis test" utilized in *Romer.* These cases, which typically analyzed the constitutionality of the United States Military's "Don't Ask, Don't Tell" policy, examined whether the forced separation from service of individuals who engage in a homosexual act or who state that they are homosexual violates the Equal Protection Clause. In concluding that the policy does not violate the Equal Protection Clause, these Courts have relied on the uniqueness of the military setting and the deference accorded to military decisions. *See, e.g., Able v. United States,* 155 F.3d 628, 632–35 (2d Cir.1998). Nevertheless, as in *Romer,* these Courts recognized that government action in a civil rather than a military setting cannot survive a rational basis review when it is motivated by irrational fear and prejudice towards homosexuals.

Under the above cases, and viewing the proof in a light most favorable to Quinn, the plaintiff has introduced more than sufficient evidence to support a claim for an Equal Protection violation based on a workplace environment that transcended hostile, coarse and boorish behavior, and which was motivated by an invidious, irrational fear and prejudice towards homosexuals. Section 1983 liability can be imposed upon the employer, the Nassau County Police Department, and the remaining defendant supervisors, for failing to properly investigate and address Quinn's complaints, and permitting the acts of harassment which the supervisors either observed or themselves perpetrated. Like the enactment at issue in *Romer,* conduct by police department officers, supervisors and policy makers contributing to, failing to address, and outright condoning harassment of homosexuals amounts to impermissible "status-based [conduct and policy] divorced from any factual context from which we could discern a relationship to legitimate state interests. Such harassment by Nassau County Police Department personnel cannot survive a rational basis review when it is motivated by irrational fear and prejudice towards homosexuals. The "inevitable inference" from the Quinn's mistreatment is that it was "born of animosity toward the class of persons affected," *Romer, supra,* at 634, namely, homosexuals.

Notes and Questions

1. Cases in which lower federal courts applied *Romer v. Evans* to protect lesbian or gay individuals from discrimination by public officials include *Stemler v. City of Florence,* 126 F.3d 856 (6th Cir. 1997); *Weaver v. Nebo School District,* 29 F. Supp. 2d 1279 (D. Utah 1998); and *Glover v. Williamsburg Local School District Board of Education,* 20 F. Supp. 2d 1160 (S.D. Ohio 1998). Although the courts did not apply heightened scrutiny, in each case they found conduct that might have passed a rationality test to be unconstitutional, on the ground that dislike or moral disapproval is not a legitimate reason for the state to disadvantage members of a particular group.

2. What impact should *Lawrence v. Texas* have on the questions raised in this section? In Chapter 2, we saw that judges of the 11th Circuit Court of Appeals were sharply divided in *Lofton,* the case challenging the Florida gay adoption ban, over whether, in light of *Romer* and *Lawrence,* some more stringent form of judicial review than rationality should be applied to government policies that disadvantage gay people. In a petition for certiorari in *Lofton* filed on October 1, 2004, the American Civil Liberties Union, representing the plaintiffs, argued that the diversity of views among lower court judges, both federal and state, about the appropriate standard for reviewing government laws and policies, required the Supreme Court to take up the issue in order to clarify the appropriate standard. The court declined that invitation early in 2005.

3. In its certiorari petition in *Lofton,* the ACLU argues that *Lawrence* was a "fundamental rights case" and that strict or heightened scrutiny should be used to evaluate anti-gay discrimination by the government. Do you agree with this interpretation of *Lawrence*? It is based on the insight that the Court relied on such cases as *Griswold* and *Eisenstadt* to hold that *Bowers v. Hardwick* was wrong when it was decided, leading to the logical conclusion that the same constitutional right that states had violated by placing restrictions on access to contraception was also violated by criminalizing private, consensual sodomy between adults of the same sex. Viewed from this perspective, the assertion in Justice Scalia's dissenting opinion that the Court had not ruled that "homosexual sodomy" was a fundamental right was an inaccurate way to characterize the majority opinion in *Lawrence.*

4. In her concurring opinion in *Lawrence,* Justice O'Connor suggested that sexual orientation discrimination claims should be evaluated under rationality review, but of a "more searching" nature because of the burden placed on intimate associations. Would such an approach produce a different result in any of the opinions included in this section?

C. Sex Discrimination and Sexual Minority Rights: Statutory Protection

When Congress debated a proposed Civil Rights Act in 1964, the bill sent to the floor of the House of Representatives did not include a ban on discrimination because of sex, enumerating only race and color, religion and national origin as forbidden grounds for discrimination. Although sex discrimination had been studied in the relevant House committees, and there was overwhelming documentation that such discrimination had an adverse impact on society (and, most saliently for purposes of Congress's legislative authority, the national economy), the bill's sponsors believed that there was insufficient political support for attacking the issue of sex discrimination to justify adding such a provision to a bill that was expected to be difficult to pass in any event. Opponents of the bill tended to agree with this conclusion, and one of their leaders, Rep. Howard Smith of Virginia, proposed a floor amendment to add "sex" to the bill, hoping that its addition would sink the bill. Rep. Smith's amendment passed, "sex" was added, and then later the House approved the bill with this additional provision. The bill was sent to the Senate floor without going through committees, under an agreement by the Congressional leaders who were committed to its passage but concerned that conservative chairmen of the pertinent Senate committees, all socially-conservative senior Southern Democrats who were staunchly opposed to civil rights legislation, would prevent it from getting to the floor for a vote. During the debate on the floor of the Senate, an amendment was added to clarify the relationship between "sex" in the Civil Rights bill and a previously enacted law, the Equal Pay Act, which forbids discrimination in compensation on account of sex when men and women are performing "equal jobs." The bill passed the Senate and was ultimately enacted, to become effective in 1965. Most attention was focused on Title VII of the bill, which deals with employment discrimination.

As a result of the way "sex" was added, there is limited legislative history to explain what Congress intended. The House Committee reports shed no light, and floor debate in the House was limited and relatively non-substantive. There are no Senate committee reports, and again the floor debate sheds little light. The statute contained no definition of "sex." When a word in common usage is not given a special definition in a statute, administrators and courts will usually give it the common, every-day definition that would have been familiar to the legislators. In such circumstances, can it be argued that the inclusion of "sex" in the Civil Rights Act of 1964 can be broadly read to encompass all aspects of gender, including sex, sexual orientation and gender identity?

At the time of passage, there was a small gay rights movement in the U.S. that had mounted some demonstrations but was not actively lobbying Congress for inclusion in the Civil Rights bill. At that time, there was no organized movement for transgender rights. The first bill proposing to amend Title VII to add "sexual orientation or affectional preference" was not introduced until the mid-1970s, and never received a floor vote in Congress. In 1993, after Congress was consumed with hearings and lengthy debates over President Bill Clinton's proposal to end the ban on military service by gay people, gay political groups settled on a new tactic in attempting to gain a federal "gay rights" bill. Noting that many members of Congress had stated in the course of that debate that they believed gay people should not suffer workplace discrimination, but that the military was "different," these strategists believed the time was right to draft a new bill, narrowly focused on the civilian workplace, and stripped of any provisions that would appear threatening to those political moderates who might be induced to endorse a simple measure against overt anti-gay discrimination.

The resulting bill, the Employment Non-Discrimination Act (ENDA), which has been reintroduced in every subsequent session of Congress, abandoned the goal of amending Title VII to add "sexual orientation." Instead, it would create a stand-alone statute banning *intentional* sexual orientation discrimination in the workplace, but disavowing affirmative action and specifically reserving to another day the question whether employers would have to afford benefits equality to their gay employees by adopting domestic partnership benefits plans.

Also, taking a narrower approach to the concept of discrimination than that developed under Title VII, ENDA does not embrace the concept of "disparate impact" discrimination. The disparate impact theory, adopted in *Griggs v. Duke Power Co.*, 401 U.S. 424 (1971), one of the earliest cases the Supreme Court decided under Title VII, extends the reach of the law to employer policies that appear neutral on their face but have the effect of discriminating on the basis of a forbidden ground under Title VII. In *Griggs*, for example, plaintiffs challenged the employer's adoption of a high school diploma requirement for certain jobs, pointing out that in the relevant labor pool, such a requirement would disproportionately disqualify African-American applicants. The Supreme Court ruled that a facially neutral policy that has a substantial disparate impact on racial minorities may not be adopted unless it is necessary to advance a legitimate non-discriminatory business interest of the employer, and once a plaintiff had demonstrated that a disparate impact existed, the burden shifted to the employer to prove the business necessity of the policy. During the 1980s, a series of Supreme Court decisions significantly weakened the disparate impact theory, but Congress responded by amending Title VII to restore the law to what it was prior to the Supreme Court decisions, adopting an express statutory requirement that employment policies having a disparate impact could only be used if the employer showed that they were "consistent with business necessity."

The decision to disavow disparate impact cases under ENDA meant that the bill was very narrowly focused to ban only the most overt types of discrimination. Nonetheless, even as narrowed and weakened, ENDA has never come to a vote on the floor of the House. In a legislative deal brokered in 1996 prior to the national elections to allow the Defense of Marriage Act to come to a vote in the Senate without any floor amendments, the Republican Senate leadership allowed ENDA to come up for a vote under the same rules. Although the Republicans narrowly controlled the Senate and the platform of the Republican Party was opposed to enactment of ENDA, the measure fell just one vote short of a tie. Prospects for ENDA in the near future are uncertain.

Since the 1996 vote, a new issue has arisen with respect to ENDA. Advocates for the rights of transsexuals have asked that ENDA be revised to extend protection on the basis of "gender identity or expression." The congressional sponsors of ENDA have opposed this request on political grounds, believing that it would make enactment of ENDA more difficult, but the leading national political organizations of the gay community, the National Gay & Lesbian Task Force and Human Rights Campaign, after a period of intense debate and well-organized educational and lobbying efforts by the transgender rights movement, have come around to endorsing the expansion of ENDA, taking the pragmatic view that in the current political climate the bill is unlikely to advance and that by the time its enactment becomes practicable, acceptance of the justice of the transgender rights movement's position may be sufficient to carry the entire package to enactment.

Thus, at the federal level, as of 2005 there is no express statutory protection against discrimination for public or private sector employees on the basis of sexual orientation or gender identity. Under a civil service reform bill enacted in 1978, however, there is a general principle governing the civilian federal workforce that has been interpreted by some as establishing a requirement that federal personnel decisions be based on job qualifications and not individual characteristics such as sexual orientation or gender identity, and of course federal employment is governed by constitutional requirements of non-discrimination, as noted in the previous section. During the 1990s, the heads of all the departments of the executive branch adopted executive orders banning sexual orientation discrimination among civilian employees of their agencies—including civilian employees of the Defense Department—and towards the end of the decade, President Bill Clinton issued an Executive Order covering all civilian employees of the executive branch, which George W. Bush did not rescind.

However, there is Title VII, with its ban on sex discrimination in employment. To what extent does the federal statutory ban on such discrimination provide some sort of workplace protection for sexual minorities? Some legal theorists have argued that as a matter of broad concept, such discrimination is a form of sex discrimination. In a frequently-cited law review article, New York University Professor Sylvia Law wrote: "My central thesis is that contemporary legal and cultural contempt for lesbian women and gay men serves primarily to preserve and reinforce the social meaning attached to gender." She goes on to argue that "the persistence of negative social and legal attitudes toward homosexuality can best be understood as preserving traditional concepts of masculinity and femininity as well as upholding the political, market and family structures premised upon gender differentiation," and that "legal censure of homosexuality violates constitutional norms of gender equality." Sylvia A. Law, *Homosexuality and the Social Meaning of Gender*, 1988 Wisconsin Law Review 187. More recently, in his book *The Gay Rights Question in Contemporary American Law* (2002), Andrew Koppelman reasserted and expanded on Law's arguments, building on two much-cited law review articles he had previously written, *The Miscegenation Analogy: Sodomy Law as Sex Discrimination*, 98 Yale Law Journal 145 (1988), and *Why Discrimination Against Lesbians and Gay Men is Sex Discrimination*, 69 N.Y.U. Law Review 197 (1994).

Beginning soon after Title VII went into effect, lesbians and gay men encountering workplace difficulties sought the protection of the sex discrimination ban. Over the forty years of Title VII's history, the judicial construction of "sex discrimination" has developed to such an extent that gay and transgender litigants are beginning to achieve some success for their claims. Understanding this development—both its promise and its limitations—requires a trip through the history of Title VII and sex.

Desantis v. Pacific Telephone & Telegraph Co., Inc.
608 F.2d 327 (9th Cir. 1979)

CHOY, Circuit Judge:

Male and female homosexuals brought three separate federal district court actions claiming that their employers or former employers discriminated against them in employment decisions because of their homosexuality. They alleged that such discrimination violated Title VII of the Civil Rights Act of 1964 and 42 U.S.C. sec. 1985(3).

I. Statement of the Case

A. *Strailey v. Happy Times Nursery School, Inc.*

Appellant Strailey, a male, was fired by the Happy Times Nursery School after two years' service as a teacher. He alleged that he was fired because he wore a small gold earloop to school prior to the commencement of the school year. He filed a charge with the Equal Employment Opportunity Commission (EEOC) which the EEOC rejected because of an alleged lack of jurisdiction over claims of discrimination based on sexual orientation. He then filed suit on behalf of himself and all others similarly situated, seeking declaratory, injunctive, and monetary relief. The district court dismissed the complaint as failing to state a claim under either Title VII or sec. 1985(3).

B. *DeSantis v. Pacific Telephone & Telegraph Co.*

DeSantis, Boyle, and Simard, all males, claimed that Pacific Telephone & Telegraph Co. (PT&T) impermissibly discriminated against them because of their homosexuality. DeSantis alleged that he was not hired when a PT&T supervisor concluded that he was a homosexual. According to appellants' brief, "BOYLE was continually harrassed by his co-workers and had to quit to preserve his health after only three months because his supervisors did nothing to alleviate this condition." Finally, "SIMARD was forced to quit under similar conditions after almost four years of employment with PT&T, but he was harrassed by his supervisors (as well)....In addition, his personnel file has been marked as not eligible for rehire, and his applications for employment were rejected by PT&T in 1974 and 1976." Appellants DeSantis, Boyle, and Simard also alleged that PT&T officials have publicly stated that they would not hire homosexuals.

These plaintiffs also filed charges with the EEOC, also rejected by the EEOC for lack of jurisdiction. They then filed suit on behalf of themselves and all others similarly situated seeking declaratory, injunctive, and monetary relief under Title VII and sec. 1985(3). They also prayed that the district court issue mandamus commanding the EEOC to process charges based on sexual orientation. The district court dismissed their complaint. It held that the court lacked jurisdiction to compel the EEOC to alter its interpretation of Title VII. It also held that appellants had not stated viable claims under either Title VII or sec. 1985(3).

C. *Lundin v. Pacific Telephone & Telegraph*

Lundin and Buckley, both females, were operators with PT&T. They filed suit in federal court alleging that PT&T discriminated against them because of their known lesbian relationship and eventually fired them. They also alleged that they endured numerous insults by PT&T employees because of their relationship. Finally, Lundin alleged that the union that represented her as a PT&T operator failed adequately to represent her interests and failed adequately to present her grievance regarding her treatment. Appellants sought monetary and injunctive relief. The district court dismissed their suit as not stating a claim upon which relief could be granted. It also refused leave to amend their complaint to add a claim under sec. 1985(3).

II. Title VII Claim

Appellants argue first that the district courts erred in holding that Title VII does not prohibit discrimination on the basis of sexual preference. They claim that in prohibiting certain employment discrimination on the basis of "sex," Congress meant to include discrimination on the basis of sexual orientation. They add that in a trial they could establish that discrimination against homosexuals disproportionately affects men and that this disproportionate impact and correlation between discrimination on the basis of sexual preference and discrimination on the basis of "sex" requires that sexual preference be considered a subcategory of the "sex" category of Title VII.

A. Congressional Intent in Prohibiting "Sex" Discrimination

In *Holloway v. Arthur Andersen & Co.*, 566 F.2d 659 (9th Cir. 1977), plaintiff argued that her employer had discriminated against her because she was undergoing a sex transformation and that this discrimination violated Title VII's prohibition on sex discrimination. This court rejected that claim, writing:

> The cases interpreting Title VII sex discrimination provisions agree that they were intended to place women on an equal footing with men. Giving the statute its plain meaning, this court concludes that Congress had only the traditional notions of "sex" in mind. Later legislative activity makes this narrow definition even more evident. Several bills have been introduced to Amend the Civil Rights Act to prohibit discrimination against "sexual preference." None have (Sic) been enacted into law. Congress has not shown any intent other than to restrict the term "sex" to its traditional meaning. Therefore, this court will not expand Title VII's application in the absence of Congressional mandate. The manifest purpose of Title VII's prohibition against sex discrimination in employment is to ensure that men and women are treated equally, absent a bona fide relationship between the qualifications for the job and the person's sex.

Id. at 662–63; See *Baker v. California Land Title Co.*, 507 F.2d 895, 896 & n.2 (9th Cir. 1974), *cert. denied*, 422 U.S. 1046 (1975); *Rosenfeld v. Southern Pacific Co.*, 444 F.2d 1219, 1225 (9th Cir. 1971).

Following *Holloway*, we conclude that Title VII's prohibition of "sex" discrimination applies only to discrimination on the basis of gender and should not be judicially extended to include sexual preference such as homosexuality. See *Smith v. Liberty Mutual Insurance Co.*, 569 F.2d 325, 326–27 (5th Cir. 1978); *Holloway*, 566 F.2d at 662–63; *Voyles v. Ralph K. Davies Medical Center*, 403 F.Supp. 456, 456–57 (N.D.Cal.1975), aff'd without published opinion, 570 F.2d 354 (9th Cir. 1978).[1]

B. Disproportionate Impact

Appellants argue that recent decisions dealing with disproportionate impact require that discrimination against homosexuals fall within the purview of Title VII. They contend that these recent decisions, like *Griggs v. Duke Power Co.*, 401 U.S. 424 (1971), establish that any employment criterion that affects one sex more than the other violates Title VII. They quote from Griggs:

> What is required by Congress (under Title VII) is the removal of artificial, arbitrary, and unnecessary barriers to employment when the barriers operate invidiously to discriminate on the basis of racial or other impermissible classifications.

---

1. Based on a similar reading of the legislative history and the principle that "words used in statutes are to be given their ordinary meaning," the EEOC has concluded "that when Congress used the word sex in Title VII it was referring to a person's gender" and not to "sexual practices." EEOC Dec. No. 76-75, (1976) Emp.Prac.Guide (CCH) P 6495, at 4266.

401 U.S. at 431. They claim that in a trial they could prove that discrimination against homosexuals disproportionately affects men both because of the greater incidence of homosexuality in the male population and because of the greater likelihood of an employer's discovering male homosexuals compared to female homosexuals.

Assuming that appellants can otherwise satisfy the requirement of *Griggs*, we do not believe that *Griggs* can be applied to extend Title VII protection to homosexuals. In finding that the disproportionate impact of educational tests on blacks violated Title VII, the Supreme Court in *Griggs* sought to effectuate a major congressional purpose in enacting Title VII: protection of blacks from employment discrimination. For as the Supreme Court noted in *Philbrook v. Goldgett*, 421 U.S. 707 (1975), in construing a statute, "(o)ur objective…is to ascertain the congressional intent and give effect to the legislative will." Id. at 713.

The *Holloway* court noted that in passing Title VII Congress did not intend to protect sexual orientation and has repeatedly refused to extend such protection. Appellants now ask us to employ the disproportionate impact decisions as an artifice to "bootstrap" Title VII protection for homosexuals under the guise of protecting men generally.

This we are not free to do. Adoption of this bootstrap device would frustrate congressional objectives as explicated in Holloway, not effectuate congressional goals as in *Griggs*. It would achieve by judicial "construction" what Congress did not do and has consistently refused to do on many occasions. It would violate the rule that our duty in construing a statute is to "ascertain…and give effect to the legislative will." *Philbrook*, 421 U.S. at 713. We conclude that the Griggs disproportionate impact theory may not be applied to extend Title VII protection to homosexuals.

C. Differences in Employment Criteria

Appellants next contend that recent decisions have held that an employer generally may not use different employment criteria for men and women. They claim that if a male employee prefers males as sexual partners, he will be treated differently from a female who prefers male partners. They conclude that the employer thus uses different employment criteria for men and women and violates the Supreme Court's warning in *Phillips v. Martin-Marietta Corp.*, 400 U.S. 542 (1971):

> The Court of Appeals therefore erred in reading this section as permitting one
> hiring policy for women and another for men.…

Id. at 544.

We must again reject appellants' efforts to "bootstrap" Title VII protection for homosexuals. While we do not express approval of an employment policy that differentiates according to sexual preference, we note that whether dealing with men or women the employer is using the same criterion: it will not hire or promote a person who prefers sexual partners of the same sex. Thus this policy does not involve different decisional criteria for the sexes.

D. Interference with Association

Appellants argue that the EEOC has held that discrimination against an employee because of the race of the employee's friends may constitute discrimination based on race in violation of Title VII. See EEOC Dec. No. 71-1902, (1972) Empl.Prac.Guide (CCH) P 6281; EEOC Dec. No. 71-969, (1972) Empl.Prac.Guide (CCH) P 6193. They contend that analogously discrimination because of the sex of the employees' sexual partner should constitute discrimination based on sex.

Appellants, however, have not alleged that appellees have policies of discriminating against employees because of the gender of their friends. That is, they do not claim that the appellees will terminate anyone with a male (or female) friend. They claim instead that the appellees discriminate against employees who have a certain type of relationship, i.e., homosexual relationship with certain friends. As noted earlier, that relationship is not protected by Title VII. Thus, assuming that it would violate Title VII for an employer to discriminate against employees because of the gender of their friends, appellants' claims do not fall within this purported rule.

E. Effeminacy

Appellant Strailey contends that he was terminated by the Happy Times Nursery School because that school felt that it was inappropriate for a male teacher to wear an earring to school. He claims that the school's reliance on a stereotype that a male should have a virile rather than an effeminate appearance violates Title VII.

In *Holloway* this court noted that Congress intended Title VII's ban on sex discrimination in employment to prevent discrimination because of gender, not because of sexual orientation or preference. Recently the Fifth Circuit similarly read the legislative history of Title VII and concluded that Title VII thus does not protect against discrimination because of effeminacy. *Smith v. Liberty Mutual Insurance Co.*, 569 F.2d at 326–27. We agree and hold that discrimination because of effeminacy, like discrimination because of homosexuality or transsexualism (Holloway), does not fall within the purview of Title VII.

F. Conclusion as to Title VII Claim

Having determined that appellants' allegations do not implicate Title VII's prohibition on sex discrimination, we affirm the district court's dismissals of the Title VII claims.

III. Sec. 1985(3) Claim

Section 1985(3) provides in relevant part:

> If two or more persons...conspire or go in disguise on the highway or on the premises of another, for the purpose of depriving, either directly or indirectly, any person or class of persons of the equal protection of the laws, or of equal privileges and immunities under the laws...in any case of conspiracy set forth in this section, if one or more persons engaged therein do, or cause to be done, any act in furtherance of the object of such conspiracy, whereby another is injured in his person or property, or deprived of having and exercising any right or privilege of a citizen of the United States, the party so injured or deprived may have an action for the recovery of damages, occasioned by such injury or deprivation, against any one or more of the conspirators.

Appellants argue that the concerted actions of various agents of their employers and others, to effectuate the discriminatory policy of the employers constituted a conspiracy in violation of sec. 1985(3). They conclude that regardless of this court's holding as to Title VII, they can assert a viable sec. 1985(3) claim.

The forerunner of sec. 1985(3) was enacted as part of the Ku Klux Klan Act of 1871. It was intended to provide special federal assistance to southern blacks and their allies in protecting their rights under the fourteenth amendment and other reconstruction legislation against the Ku Klux Klan and others organized to thwart reconstruction efforts. A century later the Supreme Court held that sec. 1985(3) applied only when there is "some racial, or perhaps otherwise class-based, invidiously discriminatory animus behind the conspirators' action." *Griffin v. Breckenridge*, 403 U.S. 88, 102 (1971). Because Griffin dealt with allegations by blacks of a conspiracy to deprive them of their civil rights, the Supreme Court did not decide "whether a conspiracy motivated by invidiously discriminatory intent other than racial bias would be actionable" under sec. 1985(3). Id. at 102 n.9.

In *Life Insurance Co. of North America v. Reichardt*, 591 F.2d 499 (9th Cir. 1979), this court held that plaintiffs alleging a conspiracy to deprive women of equal rights could invoke sec. 1985(3). Appellants here claim that since *Reichardt* moved beyond the narrow historical perspective of 1871, homosexuals (and all groups) can now claim the special protection of sec. 1985(3).

We disagree. While sec. 1985(3) has been liberated from the now anachronistic historical circumstances of reconstruction America, we may not uproot sec. 1985(3) from the principle underlying its adoption: the Governmental determination that some groups require and warrant special federal assistance in protecting their civil rights. This underlying principle must continue to determine the coverage of sec. 1985(3).

In contradistinction to southern blacks of 1871, the blacks of *Griffin*, and the women of *Reichardt*, it cannot be said that homosexuals have been afforded special federal assistance in protecting their civil rights. The courts have not designated homosexuals a "suspect" or "quasi-suspect" classification so as to require more exacting scrutiny of classifications involving homosexuals. Congress did not and has consistently refused to include homosexuals as a group within the special protection of Title VII.

We conclude that homosexuals are not a "class" within the meaning of sec. 1985(3). The district courts therefore properly rejected appellants' s 1985(3) claims.

SNEED, Circuit Judge (concurring and dissenting):

I concur in the majority's opinion save subpart B of Part II thereof. I respectfully dissent from subpart B which holds that male homosexuals have not stated a Title VII claim under the disproportionate impact theory. My position is not foreclosed by our holding, with which I agree, that Title VII does not afford protection to homosexuals, male or female. The male appellants' complaint, as I understand it, is based on the contention that the use of homosexuality as a disqualification for employment, which for Griggs' purposes must be treated as a facially neutral criterion, impacts disproportionately on males because of the greater visibility of male homosexuals and a higher incidence of homosexuality among males than females.

To establish such a claim will be difficult because the male appellants must prove that as a result of the appellee's practices there exists discrimination against males Qua males. That is, to establish a prima facie case under Griggs it will not be sufficient to show that appellees have employed a disproportionately large number of female Homosexuals and a disproportionately small number of male Homosexuals. Rather it will be necessary to establish that the use of homosexuality as a bar to employment disproportionately impacts on males, a class that enjoys Title VII protection. Such a showing perhaps could be made were male homosexuals a very large proportion of the total applicable male population.

My point of difference with the majority is merely that the male appellants in their *Griggs* claim are not using that case "as an artifice to 'bootstrap' Title VII protection for homosexuals under the guise of protecting men generally." Their claim, if established properly, would in fact protect males generally. I would permit them to try to make their case and not dismiss it on the pleadings.

With respect to the appellants' section 1985(3) claims, I should like to observe that the appellants fail because discrimination against homosexuals does not rest on the class-based, invidiously discriminatory animus required by section 1985(3), as interpreted by *Griffin v. Breckenridge*, 403 U.S. 88 (1971). Many groups, quite satisfactorily subject to identification, are not within the ambit of section 1985(3)'s protection. This section is not a writ by which the judiciary can provide comfort and succor to all groups, large and small, who feel social disapproval from time to time. Like many others, homosexuals do not enjoy section 1985(3) protection.

Notes and Questions

1. The court's decision notes that the Equal Employment Opportunity Commission, the federal agency charged with receiving Title VII complaints, investigating them, and seeking enforcement in the courts, had determined that Title VII's ban on sex discrimination involved "gender" but not "sexual practices." What does that mean, exactly? The statute refers to "sex," not "gender." The words have different meanings, and gender is usually used in a broader sense than sex to encompass more than anatomical differences between men and women.

2. Understanding cases under Title VII requires at least quick acquaintance with some basic principles work out by the courts:

Title VII: A Quick Primer

The plaintiff in a Title VII case has the ultimate burden of proving discrimination, although in some circumstances employer-defendants may have the burden of proving what amounts to an affirmative defense under the statute. Title VII cases divide into two basic types, disparate treatment and disparate impact. Disparate treatment cases are those in which the employer is charged with intentional discrimination on a forbidden ground—race or color, religion, national origin or sex. Disparate impact cases are those in which facially neutral practices have a disproportionately adverse effect on particular groups.

If a plaintiff can present direct evidence of intentional discrimination on a forbidden ground, the defendant can win the case if it can prove by a preponderance of the evidence that the trait that is the basis for the discrimination constitutes a "bona fide occupational qualification," unless that trait is race or color. (The statute admits of no defense for an employer who is found to have intentionally discriminated based on race or color.) Much "direct evidence" Title VII litigation actually revolves around employer assertions that the plaintiff's "direct evidence" does not prove discriminatory intent. The BFOQ defense is rarely successful.

If a plaintiff has no direct evidence of intentional discrimination, she may still bring a Title VII suit provided she can truthfully allege the essential elements of a prima facie case from which discriminatory intent might be inferred. As specified in *McDonnell Douglas Corp. v. Green*, 411 U.S. 792 (1973) and amplified in later cases, the elements of a prima facie case may vary depending on the nature of the case. In a hiring case such as *McDonnell*, the elements were (1) minority group status, (2) qualified job applicant, (3) rejected despite qualifications, and (4) after rejection, the employer continued to receive applications or filled the position—that is, the position was not eliminated. If the plaintiff can allege a prima facie case, an inference of discriminatory intent is raised, and a burden of production shifts to the employer to articulate a legitimate, non-discriminatory reason for its actions, to rebut the inference. If the employer meets that burden, the case is over unless the plaintiff can show that the employer's explanation was pretextual. A showing of pretext will revive the plaintiff's case. Ultimately, the plaintiff still must prove discrimination by a preponderance of the evidence, but credibly alleging a prima facie case is sufficient to survive a motion to dismiss, thus opening up the possibility of discovery and, through skill or luck, being able to uncover direct evidence of discrimination.

Disparate impact cases follow a different path. In order to bring a disparate impact case, the plaintiff must identify a specific employer rule, policy or practice that is alleged to disadvantage applicants or employees based on one of the characteristics listed in the statute, even though the rule, policy or practice is neutral on its face with respect to the characteristic. It is the plaintiff's burden to amass the necessary statistical proof to show that the practice in question has a sufficient disparate impact to raise an issue of discrimination under the statute, and the EEOC and the courts have approved various mathematical formulas for evaluating whether a disparate impact is severe enough to qualify. If the plaintiff is successful in presenting such proof, the burden shifts to the defendant to show by a preponderance of the evidence that the challenged policy is consistent with business necessity; that is, that there is a legitimate business justification for the policy. The courts have held, for example, that the obligation to comply with the terms of a valid collective bargaining agreement between the employer and a union representing its employees may constitute a business necessity, as would the requirement to comply with applicable federal or state regulations. In a disparate impact case, the plaintiff is not required to prove that the employer intended to disadvantage minorities.

In the field of sex discrimination law, the Supreme Court has recognized that various kinds of workplace harassment may rise to the level of adversely affecting an employee's working conditions. In *Meritor Savings Bank v. Vinson*, 477 U.S. 57 (1986), the Supreme Court accepted the proposition that a supervisor's sexual demands on an employee might provide the basis for a "sexual harassment" claim that would be recognized under Title VII. In this and subsequent cases, the Court recognize two broad categories of harassment claims: quid pro quo and hostile environment. Quid pro quo claims were those in which the plaintiff alleged that sexual relationships were coerced by threats (sometimes implied rather than express) of possible workplace retaliation; hiring or advancement was premised as a reward for willingness to submit to the supervisor's sexual demands. Hostile environment claims, the more common of the two, involved situations where hostility to the presence of members of one sex in the workplace had escalated to the point of making it difficult for the victims to do their jobs. In many cases, this would involve situations where things got so bad that a reasonable person under the circumstances would quit. While recognizing the possibility of liability under Title VII for a hostile environment, the Court took steps to ensure that only the most egregious cases would result in imposing liability on the employer, and then only where an employer who knew or should have known about the problem failed to address it appropriately. Vicarious liability for harassment by supervisors or co-workers presented particularly difficult issues, and ultimately the Court created a "safe harbor" for employers who adopted anti-harassment policies, established mechanisms for receiving and investigating employee complaints, and actually followed up on complaints from employees in a reasonable way.

The *DeSantis* case, above, illustrates a variety of these legal theories combined in one case, including allegations of intentional discrimination, disparate impact and hostile environment. On all of those claims, the *DeSantis* court was unwilling to find statutory protection for the plaintiffs, based on its conclusion that Congress did not intend to protect gay people from discrimination when it adopted Title VII.

* * *

Ulane v. Eastern Airlines, Inc.
742 F.2d 1081 (7th Cir. 1984),
cert. denied, 471 U.S. 1017 (1985)

HARLINGTON WOOD, Jr., Circuit Judge.

Plaintiff, as Kenneth Ulane, was hired in 1968 as a pilot for defendant, Eastern Air Lines, Inc., but was fired as Karen Frances Ulane in 1981. Ulane filed a timely charge of sex discrimination with the Equal Employment Opportunity Commission, which subsequently issued a right to sue letter. This suit followed. Counts I and II allege that Ulane's discharge violated Title VII: Count I alleges that Ulane was discriminated against as a female; Count II alleges that Ulane was discriminated against as a transsexual. The judge ruled in favor of Ulane on both counts after a bench trial. The court awarded her reinstatement as a flying officer with full seniority and back pay, and attorneys' fees. This certified appeal followed pursuant to Federal Rule of Civil Procedure 54(b). Since Ulane considers herself to be female, and appears in public as female, we will use feminine pronouns in referring to her.

FACTUAL BACKGROUND

Counsel for Ulane opens their brief by explaining: "This is a Title VII case brought by a pilot who was fired by Eastern Airlines for no reason other than the fact that she ceased being a male and became a female." That explanation may give some cause to pause, but this briefly is the story.

Ulane became a licensed pilot in 1964, serving in the United States Army from that time until 1968 with a record of combat missions in Vietnam for which Ulane received the Air Medal with eight clusters. Upon discharge in 1968, Ulane began flying for Eastern. With Eastern, Ulane progressed from Second to First Officer, and also served as a flight instructor, logging over 8,000 flight hours. Ulane was diagnosed a transsexual in 1979. She explains that although embodied as a male, from early childhood she felt like a female. Ulane first sought psychiatric and medical assistance in 1968 while in the military. Later, Ulane began taking female hormones as part of her treatment, and eventually developed breasts from the hormones. In 1980, she underwent "sex reassignment surgery." After the surgery, Illinois issued a revised birth certificate indicating Ulane was female, and the FAA certified her for flight status as a female. Ulane's own physician explained, however, that the operation would not create a biological female in the sense that Ulane would "have a uterus and ovaries and be able to bear babies." Ulane's chromosomes, all concede, are unaffected by the hormones and surgery. Ulane, however, claims that the lack of change in her chromosomes is irrelevant. Eastern was not aware of Ulane's transsexuality, her hormone treatments, or her psychiatric counseling until she attempted to return to work after her reassignment surgery. Eastern knew Ulane only as one of its male pilots.

A. *Title VII and Ulane as a Transsexual.*

The district judge first found under Count II that Eastern discharged Ulane because she was a transsexual, and that Title VII prohibits discrimination on this basis. While we do not condone discrimination in any form, we are constrained to hold that Title VII does not protect transsexuals, and that the district court's order on this count therefore must be reversed for lack of jurisdiction.

Section 2000e-2(a)(1) provides in part that: "(a) It shall be an unlawful employment practice for an employer (1) to...discharge any individual...because of such individual's...sex...." Other courts have held that the term "sex" as used in the statute is not synonymous with "sexual preference." *See, e.g., Sommers v. Budget Marketing, Inc.,* 667 F.2d 748, 750 (8th Cir.1982) (per curiam); *De Santis v. Pacific Telephone & Telegraph Co.,* 608 F.2d 327, 329–30 (9th Cir.1979); *Smith v. Liberty Mutual Insurance Co.,* 569 F.2d 325, 326–27 (5th Cir.1978); *Holloway v. Arthur Andersen & Co.,* 566 F.2d 659, 662 (9th Cir.1977); *Voyles v. Ralph K. Davies Medical Center,* 403 F.Supp. 456, 457 (N.D.Cal.1975), *aff'd mem.,* 570 F.2d 354 (9th Cir.1978). The district court recognized this, and agreed that homosexuals and transvestites do not enjoy Title VII protection, but distinguished transsexuals as persons who, unlike homosexuals and transvestites, have sexual *identity* problems; the judge agreed that the term "sex" does not comprehend "sexual preference," but held that it does comprehend "sexual identity." The district judge based this holding on his finding that "sex is not a cut-and-dried matter of chromosomes," but is in part a psychological question—a question of self-perception; and in part a social matter—a question of how society perceives the individual. The district judge further supported his broad view of Title VII's coverage by recognizing Title VII as a remedial statute to be liberally construed. He concluded that it is reasonable to hold that the statutory word "sex" literally and scientifically applies to transsexuals even if it does not apply to homosexuals or transvestites. We must disagree.

Even though Title VII is a remedial statute, and even though some may define "sex" in such a way as to mean an individual's "sexual identity," our responsibility is to interpret this congressional legislation and determine what Congress intended when it decided to outlaw discrimination based on sex. The district judge did recognize that Congress manifested an intention to exclude homosexuals from Title VII coverage. Nonetheless, the judge defended his conclusion that Ulane's broad interpretation of the term "sex" was reasonable and could therefore be applied to the statute by noting that transsexuals are different than homosexuals, and that Congress never considered whether it should include or exclude transsexuals. While we recognize distinctions among homosexuals, transvestites, and transsexuals, we believe that the same reasons for holding that the first two groups do not enjoy Title VII coverage apply with equal force to deny protection for transsexuals.

It is a maxim of statutory construction that, unless otherwise defined, words should be given their ordinary, common meaning. The phrase in Title VII prohibiting discrimination based on sex, in its plain meaning, implies that it is unlawful to discriminate against women because they are women and against men because they are men. The words of Title VII do not outlaw discrimination against a person who has a sexual identity disorder, *i.e.,* a person born with a male body who believes himself to be female, or a person born with a female body who believes herself to be male; a prohibition against discrimination based on an individual's sex is not synonymous with a prohibition against discrimination based on an individual's sexual identity disorder or discontent with the sex into which they were born. The dearth of legislative history on section 2000e-2(a)(1) strongly reinforces the view that that section means nothing more than its plain language implies.

When Congress enacted the Civil Rights Act of 1964 it was primarily concerned with race discrimination. "Sex as a basis of discrimination was added as a floor amendment one day before the House approved Title VII, without prior hearing or debate." *Holloway v. Arthur Andersen & Co.*, 566 F.2d 659, 662 (9th Cir.1977) (citations omitted); *Developments in the Law—Employment Discrimination and Title VII of the Civil Rights Act of 1964*, 84 Harv.L.Rev. 1109, 1167 (1971). This sex amendment was the gambit of a congressman seeking to scuttle adoption of the Civil Rights Act. The ploy failed and sex discrimination was abruptly added to the statute's prohibition against race discrimination. *See Bradford v. Peoples Natural Gas Co.*, 60 F.R.D. 432, 434–35 & n. 1 (W.D.Pa.1973).

The total lack of legislative history supporting the sex amendment coupled with the circumstances of the amendment's adoption clearly indicates that Congress never considered nor intended that this 1964 legislation apply to anything other than the traditional concept of sex. Had Congress intended more, surely the legislative history would have at least mentioned its intended broad coverage of homosexuals, transvestites, or transsexuals, and would no doubt have sparked an interesting debate. There is not the slightest suggestion in the legislative record to support an all-encompassing interpretation.

Members of Congress have, moreover, on a number of occasions, attempted to amend Title VII to prohibit discrimination based upon "affectational or sexual orientation." Each of these attempts has failed. While the proposed amendments were directed toward homosexuals, *see, e.g., Civil Rights Act Amendments of 1981: Hearings on H.R. 1454 Before the Subcomm. on Employment Opportunities of the House Comm. on Education and Labor,* 97th Cong., 2d Sess. 1-2 (1982) (statements of Rep. Hawkins, chairman of subcommittee, and Rep. Weiss, N.Y., author of bill); *Civil Rights Amendments Act of 1979: Hearings on H.R. 2074 Before the Subcomm. on Employment Opportunities of the House Comm. on Education and Labor,* 96th Cong., 2d Sess. 6 (1980) (statements of Rep. Hawkins, chairman of subcommittee, and Rep. Weiss, N.Y., coauthor of bill), their rejection strongly indicates that the phrase in the Civil Rights Act prohibiting discrimination on the basis of sex should be given a narrow, traditional interpretation, which would also exclude transsexuals. Furthermore, Congress has continued to reject these amendments even after courts have specifically held that Title VII does not protect transsexuals from discrimination. *Compare* H.R. 1454, 97th Cong., 2d Sess. (1982) (hearing held on Jan. 27, 1982) *with Sommers v. Budget Marketing, Inc.*, 667 F.2d 748, 750 (8th Cir. Jan. 8, 1982) (per curiam); *Holloway v. Arthur Andersen & Co.*, 566 F.2d 659, 662–63 (9th Cir.1977); *Powell v. Read's, Inc.*, 436 F.Supp. 369, 371 (D.Md.1977); *Grossman v. Board of Education,* 11 Fair Empl. Prac. Cas. (BNA) 1196, 1199 (D.N.J.1975), *aff'd mem.,* 538 F.2d 319 (3d Cir.), *cert. denied,* 429 U.S. 897, 97 S.Ct. 261, 50 L.Ed.2d 181 (1976); *Voyles v. Ralph K. Davies Medical Center,* 403 F.Supp. 456, 457 (N.D.Cal.1975), *aff'd mem.,* 570 F.2d 354 (9th Cir.1978); *see also United States v. PATCO,* 653 F.2d 1134, 1138 (7th Cir.1981) (Congress is presumed to know the law and judicial interpretations of it); *United States v. Ambrose,* 740 F.2d 505 at 514 (7th Cir.1984) (Wood, J., concurring and dissenting) (same).

Although the maxim that remedial statutes should be liberally construed is well recognized, that concept has reasonable bounds beyond which a court cannot go without transgressing the prerogatives of Congress. In our view, to include transsexuals within the reach of Title VII far exceeds mere statutory interpretation. Congress had a narrow view of sex in mind when it passed the Civil Rights Act, and it has rejected subsequent attempts to broaden the scope of its original interpretation. For us to now hold that Title VII protects transsexuals would take us out of the realm of interpreting and reviewing and into the realm of legislating. This we must not and will not do.

Congress has a right to deliberate on whether it wants such a broad sweeping of the untraditional and unusual within the term "sex" as used in Title VII. Only Congress can consider all the ramifications to society of such a broad view. We do not believe that the interpretation of the word "sex" as used in the statute is a mere matter of expert medical testimony or the credibility of witnesses produced in court. Congress may, at some future time, have some interest in testimony of that type, but it does not control our interpretation of Title VII based on the legislative history or lack thereof. If Congress believes that transsexuals should enjoy the protection of Title VII, it may so provide. Until that time, however, we decline in behalf of the Congress to judicially expand the definition of sex as used in Title VII beyond its common and traditional interpretation.

B. *Title VII and Ulane as a Female.*

The trial judge originally found only that Eastern had discriminated against Ulane under Count II as a transsexual. The judge subsequently amended his findings to hold that Ulane is also female and has been discriminated against on this basis. Even if we accept the district judge's holding that Ulane is female, he made no factual findings necessary to support his conclusion that Eastern discriminated against her on this basis. All the district judge said was that his previous "findings and conclusions concerning sexual discrimination against the plaintiff by Eastern Airlines, Inc. apply with equal force whether plaintiff be regarded as a transsexual or a female." This is insufficient to support a finding that Ulane was discriminated against because she is *female* since the district judge's previous findings all centered around his conclusion that Eastern did not want "[a] *transsexual* in the cockpit" (emphasis added).

Ulane is entitled to any personal belief about her sexual identity she desires. After the surgery, hormones, appearance changes, and a new Illinois birth certificate and FAA pilot's certificate, it may be that society, as the trial judge found, considers Ulane to be female. But even if one believes that a woman can be so easily created from what remains of a man, that does not decide this case. If Eastern had considered Ulane to be female and had discriminated against her because she was female (*i.e.*, Eastern treated females less favorably than males), then the argument might be made that Title VII applied, *cf. Holloway v. Arthur Andersen,* 566 F.2d at 664 (although Title VII does not prohibit discrimination against transsexuals, "transsexuals claiming discrimination because of their sex, male or female, would clearly state a cause of action under Title VII") (dicta), but that is not this case. It is clear from the evidence that if Eastern did discriminate against Ulane, it was not because she is female, but because Ulane is a transsexual—a biological male who takes female hormones, cross-dresses, and has surgically altered parts of her body to make it appear to be female.

Since Ulane was not discriminated against as a female, and since Title VII is not so expansive in scope as to prohibit discrimination against transsexuals, we reverse the order of the trial court and remand for entry of judgment in favor of Eastern on Count I and dismissal of Count II.

* * *

Price Waterhouse v. Hopkins
490 U.S. 228 (1989)

Justice BRENNAN announced the judgment of the Court and delivered an opinion, in which Justice MARSHALL, Justice BLACKMUN, and Justice STEVENS join.

[This case involved a charge by Ann Hopkins, a senior manager at Price Waterhouse, that the firm's decision not to make her a partner violated Title VII's prohibition on sex discrimination. Hopkins, a married woman, was known to superiors and co-workers as an abrasive character, prone to using foul language. She also did not cultivate a stereotypically feminine manner of dress, eschewing make-up and jewelry. However, clients of the firm knew her as a powerhouse who got the job done, and she was notably successful at attracting new business for the firm—substantially more successful than the men with whom she was competing for partnership. During the course of litigation, discovery uncovered "smoking gun" evidence in the form of internal memoranda showing that some partners voted against her application based on their views that she was not adequately "feminine" to meet their image of a "lady partner" at Price Waterhouse. One partner had observed on an evaluation form that she needed a course in "charm school." Her immediate supervisor, in conveying the bad news to her after her first rejection, advised that she dress and act more femininely and start wearing makeup to improve her chances in the next partnership decision round. The question was whether the information uncovered in discovery, taken together with the comments by her supervisor, would be relevant to prove an intentional sex discrimination case under Title VII. Price Waterhouse argued that Hopkins' abrasive office behavior provided a non-discriminatory reason for denying her a partnership. One of the main issues addressed in the opinion was how to allocate burdens of proof when a variety of motivations might be present in the case (a so-called "mixed motives" case). The Court struck a balance with which Congress disagreed, and that part of the opinion was overruled in amendments to Title VII. What was not overruled was the portion of the plurality opinion dealing with what would constitute evidence of a discriminatory intent under Title VII in a sex discrimination case, as follows:]

In saying that gender played a motivating part in an employment decision, we mean that, if we asked the employer at the moment of the decision what its reasons were and if we received a truthful response, one of those reasons would be that the applicant or employee was a woman. In the specific context of sex stereotyping, an employer who acts on the basis of a belief that a woman cannot be aggressive, or that she must not be, has acted on the basis of gender.

Although the parties do not overtly dispute this last proposition, the placement by Price Waterhouse of "sex stereotyping" in quotation marks throughout its brief seems to us an insinuation either that such stereotyping was not present in this case or that it lacks legal relevance. We reject both possibilities. As to the existence of sex stereotyping in this case, we are not inclined to quarrel with the District Court's conclusion that a number of the partners' comments showed sex stereotyping at work. As for the legal relevance of sex stereotyping, we are beyond the day when an employer could evaluate employees by assuming or insisting that they matched the stereotype associated with their group, for "'[i]n forbidding employers to discriminate against individuals because of their sex, Congress intended to strike at the entire spectrum of disparate treatment of men and women resulting from sex stereotypes.'" *Los Angeles Dept. of Water and Power v. Manhart*, 435 U.S. 702, 707, n. 13 (1978), quoting *Sprogis v. United Air Lines, Inc.*, 444 F.2d 1194, 1198 (CA7 1971). An employer who objects to aggressiveness in women but whose positions require this trait places women in an intolerable and impermissible catch 22: out of a job if they behave aggressively and out of a job if they do not. Title VII lifts women out of this bind.

Remarks at work that are based on sex stereotypes do not inevitably prove that gender played a part in a particular employment decision. The plaintiff must show that the employer actually relied on her gender in making its decision. In making this showing, stereotyped remarks can certainly be *evidence* that gender played a part. In any event, the stereotyping in this case did not simply consist of stray remarks. On the contrary, Hopkins proved that Price Waterhouse invited partners to submit comments; that some of the comments stemmed from sex stereotypes; that an important part of the Policy Board's decision on Hopkins was an assessment of the submitted comments; and that Price Waterhouse in no way disclaimed reliance on the sex-linked evaluations. This is not, as Price Waterhouse suggests, "discrimination in the air"; rather, it is, as Hopkins puts it, "discrimination brought to ground and visited upon" an employee. By focusing on Hopkins' specific proof, however, we do not suggest a limitation on the possible ways of proving that stereotyping played a motivating role in an employment decision, and we refrain from deciding here which specific facts, "standing alone," would or would not establish a plaintiff's case, since such a decision is unnecessary in this case....

Justice KENNEDY, dissenting.

III

The ultimate question in every individual disparate-treatment case is whether discrimination caused the particular decision at issue. Some of the plurality's comments with respect to the District Court's findings in this case, however, are potentially misleading. As the plurality notes, the District Court based its liability determination on expert evidence that some evaluations of respondent Hopkins were based on unconscious sex stereotypes, and on the fact that Price Waterhouse failed to disclaim reliance on these comments when it conducted the partnership review. The District Court also based liability on Price Waterhouse's failure to "make partners sensitive to the dangers [of stereotyping], to discourage comments tainted by sexism, or to investigate comments to determine whether they were influenced by stereotypes."

Although the District Court's version of Title VII liability is improper under any of today's opinions, I think it important to stress that Title VII creates no independent cause of action for sex stereotyping. Evidence of use by decision-makers of sex stereotypes is, of course, quite relevant to the question of discriminatory intent. The ultimate question, however, is whether discrimination caused the plaintiff's harm. Our cases do not support the suggestion that failure to "disclaim reliance" on stereotypical comments itself violates Title VII. Neither do they support creation of a "duty to sensitize." As the dissenting judge in the Court of Appeals observed, acceptance of such theories would turn Title VII "from a prohibition of discriminatory conduct into an engine for rooting out sexist thoughts." 825 F.2d 458, 477 (1987) (Williams, J., dissenting).

Employment discrimination claims require fact finders to make difficult and sensitive decisions. Sometimes this may mean that no finding of discrimination is justified even though a qualified employee is passed over by a less than admirable employer. In other cases, Title VII's protections properly extend to plaintiffs who are by no means model employees. As Justice BRENNAN notes, courts do not sit to determine whether litigants are nice. In this case, Hopkins plainly presented a strong case both of her own professional qualifications and of the presence of discrimination in Price Waterhouse's partnership process.

Notes and Questions

1. On remand from the Supreme Court, Ann Hopkins won her case against Price Waterhouse at trial, and ultimately was offered a partnership at the firm in a post-trial settlement.

2. Does the Price Waterhouse plurality opinion provide a basis for questioning the decisions in *DeSantis v. Pacific Telephone* or *Ulane v. Eastern Airlines*? Consider Prof. Law's argument that anti-gay discrimination is motivated by a desire to enforce stereotypical gender roles. If an employer refuses to hire gay men, lesbians, bisexuals, or transsexuals for a particular job, could theories about gender non-conformity provide a basis for arguing that the employer's motivations were sexist?

3. One conceptual barrier that some, almost always male, hostile environment plaintiffs encountered under Title VII was the unwillingness of some courts to entertain the proposition that Title VII might treat as sex discrimination a situation where one male worker is being harassed by other male workers or supervisors. So-called "same-sex" harassment claims began to be filed with increasing frequency during the 1990's, as part of a general increase in sexual harassment case filings due to increased public awareness of the concept of sexual harassment, at least in part due to the national attention on confirmation hearings for Supreme Court Justice Clarence Thomas, during which Anita Hill, who had been an EEOC employee when Thomas was chairman of that agency, claimed to have been sexually harassed by him. A split emerged among the lower federal courts over whether a male employee could assert a hostile environment claim under Title VII, when the harassers were all male. The Supreme Court decisively answered the question in *Oncale v. Sundowner Offshore Services, Inc.*, 523 U.S. 75 (1998), a unanimous decision holding that all discrimination because of sex was potentially actionable under Title VII, the key inquiry being whether the plaintiff was victimized because of his sex.

Spearman v. Ford Motor Company
231 F.3d 1080 (7th Cir. 2000),
cert. denied, 532 U.S. 995 (2001)

MANION, Circuit Judge.

Edison Spearman sued his current employer, Ford Motor Company, alleging that Ford violated Title VII by subjecting him to a hostile environment of sexual harassment, retaliating against him for opposing sexual harassment, and for discriminating against him on the basis of his sex. Ford moved for summary judgment, which the district court granted. Spearman appeals, and we affirm.

Edison Spearman is a black man and a homosexual who has been working for Ford since 1990. (Spearman testified at his deposition that he is a homosexual, but he claims that he never made that known to anyone at Ford.) In October 1995, Spearman worked as a "blanker operator" at Ford's Chicago Heights Stamping Plant, where he operated press machines that "blank" or "stamp" sheet metal into dimensional form. In the summer of 1997, Spearman was promoted to the position of "blanker utility" worker, and assigned to relieve two blanker operators (Gregory Curtis and Steve Neeley) for their work breaks, lunch breaks and other rotations.

Spearman filed his first of several complaints of harassment on December 8, 1995, in which he reported that since his assignment as a blanker operator in October 1995, Curtis constantly took personal items (pens, newspapers, and gloves) from him without his permission. When Spearman told Curtis to stop, Curtis (a black man) called Spearman a "nigger" and a "selfish bitch." Curtis would also hound Spearman for lunch money, and then call him a "cheap ass bitch" if his requests were occasionally denied. Following a glove-snatching incident, Spearman had two meetings with his union representative and Curtis to resolve the matter.

Spearman reported no further incidents of harassment until May 16, 1997, when he filed a written complaint concerning an altercation with Curtis over the timing of lunch breaks. Curtis confronted Spearman, called him a "little bitch," told him that he hated his "gay ass," and threatened to go to Spearman's residence in Indiana and "f—— [his] gay faggot ass up." To defuse the situation, a foreman assigned Spearman and Curtis to different press areas for the balance of the shift. The following week, labor relations investigated the matter and held two meetings with Spearman, Curtis and a union representative.

Curtis and Neeley testified that they and their co-workers at Ford suspected that Spearman was a homosexual. According to Curtis, he thought that Spearman was homosexual when they first met and Spearman supposedly took "a full look" at Curtis like a man would look at a woman. Curtis also opined that other blanker operators at Ford were uncomfortable with Spearman because they observed that he "looked [them] over" like a man would "take a full look" at a woman, that he got too close to his male co-workers when he talked to them, and even "rubbed up especially close" to some of them. Curtis also testified that one coworker started "squirming" when others teased him that Spearman had a "crush" on him. And Curtis also claimed that his brother-in-law and a coworker told him that they saw Spearman at gay nightclubs.

According to Spearman, Curtis continually harassed him after the May 1997 incident by reporting to work late and returning from his breaks late in order to disrupt Spearman's relief schedule as a utility worker, and thus deprive him of his breaks and lunches. Curtis's negative behavior toward Spearman continued until he was moved to another press machine (and away from Spearman) in October 1997.

Spearman submitted another written complaint concerning a June 21, 1997 argument with Neeley over the timing of a break. As a blanker utility worker, Spearman told Neeley to take a break, but Neeley refused, leaned into Spearman's face, and taunted him by telling Spearman to hit him. In his complaint, Spearman wrote: "[T]here's a constant problem with Steve, when it comes to breaks; since I've become utility, he rebels and insist [sic] on debating me about how and when I relieve." Labor relations responded by conducting a meeting with all of the parties involved in the matter.

In June 1997, Spearman discovered graffiti on the bulletin board that stated: "Aids kills faggots dead…RuPaul, RuSpearman." Spearman waited five months to report the incident, and when he did, labor relations representatives promptly painted over it the following day.

On October 21, 1997, Spearman delivered another complaint to Ford that involved an altercation with George Pearson (who was temporarily assigned to work with Spearman) about the timing of a break. While Pearson was leaving his work station, he said to Spearman, "You f——ing jack-off, pussy-ass," and saluted Spearman with his middle finger. Spearman reported the incident to his foreman, Anthony Perez, who assured Spearman that he would discuss the matter with Pearson and "discipline him." Shortly after Spearman filed his complaint about the incident, a labor relations representative investigated the matter and conducted a meeting with Spearman and his union representative.

In November 1997, Spearman discovered more graffiti outside a portable toilet that stated: "Ed Sperman [sic] is a fag and has AIDS" and "Edison Sperman [sic] is gay." Labor relations representatives painted over the graffiti immediately after Spearman's report.

Ford received another letter from Spearman around November 24, 1997, in which he complained that he was being harassed by Perez, who used the following instructional hypothetical at a department meeting about sexual harassment:

> Say for instance, Greg and Ed are in the back bringing in a coil, and Ed touches Greg in a way that made him feel uncomfortable, that can be a charge of sexual harassment.

Spearman believed that Perez's hypothetical was about himself (Ed) and Greg Curtis, and thus it was "totally inappropriate" and harmful to Spearman because he and Curtis had been involved in several altercations in the past. Perez testified that he was not referring to Spearman in the example, but to Ed Rolff, one of Spearman's co-workers. In the same letter, Spearman also complained that Perez had offered to give him a hug on two separate occasions. On the first occasion, Spearman admits that Perez greeted him with a hug because he showed up for work during a staff shortage in the summer of 1997. But Spearman stated that he "felt very awkward" about Perez's second offer of a hug that occurred when Spearman was confused about overtime duties and consulted Perez for advice. Perez testified that Spearman appeared to be distraught because the press machine was not working, and that Perez offered to give him a hug to lift his spirits.

During the afternoon of November 24, 1997, Perez instructed Spearman to perform housekeeping duties and wash the windows of the press machines for about an hour before the end of his shift. Spearman believed that his assignment was punitive and that Perez was retaliating against him for his November 17, 1997 harassment complaint about Perez's instructional hypothetical and offers to hug Spearman. He left work that day, went on medical leave in December 1997, and did not return to work until May 4, 1998. Perez testified that he assigned similar housekeeping tasks to other utility workers and operators to keep them busy when they were not operating the press machines.

During his medical leave, Spearman received treatment for depression. When he returned to work after a five-month absence, he discovered that his tool box was destroyed and that his tools had been stolen.

Spearman then sued Ford, alleging that it violated Title VII by subjecting him to a hostile environment of sexual harassment; by retaliating against him because he filed complaints opposing sexual harassment; and by discriminating against him because of his sex by failing to investigate his sexual harassment complaints as promptly as similar complaints from female employees. Ford moved for summary judgment. The district court granted Ford's motion, concluding that while Spearman established a reasonable inference that he was harassed because of his sex, his sexual harassment claim failed because he did not show that the harassment was severe enough to cause a change in his employment conditions. The district court also denied Spearman's retaliation claim by concluding that he failed to establish a prima facie case by showing that he suffered an adverse employment action. The court did not address Spearman's sex discrimination claim. Spearman appeals.

Title VII prohibits an employer from harassing an employee "because of [the employee's] sex." *Oncale v. Sundowner Offshore Services, Inc.*, 523 U.S. 75, 78. Same-sex sexual harassment is actionable under Title VII "to the extent that it occurs 'because of' the plaintiff's sex." *Shepherd v. Slater Steels Corp.*, 168 F.3d 998, 1007 (7th Cir.1999). We have stated that "[t]he phrase in Title VII prohibiting discrimination based on sex" means that "it is unlawful to discriminate against women because they are women and against men because they are men." *Ulane v. Eastern Airlines, Inc.*, 742 F.2d 1081, 1085 (7th Cir.1984). In other words, Congress intended the term "sex" to mean "biological male or biological female," and not one's sexuality or sexual orientation. Therefore, harassment based solely upon a person's sexual preference or orientation (and not on one's sex) is not an unlawful employment practice under Title VII.

Hostile Environment Claim

Spearman first argues on appeal that he was sexually harassed at Ford in violation of Title VII. He claims that the vulgar and sexually explicit insults and graffiti of his harassers were motivated by "sex-stereotypes" because his co-workers perceived him to be too feminine to fit the male image at Ford. His contention relies primarily on Curtis's testimony that there is a "masculine" environment at the Ford plant, implying that he questioned Spearman's masculinity. Spearman also contends that Curtis engaged in sex stereotypes when he called Spearman a "bitch," which, according to another utility worker at Ford (David Gibson), meant that Curtis called Spearman a "woman." Moreover, Spearman asserts that the graffiti associating him with a drag queen (RuPaul) proves that his co-workers perceived him to be too feminine to work at Ford. And he claims that sex stereotypes motivated Perez to harass him with the window-washing assignment, which is a function "traditionally reserved for women" (a view that could also be labeled sex stereotyping).

While sexually explicit language may constitute evidence of sexual harassment, it is not "always actionable, regardless of the harasser's sex, sexual orientation, or motivations." The plaintiff must still show that he was harassed because of his sex. Similarly, while sex stereotyping may constitute evidence of sex discrimination, "[r]emarks at work that are based on sex-stereotypes do not inevitably prove that gender played a part in a particular employment decision. The plaintiff must show that the employer actually relied on [the plaintiff's] gender in making its decision." *Price Waterhouse v. Hopkins*, 490 U.S. 228, 251 (1989). Therefore, according to *Oncale* and *Price Waterhouse*, we must consider any sexually explicit language or stereotypical statements within the context of all of the evidence of harassment in the case, and then determine whether the evidence as a whole creates a reasonable inference that the plaintiff was discriminated against because of his sex.

Here, the record clearly demonstrates that Spearman's problems resulted from his altercations with co-workers over work issues, and because of his apparent homosexuality. But he was not harassed because of his sex (i.e. not because he is a man). His harassers used sexually explicit, vulgar insults to express their anger at him over work-related conflicts. However, these conflicts did not arise because he is a man. Curtis directed insults at Spearman to irritate or provoke him during three specific arguments about lunch money, small personal items, and the timing of lunch breaks. And Pearson directed a barrage of derogatory remarks at Spearman after he unsuccessfully protested Spearman's order to take a break. It is clear that Curtis and Pearson lodged sexually explicit insults at Spearman to express their acrimony over work-related disputes, and not to harass him because he is a man; and such conduct does not constitute sexual harassment. *See Johnson v. Hondo, Inc.*, 125 F.3d 408, 412 (7th Cir.1997) (sexually explicit remarks among male co-workers were "simply expressions of animosity or juvenile provocation," and were not directed at the plaintiff because of his sex).

The record also shows that Spearman's co-workers maligned him because of his apparent homosexuality, and not because of his sex. The testimonies of Curtis and Neeley clearly demonstrate that Spearman's harassers were motivated by their suspicion of Spearman's sexual orientation and his perceived desire for some sort of physical intimacy with them. And even Spearman's understanding of Perez's instructional hypothetical indicates that Perez teased him about his homosexuality. Moreover, Spearman's coworkers directed stereotypical statements at him to express their hostility to his perceived homosexuality, and not to harass him because he is a man. Curtis called him a "bitch" which, according to Gibson, means a "woman," or a "faggot." And the graffiti that specifically stated that Spearman is "gay," a "fag," and compared him to a drag queen confirms that some of his co-workers were hostile to his sexual orientation, and not to his sex.

Title VII is not a "general civility code" for the workplace, *see Oncale*, 523 U.S. at 81, 98; it does not prohibit harassment in general or of one's homosexuality in particular. Likewise, sexually explicit insults that arise solely from altercations over work-related issues, while certainly unpleasant, do not violate Title VII. Because Spearman was not harassed because of his sex, his hostile environment claim fails.

Réné v. Mgm Grand Hotel, Inc.
305 F.3d 1061 (9th Cir. En banc 2002),
Certiorari denied, 538 U.S. 922 (2003)

W. FLETCHER, Circuit Judge.

This case presents the question of whether an employee who alleges that he was subjected to severe, pervasive, and unwelcome "physical conduct of a sexual nature" in the workplace asserts a viable claim of discrimination based on sex under Title VII of the 1964 Civil Rights Act, even if that employee also alleges that the motivation for that discrimination was his sexual orientation. We would hold that an employee's sexual orientation is irrelevant for purposes of Title VII. It neither provides nor precludes a cause of action for sexual harassment. That the harasser is, or may be, motivated by hostility based on sexual orientation is similarly irrelevant, and neither provides nor precludes a cause of action. It is enough that the harasser have engaged in severe or pervasive unwelcome physical conduct of a sexual nature. We therefore would hold that the plaintiff in this case has stated a cause of action under Title VII.

Medina Réné, an openly gay man, appeals from the district court's grant of summary judgment in favor of his employer MGM Grand Hotel in his Title VII action alleging sexual harassment by his male coworkers and supervisor. The relevant facts are not in dispute. Réné worked for the hotel, located in Las Vegas, Nevada, from December 1993 until his termination in June 1996. He worked as a butler on the 29th floor, where his duties involved responding to the requests of the wealthy, high-profile and famous guests for whom that floor was reserved. All of the other butlers on the floor, as well as their supervisor, were also male.

Réné provided extensive evidence that, over the course of a two-year period, his supervisor and several of his fellow butlers subjected him to a hostile work environment on almost a daily basis. The harassers' conduct included whistling and blowing kisses at Réné, calling him "sweetheart" and "muneca" (Spanish for "doll"), telling crude jokes and giving sexually oriented "joke" gifts, and forcing Réné to look at pictures of naked men having sex. On "more times than [Réné said he] could possibly count," the harassment involved offensive physical conduct of a sexual nature. Réné gave deposition testimony that he was caressed and hugged and that his coworkers would "touch [his] body like they would to a woman." On numerous occasions, he said, they grabbed him in the crotch and poked their fingers in his anus through his clothing. When asked what he believed was the motivation behind this harassing behavior, Réné responded that the behavior occurred because he is gay.

On June 20, 1996, Réné filed a charge of discrimination with the Nevada Equal Rights Commission. He alleged that he "was discriminated against because of my sex, male" and indicated "I believe that my sex, male, was a factor in the adverse treatment I received." On April 13, 1997, Réné filed a complaint in federal district court, alleging that he had been unlawfully sexually harassed in violation of Title VII. MGM Grand moved for summary judgment on the grounds that "claims of discrimination based on sexual orientation are not cognizable under Title VII."

The district court agreed that Réné had failed to state a cognizable Title VII claim. In granting summary judgment in favor of MGM Grand, it concluded that "Title VII's prohibition of 'sex' discrimination applies only [to] discrimination on the basis of gender and is not extended to include discrimination based on sexual preference." Réné timely appealed.

...Réné alleged that he was sexually harassed by his male supervisor and male coworkers under the hostile work environment theory of sexual harassment. *See Harris v. Forklift Sys., Inc.,* 510 U.S. 17, 22 (1993) (noting "the very fact that the discriminatory conduct was so severe or pervasive that it created a work environment abusive to employees because of their...gender...offends Title VII's broad rule of workplace equality").

In describing the kinds of sexual harassment that can create a hostile work environment, the Court in *Meritor* explicitly included "physical conduct of a sexual nature." *Meritor,* 477 U.S. at 65 (quoting EEOC Guidelines, 29 C.F.R. § 1604.11(a) (1985)). We have applied this holding on numerous occasions, "explain[ing] that a hostile environment exists when an employee can show (1) that he or she was subjected to...physical conduct of a sexual nature, (2) that this conduct was unwelcome, and (3) that the conduct was sufficiently severe or pervasive as to alter the conditions of the victim's employment and create an abusive working environment." *Ellison v. Brady,* 924 F.2d 872, 875–76 (9th Cir.1991).

It is clear that Réné has alleged physical conduct that was so severe and pervasive as to constitute an objectively abusive working environment. It is equally clear that the conduct was "of a sexual nature." Réné's tormentors did not grab his elbow or poke their fingers in his eye. They grabbed his crotch and poked their fingers in his anus.

Physical sexual assault has routinely been prohibited as sexual harassment under Title VII. The most extreme form of offensive physical, sexual conduct—rape—clearly violates Title VII. *See Little v. Windermere Relocation,* 265 F.3d at 912 ("Rape is unquestionably among the most severe forms of sexual harassment.…Being raped is, at minimum, an act of discrimination based on sex."); *Brock v. United States,* 64 F.3d 1421, 1423 (9th Cir.1995) ("Just as every murder is also a battery, every rape committed in the employment setting is also discrimination based on the employee's sex.").

In granting MGM Grand's motion for summary judgment, the district court did not deny that the sexual assaults alleged by Réné were so objectively offensive that they created a hostile working environment. Rather, it appears to have held that Réné's otherwise viable cause of action was defeated because he believed he was targeted because he is gay. This is not the law. We have surveyed the many cases finding a violation of Title VII based on the offensive touching of the genitalia, buttocks, or breasts of women. In none of those cases has a court denied relief because the victim was, or might have been, a lesbian. The sexual orientation of the victim was simply irrelevant. If sexual orientation is irrelevant for a female victim, we see no reason why it is not also irrelevant for a male victim.

The premise of a sexual touching hostile work environment claim is that the conditions of the work environment have been made hostile "because of sex." The physical attacks to which Réné was subjected, which targeted body parts clearly linked to his sexuality, were "because of sex." Whatever else those attacks may, or may not, have been "because of" has no legal consequence. "[S]o long as the environment itself is hostile to the plaintiff because of [his] sex, why the harassment was perpetrated (sexual interest? misogyny? personal vendetta? misguided humor? boredom?) is beside the point." *Doe,* 119 F.3d at 578.

Our opinion today is guided by the principles established by the Supreme Court in *Oncale v. Sundowner Offshore Servs., Inc.,* 523 U.S. 75 (1998). As recounted by the Court, the Title VII plaintiff in *Oncale* had been"forcibly subjected to sex-related, humiliating actions" and had been"physically assaulted…in a sexual manner" by other males at his place of employment. We know from the circuit court's opinion that this physical assault included, among other things, "the use of force by [one co-worker] to push a bar of soap into Oncale's anus while [another co-worker] restrained Oncale as he was showering[.]" *Oncale v. Sundowner Offshore Servs., Inc.,* 83 F.3d 118, 118–19 (5th Cir.1996). This behavior occurred, the Court noted, in an all-male workplace. Oncale was a male plaintiff who worked on an all-male off-shore oil drilling rig "as a roustabout on an eight-*man* crew." *See Oncale,* 523 U.S. at 77 (emphasis added). Oncale's employer, Sundowner, never employed women on any of its drilling rigs.

Based on these facts, the Supreme Court reversed the judgment of the Court of Appeals for the Fifth Circuit, which had affirmed a grant of summary judgment in favor of the defendant-employer on the grounds that "same-sex harassment is not cognizable under Title VII ." *Oncale,* 83 F.3d at 118. We take two lessons from the Court's decision in *Oncale.*

First, Title VII forbids severe or pervasive same-sex offensive sexual touching. The Court made clear that a plaintiff's action for sexual harassment under Title VII cannot be defeated by a showing that the perpetrator and the victim of an alleged sexual assault are of the same gender. The Court wrote,

We see no justification in the statutory language or our precedents for a categorical rule excluding same-sex harassment claims from the coverage of Title VII. As some courts have observed, male-on-male sexual harassment in the workplace was assuredly not the principal evil Congress was concerned with when it enacted Title VII. But statutory prohibitions often go beyond the principal evil to cover reasonably comparable evils, and it is ultimately the provisions of our laws rather than the principal concerns of our legislators by which we are governed.

Oncale, 523 U.S. at 79; *see also id.* at 78 ("Because of the many facets of human motivation, it would be unwise to presume as a matter of law that human beings of one definable group will not discriminate against other members of their group." (citation and internal quotation omitted)). Thus, Oncale's cause of action could not be defeated based on the fact that he was tormented *by other men.*

Second, offensive sexual touching is actionable discrimination even in a same-sex workforce. The Court in *Oncale* made clear that "discrimination" is a necessary predicate to every Title VII claim. That is, a defendant's conduct must not merely be "because of...sex"; it must be" *'discriminat[ion]*...because of...sex.' " *Oncale,* 523 U.S. at 81 (emphasis in original). The Court in *Oncale* held that"discrimina[tion]...because of...sex" can occur entirely among men, where some men are subjected to offensive sexual touching and some men are not. There were no women on Oncale's drilling rig; indeed, there were no women on any of his employer's oil rigs. Discrimination is the use of some criterion as a basis for a difference in treatment. In the context of our civil rights laws, including Title VII, discrimination is the use of a *forbidden* criterion as a basis for a *disadvantageous* difference in treatment. "Sex" is the forbidden criterion under Title VII, and discrimination is any disadvantageous difference in treatment "because of...sex." The *Oncale* Court's holding that offensive sexual touching in a same-sex workforce is actionable discrimination under Title VII necessarily means that discrimination can take place between members of the same sex, not merely between members of the opposite sex. Thus, Oncale did not need to show that he was treated worse than members of the opposite sex. It was enough to show that he suffered discrimination *in comparison to other men.*

Viewing the facts, as we must, in the light most favorable to the nonmoving party, we are presented with the tale of a man who was repeatedly grabbed in the crotch and poked in the anus, and who was singled out from his other male co-workers for this treatment. It is clear that the offensive conduct was sexual. It is also clear that the offensive conduct was discriminatory. That is, René has alleged that he was treated differently—and disadvantageously—based on sex. This is precisely what Title VII forbids: "discriminat[ion]...because of...sex."

In sum, what we have in this case is a fairly straightforward sexual harassment claim. Title VII prohibits offensive "physical conduct of a sexual nature" when that conduct is sufficiently severe or pervasive. *Meritor,* 477 U.S. at 65. It prohibits such conduct without regard to whether the perpetrator and the victim are of the same or different genders. *See Oncale,* 523 U.S. at 79. And it prohibits such conduct without regard to the sexual orientation— real or perceived—of the victim.

There will be close cases on the question of what constitutes physical conduct of a sexual nature, for there are some physical assaults that are intended to inflict physical injury, but are not intended to have (and are not interpreted as having) sexual meaning. That is, there will be some cases in which a physical assault, even though directed at a sexually identifiable part of the body, does not give rise to a viable Title VII claim. But this is not such a case. Like the plaintiff in *Oncale*, Réné has alleged a physical assault of a sexual nature that is sufficient to survive a defense motion for summary judgment.

This opinion is joined by Judges Trott, Thomas, Graber, and Fisher. Judge Pregerson, in a separate opinion joined by Judges Trott and Berzon, reaches the same result but under a different rationale. Taken together, these two opinions are joined by a majority of the en banc panel. Accordingly, the district court's grant of summary judgment to MGM Grand is REVERSED, and the case is REMANDED for further proceedings.

PREGERSON, Circuit Judge, with whom TROTT and BERZON, Circuit Judges, join, concurring.

I write separately to point out that in my view, this is a case of actionable gender stereotyping harassment. More than a decade ago, the Supreme Court held that gender stereotyping is actionable under Title VII. More recently, the Supreme Court held that "same-sex sexual harassment is actionable under Title VII." And only last year, we held that same-sex gender stereotyping of the sort suffered by Réné—*i.e.*, gender stereotyping of a male gay employee by his male co-workers—"constituted actionable harassment under...Title VII." *Nichols v. Azteca Restaurant Enterprises, Inc.*, 256 F.3d 864, 874–75 (9th Cir.2001).

Réné testified in his deposition that his co-workers teased him about the way he walked and whistled at him"[l]ike a man does to a woman." Réné also testified that his co-workers would "caress my butt, caress my shoulders" and blow kisses at him "the way...a man would treat a woman," hugged him from behind "like a man hugs a woman," and would "touch my body like they would to a woman, touch my face." Réné further testified that his co-workers called him" sweetheart" and "muneca" ("doll"), "a word that Spanish men will say to Spanish women." This conduct occurred "many times." The repeated testimony that his co-workers treated Réné, in a variety of ways, "like a woman" constitutes ample evidence of gender stereotyping.

The conduct suffered by Réné is indistinguishable from the conduct found actionable in *Nichols*. In that case,

> Male co-workers and a supervisor repeatedly referred to [the male gay plaintiff] in Spanish and English as "she" and "her." Male co-workers mocked [him] for walking and carrying his serving tray "like a woman," and taunted him in Spanish and English as, among other things, a "faggot" and a "...female whore."

256 F.3d at 870. We concluded in *Nichols* that "[the] rule that bars discrimination on the basis of sex stereotypes" set in *Price Waterhouse* "squarely applies to preclude the harassment here." *Nichols*, 256 F.3d at 874–75. More generally, we held that "this verbal abuse was closely related to gender," "occurred because of sex," and therefore "constituted actionable harassment under...Title VII." *Id.*

The similarities between *Nichols* and the present case are striking. In both cases, a male gay employee was"teased" or "mocked" by his male co-workers because he walked "like a woman." And in both cases, a male gay employee was referred to by his male-co-workers in female terms—"she," "her," and "female whore" in *Nichols;* "sweetheart" and "muneca" ("doll") in the present case—to "remind[ ][him] that he did not conform to their gender-based stereotypes." *Nichols*, 256 F.3d at 874. For the same reasons that we concluded in *Nichols* that "[the] rule that bars discrimination on the basis of sex stereotypes" set in *Price Waterhouse* "squarely applie[d] to preclude the harassment" at issue there, *Nichols*, 256 F.3d at 874–75, I conclude that this rule also squarely applies to preclude the identical harassment at issue here. Accordingly, this is a case of actionable gender stereotyping harassment.

Hug, Circuit Judge, with whom Schroeder, Chief Judge, Fernandez, and T.G. Nelson, Circuit Judges, join, dissenting.

I respectfully dissent from Judge Fletcher's plurality opinion and Judge Pregerson's opinion concurring in the result, but expressing a different rationale for the result.

The basis of Judge Fletcher's opinion is well expressed in the following statement from the first paragraph:

> This case presents the question of whether an employee who alleges that he was subjected to severe, pervasive, and unwelcome "physical conduct of a sexual nature" in the workplace asserts a viable claim of discrimination based on sex under Title VII of the 1964 Civil Rights Act....It is enough that the harassers have engaged in severe or pervasive unwelcome physical conduct of a sexual nature.

This is a mischaracterization of the pertinent section of Title VII and the Supreme Court's interpretation of that section.

The pertinent section of Title VII provides: It shall be an unlawful employment practice for an employer — (1) to fail or refuse to hire or to discharge any individual, or otherwise to discriminate against any individual with respect to his compensation, terms, conditions, or privileges of employment, *because of* such individual's race, color, religion, sex, or national origin[.] 42 U.S.C. §2000e-2(a)(1) (emphasis added). Supreme Court decisions have made it clear that the term "sex" in that section refers to "gender." The terms "sex" and "gender" have been used interchangeably to mean "gender." Thus, it is discrimination based on "gender" that is prohibited. *See Harris v. Forklift Sys ., Inc.*, 510 U.S. 17, 22 (1993); *Price Waterhouse v. Hopkins*, 490 U.S. 228, 239 (1989).

I believe the following is a proper application of the statute as interpreted by the Supreme Court.

1. Title VII provides that it is an unlawful employment practice to *discriminate* against a person because of that person's race, color, religion, sex, or national origin.

2. Harassment on the job can be a form of discrimination. *Meritor Sav. Bank v. Vinson*, 477 U.S. 57, 64 (1986).

3. Thus, Title VII protects against harassment, as a type of discrimination on the job if it is because of race, color, religion, sex, or national origin. Harassment for other reasons, for example, because a person is short, fat, bald, disfigured, belongs to an unpopular social group, belongs to a particular political party, or engages in other activities outside the work-place, including sexual activities, that the harasser disfavors, is not actionable under Title VII.

4. Harassment on the job by physical assault or humiliation because a person is Asian, Black, a Jehovah's Witness, Polish, or because of the person's gender is actionable under Title VII because it is a type of discrimination and is against the particular classes of people protected by Title VII.

5. Title VII does not protect against physical assaults as a general matter. In order for an assault to be actionable under Title VII it must be a *type of discrimination* against one of the five protected classes.

6. If a person is assaulted or otherwise harassed on the job in a sexual manner, it is a form of discrimination against that person. However, the assault or harassment is actionable under Title VII only if it is *because of* that person's race, color, religion, gender, or national origin.

7. Sexual harassment on the job can be a form of discrimination that is actionable under Title VII if it is *because of* the person's gender. For example, "when a supervisor sexually harasses a subordinate *because of the subordinate's sex,* that supervisor 'discriminate[s]' on the basis of sex." *Meritor,* 477 U.S. at 64 (emphasis added).

8. Discrimination because of sex (gender) can extend to sexual stereotyping on the job. For example, if a woman does not act on the job in the way her employers perceived she should act as a woman, as was the situation in *Price Waterhouse,* or if a man does not act on the job like it is perceived a man should, as was the situation in *Nichols v. Azteca Restaurant Enterprises, Inc.,* 256 F.3d 864 (9th Cir.2001), this can be sexual stereotyping and actionable under Title VII.

9. Discrimination in the form of harassment or assault on the job because of a man's activity *outside* the workplace, such as his sexual activities, is not a basis for discrimination based on gender stereotyping of how he is expected to work on the job. A person might conform to all the stereotypes of masculinity on the job yet have a homosexual orientation in his own private life.

10. Discrimination based on gender can extend to discrimination against a person of one sex by a person of the same sex. *Oncale v. Sundowner Offshore Servs., Inc.,* 523 U.S. 75 (1998).

It is by now clear that sexual harassment can be a form of discrimination based on sex. *Meritor,* 477 U.S. at 64. The Supreme Court stated: "Without question, when a supervisor sexually harasses a subordinate *because of the subordinate's sex,* that supervisor 'discriminate[s]' on the basis of sex." *Id.* (emphasis added). In that case the evidence that a male supervisor made unwelcome sexual advances to a woman subordinate was sufficient to constitute discrimination based on sex.

Réné alleged that he was discriminated against because he was gay. Alleging a hostile work environment theory of sexual harassment, Réné alleged that he was sexually harassed by his male co-workers and a supervisor. To succeed on that theory, Réné must first prove that he was forced to endure a subjectively and objectively abusive working environment. In this case, the parties do not dispute the existence of a hostile work environment, for there is no doubt that the harassment that Réné alleged was so objectively offensive that it created a hostile work environment. The dispute is whether he was discriminated against because of his gender.

Réné relies on *Oncale* to make his case, contending that the Supreme Court impliedly held that discrimination based on sexual orientation is actionable under Title VII. This is a misreading of *Oncale.* That case did involve harassment of the male plaintiff by his male co-workers, some of which was similar to the harassment in this case. The Fifth Circuit Court of Appeals affirmed summary judgment in favor of the employer on the ground that "Mr. Oncale, a male, has no cause of action under Title VII for harassment by male co-workers." The sole issue before the Supreme Court on certiorari was whether same-sex sexual harassment is actionable under Title VII. The Court held that it was. However, the Supreme Court explained, "Title VII does not prohibit all verbal or physical harassment in the workplace; it is directed only at '*discriminat[ion]* ... because of ... sex.'" Never has it been held "that workplace harassment, even harassment between men and women, is automatically discrimination because of sex merely because the words used have sexual content or connotations." Rather, under Title VII, the plaintiff "must always prove that the conduct at issue was not merely tinged with offensive sexual connotations, but actually constituted '*discrimina [tion]*…because of… sex.'"

Justice Thomas added a concurring opinion specifically to emphasize that the discrimination had to be "because of sex." The concurring opinion states: "I concur because the Court stresses that in every sexual harassment case, the plaintiff must plead and ultimately prove Title VII's statutory requirement that there be discrimination "because of…sex." *Id.* at 82. Thus, the Supreme Court in *Oncale* did not hold that the harassment alleged by the plaintiff in that case was actionable under Title VII. The Court, rather, simply rejected the Fifth Circuit's holding that same-sex harassment could *never* be actionable under Title VII. *See Oncale,* 523 U.S. at 82 ("Because we conclude that sex discrimination consisting of same-sex sexual harassment is actionable under Title VII, the judgment of the Court of Appeals for the Fifth Circuit is reversed.…"); *id.* at 79 (criticizing the Fifth Circuit's view that "same-sex sexual harassment claims are never cognizable under Title VII").

After clarifying that same-sex sexual harassment could be actionable under Title VII, the Court remanded to the Fifth Circuit to address the question of whether the harassment was "because of sex," that is, whether the harassment was because of Oncale's gender. That issue had not been addressed by the district court or the circuit court because of the holdings of those courts that same-sex harassment could never be actionable under Title VII. The Court gave illustrations of how same-sex harassment could be "because of sex" and thus actionable under Title VII. Oncale had alleged both quid pro quo and hostile work environment sexual harassment in the district court. *Oncale v. Sundowner Offshore Servs., Inc.,* 83 F.3d 118, 119 (5th Cir.1996). On remand, the lower courts were to address the question of whether this sexual harassment was because of his gender. There was no implication in the Supreme Court's opinion that the alleged sexual harassment was "because of sex." That determination, which had not been previously considered, was to be addressed by the lower courts on remand.

Judge Fletcher's opinion in effect interprets *Oncale* to mean that if the defendant's conduct was "sexual in nature" the statutory requirements of Title VII are met. The opinion then reasons that because the touching in this case was sexual in nature and was discriminatory, Réné has stated a claim under Title VII. This misinterprets *Oncale.* The *Oncale* Court did say that "[w]e see no justification in the statutory language or our precedents for a categorical rule excluding same-sex harassment claims from the coverage of Title VII." 523 U.S. at 79. However, the Court qualified that by stating "Title VII prohibits 'discriminat[ion]…because of…sex' in the 'terms' or 'conditions' of employment. Our holding that this includes sexual harassment must extend to sexual harassment of any kind *that meets the statutory requirements.*" *Oncale,* 523 U.S. at 79–80 (emphasis added). Thus, the Court stressed that the harassment type of discrimination must meet the statutory requirement of "because of sex." Justice Thomas' concurrence emphasized that point. *Oncale,* 523 U.S. at 82.

Differential treatment of an individual based only on conduct that is "sexual in nature" does not meet the statutory requirement .The alleged harassment in this case was not on account of the plaintiff's sex, i.e., this plaintiff was not treated differently from all the other male butlers because he was male. Réné contended that he was treated differently because he was homosexual.

Title VII is not an anti-harassment statute; it is an anti-discrimination statute against persons in five specific classifications: race, color, religion, sex, or national origin. Harassment can be a type of discrimination against persons in one of those five specific classifications. However, in order for harassment to be actionable it has to be a type of discrimination "because of" race, color, religion, sex, or national origin. There are many types of harassment in the workplace that are very offensive but are not actionable under the federal Title VII law.

While the Court held in *Oncale* that same-sex harassment can be actionable under Title VII, it did not hold that same-sex harassment because of sexual orientation is actionable under Title VII. The Court gave three examples of ways a plaintiff can prove that members of one sex can discriminate against members of the same sex because of gender. *Id.* at 80–81. These examples are not the exclusive ways, but rather are illustrative of same-sex harassment because of gender that could be actionable under Title VII.

First, the plaintiff could show that the harasser was motivated by sexual desire; this route, the Court stated, requires that there be "credible evidence that the harasser was homosexual." *Id.* at 80. Réné has presented no evidence that any of his harassers were homosexual, nor that they were in any way motivated by sexual desire. On the contrary, evidence presented by Réné suggests not that they desired him sexually, but rather that they sought to humiliate him because of his sexual orientation.

The second route identified by the Court for proving same-sex sexual harassment requires that the plaintiff demonstrate that he was "harassed in such sex-specific and derogatory terms by another [man] as to make it clear that the harasser [was] motivated by general hostility to the presence of [men] in the workplace." *Id* . Réné presented no evidence of this form of harassment. In fact, it is difficult to imagine how he could have; *all* of his co-workers on the 29th floor were male, and it would thus be strange indeed to conclude that their harassment of Réné was motivated by a "general hostility to the presence of [men] in the workplace." *Id.*

Third, the Court stated that a plaintiff may "offer direct comparative evidence about how the alleged harasser treated members of both sexes in a mixed-sex workplace." *Id.* at 80–81. Réné cannot avail himself of this route because he worked on the 29th floor of the MGM Grand Hotel, where only men were employed.

In each of these illustrations the harassment type of discrimination is directed at a person because of that person's gender. Given the facts of the *Oncale* case itself, it is significant that the Supreme Court did not indicate that one of the ways a plaintiff can prove same-sex discrimination is harassment because of sexual orientation. In Réné's case he clearly stated in his deposition that the reason for the harassment was that he was gay. No other reason was offered to the district court.

In determining the motivation for harassment, courts must be mindful of the fact that Title VII protects against discrimination only on the basis of race, color, religion, sex, or national origin. 42 U.S.C. § 2000e-2(a)(1). Discrimination based on a victim's other characteristics, no matter how unfortunate and distasteful that discrimination may be, simply does not fall within the purview of Title VII. The Court in *Price Waterhouse* specifically made that point in quoting from an interpretive memorandum entered in the Congressional Record by the co-managers in the Senate of the bill that became Title VII. The Court quoted the portion of the memorandum that stated:

> To discriminate is to make a distinction, to make a difference in treatment or favor, and those distinctions or differences in treatment or favor which are prohibited by section 704 are those which are based on any five of the forbidden

criteria: race, color, religion, sex, and national origin. *Any other criterion or qualification for employment is not affected by this title.*

490 U.S. at 244 (emphasis added).

This court recognized that fact more than twenty years ago in *DeSantis v. Pacific Telephone & Telegraph Co.*, 608 F.2d 327, 329–30 (9th Cir.1979), when we held that discrimination on the basis of sexual orientation does not subject an employer to liability under Title VII. While societal attitudes toward homosexuality have undergone some changes since *DeSantis* was decided, Title VII has not been amended to prohibit discrimination based on sexual orientation; this aspect of *DeSantis* remains good law and has been followed in other circuits. *See, e.g., Higgins v. New Balance Athletic Shoe, Inc.,* 194 F.3d 252, 259 (1st Cir.1999); *Wrightson v. Pizza Hut of Am., Inc.,* 99 F.3d 138, 143 (4th Cir.1996); *Williamson v. A.G. Edwards & Sons, Inc.,* 876 F.2d 69, 70 (8th Cir.1989) (per curiam).

More recently the Third Circuit in *Bibby v. Phila. Coca-Cola Bottling Co.,* 260 F.3d 257 (3d Cir.2001), *cert. denied,* 122 S.Ct. 1126 (2002), held that harassment based on sexual orientation is not actionable under Title VII. The allegations of harassment in that case, as in this one, were solely based on harassment because of sexual orientation. The court stated:

> [I]t is clear that "[w]hatever evidentiary route the plaintiff chooses to follow, he or she must always prove that the conduct at issue was not merely tinged with offensive sexual connotations, but actually constituted '*discrimina [tion]…because of…sex.*' " *Oncale* at 81. Bibby simply failed in this respect; indeed, *he did not even argue that he was being harassed because he was a man and offered nothing that would support such a conclusion.* There was no allegation that his alleged harassers were motivated by sexual desire, or that they possessed any hostility to the presence of men in the workplace or in Bibby's particular job. *Moreover, he did not claim that he was harassed because he failed to comply with societal stereotypes* of how men ought to appear or behave.…His claim was, pure and simple, that he was discriminated against because of his sexual orientation. *No reasonable finder of fact could reach the conclusion that he was discriminated against because he was a man.*

Id. *at 264 (some emphasis added).*

If sexual orientation is to be a separate category of protection under Title VII, this is a matter for Congress to enact. Over the years since the passage of Title VII, numerous bills have been introduced to include sexual orientation as a protected classification. None has passed.

In *Price Waterhouse,* the Supreme Court held that discrimination based on sex stereotyping was a type of gender discrimination that is actionable under Title VII. The Court held that a woman, who was denied partnership in an accounting firm in part because she did not conform to what some of the partners thought was the appropriate way a woman should act, had an actionable claim under Title VII.

Recently, we held in *Nichols v. Azteca Restaurant Enterprises, Inc.,* 256 F.3d 864 (9th Cir.2001), that harassment of a male waiter by male workers and a supervisor amounted to harassment because of sex stereotyping and thus was discrimination because of gender. In that case the plaintiff presented evidence that the harassment was because he acted too feminine on the job. He was taunted for walking and carrying his serving tray like a woman and for having feminine mannerisms. He was harassed because he did not act on the job as his co-workers perceived he should act as a man, not just because of his sexual orientation. 256 F.3d at 874–75. This corresponds to the sex stereotyping described in *Price Waterhouse.*

In Réné's case there was no contention before the district court that the harassment Réné experienced was because he acted effeminately on the job, or for any reason other than his sexual orientation. The first line of the legal argument presented to the district court in opposition to the motion for summary judgment crystalizes this point in stating: "The question raised by the motion is whether the conduct as alleged by Réné is prohibited by Title VII even though it was directed at Réné because of his sexual orientation." Réné made no claim of sexual stereotyping and there was virtually no evidentiary basis upon which Réné could have supported such a claim had it been made. In fact, at one point in his deposition in referring to another worker who had harassed him, he stated: "He's skinny. He is not masculine like I am."

The degrading and humiliating treatment Réné describes is appalling and deeply disturbing. I agree with the eloquent words of the First Circuit:

> We hold no brief for harassment because of sexual orientation; it is a noxious practice, deserving of censure and opprobrium. But we are called upon here to construe a statute as glossed by the Supreme Court, not to make a moral judgment—and we regard it as settled law that, as drafted and authoritatively construed, Title VII does not proscribe harassment simply because of sexual orientation.

Higgins, 194 F.3d at 259.

Réné's lawsuit was brought solely on the basis that he was harassed in the workplace because of his sexual orientation, which is not actionable under Title VII of the Civil Rights Act; therefore the summary judgment was properly entered. I would affirm the district court.

Smith v. City of Salem, Ohio
378 F.3d 566 (6th Cir. 2004)

COLE, Circuit Judge.

Jimmie L. Smith appeals from a judgment of the U.S. District Court for the Northern District of Ohio dismissing his claims against his employer, City of Salem, Ohio, and various City officials, and granting judgment on the pleadings to Defendants. Smith, who considers himself a transsexual and has been diagnosed with Gender Identity Disorder, alleged that Defendants discriminated against him in his employment on the basis of sex. He asserted claims pursuant to Title VII of the Civil Rights Act of 1964 and 42 U.S.C. § 1983. The district court dismissed those claims. For the following reasons, we reverse the judgment of the district court and remand the case for further proceedings consistent with this opinion.

Smith is—and has been, at all times relevant to this action—employed by the city of Salem, Ohio, as a lieutenant in the Salem Fire Department (the "Fire Department"). Prior to the events surrounding this action, Smith worked for the Fire Department for seven years without any negative incidents. Smith—biologically and by birth a male— is a transsexual and has been diagnosed with Gender Identity Disorder ("GID"), which the American Psychiatric Association characterizes as a disjunction between an individual's sexual organs and sexual identity. American Psychiatric Association, Diagnostic and Statistical Manual of Mental Disorders 576–82 (4th ed.2000). After being diagnosed with GID, Smith began "expressing a more feminine appearance on a full-time basis"— including at work—in accordance with international medical protocols for treating GID. Soon thereafter, Smith's co-workers began questioning him about his appearance and commenting that his appearance and mannerisms were not "masculine enough." As a result, Smith notified his immediate supervisor, Defendant Thomas Eastek, about his GID diagnosis and treatment. He also informed Eastek of the likelihood that his treatment would eventually include complete physical transformation from male to female. Smith had approached Eastek in order to answer any questions Eastek might have concerning his appearance and manner and so that Eastek could address Smith's co-workers' comments and inquiries. Smith specifically asked Eastek, and Eastek promised, not to divulge the substance of their conversation to any of his superiors, particularly to Defendant Walter Greenamyer, Chief of the Fire Department. In short order, however, Eastek told Greenamyer about Smith's behavior and his GID.

Greenamyer then met with Defendant C. Brooke Zellers, the Law Director for the City of Salem, with the intention of using Smith's transsexualism and its manifestations as a basis for terminating his employment. On April 18, 2001, Greenamyer and Zellers arranged a meeting of the City's executive body to discuss Smith and devise a plan for terminating his employment. The executive body included Defendants Larry D. DeJane, Salem's mayor; James A. Armeni, Salem's auditor; and Joseph S. Julian, Salem's service director. Also present was Salem Safety Director Henry L. Willard, now deceased, who was never a named defendant in this action.

Although Ohio Revised Code § 121.22(G)—which sets forth the state procedures pursuant to which Ohio municipal officials may meet to take employment action against a municipal employee—provides that officials "may hold an executive session to consider the appointment, employment, dismissal, discipline, promotion, demotion, or compensation of a public employee only after a majority of a quorum of the public body determines, by a roll call vote, to hold an executive session and only at a regular or special meeting for the sole purpose of [considering such matters]," the City did not abide by these procedures at the April 18, 2001 meeting.

During the meeting, Greenamyer, DeJane, and Zellers agreed to arrange for the Salem Civil Service Commission to require Smith to undergo three separate psychological evaluations with physicians of the City's choosing. They hoped that Smith would either resign or refuse to comply. If he refused to comply, Defendants reasoned, they could terminate Smith's employment on the ground of insubordination. Willard, who remained silent during the meeting, telephoned Smith afterwards to inform him of the plan, calling Defendants' scheme a "witch hunt."

Two days after the meeting, on April 20, 2001, Smith's counsel telephoned DeJane to advise him of Smith's legal representation and the potential legal ramifications for the City if it followed through on the plan devised by Defendants during the April 18 meeting. On April 22, 2001, Smith received his "right to sue" letter from the U.S. Equal Employment Opportunity Commission ("EEOC"). Four days after that, on April 26, 2001, Greenamyer suspended Smith for one twenty-four hour shift, based on his alleged infraction of a City and/or Fire Department policy.

At a subsequent hearing before the Salem Civil Service Commission (the "Commission") regarding his suspension, Smith contended that the suspension was a result of selective enforcement in retaliation for his having obtained legal representation in response to Defendants' plan to terminate his employment because of his transsexualism and its manifestations. At the hearing, Smith sought to elicit testimony from witnesses regarding the meeting of April 18, 2001, but the City objected and the Commission's chairman, Defendant Harry Dugan, refused to allow any testimony regarding the meeting, despite the fact that Ohio Administrative Code § 124-9-11 permitted Smith to introduce evidence of disparate treatment and selective enforcement in his hearing before the Commission.

The Commission ultimately upheld Smith's suspension. Smith appealed to the Columbiana County Court of Common Pleas, which reversed the suspension, finding that "[b]ecause the regulation [that Smith was alleged to have violated] was not effective[,] [Smith] could not be charged with violation of it."

II. ANALYSIS

A. *Title VII*

The parties disagree over two issues pertaining to Smith's Title VII claims: (1) whether Smith properly alleged a claim of sex stereotyping, in violation of the Supreme Court's pronouncements in *Price Waterhouse v. Hopkins*, 490 U.S. 228 (1989); and (2) whether Smith alleged that he suffered an adverse employment action. Defendants do not challenge Smith's complaint with respect to any of the other elements necessary to establish discrimination and retaliation claims pursuant to Title VII. In any event, we affirmatively find that Smith has made out a *prima facie* case for both claims.

To establish a *prima facie* case of employment discrimination pursuant to Title VII, Smith must show that: (1) he is a member of a protected class; (2) he suffered an adverse employment action; (3) he was qualified for the position in question; and (4) he was treated differently from similarly situated individuals outside of his protected class. *Perry v. McGinnis*, 209 F.3d 597, 601 (6th Cir.2000). Smith is a member of a protected class. His complaint asserts that he is a male with Gender Identity Disorder, and Title VII's prohibition of discrimination "because of ... sex" protects men as well as women. The complaint also alleges both that Smith was qualified for the position in question — he had been a lieutenant in the Fire Department for seven years without any negative incidents — and that he would not have been treated differently, on account of his non-masculine behavior and GID, had he been a woman instead of a man.

To establish a *prima facie* case of retaliation pursuant to Title VII, a plaintiff must show that: (1) he engaged in an activity protected by Title VII; (2) the defendant knew he engaged in this protected activity; (3) thereafter, the defendant took an employment action adverse to him; and (4) there was a causal connection between the protected activity and the adverse employment action. *DiCarlo v. Potter*, 358 F.3d 408, 420 (6th Cir.2004). Smith's complaint satisfies the first two requirements by explaining how he sought legal counsel after learning of the Salem executive body's April 18, 2001 meeting concerning his employment; how his attorney contacted Defendant DeJane to advise Defendants of Smith's representation; and how Smith filed a complaint with the EEOC concerning Defendants' meeting and intended actions. With respect to the fourth requirement, a causal connection between the protected activity and the adverse employment action, "[a]lthough no one factor is dispositive in establishing a causal connection, evidence ... that the adverse action was taken shortly after the plaintiff's exercise of protected rights is relevant to causation." *Nguyen v. City of Cleve-*

land, 229 F.3d 559, 563 (6th Cir.2000). Here, Smith was suspended on April 26, 2001, just days after he engaged in protected activity by receiving his "right to sue" letter from the EEOC, which occurred four days before the suspension, and by his attorney contacting Mayor DeJane, which occurred six days before the suspension. The temporal proximity between the events is significant enough to constitute direct evidence of a causal connection for the purpose of satisfying Smith's burden of demonstrating a *prima facie* case.

1. *Sex Stereotyping*

In his complaint, Smith asserts Title VII claims of retaliation and employment discrimination "because of...sex." The district court dismissed Smith's Title VII claims. The district court implied that Smith's claim was disingenuous, stating that he merely "invokes the term-of-art created by *Price Waterhouse,* that is, 'sex-stereotyping,'" as an end run around his "real" claim, which, the district court stated, was "based upon his transsexuality." The district court then held that "Title VII does not prohibit discrimination based on an individual's transsexualism."

Relying on *Price Waterhouse*—which held that Title VII's prohibition of discrimination "because of...sex" bars gender discrimination, including discrimination based on sex stereotypes—Smith contends on appeal that he was a victim of discrimination "because of...sex" both because of his gender non-conforming conduct and, more generally, because of his identification as a transsexual.

We first address whether Smith has stated a claim for relief, pursuant to *Price Waterhouse*'s prohibition of sex stereotyping, based on his gender non-conforming behavior and appearance. In *Price Waterhouse,* the plaintiff, a female senior manager in an accounting firm, was denied partnership in the firm, in part, because she was considered "macho." 490 U.S. at 235. She was advised that she could improve her chances for partnership if she were to take "a course at charm school," "walk more femininely, talk more femininely, dress more femininely, wear make-up, have her hair styled, and wear jewelry." *Id.* (internal quotation marks omitted). Six members of the Court agreed that such comments bespoke gender discrimination, holding that Title VII barred not just discrimination because Hopkins was a woman, but also sex stereotyping—that is, discrimination because she failed to *act* like a woman. *Id.* at 250–51, 109 S.Ct. 1775 (plurality opinion of four Justices); *id.* at 258–61, 109 S.Ct. 1775 (White, J., concurring); *id.* at 272–73, 109 S.Ct. 1775 (O'Connor, J., concurring) (accepting plurality's sex stereotyping analysis and characterizing the "failure to conform to [gender] stereotypes" as a discriminatory criterion; concurring separately to clarify the separate issues of causation and allocation of the burden of proof). As Judge Posner has pointed out, the term "gender" is one "borrowed from grammar to designate the sexes as viewed as social rather than biological classes." Richard A. Posner, Sex and Reason, 24–25 (1992). The Supreme Court made clear that in the context of Title VII, discrimination because of "sex" includes gender discrimination: "In the context of sex stereotyping, an employer who acts on the basis of a belief that a woman cannot be aggressive, or that she must not be, has acted on the basis of gender." *Price Waterhouse,* 490 U.S. at 250. The Court emphasized that "we are beyond the day when an employer could evaluate employees by assuming or insisting that they matched the stereotype associated with their group." *Id.* at 251.

Smith contends that the same theory of sex stereotyping applies here. His complaint sets forth the conduct and mannerisms which, he alleges, did not conform with his employers' and co-workers' sex stereotypes of how a man should look and behave. Smith's complaint states that, after being diagnosed with GID, he began to express a more feminine appearance and manner on a regular basis, including at work. The complaint states that his co-workers began commenting on his appearance and mannerisms as not being masculine enough; and that his supervisors at the Fire Department and other municipal agents knew about this allegedly unmasculine conduct and appearance. The complaint then describes a high-level meeting among Smith's supervisors and other municipal officials regarding his employment. Defendants allegedly schemed to compel Smith's resignation by forcing him to undergo multiple psychological evaluations of his gender non-conforming behavior. The complaint makes clear that these meetings took place soon after Smith assumed a more feminine appearance and manner and after his conversation about this with Eastek. In addition, the complaint alleges that Smith was suspended for twenty-four hours for allegedly violating an unenacted municipal policy, and that the suspension was ordered in retaliation for his pursuing legal remedies after he had been informed about Defendants' plan to intimidate him into resigning. In short, Smith claims that the discrimination he experienced was based on his failure to conform to sex stereotypes by expressing less masculine, and more feminine manner-isms and appearance.

Having alleged that his failure to conform to sex stereotypes concerning how a man should look and behave was the driving force behind Defendants' actions, Smith has suf-ficiently pleaded claims of sex stereotyping and gender discrimination. In so holding, we find that the district court erred in relying on a series of pre-*Price Waterhouse* cases from other federal appellate courts holding that transsexuals, as a class, are not entitled to Title VII protection because "Congress had a narrow view of sex in mind" and "never consid-ered nor intended that [Title VII] apply to anything other than the traditional concept of sex." *Ulane v. Eastern Airlines, Inc.,* 742 F.2d 1081, 1085, 1086 (7th Cir.1984); *see also Holloway v. Arthur Andersen & Co.,* 566 F.2d 659, 661–63 (9th Cir.1977) (refusing to extend protection of Title VII to transsexuals because discrimination against transsexuals is based on "gender" rather than "sex"). It is true that, in the past, federal appellate courts regarded Title VII as barring discrimination based only on "sex" (referring to an individ-ual's anatomical and biological characteristics), but not on "gender" (referring to socially-constructed norms associated with a person's sex). *See, e.g., Ulane,* 742 F.2d at 1084 (con-struing "sex" in Title VII narrowly to mean only anatomical sex rather than gender); *Sommers v. Budget Mktg., Inc.,* 667 F.2d 748, 750 (8th Cir.1982) (holding that transsexuals are not protected by Title VII because the "plain meaning" must be ascribed to the term "sex" in the absence of clear congressional intent to do otherwise); *Holloway,* 566 F.2d at 661–63 (refusing to extend protection of Title VII to transsexuals because discrimination against transsexualism is based on "gender" rather than "sex;" and "sex" should be given its traditional definition based on the anatomical characteristics dividing "organisms" and "living beings" into male and female). In this earlier jurisprudence, male-to-female transsexuals (who were the plaintiffs in *Ulane, Sommers,* and *Holloway*) — as biological males whose outward behavior and emotional identity did not conform to socially-pre-scribed expectations of masculinity — were denied Title VII protection by courts because they were considered victims of "gender" rather than "sex" discrimination.

However, the approach in *Holloway, Sommers,* and *Ulane* — and by the district court in this case — has been eviscerated by *Price Waterhouse. See Schwenk v. Hartford,* 204 F.3d 1187, 1201 (9th Cir.2000) ("The initial judicial approach taken in cases such as *Holloway* [and *Ulane*] has been overruled by the logic and language of *Price Water-house.*"). By holding that Title VII protected a woman who failed to conform to social expectations concerning how a woman should look and behave, the Supreme Court es-tablished that Title VII's reference to "sex" encompasses both the biological differences between men and women, and gender discrimination, that is, discrimination based on a failure to conform to stereotypical gender norms. *See Price Waterhouse,* 490 U.S. at 251, 109 S.Ct. 1775; *see also Schwenk,* 204 F.3d at 1202 (stating that Title VII encompasses instances in which "the perpetrator's actions stem from the fact that he believed that the victim was a man who 'failed to act like' one" and that "sex" under Title VII encompasses both the anatomical differences between men and women and gender); *Réné v. MGM Grand Hotel, Inc.,* 305 F.3d 1061, 1068 (9th Cir.2002) (en banc) (Pregerson, J., concurring) (noting that the Ninth Circuit had previously found that "same-sex gender stereotyping of the sort suffered by Réné—i.e. gender stereotyping of a male gay employee by his male co-workers" constituted actionable harassment under Title VII and concluding that "[t]he repeated testimony that his co-workers treated Réné, in a variety of ways, 'like a woman' constitutes ample evidence of gender stereotyping"); *Bibby v. Philadelphia Coca Cola Bottling Co.,* 260 F.3d 257, 262–63 (3d Cir.2001) (stating that a plaintiff may be able to prove a claim of sex discrimination by showing that the "harasser's conduct was motivated by a belief that the victim did not conform to the stereotypes of his or her gender"); *Nichols v. Azteca Rest. Enters., Inc.,* 256 F.3d 864, 874–75 (9th Cir.2001) (holding that harassment "based upon the perception that [the plaintiff] is effeminate" is discrimination because of sex, in violation of Title VII), *overruling DeSantis v. Pac. Tel. & Tel. Co., Inc.,* 608 F.2d 327 (9th Cir.1979); *Doe v. Belleville,* 119 F.3d 563, 580–81 (7th Cir.1997) (holding that "Title VII does not permit an employee to be treated adversely because his or her appearance or conduct does not conform to stereotypical gender roles" and explaining that "a man who is harassed because his voice is soft, his physique is slight, his hair long, or because in some other respect he exhibits his masculinity in a way that does not meet his coworkers' idea of how men are to appear and behave, is harassed 'because of his sex' "), *vacated and remanded on other grounds,* 523 U.S. 1001 (1998).

After *Price Waterhouse,* an employer who discriminates against women because, for instance, they do not wear dresses or makeup, is engaging in sex discrimination because the discrimination would not occur but for the victim's sex. It follows that employers who discriminate against men because they *do* wear dresses and makeup, or otherwise act femininely, are also engaging in sex discrimination, because the discrimination would not occur but for the victim's sex. *See, e.g., Nichols,* 256 F.3d 864 (Title VII sex discrimination and hostile work environment claim upheld where plaintiff's male co-workers and supervisors repeatedly referred to him as "she" and "her" and where co-workers mocked him for walking and carrying his serving tray "like a woman"); *Higgins v. New Balance Athletic Shoe, Inc.,* 194 F.3d 252, 261 n. 4 (1st Cir.1999) ("[J]ust as a woman can ground an action on a claim that men discriminated against her because she did not meet stereotyped expectations of femininity, a man can ground a claim on evidence that other men discriminated against him because he did not meet stereotypical expectations of masculinity." (internal citation omitted)); *see also Rosa v. Park West Bank & Trust Co.,* 214 F.3d 213 (1st Cir.2000) (applying *Price Waterhouse* and Title VII jurisprudence to an Equal Credit Opportunity Act claim and reinstating claim on behalf of biologically male plaintiff who alleged that he was denied an opportunity to apply for a loan because was dressed in "traditionally feminine attire").

Yet some courts have held that this latter form of discrimination is of a different and somehow more permissible kind. For instance, the man who acts in ways typically associated with women is not described as engaging in the same activity as a woman who acts in ways typically associated with women, but is instead described as engaging in the different activity of being a transsexual (or in some instances, a homosexual or transvestite). Discrimination against the transsexual is then found not to be discrimination "because of… sex," but rather, discrimination against the plaintiff's unprotected status or mode of self-identification. In other words, these courts superimpose classifications such as "transsexual" on a plaintiff, and then legitimize discrimination based on the plaintiff's gender non-conformity by formalizing the non-conformity into an ostensibly unprotected classification. *See, e.g., Dillon v. Frank,* No. 90-2290, 1992 WL 5436 (6th Cir. Jan.15, 1992).

Such was the case here: despite the fact that Smith alleges that Defendants' discrimination was motivated by his appearance and mannerisms, which Defendants felt were inappropriate for his perceived sex, the district court expressly declined to discuss the applicability of *Price Waterhouse.* The district court therefore gave insufficient consideration to Smith's well-pleaded claims concerning his contra-gender behavior, but rather accounted for that behavior only insofar as it confirmed for the court Smith's status as a transsexual, which the district court held precluded Smith from Title VII protection.

Such analyses cannot be reconciled with *Price Waterhouse,* which does not make Title VII protection against sex stereotyping conditional or provide any reason to exclude Title VII coverage for non-sex-stereotypical behavior simply because the person is a transsexual. As such, discrimination against a plaintiff who is a transsexual—and therefore fails to act and/or identify with his or her gender—is no different from the discrimination directed against Ann Hopkins in *Price Waterhouse,* who, in sex-stereotypical terms, did not act like a woman. Sex stereotyping based on a person's gender non-conforming behavior is impermissible discrimination, irrespective of the cause of that behavior; a label, such as "transsexual," is not fatal to a sex discrimination claim where the victim has suffered discrimination because of his or her gender non-conformity. Accordingly, we hold that Smith has stated a claim for relief pursuant to Title VII's prohibition of sex discrimination.

Finally, we note that, in its opinion, the district court repeatedly places the term "sex stereotyping" in quotation marks and refers to it as a "term of art" used by Smith to disingenuously plead discrimination because of transsexualism. Similarly, Defendants refer to sex stereotyping as "the *Price Waterhouse* loophole." (Appellees' Brief at 6.) These characterizations are almost identical to the treatment that Price Waterhouse itself gave sex stereotyping in its briefs to the U.S. Supreme Court. As we do now, the Supreme Court noted the practice with disfavor, stating:

> In the specific context of sex stereotyping, an employer who acts on the basis of a belief that a woman cannot be aggressive, or that she must not be, has acted on the basis of gender. Although the parties do not overtly dispute this last proposition, the placement by Price Waterhouse of "sex stereotyping" in quotation marks throughout its brief seems to us an insinuation either that such stereotyping was not present in this case or that it lacks legal relevance. We reject both possibilities.

Price Waterhouse, 490 U.S. at 250, 109 S.Ct. 1775.

B. *42 U.S.C. § 1983 Claims*

The district court also dismissed Smith's claims pursuant to 42 U.S.C. § 1983 on the ground that he failed to state a claim based on the deprivation of a constitutional or federal statutory right.

42 U.S.C. § 1983 provides a civil cause of action for individuals who are deprived of any rights, privileges, or immunities secured by the Constitution or federal laws by those acting under color of state law. Smith has stated a claim for relief pursuant to § 1983 in connection with his sex-based claim of employment discrimination. Individuals have a right, protected by the Equal Protection clause of the Fourteenth Amend-

ment, to be free from discrimination on the basis of sex in public employment. *Davis v. Passman*, 442 U.S. 228, 234–35 (1979). To make out such a claim, a plaintiff must prove that he suffered purposeful or intentional discrimination on the basis of gender. *Vill. of Arlington Heights v. Metro. Hous. Dev. Corp.*, 429 U.S. 252, 264–65 (1977). As this Court has noted several times, "the showing a plaintiff must make to recover on a disparate treatment claim under Title VII mirrors that which must be made to recover on an equal protection claim under section § 1983." *Gutzwiller v. Fenik*, 860 F.2d 1317, 1325 (6th Cir.1988). The facts Smith has alleged to support his claims of gender discrimination pursuant to Title VII easily constitute a claim of sex discrimination grounded in the Equal Protection Clause of the Constitution, pursuant to § 1983. *See Back v. Hastings on Hudson Union Free Sch. Dist.*, 365 F.3d 107, 117–21 (2d Cir. 2004) (holding that claims premised on *Price Waterhouse* sex stereotyping theory sufficiently constitute claim of sex discrimination pursuant to § 1983).

Notes and Questions

1. What is the significance of the Supreme Court's decision to deny the petition for certiorari in *Réné v. MGM Grand*? This decision takes a decidedly different view of the potential application of Title VII to harassment complaints by gay employees than that of the 7th Circuit in *Spearman*. Indeed, the lower federal courts are not at all unanimous about how to deal with such claims. The failure of the Supreme Court to act on the petition is striking, even though technically a denial of certiorari does not represent an expression on the merits by the Supreme Court.

2. A litigation strategy consideration: In states and localities that expressly ban discrimination on the basis of sexual orientation, it would likely be uncontroversial that harassment of an employee because of her sexual orientation is unlawful. On the other hand, the question whether such conduct is unlawful under Title VII is much disputed, and appears to turn on either some argument that the victim is a gender non-conformist or, according to some of the 9th Circuit judges, on whether the harassment is "of a sexual nature." In contemplating filing a lawsuit on behalf of an individual who has suffered such harassment, either because they are gay or are perceived as being gay, does it make sense to file the lawsuit in the federal court system, with Title VII serving as the basis for jurisdiction, or in a state or local court? What are the pros and cons to consider in forum selection? In thinking about this strategic question, keep in mind that state courts have concurrent jurisdiction to enforce federal statutes, and that federal courts may use supplementary jurisdiction to enforce state statutes in cases that are otherwise within the jurisdiction of the federal court, but that if a federal judge finds that the statutory basis for federal jurisdiction is absent, she will most likely dismiss any supplementary state law claims on prudential grounds.

3. Several federal circuit courts have accepted the argument that an employee harassed because of gender-nonconformity may bring a Title VII sex discrimination claim, although in many of those cases the courts found that the plaintiff had not made sufficient allegations to prevail on such a theory. *See, e.g., Nichols v. Azteca Restaurant Enterprises, Inc.*, 256 F.3d 864 (9th Cir.2001); *Higgins v. New Balance Athletic Shoe*, 194 F.3d 252 (1st Cir. 1999); *Simonton v. Runyon*, 232 F. 3d 33 (2nd Cir. 2000); *Schmedding v. Tnemec Company, Inc.*, 187 F. 3d 862 (8th Cir. 1999).

4. It is relatively uncontroversial among the federal courts, as suggested by Justice Scalia in *Oncale,* referred to in the dissenting opinion in *Réné,* that when a homosexual employee subjects another employee of the same sex to harassment out of sexual attraction, a violation of Title VII could be found if the harassment is sufficiently severe and pervasive. In addition, of course, the quid pro quo theory of sexual harassment law could also apply if a gay supervisor were to premise tangible working conditions on a subordinate's willingness to respond affirmatively to sexual advances, and, with the exception of the 5th Circuit in the years prior to the Oncale decision, federal courts have been nearly unanimous in finding employer liability if an employee suffers adverse workplace conditions as a result of rejecting sexual demands by a supervisor of the same sex. The earliest case on point is *Wright v. Methodist Youth Services,* 511 F. Supp. 307 (N.D.Ill. 1981).

5. If other circuits follow the decision in *Smith,* would there be any need for the transgender rights movement to continue requesting the inclusion of "gender identity or expression" in ENDA? It is ironic that the transgender rights movement has now moved ahead of the gay rights movement in achieving coverage under Title VII, when the gay rights movement persisted for several years in rebuffing the request by the transgender rights movement to be included under ENDA.

D. Express Bans on Sexuality Discrimination

Advocates for express statutory bans on sexual orientation discrimination began to achieve success in the mid-1970s with the enactment of municipal and county ordinances in a handful of jurisdictions. By the early 1980s, state legislatures began to take serious notice of the issue of sexual orientation discrimination, with Wisconsin passing the first statute. By the early 1990s, the issue of gender identity discrimination had won its way onto the legislative agenda, and Minnesota became the first state to adopt a civil rights statute that defined "sexual orientation" broadly to include issues of gender identity and expression.

By the early years of the 21st century, a sufficient number of states, counties and municipalities had adopted express bans on sexual orientation discrimination to make it possible to assert that about a third of the American population was living in state jurisdictions where such discrimination is specifically made unlawful. As of 2004, the states that banned workplace discrimination on the basis of sexual orientation were California, Connecticut, Hawaii, Maryland, Massachusetts, Minnesota, Nevada, New Hampshire, New Jersey, New Mexico, New York, Rhode Island, Vermont, and Wisconsin. Early in 2005, Illinois moved to ban sexual orientation discrimination as well, and bills were pending in several other states. The District of Columbia has also banned such discrimination. A court ruling from Oregon suggested that the state's ban on sex discrimination also applied to discrimination on the basis of sexual orientation, and a Colorado appeals court held that a law banning employment discrimination on the basis of lawful off-duty conduct could protect gay employees. See *Tanner v. Oregon Health Sciences University,* 971 P.2d 435 (Or. Ct. App. 1998); *Borquez v. Ozer,* 923 P.2d 166 (Colo. Ct. App. 1995), rev'd on other grounds, 940 P.2d 371 (Colo. 1997).

Minnesota, Rhode Island, Illinois and California statutes also forbid discrimination on the basis of gender identity or expression, Minnesota through a broad definition of sexual orientation and Rhode Island, Illinois and California through straightforward bans. The New Jersey statute has also been interpreted to ban such discrimination. See *Enriquez v. West Jersey Health Systems*, 777 A.2d 365(N.J. App. Div. 2001).

All of these state statutes extend to employment, housing, public accommodations and public services, except for Hawaii's, which is narrowly focused on employment.

The number of counties and municipalities forbidding sexual orientation discrimination surpasses a hundred, and includes many large metropolitan areas in states that have not yet enacted a discrimination ban, such as Philadelphia and Harrisburg (Pennsylvania), Atlanta (Georgia), Miami and Orlando (Florida), Houston and Dallas (Texas) and Seattle (Washington). About two dozen of the local laws also cover gender identity and expression.

If one adds all public employees protected by executive orders issued by governors and mayors, as well as the federal order issued by President Clinton and not revoked by President Bush, then it seems likely that a majority of American workers are employed under policies forbidding sexual orientation discrimination.

In addition to express statutory and administrative discrimination bans, there are privately adopted policies that apply to the employment of millions of American workers. Surveys by the National Gay and Lesbian Task Force and other organizations have found that a substantial portion of the nation's largest employers, listed in the top 500 firms compiled each year by *Fortune* magazine, have adopted policies forbidding discrimination on the basis of sexual orientation. (For a current list, visit the Task Force website, www.ngltf.org.) Similarly, hundreds of universities and colleges have adopted non-discrimination policies regarding employment, student admissions, and issues of student life, as have many major not-for-profit public institutions.

The legal enforceability of privately adopted policies depends on principles of contract law. In a majority of the states, a written policy of non-discrimination contained in an employee handbook or manual may be enforceable under an exception to the common law employment-at-will rule, and contract rules may also support enforceability of formal non-discrimination policies adopted by institutions of higher education. However, some employers and institutions attempt to render such policies as merely advisory by publishing statements, called disclaimers, that their written policies are intended as guidelines and not as binding contracts. Such disclaimers may be effective, depending on the circumstances and jurisdiction. Even where such policies are not legally enforceable, however, their adoption sends an important message of non-discrimination to managers, supervisors and employees, although the effectiveness of such a policy will depend on the degree of publicity it is given and the availability of enforcement mechanisms. Some large employers have established internal grievance procedures culminating in binding arbitration for the enforcement of internal policies.

1. The Enforcement of Discrimination Laws

The existence of laws and policies against sexual orientation (and in some cases gender identity) discrimination raises questions about the substantive content of such guarantees. In particular, to what extent do the overlapping concepts of conduct and status inherent in sexual minority issues raise special concerns under express non-discrimination laws or policies? To what extent does a non-discrimination policy mandate actual equality of treatment, especially regarding such potentially politically and financially charged issues as employee benefits eligibility for domestic partners? Cases in this section of the materials are intended to raise those issues.

Singer v. United States Civil Service Commission
530 F.2d 247 (9th Cir. 1976),
vacated, 429 U.S. 1034 (1977)

JAMESON, District Judge:

This is an appeal from a summary judgment of dismissal of an action brought by John F. Singer against the United States Civil Service Commission...The district court held that there was "substantial evidence in the administrative record to support the findings and conclusions" of the Civil Service Commission.

On August 2, 1971, Singer was hired by the Seattle Office of the Equal Employment Opportunity Commission (EEOC) as a clerk typist. Pursuant to 5 C.F.R. sec. 315.801 et seq., he was employed for one year on probationary status, subject to termination if "his work performance or conduct during this period (failed) to demonstrate his fitness or his qualifications for continued employment." At the time he was hired Singer informed the Director of EEOC that he was a homosexual.

On May 12, 1972, an investigator for the Civil Service Commission sent a letter to Singer inviting him "to appear voluntarily for an interview to comment upon, explain or rebut adverse information which has come to the attention of the Commission" as a result of its investigation to determine Singer's "suitability for employment in the competitive Federal service." The interview was set for May 19. Singer appeared at the appointed time with his counsel. Singer was advised that the investigation by the Commission disclosed that "you are homosexual. You openly profess that you are homosexual and you have received wide-spread publicity in this respect in at least two states." Specific acts were noted, which may be summarized as follows:

(1) During Singer's previous employment with a San Francisco mortgage firm Singer had "flaunted" his homosexuality by kissing and embracing a male in front of the elevator in the building where he was employed and kissing a male in the company cafeteria;

(2) The San Francisco Chronicle wrote an article on Singer in November of 1970 in which he stated his name and occupation and views on "closet queens";

(3) At the Seattle EEOC office Singer openly admitted being "gay" and indicated by his dress and demeanor that he intended to continue homosexual activity as a "way of life";

(4) On September 20, 1971, Singer and another man applied to the King County Auditor for a marriage license, which was eventually refused by the King County Superior Court;

(5) As a result of the attempt to obtain the marriage license Singer was the subject of extensive television, newspaper and magazine publicity;

(6) Articles published in the Seattle papers of September 21, 1971 included Singer's identification as a typist employed by EEOC and quoted Singer as saying, in part, that he and the man he sought to marry were "two human beings who happen to be in love and want to get married for various reasons";

(7) Singer was active as an "organizer, leader and member of the Board of Directors of the Seattle Gay Alliance, Inc."; his name accompanied by (his) "place of employment appeared as one of the individuals involved in the planning

and conducting of a symposium presented by the Seattle Gay Community"; he appeared in a radio "talk show" and displayed homosexual advertisements on the windows of his automobile;

(8) Singer sent a letter to the Civil Service Commission about a planned symposium on employment discrimination stating in part, "I work for the E.E.O.C., and am openly Gay."

Singer was offered an opportunity to comment "regarding these matters". He did not do so. On May 22 his counsel by letter requested a citation to the Civil Service regulations under which the investigation was proceeding and any regulation related to his alleged unsuitability for employment. In a response dated May 23 the Commission stated that its authority was found in Rule 5, Section 5.2 of the Civil Service Rules and Regulations; and that the "suitability standards in Section 731.201 of the Commission's regulations" cite as disqualifying factors: "Criminal, infamous, dishonest, immoral, or notoriously disgraceful conduct." Singer and his counsel were given a further opportunity to appear on Wednesday, May 24, to make a statement or give further information. Instead an affidavit was presented dated May 26 in which Singer stated that (1) he had read the investigative report; (2) the identification of his employment as a typist for the EEOC (6 above) was done by the newspaper without his "specific authorization"; (3) the use of his place of employment with respect to the symposium (7 above) was "not specifically authorized" by him and "was done without (his) knowledge or consent"; and (4) he saw nothing in the report "which in any way indicates that my conduct has been in violation of regulations pertaining to federal employees."

By letter dated June 26, 1972 the Chief of the Investigations Division of the Seattle office of the Civil Service Commission notified Singer that by reason of his "immoral and notoriously disgraceful conduct" he was disqualified under Section 731.201(b) of the Civil Service Regulations and that his agency had been directed to separate him from the service. Singer appealed the decision. Following the submission of briefs, the Hearing Examiner, on September 14, 1972 upheld the decision of the Chief of the Investigations Division. In advising Singer that instructions for his removal were being renewed, the Examiner reviewed the virtually unrefuted charges against Singer and continued in part:

"In reaching a decision on your appeal, careful consideration has been given to the written representations and evidence submitted in your behalf by Attorney Christopher E. Young on September 7, 1972, in lieu of an opportunity for personal appearance afforded to you on that date. In pertinent part, these representations contend that your supervisor and co-workers have experienced no complaint with your performance or conduct on the job, and that your removal will not promote the efficiency of the service. The appellate representations otherwise disagree with the Commission's determination that homosexual conduct is immoral in nature and does not meet requirements of suitability for the Federal service, contending that such actions based on an individual's personal sexuality and sexual activities are violative of constitutional rights of privacy and free speech.

"However, there is more to the 'efficiency of the service' than the proper performance of assigned duties. The immoral and notoriously disgraceful conduct which is established by the evidence in your case, in our view, does have a direct and material bearing upon your fitness for Federal employment. Activities of the type you have engaged in, which has not been limited to activity conducted in private, are such that general public knowledge thereof would reflect discredit upon the Federal government as your employer, impeding the efficiency of the service by lessening general public confidence in the fitness of the government to conduct the public business with which it is entrusted. The federal government, like any employer, may be judged by the character and conduct of the persons in its employ, and it will promote the efficiency of the service to remove from its employ any individual whose detrimental influence will detract from that efficiency."

Singer appealed to the United States Civil Service Commission, Board of Appeals and Review. The Board affirmed the decision of the Regional Office dated September 14, 1972, saying in part:

There is evidence in the file which indicated that appellant's actions establish that he has engaged in immoral and notoriously disgraceful conduct, openly and publicly flaunting his homosexual way of life and indicating further continuance of such activities. Activities of the type he has engaged in are such that general public knowledge thereof reflects discredit upon the Federal Government as his employer, impeding the efficiency of the service by lessening general public confidence in the fitness of the Government to conduct the public business with which it is entrusted.

On December 29, 1972 Singer filed this action on behalf of himself and other persons similarly situated, seeking injunctive and declaratory relief. The complaint was later amended to include a prayer for damages and an order restoring Singer to his Civil Service position. Summary judgment of dismissal with prejudice was entered on March 29, 1974.

Contentions of Parties

Appellant contends that he was discharged because of his status as a homosexual without the Commission showing any "rational nexus" between his homosexual activities and the efficiency of the service, in violation of the Due Process Clause of the Fifth Amendment; and that he has been denied freedom of expression and the right to petition the Government for redress of grievances, in violation of the First Amendment. The Commission argues that appellant's discharge as a probationary employee was not arbitrary, capricious, an abuse of discretion, or unconstitutional; that appellant was not discharged because of his status as a homosexual; and that appellant's repeated flaunting and advocacy of a controversial lifestyle, with substantial publicity in which he was identified as an employee of EEOC, provided a rational basis for the Commission's conclusion as to "possible embarrassment to, and loss of public confidence in (the) agency and the Federal Civil Service."

In considering these contentions, we are concerned with recent developments of the law in four related areas: (1) the extent of judicial review of agency decisions; (2) the extent of the Government's prerogative to regulate the conduct of its employees; (3) the constitutional rights of probationary employees; and (4) the dismissal of government employees for homosexual activities.

Scope of Review of Agency Action

Dismissal from federal employment is largely a matter of executive agency discretion. Particularly is this true during the probationary period. The scope of judicial review is narrow. Assuming that statutory procedures meet constitutional requirements, the court is limited to a determination of whether the agency substantially complied with its statutory and regulatory procedures, whether its factual determinations were supported by substantial evidence, and whether its action was arbitrary, capricious or an abuse of discretion.

Right of Government to Control Conduct and Speech of Employees

Courts are "increasingly re-examining and considering to what extent the Government's prerogative to employ or discharge permits it to regulate conduct of its employees" which might otherwise violate constitutional rights. It is well established, however, that the Government as an employer has interests in regulating the speech of its employees "that differ significantly from those it possesses in connection with regulation of the speech of the citizenry in general." The problem is to arrive at the proper balance between the interests of the employee, as a citizen, and the interest of the Government, as an employer, "in promoting the efficiency of the public service it performs through its employees."

Status of Probationary Employee

As a probationary employee appellant had no right per se to continued employment. However, even though a person has no "right" to a valuable governmental benefit and "even though the government may deny him the benefit for any number of reasons," it "may not deny a benefit to a person on a basis that infringes his constitutionally protected interests — especially his interest in freedom of speech." Perry v. Sindermann, 408 U.S. 593, 597 (1972). Moreover, while the Civil Service Commission has wide discretion in determining what reasons may justify removal of federal employees, that discretion is not unlimited. Due process limitations in determining what reasons justify removal may apply to those whose employment is not protected by statute.

It is clear that the Civil Service Commission complied with the statutory and regulatory procedures in its investigation of appellant's conduct and in his dismissal. It is clear also that the dismissal was not based upon unfounded and unsupported charges. Appellant in effect admitted the truth of the charges. The sole question is whether the action of the Commission in dismissing appellant on the basis of the admitted charges was arbitrary and capricious, an abuse of discretion, and in violation of appellant"s constitutional rights.

Dismissal for Homosexual Activities

With the foregoing principles and trends in mind, we turn to those cases which have considered homosexual activities as a basis for dismissal of Civil Service employees. The leading case is Norton v. Macy, 417 F.2d 1161 (1969), where a protected civil servant sought review of his discharge for "immoral conduct" and for possessing personality traits which rendered him "unsuitable for further Government employment". The employee was "competent" and doing "very good" work. He was dismissed solely because he had made an off-duty homosexual advance. The Commission found that this act amounted to "immoral, indecent, and disgraceful conduct," resulting in possible embarrassment to the employing agency. Relying on the First Amendment and the Due Process Clause the court held that the dismissal could not be sustained on the grounds relied on by the Commission, in that the employer agency had not demonstrated any "rational basis" for its conclusion that discharge would "promote the efficiency of the service." The court noted, however, that homosexual conduct cannot be ignored as a factor in determining fitness for federal employment since it might "bear on the efficiency of the service in a number of ways". More specifically the court said: "If an employee makes offensive overtures while on the job, or if his conduct is notorious, the reactions of other employees and of the public with whom he comes in contact in the performance of his official functions may be taken into account. Whether or not such potential consequences would justify removal, they are at least broadly relevant to 'the efficiency of the service.'"

The court concluded that: "A reviewing court must at least be able to discern some reasonably foreseeable, specific connection between an employee's potentially embarrassing conduct and the efficiency of the service. Once the connection is established, then it is for the agency and the Commission to decide whether it outweighs the loss to the service of a particular competent employee. In the instant case appellee has shown us no such specific connection. Indeed, on the record appellant is at most an extremely infrequent offender, who neither openly flaunts nor carelessly displays his unorthodox sexual conduct in public. Thus, even the potential for the embarrassment the agency fears is minimal. We think the unparticularized and unsubstantiated conclusion that such possible embarrassment threatens the quality of the agency's performance is an arbitrary ground for dismissal."

Norton v. Macy was construed by another panel of the Court of Appeals for the District of Columbia, in *Gayer v. Schlesinger*, 490 F.2d 740 (1973). The court concluded regarding Norton: "Thus the court said (in part) that a rational connection between an employee's homosexual conduct and the efficiency of the service may exist" justifying agency personnel action. The court noted that judicial opinion on the issue was not unanimous since in *Anonymous v. Macy*, 398 F.2d 317, 318 (5 Cir. 1968), the court rejected the contention that homosexual acts of employees do not affect the efficiency of the service and may not be the basis of discharge. The court in Gayer concluded that, "As in other decisions of importance the bearing of particular conduct must be left to a rational appraisal based on relevant facts;" that the determination of the government agency should be "explained in such manner that a reviewing court may be able to discern whether there is a rational connection between the facts relied upon and the conclusions drawn"; that some deference must be accorded the decision of the agency; and that the "degree of this deference must be the result of a nice but not—easily—definable weighing of the ingredients of which the particular case is comprised."

In *Society for Individual Rights, Inc. v. Hampton*, 63 F.R.D. 399 (N.D.Cal.1973), an organization of homosexual persons and a discharged employee brought an action to "challenge the United States Civil Service Commission's policy as stated in Federal Personnel Manual Supplement (Int.) 731–71 of excluding from government employment all persons who have engaged in or solicited others to engage in homosexual acts." The court found that the decision of the Board of Appeals and Review was "based solely upon the fact that plaintiff is presently a homosexual person and the Commission's view that the employment of such persons will bring the government service into 'public contempt.'" Following *Norton v. Macy*, the court held that the "Commission can discharge a person for immoral behavior only if that behavior actually impairs the efficiency of the service", and that the Commission had not met, or even tried to meet, this standard.

The court recognized, however, that "granting this relief will not interfere with the power of the Commission to dismiss a person for homosexual conduct in those circumstances where more is involved than the Commission's unparticularized and unsubstantiated conclusion that possible embarrassment about an employee's homosexual conduct threatens the quality of the government's performance. Thus, although the overbroad rule stated in Federal Personnel Manual Supplement cannot be enforced, the Commission is free to consider what particular circumstances might justify dismissing an employee for charges relating to homosexual conduct."

Changes in Civil Service Regulations and Personnel Manual

At oral argument counsel called attention to changes in the Personnel Manual following *Society for Individual Rights v. Hampton*, which were set forth in a bulletin issued

December 21, 1973, and also to amendments to the Civil Service Regulations relating to Suitability Disqualification, which became effective July 2, 1975 following rule making proceedings initiated on December 3, 1973. The bulletin issued on December 21, 1973 was not made a part of the record in this case, and it does not appear that it was called to the attention of the district court. The new regulations were adopted subsequent to the entry of judgment and during the pendency of this appeal. Our decision in this case is based on the record before the district court and the regulations and guidelines in effect when appellant's contract was terminated.

Reason for Termination of Employment

We conclude from a review of the record in its entirety that appellant's employment was not terminated because of his status as a homosexual or because of any private acts of sexual preference. The statements of the Commission's investigation division, hearing examiner, and Board of Appeals make it clear that the discharge was the result of appellant's "openly and publicly flaunting his homosexual way of life and indicating further continuance of such activities", while identifying himself as a member of a federal agency. The Commission found that these activities were such that "general public knowledge thereof reflects discredit upon the Federal Government as his employer, impeding the efficiency of the service by lessening public confidence in the fitness of the Government to conduct the public business with which it was entrusted."

This case is factually distinguishable from *Norton v. Macy* and the other cases discussed supra. It is apparent from their statements that the Commission and its officials appreciated the requirement of *Norton v. Macy*, decided three years earlier, that the discharge of a homosexual must be justified by a finding that his conduct affected the efficiency of the service. Norton v. Macy recognized that notorious conduct and open flaunting and careless display of unorthodox sexual conduct in public might be relevant to the efficiency of the service. The Commission set forth in detail the specified conduct upon which it relied in determining appellant"s unsuitability for continued employment in the competitive Federal service. We are able to discern "a rational connection between the facts relied upon and the conclusions drawn" and agree with the district court that there was substantial evidence to support the findings and conclusions of the Civil Service Commission.

First Amendment Rights

With respect to appellant's contention that his First Amendment rights have been violated, appellant relies on two cases which deserve comment. The first of these cases, *Gay Students Org. of University of New Hampshire v. Bonner*, 509 F.2d 652 (1 Cir. 1974), did not involve public employment, but rather the validity of a regulation prohibiting a homosexual organization from holding social activities on the campus. The court concluded that "The GSO's efforts to organize the homosexual minority, 'educate' the public as to its plight, and obtain for it better treatment from individuals and from the government, represent but another example of the associational activity unequivocally singled out for protection in the very core of association cases decided by the Supreme Court. In holding that "conduct may have a communicative content sufficient to bring it within the ambit of the First Amendment", the Court also recognized that "Communicative conduct is subject to regulation as to "time, place and manner" in the furtherance of a substantial governmental interest, so long as the restrictions imposed are only so broad as required in order to further the interest and are unrelated to the content and subject matter of the message communicated."

In *Acanfora v. Board of Education of Montgomery County*, 491 F.2d 498 (4 Cir. 1974), the Board had transferred Acanfora to a non-teaching position when they found that he was a homosexual. The Board's action was upheld on the ground that Acanfora had deliberately withheld from his application information relating to his homosexuality. In holding, however, that Acanfora's public statements on homosexuality were protected by the First Amendment, the court recognized the balancing test set forth in *Pickering v. Board of Education*, and continued:

> "At the invitation of the Public Broadcasting System, Acanfora appeared with his parents on a program designed to help parents and homosexual children cope with the problems that confront them. Acanfora also consented to other television, radio, and press interviews. The transcripts of the television programs, which the district court found to be typical of all the interviews, disclose that he spoke about the difficulties homosexuals encounter, and, while he did not advocate homosexuality, he sought community acceptance. He also stressed that he had not, and would not, discuss his sexuality with the students.

> "In short, the record discloses that press, radio and television commentators considered homosexuality in general, and Acanfora's plight in particular, to be a matter of public interest about which reasonable people could differ, and Acanfora responded to their inquiries in a rational manner. There is no evidence that the interviews disrupted the school, substantially impaired his capacity as a teacher, or gave the school officials reasonable grounds to forecast that these results would flow from what he said. We hold, therefore, that Acanfora's public statements were protected by the first amendment and that they do not justify either the action taken by the school system or the dismissal of his suit."

Bonner and Acanfora are factually distinguishable. Neither involved the open and public flaunting or advocacy of homosexual conduct. Applying the balancing test of Pickering, the Commission could properly conclude that under the facts of this case, the interest of the Government as an employer "in promoting the efficiency of the public service" outweighed the interest of its employee in exercising his First Amendment Rights through publicly flaunting and broadcasting his homosexual activities.

* * *

Singer filed a petition for certiorari with the United States Supreme Court. In response, the Civil Service Commission filed a memorandum in opposition, setting forth its revised policy to which the Circuit Court had alluded in its opinion. The Supreme Court issued the following order:

> No. 75-1459. SINGER V. UNITED STATES CIVIL SERVICE COMMISSION ET AL. C.A. 9th Cir. Certiorari granted, judgment vacated, and case remanded for reconsideration in light of the position now asserted by the Solicitor General in his memorandum filed on behalf of the United States Civil Service Commission. THE CHIEF JUSTICE, MR. JUSTICE WHITE, and MR. JUSTICE REHNQUIST dissent.

Notes and Questions

1. Singer's lawsuit seeking a marriage license was the subject of considerable discussion in the press at the time he was discharged. The Washington State Court of Appeals ultimately ruled against him, in *Singer v. Hara*, 522 P.2d 1187 (Wash. Ct. App., Div. 1, 1974).

2. Is Singer's case one of status discrimination, or was he discharged solely due to conduct? If the latter, was the conduct such as to merit discharge from a clerical job at an agency whose specified function is to enforce federal civil rights laws? Is it possible to disaggregate status from conduct and protect individuals from discrimination for their status while allowing discrimination based on conduct that violates no law but correlates with the status? Was Singer really dismissed for conduct or status? Note the comparison to *Norton v. Macy*. Mr. Norton was arrested by an undercover police officer whom he "picked up" while driving about "cruising for sex" in Washington, D.C. The court determined that his federal employer's reason for discharging him was mainly potential embarrassment to the agency, and that this would not suffice under the Due Process Clause.

* * *

The following decision is provided as an example of issues that arise in the enforcement of laws against sexual orientation discrimination. The case arises under California's Fair Employment and Housing Code, which expressly prohibits discrimination on the basis of sexual orientation. The complaint involves discrimination, hostile environment sexual harassment, and retaliation. Although the story is rather long and detailed, it provides a useful sense of the kinds of issues that arise for gay employees in the workplace, and the legal responsibilities that employers have when such issues arise.

Shelton v. City of Manhattan Beach

2004 WL 2163741 (California Court of Appeal 2004)
(Unpublished disposition)

TURNER, P.J.

This case involves alleged harassment, discrimination, and retaliation against a gay police sergeant. Shawn Shelton, plaintiff, appeals from a judgment in favor of the City of Manhattan Beach (the city), Chief of Police Ernest M. Klevesahl, Jr., Officer Eric Eccles, and Officer Donovan Sellan, defendants.

II. BACKGROUND

Plaintiff was employed by the department beginning in April 1994, following five years of unblemished service with the Los Angeles County Sheriff's Department. Due to his consistently excellent performance, former Police Chief Ted Mertens promoted plaintiff to detective after two years and sergeant after four years. Plaintiff's promotion to sergeant after four years was the most rapid such promotion in the department's history. In 1999, Chief Klevesahl promoted plaintiff to a premium pay position as head of the department's Human Resources Division. Plaintiff at all times received positive performance reviews. Plaintiff's fellow officers elected him president of their union. Prior to August 2001, when plaintiff first complained about sexual orientation harassment and discrimination, he had never been investigated for wrongdoing, had a complaint filed against him, or been disciplined. For the first seven years of plaintiff's employment, he hid his sexual orientation at work and no one in the department knew he was gay. Officers Eccles and Sellan were plaintiff's subordinates. They were not supervisory employees of the police department.

Plaintiff presented evidence the department's environment was anti-gay; further, this bias was apparent to him from his first weeks as a probationary officer. Plaintiff's declaration states, "[C]itizens perceived to be gay or lesbian were regularly referred to as 'pole smokers,' 'bat smokers,' 'rump rangers,['] 'dykes,' 'fags,' 'faggots,' 'queers,' 'fruitcakes,' 'carpet munchers,' 'muff divers,' or 'pussy munchers[.]'" Plaintiff repeatedly heard Officers Sellan and Eccles use such terms. Within the last year of his employment, plaintiff had heard the two officers use such terms. Officer Sellan frequently used the term "pole smoker" in plaintiff's presence. At various times, plaintiff had also heard Chief Klevesahl refer to people as "pole smokers." Plaintiff had personally heard roughly 40 officers repeatedly use derogatory terms in reference to homosexuals including, in addition to Officers Sellan and Eccles and Chief Klevesahl, a captain, several lieutenants, and several sergeants. An employee who had been employed by the department in various capacities (as an intern, parking control officer, police jailer, officer trainee) from 1997 to 2000, testified there were about 15 officers, sergeants, and lieutenants who routinely made disparaging and offensive remarks about gay people, including Officers Eccles and Sellan, as well as a captain. The former employee personally heard a certain captain routinely make anti-gay slurs. Plaintiff never reported the anti-gay conduct. Plaintiff stated, "I felt that there was a threat to me if I did" because "the tone of the department [was] that of not being friendly towards gay people." Plaintiff was afraid to tell anyone about Chief Klevesahl's conduct. Prior to a transfer request, which will be described shortly, plaintiff never asked not to be assigned to work with Officers Sellan or Eccles. Prior to filing his August 22, 2001, internal complaint, plaintiff never complained to Chief Klevesahl, Officer Sellan, or Officer Eccles about being upset or offended by their alleged anti-gay remarks.

Plaintiff began treatment with a psychiatrist, Dr. Donna Ehlers, in September 1999, five years after he joined the police department. (This was about two years before he filed his internal complaint on August 22, 2001.) Plaintiff told Dr. Ehlers he was suffering from severe anxiety and depression. He felt anxious and tense most of the time. He had been prescribed a variety of medications for those symptoms. In addition, plaintiff had been diagnosed as HIV positive. Dr. Ehlers's September 24, 1999, notes related: "Patient feels extremely tense because he cannot let anyone know about his disease. He is very fearful because he works…on the police force, and they have a strange or strong prejudice against homosexuals. Patient has not felt comfortable getting any support from the community." At her deposition, Dr. Ehlers was asked, "Is that an accurate reflection that he related to you that he was fearful about disclosing his sexual orientation at his workplace?" Dr. Ehlers replied, "Yes."

There was conflicting evidence whether Chief Klevesahl had discriminated against a gay applicant for lateral employment as an officer with the department. Plaintiff testified at his deposition concerning a telephone call in 1999 or 2000. A telephone call was received from an officer employed elsewhere seeking employment with the department. Plaintiff testified: "[A] lateral police officer [called] in to apply for the department, and he disclosed that…he was gay, and that he was having some problems with the department that he was with, and he wanted to make it clear before he came to another department so he didn't have to repeat those problems.…And [a lieutenant] took this call and shared the information with myself, [an officer],…, and the chief had just walked up as he was talking about it." Chief Klevesahl said, "'You're not going to send that faggot an application, are you?'" A former department employee corroborated plaintiff's testimony that Chief Klevesahl discriminated against the gay applicant. Chief Klevesahl denied referring to a gay applicant by any derogatory term. The aforementioned lieutenant likewise denied Chief Klevesahl ever made any such statement.

In August 2001, a dispute arose between plaintiff and Officers Eccles and Sellan. Officer Sellan had expressed unhappiness with the department's recent hiring decisions. Officers Sellan and Eccles hoped to become field training officers. Officers Sellan and

Eccles were willing to use their authority as field training officers to have the new officers discharged. Plaintiff discussed the attitudes of Officers Sellan and Eccles with Chief Klevesahl. Plaintiff believed Chief Klevesahl was not "real serious" about the attitudes of Officers Sellan and Eccles. Plaintiff explained Chief Klevesahl's failure to immediately respond thusly, "He had a lot of stuff going on at that time." As a result of the dispute, Officers Sellan and Eccles began to make derogatory comments about plaintiff's sexual orientation and that of certain police recruits.

Plaintiff orally complained to Chief Klevesahl on several occasions, but no action was taken. Plaintiff discussed the conduct of Officers Sellan and Eccles with Captain Paul Marshall, head of the department's Administration and Investigation Division. Captain Marshall was plaintiff's second-level supervisor. Captain Marshall told plaintiff it was a serious matter that needed to be addressed. Captain Marshall suggested plaintiff should put in writing. If the allegations concerning Officers Sellan and Eccles were not put in writing, Captain Marshall expressed a willingness to order plaintiff to do so. Captain Marshall testified as to the following: "Q Did you tell [plaintiff] that, if he didn't put it in writing to the Chief, that you would order him to do it, or words to that effect? A I believe I did."

Plaintiff described the conduct of Officers Sellan and Eccles in a memorandum addressed to Chief Klevesahl dated August 22, 2001. Captain Marshall delivered plaintiff's internal complaint to Chief Klevesahl on August 23, 2001. The August 22, 2001, written complaint began by describing the dispute between plaintiff, on one hand, and Officers Eccles and Sellan the other concerning new department hires. Officers Eccles and Sellan were critical of the recent hires by the department. Plaintiff defended the recent hiring decisions. Both sides in the dispute vigorously disagreed as to the quality of the recently hired new officers....

Plaintiff's August 22, 2001, internal complaint then stated that after the disagreement with Officers Sellan and Eccles the following occurred: "I believe Sellan and Eccles initiated the following rumors in an effort to discredit me as a person and to place discredit upon the people who I have processed to become police officers with our department. The most harmful of the rumors are: 1) I am '*Gay*' and the only reason [a certain recruit] was hired here is because his twin brother is my boyfriend. 2) I am a '*faggot*' and I am hiring all my little gay boys to be cops on our department. 3) [Four named recruits] are the beginning of the '*Homo[s]*' that I have and will continue to bring on board. 4) The only one who I have hired who has not 'sucked my dick' is [a named individual] because she is a '*Dyke*'." (Orig.emphasis.) Plaintiff also asserted, "[Officer Sellan] did not feel that any of the recent hires belong here except [one]." The new police officer recruits had approached plaintiff to express their concern about being "'black-balled'" by "the 'firm'" as Officers Sellan and Eccles called themselves. Plaintiff concluded: "I continue to do my job without bias or prejudice. I treat everyone equal and fair regardless of what some do and say to tarnish my person and reputation. *However, I demand that something be done immediately to stop Officer[s] Sellan and Eccles from continuing this behavior.* There are employee[s] (sworn/civilian) in our agency who are of an alternative lifestyle. The actions of Sellan and Eccles cannot be tolerated. The things that they have said to this point have already caused my reputation great damage. I will undoubtedly suffer long term consequences of the harmful, prejudice and most importantly untrue rumors." (Orig.emphasis.)

Plaintiff perceived that no action was being taken on his August 22, 2001, internal complaint. Plaintiff repeatedly complained to Chief Klevesahl and Captain Marshall that nothing was being done and Officers Sellan and Eccles were continuing their offensive conduct. At one point, plaintiff told Captain Marshall, "[H]e had had a conversation with [an officer] where [the officer] had indicated that Officer Sellan was saying that [plaintiff] had filed a sexual harassment complaint because he called him a fag...."

Prior to August 2001, plaintiff's relationship with Chief Klevesahl had been cordial, even friendly. Captain Marshall testified Chief Klevesahl had never complained about plaintiff. Chief Klevesahl had always spoken in a complimentary fashion about plaintiff. However, both plaintiff and Captain Marshall perceived that Chief Klevesahl's attitude and conduct changed. Plaintiff testified: "After I filed my written complaint, his whole personality and the way he treated me changed [publicly];...from being...cordial and friendly to each other as...somewhat friends...to not even making eye contact in the hallway." Plaintiff described the change in his relationship with Chief Klevesahl as "shocking" and having "changed overnight." Plaintiff felt ridiculed and intimidated. According to Captain Marshall, Chief Klevesahl gave plaintiff the "cold shoulder." Chief Klevesahl did not even exchange superficial pleasantries with plaintiff. When they discussed plaintiff, Chief Klevesahl, according to Captain Marshall, got angry and turned red.

In addition, there was testimony Chief Klevesahl began piling assignments on plaintiff. This caused plaintiff to experience additional stress. Plaintiff testified that after he submitted his August 22, 2001, internal complaint, the assignments that came directly from the chief were significantly increased. Plaintiff said, "I am talking about little things that are above and beyond my regular duties, which I was maxed out at already." Captain Marshall observed, "[T]here seemed to be a lot of increase in assignments to [plaintiff]."

On or about September 4, 2001, plaintiff met with Captain Marshall and a lieutenant. At that time, the lieutenant was plaintiff's direct supervisor. Plaintiff complained to the lieutenant that 14 days had passed with no action on the August 22, 2001, internal complaint and Officers Sellan and Eccles were continuing their campaign of verbal harassment. Captain Marshall described plaintiff during the meeting, "[Plaintiff] was very upset about what he felt was piling up of assignments by the Chief of Police and seemed very distraught, red faced, very upset." Plaintiff cried during the September 4, 2001, meeting with Captain Marshall and the lieutenant. Plaintiff said that because of the way he was being treated, he wanted to transfer to patrol. Captain Marshall and the lieutenant tried to talk plaintiff out of returning to a patrol assignment. Captain Marshall added, "[W]e expressed a desire and intent to try to gain some control over the number and nature of assignments that he received." The lieutenant was going to take responsibility for controlling the workload. During Captain Marshall's deposition, the following developed: "Q Did [plaintiff] say words to the effect the he couldn't work with the Chief anymore because the Chief was being so hateful towards him? [¶] A Something to that effect."

Later that day, September 4, 2001, plaintiff met with Chief Klevesahl. Chief Klevesahl probed to discover whether Officers Sellan and Eccles's statements about plaintiff's sexual orientation were true. As to the questions concerning his sexual orientation, plaintiff's declaration states, "I avoided directly responding to the question."

On September 6, 2001, plaintiff submitted a written request for a transfer to patrol duties. Plaintiff knew when he requested the transfer to patrol that he would be leaving a premium pay position. Captain Marshall's initial reaction to plaintiff's transfer request was not to allow it because of a staffing shortage. But following conversations with Chief Klevesahl, the two decided collectively to allow the transfer. Chief Klevesahl subsequently granted plaintiff's transfer request.

On September 10, 2001, plaintiff returned to Chief Klevesahl's office. Plaintiff voiced his displeasure with the progress of the investigation of his August 22, 2001, internal complaint. He also threatened to complain to the media. Shortly thereafter, on or about September 11, 2001, Officers Sellan and Eccles were notified they were the subjects of an investigation as a result of plaintiff's August 22, 2001, internal complaint. Later that same day, all four of plaintiff's automobile tires were punctured while his car was parked in the department's employee parking lot. Captain Marshall recommended to a lieutenant that a criminal complaint be filed and surveillance undertaken. Captain Marshall also advised Chief Klevesahl a crime report should be taken. Chief Klevesahl told plaintiff not to file a crime report. But plaintiff was ordered to e-mail Chief Klevesahl about the vandalism. This order came directly from Chief Klevesahl. Plaintiff obeyed the order. In a September 23, 2001 memorandum to Chief Klevesahl, plaintiff stated: "Remember Chief, the very day that the order was finally served to the Officers[,] all four of my tires were damaged with large contractor nails in an employee parking spot. Nothing was done despite my request to investigate. Nothing. The only action taken was against me in 'ordering' me to cancel the DR number and crime report, then 'report' the damage to my vehicle directly to you through [a lieutenant], via email. I followed my order and did what I was told. Nothing was done about it." Plaintiff was upset and frustrated by the inaction.

Between September 15 and October 7, 2001, plaintiff received dozens of crank telephone calls in the middle of the night. Plaintiff believed the calls were related to the August 22, 2001, internal complaint against Officers Sellan and Eccles. Plaintiff so advised Captain Marshall. At Captain Marshall's suggestion, plaintiff kept a log of the calls. The calls stopped only after plaintiff spread a false rumor that the telephone company had installed a trap. Chief Klevesahl was advised but took no action.

On September 23, 2001, plaintiff sent a memorandum to Chief Klevesahl. Among other things, plaintiff complained of inaction on the August 22, 2001, internal complaint and the failure to investigate the September 11, 2001, vandalism. Plaintiff asked for help in resolving the situation. Plaintiff discussed the prank telephone calls he had been receiving. Plaintiff expressed the suspicion that Officers Sellan and Eccles were involved in the prank calls. Plaintiff described the effect the calls were having on his ability to sleep.

With respect to the investigation of his August 22, 2001, internal complaint, plaintiff stated: "I know you indicated that funds were tight due to the money spent on [another investigation]. Please reconsider an outside investigator [so] as to expedite and conclude this nightmare I'm living. Money should be no object when it relates to this type of complaint and issue. In light of what you said about not 'being comfortable going to [the city manager] for more money for another outside investigation[,]' please[ ] insure that every possible 'available' internal resource is directed towards resolution of this investigation. To date, nobody has said word 'one' to me about what if anything is being done. Again, I don't have to remind you but I had to 'pester' you on a near daily basis in an effort to get you to take initial action by just issuing an order to 'seize and desist' [sic] to Officer's [sic] Eccles and Sellan; 19 (nineteen) days after I filed the 'written' complaint. I still feel that the time frame is unacceptable and I'm very concerned that it is an indication of what is yet to come. Remember Chief, the very day that the order was finally served to the Officers[,] all four of my tires were damaged...in an employee parking spot. Nothing was done despite my request to investigate. Nothing. The only action taken was against me in 'ordering' me to cancel the DR number and crime report, then 'report' the damage to my vehicle directly to you through Lieutenant Leaf, via email.... I'm afraid that you've become bias[ed] towards (against) me since our initial conversation after filing the written complaint when you stated 'these allegations can be very devastating to your career, especially if the allegations were TRUE.' If you're angry because I refused to answer you, I'm sorry you feel that way. I refuse to confirm or deny a rumor that is based upon my personal life especially with regards to my sexuality! If my refusal to confirm or deny the validity of the rumors upon your comment upsets you, I'm sorry. The reality of whether I'm heterosexual and/or homosexual is totally irrelevant! Harassment based upon 'perceived or actual' sexual orientation is what the law states. Reality has nothing to do with anything especially as to what extent of damage to me and my career might become as a result of fact or fiction! Chief, the rumors are devastating to me in either case. I don't like being put on the defensive, but as you very well know I will not stay quiet when someone is wronged. There was a time that you told me you respected me for my honesty and candor. I guess that's the case as long as it does not revolve around subject matter that you're not comfortable with. It's simply unacceptable that this department is not protecting me, no more no less."

Chief Klevesahl had promised plaintiff to speak at an October 8, 2001, union meeting. Chief Klevesahl made this promise prior to plaintiff's sexual orientation becoming known. However, Chief Klevesahl failed to appear at the October 8, 2001, union meeting. Chief Klevesahl never indicated he would not be at the meeting. The purpose of the meeting was to hear Chief Klevesahl speak. At the October 8, 2001, meeting, Officer Eccles made a motion to remove plaintiff as the union president. Plaintiff described Officer Eccles's conduct as follows, "At the meeting, [Officer] Eccles made a motion to remove me as Association President 'because of what he is doing to Sellan and me.' "

Two days after the union meeting, on October 10, 2001, plaintiff took a medical leave of absence. Plaintiff said he was suffering from "[u]ncontrolled hypertension."... Plaintiff returned from medical leave on November 13, 2001. In plaintiff's mailbox was an order from Chief Klevesahl. Chief Klevesahl had transferred plaintiff to patrol. Plaintiff stated, "[H]e waited until I was out on sick leave, and then cut my pay."

On December 4, 2001, plaintiff was required to work while the remainder of the force began attending a team-building workshop in Lake Arrowhead. Plaintiff had been primarily responsible for putting the workshop together. The offered explanation for leaving plaintiff behind was financial....Plaintiff worked the night shift in patrol, from 3 p.m. to 1 a.m., and then drove to Lake Arrowhead in bad weather and without sleep. During the following day, at the team building workshop, Captain Marshall saw Chief Klevesahl become angry and irrational toward plaintiff in front of other officers. According to Captain Marshall, Chief Klevesahl disagreed with plaintiff "in front of everybody at the department, all of the supervisors in the department," about who was responsible for initiating the officer of the year process. Captain Marshall thought Chief Klevesahl's conduct was "highly unusual" and inappropriate.

On December 11, 2001, plaintiff again complained by e-mail to Chief Klevesahl that no action was being taken on his August 22, 2001, internal complaint. In response, Chief Klevesahl asked plaintiff for a meeting. They met on December 14, 2001. Plaintiff admitted the purpose of his e-mails was to put Chief Klevesahl on notice. According to plaintiff, the e-mails were pleas to take action against Officers Eccles and Sellan. Plaintiff told Chief Klevesahl his failure to respond to the e-mails and the August 22, 2001, internal complaint was destroying plaintiff's health and career. On December 14, 2001, a lieutenant gave the following written order to plaintiff, "You are ordered not to discuss the circumstances of this investigation with anyone other than Chief Klevesahl, Marcie Glen, your chosen counsel, or myself unless authorized to do so by Chief Klevesahl, Marcie Glen, or myself." The lieutenant's December 14, 2001, written order referenced an internal affairs investigation into plaintiff's allegations involving Officers Sellan and Eccles.

On December 18, 2001, plaintiff became ill at work. He was very dizzy. The room began to spin. Plaintiff got up and walked to the Fire Department where paramedics attended to him. Plaintiff was taken to an emergency room by ambulance. This was the fourth time plaintiff had been hospitalized since September. Plaintiff took a second medical leave of absence beginning December 18, 2001. Chief Klevesahl never contacted plaintiff.

On January 13, 2002, plaintiff stopped by the police station to pick up a paycheck and speak with the new union president. In a January 17, 2002, letter, Chief Klevesahl advised plaintiff: "It has come to my attention that you were in the [p]olice station in the very early morning hours on Sunday, January 13, 2002. Since you have provided documentation from your doctor that your medical condition prevents you from working until February 4th, it is not appropriate for you to be in the station until your doctor clears you to return to duty. I am concerned about your health and want you to focus your attention on improving it. If you have any work-related issues that need immediate attention or would require your presence in the station, contact Captain Maggard or me to discuss how to resolve those issues. I hope you are on the road to recovery and will be able to return to work in early February."

City resolution No. 3590 states the city manager may grant a full time employee a leave of absence with or without pay not to exceed one year. City Manager Geoff Dolan granted plaintiff a leave of absence in excess of one year. In February 2003, the city offered to return plaintiff to work "with the accommodations described by his physician" related to his carpal tunnel syndrome. However, on February 26, 2003, plaintiff submitted a letter of "retirement" rather than return to work on modified light duty. Plaintiff had remained a city employee until he submitted his letter of retirement. Plaintiff has not returned to work and has asserted, under penalty of perjury, that he is permanently disabled from being a police officer. Plaintiff presented evidence his doctors have declared him permanently disabled from returning to his employment with the department because of stress and high blood pressure....

On August 26, 2002, five days after he filed his complaint in the trial court in this matter, plaintiff was interviewed on a Los Angeles radio station. Plaintiff discussed his sexual orientation and his allegations against the city and the individual defendants. Plaintiff testified at his deposition as follows: "Q Do you remember responding to the question from [one of the interviewers], saying, quote: 'I had no problems with the anti-gay slurs and the jokes. I understand it's a cop thing[?'] A Absolutely if that is in fact what I said. I can't tell you whether I said it or not. I wouldn't normally have a problem with it. I survived 14 years on the job listening to it. If I had a significant problem with it, I wouldn't have made it. Q And was that the truth when you said that on the...radio show? A It's the truth now."

Plaintiff's deposition testimony further included the following: "Q And anti-gay slurs never bothered you, did they? A Sure they did. Q Did you ever tell anybody that anti-gay slurs didn't bother you? A That they didn't bother me? Q Yes. A Well, what I have said is that being [a] third generation [police officer], I prepared myself for the fact that that was going to be part of the job, and you just have to accept it. But internally, of course, it bothers you. I mean, you don't jump the gun, and let everything that is said bother you or you would be crazy. It's just....Q Did you ever tell anyone that even if it was a joking matter, I can take it....A Even if [it] was a joking matter? Q The anti-gay slurs, did you ever say that? A That I can take it? Q Yes. A I can take it."; "Q Even people who made antigay slurs you were friendly with? A Sure. Q So it must not have offended you? A It offended me deeply inside."

[In a portion of the opinion omitted here, the court discussed at length the department's investigations of plaintiff's complaints, as well as a disciplinary proceeding that the police chief instituted against plaintiff on charges of submitting requests for improper reimbursements for expenses. The former investigations involved questioning some of the officers against whom plaintiff complained, who essentially denied all his charges, and the later turned up nothing untoward compared to treatment of other officers.]

III. DISCUSSION

2. The first cause of action—sexual orientation discrimination

Plaintiff's first cause of action is for sexual orientation discrimination. To recover for sexual orientation or other unlawful discrimination in violation of the Fair Employment and Housing Act, the California Supreme Court has held: "Generally, the plaintiff must provide evidence that (1) he was a member of a protected class, (2) he was...performing competently in the position he held, (3) he suffered an adverse employment action, such as termination, demotion, or denial of an available job, and (4) some other circumstance suggests discriminatory motive." The burdens of proof at trial with respect to plaintiff's sexual orientation discrimination claim are governed by the test formulated by the United States Supreme Court in *McDonnell Douglas Corp. v. Green* (1973) 411 U.S. 792, 802–3. In the case of a summary judgment or adjudication motion in the employment context, the burden of production rests with the moving employer to present evidence that shows the plaintiff cannot prevail. An employer may obtain a summary judgment either by attacking the employee's prima facie case or by establishing an absence of pretext with respect to its actions. Here, defendants attempt to show that one or more of plaintiff's prima facie elements is lacking.

Plaintiff alleges the city discriminated against him on the basis of his sexual orientation by: failing to investigate his discrimination complaints; attempting to terminate him for "job abandonment"; investigating his use of the department credit card; banning him from the station; requiring him to work when the other officers had the time off to travel to a team-building workshop; and piling assignments on him. There is no dispute as to the first element of plaintiff's claim, that he is a member of a protected class. However, the trial court found there was no triable issue of material fact as to whether plaintiff: was intentionally discriminated against because of his sexual orientation; suffered an adverse employment action; and was qualified for the position given his asserted permanent disability. On appeal, defendants contend: plaintiff did not suffer any adverse employment action; he was permanently disabled and therefore not qualified to perform peace officer duties; and any discrimination could not have been intentional because no one knew he was gay. We find there is a triable issue of material fact as to whether plaintiff suffered an adverse employment action under circumstances suggesting a discriminatory motive. We further conclude defendants' remaining arguments are without merit.

a. adverse employment action

In *Guz v. Bechtel National, Inc.,* the California Supreme Court briefly described an adverse employment action as *including* a termination, demotion, or denial of an available job. Defendants have consistently advocated that the meaning of an "adverse employment action" within the Fair Employment and Housing Act context should be limited to termination, demotion, or denial of an available job. The relevant language defendants cite to in *Guz* is, "Generally, the plaintiff must provide evidence that...he suffered an adverse employment action, such as termination, demotion, or denial of an available job...." Defendants' argument that *Guz* restricts the scope of an adverse employment action under the Fair Employment and Housing Act to "termination, demotion, or denial of an available job" is without merit. As can be noted, the Supreme Court preceded the listing of "termination, demotion, or denial of an available job" with the words "such as." Hence, the cited discussion in *Guz* was illustrative of what constitutes an adverse employment action—not restrictive. Moreover, the Supreme Court in *Guz* was not addressing the issue of the extent of an adverse employment action for purposes of the Fair Employment and Housing Act.

Moreover, two Court of Appeal cases—*Thomas v. Department of Corrections* (2000) 77 Cal.App.4th 507, 510–12 (*Thomas*), and *Akers v. County of San Diego* (2002) 95 Cal.App.4th 1441, 1455 (*Akers*)—have, subsequent to *Guz,* specifically considered the meaning of "adverse employment action" and have adopted a broader approach than that asserted by defendants. Separate divisions of the Court of Appeal for the Fourth Appellate District decided *Thomas* and *Akers.* Neither decision accepts defendants' analysis.

In *Thomas,* the Court of Appeal for the Fourth Appellate District, Division Two, observed, "[T[here appears to be no California decisions defining the scope of an adverse employment action[.]" The court further noted that federal authority on the definition of an adverse employment action varies from circuit to circuit. However, the court explained: "[M]ost circuits agree that an adverse employment action requires 'a materially adverse change in the terms of...employment.' (*Kocsis v. Multi-Care Management, Inc.* (6th Cir.1996) 97 F.3d 876, 885.)" The *Thomas* court further observed, "[M]ost circuits require that the action 'be more disruptive than a mere inconvenience or an alteration of job responsibilities. A materially adverse change might be indicated by termination of employment, a demotion evidenced by a decrease in wage or salary, a less distinguished title, a material loss of benefits, significantly diminished material responsibilities, or other indices that might be unique to a particular situation.' (*Crady v. Liberty Nat. Bank and Trust Co.* (7th Cir.1993) 993 F.2d 132, 136.) The employment action must be both detrimental and substantial. (*Bernheim v. Litt* (2d Cir.1996) 79 F.3d 318, 327 (conc. opn. of Jacobs, C.J.).)"

Whether an employment action is adverse requires a case-by-case determination based on objective evidence. The Courts of Appeal have found adverse employment action (other than termination) consisting of: denial of a comparable position (*Mathieu v. Norrell Corp.* (2004) 115 Cal.App.4th 1174, 1185–87); delayed promotion and denial of a position (*Perez v. County of Santa Clara* (2003) 111 Cal.App.4th 671, 676); a negative evaluation accusing a prosecutor of dishonesty and, in effect, precluding promotion (*Akers, supra,* 95 Cal.App.4th at p. 1455); suspension and salary reduction (*Dudley v. Department of Transportation* (2001) 90 Cal.App.4th 255, 264–65); harassment and threatened transfer (*Thompson v. Tracor Flight Systems, Inc.* (2001) 86 Cal.App.4th 1156, 1167); denial of a promotion and overtime (*Iwekaogwu v. City of Los Angeles* (1999) 75 Cal.App.4th 803, 814); work transferred and flex time eliminated (*Addy v. Bliss & Glennon* (1996) 44 Cal.App.4th 205, 217); and suspension without pay (*Garcia v. Rockwell Internat. Corp.* (1986) 187 Cal.App.3d 1556, 1562).

There is evidence in the present case that plaintiff, a police officer with a successful and unblemished record of many years, was, shortly after he lodged his August 22, 2001, internal complaint, subjected to two formal internal affairs investigations, one or more of which may have been unwarranted; further, the goal of the investigations was to demote him or terminate his employment. Until he complained in writing of sexual orientation discrimination on August 22, 2001, plaintiff, in 12 years as a law enforcement officer, had never been the subject of an internal affairs investigation or a citizen complaint. After plaintiff submitted his internal complaint, he was the subject of two formal internal affairs investigations involving his use of a police department credit card, and allegations he had harassed Officers Eccles and Sellan. Captain Marshall, who was in charge of the investigation division, believed the formal inquiries were unwarranted. While the investigations were ongoing and before they were completed, Chief Klevesahl spoke to Captain Marshall. Chief Klevesahl said he wanted to terminate or demote plaintiff based on the ongoing investigations even though they had not yet been completed. Even if the investigations resulted in findings against plaintiff, a reasonable jury would not be precluded from finding one or more of the formal investigations was motivated at least in part by plaintiff's sexual orientation because: plaintiff had a lengthy, unblemished record as a law enforcement officer; the timing of the investigations; and Chief Klevesahl expressed a desire to demote or terminate plaintiff based on the investigations even before they were completed. (See *Brandsasse v. City of Suffolk, Va.* (E.D.Va.1999) 72 F.Supp.2d 608, 619–20 [retaliatory investigation was adverse employment action under Uniformed Services Employment and Reemployment Rights Act]; compare, *Spain v. City of Winston-Salem* (M.D.N.C.2002) 199 F.Supp.2d 354, 358–59 [internal affairs investigation of police officer not adverse employment action under circumstances].) A reasonable jury could conclude: the investigations were unwarranted; they were motivated by illegal sexual orientation discrimination; the chief intended to substantially and materially obstruct plaintiff's career within the department; but for plaintiff's resignation, he would have faced discipline, and possible demotion or termination, based on the unwarranted investigations; and had plaintiff not submitted his August 22, 2001, internal complaint, his unblemished record would have remained intact and his career advanced. (See *Akers, supra,* 95 Cal.App.4th at p. 1456.) In addition, there is evidence: plaintiff was subjected to "hateful," ridiculing, and intimidating conduct by Chief Klevesahl; he was unnecessarily excluded from full participation in the team building workshop; and he was overburdened with assignments, causing him to become distraught. Taken together, all of the foregoing is evidence of adverse employment actions having a substantial and material adverse effect on the terms and conditions of plaintiff's employment. This is sufficient evidence to raise a triable issue of material fact as to whether plaintiff suffered an adverse employment action.

b. permanent disability

Defendants assert, and the trial court found, that plaintiff could not meet his prima facie burden because he was permanently disabled from performing his law enforcement duties. We disagree. Plaintiff was required to show only that, *at the time of the defendants' discriminatory actions,* he was performing competently in the position he held. There is no dispute as to that fact.

c. lack of *intentional* discrimination

Defendants argue, as the trial court found, that there could not have been any *intentional* discrimination because no one knew plaintiff was gay. All of plaintiff's allegations involve conduct occurring after it was suspected or known he was gay.

3. Sexual orientation harassment

The Fair Employment and Housing Act prohibits employment discrimination including harassment based on sexual orientation. To recover for sexual orientation harassment in violation of the Fair Employment and Housing Act on a hostile work environment theory, plaintiff must show that: he belongs to a protected group; he was subject to unwelcome sexual orientation harassment; the harassment complained of was based on sexual orientation; the harassment complained of was sufficiently severe *or* pervasive so as to alter the conditions of employment and create an abusive working environment; and respondeat superior. Plaintiff alleges as against all of the defendants that he was subjected to sexual orientation harassment in the form of a hostile work environment. On appeal, defendants argue, as the trial court found, that plaintiff did not subjectively perceive his work environment to be hostile or abusive, and the conduct in question was not objectively severe or pervasive. We find triable issues of material fact remain as to these issues.

a. plaintiff's subjective perception

Defendants contend, as the trial court found, that given plaintiff's discovery admissions there is no triable issue of material fact as to whether plaintiff subjectively perceived his work environment to be abusive. We disagree. We find plaintiff's deposition testimony was equivocal and, as a result, the rule of law on which defendants rely is inapplicable. As noted above, on August 26, 2002, five days after he filed his original complaint in this action, plaintiff appeared on a radio talk show. Plaintiff told the interviewer: "I had no problem with the anti-gay slurs and the jokes. I understand that is a cop thing." At his deposition, plaintiff explained that statement: "I wouldn't normally have a problem with [the anti-gay slurs and jokes]. I survived 14 years on the job listening to it. If I had a significant problem with it, I wouldn't have made it." Plaintiff was then asked, "And was that the truth when you said that on the radio show?" Plaintiff responded, "It's the truth now." [After quoting in full the deposition testimony about the radio interview that was previously quoted, the court continued:]

The rule of law on which defendants rely stems from the Supreme Court's decision in *D'Amico v. Board of Medical Examiners* (1974) 11 Cal.3d 1, 21–22. There the court held that a "clear and unequivocal admission" in a deposition must be accepted as conclusive as to the nonexistence of a triable issue of material fact; moreover, the discovery admission cannot be contradicted by a declaration in opposition to a summary judgment motion. However, the *D'Amico* rule is inapplicable when a discovery admission is equivocal…As the Court of Appeal explained in *Price:* "[A]n uncritical application of the *D'Amico* decision can lead to anomalous results, inconsistent with the general principles of summary judgment law. We do not interpret the decision…as saying that admissions should be shielded from careful examination in light of the entire record. A summary judgment should not be based on tacit admissions or fragmentary and equivocal concessions, which are contradicted by other credible evidence." (*Price v. Wells Fargo Bank, supra,* 213 Cal.App.3d at p. 482.)

Here, plaintiff testified he had no significant problem with the anti-gay work environment. However, he also testified at his deposition that the anti-gay slurs and jokes bothered him—he was deeply offended inside. This deposition testimony is equivocal as to whether plaintiff subjectively perceived the environment to be abusive. In addition, there was evidence that in 1999, five years after he joined the department, plaintiff sought the help of a psychiatrist, Dr. Ehlers. At that time, he was already taking medication for anxiety and tension. He told Dr. Ehlers he was anxious and tense because of the department's strong prejudice against homosexuals. Therefore, plaintiff's equivocal discovery admissions are not conclusive. Hence, there is a triable issue of material fact whether plaintiff subjectively perceived his work environment to be abusive.

b. severe or pervasive

Defendants argue, as the trial court found, that plaintiff failed to present evidence sufficient to raise a triable issue of material fact whether the harassment was sufficiently severe or pervasive to alter the conditions of his employment and create an abusive working environment. Defendants assert: no one knew plaintiff was gay until August 2001; therefore he could not have been intentionally harassed based on his sexual orientation; plaintiff admitted none of the defendants ever directed any anti-gay slurs at him; plaintiff admitted he never told any of the defendants he was upset or offended by the anti-gay remarks; and from the time plaintiff submitted his internal complaint until he went out on disability leave, none of the defendants made *any* anti-gay comments—in other words, no harassment occurred after defendants learned plaintiff was gay.

Plaintiff claims he was harassed because of his sexual orientation *after* he submitted his August 22, 2001, internal complaint and it became known or suspected that he was gay. Moreover, that he was not personally subjected to offensive remarks does not preclude a showing he was subjected to a hostile work environment. As the Court of Appeal observed in *Fisher v. San Pedro Peninsula Hospital, supra,* 214 Cal.App.3d at page 610, "'Evidence of the general work atmosphere, involving employees other than the plaintiff, is relevant to the issue of whether there existed an atmosphere of hostile work environment....'" The *Fisher* court further noted, "[A]n employee who is subjected to a hostile work environment is a victim of sexual harassment even though no offensive remarks or touchings are directed to or perpetrated upon that employee."

The totality of the circumstances shown by the evidence raises a triable issue whether the conduct in question was severe or pervasive. Plaintiff has presented evidence that from his first weeks as a probationary officer with the department, in 1994, anti-gay slurs were regularly and repeatedly used by a large number of officers and their superiors. Plaintiff repeatedly had heard Officers Sellan and Eccles use such terms throughout his employment, including within the last year with the department. Officer Sellan had frequently used the term "pole smoker" in plaintiff's presence. At various times, plaintiff had also heard Chief Klevesahl refer to people as "pole smokers." Plaintiff had personally heard roughly 40 officers repeatedly use derogatory terms in reference to homosexuals including, in addition to Officers Sellan and Eccles and Chief Klevesahl, a captain, several lieutenants, and several sergeants. A former employee who had worked in the department from 1997 to 2000, testified there were about 15 officers, sergeants, and lieutenants who routinely made disparaging and offensive remarks about gay people, including Officers Eccles and Sellan, as well as a captain. The former employee testified he had personally heard one captain routinely make anti-gay slurs. Plaintiff was afraid to report the anti-gay conduct because, "[T]he tone of the department [was] that of not being friendly towards gay people." There was evidence Chief Klevesahl had discriminated against a potential applicant for a position as a police officer who was openly gay. There was evidence Chief Klevesahl referred to the potential employee as a "faggot." In addition, gay or lesbian citizens were *regularly* referred to by derogatory terms. Five years after joining the department, in 1999, plaintiff told his psychiatrist, Dr. Ehlers, that he was anxious and fearful because the police force had a strong prejudice against homosexuals. Plaintiff testified at his deposition that he had survived 14 years as a law enforcement officer listening to anti-gay slurs and jokes. Finally, there was evidence that after plaintiff filed his internal complaint, in August 2001, Officers Sellan and Eccles referred to plaintiff as a "faggot" and to certain police recruits as "homos" and "a dyke." They described recent recruits as plaintiff's "little butt boys" or "butt buddies." They discussed becoming field training officers so that they could get rid of plaintiff's "butt boys." This evidence is sufficient to raise a triable issue whether there was an anti-gay atmosphere within the department evidenced by the repeated and regular use of crude and derogatory slurs over the seven-year period of plaintiff's employment, including the year preceding the date on which he filed his administrative complaint with the California Department of Fair Employment and Housing. If true, the use of such vulgar and derogatory terms by peace officers sworn to serve the public and enforce the law is severe conduct. A trier of fact could conclude that the regular, repeated, and routine use of anti-gay slurs over an extended period of time was pervasive. A trier of fact could find that a reasonable person in plaintiff's position would have perceived the work environment to be objectively hostile or abusive.

4. Retaliation

The Court of Appeal has identified the elements of a retaliation claim as follows: "To establish a prima facie case of retaliation, the plaintiff must show (1) he or she engaged in a protected activity; (2) the employer subjected the employee to an adverse employment action; and (3) a causal link between the protected activity and the employer's action." The *McDonnell Douglas* test applies. As the Court of Appeal held in *Akers, supra,* 95 Cal.App.4th at page 1453: "Once an employee establishes a prima facie case, the employer is required to offer a legitimate, non-retaliatory reason for the adverse employment action. If the employer produces a legitimate reason for the adverse employment action, the presumption of retaliation [then] 'drops out of the picture,' and the burden shifts back to the employee to prove intentional retaliation."

Plaintiff alleges he was the subject of retaliation for complaining of sexual orientation discrimination. The city and Chief Klevesahl are named as defendants in the retaliation cause of action. The trial court found there was no adverse employment action in that plaintiff was not terminated, demoted, suspended, or disciplined and there was no evidence of pretext. On appeal, the city and Chief Klevesahl first contend there is no triable issue of material fact as to whether plaintiff suffered a material adverse employment action. For the reasons discussed above, we conclude a triable issue of material fact exists as to whether plaintiff suffered an adverse employment action. The city and Chief Klevesahl further argue that even if adverse employment actions occurred, there is no evidence this misconduct was a pretext for retaliation. However, the city and Chief Klevesahl have not pointed to any evidence of legitimate, non-retaliatory reasons for the alleged adverse employment actions discussed above. The city and Chief Klevesahl argue only that there was no adverse employment action because plaintiff was not terminated, suspended, or demoted, and was transferred to patrol at his own request. Because defendants have not contended on appeal that there was a legitimate non-discriminatory reason for the adverse employment actions, the issue has been waived. A triable issue of material fact remains as to whether the employment actions in question were retaliatory.

5. Failure to Prevent and Correct Sexual Orientation Discrimination and Retaliation

Plaintiff's cause of action for failure to prevent and correct sexual orientation discrimination and retaliation arises under Government Code section 12940, subdivision (i), which provides it is unlawful for an employer to fail to take all reasonable steps necessary to prevent discrimination and harassment. In enacting that provision, the Legislature established a cause of action in tort. As we observed in *Northrop Grumman Corp. v. Workers' Comp. Appeals Bd.* (2002) 103 Cal.App.4th 1021, 1035–36: "The employer's duty to prevent harassment and discrimination is affirmative and mandatory. (Gov.Code,

§ 12940, subds.(j)(1) & (k).) Prompt investigation of a discrimination claim is a necessary step by which an employer meets its obligation to ensure a discrimination-free work environment." The Fair Employment and Housing Act mandates that the defendants, acting in good faith, conduct an investigation that is appropriate under the circumstances.

Plaintiff alleges the city failed to prevent and correct the sexual orientation discrimination and retaliation. Defendants assert, as the trial court found, that the undisputed facts establish as a matter of law that the city's investigation of plaintiff's internal complaint was appropriate under the circumstances. They argue any delay in the investigation was explained by plaintiff's unavailability for an interview. At the time of trial, plaintiff's lengthy refusal to submit to an interview may be dispositive. But at the summary judgment stage, it is not dispositive. At present, there is a triable issue of material fact whether the investigation of plaintiff's internal complaint was prompt and appropriate under the circumstances.

Plaintiff's August 22, 2001, complaint was not assigned to a lieutenant for investigation until eight days after it was first submitted to Chief Klevesahl. No action was taken to stop Officers Eccles and Sellan from making harassing and discriminatory statements about plaintiff during that time. Moreover, close to a month elapsed before Officers Eccles and Sellan were advised of plaintiff's August 22, 2001, complaint and were ordered to cease their alleged offending conduct. Defendants were on notice during this time period that Officers Eccles and Sellan allegedly continued to comment inappropriately about plaintiff and his internal complaint. There is also evidence Officers Eccles and Sellan ignored the order to cease discussing plaintiff's sexual orientation and his internal complaint and that, moreover, no further steps were taken to compel their compliance. Chief Klevesahl reassigned the investigation to a second lieutenant on October 24, 2001, two months after the August 22, 2001, complaint was submitted. At the time of the reassignment to the second lieutenant, Chief Klevesahl admitted that the matter had already "hung on much too long...." No witnesses were interviewed until November 27, 2001, more than three months after plaintiff submitted his August 22, 2001, internal complaint. Officers Eccles and Sellan were not interviewed until February 21, 2002, and March 7, 2002, respectively. No effort was made to interview plaintiff until April 2002, eight months after his internal complaint was filed. Captain Marshall could recall only one other investigation that had taken as long to complete. This is sufficient evidence of the city's failure to take reasonable steps necessary to prevent the misconduct from continuing and to conduct a prompt investigation appropriate under the circumstances to raise a triable issue.

* * *

Laws forbidding discrimination on the basis of gender identity or expression raise their own particular issues. The following decision illustrates courts grappling with one of those issues.

Goins v. West Group
635 N.W.2d 717 (Minn. 2001)

Russell A. Anderson, Justice.

Goins claims that West discriminated against her based upon her sexual orientation by designating restrooms and restroom use on the basis of biological gender, in violation of the Minnesota Human Rights Act (MHRA), Minn.Stat. § 363.03, subd. 1(2) (2000). Goins also claims that such discrimination created a hostile work environment. We hold that an employer's designation of employee restroom use based on biological gender is not sexual orientation discrimination in violation of the MHRA. We also conclude that Goins has not established a factual basis for the hostile work environment claim. We reverse the court of appeals and reinstate the judgment entered by the district court dismissing Goins' claims.

Respondent Julienne Goins was designated male at birth and given the name Justin Travis Goins, but Goins was confused about that sexual identity throughout much of childhood and adolescence. Since 1994, Goins has taken female hormones and, with the exception of one occasion, has presented publicly as female since 1995. In October 1995, a Texas court granted Goins' petition for a name change as well as a request for a gender change "from genetic male to reassigned female." Goins identifies as transgender or "trans-identified."[1]

In May 1997, Goins began full-time work with West in its Rochester, New York, office. Goins transferred to West's Minnesota facility in Eagan in October 1997. Prior to the actual relocation, Goins visited the Eagan facility and used the employee women's restrooms. A few of West's female employees observed Goins' use of the women's restrooms and, believing Goins to be biologically male, expressed concern to West supervisors about sharing a restroom with a male. This concern was brought to the attention of West's director of human resources who, in turn, discussed the concern with other human resources personnel and legal counsel. West's director of human resources considered the female employees' restroom use complaint as a hostile work environment concern and decided to enforce the policy of restroom use according to biological gender. After considering the options, the director decided that it would be more appropriate for Goins to use either a single-occupancy restroom in the building where she worked but on a different floor or another single-occupancy restroom in another building.

The decision on restroom use was conveyed to Goins by the director of human resources in the morning of her first day of work at the Eagan facility. The director explained that West was attempting to accommodate the conflicting concerns of Goins and the female employees who expressed uneasiness about sharing their restroom with a male. Goins objected, proposing instead education and training regarding transgender individuals so as to allay female coworker concerns. She also refused to comply with the restroom use policy, in protest in part, and continued to use the employee women's restroom closest to her workstation. In November 1997, Goins was threatened with disciplinary action if she continued to disregard the restroom use policy. In January 1998, Goins tendered her resignation, declining West's offer of a promotion and substantial salary increase, and accepted a job offer elsewhere. In her letter of resignation, Goins stated that West's human resources department had treated her in a manner that had caused undue stress and hostility.

Goins subsequently commenced an action in district court, alleging that West had engaged in discrimination based on sexual orientation in the enforcement of a policy that denied her access to the employee women's restroom. Goins further asserted that West's discriminatory treatment, as well as conduct of West employees, created a hostile

---

1. Transgender people seek to live as a gender other than that attributed to them at birth but without surgery. Susan Etta Keller, *Operations of Legal Rhetoric: Examining Transsexual and Judicial Identity,* 34 Harv. C.R.-C.L. L.Rev. 329, 332 (1999). Because Goins refers to herself as female, we will refer to her in this opinion using feminine pronouns.

work environment. The district court granted West's motion for summary judgment. The court of appeals reversed, concluding that Goins had established a prima facie showing of sexual orientation discrimination and that there were factual allegations with regard to the hostile work environment claim sufficient to raise genuine issues of material fact precluding summary judgment.

I.

The MHRA prohibits sexual orientation discrimination in the workplace. Minn.Stat. § 363.03, subd. 1(2)(c) (2000). The definition of "sexual orientation" includes "having or being perceived as having a self-image or identity not traditionally associated with one's biological maleness or femaleness." Minn.Stat. § 363.01, subd. 41a (2000). The parties agree that Goins consistently presents herself as a woman. Her discrimination claim is predicated on her self-image as a woman that is or is perceived to be inconsistent with her biological gender. Accordingly, for purposes of Goins' discrimination claim, her self-image is inconsistent with her biological gender.

Employment discrimination may be established under either a disparate impact or disparate treatment theory. Goins alleged disparate treatment. When a plaintiff alleges disparate treatment, liability "'depends on whether the protected trait actually motivated the employer's decision.'" *Reeves v. Sanderson Plumbing Prods., Inc.,* 530 U.S. 133, 141 (2000) (quoting *Hazen Paper Co. v. Biggins,* 507 U.S. 604, 610 (1993)). The plaintiff's protected trait must have "'actually played a role in the [employer's decisionmaking] process.'" *Id.* Proof of discriminatory motive is critical in a disparate treatment claim. *International Bhd. of Teamsters v. United States,* 431 U.S. 324, 335 n. 15 (1977). Of course, proof of a discriminatory motive may be established by direct evidence. *Hardin v. Stynchcomb,* 691 F.2d 1364, 1369 n. 16 (11th Cir.1982).

Direct evidence of an employer's discriminatory motive shows that the employer's discrimination was purposeful, intentional or overt. Courts have found direct evidence of discriminatory motive where a statement or a policy is discriminatory on its face. The court of appeals concluded that Goins "made a prima facie case of direct discrimination under the MHRA by showing that she was denied the use of a workplace facility based on the inconsistency between her self-image and her anatomy." *Goins,* 619 N.W.2d at 429. The evidence, however, was that West's policy of restroom designation and use was based on gender. In that Goins sought and was denied access only to those restrooms designated for women, West's enforcement of that policy was likewise grounded on gender.

Goins does not argue that an employer engages in impermissible discrimination by designating the use of restrooms according to gender. Rather, her claim is that the MHRA prohibits West's policy of designating restroom use according to biological gender, and requires instead that such designation be based on self-image of gender. Goins alleges that West engaged in impermissible discrimination by denying her access to a restroom consistent with her self-image of gender. We do not believe the MHRA can be read so broadly. As the district court observed, where financially feasible, the traditional and accepted practice in the employment setting is to provide restroom facilities that reflect the cultural preference for restroom designation based on biological gender. To conclude that the MHRA contemplates restrictions on an employer's ability to designate restroom facilities based on biological gender would likely restrain employer discretion in the gender designation of workplace shower and locker room facilities, a result not likely intended by the legislature. We believe, as does the Department of Human Rights, that the MHRA neither requires nor prohibits restroom designation according to self-image of gender or according to biological gender. *See Cruzan v. Special Sch. Dist. No. 1,* No. 31706 (Dep't of Human Rights Aug. 26, 1999). While an employer may elect to offer education and training as proposed by Goins, it is not for us to condone or condemn the manner in which West enforced the disputed employment policy. Bearing in mind that the obligation of the judiciary in construing legislation is to give meaning to words accorded by common experience and understanding, to go beyond the parameters of a legislative enactment would amount to an intrusion upon the policy-making function of the legislature. Accordingly, absent more express guidance from the legislature, we conclude that an employer's designation of employee restroom use based on biological gender is not sexual orientation discrimination in violation of the MHRA.[2]

Even though West's restroom policy is permissible under the MHRA, Goins could still establish discriminatory motive by circumstantial evidence. Disparate treatment claims based on circumstantial evidence are governed by the burden-shifting framework established in *McDonnell Douglas Corp. v. Green,* 411 U.S. 792 (1973). The *McDonnell Douglas* scheme allocates the burden of producing evidence between the parties and establishes the order of presentation of proof. A plaintiff must establish a prima facie case of discriminatory motive. If the plaintiff makes this showing, the burden of production then shifts to the employer to articulate a legitimate, nondiscriminatory reason for its adverse employment action. If the employer articulates such a reason, the plaintiff must then put forward sufficient evidence to demonstrate that the employer's proffered explanation was a pretext for discrimination. The burden of persuasion, however, remains with the plaintiff at all stages.

In the context of a discriminatory discharge claim, to establish a prima facie case as that term is used in *McDonnell Douglas,* a plaintiff typically must demonstrate that she " '(1) is a member of [a] protected class; (2) was qualified for the position from which she was discharged; and (3) was replaced by a non-member of the protected class.' " *Hoover v. Norwest Private Mortgage Banking,* 632 N.W.2d 534, 542 (Minn.2001). The *McDonnell Douglas* elements "vary with the circumstances of the alleged discrimination." *Jones v. Frank,* 973 F.2d 673, 676 (8th Cir.1992) (citing *McDonnell Douglas,* 411 U.S. at 802 n. 13).

Under the circumstances presented here, Goins must demonstrate that (1) she is a member of a protected class; (2) she is qualified—which, in the context of the issues presented in this case, means that she must establish that she is eligible to use the restrooms designated for her biological gender; and (3) West denied her access to such a restroom. Under the *McDonnell Douglas* framework, if Goins fails to establish any one of the elements of the prima facie case, no additional analysis is required and West is entitled to dismissal of her claim as a matter of law.

The MHRA prohibits an employer, because of sex or sexual orientation, from discriminating against a person "with respect to conditions, facilities, or privileges of employment." Minn.Stat. § 363.03, subd. 1(2)(c). The MHRA defines "sexual orientation" as including "having or being perceived as having a self-image or identity not traditionally associated with one's biological maleness or femaleness." § 363.01, subd. 41a. Goins alleges that she has such a self-image and West does not contend that she is not a mem-

---

2. Nonetheless, in concluding that the MHRA does not cover workplace restroom designation and use according to biological gender or according to the employee's self-image of gender, we by no means imply that workplace restrooms are, in other respects, beyond the coverage of the Act. Typically, workplace restroom discrimination claims have more to do with an employer's obligation to provide appropriate and sanitary facilities. While the MHRA does not go so far as to protect Goins' choice of restroom use, it does protect her right to be provided an adequate and sanitary restroom.

ber of the class protected by this statutory provision. Accordingly, Goins has successfully made out the first element of her prima facie case.

Having established that she is a member of the class protected by the MHRA, Goins next bears the burden of establishing that she is qualified. As discussed above, West's designation of restroom facilities based solely on biological gender does not violate the MHRA. Thus, to meet that burden, Goins must establish that she was eligible to use the restrooms that West designated for use according to biological gender. On the record before us, she has not done so. As a result, she has failed to make out the second element of her prima facie case under *McDonnell Douglas*. Having failed to establish that she was qualified, no further inquiry is necessary. Goins' disparate treatment sexual orientation discrimination claim fails as a matter of law.

II.

Goins also claims that West created a hostile work environment based on her sexual orientation. To prevail on a hostile work environment claim, a plaintiff must establish that (1) she is a member of a protected group; (2) she was subject to unwelcome harassment; (3) the harassment was based on membership in a protected group; (4) the harassment affected a term, condition or privilege of her employment; and (5) the employer knew of or should have known of the harassment and failed to take appropriate remedial action. *Carter v. Chrysler Corp.*, 173 F.3d 693, 700 (8th Cir.1999). Even if a plaintiff demonstrates discriminatory harassment, such conduct is not actionable unless it is "so severe or pervasive" as to "'alter the conditions of the [plaintiff's] employment and create an abusive working environment.'" *Meritor Sav. Bank, FSB v. Vinson*, 477 U.S. 57, 67 (1986) The objectionable environment "must be both objectively and subjectively offensive, one that a reasonable person would find hostile or abusive, and one that the victim did in fact perceive to be so." *Faragher v. City of Boca Raton*, 524 U.S. 775, 787 (1998) (citing *Harris v. Forklift Systems, Inc.*, 510 U.S. 17, 21–22 (1993)). In ascertaining whether an environment is sufficiently hostile or abusive to support a claim, courts look at the totality of the circumstances, including the "'frequency of the discriminatory conduct; its severity; whether it is physically threatening or humiliating, or a mere offensive utterance; and whether it unreasonably interferes with an employee's work performance.'" *Faragher*, 524 U.S. at 787–88 (quoting *Harris*, 510 U.S. at 23).

Assuming that the MHRA contemplates a hostile work environment claim based on sexual orientation and that Goins otherwise carried her burden, we find that summary judgment was appropriate. Goins' hostile work environment claim was predicated on allegations that she was the subject of scrutiny, gossip, stares, glares and restrictions on the use of the restroom near her workstation because of her sexual orientation. The restroom policy, as we have concluded, was not based on sexual orientation. As for the remaining allegations, we agree with the district court's conclusion that Goins' claim fails because the alleged conduct of coworkers, however inappropriate, was not of the type of severe or pervasive harassment required to sustain an actionable hostile work environment claim. We therefore reverse the court of appeals decision and reinstate judgment for West on all claims. Reversed and judgment reinstated.

PAGE, Justice (concurring specially).

I concur in the result reached by the court. I write separately to clarify one point with respect to the court's conclusion that Goins has failed to establish that "she is eligible to use the restrooms designated for her biological gender." To satisfy this element, Goins must establish that she is biologically female. Because she has failed to do so, her disparate treatment discrimination claim fails as a matter of law. ANDERSON, PAUL H., Justice (concurring specially). I join in the special concurrence of Justice Page.

Notes and Questions

1. Does the court's decision exhibit an understanding of the problems faced by transsexual persons in the workplace? Does the court's decision effectuate the legislative intention to forbid discrimination in working conditions on the basis of gender identity (as encompassed within the statutory definition of "sexual orientation")?

2. In some areas of employment discrimination law, employers are required to make "reasonable accommodations" to ensure that particular kinds of workers can function in the workplace. For example, workplace modification may be necessary to make it possible for persons with disabilities to function in a workplace, under the Americans with Disabilities Act. The requirement of reasonable accommodation in the context of Title VII usually refers to religious discrimination, and particularly scheduling around the Sabbath observance of persons whose religious faith requires total abstention from work on their Sabbath. Should laws dealing with gender identity discrimination require reasonable accommodations? What sort of accommodation would be reasonable regarding restroom facilities in the workplace?

2. Discrimination in Employee Benefits

A significant portion of the income earned by wage-earners in the United States comes in the form of employee benefits rather than direct payment of wages. Although the proportion of compensation attributable to employee benefits varies widely among employers, among those who provide health insurance and pension benefits as much as a quarter to a third of their employee compensation costs may go to benefits. Many employee benefit plans extend to spouses and offspring of employees, and for married employees the ability to include their families within health coverage in particular can be a significant part of their compensation. To what extent would the failure of an employer to extend such benefit rights to the same-sex domestic partners of employees, and the children of such partners being raised by the employee, constitute unlawful discrimination?

The question is complicated in the private sector by the existence of the federal Employee Retirement Income Security Act (ERISA), a statute that broadly preemptions state and local laws affecting employee benefit plans. As a result of ERISA, attempts by sexual minority employees to secure equal compensation in the non-governmental workplace have focused on collective bargaining through unions (in those relatively rare private sector workplaces where the employees have union representation—less than ten percent of the private civilian workforce) and on lobbying employers to extend such benefits voluntarily, under no legal compulsion. Such attempts by employees have actually been surprisingly successful in recent years, at least in situations involving skilled workers, mainly due to employers' desires to maintain competitive advantages in recruiting such workers. As soon as one or two major employers in a particular field decide to extend such benefits voluntarily or in response to union bargaining demands, the perception of competitive advantage may cause others to follow suit, resulting in major portions of significant economic sectors quickly embracing domestic partnership benefits, and leaving the occasional laggard employer to be the subject of public scorn by gay rights organizations. From modest beginnings in the 1970s, when the Village Voice newspaper in New York City became the first private employer to adopt a domestic partnership plan for health care, a movement for such benefits expansion grew through the next two decades and spread through the non-profit sector (including major universities and public interest organizations), banking, media and communications, and even the auto and energy industries. Most heavy manufacturing industries stayed aloof.

The question is quite different in the public sector, where ERISA is inapplicable, and many state and local governments have faced litigation over the question whether employees are entitled to such benefits, either under general equal protection requirements or specific civil rights statutes, banning workplace discrimination on the basis of sex, sexual orientation, or in a few dozen states, marital status. The results of such litigation were mixed, and a detailed consideration of the case law falls beyond the realistic scope of this casebook. The leading case in favor of finding an entitlement of benefits is *Tanner v. Oregon Health Sciences University*, 971 P.2d 435 (Or. Ct. App. 1998), in which the court found constitutional and statutory grounds supporting a domestic partnership benefits claim. The state government decided not to appeal the case to the state supreme court, instead legislating to authorize state agency employers to adopt domestic partnership benefits programs. In some states, such as New York, benefits programs were adopted through collective bargaining with public employee unions, while in others, such as Hawaii and California, the benefits were provided as a result of statutes. Numerous municipalities and counties have adopted domestic partnership benefits programs through legislation or collective bargaining, including many of the country's largest cities and the District of Columbia.

A new wrinkle in such benefits programs emerged during the 1990s, when San Francisco's Board of Supervisors adopted an ordinance requiring the city to avoid contracting with private sector employers who do not provide domestic partnership benefits. Opponents of the legislation raised serious questions about whether this attempt by the city to influence the employee benefit plan coverage of private employers might be preempted by ERISA. In subsequent litigation involving recalcitrant employers who wished to bid on or retain city contracts, the federal courts found partial preemption, upholding portions of the program while striking down others. *Air Transportation Association v. City of San Francisco*, 1999 U.S.Dist.Lexis 8747 (U.S.Dist.Ct., N.D.Cal., Wilken, J., May 27, 1999); *S.D. Myers v. City of San Francisco*, 1999 U.S.Dist.Lexis 8748 (U.S.Dist.Ct., N.D.Cal., Wilken, J., May 27, 1999); *Air Transport Association of America v. City and County of San Francisco*, 266 F.3d 1064 (9th Cir., Sept. 11, 2001). ERISA does not regulate or preempt with respect to all employee benefits, just those that are maintained as part of funded plans, thus ERISA preemption was found not to be complete in the California cases. The Supreme Court has yet to pass on the issue, which will certainly arise in other places, as municipalities have adopted similar measures in Los Angeles, Seattle, Portland (Maine) and New York City.

In New York City, the city council enacted the Equal Benefits Law over the mayor's veto. Subsequent litigation resulted early in 2005 in an intermediate appellate decision holding that the measure was preempted by state and federal law, but the council immediately appealed to the state's highest court. See *Council of the City of New York v. Bloomberg*, 2005 N.Y. Slip Op. 01843, 2005 Westlaw 589606 (N.Y. App. Div., 1st Dept. 2005).

3. Exceptions to the Non-discrimination Requirement

Hurley v. Irish-American Gay, Lesbian and Bisexual Group
515 U.S. 557 (1995)

Justice SOUTER delivered the opinion of the Court.

The issue in this case is whether Massachusetts may require private citizens who organize a parade to include among the marchers a group imparting a message the organizers do not wish to convey. We hold that such a mandate violates the First Amendment.

March 17 is set aside for two celebrations in South Boston. As early as 1737, some people in Boston observed the feast of the apostle to Ireland, and since 1776 the day has marked the evacuation of royal troops and Loyalists from the city, prompted by the guns captured at Ticonderoga and set up on Dorchester Heights under General Washington's command. Washington himself reportedly drew on the earlier tradition in choosing "St. Patrick" as the response to "Boston," the password used in the colonial lines on evacuation day. Although the General Court of Massachusetts did not officially designate March 17 as Evacuation Day until 1938, the City Council of Boston had previously sponsored public celebrations of Evacuation Day, including notable commemorations on the centennial in 1876, and on the 125th anniversary in 1901, with its parade, salute, concert, and fireworks display.

The tradition of formal sponsorship by the city came to an end in 1947, however, when Mayor James Michael Curley himself granted authority to organize and conduct the St. Patrick's Day-Evacuation Day Parade to the petitioner South Boston Allied War Veterans Council, an unincorporated association of individuals elected from various South Boston veterans groups. Every year since that time, the Council has applied for and received a permit for the parade, which at times has included as many as 20,000 marchers and drawn up to 1 million watchers. No other applicant has ever applied for that permit. Through 1992, the city allowed the Council to use the city's official seal, and provided printing services as well as direct funding.

In 1992, a number of gay, lesbian, and bisexual descendants of the Irish immigrants joined together with other supporters to form the respondent organization, GLIB, to march in the parade as a way to express pride in their Irish heritage as openly gay, lesbian, and bisexual individuals, to demonstrate that there are such men and women among those so descended, and to express their solidarity with like individuals who sought to march in New York's St. Patrick's Day Parade. Although the Council denied GLIB's application to take part in the 1992 parade, GLIB obtained a state-court order to include its contingent, which marched "uneventfully" among that year's 10,000 participants and 750,000 spectators.

In 1993, after the Council had again refused to admit GLIB to the upcoming parade, the organization and some of its members filed this suit against the Council, the individual petitioner John J. "Wacko" Hurley, and the city of Boston, alleging violations of the State and Federal Constitutions and of the state public accommodations law, which prohibits "any distinction, discrimination or restriction on account of...sexual orientation...relative to the admission of any person to, or treatment in any place of public accommodation, resort or amusement." Mass.Gen.Laws § 272:98 (1992). After finding that "[f]or at least the past 47 years, the Parade has traveled the same basic route along the public streets of South Boston, providing entertainment, amusement, and recreation to participants and spectators alike," the state trial court ruled that the parade fell within the statutory definition of a public accommodation, which includes "any place...which is open to and accepts or solicits the patronage of the general public and, without limiting the generality of this definition, whether or not it be...(6) a boardwalk or other public highway [or]...(8) a place of public amusement, recreation, sport, exercise or entertainment," Mass.Gen.Laws § 272:92A (1992). The court found that the Council had no written criteria and employed no particular procedures for admission, voted on new applications in batches, had occasionally admitted groups who simply showed up at the parade without having submitted an application, and did "not generally inquire into the specific messages or views of each applicant." The court consequently rejected the Council's contention that the parade was "private" (in the sense of being exclusive), holding instead that "the lack of genuine selectivity in choosing participants and sponsors demonstrates that the Parade is a public event." It found the parade to be "eclectic," containing a wide variety of "patriotic, commercial, political, moral, artistic, religious, athletic, public service, trade union, and eleemosynary themes," as well as conflicting messages. While noting that the Council had indeed excluded the Ku Klux Klan and ROAR (an antibusing group), it attributed little significance to these facts, concluding ultimately that "[t]he only common theme among the participants and sponsors is their public involvement in the Parade."

The court rejected the Council's assertion that the exclusion of "groups with sexual themes merely formalized [the fact] that the Parade expresses traditional religious and social values," and found the Council's "final position [to be] that GLIB would be excluded because of its values and its message, *i.e.*, its members' sexual orientation." This position, in the court's view, was not only violative of the public accommodations law but "paradoxical" as well, since "a proper celebration of St. Patrick's and Evacuation Day requires diversity and inclusiveness." The court rejected the notion that GLIB's admission would trample on the Council's First Amendment rights since the court understood that constitutional protection of any interest in expressive association would "requir[e] focus on a specific message, theme, or group" absent from the parade. "Given the [Council's] lack of selectivity in choosing participants and failure to circumscribe the marchers' message," the court found it "impossible to discern any specific expressive purpose entitling the Parade to protection under the First Amendment." It concluded that the parade is "not an exercise of [the Council's] constitutionally protected right of expressive association," but instead "an open recreational event that is subject to the public accommodations law."

The court held that because the statute did not mandate inclusion of GLIB but only prohibited discrimination based on sexual orientation, any infringement on the Council's right to expressive association was only "incidental" and "no greater than necessary to accomplish the statute's legitimate purpose" of eradicating discrimination, citing *Roberts v. United States Jaycees*, 468 U.S. 609, 628–29 (1984). Accordingly, it ruled that "GLIB is entitled to participate in the Parade on the same terms and conditions as other participants." The Supreme Judicial Court of Massachusetts affirmed...

We granted certiorari to determine whether the requirement to admit a parade contingent expressing a message not of the private organizers' own choosing violates the First Amendment. We hold that it does and reverse.

If there were no reason for a group of people to march from here to there except to reach a destination, they could make the trip without expressing any message beyond the fact of the march itself. Some people might call such a procession a parade, but it would not be much of one. Real "[p]arades are public dramas of social relations, and in them performers define who can be a social actor and what subjects and ideas are available for communication and consideration." S. Davis, Parades and Power: Street Theatre in Nineteenth-Century Philadelphia 6 (1986). Hence, we use the word "parade" to indicate marchers who are making some sort of collective point, not just to each other but to bystanders along the way. Indeed, a parade's dependence on watchers is so extreme that nowadays, as with Bishop Berkeley's celebrated tree, "if a parade or demonstration receives no media coverage, it may as well not have happened." Parades are thus a form of expression, not just motion, and the inherent expressiveness of marching to make a point explains our cases involving protest marches. In *Gregory v. Chicago,* 394 U.S. 111, 112 (1969), for example, petitioners had taken part in a procession to express their grievances to the city government, and we held that such a "march, if peaceful and orderly, falls well within the sphere of conduct protected by the First Amendment." Similarly, in *Edwards v. South Carolina, supra,* 372 U.S., at 235, where petitioners had joined in a march of protest and pride, carrying placards and singing The Star Spangled Banner, we held that the activities "reflect an exercise of these basic constitutional rights in their most pristine and classic form."

The protected expression that inheres in a parade is not limited to its banners and songs, however, for the Constitution looks beyond written or spoken words as mediums of expression. Noting that "[s]ymbolism is a primitive but effective way of communicating ideas," *West Virginia Bd. of Ed. v. Barnette,* 319 U.S. 624, 632 (1943), our cases have recognized that the First Amendment shields such acts as saluting a flag (and refusing to do so), wearing an armband to protest a war, displaying a red flag, and even "[m]arching, walking or parading" in uniforms displaying the swastika. As some of these examples show, a narrow, succinctly articulable message is not a condition of constitutional protection, which if confined to expressions conveying a "particularized message,"would never reach the unquestionably shielded painting of Jackson Pollock, music of Arnold Schoenberg, or Jabberwocky verse of Lewis Carroll.

Not many marches, then, are beyond the realm of expressive parades, and the South Boston celebration is not one of them.... To be sure, we agree with the state courts that in spite of excluding some applicants, the Council is rather lenient in admitting participants. But a private speaker does not forfeit constitutional protection simply by combining multifarious voices, or by failing to edit their themes to isolate an exact message as the exclusive subject matter of the speech. Nor, under our precedent, does First Amendment protection require a speaker to generate, as an original matter, each item featured in the communication....

Respondents' participation as a unit in the parade was equally expressive. GLIB was formed for the very purpose of marching in it, as the trial court found, in order to celebrate its members' identity as openly gay, lesbian, and bisexual descendants of the Irish immigrants, to show that there are such individuals in the community, and to support the like men and women who sought to march in the New York parade. The organization distributed a fact sheet describing the members' intentions, and the record otherwise corroborates the expressive nature of GLIB's participation. In 1993, members of

GLIB marched behind a shamrock-strewn banner with the simple inscription "Irish American Gay, Lesbian and Bisexual Group of Boston." GLIB understandably seeks to communicate its ideas as part of the existing parade, rather than staging one of its own.

The Massachusetts public accommodations law under which respondents brought suit has a venerable history. At common law, innkeepers, smiths, and others who "made profession of a public employment," were prohibited from refusing, without good reason, to serve a customer. *Lane v. Cotton,* 12 Mod. 472, 484–85, 88 Eng.Rep. 1458, 1464–65 (K.B.1701) (Holt, C.J.); see *Bell v. Maryland,* 378 U.S. 226, 298, n. 17 (1964) (Goldberg, J., concurring); *Lombard v. Louisiana,* 373 U.S. 267, 277 (1963) (Douglas, J., concurring). As one of the 19th-century English judges put it, the rule was that "[t]he innkeeper is not to select his guests[;] [h]e has no right to say to one, you shall come into my inn, and to another you shall not, as every one coming and conducting himself in a proper manner has a right to be received; and for this purpose innkeepers are a sort of public servants." *Rex v. Ivens,* 7 Car. & P. 213, 219, 173 Eng.Rep. 94, 96 (N.P.1835); M. Konvitz & T. Leskes, A Century of Civil Rights 160 (1961).

After the Civil War, the Commonwealth of Massachusetts was the first State to codify this principle to ensure access to public accommodations regardless of race. See Act Forbidding Unjust Discrimination on Account of Color or Race, 1865 Mass. Acts, ch. 277 (May 16, 1865). In prohibiting discrimination "in any licensed inn, in any public place of amusement, public conveyance or public meeting," 1865 Mass.Acts, ch. 277, §1, the original statute already expanded upon the common law, which had not conferred any right of access to places of public amusement. As with many public accommodations statutes across the Nation, the legislature continued to broaden the scope of legislation, to the point that the law today prohibits discrimination on the basis of "race, color, religious creed, national origin, sex, sexual orientation..., deafness, blindness or any physical or mental disability or ancestry" in "the admission of any person to, or treatment in any place of public accommodation, resort or amusement." Mass.Gen.Laws §272:98 (1992). Provisions like these are well within the State's usual power to enact when a legislature has reason to believe that a given group is the target of discrimination, and they do not, as a general matter, violate the First or Fourteenth Amendments. Nor is this statute unusual in any obvious way, since it does not, on its face, target speech or discriminate on the basis of its content, the focal point of its prohibition being rather on the act of discriminating against individuals in the provision of publicly available goods, privileges, and services on the proscribed grounds.

In the case before us, however, the Massachusetts law has been applied in a peculiar way. Its enforcement does not address any dispute about the participation of openly gay, lesbian, or bisexual individuals in various units admitted to the parade. Petitioners disclaim any intent to exclude homosexuals as such, and no individual member of GLIB claims to have been excluded from parading as a member of any group that the Council has approved to march. Instead, the disagreement goes to the admission of GLIB as its own parade unit carrying its own banner. Since every participating unit affects the message conveyed by the private organizers, the state courts' application of the statute produced an order essentially requiring petitioners to alter the expressive content of their parade. Although the state courts spoke of the parade as a place of public accommodation, once the expressive character of both the parade and the marching GLIB contingent is understood, it becomes apparent that the state courts' application of the statute had the effect of declaring the sponsors' speech itself to be the public accommodation. Under this approach any contingent of protected individuals with a message would have the right to participate in petitioners' speech, so that the communication produced by the private organizers would be shaped by all those protected by the law who wished to join in with some expressive demonstration of their own. But this use of the State's power violates the fundamental rule of protection under the First Amendment, that a speaker has the autonomy to choose the content of his own message.

"Since *all* speech inherently involves choices of what to say and what to leave unsaid," *Pacific Gas & Electric Co. v. Public Utilities Comm'n of Cal.,* 475 U.S. 1, 11 (1986) (plurality opinion) (emphasis in original), one important manifestation of the principle of free speech is that one who chooses to speak may also decide "what not to say." Although the State may at times "prescribe what shall be orthodox in commercial advertising" by requiring the dissemination of "purely factual and uncontroversial information," *Zauderer v. Office of Disciplinary Counsel of Supreme Court of Ohio,* 471 U.S. 626, 651 (1985); see *Pittsburgh Press Co. v. Pittsburgh Comm'n on Human Relations,* 413 U.S. 376, 386–87 (1973), outside that context it may not compel affirmance of a belief with which the speaker disagrees. Indeed this general rule, that the speaker has the right to tailor the speech, applies not only to expressions of value, opinion, or endorsement, but equally to statements of fact the speaker would rather avoid, subject, perhaps, to the permissive law of defamation. Nor is the rule's benefit restricted to the press, being enjoyed by business corporations generally and by ordinary people engaged in unsophisticated expression as well as by professional publishers. Its point is simply the point of all speech protection, which is to shield just those choices of content that in someone's eyes are misguided, or even hurtful.

Petitioners' claim to the benefit of this principle of autonomy to control one's own speech is as sound as the South Boston parade is expressive. Rather like a composer, the Council selects the expressive units of the parade from potential participants, and though the score may not produce a particularized message, each contingent's expression in the Council's eyes comports with what merits celebration on that day. Even if this view gives the Council credit for a more considered judgment than it actively made, the Council clearly decided to exclude a message it did not like from the communication it chose to make, and that is enough to invoke its right as a private speaker to shape its expression by speaking on one subject while remaining silent on another. The message it disfavored is not difficult to identify. Although GLIB's point (like the Council's) is not wholly articulate, a contingent marching behind the organization's banner would at least bear witness to the fact that some Irish are gay, lesbian, or bisexual, and the presence of the organized marchers would suggest their view that people of their sexual orientations have as much claim to unqualified social acceptance as heterosexuals and indeed as members of parade units organized around other identifying characteristics. The parade's organizers may not believe these facts about Irish sexuality to be so, or they may object to unqualified social acceptance of gays and lesbians or have some other reason for wishing to keep GLIB's message out of the parade. But whatever the reason, it boils down to the choice of a speaker not to propound a particular point of view, and that choice is presumed to lie beyond the government's power to control....

The statute, Mass.Gen.Laws § 272:98 (1992), is a piece of protective legislation that announces no purpose beyond the object both expressed and apparent in its provisions, which is to prevent any denial of access to (or discriminatory treatment in) public accommodations on proscribed grounds, including sexual orientation. On its face, the object of the law is to ensure by statute for gays and lesbians desiring to make use of public accommodations what the old common law promised to any member of the public wanting a meal at the inn, that accepting the usual terms of service, they will not be turned away merely on the proprietor's exercise of personal preference. When the law is applied to expressive activity in the way it was done here, its apparent object is simply to require speakers to modify the content of their expression to whatever extent beneficiaries of the law choose to alter it with messages of their own. But in the absence of some further, legitimate end, this object is merely to allow exactly what the general rule of speaker's autonomy forbids.

It might, of course, have been argued that a broader objective is apparent: that the ultimate point of forbidding acts of discrimination toward certain classes is to produce a society free of the corresponding biases. Requiring access to a speaker's message would thus be not an end in itself, but a means to produce speakers free of the biases, whose expressive conduct would be at least neutral toward the particular classes, obviating any future need for correction. But if this indeed is the point of applying the state law to expressive conduct, it is a decidedly fatal objective. Having availed itself of the public thoroughfares "for purposes of assembly [and] communicating thoughts between citizens," the Council is engaged in a use of the streets that has "from ancient times, been a part of the privileges, immunities, rights, and liberties of citizens." Our tradition of free speech commands that a speaker who takes to the street corner to express his views in this way should be free from interference by the State based on the content of what he says. The very idea that a noncommercial speech restriction be used to produce thoughts and statements acceptable to some groups or, indeed, all people, grates on the First Amendment, for it amounts to nothing less than a proposal to limit speech in the service of orthodox expression. The Speech Clause has no more certain antithesis. While the law is free to promote all sorts of conduct in place of harmful behavior, it is not free to interfere with speech for no better reason than promoting an approved message or discouraging a disfavored one, however enlightened either purpose may strike the government.

New York State Club Assn. is also instructive by the contrast it provides. There, we turned back a facial challenge to a state anti-discrimination statute on the assumption that the expressive associational character of a dining club with over 400 members could be sufficiently attenuated to permit application of the law even to such a private organization, but we also recognized that the State did not prohibit exclusion of those whose views were at odds with positions espoused by the general club memberships. 487 U.S., at 13. In other words, although the association provided public benefits to which a State could ensure equal access, it was also engaged in expressive activity; compelled access to the benefit, which was upheld, did not trespass on the organization's message itself. If we were to analyze this case strictly along those lines, GLIB would lose. Assuming the parade to be large enough and a source of benefits (apart from its expression) that would generally justify a mandated access provision, GLIB could nonetheless be refused admission as an expressive contingent with its own message just as readily as a private club could exclude an applicant whose manifest views were at odds with a position taken by the club's existing members.

Our holding today rests not on any particular view about the Council's message but on the Nation's commitment to protect freedom of speech. Disapproval of a private speaker's statement does not legitimize use of the Commonwealth's power to compel the speaker to alter the message by including one more acceptable to others. Accordingly, the judgment of the Supreme Judicial Court is reversed, and the case is remanded for proceedings not inconsistent with this opinion. It is so ordered.

Notes & Questions

1. The Massachusetts statute had no express exemption for those whose refusal to allow participation in a "public accommodation" was motivated by expressive concerns. Constitutional claims of this sort can be held to override statutory language, as the enforceability of the statute depends upon the existence of the Constitutional structure (and also because the Supremacy Clause of the Constitution provides that constitutional provisions take priority over state statutes).

2. A recurring question under state public accommodations laws is whether a particular entity charged with discrimination is a public accommodation. Many such laws are phrased in terms of "place of public accommodation," leaving open the defensive argument that a particular alleged discriminating entity does not have a fixed place and is thus not covered. For example, supposed that the publisher of a Yellowpages phone directory refused to accept for publication an advertisement from a gay-owned business that would be specifically targeted to gay consumers? The publisher states that use of the words "lesbian" and "gay" in the advertisement violates its standards, and that it prefers to avoid publishing controversial advertisements. If the business sued under a state law forbidding discrimination on the basis of sexual orientation in public accommodations, could the defendant win a dismissal motion on the argument that the Yellowpages is not a "place of public accommodation?" See *Hatheway v. Gannett Satellite Information Network, Inc.*, 459 N.W.2d 873 (Wis.App. 1990), rev. denied. Would a private dentist's office be considered a place of public accommodation, such that a dentist who terminated a patient relationship after learning the patient was gay would be faced with a discrimination charge? See *Cahill v. Rosa*, 89 N.Y.2d 14, 674 N.E.2d 274, 651 N.Y.S.2d 344 (1996).

* * *

The "public accommodations" issue took on major proportions in state litigation during the 1990s over the refusal of the Boy Scouts of America to allow openly-gay boys and men to participate in its activities. In conflicting decisions, the California and New Jersey Supreme Courts came to opposite conclusions over whether a Boy Scout troop is subject to non-discrimination laws. Compare *Curran v. Mount Diablo Council of the Boy Scouts of America*, 952 P.2d 218 (Cal. 1998) with *Dale v. Boy Scouts of America*, 734 A.2d 1196, 160 N.J. 562 (N.J. Supreme Ct. 1999). The New Jersey decision, which went on to determine the merits of whether the Boy Scouts could raise a First Amendment defense, ultimately generated the following decision.

Boy Scouts of America v. Dale
530 U.S. 640 (2000)

CHIEF JUSTICE REHNQUIST delivered the opinion of the Court.

I

James Dale entered scouting in 1978 at the age of eight by joining Monmouth Council's Cub Scout Pack 142. Dale became a Boy Scout in 1981 and remained a Scout until he turned 18. By all accounts, Dale was an exemplary Scout. In 1988, he achieved the rank of Eagle Scout, one of Scouting's highest honors. Dale applied for adult membership in the Boy Scouts in 1989. The Boy Scouts approved his application for the position of assistant scoutmaster of Troop 73. Around the same time, Dale left home to attend Rutgers University. After arriving at Rutgers, Dale first acknowledged to himself and others that he is gay. He quickly became involved with, and eventually became the co-president of, the Rutgers University Lesbian/Gay Alliance.

In 1990, Dale attended a seminar addressing the psychological and health needs of lesbian and gay teenagers. A newspaper covering the event interviewed Dale about his advocacy of homosexual teenagers' need for gay role models. In early July 1990, the newspaper published the interview and Dale's photograph over a caption identifying him as the co-president of the Lesbian/Gay Alliance. Later that month, Dale received a letter from Monmouth Council Executive James Kay revoking his adult membership. Dale wrote to Kay requesting the reason for Monmouth Council's decision. Kay responded by letter that the Boy Scouts "specifically forbid membership to homosexuals."

In 1992, Dale filed a complaint against the Boy Scouts in the New Jersey Superior Court. The complaint alleged that the Boy Scouts had violated New Jersey's public accommodations statute and its common law by revoking Dale's membership based solely on his sexual orientation. New Jersey's public accommodations statute prohibits, among other things, discrimination on the basis of sexual orientation in places of public accommodation. The New Jersey Superior Court's Chancery Division granted summary judgment in favor of the Boy Scouts. The New Jersey Superior Court's Appellate Division affirmed the dismissal of Dale's common-law claim, but otherwise reversed and remanded for further proceedings. The New Jersey Supreme Court affirmed the judgment of the Appellate Division. It held that the Boy Scouts was a place of public accommodation subject to the public accommodations law, that the organization was not exempt from the law under any of its express exceptions, and that the Boy Scouts violated the law by revoking Dale's membership based on his avowed homosexuality. With respect to the right to intimate association, the court concluded that the Boy Scouts' "large size, non-selectivity, inclusive rather than exclusive purpose, and practice of inviting or allowing nonmembers to attend meetings, establish that the organization is not 'sufficiently personal or private to warrant constitutional protection' under the freedom of intimate association." With respect to the right of expressive association, the court "agree[d] that Boy Scouts expresses a belief in moral values and uses its activities to encourage the moral development of its members." But the court concluded that it was "not persuaded that a shared goal of Boy Scout members is to associate in order to preserve the view that homosexuality is immoral." Accordingly, the court held "that Dale's membership does not violate the Boy Scouts' right of expressive association because his inclusion would not 'affect in any significant way [the Boy Scouts'] existing members' ability to carry out their various purposes.'" The court also determined that New Jersey has a compelling interest in eliminating "the destructive consequences of discrimination from our society," and that its public accommodations law abridges no more speech than is necessary to accomplish its purpose. Finally, the court addressed the Boy Scouts' reliance on *Hurley v. Irish-American Gay, Lesbian and Bisexual Group of Boston, Inc.*, 515 U.S. 557 (1995). The court determined that *Hurley* did not require deciding the case in favor of the Boy Scouts because "the reinstatement of Dale does not compel Boy Scouts to express any message."

II

In *Roberts v. United States Jaycees*, 468 U.S. 609, 622 (1984), we observed that "implicit in the right to engage in activities protected by the First Amendment" is "a corresponding right to associate with others in pursuit of a wide variety of political, social, economic, educational, religious, and cultural ends." This right is crucial in preventing the majority from imposing its views on groups that would rather express other, perhaps unpopular, ideas. Government actions that may unconstitutionally burden this freedom may take many forms, one of which is "intrusion into the internal structure or affairs of an association" like a "regulation that forces the group to accept members it does not desire." Forcing a group to accept certain members may impair the ability of the group to express those views, and only those views, that it intends to express. Thus, "[f]reedom of association plainly presupposes a freedom not to associate."

The forced inclusion of an unwanted person in a group infringes the group's freedom of expressive association if the presence of that person affects in a significant way the group's ability to advocate public or private viewpoints. But the freedom of expressive association, like many freedoms, is not absolute. We have held that the freedom could be overridden "by regulations adopted to serve compelling state interests, unrelated to the suppression of ideas, that cannot be achieved through means significantly less restrictive of associational freedoms."

To determine whether a group is protected by the First Amendment's expressive associational right, we must determine whether the group engages in "expressive association." The First Amendment's protection of expressive association is not reserved for advocacy groups. But to come within its ambit, a group must engage in some form of expression, whether it be public or private.

The Boy Scouts is a private, nonprofit organization. According to its mission statement:

> "It is the mission of the Boy Scouts of America to serve others by helping to instill values in young people and, in other ways, to prepare them to make ethical choices over their lifetime in achieving their full potential.

> "The values we strive to instill are based on those found in the Scout Oath and Law:

> "Scout Oath
> "On my honor I will do my best To do my duty to God and my country and to obey the Scout Law; To help other people at all times; To keep myself physically strong, mentally awake, and morally straight.
> "Scout Law
> "A Scout is:
> "Trustworthy Obedient
> Loyal Cheerful
> Helpful Thrifty
> Friendly Brave
> Courteous Clean
> Kind Reverent."

Thus, the general mission of the Boy Scouts is clear: "[T]o instill values in young people." The Boy Scouts seeks to instill these values by having its adult leaders spend time with the youth members, instructing and engaging them in activities like camping, archery, and fishing. During the time spent with the youth members, the scoutmasters and assistant scoutmasters inculcate them with the Boy Scouts' values—both expressly and by example. It seems indisputable that an association that seeks to transmit such a system of values engages in expressive activity.

Given that the Boy Scouts engages in expressive activity, we must determine whether the forced inclusion of Dale as an assistant scoutmaster would significantly affect the Boy Scouts' ability to advocate public or private viewpoints. This inquiry necessarily requires us first to explore, to a limited extent, the nature of the Boy Scouts' view of homosexuality. The values the Boy Scouts seeks to instill are "based on" those listed in the Scout Oath and Law. The Boy Scouts explains that the Scout Oath and Law provide "a positive moral code for living; they are a list of 'do's' rather than 'don'ts.'" The Boy Scouts asserts that homosexual conduct is inconsistent with the values embodied in the Scout Oath and Law, particularly with the values represented by the terms "morally straight" and "clean." Obviously, the Scout Oath and Law do not expressly mention sexuality or sexual orientation. And the terms "morally straight" and "clean" are by no means self-defining. Different people would attribute to those terms very different meanings. For example, some people may believe that engaging in homosexual conduct is not at odds with being "morally straight" and "clean." And others may believe that engaging in homosexual conduct is contrary to being "morally straight" and "clean." The Boy Scouts says it falls within the latter category.

The New Jersey Supreme Court analyzed the Boy Scouts' beliefs and found that the "exclusion of members solely on the basis of their sexual orientation is inconsistent with Boy Scouts' commitment to a diverse and 'representative' membership... [and] contradicts Boy Scouts' overarching objective to reach 'all eligible youth.'" The court concluded that the exclusion of members like Dale "appears antithetical to the organization's goals and philosophy." But our cases reject this sort of inquiry; it is not the role of the courts to reject a group's expressed values because they disagree with those values or find them internally inconsistent.

The Boy Scouts asserts that it "teach[es] that homosexual conduct is not morally straight," and that it does "not want to promote homosexual conduct as a legitimate form of behavior." We accept the Boy Scouts' assertion. We need not inquire further to determine the nature of the Boy Scouts' expression with respect to homosexuality. But because the record before us contains written evidence of the Boy Scouts' viewpoint, we look to it as instructive, if only on the question of the sincerity of the professed beliefs.

A 1978 position statement to the Boy Scouts' Executive Committee, signed by Downing B. Jenks, the President of the Boy Scouts, and Harvey L. Price, the Chief Scout Executive, expresses the Boy Scouts' "official position" with regard to "homosexuality and Scouting":

"Q. May an individual who openly declares himself to be a homosexual be a volunteer Scout leader?

"A. No. The Boy Scouts of America is a private, membership organization and leadership therein is a privilege and not a right. We do not believe that homosexuality and leadership in Scouting are appropriate. We will continue to select only those who in our judgment meet our standards and qualifications for leadership."

Thus, at least as of 1978—the year James Dale entered Scouting—the official position of the Boy Scouts was that avowed homosexuals were not to be Scout leaders. A position statement promulgated by the Boy Scouts in 1991 (after Dale's membership was revoked but before this litigation was filed) also supports its current view:

"We believe that homosexual conduct is inconsistent with the requirement in the Scout Oath that a Scout be morally straight and in the Scout Law that a Scout be clean in word and deed, and that homosexuals do not provide a desirable role model for Scouts."

This position statement was redrafted numerous times but its core message remained consistent. For example, a 1993 position statement, the most recent in the record, reads, in part:

> "The Boy Scouts of America has always reflected the expectations that Scouting families have had for the organization. We do not believe that homosexuals provide a role model consistent with these expectations. Accordingly, we do not allow for the registration of avowed homosexuals as members or as leaders of the BSA."

The Boy Scouts publicly expressed its views with respect to homosexual conduct by its assertions in prior litigation. For example, throughout a California case with similar facts filed in the early 1980's, the Boy Scouts consistently asserted the same position with respect to homosexuality that it asserts today. See *Curran v. Mount Diablo Council of Boy Scouts of America*, No. C-365529 (Cal.Super.Ct., July 25, 1991); 29 Cal.Rptr.2d 580 (1994); 17 Cal.4th 670, 72 Cal.Rptr.2d 410, 952 P.2d 218 (1998). We cannot doubt that the Boy Scouts sincerely holds this view.

We must then determine whether Dale's presence as an assistant scoutmaster would significantly burden the Boy Scouts' desire to not "promote homosexual conduct as a legitimate form of behavior." As we give deference to an association's assertions regarding the nature of its expression, we must also give deference to an association's view of what would impair its expression. That is not to say that an expressive association can erect a shield against anti-discrimination laws simply by asserting that mere acceptance of a member from a particular group would impair its message. But here Dale, by his own admission, is one of a group of gay Scouts who have "become leaders in their community and are open and honest about their sexual orientation." Dale was the co-president of a gay and lesbian organization at college and remains a gay rights activist. Dale's presence in the Boy Scouts would, at the very least, force the organization to send a message, both to the youth members and the world, that the Boy Scouts accepts homosexual conduct as a legitimate form of behavior.

Hurley is illustrative on this point. There we considered whether the application of Massachusetts' public accommodations law to require the organizers of a private St. Patrick's Day parade to include among the marchers an Irish—American gay, lesbian, and bisexual group, GLIB, violated the parade organizers' First Amendment rights. We noted that the parade organizers did not wish to exclude the GLIB members because of their sexual orientations, but because they wanted to march behind a GLIB banner. We observed:

> [A] contingent marching behind the organization's banner would at least bear witness to the fact that some Irish are gay, lesbian, or bisexual, and the presence of the organized marchers would suggest their view that people of their sexual orientations have as much claim to unqualified social acceptance as heterosexuals.... The parade's organizers may not believe these facts about Irish sexuality to be so, or they may object to unqualified social acceptance of gays and lesbians or have some other reason for wishing to keep GLIB's message out of the parade. But whatever the reason, it boils down to the choice of a speaker not to propound a particular point of view, and that choice is presumed to lie beyond the government's power to control."

Here, we have found that the Boy Scouts believes that homosexual conduct is inconsistent with the values it seeks to instill in its youth members; it will not "promote homosexual conduct as a legitimate form of behavior." As the presence of GLIB in Boston's St. Patrick's Day parade would have interfered with the parade organizers' choice not to propound a particular point of view, the presence of Dale as an assistant scoutmaster would just as surely interfere with the Boy Scout's choice not to propound a point of view contrary to its beliefs.

The New Jersey Supreme Court determined that the Boy Scouts' ability to disseminate its message was not significantly affected by the forced inclusion of Dale as an assistant scoutmaster because of the following findings:

> "Boy Scout members do not associate for the purpose of disseminating the belief that homosexuality is immoral; Boy Scouts discourages its leaders from disseminating *any* views on sexual issues; and Boy Scouts includes sponsors and members who subscribe to different views in respect of homosexuality."

We disagree with the New Jersey Supreme Court's conclusion drawn from these findings.

First, associations do not have to associate for the "purpose" of disseminating a certain message in order to be entitled to the protections of the First Amendment. An association must merely engage in expressive activity that could be impaired in order to be entitled to protection. For example, the purpose of the St. Patrick's Day parade in *Hurley* was not to espouse any views about sexual orientation, but we held that the parade organizers had a right to exclude certain participants nonetheless.

Second, even if the Boy Scouts discourages Scout leaders from disseminating views on sexual issues—a fact that the Boy Scouts disputes with contrary evidence—the First Amendment protects the Boy Scouts' method of expression. If the Boy Scouts wishes Scout leaders to avoid questions of sexuality and teach only by example, this fact does not negate the sincerity of its belief discussed above.

Third, the First Amendment simply does not require that every member of a group agree on every issue in order for the group's policy to be "expressive association." The Boy Scouts takes an official position with respect to homosexual conduct, and that is sufficient for First Amendment purposes. In this same vein, Dale makes much of the claim that the Boy Scouts does not revoke the membership of heterosexual Scout leaders that openly disagree with the Boy Scouts' policy on sexual orientation. But if this is true, it is irrelevant.[1] The presence of an avowed homosexual and gay rights activist in an assistant scoutmaster's uniform sends a distinctly different message from the presence of a heterosexual assistant scoutmaster who is on record as disagreeing with Boy Scouts policy. The Boy Scouts has a First Amendment right to choose to send one message but not the other. The fact that the organization does not trumpet its views from the housetops, or that it tolerates dissent within its ranks, does not mean that its views receive no First Amendment protection.

Having determined that the Boy Scouts is an expressive association and that the forced inclusion of Dale would significantly affect its expression, we inquire whether the application of New Jersey's public accommodations law to require that the Boy Scouts

---

1. The record evidence sheds doubt on Dale's assertion. For example, the National Director of the Boy Scouts certified that "*any* persons who advocate to Scouting youth that homosexual conduct is" consistent with Scouting values will not be registered as adult leaders. And the Monmouth Council Scout Executive testified that the advocacy of the morality of homosexuality to youth members by any adult member is grounds for revocation of the adult's membership.

accept Dale as an assistant scoutmaster runs afoul of the Scouts' freedom of expressive association. We conclude that it does.

State public accommodations laws were originally enacted to prevent discrimination in traditional places of public accommodation—like inns and trains. Over time, the public accommodations laws have expanded to cover more places. New Jersey's statutory definition of " '[a] place of public accommodation' " is extremely broad. The term is said to "include, but not be limited to," a list of over 50 types of places. N.J. Stat. Ann. § 10:5-5(*l*) (West Supp. 2000). Many on the list are what one would expect to be places where the public is invited. For example, the statute includes as places of public accommodation taverns, restaurants, retail shops, and public libraries. But the statute also includes places that often may not carry with them open invitations to the public, like summer camps and roof gardens. In this case, the New Jersey Supreme Court went a step further and applied its public accommodations law to a private entity without even attempting to tie the term "place" to a physical location. As the definition of "public accommodation" has expanded from clearly commercial entities, such as restaurants, bars, and hotels, to membership organizations such as the Boy Scouts, the potential for conflict between state public accommodations laws and the First Amendment rights of organizations has increased.

We [have] recognized that States have a compelling interest in eliminating discrimination against women in public accommodations. But in each of these cases we went on to conclude that the enforcement of these statutes would not materially interfere with the ideas that the organization sought to express. We thereupon concluded in each of these cases that the organizations' First Amendment rights were not violated by the application of the States' public accommodations laws.

In *Hurley*, we said that public accommodations laws "are well within the State's usual power to enact when a legislature has reason to believe that a given group is the target of discrimination, and they do not, as a general matter, violate the First or Fourteenth Amendments." But we went on to note that in that case "the Massachusetts [public accommodations] law has been applied in a peculiar way" because "any contingent of protected individuals with a message would have the right to participate in petitioners' speech, so that the communication produced by the private organizers would be shaped by all those protected by the law who wish to join in with some expressive demonstration of their own." And in the associational freedom cases such as *Roberts, Duarte*, and *New York State Club Assn.*, after finding a compelling state interest, the Court went on to examine whether or not the application of the state law would impose any "serious burden" on the organization's rights of expressive association. So in these cases, the associational interest in freedom of expression has been set on one side of the scale, and the State's interest on the other.

Dale contends that we should apply the intermediate standard of review enunciated in *United States v. O'Brien*, 391 U.S. 367 (1968), to evaluate the competing interests. There the Court enunciated a four-part test for review of a governmental regulation that has only an incidental effect on protected speech—in that case the symbolic burning of a draft card. A law prohibiting the destruction of draft cards only incidentally affects the free speech rights of those who happen to use a violation of that law as a symbol of protest. But New Jersey's public accommodations law directly and immediately affects associational rights, in this case associational rights that enjoy First Amendment protection. Thus, *O'Brien* is inapplicable.

In *Hurley*, we applied traditional First Amendment analysis to hold that the application of the Massachusetts public accommodations law to a parade violated the First

Amendment rights of the parade organizers. Although we did not explicitly deem the parade in Hurley an expressive association, the analysis we applied there is similar to the analysis we apply here. We have already concluded that a state requirement that the Boy Scouts retain Dale as an assistant scoutmaster would significantly burden the organization's right to oppose or disfavor homosexual conduct. The state interests embodied in New Jersey's public accommodations law do not justify such a severe intrusion on the Boy Scouts' rights to freedom of expressive association. That being the case, we hold that the First Amendment prohibits the State from imposing such a requirement through the application of its public accommodations law.

Justice STEVENS' dissent makes much of its observation that the public perception of homosexuality in this country has changed. Indeed, it appears that homosexuality has gained greater societal acceptance. But this is scarcely an argument for denying First Amendment protection to those who refuse to accept these views. The First Amendment protects expression, be it of the popular variety or not. And the fact that an idea may be embraced and advocated by increasing numbers of people is all the more reason to protect the First Amendment rights of those who wish to voice a different view.

Justice STEVENS' extolling of Justice Brandeis' comments in *New State Ice Co. v. Liebmann*, 285 U.S. 262 (1932) (dissenting opinion), confuses two entirely different principles. In *New State Ice,* the Court struck down an Oklahoma regulation prohibiting the manufacture, sale, and distribution of ice without a license. Justice Brandeis, a champion of state experimentation in the economic realm, dissented. But Justice Brandeis was never a champion of state experimentation in the suppression of free speech. To the contrary, his First Amendment commentary provides compelling support for the Court's opinion in this case. In speaking of the Founders of this Nation, Justice Brandeis emphasized that they "believed that the freedom to think as you will and to speak as you think are means indispensable to the discovery and spread of political truth." *Whitney v. California*, 274 U.S. 357, 375 (concurring opinion). He continued:

> "Believing in the power of reason as applied through public discussion, they eschewed silence coerced by law—the argument of force in its worst form. Recognizing the occasional tyrannies of governing majorities, they amended the Constitution so that free speech and assembly should be guaranteed."

We are not, as we must not be, guided by our views of whether the Boy Scouts' teachings with respect to homosexual conduct are right or wrong; public or judicial disapproval of a tenet of an organization's expression does not justify the State's effort to compel the organization to accept members where such acceptance would derogate from the organization's expressive message. "While the law is free to promote all sorts of conduct in place of harmful behavior, it is not free to interfere with speech for no better reason than promoting an approved message or discouraging a disfavored one, however enlightened either purpose may strike the government." *Hurley,* 515 U.S., at 579. The judgment of the New Jersey Supreme Court is reversed, and the cause remanded for further proceedings not inconsistent with this opinion.

Justice STEVENS, with whom Justice SOUTER, Justice GINSBURG and Justice BREYER join, dissenting.

New Jersey "prides itself on judging each individual by his or her merits" and on being "in the vanguard in the fight to eradicate the cancer of unlawful discrimination of all types from our society." *Peper v. Princeton Univ. Bd. of Trustees,* 77 N.J. 55, 80, 389

A.2d 465, 478 (1978). Since 1945, it has had a law against discrimination. The law broadly protects the opportunity of all persons to obtain the advantages and privileges "of any place of public accommodation." The New Jersey Supreme Court's construction of the statutory definition of a "place of public accommodation" has given its statute a more expansive coverage than most similar state statutes. And as amended in 1991, the law prohibits discrimination on the basis of nine different traits including an individual's "sexual orientation." The question in this case is whether that expansive construction trenches on the federal constitutional rights of the Boy Scouts of America (BSA).

Because every state law prohibiting discrimination is designed to replace prejudice with principle, Justice Brandeis' comment on the States' right to experiment with "things social" is directly applicable to this case.

> "To stay experimentation in things social and economic is a grave responsibility. Denial of the right to experiment may be fraught with serious consequences to the Nation. It is one of the happy incidents of the federal system that a single courageous State may, if its citizens choose, serve as a laboratory; and try novel social and economic experiments without risk to the rest of the country. This Court has the power to prevent an experiment. We may strike down the statute which embodies it on the ground that, in our opinion, the measure is arbitrary, capricious or unreasonable. We have power to do this, because the due process clause has been held by the Court applicable to matters of substantive law as well as to matters of procedure. But in the exercise of this high power, we must be ever on our guard, lest we erect our prejudices into legal principles. If we would guide by the light of reason, we must let our minds be bold." *New State Ice Co. v. Liebmann*, 285 U.S. 262, 311 (1932) (dissenting opinion).

In its "exercise of this high power" today, the Court does not accord this "courageous State" the respect that is its due. The majority holds that New Jersey's law violates BSA's right to associate and its right to free speech. But that law does not "impos[e] any serious burdens" on BSA's "collective effort on behalf of [its] shared goals," *Roberts v. United States Jaycees*, 468 U.S. 609, 622, 626–27 (1984), nor does it force BSA to communicate any message that it does not wish to endorse. New Jersey's law, therefore, abridges no constitutional right of the Boy Scouts.

I

In this case, Boy Scouts of America contends that it teaches the young boys who are Scouts that homosexuality is immoral. Consequently, it argues, it would violate its right to associate to force it to admit homosexuals as members, as doing so would be at odds with its own shared goals and values. This contention, quite plainly, requires us to look at what, exactly, are the values that BSA actually teaches.

BSA's mission statement reads as follows: "It is the mission of the Boy Scouts of America to serve others by helping to instill values in young people and, in other ways, to prepare them to make ethical choices over their lifetime in achieving their full potential." Its federal charter declares its purpose is "to promote, through organization, and cooperation with other agencies, the ability of boys to do things for themselves and others, to train them in scoutcraft, and to teach them patriotism, courage, self-reliance, and kindred values, using the methods which were in common use by Boy Scouts on June 15, 1916." 36 U.S.C. §23. BSA describes itself as having a "representative membership," which it defines as "boy membership [that] reflects proportionately the characteristics of the boy population of its service area." In particular, the group emphasizes that "[n]either the charter nor the bylaws of the Boy Scouts of America permits the exclusion of any boy.... To meet these responsibilities we have made a commitment that our membership shall be representative of *all* the population in every community, district, and council." (emphasis in original).

To instill its shared values, BSA has adopted a "Scout Oath" and a "Scout Law" setting forth its central tenets. For example, the Scout Law requires a member to promise, among other things, that he will be "obedient." Accompanying definitions for the terms found in the Oath and Law are provided in the Boy Scout Handbook and the Scoutmaster Handbook. For instance, the Boy Scout Handbook defines "obedient" as follows:

> "A scout is OBEDIENT. A Scout follows the rules of his family, school, and troop. He obeys the laws of his community and country. If he thinks these rules and laws are unfair, he tries to have them changed in an orderly manner rather than disobey them."

To bolster its claim that its shared goals include teaching that homosexuality is wrong, BSA directs our attention to two terms appearing in the Scout Oath and Law. The first is the phrase "morally straight," which appears in the Oath ("On my honor I will do my best...To keep myself...morally straight"); the second term is the word "clean," which appears in a list of 12 characteristics together comprising the Scout Law.

The Boy Scout Handbook defines "morally straight," as such:

> To be a person of strong character, guide your life with honesty, purity, and justice. Respect and defend the rights of all people. Your relationships with others should be honest and open. Be clean in your speech and actions, and faithful in your religious beliefs. The values you follow as a Scout will help you become virtuous and self-reliant."

The Scoutmaster Handbook emphasizes these points about being "morally straight":

> "In any consideration of moral fitness, a key word has to be 'courage.' A boy's courage to do what his head and his heart tell him is right. And the courage to refuse to do what his heart and his head say is wrong. Moral fitness, like emotional fitness, will clearly present opportunities for wise guidance by an alert Scoutmaster."

As for the term "clean," the Boy Scout Handbook offers the following:

> "A Scout is CLEAN. *A Scout keeps his body and mind fit and clean. He chooses the company of those who live by these same ideals. He helps keep his home and community clean.*
>
> "You never need to be ashamed of dirt that will wash off. If you play hard and work hard you can't help getting dirty. But when the game is over or the work is done, that kind of dirt disappears with soap and water.
>
> "There's another kind of dirt that won't come off by washing. It is the kind that shows up in foul language and harmful thoughts.
>
> "Swearwords, profanity, and dirty stories are weapons that ridicule other people and hurt their feelings. The same is true of racial slurs and jokes making fun of ethnic groups or people with physical or mental limitations. A Scout knows there is no kindness or honor in such mean-spirited behavior. He avoids it in his own words and deeds. He defends those who are targets of insults."

It is plain as the light of day that neither one of these principles — "morally straight" and "clean" — says the slightest thing about homosexuality. Indeed, neither term in the Boy Scouts' Law and Oath expresses any position whatsoever on sexual matters.

BSA's published guidance on that topic underscores this point. Scouts, for example, are directed to receive their sex education at home or in school, but not from the organization: "Your parents or guardian or a sex education teacher should give you the facts about sex that you must know." Boy Scout Handbook (1992). To be sure, Scouts are not forbidden from asking their Scoutmaster about issues of a sexual nature, but Scoutmasters are, literally, the last person Scouts are encouraged to ask: "If you have questions about growing up, about relationships, sex, or making good decisions, ask. Talk with your parents, religious leaders, teachers, or Scoutmaster." Moreover, Scoutmasters are specifically directed to steer curious adolescents to other sources of information:

> "If Scouts ask for information regarding sexual activity, answer honestly and factually, but stay within your realm of expertise and comfort. If a Scout has serious concerns that you cannot answer, refer him to his family, religious leader, doctor, or other professional." Scoutmaster Handbook (1990).

More specifically, BSA has set forth a number of rules for Scoutmasters when these types of issues come up:

> "You may have boys asking you for information or advice about sexual matters....

> "How should you handle such matters?

> "Rule number 1: *You do not undertake to instruct Scouts, in any formalized manner, in the subject of sex and family life. The reasons are that it is not construed to be Scouting's proper area*, and that you are probably not well qualified to do this.

> "Rule number 2: If Scouts come to you to ask questions or to seek advice, you would give it within your competence. A boy who appears to be asking about sexual intercourse, however, may really only be worried about his pimples, so it is well to find out just what information is needed.

> "Rule number 3: You should refer boys with sexual problems to persons better qualified than you [are] to handle them. If the boy has a spiritual leader or a doctor who can deal with them, he should go there. If such persons are not available, you may just have to do the best you can. But don't try to play a highly professional role. And at the other extreme, avoid passing the buck." Scoutmaster Handbook (1972) (emphasis added).

In light of BSA's self-proclaimed ecumenism, furthermore, it is even more difficult to discern any shared goals or common moral stance on homosexuality. Insofar as religious matters are concerned, BSA's bylaws state that it is "absolutely nonsectarian in its attitude toward...religious training." "The BSA does not define what constitutes duty to God or the practice of religion. This is the responsibility of parents and religious leaders." In fact, many diverse religious organizations sponsor local Boy Scout troops. Because a number of religious groups do not view homosexuality as immoral or wrong and reject discrimination against homosexuals, it is exceedingly difficult to believe that BSA nonetheless adopts a single particular religious or moral philosophy when it comes to sexual orientation. This is especially so in light of the fact that Scouts are advised to seek guidance on sexual matters from their religious leaders (and Scoutmasters are told to refer Scouts to them); BSA surely is aware that some religions do not teach that homosexuality is wrong.

II

The Court seeks to fill the void by pointing to a statement of "policies and procedures relating to homosexuality and Scouting" signed by BSA's President and Chief Scout Executive in 1978 and addressed to the members of the Executive Committee of the national organization. The letter says that the BSA does "not believe that homosexuality and leadership in Scouting are appropriate." But when the *entire* 1978 letter is read, BSA's position is far more equivocal:

"4. Q. May an individual who openly declares himself to be a homosexual be employed by the Boy Scouts of America as a professional or non-professional?

"A. Boy Scouts of America does not knowingly employ homosexuals as professionals or non-professionals. We are unaware of any present laws which would prohibit this policy.

"5. Q. Should a professional or non-professional individual who openly declares himself to be a homosexual be terminated?

"A. Yes, *in the absence of any law to the contrary.* At the present time we are unaware of any statute or ordinance in the United States which prohibits discrimination against individual's employment upon the basis of homosexuality. *In the event that such a law was applicable, it would be necessary for the Boy Scouts of America to obey it, in this case as in Paragraph 4 above.* It is our position, however, that homosexuality and professional or non-professional employment in Scouting are not appropriate." (emphasis added).

Four aspects of the 1978 policy statement are relevant to the proper disposition of this case. First, at most this letter simply adopts an exclusionary membership policy. But simply adopting such a policy has never been considered sufficient, by itself, to prevail on a right to associate claim.

Second, the 1978 policy was never publicly expressed—unlike, for example, the Scout's duty to be "obedient." It was an internal memorandum, never circulated beyond the few members of BSA's Executive Committee. It remained, in effect, a secret Boy Scouts policy. Far from claiming any intent to express an idea that would be burdened by the presence of homosexuals, BSA's *public* posture—to the world and to the Scouts themselves—remained what it had always been: one of tolerance, welcoming all classes of boys and young men. In this respect, BSA's claim is even weaker than those we have rejected in the past.

Third, it is apparent that the draftsmen of the policy statement foresaw the possibility that laws against discrimination might one day be amended to protect homosexuals from employment discrimination.

Fourth, the 1978 statement simply says that homosexuality is not "appropriate." It makes no effort to connect that statement to a shared goal or expressive activity of the Boy Scouts. Whatever values BSA seeks to instill in Scouts, the idea that homosexuality is not "appropriate" appears entirely unconnected to, and is mentioned nowhere in, the myriad of publicly declared values and creeds of the BSA. That idea does not appear to be among any of the principles actually taught to Scouts. Rather, the 1978 policy appears to be no more than a private statement of a few BSA executives that the organization wishes to exclude gays—and that wish has nothing to do with any expression BSA actually engages in.

The majority also relies on four other policy statements that were issued between 1991 and 1993. All of them were written and issued *after* BSA revoked Dale's membership. Accordingly, they have little, if any, relevance to the legal question before this Court. In any event, they do not bolster BSA's claim.

The only policy written before the revocation of Dale's membership was an equivocal, undisclosed statement that evidences no connection between the group's discriminatory intentions and its expressive interests. The later policies demonstrate a brief— though ultimately abandoned—attempt to tie BSA's exclusion to its expression, but other than a single sentence, BSA fails to show that it ever taught Scouts that homosexuality is not "morally straight" or "clean," or that such a view was part of the group's collective efforts to foster a belief. Furthermore, BSA's policy statements fail to establish any clear, consistent, and unequivocal position on homosexuality. Nor did BSA have any reason to think Dale's sexual *conduct,* as opposed to his orientation, was contrary to the group's values.

BSA's inability to make its position clear and its failure to connect its alleged policy to its expressive activities is highly significant. By the time Dale was expelled from the Boy Scouts in 1990, BSA had already been engaged in several suits under a variety of state anti-discrimination public accommodation laws challenging various aspects of its membership policy. Indeed, BSA had filed *amicus* briefs before this Court in two earlier right to associate cases (*Roberts v. United States Jaycees,* 468 U.S. 609 (1984), and *Board of Directors of Rotary Int'l v. Rotary Club of Duarte,* 481 U.S. 537 (1987)) pointing to these very cases; it was clearly on notice by 1990 that it might well be subjected to state public accommodation anti-discrimination laws, and that a court might one day reject its claimed right to associate. Yet it took no steps prior to Dale's expulsion to clarify how its exclusivity was connected to its expression. It speaks volumes about the credibility of BSA's claim to a shared goal that homosexuality is incompatible with Scouting that since at least 1984 it had been aware of this issue—indeed, concerned enough to twice file *amicus* briefs before this Court—yet it did nothing in the intervening six years (or even in the years after Dale's expulsion) to explain clearly and openly why the presence of homosexuals would affect its expressive activities, or to make the view of "morally straight" and "clean" taken in its 1991 and 1992 policies a part of the values actually instilled in Scouts through the Handbook, lessons, or otherwise.

III

BSA's claim finds no support in our cases. We have recognized "a right to associate for the purpose of engaging in those activities protected by the First Amendment— speech, assembly, petition for the redress of grievances, and the exercise of religion." *Roberts,* 468 U.S., at 618. And we have acknowledged that "when the State interferes with individuals' selection of those with whom they wish to join in a common endeavor, freedom of association may be implicated." But "[t]he right to associate for expressive purposes is not absolute"; rather, "the nature and degree of constitutional protection afforded freedom of association may vary depending on the extent to which... the constitutionally protected liberty is at stake in a given case." Indeed, the right to associate does not mean "that in every setting in which individuals exercise some discrimination in choosing associates, their selective process of inclusion and exclusion is protected by the Constitution." *New York State Club Assn., Inc. v. City of New York,* 487 U.S. 1, 13 (1988). For example, we have routinely and easily rejected assertions of this right by expressive organizations with discriminatory membership policies, such as private schools, law firms, and labor organizations. In fact, until today, we have never once found a claimed right to associate in the selection of members to prevail in the face of a

State's anti-discrimination law. To the contrary, we have squarely held that a State's anti-discrimination law does not violate a group's right to associate simply because the law conflicts with that group's exclusionary membership policy.

Several principles are made perfectly clear by *Jaycees* and *Rotary Club.* First, to prevail on a claim of expressive association in the face of a State's anti-discrimination law, it is not enough simply to engage in *some kind* of expressive activity. Both the Jaycees and the Rotary Club engaged in expressive activity protected by the First Amendment, yet that fact was not dispositive. Second, it is not enough to adopt an openly avowed exclusionary membership policy. Both the Jaycees and the Rotary Club did that as well. Third, it is not sufficient merely to articulate *some* connection between the group's expressive activities and its exclusionary policy. The Rotary Club, for example, justified its male-only membership policy by pointing to the " 'aspect of fellowship that is enjoyed by the [exclusively] male membership' " and by claiming that only with an exclusively male membership could it "operate effectively" in foreign countries.

Rather, in *Jaycees,* we asked whether Minnesota's Human Rights Law requiring the admission of women "impose[d] any *serious burdens* " on the group's "collective effort on behalf of [its] *shared goals.*" Notwithstanding the group's obvious publicly stated exclusionary policy, we did not view the inclusion of women as a "serious burden" on the Jaycees' ability to engage in the protected speech of its choice. Similarly, in *Rotary Club,* we asked whether California's law would "affect in any *significant way* the existing members' ability" to engage in their protected speech, or whether the law would require the clubs "to abandon their *basic goals.*" The relevant question is whether the mere inclusion of the person at issue would "impose any serious burden," "affect in any significant way," or be "a substantial restraint upon" the organization's "shared goals," "basic goals," or "collective effort to foster beliefs." Accordingly, it is necessary to examine what, exactly, are BSA's shared goals and the degree to which its expressive activities would be burdened, affected, or restrained by including homosexuals.

The evidence before this Court makes it exceptionally clear that BSA has, at most, simply adopted an exclusionary membership policy and has no shared goal of disapproving of homosexuality. As in *Jaycees,* there is "no basis in the record for concluding that admission of [homosexuals] will impede the [Boy Scouts'] ability to engage in [its] protected activities or to disseminate its preferred views" and New Jersey's law "requires no change in [BSA's] creed." 468 U.S., at 626–27. And like *Rotary Club,* New Jersey's law "does not require [BSA] to abandon or alter any of" its activities. 481 U.S., at 548. The evidence relied on by the Court is not to the contrary.

Equally important is BSA's failure to adopt any clear position on homosexuality. BSA's temporary, though ultimately abandoned, view that homosexuality is incompatible with being "morally straight" and "clean" is a far cry from the clear, unequivocal statement necessary to prevail on its claim.

IV

The majority pretermits this entire analysis. It finds that BSA in fact " 'teach[es] that homosexual conduct is not morally straight.' " This conclusion, remarkably, rests entirely on statements in BSA's briefs. Moreover, the majority insists that we must "give deference to an association's assertions regarding the nature of its expression" and "we must also give deference to an association's view of what would impair its expression."

So long as the record " contains written evidence" to support a group's bare assertion, "[w]e need not inquire further." Once the organization "asserts" that it engages in particular expression, *ibid.*, "[w]e cannot doubt" the truth of that assertion.

This is an astounding view of the law. I am unaware of any previous instance in which our analysis of the scope of a constitutional right was determined by looking at what a litigant asserts in his or her brief and inquiring no further. It is even more astonishing in the First Amendment area, because, as the majority itself acknowledges, "we are obligated to independently review the factual record." It is an odd form of independent review that consists of deferring entirely to whatever a litigant claims. But the majority insists that our inquiry must be "limited," because "it is not the role of the courts to reject a group's expressed values because they disagree with those values or find them internally inconsistent."

But nothing in our cases calls for this Court to do any such thing. An organization can adopt the message of its choice, and it is not this Court's place to disagree with it. But we must inquire whether the group is, in fact, expressing a message (whatever it may be) and whether that message (if one is expressed) is significantly affected by a State's anti-discrimination law. More critically, that inquiry requires our *independent* analysis, rather than deference to a group's litigating posture. Reflection on the subject dictates that such an inquiry is required.

V

Even if BSA's right to associate argument fails, it nonetheless might have a First Amendment right to refrain from including debate and dialogue about homosexuality as part of its mission to instill values in Scouts. It can, for example, advise Scouts who are entering adulthood and have questions about sex to talk "with your parents, religious leaders, teachers, or Scoutmaster," and, in turn, it can direct Scoutmasters who are asked such questions "not undertake to instruct Scouts, in any formalized manner, in the subject of sex and family life" because "it is not construed to be Scouting's proper area." Dale's right to advocate certain beliefs in a public forum or in a private debate does not include a right to advocate these ideas when he is working as a Scoutmaster. And BSA cannot be compelled to include a message about homosexuality among the values it actually chooses to teach its Scouts, if it would prefer to remain silent on that subject.

In its briefs, BSA implies, even if it does not directly argue, that Dale would use his Scoutmaster position as a "bully pulpit" to convey immoral messages to his troop, and therefore his inclusion in the group would compel BSA to include a message it does not want to impart. Even though the majority does not endorse that argument, I think it is important to explain why it lacks merit, before considering the argument the majority does accept.

BSA has not contended, nor does the record support, that Dale had ever advocated a view on homosexuality to his troop before his membership was revoked. Accordingly, BSA's revocation could only have been based on an assumption that he would do so in the future. But the only information BSA had at the time it revoked Dale's membership was a newspaper article describing a seminar at Rutgers University on the topic of homosexual teenagers that Dale attended. The relevant passage reads:

> "James Dale, 19, co-president of the Rutgers University Lesbian Gay Alliance with Sharice Richardson, also 19, said he lived a double life while in high school, pretending to be straight while attending a military academy.

"He remembers dating girls and even laughing at homophobic jokes while at school, only admitting his homosexuality during his second year at Rutgers.

" 'I was looking for a role model, someone who was gay and accepting of me,' Dale said, adding he wasn't just seeking sexual experiences, but a community that would take him in and provide him with a support network and friends."

Nothing in that article, however, even remotely suggests that Dale would advocate any views on homosexuality to his troop. The Scoutmaster Handbook instructs Dale, like all Scoutmasters, that sexual issues are not their "proper area," and there is no evidence that Dale had any intention of violating this rule. Indeed, from all accounts Dale was a model Boy Scout and Assistant Scoutmaster up until the day his membership was revoked, and there is no reason to believe that he would suddenly disobey the directives of BSA because of anything he said in the newspaper article.

To be sure, the article did say that Dale was co-president of the Lesbian/Gay Alliance at Rutgers University, and that group presumably engages in advocacy regarding homosexual issues. But surely many members of BSA engage in expressive activities outside of their troop, and surely BSA does not want all of that expression to be carried on inside the troop. For example, a Scoutmaster may be a member of a religious group that encourages its followers to convert others to its faith. Or a Scoutmaster may belong to a political party that encourages its members to advance its views among family and friends. Yet BSA does not think it is appropriate for Scoutmasters to proselytize a particular faith to unwilling Scouts or to attempt to convert them from one religion to another. Nor does BSA think it appropriate for Scouts or Scoutmasters to bring politics into the troop. From all accounts, then, BSA does not discourage or forbid outside expressive activity, but relies on compliance with its policies and trusts Scouts and Scoutmasters alike not to bring unwanted views into the organization. Of course, a disobedient member who flouts BSA's policy may be expelled. But there is no basis for BSA to presume that a homosexual will be unable to comply with BSA's policy not to discuss sexual matters any more than it would presume that politically or religiously active members could not resist the urge to proselytize or politicize during troop meetings. As BSA itself puts it, Its rights are "not implicated *unless* a prospective leader *presents himself* as a role model inconsistent with Boy Scouting's understanding of the Scout Oath and Law."

The majority, though, does not rest its conclusion on the claim that Dale will use his position as a bully pulpit. Rather, it contends that Dale's mere presence among the Boy Scouts will itself force the group to convey a message about homosexuality—even if Dale has no intention of doing so. The majority holds that "[t]he presence of an avowed homosexual and gay rights activist in an assistant scoutmaster's uniform sends a distinc[t] message," and, accordingly, BSA is entitled to exclude that message. In particular, "Dale's presence in the Boy Scouts would, at the very least, force the organization to send a message, both to the youth members and the world, that the Boy Scouts accepts homosexual conduct as a legitimate form of behavior." See also Brief for Petitioners 24 ("By donning the uniform of an adult leader in Scouting, he would 'celebrate [his] identity' as an openly gay Scout leader").

The majority's argument relies exclusively on *Hurley v. Irish-American Gay, Lesbian and Bisexual Group of Boston.* Though *Hurley* has a superficial similarity to the present case, a close inspection reveals a wide gulf between that case and the one before us today. First, it was critical to our analysis that GLIB was actually conveying a message by participating in the parade—otherwise, the parade organizers could hardly claim that they were being forced to include any unwanted message at all. Second, we found it relevant that GLIB's message "would likely be perceived" as the parade organizers' own speech.

Dale's inclusion in the Boy Scouts is nothing like the case in *Hurley.* His participation sends no cognizable message to the Scouts or to the world. Unlike GLIB, Dale did not carry a banner or a sign; he did not distribute any fact sheet; and he expressed no intent to send any message. If there is any kind of message being sent, then, it is by the mere act of joining the Boy Scouts. Such an act does not constitute an instance of symbolic speech under the First Amendment.

It is true, of course, that some acts are so imbued with symbolic meaning that they qualify as "speech" under the First Amendment. At the same time, however, "[w]e cannot accept the view that an apparently limitless variety of conduct can be labeled 'speech' whenever the person engaging in the conduct intends thereby to express an idea." Though participating in the Scouts could itself conceivably send a message on some level, it is not the kind of act that we have recognized as speech. Indeed, if merely joining a group did constitute symbolic speech; and such speech were attributable to the group being joined; and that group has the right to exclude that speech (and hence, the right to exclude that person from joining), then the right of free speech effectively becomes a limitless right to exclude for every organization, whether or not it engages in *any* expressive activities. That cannot be, and never has been, the law.

The only apparent explanation for the majority's holding, then, is that homosexuals are simply so different from the rest of society that their presence alone—unlike any other individual's—should be singled out for special First Amendment treatment. Under the majority's reasoning, an openly gay male is irreversibly affixed with the label "homosexual." That label, even though unseen, communicates a message that permits his exclusion wherever he goes. His openness is the sole and sufficient justification for his ostracism. Though unintended, reliance on such a justification is tantamount to a constitutionally prescribed symbol of inferiority. As counsel for the Boy Scouts remarked, Dale "put a banner around his neck when he got himself into the newspaper. He created a reputation. He can't take that banner off. He put it on himself and, indeed, he has continued to put it on himself."

Another difference between this case and *Hurley* lies in the fact that *Hurley* involved the parade organizers' claim to determine the content of the message they wish to give at a particular time and place. The standards governing such a claim are simply different from the standards that govern BSA's claim of a right of expressive association. Generally, a private person or a private organization has a right to refuse to broadcast a message with which it disagrees, and a right to refuse to contradict or garble its own specific statement at any given place or time by including the messages of others. An expressive association claim, however, normally involves the avowal and advocacy of a consistent position on some issue over time. This is why a different kind of scrutiny must be given to an expressive association claim, lest the right of expressive association simply turn into a right to discriminate whenever some group can think of an expressive object that would seem to be inconsistent with the admission of some person as a member or at odds with the appointment of a person to a leadership position in the group.

Furthermore, it is not likely that BSA would be understood to send any message, either to Scouts or to the world, simply by admitting someone as a member. Over the years, BSA has generously welcomed over 87 million young Americans into its ranks. In 1992 over one million adults were active BSA members. The notion that an organization of that size and enormous prestige implicitly endorses the views that each of those adults may express in a non-Scouting context is simply mind boggling. Indeed, in this case there is no evidence that the young Scouts in Dale's troop, or members of their families, were even aware of his sexual orientation, either before or after his public statements at Rutgers University. It is equally farfetched to assert that Dale's open declaration of his homosexuality, reported in a local newspaper, will effectively force BSA to send a message to anyone simply because it allows Dale to be an Assistant Scoutmaster. For an Olympic gold medal winner or a Wimbledon tennis champion, being "openly gay" perhaps communicates a message — for example, that openness about one's sexual orientation is more virtuous than concealment; that a homosexual person can be a capable and virtuous person who should be judged like anyone else; and that homosexuality is not immoral — but it certainly does not follow that they necessarily send a message on behalf of the organizations that sponsor the activities in which they excel. The fact that such persons participate in these organizations is not usually construed to convey a message on behalf of those organizations any more than does the inclusion of women, African-Americans, religious minorities, or any other discrete group. Surely the organizations are not forced by anti-discrimination laws to take any position on the legitimacy of any individual's private beliefs or private conduct.

The State of New Jersey has decided that people who are open and frank about their sexual orientation are entitled to equal access to employment as school teachers, police officers, librarians, athletic coaches, and a host of other jobs filled by citizens who serve as role models for children and adults alike. Dozens of Scout units throughout the State are sponsored by public agencies, such as schools and fire departments, that employ such role models. BSA's affiliation with numerous public agencies that comply with New Jersey's law against discrimination cannot be understood to convey any particular message endorsing or condoning the activities of all these people.

VI

Unfavorable opinions about homosexuals "have ancient roots." *Bowers v. Hardwick,* 478 U.S. 186, 192 (1986). Like equally atavistic opinions about certain racial groups, those roots have been nourished by sectarian doctrine. Over the years, however, interaction with real people, rather than mere adherence to traditional ways of thinking about members of unfamiliar classes, have modified those opinions. A few examples: The American Psychiatric Association's and the American Psychological Association's removal of "homosexuality" from their lists of mental disorders; a move toward greater understanding within some religious communities; Justice Blackmun's classic opinion in *Bowers*; Georgia's invalidation of the statute upheld in *Bowers*; and New Jersey's enactment of the provision at issue in this case.

That such prejudices are still prevalent and that they have caused serious and tangible harm to countless members of the class New Jersey seeks to protect are established matters of fact that neither the Boy Scouts nor the Court disputes. That harm can only be aggravated by the creation of a constitutional shield for a policy that is itself the product of a habitual way of thinking about strangers. As Justice Brandeis so wisely advised, "we must be ever on our guard, lest we erect our prejudices into legal principles." If we would guide by the light of reason, we must let our minds be bold. I respectfully dissent. [Justice SOUTER, with whom Justice GINSBURG and Justice BREYER joined, offered a separate brief dissenting opinion, omitted here.]

Notes & Questions

1. What is the holding of the Supreme Court concerning the circumstances in which a state law forbidding discrimination on the basis of sexual orientation (or, possibly, gender identity) must give way before an organization's desire not to be perceived to be expressing particular views? What is the relevance of the issue, as to which Chief Justice Rehnquist and Justice Stevens so strongly disagreed, of whether the Boy Scouts of America has a strongly-articulated public stance on the issue of homosexuality, or had such a stance at the time when Dale's membership was revoked?

2. Does the decision in *Dale* provide a basis for any other organization or employer to claim an exemption from anti-discrimination laws on expressive association grounds? Suppose the employer is a not-for-profit organization (in a state that bans sexual orientation discrimination) that was formed to advocate on behalf of the right to life of the unborn fetus, and the director of the organization discovers that a member of the staff has become active in a local gay rights organization. Could the director discharge the employee on the ground that the organization does not want to be perceived as communicating to the public any positions on the subject of gay rights, because many supporters of the organization may be offended by such a message?

3. How broad a holding is *Dale*? Would the Boy Scouts be privileged to exclude gay people from administrative positions that do not involve direct dealings with members of the public or boys enrolled in the program? See *Chicago Area Council of Boy Scouts of America v. City of Chicago Commission on Human Relations*, 748 N.E. 2d 759 (Ill. Ct. App., 1st Dist., 2001) (Held, no).

4. If a public authority that has adopted a policy against sexual orientation discrimination decides that it should not make available its meeting facilities to any organization that does not comport with that policy, would the resulting exclusion of the discriminatory organization be unlawful? See *Boy Scouts of America v. Till*, 136 F.Supp.2d 1295 (S.D.Fla. 2001) (Held, yes, where the meeting facilities were found to be a "limited public forum" because they were generally made available to outside groups).

* * *

Another part of the First Amendment, which protects the free exercise of religion, has been cited as requiring a constitutional exception to laws forbidding sexual orientation discrimination. Anti-discrimination laws may not be used to contest a church's decision in hiring ministers or other personnel whose functions are to advance the religious goals of the organization. For example, early in the history of San Francisco's civil rights ordinance, which contained at the time no express exemption on religious grounds, a trial court held that a church could discharge its choir director/organist after it found out he was gay, because of a constitutionally mandated exemption under the Free Exercise Clause. *Walker v. First Presbyterian Church*, 22 Fair Empl.Prac.Cas. (BNA) 762 (Cal.Super.Ct.1980). The issue is more difficult, however, when the employee is not performing functions directly related to the organization's religious goals, such as clerical or maintenance duties for a church. Even more vexing is the application of anti-discrimination laws to largely secular activities that are under church ownership, or to secular businesses whose owners are devoutly religious.

Some jurisdictions have responded to these concerns by including specific exemption language in their civil rights statutes, sometimes specifically focusing on sexual orientation discrimination as presenting a special challenge due to religiously-based objections to homosexuality. The following case provides an example of the difficulties of construing such provisions.

Thorson v. Billy Graham Evangelistic Association

687 N.W.2d 652 (Minn. App. 2004), review denied

WRIGHT, Judge.

Respondent Billy Graham Evangelistic Association (BGEA) promotes Christianity through a combination of live events, productions for film and television, and publication of books, pamphlets, and magazines. Its employees are required to profess Christianity and participate in devotional activities. Appellant Sarah Thorson is a professed Christian who has worked at BGEA since June 1971. She started as a mailroom clerk and has continued in mailroom functions over the course of her career. In one position, as a night supervisor, she led other employees in prayer during meetings. Thorson's most recent position was as a bulk-mail services coordinator, in which she prepared mail and reported shipping for various BGEA departments. Her responsibilities have never involved development or production of evangelical media.

In February 2002, two employees reported seeing Thorson kissing another woman in the parking lot at work. At a meeting on February 21, 2002, two supervisors confronted Thorson with the allegations. Thorson admitted that she is a lesbian. One of her supervisors advised that, unless Thorson reconsidered her "lifestyle," she would be terminated. Following the meeting, Thorson was placed on leave. Thorson sent a letter to BGEA on March 7, 2002, asserting that her sexual orientation did not affect her employment and requesting that she be allowed to continue working for BGEA. BGEA did not respond to this request. Based on a determination that Thorson's sexual orientation was inconsistent with BGEA's mission, BGEA terminated Thorson's employment on June 24, 2002.

Thorson brought a lawsuit against BGEA, claiming that BGEA had discriminated against her on the basis of sexual orientation, in violation of the MHRA, Minn.Stat. § 363A.08, subds. 2 (barring discharge of employee because of sexual orientation), 4 (barring employer from requesting that employee furnish information as to sexual orientation) (Supp.2003). BGEA moved for summary judgment, contending that it was exempt from the sexual-orientation provisions of the MHRA. The district court entered summary judgment in favor of BGEA. This appeal followed.

Thorson argues that, because she was engaged in a secular business activity as a mailroom employee, BGEA is not exempt from the operation of the MHRA. On appeal from summary judgment, we determine whether there are any genuine issues of material fact and whether the district court erred in its application of the law.

Under limited circumstances, nonprofit religious associations are exempt from the MHRA's prohibition against discrimination based on sexual orientation. The exemption provides in relevant part:

> Nothing in this chapter prohibits any religious association...that is not organized for private profit, or any institution organized for educational purposes that is operated...by a religious association...that is not organized for private profit, from:...
>
> (2) in matters relating to sexual orientation, taking any action with respect to education, employment, housing and real property, or use of facilities. This

clause shall not apply to secular business activities engaged in by the religious association…the conduct of which is unrelated to the religious and educational purposes for which it is organized.

Minn.Stat. § 363A.26 (Supp.2003). The critical question for our consideration is the meaning of "secular business activities…the conduct of which is unrelated to the religious and educational purposes for which [a nonprofit religious association] is organized."

Our primary purpose, when considering the meaning of this statute, is to give effect to legislative intent as expressed in the statutory language. When the meaning of a statute's language is clear, we interpret the language according to its plain meaning without resorting to further construction. But when the language of a statute is reasonably susceptible of more than one meaning, we may employ principles of construction to resolve the ambiguity.

To determine whether a workplace activity is a secular business activity, Thorson asserts that the activity should be evaluated according to the job responsibilities of the particular employee. BGEA counters that the activity should be viewed in the context of the employer's purpose and mission as a whole to determine whether the business activity is secular or religious. Because we conclude that the statutory phrase "secular business activities" is reasonably susceptible to more than one interpretation, we employ applicable principles of construction to determine its meaning here.

Legislative history, including records of legislative hearings and changes in statutory language, may be used to resolve ambiguity in statutory language. Of relevance here are the statements made by the bill's sponsors during legislative floor debates. One of the House sponsors, Representative Ron Abrams, offered this observation regarding the statutory language at issue here:

> [U]pon receiving a complaint…dealing with, let's say, the termination of a pastor's secretary because of her [sexual orientation], ought to have the right not to be investigated.…[W]hat the intention here is is to give the broadest possible recognition and scope to the fundamental American value of separation of church and state.…
>
> I asked the Commissioner of Human Rights…under [a prior version of the bill], if they received a complaint dealing with a secretary or a choir director or a janitor, and they found probable cause that the person was terminated solely based upon sexual orientation, would the department prosecute? And his unequivocal answer was "yes." This language changes it to "no."

Floor Debate on H.F. 585, 78th Legis. (Mar. 18, 1993). He also explained that certain secular activities of a religious association, such as running a "for-profit printing press" or a hospital would remain subject to the MHRA.

Similar concerns were raised in the Senate, leading to these comments by the Senate sponsor, Senator Allen Spear:

> The religious exemption that's in the bill was worked out with the joint religious legislative coalition and other interested religious groups. Since then we've had more discussions, and have decided to broaden the amendment and make it absolutely clear that religious organizations would not be forced to hire people who adhere to a lifestyle that is contrary to their religious beliefs.
>
> ….
>
> Some few people did come to me and say, "Why don't we just make it an absolute exemption." And this is what this amendment does. There is one clause

in there that simply clarifies that while we are giving absolute exemption to churches, synagogues, religious institutions and societies, we would not be covering secular business activities that are not related to the purpose of the church. So we're talking about things, perhaps, like Augsburg Publishing, or something like that, which is a commercial secular business enterprise. But all the hiring, the renting of facilities, that are done by the church or the religious organizations would be exempt under this amendment.

Floor Debate on S.F. 444, 86th Legis. (Mar. 18, 1993). Later in the debate Senator Joann Benson asked Senator Spear:

> In those religious organizations, let's say a school or whatever, [the religious association exemption] then allows the person who hires to hire everyone in that school, from top to bottom, whether they're teachers or cooks or whatever, if they look at this as a whole entity?

Senator Spear responded:

> Madame Chair, that's correct. It would allow them to hire as they choose without regard to the restrictions of this bill for everyone that they hire.

> The question had been raised...about what the words meant [under a prior version of the bill] that it is "necessary to promote the religious tenets, teachings or principles for which it is established or maintained." And there was some confusion whether that meant just the ministers or the teachers but it would also include the cooks and the janitors. By removing that language we make it clear that the exemption includes everybody.

The MHRA's prohibition against discrimination in employment based on sexual orientation applies to the secular business activities of a nonprofit religious association that are "*unrelated* to the religious and educational purposes for which [the religious association] is organized." Minn.Stat. § 363A.26(2) (emphasis added). In accordance with legislative intent, we conclude that the phrase "secular business activities" is properly considered in light of the purpose and mission of the entire entity, not the job responsibilities of the individual employee. Here, BGEA's activities are exclusively evangelical and are entirely related to the religious purpose for which it is organized. It is, therefore, exempt from the sexual orientation provisions of the MHRA.

Thorson maintains that, because any activity of a nonprofit religious association may be deemed to serve a religious purpose, under the construction adopted here, there are no secular business activities that are governed by the MHRA. In effect, Thorson argues, the exception swallows the rule. We disagree. Indeed, the statute must be construed, whenever possible, in a manner that gives effect to all its provisions. It is evident from the legislative history that, when a nonprofit religious association is engaged in ordinary commerce, such as operating a hospital or printing press, the exemption will not cover these secular activities. Conversely, BGEA's business is the promotion of its evangelical ministry. Its business activities are not a matter of ordinary commerce. Rather, they are exclusively in furtherance of BGEA's religious purpose. Even though we determine that BGEA is not engaged in a secular business activity, our holding does not preclude a contrary result when a nonprofit religious association's business activity cannot be attributed to its religious purpose.

Citing our recent holding in *Egan v. Hamline United Methodist Church,* 679 N.W.2d 350, 355–56 (Minn.App.2004), *review denied* (Minn. June 29, 2004), Thorson also argues that we should apply the "ministerial exception" of Title VII of the Civil Rights Act to determine whether her employment is a secular business activity. This federal constitutional doctrine, developed in accordance with the Free Exercise Clause, prevents the operation of Title VII of the Civil Rights Act when it potentially encroaches on matters of religious practice. *See Rayburn v. Gen. Conference of Seventh-Day Adventists,* 772 F.2d 1164, 1168–69 (4th Cir.1985) (applying exception to bar suit by woman denied pastoral position because state's scrutiny of church's choice violates the free exercise clause); *McClure v. Salvation Army,* 460 F.2d 553, 560 (5th Cir.1972) (establishing exception because applying Title VII to employment relationships between church and minister results in an unconstitutional encroachment into religious freedom). But in *Egan* we did not conclusively adopt the ministerial exception, noting that it "is more demanding than the Minnesota statutory test." 679 N.W.2d at 356. To effectuate legislative intent and give proper effect to the religious-association exemption of the MHRA, we decline to apply the ministerial exception here.

Because BGEA's business activities are exclusively related to its evangelical ministry, they are not secular business activities unrelated to the religious and educational purposes for which BGEA is organized. Accordingly, BGEA is exempt from the sexual-orientation provisions of the Minnesota Human Rights Act. The district court applied the law correctly when it entered summary judgment in favor of BGEA.

Notes and Questions

The Thorson case illustrates the recurring phenomenon of the long-time closeted gay employee who provides decades of loyal, uncontroversial service to an organization and then is dismissed when they "slip up" and do something in an unguarded moment that reveals their sexual minority status to a disapproving employer. Ms. Thorson had worked in the mailroom for over thirty years, but an unguarded kiss in the parking lot "did her in." Are you persuaded by the court's reading of the legislative history of Minnesota's statutory exemption for religious organizations?

E. Immigration and Asylum

From the 1950s until 1990, federal law expressly required the exclusion of applicants for immigration to the United States who were found to be "afflicted" with a "psychopathic personality," interpreted by the courts to require exclusion of homosexuals or bisexuals. The word "afflicted" signifies that this was in the "medical exclusions" section of the Immigration and Naturalization Act. When litigation raised doubts about this interpretation of "psychopathic personality," Congress amended the law to add "sexual deviation" in order to clarify the exclusionary intent. (The Supreme Court meanwhile resolved those doubts in *Boutilier v. Immigration & Naturalization Service,* 387 U.S. 118 (1967), finding that clear congressional intent would support the Immigration Service's reading of the statute.)

In 1979, responding to the majority view of the medical profession that homosexuality and bisexuality were not mental illnesses, the Surgeon General of the U.S. Public Health Service, Dr. Julius Richmond, announced that PHS medical examiners would no longer diagnose homosexuality for immigration purposes. Federal appeals courts split over whether such a diagnosis was a prerequisite for exclusion. In addition, the law requires a finding of "good character" for all immigrants who applied to become U.S. citizens, and courts were split over whether homosexual immigrants could qualify. The case law was complex and confusing on both questions, but has become moot as a result of a 1990 amendment co-sponsored by Rep. Barney Frank (D-Mass) and Rep. Tom Campbell (R-Calif.) that removed "psychopathic personality or sexual deviation" from the medical exclusions and, in effect, dropped the legal ban on immigration to the U.S. by sexual minorities. For those interested in the pre-reform cases, see *Nemetz v. Immigration and Naturalization Service*, 647 F.2d 432 (4th Cir. 1981); *Hill v. U.S. Immigration and Naturalization Service*, 714 F.2d 1470 (9th Cir. 1983); *Petition of Longstaff*, 716 F.2d 1439 (5th Cir. 1983), cert. denied, 467 U.S. 1219 (1984).

1. Immigration of Same-sex Partners

Should same-sex partners of U.S. citizens be recognized as immediate family members for purposes of the immigration law? Immediate family members have a preferred status under the law for purposes of being allowed to stay in the United States or to travel here. Some other countries—most notably Australia, New Zealand, Canada, South Africa, as well as the European countries that now have either same-sex marriage or some form of registered partnership for same-sex couples—recognize the same-sex partners of their lawful residents as family members for purposes of permission to emigrate and obtain citizenship status, but the United States has as yet made no move in that direction. See *Adams v. Howerton*, 673 F.2d 1036 (9th Cir.), cert. denied, 458 U.S. 1111 (1982), and *Sullivan v. Immigration and Naturalization Service*, 772 F.2d 609 (9th Cir. 1985).

U.S. Rep. Jerrold Nadler (D.-N.Y.) introducing legislation in 2001 to allow "permanent partners" of U.S. residents to have the same rights as spouses under U.S. immigration law. The measure has been reintroduced in subsequent sessions of Congress in both houses, but has yet to receive a committee vote. The *Permanent Partners Immigration Act of 2001,* HR 690 (107th Cong., 1st Session), defines "permanent partners" as follows:

The term 'permanent partner' means an individual 18 years of age or older who-

'(A) is in a committed, intimate relationship with another individual 18 years of age or older in which both parties intend a lifelong commitment;

'(B) is financially interdependent with that other individual;

'(C) is not married to or in a permanent partnership with anyone other than that other individual;

'(D) is unable to contract with that other individual a marriage cognizable under this Act; and

'(E) is not a first, second, or third degree blood relation of that other individual.

The term 'permanent partnership' means the relationship that exists between two permanent partners.'

The bill would amend existing immigration law to insert the term "permanent partner" or "permanent partnership" into the statute wherever reference is made to marital partners or spouses or other family members recognized under the law. The bill makes no distinction between same-sex partners and opposite-sex partners, thus realizing that many people, regardless of sexual orientation, live in long-term partnerships that should be respected by the law.

The Defense of Marriage Act (1996) provides that same-sex couples cannot be treated as spouses for purposes of federal law, including immigration and naturalization law. Although doubts have been expressed about the constitutionality of DOMA, prior to the possibility of same-sex marriage in Canada and Massachusetts, which occurred in 2003, there was little likelihood that DOMA could be challenged in an immigration law context. However, challenges are now likely as mixed-nationality couples marry in these jurisdictions and then seek permanent residency status for the non-U.S.-citizen member of the couple.

As shown by the Supreme Court's decision in *Lawrence v. Texas*, some of the justices have become sensitive to international opinion on matters of human rights law. Consequently, the following decision by the Constitutional Court of South Africa on the issue of partner immigration rights might be persuasive.

National Coalition for Gay and Lesbian Equality v. the Minister of Home Affairs
Case CCT 10/99 (1999)
CONSTITUTIONAL COURT OF SOUTH AFRICA

ACKERMANN J:

This matter raises two important questions. The first is whether it is unconstitutional for immigration law to facilitate the immigration into South Africa of the spouses of permanent South African residents but not to afford the same benefits to gays and lesbians in permanent same-sex life partnerships with permanent South African residents. The second is whether, when it concludes that provisions in a statute are unconstitutional, the Court may read words into the statute to remedy the unconstitutionality. These questions arise from the provisions of section 25(5) ("section 25(5)") of the Aliens Control Act 96 of 1991 (the "Act") and the application of the provisions of section 172(1)(b) of the 1996 Constitution (the "Constitution") should section 25(5) be found to be inconsistent with the Constitution. Section 25(5) reads: "Notwithstanding the provisions of subsection (4), but subject to the provisions of subsections (3) and (6), a regional committee may, upon application by the spouse or the dependent child of a person permanently and lawfully resident in the Republic, authorize the issue of an immigration permit."

Section 25(5) was declared constitutionally invalid and consequential relief granted by the Cape of Good Hope High Court (the "High Court").

The statutory framework and relevant facts

The Act is wide-ranging and provides for "the control of the admission of persons to, their residence in, and their departure from, the Republic; and for matters connected therewith." Section 24(1) of the Act establishes an Immigrants Selection Board which consists of the central committee and at least one regional committee (a "regional committee") for each of the provinces of the Republic. An important provision, for purposes of this case, is section 23 which deals with "aliens", an "alien" being defined in section 1(1) as "a person who is not a South African citizen", and which provides as follows:

"Subject to the provisions of sections 28 and 29, no alien shall-

(a) enter or sojourn in the Republic with a view to permanent residence therein, unless he or she is in possession of an immigration permit issued to him or her in terms of section 25; or

(b) enter or sojourn in the Republic with a view to temporary residence therein, unless he or she is in possession of a permit for temporary residence issued to him or her in terms of section 26."

The attack on the constitutional validity of section 25(5) concentrated on the fact that it enables preferential treatment to be given to a foreign national applying for an immigration permit who is "the spouse...of a person permanently and lawfully resident in the Republic", but not to a foreign national who, though similarly placed in all other respects, is in a same-sex life partnership with a person permanently and lawfully resident in the Republic.

The constitutional validity of section 25(5)

[The Respondents] submitted that the Republic, as a sovereign independent state, was lawfully entitled to exclude any foreign nationals from the Republic; that it had an absolute discretion to do so which was beyond the reach of the Constitution and the courts; and that, to the extent that Parliament legislated to permit foreign nationals to reside in South Africa, it did so in the exercise of such discretion and that the provisions of such legislation were equally beyond the reach of the Constitution and the courts. [The Respondents] submitted that this was recognised by the Constitution in that certain provisions of the Bill of Rights conferred significant rights only on citizens of the Republic. Thus only a citizen has the right to "enter, to remain in and to reside anywhere in the Republic"; to "a passport"; to certain political rights; and to choose a "trade, occupation or profession freely".

Such an argument, even if correct, would not assist the respondents, because in the present case we are not dealing with such a category of foreign nationals, but with persons who are in intimate life partnerships with persons who are permanently and lawfully resident in the Republic (to whom I shall refer as "South Africans"). This is a significant and determinative difference. The failure of the Act to grant any recognition at all to same-sex life partnerships impacts in the same way on the South African partners as it does on the foreign national partners. In my view this case can, and ought properly to be decided, on the basis of whether section 25(5) unconstitutionally limits the rights of the South African partners.

Section 9 of the Constitution provides:

"**Equality**

(1) Everyone is equal before the law and has the right to equal protection and benefit of the law.

(2) Equality includes the full and equal enjoyment of all rights and freedoms. To promote the achievement of equality, legislative and other measures designed to protect or advance persons, or categories of persons, disadvantaged by unfair discrimination may be taken.

(3) The state may not unfairly discriminate directly or indirectly against anyone on one or more grounds, including race, gender, sex, pregnancy, marital status, ethnic or social origin, colour, sexual orientation, age, disability, religion, conscience, belief, culture, language and birth.

(4) No person may unfairly discriminate directly or indirectly against anyone on one or more grounds in terms of subsection (3). National legislation must be enacted to prevent or prohibit unfair discrimination.

(5) Discrimination on one or more of the grounds listed in subsection (3) is unfair unless it is established that the discrimination is fair."

Section 10 provides:

"**Human dignity**

Everyone has inherent dignity and the right to have their dignity respected and protected."

Davis J found that section 25(5) constituted a clear limitation of the section 9 guarantee against unfair discrimination because it differentiated on the grounds of sexual orientation; under section 9(5) such differentiation, being a ground specified in section 9(3), is presumed to be unfair unless the contrary is established; and that the contrary had not been established. The High Court considered it unnecessary to deal with the other grounds on which section 25(5) had been attacked. In National Coalition for Gay and Lesbian Equality and Another v Minister of Justice and Others (the "*Sodomy* case") this Court pointed out that in particular circumstances the rights of equality and dignity are closely related and found the criminal offence of sodomy to be unconstitutional because it breached both rights. In the present case the rights of equality and dignity are also closely related and it would be convenient to deal with them in a related manner.

The differentiation brought about by section 25(5) is of a negative kind. It does not proscribe conduct of same-sex life partners or enact provisions that in themselves prescribe negative consequences for them. The differentiation lies in its failure to extend to them the same advantages or benefits that it extends to spouses.

Before this Court the respondents challenged the conclusion reached by the High Court that the omission in section 25(5) of spousal benefits to same-sex life partners was a differentiation based on the ground of sexual orientation. It was submitted on their behalf that the differentiation was based on the ground that they were non-spouses, which had nothing to do with their sexual orientation, and that accordingly, because the differentiation was on "non-spousal" grounds, rather than on marital status, it did not constitute unfair discrimination. There is no merit in this submission, because as indicated above in paragraph 25, spouse is defined with regard to marriage and is but the name given to the partners to a marriage.

In the alternative it was argued that, even if the differentiation was on grounds of marital status, there was nothing that prevented gays and lesbians from contracting marriages with persons of the opposite sex, thus becoming and acquiring spouses and accordingly being entitled to the spousal benefits under section 25(5). Therefore, so the submission proceeded, the fact that they did not enjoy the advantages of a spousal relationship was of their own choosing. What the submission implies is that same-sex life partners should ignore their sexual orientation and, contrary thereto, enter into marriage with someone of the opposite sex.

I am unable to accede to this line of argument. It confuses form with substance and does not have proper regard for the operation, experience or impact of discrimination in society. Discrimination does not take place in discrete areas of the law, hermetically sealed from one another, where each aspect of discrimination is to be examined and its impact evaluated in isolation. Discrimination must be understood in the context of the experience of those on whom it impacts. As recognised in the *Sodomy* case — "[t]he experience of subordination — of personal subordination, above all — lies behind the vision of equality."

Moreover, the submission fails to recognise that marriage represents but one form of life partnership. The law currently only recognises marriages that are conjugal relationships between people of the opposite sex. Suffice it to say that there is another form of life partnership which is different from marriage as recognised by law. This form of life partnership is represented by a conjugal relationship between two people of the same sex. The law currently does not recognise permanent same-sex life partnerships as marriages. It follows that section 25(5) affords protection only to conjugal relationships between heterosexuals and excludes any protection to a life partnership which entails a conjugal same-sex relationship, which is the only form of conjugal relationship open to gays and lesbians in harmony with their sexual orientation.

A notable and significant development in our statute law in recent years has been the extent of express and implied recognition the legislature has accorded same-sex partnerships. A range of statutory provisions have included such unions within their ambit. While this legislative trend is significant in evincing Parliament's commitment to equality on the ground of sexual orientation, there is still no appropriate recognition in our law of the same-sex life partnership, *as a relationship*, to meet the legal and other needs of its partners.

It follows that same-sex partners are in a different position from heterosexual partners who have not contracted a marriage and have not become spouses. The respondents' submission that gays and lesbians are free to marry in the sense that nothing prohibits them from marrying persons of the opposite sex, is true only as a meaningless abstraction. This submission ignores the constitutional injunction that gays and lesbians cannot be discriminated against on the grounds of their own sexual orientation and the constitutional right to express that orientation in a relationship of their own choosing.

There is much to be said for the view that the discrimination in section 25(5) is on the ground of sexual orientation. As previously pointed out, the section 25(5) protection is not extended to the only form of conjugal relationship in which gays and lesbians are able to participate in harmony with their sexual orientation, namely, same-sex life partnerships.

The better view, however, in my judgment, is that the discrimination in section 25(5) constitutes overlapping or intersecting discrimination on the grounds of sexual orientation and marital status, both being specified in section 9(3) and presumed to constitute unfair discrimination by reason of section 9(5) of the Constitution. The prerequisite of marriage before the benefit is available points to that element of the discrimination concerned with marital status, while the fact that no such benefit is available to gays and lesbians engaged in the only form of conjugal relationship open to them in harmony with their sexual orientation represents discrimination on the grounds of sexual orientation. I propose dealing with the present case on this basis.

The impact of the discrimination on the affected applicants

The determining factor regarding the unfairness of discrimination is, in the final analysis, the impact of the discrimination on the complainant or the members of the affected group. The approach to this determination is a nuanced and comprehensive one in which various factors come into play which, when assessed cumulatively and objectively, will assist in elaborating and giving precision to the constitutional test of unfairness. Important factors to be assessed in this regard (which do not however constitute a closed list) are: (a) the position of complainants in society and whether they have suffered in the past from patterns of disadvantage; (b) the nature of the provision or power and the purpose sought to be achieved by it. If its purpose is manifestly not directed, in the first instance, at impairing the complainants in their fundamental human dignity or in a comparably serious respect, but is aimed at achieving a worthy and important societal goal, such as, for example, the furthering of equality for all, this purpose may, depending on the facts of the particular case, have a significant bearing on the question whether the complainants have in fact suffered the impairment in question. (c) with due regard to (a) and (b) above, and any other relevant factors, the extent to which the discrimination has affected the rights or interests of complainants and whether it has led to an impairment of their fundamental human dignity or constitutes an impairment of a comparably serious nature. It is noteworthy how the Canadian Supreme Court has, in the development of its equality jurisprudence under section 15(1) of the Canadian Charter, come to see the central purpose of its equality guarantee as the protection and promotion of human dignity.

In the *Sodomy* case this Court dealt with the seriously negative impact that societal discrimination on the ground of sexual orientation has had, and continues to have, on gays and their same-sex partnerships, concluding that gay men are a permanent minority in society and have suffered in the past from patterns of disadvantage. Although the main focus of that judgment was on the criminalisation of sodomy and on other proscriptions of erotic expression between men, the conclusions regarding the minority status of gays and the patterns of discrimination to which they have been and continue to be subject are also applicable to lesbians. Society at large has, generally, accorded far less respect to lesbians and their intimate relationships with one another than to heterosexuals and their relationships. The sting of past and continuing discrimination against both gays and lesbians is the clear message that it conveys, namely, that they, whether viewed as individuals or in their same-sex relationships, do not have the inherent dignity and are not worthy of the human respect possessed by and accorded to heterosexuals and their relationships. This discrimination occurs at a deeply intimate level of human existence and relationality. It denies to gays and lesbians that which is foundational to our Constitution and the concepts of equality and dignity, which at this point are closely intertwined, namely that all persons have the same inherent worth and dignity as human beings, whatever their other differences may be. The denial of equal dignity and worth all too quickly and insidiously degenerates into a denial of humanity and leads to inhuman treatment by the rest of society in many other ways. This is deeply demeaning and frequently has the cruel effect of undermining the confidence and sense of self-worth and self-respect of lesbians and gays.

This Court has recognised that "[t]he more vulnerable the group adversely affected by the discrimination, the more likely the discrimination will be held to be unfair." Vulnerability in turn depends to a very significant extent on past patterns of disadvantage, stereotyping and the like. This is why an enquiry into past disadvantage is so important. In the present case, there is significant pre-existing disadvantage and vulnerability.

I turn now to deal with the discriminatory impact of section 25(5) on same-sex life partners. I agree with the submission advanced on respondents' behalf that section 25(5) is manifestly aimed at achieving the societal goal of protecting the family life of "lawful marriages" (which I understand to mean marriages which are formally valid and contracted in good faith and not sham marriages for the purposes of circumventing the Act) and certain recognised customary unions, by making provision for family reunification and in particular by entitling spouses of persons permanently and lawfully resident in the Republic to receive permanent residence permits. The pertinent question that immediately arises is what the impact of being excluded from these protective provisions is on same-sex life partners.

The starting point is to enquire what the nature of such family life is in the case of spouses that section 25(5) specially protects and benefits. For purposes of this case it is unnecessary to consider comprehensively the nature of traditional marriage and the spousal relationship. It is sufficient to indicate that under South African common law a marriage "creates a physical, moral and spiritual community of life, a consortium omnis vitae" which has been described as: "…an abstraction comprising the totality of a number of rights, duties and advantages accruing to spouses of a marriage…These embrace intangibles, such as loyalty and sympathetic care and affection, concern…as well as the more material needs of life, such as physical care, financial support, the rendering of services in the running of the common household or in a support-generating business…." As Sinclair and Heaton point out, the duties of cohabitation and fidelity flow from this relationship. In *Grobbelaar v Havenga* it was held that "[c]ompanionship, love, affection, comfort, mutual services, sexual intercourse—all belong to the married state. Taken together, they make up the *consortium*."

It is important to emphasise that over the past decades an accelerating process of transformation has taken place in family relationships as well as in societal and legal concepts regarding the family and what it comprises. Sinclair and Heaton, after alluding to the profound transformations of the legal relationships between family members that have taken place in the past, comment as follows on the present: "But the current period of rapid change seems to 'strike at the most basic assumptions' underlying marriage and the family.….Itself a country where considerable political and socio-economic movement has been and is taking place, South Africa occupies a distinctive position in the context of developments in the legal relationship between family members and between the state and the family. Its heterogeneous society is 'fissured by differences of language, religion, race, cultural habit, historical experience and self-definition' and, consequently, reflects widely varying expectations about marriage, family life and the position of women in society." [Internal citations omitted]

In other countries a significant change in societal and legal attitudes to same-sex partnerships in the context of what is considered to constitute a family has occurred. Evidence of these changes are to be found in the jurisprudence dealing with equality issues in countries such as Canada, Israel, the United Kingdom and the United States. In referring to these judgments from the highest courts of other jurisdictions I do not overlook the different nature of their histories, legal systems and constitutional contexts nor that, in the last two cases, the issue was one essentially of statutory construction and not constitutional invalidity. Nevertheless, these judgments give expression to norms and values in other open and democratic societies based on human dignity, equality and freedom which, in my view, give clear expression to the growing concern for, understanding of, and sensitivity towards human diversity in general and to gays and lesbians and their relationships in particular. This is an important source from which to illuminate our understanding of the Constitution and the promotion of its informing norms.

The impact of section 25(5) is to reinforce harmful and hurtful stereotypes of gays and lesbians. At the heart of these stereotypes whether expressly articulated or not, lie misconceptions based on the fact that the sexual orientation of lesbians and gays is such that they have an erotic and emotional affinity for persons of the same sex and may give physical sexual expression thereto with same-sex partners.

A second stereotype, often used to bolster the prejudice against gay and lesbian sexuality, is constructed on the fact that a same-sex couple cannot procreate in the same way as a heterosexual couple. Gays and lesbians are certainly individually permitted to adopt children under the provisions of section 17(b) of the Child Care Act 74 of 198373 and nothing prevents a gay couple or a lesbian couple, one of whom has so adopted a child, from treating such child in all ways, other than strictly legally, as their child. They can certainly love, care and provide for the child as though it was their joint child.

From a legal and constitutional point of view procreative potential is not a defining characteristic of conjugal relationships. Such a view would be deeply demeaning to couples (whether married or not) who, for whatever reason, are incapable of procreating when they commence such relationship or become so at any time thereafter. It is likewise demeaning to couples who commence such a relationship at an age when they no longer have the desire for sexual relations. It is demeaning to adoptive parents to suggest that their family is any less a family and any less entitled to respect and concern than a family with procreated children. I would even hold it to be demeaning of a couple who voluntarily decide not to have children or sexual relations with one another; this being a decision entirely within their protected sphere of freedom and privacy.

The message that the total exclusion of gays and lesbians from the provisions of the sub-section conveys to gays and lesbians and the consequent impact on them can in my view be conveniently expressed by comparing (a) the facts concerning gays and lesbians and their same-sex partnerships which must be accepted, with (b) what the subsection in effect states: (a) (i) Gays and lesbians have a constitutionally entrenched right to dignity and equality; (ii) Sexual orientation is a ground expressly listed in section 9(3) of the Constitution and under section 9(5) discrimination on it is unfair unless the contrary is established; (iii) Prior criminal proscription of private and consensual sexual expression between gays, arising from their sexual orientation and which had been directed at gay men, has been struck down as unconstitutional; (iv) Gays and lesbians in same-sex life partnerships are as capable as heterosexual spouses of expressing and sharing love in its manifold forms including affection, friendship, eros and charity; (v) They are likewise as capable of forming intimate, permanent, committed, monogamous, loyal and enduring relationships; of furnishing emotional and spiritual support; and of providing physical care, financial support and assistance in running the common household; (vi) They are individually able to adopt children and in the case of lesbians to bear them; (vii) In short, they have the same ability to establish a consortium omnis vitae; (viii) Finally, and of particular importance for purposes of this case, they are capable of constituting a family, whether nuclear or extended, and of establishing, enjoying and benefiting from family life which is not distinguishable in any significant respect from that of heterosexual spouses. (b) The subsection, in this context, in effect states that all gay and lesbian permanent residents of the Republic, who are in same-sex relationships with foreign nationals, are not entitled to the benefit extended by the subsection to spouses married to foreign nationals in order to protect their family and family life. This is so stated, notwithstanding that the family and family life which gays and lesbians are capable of establishing with their foreign national same-sex partners are in all significant respects indistinguishable from those of spouses and in human terms as important to gay and lesbian same-sex partners as they are to spouses.

The message and impact are clear. Section 10 of the Constitution recognises and guarantees that everyone has inherent dignity and the right to have their dignity respected and protected. The message is that gays and lesbians lack the inherent humanity to have their families and family lives in such same-sex relationships respected or protected. It serves in addition to perpetuate and reinforce existing prejudices and stereotypes. The impact constitutes a crass, blunt, cruel and serious invasion of their dignity. The discrimination, based on sexual orientation, is severe because no concern, let alone anything approaching equal concern, is shown for the particular sexual orientation of gays and lesbians.

We were pressed with an argument that it was of considerable public importance to protect the traditional and conventional institution of marriage and that the government accordingly has a strong and legitimate interest to protect the family life of such marriages and was entitled to do so by means of section 25(5). Even if this proposition were to be accepted it would be subject to two major reservations. In the first place, protecting the traditional institution of marriage as recognised by law may not be done in a way which unjustifiably limits the constitutional rights of partners in a permanent same-sex life partnership. In the second place there is no rational connection between the exclusion of same-sex life partners from the benefits under section 25(5) and the government interest sought to be achieved thereby, namely the protection of families and the family life of heterosexual spouses.

There is nothing in the scales to counteract such conclusion. I accordingly hold that section 25(5) constitutes unfair discrimination and a serious limitation of the section 9(3) equality right of gays and lesbians who are permanent residents in the Republic and who are in permanent same-sex life partnerships with foreign nationals. I also hold, for the reasons appearing throughout this judgment and culminating in the conclusion reached at the beginning of this paragraph, that section 25(5) simultaneously constitutes a severe limitation of the section 10 right to dignity enjoyed by such gays and lesbians.

I now apply the section 36(1) justification analysis...The rights limited, namely equality and dignity, are important rights going to the core of our constitutional democratic values of human dignity, equality and freedom. The forming and sustaining of intimate personal relationships of the nature here in issue are for many individuals essential for their own self-understanding and for the full development and expression of their human personalities.

There is no interest on the other side that enters the balancing process. It is true, as previously stated, that the protection of family and family life in conventional spousal relationships is an important governmental objective, but the extent to which this could be done would in no way be limited or affected if same-sex life partners were appropriately included under the protection of section 25(5). There is in my view no justification for the limitation in the present case and it therefore follows that the provisions of section 25(5) are inconsistent with the Constitution and invalid. [As a remedy, the Court concluded that it could "read in" to the statute a requirement to extend its benefits to same-sex couples.]

Notes and Questions

1. The South Africa Constitution specifically prohibits sexual orientation discrimination by reference on the list of forbidden grounds of discrimination. By contrast, the U.S. Con-

stitution adopts a general equal protection requirement without mentioning any specific forbidden grounds of discrimination. However, in *Romer v. Evans*, the Supreme Court held that sexual orientation discrimination may violate the Equal Protection Clause. In litigation over the refusal to grant spousal preferences to same-sex partners of legal American permanent residents or citizens, should this difference produce a different outcome?

2. One of the important barriers to asserting constitutional claims in the United States on behalf of "aliens" is the Supreme Court's view that aliens do not, in general, have rights under the U.S. Constitution, and that Congress has plenary power to control immigration policy. The South Africa Constitutional Court was confronted with much the same argument, but opined that the constitutional rights at stake were those of South African residents who were being denied the right to live together with their desired same-sex partners. Consider the possibility of raising this argument in U.S. litigation. Does it take on enhanced resonance in light of the following statement in the Supreme Court's decision in *Lawrence v. Texas*?

> The *Casey* decision again confirmed that our laws and tradition afford constitutional protection to personal decisions relating to marriage, procreation, contraception, family relationships, child rearing, and education. *Id.*, at 851. In explaining the respect the Constitution demands for the autonomy of the person in making these choices, we stated as follows: 'These matters, involving the most intimate and personal choices a person may make in a lifetime, choices central to personal dignity and autonomy, are central to the liberty protected by the Fourteenth Amendment. At the heart of liberty is the right to define one's own concept of existence, of meaning, of the universe, and of the mystery of human life. Beliefs about these matters could not define the attributes of personhood were they formed under compulsion of the State.' *Ibid.* Persons in a homosexual relationship may seek autonomy for these purposes, just as heterosexual persons do.

3. In common with courts of other British Commonwealth countries, the South African Constitutional Court makes frequent reference to, and indulges in extensive quotations from, opinions by court of other English-speaking countries. For reasons of length, the version of the National Coalition decision reproduced above omits lengthy discussion and quotations from Canadian Supreme Court opinions, as well as some references to decisions by the courts of other Commonwealth countries.

2. Asylum for Sexual Minorities

Once it became possible for sexual minorities to immigrate openly to the United States, questions arose about persons seeking asylum here due to persecution in their home country on grounds of sexual orientation or identity. This led to interesting cases about the nature of human sexuality, the concept of a "social group" for purposes of international human rights law, and what constitutes "persecution" in the context of governmental or societal treatment of sexual minorities.

This was first explored legally in cases involving refugees from the Cuban Mariel boatlift to the U.S., many of whom were gay prisoners of the Castro regime. In *Toboso-Alfonso,* 20 I. & N. Dec. 819, 820–23, 1990 WL 547189 (BIA 1990), the Board of Immigration Appeals concluded that homosexuals can be considered a member of a "social group," a decision that Attorney General Janet Reno subsequently designated as precedential within the Immigration Service. But the meaning of "persecution" remained contested, as did the scope of the "social group" determination.

Pitcherskaia v. Immigration and Naturalization Service
118 F.3d 641 (9th Cir. 1997)

FLETCHER, Circuit Judge:

Alla Pitcherskaia is a 35 year old native and citizen of Russia. She entered the United States as a visitor for pleasure on March 22, 1992, with authorization to remain for six months. On June 2, 1992, she applied for asylum on the basis that she feared persecution on account of her own and her father's anti-Communist political opinions. After a complete interview, the Immigration and Naturalization Service Asylum Office found that she was credible and that she had suffered past persecution. However, it found that she failed to establish a well-founded fear of future persecution and denied her application. She was placed in deportation proceedings for overstaying her visa.

Pitcherskaia renewed her request for asylum and withholding of deportation, under sections 208(a) and 243(h) of the Immigration and Nationality Act ("INA" or "Act"), 8 U.S.C. §§ 1158(a) and 1243(h). In this application, she claimed an additional basis for granting her petition—that she was persecuted and feared future persecution on account of her political opinions in support of lesbian and gay civil rights in Russia, and on account of her membership in a particular social group: Russian lesbians. Pitcherskaia alleges that she did not include a claim for persecution on account of her lesbianism and her political activism for lesbian and gay rights in her original application because she did not know that it was a possible ground for an asylum claim.]

Pitcherskaia's father was an artist and political dissident. As a result of his anti-government activities, he was arrested and imprisoned numerous times during Pitcherskaia's childhood until 1972 when he died in prison. Pitcherskaia testified that, because of her father's anticommunist activities, she has been under the control and surveillance of the police for her entire life. Pitcherskaia was first arrested by the militia in 1980, when she was eighteen years old. She was charged with the crime of "hooliganism" and detained for fifteen days because she protested her former school director's beating of a gay friend. At the time of this arrest, the director was unaware Pitcherskaia was herself a lesbian.

In 1981, Pitcherskaia was arrested again, imprisoned for fifteen days, and beaten for participating in an illegal demonstration demanding the release of the leader of a lesbian youth organization which she belonged to. Pitcherskaia claims that, at the time of this arrest, the Russian militia warned her not to continue to associate with other women in the organization and threatened her with involuntary psychiatric confinement if she continued "to see women."

Over the next two years Pitcherskaia claims that she was detained by the militia for short periods, interrogated, and on occasion beaten. On several occasions she was pressed to identify gay and lesbian friends. In May 1983, she was again arrested, charged with "hooliganism," and detained for ten days. Pitcherskaia maintains that the sole reason for her arrest was the arresting officer's knowledge of her sexual identity and political opinions.

In 1985 or 1986, Pitcherskaia's ex-girlfriend was forcibly sent to a psychiatric institution for over four months, during which time she was subjected to electric shock treatment and other so-called "therapies" in an effort to change her sexual orientation. Pitcherskaia testified that while she was visiting this woman at the psychiatric institution, she was grabbed by the militia, forcibly taken to a doctor's office and questioned about her sexual orientation. She was permitted to leave only after she provided a false address outside the jurisdiction of the clinic. Although she denied being a lesbian, the clinic registered her as a "suspected lesbian" and told her she must undergo treatment at her local clinic every six months. When she failed to show up for these outpatient sessions, she received a "Demand for Appearance." She testified that if she failed to comply, the militia would threaten her with forced institutionalization and forcibly take her from her home to the sessions.

Pitcherskaia testified that she attended eight of these "therapy" sessions. During these sessions, Pitcherskaia continued to deny that she was a lesbian. However, she was officially diagnosed with "slow-going schizophrenia," a catchall phrase often used in Russia to "diagnose" homosexuals. The psychiatrist prescribed sedative drugs, which Pitcherskaia never took. On one occasion, the psychiatrist tried to hypnotize her.

On two separate occasions, in 1990 and 1991, Pitcherskaia was arrested while in the homes of gay friends and taken to prison overnight. She received several "Demands for Appearance" when the militia sought to interrogate her about her sexual orientation and political activities. In 1991, she was interrogated about her activities with a gay and lesbian political organization—the "Union of Coming Out"—that had been denied legal recognition by the government. Since her arrival in the United States, Pitcherskaia has received two more "Demands for Appearance" from the militia that were delivered at her mother's residence. Since she did not respond to the two recent Demands, Pitcherskaia fears that the militia will carry out their previous threats and forcibly institutionalize her if she returns to Russia.

After hearing testimony and reviewing an advisory opinion from the State Department, the IJ [Immigration Judge] denied Pitcherskaia's applications for asylum and withholding of deportation and granted 30-days voluntary departure. The IJ did not render a specific finding with respect to Pitcherskaia's credibility, but simply proceeded as if her testimony was essentially credible. The IJ found that, "based upon the entire record including the Court's observation of the demeanor of the respondent as well as her witness while testifying and after consideration of the arguments of counsel," Pitcherskaia had not established that she was eligible for asylum.

Pitcherskaia appealed to the Board of Immigration Appeals ("BIA" or "Board"). In a divided opinion, the Board denied her appeal. The BIA majority did not make a finding as to Pitcherskaia's credibility because it found that, "even if her testimony is essentially credible," she had failed to meet her burden in establishing eligibility for relief. The BIA majority concluded that Pitcherskaia had not been persecuted because, although she had been subjected to involuntary psychiatric treatments, the militia and psychiatric institutions intended to "cure" her, not to punish her, and thus their actions did not constitute "persecution" within the meaning of the Act. The BIA majority also concluded that recent political and social changes in the former Soviet Union make it unlikely that she would be "subject to psychiatric treatment with persecutory intent upon [her] return to the present-day Russia."

In dissent, Chairman Schmidt concluded that Pitcherskaia had established a well-founded fear of persecution on account of her membership in a particular social group. He rejected both the BIA majority's legal holding that an alien must prove that her persecutor had an "intent to punish" as well as its factual finding that the situation had improved markedly for gays and lesbians in Russia. Because both the IJ and the BIA assumed, for purposes of their decisions, that Pitcherskaia's testimony was credible, we will also, for purposes of this appeal, assume that the testimony was credible.

II.

A. Statutory Scheme

The Attorney General may grant asylum to an alien present in the United States who is a "refugee." A "refugee" is an alien who is unable or unwilling to return to her or his country of origin "because of persecution or well-founded fear of persecution on account of race, religion, nationality, membership in a particular social group, or political opinion." In order for Pitcherskaia to qualify for asylum based on persecution or fear of persecution on account of her membership in a "particular social group," Russian lesbians must constitute a "particular social group" within the meaning of the INA. In its opinion, the IJ assumed lesbians constitute a "particular social group." Before the BIA, the majority specifically declined to reach the issue because it concluded that Pitcherskaia had not established that she had been persecuted or had a well-founded fear of persecution. We also do not reach the issue.] Either past persecution or a well-founded fear of future persecution provide eligibility for a discretionary grant of asylum. *Lopez-Galarza v. INS,* 99 F.3d 954, 958 (9th Cir.1996).

To establish a well-founded fear of persecution requires "subjectively genuine" and "objectively reasonable" fear of persecution "on account of" political opinion or membership in a particular social group. "The subjective component requires that the applicant have a genuine concern that he will be persecuted," and may be satisfied by the applicant's testimony that she genuinely fears persecution. The objective component requires that the alien establish a reasonable fear of persecution by credible, direct, and specific evidence. An alien is not, however, required to present proof that persecution is more likely than not. "One can certainly have a well-founded fear of an event happening when there is less than a 50% chance of the occurrence taking place."

An alien who establishes past persecution is presumed to have a well-founded fear of persecution. However, this presumption may be rebutted where the conditions in the country have significantly changed. The INS bears the burden to rebut this presumption by a preponderance of the evidence. Eligibility for asylum also may be established on the basis of past persecution alone.

Pitcherskaia claims, *inter alia,* that the BIA applied an erroneous legal standard by insisting that intent to punish is a necessary element of "persecution." The meaning of "persecution" under section 101(a)(42)(A) of the Act is a legal question reviewed *de novo.* However, the BIA's interpretations are generally entitled to deference. Because the Act does not define "persecution," we defer to the Board's interpretation unless it is "arbitrary, capricious, or manifestly contrary to the statute." The Board is also bound by our prior decisions interpreting the Act.

B. The Definition of Persecution is Objective

The majority of the Board required that Pitcherskaia prove that the Russian authorities intended to harm or punish her. While acknowledging that forced institutionalization, electroshock treatments, and drug injections could constitute persecution, the BIA majority concluded that because here the "[i]nvoluntary treatment and confinement [were] intended to treat or cure the supposed illness, not to punish," Pitcherskaia had not been persecuted nor did she have a well-founded fear of persecution. For the following reasons we conclude that in requiring Pitcherskaia to prove intent to harm or punish as an element of persecution, the BIA majority erred.

Although many asylum cases "involve actors who had a subjective intent to punish their victims this subjective 'punitive' or 'malignant' intent is not required for harm to constitute persecution." *In re Fauziya Kasinga*, Int. Dec. 3278 at 12 (BIA June 13, 1996) (en banc) (designated as precedent by the BIA). Neither the Supreme Court nor this court has construed the Act as imposing a requirement that the alien prove that her persecutor was motivated by a desire to punish or inflict harm. We have defined "persecution" as "the infliction of suffering or harm upon those who differ in a way regarded as offensive." *Sangha v. INS*, 103 F.3d 1482, 1487 (9th Cir.1997) This definition of persecution is objective, in that it turns not on the subjective intent of the persecutor but rather on what a reasonable person would deem "offensive." That the persecutor inflicts the suffering or harm in an attempt to elicit information, for his own sadistic pleasure, to "cure" his victim, or to "save his soul" is irrelevant. Persecution by any other name remains persecution.

Motive of the alleged persecutor is a relevant and proper consideration only insofar as the alien must establish that the persecution is inflicted on him or her "on account of" a characteristic or perceived characteristic of the alien. *See Elias-Zacarias*, 502 U.S. at 481, 112 S.Ct. at 815. The BIA majority misconstrues this motive requirement. *Elias-Zacarias* does not require an alien to provide evidence that his persecutor's motive was to inflict harm and suffering in an effort to punish. It is the characteristic of the victim (membership in a group, religious or political belief, racial characteristic, etc.), not that of the persecutor, which is the relevant factor.

The Board has defined "persecution" as "the infliction of harm or suffering by a government, or persons a government is unwilling or unable to control, to overcome a characteristic of the victim." This "'seeking to overcome' formulation has its antecedents in concepts of persecution that predate the Refugee Act of 1980." The BIA majority, however invokes two prior BIA rulings, *Matter of Mogharrabi*, 19 I & N Dec. 439, 446 (BIA 1987) and *Matter of Acosta*, 19 I & N Dec. 211, 226 (BIA 1985), both of which speak in terms of an "intent to punish." To establish a well-founded fear of persecution, these cases require that an applicant for asylum establish that: "(1) the alien possesses a belief or characteristic a persecutor seeks to overcome in others by means of *punishment* of some sort; (2) the persecutor is already aware, or could become aware, that the alien possesses this belief or characteristic; (3) the persecutor has the capability of *punishing* the alien; and (4) the persecutor has the inclination to *punish* the alien." *Mogharrabi*, 19 I & N Dec. at 446 (quoting *Acosta*, 19 I & N Dec. at 226) (emphasis added). This test confuses *punishment* and *persecution*. The two concepts are not coterminous.

Although we have held that unreasonably severe punishment can constitute "persecution," "punishment" is neither a mandatory nor a sufficient aspect of persecution. Webster defines to *punish* as "(1) To afflict with pain, loss, or suffering for a crime or fault; to chasten. (2) To inflict a penalty for (an offense) upon the offender." *Webster's New Collegiate Dictionary* 685 (Second Edition 1956). To *persecute*, in contrast, is defined as "(1) To pursue in a manner to injure; to cause to suffer because of belief, esp. religious belief. (2) To afflict, harass, or annoy." Hence, punishment implies that the perpetrator believes the victim has committed a crime or some wrong; whereas persecution simply requires that the perpetrator cause the victim suffering or harm. To the extent that *Acosta* and *Mogharrabi* require an alien to prove the persecutor harbored a subjective intent to punish, we reject their holdings.

The current requirement that an alien have been persecuted or have a well-founded fear of persecution was part of the Refugee Act of 1980. Congress passed the Refugee Act to conform the INA to the 1967 Protocol Relating to the Status of Refugees ("Protocol"). The United States acceded to the Protocol in 1968. Because Congress intended the definition of "refugee" to conform to the Protocol, we often refer to the *Handbook on Procedures and Criteria for Determining Refugee Status Under the 1951 Convention and the 1967 Protocol Relating to the Status of Refugees* ("Handbook") (interpreting the Protocol) when construing the Act. The definition of "persecution" in the Handbook does not include a subjective intent to punish or harm. Indeed, it acknowledges that "often the applicant himself may not be aware of the reasons for the persecution feared."

The fact that a persecutor believes the harm he is inflicting is "good for" his victim does not make it any less painful to the victim, or, indeed, remove the conduct from the statutory definition of persecution. The BIA majority's requirement that an alien prove that her persecutor's subjective intent was punitive is unwarranted. Human rights laws cannot be sidestepped by simply couching actions that torture mentally or physically in benevolent terms such as "curing" or "treating" the victims.

In light of our holding that the definition of persecution applied by the BIA majority is erroneous, we do not reach Pitcherskaia's other claims; whether she established the requisite subjective and objective components for her asylum claim should be determined on remand. We express no view on whether the evidence established a valid claim of asylum when the appropriate definition of persecution is applied. We grant the petition for review and reverse the BIA's order denying asylum and withholding of deportation. We remand to the BIA for reconsideration consistent with this opinion.

* * *

Hernandez-Montiel v. Immigration and Naturalization Service
225 F.3d 1084 (9th Cir. 2000)

Tashima, Circuit Judge:

Geovanni Hernandez-Montiel ("Geovanni"), a native and citizen of Mexico, seeks review of a decision of the Board of Immigration Appeals ("BIA"), denying his application for both asylum and withholding of deportation. The BIA dismissed Geovanni's appeal because it agreed with the immigration judge ("IJ") that Geovanni failed to show that he was persecuted, or that he had a well-founded fear of future persecution, on account of his membership in a particular social group. We conclude as a matter of law that gay men with female sexual identities in Mexico constitute a "particular social group" and that Geovanni is a member of that group. His female sexual identity is immutable because it is inherent in his identity; in any event, he should not be required to change it. Because the evidence compels the conclusion that Geovanni suffered past persecution and has a well-founded fear of future persecution if he were forced to return to Mexico, we conclude that the record compels a finding that he is entitled to asylum and withholding of deportation.

Geovanni testified that, at the age of eight, he "realized that [he] was attracted to people of [his] same sex." At the age of 12, Geovanni began dressing and behaving as a woman. He faced numerous reprimands from family and school officials because of his sexual orientation. His mother registered him in a state-run Mexican school and informed the school authorities about what she deemed to be his "problem," referring to his sexual orientation. School authorities directed Geovanni to stop socializing with two gay friends. The father of a schoolmate grabbed Geovanni by the arm and threatened to kill him for "perverting" his son. He was even prevented from attending a school dance because of the way he was dressed. Shortly after the dance, the school asked Geovanni's mother to consent to his expulsion because he was not acting appropriately. He could not enroll in another school because the school refused to transfer his paperwork until he agreed to change his sexual orientation. Geovanni's parents threw him out of their home the day after his expulsion.

Beyond his school and family, Geovanni also suffered harassment and persecution at the hands of Mexican police officers. On numerous occasions, the Mexican police detained and even strip-searched Geovanni because he was walking down the street or socializing with other boys also perceived to be gay. In 1992, the Mexican police twice arrested Geovanni and a friend. The police told them that it was illegal for homosexuals to walk down the street and for men to dress like women. The police, however, never charged Geovanni with any crime. Police officers sexually assaulted Geovanni on two separate occasions. In November 1992, when Geovanni was 14 years old, a police officer grabbed him as he was walking down the street, threw him into the police car, and drove to an uninhabited area. The officer demanded that Geovanni take off his clothes. Threatening him with imprisonment if he did not comply, the officer forced Geovanni to perform oral sex on him. The officer also threatened to beat and imprison Geovanni if he ever told anyone about the incident.

Approximately two weeks later, when Geovanni was at a bus stop with a gay friend one evening, the same officer pulled up in a car, accompanied by a second officer. The officers forced both boys into their car and drove them to a remote area, where they forced the boys to strip naked and then separated them. One of the officers grabbed Geovanni by the hair and threatened to kill him. Holding a gun to his temple, the officer anally raped Geovanni. Geovanni believes that his friend was also raped, although his friend refused to talk about the incident. Even before the boys could get dressed, the police officers threatened to shoot if they did not start running. The boys were left stranded in an abandoned area. A few months after the second assault, in February 1993, Geovanni was attacked with a knife by a group of young men who called him names relating to his sexual orientation. He was hospitalized for a week while recovering from the attack.

Geovanni fled to the United States in October 1993, when he was 15 years old. He was arrested within a few days of his October 1993 entry. Geovanni testified that while he was walking down the street in San Diego dressed in women's clothing, a man in a car pulled up and offered money in exchange for sex. Geovanni said he would not have sex, but asked the man for a ride. When the car turned the corner, police officers were waiting to arrest him. Geovanni was held in jail in San Diego for a week. There is no documentary evidence concerning the arrest in the record.] When Geovanni returned to Mexico to live with his sister, she enrolled him in a counseling program, which ostensibly attempted to "cure" his sexual orientation by altering his female appearance. The program staff cut his hair and nails, and forced him to stop taking female hormones. Geovanni remained in the program from late January to late March 1994. Because his sister saw no changes in him, she brought Geovanni home to live with her. Soon thereafter, however, she forced Geovanni out of her house because he was not "cured" of his gay sexual orientation, despite his change in appearance. He again sought refuge in the United States.

> After a number of attempts to re-enter the United States, Geovanni last entered on or around October 12, 1994, without inspection. He filed an application for asylum and withholding of deportation on February 22, 1995. At his asylum hearing, Geovanni presented the testimony of Thomas M. Davies, Jr., a profes-

sor at San Diego State University and an expert in Latin American history and culture. Professor Davies, who has lived for extended periods of time in Mexico and elsewhere in Latin America, testified that certain homosexuals in Latin America are subjected to greater abuse than others. Professor Davies testified that it is "accepted" that "in most of Latin America a male before he marries may engage in homosexual acts as long as he performs the role of the male." A male, however, who is perceived to assume the stereotypical "female," *i.e.,* passive, role in these sexual relationships is "ostracized from the very beginning and is subject to persecution, gay bashing as we would call it, and certainly police abuse." Professor Davies testified that these gay men with "female" sexual identities in Mexico are "heavily persecuted by the police and other groups within the society. [They are] a separate social entity within Latin American society and in this case within the nation of Mexico." According to Professor Davies, it is commonplace for police to "hit the gay street and not only brutalize but actually rape with batons homosexual males that are dressed or acting out the feminine role."

Professor Davies testified that gay men with female sexual identities are likely to become scapegoats for Mexico's present economic and political problems, especially since the recent collapse of the Mexican economy. Professor Davies specifically noted that Geovanni is "a homosexual who has taken on a primarily 'female' sexual role." Based on his expert knowledge, review of Geovanni's case, and interaction with Geovanni, Professor Davies opined that Geovanni would face persecution if he were forced to return to Mexico.

The IJ denied Geovanni asylum on both statutory and discretionary grounds. The IJ determined that Geovanni's testimony was "credible," "sincere," "forthright," "rational," and "coherent." The IJ found, however, that Geovanni had failed to demonstrate persecution "on account of a particular social group," classifying his social group as "homosexual males who wish to dress as a woman [sic.]." The IJ noted that Geovannni "has altered certain outward physical attributes and his manner of dress to resemble a woman." The IJ found Geovanni's female gender identity not to be immutable, explaining:

> If he wears typical female clothing sometimes, and typical male clothing other times, he cannot characterize his assumed female persona as immutable or fundamental to his identity. The record reflects that respondent's decision to dress as a women [sic] is volitional, not immutable, and the fact that he sometimes dresses like a typical man reflects that respondent himself may not view his dress as being so fundamental to his identity that he should not have to change it.

The IJ further found that Geovanni was not entitled to discretionary eligibility and denied voluntary departure in the exercise of discretion. The BIA dismissed Geovanni's appeal from the IJ's decision.

Because the BIA conducted an independent review of the record, our review is limited to the BIA's decision. We review de novo determinations by the BIA of purely legal questions concerning requirements of the INA. We examine the BIA's factual findings under the substantial evidence standard. Under the substantial evidence standard, "[w]e will uphold the BIA's determination unless the evidence compels a contrary conclusion."

The Attorney General may, in her discretion, grant asylum to an applicant determined to be a refugee. An alien establishes refugee status if he is unable or unwilling to return to his country of nationality either because: (1) he was persecuted in the past; or

(2) he has a well-founded fear of future persecution "on account of race, religion, nationality, membership in a *particular social group,* or political opinion"(emphasis added). The Attorney General must withhold deportation of any asylum applicant who establishes a "clear probability of persecution," which is a stricter standard than the "well-founded fear" standard for asylum.

The applicant has the burden of proving his eligibility with "credible, direct, and specific evidence." We have held that where "the IJ expressly finds certain testimony to be credible, and where the BIA makes no contrary finding, we accept as undisputed the testimony given at the hearing before the IJ." Here, the IJ found Geovanni's testimony to be "credible," "sincere," "forthright," "rational," and "coherent." The BIA agreed that "the respondent testified credibly regarding the events that occurred in his life." Thus, we also accept Geovanni's testimony.

This case turns on the legal question of whether Geovanni was persecuted on account of his membership in a "particular social group." There is no definition of "particular social group" in the INA. The BIA, however, has recognized that the language comes directly from the United Nations Protocol Relating to the Status of Refugees. When Congress ratified the Protocol on October 4, 1968, it did not shed any further light on the definition of "particular social group." The case law regarding the definition of "particular social group" is not wholly consistent. In *Acosta,* 19 I. & N. Dec. at 233, 1985 WL 56042 the BIA interpreted "persecution on account of membership in a particular social group" to mean "persecution that is directed toward an individual who is a member of a group of persons all of whom share a common, immutable characteristic." The BIA explained that:

> The shared characteristic might be an innate one such as sex, color, or kinship ties, or in some circumstances it might be a shared past experience such as former military leadership or land ownership. The particular kind of group characteristic that will qualify under this construction remains to be determined on a case-by-case basis. However, whatever the common characteristic that defines the group, it must be one that the members of the group either cannot change, or should not be required to change because it is fundamental to their individual identities or consciences.

The BIA held that a group of taxi drivers did not meet the immutable characteristic requirement because an occupation can change; thus, driving a taxi is not fundamental to a person's identity. The BIA's interpretation is entitled to some deference. The First, Third, and Seventh Circuits have adopted *Acosta*'s immutability analysis.

In *Sanchez-Trujillo,* 801 F.2d at 1576, we acknowledged that the social group category "is a flexible one which extends broadly to encompass many groups who do not otherwise fall within the other categories of race, nationality, religion, or political opinion." We stated that:

> "particular social group" implies a collection of people closely affiliated with each other, who are actuated by some common impulse or interest. Of central concern is the existence of a voluntary associational relationship among the purported members, which imparts some common characteristic that is fundamental to their identity as a member of that discrete social group.

The *Sanchez-Trujillo* court held that the class of working class, urban males of military age who maintained political neutrality in El Salvador did not constitute a "particular social group" for which the immigration laws provide protection from persecution.

We are the only circuit to suggest a "voluntary associational relationship" require-ment. The Seventh Circuit has noted that this requirement "read literally, conflicts with *Acosta* 's immutability requirement." Moreover, in *Sanchez-Trujillo,* we recog-nized a group of family members as a "prototypical example" of a "particular social group." 801 F.2d at 1576. Yet, biological family relationships are far from "voluntary." We cannot, therefore, interpret *Sanchez-Trujillo*'s "central concern" of a voluntary as-sociational relationship strictly as applying to every qualifying "particular social group." For, as *Sanchez-Trujillo* itself recognizes, in some particular social groups, members of the group are not voluntarily associated by choice. We thus hold that a "particular social group" is one united by a voluntary association, including a former association, *or* by an innate characteristic that is so fundamental to the identities or consciences of its members that members either cannot or should not be required to change it.

Sexual orientation and sexual identity are immutable; they are so fundamental to one's identity that a person should not be required to abandon them. Many social and behavioral scientists "generally believe that sexual orientation is set in place at an early age." Suzanne B. Goldberg, *Give Me Liberty or Give Me Death: Political Asylum and the Global Persecution of Lesbians and Gay Men,* 26 Cornell Int'l L.J. 605, 614 n. 56 (1993). The American Psychological Association has condemned as unethical the attempted "conversion" of gays and lesbians. Further, the American Psychiatric Association and the American Psychological Association have removed "homosexuality" from their lists of mental disorders.

Sexual identity is inherent to one's very identity as a person. *See* Alfred Kinsey, et al., "Sexual Behavior in the Human Male," in *Cases and Materials on Sexual Orientation and the Law* 1, 7 (William B. Rubenstein ed., 2d ed., 1997) ("Even psychiatrists discuss 'the homosexual personality' and many of them believe that preferences for sexual partners of a particular sex are merely secondary manifestations of something that lies much deeper in the totality of that intangible which they call the personality."); *cf. Gay Rights Coalition of Georgetown Univ. Law Ctr. v. Georgetown Univ.,* 536 A.2d 1, 35 (D.C.1987) (observing that "homosexuality encompasses far more than people's sexual proclivities. Too often homosexuals have been viewed simply with reference to their sexual interests and activity. Usually the social context and psychological correlates of homosexual ex-perience are largely ignored"). Sexual identity goes beyond sexual conduct and mani-fests itself outwardly, often through dress and appearance. *See* Kenji Yoshino, *Suspect Symbols: The Literary Argument for Heightened Scrutiny for Gays,* 96 Colum. L.Rev. 1753, 1775 n. 3 (1996) (defining gay identity as "the shared experience of having a sex-ual attachment to persons of the same sex and the oppression experienced because of that attachment"); Naomi Mezey, *Dismantling the Wall: Bisexuality and the Possibilities of Sexual Identity Classification Based on Acts,* 10 Berkeley Women's L.J. 98, 100–3 (1995) (discussing the relationship of identity and conduct in arguing that "[s]eparat-ing the way we speak of sexual acts and sexual identities is crucial" and arguing that the traditional binary system of heterosexuals and homosexuals is too restrictive); *see also* Gilbert Herdt, *Same Sex, Different Cultures: Exploring Gay and Lesbian Lives* 20 (1997).

In *Gay Rights Coalition*, the District of Columbia Court of Appeals noted that "[H]omosexuality is as deeply ingrained as heterosexuality. [E]xclusive homosexuality probably is so deeply ingrained that one should not attempt or expect to change it. Rather, it would probably make far more sense simply to recognize it as a basic component of a person's core identity." 536 A.2d at 34–35 (quoting A. Bell, M. Weinberg & S. Hammer-smith, Sexual Preference—Its Development in Men and Women 190, 211 (1981)).

Under the BIA's decision in *Toboso-Alfonso,* 20 I. & N. Dec. 819, 820–23, 1990 WL 547189 (BIA 1990), sexual orientation can be the basis for establishing a "particular social group" for asylum purposes. In *Toboso-Alfonso,* the Cuban government had registered and tracked homosexual men for investigation over many years. The INS did not contest that homosexuality is an immutable characteristic, and the BIA held that sexual orientation establishes membership in a "particular social group." The Attorney General has designated the decision in *Toboso-Alfonso* to be "precedent in all proceedings involving the same issue or issues." Attorney General Order No. 1895 (June 19, 1994).

In determining that sexual orientation and sexual identity can be the basis for establishing a "particular social group," we also find persuasive the reasoning in *Matter of Tenorio,* No. A72-093-558 (IJ July 26, 1993). In *Tenorio,* the IJ granted asylum to a Brazilian gay man who had been beaten and stabbed by a group of people in Rio de Janeiro, who repeatedly used anti-gay epithets. The IJ found that Tenorio had a well-founded fear of future persecution due to his membership in a "particular social group" based on his sexual orientation. The BIA adopted the IJ's reasoning and dismissed the INS' appeal. *See Matter of Tenorio,* No. A72-093-558 (BIA 1999) (per curiam). The BIA held that the IJ's decision "correctly concludes that the respondent has established persecution or a well-founded fear of future persecution on account of one of the five grounds enumerated" in the INA.

Based on the reasoning of the authorities discussed above, we conclude that the appropriate "particular social group" in this case is composed of gay men with female sexual identities in Mexico. Although not necessary to establish the "particular social group," the testimony of Professor Davies is helpful to our analysis. Professor Davies testified that gay men with female sexual identities in Mexico are "heavily persecuted by the police and other groups within the society. [T]hey are a separate social entity within Latin American society and in this case within the nation of Mexico." Professor Davies expressly noted that as a subset of the gay male population, men with female sexual identities, are "ostracized from the beginning and [ ] subject to persecution, gay bashing as we would call it, and certainly police abuse."

We thus conclude that the BIA erred in defining the "particular social group" as "homosexual males who dress as females." Professor Davies did not testify that homosexual males are persecuted simply because they may dress as females or because they engage in homosexual acts. Rather, gay men with female sexual identities are singled out for persecution because they are perceived to assume the stereotypical "female," *i.e.,* passive, role in gay relationships. Gay men with female sexual identities outwardly manifest their identities through characteristics traditionally associated with women, such as feminine dress, long hair and fingernails. Gay men with female sexual identities in Mexico are a "small, readily identifiable group." Their female sexual identities unite this group of gay men, and their sexual identities are so fundamental to their human identities that they should not be required to change them. We therefore conclude as a matter of law that the "particular social group" in this case is comprised of gay men with female sexual identities in Mexico.

We find that the evidence compels the conclusion that Geovanni is a member of the "particular social group" of gay men in Mexico with female sexual identities. Professor Davies specifically classified Geovanni as "a homosexual who has taken on a primarily 'female' sexual role." In addition to being a gay man with a female sexual identity, Geovanni's brief states that he "may be considered a transsexual." A transsexual is "a person who is genetically and physically a member of one sex but has a deep-seated psychological conviction that he or she belongs, or ought to belong, to the opposite sex, a conviction which may in some cases result in the individual's decision to undergo surgery in order to physically modify his or her sex organs to resemble those of the opposite sex." Deborah Tussey, *Transvestism or Transsexualism of Spouse as Justifying Divorce*, 82 A.L.R.3d n. 2 (2000); *see Farmer v. Haas*, 990 F.2d 319, 320 (7th Cir.1993) (Posner, J.) ("The disjunction between sexual identity and sexual organs is a source of acute psychological suffering that can, in some cases anyway, be cured or at least alleviated by sex reassignment—the complex of procedures loosely referred to as 'a sex-change operation.' "). We need not consider in this case whether transsexuals constitute a particular social group.] Geovanni has known that he was gay from the age of eight and began dressing as a woman when he was 12. He socialized with other gay boys in school, which led to his eventual expulsion. The BIA found that the police "temporarily detained [him] for walking the street and socializing with other young homosexual men." He was sexually assaulted twice by the police. After placing him in a therapy program to "convert" his sexuality, his sister eventually "realized that I was the same and the only thing that had changed was the fact that they had cut my hair and cut my nails." Geovanni's female sexual identity must be fundamental, or he would not have suffered this persecution and would have changed years ago.

Because we conclude that Geovanni should not be required to change his sexual orientation or identity, we need not address whether Geovanni could change them. Geovanni's credible and uncontradicted testimony about the inherent and immutable nature of his sexual identity compels the conclusion that Geovanni was a member of the particular social group of gay men in Mexico with female sexual identities.

The BIA erroneously concluded that "tenor of [Geovanni's] claim is that he was mistreated because of the way he dressed (as a male prostitute) and not because he is a homosexual." This statement is not supported by substantial evidence; in fact, it is wholly unsupported by any evidence in the record. There is no evidence that Geovanni was a male prostitute, and we do not venture to guess the non-record basis of the BIA's assumption of how a male prostitute dresses.

The BIA stressed that Geovanni could not remember how he was dressed on one occasion when he was arrested crossing the border between the United States and Mexico. The BIA, therefore, agreed with the IJ that "the decision to dress as a female was a volitional act, not an immutable trait." Geovanni did testify that he dresses as a man when he is going to a place where an effeminate style of dress would not be appropriate. That Geovanni could not remember how he was dressed on one occasion several years before does not support the BIA's conclusion that, because Geovanni can change his clothes, he can change his identity as quickly as the taxi drivers in *Acosta* can change jobs.

This case is about sexual identity, not fashion. Geovanni is not simply a transvestite "who dresses in clothing of the opposite sex for psychological reasons." *American Heritage Dictionary* 1289 (2d Coll. Ed.) (1985). Rather, Geovanni manifests his sexual orientation by adopting gendered traits characteristically associated with women.

Geovanni must show that he was persecuted "on account of" his "membership in the particular social group." In satisfying the "on account of" requirement, the evidence compels a finding that Geovanni's sexual identity was a significant motivation for the violence and abuse he endured. The BIA explicitly noted that Geovanni was "stopped on numerous occasions and temporarily detained for walking the street and socializing with other young homosexual men." The police were not going after people with long hair and nails, or everyone dressed in female clothing. Geovanni was sexually assaulted because of his outward manifestations of his sexual orientation.

The government's legal reasoning is unpersuasive when it argues that "the evidence does not compel the conclusion that the mistreatment [Geovanni] suffered by Mexican authorities was solely on account of his homosexual status." Geovanni is not required to prove that his persecutors were motivated by his sexual orientation to the exclusion of all other possible motivations. We have recognized that "persecutory conduct may have more than one motive, and so long as one motive is of one of the statutorily enumerated grounds, the requirements [for asylum] have been satisfied." *Singh v. Ilchert*, 63 F.3d 1501, 1509–10 (9th Cir.1995).

Professor Davies' testimony and the accompanying evidence highlight that the persecution Geovanni suffered was "on account of" his membership in the "particular social group" of men with female sexual identities in Mexico. Professor Davies testified that gay men with female sexual identities are recognized in Mexico as a distinct and readily identifiable group and are persecuted for their membership in that group. He testified that the police attack and even rape men with female sexual identities. Attached to Professor Davies's declaration are numerous articles and reports documenting the violence against gay men in Mexico and throughout Latin America. A co-founder and general coordinator of a Mexican human rights organization stated: "The government has said it will not protect transvestites unless they are dressed like men, insinuating that it is okay to kill homosexuals if they are visible." *Anti-Queer Violence Continues in Mexico*, S.F. Bay Times, Feb. 25, 1993. There was also a *New York Times* article, documenting the granting of asylum to a gay man from Mexico. *See Gay Man Who Cited Abuse in Mexico is Granted Asylum*, N.Y. Times, March 26, 1994 at A5. The man had been arrested in Mexico for going to certain neighborhoods, attending certain parties and patronizing certain bars. The police falsely accused him of crimes, extorted him, and on one occasion, raped him.

Also in evidence was an advisory opinion about Geovanni's case by the Office of Asylum Affairs of the United States Department of State, claiming that: "[o]ur Embassy in Mexico advises us that it has no evidence of the systematic persecution of homosexuals there although *random violence against homosexuals has occurred.*" (emphasis added). This evidence along with Geovanni's testimony compels the conclusion that Geovanni was persecuted "on account of" his membership in the "particular social group." The evidence is susceptible of no other conclusion.

The BIA legally erred in finding that Geovanni failed to establish both past persecution and a well-founded fear of future persecution upon return to Mexico. We have held that persecution involves "the infliction of suffering or harm upon those who differ in a way regarded as offensive." Geovanni must show that the persecution he suffered was "inflicted either by the government or by persons or organizations which the government is unable or unwilling to control." The BIA was misguided when it concluded that Geovanni was not persecuted "even if the Mexican authorities give low priority to protection of gays." In this case, it was the police who actually perpetrated the violence. During the first sexual attack, Geovanni was abducted, ordered to remove his clothes, and forced to perform oral sex on the officer. The officer then told Geovanni that he would go to jail if he told anyone about the rape. During the second assault, Geovanni and a friend were abducted by two officers, driven to a secluded area, and ordered to remove their clothing. One officer sodomized Geovanni as he held a gun to his temple. Given these past assaults, Geovanni "is at risk of persecution at the hand of the very agency which purports to protect him by law." The sexual assaults Geovanni suffered at the hands of police officers undoubtedly constitute persecution. We have held that "rape or sexual assault may constitute persecution." In *Lopez-Galarza,* we took note of: "the numerous studies revealing the physical and psychological harms rape causes. A recent article in the *Journal of the American Medical Association* summarized several studies of the effects of rape," and concluded:

> Rape commonly results in severe and long-lasting psychological sequelae that are complex and shaped by the particular social and cultural context in which the rape occurs....Commonly reported feelings at the time of the rape include shock, a fear of injury or death that can be paralyzing, and a sense of profound loss of control over one's life. Longer-term effects can include persistent fears, avoidance of situations that trigger memories of the violation, profound feelings of shame, difficulty remembering events, intrusive thoughts of the abuse, decreased ability to respond to life generally, and difficulty reestablishing intimate relationships.

Lopez-Galarza, 99 F.3d at 962 (citation omitted). There is no reason to believe that the trauma for male victims of rape is any less severe than for female victims.

The BIA gave the convoluted, inapposite, and irrelevant reasoning that "[w]hile *Toboso-Alfonso, supra,* provides a basis for finding that homosexuality is a basis for asylum, anti-sodomy laws are not persecution. *Bowers v. Hardwick,* 478 U.S. 186 (1986)." Geovanni did not argue, however, that he was being persecuted because of the prohibition of any anti-sodomy laws. Instead, he was raped twice by police officers who forced him to engage in sodomy. *Bowers* has no relevance to this case, and the BIA's reliance on that case is completely misplaced.

Further, the BIA erroneously reasoned that "the respondent's mistreatment arose from his conduct, thus the rape by the policemen, and the attack by a mob of gay bashers are not necessarily persecution." We are uncertain whether by "conduct" the BIA was referring to some alleged criminal conduct or to Geovanni's appearance and style of dress. Either way, substantial evidence compels a contrary result. There is absolutely no evidence in the record that Geovanni's "mistreatment arose from his conduct," if conduct refers to criminal activity. There is no evidence in the record of any past convictions. In fact, the IJ explicitly noted that, despite police harassment in Mexico, Geovanni had "never been formally charged or convicted of any offense." Perhaps, then, by "conduct," the BIA was referring to Geovanni's effeminate dress or his sexual orientation as a gay man, as a justification for the police officers' raping him. The "you asked for it" excuse for rape is offensive to this court and has been discounted by courts and commentators alike.

Further, the BIA had no basis for concluding that Geovanni's failure to respond to questions regarding his arrests in the United States "casts further doubt on his claim of persecution." It is true that "[t]here is no rule of law which prohibits officers charged with the administration of the immigration law from drawing an inference from the silence of one who is called upon to speak." Any inference to be drawn, however, must be reasonable. There simply is no logical connection between Geovanni's failure to answer questions regarding arrests in the United States and the rapes by police officers in Mexico.

Because Geovanni has established past persecution, there is a presumption that he has a well-founded fear of future persecution, which the INS must overcome by a preponderance of the evidence that country conditions have changed. The INS presented no evidence that Mexico has taken effective steps to curb sexual orientation-based violence, including that perpetrated by the police. To the contrary, Professor Davies testified that the situation for gay men in Mexico has worsened because of the decline of the economy. Thus, the presumption must be given its full force.

Our analysis of past persecution also triggers a presumption that Geovanni has shown a "clear probability" of future persecution with respect to his withholding claim—a presumption that the INS may also rebut by an individualized showing of changed country conditions. Again, there is nothing in the record to rebut that presumption. Accordingly, we conclude that Geovanni is also entitled to withholding of deportation.

We hold that the BIA's decision denying Geovanni asylum on statutory grounds is fatally flawed as a matter of law and is not supported by substantial evidence. We therefore grant the petition for review and remand the case to the BIA with instructions to grant his application for withholding of deportation and to present this case to the Attorney General for the exercise of her discretion to grant asylum.

Notes and Questions

1. What sorts of conditions prevailing in a country should be sufficient to support a finding that an openly lesbian, gay, bisexual or transgendered person in that country would be subject to persecution sufficient to qualify them for refugee status in the U.S.? Do the above cases suggest general guidelines? To what degree is this a very case-specific determination? Cases since *Hernandez-Montiel* suggest that immigration authorities remain very skeptical about asylum claims from gay people, especially when the claims are not raised immediately upon entry in the U.S. See, e.g., *Abdul-Karim v. Ashcroft*, 2004 WL 1435149 (9th Cir., June 24, 2004) (not selected for publication); *Andreasian v. Ashcroft*, 2004 WL 785064 (9th Cir., April 12, 2004) (not selected for publication); *Burog-Perez v. Immigration and Naturalization Service*, 2004 WL 856766 (9th Cir., April 21, 2004) (not selected for publication); *Lin v. Ashcroft*, 2004 WL 1153699 (9h Cir., May 24, 2004) (not selected for publication); *Pereira-Lima v. Ashcroft*, 2004 WL 816900 (4th Cir., April 15, 2004) (not selected for publication). A common element to many of these cases is the failure of the applicant to show that the government is responsible for anti-gay harassment, or officially tolerates or encourages such harassment by private individuals.

2. One of the most difficult problems for attorneys representing sexual minority asylum applicants is the need to document the conditions prevailing in the applicant's home country. Gathering such information can be difficult and costly. The International Lesbian and Gay Human Rights Commission was formed, among many reasons, to become a central repository for such information, so that attorneys would have one place to which they could turn to obtain the necessary documentation. In addition, the Commission attempts to mobilize international protest around particular human rights violations involving sexual minorities. Another major problem for attorneys representing sexual minority asylum applicants is the tight time-frame imposed by Congress for asserting asylum claims; it is a common experience for attorneys in this field to discover that their client may have been in the U.S. too long before asserting their claims, usually due to their failure to realize that it was possible for a member of a sexual minority to seek asylum in the U.S. based on persecution due to sexuality in their home country, or to their fear of revealing their sexuality to U.S. immigration officials, a logical fear in light of the treatment they may have suffered from government officials in their native lands.

3. It is common for ethnocentric Americans to believe that the human rights situation for sexual minorities is better in the United States than anywhere else. However, a cursory review of the legal and social status of sexual minorities in other parts of the world shows that the U.S. is not necessarily in the vanguard of respect for equal human rights for sexual minorities. The Scandinavian countries, the Netherlands and some other countries in the European Community, Australia, New Zealand, Canada and Israel have all made advances in legal recognition of rights for sexual minorities that in some respects surpass what has been accomplished in the United States, and South Africa, under its progressive post-apartheid constitution, is rapidly becoming one of the most progressive societies on the relevant legal and social issues, as the *National Coalition* case included above demonstrates. On the other hand, there are significant portions of the world where people are subjected to serious, ongoing persecution, including in some areas the death penalty, for being a member of a sexual minority or engaging in sexual activity outside of heterosexual marriage.

Chapter Seven

Sexual Expression, Free Speech and Association

A. Introduction: The Constitutional Framework

The First Amendment of the United States Constitution provides:

> Congress shall make no law respecting an establishment of religion, or prohibiting the free exercise thereof; or abridging the freedom of speech, or of the press; or the right of the people peaceably to assemble and to petition the Government for a redress of grievances.

By its terms, this refers only to laws made by Congress, but the Supreme Court quickly expanded the meaning to include actions of the federal government generally. During the first half of the 20th century, the Supreme Court developed the doctrine of "selective incorporation" under which the First Amendment and other portions of the Bill of Rights (first ten amendments) were held to be binding upon state and local governments by virtue of the Fourteenth Amendment's requirement that the states guarantee "due process of law" to all those resident in the United States. It is now accepted that the rights articulated in the First Amendment are fully binding on the entire federal government (not just the Congress) as well as state and local governments.

While there are a broad range of First Amendment issues that could be explored in considering the relation of sexuality and law, this chapter focuses on three: sexually-oriented communication; communication about sexuality and related issues; and expressive associational rights of sexual minorities. In the prior chapter, we explored the role of the 1st Amendment in privileging certain entities to avoid complying with anti-discrimination laws.

B. Sexually-Oriented Expression

This section examines how the law affects sexual expression through speech, print and other media, apart from actual sexual conduct. Most of the cases concern attempts by legislators and law enforcement officials to repress forms of sexual communication intended to stimulate the listener, viewer or reader to experience sexual enjoyment.

The Supreme Court held in *Roth v. United States*, 354 U.S. 476 (1957), that obscenity, however defined, is beyond the protection of the First Amendment, and thus that pornographers whose products were judged obscene could be subjected to criminal prosecution. However, non-obscene communication, although sexually-related, enjoys First Amendment protection. In other cases, the Court upheld postal regulations banning the mailing of obscene matter, although, in an important application of *Roth*, the Court concluded in the first cases ever won by gay rights advocates in the high court that printed material pertaining to homosexuality was not necessarily obscene. See *One, Inc. v. Oleson*, 355 U.S. 371 (1958) and *Manual Enterprises, Inc. v. Day*, 370 U.S. 478 (1962). The Court ruled in *Stanley v. Georgia*, 394 U.S. 557 (1969), that adults have a right protected under the 1st Amendment to possess and view obscene materials in their homes, but the state could regulate commerce in sexually-oriented material and ban obscene material from commerce. To the extent that regulation of sexually-oriented material and obscenity rests largely on the desire of legislators to express moral disapproval, however, the continuing vitality of these older precedents might be questioned in light of *Lawrence v. Texas*. Early in 2005, a federal district court ruled in reliance on *Lawrence* that a federal obscenity statute could not be used to prosecute a business for distribution of obscene materials on the internet, when such distribution was limited to consenting adults. See *United States v. Extreme Associates, Inc.*, 352 F. Supp. 2d 578 (W.D. Pa. 2005), below. The Justice Department promptly announced that it would appeal the ruling.

The Court has long grappled with the problem of defining obscenity and the resultant exception from constitutional protection; the results of the grappling can be detected in the following cases. However, these cases are selected not primarily to illustrate that process, but mainly to show how the interrelated concepts of privacy, sexuality, and individual autonomy have combined to extend protection, in some circumstances, to communications that appeal almost solely to sexual interests, a category of protection that the Court has purportedly disavowed in its obscenity cases.

In considering the constitutionality of lawmakers' attempts to prevent or punish sexually explicit communication, courts must balance the free speech rights embodied in absolutist language in the First Amendment of the Bill of Rights ("Congress shall make no law abridging the freedom of speech or of the press…") with the undoubted authority of government to regulate or prohibit conduct that may have a negative effect on the public welfare and the interests of those who object to sexually explicit communication, as well as the "secondary effects" sometimes associated with such speech. Observe how the balance is struck in the cases in this chapter, and consider whether the balance has been struck in such a way as to preserve First Amendment freedom consistent with maintaining a "decent" society.

Stanley v. Georgia
394 U.S. 557 (1969)

Justice MARSHALL delivered the opinion of the Court.

An investigation of appellant's alleged bookmaking [i.e., gambling] activities led to the issuance of a search warrant for appellant's home. Under authority of this warrant, federal and state agents secured entrance. They found very little evidence of bookmaking activity, but while looking through a desk drawer in an upstairs bedroom, one of the federal agents, accompanied by a state officer, found three reels of eight-millimeter film. Using a projector and screen found in an upstairs living room, they viewed the films. The state officer concluded that they were obscene and seized them. Since a further examination of the bedroom indicated that appellant occupied it, he was charged with possession of obscene matter and placed under arrest. He was later indicted for "knowingly hav(ing) possession of obscene matter" in violation of Georgia law. Appellant was tried before a jury and convicted. The Supreme Court of Georgia affirmed.

Appellant argues that the Georgia obscenity statute, insofar as it punishes mere private possession of obscene matter, violates the First Amendment, as made applicable to the States by the Fourteenth Amendment. The State and appellant both agree that the question here before us is whether "a statute imposing criminal sanctions upon the mere (knowing) possession of obscene matter" is constitutional. In this context, Georgia concedes that the present case appears to be one of "first impression on this exact point," but contends that since "obscenity is not within the area of constitutionally protected speech or press," the States are free, subject to the limits of other provisions of the Constitution, to deal with it any way deemed necessary, just as they may deal with possession of other things thought to be detrimental to the welfare of their citizens. If the State can protect the body of a citizen, may it not, argues Georgia, protect his mind?

We do not believe that this case can be decided simply by citing *Roth*. *Roth* and its progeny certainly do mean that the First and Fourteenth Amendments recognize a valid governmental interest in dealing with the problem of obscenity. But the assertion of that interest cannot, in every context, be insulated from all constitutional protections. Neither *Roth* nor any other decision of this Court reaches that far. As the Court said in *Roth* itself, "ceaseless vigilance is the watchword to prevent erosion (of First Amendment rights) by Congress or by the States. The door barring federal and state intrusion into this area cannot be left ajar; it must be kept tightly closed and opened only the slightest crack necessary to prevent encroachment upon more important interests." Roth and the cases following it discerned such an "important interest" in the regulation of commercial distribution of obscene material. That holding cannot foreclose an examination of the constitutional implications of a statute forbidding mere private possession of such material.

It is now well established that the Constitution protects the right to receive information and ideas. This right to receive information and ideas, regardless of their social worth, is fundamental to our free society. Moreover, in the context of this case—a prosecution for mere possession of printed or filmed matter in the privacy of a person's own home—that right takes on an added dimension. For also fundamental is the right to be free, except in very limited circumstances, from unwanted governmental intrusions into one's privacy.

> The makers of our Constitution undertook to secure conditions favorable to the pursuit of happiness. They recognized the significance of man's spiritual nature, of his feelings and of his intellect. They knew that only a part of the pain, pleasure and satisfactions of life are to be found in material things. They sought to protect Americans in their beliefs, their thoughts, their emotions and their sensations. They conferred, as against the government, the right to be let alone—the most comprehensive of rights and the right most valued by civilized man. *Olmstead v. United States* (Brandeis, J., dissenting).

These are the rights that appellant is asserting in the case before us. He is asserting the right to read or observe what he pleases—the right to satisfy his intellectual and emotional needs in the privacy of his own home. He is asserting the right to be free from state inquiry into the contents of his library. Georgia contends that appellant does not have these rights, that there are certain types of materials that the individual may not read or even possess. Georgia justifies this assertion by arguing that the films in the present case are obscene. But we think that mere categorization of these films as "obscene" is insufficient justification for such a drastic invasion of personal liberties guaranteed by the First and Fourteenth Amendments. Whatever may be the justifications for other statutes regulating obscenity, we do not think they reach into the privacy of one's own home. If the First Amendment means anything, it means that a State has no business telling a man, sitting alone in his own house, what books he may read or what films he may watch. Our whole constitutional heritage rebels at the thought of giving government the power to control men's minds.

And yet, in the face of these traditional notions of individual liberty, Georgia asserts the right to protect the individual's mind from the effects of obscenity. We are not certain that this argument amounts to anything more than the assertion that the State has the right to control the moral content of a person's thoughts. To some, this may be a noble purpose, but it is wholly inconsistent with the philosophy of the First Amendment. As the Court said in *Kingsley International Pictures Corp. v. Regents*, "(t)his argument misconceives what it is that the Constitution protects. Its guarantee is not confined to the expression of ideas that are conventional or shared by a majority. And in the realm of ideas it protects expression which is eloquent no less than that which is unconvincing." Nor is it relevant that obscene materials in general, or the particular films before the Court, are arguably devoid of any ideological content. The line between the transmission of ideas and mere entertainment is much too elusive for this Court to draw, if indeed such a line can be drawn at all. Whatever the power of the state to control public dissemination of ideas inimical to the public morality, it cannot constitutionally premise legislation on the desirability of controlling a person's private thoughts.

Perhaps recognizing this, Georgia asserts that exposure to obscene materials may lead to deviant sexual behavior or crimes of sexual violence. There appears to be little empirical basis for that assertion. But more important, if the State is only concerned about printed or filmed materials inducing antisocial conduct, we believe that in the context of private consumption of ideas and information we should adhere to the view that "among free men, the deterrents ordinarily to be applied to prevent crime are education and punishment for violations of the law." *Whitney v. California* (Brandeis, J., concurring). Given the present state of knowledge, the State may no more prohibit mere possession of obscene matter on the ground that it may lead to antisocial conduct than it may prohibit possession of chemistry books on the ground that they may lead to the manufacture of homemade spirits.

It is true that in *Roth* this Court rejected the necessity of proving that exposure to obscene material would create a clear and present danger of antisocial conduct or would probably induce its recipients to such conduct. But that case dealt with public distribution of obscene materials and such distribution is subject to different objections.

Finally, we are faced with the argument that prohibition of possession of obscene materials is a necessary incident to statutory schemes prohibiting distribution. That argument is based on alleged difficulties of proving an intent to distribute or in producing evidence of actual distribution. We are not convinced that such difficulties exist, but even if they did we do not think that they would justify infringement of the individual's right to read or observe what he pleases. Because that right is so fundamental to our scheme of individual liberty, its restriction may not be justified by the need to ease the administration of otherwise valid criminal laws.

We hold that the First and Fourteenth Amendments prohibit making mere private possession of obscene material a crime. *Roth* and the cases following that decision are not impaired by today's holding. As we have said, the States retain broad power to regulate obscenity; that power simply does not extend to mere possession by the individual in the privacy of his own home. Accordingly, the judgment of the court below is reversed.

[Justices Stewart, Brennan and White concurred in the result, but based their decision on 4th Amendment search and seizure doctrine. They argued that this seemed to be a clear instance of police officials going beyond the scope of a search warrant to uncover and seize materials that had no plausible relationship to the basis for the warrant.]

Questions

1. What is the basis for the constitutional right identified in *Stanley v. Georgia*? The First Amendment? The Fourth Amendment? The Ninth Amendment? The Fourteenth Amendment? Justice Douglas's "right of privacy" as identified in *Griswold v. Connecticut*, derived generally from the constitutional provisions suggesting some aspect of personal privacy in the home? (This case was decided just a few years after *Griswold*.)

2. To what extent is the holding in Stanley premised on possession and use in the home and the solitary presence of the owner and possessor of the material? If Stanley invited a group of friends to his home to view the pornographic films, would constitutional privacy still apply? What if he asked each friend to make a voluntary donation toward the maintenance expenses of his projection equipment and acquisition of films? What if he charged admission?

Paris Adult Theatre I v. Slaton
413 U.S. 49 (1973)

Chief Justice BURGER delivered the opinion of the Court.

Petitioners are two Atlanta, Georgia, movie theaters and their owners and managers, operating in the style of "adult" theaters. On December 28, 1970, respondents, the local state district attorney and the solicitor for the local state trial court, filed civil complaints in that court alleging that petitioners were exhibiting to the public for paid admission two allegedly obscene films, contrary to Georgia Code Ann. § 26-2101.

The two films were exhibited to the trial court. The only other state evidence was testimony by criminal investigators that they had paid admission to see the films and that nothing on the outside of the theater indicated the full nature of what was shown. In particular, nothing indicated that the films depicted—as they did—scenes of simulated fellatio, cunnilingus, and group sex intercourse. There was no evidence presented that minors had ever entered the theaters. Nor was there evidence presented that petitioners had a systematic policy of barring minors, apart from posting signs at the entrance. On April 12, 1971, the trial judge dismissed respondents' complaints. He assumed "that obscenity is established," but stated: "It appears to the Court that the display of these films in a commercial theater, when surrounded by requisite notice to the public of their nature and by reasonable protection against the exposure of these films to minors, is constitutionally permissible."

On appeal, the Georgia Supreme Court unanimously reversed. It assumed that the adult theaters in question barred minors and gave a full warning to the general public of the nature of the films shown, but held that the films were without protection under the First Amendment. The Georgia court stated that "the sale and delivery of obscene material to willing adults is not protected under the first amendment." The Georgia court also held *Stanley v. Georgia* to be inapposite since it did not deal with "the commercial distribution of pornography, but with the right of Stanley to possess, in the privacy of his home, pornographic films." After viewing the films, the Georgia Supreme Court held that their exhibition should have been enjoined, stating: "The films in this case leave little to the imagination. It is plain what they purport to depict, that is, conduct of the most salacious character. We hold that these films are also hard core pornography, and the showing of such films should have been enjoined since their exhibition is not protected by the first amendment."

I

It should be clear from the outset that we do not undertake to tell the States what they must do, but rather to define the area in which they may chart their own course in dealing with obscene material. This Court has consistently held that obscene material is not protected by the First Amendment as a limitation on the state police power by virtue of the Fourteenth Amendment.

> [On the same date this opinion was issued, the Court announced a new standard for determining whether sexually explicit material is obscene in *Miller v. California*, 413 U.S. 15 (1973). The Court remanded this case to the Georgia Supreme Court for an application of its new *Miller* standards, articulated in the notes and comments following this case, to the films in question.]

II

We categorically disapprove the theory, apparently adopted by the trial judge, that obscene, pornographic films acquire constitutional immunity from state regulation simply because they are exhibited for consenting adults only. Although we have often pointedly recognized the high importance of the state interest in regulating the exposure of obscene materials to juveniles and unconsenting adults, this Court has never declared these to be the only legitimate state interests permitting regulation of obscene material. The States have a long-recognized legitimate interest in regulating the use of obscene material in local commerce and in all places of public accommodation, as long as these regulations do not run afoul of specific constitutional prohibitions.

In particular, we hold that there are legitimate state interests at stake in stemming the tide of commercialized obscenity, even assuming it is feasible to enforce effective safeguards against exposure to juveniles and to passersby. Rights and interests "other than those of the advocates are involved." These include the interest of the public in the quality of life and the total community environment, the tone of commerce in the great city centers, and, possibly, the public safety itself. The Hill-Link Minority Report of the Commission on Obscenity and Pornography indicates that there is at least an arguable correlation between obscene material and crime. Quite apart from sex crimes, however, there remains one problem of large proportions aptly described by Professor Bickel:

> "It concerns the tone of the society, the mode, or to use terms that have perhaps greater currency, the style and quality of life, now and in the future. A man may be entitled to read an obscene book in his room, or expose himself

indecently there. We should protect his privacy. But if he demands a right to obtain the books and pictures he wants in the market, and to foregather in public places—discreet, if you will, but accessible to all—with others who share his tastes, then to grant him his right is to affect the world about the rest of us, and to impinge on other privacies. Even supposing that each of us can, if he wishes, effectively avert the eye and stop the ear (which, in truth, we cannot), what is commonly read and seen and heard and done intrudes upon us all, want it or not." 22 *The Public Interest* 25—26 (Winter 1971).

As Mr. Chief Justice Warren stated, there is a "right of the Nation and of the States to maintain a decent society," *Jacobellis v. Ohio*, 378 U.S. 184, 199 (1964) (dissenting opinion).

But, it is argued, there are no scientific data which conclusively demonstrate that exposure to obscene material adversely affects men and women or their society. It is urged on behalf of the petitioners that, absent such a demonstration, and kind of state regulation is "impermissible." We reject this argument. Although there is no conclusive proof of a connection between antisocial behavior and obscene material, the legislature of Georgia could quite reasonably determine that such a connection does or might exist. In deciding *Roth*, this Court implicitly accepted that a legislature could legitimately act on such a conclusion to protect "the social interest in order and morality."

From the beginning of civilized societies, legislators and judges have acted on various unprovable assumptions. Such assumptions underlie much lawful state regulation of commercial and business affairs. The same is true of the federal securities and antitrust laws and a host of federal regulations. On the basis of these assumptions both Congress and state legislatures have, for example, drastically restricted associational rights by adopting antitrust laws, and have strictly regulated public expression by issuers of and dealers in securities, profit sharing "coupons," and "trading stamps," commanding what they must and must not publish and announce. Understandably those who entertain an absolutist view of the First Amendment find it uncomfortable to explain why rights of association, speech, and press should be severely restrained in the marketplace of goods and money, but not in the marketplace of pornography.

If we accept the unprovable assumption that a complete education requires the reading of certain books, and the well nigh universal belief that good books, plays, and art lift the spirit, improve the mind, enrich the human personality, and develop character, can we then say that a state legislature may not act on the corollary assumption that commerce in obscene books, or public exhibitions focused on obscene conduct, have a tendency to exert a corrupting and debasing impact leading to antisocial behavior? "Many of these effects may be intangible and indistinct, but they are nonetheless real." Mr. Justice Cardozo said that all laws in Western civilization are "guided by a robust common sense." *Steward Machine Co. v. Davis*, 301 U.S. 548, 590 (1937). The sum of experience, including that of the past two decades, affords an ample basis for legislatures to conclude that a sensitive, key relationship of human existence, central to family life, community welfare, and the development of human personality, can be debased and distorted by crass commercial exploitation of sex. Nothing in the Constitution prohibits a State from reaching such a conclusion and acting on it legislatively simply because there is no conclusive evidence or empirical data.

It is argued that individual "free will" must govern, even in activities beyond the protection of the First Amendment and other constitutional guarantees of privacy, and that government cannot legitimately impede an individual's desire to see or acquire obscene plays, movies, and books. We do indeed base our society on certain assumptions that people have the capacity for free choice. Most exercises of individual free choice—those in politics, religion, and expression of ideas—are explicitly protected by the Constitution. Totally unlimited play for free will, however, is not allowed in our or any other society. We have just noted, for example, that neither the First Amendment nor "free will" precludes States from having "blue sky" laws to regulate what sellers of securities may write or publish about their wares. Such laws are to protect the weak, the uninformed, the unsuspecting, and the gullible from the exercise of their own volition. Nor do modern societies leave disposal of garbage and sewage up to the individual "free will," but impose regulation to protect both public health and the appearance of public places. States are told by some that they must await a "laissez-faire" market solution to the obscenity-pornography problem, paradoxically "by people who have never otherwise had a kind word to say for laissez-faire," particularly in solving urban, commercial, and environmental pollution problems. The States, of course, may follow such a "laissez-faire" policy and drop all controls on commercialized obscenity, if that is what they prefer, just as they can ignore consumer protection in the marketplace, but nothing in the Constitution compels the States to do so with regard to matters falling within state jurisdiction.

It is asserted, however, that standards for evaluating state commercial regulations are inapposite in the present context, as state regulation of access by consenting adults to obscene material violates the constitutionally protected right to privacy enjoyed by petitioners' customers. Even assuming that petitioners have vicarious standing to assert potential customers' rights, it is unavailing to compare a theater, open to the public for a fee, with the private home of *Stanley v. Georgia* and the marital bedroom of *Griswold v. Connecticut*. This Court, has, on numerous occasions, refused to hold that commercial ventures such as a motion-picture house are "private" for the purpose of civil rights litigation and civil rights statutes. The Civil Rights Act of 1964 specifically defines motion-picture houses and theaters as places of "public accommodation" covered by the Act as operations affecting commerce.

Our prior decisions recognizing a right to privacy guaranteed by the Fourteenth Amendment included "only personal rights that can be deemed 'fundamental' or 'implicit in the concept of ordered liberty.' Palko v. Connecticut, 302 U.S. 319, 325." This privacy right encompasses and protects the personal intimacies of the home, the family, marriage, motherhood, procreation, and child rearing. Nothing, however, in this Court's decisions intimates that there is any "fundamental" privacy right "implicit in the concept of ordered liberty" to watch obscene movies in places of public accommodation.

If obscene material unprotected by the First Amendment in itself carried with it a "penumbra" of constitutionally protected privacy, this Court would not have found it necessary to decide *Stanley* on the narrow basis of the "privacy of the home," which was hardly more than a reaffirmation that "a man's home is his castle." Moreover, we have declined to equate the privacy of the home relied on in *Stanley* with a "zone" of "privacy" that follows a distributor or a consumer of obscene materials whatever he goes. The idea of a "privacy" right and a place of public accommodation are, in this context, mutually exclusive. Conduct or depictions of conduct that the state police power can prohibit on a public street do not become automatically protected by the Constitution merely because the conduct is moved to a bar or a "live" theater stage, any more than a "live" performance of a man and woman locked in a sexual embrace at high noon in Times Square is protected by the Constitution because they simultaneously engage in a valid political dialogue.

It is also argued that the State has no legitimate interest in "control (of) the moral content of a person's thoughts," and we need not quarrel with this. But we reject the claim that the State of Georgia is here attempting to control the minds or thoughts of those who patronize theaters. Preventing unlimited display or distribution of obscene material, which by definition lacks any serious literary, artistic, political, or scientific value as communication, *Miller v. California*, 413 U.S., at 24, 34, is distinct from a control of reason and the intellect. Where communication of ideas, protected by the First Amendment, is not involved, or the particular privacy of the home protected by *Stanley*, or any of the other "areas or zones" of constitutionally protected privacy, the mere fact that, as a consequence, some human "utterances" or "thoughts" may be incidentally affected does not bar the State from acting to protect legitimate state interests. The fantasies of a drug addict are his own and beyond the reach of government, but government regulation of drug sales is not prohibited by the Constitution.

Finally, petitioners argue that conduct which directly involves "consenting adults" only has, for that sole reason, a special claim to constitutional protection. Our Constitution establishes a broad range of conditions on the exercise of power by the States, but for us to say that our Constitution incorporates the proposition that conduct involving consenting adults only is always beyond state regulation, is a step we are unable to take. Commercial exploitation of depictions, descriptions, or exhibitions of obscene conduct on commercial premises open to the adult public falls within a State's broad power to regulate commerce and protect the public environment. The issue in this context goes beyond whether someone, or even the majority, considers the conduct depicted as "wrong" or "sinful." The States have the power to make a morally neutral judgment that public exhibition of obscene material, or commerce in such material, has a tendency to injure the community as a whole, to endanger the public safety, or to jeopardize in Mr. Chief Justice Warren's words, the States' "right to maintain a decent society."

> [Four members of the Court dissented, but focused their arguments (in opinions by Justices Brennan and Douglas) on the substantive standard for determining whether particular material is obscene rather than on the privacy issue for which the decision is included here.]

Notes and Questions

1. In *Miller v. California*, 413 U.S. 15 (1973), announced the same day as *Paris Adult Theatre v. Slaton*, the Supreme Court decided that juries, rather than the Supreme Court justices themselves, should be deciding whether particular material is obscene based on "community standards" rather than some national constitutional standard. According to the Court, government regulation of expression as "obscene" is limited to "works which depict or describe sexual conduct" that is specifically defined in the statute proscribing it, and such government proscription may only apply to "works which, taken as a whole, appeal to the prurient interest in sex, which portray sexual conduct in a patently offensive way, and which, taken as a whole, do not have serious literary, artistic, political, or scientific value." A jury is to be told that it should apply these tests from the viewpoint of "the average person, applying contemporary community standards," and the relevant community is the one in which the juror lives and the

challenged work was being exhibited or distributed. Does this standard strike the appropriate balance between the First Amendment rights of publishers, distributors and willing consumers of pornography, and those of the community members who find such material distasteful and offensive? How meaningful is a concept of "community standards" in dealing with national communications media such as television, radio, movies, and nationally distributed books, magazines and newspapers? Does such an approach, devised prior to the invention of the Internet, fit comfortably with a new system of distribution over telephone lines and wireless transmission directly into private homes without respect for state or national borders?

2. Should the Constitution protect from state prohibition the operation of "adult" movie theaters? Would it be sufficient to meet the state interests identified in the opinion for states and localities to be able to restrict the location of such theaters through zoning ordinances? See *City of Renton v. Playtime Theatres, Inc.*, 475 U.S. 41 (1986), in which the Court upheld zoning rules limiting the location of "adult" businesses due to the "secondary effects" attributable to the presence of such businesses in a neighborhood. In New York City during the 1990s, the City Council amended the municipal zoning ordinance to sharply restrict the areas within the city where "adult" businesses could operate. Adult businesses were defined with respect to the proportion of their physical premises that were devoted to sexually-explicit communication (live performances and/or sale of sexual aids, such as pornography and sex toys). Passage of the zoning amendment led to prolonged litigation as owners of such businesses sought to comply by setting off portions of their premises where adult-related uses were excluded. When the city administration attacked these arrangements as "shams" the courts ruled that a good-faith attempt to comply with the letter of the ordinance was sufficient to protect the business. See *City of New York v. Les Hommes*, 94 N.Y.2d 267, 724 N.E.2d 368 (1999).

3. To what extent is *Paris Adult Theater* consistent with *Stanley v. Georgia*?

4. During the 1980s, feminist activists under the intellectual leadership of Professor Catharine A. MacKinnon propounded the theory that pornography could be particularly harmful to the interests of women. They were able to secure the introduction of legislative proposals in several cities that would deem certain kinds of pornography, in which women were treated as sex-objects and subjected to degrading violence, as civil rights violations. The city of Indianapolis, Indiana, passed such an ordinance, but it was held to violate the 1st Amendment. See *American Booksellers Association v. Hudnut*, 771 F.2d 323 (7th Cir. 1985), summarily aff'd, 475 U.S. 1001 (1986). By contrast, the Supreme Court of Canada rejected a constitutional challenge to a similar statute, finding that the government had a compelling interest in preventing the harms to the equality of women identified by Professor MacKinnon in her work. See *Regina v. Donald Victor Butler*, 1 S.C.R. 452 (1992). The resulting laws have been used to prosecute sellers of feminist and lesbian and gay literature with explicit sexual content, but the Canadian court recently ruled that discriminatory enforcement would not be permitted. *Little Sisters Book and Art Emporium v. Canada (Minister of Justice)*, 2 S.C.R. 1120 (2000).

* * *

While it was clear under Miller and Paris Adult Theater that Congress and the states could use criminal and regulatory statutes to ban commercial distribution of obscene matter, what of non-obscene sexually-oriented speech? Before the Internet became the main conduit for the distribution of pornography to a mass public, telephone sex lines emerged during the 1980s as a premier venue for such distribution, attracting the atten-

tion of legislatures. Which was the more relevant precedent to the 1st Amendment issues raised by such laws, *Stanley v. Georgia* or *Paris Adult Theater*?

Sable Communications v. Federal Communications Commission
492 U.S. 115 (1989)

Justice WHITE delivered the opinion of the Court.

The issue before us is the constitutionality of § 223(b) of the Communications Act of
1934, 47 U.S.C. § 223(b) (as amended in 1988). The statute imposes an outright ban on
indecent as well as obscene interstate commercial telephone messages.

I

In 1983, Sable Communications, Inc., a Los Angeles-based affiliate of Carlin Communications, Inc., began offering sexually-oriented pre-recorded telephone messages
(popularly known as "dial-a-porn") through the Pacific Bell telephone network. In order
to provide the messages, Sable arranged with Pacific Bell to use special telephone lines,
designed to handle large volumes of calls simultaneously. Those who called the adult
message number were charged a special fee. The fee was collected by Pacific Bell and divided between the phone company and the message provider. Callers outside the Los Angeles metropolitan area could reach the number by means of a long-distance toll call to
the Los Angeles area code. [After Congress amended the Communications Act in 1988,
Sable sought a declaratory judgment and injunctive relief against its enforcement. The
district court refused to enjoin enforcement with respect to obscene speech, but declared
that the 1988 amendment's application to "indecent" speech was unconstitutional.]

II

While dial-a-porn services are a creature of this decade, the medium, in its brief history, has been the subject of much litigation and the object of a series of attempts at
regulation. The first litigation involving dial-a-porn was brought under 82 Stat. 112,
which proscribed knowingly "permitting a telephone under [one's] control" to be used
to make "any comment, request, suggestion or proposal which is obscene, lewd, lascivious, filthy, or indecent." However, the FCC concluded in an administrative action that
the existing law did not cover dial-a-porn.

In reaction to that FCC determination, Congress made its first effort explicitly to address "dial-a-porn" when it added a subsection 223(b) to the 1934 Communications
Act. The provision, which was the predecessor to the amendment at issue in this case,
pertained directly to sexually-oriented commercial telephone messages, and sought to
restrict the access of minors to dial-a-porn. The relevant provision of the Act made it a
crime to use telephone facilities to make "obscene or indecent" interstate telephone
communications "for commercial purposes to any person under eighteen years of age
or to any other person without that person's consent." The statute criminalized commercial transmission of sexually oriented communications to minors and required the
FCC to promulgate regulations laying out the means by which dial-a-porn sponsors
could screen out under-aged callers. The enactment provided that it would be a defense
to prosecution that the defendant restricted access to adults only, in accordance with
procedures established by the FCC. The statute did not criminalize sexually-oriented
messages to adults, whether the messages were obscene or indecent.

The FCC initially promulgated regulations that would have established a defense to message providers operating only between the hours of 9:00 p.m. and 8:00 a.m. Eastern Time (time channeling) and to providers requiring payment by credit card (screening) before transmission of the dial-a-porn message. In Carlin Communications, Inc. v. FCC, 749 F.2d 113 (2nd Cir. 1984) (Carlin I), the Court of Appeals for the Second Circuit set aside the time channeling regulations and remanded to the FCC to examine other alternatives, concluding that the operating hours requirement was "both overinclusive and underinclusive" because it denied "access to adults between certain hours, but not to youths who can easily pick up a private or public telephone and call dial-a-porn during the remaining hours." The Court of Appeals did not reach the constitutionality of the underlying legislation.

In 1985, the FCC promulgated new regulations which continued to permit credit card payment as a defense to prosecution. Instead of time restrictions, however, the Commission added a defense based on use of access codes (user identification codes). Thus, it would be a defense to prosecution under § 223(b) if the defendant, before transmission of the message, restricted customer access by requiring either payment by credit card or authorization by access or identification code. The regulations required each dial-a-porn vendor to develop an identification code database and implementation scheme. Callers would be required to provide an access number for identification (or a credit card) before receiving the message. The access code would be received through the mail after the message provider reviewed the application and concluded through a written age ascertainment procedure that the applicant was at least eighteen years of age. The FCC rejected a proposal for "exchange blocking" which would block or screen telephone numbers at the customer's premises or at the telephone company offices. In Carlin Communications, Inc. v. FCC, 787 F.2d 846 (2nd Cir. 1986) (Carlin II), the Court of Appeals set aside the new regulations because of the FCC's failure adequately to consider customer premises blocking. Again, the constitutionality of the underlying legislation was not addressed.

The FCC then promulgated a third set of regulations, which again rejected customer-premises blocking but added to the prior defenses of credit card payment and access-code use a third defense: message scrambling. Under this system, providers would scramble the message, which would then be unintelligible without the use of a descrambler, the sale of which would be limited to adults. On January 15, 1988, in Carlin Communications, Inc. v. FCC, 837 F.2d 546 (Carlin III), cert. denied, 109 S.Ct. 305 (1988), the Court of Appeals for the Second Circuit held that the new regulations, which made access codes, along with credit card payments and scrambled messages, defenses to prosecution under § 223(b) for dial-a-porn providers, were supported by the evidence, had been properly arrived at, and were a "feasible and effective way to serve [the] compelling state interest" in protecting minors; but the Court directed the FCC to reopen proceedings if a less restrictive technology became available. The Court of Appeals, however, this time reaching the constitutionality of the statute, invalidated § 223(b) insofar as it sought to apply to nonobscene speech.

Thereafter, in April 1988, Congress amended § 223(b) of the Communications Act to prohibit indecent as well as obscene interstate commercial telephone communications directed to any person regardless of age. The amended statute, which took effect on July 1, 1988, also eliminated the requirement that the FCC promulgate regulations for restricting access to minors since a total ban was imposed on dial-a-porn, making it illegal for adults, as well as children, to have access to the sexually explicit messages. It was this version of the statute that was in effect when Sable commenced this action.

III

In the ruling at issue, the District Court upheld § 223(b)'s prohibition of obscene telephone messages as constitutional. We agree with that judgment. In contrast to the prohibition on indecent communications, there is no constitutional barrier to the ban on obscene dial-a-porn recordings. We have repeatedly held that the protection of the First Amendment does not extend to obscene speech. The case before us today does not require us to decide what is obscene or what is indecent but rather to determine whether Congress is empowered to prohibit transmission of obscene telephonic communications.

In its facial challenge to the statute, Sable argues that the legislation creates an impermissible national standard of obscenity, and that it places message senders in a "double bind" by compelling them to tailor all their messages to the least tolerant community.

We do not read § 223(b) as contravening the "contemporary community standards" requirement of *Miller v. California*. Section 223(b) no more establishes a "national standard" of obscenity than do federal statutes prohibiting the mailing of obscene materials, or the broadcasting of obscene messages. In *United States v. Reidel*, 402 U.S. 351 (1971), we said that Congress could prohibit the use of the mails for commercial distribution of materials properly classifiable as obscene, even though those materials were being distributed to willing adults who stated that they were adults. Similarly, we hold today that there is no constitutional stricture against Congress' prohibiting the interstate transmission of obscene commercial telephone recordings.

We stated in *United States v. 12 200-ft. Reels of Film*, 413 U.S. 123 (1973), that the *Miller* standards, including the "contemporary community standards" formulation, apply to federal legislation. As we have said before, the fact that "distributors of allegedly obscene materials may be subjected to varying community standards in the various federal judicial districts into which they transmit the materials does not render a federal statute unconstitutional because of the failure of application of uniform national standards of obscenity." *Hamling v. United States*, 418 U.S., at 106.

Furthermore, Sable is free to tailor its messages, on a selective basis, if it so chooses, to the communities it chooses to serve. While Sable may be forced to incur some costs in developing and implementing a system for screening the locale of incoming calls, there is no constitutional impediment to enacting a law which may impose such costs on a medium electing to provide these messages. There is no constitutional barrier under Miller to prohibiting communications that are obscene in some communities under local standards even though they are not obscene in others. If Sable's audience is comprised of different communities with different local standards, Sable ultimately bears the burden of complying with the prohibition on obscene messages.

IV

The District Court concluded that while the government has a legitimate interest in protecting children from exposure to indecent dial-a-porn messages, § 223(b) was not sufficiently narrowly drawn to serve that purpose and thus violated the First Amendment. We agree.

Sexual expression which is indecent but not obscene is protected by the First Amendment; and the government does not submit that the sale of such materials to adults could be criminalized solely because they are indecent. The government may, however, regulate the content of constitutionally protected speech in order to promote a compelling interest if it chooses the least restrictive means to further the articulated interest.

We have recognized that there is a compelling interest in protecting the physical and psychological well-being of minors. This interest extends to shielding minors from the influence of literature that is not obscene by adult standards. The government may serve this legitimate interest, but to withstand constitutional scrutiny, it must do so by narrowly drawn regulations designed to serve those interests without unnecessarily interfering with First Amendment freedoms. It is not enough to show that the government's ends are compelling; the means must be carefully tailored to achieve those ends.

In *Butler v. Michigan*, 352 U.S. 380 (1957), a unanimous Court reversed a conviction under a statute which made it an offense to make available to the general public materials found to have a potentially harmful influence on minors. The Court found the law to be insufficiently tailored since it denied adults their free speech rights by allowing them to read only what was acceptable for children. As Justice Frankfurter said in that case, "Surely this is to burn the house to roast the pig." In our judgment, this case, like Butler, presents us with "legislation not reasonably restricted to the evil with which it is said to deal."

In attempting to justify the complete ban and criminalization of the indecent commercial telephone communications with adults as well as minors, the government relies on *FCC v. Pacifica Foundation*, 438 U.S. 726 (1978), a case in which the Court considered whether the FCC has the power to regulate a radio broadcast that is indecent but not obscene. In an emphatically narrow holding, the *Pacifica* Court concluded that special treatment of indecent broadcasting was justified.

Pacifica is readily distinguishable from this case, most obviously because it did not involve a total ban on broadcasting indecent material. The FCC rule was not "intended to place an absolute prohibition on the broadcast of this type of language, but rather sought to channel it to times of day when children most likely would not be exposed to it." The issue of a total ban was not before the Court.

The *Pacifica* opinion also relied on the "unique" attributes of broadcasting, noting that broadcasting is "uniquely pervasive," can intrude on the privacy of the home without prior warning as to program content, and is "uniquely accessible to children, even those too young to read." The private commercial telephone communications at issue here are substantially different. The context of dial-in services, where a caller seeks and is willing to pay for the communication, is manifestly different from a situation in which a listener does not want the received message. Placing a telephone call is not the same as turning on a radio and being taken by surprise by an indecent message.

The Government nevertheless argues that the total ban on indecent commercial telephone communications is justified because nothing less could prevent children from gaining access to such messages. We find the argument quite unpersuasive. The FCC, after lengthy proceedings, determined that its credit card, access code, and scrambling rules were a satisfactory solution to the problem of keeping indecent dial-a-porn messages out of the reach of minors. The Court of Appeals, after careful consideration, agreed that these rules represented a "feasible and effective" way to serve the Government's compelling interest in protecting children.

The Government now insists that the rules would not be effective enough—that enterprising youngsters could and would evade the rules and gain access to communications from which they should be shielded. There is no evidence in the record before us to that effect, nor could there be since the FCC's implementation of §223(b) prior to its 1988 amendment has never been tested over time. In this respect, the Government asserts that in amending §223(b) in 1988, Congress expressed its view that there was not a sufficiently effective way to protect minors short of the total ban that it enacted. The Government claims that we must give deference to that judgment.

There is no doubt Congress enacted a total ban on both obscene and indecent telephone communications. But aside from conclusory statements during the debates by proponents of the bill, as well as similar assertions in hearings on a substantially identical bill the year before, H.R. 1786, that under the FCC regulations minors could still have access to dial-a-porn messages, the Congressional record presented to us contains no evidence as to how effective or ineffective the FCC's most recent regulations were or might prove to be. It may well be that there is no fail-safe method of guaranteeing that never will a minor be able to access the dial-a-porn system. The bill that was enacted, however, was introduced on the floor; nor was there a committee report on the bill from which the language of the enacted bill was taken. No Congressman or Senator purported to present a considered judgment with respect to how often or to what extent minors could or would circumvent the rules and have access to dial-a-porn messages. On the other hand, in the hearings on H.R. 1786, the committee heard testimony from the FCC and other witnesses that the FCC rules would be effective and should be tried out in practice. Furthermore, at the conclusion of the hearing, the chairman of the subcommittee suggested consultation looking toward "drafting a piece of legislation that will pass constitutional muster, while at the same time providing for the practical relief which families and groups are looking for." The bill never emerged from Committee.

For all we know from this record, the FCC's technological approach to restricting dial-a-porn messages to adults who seek them would be extremely effective, and only a few of the most enterprising and disobedient young people will manage to secure access to such messages. If this is the case, it seems to us that §223(b) is not a narrowly tailored effort to serve the compelling interest of preventing minors from being exposed to indecent telephone messages. Under our precedents, §223(b), in its present form, has the invalid effect of limiting the content of adult telephone conversations to that which is suitable for children to hear. It is another case of "burn[ing] up the house to roast the pig."

Because the statute's denial of adult access to telephone messages which are indecent but not obscene far exceeds that which is necessary to limit the access of minors to such messages, we hold that the ban does not survive constitutional scrutiny. [Justice Scalia concurred in a separate opinion, omitted here.]

Justice BRENNAN, with whom Justice MARSHALL and Justice STEVENS join, concurring in part and dissenting in part.

I agree that a statute imposing criminal penalties for making, or for allowing others to use a telephone under one's control to make, any indecent telephonic communication for a commercial purpose is patently unconstitutional. In my view, however, §223(b)(1)(A)'s parallel criminal prohibition with regard to obscene commercial communications likewise violates the First Amendment. I have long been convinced that the exaction of criminal penalties for the distribution of obscene materials to consenting adults is constitutionally intolerable. In my judgment, "the concept of 'obscenity' cannot be defined with sufficient specificity and clarity to provide fair notice to persons who create and distribute sexually oriented materials, to prevent substantial erosion of protected speech as a byproduct of the attempt to suppress unprotected speech, and to avoid very costly institutional harms." *Paris Adult Theatre I v. Slaton*, 413 U.S. 49, 103 (1973) (BRENNAN, J., dissenting). To be sure, the Government has a strong interest in protecting children against exposure to pornographic material that might be harmful to them.

But a complete criminal ban on obscene telephonic messages for profit is 'unconstitutionally overbroad, and therefore invalid on its face," as a means for achieving this end.

The very evidence the Court adduces to show that denying adults access to all indecent commercial messages "far exceeds that which is necessary to limit the access of minors to such messages," also demonstrates that forbidding the transmission of all obscene messages is unduly heavy-handed. After painstaking scrutiny, both the FCC and the Second Circuit found that "a scheme involving access codes, scrambling, and credit card payment is a feasible and effective way to serve this compelling state interest" in safeguarding children. And during the 1987 Hearings on H.R. 1786, a United States Attorney speaking on behalf of the Justice Department described the FCC's proposed regulations as "very effective," because they would "dramatically reduc[e] the number of calls from minors in the United States, almost eliminating them." In addition, as the Court notes, no contrary evidence was before Congress when it voted to impose a total prohibition on obscene telephonic messages for profit. Hence, the Government cannot plausibly claim that its legitimate interest in protecting children warrants this draconian restriction on the First Amendment rights of adults who seek to hear the messages that Sable and others provide. Section 223(b)(1)(A) unambiguously proscribes all obscene commercial messages, and thus admits of no construction that would render it constitutionally permissible.

Notes and Questions

1. Assuming that consumers of dial-a-porn are in their homes when they place calls to such a service, and their activities while listening to the message are not exposed to public view or hearing, is this situation distinguishable in any way relevant for purposes of constitutional analysis from the situation of the private consumer of pornographic books, pictures or films considered in *Stanley v. Georgia*? Based on this ruling, could you predict how the Supreme Court would consider the issue of attempts by Congress to restrict the distribution of pornographic material, either obscene or non-obscene, to consenting adults through the Internet?

2. As a result of the *Sable Communications* ruling, Congress subsequently passed a new amendment to the Communications Act seeking to limit the availability of telephone company "billing services" for sexually oriented telephone messages while requiring that access to such services be limited to adults who requested access in writing from the telephone company. Due to the nature of technology in this industry, such limitations would make it impossible for "dial-a-porn" services to operate at a profit. Are such limitations constitutional? The Court has decisively answered in the negative.

3. How would a judge or jury determine whether the message conveyed by a particular dial-a-porn service is obscene or merely indecent? Why should such distinctions make any difference for purposes of the First Amendment? Justice Brennan argued in his dissent that they should not.

4. The notion that indecent speech has constitutional protection may be significant in other connections. Consider the constitutional issues raised by the following statutory proposals:

(1) Congress includes in the appropriations bill for the National Endowment for the Arts a provision banning financial assistance for any art that is consid-

ered "indecent" or "offensive" to the majority of the community. See *National Endowment for the Arts v. Finley*, 524 U.S. 569 (1998).

(2) Congress includes in the appropriations for the Public Health Service a provision banning financial assistance for any educational materials that might be seen as "indecent" or "offensive" or that might be considered to "promote homosexuality or sexual promiscuity." This provision is inspired by concern about federal funding of "safe-sex" information targeted at gay men to stem the spread of HIV. See *Gay Men's Health Crisis v. Sullivan*, 792 F.Supp. 278 (S.D.N.Y. 1992).

(3) Congress mandates federal criminal penalties for individuals who transmit "indecent" materials on the Internet that can be seen by minors. See *Ashcroft v. Free Speech Coalition*, 535 U.S. 234 (2002), below.

Osborne v. Ohio
495 U.S. 103 (1990)

Justice WHITE delivered the opinion of the Court.

In order to combat child pornography, Ohio enacted Rev. Code Ann. § 2907.323(A)(3) (Supp.1989), which provides in pertinent part [criminal penalties for the possession or viewing of] "any material or performance that shows a minor who is not the person's child or ward in a state of nudity, unless one of the following applies: (a) The material or performance is sold, disseminated, displayed, possessed, controlled, brought or caused to be brought into this state, or presented for a bona fide artistic, medical, scientific, educational, religious, governmental, judicial, or other proper purpose, by or to a physician, psychologist, sociologist, scientist, teacher, person pursuing bona fide studies or research, librarian, clergyman, prosecutor, judge, or other person having a proper interest in the material or performance; (b) The person knows that the parents, guardian, or custodian has consented in writing to the photographing or use of the minor in a state of nudity and to the manner in which the material or performance is used or transferred."

Petitioner, Clyde Osborne, was convicted of violating this statute and sentenced to six months in prison, after the Columbus, Ohio, police, pursuant to a valid search, found four photographs in Osborne's home. Each photograph depicts a nude male adolescent posed in a sexually explicit position.

I

The threshold question in this case is whether Ohio may constitutionally proscribe the possession and viewing of child pornography or whether, as Osborne argues, our decision in *Stanley v. Georgia* compels the contrary result. In *Stanley*, we struck down a Georgia law outlawing the private possession of obscene material. We recognized that the statute impinged upon Stanley's right to receive information in the privacy of his home, and we found Georgia's justifications for its law inadequate.

Stanley should not be read too broadly. We have previously noted that *Stanley* was a narrow holding, and, since the decision in that case, the value of permitting child pornography has been characterized as "exceedingly modest, if not de minimis." *New York v. Ferber*, 458 U.S. 747, 762 (1982). But assuming, for the sake of argument, that Osborne has a First Amendment interest in viewing and possessing child pornography, we nonetheless find this case distinct from *Stanley* because the interests underlying child pornography prohibitions far exceed the interests justifying the Georgia law at issue in *Stanley*.

In *Stanley*, Georgia primarily sought to proscribe the private possession of obscenity because it was concerned that obscenity would poison the minds of its viewers. We responded that "[w]hatever the power of the state to control public dissemination of ideas inimical to the public morality, it cannot constitutionally premise legislation on the desirability of controlling a person's private thoughts." The difference here is obvious: the State does not rely on a paternalistic interest in regulating Osborne's mind. Rather, Ohio has enacted § 2907.323(A)(3) in order to protect the victims of child pornography; it hopes to destroy a market for the exploitative use of children.

"It is evident beyond the need for elaboration that a State's interest in 'safeguarding the physical and psychological well-being of a minor' is 'compelling.' The legislative judgment, as well as the judgment found in relevant literature, is that the use of children as subjects of pornographic materials is harmful to the physiological, emotional, and mental health of the child. That judgment, we think, easily passes muster under the First Amendment." *Ferber*, 458 U.S., at 756–58 (citations omitted). It is also surely reasonable for the State to conclude that it will decrease the production of child pornography if it penalizes those who possess and view the product, thereby decreasing demand. In *Ferber*, where we upheld a New York statute outlawing the distribution of child pornography, we found a similar argument persuasive: "the advertising and selling of child pornography provide an economic motive for and are thus an integral part of the production of such materials, an activity illegal throughout the Nation. 'It rarely has been suggested that the constitutional freedom for speech and press extends its immunity to speech or writing used as an integral part of conduct in violation of a valid criminal statute.'"

Osborne contends that the State should use other measures, besides penalizing possession, to dry up the child pornography market. Osborne points out that in *Stanley* we rejected Georgia's argument that its prohibition on obscenity possession was a necessary incident to its proscription on obscenity distribution. This holding, however, must be viewed in light of the weak interests asserted by the State in that case. *Stanley* itself emphasized that we did not "mean to express any opinion on statutes making criminal possession of other types of printed, filmed, or recorded materials. In such cases, compelling reasons may exist for overriding the right of the individual to possess those materials."

Given the importance of the State's interest in protecting the victims of child pornography, we cannot fault Ohio for attempting to stamp out this vice at all levels in the distribution chain. According to the State, since the time of our decision in *Ferber*, much of the child pornography market has been driven underground; as a result, it is now difficult, if not impossible, to solve the child pornography problem by only attacking production and distribution. Indeed, 19 States have found it necessary to proscribe the possession of this material.

Other interests also support the Ohio law. First, as *Ferber* recognized, the materials produced by child pornographers permanently record the victim's abuse. The pornography's continued existence causes the child victims continuing harm by haunting the children in years to come. The State's ban on possession and viewing encourages the possessors of these materials to destroy them. Second, encouraging the destruction of these materials is also desirable because evidence suggests that pedophiles use child pornography to seduce other children into sexual activity.

Given the gravity of the State's interests in this context, we find that Ohio may constitutionally proscribe the possession and viewing of child pornography.

II

Osborne next argues that even if the State may constitutionally ban the possession of child pornography, his conviction is invalid because § 2907.323(A)(3) is unconstitutionally overbroad in that it criminalizes an intolerable range of constitutionally protected conduct. In our previous decisions discussing the First Amendment overbreadth doctrine, we have repeatedly emphasized that where a statute regulates expressive conduct, the scope of the statute does not render it unconstitutional unless its overbreadth is not only "real, but substantial as well, judged in relation to the statute's plainly legitimate sweep." Even where a statute at its margins infringes on protected expression, "facial invalidation is inappropriate if the 'remainder of the statute covers a whole range of easily identifiable and constitutionally proscribable conduct.'" *New York v. Ferber.*

The Ohio statute, on its face, purports to prohibit the possession of "nude" photographs of minors. We have stated that depictions of nudity, without more, constitute protected expression. Relying on this observation, Osborne argues that the statute as written is substantially overbroad. We are skeptical of this claim because, in light of the statute's exemptions and "proper purposes" provisions, the statute may not be substantially overbroad under our cases. However that may be, Osborne's overbreadth challenge, in any event, fails because the statute, as construed by the Ohio Supreme Court on Osborne's direct appeal, plainly survives overbreadth scrutiny. Under the Ohio Supreme Court reading, the statute prohibits "the possession or viewing of material or performance of a minor who is in a state of nudity, where such nudity constitutes a lewd exhibition or involves a graphic focus on the genitals, and where the person depicted is neither the child nor the ward of the person charged." By limiting the statute's operation in this manner, the Ohio Supreme Court avoided penalizing persons for viewing or possessing innocuous photographs of naked children. We have upheld similar language against overbreadth challenges in the past.

The Ohio Supreme Court also concluded that the State had to establish scienter in order to prove a violation of § 2907.323(A)(3) based on the Ohio default statute specifying that recklessness applies when another statutory provision lacks an intent specification. The statute on its face lacks a mens rea requirement, but that omission brings into play and is cured by another law that plainly satisfies the requirement laid down in *Ferber* that prohibitions on child pornography include some element of scienter. [The Court agreed with Osborne's argument that the charge to the jury in his case was inadequately protective of his due process rights, and remanded for a new trial.]

Justice BRENNAN, with whom Justice MARSHALL and Justice STEVENS join, dissenting.

In my view, the state law, even as construed authoritatively by the Ohio Supreme Court, is still fatally overbroad, and our decision in *Stanley v. Georgia* prevents the State from criminalizing appellant's possession of the photographs at issue in this case. I therefore respectfully dissent.

As written, the Ohio statute is plainly overbroad. In short, §§ 2907.323 and 2907.01(H) use simple nudity, without more, as a way of defining child pornography.

But as our prior decisions have made clear, "'nudity alone' does not place otherwise protected material outside the mantle of the First Amendment." *Schad v. Mount Ephraim*, 452 U.S. 61, 66 (1981) (quoting *Jenkins v. Georgia*, 418 U.S. 153, 161 (1974)).

Wary of the statute's use of the "nudity" standard, the Ohio Supreme Court construed [it] to apply only "where such nudity constitutes a lewd exhibition or involves a graphic focus on the genitals." The "lewd exhibition" and "graphic focus" tests not only fail to cure the overbreadth of the statute, but they also create a new problem of vagueness.

The Court dismisses appellant's overbreadth contention in a single cursory paragraph. Relying exclusively on our previous decision in *New York v. Ferber*, the majority reasons that the "lewd exhibition" standard adequately narrows the statute's ambit because "we have upheld similar language against overbreadth challenges in the past." The Court's terse explanation is unsatisfactory, since *Ferber* involved a law that differs in crucial respects from the one here.

The New York law at issue in *Ferber* criminalized the use of a child in a "sexual performance," defined as "any performance or part thereof which includes sexual conduct by a child less than sixteen years of age." "Sexual conduct" was in turn defined as "actual or simulated sexual intercourse, deviate sexual intercourse, sexual bestiality, masturbation, sado-masochistic abuse, or lewd exhibition of the genitals." Although we acknowledged that "nudity, without more, is protected expression," we found that the statute was not overbroad because only "a tiny fraction of materials within the statute's reach" was constitutionally protected. We therefore upheld the conviction of a bookstore proprietor who sold films depicting young boys masturbating.

The Ohio law is distinguishable for several reasons. First, the New York statute did not criminalize materials with a "graphic focus" on the genitals, and, as discussed further below, Ohio's "graphic focus" test is impermissibly capacious. Even setting aside the "graphic focus" element, the Ohio Supreme Court's narrowing construction is still overbroad because it focuses on "lewd exhibitions of nudity" rather than "lewd exhibitions of the genitals" in the context of sexual conduct, as in the New York statute at issue in *Ferber*. Ohio law defines "nudity" to include depictions of pubic areas, buttocks, the female breast, and covered male genitals "in a discernably turgid state," as well as depictions of the genitals. On its face, then, the Ohio law is much broader than New York's.

In addition, whereas the Ohio Supreme Court's interpretation uses the "lewd exhibition of nudity" test standing alone, the New York law employed the phrase "lewd exhibition of the genitals" in the context of a longer list of examples of sexual conduct: "actual or simulated sexual intercourse, deviate sexual intercourse, sexual bestiality, masturbation, [and] sado-masochistic abuse." This syntax was important to our decision in *Ferber*. We recognized the potential for impermissible applications of the New York statute, but in view of the examples of "sexual conduct" provided by the statute, we were willing to assume that the New York courts would not "widen the possibly invalid reach of the statute by giving an expansive construction to the proscription on 'lewd exhibition[s] of the genitals.'" In the Ohio statute, of course, there is no analog to the elaborate definition of "sexual conduct" to serve as a similar limit. Hence, while the New York law could be saved at least in part by the notion of ejusdem generis, the Ohio Supreme Court's construction of its law cannot.

Indeed, the broad definition of nudity in the Ohio statutory scheme means that "child pornography" could include any photograph depicting a "lewd exhibition" of even a small portion of a minor's buttocks or any part of the female breast below the nipple. Pictures of topless bathers at a Mediterranean beach, of teenagers in revealing dresses, and even of toddlers romping unclothed, all might be prohibited. Furthermore, the Ohio law forbids not only depictions of nudity per se, but also depictions of the buttocks, breast, or pubic area with less than a "full, opaque covering." Thus, pictures of fashion models wearing semitransparent clothing might be illegal, as might a photograph depicting a fully clad male that nevertheless captured his genitals "in a discernably turgid state." The Ohio statute thus sweeps in many types of materials that are not "child pornography," as we used that term in *Ferber*, but rather that enjoy full First Amendment protection.

It might be objected that many of these depictions of nudity do not amount to "lewd exhibitions." But in the absence of any authoritative definition of that phrase by the Ohio Supreme Court, we cannot predict which ones. Many would characterize a photograph of a seductive fashion model or alluringly posed adolescent on a topless European beach as "lewd," although such pictures indisputably enjoy constitutional protection. Indeed, some might think that any nudity, especially that involving a minor, is by definition "lewd," yet this Court has clearly established that nudity is not excluded automatically from the scope of the First Amendment. The Court today is unable even to hazard a guess as to what a "lewd exhibition" might mean; it is forced to rely entirely on an inapposite case—*Ferber*—that simply did not discuss, let alone decide, the central issue here.

The Ohio Supreme Court provided few clues as to the meaning of the phrase "lewd exhibition of nudity." The court distinguished "child pornography" from "obscenity," thereby implying that it did not believe that an exhibition was required to be "obscene" in order to qualify as "lewd." But it supplied no authoritative definition—a disturbing omission in light of the absence of the phrase "lewd exhibition" from the statutory definition section of the Sex Offenses chapter of the Ohio Revised Code. In fact, the word "lewd" does not appear in the statutory definition of any crime involving obscenity or other sexually oriented materials in the Ohio Revised Code. Thus, when the Ohio Supreme Court grafted the "lewd exhibition" test onto the definition of nudity, it was venturing into uncharted territory.

Moreover, there is no longstanding, commonly understood definition of "lewd" upon which the Ohio Supreme Court's construction might be said to draw that can save the "lewd exhibition" standard from impermissible vagueness. At common law, the term "lewd" included "any gross indecency so notorious as to tend to corrupt community morals," an approach that was "subjective" and dependent entirely on a speaker's "social, moral, and cultural bias." Not surprisingly, States with long experience in applying indecency laws have learned that the word "lewd" is "too indefinite and uncertain to be enforceable." *Courtemanche v. State*, 507 S.W.2d 545, 546 (Tex.Cr.App.1974). The term is often defined by reference to such pejorative synonyms as "lustful, lascivious, unchaste, wanton, or loose in morals and conduct." *People v. Williams*, 59 Cal.App.3d 225, 229 (1976). But "the very phrases and synonyms through which meaning is purportedly ascribed serve to obscure rather than clarify." *State v. Kueny*, 215 N.W.2d 215, 217 (Iowa 1974). "To instruct the jury that a 'lewd or dissolute' act is one which is morally 'loose,' or 'lawless,' or 'foul' piles additional uncertainty upon the already vague words of the statute. In short, vague statutory language is not rendered more precise by defining it in terms of synonyms of equal or greater uncertainty." *Pryor v. Municipal Court for Los Angeles*, 25 Cal.3d 238, 249 (1979).

The Ohio Supreme Court, moreover, did not specify the perspective from which "lewdness" is to be determined. A "reasonable" person's view of "lewdness"? A reasonable pedophile's? An "average" person applying contemporary local community standards? Statewide standards? Nationwide standards? Cf. *Sable Communications of California, Inc. v. FCC*, 109 S.Ct. 2829 (1989). In sum, the addition of a "lewd exhibition" standard does not narrow adequately the statute's reach. If anything, it creates a new problem of vagueness, affording the public little notice of the statute's ambit and providing an avenue for "policemen, prosecutors, and juries to pursue their personal predilections." *Kolender v. Lawson*, 461 U.S. 352, 358 (1983) (quoting *Smith v. Goguen*, 415 U.S. 566, 575 (1974)). Given the important First Amendment interests at issue, the vague, broad sweep of the "lewd exhibition" language means that it cannot cure § 2907.323(A)(3)'s overbreadth.

The Ohio Supreme Court also added a "graphic focus" element to the nudity definition. This phrase, a stranger to obscenity regulation, suffers from the same vagueness difficulty as "lewd exhibition."…In sum, the "lewd exhibition" and "graphic focus" tests are too vague to serve as any workable limit. Because the statute, even as construed authoritatively by the Ohio Supreme Court, is impermissibly overbroad, I would hold that appellant cannot be retried under it.

Even if the statute was not overbroad, our decision in *Stanley v. Georgia* forbids the criminalization of appellant's private possession in his home of the materials at issue. "If the First Amendment means anything, it means that the State has no business telling a man, sitting alone in his own house, what books he may read or what films he may watch." Appellant was convicted for possessing four photographs of nude minors, seized from a desk drawer in the bedroom of his house during a search executed pursuant to a warrant. Appellant testified that he had been given the pictures in his home by a friend. There was no evidence that the photographs had been produced commercially or distributed. All were kept in an album that appellant had assembled for his personal use and had possessed privately for several years.

In these circumstances, the Court's focus on *Ferber* rather than *Stanley* is misplaced. *Ferber* held only that child pornography is "a category of material the production and distribution of which is not entitled to First Amendment protection;" our decision did not extend to private possession. The authority of a State to regulate the production and distribution of such materials is not dispositive of its power to penalize possession

The Court today finds *Stanley* inapposite. The majority's analysis does not withstand scrutiny. While the sexual exploitation of children is undoubtedly a serious problem, Ohio may employ other weapons to combat it. Indeed, the State already has enacted a panoply of laws prohibiting the creation, sale, and distribution of child pornography and obscenity involving minors. Ohio has not demonstrated why these laws are inadequate and why the State must forbid mere possession as well.

At bottom, the Court today is so disquieted by the possible exploitation of children in the production of the pornography that it is willing to tolerate the imposition of criminal penalties for simple possession. While I share the majority's concerns, I do not believe that it has struck the proper balance between the First Amendment and the State's interests.

When speech is eloquent and the ideas expressed lofty, it is easy to find restrictions on them invalid. But were the First Amendment limited to such discourse, our freedom would be sterile indeed. Mr. Osborne's pictures may be distasteful, but the Constitution guarantees both his right to possess them privately and his right to avoid punishment under an overbroad law. I respectfully dissent.

Notes and Questions

1. The precedential prerequisite for this decision was the Court's prior ruling in *New York v. Ferber*, 458 U.S. 747, 762 (1982), upholding a state law that made it a crime to produce or distribute pornographic material depicting minors. The key distinction between this statute and earlier laws against pornography that had been upheld by the Court was that this statute did not require a finding that the materials be obscene in order to lose First Amendment protection. The Court theorized that the state was penalizing their production and distribution in order to protect children from harm, a compelling interest, and that this interest would not be served by restricting application of the law to obscene matter. Any sexually-explicit matter depicting minors could be banned due to the impact upon minors of their involvement in the production and of the subsequent circulation of their images.

2. In a footnote, Justice Brennan describes the particular impact of this kind of law on members of sexual minorities:

> The danger of discriminatory enforcement assumes particular importance of the context of the instant case, which involves child pornography with male homosexual overtones. Sadly, evidence indicates that the overwhelming majority of arrests for violations of "lewdness" laws involve male homosexuals. "Such uneven application of the law is the natural consequence of a statute which as judicially construed measure[s] the criminality of conduct by community or even individual notions of what is distasteful behavior." *Pryor*, 25 Cal.3d at 252, 599 P.2d, at 644. The "lewd exhibition" standard "'furnishes a convenient tool for "harsh and discriminatory enforcement by local prosecuting officials, against particular groups deemed to merit their displeasure."'" *Kolender v. Lawson*, 461 U.S., at 360 (quoting Papachristou, 405 U.S., at 170, in turn quoting *Thornhill v. Alabama*, 310 U.S. 88, 97–98 (1940)).

3. Are you persuaded by the Court's distinction between the Georgia law held unconstitutional in *Stanley v. Georgia* and the Ohio law upheld as to constitutionality in the instant case? Should the motivation of the legislature play such a crucial role in evaluating the constitutionality of the statute? How much of the *Stanley* holding survives the decision in *Osborne*?

4. Consider the constitutionality of the following government activity: The government wants to destroy the profitability of businesses that sell pornographic photos of minors through the mail. To this end, the government plans to target customers of such businesses by directly prosecuting them for ordering and possessing such materials. When the government comes into possession of the mailing list of such a company, it sends out questionnaires to all those on the mailing list. The questionnaires state that they are from a private company which specializes in supplying sexually-oriented materials to consenting adults who request them, and ask the recipients to indicate by their answers to the questionnaire the types of materials in which they are interested. Any recipient who responds receives follow-up mailings with catalogs for erotic materials. Any recipient who then orders materials which include the depiction of minors receives a

surprise search of their home pursuant to a warrant approved by a federal magistrate on the basis of the order for materials, and is subsequently prosecuted. Do these activities constitute entrapment? To what extent is the government's program justified under the rationale of the Court in *Osborne*? See *Jacobson v. United States*, 503 U.S. 540 (1992), reversing 916 F.2d 467 (8th Cir. en banc 1990).

5. The technology now exists to produce realistic pornographic images depicting children without using real children as models, through computer manipulation of the images. Congress passed a law criminalizing the production and distribution of such material, which the Supreme Court concluded was unconstitutional in *Ashcroft v. The Free Speech Coalition*, 535 U.S. 234 (2002). The Court found that the main justification for upholding child porn laws was the protection of children who were involved in their production. Since no children were involved in the production of "virtual" child porn, sufficient justification was missing in light of the First Amendment issues.

* * *

The emergence of the Internet as a mass medium during the 1990s gave rise to new Congressional attempts to restrict access to sexual speech. As it became strikingly clear that the Internet would provide an extraordinary new means to disseminate sexually-oriented materials, concerns emerged about the ease with which minors could access such materials "on line." At the same time, the emergence of "virtual communities" with special interests on the Internet had made it possible for lesbian, gay, bisexual and transgender youth to use this medium as a way of "coming out" and finding communal support, and also provided new mechanisms for various other sexual minority communities to organize for political as well as sexual purposes (for example, the transgendered community's political organization was greatly facilitated by the ability to communicate through websites, chatrooms, and listserves, as were the various sexual fetish communities). It is not surprising that groups concerned with lesbian and gay rights joined the coalitions of plaintiffs that formed to challenge new federal restrictions to Internet access. What was surprising was the degree to which the Supreme Court quickly became sensitive to the significant First Amendment issues posed by such restrictions.

Reno v. American Civil Liberties Union
521 U.S. 844 (1997)

Justice STEVENS delivered the opinion of the Court.

At issue is the constitutionality of two statutory provisions enacted to protect minors from "indecent" and "patently offensive" communications on the Internet. Notwithstanding the legitimacy and importance of the congressional goal of protecting children from harmful materials, we agree with the three-judge District Court that the statute abridges "the freedom of speech" protected by the First Amendment.

I

The District Court made extensive findings of fact, most of which were based on a detailed stipulation prepared by the parties. The findings describe the character and the dimensions of the Internet, the availability of sexually explicit material in that medium, and the problems confronting age verification for recipients of Internet communications. [Omitted here are the court's detailed descriptions of email, websites, links, and the other salient features of how the Internet works.]

Sexually Explicit Material

Sexually explicit material on the Internet includes text, pictures, and chat and "extends from the modestly titillating to the hardest-core." These files are created, named, and posted in the same manner as material that is not sexually explicit, and may be accessed either deliberately or unintentionally during the course of an imprecise search. "Once a provider posts its content on the Internet, it cannot prevent that content from entering any community." Thus, for example,

> when the UCR/California Museum of Photography posts to its Web site nudes by Edward Weston and Robert Mapplethorpe to announce that its new exhibit will travel to Baltimore and New York City, those images are available not only in Los Angeles, Baltimore, and New York City, but also in Cincinnati, Mobile, or Beijing—wherever Internet users live. Similarly, the safer sex instructions that Critical Path posts to its Web site, written in street language so that the teenage receiver can understand them, are available not just in Philadelphia, but also in Provo and Prague.

Some of the communications over the Internet that originate in foreign countries are also sexually explicit.

Though such material is widely available, users seldom encounter such content accidentally. "A document's title or a description of the document will usually appear before the document itself and in many cases the user will receive detailed information about a site's content before he or she need take the step to access the document. Almost all sexually explicit images are preceded by warnings as to the content." For that reason, the "odds are slim" that a user would enter a sexually explicit site by accident. Unlike communications received by radio or television, "the receipt of information on the Internet requires a series of affirmative steps more deliberate and directed than merely turning a dial. A child requires some sophistication and some ability to read to retrieve material and thereby to use the Internet unattended."

Systems have been developed to help parents control the material that may be available on a home computer with Internet access. A system may either limit a computer's access to an approved list of sources that have been identified as containing no adult material, it may block designated inappropriate sites, or it may attempt to block messages containing identifiable objectionable features. "Although parental control software currently can screen for certain suggestive words or for known sexually explicit sites, it cannot now screen for sexually explicit images." Nevertheless, the evidence indicates that "a reasonably effective method by which parents can prevent their children from accessing sexually explicit and other material which parents may believe is inappropriate for their children will soon be widely available."

Age Verification

The problem of age verification differs for different uses of the Internet. The District Court categorically determined that there "is no effective way to determine the identity or the age of a user who is accessing material through e-mail, mail exploders, newsgroups or chat rooms." The Government offered no evidence that there was a reliable way to screen recipients and participants in such forums for age. Moreover, even if it were technologically feasible to block minors' access to newsgroups and chat rooms containing discussions of art, politics, or other subjects that potentially elicit "indecent" or "patently offensive" contributions, it would not be possible to block their access to that material and "still allow them access to the remaining content, even if the overwhelming majority of that content was not indecent."

Technology exists by which an operator of a Web site may condition access on the verification of requested information such as a credit card number or an adult password. Credit card verification is only feasible, however, either in connection with a commercial transaction in which the card is used, or by payment to a verification agency. Using credit card possession as a surrogate for proof of age would impose costs on non-commercial Web sites that would require many of them to shut down. For that reason, at the time of the trial, credit card verification was "effectively unavailable to a substantial number of Internet content providers." Moreover, the imposition of such a requirement "would completely bar adults who do not have a credit card and lack the resources to obtain one from accessing any blocked material."

Commercial pornographic sites that charge their users for access have assigned them passwords as a method of age verification. The record does not contain any evidence concerning the reliability of these technologies. Even if passwords are effective for commercial purveyors of indecent material, the District Court found that an adult password requirement would impose significant burdens on noncommercial sites, both because they would discourage users from accessing their sites and because the cost of creating and maintaining such screening systems would be "beyond their reach."

In sum, the District Court found:

> Even if credit card verification or adult password verification were implemented, the Government presented no testimony as to how such systems could ensure that the user of the password or credit card is in fact over 18. The burdens imposed by credit card verification and adult password verification systems make them effectively unavailable to a substantial number of Internet content providers.

II

The Telecommunications Act of 1996 was an unusually important legislative enactment. Title V—known as the "Communications Decency Act of 1996" (CDA)—contains provisions that were either added in executive committee after the hearings were concluded or as amendments offered during floor debate on the legislation. An amendment offered in the Senate was the source of the two statutory provisions challenged in this case. They are informally described as the "indecent transmission" provision and the "patently offensive display" provision.

The first, 47 U.S.C. § 223(a), prohibits the knowing transmission of obscene or indecent messages to any recipient under 18 years of age. It provides in pertinent part:

> a) Whoever—(1) in interstate or foreign communications- (B) by means of a telecommunications device knowingly—(i) makes, creates, or solicits, and (ii) initiates the transmission of, any comment, request, suggestion, proposal, image, or other communication which is obscene or indecent, knowing that the recipient of the communication is under 18 years of age, regardless of whether the maker of such communication placed the call or initiated the communication; (2) knowingly permits any telecommunications facility under his control to be used for any activity prohibited by paragraph (1) with the intent that it be used for such activity, shall be fined under Title 18, or imprisoned not more than two years, or both.

The second provision, § 223(d), prohibits the knowing sending or displaying of patently offensive messages in a manner that is available to a person under 18 years of age. It provides:

> (d) Whoever—(1) in interstate or foreign communications knowingly—(A) uses an interactive computer service to send to a specific person or persons under 18 years of age, or (B) uses any interactive computer service to display in a manner available to a person under 18 years of age, any comment, request, suggestion, proposal, image, or other communication that, in context, depicts or describes, in terms patently offensive as measured by contemporary community standards, sexual or excretory activities or organs, regardless of whether the user of such service placed the call or initiated the communication; or (2) knowingly permits any telecommunications facility under such person's control to be used for an activity prohibited by paragraph (1) with the intent that it be used for such activity, shall be fined under Title 18, or imprisoned not more than two years, or both.

The breadth of these prohibitions is qualified by two affirmative defenses. One covers those who take "good faith, reasonable, effective, and appropriate actions" to restrict access by minors to the prohibited communications. § 223(e)(5)(A). The other covers those who restrict access to covered material by requiring certain designated forms of age proof, such as a verified credit card or an adult identification number or code. § 223(e)(5)(B).

III

[Immediately after the president signed the bill, lawsuits were filed challenging its constitutionality. A three-judge district court, as provided in the Act, was convened and stopped the challenged provisions from going into effect on the ground that they were unconstitutional.]

IV.

In arguing for reversal, the Government contends that the CDA is plainly constitutional under three of our prior decisions: (1) *Ginsberg v. New York*, 390 U.S. 629 (1968); (2) *FCC v. Pacifica Foundation*, 438 U.S. 726 (1978); and (3) *Renton v. Playtime Theatres, Inc.*, 475 U.S. 41 (1986). A close look at these cases, however, raises—rather than relieves—doubts concerning the constitutionality of the CDA.

In *Ginsberg*, we upheld the constitutionality of a New York statute that prohibited selling to minors under 17 years of age material that was considered obscene as to them even if not obscene as to adults. We rejected the defendant's broad submission that "the scope of the constitutional freedom of expression secured to a citizen to read or see material concerned with sex cannot be made to depend on whether the citizen is an adult or a minor." In rejecting that contention, we relied not only on the State's independent interest in the well-being of its youth, but also on our consistent recognition of the principle that "the parents' claim to authority in their own household to direct the rearing of their children is basic in the structure of our society."

In four important respects, the statute upheld in *Ginsberg* was narrower than the CDA. First, we noted in *Ginsberg* that "the prohibition against sales to minors does not bar parents who so desire from purchasing the magazines for their children." Under the CDA, by contrast, neither the parents' consent—nor even their participation—in the communication would avoid the application of the statute. Second, the New York statute applied only to commercial transactions, whereas the CDA contains no such limitation. Third, the New York statute cabined its definition of material that is harmful to minors with the requirement that it be "utterly without redeeming social importance for minors." The CDA fails to provide us with any definition of the term "indecent" as used in §223(a)(1) and, importantly, omits any requirement that the "patently offensive" material covered by §223(d) lack serious literary, artistic, political, or scientific value. Fourth, the New York statute defined a minor as a person under the age of 17, whereas the CDA, in applying to all those under 18 years, includes an additional year of those nearest majority.

In *Pacifica*, we upheld a declaratory order of the Federal Communications Commission, holding that the broadcast of a recording of a 12-minute monologue entitled "Filthy Words" that had previously been delivered to a live audience "could have been the subject of administrative sanctions." The Commission had found that the repetitive use of certain words referring to excretory or sexual activities or organs "in an afternoon broadcast when children are in the audience was patently offensive" and concluded that the monologue was indecent "as broadcast." The respondent did not quarrel with the finding that the afternoon broadcast was patently offensive, but contended that it was not "indecent" within the meaning of the relevant statutes because it contained no prurient appeal. After rejecting respondent's statutory arguments, we confronted its two constitutional arguments: (1) that the Commission's construction of its authority to ban indecent speech was so broad that its order had to be set aside even if the broadcast at issue was unprotected; and (2) that since the recording was not obscene, the First Amendment forbade any abridgment of the right to broadcast it on the radio.

In the portion of the lead opinion not joined by Justices Powell and Blackmun, the plurality stated that the First Amendment does not prohibit all governmental regulation that depends on the content of speech. Accordingly, the availability of constitutional protection for a vulgar and offensive monologue that was not obscene depended on the context of the broadcast. Relying on the premise that "of all forms of communication" broadcasting had received the most limited First Amendment protection, the Court concluded that the ease with which children may obtain access to broadcasts, "coupled with the concerns recognized in *Ginsberg*," justified special treatment of indecent broadcasting.

As with the New York statute at issue in *Ginsberg*, there are significant differences between the order upheld in *Pacifica* and the CDA. First, the order in *Pacifica*, issued by an agency that had been regulating radio stations for decades, targeted a specific broadcast that represented a rather dramatic departure from traditional program content in order to designate when—rather than whether—it would be permissible to air such a program in that particular medium. The CDA's broad categorical prohibitions are not limited to particular times and are not dependent on any evaluation by an agency familiar with the unique characteristics of the Internet. Second, unlike the CDA, the Commission's declaratory order was not punitive; we expressly refused to decide whether the indecent broadcast "would justify a criminal prosecution." Finally, the Commission's order applied to a medium which as a matter of history had "received the most limited First Amendment protection," in large part because warnings could not adequately protect the listener from unexpected program content. The Internet, however, has no comparable history. Moreover, the District Court found that the risk of encountering indecent material by accident is remote because a series of affirmative steps is required to access specific material.

In *Renton*, we upheld a zoning ordinance that kept adult movie theaters out of residential neighborhoods. The ordinance was aimed, not at the content of the films shown in the theaters, but rather at the "secondary effects"—such as crime and deteriorating property values—that these theaters fostered. According to the Government, the CDA is constitutional because it constitutes a sort of "cyberzoning" on the Internet. But the CDA applies broadly to the entire universe of cyberspace. And the purpose of the CDA is to protect children from the primary effects of "indecent" and "patently offensive" speech, rather than any "secondary" effect of such speech. Thus, the CDA is a content-based blanket restriction on speech, and, as such, cannot be "properly analyzed as a form of time, place, and manner regulation."

These precedents, then, surely do not require us to uphold the CDA and are fully consistent with the application of the most stringent review of its provisions.

V

In *Southeastern Promotions, Ltd. v. Conrad*, 420 U.S. 546, 557 (1975), we observed that "each medium of expression may present its own problems." Thus, some of our cases have recognized special justifications for regulation of the broadcast media that are not applicable to other speakers. In these cases, the Court relied on the history of extensive Government regulation of the broadcast medium; the scarcity of available frequencies at its inception; and its "invasive" nature. Those factors are not present in cyberspace. Neither before nor after the enactment of the CDA have the vast democratic forums of the Internet been subject to the type of government supervision and regulation that has attended the broadcast industry. Moreover, the Internet is not as "invasive" as radio or television. The District Court specifically found that "communications over the Internet do not 'invade' an individual's home or appear on one's computer screen unbidden. Users seldom encounter content 'by accident.'" It also found that "almost all sexually explicit images are preceded by warnings as to the content," and cited testimony that "'odds are slim' that a user would come across a sexually explicit sight by accident."

We distinguished *Pacifica* in *Sable*, 492 U.S., at 128, on just this basis. In *Sable*, a company engaged in the business of offering sexually oriented prerecorded telephone messages (popularly known as "dial-a-porn") challenged the constitutionality of an amendment to the Communications Act of 1934 that imposed a blanket prohibition on indecent as well as obscene interstate commercial telephone messages. We held that the statute was constitutional insofar as it applied to obscene messages but invalid as applied to indecent messages. In attempting to justify the complete ban and criminalization of indecent commercial telephone messages, the Government relied on *Pacifica*, arguing that the ban was necessary to prevent children from gaining access to such messages. We agreed that "there is a compelling interest in protecting the physical and psychological well-being of minors" which extended to shielding them from indecent messages that are not obscene by adult standards, but distinguished our "emphatically narrow holding" in *Pacifica* because it did not involve a complete ban and because it involved a different medium of communication. We explained that "the dial-it medium requires the listener to take affirmative steps to receive the communication." "Placing a telephone call," we continued, "is not the same as turning on a radio and being taken by surprise by an indecent message."

Finally, unlike the conditions that prevailed when Congress first authorized regulation of the broadcast spectrum, the Internet can hardly be considered a "scarce" expressive commodity. It provides relatively unlimited, low-cost capacity for communication of all kinds. The Government estimates that "[a]s many as 40 million people use the Internet today, and that figure is expected to grow to 200 million by 1999." This dynamic, multifaceted category of communication includes not only traditional print and news services, but also audio, video, and still images, as well as interactive, real-time dialogue. Through the use of chat rooms, any person with a phone line can become a town crier with a voice that resonates farther than it could from any soapbox. Through the use of Web pages, mail exploders, and newsgroups, the same individual can become a pamphleteer. As the District Court found, "the content on the Internet is as diverse as human thought." We agree with its conclusion that our cases provide no basis for qualifying the level of First Amendment scrutiny that should be applied to this medium.

VI

Regardless of whether the CDA is so vague that it violates the Fifth Amendment, the many ambiguities concerning the scope of its coverage render it problematic for purposes of the First Amendment. For instance, each of the two parts of the CDA uses a different linguistic form. The first uses the word "indecent," while the second speaks of material that "in context, depicts or describes, in terms patently offensive as measured by contemporary community standards, sexual or excretory activities or organs," §223(d). Given the absence of a definition of either term, this difference in language will provoke uncertainty among speakers about how the two standards relate to each other and just what they mean. Could a speaker confidently assume that a serious discussion about birth control practices, homosexuality, the First Amendment issues raised by the Appendix to our *Pacifica* opinion, or the consequences of prison rape would not violate the CDA? This uncertainty undermines the likelihood that the CDA has been carefully tailored to the congressional goal of protecting minors from potentially harmful materials.

The vagueness of the CDA is a matter of special concern for two reasons. First, the CDA is a content-based regulation of speech. The vagueness of such a regulation raises special First Amendment concerns because of its obvious chilling effect on free speech. Second, the CDA is a criminal statute. In addition to the opprobrium and stigma of a criminal conviction, the CDA threatens violators with penalties including up to two years in prison for each act of violation. The severity of criminal sanctions may well cause speakers to remain silent rather than communicate even arguably unlawful words, ideas, and images. As a practical matter, this increased deterrent effect, coupled with the "risk of discriminatory enforcement" of vague regulations, poses greater First Amendment concerns than those implicated by the civil regulation reviewed in *Denver Area Ed. Telecommunications Consortium, Inc. v. FCC*, 518 U.S. 727 (1996).

The Government argues that the statute is no more vague than the obscenity standard this Court established in *Miller v. California*. But that is not so. In *Miller*, this Court reviewed a criminal conviction against a commercial vendor who mailed brochures containing pictures of sexually explicit activities to individuals who had not requested such materials. Having struggled for some time to establish a definition of obscenity, we set forth in *Miller* the test for obscenity that controls to this day: "(a) whether the average person, applying contemporary community standards would find that the work, taken as a whole, appeals to the prurient interest; (b) whether the work depicts or describes, in a patently offensive way, sexual conduct specifically defined by the applicable state law; and (c) whether the work, taken as a whole, lacks serious literary, artistic, political, or scientific value."

Because the CDA's "patently offensive" standard (and, we assume, *arguendo,* its synonymous "indecent" standard) is one part of the three-prong *Miller* test, the Government reasons, it cannot be unconstitutionally vague.

The Government's assertion is incorrect as a matter of fact. The second prong of the *Miller* test—the purportedly analogous standard—contains a critical requirement that is omitted from the CDA: that the proscribed material be "specifically defined by the applicable state law." This requirement reduces the vagueness inherent in the open-ended term "patently offensive" as used in the CDA. Moreover, the *Miller* definition is limited to "sexual conduct," whereas the CDA extends also to include (1) "excretory activities" as well as (2) "organs" of both a sexual and excretory nature.

The Government's reasoning is also flawed. Just because a definition including three limitations is not vague, it does not follow that one of those limitations, standing by itself, is not vague. Each of *Miller*'s additional two prongs—(1) that, taken as a whole, the material appeal to the "prurient" interest, and (2) that it "lac[k] serious literary, artistic, political, or scientific value"—critically limits the uncertain sweep of the obscenity definition. The second requirement is particularly important because, unlike the "patently offensive" and "prurient interest" criteria, it is not judged by contemporary community standards. This "societal value" requirement, absent in the CDA, allows appellate courts to impose some limitations and regularity on the definition by setting, as a matter of law, a national floor for socially redeeming value. The Government's contention that courts will be able to give such legal limitations to the CDA's standards is belied by *Miller*'s own rationale for having juries determine whether material is "patently offensive" according to community standards: that such questions are essentially ones of *fact.*

In contrast to *Miller* and our other previous cases, the CDA thus presents a greater threat of censoring speech that, in fact, falls outside the statute's scope. Given the vague contours of the coverage of the statute, it unquestionably silences some speakers whose messages would be entitled to constitutional protection. That danger provides further reason for insisting that the statute not be overly broad. The CDA's burden on protected speech cannot be justified if it could be avoided by a more carefully drafted statute.

VII

We are persuaded that the CDA lacks the precision that the First Amendment requires when a statute regulates the content of speech. In order to deny minors access to potentially harmful speech, the CDA effectively suppresses a large amount of speech that adults have a constitutional right to receive and to address to one another. That burden on adult speech is unacceptable if less restrictive alternatives would be at least as effective in achieving the legitimate purpose that the statute was enacted to serve.

In evaluating the free speech rights of adults, we have made it perfectly clear that "[s]exual expression which is indecent but not obscene is protected by the First Amendment." Indeed, *Pacifica* itself admonished that "the fact that society may find speech offensive is not a sufficient reason for suppressing it." 438 U.S., at 745.

It is true that we have repeatedly recognized the governmental interest in protecting children from harmful materials. But that interest does not justify an unnecessarily broad suppression of speech addressed to adults. As we have explained, the Government may not "reduc[e] the adult population...to...only what is fit for children." "[R]egardless of the strength of the government's interest" in protecting children, "[t]he level of discourse reaching a mailbox simply cannot be limited to that which would be suitable for a sandbox." *Bolger v. Youngs Drug Products Corp.,* 463 U.S. 60, 74–75 (1983).

The District Court was correct to conclude that the CDA effectively resembles the ban on "dial-a-porn" invalidated in *Sable.* In *Sable,* this Court rejected the argument that we should defer to the congressional judgment that nothing less than a total ban would be effective in preventing enterprising youngsters from gaining access to indecent communications. *Sable* thus made clear that the mere fact that a statutory regulation of speech was enacted for the important purpose of protecting children from exposure to sexually explicit material does not foreclose inquiry into its validity. That inquiry embodies an "overarching commitment" to make sure that Congress has designed its statute to accomplish its purpose "without imposing an unnecessarily great restriction on speech."

In arguing that the CDA does not so diminish adult communication, the Government relies on the incorrect factual premise that prohibiting a transmission whenever it is known that one of its recipients is a minor would not interfere with adult-to-adult communication. The findings of the District Court make clear that this premise is untenable. Given the size of the potential audience for most messages, in the absence of a viable age verification process, the sender must be charged with knowing that one or more minors will likely view it. Knowledge that, for instance, one or more members of a 100-person chat group will be a minor—and therefore that it would be a crime to send the group an indecent message—would surely burden communication among adults.

The District Court found that at the time of trial existing technology did not include any effective method for a sender to prevent minors from obtaining access to its communications on the Internet without also denying access to adults. The Court found no effective way to determine the age of a user who is accessing material through e-mail, mail exploders, newsgroups, or chat rooms. As a practical matter, the Court also found that it would be prohibitively expensive for noncommercial—as well as some commercial—speakers who have Web sites to verify that their users are adults. These limitations must inevitably curtail a significant amount of adult communication on the Internet. By contrast, the District Court found that "[d]espite its limitations, currently available *user-based* software suggests that a reasonably effective method by which *parents* can prevent their children from accessing sexually explicit and other material which *parents* may believe is inappropriate for their children will soon be widely available."

The breadth of the CDA's coverage is wholly unprecedented. Unlike the regulations upheld in *Ginsberg* and *Pacifica,* the scope of the CDA is not limited to commercial speech or commercial entities. Its open-ended prohibitions embrace all nonprofit entities and individuals posting indecent messages or displaying them on their own computers in the presence of minors. The general, undefined terms "indecent" and "patently offensive" cover large amounts of nonpornographic material with serious educational or other value. Moreover, the "community standards" criterion as applied to the Internet means that any communication available to a nation wide audience will be judged by the standards of the community most likely to be offended by the message. The regulated subject matter includes any of the seven "dirty words" used in the *Pacifica* monologue, the use of which the Government's expert acknowledged could constitute a felony. It may also extend to discussions about prison rape or safe sexual practices, artistic images that include nude subjects, and arguably the card catalog of the Carnegie Library.

For the purposes of our decision, we need neither accept nor reject the Government's submission that the First Amendment does not forbid a blanket prohibition on all "indecent" and "patently offensive" messages communicated to a 17-year-old—no matter how much value the message may contain and regardless of parental approval. It is at least clear that the strength of the Government's interest in protecting minors is not equally strong throughout the coverage of this broad statute. Under the CDA, a parent allowing her 17-year-old to use the family computer to obtain information on the Internet that she, in her parental judgment, deems appropriate could face a lengthy prison term. Similarly, a parent who sent his 17-year-old college freshman information on birth control via e-mail could be incarcerated even though neither he, his child, nor anyone in their home community found the material "indecent" or "patently offensive," if the college town's community thought otherwise.

The breadth of this content-based restriction of speech imposes an especially heavy burden on the Government to explain why a less restrictive provision would not be as effective as the CDA. It has not done so. The arguments in this Court have referred to possible alternatives such as requiring that indecent material be "tagged" in a way that facilitates parental control of material coming into their homes, making exceptions for messages with artistic or educational value, providing some tolerance for parental choice, and regulating some portions of the Internet—such as commercial Web sites— differently from others, such as chat rooms. Particularly in the light of the absence of any detailed findings by the Congress, or even hearings addressing the special problems of the CDA, we are persuaded that the CDA is not narrowly tailored if that requirement has any meaning at all.

VIII

In an attempt to curtail the CDA's facial overbreadth, the Government advances three additional arguments for sustaining the Act's affirmative prohibitions:

The Government first contends that, even though the CDA effectively censors discourse on many of the Internet's modalities—such as chat groups, newsgroups, and mail exploders—it is nonetheless constitutional because it provides a "reasonable opportunity" for speakers to engage in the restricted speech on the World Wide Web. This argument is unpersuasive because the CDA regulates speech on the basis of its content. A "time, place, and manner" analysis is therefore inapplicable. It is thus immaterial whether such speech would be feasible on the Web (which, as the Government's own expert acknowledged, would cost up to $10,000 if the speaker's interests were not accommodated by an existing Web site, not including costs for data base management and age verification). The Government's position is equivalent to arguing that a statute could ban leaflets on certain subjects as long as individuals are free to publish books. In invalidating a number of laws that banned leafletting on the streets *regardless of* their content, we explained that "one is not to have the exercise of his liberty of expression in appropriate places abridged on the plea that it may be exercised in some other place." *Schneider v. State of N.J. (Town of Irvington)*, 308 U.S. 147, 163 (1939).

The Government also asserts that the "knowledge" requirement of both §§ 223(a) and (d), especially when coupled with the "specific child" element found in § 223(d), saves the CDA from overbreadth. Because both sections prohibit the dissemination of indecent messages only to persons known to be under 18, the Government argues, it does not require transmitters to "refrain from communicating indecent material to adults; they need only refrain from disseminating such materials to persons they know to be under 18." This argument ignores the fact that most Internet forums—including chat rooms, newsgroups, mail exploders, and the Web—are open to all comers. The Government's assertion that the knowledge requirement somehow protects the communications of adults is therefore untenable. Even the strongest reading of the "specific person" requirement of § 223(d) cannot save the statute. It would confer broad powers of censorship, in the form of a "heckler's veto," upon any opponent of indecent speech who might simply log on and inform the would-be discoursers that his 17-year-old child—a "specific person…under 18 years of age,"—would be present.

Finally, we find no textual support for the Government's submission that material having scientific, educational, or other redeeming social value will necessarily fall outside the CDA's "patently offensive" and "indecent" prohibitions.

IX

The Government's three remaining arguments focus on the defenses provided in § 223(e)(5). First, relying on the "good faith, reasonable, effective, and appropriate actions" provision, the Government suggests that "tagging" provides a defense that saves the constitutionality of the CDA. The suggestion assumes that transmitters may encode their indecent communications in a way that would indicate their contents, thus permitting recipients to block their reception with appropriate software. It is the requirement that the good-faith action must be "effective" that makes this defense illusory. The Government recognizes that its proposed screening software does not currently exist. Even if it did, there is no way to know whether a potential recipient will actually block the encoded material. Without the impossible knowledge that every guardian in America is screening for the "tag," the transmitter could not reasonably rely on its action to be "effective."

For its second and third arguments concerning defenses—which we can consider together—the Government relies on the latter half of § 223(e)(5), which applies when the transmitter has restricted access by requiring use of a verified credit card or adult identification. Such verification is not only technologically available but actually is used by commercial providers of sexually explicit material. These providers, therefore, would be protected by the defense. Under the findings of the District Court, however, it is not economically feasible for most noncommercial speakers to employ such verification. Accordingly, this defense would not significantly narrow the statute's burden on noncommercial speech. Even with respect to the commercial pornographers that would be protected by the defense, the Government failed to adduce any evidence that these verification techniques actually preclude minors from posing as adults. Given that the risk of criminal sanctions "hovers over each content provider, like the proverbial sword of Damocles," the District Court correctly refused to rely on unproven future technology to save the statute. The Government thus failed to prove that the proffered defense would significantly reduce the heavy burden on adult speech produced by the prohibition on offensive displays.

The CDA places an unacceptably heavy burden on protected speech, and the defenses do not constitute the sort of "narrow tailoring" that will save an otherwise patently invalid unconstitutional provision. In *Sable,* we remarked that the speech restriction at issue there amounted to "burn[ing] the house to roast the pig." The CDA, casting a far darker shadow over free speech, threatens to torch a large segment of the Internet community.

X

At oral argument, the Government relied heavily on its ultimate fall-back position: If this Court should conclude that the CDA is insufficiently tailored, it urged, we should save the statute's constitutionality by honoring the severability clause, and construing nonseverable terms narrowly. In only one respect is this argument acceptable. [The Court held that the statute was valid as applied to "obscene" speech, but that apart from this, the government's severability arguments were invalid.]

XI

In this Court, though not in the District Court, the Government asserts that—in addition to its interest in protecting children—its "equally significant" interest in fostering the growth of the Internet provides an independent basis for upholding the constitutionality of the CDA. The Government apparently assumes that the unregulated availability of "indecent" and "patently offensive" material on the Internet is driving countless citizens away from the medium because of the risk of exposing themselves or their children to harmful material.

We find this argument singularly unpersuasive. The dramatic expansion of this new marketplace of ideas contradicts the factual basis of this contention. The record demonstrates that the growth of the Internet has been and continues to be phenomenal. As a matter of constitutional tradition, in the absence of evidence to the contrary, we presume that governmental regulation of the content of speech is more likely to interfere with the free exchange of ideas than to encourage it. The interest in encouraging freedom of expression in a democratic society outweighs any theoretical but unproven benefit of censorship.

For the foregoing reasons, the judgment of the District Court is affirmed. *It is so ordered.*

Notes and Questions

1. Suppose that Congress, in reaction to the Court's decision in *Reno*, decided to try to craft a carefully-drawn measure to protect children from exposure to sexually "indecent" materials on the internet by narrowly focusing on commercial websites, and by refraining from imposing absolute bans? For example, would the requirements of the First Amendment be met if Congress provided criminal penalties for anybody posting sexually-oriented material deemed harmful to children on the basis of community standards unless access to the material was made contingent on some adult identification process such as the presentation of an adult verification code or a credit card? See *Ashcroft v. American Civil Liberties Union*, 124 S.Ct. 2783 (2004), holding that Internet content providers and civil liberties groups were likely to prevail on their claim that the Child Online Protection Act violated the 1st Amendment by burdening adults' access to some protected speech.

2. Congress has continued to be concerned with the accessibility of sexually-oriented material on cable television. One legislative solution was to require that channels carrying such material either be scrambled such that only adult-verified subscribers could access them, or only carried at hours when it was deemed unlikely that minors would be viewing. Is this an appropriate solution, or would the obvious content-based regulation of communication not be deemed narrowly-enough tailored to survive strict scrutiny? See *United States v. Playboy Entertainment Group, Inc.*, 529 U.S. 803 (2000) (held, 5-4, that provision violates 1st Amendment rights of broadcasters and adult viewers).

* * *

When the Supreme Court ruled in *Lawrence v. Texas*, 539 U.S. 558 (2003), that moral objections to homosexual conduct could not provide a legitimate justification for restricting liberty protected by the 1st Amendment, it potentially placed into question half a century of case law development concerning sexually-oriented speech, and particularly the prior holdings that obscene speech enjoyed no constitutional protection. To what extent do laws against the distribution of obscene material rest solely on moral concerns, and under what circumstances might they be subject to constitutional challenge? The following decision constitutes a first tentative answer to this question, subject to consideration in the appellate courts.

United States v. Extreme Associates, Inc.
352 F.Supp.2d 578 (W.D. Pa. 2005)

LANCASTER, District Judge.

This is a criminal prosecution charging nine counts of violating the federal obscenity statutes and one count of conspiracy based on that conduct. 18 U.S.C. §§ 371, 1461, 1462 and 1465. The United States has charged defendants Extreme Associates, Inc., Robert Zicari, and Janet Romano with distribution of obscene material via the mails and the Internet. Defendants have filed a motion to dismiss the indictment arguing that the federal obscenity laws infringe on the rights of liberty and privacy guaranteed by the due process clause of the United States Constitution.

[In a joint stipulation of facts, the parties agreed that the defendants operated a website through which individuals with credit cards could obtain "memberships" entitling them to view obscene film clips on the website and to order obscene films from which the clips were excerpted to be delivered by mail. A postal inspector "joined" the website under an assumed name, viewed the clips, and ordered some of the films. The defendants were indicted for distributing obscene matter over the internet and through the mails, and moved to dismiss, contending the federal obscenity statutes were unconstitutional as applied to them.]

Defendants contend that the federal obscenity statutes are unconstitutional because they infringe on the fundamental rights of liberty and privacy guaranteed by the United States Constitution. Specifically, defendants contend that there is a broad fundamental right to sexual privacy, which encompasses a right to possess and view sexually explicit material in the privacy of one's own home. Defendants argue that this right is not diminished by the fact that the material viewed is without literary or artistic merit or inspires lewd or lascivious thoughts in the mind of the viewer. Defendants contend that this right arises from the holdings in two Supreme Court cases: *Lawrence v. Texas*, 539 U.S. 558 (2003) and *Stanley v. Georgia*, 394 U.S. 557 (1969). Defendants further argue that because the federal obscenity laws place a complete ban on the distribution of materials that an individual has the fundamental right to possess and view in private, the statutes should be subjected to the strict scrutiny test. Finally, defendants contend that the federal obscenity statutes fail both the strict scrutiny test and the rational basis test because, after *Lawrence*, the government can no longer justify legislation with enforcement of a "moral code."

The government contends that because the federal obscenity statutes have withstood constitutional attack for more than thirty-five years, this court lacks the authority to find that they are unconstitutional. On the merits, the government argues that there is no fundamental right involved in this case and that this court should not create a "new" fundamental right to commercially distribute obscene material. According to the government, the Supreme Court did not subject Texas' sodomy law to the strict scrutiny test in *Lawrence*, and therefore, there is no basis to subject the federal obscenity statutes to that exacting level of constitutional scrutiny. Instead, the government argues that the rational basis test should be applied, and that under that test, legitimate governmental interests justify the law.

In 1957 the Supreme Court announced that "obscenity is not within the area of constitutionally protected speech" under the First Amendment. *Roth v. United States*, 354 U.S. 476, 485 (1957). Twelve years later, however, the Supreme Court held that a state could not make the mere private possession of obscene material in one's home a crime. *Stanley v. Georgia*, 394 U.S. 557, 568 (1969). In doing so, the Court did not hold that obscene material had become protected speech. Rather, the Court recognized that freedom of speech goes beyond self-expression and includes the fundamental right to "receive information and ideas regardless of their social worth."

The Supreme Court also determined that the Georgia statute, which criminalized the mere private possession of obscene material, raised a privacy issue as well. The Court stated, "[i]f the First Amendment means anything, it means that a State has no business telling a man, sitting alone in his own house, what books he may read or what films he may watch." To permit the government to do so would support the "...assertion that the State has the right to control the moral content of a person's thoughts. To some, this may be a noble purpose, but it is wholly inconsistent with the philosophy of the First Amendment." Moreover, the Supreme Court explicitly found that this right to read or observe or think about what one pleases in his own home was "fundamental to our scheme of individual liberty."

Although the Georgia statute in *Stanley* prohibited possessing material of a sexually explicit nature, the analysis and result would have been the same had the Georgia statute criminalized the possession of Communist tract literature, or racist hate literature, or a copy of George Orwell's *1984*, or any other material the government deemed inappropriate for citizens to learn or think about. Therefore, *Stanley* represents a unique intersection between the substantive due process clause's protection of personal liberty and privacy and the First Amendment's protection of an individual's right to receive, and consider, information and ideas.

The government correctly notes that after *Stanley* established the right to privately possess obscenity in one's home, the Supreme Court repeatedly refused to recognize a correlative First Amendment right to distribute such material. Each holding, however, was based on the settled rule established in *Roth* that obscenity is not protected speech under the First Amendment. The motion in this case, however, does not raise a First Amendment challenge to the federal obscenity statutes; it raises a substantive due process challenge. The fact that the obscenity statutes have been upheld under one constitutional provision does not mean that they are immune from all constitutional attack.

Neither the Supreme Court nor the Court of Appeals for the Third Circuit has considered a substantive due process challenge to the federal obscenity statutes by a vendor arguing that the laws place an unconstitutional burden, in the form of a complete ban on distribution, on an individual's fundamental right to possess and view what he pleases in his own home, as established in *Stanley.* Therefore, contrary to the government's position, defendants' challenge is not precluded by *Roth*, but is instead guided by cases such as *Stanley, Griswold v. Connecticut, Roe v. Wade*, and *Lawrence v. Texas*.

The Supreme Court relied on a substantive due process analysis to strike down Texas' homosexual sodomy law. The decision opens with the Court's declaration that "[l]iberty protects the person from unwarranted government intrusions into a dwelling or other private places." After a discussion of *Griswold, Eisenstadt, Roe v. Wade* and other right of privacy cases, the Supreme Court found that a person's decisions about what personal relationships, including homosexual relationships, he will have in his own home are not to be controlled or criminalized by the government because the government finds such relationships to be immoral. Instead, the Court deemed such decisions to lie within a "realm of personal liberty which the government may not enter." Because the case involved two consenting adults engaged in sexual activity in the privacy of their own home and not minors, persons who might be coerced or injured, public conduct, or prostitution, the Court found that no state interest - including promoting a moral code - could justify the law's intrusion into the personal and private life of the individuals involved.

In a dissenting opinion joined by Chief Justice Rehnquist and Justice Thomas, Justice Scalia opined that the holding in *Lawrence* calls into question the constitutionality of the nation's obscenity laws, among many other laws based on the state's desire to establish a "moral code" of conduct. *Lawrence*, 539 U.S. at 590 (Scalia, J., dissenting). It is reasonable to assume that these three members of the Court came to this conclusion only after reflection and that the opinion was not merely a result of over-reactive hyperbole by those on the losing side of the argument.

In any event, there are other constitutional scholars who have reached the same conclusion, *i.e.*, that the nation's obscenity laws cannot stand in light of *Lawrence*. Laurence H. Tribe, *Lawrence v. Texas: The "Fundamental Right" that Dare not Speak its Name*, 117 HARV. L. REV. 1893, 1945 (2004) (stating that "...the Court's holding in *Lawrence* is hard to reconcile with retaining the state's authority to ban the distribution to adults of sexually explicit materials identified by, among other things, their supposed appeal to what those in power regard as 'unhealthy' lust, or the state's power to punish adults for enjoying such materials in private, whether alone or in the company of other adults"); James W. Paulsen, *The Significance of Lawrence*, 41 HOUS. LAW. 32, 37 (2004) (stating that, "[a]fter *Lawrence*, any law that can be justified only because 'most people think that sort of thing is immoral' may be in constitutional trouble"); Calvin Massey, *The New Formalism: Requiem for Tiered Scrutiny*, 6 U. Pa. J. Const. L. 945, 964-65 (2004) (noting that obscenity laws will be void under *Lawrence* if the decision stands for the idea that moral disapproval is insufficient justification to infringe upon an individual's liberty); Mark Cenite, *Federalizing or Eliminating Online Obscenity Law as an Alternative to Contemporary Community Standards*, 9 Comm. L. & Pol'y 25, 25 (2004) (stating that First Amendment principles favoring autonomy and the *Lawrence* decision "... point toward elimination of obscenity law entirely"); *see also* Gary D. Allison, *Sanctioning Sodomy: The Supreme Court Liberates Gay Sex and Limits State Power to Vindicate the Moral Sentiments of the People*, 39 Tulsa L. Rev. 95, 145-48 (2003) (noting Justice Scalia's prediction, but stating that *Lawrence* will not serve as the basis to invalidate all "morality" laws; however, upon application of the decision to the area of obscenity laws, the author concludes that after *Lawrence* the government could only proscribe child pornography due to the independent governmental interest in protecting the children involved in its production).

Despite defendants' urging, we do not find that *Lawrence* created a "new" and/or "broad" fundamental right to engage in private sexual conduct. Although the *Lawrence* opinion is mixed, certain language suggests that the Court engaged in a rational basis review of the challenged statute. In that light, it is reasonable to find that the court itself did not consider it was addressing a fundamental right. However, that lack of clarity in *Lawrence* need not be resolved here because we are analyzing the burden that the obscenity laws place on the fundamental rights of privacy and speech of the viewer, which have already been explicitly established in *Stanley v. Georgia.*

The *Lawrence* decision, however, is nevertheless important to this case. It can be reasonably interpreted as holding that public morality is not a legitimate state interest sufficient to justify infringing on adult, private, consensual, sexual conduct even if that conduct is deemed offensive to the general public's sense of morality. Such is the import of *Lawrence* to our decision.

A court may hold a statute unconstitutional either because it is invalid "on its face" or because it is unconstitutional "as applied" to a particular set of circumstances. *Ada v. Guam Soc'y of Obstetricians and Gynecologists,* 506 U.S. 1011, 1012 (1992) (Scalia, J., dissenting). If a statute is unconstitutional as applied, the government may continue to enforce the statute in different circumstances under which it is not unconstitutional. If a statute is unconstitutional on its face, the government may not enforce the statute under any circumstances. A challenger's argument in an as-applied challenge is different from that in a facial challenge. In an as-applied challenge, "the [challenger] contends that application of the statute in the particular context in which he has acted, or in which he proposes to act, would be unconstitutional." Therefore, the constitutional inquiry in an as-applied challenge is limited to the challenger's particular situation. For the reasons that follow, we have considered defendants' challenge to the obscenity statutes to be an as-applied challenge. Under those standards, we find that the obscenity statutes are unconstitutional as applied to the defendants' conduct in this case.

In *Stanley,* the Supreme Court explicitly stated that the right to read, observe, or think about what one pleases in his own home, including obscene material, is "fundamental to our scheme of individual liberty." That principle of law is not in dispute. Nor has it been disputed by the government that this right is burdened by the federal obscenity statutes, which criminalize the distribution of such material. Thus, the statutes are properly subjected to the strict scrutiny test. The statutes do not survive that level of exacting constitutional scrutiny as applied to the facts of this case.

Although the government requested and was granted more time to brief the limited issue of the application of the strict scrutiny test to this case, it has failed to identify a compelling state interest justifying the total ban on distribution of obscene material, even in the form of an "in the alternative" argument. Instead, the government states that the rational basis test should be applied, and that under that test, the dual legitimate state interests of: 1) protecting children from viewing obscene materials; and, 2) protecting unwitting adults from inadvertent exposure to obscene materials, justify a complete ban on its distribution.

A fair reading of the government's brief leads to the conclusion that the government approached this case by focusing on whether the courts have recognized, or should recognize, a fundamental right to commercially distribute obscene material, which is not the issue in this case. As stated above, the issue in this case is whether the federal obscenity statutes place a sustainable burden on an individual's fundamental right, as clearly established in *Stanley,* to read, view, or think what one wants to in the privacy of his own home. Although we could assume that the government concedes that no compelling interest justifies the federal obscenity laws and end our analysis there, we will give the government the benefit of the doubt and analyze its asserted "legitimate" state interests under the strict scrutiny test.

It cannot be seriously disputed that, historically, the government's purpose in completely banning the distribution of sexually explicit obscene material, including to consenting adults, was to uphold the community sense of morality. That is, to prevent, to the extent possible, individuals from entertaining lewd or lustful thoughts stimulated by viewing material that appeals to one's prurient interests. Harboring such thoughts, the government deems, is immoral conduct even when done by consenting adults in private. Indeed, one of, if not the, principal underpinning of *Roth v. U.S.*, in which the Supreme Court held that obscenity is not within the area of constitutionally protected speech, was the Court's unquestioned assumption that such material offends the community sense of morality. *Roth*, 354 U.S. at 485 ("…any benefit that may be derived from [lewd and obscene material] is clearly outweighed by the social interest in order and morality"). After *Lawrence*, however, upholding the public sense of morality is not even a legitimate state interest that can justify infringing one's liberty interest to engage in consensual sexual conduct in private. Therefore, this historically asserted state interest certainly cannot rise to the level of a compelling interest, as is required under the strict scrutiny test.

Even if the government's asserted interest in keeping unwitting adults from inadvertently viewing this material could rise to the level of being a compelling state interest, the obscenity laws, as applied to these defendants, are not narrowly tailored to advance that interest. As such, they would nevertheless fail the strict scrutiny test. Access to the video clips for which defendants are being prosecuted is limited to those people who: 1) access defendants' website; 2) join the members-only section of defendants' website, which requires a name and address; 3) pay a membership fee, which requires a credit card; 4) are issued a password; 5) use the password to gain access to the obscene material; and, finally, 6) either view or download the material that they wish to view on a computer. Similarly, the video tapes for which defendants are being prosecuted in this case could only be accessed by an individual who: 1) accessed defendants' website; 2) reviewed the inventory of videos that were for sale; 3) selected a title to order; 4) inputted personal information, such as a name and an address; 5) submitted credit card information for payment; and 6) executed an order. Therefore, due to the Internet access technology used by these defendants to distribute the video tapes and video clips charged in this case, the interest of protecting unwitting adults from inadvertent exposure to their material is not advanced at all, let alone by the least restrictive means possible. That is, defendants' mechanism of distributing the materials charged in this case dictate that only those individuals who want to see defendants' films, indeed, want to see them badly enough that they are willing to pay to see them, are able to do so. Therefore, because of the manner in which the charged video tapes and video clips are accessed, the federal obscenity statutes, as applied to these defendants, cannot withstand analysis under the strict scrutiny test.

We are not persuaded by the government's argument that a total ban is necessary because, even if the material is initially received for private use, it might later be distributed for viewing other than in private. First, the government can create laws that punish those who distribute obscene material to be viewed other than in private. Second, there are many activities that the law recognizes a person may constitutionally engage in in his home that could be made criminal if done in public. For instance, a person is free to drink alcohol to the point of inebriation in his home, but could be cited for public intoxication if he left the house. A person can possess a firearm without a license in his home, but could be cited for carrying that same item in public. A person can walk around naked in his home, but could be cited for public indecency if he left his house in that condition.

Finally, the government asserts that protecting minors from exposure to obscene material is a governmental interest justifying a total ban on its distribution. We find that even if this interest qualifies as a compelling one, as applied to this case, the federal obscenity statutes are not narrowly drawn to serve that interest. As a general rule, the Supreme Court has not allowed the fact that a determined minor might access inappropriate materials to justify a complete ban on their distribution, thus reducing the adult population to only what is fit for children. *Denver Area Educ. Telecommunications Consortium, Inc. v. Federal Comm. Comm'n*, 518 U.S. 727, 759 (1996); *see also United States v. Playboy Entertainment Group, Inc.*, 529 U.S. 803, 814 (2000) ("the objective of shielding children does not suffice to support a blanket ban if the protection can be obtained by a less restrictive alternative"). Rather, along with such appropriate restrictions imposed by the government, such as age requirements, parents are expected to control their children's access to inappropriate items, such as alcohol, tobacco, firearms, and sexually explicit movies. As the Supreme Court recognized in *Ashcroft v. American Civil Liberties Union*, a total ban on the distribution of materials cannot be justified on the assumption that parental supervision of their minor children's activities is an ineffective means of protecting minors from viewing inappropriate material. *Ashcroft v. American Civil Liberties Union*, 124 S.Ct. 2783, 2793 (2004) (citing *Playboy*, 529 U.S. at 824).

In addition to this case law, upon application of the strict scrutiny test to the facts of this case, a complete ban on the distribution of obscene materials for the purpose of keeping them out of the hands of minors is not the least restrictive means of achieving that goal. There are numerous ways to protect minors from exposure to obscene materials that are less restrictive than a complete ban on the distribution of such material to consenting adults. Access by minors can be limited by regulations that direct when, where and how obscene materials can be displayed commercially and sold. For instance, exposure to minors could be controlled by establishing age limits, as is done with innumerable other products in the marketplace that are deemed inappropriate for minors, such as alcohol, tobacco, and firearms. In addition, computer software is available that parents, or other supervising adults, can install on their computers that would effectively filter sexually explicit material when minors are surfing the Internet. This software allows the adult user to disable the filtering device when the computer is being used by an adult, if desired. Such software was recognized as an effective means of shielding minors from exposure to inappropriate material by the Supreme Court in *United States v. American Library Ass'n, Inc.*, 539 U.S. 194 (2003). In that case, the Supreme Court upheld, against a First Amendment challenge, the Children's Internet Protection Act, which provided that a public library may not receive federal assistance to provide Internet access unless it installed filtering software to block obscene or pornographic images from access by minors. The Court noted that the library had the ability to easily disable the filter upon the request of an adult patron who wished to view material inappropriate for minors, thereby making the restriction constitutional.

Finally, as was required by these defendants, prepayment with credit cards is another effective way to restrict access to inappropriate materials by minors. Significantly, the Federal Communications Commission has already determined that requiring prepayment by credit card effectively restricts minors' access to live "dial-a-porn" messages. The Commission reasoned that because credit cards are not routinely issued to minors, services which require credit card payment are usually limited to adults. The Commission assumed that minors who are issued credits cards in their own names, such as those who are issued a supplementary card to a parent's account, are supervised by adults as to their use of the cards. Defendants themselves have restricted access to the charged materials by minors by requiring that credit card information be entered before viewing the video clips, or ordering the video tapes.

Assuming that protecting minors from exposure to obscene materials is a compelling interest, the federal obscenity statutes, which completely ban the distribution of all such material, including to consenting adults, are not narrowly drawn to advance that interest. Therefore, the federal obscenity statutes, as applied to defendants, do not survive the strict scrutiny test.

Because the federal obscenity statutes are unconstitutional as applied, defendants' indictment must be dismissed.

Questions

Are you persuaded by the Court's contention that federal obscenity laws are subject to strict scrutiny, and that "morality" may not be cited as a legitimate state interest after *Lawrence*? Can you think of arguments that the government might make on appeal to provide alternative justifications for the obscenity laws and thus escape the "morality" problem?

C. Speaking Out

Advocacy, or political speech, is at the core of the speech protected by the First Amendment, while commercial speech is of lesser value entitled to lesser protection. Somewhere in between might come speech intended to enlighten or inform with no explicit purpose of advocating or selling. This section contains cases that present speech about homosexuality in different contexts: discipline of a public employee for testifying at a public hearing on homosexuality; adoption of a legislative policy barring employment of public school teachers who "advocate" for or "promote" homosexuality; exclusion of advertising appealing to lesbian and gay consumers from the "yellow pages" telephone directory; and municipal restrictions on a political demonstration. In each instance, the case should be viewed as a springboard for discussion of competing values of communication and public order.

Van Ooteghem v. Gray
628 F.2d 488 (5th Cir. 1980),
cert. denied, 455 U.S. 909 (1982)

GOLDBERG, Circuit Judge:

I. The Factual Background

In January 1975, plaintiff John Van Ooteghem was hired by defendant Hartsell Gray, the Treasurer of Harris County, Texas, to serve first as Cashier Assistant County Treasurer, and later as Assistant County Treasurer. Van Ooteghem performed his job in a professional manner: he was recognized to be both hard-working and quite brilliant. Accordingly, Treasurer Gray treated the plaintiff with the respect due to a professional: Van Ooteghem was allowed to set his own hours and to take time off as needed.

On July 28, 1975, Van Ooteghem informed Gray that he was a homosexual and, shortly thereafter, related his plans to address the Commissioners Court on the subject of the civil rights of homosexuals. On July 31, 1975, Gray forwarded a letter to Van Ooteghem which purported to restrict the latter to his office between the hours of eight a. m. and twelve noon and from one p.m. until five p.m., Monday through Friday. These hours corresponded to the times during which citizens were allowed to address the Commissioners Court. Van Ooteghem was instructed to acknowledge his agreement with the new schedule by signing the letter; upon his refusal to do so, Van Ooteghem was dismissed. In response, Van Ooteghem filed suit…alleging that he was dismissed as Assistant County Treasurer in violation of his constitutional right to free speech.

II. The Constitutional Violation

While it is true that Van Ooteghem, a nontenured employee, could have been fired for no reason whatsoever, it is also true that no public employee can be dismissed from his job for a constitutionally infirm reason. No governmental benefit can be denied for a reason that infringes constitutionally protected interests, including freedom of speech. In assessing whether Van Ooteghem's dismissal constituted a violation of his First Amendment right to free speech, the district court was faced with a tripart inquiry:

1. Was Van Ooteghem's speech to the Commissioners Court a "substantial" or "motivating" factor in his being dismissed;

2. Was this speech constitutionally protected; and

3. Would Van Ooteghem have been fired, in the absence of his decision to address the Commissioners Court?

The court below decided each of these three questions in favor of Van Ooteghem and we have been asked by appellant to review all three findings. But our review is no easy task as substantial confusion exists as to the proper scope of appellate review and the standards to be employed in addressing each of these three questions.

Many appellate decisions — especially in Title VII discrimination suits — have characterized the issue of an employer's motivation in dismissing an employee as one of ultimate fact, subject to plenary review. On the other hand, recent Supreme Court cases in the area have treated the question of the employer's motivation as one of "subsidiary" fact, subject only to "clearly erroneous" review. In the majority of cases, the appellate court never articulates the standard it is employing in reviewing this question.…

Both parties in this action admit that Van Ooteghem's insistence on addressing the Commissioners Court (which could only occur during the normal working day) precipitated the dismissal. However, the two sides characterize this one issue quite differently. Appellant argues that the event represented clear insubordination by an employee in unilaterally choosing to violate assigned working hours. Appellee responds that the institution of assigned hours and the subsequent dismissal for their breach were aimed solely at stymieing Van Ooteghem's free speech. The district court agreed with Van Ooteghem, finding that his speech to the Commissioners Court was a substantial factor in the decision to dismiss.

In making this finding, the district court was faced with a clear factual choice: was Van Ooteghem fired for his mere absence from work regardless of the purpose of this absence, or, alternatively, was the establishment of set working hours and the dismissal for their violation an attempt to prevent and punish his decision to speak to a political body on a controversial, political issue? Pursuant to Federal Rule of Civil Procedure 52, the district court's finding on this factual issue cannot be set aside absent clear error.

We cannot say that the trial judge's finding that Van Ooteghem's speech to the Commissioners Court was a substantial or motivating factor in his dismissal was clearly erroneous. Immediately after Van Ooteghem's announcement of his plan to address the Commissioners Court, Gray imposed a time schedule restricting Van Ooteghem to his office between set hours. Although the time schedule did not appear to be overly burdensome on its face, the new regulation was completely inconsistent with the professionalism that had previously typified Van Ooteghem's relationship with Gray and the Treasurer's Office. Van Ooteghem's compliance with the schedule would have necessitated the abandonment of his plan to address the Commissioners Court. The stipulated facts provide no basis from which any justification for the new schedule can be reasonably inferred, other than the desire to thwart Van Ooteghem's lobbying on behalf of homosexuals.

Having concluded that Van Ooteghem's speech was a substantial factor in his dismissal, we turn to the second part of our inquiry — whether the speech was constitutionally protected. The applicable test originates from the Supreme Court's opinion in *Pickering v. Board of Education*, 391 U.S. 563, 568 (1968):

> The problem in any case is to arrive at a balance between the interests of the (employee), as a citizen, in commenting upon matters of public concern and the interest of the State, as an employer, in promoting the efficiency of the public services it performs through its employees.

Employing this test, the district court concluded that, on balance, Van Ooteghem's address was constitutionally protected.

We regard the ultimate determination of whether an individual's speech was "constitutionally protected" to be a question of law. However, in balancing the interests discussed in *Pickering* in order to assess the protected nature of a given speech, an appellate court is constrained, absent clear error, to follow the trial court's findings as to the amount of disruption in the workplace caused by the employee's speech. In the present case, the trial court found that Van Ooteghem's speech did not significantly interfere with the operation of the Treasury nor did it impede Van Ooteghem's performance of his daily duties. Based on the stipulated facts of this case, we cannot find these conclusions to be clearly erroneous.

Having accepted the trial court's finding as to the insignificance of the disruption caused by Van Ooteghem's speech, we are clearly led to the conclusion that, as a matter of law, Van Ooteghem's speech was "constitutionally protected." The state cannot prevent the speech of its citizen absent a compelling state interest. In the employment context, this compelling state interest standard is satisfied only upon proof that the regulation of speech was necessary to prevent "a material and substantial interference" with the operation of the public department. *Hastings v. Bonner*, 578 F.2d 136 (5th Cir. 1978). Gray's imposition of a restricted schedule was not justified by the need to prevent a material and substantial interference with the Treasury. It may be true that some treasury workers, or Gray himself, found the prospect of an employee addressing the Commissioners Court on homosexual rights to be distressing. However, the ability of a member of a disfavored class to express his views on civil rights publicly and without hesitation — no matter how personally offensive to his employer or majority of his co-employees — lies at the core of the Free Speech Clause of the First Amendment.[1] Thus, the type of disturbance possibly present here, as a matter of law, cannot present a "substantial and material interference."

Up to this point, we have concluded that Van Ooteghem's constitutionally protected speech was a substantial factor in his dismissal. While it is clear that a dismissal of an employee, which is substantially based on protected speech, constitutes a violation of the Constitution, the Supreme Court has recently concluded that such a violation does not justify remedial action[2] absent proof that "but for" the protected speech the employee would not have been dismissed. *Mt. Healthy City School District v. Doyle*, 429 U.S. 274 (1977). The Court considered the issue of causation to be one of fact, and remanded the *Mt. Healthy* case for a determination whether the employee in that case would have been dismissed absent the protected conduct.

In the case at bar, the district court found that Van Ooteghem would not have been dismissed but for his speech to the Commissioners Court. We cannot say that such a finding was clearly erroneous. Van Ooteghem was shown to be brilliant and hard working. The record is absolutely devoid of any collateral justification for his discharge.

> [A substantial portion of the opinion, dealing with the technical questions of whether Gray or the government should bear the cost of damages and the amount of attorneys fees to be awarded to Van Ooteghem, is omitted here.]

Defendant Hartsell Gray, while acting in his official capacity, dismissed plaintiff John Van Ooteghem in violation of the latter's right to free speech. Damages were properly assessed against Harris County. Finding no error in the proceedings below on the issues of liability and damages, we affirm those sections of the lower court's opinion. The district court failed to make adequate findings in awarding attorney's fees. We vacate the award of $7,500 in attorney's fees and remand the case for reconsideration of this one issue.

REAVLEY, Circuit Judge, specially concurring:

...I cannot agree with the majority's conclusion in part II of the opinion that the balancing test enunciated by the Supreme Court in *Pickering* has somehow been transformed or "refined" into a compelling state interest test by the Court's subsequent decisions...

Branti v. Finkel and *Elrod v. Burns* involved discharges of governmental employees for patronage reasons. In each case, the Court clearly indicated that when political patron-

---

1. In affirming the district court's finding that Van Ooteghem's speech was constitutionally protected, we add a note of caution concerning the test, first announced in Pickering, as to whether speech is "constitutionally protected." Since the formulation of the Pickering test in 1968, the Supreme Court has refined the analysis employed to accommodate the interests of the State and those of its citizenry under the First Amendment. Although the court in Pickering, pursued this inquiry in terms of whether the speech in question was, "on balance", "constitutionally protected", subsequent cases have clearly established that the analysis is more properly phrased as to whether the government's regulation of constitutionally-protected speech is justified by a compelling state interest. See, e. g.; Branti v. Finkel, 100 S.Ct. at 1293. Elrod v. Burns, 427 U.S. 347 (1976); Buckley v. Valeo, 424 U.S. 1, 64–65 (1976).

2. It is likely that the Supreme Court would permit an award of nominal damages to rectify a constitutional violation that was not proven to be the cause of the dismissal. Cf. Carey v. Piphus, 435 U.S. 247 (1978) (nominal damages recoverable for violation of procedural due process in the absence of proof of actual damages).

age is practiced the First Amendment rights of belief and association are restricted. In these cases, the Court held that in order for government to impose a restriction on public employment based on party identification, the restriction must survive "exacting scrutiny," which is synonymous with the "compelling state interest" test.

In this case, however, we deal not with a governmental employee's rights of belief and association, but with his right of free speech. The Supreme Court has chosen to employ different levels of judicial scrutiny with respect to a government's restrictions on its employees' First Amendment rights: the constitutionality of an impairment on a public employee's rights of belief and association is determined by applying the compelling state interest test, while the constitutionality of an impairment on his right of speech is determined by application of a balancing test....I fail to find any mention, either express or implied, of a refinement or metamorphosis of the *Pickering* balancing test into a compelling state interest analysis; instead,...the Court restates the *Pickering* test without modification.[3]....

The Court, by employing different standards to test governmental action that interferes with public employees' First Amendment rights, apparently differentiates between the primacy of the values protected by the rights of belief and association on one hand and the right of speech on the other. Freedom of "political belief and association constitute the core of those activities protected by the First Amendment." *Elrod v. Burns*, 427 U.S. at 356. They are the keystone rights of the First Amendment — the most preferred of the preferred rights. A public employee's belief and association rights rarely would result in a material and substantial interference with the interest of government "in promoting the efficiency of the public services it performs through its employees." *Pickering v. Board of Education*, 391 U.S. at 568. However, the possibility for such interference is greater when the public employee transmits his beliefs in the form of speech.[4] Therefore, it is appropriate that a more lenient — from the governmental employer's perspective — balancing test is applied to restraints on public employees' speech, while a more stringent compelling state interest test is applied to restraints on their rights of belief and association.

The imposition of the compelling state interest test to the area of public employee free speech would work too onerous a burden on the governmental employer. Under the compelling state interest test, the burden is on the government to show the existence of a paramount, vital or compelling interest in conditioning a public employee's continued employment on a restraint of his First Amendment rights, which will further "some

---

3. It is significant to note the following language from Givhan, 439 U.S. at 415 n.4: "Although the First Amendment's protection of government employees extends to private as well as public expression, striking the Pickering balance in each context may involve different considerations. When a teacher speaks publicly, it is generally the content of his statements that must be assessed to determine whether they 'in any way either impeded the teacher's proper performance of his daily duties in the classroom or...interfered with the regular operation of the schools generally.' Pickering v. Board of Education, 391 U.S. at 572–73. Private expression, however, may in some situations bring additional factors to the Pickering calculus. When a government employee personally confronts his immediate superior, the employing agency's institutional efficiency may be threatened not only by the content of the employee's message, but also by the manner, time, and place in which it is delivered."

4. I recognize that association is to some extent the outward indicia of belief, as is speech. Association, however, involves subjective elements as well, unlike speech which is purely objective. I also recognize that the line between association and speech is fine and often difficult to discern. Nonetheless, the Supreme Court has decided to test restraints on these rights with different standards. It is not our prerogative to disregard the Court's decision.

vital government end by a means that is least restrictive of freedom of belief and association in achieving that end, and the benefit gained must outweigh the loss of constitutionally protected rights." *Elrod v. Burns*, 427 U.S. at 362–63. A compelling state interest is most often present when the regulated conduct, normally protected by the First Amendment, poses "some substantial threat to public safety, peace or order." *Sherbert v. Verner*, 374 U.S. at 403....

I conclude that Van Ooteghem's speech was constitutionally protected under the balancing test of *Pickering*. In balancing the interests of Van Ooteghem in commenting on matters of public concern against the interest of Harris County as an employer in promoting the efficiency of public services performed by the county treasurer's office, I look to the values of the First Amendment in "having free and unhindered debate on matters of public importance," *Pickering*, 391 U.S. at 573, and whether addressing the commissioners court would "substantially and materially interfere" with the discharge of the duties and responsibilities inherent in Van Ooteghem's employment. The district court found that Van Ooteghem's "temporary absence to address the Commissioners Court could not have substantially impeded the functioning of the Treasury." I agree with the majority that this finding is not "clearly erroneous." On this basis I concur in the judgment of the court.

Notes and Questions

1. Subsequent to this decision, the Supreme Court adopted a narrower view of protected speech by public employees. In *Connick v. Myers*, 461 U.S. 138 (1983), the Court held that there was little, if any, First Amendment protection for an assistant district attorney who had circulated a questionnaire within the district attorney's office suggesting criticism of various internal personnel policies:

> *Pickering*, its antecedents, and its progeny lead us to conclude that if Myers' questionnaire cannot be fairly characterized as constituting speech on a matter of public concern, it is unnecessary for us to scrutinize the reasons for her discharge. When employee expression cannot be fairly considered as relating to any matter of political, social, or other concern to the community, government officials should enjoy wide latitude in managing their offices, without intrusive oversight by the judiciary in the name of the First Amendment.... Whether an employee's speech addresses a matter of public concern must be determined by the content, form, and context of a given statement, as revealed by the whole record.

2. Given the narrower view of *Connick v. Myers*, how do you think the following case would be decided?

> Marjorie Rowland, a non-tenured guidance counselor at Stebbins High School in Montgomery County, Ohio, was suspended with pay for the duration of her one-year contract after she confided in a co-worker, and told a student who had come to her for counseling, that she was bisexual. A federal trial judge enjoined her suspension and she was reassigned to a position without student contact. At the end of the year, her contract was not renewed. Rowland claims that her discharge violates First Amendment rights of free speech.

See *Rowland v. Mad River Local School District*, 730 F.2d 444 (6th Cir. 1984), cert. denied, 470 U.S. 1009 (1985)(Dissent by Brennan and Marshall).

* * *

As the lesbian and gay rights movement became more visible in the United States during the 1970s and municipalities began to debate proposals for ordinances forbidding discrimination on the basis of sexual orientation, opponents of such legislation began to mobilize to preserve "traditional values." One of their vehicles was the process of initiative and referendum, either to repeal non-discrimination laws—as was first done in Dade County, Florida, in 1977, under the leadership of Anita Bryant—or to attempt to enact laws specifically authorizing discrimination—as was attempted in California in 1980 through the Briggs Initiative, Proposition 6. Proposition 6 authorized California school districts to discharge teachers who were known to be gay or to have taken public stands of "advocating or promoting" homosexuality. The hard fought referendum campaign became embroiled in national presidential politics, as both candidates for the presidency came out in opposition. Proposition 6 was narrowly defeated, but the Oklahoma legislature subsequently enacted a "clone" of Proposition 6 as a state law. A legal challenge was promptly filed:

National Gay Task Force v. Board of Education of City of Oklahoma City
729 F.2d 1270 (10th Cir. 1984),
affirmed, 470 U.S. 903 (1985)*

LOGAN, Circuit Judge.

The National Gay Task Force (NGTF), whose membership includes teachers in the Oklahoma public school system, filed this action in the district court challenging the facial constitutional validity of Okla.Stat. tit. 70, sec. 6-103.15. The district court held that the statute was constitutionally valid....

The challenged statute provides:

A. As used in this section:

1. 'Public homosexual activity' means the commission of an act defined in Section 886 of Title 21 of the Oklahoma Statutes, if such act is:

a. committed with a person of the same sex, and

b. indiscreet and not practiced in private;

2. 'Public homosexual conduct' means advocating, soliciting, imposing, encouraging or promoting public or private homosexual activity in a manner that creates a substantial risk that such conduct will come to the attention of school children or school employees; and

3. 'Teacher' means a person as defined in Section 1-116 of Title 70 of the Oklahoma Statutes.

B. In addition to any ground set forth in Section 6-103 of Title 70 of the Oklahoma Statutes, a teacher, student teacher or a teachers' aide may be refused employment, or reemployment, dismissed, or suspended after a finding that the teacher or teachers' aide has:

---

* Affirmed without opinion by equally divided Supreme Court.

SEXUAL EXPRESSION, FREE SPEECH AND ASSOCIATION

1. Engaged in public homosexual conduct or activity; and

2. Has been rendered unfit, because of such conduct or activity, to hold a position as a teacher, student teacher or teachers' aide.

C. The following factors shall be considered in making the determination whether the teacher, student teacher or teachers' aide has been rendered unfit for his position:

1. The likelihood that the activity or conduct may adversely affect students or school employees;

2. The proximity in time or place the activity or conduct to the teacher's, student teacher's or teachers' aide's official duties;

3. Any extenuating or aggravating circumstances; and

4. Whether the conduct or activity is of a repeated or continuing nature which tends to encourage or dispose school children toward similar conduct or activity.

The trial court held that the statute reaches protected speech but upheld the constitutionality of the statute by reading a "material and substantial disruption" test into it. We disagree. The statute proscribes protected speech and is thus facially overbroad, and we cannot read into the statute a "material and substantial disruption" test. Therefore, we reverse the judgment of the trial court.

I

We see no constitutional problem in the statute's permitting a teacher to be fired for engaging in "public homosexual activity." Section 6-103.15 defines "public homosexual activity" as the commission of an act defined in Okla.Stat. tit. 21, sec. 886, that is committed with a person of the same sex and is indiscreet and not practiced in private. In support of their argument that this provision violates their members' right of privacy, plaintiff cites *Baker v. Wade*, 553 F.Supp. 1121 (N.D.Tex. 1982), and *New York v. Onofre*, 51 N.Y.2d 476 (1980), cert. denied, 451 U.S. 987 (1981). Both of those cases held that the constitution protects consensual, noncommercial sexual acts in private between adults. *Baker* and *Onofre* are inapplicable to the instant case. Section 6-103.15 does not punish acts performed in private. Thus, the right of privacy, whatever its scope in regard to homosexual acts, is not implicated.

The trial court correctly rejected plaintiff's contention that the Oklahoma statute is vague in regard to "public homosexual activity." In *Village of Hoffman Estates v. The Flipside, Hoffman Estates, Inc.*, 455 U.S. 489 (1982), the Court outlined the doctrines of facial overbreadth and vagueness. Regarding vagueness the Court said:

A law that does not reach constitutionally protected conduct and therefore satisfies the overbreadth test may nevertheless be challenged on its face as unduly vague, in violation of due process. To succeed, however, the complainant must demonstrate that the law is impermissibly vague in all of its applications.

Plaintiff makes no such showing. The Oklahoma cases construing the "crime against nature" statute have clearly defined the acts that the statute proscribes.[1]

---

1. Section 886 provides: "Every person who is guilty of the detestable and abominable crime against nature, committed with mankind or with a beast, is punishable by imprisonment in the

Plaintiff also argues that the statute violates its members' right to equal protection of the law. We cannot find that a classification based on the choice of sexual partners is suspect, especially since only four members of the Supreme Court have viewed gender as a suspect classification. *Frontiero v. Richardson*, 411 U.S. 677 (1973). Thus something less than a strict scrutiny test should be applied here. Surely a school may fire a teacher for engaging in an indiscreet public act of oral or anal intercourse. We also agree that the district court correctly rejected the Establishment Clause claim.

II

The part of sec. 6-103.15 that allows punishment of teachers for "public homosexual conduct" does present constitutional problems. To be sure, this is a facial challenge, and facial challenges based on First Amendment overbreadth are "strong medicine" and should be used "sparingly and only as a last resort." Nonetheless, invalidation is an appropriate remedy in the instant case because this portion of sec. 6-103.15 is overbroad, is "not readily subject to a narrowing construction by the state courts," and "its deterrent effect on legitimate expression is both real and substantial." Also, we must be especially willing to invalidate a statute for facial overbreadth when, as here, the statute regulates "pure speech."

Section 6-103.15 allows punishment of teachers for "public homosexual conduct," which is defined as "advocating, soliciting, imposing, encouraging or promoting public or private homosexual activity in a manner that creates a substantial risk that such conduct will come to the attention of school children or school employees." The First Amendment protects "advocacy" even of illegal conduct except when "advocacy" is "directed to inciting or producing imminent lawless action and is likely to incite or produce such action." The First Amendment does not permit someone to be punished for advocating illegal conduct at some indefinite future time.

"Encouraging" and "promoting," like "advocating," do not necessarily imply incitement to imminent action. A teacher who went before the Oklahoma legislature or appeared on television to urge the repeal of the Oklahoma anti-sodomy statute would be "advocating," "promoting," and "encouraging" homosexual sodomy and creating a substantial risk that his or her speech would come to the attention of school children or school employees if he or she said, "I think it is psychologically damaging for people with homosexual desires to suppress those desires. They should act on those desires and should be legally free to do so." Such statements, which are aimed at legal and social change, are at the core of First Amendment protections.... [T]he statute by its plain terms is not easily susceptible of a narrowing construction. The Oklahoma legislature chose the word "advocacy" despite the Supreme Court's interpretation of that word... Finally, the deterrent effect of sec. 6-103.15 is both real and substantial. It applies to all teachers, substitute teachers, and teachers aides in Oklahoma. To protect their jobs they

---

penitentiary not exceeding ten (10) years." The Oklahoma Court of Criminal Appeals has held that sec. 886 proscribes oral and anal copulation. In *Wainwright v. Stone*, 414 U.S. 21 (1973), the Court held that an almost identical Florida statute was not unconstitutionally vague because the Florida courts had specified that the statute applied to oral and anal copulation. "When a state statute has been construed to forbid identifiable conduct so that 'interpretation by [the state court] puts these words in the statute as definitely as if it had been so amended by the legislature,' claims of impermissible vagueness must be judged in that light."

must restrict their expression. Thus, the proscription of advocating, encouraging, or promoting homosexual activity is unconstitutionally overbroad.

We recognize that a state has interests in regulating the speech of teachers that differ from its interests in regulating the speech of the general citizenry. *Pickering v. Board of Education*, 391 U.S. 563 (1968). But a state's interests outweigh a teacher's interests only when the expression results in a material or substantial interference or disruption in the normal activities of the school. See *Tinker v. Des Moines Independent Community School District*, 393 U.S. 503 (1969). This Court has held that a teacher's First Amendment rights may be restricted only if "the employer shows that some restriction is necessary to prevent the disruption of official functions or to insure effective performance by the employee." Defendant has made no such showing.

The statute declares that a teacher may be fired under sec. 6-103.15 only if there is a finding of "unfitness" and lists factors that are to be considered in determining "unfitness"…An adverse effect on students or other employees is the only factor among those listed that is even related to a material and substantial disruption. And although a material and substantial disruption is an adverse effect, many adverse effects are not material and substantial disruptions. The statute does not require that the teacher's public utterance occur in the classroom. Any public statement that would come to the attention of school children, their parents, or school employees that might lead someone to object to the teacher's social and political views would seem to justify a finding that the statement "may adversely affect" students or school employees. The statute does not specify the weight to be given to any of the factors listed. An adverse effect is apparently not even a prerequisite to a finding of unfitness. A statute is saved from a challenge to its overbreadth only if it is "readily subject" to a narrowing construction. It is not within this Court's power to construe and narrow state statutes. The unfitness requirement does not save sec. 6-103.15 from its unconstitutional overbreadth.

III

The parts of §6-103.15 that deal with "public homosexual conduct" can be severed from the rest of the statute without creating a result that the legislature did not intend or contemplate. We reverse the judgment of the district court, holding that the statute, insofar as it punishes "homosexual conduct," as that phrase is defined in the statute to include "advocating…encouraging or promoting public or private homosexual activity" is unconstitutional. We also hold that the unconstitutional portion is severable from the part of the statute that proscribes "homosexual activity," and we find that portion constitutional.

BARRETT, Circuit Judge, dissenting:

I would affirm the district court's finding that 70 O.S. sec. 6-103.15 passes constitutional muster on every "front" challenged. The majority opinion renders the statute ineffective. It upholds the sanctions of the statute only if there is evidence proving that a teacher has engaged in "public homosexual activity" defined in 70 O.S. §6-103.15(A.)(1.)(a.) and (b.).

The "punishment" referred to in the majority opinion which the majority holds may not be imposed on Oklahoma teachers is refusal of employment or reemployment, or dismissal or suspension if a teacher advocates, solicits, imposes, encourages or promotes "Public homosexual activity" (which, by specific reference to the Oklahoma criminal code is distinctly identified as "the unnatural, perverse, detestable and abominable act of sodomy") in a manner that creates a substantial risk that such conduct will come to the attention of school children or school employees.

It is fundamental that state legislative bodies, in the exercise of state police power, may enact reasonable regulations in the interest of public health, safety, morals and welfare over persons within state limits. Oklahoma has, by enactment of the subject statute, endeavored to protect its school children and school employees from any teacher who advocates, solicits, encourages or promotes public or private homosexual activity pinpointed as the commission of the unnatural and detestable act of sodomy. 21 Okla.Stat.Ann. sec. 886 entitled "Crime against nature" provides: "Every person who is guilty of the detestable and abominable crime against nature, committed with mankind or with a beast, is punishable by imprisonment in the penitentiary not exceeding ten (10) years." Oklahoma has held that this section is not unconstitutionally vague even though it is general in its terms and circumstances, inasmuch as the terms convey adequate description of prohibited act or conduct to persons of ordinary understanding. Oklahoma has clearly announced that the offense of sodomy is not to be countenanced within its borders. Federal courts should not function as superlegislatures in order to judge the wisdom or desirability of legislative policy determinations in areas that neither affect fundamental rights nor proceed along suspect lines.

In *Wainwright v. Stone*, 414 U.S. 21 (1973), the Supreme Court upheld a Florida statute which proscribed "the abominable and detestable crime against nature, either with mankind or with beast" against a constitutional challenge of void for vagueness. The Fifth Circuit had held the statute infirm as unconstitutionally vague and void on its face for failure to give adequate notice of the conduct forbidden by law. In reversing, the Supreme Court observed that copulation per os and per anum had long been held by Florida courts violative of the challenged statute as the "abominable and detestable" crimes against nature referred to in the statute. Hence, the Supreme Court found that the statute was subject to a narrowing construction.

The majority, unlike the district court, holds that portion of the statute which allows "punishment" for teachers for advocating "public homosexual conduct" to be overbroad because it is "not readily subject to a narrowing construction by the state courts" and "its deterrent effect on legitimate expression is both real and substantial." I disagree. Sodomy is *malum in se*, i.e., immoral and corruptible in its nature without regard to the fact of its being noticed or punished by the law of the state. It is not *malum prohibitum*, i.e., wrong only because it is forbidden by law and not involving moral turpitude. It is on this principle that I must part with the majority's holding that the "public homosexual conduct" portion of the Oklahoma statute is overbroad.

Any teacher who advocates, solicits, encourages or promotes the practice of sodomy "in a manner that creates a substantial risk that such conduct will come to the attention of school children or school employees" is in fact and in truth inciting school children to participate in the abominable and detestable crime against nature. Such advocacy by school teachers, regardless of the situs where made, creates a substantial risk of being conveyed to school children. In my view, it does not merit any constitutional protection. There is no need to demonstrate that such conduct would bring about a material or substantial interference or disruption in the normal activities of the school. A teacher advocating the practice of sodomy to school children is without First Amendment protection. This statute furthers an important and substantial government interest, as determined by the Oklahoma legislature, unrelated to the suppression of free speech. The incidental restriction on alleged First Amendment freedom is no greater than is essential to the furtherance of that interest.

Tinker v. Des Moines Independent Community School District, 393 U.S. 503 (1969), is a poor vehicle for the majority to rely upon. There, the Supreme Court simply held that school children opposed to the Vietnam conflict were protected under the First Amendment in their practice of wearing black arm bands in protest thereto, unless that conduct could be shown to substantially interfere or disrupt normal school activities. *Tinker* involved a symbolic demonstration involving a matter of national political significance. Political expression and association is at the very heart of the First Amendment. The advocacy of a practice as universally condemned as the crime of sodomy hardly qualifies as such. There is no need to establish that such advocacy will interfere, substantially or otherwise, in normal school activities. It is sufficient that such advocacy is advanced in a manner that creates a substantial risk that such conduct will encourage school children to commit the abominable crime against nature. This finds solid support in *Tinker*, where the Court said "First Amendment rights must always be applied 'in light of the special characteristics of the...environment' in the particular case."

The Oklahoma legislature has declared that the advocacy by teachers of homosexual acts to school children is a matter of statewide concern. The Oklahoma statute does not condemn or in anywise affect teachers, homosexual or otherwise, except to the extent of the non-advocacy restraint aimed at the protection of school children. It does not deny them any rights as human beings. To equate such "restraint" on First Amendment speech with the Tinker armband display and to require proof that advocacy of the act of sodomy will substantially interfere or disrupt normal school activities is a bow to permissiveness. To the same extent, the advocacy of violence, sabotage and terrorism as a means of effecting political reform held in *Brandenburg v. Ohio*, 395 U.S. 444 (1969) to be protected speech unless demonstrated as directed to and likely to incite or produce such action did not involve advocacy of a crime malum in se to school children by a school teacher.

Facial overbreadth challenges are "manifestly strong medicine" which must be employed "sparingly and only as a last resort." When a party asserts such a challenge, the overbreadth "must not only be real, but substantial as well, judged in relation to the statute's plainly legitimate sweep." A statute's "plainly legitimate sweep" usually includes "controls over harmful, constitutionally unprotected conduct." A broadly-worded statute which does deter some protected speech or conduct may not require invalidation if that deterrence can, with confidence, justify such action.

In *Keyishian v. Board of Regents*, 385 U.S. 589 (1967), the Supreme Court set down its initial guidelines for determining when deterrence of speech or conduct does or does not justify invalidation of a statute. The Court held that a statute is overbroad if it proscribes speech or conduct which "merely advocates the doctrine in the abstract without any attempt to indoctrinate others, or incite others to action in furtherance of unlawful aims." The Court drew a distinction between speech or conduct advocating an abstract doctrine or belief, which demands constitutional protection, and advocacy of unlawful action or acts, with the intent to incite, which deserves no such protection. I submit that in the context of the Oklahoma public school system, the advocacy of sodomy by a teacher in a manner "that creates a substantial risk" it will come to the attention of school children deserves no First Amendment protection.

There is nothing abstract about a teacher advocating to school children the commission of the criminal act proscribed by section 886. The expression proscribed by sec. 6-

103.15 is the advocacy of the commission of the very act held to be a criminal act... Thus, the deterred speech or conduct concerns "advocating," "promoting" and "encouraging" school children to commit the crime of sodomy. In the context of the public school system involving the teacher-student relationship, it cannot be said that the advocacy of such action is mere advocacy of an abstract doctrine or belief. To hold otherwise ignores the difference between children and adults.

> [The cross-appeals in this case were argued before the Supreme Court when Justice Powell was absent due to surgery. The Court deadlocked 4-4 on this and many other cases. Some were set down for reargument before a full Court; in others, including this case, the circuit opinion was left standing by the Supreme Court tie vote. Presumably, Justice Powell was satisfied by the 10th Circuit's decision, or he would have asked for a new hearing so that he could participate in deciding the appeal.]

* * *

Before the telephone became an ubiquitous instrument of communication, publishers in most towns and cities (sometimes affiliated with newspaper companies) published "city directories" in which businesses and residents were listed. By the middle of the twentieth century, such directories had been supplanted in most communities by the "white pages" and "yellow pages" directories published by telephone companies and distributed at no charge to all telephone subscribers. Both the city directories of pre-telephone America and the telephone directories were published by private companies, but they served important public functions. Indeed, exclusion from such a directory could have significant economic consequences for a business.

The issue of inclusion in directories is particularly significant for businesses that seek to reach a widely dispersed, and hard to identify, audience. The "yellow pages" controversy discussed in the following case has recurred in many different locations. In New York City, public pressure exerted by lesbian and gay organizations and government officials persuaded the regional telephone company to change its policy and establish a category of "lesbian and gay organizations" under the Social Services heading in the "yellow pages" directory.

Loring v. Bellsouth Advertising & Publishing Corporation
339 S.E.2d 372 (Ga. App. 1985),
certiorari denied Jan. 29, 1986.

SOGNIER, Judge.

Gene Loring, d/b/a Christopher's Kind Bookseller, brought this action against BellSouth Advertising & Publishing Corporation (BA & P) seeking injunctive and declaratory relief from BA & P's refusal to accept for publication in its classified advertisement directory ("yellow pages") Loring's advertisement which contained the words "lesbian" and "gay male."...

...Southern Bell is a public utility which enjoys a monopoly in local telephonic communication and is regulated by the Georgia Public Service Commission (PSC). Southern Bell published both the white and the yellow pages directories until the breakup of A.T. & T. in January 1984 at which time appellee assumed the publication duties pursuant to a written agreement between it and Southern Bell. Appellant's bookstore, which opened in 1980 was contacted that same year by a representative of Southern Bell about advertising in its yellow pages. Although Southern Bell rejected a draft advertisement from appellant at that time, appellant was again contacted in 1981 and, after the Southern Bell representative obtained specific authorization, Loring's advertisement was accepted by Southern Bell. The text of the advertisement as published is as follows:

CHRISTOPHER'S KIND BOOKSELLER
Lesbian and Gay Male Literature
Periodicals, Cards and Records, etc.

together with the address and telephone number of the store. For the next three years this advertisement was run in the yellow pages under the heading "Book Dealers—Retail." The cost for such advertisement was billed to appellant each month on his telephone service bill; there is no evidence that such cost has not been timely paid.

In May 1984, appellee notified appellant that his advertisement would not be accepted for the 1984–1985 yellow pages directory, so long as it contained the words "lesbian" and "gay," because the advertisement was said to violate the "Yellow Pages Standards (Ethics)." Section 5.26 of such policy is as follows:

"The Company may determine, as a matter of policy, not to accept advertisement with respect to homosexuals on the grounds that to do so may at this time be offensive to a segment of its directory users who fully utilize the telephone and directory as a means of communication."

The ethics policy in question is identical to the ethics policy of Southern Bell in effect at the time appellant's advertisement was first accepted and published. The trial court found that appellee's ethics committee made an internal business decision to reject advertisements concerning homosexuals, including appellee's advertisement, on the rationale that "such an advertisement may be considered controversial by, or may offend, a certain segment of its customers." Appellee also asserts this standard seeks to uphold the prestige of its directory. Appellee admits that in the three years in which the advertisement has run in the Southern Bell published yellow pages directory, not one complaint from the public or a customer has been received.

The threshold issue in this case is whether appellee's directory publication business is that of a private enterprise with an unqualified right to reject appellant's advertisement or that of a public enterprise subject to public regulation by the courts in its business decisions regarding the advertising it will accept. We agree with the trial court's finding that appellee is a private enterprise. As noted by the trial court, Southern Bell and appellee are both wholly owned subsidiaries of BellSouth but while Southern Bell is a public utility, appellee is not a public utility and its connection with Southern Bell is not enough in itself to make the service appellee provides necessarily a public service. While the PSC requires alphabetical listing of telephone numbers in the white pages be published and regulates the publication of the white pages as being within the realm of Southern Bell's responsibilities as a public utility, it is uncontroverted that the PSC does not require Southern Bell to publish a yellow pages directory and does not regulate any phase of appellee's yellow pages directory publication business. Although appellant argues, and the trial court noted, that "[f]or all practical purposes, if not for all purposes, there is no other 'yellow pages' publication which services the City of Atlanta" and that four out of five adults use appellee's directory in the metro Atlanta market, appellee does not have a monopoly in the directory publication business as demonstrated by evidence in the record that any and all businesses interested in entering the market for these directories have equal access to all phases of the business, including equal access to the type of licensing agreement between appellee and Southern Bell regarding telephone number lists. Appellee is operating in a competitive market, and while we recognize the difficulty a fledgling business may experience in entering that market in competition with appellee because of the public's familiarity with appellee's directory and appellee's advantage in being able to utilize the distribution system set up by Southern Bell for its white pages, those advantages do not convert appellee's private enterprise into a public enterprise. Appellee's position in its market is comparable to that held by an editor-owner in a one-newspaper town and its business decisions are no more subject to public regulation than those decisions of its marketplace competitors.

While appellant articulately argues that appellee's rejection of his advertisement because some directory users might be offended is unreasonable in view of the total absence of complaints over a three-year period and appellee's inclusion in its directory of advertisements for massage parlors, escort services and abortion clinics, as judges we cannot interject our personal response to appellee's decision but instead must address the legal issues before the court and apply the applicable standard of review. Thus, we are bound by the trial court's findings.

DEEN, Presiding Judge, concurring specially.

"'Let your fingers do the walking' is a commercial jingle urging use of the yellow pages of telephone directories. That such classified sections are regarded as valuable by business is shown in the instant case." In another exemplary case, which highlights judicial deference to an exercise of broad discretion, an advertiser, with an AAA alphabetic and almost addictive alliterative affliction or affinity analysis, actually attempted to attain, achieve and accomplish arithmetically an acme, apex, and alpha position in the directory by adding twenty-three A's to form its name. AAAAAAAAAAAAAAAAAAAAAAAAA v. Southwestern Bell Tel. Co., 373 P2d 31 (Okl. 1962).

1. There seems to be no dispute that the threshold question in the instant case concerned classifying publication of the yellow pages as a purely private enterprise or as a matter connected with the telephone company's responsibilities as a public utility.... This court in fact once suggested by obiter dictum that "publication of the yellow pages is apart from Southern Bell's public service..." I find preferable the view that "[t]he telephone company has an exclusive private advertising business which, if not legally monopolistic, is tied to its public utility service of providing telephone service." Mere nomenclature or form (technically private) must always yield to substance or reality (partly public). Thus, "[i]n the absence of regulation by the State [as in the instant case with the yellow pages directory], the whole subject of the making of rules and regulations is left to the [public utility], subject only to control by the courts of their reasonableness or discriminatory character." Accordingly, the appellee has considerable discretion in selecting the contents of the yellow pages advertising, although that exercise of discretion may be controlled by the courts if it is unreasonable or discriminatory. AAAAAAAAAAAAAAAAAAAAAAAA in particular emphasizes judicial deference to the exercise of this broad discretion unless it is arbitrary, unjust, or unreasonable.

I believe that the trial court (as well as the majority opinion) incorrectly classified the appellee's publication of the yellow pages directory as a private enterprise, although the trial court did, nevertheless, ultimately review the decision to reject the appellant's advertisement as if the appellee were a public utility. In doing so, the trial court concluded that the appellee's decision to exclude the specific advertisement was based upon a valid and rational business determination, and I agree....

The appellee maintained a set of standards for determining whether to accept an advertisement, and section 5.26 of those standards provided that advertisements with regard to homosexuals may be rejected on the grounds that such may be offensive to a segment of the directory users. The appellee obviously was not discriminatory in its application of this standard, as no other advertisements similar to that of the appellant were accepted for publication. The sole issue is whether the appellee's decision to reject the advertisement was arbitrary.

Certainly the general reason to exclude, i.e., the policy of not publishing an advertisement that may be offensive to a segment of society, is not irrational or arbitrary. The appellant contends that the specific application of that policy in this case was arbitrary, claiming that no evidence exists to support the appellee's determination that the appellant's advertisement may be offensive, in view of the absence of any complaints when the same advertisement had been published some time earlier. That assertion, however, is based upon pure speculation. The tenor of the times cannot be conclusively measured by the number of complaints; it is just as likely (and speculative) that some silent portion of the populace grimaced and bore the offense. This court should not impose upon the appellee a burden of conducting a certified statewide poll to measure societal approval of an advertisement.

This writer notes with great interest the appellant's contention that some people may consider the words "Christian," "Mormon," and "Islamic," which are printed in the directory, to be just as controversial or offensive as the words "gay" and "lesbian." This argument is not advanced to equate the last two quoted words on parity as a religion seeking equal treatment, exercise and protection with the first three quoted religions, but is articulated that similar treatment of advertisement in the yellow pages is sought because the latter is thought no less controversial and offensive to some than the former. In any event, the limited test to be applied in this case should be whether the publisher exercised good faith in making its determination that a particular advertisement may be offensive to a segment of society.

In the instant case, Edmund Gay (who was in charge of the directory) and the appellee's ethics committee considered the interests of both the gay community and the non-gay community. Based upon their experience and perception of societal attitudes, Gay and the committee decided that the appellant's advertisement may be offensive to some people. There is absolutely no indication in the record that Gay and the committee were anything but sincere in that determination.... The accuracy of the appellee's perception of societal reaction is another issue, and one that is immaterial in the review of the publisher's exercise of discretion.

2. Where First Amendment speech interests are involved, radio and television broadcasters may be required to provide equal access, under a "fairness doctrine." This is because they use public airwaves and, with only limited, regulated competition, are essentially monopolistic. A newspaper publisher is not subject to similar regulation.... [T]he position of the appellee as a publisher of the yellow pages directory surely would lie somewhere between that of a radio/television broadcaster and a newspaper, although it would appear that the appellee is more akin to the former since some extra public duty exists. A parallel might be drawn with the responsibility and position of trustees of a public library. Such trustees obviously have a public duty to make available a broad selection of books. Nevertheless, certain limitations are obvious. Limited financial resources necessitate exclusion of some books, and the trustees may also exclude books

which they determine in their discretion to be objectionable, provided that decision has a rational basis and is not discriminatory.

Since the appellee is a private entity, however, the First Amendment to the United States Constitution provides the appellant no basis or right to have its advertisement included in the yellow page directory. (Assuming arguendo that it did, commercial speech interests would be at issue, which do not enjoy the degree of protection extended to pure speech interests.) It should be emphasized nevertheless that the present generation of "lawyers has an unparalleled opportunity to aid in the formulation of a state constitutional jurisprudence that will protect the rights and liberties of our people, however the philosophy of the U.S. Supreme Court may ebb and flow." Art. I, Sec. I, Par. 5 of the Ga. Constitution provides that "[e]very person may speak, write, or publish sentiments on all subjects but shall be responsible for the abuse of that liberty." It may very well be that this state constitutional provision would have some bearing on the instant case, but unfortunately neither party raised this matter in the proceedings below, thus precluding this court from addressing it.....

Pope, Judge, dissenting.

The majority holds that defendant, as a private publisher, has an unqualified right to reject plaintiff's advertisement. I respectfully disagree.... [B]oth Southern Bell and defendant are wholly owned subsidiaries of BellSouth Corporation, one of the regional telephone operating companies formed as the result of the breakup of American Telephone & Telegraph Company. Southern Bell is a public utility; defendant is not a public utility. Prior to the breakup of A.T. & T., Southern Bell itself undertook the publication of the white and yellow pages directories. Since the breakup this function has been performed by defendant pursuant to a written agreement with Southern Bell. Defendant does not contend that this agreement has removed the white pages (alphabetical) directory from the realm of Southern Bell's responsibilities as a public utility (and consequently from regulation by the PSC, see Rule 515-12-1-.10, Rules of the Georgia Public Service Commission), yet it argues that said agreement effectively removes the yellow pages (classified) directory therefrom. This argument misses the point. If publication of the yellow pages directory is a service provided by Southern Bell which touches upon its responsibilities and obligations as a public utility, it may not avoid same merely by contracting with another not a public utility to provide the service. It follows that defendant, by contractually assuming Southern Bell's responsibilities and obligations in this regard, may not pursue same in a manner different from that required of Southern Bell.... What, if any, responsibilities and obligations does defendant have in regard to the publication of advertisements in the yellow pages...? "The weight of authority seems to treat the publication—including advertising—of a classified telephone directory [yellow pages] as being more nearly a private matter than one of public interest so as to make it subject to regulation by a Public Service Commission. However, a telephone company enjoys the advantage of being a monopoly for its area in the field of telephonic communication. As a subscriber for a private telephone I am entitled to have my name and telephone number listed in the regular directory. It is part of the service furnished in return for my payment. Without such a current alphabetical directory, the utility value of my telephone would be infinitely less. Apparently all the court and commission authorities agree that this regular directory is subject to the jurisdiction of and regulation by the Public Service regulatory bodies. A greater charge is paid for a business telephone than for a private telephone and in partial return therefor the customer is entitled to be listed under the proper business or professional grouping in the Classified Directory. Such subscriber also has what might be termed an option to buy advertising therein subject to the reasonable rules and regulations of the Telephone Company...The Classified Directory, like the regular directory...is provided by a company which enjoys an absolute monopoly. A business dependent even partially upon the telephone—and many businesses are to a great extent so dependent—is at a tremendous disadvantage with no telephone. It is prejudiced if not listed in the Classified Directory and the business is damaged if it is denied the right to advertise in the Classified Section, especially if competitors do advertise there. There is no comparable advertising media." *Videon Corp. v. Burton*, 369 S.W.2d 264, 269 (Mo.App.1963). "The yellow pages are a very useful and beneficial component in providing telephone service to the public...Indeed, the yellow pages are more than a convenience to newcomers in town who need a doctor, lawyer, plumber, electrician or any number of services. Newcomers could not be expected to begin in the front of the alphabetical listings and search until they find the desired service." *State ex rel. Utilities Comm. v. Southern Bell Tel. etc. Co.*, 307 N.C. 541, 299 S.E.2d 763, 765–66 (1983), overruling *Gas House, Inc. v. Southern Bell Tel. etc. Co.*, 289 N.C. 175, 221 S.E.2d 499 (1976). "Although there are 'yellow pages' published by independent publishers, the telephone company's yellow pages is the only one distributed to everyone with a telephone." *Discount Fabric House v. Wis. Tel. Co.*, 117 Wis.2d 587, 345 N.W.2d 417, 419 (1984).

Yellow pages advertising "arises out of a private business transaction of the telephone company which in all other respects has been recognized as a monopoly and has been regulated by the Public Service Commission in performing its services. Certainly, the telephone company would not argue that it is engaged in a business other than one which performs a service of great importance to the public when it distributes a yellow pages book without cost to every telephone customer. The telephone company without question holds itself out as willing to give reasonable public service to all who apply for an advertisement in the yellow pages...The telephone company has wisely and responsibly taken advantage of an energy conserving society, both as to time and natural resources, by advertising that persons should determine the availability of products before traveling to shopping areas by letting their fingers do the walking through the yellow pages. The telephone company has an exclusive private advertising business which, if not legally monopolistic, is tied to its public utility service of providing telephone service. Without additional or identifiable charges, every telephone customer receives the yellow pages free with the telephone service. There is nothing in this record to show that there is any other mode of advertising available to [plaintiff] which reaches as many customers, is of a similar nature as the yellow pages, and is inexorably tied to the telephone service." *Discount Fabric House v. Wis. Tel. Co., supra* 345 N.W.2d at 420–21. "The company derives revenue from this source which should be and is considered in fixing the over-all rates...We believe that the publication of the Classified Directory and the advertising thereunder is a method, procedure and operation which is designed for and actually does facilitate the business of affording telephonic communication, is truly a monopoly in that advertising field and is public business insofar as its business subscribers are concerned. Such a publication sui generis ought to be subject to reasonable rules and regulations." *Videon Corp. v. Burton, supra* at 269–70.

The yellow pages have never been and are not now regulated by the PSC. However, as noted above, yellow pages advertising is not an enterprise entirely separate from the telephone company's responsibilities and obligations as a public utility....A public utility may not enforce arbitrary requirements, but "should be given great leniency in restricting the contents of advertising, not only for the protection and preservation of its own good name but also to shield the public from pillage and misunderstandings."

It follows from the foregoing that defendant has considerable discretion regarding the contents of yellow pages advertising. The exercise of that discretion should be controlled by the courts, in the absence of regulation by the PSC, only to the extent that it is unreasonable or discriminatory.

The trial court concluded that the business judgment of defendant to exclude the words "gay" and "lesbian" was based on a valid and rational business determination that some segment of the readers of the yellow pages "could perhaps" be offended by such words in the context used. This finding is apparently premised upon defendant's "ethics" policy (advertisement with respect to homosexuals "may at this time be offensive" to users of the yellow pages) and defendant's testimony that plaintiff's advertisement "may be considered controversial by, or may offend, a certain segment of its customers" and that defendant also seeks to uphold the "prestige" of the yellow pages directory. Defendant's "evidence" in this regard can only be fairly described as mere opinion or belief, affording no hint as to the factual basis for its conclusion. There are no facts in this case which support defendant's conclusion that the subject advertisement "may be" offensive to users of the yellow pages, only patent speculation. Indeed, the positive evidence of record compels a finding contrary to defendant's conclusion—during the three years in which the subject advertisement appeared in the yellow pages, not one complaint was received from the public or a customer. Cf. *Boyer v. Southwestern Bell Tel. Co.* (10 complaints received over a year's time by master plumbers concerning classification of sewer and drain cleaners under the general heading "plumbing" in yellow pages were de minimis and did not establish that the public was confused or misled to its detriment). Compare *Videon Corp. v. Burton* (177 complaints received by the Better Business Bureau considered as part of the substantial evidence supporting PSC's finding of no unlawful discrimination and no unreasonableness in telephone company's refusing to accept Videon's advertising in the yellow pages as submitted because of the implication that Videon was rendering free service).

A "rational" business decision is necessarily one "of, relating to, or based upon reason." Webster's Third New Intl. Dictionary at 1885. "Conclusions of witnesses are of no probative value unless the facts on which the opinions are based sustain the opinions rendered." Findings of fact of a court sitting without a jury are not to be disturbed on appeal unless clearly erroneous. OCGA s 9-11-52(a). The 'clearly erroneous' standard requires reversal of a trial court's findings of fact if there is no evidence to support them." *Richmond County Hosp. Auth. v. Richmond County*, 255 Ga. 183, 191, 336 S.E.2d 562 (1985). " 'If the court's judgment is based upon a stated fact for which there is no evidence, it should be reversed.' " *Lamas v. Baldwin*, 140 Ga.App. 37, 39, 230 S.E.2d 13 (1976). There being no probative evidence to support the trial court's finding that defendant's refusal of the subject advertising was based on a valid and rational business determination (i.e., that such refusal was not arbitrary and capricious), the judgment of the trial court should be reversed.

In light of the foregoing discussion, I find no merit in defendant's assertion that compelling it to accept the subject advertisement violates its rights under the First Amendment to the United States Constitution.

Notes and Questions

1. Would the First Amendment analysis be any different if the same exclusionary policy was adopted by a daily newspaper? monthly newsmagazine? special interest maga-

zine published by a professional association or hobby club? radio or television station? What if the radio or television station was not-for-profit, listener-supported "public" radio or television, and the rejected advertisement was a "public service announcement" in support of sex education programs in the schools? What if the radio or television station was operated by a municipality?

2. Apart from the First Amendment issues, could a business such as the Yellowpages publisher, a radio station or a newspaper refuse to carry advertising for a business aimed at lesbian and gay consumers, or refuse to carry advertising by an organization promoting lesbian and gay rights, in a jurisdiction that outlaws discrimination based on sexual orientation?

* * *

Olivieri v. Ward
801 F.2d 602 (2nd Cir. 1986)
cert. denied, 480 U.S. 917 (1987)

CARDAMONE, Circuit Judge:

This expedited appeal arises from one aspect of the "Gay Pride Parade" held in Manhattan on Sunday June 29, 1986. Plaintiffs are Dignity-New York, a not-for-profit New York Corporation (Dignity), Michael Olivieri, its president, and 21 other gay Catholic members of Dignity-New York. Defendants are Benjamin Ward, as Police Commissioner of the City of New York, Edward I. Koch, as Mayor of New York, and the New York City Police Department. Plaintiffs, who instituted suit in the United States District Court for the Southern District of New York (Motley, C.J.) claiming infringement of their civil rights under 42 U.S.C. sec. 1983, sought a declaratory judgment and a permanent injunction. Following trial, Chief Judge Motley handed down a thorough opinion and a brief order that in substance granted plaintiffs the relief they sought.

BACKGROUND

The focus of this controversy is the public sidewalk in front of St. Patrick's Cathedral on the east side of 5th Avenue between 50th-51st Streets in midtown Manhattan. Plaintiffs sought to conduct a peaceful demonstration there during the hours from 1 P.M. to 3 P.M. while the Annual Gay Pride Parade passed in its march south from Central Park to Greenwich Village. Defendants refused plaintiffs unlimited access to the sidewalk because they thought it was a focal point for potential confrontation with counterdemonstrators formed loosely into a Committee for the Defense of St. Patrick's Cathedral (Committee). This group, whose president is Herbert McKay, draws its members from the Knights of Columbus, Ancient Order of Hibernians, Catholic War Veterans, groups of Orthodox Jews and other organizations. These counterdemonstrators have been present behind police barricades on the west side of 5th Avenue across the street from the Cathedral for the past five annual Gay Pride Parades. As a result of their fears, Commissioner Ward and the City Police Department planned to close the sidewalk in front of the Cathedral to plaintiffs, other demonstrators and counterdemonstrators, and the public at large for the duration of the 1986 parade. It was that decision that prompted the instant lawsuit before Chief Judge Motley.

PROCEEDINGS BELOW

During the eight days of trial—that commenced on May 12 and concluded May 21, 1986—the trial court heard testimony from 11 witnesses and reviewed and received a number of exhibits into evidence. Among those testifying were the police officials in charge of this and past year's parades, a member of Dignity-New York serving as coordinator of this year's parade, the Rector of St. Patrick's Cathedral, and leaders of the counterdemonstrators. The trial judge handed down an opinion on June 13, 1986, which concluded that freezing the sidewalk was not a reasonable time, place and manner restriction on the exercise of plaintiffs' rights of free speech because it was not content-neutral. The district court believed that the police had given the counterdemonstrators a "heckler's veto" and that the Police Department's estimations of violence were not credible, and hence were pretextual. The district court found "a certain excessive sensitivity to the Catholic Church on the part of police officials" that supported its conclusion that the speech restriction was not content neutral. The trial court also stated that the limitation imposed was not adequately tailored to further any significant governmental interest. No analysis was undertaken regarding whether the sidewalk freeze allowed plaintiffs adequate alternatives to express their message.

Chief Judge Motley declared defendants' decision to prohibit Dignity access to the sidewalk adjacent to St. Patrick's an unconstitutional restraint on plaintiffs' First Amendment rights. The district court thereupon granted a permanent injunction enjoining defendants from preventing up to 100 members of Dignity from peacefully demonstrating on the public walk before the Cathedral for the duration of the "Gay Pride Parade" on June 29, 1986 and "during subsequent annual Gay Pride Parades." Defendants were granted the right to apply for modification of the injunction based on a substantial change in circumstances.

PROCEEDINGS BEFORE THIS PANEL

Five days after the trial court handed down its June 13 opinion defendants appealed, and the matter was ordered expedited to this panel for an oral argument that was heard on Thursday June 26, 1986. The three days available until the June 29 parade provided an insufficient time to draft an opinion adequately resolving the significant issues raised. We therefore attempted at the argument to induce the parties to agree on a limited number that would demonstrate in front of the Cathedral. In response to this suggestion, the City of New York proposed that 20 of plaintiffs' members remain in an enclosed area depicted in trial exhibit # 193 for 45 minutes and—after a 30 minute interval—a similar number of counterdemonstrators occupy the same area for the same period of time.

Trial exhibit # 193 is a photo taken during the 1985 parade and was referred to by the panel and counsel during oral argument. The view is one looking down on a barricaded area—resembling a chute—leading from the 5th Avenue curb to the foot of the steps at the main entrance of St. Patrick's Cathedral. In response to the City's proposal, a letter from plaintiffs' counsel of Friday June 27 stated that plaintiffs would agree to limit its demonstrators to 75 persons in a "pen located in the center of the sidewalk" for 45 minutes and would also agree to counterdemonstrators coming into the area during the second half of the parade. The smaller number proposed by the City was not acceptable.

In view of the impasse, we handed down an order on Friday June 27 which, on our own motion, stayed the injunction issued by the district court, subject to certain conditions. Principal among the conditions was that defendants permit 25 members of Dignity to demonstrate peacefully for 30 minutes during the parade within the confines of the police barricade shown on exhibit # 193 and that defendants permit the same number of those opposed to Dignity to demonstrate for the same time in the same area, separated by a 30 minute interval. The police were granted authority to close the sidewalk to the general public during the parade and to impose more restrictive measures if in their professional judgment circumstances at or near the site posed a danger to public safety.

According to news reports the parade went off as scheduled with more than 12,000 marching by St. Patrick's Cathedral. The scenario fashioned by the order apparently went smoothly as both Dignity and the Committee demonstrated for their allotted times in front of the Cathedral without serious incident.[1]

Discussion

A. General Rules

In considering the general rules applicable to the present litigation we begin on common ground. The right of defendants as city officials to limit freedom of speech on a public sidewalk — held since time immemorial for the use of the public — is sharply restricted to those regulations that are necessary to serve a compelling state interest and that are narrowly drawn to achieve that end. Yet the First Amendment does not guarantee an absolute right to anyone to express their views any place, at any time, and in any way they want. The activities of Dignity and the Committee are subject to reasonable time, place and manner restrictions to further significant government interests. The well-established tests for assessing the validity of such a restriction require that it (1) be content-neutral, (2) be narrowly tailored to meet a significant governmental interest, and (3) leave open ample alternative means of communication. *Clark v. Community for Creative Non-Violence*, 468 U.S. 288, 293 (1984).

B. Scope of Review

Before considering the validity of the restriction imposed here, it is necessary to examine a court's power to review a department rule or regulation. In *Clark v. Community For Creative Non-Violence*, the Supreme Court sustained a National Parks Service Regulation that prohibited overnight sleeping in Lafayette Park and The Mall in Washington, D.C., over claims that the regulation violated demonstrators' right to free speech. In reversing the District of Columbia Circuit Court of Appeals, the Supreme Court noted that the circuit court's suggestions respecting reducing the size or duration of the demonstration represented no more than fine-tuning of the regulation in an area where courts have no expertise. That Court of Appeals now views the judiciary's role as confined to upholding regulations that are constitutional and striking down those that are

---

1. Counsel submitted a Joint Statement of Agreed Facts dated August 30, 1986 following the 1986 Gay Pride Parade. It revealed that the barricaded demonstration pen was not as depicted in trial exhibit # 193, but rather on the north end of the east sidewalk in front of St. Patrick's Cathedral. It further appears from the Joint Statement that when Dignity came onto the Cathedral sidewalk there were 150 police officers in front of the Cathedral. Counterdemonstrators, identified as members of Orthodox Jewish groups, Catholic War Veterans and the "Bayside" group, reached a peak number of 150. Although as Parade participants passed in front of counter-demonstrators, they directed derogatory obscenities at Catholic nuns, priests and Cardinal O'Connor, there were no reported incidents of violence, nor were there any attempts by counter-demonstrators to break the line of march.

not. *White House Vigil v. Clark*, 746 F.2d 1518, 1531–32 (D.C.Cir.1984). Based upon this view defendants urge that the district court's findings on the potential for violence are beyond judicial competence. We cannot agree.

A court's power to review government restrictions imposed on the exercise of a First Amendment right occupies middle ground between extremes. It does not kowtow without question to agency expertise, nor does it dispense justice according to notions of individual expediency "like a kadi under a tree." *Terminiello v. Chicago*, 337 U.S. 1, 11 (1949) (Frankfurter, J., dissenting). "Because the excuses offered for refusing to permit the fullest scope of free speech are often disguised, a court must carefully sort through the reasons offered to see if they are genuine." *Olivieri v. Ward*, 766 F.2d 690, 691 (2d Cir.1985). The district court performed that sorting process by means of the full trial that it conducted and the thorough opinion it handed down.

When First Amendment concerns are involved a court " 'may not simply assume that [a decision by local officials] will always advance the asserted state interests sufficiently to justify its abridgement of expressive activity.' " *City of Los Angeles v. Preferred Communications, Inc.*, 106 S.Ct. 2034, 2037 (1986) (quoting with approval *Members of the City Council v. Taxpayers for Vincent*, 466 U.S. 789, 803 n. 22 (1984)). When reviewing the reasonableness of time, place and manner restrictions on First Amendment rights, a court must independently determine the rationality of the government interest implicated and whether the restrictions imposed are narrowly drawn to further that interest. In the instant case, we agree with the district court that the restrictions imposed were not drawn solely to further the government's conceded interest in public safety.

C. Fashioning a Rule for the Instant Case

Thus, here the district court properly reviewed the proposed restriction and correctly concluded that Dignity's presence on the walk is assured as an exercise of its members' constitutional rights. Insofar as the trial court went on to find that the counterdemonstrators had no real interest of their own in being on the sidewalk—but simply wanted to keep Dignity's members off—its opinion and order did not protect the constitutional rights of the Committee as counterdemonstrators to convey their message in opposition to that expressed by Dignity. In this respect, we believe the district court erred.

The message that plaintiffs seek to convey is that they are members of the Catholic Church which they do not forsake because of their homosexuality. Since St. Patrick's Cathedral is the see for the Roman Catholic Archdiocese of New York and serves, the Committee believes, as a symbol of religious and family values they think is under attack by the gay demonstrators, the potential for confrontation and violence is obviously present when the opposing groups share the same public forum at the same time. It is not up to the city or its officials to determine those issues worth debating in a public forum. In the field of expression all ideas are considered equal. "Once a forum is opened up to assembly or speaking by some groups, government may not prohibit others from assembling or speaking on the basis of what they intend to say." Thus, both groups are entitled to be present before St. Patrick's Cathedral during the Gay Pride Parade.

The questions—which now apparently arise each year—are how much of a presence, where on the walk, and for how long a period are Dignity and the Committee entitled to? Ordinarily, a court would simply rule on the constitutional validity of the restraints imposed and refrain from devising its own plan. Yet here time constraints forced the district court—and this Court, too—to choose between striking down defendants' order freezing the sidewalk or deferring to government imposed limitations on First Amendment rights. Neither alternative was desirable: to choose the former risks ignoring public safety concerns because demonstrators and counterdemonstrators would at the same time occupy the sidewalk with the public; by choosing the latter, a court abdicates its independent responsibility to examine the constitutionality of First Amendment restrictions—it simply adopts them. The scheme devised by the district court steered a middle course between these extremes—limiting Dignity's members, yet upholding the exercise of their communicative rights. Obviously under such circumstances courts must and do have the power to rule in this fashion. Appellate review is limited to the question of whether the district court abused its discretion.

The critical questions—as a practical matter—are (1) how many individuals need be on the sidewalk to convey Dignity's and the Committee's messages with some impact to the line of marchers and to the public, and (2) how can the size, positioning, and timing of these competing groups be accommodated to legitimate public safety concerns. Concededly, permitting two individuals to occupy the sidewalk as in past parades is *de minimis*, constituting more of a symbolic than an actual presence. Yet because the district court's order that permitted 100 members of Dignity to occupy the entire sidewalk from 50th to 51st Street for the duration of the Parade was issued without consideration of the rights of the Committee, it is subject to modification. Those portions of a decree that are disapproved of may be modified by an appellate court. In our view it is preferable at present that each group have an equal time of 30 minutes on the walk, separated by 30 minutes during the two hour march. Such plan accommodates Dignity, the Committee, and public safety concerns, at least for the 1986 parade. Moreover, the idea of sharing the walk is one that plaintiffs and defendants agreed to in separate letters addressed to the Court following oral argument.

Further, the police suggestion of a barricaded enclosure for demonstrators and counterdemonstrators was not intended to limit the exercise of free speech. Instead, it is a practical device used by the police to protect those actively exercising their rights from those who would prevent its exercise. We conclude that this type of manner and place restriction is content-neutral since it is applicable to both groups. Further, it is adequately tailored to promote the significant governmental interest in public order. It also provides a reasonable alternative for communication, rather than the requested use of the entire block-long stretch of the sidewalk. In addition, the suggestion to confine the demonstrators to this enclosure was also accepted by plaintiffs. Again, with the luxury of hindsight—denied the district court because we write after the parade is over—we now know that both demonstrators and counterdemonstrators appeared and used this enclosure for their allotted time. This speaks well for all concerned, not the least of whom are the New York City police who over the years have guarded successfully the safety of demonstrators and the public during this parade.

Having agreed to the duration and a specific place on the sidewalk, the number to be permitted becomes somewhat easier to determine as that is limited both by the space available and the logistics of moving one group out and another into the area. Granted 100 people would make a bigger impact in conveying the message of demonstrators than 25, but the incremental impact of 75 more people is not justified by the added risks defendants encounter in dealing with four times as many individual demonstrators.

D. Permanent Injunction

...If interested parties seek to modify this order, they will have the burden of showing to the district court that significantly changed circumstances warrant it. Over the past several years counsel, the trial court, and this Court have devoted considerable time to the significant constitutional issues raised by this litigation. The parties now have the considered judgment of this Court in the resolution of the issues presented. We do not think therefore that our order should be modified readily or that this litigation should—like the Gay Rights Parade—become an annual event.....

D. Forming Ranks

Courts have recognized that the rights specified in the First Amendment carry by implication a right of association, especially for political and communitarian purposes. The concept of associational rights flowing from the First Amendment was perhaps most notably developed in cases involving the organization of persons of color to fight segregation during the first half of this century, and of workers to form associations (labor organizations or unions) to improve their terms and conditions of employment. Associational rights may take many forms. As we saw in the case of *Boy Scouts of America v. Dale*, such rights may be used to exclude persons from participating in a particular activity on the theory that individuals may choose with whom they wish to associate, or may be used to stop the government from interfering with associational activity. The cases selected for this section involve instances where government agencies refused to respect associational rights of persons seeking to organize to combat the stigma and discrimination imposed by society on sexual minorities.

In re William J. Thom
(Lambda Legal Defense & Education Fund, Inc.)
337 N.Y.S.2d 588 (App. Div. 1972)

PER CURIAM.

Application for approval as a legal assistance corporation denied and petition dismissed, without costs and without disbursements. The Application states: "The attorneys employed by the Corporation will render, provide and carry out the practice of law activities of the Corporation as set forth in this paragraph. These activities include providing without charge legal services in those situations which give rise to legal issues having a substantial effect on the legal rights of homosexuals; to promote the availability of legal services to homosexuals by encouraging and attracting homosexuals into the legal profession; to disseminate to homosexuals general information concerning their legal rights and obligations, and to render technical assistance to any legal services corporation or agency in regard to legal issues affecting homosexuals." The stated purposes are on their face neither benevolent nor charitable, nor, in any event, is there a demonstrated need for this corporation. It is not shown that the private sector of the profession is not available to serve this clientele, nor that, as to indigents, the existing legal assistance corporations are not available. A supplemental affidavit does indicate a lack of desire on the part of some attorneys who work *pro bono publico* to take the cases of homosexuals, but this appears to be no more than a matter of taste, and it is not established that lawyers are completely lacking. The averment does not show that the persons concerned will be without legal services unless this corporation is approved for the purpose.

It is sought in the papers to demonstrate a likeness to the Application of Puerto Rican Legal Defense & Education Fund, Inc., heretofore approved by us, but there is no parallel: the latter's Application demonstrated clearly that indigence is rife amongst the intended clientele. It does not appear that discrimination against homosexuals, which undoubtedly exists, operates to deprive them of legal representation.

The lack of merit in this Application leads us to comment further. We are not told whence the funds to finance the corporation are expected to come, except that they will be solicited. It is well known that there has not been a lack of public and private moneys available to support corporations of this nature, and this free flowing of finance has undoubtedly led to the proliferation of those similar corporations which now exist. While we have not approved any except those which in our opinion fill a real need, we shall require of each such corporation, on application for continued approval, that it demonstrate continuance of that need. Perhaps the legislature should speak again with clarity as to what the words "benevolent or charitable purposes" mean…We invite such a clarification. Meanwhile, it seems to us that we should not put our imprimatur upon any corporation which seeks approval to practice law for no more reason than that it claims to represent a minority.

Application of William J. Thom, Appellant,

for Approval of the Incorporation of
Lambda Legal Defense & Education Fund, Inc.
301 N.E.2d 542(N.Y. 1973)

PER CURIAM.

The order of the Appellate Division should be reversed and the matter remitted to that court for reconsideration of the Application. The determination of that court was unsupportable in finding that the Lambda Corporation was neither benevolent nor charitable in ostensible purpose and that there was no demonstrated need for the corporation. We do not agree, however, that the Appellate Division is without discretion in considering Applications for approval under § 495 of the Judiciary Law…There may be and will undoubtedly arise in the future many applications on behalf of corporations which will not merit approval because of factors related to the responsibility of the sponsors, the method of financing, the scope of activities proposed, and still others not predictable or definable in advance, any or all of which may affect the public interest. Moreover, section 608.2 setting forth the requirements and standards for Applications would be senseless unless the several matters required to be included in the Application were not subject to discretionary review. Nor do we find any lack of standards, if standards be required, implied or expressed, in the variously detailed rules.

BURKE, Judge (concurring).

The appellant seeks to reverse an order of the Appellate Division which denied his Application for approval of "the * * * existence * * * and incorporation" of the Lambda Legal Defense & Education Fund, Inc. (hereafter Lambda) as a legal assistance corporation and dismissed the petition.

Section 495 of the Judiciary Law prohibits the practice of law in New York by corporations or voluntary associations, subject to certain limited exceptions set forth in subdivision 5 of § 495 which provides, in relevant part: "This section shall not apply * * * to organizations organized for benevolent or charitable purposes, or for the purpose of assisting persons without means in the pursuit of any civil remedy, whose existence, organization or incorporation may be approved by the appellate division of the supreme court of the department in which the principal office of such corporation or voluntary association may be located."

In furtherance of the authority thus vested in the Appellate Divisions by subdivision 5 to approve or disapprove the practice of law by "benevolent or charitable" organizations or by organizations rendering legal services to "persons without means," the First Department promulgated part 608 of its Rules which sets forth the procedural rules for Application and practice pursuant to § 495 of the Judiciary Law. Actually, Rule 608 is a codification of the principles set forth in *Matter of Community Action for Legal Servs.*, 26 A.D.2d 354, 274 N.Y.S.2d 779 (hereafter CALS), wherein, noting the Appellate Division's concern for the protection of the public from the potential abuses of the corporate practice of law, minimal standards were called for which would insure that, in dealing with authorized corporate practitioners, "the public will receive the best available legal services in the same way as those who retain their own private lawyers, with effective recourse to the Court for gross professional failure." Among the safeguards suggested in CALS were the requirements that lay control over the operation of the legal assistance corporation be held to a minimum, and that the lawyer-employee of the corporation "maintain full professional and direct responsibility to his clients for the information and services so received" thus insuring the independence and inviolability of the lawyer-client relationship.

The petition gave to Lambda, which had previously been approved by the Commissioner of Education as a not-for-profit corporation, the following corporate purpose: "The Corporation is organized to seek, through the legal process, to insure equal protection of the laws and the protection of civil rights of homosexuals." In the petition, which was modeled upon the previously approved Application of the Puerto Rican Legal Defense and Education Fund, Inc., Lambda proposed, among other things "(a) to initiate or join in judicial and administrative proceedings whenever legal rights and interests of significant numbers of homosexuals may be affected; (b) to provide to homosexuals information which will broaden their awareness of their legal rights and obligations; (c) to inform the legal community and the public of the goals, methods and accomplishments of the Corporation." Additionally, it was proposed that Lambda would provide legal services without charge "in those situations which give rise to legal issues having a substantial effect on the legal rights of homosexuals." It is not disputed that Lambda's petition complied in all respects with the requirements of Rule 608, pursuant to which other legal assistance organizations have been authorized to practice law.

Despite the compliance of Lambda's petition with Rule 608, and the recommendation of various bar associations that Lambda's Application be approved,[1] the Appellate

---

1. Section 608.2 requires submission of each petition to the Association of the Bar of the City of New York, the New York County Lawyers Association and the Bronx County Bar Association for consideration. In regards the Lambda petition, both the New York County Lawyers Association and the Association of the Bar recommended approval of the Application. In a Memorandum submitted by the Committee on Professional Responsibility of the Association of the Bar, it was noted: "We have carefully reviewed New York cases interpreting the terms 'benevolent or charitable' and have concluded that the purposes of the LAMBDA Legal Defense & Education Fund are within the meaning of Judiciary Law sec. 495. It seems established that all the purposes of an accepted charitable institution need not be charitable, nor need its services be limited to the poor."

Division denied and dismissed the Application.... For reasons set forth hereinafter, we reverse.

The threshold issue on this appeal concerns the validity of the Appellate Division's determination that Lambda did not qualify for § 495 (subd. 5) approval since its stated purpose — to protect the legal rights of homosexuals, a minority — was "neither benevolent nor charitable." Petitioner contends, with justification, that the disapproval of Lambda's Application on the ground that its purpose was not charitable or benevolent was inconsistent with the Appellate Division's prior approval of the Puerto Rican Legal Defense and Education Fund, Inc. (PRLDEF), and that the equal protection clause thus requires consideration of Lambda as a charitable organization.

Section 495 (subd. 5) excepts from the proscription against the corporate practice of law organizations organized "for benevolent or charitable purposes" or "for the purpose of assisting persons without means." In February of 1972, the Appellate Division approved the § 495 (subd. 5) Application of the PRLDEF, which set forth the following as its corporate purpose: "To initiate or join in judicial and administrative proceedings affecting legal rights and interests of substantial numbers of Puerto Ricans and to conduct related informational and research programs." The PRLDEF petition did not purport to limit its services to indigents; it must, therefore, be concluded that its Application was approved as being that of an organization organized for "benevolent or charitable" purposes — that the Appellate Division considered the rendering of free legal services in furtherance of the rights of a minority to be a charitable or benevolent purpose. As the petitioner points out, the characterization of such free legal services as charitable finds support in decisional law.

The stated purpose of the Lambda petition was substantially identical to that of the Puerto Rican Defense Fund; indeed the petitioner admits having modeled the Lambda petition on the PRLDEF Application. There is thus no justification for a finding that one was motivated by charitable goals while the other was not. Accordingly, the Appellate Division erred in finding the purpose of Lambda neither "benevolent nor charitable."

Upon concluding that Lambda was a charitable organization, a more troublesome issue arises — whether in the case of a properly submitted Application, which fully complies with Rule 608 in a case such as this, there remains in the Appellate Division any discretion as to the approval or disapproval thereof. We think not. The petitioner contends that Lambda's proposed activities are protected by the First Amendment, and that under the United States Supreme Court's decisions the Appellate Division may not restrict or prohibit such activities. Were this merely a cause of the State prohibiting a group such as Lambda from employing or selecting attorneys to represent them and then soliciting and referring cases for litigation in furtherance of the groups rights, *Button* and its progeny would be dispositive, for, as the Supreme Court recently stated: "The common thread running through our decisions in *NAACP v. Button*, *Trainmen*, and *United Mine Workers* is that collective activity undertaken to obtain meaningful access to the courts is a fundamental right within the protection of the First Amendment" (*United Transp. Union v. Michigan Bar*, 401 U.S. 576, 585). Accordingly, based upon First Amendment principles, Lambda, or any such group formed to further common legal rights, is entitled to employ attorneys to represent them and to seek out cases which will advance their common goals. To the extent that § 495 of the Judiciary Law would frustrate such activity by undue restriction or prohibition, it runs afoul of the First Amendment.

There is involved here, however, more than the mere employment of attorneys or solicitation of cases in furtherance of group rights. The petitioner is seeking permission to practice law as a corporate entity. While the practice of law has always been subject to State regulation and is not, per se, protected by the First Amendment, State regulation of the practice of law is, of course, subject to constitutional strictures; any qualification upon the practice of law must have a rational connection with the applicant's fitness or capacity to practice law, and must be applied in such a manner as to comport with the equal protection clause of the Fourteenth Amendment. As Mr. Justice Black stated for the majority in *Konigsberg*: "We recognize the importance of leaving States free to select their own bars, but it is equally important that the State not exercise this power in an arbitrary or discriminatory manner nor in such way as to impinge on the freedom of political expression or association."

In enacting §495 (subd. 5) of the Judiciary Law, the Legislature has extended the right to practice law to certain groups and corporations, and has placed in the Appellate Division the authority and responsibility to oversee the enforcement thereof. In setting forth Rule 608, a regulatory scheme which, as suggested in *CALS*, is designed to protect the public from abuses by prohibiting lay control over the legal functions of corporately-employed attorneys and by fixing client responsibility in the individual attorney rather than in the corporate practitioner, the Appellate Division has effected controls over the corporate practice of law which, on their face, may be applied in a nondiscriminatory fashion. Once, however, an applicant has complied with Rule 608, in a case such as this, by filing a petition specifying all the requisite information, the Appellate Division may not, as it attempted to do here, exercise its discretion by selectively approving Applications based upon a determination as to whether there is a need for the legal services sought to be offered by each applicant. It is of no consequence—it bears no rational connection to the valid regulation of the practice of law—that there exists in "the private sector" attorneys who are willing to handle the class of cases with which the applicant proposes to deal. Accordingly, it would violate equal protection of the law to distinguish between similarly situated minorities on such an irrational basis.

Furthermore, such a subjective determination as is proposed here lacks the necessary standards to insure a nondiscriminatory result. The danger of discrimination which inheres in such a standardless approval is, in our opinion, evidenced by the determination in question here. We can perceive no rational distinction in the need for group legal services as between Puerto Ricans and homosexuals. Both groups are minorities subject to varied discriminations and in need of legal services. Absent evidence to the contrary, it must be assumed that the services of private attorneys are equally available or unavailable to both groups....

Regarding the petitioner's contention that the §495 delegation of authority to the Appellate Division to Approve the Applications lacks adequate standards to govern such determinations,[2] suffice it to say that if, as suggested above, the statute is construed to leave no discretion in the Appellate Division—if approval is granted in a nondiscriminatory manner—then the lack of standards will not render the statute constitutionally infirm. The order appealed from should be reversed, the petition reinstated and the matter remitted to the Appellate Division.

---

2. At least one commentator has also suggested that the section 495 delegation of authority to "approve" may be unconstitutional for lack of adequate standards. (See Botein, The Constitutionality of Restrictions on Poverty Law Firms: A New York Case Study, 46 NYU L.Rev. 748, 751–52.) However, as Professor Botein points out, the Supreme Court has recently upheld a similarly vague delegation to the Appellate Division vis-a-vis the admission of individuals to practice law (see Law Students, etc., Research Council v. Wadmond, 401 U.S. 154).

GABRIELLI, Judge (dissenting).

In ruling that the Appellate Division's unanimous determination is "unsupportable," the majority is according that court, which was acting in an administrative capacity, a narrower ranger of discretion than normally is accorded an administrative agency. The test applied by a court exercising the administrative review function is whether a rational basis undergirds the determination appealed from. Section 495 of the Judiciary Law clearly gives the Appellate Division discretion to approve or not to approve organizations applying to practice law for benevolent or charitable purposes. This is recognized in the majority's Per Curiam statement which proceeds abruptly to the conclusion of unsupportability without advising as to how or why a rational basis is lacking.

The Appellate Division has fully explained its determination in a detailed statement. The finding that the organization's stated purposes "are on their face neither benevolent nor charitable" is fully supported in the record unless the operative words "benevolent" and "charitable" are to be accorded other than their well-understood meaning. In the last two paragraphs of its statement, the court has laid down the factor of financial inability to afford legal representation as at least one important guideline to be applied. The concurring opinion in this court makes much of the assertion that in a prior Application invoking the Puerto Rican Legal Defense and Education Fund, Inc., the court's approval was based solely on the charitable purpose of helping a minority ethnic group, not because of the members' indigency, but solely because of their minority status in the society. However, the Appellate Division in its statement here appealed from noted there is no parallel since "the latter's (PRLDEF) Application demonstrated clearly that indigence is rife amongst the intended clientele. It does not appear that discrimination against homosexuals, which undoubtedly exists, operates to deprive them of legal representation." I am unable to see why that distinction is without effect, as much the rest of this court. And even assuming, without agreeing, that there is some measure of inconsistency between the determination in the Puerto Rican case and the one now before us, at least on the question of indigency as a criterion, we again find the Appellate Division accorded lesser powers by the majority than would be accorded any other administrative agency exercising discretionary and regulatory powers. The Appellate Division in regulating these matters has seen fit to draw some lines which are not without rational bases. The court is normally loath to interfere with agency regulation in areas delegated to the agency by the Legislature. Yet here the signatories to the concurring opinion have substituted their judgment in the matter for the judgment of those to whom the responsibility was delegated; and those subscribing to the Per Curiam statement, although remitting the case for reconsideration, seem to have given the court below very little to reconsider.

The majority has, in effect, taken the regulatory function away from the Appellate Division in this case and for that reason I must dissent.

Application of William J. Thom, Petitioner,

For Approval of the Incorporation of
Lambda Legal Defense & Education Fund, Inc.
350 N.Y.S.2d 1 (App. Div. 1973)

PER CURIAM:

...Having been instructed that the determination in which we exercised that discretion was "unsupportable," we now grant the Application, but we now exercise discretion to strike from the order presented a paragraph not concerned with the practice of law and which does not, in our view, fall within § 495 of the Judiciary Law as descriptive of powers which we should authorize legal assistance corporations to exercise. We do not deem it appropriate to lend our approval to paragraph (g): "to promote legal education among homosexuals by recruiting and encouraging potential law students who are homosexuals and by providing assistance to such students after admission to law school."

In making this disposition, we repeat the observation made in our November, 1972 decision: "Perhaps the Legislature should speak again with clarity as to what the words 'benevolent or charitable purposes' mean as they are used in § 495. We invite such a clarification." Clarification seems to be needed now more than ever. Indeed, the whole subject of legal representation by associations, organizations and corporations requires careful and analytical re-examination by our Legislature in the light of the many developments and new thinking in this area, including studies of bar associations and others, court decisions and statutory changes which have occurred during the two-thirds of a century which has elapsed since section 495, Judiciary Law, was enacted in 1909, as section 280 of the then Penal Law, in substantially its present form.

Notes and Questions

1. A subsequent decision by the Internal Revenue Service to recognized Lambda Legal Defense & Education Fund as exempt from federal income taxation under Section 501(c)(3) of the Internal Revenue Code marked a major breakthrough for organizations advocating for equal rights for sexual minorities. Recognition as a tax-exempt charitable or educational organization had been achieved by some prior groups, but only by adopting non-controversial names and statements of purpose that did not disclose the organization's lesbian or gay nature. In 1978, after years of internal debate, the IRS finally issued a public ruling in which it declared that a "nonprofit organization formed to educate the public about homosexuality in order to foster an understanding and tolerance of homosexuals and their problems qualifies for exemption under section 501(c)(3) of the Code." See Rev. Rul. 78-305, 1978-2 C.B. 172.

2. At the time this case was decided, consensual sodomy between adults was a misdemeanor in New York. (The law was subsequently declared unconstitutional as applied to consenting adults in private by New York's courts, and ultimately the Supreme Court declared all laws against private, adult consensual sodomy unconstitutional in 2003 in *Lawrence v. Texas*.) Would the result have been different if the state's Penal Code treated consensual sodomy as a serious felony?

* * *

Many of the most important precedents on the associational rights of sexual minorities have been achieved by lesbian and gay student groups at public universities. In successive cases, such groups have won the right to hold events on campus, the right to obtain official university recognition on the same basis as other student organizations, and the right to received student activity funds on the same basis as other organizations. However, the United States Supreme Court has never granted certiorari in a case involving lesbian and gay student organizations, leaving open the question whether the various court of appeals precedents would stand up in the current conservative Supreme Court.

Gay Students Organization v. Bonner

509 F.2d 652 (1st Cir. 1974)

COFFIN, Chief Judge.

The Gay Students Organization (GSO) was officially recognized as a student organization at the University of New Hampshire in May, 1973,[1] and on November 9, 1973 the group sponsored a dance on campus. The dance itself was held without incident, but media coverage of the event and criticism by Governor Meldrim Thomson, Jr., led the University's Board of Trustees to reconsider its treatment of the organization. The next day, November 10, 1973, the Board issued a "Position Statement" which indicated that the University would attempt to have determined the "legality and appropriateness of scheduling social functions by the Gay Students Organization" and which "directed that in the interim the University administration would schedule no further social functions by the Gay Students Organization until the matter is legally resolved." The University subsequently filed a declaratory judgment action in Strafford County Superior Court on November 21, 1973.

When the GSO requested permission to sponsor a play on December 7 and have a social function afterward, the University permitted the play but denied permission for the social function. The play was given as scheduled, and the GSO held a meeting following it. Sometime during the evening copies of two "extremist" homosexual publications were distributed by individuals over whom the GSO claims it had no control. Governor Thomson wrote an open letter to the trustees after the play, warning that if they did not "take firm, fair and positive action to rid your campuses of socially abhorrent activities" he would "stand solidly against the expenditure of one more cent of taxpayers' money for your institutions." Dr. Thomas N. Bonner, President of the University, then issued a public statement condemning the distribution of the homosexual literature and announcing that a repetition of the behavior would cause him to seek suspension of the GSO as a student organization. Bonner also revealed that he had "ordered that the current Trustee ban on GSO social functions be interpreted more strictly by administrative authorities than had been the case before December 7, 1973."

The lawsuit which is the subject of this appeal was filed in federal district court by the GSO on November 29, 1973. The complaint alleged First and Fourteenth Amendment violations giving rise to a cause of action under 42 U.S.C. sec. 1983, and sought

---

1. The organization filed the following Statement of Purpose:

"1) The primary purpose of the UNH Gay Students Organization is to promote the recognition of Gay people on campus and to form a viable organization through which bisexual and homosexual people may express themselves.

"2) Through this organization social functions will be organized in which both Gay and straight people can learn about the others' thoughts and feelings concerning sexuality and sexual roles.

"3) In an effort to educate the public about bisexuality and homosexuality, this organization will attempt to affect social changes through public relation measures such as guest lecturers, free literature, films, newspaper articles and radio programs.

"4) Not the least important reason for establishing a Gay organization is to give bisexual and homosexual members of the college community a place to communicate with each other and form discussion groups so that a healthy Gay consciousness can evolve among students."

injunctive and declaratory relief. A hearing was held on December 10 on the GSO's request for a preliminary injunction, and the parties agreed that the hearing would serve as a final hearing on the merits. Defendants, hereinafter "appellants," requested that the proceeding be reopened for the submission of additional evidence, and a second hearing was held on December 28. On January 16, 1974, the district court held for the GSO (sometimes hereinafter referred to as "appellees") on the ground that its members had been denied their First Amendment right of association. The court found no direct impairment of the GSO's "more traditional First Amendment rights," presumably the freedoms of speech, assembly and petition from which the right of association is derived. The court also indicated that in its view substantial equal protection questions were raised by defendants' policy, and that, First Amendment considerations aside, the state could not demonstrate that the classification rationally furthered a legitimate state interest. The court enjoined appellants "from prohibiting or restricting the sponsorship of social functions or use of University facilities for such functions by the Gay Students Organization" and "from treating the Gay Students Organization differently than other University student organizations."....

> [Omitted here is the court's lengthy consideration of procedural defenses raised by the defendants with regard to applicability of Section 1983 and service of process on individual defendants.]

Coming to the merits, we are conscious of the tension between deeply felt, conflicting values or moral judgments, and the traditional legal method of extracting and applying principles from decided cases. First, this case deals with a university attempting to regulate student activity—in the *in loco parentis* tradition which most judges, being over thirty, acknowledged without much question during their years of matriculation. Second, the campus group sought to be regulated stands for sexual values in direct conflict with the deeply imbued moral standards of much of the community whose taxes support the university.

The underlying question, usually not articulated, is whether, whatever may be Supreme Court precedent in the First Amendment area, group activity promoting values so far beyond the pale of the wider community's values is also beyond the boundaries of the First Amendment, at least to the extent that university facilities may not be used by the group to flaunt its credo. If visceral reactions suggest an affirmative answer, the next task for judges is to devise a standard which, while damping down the First Amendment on a university campus, is generally applicable and free from the dangers of arbitrariness. At this point troubles arise. How are the deeply felt values of the community to be identified? On an issue such as permissive abortion, the wider community may well be divided among those believing in "the right to life," those believing in "the right to control over one's body," and those who do not feel deeply either way. Assuming that "community-wide values" could be confidently identified, and that a university could limit the associational activity of groups challenging those values, such an approach would apply also to socialists, conscientious objectors, vivisectionists, those favoring more oil refineries. As to each group, there are sectors of the community to whom its values are anathema. Or, if values be limited to morals, the barrier would reach those attracted to pre-marital sex, atheism, the consumption of alcoholic beverages, esoteric heterosexual activity, violence on television, or dirty books. This is not to suggest that a university is powerless to proscribe either harmful activity or incitement of illegal activity, but it is to say that we are unable to devise a tolerable standard exempting this case at the threshold from general First Amendment precedents.

We address first one of the questions we have alluded to: is there something different about a university that makes it an enclave sheltered from the full play of the First Amendment? The Supreme Court's recent decisions in *Healy v. James*, 408 U.S. 169 (1972), and *Papish v. Board of Curators*, 410 U.S. 667 (1973), indicate in no uncertain terms that the First Amendment applies with full vigor on the campuses of state universities. In *Healy* the Court rejected the notion that First Amendment protections apply with less force on campus than in the community at large, and the Papish Court made it clear that there is no "dual standard" to be applied in scrutinizing restrictions upon speech. Indeed, the Court has recognized that the "vigilant protection of constitutional freedoms is nowhere more vital than in the community of American schools." *Shelton v. Tucker*, 364 U.S. at 487. Thus we proceed as if the state itself, or one of its instrumentalities other than a university, had promulgated the regulation at issue.

Given this standard by which a university regulation should be judged, we now must ask whether, even though GSO was recognized as a campus organization, its members' right of association was abridged. Here again, *Healy v. James* is controlling. It is true that there the university had refused to recognize the campus organization altogether rather than denying it the use of campus facilities for certain activities. But the Court's analysis in *Healy* focused not on the technical point of recognition or nonrecognition, but on the practicalities of human interaction. While the Court concluded that the SDS members' right to further their personal beliefs had been impermissibly burdened by nonrecognition, this conclusion stemmed from a finding that the "primary impediment to free association flowing from nonrecognition is the denial of use of campus facilities for meetings and other appropriate purposes." The ultimate issue at which inquiry must be directed is the effect which a regulation has on organizational and associational activity, not the isolated and for the most part irrelevant issue of recognition per se.

Despite the language of *Healy* cited above, appellants argue that "social events" are not among the class of protected associational activities. One aspect of this argument is the suggestion that the ban on social events is permissible because other GSO activities such as discussions are allowed. A very similar contention was rejected in *Healy*. The university had pointed out that nonrecognition affected only on-campus activities, and that therefore the individuals wishing to form an SDS group could meet and distribute literature off campus, and even meet on campus if they did so informally. The Court was thus invited to find that the individuals were free to associate even though their on-campus activities were restricted. It held, however, that the other associational opportunities available to the individuals did not ameliorate significantly the disabilities imposed by the university. Once again, its standard was expressed in the clearest of terms—"(T)he Constitution's protection is not limited to direct interference with fundamental rights." Although the Supreme Court refused in *Healy* to characterize as insubstantial the impediments to association resulting from denial of access to campus bulletin boards and the school newspaper, that case could conceivably be read to shelter only those group efforts at self-promotion which utilize such conventional approaches.

There are, however, many other ways in which an organization might wish to go about attracting members and promoting its point of view. *Healy* has been interpreted to extend to the use of campus facilities for social events in the one case of which we are aware which has considered the issue. We are also led to this conclusion by the realization that efforts by a state to restrict groups other than the GSO to gatherings that were in no sense "social events" would be rejected out of hand. Even a lecture or discussion, which appear to be the only types of meetings which the appellants would allow the GSO to hold, becomes a social event if beer is served beforehand or coffee afterward.

Teas, coffees and dinners form the backbone of many a political candidate's campaign, and yet these activities would seemingly be subject to prohibition. While a university may have some latitude in regulating organizations such as fraternities or sororities which can be purely social, its efforts to restrict the activities of a cause-oriented group like the GSO stand on a different footing. See Note, Freedom of Political Association on the Campus: The Right to Official Recognition, 46 N.Y.U.L.Rev. 1149, 1158 61 (1971). Considering the important role that social events can play in individuals' efforts to associate to further their common beliefs, the prohibition of all social events must be taken to be a substantial abridgment of associational rights, even if assumed to be an indirect one.

What we have been considering is appellants' contention that, so long as an association is allowed to meet, restrictions on some of its activities are permissible — i.e., that it is enough that the glass is half full. We now address appellants' contention that when we examine the other half of the glass, the activities barred by the campus regulation, we must conclude that the First Amendment offers no protection because the activities barred are not speech related. Putting aside for a moment the question of whether GSO social events constitute "speech" in their own right, we note the district court's conclusion, not disputed by appellants, that the GSO is a political action organization. The GSO's efforts to organize the homosexual minority, "educate" the public as to its plight, and obtain for it better treatment from individuals and from the government thus represent but another example of the associational activity unequivocally singled out for protection in the very "core" of association cases decided by the Supreme Court.[2] Moreover, the activity engaged in by the GSO would be protected even if it were not so intimately bound up with the political process, for "it is immaterial whether the beliefs sought to be advanced by association pertain to political, economic, religious or cultural matters." *NAACP v. Alabama ex rel. Patterson*, 357 U.S. at 460.

While we accept the district court's conclusion that the associational rights of GSO members have been impermissibly regulated, we cannot agree that their "more traditional First Amendment rights," have not been abridged as well. Certainly GSO social functions do not constitute "pure speech," but conduct may have a communicative content sufficient to bring it within the ambit of the First Amendment. *Tinker v. Des Moines Indep. Community School Dist.*, 393 U.S. 503 (1969); . . . Communicative conduct is subject to regulation as to "time, place and manner" in the furtherance of a substantial governmental interest, so long as the restrictions imposed are only so broad as required in order to further the interest and are unrelated to the content and subject matter of the message communicated.

There can be no doubt that expression, assembly and petition constitute significant aspects of the GSO's conduct in holding social events.[3] The GSO was created, as its Statement of Purpose attests, to promote the free exchange of ideas among homosexuals and between homosexuals and heterosexuals, and to educate the public about bi-

---

2. As we have indicated at the outset, we see no sanction in reason or law for saying that, absent a direct threat to safety or the enforcement of law, certain groups lack a right of association. Many of the groups whose associational rights have been recognized by the Supreme Court have stood for propositions which must have seemed as outrageous as the GSO's positions today must seem to many.

3. Indeed, there is some support for the proposition that dancing, the activity which the appellants are most confident in asserting their right to regulate, is itself a form of expression protected by the First Amendment. See *Salem Inn, Inc. v. Frank*, 501 F.2d 18, 20 (2d Cir. 1974); cf. *California v. LaRue*, 409 U.S. 109, 118 (1972).

sexuality and homosexuality. GSO claims that social events in which discussion and exchange of ideas can take place in an informal atmosphere can play an important part in this communication. It would seem that these communicative opportunities are even more important for it than political teas, coffees, and dinners are for political candidates and parties, who have much wider access to the media, being more highly organized and socially accepted. And beyond the specific communications at such events is the basic "message" GSO seeks to convey—that homosexuals exist, that they feel repressed by existing laws and attitudes, that they wish to emerge from their isolation, and that public understanding of their attitudes and problems is desirable for society.

Perhaps these claims, being self serving, fall short of establishing the speech-relatedness of GSO social events. But they receive the strongest corroboration from the interpretation placed on these events by the outside community, as related by appellants. Appellants have relied heavily on their obligation and right to prevent activities which the people of New Hampshire find shocking and offensive. In the brief for President Bonner and the University administrators we are told that the "activity of the GSO was variously labelled a spectacle, an abomination and similar terms of disapprobation" after the GSO dance on November 8, 1973; that the University has an obligation to prevent activity which affronts the citizens of the University and the town and which violates breach of the peace statutes; that the GSO dance constituted "grandstanding;" that recognition of the GSO inflamed a large segment of the people of the state; that the organization cannot be permitted to use its unpopularity without restriction to undermine the University within the state; and that "the ban on social functions reflects the distaste with which homosexual organizations are regarded in the State."

We do not see how these statements can be interpreted to avoid the conclusion that the regulation imposed was based in large measure, if not exclusively, on the content of the GSO's expression. It is well established that "above all else, the First Amendment means that government has no power to restrict expression because of its message, its ideas, its subject matter, or its content." *Police Dept. v. Mosley*, 408 U.S. at 95. Not only do appellants' statements indicate that the prohibition reflects a distaste both for the ideas held and communicated by GSO members and for the larger message conveyed by the very holding of such public events, but the fact that the GSO alone was made subject to the regulation indicates that the ban is content-related. Nor do the events of November 8 leave room for the conclusion that the disapproval of the GSO event was due to the occurrence of violently disruptive or otherwise illegal activities. The adverse reaction must be viewed as precipitated by the GSO's program and the fact that the organization was aggressively presenting it to the public.

With the expressive quality of the GSO activities established, the appellants' policy regulating the activities must be measured against the detailed standard articulated in *United States v. O'Brien*. The Supreme Court there upheld a conviction based upon the burning of a draft card by one who claimed to be demonstrating against the war and against the draft. The Court recognized that such conduct could be regulated despite its "speech" element because (1) the regulation was within the constitutional power of the government; (2) it furthered an important or substantial governmental interest; (3) the governmental interest was unrelated to the suppression of free expression; and (4) the incidental restriction on alleged First Amendment freedoms was no greater than essential to the furtherance of that interest.

As is apparent from our discussion above of the extent to which appellants' policy toward the GSO is content-related, the curtailing of expression which they find abhorrent or offensive cannot provide the important governmental interest upon which impairment of First Amendment freedoms must be predicated. "Once a forum is opened up to assembly or speaking by some groups, government may not prohibit others from assembling or speaking on the basis of what they intend to say. Selective exclusions from a public forum may not be based on content alone, and may not be justified by reference to content alone." *Police Dept. v. Mosley*, 408 U.S. at 96.

Another interest asserted by appellants is that in preventing illegal activity, which may include "deviate" sex acts, "lascivious carriage," and breach of the peace. But there has been no allegation that any such illegal acts took place at the GSO social events held on November 8 and December 7, 1973. Indeed, we emphasize the finding of the district court that "There were no official complaints about the dance, and no evidence was adduced to show that improper or illegal activities had taken place" at the dance. The only activity of even questionable legality discussed in the record involved the distribution of printed materials alleged to be obscene, and the district court found that no University of New Hampshire students were responsible for the distribution. Mere "undifferentiated fear or apprehension" of illegal conduct, is not enough to overcome First Amendment rights, and speculation that individuals might at some time engage in illegal activity is insufficient to justify regulation by the state.

The University is by no means bereft of power to regulate conduct on campus. Not only may it act to prevent criminal conduct by policies focused on real and established dangers, but it can proscribe advocacy of illegal activities falling short of conduct, or conduct in itself noncriminal, if such advocacy or conduct is directed at producing or is likely to incite imminent lawless action.

Finally there is a residual power going beyond the prevention of criminal conduct and the kind of advocacy of such conduct we have described. In *Healy v. James*, 408 U.S. 169, 189 (1971), the Supreme Court said that in a school environment, the power to prohibit lawless action is not limited to acts of a criminal nature: "Also prohibitable are actions which 'materially and substantially disrupt the work and the discipline of the school.'" We would assume that a university, so minded, would not be powerless to regulate public petting (heterosexual or otherwise), drinking in university buildings, or many other noncriminal activities which those responsible for running the institution rightly or wrongly think necessary "to assure that the traditional academic atmosphere is safeguarded." Thus, if a university chose to do so, it might well be able to regulate overt sexual behavior, short of criminal activity, which may offend the community's sense of propriety, so long as it acts in a fair and equitable manner. The point in this case is that the district court has found no improper conduct, and it does not appear that the university ever concerned itself with defining or regulating such behavior. Defendants sought to cut back GSO's social activities simply because sponsored by that group. The ban was not justified by any evidence of misconduct attributable to GSO, and it was altogether too sweeping....

Gay Lib v. University of Missouri

558 F.2d 848 (8th Cir. 1977),
cert. denied, 434 U.S. 1080 (1978)

LAY, Circuit Judge.

The issue before us is whether officials of a state university may lawfully withhold formal recognition of a student organization, comprised largely of homosexuals, whose basic purpose is to provide a forum for discussion about homosexuality. Gay Lib, an organization at the University of Missouri, and four of its members appeal from the denial of their request for injunctive relief by the United States District Court....In denying the 42 U.S.C. sec. 1983 claim the district court sustained the University administration's refusal to recognize Gay Lib as a campus organization. The court conceded that the question was a close one, but ruled that the school officials justified their action on the ground that recognition of Gay Lib would probably result in the commission of felonious acts of sodomy in violation of Missouri law.[1] The district court also rejected plaintiffs' claim that nonrecognition denied them equal protection of the laws....

Formal recognition of a student organization by the University of Missouri entitles the group to use campus facilities for meetings and to apply for financial support from student activities funds. Written University policies with respect to recognition of campus groups provide that:

> Groups are recognized on the basis of their own statements as to name, aims, nature and program. Recognition of an organization by the Committee does not constitute approval or endorsement of the organization's aims and activities * * *.

Gay Lib began its efforts to gain formal recognition in early 1971. In accordance with established University procedures, the group submitted a petition for recognition to the Missouri Students Association (MSA). A statement of purposes accompanying the petition set forth the proposed organization's aims as follows:

(a) To provide a dialogue between the homosexual and heterosexual members of the university community.

(b) To dispel the lack of information and develop an understanding of the homosexual at the University of Missouri.

(c) To alleviate the unnecessary burden of shame felt by the local homosexual population.

(d) To help education, the community and the homosexual to understand the social roles that the homosexual now plays in the community.

(e) To work closely with established university and community groups for a broader sharing of knowledge and information.

Both the MSA Rules Committee and the Senate approved Gay Lib's petition. The matter was then referred to the Committee on Student Organizations, Government

---

1. MO. Ann. Stat. sec. 563.230 (Vernon) provides: Every person who shall be convicted of the detestable and abominable crime against nature, committed with mankind or with beast, with the sexual organs or with the mouth, shall be punished by imprisonment in the penitentiary not less than two years.

and Activities (SOGA), which was comprised of students and faculty. While the matter was pending before SOGA, Gay Lib submitted a revised, more detailed statement of purposes.[2]

In December, 1971, SOGA voted to recommend recognition of Gay Lib. The recommendation, however, was vetoed by Edwin Hutchins, then Dean of Student Affairs. Hutchins based his veto on "a concern for the impact of recognition on the general relationship of the University to the public at large."

Gay Lib appealed the nonrecognition decision to successive levels of the University hierarchy, ending with the President of the University. Each level sustained Hutchins' ruling. Thereafter, Gay Lib appealed the decision to the University's Board of Curators. The Board consolidated the appeal with a related matter arising out of the University of Missouri at Kansas City, and appointed a hearing officer, Cullen Coil, a Jefferson City attorney and former Commissioner of the Missouri Supreme Court, to develop the facts. At the hearings substantial lay and expert testimony was adduced. Following the hearings, Coil recommended that the University deny formal recognition to the organization.[3] Subsequently, the Board denied Gay Lib'S appeal, adopting the following resolution:

---

2. The revised statement provided: 1. Gay Lib intends to create a forum for the study of the sexual statutes of this state and especially of the sodomy law now in effect. Through study of the intent of the law and of its psychological and sociological implications, it will be possible to more fully understand what the full meaning is of being Gay. Through knowledge of the law, it becomes possible to create an atmosphere within which the present statute may be revised or eliminated through an educational and candid look at all ramifications of such laws and their rationale. Changes of other such laws outside of Missouri and in nations such as Great Britain will provide a fuller context. 2. Gay Lib seeks to promote meaningful communication between all members of the University community, whether homosexual or heterosexual. With candor and compassion on both sides, much of the fear of the unknown can be eliminated and scars of past repression may be healed. This communication is specifically intended to be two-way in nature. The Gay world has just as much to learn from the straight world as they have to offer it. We seek to develop an atmosphere in which people are themselves first and sexual entities second. 3. Gay Lib wants to provide information to the vast majority of those who really don't know what homosexuality or bisexual behavior is. Too much of the same prejudice is now directed at Gay people just as it is directed at ethnic minorities. 4. Gay Lib does not seek to proselytize, convert, or recruit. On the other hand, people who have already established a pattern of homosexuality when they enter college must adjust to this fact. 5. Gay Lib hopes to help the Gay community to rid itself of its subconscious burden of guilt. Society imprints this self-image on homosexuals and makes adjustment with the straight world more difficult. 6. Gay Lib hopes to function as a channel for those who find difficulty in sexual adjustment. While we do not pretend to have psychiatric expertise, we can reach people who do not trust normal channels for such help and enable them to contact professional help as required. 7. As an educational group, Gay Lib does not advocate any violation of state statutes. We serve as a forum for understanding and knowledge where this is now lacking.

3. Coil found that formal recognition of Gay Lib would: (1) give a formal status to and tend to reinforce the personal identities of the homosexual members of those organizations and will perpetuate and expand an abnormal way of life, unless contrary to their intention as stated in their written purposes, the homosexual members make a concerted effort to seek treatment, recognize homosexuality as abnormal and attempt to cease their homosexual practices; (2) tend to cause latent or potential homosexuals who become members to become overt homosexuals; (3) tend to expand homosexual behavior which will cause increased violations of section 563.230 of the Revised Statutes of Missouri; (4) be undesirable insofar as homosexuals will counsel other homosexuals, i. e., the sick and abnormal counseling others who are similarly ill and abnormal; and (5) constitute an implied approval by the University of the abnormal homosexual life-style as a normal way of life and would be so understood by many students and other members of the public, even though, and despite the fact that, the University's regulations for student organizations provide that recognition of

Be it hereby resolved that the Board of Curators of the University of Missouri concurs with and hereby adopts the Hearing Officer's Recommended Findings of Fact made by the Honorable Cullen Coil and further makes the following specific findings of fact:

1. The Gay Lib movement as exemplified by the Gay Lib Organization at UMC and the Gay People's Union at UMKC is premised upon homosexuality being normal behavior, contrary to the further findings herein.

2. A homosexual is one who seeks to satisfy his or her sexual desires by practicing some or all of the following: fellatio, cunnilingus, masturbation, anal eroticism and perhaps in other ways.

3. Homosexuality is a compulsive type of behavior.

4. There are potential or latent homosexuals, i. e. persons who come into adolescence or young adulthood unaware that they have homosexual tendencies, but who have fears of sexual relations with a member of the opposite sex.

5. What happens to a latent or potential homosexual from the standpoint of his environment can cause him to become or not to become a homosexual.

6. That homosexuality is an illness and should and can be treated as such and is clearly abnormal behavior.

7. Certain homosexual practices violate provisions of Section 563.230 of the Revised Statutes of Missouri.

8. That formal recognition by the University of either or both the proposed Gay Lib and Gay People's Union will: (The Board of Curators here adopted verbatim Mr. Coil's above-cited conclusions as to the effect of formal recognition.)

Plaintiffs filed this civil rights action to compel the University to formally recognize Gay Lib, alleging that nonrecognition infringed their First Amendment freedom of association and denied them equal protection....

First Amendment.

Although the district court denied plaintiffs relief, Judge Hunter, recognizing *Healy v. James*, 408 U.S. 169 (1972), stated:

(T)he University, acting here as an instrumentality of the State, has no right to restrict speech or association "simply because it finds the views expressed to be abhorrent."

Since the Supreme Court's decision in Healy, the First and Fourth Circuits have sustained the rights of groups similar to Gay Lib to sponsor social functions involving the use of university facilities, *Gay Students Org. of Univ. of New Hampshire v. Bonner*, 509 F.2d 652 (1st Cir. 1974); and to register as a student organization. *Gay Alliance of Students v. Matthews*, 544 F.2d 162 (4th Cir. 1976). The analytical discussion offered by these two courts strongly supports recognition of Gay Lib here.[4]

---

an organization by the University does not constitute approval or endorsement of the organization's aims or activities.

4. As Judge Winter of the Fourth Circuit observes: If the University is attempting to prevent homosexuals from meeting one another to discuss their common problems and possible solutions to those problems, then its purpose is clearly inimical to basic first amendment values. Individuals of whatever sexual persuasion have the fundamental right to meet, discuss current problems, and to advocate changes in the status quo, so long as there is no "incitement to imminent lawless action." If, on the other hand, VCU's concern is with a possible rise in the incidence of actual homosexual conduct between students, then a different problem is presented. We have little doubt that the Uni-

Notwithstanding these decisions, defendants assert that the record in this case contains expert medical testimony which provides a legal justification for withholding formal recognition from Gay Lib. They argue, and the district court found, that recognition of Gay Lib would likely result in imminent violations of Missouri sodomy laws.

The district court placed reliance on the testimony of two psychiatrists, Dr. Harold Voth and Dr. Charles Socarides. Dr. Voth testified that formal recognition would tend to "perpetuate" or "expand" homosexual behavior. However, on cross-examination, Dr. Voth further testified that his conclusion was "an inference," and "(t)here is no way in the world for me or anyone else to know." Dr. Socarides stated that he believed "that wherever you have a convocation of homosexuals, that you are going to have increased homosexual activities which, of course includes sodomy." He concluded that "any gathering would certainly promote such sexual contact."

Also relevant to the district court's determination was the medical opinion proffered by defendants' experts that homosexual behavior is compulsive. However, as demonstrated by the substantial body of professional medical opinion conflicting with defendants' case, it must be acknowledged that there is no scientific certitude to the opinions offered.[5]

The district court noted testimony from Dr. Robert Kolodny, a medical doctor with some training in psychiatry. Dr. Kolodny testified that he believed recognition would not have "any discernible effect upon the sexual behavior of the student population." He based his conclusion on his clinical knowledge of human sexual behavior and "from actual knowledge of what, in fact has occurred on several campuses where homosexual groups have been allowed to acquire office space, hold social functions, and sponsor university activities."

Defendants urge that their experts are more worthy of belief because of their outstanding professional credentials. We need not pause here since defendants' evidence turns solely on Dr. Voth's conclusory "inference" and Dr. Socarides' "belief," for which no historical or empirical basis is disclosed.

Even accepting the opinions of defendants' experts at face value, we find it insufficient to justify a governmental prior restraint on the right of a group of students to associate for the purposes avowed in their statement and revised statement of purposes. While it is difficult to articulate generalized standards as to the quantum and quality of proof necessary to justify the abridgment of First Amendment rights, the many

---

versity could constitutionally regulate such conduct. Additionally, it may regulate any conduct (homosexual or otherwise) which "materially and substantially disrupt(s) the work and discipline of the school." But denial of registration is overkill. "(T)he critical line for First Amendment purposes must be drawn between advocacy, which is entitled to full protection, and action, which is not." There is no evidence that GAS is an organization devoted to carrying out illegal, specifically proscribed sexual practices. While Virginia law proscribes the practice of certain forms of homosexuality, Va.Code sec. 18.2-361, Virginia law does not make it a crime to be a homosexual. Indeed, a statute criminalizing such status and prescribing punishment therefor would be invalid. It follows that even if affording GAS registration does increase the opportunity for homosexual contacts, that fact is insufficient to overcome the associational rights of members of GAS. Given the right to exclude individuals who are convicted of practicing proscribed forms of homosexuality, or whose homosexual conduct, although not proscribed, materially and substantially disrupts the work and discipline at VCU, the suppression of associational rights because the opportunity for homosexual contacts is increased constitutes prohibited overbreadth....

5. Of further significance is the fact that recognition of Gay Lib is not determinative of whether its members will be allowed to meet or associate, but only of whether the group may use school facilities and become eligible for student activities funds.

Supreme Court cases dealing with prior restraints and other First Amendment issues make clear that the restriction of First Amendment rights in the present context may be justified only by a far greater showing of a likelihood of imminent lawless action than that presented here.

Mr. Justice Harlan, in delivering the opinion of the Supreme Court in *NAACP v. Alabama*, 357 U.S. 449 (1958), emphasized the importance of freedom to engage in association:

> Effective advocacy of both public and private points of view, particularly controversial ones, is undeniably enhanced by group association, as this Court has more than once recognized by remarking upon the close nexus between the freedoms of speech and assembly. It is beyond debate that freedom to engage in association for the advancement of beliefs and ideas is an inseparable aspect of the "liberty" assured by the Due Process Clause of the Fourteenth Amendment, which embraces freedom of speech. Of course, it is immaterial whether the beliefs sought to be advanced by association pertain to political, economic, religious or cultural matters, and state action which may have the effect of curtailing the freedom to associate is subject to the closest scrutiny.

In the present case, none of the purposes or aims of Gay Lib, at least in this record, evidences advocacy of present violations of state law[6] or of university rules or regulations, and the district court made no finding of such advocacy. The district court further made no finding that Gay Lib would "infringe reasonable campus rules, interrupt classes, or substantially interfere with the opportunity of other students to obtain an education." So far as the avowed purposes and aims of this association are concerned, in the words of the Fourth Circuit:

> (I)t is, at most, a "pro-homosexual" political organization advocating a liberalization of legal restrictions against the practice of homosexuality and one seeking, by the educational and informational process, to generate understanding and acceptance of individuals whose sexual orientation is wholly or partly homosexual.

It is difficult to singularly ascribe evil connotations to the group simply because they are homosexuals. An interesting fact is that not all members of the group are homosexuals.[7] Furthermore, this approach blurs the constitutional line between mere advocacy

---

6. Surely, it is no longer a valid argument to suggest that an organization cannot be formed to peaceably advocate repeal of certain criminal laws. See *Street v. New York*, 394 U.S. 576, 591 (1969). Chief Judge Markey of the Court of Customs and Patent Appeals, sitting by designation, concurred in Judge Winter's analysis in *Gay Alliance of Students v. Matthews*, and cogently added: Consistent with the present decision, associations advocating any idea, any change in the law or policy of the general society, are as fully entitled to registration as is the plaintiff. Thus, associations devoted to peaceful advocacy of decriminalization or social acceptance of sadism, euthanasia, masochism, murder, genocide, segregation, master-race theories, gambling, voodoo, and the abolishment of all higher education, to list a few, must be granted registration, upon proper application and indicated compliance with reasonable regulations, if VCU continues to "register" associations. It is of no moment, in First Amendment jurisprudence, that ideas advocated by an association may to some or most of us be abhorrent, even sickening. The stifling of advocacy is even more abhorrent, even more sickening. It rings the death knell of a free society. Once used to stifle "the thought that we hate," in Holmes' phrase, it can stifle ideas we love. It signals a lack of faith in people, in its supposition that they are unable to choose in the market place of ideas.

7. Would defendants allow a group of heterosexual students to meet to discuss the problems of homosexuals and the repeal of the sodomy laws? Presumably so, since there would be no basis to "infer" that the compulsive behavior of the students would incite violations of the law. However, assuming this to be so, it is obvious that equal protection principles become more sharply focused.

and advocacy directed to inciting or producing imminent lawless action. Finally, such an approach smacks of penalizing persons for their status rather than their conduct, which is constitutionally impermissible. See *Robinson v. California*, 370 U.S. 660 (1962)....

Plaintiffs also seek an award of attorneys' fees, to be assessed against the defendants as costs, pursuant to the Civil Rights Attorney's Fees Awards Act of 1976, Pub.L.No.94-559 (Oct. 19, 1976), 90 Stat. 2641, 42 U.S.C.A. sec. 1988 (Dec. 1976 Supp.), which provides in pertinent part:

> In any action or proceeding to enforce a provision of sections 1981 to 1983, 1985, and 1986 of this title * * * the court, in its discretion, may allow the prevailing party, other than the United States, a reasonable attorney's fee as part of the costs.

The Act did not become effective until October 19, 1976, subsequent to the conclusion of the district court proceedings; however, we have held that the Act may be applied retroactively in cases in which an appeal was pending on the effective date of the Act. We feel that this is an appropriate case for an award of attorneys' fees. Accordingly, we award plaintiffs' attorneys fees for the appellate portion of this litigation in the sum of $1,000. We remand the cause to the district court for the determination and entry of an award of reasonable attorneys' fees for the district court phase of this case.

....

WEBSTER, Circuit Judge, concurring.

....Of particular significance to me is the prior restraint of First Amendment rights on such skimpy and speculative evidence as appellees advanced below. There is absolutely no evidence that appellants intend to violate any state law or regulation of the university or even that they will advocate such violations. Until such time as imminent overt lawless activity can be shown, the organization may not be excluded from recognition if it is otherwise in compliance with university regulations.

I have no doubt that the ancient halls of higher learning at Columbia will survive even the most offensive verbal assaults upon traditional moral values; solutions to tough problems are not found in repression of ideas. I am equally certain that the university possesses the power and the right to deal with individuals and organizations, "recognized" or not, that violate either its lawful regulations or the laws of the state. There will be time for that if appellees' dire predictions should somehow prove to be correct. The nature of our government demands that we abide that time.

REGAN, District Judge, dissenting.

I recognize, as did the District Court, that the denial of official recognition to a college organization is a form of prior restraint of the First Amendment of right of association, as held in Healy v. James....

Having said this, I am nevertheless convinced, after a careful study of the record, that the District Court correctly held that the evidence amply justified the considered decision of the University officials to deny recognition to Gay Lib.

What *Healy v. James* held was that "denial of official recognition, without justification, to college organizations burdens or abridges the right of individuals to associate to further their personal beliefs." Healy involved a "left wing" group (Students for a Democratic Society) which sought recognition at a time when "(t)here had been widespread civil disobedience on some (college) campuses, accompanied by the seizure of buildings, vandalism and arson," with respect to which "SDS chapters on some of these campuses had been a catalytic force during this period." However, inasmuch as there was a total absence of any evidence that the organization seeking recognition itself actually "posed a substantial threat" that it would constitute a disruptive force on campus, there was, on the record, "no justification" for denying recognition to that group.

I do not read *Healy* as mandating that in every case involving non-recognition of a campus group a showing of the certitude of imminent overt lawless or disruptive activity must be made. Rather, the issue is whether, under the circumstances, justification of the appropriateness of denial of recognition has sufficiently been shown.

The credible testimony of highly qualified psychiatrists persuasively demonstrates to me, as it did to the District Court, that homosexual behavior is compulsive and that homosexuality is an illness and clearly abnormal. In view of the expert testimony which in my view is neither "skimpy (nor) speculative," defendants were warranted in concluding that formal recognition of Gay Lib would tend to expand homosexual behavior and activity on campus and likely result in felonious acts of sodomy proscribed by Missouri law. As the District Court stated: "The legitimate interest of the University as a state institution includes the right to refuse the requested recognition and its concomitants where the result predictably is to bring on the commission of crimes against the sodomy statutes of the State of Missouri."

With all due respect to the majority, I do not agree that the combined testimony of the psychiatrists testifying for the defendants stands on no different footing than that of the school principal in *Tinker v. Des Moines Independent Community School District*. In light of the admittedly "outstanding professional credentials" of the psychiatrists, they were eminently qualified by training and experience to express expert opinions on the subject of homosexuality and the effect of recognition of Gay Lib by the University.

As for *Tinker*, it held only that individuals had the right to wear black armbands as a silent, passive expression of their disapproval of this country's Viet Nam policy. Such a purely symbolic act was "unaccompanied by any disorder or disturbance" on their part or any "interference, actual or nascent, with the schools' work or...collision with the rights of other students to be secure and to be let alone." The case was not ruled in the context of group action. It involved only the school authorities' disagreement with the philosophy being expressed by the wearers of the black armbands. It is totally unlike the situation here present. Here, the officials' denial of recognition to Gay Lib was not based on "mere disagreement" with the group's "philosophy."

Moreover, state university officials have a responsibility not only to taxpayers but to all students on campus, and that responsibility encompasses a right to protect latent or potential homosexuals from becoming overt homosexual students. In carrying out these responsibilities, they were aware that unlike recognition of political associations, whether of the right, center or left, an organization dedicated to the furtherance and advancement of homosexuality would, in any realistic sense, certainly so to impressionistic students, imply approval not only of the organization per se but of homosexuality and the normality of such conduct, and thus adversely affect potential homosexual students. In my opinion, the University was entitled to protect itself and the other students on campus, in this small way, against abnormality, illness and compulsive conduct of the kind here described in the evidence....

I am firmly of the view that Rule 52, FRCP, which mandates that the district court's "(f)indings of fact shall not be set aside unless clearly erroneous," precludes reversal in this case. Granted that the trial court had no better opportunity than this panel to judge the credibility of the witnesses, a factor which may not be ignored, nevertheless, the plain language of the Rule makes the clearly erroneous principle here applicable. And since I do not have a firm conviction that the trial court reached a fundamentally wrong result, I would affirm.

On Petition for Rehearing En Banc: The petition for rehearing en banc is denied by an evenly divided court. GIBSON, Chief Judge, joined by HENLEY, Circuit Judge, files the following statement in regard to the denial of the petition for rehearing en banc:

GIBSON, Chief Judge.

I dissent from the denial of the petition for rehearing en banc. In my opinion, Fed.R.Civ.P. 52 has been misapplied in this case and the District Court's findings of fact, which are supported by the record, have been improperly displaced by appellate findings of fact.... The District Court, accepting the testimony of two highly qualified psychiatrists, found that recognition of Gay Lib would likely result in imminent violations of the Missouri sodomy laws. To rebut this expert psychiatric testimony, Gay Lib relies on the testimony of a medical doctor who is not a psychiatrist; an assistant professor of psychology who stated that he had not undertaken any in-depth research into the etiologies of homosexuality, but "doubt(ed)" that recognition of Gay Lib would increase actual homosexual behavior; and a professor of psychology who admitted in his testimony that "I'm not saying that the existence of such a (homosexual) group wouldn't" increase the incidence of homosexuality on the campus.

The District Court, confronted with this conflicting testimony, accepted the testimony of the psychiatric experts rather than the above testimony of non-psychiatrists. Lacking training in the psychiatric discipline, appellate judges are ill-prepared to conclude that these expert psychiatric opinions lack an historical or empirical basis. Maybe an appellate court, reviewing this case de novo, would have made a finding different than the District Court's. But our review is not so unbridled that we can reject the District Court's findings on that basis....

Given the finding that recognition of Gay Lib would likely result in imminent violations of Missouri sodomy laws, there is no prior restraint issue in this case. There is "little doubt that the University could constitutionally regulate such conduct," *Gay Alliance of Students v. Matthews*, 544 F.2d 162, 166 (4th Cir. 1976), and the First Amendment does not require a University to extend formal recognition to a campus organization that will engage in criminal activity, *Healy v. James*, 408 U.S. 169, 188–89 (1972). Citizens possess no First Amendment right to engage in illegal activity and, in light of the District Court's findings, the University officials' action did not constitute an impermissible prior restraint.

This case involves the sensitive and polemical issue of homosexual rights, an issue which has spawned nationwide debate and attention. The limited question here is whether a homosexual group has a First Amendment right to be recognized by a university and thus to be entitled to use school facilities and to be eligible for student activities funds. These First Amendment arguments must be considered in light of the special characteristics and interests of an educational institution. These institutions are populated by young, often impressionable students; school officials have a responsibility to shield these students from exposure to probable illegal conduct on the campus. Missouri law has criminalized sodomy and the District Court found that recognition of Gay Lib would result in imminent violations of that law. Under these circumstances, it was permissible for school officials to withhold recognition of Gay Lib. Requiring the school to recognize Gay Lib places school officials in the unseemly position of officially sanctioning this conduct and making school funds and facilities available for the use of a homosexual organization, whose members will likely engage in criminal activity, a situation not mandated by the First Amendment.

This is yet another example of unwarranted judicial intrusion into the internal operations of an educational institution....We are not school administrators and have no authority to dictate school policy unless there is a clear showing of a constitutional violation. I find no such violation here. I am in accord with Judge Regan's dissenting opinion and would affirm the District Court's Judgment.

Ratchford v. Gay Lib
434 U.S. 1080 (1978)

Petition for writ of certiorari to the United States Court of Appeals for the Eighth Circuit. Feb. 21, 1978. Denied.

THE CHIEF JUSTICE [Warren Burger] would grant the petition and give plenary consideration to this case.

Justice REHNQUIST, with whom Justice BLACKMUN joins, dissenting.

There is a natural tendency on the part of any conscientious court to avoid embroiling itself in a controversial area of social policy unless absolutely required to do so. I therefore completely understand, if I do not agree with, the Court's decision to deny certiorari in this case....

Courts by nature are passive institutions and may decide only those issues raised by litigants in lawsuits before them. The obverse side of that passivity is the requirement that they do dispose of those lawsuits that are before them and entitled to attention. The District Court and the Court of Appeals were doubtless as chary as we are of being thrust into the middle of this controversy but were nonetheless obligated to decide the case. Unlike the District Court and the Court of Appeals, Congress has accorded to us through the Judiciary Act of 1925, 28 U.S.C. sec. 1254, the discretion to decline to hear a case such as this on the merits without explaining our reasons for doing so. But the existence of such discretion does not imply that it should be used as a sort of judicial storm cellar to which we may flee to escape from controversial or sensitive cases. Our Rules provide that one of the considerations governing review on certiorari is whether a Court of Appeals "has decided an important question of federal law which has not been, but should be, settled by this [C]ourt; or has decided a federal question in a way in conflict with applicable decisions of this [C]ourt." Rule 19(1)(b). In my opinion the panel decision of the Court of Appeals meets both of these tests, and I would therefore grant certiorari and hear the case on the merits.

The sharp split amongst the judges who considered this case below demonstrates that our past precedents do not conclusively address the issues central to this dispute. In the same manner that we expect considered and deliberate treatment of cases by these courts, we have a concomitant responsibility to aid them where confusion or uncertainty in the law prevails. By refusing to grant certiorari in this case, we ignore our function and responsibility in the framework of the federal court system and place added burdens on other courts in that system.

Writ large, the issue posed in this case is the extent to which a self-governing democracy, having made certain acts criminal, may prevent or discourage individuals from engaging in speech or conduct which encourages others to violate those laws. The Court of Appeals holds that a state university violates the First and Fourteenth Amendments when it refuses to recognize an organization whose activities both a University factfinder and the District Court found were likely to incite violations of an admittedly valid criminal statute. Neither the Court of Appeals nor respondents contend that the testimony of the expert psychologists at these hearings was insufficient to support such a finding. They appear to take instead the position that such a finding is not governed by the normal "clearly erroneous" test established in Fed.Rule Civ.Proc. 52(a). This unusual conclusion, in itself, would seem to me to be sufficient to warrant a grant of certiorari.

But lurking behind this procedural question is one which surely goes to the heart of the inevitable clash between the authority of a State to prevent the subversion of the lawful rules of conduct which it has enacted pursuant to its police power and the right of individuals under the First and Fourteenth Amendments who disagree with various of those rules to urge that they be changed through democratic processes. The University in this case did not ban the discussion in the classroom, or out of it, of the wisdom of repealing sodomy statutes. The State did not proscribe membership in organizations devoted to advancing "gay liberation." The University merely refused to recognize an organization whose activities were found to be likely to incite a violation of a valid state criminal statute. While respondents disavow any intent to advocate present violations of state law, the organization intends to engage in far more than political discussion. Among respondent Gay Lib's asserted purposes are the following: "3. Gay Lib wants to provide information to the vast majority of those who really don't know what homosexuality or bi-sexual behavior really is. Too much of the same prejudice is now directed at Gay people just as it is directed at ethnic minorities. "4. Gay Lib does not seek to proselytize, convert, or recruit. On the other hand, people who have already established a pattern of homosexuality when they enter college must adjust to this fact. "5. Gay lib hopes to help the Gay community to rid itself of its subconscious burden of guilt. Society imprints this self-image on homosexuals and makes adjustment with the straight world more difficult."

Expert psychological testimony below established the fact that the meeting together of individuals who consider themselves homosexual in an officially recognized university organization can have a distinctly different effect from the mere advocacy of repeal of the State's sodomy statute. As the University has recognized, this danger may be particularly acute in the university setting where many students are still coping with the sexual problems which accompany late adolescence and early adulthood.

The University's view of respondents' activities and respondents' own view of them are diametrically opposed. From the point of view of the latter, the question is little different from whether university recognition of a college Democratic club in fairness also requires recognition of a college Republican club. From the point of view of the University, however, the question is more akin to whether those suffering from measles have a constitutional right, in violation of quarantine regulations, to associate together and with others who do not presently have measles, in order to urge repeal of a state law providing that measle sufferers be quarantined. The very act of assemblage under these circumstances undercuts a significant interest of the State which a plea for the repeal of the law would nowise do. Where between these two polar characterizations of the issue the truth lies is not as important as whether a federal appellate court is free to reject the University's characterization, particularly when it is supported by the findings of the District Court.

As the split among the lower court judges shows, *Healy v. James* did not directly address these questions. There we remanded the decision of the Court of Appeals of the Second Circuit to decide whether the University's refusal to recognize a local branch of the Students for a Democratic Society was motivated by a factual conclusion that the organization would not abide by reasonable campus regulations of the sort held valid in *Esteban v. Central Missouri State College*, 415 F.2d 1077, 1089 (CA8 1969) (Blackmun, J.). Here the question is not whether Gay Lib as an organization will abide by university regulations. Nor it is really whether Gay Lib will persuasively advocate violations of the sodomy statute. Instead, the question is whether a university can deny recognition to an organization the activities of which expert psychologists testify will in and of themselves lead directly to violations of a concededly valid state criminal law.

As our cases establish from *Schenck v. United States*, 249 U.S. 47 (1919), in which Mr. Justice Holmes, speaking for a unanimous Court, held that the Government has a right to criminally punish words which are "used in such circumstances and are of such a nature as to create a clear and present danger that they will bring about the substantive evils that Congress has a right to prevent," to *Brandenburg v. Ohio*, 395 U.S. 444 (1969), some speech that has a propensity to induce action prohibited by the criminal laws may itself be prohibited. A fortiori, speech and conduct combined which have that effect may surely be placed off limits of a university campus without doing violence to the First or Fourteenth Amendments.

Healy was decided by the lower courts in what may fairly be described as a factual vacuum. There this Court stated that a student organization need not be recognized if such recognition is likely to incite criminal violations, but did not have to consider how that standard would be applied to a particular factual situation. No attempt had been made by the University to demonstrate that imminent lawless action was likely as a result of the speech in question, nor was there any hint that any such effort was likely to have been successful. Here, such a demonstration was undertaken, and the District Court sitting as a finder of fact concluded that petitioners had made out their case. The Court of Appeals' panel opinion, for me at least, sheds no light on why this conclusion of the District Court could be rejected. By denying certiorari, we must leave university officials in complete confusion as to how, if ever, they may meet the standard that we laid out in *Healy*.

The mathematically even division of the Court of Appeals on the petition for rehearing en banc gives some indication of the divergence of judicial views which may be expected from conscientious judges on difficult constitutional questions such as this. Our views may be no less divergent, and no less persuasive to one another, than were the views of the eight judges of the Court of Appeals. But believing as I do that we cannot under our Rules properly leave this important question of law in its present state, I would grant the petition for certiorari.

Gay and Lesbian Students Association v. Gohn
850 F.2d 361 (8th Cir. 1988)

ARNOLD, Circuit Judge.

The Gay and Lesbian Students Association of the University of Arkansas at Fayetteville brought this sec. 1983 action after its funding request was denied by the Student Senate. The GLSA alleged that it was denied funds because of the content of its message, in violation of the First Amendment. The District Court ruled that while the case was not moot, and state action was present, the GLSA's First Amendment right of free speech was not violated by the Senate's action....

In brief, we hold that a public body that chooses to fund speech or expression must do so even-handedly, without discriminating among recipients on the basis of their ideology. The University need not supply funds to student organizations; but once having decided to do so, it is bound by the First Amendment to act without regard to the content of the ideas being expressed. This will mean, to use Holmes's phrase, that the taxpayers will occasionally be obligated to support not only the thought of which they approve, but also the thought that they hate. That is one of the fundamental premises of American law.

I.

The University of Arkansas is a publicly funded university governed by a Board of Trustees. Student government is carried out through an organization called the Associated Student Government (ASG), which was created by a constitution adopted by the Board of Trustees in 1943. Under this constitution the Student Senate, the legislative branch of the ASG, has been delegated the function of appropriating money from student service funds to student organizations, subject to administrative approval. These funds come from tuition, state tax money, and general fees collected from students.

The GLSA has been a registered student organization on the Fayetteville campus of the University since 1983. Its stated purpose then and now is to educate people about homosexuality and to provide a support group for homosexuals. The group's typical activities include sponsoring workshops, films, and panel discussions on homosexuality. As a registered student organization, the GLSA is entitled to certain benefits, such as using University facilities for its meetings and projects, and being listed in University publications.

Registered student organizations also have the right to petition the Student Senate for University funds. A group may apply for "A" funds to supply large, ongoing enterprises like the school newspaper, or "B" funds to support special needs or projects. "B" funds are often granted for speech-related purposes. For example, Amnesty International used "B" funds to sponsor films, and the Nuclear Awareness Group used them to bring in a speaker. The denial of "B" funds is at issue in this case.

To receive "B" funds, a student group must first submit an application to the Finance Committee of the Student Senate. The Committee reviews the application, checking to see whether the group complies with the criteria laid out in the constitution. If one of these technical requirements[3] is not met, the group's request is rejected, usually with an explanation attached. After this initial objective evaluation, the Committee then determines whether the group's planned events would be educational and would benefit the entire community.[4] Besides accepting or rejecting the funding requests, the Finance Committee may also modify them. For example, the Committee may strike from the application requests for office supplies, or change the estimate of the cost of obtaining a film. The Committee delivers its recommendations to the Senate, which then votes on them. Though time is set aside at the Senate meeting to discuss and debate the funding

---

3. Technical requirements include holding a fundraiser before asking for University funds and setting forth in detail the organization's planned activities. In addition, some events, such as beauty pageants, can never be funded with University money.

4. GLSA contends this second test was added in order to block its receipt of funds.

requests, receiving a recommendation from the Finance Committee has historically been tantamount to being funded.

The GLSA first applied for "B" funds in January of 1983 in order to present two films and hold a panel discussion. The Finance Committee recommended it receive $136.00. Senate debate on the measure was described as "heated." One Senator argued, "The key word is 'support.'...This is a group that supports Gay and lesbian homosexuality. We cannot use state money to support a homosexual group. What if a group of students/arsonists wanted to start an arsonists club and start fires. Would you fund them?...It's the same thing as funding homosexuals." However, another remarked, "Why is it that this group is being subjected to a review...[when] [o]ther groups on campus who request funding are not treated like this." The proposal was defeated by a vote of 35 to 17.

The GLSA appealed to Lyle Gohn, Vice Chancellor for Student Services and the official charged with oversight of student organizations. Gohn denied relief, stating "I would hope that you...would accept the decision of your fellow student senators." He disavowed knowledge of why the Senate voted the way it did.[5] The GLSA next appealed to then-Chancellor B.A. Nugent. He claimed to "have no evidence that discrimination was present among those who voted against funding," and that "[d]etermining the motives or rationale of the individual student senators...has no relevancy." He believed that the Senate made its choice on purely fiscal considerations.[6] Finally, the GLSA took its case to the Vice President for Academic Affairs, Charles Oxford. He too denied the appeal, finding no "procedural error."

During this same period of time, the Arkansas State Legislature was in session. Representative Travis Dowd of Texarkana introduced two resolutions dealing with state universities and homosexuals. The first, House Resolution 16, urged the University "to refrain from assisting in any manner the Gay community on campus." The second, House Resolution 25, went further, urging University officials "not only [to] refrain from assisting in any manner whatsoever the homosexual community of their campuses, but to institute any and all lawful measures to stem the tide of homosexuality on the campuses of our colleges and universities." Both resolutions were narrowly defeated in committee. Gohn was aware of the resolutions, and kept copies of them in the same file where he stored his correspondence with the GLSA.

In the fall of 1984 the GLSA again applied for "B" funds and secured the approval of the Finance Committee. However, the procedure the Committee followed in submitting funding recommendations to the Senate was different that year. Funding requests were put before the Senate in packages, so that three or four were voted on at a time. Thus, the GLSA's application was presented along with several others. Various Senators did attempt to separate out the GLSA's request. However, despite what was described as a "horrible," "emotional," and "vulgar" debate, these parliamentary maneuvers failed, and the GLSA received $70.00 that fall.

Campus reaction to the GLSA's receipt of $70.00 was swift and severe. The Student Senate passed a rule prohibiting the funding of any group organized around sexual preference. The measure was vetoed by the ASG president, who called it discriminatory, and analogized it to seemingly reasonable laws once used to disenfranchise blacks. She was particularly appalled that such an attitude would be found at a university, "traditionally [a] place[ ] of open-mindedness and growth."

---

5. We note, however, that Gohn attended all Senate meetings, including this one.
6. But in his letter to the GLSA Nugent also noted that some "B" funds were left over that year.

Events on campus did not escape the notice of University officials or state legislators. In June of 1985 University officials, including the President and two members of the Board of Trustees, met with a dozen state representatives and senators in Fayetteville. It appears that the funding of the GLSA was discussed, and that all present were concerned about the adverse publicity that funding the GLSA had brought to the University.

Later in June of 1985, Chancellor Willard Gatewood attended a meeting about the University's Staff Development Program. Discussion centered on a series of workshops on stereotyping and prejudice to be held in the fall. The workshops, designed around seven vignettes, were to be held for University faculty and staff. One of the scenarios was about homosexuality. Gatewood told members of the group that no state money would go to the workshops as long as the segment on Gays and lesbians was included. Apparently, Gatewood insinuated that University support would be withdrawn as well.

In the fall of 1985, the GLSA once more submitted an application for "B" funds. The group planned to show a historical documentary, "Before Stonewall," and sponsor two workshops, one on racism and one on homophobia. The GLSA initially requested $295.00, but after conferring with the Finance Committee trimmed its request to $165.00. The Finance Committee found the GLSA met all the funding criteria, and recommended that it receive "B" funds.   The student chairman of the Committee, though confident the GLSA deserved funding, was apprehensive about presenting the Committee's recommendation to the Senate. Fearing a repeat of the events from the year before, she sought Gohn's advice. He told her to handle it as best she could. She decided to present the funding requests individually, as had been done before 1984. After some initial confusion, the GLSA representative made a short speech on why the group should be funded. The GLSA was the only organization which made such a presentation. When the group's representative stood up, one senator expressed surprise at how normal she looked. Debate on the measure was brief; students argued that funding the GLSA would be illegal or contrary to religious beliefs. The GLSA was denied funds by a 34 to 21 vote.

The GLSA was the only group recommended by the Finance Committee that was not funded. The Finance Committee chairman believed it was the first time a recommended group had been denied money. Indeed, three groups who did not receive the Finance Committee's recommendation received "B" funds, and money was still left over at the end of the year.

The GLSA appealed to Vice Chancellor Gohn. Gohn conceded that the GLSA had met all technical requirements, while other groups which had not were nevertheless given funds, but denied the appeal, arguing that the decision of the Student Senate should be respected. Though in his letter to the GLSA Gohn claimed not to know why the Senate voted as it did, he later seemed to admit the GLSA had been discriminated against. The GLSA then appealed to Chancellor Ferritor, who upheld Gohn's decision in a brief statement. Finally, the GLSA wrote to the President for help. He too denied relief, stating first that he lacked jurisdiction to reverse funding decisions, as that was within the province of the Vice Chancellor, and second that in any case he agreed with Gohn's analysis. The GLSA then brought this lawsuit, alleging its First Amendment rights were violated when it was denied "B" funds because of the content of its speech. Before we reach this question, we must deal with two preliminary issues.

I.

The District Court held that this case involves a live controversy, since the funding denial was an issue capable of repetition yet evading review. The University contests this conclusion, arguing that the problem might not recur, and, if it did, there would be ample time to seek judicial review. In support of its first contention, the University notes that the composition of the Student Senate has changed since 1985; senators have graduated or retired. It is possible that a subsequent Senate would vote to fund the GLSA. After all, a Senate did so in 1984. The University claims no one can accurately predict the vagaries of student government.

We observe first that the funding cycle for student organizations is one year. That is too short a period for the GLSA to appeal to the proper University officials and then fully litigate its claim. Second, we note that it need not be proved with certainty that the situation will recur; GLSA must show only a reasonable expectation of repetition. The District Court laid out a litany of facts that point to a probable recurrence: University officials continue to support the Senate's denials of funding; the Senate has a policy of granting funds to all organizations who meet the requirements, yet has denied funding to a properly qualified GLSA on two occasions; and the one time the GLSA received funds, the Senate tried to enact a proposal that would prevent it from ever again receiving funds. The case is not moot.

III.

The University contests the District Court's determination that state action was present in the denial of funding to the GLSA. Conceding that the University and through it the Student Senate are creations of the State, and that "B" funds originate in state coffers, the appellees nonetheless contend that because University officials had no control over the Student Senate, state action was not present. The University relies on *Sinn v. The Daily Nebraskan*, 829 F.2d 662 (8th Cir.1987), a case in which state action was held to be lacking where a university exercised no editorial control over a student newspaper.

However, a review of the facts in this case demonstrates that the University did have final say over Senate funding decisions. The student handbook, which discusses, among other things, how University funds are allocated, states that "[d]ecisions concerning financing of student organizations may be appealed to the Vice Chancellor for Student Services."...

IV.

The GLSA appeals the District Court's holding that the Student Senate's denial of funding to the group did not violate its First Amendment rights. Because we believe the record is replete with evidence that the Senate's action was based on viewpoint discrimination, we reverse.

The District Court aptly concluded that the GLSA had no right to receive "B" funds. First, the Court observed that while student organizations have the right to university recognition and to use of university facilities on a nondiscriminatory basis, they have no clearly established right to receive university funds. Second, the Court reasoned that since "B" funds are finite, student organizations logically could not have a right to receive them, at least not in whatever amounts they may request. Resource constraints necessarily impose some limit.

The District Court went on to recognize that, while the GLSA has no right to receive "B" funds, it may not be denied them for a reason which violates its First Amendment rights:

> [The government] may not deny a benefit to a person on a basis that infringes his constitutionally protected interests—especially, his interest in freedom of

speech. For if the government could deny a benefit to a person because of his constitutionally protected speech or associations, his exercise of those freedoms would in effect be penalized and inhibited. This would allow the government to "produce a result which [it] could not command directly." Such interference with constitutional rights is impermissible.

Content-based discrimination can be justified only if the government demonstrates that its regulation is narrowly drawn and is necessary to effectuate a compelling state interest. This is an extremely difficult standard for government to meet.

We agree with the District Court's enunciation of these two basic premises: that a group has no right to funding, but when funds are made available, they must be distributed in a viewpoint-neutral manner, absent other considerations. If these two principles had been applied to the facts in this case, the GLSA would have prevailed, as will be shown. Obviously, the District Court's analysis did not stop after these two steps.

The District Court erred in overemphasizing the first proposition, that the GLSA has no right to funding. Noting that the GLSA had no right to have its speech subsidized, the Court cited *Regan v. Taxation With Representation*, 461 U.S. 540 (1983) (TWR), and *Cammarano v. United States*, 358 U.S. 498 (1959). In this pair of cases, the Supreme Court held that the state need not aid a taxpayer in exercising his First Amendment rights by granting him deductions for speech-related activities. But these cases dealt with content-neutral tax provisions. As Justice (as he then was) Rehnquist stated, "[t]he case would be different if Congress were to discriminate inviously in its subsidies in such a way as to "'ai[m] at the suppression of dangerous ideas".'" TWR, at 548 (citations omitted).

The District Court also overstated the role legitimate discretion played in the Senate's funding decision. Relying on *Advocates for Arts v. Thomson*, 532 F.2d 792 (1st Cir.), cert. denied, 429 U.S. 894 (1976), the Court stated that "a [funding] decision can to a certain extent rest on intrinsic matters or the 'value' of the subject matter itself." The Court went on to say that "[t]o date there has not developed any firm policy concerning the constitutional value in sexual preference nondiscrimination." Thus, the Court concluded, after weighing the merits of competing funding proposals, the Student Senate might choose not to fund the GLSA, concluding its message was less worthy than that of some other group. In its brief, the University argues along similar lines, claiming that the Senate may have chosen not to fund the group because it was not so educational and beneficial to the campus as other groups.

Advocates for Arts, however, dealt with state grants for literary magazines. The competition for funds was judged on artistic, not political or ideological grounds. The First Circuit recognized this distinction, noting that "distribution of arts grants on the basis of such extrinsic considerations as the applicants' political views, associations, or activities would violate the equal protection clause, if not the first amendment, by penalizing the exercise of those freedoms." What is at issue here is not the value of a short story or the constitutional status of sexual preferences, but speech on the subject of nondiscrimination.

The University claims the denial of funding was for a number of valid reasons related to the educational merit and benefit to the community of the GLSA's planned activities. But these reasons were not mentioned in the course of the denial of funds. Indeed, there is evidence that many senators voted against funding for other reasons, such as their disagreement with the GLSA's beliefs. In response to this, the University argues that the motive of the Student Senate is irrelevant, and in any case cannot be determined, since each senator may have a different rationale. Every claim of viewpoint discrimination requires, by its very nature, that the purposes or motives of governmental officials be determined. When the body involved has many members, the question is harder to answer, but it still must be faced.

When the original two premises are applied to the facts in this case, the First Amendment violation is apparent. The GLSA met all objective criteria for funding and received the Finance Committee's recommendation, yet was denied funds twice. The one time the GLSA received funds, an unusual procedure was followed in presenting requests before the Senate. And, immediately after the granting of funds, the Senate voted never to fund the GLSA again. All other qualified groups received money. There was no shortage of resources, since unqualified organizations were given funds, and money was left over at the end of the appropriations period. Some student senators freely admitted they voted against the group because of its views. University officials were feeling pressure from state legislators not to fund the GLSA or to allow in any way the dissemination of opinions tolerant towards homosexuals. It is apparent that the GLSA was denied "B" funds because of the views it espoused. Nor is there a compelling state interest justifying the Senate's denial of funds. The University provides no argument, and we can think of none. True, sodomy is illegal in Arkansas. However, the GLSA does not advocate sodomy, and, even if it did, its speech about an illegal activity would still be protected by the First Amendment. People may extol the virtues of arson or even cannibalism. They simply may not commit the acts. Thus, we reverse the District Court on the First Amendment issue. Conduct may be prohibited or regulated, within broad limits. But government may not discriminate against people because it dislikes their ideas, not even when the ideas include advocating that certain conduct now criminal be legalized.

We realize that the District Court made no explicit finding as to the reason for denial of funding, that this is a question of fact, and that appellate courts are not fact-finding forums. We think, though, that the District Court's opinion, when read in full and in context, includes an implicit finding that funds were denied because of distaste for the GLSA's ideas. Otherwise, there would have been no need to resort to the legal doctrines (e.g., that there is no "right" to public money) used by the Court to justify dismissing the complaint. A finding of fact that funds were denied for some content-neutral reason would have sufficed completely to dispose of the case. In any event, the facts of this case are so obvious that a remand for an explicit finding would be a waste of time. This record leaves no reasonable doubt that funds were denied because of disagreement with the GLSA's speech. A finding the other way would be clearly erroneous....

The judgment of the District Court is reversed, and the case is remanded with directions to provide the appellant with appropriate relief in accordance with this opinion.

Notes and Questions

1. The *Gohn* decision was seen by some commentators as particularly significant because Arkansas was one of a handful of states with a sodomy law that only applied to same-sex activity. (The other such states at that time were Kansas, Montana, Nevada, Tennessee and Texas. State courts subsequently declared the Montana and Tennessee laws unconstitutional, and the Texas law was invalidated in *Lawrence v. Texas* (2003), in which the U.S. Supreme Court struck down all remaining sodomy laws on due process grounds.)

2. To what extent would the First Amendment principles developed in *Bonner, Gay Lib*, and *Gohn* apply to a group of students organized purely for social purposes, such as a "gay fraternity" or "lesbian sorority"? What weight might a court give to the arguments (rejected in the above cases) that the university had a responsibility to prevent the students from engaging in unlawful sexual activities which might be promoted by the existence of such organizations in states with laws barring consensual sodomy?

3. Could a state university, required under the First Amendment to recognize and afford funding to a gay and lesbian student group on the same basis as it recognizes and funds other student groups, refuse to fund a group of transvestite students or transsexual students? Could a state university which recognizes an African American or Native American alumni association refuse to recognize a gay and lesbian alumni association?

4. Governor Guy Hunt of Alabama signed legislation on May 14, 1992, making it illegal for state schools either to give money or allow their buildings to be used by any group "that fosters or promotes a life style or actions prohibited by the sodomy and sexual misconduct laws." The measure was intended to cut off funding of gay and lesbian groups on state campuses, in reaction to an incident at Auburn University where administrators overruled a vote by the student government and extended recognition and campus privileges to such an association. The governor and legislature acted after receiving an advisory opinion from Attorney General Jimmy Evans asserting that such a law would be constitutional. Evans apparently believed that the Supreme Court and the 11th Circuit would not follow the 8th Circuit's decision in *Gay and Lesbian Student Association v. Gohn*, supra.

Following is the text of the Alabama law enacted on May 14, 1992, referenced in the main text:

CODE OF ALABAMA 1975
Title 16. Education.
Chapter 1. General Provisions.

§ 16-1-28 No public funds or public facilities to be used to promote lifestyle or activities prohibited by sodomy and sexual misconduct laws.

(a) No public funds or public facilities shall be used by any college or university to, directly or indirectly, sanction, recognize, or support the activities or existence of any organization or group that fosters or promotes a lifestyle or actions prohibited by the sodomy and sexual misconduct laws of Sections 13A-6-63 to 13A-6-65, inclusive.

(b) No organization or group that receives public funds or uses public facilities, directly or indirectly, at any college or university shall permit or encourage its members or encourage other persons to engage in any such unlawful acts or provide information or materials that explain how such acts may be engaged in or performed.

(c) This section shall not be construed to be a prior restraint of the first amendment protected speech. It shall not apply to any organization or group whose activities are limited solely to the political advocacy of a change in the sodomy and sexual misconduct laws of this state.

(Acts 1992, No. 92-439, §§ 1-3.)

CODE OF ALABAMA 1975
Title 16. Education.
Chapter 40a. Responsible Sexual Behavior and Prevention of Illegal Drug Use.

§ 16-40A-2 Minimum contents to be included in sex education program or curriculum.

(a) Any program or curriculum in the public schools in Alabama that includes sex education or the human reproductive process shall, as a minimum, include and emphasize the following:

(1) Abstinence from sexual intercourse is the only completely effective protection against unwanted pregnancy, sexually transmitted diseases, and acquired immune deficiency syndrome (AIDS) when transmitted sexually.

(2) Abstinence from sexual intercourse outside of lawful marriage is the expected social standard for unmarried school-age persons.

(b) Course materials and instruction that relate to sexual education or sexually transmitted diseases should be age-appropriate.

(c) Course materials and instruction that relate to sexual education or sexually transmitted diseases should include all of the following elements:

(1) An emphasis on sexual abstinence as the only completely reliable method of avoiding unwanted teenage pregnancy and sexually transmitted diseases.

(2) An emphasis on the importance of self-control and ethical conduct pertaining to sexual behavior.

(3) Statistics based on the latest medical information that indicate the degree of reliability and unreliability of various forms of contraception, while also emphasizing the increase in protection against pregnancy and protection against sexually transmitted diseases, including HIV and AIDS infection, which is afforded by the use of various contraceptive measures.

(4) Information concerning the laws relating to the financial responsibilities associated with pregnancy, childbirth, and child rearing.

(5) Information concerning the laws prohibiting sexual abuse, the need to report such abuse, and the legal options available to victims of sexual abuse.

(6) Information on how to cope with and rebuff unwanted physical and verbal sexual exploitation by other persons.

(7) Psychologically sound methods of resisting unwanted peer pressure.

(8) An emphasis, in a factual manner and from a public health perspective, that homosexuality is not a lifestyle acceptable to the general public and that homosexual conduct is a criminal offense under the laws of the state.

(9) Comprehensive instruction in parenting skills and responsibilities, including the responsibility to pay child support by non-custodial parents, the penalties for non-payment of child support, and the legal and ethical responsibilities of child care and child rearing.

(Acts 1992, No. 92-590, § 2.)

§ 16-40A-4 Illegal conduct not to be encouraged or proposed to public school children.

Conduct that is illegal under state or federal law, including but not limited to, illegal use or distribution of controlled substances, under-age alcohol use or distribution, sexual intercourse imposed by means of force, or sexual actions which are otherwise illegal, shall not be encouraged or proposed to public school children in such a manner as to indicate that they have a legitimate right to decide or choose illegal conduct.

(Acts 1992, No. 92-590, §4.)

Evaluate the constitutionality of these enactments in light of the foregoing cases. For the outcome of subsequent litigation brought by the ACLU, see *Gay Lesbian Bisexual Alliance v. Pryor*, 110 F.3d 1543 (11th Cir.1997).

* * *

The right of high school students to form associations based on common interests in sexual minority issues began to arise and be litigated during the 1990s, after the rights of college and university students had become reasonably well established. During the Vietnam War era, the Supreme Court had affirmed that high school students do have constitutional rights of political expression and protest, but that high school administrators may restrict those rights as necessary to prevent disruption of the educational mission of the school. In a move calculated to support efforts by religious students to form clubs on high school campuses, Congress passed an Equal Access Act that was primary intended to prevent discrimination against religious clubs by adopting a non-discrimination policy, which ultimately assisted sexual minority student groups seeking equal rights on college campuses.

Achieving a balance in this frequently hotly-contested area has proved challenging for school administrators and courts, especially when prominent community religious leaders decide to lead crusades against "homosexuality in the schools." The following decision is just one example of a growing body of case law about the associational rights of sexual minority high school students.

Boyd County High School Gay Straight Alliance v. Board of Education of Boyd County, Ky.
258 F.Supp.2d 667 (E.D. Ky. 2003)

Bunning, District Judge.

I. Introduction

This matter is before the Court on Plaintiffs' Motion for a Preliminary Injunction. Plaintiffs claim that Defendants violated their rights under the Equal Access Act, 20 U.S.C. §4071, *et seq.*, and their First Amendment rights of expression and association by denying the Boyd County High School Gay Straight Alliance the same access to school facilities given to other student groups. Plaintiffs also claim that Defendants violated the Kentucky Education Reform Act (hereinafter KERA).

II. Findings of Fact

Plaintiffs are a student organization known as the Boyd County High School Gay Straight Alliance ("GSA"), seven student members of the GSA, and the GSA's faculty advisor, Kaye King. The student members attend Boyd County High School ("BCHS") in

Cannonsburg, Kentucky. Defendants are the Board of Education of Boyd County, Kentucky (the "Board"); Board members Chester Tackett, Theresa Jackson, Randall Stapleton, Sheri Bryan and Teresa Cornette, in their official capacities; the Boyd County School District Superintendent Dr. William Capehart, in his official capacity; and BCHS Principal Jerry Johnson, in his official capacity.

In January or February of 2002, students at BCHS circulated a petition to create a GSA Club. The purpose of the GSA Club is to provide students with a safe haven to talk about anti-gay harassment and to work together to promote tolerance, understanding and acceptance of one another regardless of sexual orientation. Plaintiff Tyler McClelland testified that the GSA's core principle is that people should be treated equally as human beings regardless of their sexual orientation.

Anti-gay harassment, homophobia, and use of anti-gay epithets have been and continue to be serious problems at BCHS. One student dropped out of BCHS because of harassment based on sexual orientation and another student dropped out because of both anti-gay harassment at school as well as problems at home. One example of the harassment includes students in Plaintiff Fugett's English class stating that they needed to take all the fucking faggots out in the back woods and kill them. During a basketball game in January 2003, students with megaphones chanted at Plaintiff Reese: "faggot-kisser," "GSA" and "fag-lover." On a regular basis, students call out "homo," "fag," and "queer" behind Plaintiff McClelland's back as he walks in the hallway between classes. On April 10, 2002, during an observance of National Day of Silence, about 25 participants sat in a circle in the front lobby of BCHS. During the lunch hour observance, protesters used anti-gay epithets and threw things at them.

During the Spring 2002 semester, Kaye King, a BCHS English teacher, was made aware of a petition being circulated among the students to start a GSA Club at the high school. King discussed the GSA petition with BCHS Principal Jerry Johnson. He informed her that the student who started the petition had already come to see him and that BCHS would have a GSA Club because the student knew a great deal about the legal issues. Principal Johnson's only concern at that time was the need to approve the GSA Club in order to prevent a lawsuit against the School District. King also discussed the idea of a GSA Club with Superintendent Bill Capehart. Dr. Capehart told King that having a GSA Club was the right thing to do for all students and that the School District needed the students to follow through with starting the GSA Club at BCHS. The student who started the GSA Club petition later approached King, who agreed to be the GSA Club faculty sponsor.

After it became known that a group of BCHS students were trying to start a GSA Club, some controversy ensured in the school hallways which continued for about a month. Students who opposed the GSA wore shirts to school that said, "Adam and Eve, not Adam and Steve" or "I'm straight." In February 2002, a group of students decided to apply for club status for the GSA. School administrators asked them to wait until the controversy about the GSA died down in the community and the school. The students agreed to wait a month before submitting their GSA Club application.

In late February or early March 2002, the BCHS Diversity Awareness Council ("DAC"), a special advisory group on diversity and equity issues, held two meetings that included discussion of anti-gay harassment at BCHS and the proposed GSA Club. During the first meeting, student safety was discussed, prompting a suggestion that the GSA Club use a different name. Students who supported formation of the GSA Club unanimously rejected the suggested name change. Plaintiff McClelland testified: "[w]e felt that the aim of the club was to...promote understanding and tolerance; and if we were to exclude the word 'gay' from the name, then that would be a very defeatist thing to do." During the second DAC meeting, Board Member Chester Tackett stated that the GSA Club might be necessary to help deal with the harassment problem.

BCHS requires all clubs to apply to its governing body, the Site-Based Decision Making Council (the "Council"), for official recognition. The Council consists of three teachers, two parents, and Principal Jerry Johnson. In late March 2002, the GSA submitted its first club application. Although Principal Johnson had asked the students to wait a month before applying for club status, the Council denied the GSA's application because it came too late in the school year. Faculty Advisor King spoke with Principal Johnson one week later. He assured her that all clubs would be reapplying in the fall of the new school year and that, in a stack of club applications, no one would notice the GSA's application and it would slide right through.

In September 2002, the GSA's application for club status was resubmitted. During its first meeting for the 2002–03 school year, the council approved 20 club applications. Plaintiff GSA was the only application not approved. Among the clubs which were approved were the Human Rights Club, 4-H, Future Business Leaders of America ("FBLA"), Beta Club, Future Farmers of America ("FFA"), Future Career and Community Leaders of America ("FCCLA"), Health Occupation Student Organizations ("HOSA"), and Y-Club. The Fellowship of Christian Athletes ("FCA") was also approved. The FCA is synonymous with the Christian Fellow Club and the Bible Club. The Drama, Key and Pep Clubs were not approved at that time because of late submissions. With the exception of HOSA, each approved organization was identified as a club by BCHS in its 2001–02 student handbook list of extra-curricular activities.

Following this denial of the GSA's application for club status, the ACLU wrote a letter to the Council on behalf of the GSA. That letter set forth the requirements of the Equal Access Act. GSA members asked the Council to reconsider GSA's application at its next meeting. Although the Council received the ACLU's letter before it met at the end of September, the Council tabled reconsideration of the GSA's application until the Council's October 28, 2002, meeting.

The Board's policy on use of school facilities by noncurriculum-related student groups is tailored after the language of the Equal Access Act, 20 U.S.C. §4071, *et seq.* The Board's policy does not reference the Site Based Decision Making Council. On October 28, 2002, the Council held its meeting in the BCHS auditorium. The Council went immediately into executive session. When it returned, the Council approved the applications of three organizations: Key Club, Drama Club and the GSA Club. GSA members in the audience remained silent after the announcement. Local ministers appealed the Council decision to approve the GSA Club to the Superintendent and circulated a petition to stop the GSA Club. The Council's decision was affirmed by Superintendent Capehart.]

After the Council announced its decision approving the GSA Club, the reaction from GSA opponents was acrimonious. Principal Johnson described the reaction as one of "open hostility." The crowd directly confronted the GSA supporters "with facial expressions, hand gestures...some very uncivil body language...people were using loud voices and angry voices and, again, beginning to point...it took some effort just to calm the meeting down and get through it and get out of there...that was the first time that I stared into the face of someone that I thought would hurt someone involved in this issue if given the opportunity. That was alarming to me and frightening and disheartening."

Board Member Teresa Cornette's observations from the October 28, 2002, meeting were similar. Cornette "was appalled at the reaction of the group, the audience. There was nothing but hatred in that room and ignorance showed by moms and dads and grandparents. When I left that meeting, I honestly thought that, you know, yes, a GSA is very much needed in our community, and these people right here needed to be mandated to go to it. It was horrible. And I literally left that meeting with a fear of what was going to happen in our school the next few days. I believe that we can teach tolerance and we can teach it until we are blue in the face, but if our parents don't teach it to our children also, then it's almost like a losing battle."

In response to a GSA opponent's questioning of why the GSA Club was approved, the Council explained that it thought it was doing the right thing based on the law and in light of the hostile environment in the school.

After the Council's October 28, 2002, decision to approve the GSA Club's application, the school sent a letter to all staff and parents of BCHS children, explaining its rationale for approving the GSA Club. In that letter, the school stated:

> [I]n accordance with the federal Equal Access Act, all clubs that had submitted a request to organize were approved, including the Gay-Straight Alliance. Personal feelings aside, the Council cannot knowingly and in good faith violate the law....

In that correspondence, the BCHS identified several clubs as noncurricular, including 4-H, Key Club, Beta Club, Fellowship of Christian Athletes, and Christian Fellowship Club. FBLA, FFA, FCCLA, HOSA, and Drama club were among the clubs identified as curricular.

On October 30, 2002, two days after the Council approved the GSA Club and before the GSA Club was able to conduct its first official meeting, a group of students congregated outside the school doors in the morning before school to protest the Council's decision and the existence of the GSA Club. The protesters shouted at other students as they arrived at school, "If you go inside, you're supporting the GSA;" "We don't want something like that in our school;" and "If you go inside, you're supporting faggots." Approximately 100 of BCHS's 974 enrolled students remained outside during the protest. This protest did not, however, prevent students from entering the school.

During that protest no GSA member spoke to any protester or engaged in any sort of counter-demonstration. Rather, members proceeded into school when the bell rang. Several GSA members talked about the protest going on outside and decided that they should remain calm and ignore it in order to avoid provoking the protestors.

Principal Johnson and Assistant Principal Richard Cyrus spoke to the crowd outside the school. They granted them amnesty for refusing to go to home room, saying, "You had your picket here. You've had your disagreement, but now it's time to go back to class." Principal Johnson and Assistant Principal Cyrus also allowed students who did not want to come into the school building to move to the parking lot to continue their protest. One group moved to the parking lot to continue their protest; the rest entered the school building. Classes proceeded as scheduled that day without any disruption. On November 4, 2002, approximately one-half of the BCHS student body was absent from school.

Neither the October 30, 2002, on-campus protest nor the November 4, 2002, school boycott disrupted regularly-scheduled classroom activities, prevented teachers from teaching, or prevented students who came to school from learning. Faculty Advisor

King reported that in November she received threatening notes from students and her car was "keyed." But that harassment did not disrupt classroom activities, prevent her from teaching or prevent students from learning.

After the Council's decision to approve the GSA Club, hostility from the anti-GSA faction in the community increased. The hostility shifted from Principal Johnson and the Council to members of the Board of Education and Dr. Capehart. Superintendent Capehart, School Board members, and BCHS administrative staff received many telephone calls from parents regarding the formation of the GSA Club. Many of these parents expressed concern over the education and safety of students and staff. Additionally, according to Assistant Principal Cyrus, many parents were irate and wanted to remove their children from BCHS immediately. Cyrus spent a great deal of time dealing with those angry parents and teachers who, like many in the general public, opposed the school's approval of the GSA Club. Nevertheless, Defendants are unable to identify a single student taken out of the school district because the GSA Club was formally recognized.

The record reflects only one documented instance of classroom disruption caused by GSA members or supporters—an incident where a student left a particular classroom because of supposed pressure from GSA supporters. Other than this one instance, Defendants have not elicited any evidence that GSA members or GSA Club meetings were disruptive.

On December 16, 2002, Dr. Capehart proposed that the Council ban all noncurricular clubs for the remainder of the 2002–03 school year. Although Defendants had described Beta and Key Clubs as noncurricular clubs just six weeks earlier, Dr. Capehart listed those clubs as curricular in his proposal. Dr. Capehart admitted that he came up with the proposal to ban all noncurricular clubs to put an end to the fury surrounding the GSA. That same day, the Board met and considered a motion to stop acknowledging all noncurricular clubs, in keeping with Dr. Capehart's proposal, and to write a "closed forum" policy to be implemented in July 2003. On December 17, 2002, the Council met and declined to vote on Dr. Capehart's proposal, effectively defeating it and allowing the GSA Club to continue to meet at BCHS.

On December 20, 2002, the Board held an emergency meeting and voted unanimously to suspend all clubs, both curricular and noncurricular, at BCHS for the remainder of the school year, effective immediately until July 1, 2003. Defendants' decision to ban all clubs at BCHS was motivated by a desire, in part, to stop the disruption surrounding the existence of the GSA Club at BCHS. The disruption to which Defendants were responding when they acted to ban all clubs on December 20, 2002, was caused by opponents of the GSA rather than by supporters of the GSA. Cyrus testified that none of the controversies or issues surrounding the GSA were provoked or instigated in any way by GSA supporters. Throughout the controversy over the GSA, Cyrus's concerns about any threat or danger to students or staff were "[m]ainly from the people who were rallying, you know, against the GSA[.]" Unlike most "hot topics" at BCHS over the past 18 years, the dispute over the GSA was "more of a community issue" rather than a "student on student" issue.

On January 2, 2003, Principal Johnson visited King in her classroom and told her that the GSA Club could apply to use school facilities as an outside organization before and after school hours but would not be permitted to meet during home room. On behalf of the GSA Club, King submitted a request for permission to use her classroom for GSA Club meetings once a week before school. On January 7, 2003, Principal Johnson and Dr. Capehart denied the GSA Club's facilities use application. Principal Johnson told King that no "groups" or "clubs" would be allowed to meet on school grounds.

Since the Board's action purportedly banning all clubs, the GSA Club has not held meetings at school, made announcements over the intercom, posted notices in the hallways or listed activities in the school newspaper. While students who were GSA Club members have gathered at times in King's classroom before and during home room, no GSA Club business has been conducted during that time or on BCHS premises since December 20, 2002. Although 20 to 30 GSA Club members regularly attended GSA Club meetings at BCHS prior to the purported ban on club meetings, only 6 members have been able to attend off-campus meetings since December 20, 2002.

Despite the Board's December 20, 2002 action purporting to suspend all clubs, Defendants have permitted and continue to permit many student groups to meet at BCHS during noninstructional time; that is, before school, after school, and during home room. Home room is a 20 to 25 minute period in which teachers take attendance and any flyers or announcements can be handed out to students. There is no formal teaching during home room and it is noninstructional time. Many student organizations have continued to use BCHS facilities during noninstructional time since December 20, 2002. They include the Kentucky United Nations Assembly ("KUNA"), formerly known as the Y-club, Mock Trial and Teen Court, Academic Teams, Athletics Teams, and Cheerleading squads. Additional groups using the school facilities since December 20, 2002, are: Future Farmers of America (FFA), Future Career and Community Leaders of America (FCCLA), Future Business Leaders of America (FBLA), and Health Occupation Student Organizations (HOSA). Defendants concede this fact. According to Boyd County Assistant Superintendent Dr. Dawn Tackett, maintenance of these student organizations is required for the career and technical education program to be in compliance with state regulation. The curriculum guide for the Boyd County Career and Technical Education Center, described during the injunction hearing as "East Campus", includes a reference to FFA, FCCLA, and HOSA as opportunities for student involvement. Dr. Tackett explained that curriculum courses such as marketing or home economics require student organizations to be in compliance with state regulation on technical education programs. Indeed, participation in an agriculture class requires participation in FFA activities.

The pre and post December 20, 2002, activities of four student groups—Drama Club, Bible Club, Executive Councils, and Beta Club—are of particular relevance for purposes of the pending motion for preliminary injunctive relief. Review of the activities of each of these groups is pertinent to subsequent analysis of the merits of Plaintiffs' motion. [The court found that each of these clubs were noncurricular but had continued to meet on the premises of the school and to carry out their regular activities of preparing the school play, holding Bible Reading sessions, planning class activities, and undertaking community service activities. The court noted that there was no academic credit associated with any of these activities, and that they did not relate to subjects taught in the curriculum.]

III. Analysis

In view of the paucity of Sixth Circuit case law interpreting the federal Equal Access Act ("EAA"), 20 U.S.C. § 4071, *et seq.,* an understanding of why and how the law came into being is helpful in understanding its operation and whether it has been violated in this case. In 1984, Congress passed the EAA to both guarantee and protect the rights of public high school students. The EAA was passed by wide, bipartisan majorities in both chambers of Congress. Its purpose was to counteract perceived discrimination against content-based religious speech in public high schools, while balancing the Establishment Clause interests at stake. *See Board of Educ. of Westside Community Schools v. Mergens,* 496 U.S. 226, 239 (1990). The legislative history also shows that the EAA was enacted in part in response to two federal appellate court decisions which had held that student religious groups could not, consistent with the Establishment Clause, meet on school premises during noninstructional time. The constitutionality of the EAA was upheld by the U.S. Supreme Court in *Mergens.*

Under the EAA, if a public school which receives federal financial assistance has created a limited open forum, it is unlawful for that school to deny equal access to, or a fair opportunity to, or to discriminate against, any students who wish to conduct a meeting within such limited open forum on the basis of the religious, political, philosophical, or other content of the speech at such meetings. 20 U.S.C. § 4071(a). A public secondary school has a "limited open forum" whenever it grants an offering to, or opportunity for, one or more noncurriculum-related student groups to meet on school premises during noninstructional time. 20 U.S.C. § 4071(b).

The Court recognizes that "the education of the Nation's youth is primarily the responsibility of parents, teachers, and state and local school officials, and not of federal judges." While the daily operation of school systems is traditionally reserved to the states and local school boards, by enacting the EAA Congress "made a matter once left to the discretion of local school officials the subject of comprehensive regulation by federal law." *Mergens,* 496 U.S. at 259.

Despite the mandates of the EAA, school districts retain significant discretion and authority over the type of activities, groups, and/or clubs in which students will be permitted to participate during noninstructional time. School districts retain the authority and latitude to establish their own courses and curriculum. In the exercise of that discretion, schools may structure their course offerings in such a way as to avoid application of the EAA. For instance, so long as the activities, groups, and/or clubs meeting at the school directly relate to the curriculum taught in those courses, the school district has not created a limited open forum and so the EAA has not been violated.

Even in those circumstances where a limited open forum has been created, the EAA does not limit a school's authority to prohibit meetings that would "materially and substantially interfere with the orderly conduct of educational activities within the school." *(emphasis added)* Id.; 20 U.S.C. § 4071(c)(4). The EAA further preserves "the authority of the school, its agents and employees, to maintain order and discipline on school premises, to protect the well-being of students and faculty, and to assure that attendance of students at meetings is voluntary." 20 U.S.C. § 4071(f).

Finally, the EAA applies only to public secondary schools which receive federal funding. 20 U.S.C. § 4071(a). Therefore, a school district seeking to avoid the obligations of the statute could simply choose to forego federal funding. Although that option is ordinarily unrealistic to most, if not all, local school districts, by passing the EAA Congress clearly "sought to prohibit schools from discriminating on the basis of the content of a student group's speech, and that obligation is the price a federally funded school must pay if it opens its facilities to noncurriculum related student groups." *Mergens,* 496 U.S. at 240.

In *Mergens,* the Supreme Court examined whether three student groups (Subsurfers, Chess, and Peer Advocates) were sufficiently related to the curriculum that a limited open forum was therefore not created. The Court rejected the school district's efforts to relate Subsurfers (scuba diving) to physical education and to relate Chess to math because neither chess nor scuba diving were "taught in any regularly offered course at the school" nor did either "result in extra academic credit." Likewise, a special education service group, known as Peer Advocates, was not required by "any courses offered by the school," did not figure as part of a required participation for any course, and did "not result in extra credit in any course." Efforts by school officials to link Subsurfers to swimming which was taught as part of physical education and to link Chess to math based on encouragement by math teachers to play the game were specifically rejected by the Court. The Court explained that curriculum related must mean something other than being "remotely related to abstract educational goals;" otherwise, "no schools [would have] limited fora…and schools could evade the Act by strategically describing existing student groups." "The logic of the EAA also supports [the] view…that a curriculum-related student group is one that has more than just a tangential or attenuated relationship to courses offered by the school." Because Congress intended a "low threshold for triggering the Act's requirements," the term "noncurriculum related student group" is to be "interpreted *broadly* to mean any student group that does not *directly* relate to the body of courses offered by the school." *Mergens,* 496 U.S. at 239–40 (emphasis added).

Because Congress did not expressly define "noncurricular" when it enacted the EAA, the Supreme Court in *Mergens* spent considerable time discussing the factors lower courts should use in deciding whether a group is "noncurricular," thereby creating a "limited open forum" that, in turn, triggers the obligations of the EAA. The Supreme Court provided guidance to determining what constitutes a "noncurriculum related student group" by setting forth the criteria for what constitutes a "curriculum related student group." According to *Mergens,* a student group directly relates to a school's curriculum if: (1) the subject matter of the group is actually taught, or will soon be taught, in a regularly-offered course; (2) the subject matter of the group concerns the body of courses as a whole; (3) participation in the group is required for a particular course; or (4) participation in the group results in academic credit. "Whether a specific student group is a 'noncurriculum related student group' will therefore depend on a particular school's curriculum, but such determinations would be subject to factual findings well within the competence of trial courts to make." Moreover, in determining whether a student group is curricular versus noncurricular, the Court favored a substance over form analysis, stating that the proper inquiry is for trial courts to look at a school's actual practice rather than its stated policy. Numerous federal courts since *Mergens* have adopted the same narrow interpretation of curriculum relatedness when addressing access by student religious groups to school facilities.

Once a court determines, using the factors outlined above, that even one "noncurriculum-related student group" has been permitted to meet, a limited open forum has been created and the EAA's obligations are triggered. The school may not deny other clubs, on the "basis of the content of their speech, equal access to meet on school premises during noninstructional time."

In *Garnett v. Renton School District,* the district court determined that Future Business Leaders of America (FBLA) was a noncurriculum-related student group meeting at the school and, therefore, the school's refusal to also permit a Bible Club to meet during noninstructional time violated the EAA. School district and state guidelines required that FBLA be offered, but business class students were not required to attend and no academic credit was awarded for participation. The court stated that in such a circumstance where a club such as FBLA is required to be offered, the options open to a school to avoid a limited open forum under the EAA are restricted: "adjust class requirements, provide instruction in FBLA meetings, or drop business classes." 772 F.Supp. at 534.

What constitutes the statutory "equal access" required by the EAA is also worth noting. Equal access "to meet" is broadly defined under the EAA to include all activities in which student groups are permitted to engage in a particular school. Thus, once a court determines that a limited open forum has been created because school access has been provided to at least one noncurriculum-related group, the access afforded must be equal to that provided to all groups, both curricular and noncurricular.

Although the majority of cases defining and interpreting the EAA involve requests by religious groups to meet on school property during noninstructional time, several district courts have specifically addressed the more contentious issue of permitting gay rights groups to meet during noninstructional time. For example, in *Colin v. Orange Unified School Dist.*, 83 F.Supp.2d 1135 (C.D.Cal.2000), the court was asked to determine whether a student "Gay-Straight Alliance" club seeking recognition by the public high school for purposes of access to school premises for meetings was a "noncurriculum-elated" group under the Equal Access Act. The school district argued that the GSA related to human sexuality, which was taught in Health, Biology, and Family Planning courses, since the club intended to discuss issues related to tolerance, respect, sexual orientation, and homophobia. Following the four-step analysis of *Mergens,* the court found that, even if there was some overlap between what the plaintiffs wished to discuss and what was taught in the sex education curriculum, that overlap was not a sufficient nexus to the regularly-offered sex education curriculum to cause the club to be curriculum related and remove it from the protection of the Equal Access Act.

The Court specifically found that the school district had maintained a limited open forum in word and deed because several other noncurriculum-related groups had been recognized by the school district. These noncurriculum-related groups included a Christian Club and Red Cross/Key Club. Since the defendant had maintained a limited open forum, and because the club met other requirements of the Act, the court ruled that the GSA Club had been denied access to the school's limited open forum, holding this denial is "exactly the type of content-based restriction that is forbidden by the Equal Access Act." The court granted the injunction, ordering the school district to provide equal access to the GSA Club.

In *East High Gay/Straight Alliance v. Board of Education of Salt Lake City School Dist.,* a GSA club was granted injunctive relief, thereby permitting it to meet at the defendant high school. *East High Gay/Straight Alliance v. Board of Education of Salt Lake City School Dist.,* 81 F.Supp.2d 1166, 1184 (D.Utah 1999). In *East High,* the school district had a policy of allowing school access only to curriculum-related student groups, which policy specifically stated that it was defendant's intent not to create a limited open forum for Equal Access Act purposes. Plaintiffs, who wished to form a support group for homosexual students, argued they had been denied equal access to the defendant's facilities, including the public address system, bulletin boards, and the school fair. They asserted that regardless of the school district's policy, in actual practice the defendant had provided access to noncurriculum-related as well as curriculum-related student groups.

The plaintiffs in *East High* argued that five student groups, Improvement Council of East ("ICE"), Future Homemakers of America, Future Business Leaders of America, National Honor Society, and Odyssey of the Mind, were noncurriculum related. The stated purpose of ICE was to create a caring, positive school environment. Applying the

Mergens test, the Court found only one student group, ICE, to be noncurriculum related because this group's activities could not be tied to the subject matter of any course, did not relate to the body of courses, and no academic credit was given. The court found the school district had thereby created a limited open forum and, consequently, by denying the plaintiffs access, violated the Equal Access Act. Plaintiffs' motion for partial summary judgment was granted.

The Court must first determine if any of the groups which the Court has found to be meeting during noninstructional time since December 20, 2002 are noncurricular. If Defendants have permitted *any* noncurriculum-related student group to meet at BCHS during noninstructional time since December 20, 2002, then they must allow *every* student group, whether curriculum related or noncurriculum related, to meet on the same terms.

Bible Club

Defendants have already identified the Bible Club/Christian Fellowship Club as noncurricular Defendants seek to distinguish the Bible Club, despite conceding its noncurricular status, by contending that school administrators were unaware that members of the Bible Club had been meeting on a regular basis in the hallway before home room. Notably, however, Defendants did not elicit clear testimony that school administrators did not know about the Bible Club meetings. Regardless of Defendants' purported lack of knowledge of these meetings, the Equal Access Act does not permit schools to use their lack of knowledge as a defense. By opening their doors to students prior to school, the BCHS gave Bible Club students the opportunity to meet. This is all that is required by the statute. Given the conspicuous location and number of the meetings, the Court finds Defendants either knew or should have known the meetings were occurring. School officials "grant" an offering or opportunity to a student group when they know or should know the group is violating administration rules but take no action to prevent further meetings. The Court concludes that the Bible Club is a noncurriculum-related student group.

Drama Club

Although perhaps not meeting as the "Drama Club" per se, a group of students has met frequently in the BCHS auditorium after school to rehearse for a play that will be performed at school, has used the intercom during home room to call participating students to meetings related to play practice, and has listed the names of people in the drama group on a bulletin board in the hallway outside Ms. Thornbury's classroom. BCHS is currently offering an Arts & Humanities class in the Spring 2003 semester, which includes a section on theater history. However, acting is not one of the primary objectives of the class. In the theater history section of the Arts & Humanities class, students are taught about costumes in early French theater, about Greek and Roman mythology and about vocabulary words relevant to the theater. Students also spend approximately one and a half days on oral presentations in which students read a story aloud and tell a story from their own personal experience. The theater section of Arts & Humanities does not actually teach students acting or any of the other skills students would need to put on a play.

A close review of BCHS's 2002–03 curriculum guide reveals that the Arts and Humanities Class does include a section on drama. However, participation in the student group practicing to perform a play is not required by the Arts and Humanities Class and does not result in academic credit, despite the fact that teachers have the option of requiring their students to *watch* a performance of the play during instructional time, and may assign course work based on discussion questions provided to students who *watch* the play. Moreover, despite the fact that drama is listed as being taught in the Arts and Humanities Class, the subject matter of the drama group is not actually taught and will not soon be taught in any regularly offered course at BCHS. Additionally, although the BCHS Curriculum Guide lists a Speech/Drama course, that course was not offered in the 2001–02 academic year and is not being offered for the 2002–03 academic year, nor does BCHS have any plans to teach Speech/Drama next year.

Interpreting the term "noncurriculum-related student group" broadly, as is required by *Mergens,* the court concludes that the Drama Club is a noncurriculum-related student group. [The court reached similar conclusions about the Executive Councils and the Beta Club.]

There are, therefore, four noncurriculum-related student groups at BCHS. As a result of these findings, the Court concludes that Defendants, despite their attempts to close the forum with their December 20, 2002 action, have allowed and are continuing to allow numerous student activities, both curricular and noncurricular, to meet at school during noninstructional time, to use the public address system, and to publish information about their activities in the school newspaper paper. Accordingly, the Court finds that Defendants are maintaining a "limited open forum" by allowing at least one noncurriculum-related student group to meet at the BCHS during noninstructional time.

Thus, having found that the Defendants are subject to the EAA by virtue of permitting at least one noncurriculum-related group to meet or use the facilities at BCHS, in order to properly exclude the GSA from having equal access as required by the EAA, Defendants must show that the GSA Club will "materially and substantially interfere with the orderly conduct of educational opportunities within the school," 20 U.S.C. §4071(c)(4), or will limit the school's ability "to maintain order and discipline on school premises, to protect the well-being of students and faculty...." 20 U.S.C. §4071(f).

In this case, it is obvious that the proposed creation of a GSA Club at BCHS has caused some level of uproar within the local community. It is equally apparent that several school administrators and board members received numerous complaints and questions from parents who were concerned about the approval of the GSA Club and how that approval might affect the safety of their children. Additionally, there were two student protests regarding the approval of the GSA Club, one on October 30, 2002, and the other on November 4, 2002. In short, the disruption to which Defendants were responding when they voted to ban all clubs was caused by GSA opponents, not GSA Club members themselves.

Although there is a relative paucity of case law interpreting what level of disruption is necessary before a school, subject to the obligations of the EAA can deny equal access without violating the Act, a review of what little case law does exist is helpful. The leading case on attempts to suppress speech within the high school setting is *Tinker v. Des Moines Independent Community School Dist.,* 393 U.S. 503 (1969). It is axiomatic that students do not shed their First Amendment rights at the schoolhouse gate. In *Tinker,* the Supreme Court verified the rights of junior high and high school students to engage in nondisruptive expression on school premises, in particular the wearing of black armbands to protest the Vietnam War. The Des Moines school administrators had suspended three students for wearing the armbands because they feared a disturbance would otherwise result. The United States Supreme Court disagreed and delimited the school officials' authority to restrict student expression only where such expression would "materially and substantially interfere with the requirements of appropriate discipline in the operation of the school."

In *Tinker*, the Supreme Court concluded that school officials violated the First Amendment when they prohibited students from wearing black armbands to protest the Vietnam War. *Tinker*, 393 U.S. at 514. The Court rejected arguments that the students could be punished for wearing their armbands because school authorities had an "urgent wish to avoid the controversy which might result from the expression," because other students made hostile remarks to the children wearing armbands, because students argued in class about the armbands instead of paying attention, or because responses to the armbands might lead other students to start an argument or cause a disturbance.

Refusing to allow a "heckler's veto" to justify suppression of student speech, the Court in *Tinker* was careful to focus on whether "*engaging in the forbidden conduct would materially and substantially interfere with the requirements of appropriate discipline*," and concluded that the protesting students' speech was protected because it was "entirely divorced from actually or potentially disruptive conduct *by those participating in it*." *Tinker* expressly relied on the leading heckler's veto case, *Terminiello v. Chicago*, 337 U.S. 1 (1949). The Court explained that:

> [a]ny departure from the majority's opinion may inspire fear. Any word spoken, in class, in the lunchroom, or on the campus, that deviates from the views of another person may start an argument or cause a disturbance. But our Constitution says we must take this risk, *Terminiello v. Chicago*, 337 U.S. 1 (1949), and our history says that it is this sort of hazardous freedom—this kind of openness—that is the basis of our national strength and of the independence and vigor of Americans who grow up and live in this relatively permissive, often disputatious, society.

Tinker, 393 U.S. at 509, 89 S.Ct. 733.

In *Terminiello*, the Court held that officials violated the First Amendment when they arrested a speaker for disorderly conduct because of the disruption caused by others in response to his message. The Supreme Court held that the First Amendment prohibits the government from punishing a speaker merely because his speech "stir[s] people to anger, invite[s] public dispute, or [brings] about a condition of unrest."

Incorporation of the *Tinker* rule into 20 U.S.C. §4071(f) means that a school may not deny equal access to a student group because student and community opposition to the group substantially interferes with the school's ability to maintain order and discipline, even though equal access is not required if the student group itself substantially interferes with the school's ability to maintain order and discipline. Consistent with the holdings of *Tinker* and *Terminiello*, the Equal Access Act permits Defendants to prohibit Plaintiffs from meeting on equal terms with the noncurriculum-related student groups that have been permitted to meet since December 20, 2002 only upon a showing that Plaintiffs' *own* disruptive activities have interfered with Defendants ability to maintain order and discipline. Defendants have made no such showing in this case.

Assuming *arguendo* that the anti-GSA faction at BCHS was sufficiently disruptive to "materially and substantially interfere with the requirements of appropriate discipline," Defendants are not permitted to restrict Plaintiffs' speech and association as a means of preventing disruptive responses to it. The Court further finds that the "heckler's veto" rule does not limit Defendants' authority to maintain order and discipline on school premises or to protect the well-being of students and faculty. There was no proof elicited during the hearing that, if the GSA Club were provided equal access, Defendants' ability to discipline any student who is disruptive would be diminished in any way. *Tinker* and *Terminiello* are designed to prevent Defendants from punishing students who express unpopular views instead of punishing the students who react to those views in a disruptive manner.

While Defendants argue that these protests and the public uproar surrounding the GSA Club have materially and substantially interfered with the orderly conduct of educational activities at BCHS, limited their authority to maintain order and discipline, and limited their ability to protect the well-being of students and faculty, the facts simply do not support such a conclusion. The evidence presented during the hearing reveals that despite these protests, school officials did an excellent job maintaining the educational environment at BCHS. For instance, regularly scheduled classroom activities were not altered in any way, teachers were not prevented from teaching, and students who attended school were not prevented from learning.

For these reasons, the Court finds that Plaintiffs have shown a strong likelihood of succeeding on their claim that Defendants violated their rights under the Equal Access Act. Since the Court has found that Defendants likely violated the Equal Access Act, the Court need not at this time address either Plaintiffs' First Amendment claim or KERA claim for purposes of the pending motion.

It is well settled that "the loss of First Amendment freedoms, for even minimal periods of time unquestionably constitutes irreparable injury." *Elrod v. Burns,* 427 U.S. 347, 373 (1976). This same presumption of irreparable harm has been applied in cases of violations of the Equal Access Act because it protects "expressive liberties." This same sound reasoning applies in this case. Absent a preliminary injunction, Plaintiffs will be unable to meet at school, unable to benefit from a forum for discussion with other students who are suffering the effects of harassment based on sexual orientation, and unable to work with other students to foster tolerance among all students. In this case, Plaintiffs have already been prevented from meeting for more than three months of the Spring 2003 semester. Because two Plaintiffs (Fannin and McClelland) are seniors and three Plaintiffs (Alcorn, Carter, and Duarte) are juniors, by the time this matter is resolved on the merits, these five Plaintiffs may have graduated and would therefore receive no benefit.

The balance of the hardships also favors Plaintiffs. Compliance with an injunction will not require much effort or expense, nor will allowing the GSA Club to meet harm others. In fact, most students at BCHS are likely to benefit from a preliminary injunction because all other noncurriculum-related student activities are likely to be reinstated when the GSA Club is reinstated. This would include one or more religion or community-service based clubs.

Allowing the GSA Club to meet is unlikely to cause substantial disruption to the educational process. While the GSA Club meetings at BCHS last semester may have caused community controversy, there was no evidence that the meetings themselves caused disruptions.

Just as constitutional violations—and by extension Equal Access Act violations—constitute irreparable harm, the exoneration of any such violations would serve to satisfy the public interest requirement. The Sixth Circuit has consistently held that "[i]t is always in the public interest to prevent the violation of a party's constitutional rights."

See G & V Lounge, Inc. v. Michigan Liquor Control Com'n, 23 F.3d 1071, 1079 (6th Cir.1994); *Dayton Area Visually Impaired Persons, Inc. v. Fisher,* 70 F.3d 1474, 1490 (6th Cir.1995).

Additionally, while the primary teachers of tolerance should always be the parents and not the teachers and school administrators, school officials can play a vital role in fostering tolerance to its students. If, by permitting the GSA Club to meet, students are less likely to be the subject of hate crimes by fostering tolerance in the school community, the public interest is served. *See Colin,* 83 F.Supp.2d at 1150–51 (providing a safe and respectful environment for students to talk about "the hardships they encounter at school every day" serves the public interest).

Balancing the four factors set forth, the Court concludes that each of the four factors favors the issuance of a preliminary injunction in this case.

Notes and Questions

1. Can you imagine any circumstances in which a court could legitimately find that a proposed student GSA club is not entitled to meet on campus?

2. In the East High School case, discussed above, school officials attempted the same strategy as those in Boyd County—officially to ban all noncurricular clubs from meeting at the high school. Student outcry at the cancellation of virtually all extracurricular activities made such a ban practically impossible to enforce, and ultimately East High had to concede that it still had a limited public forum. In the only case that denied relief to a GSA, *Caudillo v. Lubbock Independent School District,* 311 F.Supp.2d 550 (N.D. Tex. 2004), the court found that school administrators were justified in denying access to a GSA that included links on its website and in its promotional literature to websites with sexually explicit content.

Subject Index

Index does not include names of cases (see Table of Cases), individual people or places.

	DATE DUE		
223-07			

THE LIBRARY STORE   #47-0120